EVANGELICA
III

BIBLIOTHECA EPHEMERIDUM THEOLOGICARUM LOVANIENSIUM

CL

EVANGELICA
III

1992-2000

COLLECTED ESSAYS

BY

FRANS NEIRYNCK

LEUVEN
UNIVERSITY PRESS

UITGEVERIJ PEETERS
LEUVEN – PARIS – STERLING, VA

2001

ISBN 90 5867 115 1 (Leuven University Press)
D/2001/1869/22
ISBN 90-429-0974-9 (Peeters Leuven)
ISBN 2-87723-550-5 (Peeters France)
D/2000/0602/180

Library of Congress Cataloging-in-Publication Data
available from the Library of Congress

Leuven University Press / Presses Universitaires de Louvain
Universitaire Pers Leuven
Blijde-Inkomststraat 5, B-3000 Leuven (Belgium)

© 2001 – Peeters, Bondgenotenlaan 153, B-3000 Leuven (Belgium)

PREFACE

Omne trinum perfectum. This adage was used in 1992 by a good colleague of mine encouraging me to prepare the publication of a third volume of *Evangelica*. Not unlike volumes I and II the preparation of the new collection was spread over a period of nine years. Again, the title *Evangelica* stands for Gospel studies, a variety of essays on the Four Gospels.

Evangelica [I]. Gospel Studies – Études d'évangile. Collected Essays, ed. F. Van Segbroeck (BETL, 60), 1982, xix-1036 p.: i. The Four Gospels. ii. The Empty Tomb Stories. iii. The Gospel of Mark. iv. Matthew and Luke. v. The Text of the Gospels. Nos. 1-43.

Evangelica II: 1982-1991. Collected Essays, ed. F. Van Segbroeck (BETL, 99), 1991, xix-874 p.: i. The Minor Agreements. ii. Matthew and Luke. iii. Mark and the Synoptic Problem. iv. The Sayings of Jesus. v. The Fourth Gospel. vi. The Apocryphal Gospels. Nos. 1-40.

Evangelica III: 1992-2000. Collected Essays (BETL, 150), 2001, xvii-666 p.: i. Colloquium Biblicum Lovaniense. ii. The Minor Agreements. iii. The Synoptic Problem. iv. The Sayings Source Q. v. John and the Synoptics Revisited. vi. The Gospels and Jesus. Nos. 1-32.

A significant number of these essays rely on papers I delivered at the meetings of the *Colloquium Biblicum Lovaniense* (= CBL): nos. 1, 2, 3, 13, 21, 25, 27, 36 in *Evangelica I*; nos. 24, 29, 38 in *Evangelica II*; and now, as one group in chronological order, nos. 1-5 in *Evangelica III* (first published in BETL 101, 110, 125, 131, and 142)[1]. The new volume begins with "John and the Synoptics: 1975-1990", a survey article extending from the CBL session on the Gospel of John (and my first paper on "John and the Synoptics") in 1975, via "John and the Synoptics: The Empty Tomb Stories" (SNTS, Leuven 1982), up to the CBL meeting on John and the Synoptics in 1990. Published in 1992, the article now receives a further supplement in Part V, John and the Synoptics Revisited, with updating notes on Jn 20,1-18 / Lk 24,12 and Mt 28,9-10.

"Literary Criticism, Old and New" (CBL 1992) is more directly devoted to my redaction-critical approach in studying the Synoptic

---

1. All volumes are indexed and indexes of Biblical References are not repeated in the present volume.

Gospels[2], with concentration on the Minor Agreements and the Sayings Source Q. Throughout the three volumes of *Evangelica* the Minor Agreements are treated in accordance with the two-source hypothesis, though with due consideration of alternative theories: nos. 31-33 in *Evangelica I*, nos. 1-6 in *Evangelica II*, and now nos. 6-13 in *Evangelica III*.

In the section on the Sayings Source Q, nos. 18-24 (and 6-7), three types of questions are discussed: Q called Source or Gospel; the origin of Lk 17,33 in Q or Mk; and overlaps evidence for Mark's use of Q or pre-Markan tradition. The question of the influence of Isaiah 61 in the Beatitudes Q 6,20b-21 is debated in no. 4: Q or MtR. A more detailed study of the reconstruction of Q is provided elsewhere[3].

For both the phenomenon of the minor agreements and the extent of Q, my approach can be evaluated by comparison with U. Luz's position(s) and with the recent developments of M.-É. Boismard's proto-Gospel hypotheses (nos. 16 and 17). In both cases book reviews (in French) are included as they were published in ETL.

The original pagination of all essays is marked in the text by the sign I and the page numbers are indicated in the headlines (in small print). Where relevant, supplementary notes referring to recent publications (up to the year 2000) are added at the conclusion of the essays.

---

2. With two bibliographic tools as companion volumes: *The Gospel of Mark: A Cumulative Bibliography 1950-1990*, by F. Neirynck, J. Verheyden, F. Van Segbroeck, G. Van Oyen, and R. Corstjens (BETL, 102), 1992; *The Gospel of Matthew and the Sayings Source Q: A Cumulative Bibliography 1950-1995*, by F. Neirynck, J. Verheyden, and R. Corstjens (BETL, 140), 1998.

3. *The Reconstruction of Q and IQP/CritEd Parallels*, in A. LINDEMANN (ed.), *The Sayings Source Q and the Historical Jesus* (BETL, 158), Leuven, 2001, pp. 53-147.

CONTENTS

I
COLLOQUIUM BIBLICUM LOVANIENSE

II
THE MINOR AGREEMENTS

III

THE SYNOPTIC PROBLEM

IV
THE SAYINGS SOURCE Q

V
JOHN AND THE SYNOPTICS REVISITED

VI

THE GOSPELS AND JESUS

INDEXES

FIRST PUBLICATION

1. John and the Synoptics: 1975-1990.
   — A. DENAUX (ed.), *John and the Synoptics* (BETL, 101), Leuven, University Press - Peeters, 1992, 3-62.
   Colloquium Biblicum Lovaniense 39, 1990

2. Literary Criticism, Old and New.
   — C. FOCANT (ed.), *The Synoptic Gospels: Source Criticism and the New Literary Criticism* (BETL, 110), Leuven, University Press - Peeters, 1993, 11-90.
   Colloquium Biblicum Lovaniense 41, 1992

3. The Sayings of Jesus in 1 Corinthians.
   — R. BIERINGER (ed.), *The Corinthian Correspondence* (BETL, 125), Leuven, University Press - Peeters, 1996, 141-176.
   Colloquium Biblicum Lovaniense 43, 1994

4. Q 6,20b-21; 7,22 and Isaiah 61.
   — C.M. TUCKETT (ed.), *The Scriptures in the Gospels* (BETL, 131), Leuven, University Press - Peeters, 1997, 27-64.
   Colloquium Biblicum Lovaniense 45, 1996

5. Luke 4,16-30 and the Unity of Luke-Acts.
   — J. VERHEYDEN (ed.), *The Unity of Luke-Acts* (BETL, 142), Leuven, University Press - Peeters, 1999, 357-203.
   Colloquium Biblicum Lovaniense 47, 1998

6. The First Synoptic Pericope: The Appearance of John the Baptist in Q?
   — *ETL* 72 (1996) 41-74.

7. The Minor Agreements and Q.
   — R.A. PIPER (ed.), *The Gospel Behind the Gospels. Current Studies on Q* (Supplements to Novum Testamentum, 75), Leiden, Brill, 1995, 49-72.

8. Luke 10:25-28: A Foreign Body in Luke?
   — S.E. PORTER, P. JOYCE, and D.E. ORTON (eds.), *Crossing the Boundaries. Essays in Biblical Interpretation in Honour of Michael D. Goulder* (Biblical Interpretation Series, 8), Leiden, Brill, 1994, 149-165.

9. The Minor Agreements and Lk 10,25-28.
   — *ETL* 71 (1995) 151-160.

10. Luke 9,22 and 10,25-28: The Case for Independent Redaction.
    — *ETL* 75 (1999) 123-132.

11. Goulder and the Minor Agreements.
    — *ETL* 73 (1997) 84-93.

12. Gospel Issues in the Passion Narratives.
    — *ETL* 70 (1994) 406-416.

13. A Symposium on the Minor Agreements.
    — *ETL* 67 (1991) 361-372; 69 (1993) 428-429.

14. The Two-Source Hypothesis: Introduction.
    — D.L. DUNGAN (ed.), *The Interrelations of the Gospels. A Symposion Led by M.-É. Boismard – W.R. Farmer – F. Neirynck: Jerusalem 1984* (BETL, 95), Leuven, University Press & Peeters, 1990, 3-22.

Thanks are due to the original publishers and editors who have granted permission to reprint the articles.

CONTENTS EVANGELICA I & II

EVANGELICA I, 1982

Collected Essays 1966-1981

EVANGELICA II, 1991

Collected Essays 1982-1991

I

COLLOQUIUM BIBLICUM LOVANIENSE

Notes on essays in "the present volume" (or "this volume") in Part I refer to one of the five CBL volumes. Cf. below, p. 206.

BETL 101 (1992) 3-62

1

JOHN AND THE SYNOPTICS: 1975-1990

I

INTRODUCTION

At the 1975 Colloquium I had the opportunity to deliver a paper on John and the Synoptics, 1965-1975. In the first part, I gave a description of the state of the problem: the then predominant theory of Johannine independence and what I thought to be the beginnings of a new development in the works of M.-É. Boismard and A. Dauer, both published in 1972, viz., on the one hand, John's extensive use of the sources of the Synoptic Gospels, and the Johannine redaction influenced by Matthew, and on the other, the influence of the three Synoptics on the pre-Johannine Vorlage of the passion narrative. In the second part, I developed my own approach relying on previous investigation of the synoptic parallels to Jn 20,1-18, i.e., Mk 16 and parallels, and in particular the editorial verses in Mt 28,9-10 and Lk 24,12. I concluded with a reformulation of B. Lindars's thesis regarding Jn 20: "not the traditions behind the Synoptic Gospels but the Synoptic Gospels themselves are the sources of the Fourth Evangelist". The text of my lecture, updated with footnotes, was published in 1977 in the volume of the Colloquium[1], which also included M. Sabbe's critique of Dauer's hypothesis (in an analysis of the arrest of Jesus, Jn 18,1-11)[2]. The general conversion of Johannine scholars did not follow immediately, but the Leuven paper, or at least its title, is widely used to signal the reemergence of the thesis of John's dependence on the Synoptics[3].

---

1. F. NEIRYNCK, *John and the Synoptics*, in M. DE JONGE (ed.), *L'Évangile de Jean. Sources, rédaction, théologie* (BETL, 44), Leuven, 1977, ²1987, pp. 73-106. Reprinted in F. NEIRYNCK, *Evangelica. Gospel Studies - Études d'évangile. Collected Essays*, ed. F. Van Segbroeck (BETL, 60), Leuven, 1982, pp. 365-398, with Additional Note, 398-400. Cf. *Evangelica II* (BETL, 99), 1991, pp. 798-799. — I refer to this paper as *JohnSyn* (in the original pagination), and to *Jean et les Synoptiques* (cf. below, n. 15) as *JeanSyn*.

2. M. SABBE, *The Arrest of Jesus in Jn 18,1-11 and Its Relation to the Synoptic Gospels. A Critical Evaluation of A. Dauer's Hypothesis*, in *L'Évangile de Jean* (n. 1), pp. 203-234; reprinted in ID., *Studia Neotestamentica. Collected Essays* (BETL, 98), Leuven, 1991, pp. 355-386 (Additional Note, 387-388). See also F. NEIRYNCK, *The 'Other Disciple' in Jn 18,15-16*, in *ETL* 51 (1975) 113-141 (= *Evangelica*, pp. 335-363, with Additional Note, 363-364; cf. *Evangelica II*, p. 798), esp. pp. 127ff.: "Jn 18,15-16 and the Synoptics".

3. See, e.g., J.L. MARTYN, *History and Theology in the Fourth Gospel*, Nashville, TN, ²1979, p. 20, n. 5: "Up to the present, however, I have to say that the impressive arguments of Neirynck have not proved convincing to me because the thesis of John's

Much has happened since 1975. In the first place, I should refer to N. Perrin († 1976), not yet mentioned in my earlier survey. In his Introduction (1974)[4], he observed that the "combination of agreement and disagreement ... makes the question of John's knowledge of the synoptic gospels very difficult"[5]. He added, however, a particular consideration: the intercalation of the trial before the High Priest into the denial story (Jn 18,19-24 at 15-18/25-27) indicates that John "must have known the gospel of Mark"[6]. And elsewhere he made a similar observation on John's use of the ἐξουσία of the Son of Man in 5,27 (cf. Mk 2,10: "characteristically Markan")[7]. Members of "the Perrin school" who published the volume on *The Passion in Mark* (1976)[8] have prolonged this view (I mention W.H. Kelber, J.R. Donahue, K.E. Dewey, J.D. Crossan)[9], and Perrin's suggestion gave rise to an intense discussion on "John and Mark" in the SBL Seminar Papers of 1978 and 1979[10], pro

dependence on the Synoptics still seems to create more problems than it solves". See also below, nn. 16, 41, 46.

4. N. PERRIN, *The New Testament. An Introduction. Proclamation and Parenesis, Myth and History*, New York, 1974, pp. 226-229 (²1982, pp. 332-335): "The Gospel of John and the Synoptic Gospels". See esp. p. 229, on the verbal parallels at Jn 5,8; 6,7; 12,3 (par. Mk) and 12,3-8 (par. Lk), and his conclusion: "they have convinced the present writer that the gospel of John shows knowledge of the gospel of Mark, and perhaps also of the gospel of Luke" (slightly adapted by D.C. Duling in the second edition, p. 335).

5. *Ibid.*, p. 227 (= 332).

6. *Ibid.*, p. 229 (= 335).

7. N. PERRIN, *A Modern Pilgrimage in New Testament Christology*, Philadelphia, 1974, pp. 122-128 ("The Use of the Son of Man in the Gospel of John"), esp. 128. He refers to Jn 1,51 "and its relationship to Mark 14:62": "distinctively Markan" (*ibid.*).

8. W.H. KELBER (ed.), *The Passion in Mark. Studies on Mark 14–16*, Philadelphia, 1976.

9. *Ibid.*, pp. 55-56 and 158-159 (W.H. Kelber), 9-10 (J.R. Donahue), 104-105 (K.E. Dewey), 144 (J.D. Crossan). On J.D. Crossan, see below, n. 36.

10. SBL 1978 Seminar Papers, vol. II, pp. 238-249: E.F. GLUSMAN, *Criteria for a Study of the Outlines of Mark and John*; 251-260: A.M. MAYNARD, *Common Elements in the Outlines of Mark and John*; 261-267: L.T. BRODIE, *Creative Rewriting: Key to a New Methodology*; 269-279: L.R. KITTLAUS, *John and Mark: A Methodological Evaluation of Norman Perrin's Suggestion*; 281-287: M. SMITH, *Mark 6:32–15:47 and John 6:1–19:42.* — SBL 1979 Seminar Papers, vol. I, pp. 105-108: M.H. SMITH, *Collected Fragments: On the Priority of John 6 to Mark 6–8*; 109-112: K.E. DEWEY, *Peter's Denial Reexamined: John's Knowledge of Mark's Gospel*; 113-117: E.F. GLUSMAN, *The Cleansing of the Temple and the Anointing at Bethany: The Order of Events in Mark 11 / John 11–12*; 119-122: L.R. KITTLAUS, *Evidence from Jn. 12 that the Author of John Knew the Gospel of Mark*; 123-125: A.B. KOLENKOW, *Two Changing Patterns: Conflicts and the Necessity of Death. John 2 and 12 and Markan Parallels*; 127-130: W. MUNRO, *The Anointing in Mark 14:3-9 and John 12:1-8.* — K.E. Dewey's contribution (1979) is a reply to R.T. FORTNA, *Jesus and Peter at the High Priest's House: A Test Case for the Question of the Relation between Mark's and John's Gospel*, in NTS 24 (1977-78) 371-383 (in response to Perrin).

and contra, with L.T. Brodie, K.E. Dewey, L.R. Kittlaus, and A.M. Maynard defending Johannine dependence.

⎮ On the European scene, I recall that my previous survey contained three announcements: the new edition of C.K. Barrett's commentary (1978)[11], the modification of Boismard's theory in *L'évangile de Jean* (1977)[12], and Dauer's promise to treat the synoptic-like sections outside the passion narrative (*Johannes und Lukas*, 1984)[13]. To these three books, now published, can be added B. de Solages's *Jean et les Synoptiques* (1979)[14] and my own work, published in the same year, with the same title, though with a rather different approach[15].

See also L.R. KITTLAUS, *The Fourth Gospel and Mark: John's Use of Markan Redaction and Composition*, Diss., Chicago, 1978; N.H. BRICKHAM, *The Dependence of the Fourth Gospel on the Gospel of Mark. A Redaction-Critical Approach*, Diss., Washington, DC, 1982. Contrast the dissertations by D.G. BOYD, *The Sources Used by John and Their Relation to the Synoptic Gospels*, Diss., McGill University, Montreal, 1972; P.A. PHARR, *The Passion Narrative in the Fourth Gospel. A Study of Sources in John 18:1–19:42*, Diss., Duke University, Durham, NC, 1972; E.F. GLUSMAN, *The Shape of Mark and John: A Primitive Gospel Outline*, Diss., Duke University, 1978. On D.M. Smith, see below, n. 15 and nn. 45-56.

11. C.K. BARRETT, *The Gospel according to St John*, London-Philadelphia, ²1978, esp. pp. 42-46: "The Christian Background of the Gospel: 1. The Synoptic Tradition, (i) Literary" (cf. 1955, pp. 34-37); now in German translation: *Das Evangelium nach Johannes* (KEK, Sonderband), Göttingen, 1990, pp. 59-71 (and p. 160: cf. below, n. 34). See also ID., *John and the Synoptic Gospels*, in *ExpT* 85 (1973-74) 228-233; cf. *JohnSyn*, p. 79 (and 73).

12. M.-É. BOISMARD – A. LAMOUILLE, *L'évangile de Jean. Commentaire* (Synopse des quatre évangiles en français, 3), Paris, 1977. Cf. *JohnSyn*, p. 93, n. 84. See below, n. 15.

13. A. DAUER, *Johannes und Lukas. Untersuchungen zu den johanneisch-lukanischen Parallelperikopen* Joh 4,46-54 / Lk 7,1-10 – Joh 12,1-8 / Lk 7,36-50; 10,38-42 – Joh 20,19-29 / Lk 24,36-49 (Forschung zur Bibel, 50), Würzburg, 1984. On Jn 4,46-54 (pp. 39-125; 315-366: notes), cf. F. NEIRYNCK, *John 4,46-54: Signs Source and/or Synoptic Gospels*, in *ETL* 60 (1984) 367-375 (reprinted in *Evangelica II*, pp. 679-687, with Additional Note, 687-688). On Jn 20,19-29 (pp. 207-296; 411-471: notes), cf. F. NEIRYNCK, *Lc 24,36-43: Un récit lucanien*, in *À cause de l'Évangile*. FS J. Dupont (Lectio Divina, 123), Paris, 1985, pp. 655-680, esp. 657-665: "Jn 20,19-20" (reprinted in *Evangelica II*, pp. 205-225, with Additional Note, 226). On Jn 12,1-8 (pp. 126-206; 367-410: notes), compare, in this volume, the contributions by C. Breytenbach and I. Dunderberg.

14. B. DE SOLAGES, *Jean et les Synoptiques*, Leiden, 1979. Cf. F. NEIRYNCK, in *ETL* 56 (1980) 176-179. See below, n. 15 (D.M. Smith) and n. 69 (end). — I mention here also É. DELEBECQUE, *Évangile de Jean. Texte traduit et annoté* (Cahiers de la Revue Biblique, 23), Paris, 1987. Cf. p. 17: "il reste à Jean à faire une sélection parmi les actes qu'ils [les Synoptiques] ont relatés, selon l'ordre qu'il tient d'une mémoire jamais défaillante"; n. 3: "Jean évite de répéter ce qui est dans les Synoptiques".

15. F. NEIRYNCK (avec la collaboration de J. DELOBEL, T. SNOY, G. VAN BELLE, F. VAN SEGBROECK), *Jean et les Synoptiques. Examen critique de l'exégèse de M.-É. Boismard* (BETL, 49), Leuven, 1979. The chapters I-VI (pp. 3-120) are reprinted from *ETL* 55 (1977) 363-478 ("L'évangile de Jean. Examen critique du commentaire de M.-É. Boismard et A. Lamouille"). — Cf. M. SABBE, *John and the Synoptists: Neirynck vs.*

Some recent Introductions to the New Testament continue to speak
| of the consensus on John's independence of the Synoptic Gospels and
simply mention one or two exceptions to that consensus[16]. The names of
a few more European scholars can be collected from monographs on
particular topics and from the periodical literature. I begin with the latest one, M. Hengel (1989), for whom "this old disputed question now
seems ... to be coming closer to a consensus"[17]: "As for dependence on
the Synoptics, we are to presuppose knowledge of them and sometimes
also their direct influence—but in a very free manner"[18]. Without leaving the Tübingen area, we note that K.T. Kleinknecht (1985), in partial
agreement with M. Sabbe's article on the Footwashing[19], emphasizes
"die Kontinuität mit den synoptischen Evangelien auch im Aufbau",
and concludes "daß man Joh 13 auch als eine produktive re-lecture von
Mk 14 (/ Mt 26) und Lk 22 nachvollziehen kann, als ein Neuerzählen
der Überlieferung, das sich auf sie zurückbezieht, ohne sich von
ihr abhängig zu machen"; "Joh geht auf dem bei Lk vorgezeichneten

Boismard, in ETL 56 (1980) 125-131 (= Studia Neotestamentica, n. 2, pp. 389-395; Additional Note, 396-397); D.M. SMITH, John and the Synoptics, in Biblica 63 (1982) 102-113
(pp. 102-106: de Solages; 106-111: Neirynck); reprinted in ID., Johannine Christianity.
Essays on Its Settings, Sources, and Theology, Columbia, SC, 1984, pp. 128-144 ("John
and the Synoptics: de Solages and Neirynck").
    16. R.F. COLLINS, Introduction to the New Testament, Garden City, NY, 1983, p. 146:
"Demurrers to the consensus have been raised by Frans Neirynck and a number of North
American scholars..."; E.D. FREED, The New Testament. A Critical Introduction, Bel-
mont, CA, 1986, p. 213, n. 8: "Among exceptions to this consensus are the views of C.K.
Barrett of Durham, England, and F. Neirynck and M. Sabbe of the University of Leuven
in Belgium". Cf. J. BEUTLER, Méthodes et problèmes de la recherche johannique
aujourd'hui [1987], in J.-D. KAESTLI, et al. (eds.), La communauté johannique et son histoire (Le Monde de la Bible), Genève, 1990, pp. 15-38, esp. p. 17: "La première
hypothèse, à savoir que l'évangéliste lui-même aurait employé les évangiles synoptiques
lors de la rédaction de son texte, est représentée ... par deux grandes variantes: celle de
M.-É. Boismard et de ses collaborateurs de Jérusalem d'une part; celle de F. Neirynck et
de ses collègues et collaborateurs de Louvain d'autre part". See also R.T. FORTNA, The
Fourth Gospel and Its Predecessor. From Narrative Source to Present Gospel, Philadelphia, 1988, pp. 216-218: "The Source and the Synoptic Gospels", esp. p. 217, n. 526:
"Since then [1975] the Leuven school has led the way in usefully questioning what had
become an unconsidered assumption in Johannine studies".
    17. M. HENGEL, The Johannine Question, London-Philadelphia, 1989, p. 193, n. 8.
    18. Ibid., p. 91. "F. Neirynck [JeanSyn] presupposes the use of all three Synoptic
Gospels by John and at the same time stresses 'the originality with which the evangelist
edits his work, borrowing various elements from his sources, but combining them and
transposing them in his own way' (286). We would need to add the fact that the Synoptic material which he takes over has usually gone through the transforming filter of his
own oral teaching" (p. 194, n. 8; cf. p. 75). See also below, nn. 86-88, 126.
    19. M. SABBE, The Footwashing in Jn 13 and Its Relation to the Synoptic Gospels, in
ETL 58 (1982) 279-308 (cf. Kleinknecht's reference, Johannes 13, pp. 363-364); now
reprinted in Studia Neotestamentica (n. 2), pp. 409-438 (Additional Note, 439-441). See
also below, nn. 70 and 210.

Weg einen Schritt weiter als Lk"[20]. And this has | been taken up by P. Stuhlmacher (1988): "Kleinknechts These ... bestätigt sich auch für Joh 6"[21]. No less significant is the observation made by G. Strecker in his essay on the Johannine school (1986): "Von größter Bedeutung ist in diesem Zusammenhang eine Beobachtung, die durch die Anwendung der redaktionsgeschichtlichen Methode auf das vierte Evangelium erneut ins Bewußtsein gerückt worden ist, daß nämlich der Verfasser des Johannesevangeliums nicht einfach vorsynoptische Traditionen verarbeitete, sondern die synoptischen Evangelien insgesamt oder teilweise voraussetzt"[22]. For U. Schnelle (1987), it is most improbable that the gospel genre was created by John independently of Mark[23]. "In der neueren Forschung wird wieder zu Recht vermehrt mit einer Kenntnis der Synoptiker durch Johannes gerechnet"[24]; in particular, verbal agreements in the feeding story (Jn 6,1-15) and its combination with the walking on the sea suggest literary dependence on Mark: "Speisung und Seewandel lassen erkennen, daß die joh. Tradition das Markusevangelium kannte, so daß auch für den Evangelisten diese Annahme nicht abwegig ist"[25].

R. Baum-Bodenbender's dissertation on the passion narrative (1984, under L. Schenke) proposes an alternative to Dauer's hypothesis: "die Annahme einer *literarischen* Beziehung zwischen Joh und die Synoptikern (ist) unausweichlich"[26]; she situates the synoptic influences on the

---

20. K.T. KLEINKNECHT, *Johannes 13, die Synoptiker und die "Methode" der johanneischen Evangelienüberlieferung*, in *ZTK* 82 (1985) 361-388, pp. 384, 385. Cf. p. 382: "eine Erklärung der angesprochenen Konvergenzen, Übereinstimmungen und Berührungen scheint mir ausgesprochen schwierig, wenn man die Benutzung der markinischen, (vor)lukanischen (und evtl. auch der matthäischen) Paralleltexte nicht unterstellt" (see also *ibid.*, n. 67, on the "literarische Einheitlichkeit des Kapitels"). Cf. below, n. 114.

21. P. STUHLMACHER, *Jesus von Nazareth - Christus des Glaubens*, Stuttgart, 1988, pp. 87-94 ("Die johanneische Mahltradition"), esp. pp. 88-89 (and 104, n. 28). Cf. p. 94: "die Einsicht, daß Johannes in beiden Kapiteln [Jn 13 und 6] von einer Neubearbeitung der lukanischen und markinischen Abendmahlstradition ausgeht" (Jn 6,51b: cf. Lk 22,19; Jn 6,53ff.: Mk 14,24).

22. G. STRECKER, *Die Anfänge der johanneischen Schule*, in *NTS* 32 (1986) 31-47, p. 42; and p. 46, n. 47 (with reference to *JohnSyn* and *JeanSyn*).

23. U. SCHNELLE, *Antidoketische Christologie im Johannesevangelium* (FRLANT, 44), Göttingen, 1987, pp. 250-251.

24. *Ibid.*, p. 130, n. 226 (with reference to *JohnSyn* and *JeanSyn*).

25. *Ibid.*, p. 130. See also p. 170: "traditionsgeschichtlich und literarisch von Mk 6,32-52 abhängig". Cf. my *JohnSyn*, p. 89, with reference to the doctoral dissertations by T. Snoy (1967: editorial connection of the stories in Mark) and J. Konings (1972: Johannine dependence). — See now also U. SCHNELLE, *Perspektiven der Johannesexegese*, in *SNTU* 15 (1990) 59-72, esp. p. 72: "Einer Neubestimmung bedarf die Stellung des Johannesevangeliums zu den Synoptikern ..." (with reference to *JeanSyn*).

26. R. BAUM-BODENBENDER, *Hoheit in Niedrigkeit. Johanneische Christologie im Prozeß Jesu vor Pilatus (Joh 18,28–19,16a)* (Forschung zur Bibel, 49), Würzburg, 1984

level of the Johannine redaction and not on that of the pre-Johannine source[27]. L. Schenke likewise reckons with synoptic influence in a study on Jn 6,1-25[28].

| Last but not least I should mention H. Thyen, who at the Colloquium in 1975 made known his conviction that the Johannine redaction was influenced by Luke in Jn 21[29] and supported the view that Lk 24,12 forms the basis (*Grundlage*) of Jn 20,2-10[30]. He added in the published text: "M.E. bedarf die Frage 'Johannes und die Synoptiker' unter dieser Perspektive dringend erneuter Untersuchung"[31]. As the author of the article *Johannesevangelium* in *TRE* (1988) he could now write: "so bahnt sich doch ein neuer Konsensus darüber an, daß jedenfalls derjenige, dem wir das Evangelium in seiner überlieferten Gestalt verdanken, die Synoptiker kannte und benutzte"[32].

(Diss., Mainz, 1984), p. 217. Cf. F. NEIRYNCK, in *ETL* 62 (1986) 427-430. See below, n. 70.

27. *Ibid.*, p. 218: "gerade die Verse, in denen eine besonders *enge Verbindung zwischen Joh und den Synoptikern* festzustellen ist (also neben 18,39–19,6 in 18,28a.b.29b.30.35b; 19,11b.12.16a), wurden bei der literarkritischen Analyse des Textes als *redaktionelle Schicht B* identifiziert". See also pp. 227-228, and 10-16 (on A. Dauer). For a reply, cf. A. DAUER, in *Theologische Revue* 81 (1985) 464-466.

On the passion narrative, compare T.A. MOHR, *Markus- und Johannespassion. Redaktions- und traditionsgeschichtliche Untersuchung der Markinischen und Johanneischen Passionstradition* (ATANT, 70), Zürich, 1982 (Diss., Basel, 1980): the post-Johannine redaction (13,36-38; 16,32; 18,15-18.25-27; 20,2-11a; 21: cf. p. 407) depends on the Synoptics; see esp. pp. 225 (13,36-38: par. Lk 22,31-34); 277 (18,15-18.25-27: "in Angleichung an die Syn."; "von diesen höchstwahrscheinlich abhängig", with reference to G. Klein and G. Schneider in n. 7); 394 (20,9: "unjoh. sc. lkn."). But see also p. 250: "Eine Abhängigkeit des joh. Textes von den Syn. scheint mir in V 11 vorzuliegen. Dass Joh die Syn. kannte und bewusst ergänzte bzw. korrigierte, wird auch an ... [18,4-9] greifbar" (the Evangelist's dependence?).

28. L. SCHENKE, *Das Szenarium von Joh 6,1-25*, in *TriererTZ* 92 (1983) 191-203. On Jn 6,1-15, see also J.-M. SEVRIN, *L'écriture du IVᵉ évangile comme phénomène de réception: L'exemple de Jn 6*, in ID. (ed.), *The New Testament in Early Christianity* (BETL, 86), Leuven, 1989, pp. 69-83, esp. 77-81: "cette hypothèse [Johannine dependence] fait mieux ressortir les caractères propres de la rédaction johannique" (p. 77); "Il n'est donc point nécessaire à l'intelligence du texte de supposer d'autres sources que les synoptiques" (p. 81).

29. H. THYEN, *Entwicklungen innerhalb der johanneischen Theologie und Kirche im Spiegel von Joh. 21 und der Lieblingsjüngertexte des Evangeliums*, in *L'Évangile de Jean* (n. 1), 1977, pp. 259-299, esp. p. 263 (Lk 5,1-11; 24,41). See also *TR* 42 (1977) 213-261: "Joh 21 und die Lieblingsjüngertexte des Evangeliums", esp. p. 247 (see also pp. 226-227, 234).

30. *Entwicklungen*, p. 289; *TR* 42 (1977), pp. 251-252.

31. *Entwicklungen*, p. 289, n. 79; *TR* 42 (1977), p. 252.

32. *Johannesevangelium*, in *TRE* 17 (1988) 200-225, esp. p. 208. See also p. 214 (knowledge of the Synoptics), and 215: "Als Datierungsanhalt bleibt (darum) nur die Abfassung des lukanischen Werkes, das Johannes kennt und an einigen Stellen sicher benutzt". Compare M. DE JONGE, *The Beloved Disciple and the Date of the Gospel of John*, in E. BEST – R. McL. WILSON (eds.), *Text and Interpretation*. FS M. Black,

My list is not complete, but this can suffice to show that Johannine dependence on the Synoptics is not an idiosyncrasy of Leuven. Those who call it the thesis of "the Leuven school" should realize that this I "school" has its ramifications in Heidelberg, Mainz, Göttingen, Erlangen, Tübingen, and elsewhere[33]. From his earlier work on the Gospel of John, E. Haenchen († 1975) was known to us as the propagator of P. Gardner-Smith in Germany (1955, 1959). In the posthumous publication of his papers (edited by U. Busse, 1980), this is mixed up with an approach that, at least with regard to Jn 20,2-10 and 21,1-14, scarcely differs from that of H. Thyen (1977): the redactor (*Ergänzer*) knew the Gospel of Luke[34]. A similar

Cambridge, 1979, pp. 99-114, esp. 113, n. 4: "The most promising approach may well be a new study of the literary dependence of the Fourth Gospel on the Synoptics [with reference to *JohnSyn*]... Even if this dependence cannot be proved in all cases where parallels occur, a few clear instances are sufficient to prove the case".

33. U. BORSE, *Der Evangelist als Verfasser der Emmauserzählung*, in *SNTU* 12 (1987) 35-67, p. 39, n. 11: "Demgegenüber scheint mir der Verfasser die synoptischen Evangelien nicht nur gekannt, sondern auch eingesehen zu haben. Eine Parallele wie Lk 24,12; Joh 20,3-6.10 setzt m. E. literarische Abhängigkeit voraus" (with reference to *JohnSyn*). See also p. 42, n. 26: Jn 20,19-29 ("Abhängigkeit von Lk ... wäre zu prüfen"); p. 43, n. 28: Jn 20,14-18 ("vielleicht ... eine direkte Abhängigkeit von Mt"); p. 44: Jn 20,17 ("Eine Beeinflussung dürfte von Mt aus in Richting Joh gehen", with reference to my contributions in *NTS* 15, 1969; 30, 1984).

A. ENNULAT, *Die 'Minor Agreements' – ein Diskussionsbeitrag zur Erklärung einer offenen Frage des synoptischen Problems*, Diss. (under U. Luz), Bern, 1990, p. 20: "Ich neige am ehesten der Position von Neirynck zu, der eine Abhängigkeit des Joh von den Synoptikern vertritt".

P. DSCHULNIGG, *Sprache, Redaktion und Intention des Markus-Evangeliums. Eigentümlichkeiten der Sprache des Markus-Evangeliums und ihre Bedeutung für die Redaktionskritik* (SBB, 11), Stuttgart, 1984, ²1986 (Diss., Luzern, under E. Ruckstuhl). Cf. pp. 311-316: "Wir erachten es ... als wahrscheinlich, dass der Verfasser des Joh das Mk gekannt hat" (p. 313); he notes the following instances of Markan *Sprachmerkmale* with relevant parallels in John: no. 88 πρωῒ 20,1 (Mk 16,2); 18,28 (cf. Mk 15,1); no. 151 κλάσμα 6,12.13 (Mk 6,45); no. 202 περιτίθημι 19,29 (Mk 15,36); no. 243 ἄνεμος 6,18 (Mk 6,48); no. 257 διδόναι (τοῖς) πτωχοῖς 12,5 (Mk 14,5), cf. 13,29; no. 262 καθίζειν ἐπί + acc 12,14 (Mk 11,7). "Das Vorkommen dieser Wörter und Wendungen an Parallelen des Joh spricht insgesamt wohl dafür..., dass der Verfasser des Joh das Mk gekannt hat" (pp. 315-316; Mark rather than Matthew: cf. p. 683, n. 130). See now E. RUCKSTUHL – P. DSCHULNIGG, *Stilkritik und Verfasserfrage im Johannesevangelium* (NTOA, 17), Freiburg, Schw. - Göttingen, 1991, pp. 15-16 ("Setzt das Joh die Kenntnis synopt. Evv. voraus?"), esp. p. 16: "Es scheint nun aber, dass die einfachere Annahme einer direkten Kenntnis der Synoptiker durch den Verfasser des Joh erneut namhafte Unterstützung gewinnt. Hier wären mehrere Untersuchungen von Neirynck (1977ff) zu erwähnen und Sabbe (1977), de Solages (1979) und Thyen (1988) zu nennen. Vielleicht zeichnet sich so gegen Ende unseres Jh. ein erneuter Meinungsumschwung in dieser Frage ab, der einen besser begründeten Anschluss an die Annahmen am Beginn des 20. Jh. ermöglicht".

34. E. HAENCHEN, *Das Johannesevangelium*. Ein Kommentar aus den nachgelassenen Manuskripten herausgegeben von U. BUSSE, Tübingen, 1980 (cf. U. BUSSE, in *ETL* 57, 1981, 125-143); ET, Philadelphia, 2 vols., 1984. On the "insertion" of Jn 20,2-10, see pp. 568-569: Lk 24,12.24 was "die Anregung" (p. 568), "ein Anknüpfungspunkt"

view has been developed more recently by Busse's student J. Kügler[35]. My own paper at the Leuven meeting of SNTS in 1982 was an attempt to show that the Synoptic influence in Jn 20 cannot be restricted to interpolations, 20,2-10 (for Thyen, *et al.*), or 20,11b-14a (for Boismard, *et al.*): "It may have been determinative for the whole of the composition of Jn 20,1-18. The Johannine writer who depends on the Synoptics is not a secondary redactor but none other than the Fourth Evangelist"[36]. At

(p. 602), "der Anlaß" (p. 604). Other insertions "von dem mit der synoptischen Tradition vertrauten Ergänzer" are 20,12 (p. 570) and 20,23 (p. 573); see also 19,29 (p. 552). On Jn 21,1-14 (par. Lk 5,1-11), see p. 585: "Der Autor unseres Kapitels dürfte mindestens das Lukasevangelium gekannt haben".

The Evangelist's dependence on the Synoptics is rejected by Haenchen: "Der Evangelist hat bei den Erzählungsstücken keines der drei anderen kanonischen Evangelien benutzt" (p. 102; cf. p. 80). Note, however, C.K. Barrett's recent comment, in "Wichtige neuere Beiträge zum Verständnis des vierten Evangeliums" (*Das Evangelium nach Johannes*, 1990, 159-172): "Haenchen geht meiner Meinung nach zu schnell über den Beitrag der synoptischen Evangelien zum vierten Evangelium hinweg. ... Zum Redenstoff macht er geltend, daß der Evangelist 'in den Reden selbst zu Wort' kommt. Diese Ansicht scheint mir soweit gerechtfertigt. Aber joh Denken schwappt von den Reden auch in die Erzählungen über; und wenn man dies einmal erkennt, dann bekommt die ganze Frage nach 'Johannes und den Synoptikern' ein neues Gesicht" (p. 160; with n. 175: reference to my contributions).

35. J. KÜGLER, *Der Jünger, den Jesus liebte. Literarische, theologische und historische Untersuchungen zu einer Schlüsselgestalt johanneischer Theologie und Geschichte* (SBB, 16), Stuttgart, 1988: he observes similarities with the Synoptics in Jn 6 (p. 229) and Jn 13 (p. 179), not necessarily implying knowledge of the Synoptics (p. 176, ctr. M. Sabbe's "wagehalsige Behauptung", and p. 178, ctr. H. Thyen), but accepts the dependence on the Gospel of Luke in Jn 20,2-10 (par. Lk 24,12: pp. 347-348, with reference to my argument in *NTS* 1984) and in Jn 21,1-14 (par. Lk 5,1-11 and 24,13-35: pp. 415-417), in accord with H. Thyen (1977): "War schon in Joh 6 und Joh 13 eine besondere Nähe der redaktionellen Textschicht zu synoptischen Texten aufgefallen, so ergab sich in Joh 20 die Notwendigkeit, eine *Kenntnis des Lk* anzunehmen. Mit dieser Annahme konnte auch die Entstehungsgeschichte von Joh 21,1-14 hinreichend erklärt werden" (p. 418).

36. F. NEIRYNCK, *John and the Synoptics: The Empty Tomb Stories*, in *NTS* 30 (1984) 161-187 (quotation from the conclusion, p. 179); reprinted in *Evangelica II*, pp. 571-597 (esp. 597), with Additional Note, 597-600. On Jn 20,19-20, see my *Lc 24,36-43* (1985); cf. above, n. 13. — With regard to my view on the composition of Jn 20,1-18 ("convincing" for C.K. Barrett, letter of 7 July 1984), I mention here that explicit support came from J.D. Crossan (Chicago) and M.D. Goulder (Birmingham).

J.D. CROSSAN, *Four Other Gospels. Shadows on the Contours of Canon*, Minneapolis, MN, 1985, pp. 162-164; *The Cross that Spoke. The Origins of the Passion Narrative*, San Francisco, CA, 1988, pp. 281-283. See also, already in 1976, *Empty Tomb and Absent Lord (Mark 16:1-8)*, in *The Passion in Mark* (n. 8), pp. 135-152, esp. 139, 142, 144 (on the influence of Mt 28,9-10 on Jn 20,14-18; with reference to my *Les femmes au tombeau*, 1969). Crossan's suggestion of dependence on the Johannine GS in Lk 24,1-11.12 (1976, pp. 141 and 142) is corrected in his later studies. Regarding "the first gospel" in the extra-canonical Gospel of Peter, see my reservations in *The Apocryphal Gospels and the Gospel of Mark*, in J.-M. SEVRIN (ed.), *The New Testament in Early Christianity* (BETL, 86), Leuven, 1989, pp. 123-175 (= *Evangelica II*, pp. 715-767, with Additional Notes, 768-772).

the Dublin meeting in 1989, in my paper on *John 21*, | I investigated the Lukan influences in 21,1-14[37]. This last topic has been pursued in 1990 in the Seminar on John at the SNTS meeting in Milan[38] and in some of the papers at our Colloquium[39].

It is clear enough that the tone has changed in recent surveys of Johannine studies. In 1978 D.A. Carson, unaware of some recent developments, could write: "A few scholars believe that John depends on Mark, Luke, or both. ... More commonly, scholars follow the line of P. Gardner-Smith"[40]. In 1983 he reported: "But now the critical orthodoxy is being assailed", and: "it is quite clear that this question [John and the Synoptics] will dominate a certain amount of scholarship on John for some time to come"[41]. A new statement followed in his 1989 survey: "The relation of the fourth gospel to the synoptics is ripe for a fresh examination, based especially on contributions by Barrett and Neirynck.

M.D. GOULDER, *Luke. A New Paradigm* (JSNT SS, 20), Sheffield, 1989, esp. 323-326 (Lk 5,1-11) and 776-777 (Lk 24,12); cf. pp. 24-25. See already his *Midrash and Lection in Matthew*, London, 1974, p. 392: "I suppose that John had read all the Synoptic Gospels, and was writing a concentrated midrashic version of his own"; and *From Ministry to Passion in John and Luke*, in NTS 29 (1983) 561-568 (on Jn 12,44ff.).

A critical reaction came from D. Zeller, 1986 (cf. below, nn. 62 and 162) and, regarding the influence of Mt 28,9-10, from J. Kügler, 1988 (but see above, n. 35, on Lk 24,12); cf. below, n. 162.

37. *John 21*, in NTS 36 (1990) 321-336; reprinted in *Evangelica II*, pp. 601-616, with Additional Note, 616. On Jn 21,1-14, see already *JeanSyn*, 1979, pp. 122-160 (esp. 140-144: "Jn 21 et Lc 5,1-11"); and *Note sur Jn 21,14*, in ETL 64 (1988) 429-432 (= *Evangelica II*, pp. 689-692).

38. Cf. W. SCHENK, *Interne Strukturierungen im Schlußsegment Joh 21:* Ἐπίλογος, Σατυρικόν, Συγγραφή (Seminar paper), Section 2: "Narrative Interaktionsstrukturen" (p. 7 and n. 57: "die kombinatorische Technik der Synoptiker-Collage", Schenk's working hypothesis); see already *JohnSyn*, p. 80, n. 30 (his study on the passion narrative). P. HOFRICHTER, *Joh 21 im Makrotext des Vierten Evangeliums* (Seminar Paper), Section 2.2: "Die Petrus-Schicht" (p. 10: "Das Muster der Erscheinung beim Fischfang [pseudo-johanneisch!] ist vermutlich Lukas 5,1-11"; p. 13: "Die Frage Jesu nach einer Speise [v. 5] hat ein Vorbild in der Erscheinungsgeschichte Lk 24,41").

39. Cf. R.T. FORTNA, *Diachronic/Synchronic: Reading Jn 21 and Lk 5*; and the short papers by C. Bammel and B. Standaert.

40. D.A. CARSON, *Current Source Criticism of the Fourth Gospel: Some Methodological Questions*, in JBL 97 (1978) 411-429, p. 411.

41. *Recent Literature on the Fourth Gospel: Some Reflections*, in Themelios 9 (1983) 8-18, p. 11. — Compare, in the same year, R. KYSAR, *The Gospel of John in Current Research*, in Religious Studies Review 9 (1983) 314-323, esp. pp. 315-316: "the issue of the relationship between John and the synoptics is once again a hotly debated question". Contrast his *The Fourth Evangelist and His Gospel*, Minneapolis, MN, 1975, pp. 54-66 (p. 59: "the demise of efforts to demonstrate literary dependence of John upon the synoptics"); *The Fourth Gospel. A Report on Recent Research* [until 1977], in ANRW II.25.3 (1985) 2389-2480, esp. pp. 2407-2411 (2407). Kysar's 1983 survey is the latest assessment that is mentioned by J. Ashton (1991): "John's dependence upon one or more of the Synoptics ... is held today by a number of experts, including J. Blinzler, C.K. Barrett, and F. Neirynck" (n. 39 refers to their works published in 1965, 1974, 1977). Cf. J. ASHTON, *Understanding the Fourth Gospel*, Oxford, 1991, p. 81.

Since so many reconstructions have depended on the assumption of a Johannine tradition hermetically sealed off from the rest of the church, the potential for reshaping Johannine scholarship is considerable"[42]. In his recent commentary (1991) he now writes: "My views on the dating and authorship of the various Gospels, coupled with the alignment of such literary evidence as we have (in particular the parallels between John and Mark, and to some extent between John and Luke), suggest that John had read Mark, and probably | Luke. It is not impossible that he read Matthew, but that is harder to prove"[43]. But he adds his reservations: "if he had them before him as he wrote, he did not consult them, or at least he did *not* make *verbatim use* of them. John wrote his own book"[44].

Over a number of years, D.M. Smith has been an attentive observer and promoter of the study of "John and the Synoptics". Up to 1975 he speaks of a growing consensus among Johannine scholars in the generation following Gardner-Smith[45]. In his SNTS paper of 1979, however, he refers to my 1975 (1977) article, devoted, he says, "to a sharp attack upon the grounds for such a consensus. And Neirynck is not alone"[46]: "The consensus did not rest long"[47]. It is said in the conclusion: "I am beginning to be able to conceive of a scenario in which John knew, or knew of, the synoptics and yet produced so dissimilar a gospel as the one which now follows them in the New Testament. ... Possibly the Fourth Gospel can be adequately explained without primary or fundamental reference to the synoptic gospels, but also without denying the Fourth Evangelist's awareness of them"[48]. I thought I could welcome "this very prudently formulated statement" as "somewhat of a semi-conversion"[49]. In the same conclusion it was also said: "The influence of the synoptics was at best secondary and perhaps in some cases even second-hand", but he added: this is not "the position being developed by Neirynck and his school"[50]. In my reexamination of "the empty tomb stories" in 1982 (1984) I tried to show how, at least in Jn 20,1-18, the influence of the synoptics is far from "secondary" or "even second-hand"[51]. In the same year, Smith wrote a reply in the Preface to his collected

42. *Selected Recent Studies of the Fourth Gospel*, in *Themelios* 14 (1989) 57-64, p. 64.

43. *The Gospel according to John*, Leicester - Grand Rapids, MI, 1991, pp. 49-58: "The relation between the Fourth Gospel and the Synoptics", esp. p. 51.

44. *Ibid.* (my emphasis). Compare D.M. SMITH, *Johannine Studies*, 1989 (below, n. 55), p. 281: "In that case [i.e., if John knew the Synoptics] one might well suppose that in composing his Gospel the Fourth Evangelist chose, for whatever reason, largely to go his own way"; J. ASHTON, 1991 (n. 41), p. 81: "although John almost certainly knew Mark, and possibly Matthew and Luke as well, his differences from the Synoptists are so great that they cannot be satisfactorily explained by a simple theory of literary dependence".

45. Cf. *JohnSyn*, p. 73 (= 366), n. 1.

46. *John and the Synoptics: Some Dimensions of the Problem*, in *NTS* 26 (1979-80) 425-444, p. 426 (= *Johannine Christianity*, 1984, pp. 145-172, esp. 147).

47. *Ibid.* Compare now his comment during the 1990 Colloquium: "The consensus is gone!" (reported by A. Denaux, in *ETL* 67, 1991, p. 196).

48. *Some Dimensions*, pp. 443-444 (= 170-171).

49. *NTS* 30 (1984), p. 161 (= *Evangelica II*, p. 572).

50. *Some Dimensions*, p. 443 (= 170-171), n. 40, referring to *Jean et les Synoptiques*, 1979. Cf. above, n. 15, the reference to Smith's detailed analysis of the book (1982).

51. Cf. above, n. 36.

essays: "Despite my willingness to concede that John may have known one or more of the synoptics (a possibility which I think I have never denied), I remain essentially unconverted to the position of Neirynck, whose efforts to understand John as essentially derivative from the synoptics seem to me to be much more plausible in the case of certain episodes from the passion and resurrection narratives than on consideration of the gospel as a whole. Thus I cannot accept his description of me as semi-converted; I fear I remain at I most among the *sebomenoi* in the weaker sense of that term!"[52]. The Preface ends, however, with a notable observation on R.A. Culpepper's literary-critical approach: "on the basis of Culpepper's analysis one could argue for John's knowledge of the other gospels. The implied reader knows the story of Jesus, or major aspects and parts of it (pp. 222f.). As *we* read John, we know these things from the synoptic gospels. Whether John's first readers knew them from that, or another, source is a good, and moot, question"[53]. More recently, this reference to Culpepper appears again in a critical presentation of B.S. Childs's "canonical" exegesis[54]. Two new survey articles were published in 1989 and 1990 (without taking into account work later than 1984): a general survey of "Johannine Studies", with a two-page passage on Johannine-Synoptic relations: "in very recent years there has appeared a vigorous, renewed advocacy of John's knowledge of one or more of the Synoptics"[55]; and, more significantly, a specific study of "John and the Synoptics" and the problem of "faith and history"[56].

52. *Johannine Christianity*, p. xiii. Cf. my review in *ETL* 61 (1985) 400-402.

53. *Ibid.*, p. xv.

54. *John, the Synoptics, and the Canonical Approach to Exegesis*, in G.F. HAWTHORNE – O. BETZ (eds.), *Tradition and Interpretation in the New Testament*. FS E.E. Ellis, Grand Rapids, MI - Tübingen, 1987, pp. 167-180, esp. 169 and 179, n. 16: cf. R.A. CULPEPPER, *Anatomy of the Fourth Gospel*, 1983, pp. 59, 213-216, 222.

55. *Johannine Studies*, in E.J. EPP – G.W. MACRAE (eds.), *The New Testament and Its Modern Interpreters* (SBL: The Bible and Its Modern Interpreters, 3), Philadelphia-Atlanta, 1989, pp. 271-296, esp. 280. *Ibid.*, pp. 280-281: "The whole question of John's relationship to the Synoptic Gospels may be more difficult or at least capable of more permutations than at first appears. ... In deciding whether John knew the Marcan or other synoptic accounts, a crucial consideration may well be whether or not evidence of Marcan or other synoptic redaction can be found in John".

56. *John and the Synoptics in Light of the Problem of Faith and History*, in J.T. CARROLL – C.H. COSGROVE – E.E. JOHNSON, *Faith and History*. FS P.W. Meyer, Atlanta, GA, 1990, pp. 74-89. The passage on the resurrection narratives deserves to be quoted in full: "With respect to the resurrection narratives an even more striking phenomenon may be observed. On the one hand, every Johannine resurrection narrative has a synoptic parallel. On the other, the discovery of the empty tomb aside, no synoptic resurrection narrative has a parallel in another synoptic gospel. There is an interesting general analogy between the Johannine resurrection narratives and the specious longer ending of Mark (16:9-20). That longer ending seems to gather together and summarize what is reported in the other canonical gospels. John's resurrection narratives could be viewed as a conflation and/or expansion of those found in the synoptics. Even John 21:1-14 has a non-resurrection parallel in Luke 5:1-11. Yet that episode also answers to the anticipation of a resurrection appearance in Galilee raised by Mark 14:28 and 16:7. Mark, of course, contains no such story. To be sure, John 20:26-29 has no synoptic parallel, but it is probably a doublet of 20:19-23 (par. Luke 24:36-43). John 21:15-23 also appears to lack any synoptic parallel, but it may be viewed as the Johannine continuation of 21:1-14. Moreover, it corresponds to the expectation aroused by the singling out of Peter in Mark 16:7, as well as to the

At the end of this Introduction, I return once more to 1975 and conclude with a clarification on my own position. You may have read I that "F. Neirynck rejects theories of 'unknown' and 'hypothetical' sources behind John, whether they are supposed to be written or oral" (P. Borgen, 1987)[57]. The truth is that I am skeptical with regard to the classic source theories such as the signs source and a continuous pre-Johannine passion narrative[58], or the combination of both in a *Grundschrift* or signs gospel[59]. But I am not aware that I ever gave such an exclusiveness to the Synoptic Gospels as to exclude John's use of oral-tradition or source material. In my reply to Dauer (1975) I expressly made the observation that "direct dependence on the Synoptic Gospels does not preclude the possibility of supplementary information"[60]. The phrase "not the

clear indication of the restoration of Peter and his task in Luke 22:31-32. Thus on the basis of the resurrection narratives alone there would be some reason to contend that John is a conflation of the synoptic gospels" (pp. 84-85).

57. P. BORGEN, *John and the Synoptics: Can Paul Offer Help?*, in G.F. HAWTHORNE – O. BETZ (eds.), *Tradition and Interpretation in the New Testament*. FS E.E. Ellis, Grand Rapids, MI - Tübingen, 1987, pp. 80-94, esp. 80. The published text is the first part of the paper P. Borgen submitted to the Jerusalem Conference in 1984. Cf. D.L. DUNGAN (ed.), *The Interrelations of the Gospels. A Symposium led by M.-É. Boismard - W.R. Farmer - F. Neirynck, Jerusalem 1984* (BETL, 95), Leuven, 1990, pp. 408-437, esp. 409 (with a slight variation in the sentence quoted above: "F. Neirynck and M. Sabbe"). See also pp. 438-450: F. NEIRYNCK, *John and the Synoptics: Response to P. Borgen*. This Reply is reprinted in *Evangelica II*, pp. 699-711: *John 5,1-18 and the Gospel of Mark. A Response to P. Borgen* (with Additional Note, pp. 711-712).

See also R.T. FORTNA, *The Fourth Gospel*, 1988 (cf. above, n. 16), p. 46, n. 95: "Neirynck holds here [1,43] *as everywhere* that 4E is dependent not on any pre-Johannine source, but simply on the Synoptics" (italics mine); J. BEUTLER, *Méthodes*, 1990 (cf. above, n. 16), p. 19: "(les) travaux de Neirynck ... contribuent à étayer sa propre thèse, selon laquelle les synoptiques constituent la seule source de Jn". Compare Beutler's own position: "on peut se rallier à l'opinion de D.M. Smith pour qui une influence des évangiles synoptiques sur la couche principale du quatrième évangile est redevenue aujourd'hui plus vraisemblable. Cela ne signifie pas pour autant que les synoptiques ont dû être la seule source du quatrième évangile" (p. 21).

58. See, e.g., J. BECKER, *Das Evangelium nach Johannes* (ÖTK, 4/1-2), Gütersloh, 1979, 1981. On John and the Synoptics, see also *Aus der Literatur zum Johannesevangelium (1978-1980)*, in *TR* 47 (1982) 279-301, pp. 289-294: "Johannes und die Synoptiker" (esp. p. 292); *Das Johannesevangelium im Streit der Methoden (1980-1986)*, in *TR* 51 (1986) 1-78, pp. 21-28: "Der Ansatz beim Verhältnis zu den Synoptikern" (esp. pp. 22-24).

On the signs source, see my *JeanSyn*, pp. 121-174 ("Les trois signes en Galilée"); *De semeia-bron in het vierde evangelie. Kritiek van een hypothese* (1983), reprinted in English translation in *Evangelica II*, pp. 651-677: *The Signs Source in the Fourth Gospel. A Critique of the Hypothesis* (with Additional Note, pp. 677-678).

59. R.T. FORTNA, *The Fourth Gospel* (n. 16). See now also U.C. VON WAHLDE, *The Earliest Version of John's Gospel. Recovering the Gospel of Signs*, Wilmington, DE, 1989; L. COPE, *The Earliest Gospel Was the "Signs Gospel"*, in E.P. SANDERS (ed.), *Jesus, the Gospels, and the Church*. FS W.R. Farmer, Macon, GA, 1987, pp. 17-24.

60. *JohnSyn*, p. 94 (= *Evangelica*, 1982, p. 386).

sources of the Synoptic Gospels but the Synoptic Gospels themselves" has been used with reference to Jn 20,1-18[61], and I continue to regard this section as a pertinent test case for the thesis of Johannine dependence. I Another clarification concerns the objection that in my approach the fourth evangelist wrote his gospel as "ein Schreibtischgelehrte, [der] zwischen den dreien kurzfristig hin- und herpendelnd, sein Evangelium schrieb" (J. Becker, 1986)[62]. First of all, we can say, I think, that the phenomenon of conflation and harmonization is already found in the Synoptic Gospels (in overlappings of Mark and Q) and that it is undeniably one of the characteristics of the early use of the canonical gospels in the apocryphal literature[63]. The identity of the fourth evangelist is unknown to me, but, if we can suppose that he was a teacher and preacher in his community who knew the earlier gospels, conflation and harmonization may have been quite natural to him.

D.M. Smith recently declared that "it is not feasible to do redaction criticism on the premise of John's having written with the synoptic text(s) in view"[64]. This is, I think, a central issue in the debate. Hypothetical source-reconstruction makes it possible to give a precise description of the Johannine redaction, words and phrases. This may be attractive, but it is no less hypothetical than the reconstruction of the source(s). Such a delineation of a redactional text in John cannot be expected in the hypothesis of dependence on the Synoptics. The Johannine redaction will appear to be a more complex process of gospel writing, but this complexity has its own attractiveness, at least to me.

---

61. *JohnSyn*, p. 106 (= *Evangelica*, p. 398). This phrase has been generalized by Borgen far beyond the meaning it had in my paper. Cf. *Evangelica II*, pp. 711-712.

62. *TR* 51 (1986), p. 22 (and 24). See also D. ZELLER, *Der Ostermorgen im 4. Evangelium (Joh 20,1-18)*, in L. OBERLINNER (ed.), *Auferstehung Jesu - Auferstehung der Christen. Deutungen des Osterglaubens* (Quaestiones Disputatae, 105), Freiburg, 1986, pp. 145-161, esp. pp. 149-150: "Kann man sich einen Evangelisten denken, der die ersten drei Evangelien wie Farbkästen vor sich hatte und bei einzelnen Versen aus allen Töpfchen kräftig mischte, an anderen Stellen wieder mit eigenen Farben frei darauflos malte?". See my reply in *Note sur Jn 20,1-18*, in *ETL* 62 (1986) 404 (= *Evangelica II*, p. 600; see also *ibid.*, p. 712). — See now M. MYLLYKOSKI, *The Material Common to Luke and John. A Sketch*, in P. LUOMANEN (ed.), *Luke-Acts. Scandinavian Perspectives* (PFES, 54), Helsinki-Göttingen, 1991, pp. 115-156, esp. 131-132: "the whole hypothesis that John had two or three Gospel scrolls on his desk ... is ... very artificial"; cf. p. 119, on John's composing: "interrupting it now and then in order to add details and ideas from two or more scrolls lying on his desk – *or which are all the time in his mind*" (my emphasis). Another echo of Becker's critique, in the same style, is found in J.P. MEIER, *A Marginal Jew. Rethinking the Historical Jesus*, New York, 1991, p. 53, n. 17.

63. Cf. F. NEIRYNCK, *The Apocryphal Gospels and the Gospel of Mark*, 1989 (cf. above, n. 36), p. 169: "'Harmonization' is a general characteristic of the extracanonical gospel literature in the second century".

64. Review: *R.T. Fortna, The Fourth Gospel*, in *JBL* 109 (1990) 352-354, p. 354.

II

JOHN AND MATTHEW

The independence of John from the Synoptics was the prevailing view among Johannine scholars in the 1960's, with a minority opinion assuming that John knew and used Mark and, probably also, Luke (C.K. Barrett, W.G. Kümmel, J. Blinzler, *et al.*)[65]. Dependence on Matthew was regarded as much more problematic: "sehr fragwürdig" (J. Blinzler). If contacts with Matthew were taken into consideration, they were either located in the final, in fact post-Johannine, redaction[66], or, following the suggestion made by N.A. Dahl and P. Borgen, seen as fused together with the Johannine tradition[67]. This last type of solution was adopted by A. Dauer in his dissertation on the passion narrative (1969, published in 1972)[68]. In the segment Jn 18,1–19,30 he noted parallels to editorial phrases in Matthew (diff. Mk) at 18,2.11a.11b.15.24.25.27.39; 19,2.13.17.19.30[69]. One of the objections | against Dauer's solution

65. Cf. *JohnSyn*, p. 73 (= 365).
66. Cf. *JohnSyn*, pp. 90-93 (= 382-385), and especially Boismard's list of 11 instances: p..90 (= 384), n. 69.
67. At that time, this was the only practicable hypothesis with regard to dependence on Matthew. In 1967, I myself wrote at the conclusion of an examination of the similarities with Matthew in the burial and empty tomb stories: "Ainsi, il me paraît une hypothèse raisonnable que les récits de l'ensevelissement et du tombeau vide reposent sur une tradition semblable à celle des Synoptiques, et même, comme certaines ressemblances précises semblent le suggérer, une tradition qui s'est formée en partie à partir de nos évangiles synoptiques". Cf. *NTS* 15 (1968-69), p. 189 (= *Evangelica*, p. 294). Compare also J. DELOBEL, in *ETL* 42 (1966), p. 470, n. 210: "la matière synoptique ... parvenue à Jean, après l'achèvement de nos synoptiques, et à travers une période de mélange de leurs matériaux dans la tradition orale".
68. Cf. *JohnSyn*, pp. 93-95 (= 385-387). On "The Borgen-Dauer Thesis", see also *Evangelica II*, pp. 700-701 (= *The Interrelations*, pp. 439-440); cf. above, n. 57.
69. See *Die Passionsgeschichte*, pp. 50-53 (Jn 18,1-11), 96-97 (Jn 18,12-27), 154-155 (Jn 18,28–19,16a), 217-222 (Jn 19,16b-30). Detailed references to these lists and to the commentary (cf.) are added here within brackets. The names of N.A. Dahl (1955, p. 32) and P. Borgen (1959) refer to their lists of John-Matthew agreements: cf. *JohnSyn*, p. 93 (= 385), nn. 86 and 87; see below, n. 146. On B. de Solages, see below in this note.
18,2   Ἰούδας ὁ παραδιδοὺς αὐτόν
        Mt 26,25 Ἰούδας ὁ παραδιδοὺς αὐτόν (cf. 27,3)
        [p. 50, cf. 25] Dahl
18,11a βάλε τὴν μάχαιραν εἰς τὴν θήκην
        Mt 26,52a ἀπόστρεψον τὴν μάχαιράν σου εἰς τὸν τόπον αὐτῆς
        [51, cf. 47] Dahl, Borgen 249 (cf. 250!), de Solages 105
18,11b τὸ ποτήριον ὃ δέδωκέν μοι ὁ πατὴρ οὐ μὴ πίω αὐτό;
        Mt 26,39 παρελθάτω ἀπ᾽ ἐμοῦ τὸ ποτήριον τοῦτο. 42 πάτερ μου, εἰ οὐ δύναται τοῦτο παρελθεῖν ἐὰν μὴ αὐτὸ πίω, γενηθήτω τὸ θέλημά σου
        [52, cf. 48] Dahl, Borgen 249, de Solages 106

concerns his acceptance of Synoptic influences at an early pre-Johannine stage. Harmonization with the Synoptics is | more easily conceivable in

18,15   καὶ συνεισῆλθεν ... εἰς τὴν αὐλήν...
        Mt 26,58 ἕως τῆς αὐλῆς ... καὶ *εἰσελθών*
        [96, cf. 73]
18,24   πρὸς Καϊάφαν τὸν ἀρχιερέα Cf. 18,13b-14
        Mt 26,57 πρὸς *Καϊάφαν* τὸν ἀρχιερέα (cf. 26,3)
        [96, cf. 70] Dahl, Borgen 256, de Solages 100
18,25   ἠρνήσατο (second denial)
        Mt 26,72 *ἠρνήσατο*
        [96, cf. 89] Borgen 256
18,27   καὶ εὐθέως ἀλέκτωρ ἐφώνησεν
        Mt 26,74 καὶ *εὐθέως* ἀλέκτωρ ἐφώνησεν
        [97, cf. 90] Borgen 256
18,39   ἔστιν δὲ συνήθεια ὑμῖν ἵνα ἕνα ἀπολύσω
        Mt 27,15 *εἰώθει* ... ἀπολύειν ἕνα
        [154, cf. 124] Borgen 254
19,2   καὶ οἱ στρατιῶται πλέξαντες στέφανον ἐξ ἀκανθῶν ἐπέθηκαν αὐτοῦ τῇ κεφαλῇ
        Mt 27,27 τότε οἱ στρατιῶται ... 29 καὶ *πλέξαντες στέφανον ἐξ ἀκανθῶν ἐπέθηκαν ἐπὶ τῆς κεφαλῆς αὐτοῦ*
        [154, cf. 126] Dahl, Borgen 250 (cf. 252!), de Solages 100
19,13   ὁ οὖν Πιλᾶτος ... καὶ ἐκάθισεν ἐπὶ βήματος
        Mt 27,19 *καθημένου δὲ αὐτοῦ ἐπὶ τοῦ βήματος*
        [155, cf. 129] Borgen 254
19,17   ἐξῆλθεν εἰς τὸν λεγόμενον Κρανίου Τόπον, ὃ λέγεται Ἑβραϊστὶ Γολγοθα
        Mt 27,32 *ἐξερχόμενοι* ... 33 καὶ *ἐλθόντες εἰς τόπον λεγόμενον* Γ., ὅ ἐστιν Κρανίου Τόπος λεγόμενος
        [217, cf. 170]
19,19   τίτλον ... ἔθηκεν ἐπὶ τοῦ σταυροῦ· ἦν δὲ γεγραμμένον· Ἰησοῦς...
        Mt 27,37 καὶ *ἐπέθηκαν ἐπάνω* τῆς κεφαλῆς αὐτοῦ τὴν αἰτίαν αὐτοῦ *γεγραμμένην· οὗτός ἐστιν Ἰησοῦς*...
        [221, cf. 176] Dahl, Borgen 253, de Solages 101
19,30   παρέδωκεν τὸ πνεῦμα
        Mt 27,50 *ἀφῆκεν τὸ πνεῦμα*
        [222, cf. 215] Borgen 253

Unlike Dauer, both Dahl and Borgen include the burial and resurrection stories in their study of the "passion narrative":

19,38   ὢν μαθητὴς τοῦ Ἰησοῦ, 40 ἔλαβον τὸ σῶμα, 41 μνημεῖον καινόν
        Mt 27,57 *ἐμαθητεύθη τῷ Ἰησοῦ*, 59 *λαβών*, 60 *ἐν τῷ καινῷ αὐτοῦ μνημείῳ*
        Dahl, Borgen 248(!), de Solages 101-103
20,17   μή μου ἅπτου, πρὸς τοὺς ἀδελφούς μου
        Mt 28,9 *ἐκράτησαν αὐτοῦ τοὺς πόδας*, 10 *τοῖς ἀδελφοῖς* μου.
        Dahl, Borgen 258, de Solages 107, 109.

The John-Matthew parallels in de Solages's list (cf. above, n. 14) are almost exclusively from the passion narrative (pp. 99-113: "Jean et Matthieu"). The parallels are displayed in two groups: first, "de brèves convergences d'expressions" in passages with parallel in Mark: a. 18,13 (24); b. 19,2b; c. 19,19; d. 19,38a; e. 19,40a; f. 19,41b (no literary dependence); second, passages without parallel in Mark: a. 5,29; b. 6,3; c. 18,11a; d. 18,11b; e. 20,14-17; f. 20,23; "Les trois premiers cas (a, b, c) ... peuvent peut-être laisser un doute sur l'ignorance où se trouvait Jean du texte de Matthieu. En tout cas, même s'il l'a connu, il en a tiré bien peu de choses" (p. 113). For a more recent critical opinion, cf.

a later redaction. Thus, R. Baum-Bodenbender, in her study of Jn 18,28–19,16a, accepts dependence on Matthew in a secondary redactional *Schicht B* at Jn 18,28 (v. 24: Caiaphas); 18,39; 19,2; 19,13 (uncertain)[70].

In this respect, Boismard's commentary (B-L 1977) shows a remarkable new development. In 1972 he had already noted specific agreements with Matthew at Jn 18,39; 19,2.17.19.30, but then assigned these phrases to Proto-Matthew (*Mt-intermédiaire*), known by John through Proto-Luke (but omitted by Luke)[71]. In 1977 Proto-Luke is abandoned, and the striking similarities in 19,2 (the mocking scene)[72] and in 19,19 (the inscription on the cross)[73] are now explained by direct dependence on (canonical) Matthew at a second stage in the composition of John. Dependence on the three Synoptic gospels and harmonization are typical of this second stage (Jn II-B, and also the redactional Jn III), in contrast to the interrelations of gospel sources in the earlier stages of Jn I (Document C) and Jn II-A[74].

M. MYLLYKOSKI, *The Material*, 1991 (n. 62), p. 116: "John has only a few special agreements with Mt, and it is not likely that he had used this gospel at all when writing his work" (in n. 3, he refers to *JohnSyn*, but only to my observations on pp. 81-82 [= 373-374]).

Only two passages of Dauer's list, 18,11 and 19,2 (and 19,38.40.41), are accepted by Borgen as "dependent on the Synoptics" (pp. 247-252). See also my critical remarks in *JohnSyn*, p. 95 (= 387): "The similarities with the Synoptics listed by Dauer are not always so significant as he seems to suggest. Some of the verbal resemblances are *minor agreements*" (see n. 94: e.g., Jn 18,15.25.27.39; 19,17). With respect to 19,17, Dauer refers to the contacts with Mt in the context (p. 170: "Beziehungen..., die sich in diesem Abschnitt schon öfters aufgedrängt haben"; but see also n. 33: rejected by Borgen and Buse, "die aber beide die ungewöhnliche Stellung von λεγόμενος [in Jn: before κ. τ.] nicht berücksichtigen"). Note also Dauer's own differentiation: in 18,1-11, "mehr (Lk) oder weniger (Mk und Mt)" (p. 60); in 18,28–19,16a, "auch mt Einfluß, besonders in der Verspottungsszene" (p. 164); in 19,16b-30 "scheint vor allem die mt Version von Einfluß gewesen zu sein" (p. 226).

70. *Hoheit*, 1984 (n. 26), pp. 202, 109, 193, 214. See also p. 74, n. 121 (Jn 18,11b). On Baum-Bodenbender, compare M. SABBE, *The Trial of Jesus before Pilate in John and Its Relation to the Synoptics*, in this volume, pp. 341-385 (= *Studia Neotestamentica*, 1991, pp. 467-513).

71. Cf. *JohnSyn*, p. 92 (= 384), n. 80.

72. B-L, p. 418b: "Ici, les contacts entre Jn et Mt sont si forts qu'une dépendance de l'un par rapport à l'autre ne peut être niée". Cf. DAUER, p. 127: "Diese Übereinstimmungen dürften kaum zufällig sein". — Both regard ἱμάτιον πορφυροῦν in v. 2b as a contact with Mk 15,17 (πορφύραν). But see R.E. BROWN, *John II*, p. 875: "In this scene only John and Matthew specifically name a garment": ἱμάτιον (πορφυροῦν) in Jn and χλαμύδα (κοκκίνην) in Mt 27,28 (cf. v. 31 τὴν χλαμύδα, par. Mk 15,20 τὴν πορφύραν).

73. B-L, p. 438b: "il se rapproche de Mt par plusieurs détails. ... Ces contacts ... nous placent au niveau de Jean II-B".

74. Other contacts with Matthew in Jn II-B (cf. Dauer's list): Jn 18,11a.b (p. 404a); 18,24 "Caiaphas", cf. 18,13b-14.28 (p. 415a, cf. 410b and 432; p. 416: "Jean II-B a

Dauer's development in his more recent study on *Johannes und Lukas* (1984) is no less remarkable. He maintains the theory of an intermediate stage between the Synoptics and John and finds direct literary dependence less probable ("nicht sehr wahrscheinlich")[75]. There is, however, a significant change in his position regarding the pre-Johannine source[76]. The first case he studies is that of the Healing of the Official's Son (4,46-54) with the parallel story of the centurion in Matthew and Luke. His conclusion is quite clear: "Die vor-joh Fassung ist eine *freie Wiedergabe* von Mt 8,5-13 unter Verwendung von Erzählzügen aus Lk 7,1-10"[77]. That means, the pre-Johannine source he proposes here is strictly post-Synoptic, relying on the Synoptics, and he dispenses with the unnecessary hypothesis of a primitive Johannine, or pre-Johannine, tradition[78].

For Boismard and Dauer, the dependence on the Synoptics, and in particular on Matthew, is becoming increasingly important. Both are convinced, for instance, of the editorial character of Mt 8,13 and of its influence on the parallel in John[79]:

voulu harmoniser l'évangile de Jn avec les Synoptiques, plus particulièrement avec Mt"); 18,39 (p. 418b, 423: less important, not impossible); and some other less evident instances, not mentioned by Dauer, at 18,31b, cf. Mt 27,1 ("même volonté des autorités juives de mettre Jésus à mort": p. 418b, 422a); 19,9b-10, Jesus' silence, cf. Mt 27,12b-13 ("une structure identique": p. 418b, 424b); 19,16a, cf. Mt 27,26b (ἵνα σταυρωθῇ: p. 425a). B-L also note ὁ παραδούς με in 19,11: "la formule ne se lit ailleurs dans le NT qu'en Mt 10,4 et surtout 27,3" (p. 424b); but see Mt 27,3 reads παραδιδούς in N²⁶, Greeven (and B-L, *Synopsis*, 1986!).

Other phrases from Dauer's list are not treated as Matthew-John agreements and assigned to the earlier stages of Document C (18,15.27; 19,17.30) or Jn II-A (19,13). In this last instance, B-L compare ἐκάθισεν (transitive!) to ἐκάθισεν (intransitive) in 12,14: "Les expressions 'l'assit sur le tribunal' ont une forme littéraire très proche de celles de 12,14: '... Jésus s'assit sur lui', addition de Jean II-A" (p. 428a; cf. 430b).

75. *Johannes und Lukas* (n. 13), p. 288 (regarding Jn 20,19-29). On Jn 12,1-8, see p. 204: "ziemlich sicher ausschließen", but also "mit größter, wenn auch nicht letzter Sicherheit" (*ibid.*), and his cautious note 526 (p. 410).

76. Cf. *ETL* 60 (1984), p. 375 (= *Evangelica II*, p. 687).

77. *Johannes und Lukas*, p. 121. See also p. 288: Jn 20,19-23(-29) "setzt eine Erzählung voraus, deren *Grundlage* Lk 24,36-49 war", and p. 206, where he takes his interpretation of 4,46-54 as the model that can be applied to 12,1-8.

78. See esp. pp. 122-125 (with explicit reference to Boismard-Lamouille's Document C).

79. Cf. *ETL* 60 (1984), p. 373 (= 685): my own presentation of the parallels (including Mt 8,15b, not taken into account by Dauer). For a negative reaction, cf. U. WEGNER, *Der Hauptmann von Kafarnaum (Mt 7,28a; 8,5-10.13 par Lk 7,1-10). Ein Beitrag zur Q-Forschung* (WUNT, 2/14), Tübingen, 1985, pp. 18-74 ("Mt 8,5-10.13 / Lk 7,1-10 im Vergleich mit Joh 4,46-54"): the resemblances "in der Wortlaut-, Satz- und Syntaxebene" are insufficient (p. 36). But see my reply in *Evangelica II*, pp. 687-688.

Jn 4   Mt 8
50a λέγει αὐτῷ ὁ Ἰησοῦς·   13a καὶ εἶπεν ὁ Ἰησοῦς τῷ ἑκατοντάρχῃ·
  b πορεύου, ὁ υἱός σου ζῇ.   ὕπαγε,
  c ἐπίστευσεν ...   ὡς ἐπίστευσας γενηθήτω σοι.
51c ὁ παῖς αὐτοῦ ζῇ.   b καὶ ἰάθη ὁ παῖς [αὐτοῦ]
52a τὴν ὥραν ... ἐν ᾗ ...   ἐν τῇ ὥρᾳ ἐκείνῃ.
  b ἀφῆκεν αὐτὸν ὁ πυρετός   15b καὶ ἀφῆκεν αὐτὴν ὁ πυρετός.

Both defend a two-stage composition and locate the Synoptic influences either in the *Vorlage* of John (Dauer) or in the second stage of Jn II-B (Boismard). I have indicated elsewhere that each of these two positions I has its own weaknesses[80], but Boismard and Dauer do concur in the sound observation of dependence on Matthew's editorial text.

In M.D. Goulder's paradigm there is no place for pre-Johannine stages: "He [John] drew on all three Synoptists, but especially Matthew, and developed them freely"[81]. In his opinion, Jn 4,46-54 is "most easily explained as a Johannine version of the earlier two Gospels"[82]. A more unusual argument for John's use of Matthew was suggested by A. Farrer (in a letter posthumously published by J. Muddiman)[83]. The argument of corresponding passages in the same order has always played an important role in the discussion of John's use of Mark (or, especially in Jn 6, the use of a pre-Markan source)[84]. In Farrer's view, structural parallels can be perceived between Matthew and John, in the original gospel text (ch. 6–5) and in the "redactional" order of Jn 4,46-54; 5,2-9; 6,1-21 (Mt 8,5-13; 9,1-8; 14,13-32)[85].

---

80. On Dauer, see *ETL*, 1984 (cf. above, n. 13); on Boismard, see *ETL* 53 (1977) 451-478; = *JeanSyn*, 1979, pp. 93-120: "Foi et miracle: le fonctionnaire royal en [Jn] 4,46-54". For further discussion, see M.-É. BOISMARD, *Jean 4,46-54 et les parallèles synoptiques*, in this volume, pp. 239-259.

81. *Luke*, 1989 (n. 36), p. 23. On John's use of Matthew, see also p. 323 (Mt 28,8-10: with reference to *JohnSyn*, pp. 96-98) and p. 326 (Jn 21 and "a matrix in Mt 28,16-20"; Jn 21,7b: cf. Mt 14,29).

82. *Luke*, p. 379 (with reference to *ETL*, 1984).

83. J. MUDDIMAN, *John's Use of Matthew: A British Exponent of the Theory*, in *ETL* 59 (1983) 333-337 (fragment of the letter [1968] quoted on p. 335).

84. See *JohnSyn*, pp. 87-89 (= 379-381). Cf. C.K. BARRETT, *John*, ²1978, pp. 43-45 (1955, pp. 34-36), with a supplementary paragraph (p. 45): "[we do have Mark,] and in Mark are the stories that John repeats, sometimes at least with similar or even identical words, sometimes at least in substantially the same order - which is not in every case as inevitable as is sometimes suggested" (*ibid.*).

85. "The later Johannine redactor or scribe understandably mistook 5,2-9 as the parallel to Matthew 9,1-8 (failing to see its connection with Matt. 21,14) and therefore swapped the chapters around" (Muddiman's comment, p. 335).

Mention can be made here of G. MAIER, *Johannes und Matthäus – Zwiespalt oder Viergestalt des Evangeliums?*, in *Gospel Perspectives* 2 (1981) 267-291. Without discussing John's knowledge and use of Mt, Maier draws attention to the similarities (*Gemeinsamkeiten*) between Jn and Mt. Starting with the structure of the Gospel ("Duktus

In my Introduction, I already mentioned M. Hengel's statement: the Fourth Gospel "presupposes" the Synoptic Gospels; but with a qualification regarding Matthew: "he [the author of the Fourth Gospel] rather ignored Matthew, which he very probably also knew: it was really at the opposite pole"[86]; and: "By idealizing the unknown | 'Nathanael' and ignoring 'Matthew'[87], the author of the Fourth Gospel could show his distance from the Greek Gospel according to 'Matthew', which ... in many respects seemed to be the precise opposite of his own work": the "Matthean" Son of David title is significantly absent from the messianic confessions at 1,41-49[88]. From both Goulder and Hengel one may expect further documentation of their respective theses: on the one hand, John using especially Matthew, and on the other, John knowing but ignoring Matthew.

*

1. Earlier attempts to show dependence on Matthew in individual passages are mostly cited with an accompanying reference to their critique. First of all, I think of H.F.D. Sparks's article on the servant-master saying in Jn 13,16 and 15,20 (1952)[89] and the reply by Gardner-Smith (1953). The judgment expressed by P. Gardner-Smith was quite clear: "This is one of those cases in which literary dependence is a superfluous hypothesis"[90]. This verdict was reiterated two years later by C.H. Dodd in

und Struktur"), he notes "einen weithin gemeinsamen Aufriß der Jesusgeschichte" (p. 270). His conclusion: "Das Feld der Gemeinsamkeiten zwischen Johannes und den Synoptikern ist beträchtlich größer, als man bis heute gemeinhin annimmt", and in reaction to R. Schnackenburg (I, p. 19): "(man) kann die Frage aufwerfen, ob Johannes mit Lukas oder Markus wirklich enger verbunden ist als mit Matthäus" (pp. 286-287).

86. *The Johannine Question*, 1989 (n. 17), p. 75.

87. On the identification Nathanael-Matthew, see p. 156, n. 110. Cf. *JohnSyn*, p. 82 (= 374), n. 36 (K. Hanhart, 1970). Contrast HENGEL, p. 19: "a connection..., but this need not be a simple identification".

88. *Ibid.*, p. 19. Note, however, some hesitation with regard to Luke: pp. 75 ("he also seems to use Luke"), 95 ("written sources"), 102 ("literary 'sources'"); but see p. 218, n. 94: "I think that *direct* literary dependence of John on Luke is improbable, even if he knows the Second Gospel".

89. H.F.D. SPARKS, *St. John's Knowledge of Matthew: The Evidence of John 13,16 and 15,20*, in *JTS* 3 (1952) 58-61. Cf. *JohnSyn*, p. 82 (= 374), n. 35.

90. P. GARDNER-SMITH, *St. John's Knowledge of Matthew*, in *JTS* 4 (1953) 31-35, p. 35. Both Kümmel and Blinzler refer to Gardner-Smith and Dodd: W.G. KÜMMEL, *Einleitung*, 1963, p. 138 (= 1973, p. 169); ET, p. 203: "The saying ... has a clear link not only with Mt 10,24f but also with its wider context (see Sparks), but this link is not close enough ("nicht eng genug") to be considered evidence for literary dependence"; J. BLINZLER, *Johannes und die Synoptiker*, 1965, p. 47 ("diese Basis ist doch wohl zu schmal..."). See also p. 59: for parallels with Matthew he mentions Dahl's list (passion narrative) and Jn 15,20; 12,15; 18,11; 20,23 ("Der Wortlaut ist in allen diesen Stellen bei Joh ein anderer als bei Mt").

his article on "Some Johannine 'Herrenworte' with Parallels in the Synoptic Gospels" (1955). He treated this case as the first of four examples of common sayings (he calls them the four "instantiae praerogativae") "in which John is not dependent on the Synoptic Gospels, but is transmitting independently a special form of the common oral tradition"[91]. Dodd's conclusion was repeated in the I major commentaries on John by Brown[92] and Schnackenburg[93]. At least an echo of Sparks can be heard in B. Lindars's comment: "a traditional saying, which has a close parallel in Mt. 10.24 (cf. also Lk. 6.40). The Matthean context is persecution, ... John knows that this is its context, as he uses the saying again to teach precisely this lesson in 15.20"[94]. Not unexpectedly, J. Becker formulates his caveat: "Nicht, daß er unmittelbar die Aussendungsrede kennt, wohl aber dürfte auch *der joh Tradition* für dieses Wort solcher Zusammenhang vertraut gewesen sein"[95].

The Synoptic parallel is found in Mt 10,24-25a:

24　οὐκ ἔστιν μαθητὴς ὑπὲρ τὸν διδάσκαλον
　　οὐδὲ δοῦλος ὑπὲρ τὸν κύριον αὐτοῦ.
25a　ἀρκετὸν τῷ μαθητῇ ἵνα γένηται ὡς ὁ διδάσκαλος αὐτοῦ
　　καὶ ὁ δοῦλος ὡς ὁ κύριος αὐτοῦ.

with a partial parallel of this double saying in Lk 6,40:

οὐκ ἔστιν μαθητὴς ὑπὲρ τὸν διδάσκαλον·
κατηρτισμένος δὲ πᾶς ἔσται ὡς ὁ διδάσκαλος αὐτοῦ[96].

Although Schürmann, Kloppenborg, *et al.*, in their reconstruction of Q, retain the sayings of Lk 6,39 (= Mt 15,14) and 6,40 (= Mt 10,24-25a) in

---

91. *NTS* 2 (1955-56) 75-86 (cf. p. 86), reprinted in *Historical Tradition*, 1963, pp. 335-365 ("Sayings common to John and the Synoptics"): 1. Jn 13,16, pp. 335-338 (= 75-78); 2. Jn 12,25, pp. 338-343 (= 78-81); 3. Jn 13,20, pp. 343-347 (= 81-85); 4. 20,23, pp. 347-349 (= 85-86); supplemented with ten "less strong" cases, pp. 349-365. – For Schnackenburg's new examination of this sayings material, cf. below, n. 93.

92. *John* II, 1970, pp. 569-570: "the original saying of Jesus probably circulated in variant forms, and these were reported independently by the different evangelists" (p. 570). Nevertheless, he notes several parallels to the material in Mt 10: Jn 12,25 (Mt 10,39); Jn 12,26 (Mt 10,38); Jn 12,44 (Mt 10,40); Jn 13,16 (Mt 10,24-25); Jn 13,20 (Mt 10,40); Jn 15,18–16,4a (Mt 10,17-25), and concludes: "Both Gospels are drawing on a common collection of material which each uses in its own way" (*ibid.*).

93. *Das Johannesevangelium* III, 1975, pp. 28-29 (esp. n. 70). – On "Synoptic sayings in John", cf. *Tradition und Interpretation im Spruchgut des Johannesevangeliums* (1980), in *Das Johannesevangelium* IV, 1984, pp. 72-89. Jn 13,16; 15,20 and 13,20 (par. Mt) are listed in the first group, "Synoptische Logien im Johannesevangelium" (p. 74), without being discussed. Cf. p. 73: "wir (wollen) nicht das literarische Verhältnis von Joh und Synoptikern untersuchen, das weiter strittig bleibt".

94. *John*, 1972, p. 453.

95. *Johannes* II, 1981, p. 491.

96. Κατηρτισμένος δὲ πᾶς is probably Lukan, but the nominative may be original (ctr. Mt 10,25a): see Mt 10,25b!

the Lukan order (at Mt 7,2/3)[97], the original location of the two sayings, or at least of Lk 6,40, remains uncertain[98]. The context in the I mission discourse of Mt 10 is almost certainly editorial and, *pace* S. Schulz[99], the δοῦλος-κύριος image was probably not part of the original saying. Both the Matthean form of the saying and the Matthean context show similarities with the saying in John.

Jn 13,16   ἀμὴν ἀμὴν λέγω ὑμῖν,
οὐκ ἔστιν δοῦλος μείζων τοῦ κυρίου αὐτοῦ
οὐδὲ ἀπόστολος μείζων τοῦ πέμψαντος αὐτόν.

Like Mt 10,24, Jn 13,16 is a double saying, οὐκ ἔστιν ... οὐδέ, and has the same image of δοῦλος-κύριος. "Since John never uses ὑπέρ with the accusative, while he is rather addicted to locutions with μείζων, he might himself have been responsible for the change ... It might be urged that since διδάσκαλος and κύριος (in that order) are the titles which the evangelist has just given as those acceptable to Jesus from his followers [13,13], we should conclude that he was acquainted with the Matthaean couplet, which has the same titles in the same order": I am quoting C.H. Dodd[100]. But at this point Dodd reverses the argument: in this context, where the Matthean form of the saying "would seem

97. See the survey of opinions in J.S. KLOPPENBORG, *Q Parallels*, Sonoma, CA, 1988, p. 38. Both Schürmann and Kloppenborg (*The Formation of Q*, Philadelphia, 1987, p. 182) accept a pre-Q sequence of sayings: Lk 6,39.40.41-42. Compare J. WANKE, *"Bezugs- und Kommentarworte" in den synoptischen Evangelien* (Erfurter Theol. Studien, 44), Leipzig, 1981, pp. 21-25: the unity of Lk 6,39 (Mt 15,24) and its commentary, Lk 6,40 (Mt 10,24-25). But see n. 98.

98. For both Lk 6,39 and 40 inserted here by Luke (from another part of Q), see, e.g., J.A. FITZMYER, *Luke*, p. 641; Lk 6,40 inserted by Luke at 6,39/41-42, cf. D. CATCHPOLE, *Jesus and the Community of Israel - The Inaugural Discourse in Q*, in *BJRL* 68 (1986) 296-316, pp. 313-314; R.A. PIPER, *Wisdom in the Q-Tradition. The Aphoristic Teaching of Jesus* (SNTS MS, 61), Cambridge, 1988, pp. 41-42 (although "it is not possible to make a decision with confidence about Lk 6:40": p. 41); L.E. VAAGE, *Composite Texts and Oral Myths: The Case of the "Sermon" (6,20b-49)*, in *SBL 1989 Seminar Papers*, pp. 424-439, esp. 431.

99. *Q*, pp. 449 (n. 336), 450 (n. 347). Contrast, e.g., R.H. GUNDRY, *Matthew*, 1982, p. 195; J. GNILKA, *Matthäusevangelium*, 1986, p. 374.
For W.D. Davies - D.C. Allison (*Matthew* II, 1991, pp. 192-193), Mt 10,24-25 came to the evangelist as an isolated tradition (cf. U. LUZ, *Matthäus* II, p. 119: "die Langform (ist) eine von Mt übernommene Sondertradition") and Jn 13,16 preserves an independent oral variant. They refer to Dodd and Brown, but add a footnote: "If Mt 10.24-5 be considered, against our judgement, as mostly redactional, then one would almost be forced to conclude that Matthew's gospel has influenced John: the parallels between Mt 10.24-5 and Jn 13.16 and 15.20 are too close to be accidental" (p. 193, n. 101). See also their observation on Mt 10,40: "Perhaps the positive formulation is due to Matthew's desire to give both thematic and formal consistency to vv. 40-2. But if so, then Jn 13.20 almost certainly shows the influence of Matthew" (p. 225).

100. *Historical Tradition*, pp. 336 and 337 (= 76-77).

eminently appropriate", it is not easy to understand why John eliminated the relation of disciple and teacher and "substituted the relation of apostle and sender"[101]. This last observation is repeated by Brown and Schnackenburg[102], but Brown and Schnackenburg rightly emphasize the connection between 13,16 (with ἀπόστολος = the one sent) and the saying in 13,20, both beginning with ἀμὴν ἀμὴν λέγω ὑμιν and both dealing with sending.

| Jn 13,20 ἀμὴν ἀμὴν λέγω ὑμῖν,
        ὁ λαμβάνων ἄν τινα πέμψω ἐμὲ λαμβάνει,
        ὁ δὲ ἐμὲ λαμβάνων λαμβάνει τὸν πέμψαντά με.
Mt 10,40 ὁ δεχόμενος ὑμᾶς ἐμὲ δέχεται,
        καὶ ὁ ἐμὲ δεχόμενος δέχεται τὸν ἀποστείλαντά με.

Dodd himself notes that the two propositions in Jn 13,16 and 20 "stand out as general statements, presupposing a traditional form"[103] and he suggests that "the sayings came to him [the evangelist] already roughly grouped"[104]. I do not think that there is any convincing evidence for the existence of a sequence of these sayings in the pre-Synoptic tradition, but John may have found a "rough grouping" of the Synoptic parallels to Jn 13,16.20 in the Matthean Mission Discourse (Mt 10,24-25.40).

The contact with Mt 10 is even more likely in the case of Jn 15,20, where, as was stressed by Sparks, "we are dealing with a whole complex of ideas and material, of which the saying itself forms but a part"[105]. These parallels can be visualized in the following chart[106]:

Jn 15,18-21	Mt 10
18 εἰ ὁ κόσμος ὑμᾶς *μισεῖ*,	22a καὶ ἔσεσθε *μισούμενοι* ὑπὸ πάντων
... ἐμὲ πρῶτον ὑμῶν μεμίσηκεν.	διὰ τὸ ὄνομά μου·
19 ...	23 ὅταν δὲ διώκωσιν ὑμᾶς ...
20 μνημονεύετε τοῦ λόγου οὗ ἐγὼ εἶπον ὑμῖν·	
οὐκ ἔστιν δοῦλος	24 οὐκ ἔστιν ... οὐδὲ δοῦλος
μείζων τοῦ κυρίου αὐτοῦ.	ὑπὲρ τὸν κύριον αὐτοῦ.
εἰ ἐμὲ ἐδίωξαν,	25b εἰ τὸν οἰκοδεσπότην ...,
καὶ ὑμᾶς διώξουσιν·	...πόσῳ μᾶλλον τοὺς οἰκιακοὺς αὐτοῦ.

101. *Ibid.*, p. 337 (= 77). "Indeed, ἀπόστολος is not a Johannine word at all; this is the only place in the Fourth Gospel where it is used. Μαθητής ... [is] his favourite word" (*ibid.*).

102. BROWN, p. 570; SCHNACKENBURG, p. 29: "Die matthäische Version ... hätte sich für unsere Stelle besonders empfohlen, weil sie das doppelte Bild von Jünger-Meister und Knecht-Herr enthält".

103. *Historical Tradition*, p. (344-)345, n. 1 (= 82, n. 1).

104. *Ibid.*, p. 391. Jn 13,16 (Mt 10,24) and Jn 13,20 (Mt 10,40) are treated there in the section on "Sequences of sayings" (pp. 388-405, esp. 390-391).

105. *St. John's Knowledge of Matthew* (n. 89), p. 61.

106. Compare BROWN, *John*, p. 694; B-L, pp. 373-374. Both consider the larger section of 15,18–16,4a and include the parallels between Jn 15,26.27 and Mt 10,20.18.

21 ἀλλὰ ταῦτα πάντα ποιήσουσιν εἰς ὑμᾶς
    διὰ τὸ ὄνομά μου,   [22a]
    ὅτι οὐκ οἴδασιν τὸν πέμψαντά με.

Brown's comment on the chart of parallels is rather confusing: both John and Matthew independently preserve early tradition and the repetition of the saying in 15,20 is explained by John's desire to keep this traditional material together[107]. I personally prefer to return to I Sparks and "to suppose, as nearly everyone does, that St. Matthew himself 'agglomerated' the [Mission] Charge; and that in so doing he, and none other, was responsible for the complex which was known to St. John"[108].

Boismard-Lamouille (1977) propose a more sophisticated analysis of Jn 13,12-20 (Doc C: 12.17; Jn II-A: 18; Jn II-B: 13-15.19; Jn III: 16.20)[109] and Jn 15,18–16,4a (Jn II-A: 22-25.3-4a; Jn II-B: 18.20b.2.21.26-27.1; Jn III: 19.20a.c)[110]. They recognize the parallels in Jn 15,18-21 and the dependence of the evangelist (Jn II-B) on Mt 10. In their view, however, Jn III is responsible for the insertion of the saying in 13,16 (and 20) and for the formula of remembering in 15,20a (μνημονεύετε τοῦ λόγου οὗ ἐγὼ εἶπον ὑμῖν). But their stylistic argument (the attraction of the relative οὗ instead of ὅν: "Jean II-B l'aurait mis à l'accusatif")[111] is hardly convincing[112]. That 13,16 is not "un corps

---

107. *John*, p. 695. One can read there that "if the fourth evangelist had copied from Matthew, he would have had to anticipate the era of modern criticism by recognizing that Matt x 17-25 and xxiv 9-10 belong together" (*ibid.*). Note that this observation does not concern the section we consider here (Jn 15,18-21). Moreover, Brown's own chart of parallels (Jn 15,18–16,4a) only includes two parallels from ch. 24: Jn 16,2, par. Mt 24,9, but see Mt 10,21 (θανατόω, never in Jn); Jn 16,1, par. Mt 24,10, but does he really mean that Matthew has kept "early tradition" in 24,10-12? Two other, more noteworthy, comments by Brown: "no other long section of Johannine discourse resembles a section of Synoptic discourse so closely as does John xv 18 – xvi 4a"; and, on the move of the warnings about persecution from the Eschatological Discourse to the discourse on Christian mission in Mt 10: "John uses the material with partially the same realized outlook as Matthew" (*ibid.*).
    108. Cf. above, n. 105.
    109. B-L, pp. 331-333, 339-341.
    110. B-L, pp. 373-374; see also p. 375.
    111. B-L, p. 374a. Cf. p. 494a (A36; cf. Ruckstuhl-Dschulnigg: A18 ὁ λόγος ὃν εἶπεν). — On Jn 13,16, cf. pp. 338-339: "reprend, en l'amplifiant, une parole que Jésus prononcera en 15,20". It is less evident that the title *Apôtre* is a correct translation of ἀπόστολος (unique in John).
    112. Cf. *JeanSyn*, p. 68 (= *ETL* 53, 1977, p. 427). B-L refer to the (irrelevant) parallels in 12,38 and 18,32 with ὁ λόγος in the nominative. In fact, there is no occurrence of τοῦ λόγου ὅν. There are four instances with the antecedent in the nominative (7,36; 12,38; 18,9.32); and two instances with the antecedent in the dative (2,22; 4,50), but both have a significant variant reading with the attraction of the relative (ᾧ in the printed text: TR S V). Cf. BLASS, *Grammatik*, § 50,2 (²1902, p. 177): non-attraction "sonst nicht ohne v. l." (Jn 2,22; 4,50; also 4,5; 7,39); in Debrunner's (and Funk's) less correct rendering: "non-attraction elsewhere only as v. l." (§ 294,1; BDR § 294, n. 3). See Jn 7,39, with antecedent in the genitive: περὶ τοῦ πνεύματος ὅ (N²⁶), but T (H) S V M B N: οὗ!

étranger qui rompt la suite du développement"[113] is well indicated by
K.T. Kleinknecht[114]:

> Der in 13,12-15 formulierte Gedankengang betont die Pflicht der Jünger zu
> einen dem Sklavendienst ihres Herrn und Lehrers analogen Verhalten. Das
> Logion aus Mt 10,24 bringt genau diesen Gedankengang prägnant und ver-
> allgemeinernd zum Ausdruck: Der Knecht/Schüler ist nicht mehr | als der
> Herr/Lehrer. Joh nimmt es deshalb auf, paßt es aber sprachlich der – für
> sein Jüngerverständnis kennzeichnenden – Konzeption an, wonach der
> Jünger šalîaḥ des mašliaḥ: bevollmächtigter Bote des ihn sendenden Herrn
> ist und deshalb gemäß jüdischen Vertretungsrecht nicht mehr als dieser.
> Die narrativ entfaltete Erfahrung der Fußwaschung wird so zum theologis-
> chen Grundsatz verdichtet.

2. A second earlier attempt to show dependence on Matthew is E.D.
Freed's article on the quotation in Jn 12,15 (1961)[115], with a response by
D.M. Smith (1963)[116].

Jn 12,15   μὴ φοβοῦ, θυγάτηρ Σιών·
          ἰδοὺ ὁ βασιλεύς σου ἔρχεται,
          καθήμενος ἐπὶ πῶλον ὄνου.

In a recent study of this quotation, M.J.J. Menken has presented a careful
analysis of the Johannine redaction[117]. The question of the parallel in
Matthew is treated in one sentence: "Die Möglichkeit der Entlehnung aus
Mt 21,5 erscheint mir abwegig" (with reference to D.M. Smith)[118]. As
usual[119], verses 16 and 17-19 (and 9-11) are attributed to the evangelist.

---

113. B-L, p. 332. Cf. p. 339 (13,16 and 13,20).
114. *Johannes 13*, 1985 (n. 20), p. 386. Cf. pp. 380-381: "Joh 13,16.20 und Mt 10"
(p. 381: "eine plausible Erklärung (ergibt sich), wenn man die Kenntnis von Mt 10,24
unterstellt"). With respect to the Johanine *Lieblingsvokabel* λαμβάνειν and πέμπειν in
13,20 (*ibid.*), cf. B-L, p. 339: "Son vocabulaire et son style sont toutefois très johanniques" (!).
115. E.D. FREED, *The Entry into Jerusalem in the Gospel of John*, in *JBL* 80 (1961)
329-338; ID., *Old Testament Quotations in the Gospel of John* (SupplNT, 11), Leiden,
1965, pp. 66-81 ("in essentially the same form" as the original publication). For Freed,
the quotation in Jn 12,15 is "a free artistic composition on the basis of Mt" (p. 80). Cf.
JohnSyn, p. 91 (= 383), n. 75.
116. D.M. SMITH, *John 12:12ff. and the Question of John's Use of the Synoptics*, in
JBL 82 (1963) 58-64; reprinted in *Johannine Christianity*, 1984 (n. 15), pp. 97-105 (cf.
p. xii: "my earliest scholarly publication"); on Jn 12,15, see esp. pp. 102-104.
117. M.J.J. MENKEN, *Die Redaktion des Zitates aus Sach 9,9 in Joh 12,15*, in *ZNW* 80
(1989) 193-209.
118. *Ibid.*, p. 196. When I wrote this paragraph in 1990, I had no knowledge of
Menken's more recent investigation, *The Quotations from Zech 9,9 in Mt 21,5 and in Jn
12,15*, in this volume, pp. 571-578. Cf. below, nn. 128-130.
119. See, e.g., J. BECKER, 1981, p. 376; R.T. FORTNA, *The Fourth Gospel* (cf. above,
n. 16), pp. 146-148 (and 143): 12,16-19 (and 12,9-11) assigned to the Evangelist and
12,12-15 to the pre-Johannine source. Contrast the exceptional position in U.C. VON
WAHLDE, *The Earliest Version of John's Gospel*, 1989 (n. 59), pp. 127-129: 12,9-11 and

In the quotation, the change to μὴ φοβοῦ (v. 15a) and the omission of σοι (v. 15b) are also attributable to the evangelist, and possibly also the use of καθήμενος and πῶλον ὄνου (cf. Gen 49,11) in v. 15c. The acceptance of such a creative intervention by the evangelist in the quotation itself may invite us to a reconsideration of the pre-Johannine source in 12,12-15, or at least in vv. 14-15. The very presence of the same explicit quotation in the parallel stories of John and Matthew is by itself a remarkable resemblance. In addition, the text of Zech 9,9 is quoted in a similar, abbreviated form. Both omit δίκαιος καὶ σῴζων. At the beginning, both omit the opening with I "rejoice" but retain θυγάτηρ Σιών in combination with another biblical passage[120]. At the end, they describe the animal as an ass (diff. Mark) with correspondences in their respective stories: πῶλος ὄνου in Jn 12,15 (v. 14: ὀνάριον), ὄνος and πῶλος in Mt 21,5 (v. 2: ὄνον ... καὶ πῶλον; v. 7: τὴν ὄνον καὶ τὸν πῶλον). It has been said that dependence on Matthew is excluded because of the introductory formula καθὼς ἦν γεγραμμένον: "Si Jn dépendait de Mt, on comprendrait mal qu'il n'ait pas utilisé sa formule habituelle: *afin que l'Écriture fût accomplie*"[121]. But it is well known that the fulfilment formula does not appear in John before 12,38[122]. Moreover, ἵνα πληρωθῇ is not used in John in connection with the theme of remembering. Καθώς ἐστιν γεγραμμένον in 12,14 (cf. 6,31) is resumed in v. 16: τότε ἐμνήσθησαν ὅτι ταῦτα ἦν ἐπ᾽ αὐτῷ γεγραμμένα (cf. 2,17.22).

The last element in v. 16 also deserves our attention: καὶ ταῦτα ἐποίησαν αὐτῷ. This can mean: that they, i.e. the crowd, had done these things to him ("das Handeln des Volkes")[123]. But is it not a more obvious reading of v. 16 to take "his disciples", the subject of ἐμνήσθησαν, as also the subject of ἐποίησαν (in Wilckens's translation: "und sie

18-19 are identified as "signs material" (the earliest version) and 12,12-16 as "editorial additions" (with v. 17 as an editorial resumptive: p. 129).

120. Isa 62,11 in Mt 21,5; Zeph 3,16 or Isa 40,9 (MENKEN, p. 198) in Jn 12,15.

121. B-L, p. 307: Matthew depends on Jn II-A and changed the Johannine formula to his usual fulfilment formula. Contrast *Synopse II*: the quotation in Mt 26,4-5 is inserted by the final redactor and the quotation in Jn 21,14b-15 is one of the "contacts évidents avec Mt ... au niveau de l'ultime rédaction johannique" (p. 331).

122. A. Faure, *et al.* Cf. M. HENGEL, *Die Schriftauslegung des 4. Evangeliums auf dem Hintergrund der urchristlichen Exegese*, in *Jahrbuch für Biblische Theologie* 4 (1989) 249-288, p. 276.

123. J. BECKER, p. 379. Cf. R. SCHNACKENBURG (III, p. 473: "was die Menge tat"), *et al.* See especially C.-P. MÄRZ, *"Siehe, dein König kommt zu dir..." . Eine traditionsgeschichtliche Untersuchung zur Einzugsperikope* (Erfurter Theol. Studien, 43), Leipzig, 1981, p. 240, n. 691: "kann sich im Zusammenhang nur auf die Jubelszene beziehen"; MENKEN, p. 200, n. 29.

selbst es an ihm erfüllt hatten")? Not a few prefer this interpretation[124]: "The Evangelist assumes as known the part which the disciples have taken" (Westcott, 1880)[125]; "Er setzt die Kenntnis der synoptischen Erzählung, wie er es auch sonst tut, einfach voraus" (Hengel, 1989)[126]. Freed rightly observes that in Jn "there is no effort to convey the idea of a procession": "Jn clearly thinks that Jesus' mere sitting on | the ass fulfills the prophecy of his kingship: 'He sat on it, as it is written' (vs. 14). This factor alone is enough to account for the use of the word καθή-μενος in the quotation"[127].

John's dependence on Mt 21,5 is firmly rejected in Menken's new contribution: "The answer to this question can only be in the negative"[128]. His argument of "the lack of agreement in the narrative" and the different place of the quotation in the narrative is not very impressive[129]. If he can say that "the two quotations agree with the LXX, which in turn agrees with the Hebrew", is it not because Jn 12,15 agrees,

124. Some prefer a more neutral translation in the passive: "and that this had happened to him" (NEB); "that this had been written of him and had been done to him" (RSV). This nice correspondence to the passive γεγραμμένα, as such, is not found in the Greek text. Note, however, the threefold ταῦτα, referring to the preceding scripture quotation: "They do not recognize in Jesus' use of the ass the fulfilment of prophecy" (BARRETT, p. 419).

125. Cf. P. SCHANZ, Johannes, Tübingen, 1885, p. 433; J.H. BERNARD, 1928, p. 427: "It seems likely that the comment ... is due to some one who was thinking of the Synoptic narrative"; BARRET, p. 419: "John's words show awareness of the older tradition, probably Mark".

126. M. HENGEL, Die Schriftauslegung (n. 122), p. 273 (and n. 88).

127. Old Testament Quotations (n. 115), p. 80. Menken's reply is hardly to the point: "die Frage ist dann, warum die Andeutungen für das Reittier nicht aneinander angeglichen worden sind" (Die Redaktion, p. 205). Is then John's use of the diminutive ὀνάριον not assimilation to πῶλος ὄνου and "sufficient variation of style" (Freed) comparable to ἐκάθισεν-καθήμενος? And is it not a long shot to explain καθήμενος (rokēb) in Jn 12,15 by ἐπικαθίζω in 1 Kings 1,38.44 LXX (for rkb hiph'il) (ibid., p. 206)? Menken's explanation of other redactional changes in Jn 12,15 is not more convincing: μὴ φοβοῦ connected with the motif of fear in the miracle stories (pp. 198-201) and the omission of σοι connected with Jesus' coming in the world (pp. 203-204).

128. The Quotations (n. 118), p. 577.

129. A few quotations will suffice, first from D.M. Smith's article: "It is quite true that the kingship of Jesus is here and throughout the Gospel of John a more important theme than in the synoptics, and it is possible, as Freed contends, that John places this quotation at the beginning [Ps 118,25 in Jn 12,13] to emphasize Jesus' kingly role" (Johannine Christianity, p. 101); and from a recent commentary: "The event is described with unusual brevity, ... No mention is made of the crowd of pilgrims that accompanied Jesus, only of those who went out of the city to meet him (vv 12-13). V 14 could imply that Jesus did not find the donkey till the crowds welcomed him, but that may be an unintended result of the Evangelist's mode of description in vv 12-13. The spreading of branches and clothes on the road by the crowd is not mentioned; this again may be due to the Evangelist's concentration of purpose". Cf. G.R. BEASLEY-MURRAY, John (Word Biblical Commentary, 36), Waco, TX, 1987, p. 206.

in content and form, with the central statement of the quotation in Mt 21,5? It is not quite correct that all identical words have "a different place and function": εἴπατε τῇ θυγατρὶ Σιών· ἰδοὺ ὁ βασιλεύς σου ἔρχεται σοι πραῢς καὶ ἐπιβεβηκὼς ἐπὶ ὄνον καὶ ἐπὶ πῶλον υἱὸν ὑπο-ζυγίου? With respect to the influence of Zech 9,9 in "the tradition before Mk and Jn", he refers to C.-P. März's tentative reconstruction of the traditional story. But in this reconstruction of "die von Sach 9,9f bestimmte Frühfassung" (Mk 11,1a.X.7c.8-10) the element X (Jesus' finding of the animal followed by v. 7c καὶ ἐκάθισεν ἐπ' αὐτόν) is taken from Jn 12,14a: εὑρὼν δὲ ὁ Ἰησοῦς (ὀνάριον) ἐκάθισεν ἐπ' αὐτό[130].

| 3. B. Lindars has taken the saying in Jn 3,3.5 as his test case in the question whether John used the Synoptic Gospels (1981)[131]:

Jn 3,3	3,5	Mt 18,3	Mk 10,15 = Lk 18,17
ἀμὴν ἀμὴν		ἀμὴν	ἀμὴν
λέγω σοι,		λέγω ὑμῖν,	λέγω ὑμῖν,
ἐὰν μή τις		ἐὰν μὴ	ὃς ἂν μὴ
γεννηθῇ		στραφῆτε	δέξηται
ἄνωθεν,	/ ἐξ ὕδατος	καὶ γένησθε	τὴν βασιλείαν τοῦ θεοῦ
	καὶ πνεύματος	ὡς τὰ παιδία,	ὡς παιδίον,
οὐ δύναται		οὐ μὴ	οὐ μὴ
ἰδεῖν	/ εἰσελθεῖν εἰς	εἰσέλθητε εἰς	εἰσέλθῃ εἰς
τὴν βασιλείαν		τὴν βασιλείαν	αὐτήν.
τοῦ θεοῦ.		τῶν οὐρανῶν.	

For Lindars, Mt 18,3 and Mk 10,15 are independent versions of the same saying, and the original form is best preserved by Matthew: "Matthew preserves [in στραφῆτε καὶ γένησθε] the saying as it was translated from the underlying Aramaic untouched"[132]. The saying came to John in an independent Greek form, an alternative translation of the Aramaic original, reconstructed by Lindars as follows: γένηται ἄνωθεν ὡς παιδίον (parallel to Matthew's στραφῆτε καὶ γένησθε ὡς τὰ παιδία). John replaced γένηται ... ὡς παιδίον by γεννηθῇ (the verb γεννάω) and εἰσελθεῖν εἰς by ἰδεῖν.

130. C.-P. MÄRZ (n. 123), p. 103-104. Cf. above, n. 33, Dschulnigg's note on καθίζειν ἐπί + acc in Mk/Jn. Concerning Jn 12,14a, cf. B-L, pp. 306-308: "La phrase reprend, moyennant un changement de sujet, les expressions attestées en Mc 11,4.7. ... L'emprunt de Jn à la tradition synoptique est difficile à nier" (pp. 306, 307). Cf. p. 308, on the source of Jn 12,14: "Nous ne pouvons évidemment pas prouver que ce n'est pas Mc! ... Une dépendance directe à l'égard de Mc conduirait à multiplier sans raison les sources de Jean II-A". But is it then not "multiplier sans raison" to suggest Jn II-A instead of Jn II-B (the Evangelist), and Document A instead of Mark?

131. *John and the Synoptic Gospels: A Test Case*, in NTS 27 (1980-81) 287-294.

132. *Ibid.*, p. 289.

Lindars has presented an attractive theory on John's use of traditional sayings and the composition of the discourses on the basis of the evangelist's own homilies[133]. I am on his side when he writes that "full recognition must be accorded to the evangelist as a creative writer"[134]; that "sayings from the tradition occur at strategic points in the discourses", they "have been adapted for their present context", and "are sufficiently close to sayings which have survived in the Synoptic tradition to be recognized as source material"[135]. His discussion of Mt 18,3, however, is symptomatic of the way the Synoptic parallels were treated I by a number of Johannine scholars in the 1960's. Of course, in the case of Mt 18,3, the name of J. Jeremias can be cited[136], but one could also mention that Jeremias refers to the dissenting opinion of J. Dupont, "der Mt 18,3 für eine Bearbeitung von Mk 10,15 hält"[137]. In 1985 Dupont republished his 1969 essay with an additional note: "l'interprétation que nous avons défendue est celle qu'on retrouve le plus souvent chez les auteurs récents"[138].

Lindars assumes that John uses ἄνωθεν in 3,3 with the meaning "from above". The word was found in the Greek saying as it came to John and there its meaning was "again": "the relationship with Mt. 18.3

---

133. B. LINDARS, *Traditions behind the Fourth Gospel*, in *L'Évangile de Jean*, 1977 (n. 1), pp. 107-124; *Discourse and Tradition. The Use of the Sayings of Jesus in the Discourses of the Fourth Gospel*, in *JSNT* 13 (1981) 83-101; and his more recent *John* (New Testament Guides), Sheffield, 1990. He repeats his view on Mt 18,3 "which may be an independent version of the saying in John 3.3,5" (p. 28); see also p. 57 and pp. 36-37 ("The Homilies of John").

134. *John*, 1990, p. 31.

135. *Ibid.*, p. 37. In reaction to Fortna, Lindars emphasizes that "the material which is common to John and the Synoptics extends to a number of sayings": cf. *SJT* 43 (1990) 526-527 (review of Fortna's *The Fourth Gospel*). Note his statement: "The proper starting-point should be passages where there are clear links with the synoptic tradition. John's source in any given instance was not necessarily identical with a Synoptic version, but the Synoptic parallel is the safest guide for reconstruction" (p. 527).

136. *Neutestamentliche Theologie*, Gütersloh, 1971, pp. 153-154 (ET, London, 1971, p. 155).

137. Note 13. Cf. J. DUPONT, Ἐὰν μὴ στραφῆτε καὶ γένησθε ὡς τὰ παιδία *(Mt 18,3)*, in *Neotestamentica et Semitica*. FS M. Black, Edinburgh, 1969, pp. 50-60; reprinted in *Études sur les évangiles synoptiques* (BETL, 70), Leuven, 1985, pp. 940-950.

138. *Études*, p. 950. Cf. S. Légasse, 1969; J. Zumstein, 1977; J. Schlosser, 1980. His view is supported by R. PESCH, *Markusevangelium*, II, p. 134, n. 15: "Mt 18,3 ist das Wort redaktionell neu formuliert"; J. SAUER, *Der ursprüngliche "Sitz im Leben" von Mk 10,13-16*, in *ZNW* 72 (1981) 27-50, p. 37, n. 53: "keine Sonderüberlieferung, sondern matthäische Überarbeitung von Mk 10,15"; R.H. GUNDRY, *Matthew*, p. 360; D. LÜHRMANN, *Markusevangelium*, p. 181. See also J. GNILKA, *Matthäusevangelium*, II, 1988, p. 120 (tacit correction of his *Markus*, II, p. 80: "die alte Fassung" in Mt 18,3); R. SCHNACKENBURG, *Großsein im Gottesreich. Zu Mt 18,1-5*, in L. SCHENKE (ed.), *Studien zum Matthäusevangelium*. FS W. Pesch, Stuttgart, 1988, pp. 269-282, esp. 273 and 277-279.

shows conclusively that it was intended to mean 'again'"[139]. But, if that is so, how can it then be said that "it would not be possible ... to derive ἄνωθεν from the Greek of Mt. 18.3"[140]? Although the meaning of ἄνωθεν in Jn 3,3 is still debated[141], we can agree with Lindars that John intended the meaning "from above", at least as the primary meaning of the word because the reaction of Nicodemus in v. 4 makes it extremely difficult to exclude deliberate ambiguity in John's use of ἄνωθεν[142]. The word is not found in Mt 18,3, but when this saying is taken out of its context in Mt 18,1-4, the phrase "unless you turn (= change) and become like children" (i.e., become comparable to children) "can easily be glossed with the phrase 'be born again'" (compare | Lindars's own explanation of the change to γεννηθῇ, to be sought in "John's interpretative licence")[143]. Lindars's position is severely criticized in a recent article by J.W. Pryor[144]:

> Jn 3.3 with its γεννηθῇ is John's re-interpretation of what eventually comes to us in Mt.18.3 as στραφῆτε καὶ γένησθε ὡς τὰ παιδία ; and 3.5, with its εἰσελθεῖν εἰς τὴν βασιλείαν τοῦ θεοῦ is more faithful to both the Markan and Matthean traditions than 3.3.
> The implications of this judgment are far-reaching for Johannine studies. ... The child/birth saying never existed independently in the Johannine community in the Johannine form... At the point when the Nicodemus story was created, the Gospel saying was *then* radically reshaped into the forms as we now have them, forming part of a larger narrative.

---

139. *Art. cit.*, p. 291.

140. *Ibid.*, p. 290.

141. For two extreme positions in recent commentaries, see, on the one hand, "from above": R. SCHNACKENBURG, I, 1965, pp. 381-382 (followed by B. Lindars and many others, e.g., J. BECKER, I, 1979, p. 134), and on the other, "anew": BOISMARD-LAMOUILLE, 1977, p. 118.

142. It is not a very convincing argument to separate Nicodemus' first question (πῶς δύναται ἄνθρωπος γεννηθῆναι γέρων ὤν;) from his second question (p. 291; cf. Schnackenburg). Nor is it correct to separate γεννηθῆναι from εἰσελθεῖν which is qualified by δεύτερον (*ibid.*). Lindars expects too much: "if ἄνωθεν means 'again' there is no reason why he should not have used it in both questions to qualify γεννηθῆναι. There is no necessity to leave it out" (*ibid.*). Should we not rather say that, after the use of ἄνωθεν in v. 3, there is no need to repeat it?

143. *Ibid.*, p. 290. On the context of Jn 3,3.5, I refer to M. MORGEN, *Jean 3 et les Synoptiques*, in this volume, pp. 514-522.

144. J.W. PRYOR, *John 3.3,5. A Study in the Relation of John's Gospel to the Synoptic Tradition*, in *JSNT* 41 (1991) 71-95; the quotations are taken from the conclusion, pp. 94-95. Pryor concurs with Lindars on one point: Mt 18,3 is not a redaction of Mk 10,15; the verse has been heavily redacted by the evangelist, but "another tradition beside Mark lies behind Matthew's redaction" (p. 87). By accepting pre-Matthean tradition in Mt 18,3, he avoids the conclusion of John's literary dependence on the Gospel of Matthew (pp. 93-94).

4. A. Dauer's list of John-Matthew agreements in the passion narrative includes one saying of Jesus, at the conclusion of the account of the arrest[145]:

Jn 18,11 a βάλε τὴν μάχαιραν εἰς τὴν θήκην·
      b τὸ ποτήριον ὃ δέδωκέν μοι ὁ πατὴρ οὐ μὴ πίω αὐτό;

Before Dauer, P. Borgen had noted that (in the passion narrative) "the parallels between John and Matthew are especially interesting", but, with only a few exceptions, he understood these parallels as "similarities between mutually independent traditions"[146]. The case of 18,11 was one of those he classified as "passages dependent on the Synoptics"[147]. A new step was made by Dauer emphasizing the editorial character of the parallels in Matthew (a: 26,52; b: 26,39.42). The debate is now no longer about dependence or independence. The question to be discussed is whether the acceptance of dependence on | Matthew (and on the Synoptics in general) should imply a two-stage composition of the Fourth Gospel[148].

Sabbe and Boismard-Lamouille assign Jn 18,11 to the evangelist and accept the evangelist's dependence on Mt 26,52 and 26,39b.42[149]. But Barrett ([2]1978) did not change his comment: the parallel in Mt 26,52 has no words in common (except μάχαιρα) and "it would be unwise to infer knowledge of Matthew on the part of John"[150]. Other scholars prefer to ignore the specific contacts with Matthew and assign 18,11 to "the earliest gospel": R.T. Fortna (1988)[151] and U.C. von Wahlde (1989)[152]. In this

145. Cf. above, n. 69.
146. P. BORGEN, *John and the Synoptics in the Passion Narrative*, in *NTS* 5 (1958-59) 246-259; reprinted in ID., *Logos Was the True Light and Other Essays on the Gospel of John*, Trondheim, 1983, pp. 67-80. See esp. his "Conclusions", p. 259 (= 80). "Both [John and Matthew] witness to traditions about Caiaphas and the decision in the council; a Christophany to the women (woman) after the resurrection; ..." (*ibid.*).
147. *Art. cit.*, pp. 247-252, esp. 250 (= 68-73, esp. 71); cf. above, n. 69. In the 1983 volume, Borgen repeats that "at some points influence from the Synoptics is probable" (p. 87; and p. 91, n. 29, with reference to A. Dauer: "the same hypothesis"); cf. his Preface: "A. Dauer uses this thesis and builds further on my studies..." (p. 6). On variations in the Borgen-Dauer thesis, cf. *Evangelica II*, pp. 700-701 (above, n. 68).
148. See the Dauer-Sabbe debate. Cf. M. SABBE, *The Arrest* (n. 2), pp. 228-232 (= 380-384), and Dauer's reply in the (still unpublished?) SNTS Seminar paper, Rome, 1981.
149. SABBE, *The Arrest*, p. 230: "directly dependent on Mt 26,52"; p. 232: "directly inspired by these Matthean verses 39 and 42"; B-L, p. 440: "Au v. 11, les affinités de Jn sont plus nettes, mais c'est avec Mt!"; see also p. 406: "Jean II-B développe, d'une façon beaucoup plus profonde, le thème de Mt 26,53" (Jn II-B = 18,1b.2.4b.5b-8a.9.10-11).
150. *John*, [2]1978, p. 522 (= 1955, p. 436).
151. *The Fourth Gospel* (n. 16), pp. 149-151: vv. 5b-9 are redactional and the pre-Johannine source resumes in vv. 10-12. Cf. p. 155: "the phrase 'which the Father [sic]

case (18,11), Dauer's position is adopted by J. Becker (1981): Jesus'
word to Peter first relies on Mt 26,52 and then uses the Gethsemane
motif: "Dieser Zusammenhang ist wohl nicht erst von E geschaffen (wie
Dauer sprachlich begründet)"[153]. In fact, Dauer has only one argument
with respect to Jn 18,11a: "die Ungewöhnlichkeit von θήκη"[154]. But if
the substitution of εἰς τὴν θήκην for εἰς τὸν τόπον αὐτῆς is unexplainable on the level of the Johannine redaction, why is this same substitution considered less unexplainable on the level of the pre-Johannine
source? Is it not because of Dauer's (but not Becker's) general assumption that this source is supposed to be "in gewisser Nähe zu Mt"[155]? The
word θήκη for sheath is less unusual I than Dauer seems to suggest[156]
and can be a correction of Matthew's too general expression: "au lieu
du vague 'à sa place' de Mt, Jn donne le terme plus technique de 'four-
reau', ce qui pourrait être une correction du texte matthéen"[157].

has given me' has a Johannine ring—but the rough parallel in Mark 14:36 ('Father ... this
cup') suggests that it is traditional"; no comment on v. 11a. But see *The Gospel of Signs*,
1970, p. 116: "Jesus' rebuke (11*a*) resembles Mt 26:52 (*cf.* Lk 22:51)".

152. *The Earliest Gospel* (n. 59), p. 136: vv. 7-8 are assigned to the source and "The
signs material continues in vv 10-11". — Concerning vv. 7-8 (traditional), contrast
Fortna (n. 151), *et multi alii* (including Schnackenburg and Becker). Cf. DAUER, pp. 29-
43: vv. 4-9 from the evangelist; on the Synoptic background, cf. SABBE, pp. 216-222.

153. *Johannes*, p. 544. — Becker recognizes as "das bleibende Verdienst von Dauer"
to have shown the influence of the Synoptics on the pre-Johannine oral tradition(s) of the
passion narrative (p. 537: "unter Quereinfluß aus den indessen literarisch festgelegten PB
bei Mt, Mk und Lk"). But in contrast to Luke's passion narrative, "Die Nähe zum Besonderen des Mt ist dabei viel weniger markant" (p. 536). Other instances of John-Matthew
agreement listed by Dauer are not even mentioned by Becker, with two exceptions, where
he explicitly rejects Dauer's explication: Jn 18,24 Caiaphas, cf. Mt 26,57 (p. 548: "keine
Angleichung an Mt"); Jn 19,19, cf. Mt 27,37 (p. 587: "doch unabhängig von ihm, da:
'dieser ist...' fehlt"). As far as I see, the case of Jesus' word in Jn 18,11a, "das am
Anfang Mt 26,52 folgt", is unique in Becker's commentary. Regarding v. 11b, he refers
to "Mk 14,36 parr", not specifically "Mt".

154. *Die Passionsgeschichte*, p. 47.

155. *Ibid.* (in contrast to Becker: see n. 153).

156. Compare κολεόν in LXX and θήκη in Josephus: μάχαιραν ... ἐν κολεῷ
αὐτῆς, καὶ ἡ μάχαιρα ἐξῆλθεν καὶ ἔπεσεν (2 Reg 20,8) and τὴν μάχαιραν ... ἐκ τῆς
θήκης ἐκπεσεῖν (Ant. 7,284).

157. BL, p. 404. See also SABBE, *The Arrest*, pp. 229-230. — For a recent analysis of
Jn 18,1-11, cf. M. MYLLYKOSKI, *Die letzten Tage Jesu. Markus und Johannes, ihre Traditionen und die historische Frage*, Bd I (AASF, B-256), Helsinki, 1991, pp. 167-172
(notes, 205-208): "Die Analyse von Joh 18,1-11". He finds elements of a traditional pas-
sion narrative in Jn 18,1a*.3*.10* (cf. Mk 14,43*.45.46.47*.50); 18,4-8 is "eine vom
Evangelisten selbst ... gebildete Sequenz", v. 9 is inserted by KR, and "In V 10-11 hat er
[Johannes] sowohl seine Gemeindetradition als auch das Gebet Jesu aus Mk 14,36
benutzt" (p. 172). With regard to Jn 18,11a, he rejects both the pre-Johannine source
(Dauer) and direct dependence on Mt 26,52 (Sabbe): "Es ist wahrscheinlicher, daß
Johannes einen in diesem Zusammenhang bekannten und üblichen Einzelspruch aufge-
griffen hat" (p. 171). Cf. ID., *Luke and John*, 1991 (n. 62), p. 132: "John used the oral
tradition of his own congregation, which had one point in common with the oral tradition

With respect to Jn 18,11b, Barrett emphasizes "the freedom with which John handles the synoptic material. (*a*) He uses the expression not in a prayer that the cup may pass, but in a calm determined acceptance of it. (*b*) The cup is the Father's gift"[158]. John's transformation of the Gethsemane prayer in 18,11b is introduced by v. 11a and takes here the form of a word of Jesus addressed to his disciples, in line with Mt 26,52-54[158a].

5. If I were asked to advance my own test case for the relationship to Matthew[159] I would take once more, I think, the appearance to the women at the tomb in Mt 28,9-10. This passage is sufficiently different from Mark to be taken as special material in Matthew, and sufficiently close to Mark to be accepted as Matthew's editorial composition. The parallel in Jn 20,14-18 is substantial and shows specific contacts with Matthew. I will not rehearse my argumentation (1969, 1977, 1984)[160], but at least one critical voice, following the 1984 article in *NTS*, should be heard. D. Zeller, in a formal confrontation with my approach (1986)[161], has suggested a *traditionsgeschichtlich* alternative: John depends on a pre-Johannine sequence (A C C' B) of the women's discovery of the

... used by Matthew (v. 11a; cf. Mt 26:52-53)". But see *Die letzten Tage Jesu*, p. 171, on Mt 26,52: "Bei Mt geht es deutlich um einen die markinische Vorlage weiterführenden Zusatz und nicht um eine alte Tradition, die einen festen Platz in der Passionsgeschichte gehabt hätte" (sic).

158. *John*, p. 522. Cf. M. MYLLYKOSKI, *Die letzten Tage Jesu*, p. 171: "Der vierte Evangelist kennt Mk, verwendet es aber kritisch, um das dort dargestellte Verständnis des Leidens Jesu zu widerlegen".

158a. Cf. H.-J. KLAUCK, in *BZ* 35 (1991) 271-272 (review of Barrett's Commentary in German translation): "Sie paßt sich insofern gut in einen neuerdings wieder erstarkenden Forschungstrend ein, als Barrett entgegen der Mehrheitsmeinung immer entschlossen daran festgehalten hat, daß der Autor des Johannesevangeliums die synoptischen Evangelien kannte, auf jeden Fall Mk und in geringerem Umfang auch Lk (aber kommt man dann an Mt vorbei? Die Verwandtschaft von Joh 18,10-11 mit Mt 26,51-54, die über das Schwertwort hinausreicht, gibt mir immer mehr zu denken, gegen Barrett 504)" (p. 271).

159. Not a few commentators have suggested that the prayer in Jn 17 is written around the themes of the Lord's Prayer. See, e.g., J.C. FENTON, *Towards an Understanding of John*, in *Studia Evangelica* 4 (1968) 28-37, p. 30. For W.O. Walker, "the High Priestly Prayer represents a type of 'midrash' on the Matthean version of the Lord's Prayer". Cf. W.O. WALKER, Jr., *The Lord's Prayer in Matthew and John*, in *NTS* 28 (1982) 237-256. The question is treated in this volume by W. SCHENK, *Die Umcodierungen der matthäischen Unser-Vater-Redaktion in Joh 17*, pp. 587-607.

160. F. NEIRYNCK, *Les femmes au tombeau. Étude de la rédaction matthéenne (Matt. xxviii.1-10)*, in *NTS* 15 (1968-69) 168-190, pp. 176-190 (= *Evangelica*, 273-295, esp. 281-295, with additional note on Mt 28,9-10); *John and the Synoptics*, 1977 (n. 1), esp. pp. 96-98 (= *Evangelica*, 388-390); *John and the Synoptics: The Empty Tomb Stories*, 1984 (n. 36), esp. pp. 166-172: "Jn. 20.11-18 and Mt. 28.9-10" (= *Evangelica II*, 579-588, with Additional Note, p. 600).

161. *Der Ostermorgen im 4. Evangelium (Joh 20,1-18)* (n. 62).

empty tomb (A: 20,1), the angelophany (C: 20,12-13), the angelic message (C': om.), Peter's visit to the tomb (B: 20,3-10*). The evangelist is responsible for the inversion of order (to A B C) and for the introduction of the Beloved Disciple in 20,2-10 (B). The continuation of the angelophany (C') is replaced by the christophany in 20,14-18, taken by the evangelist from a different *Überlieferungsstrang* (D). One will easily recognize in A C C' B the sequence of Lk 24,1-3.4-11.12, and in D the account of Mt 28,9-10; apart from his use of the term "traditions", Zeller's solution scarcely differs from my own interpretation of Jn 20,1-18[162]:

> [Jn 20,14-18] eine auch Mt 28,9f greifbare Tradition. ... Das Verbot des Anfassens könnte ... wegen Mt 28,9b vorgegeben sein... Der Inhalt des Botenauftrags V. 17c dürfte ... aufs Konto des Evangelisten zu setzen sein. [V. 18] Vielleicht sollte sie [ursprünglich] ihnen wie Mt 28,10 eine Erscheinung Jesu in Galiläa ankündigen.

With regard to Jn 20,17, the suggestion (and reconstruction) of a pre-Johannine Vorlage similar to, but independent of, Mt 28,9-10[163], is no more satisfactory than the acceptance of "un double souvenir d'un même fait" (de Solages)[164].

I come to a concluding remark on Matthew. A great deal of the similarities between Matthew and John, in the passion and elsewhere, are found in material that is parallel to Mark, and they are explicable

---

162. *Ibid.*, pp. 155 and 156. — J. Kügler, in *Der Jünger, den Jesus liebte*, 1988 (n. 35), pp. 348-349, makes a curious distinction between Jn 20,2-10 (dependent on Lk 24) and Jn 20,11-18: "Selbst wenn solche Veränderungen [in John] plausibel gemacht und ihre Basis im Mt-Text aufgezeigt werden kann, liegt hier doch kein Argument für eine literarische Abhängigkeit vor" (p. 348). — J. Gnilka, in *Matthäusevangelium*, II, 1988, pp. 492-493, notes the contacts with Jn 20,14-18 but concludes (with T.A. Mohr) that "Mt auch in den VV 8-10 von einer Überlieferung abhängig ist, die Johannes wahrscheinlich relativ besser bewahrte [sic]. Mt hat sie dem Kontext und seinem Stil angepaßt" (p. 493; not one word on Johannine redaction in Jn 20,14-18).

163. Cf. *NTS* 30 (1984), pp. 160-171. In *The Fourth Gospel* (1988), R.T. Fortna repeats his reconstruction of the source behind Jn 20,11-18 (he now adds v. 13a), with the word of Jesus: "Do not cling to me, but go to my brothers and tell them..." (v. 17). Cf. p. 189: "Evidently Mary falls down before him to embrace his feet (see Matt. 28:9)"; p. 199: the Johannine v. 17d "may have replaced something in the source, such as the promise that the disciples will see Jesus in Galilee" (cf. Mt 28,10); "That the disciples to whom Mary is sent are called by Jesus his *brothers* is found at Matt. 28:10".

164. *Jean et les Synoptiques* (n. 14), p. 113. "Un double souvenir d'un trait historique" is again de Solages's solution in the case of Jn 6,3:
Jn 6,3 ἀνῆλθεν δὲ εἰς τὸ ὄρος Ἰησοῦς καὶ ἐκεῖ ἐκάθητο μετὰ τῶν μαθητῶν αὐτοῦ. 5 ... θεασάμενος ὅτι πολὺς ὄχλος ἔρχεται πρὸς αὐτόν.
Mt 15,29b καὶ ἀναβὰς εἰς τὸ ὄρος ἐκάθητο ἐκεῖ. 30 καὶ προσῆλθον αὐτῷ ὄχλοι πολλοί. (14,14 εἶδεν πολὺν ὄχλον, par. Mk 6,34).

as independent *minor* agreements. Not unlike the Synoptic minor agreements, some of theses similarities may possibly point to independent use of Mark, the common Gospel source of Matthew and John. But for agreements beween John and Mark/Matthew there is at least a theoretical possibility that the contact with Mark took place via Matthew.

III

JOHN AND LUKE

The situation is, of course, different with Luke. The John-Luke agreements constitute a privileged theme in the study of John and the Synoptics. If we put it in very general terms we can say that most scholars accept that "some type of relationship exists between Luke and John". F.L. Cribbs, who specialises in the listing of the agreements, starts his 1979 presentation with this statement: "it seems to us that the extent and preciseness of many of these verbal/factual/sequential/conceptual agreements suggest that some type of relationship exists between Luke and John"[165]. He is more precise in his conclusion: "some type of *direct* relationship", but he still leaves open several possibilities: "John may have known some form of Luke, Luke may have known some *early* form of John, both evangelists may have been | influenced by some other common source or sources"[166]. It is quite clear that "comprehensiveness" is one of the characteristics of Cribbs's work. Unfortunately, with the exception of I.H. Marshall's commentary on Luke (1978), his bibliography does not extend beyond 1970, and there is no reference to Dauer's study of the passion narrative.

Dauer's dissertation was yet unknown to H. Klein in 1976, when he published his essay on "Die lukanisch-johanneische Passions-

---

165. F.L. CRIBBS, *The Agreements that Exist between Luke and John*, in *SBL 1979 Seminar Papers*, vol. I, pp. 215-261, esp. p. 217. Cribbs's list is an adaptation of his earlier presentations, *St. Luke and the Johannine Tradition*, in *JBL* 90 (1971) 422-450; *A Study of the Contacts that Exist between St. Luke and St. John*, in *SBL 1973 Seminar Papers*, vol. II, pp. 1-93. Compare also *The Agreements that Exist between Acts and John*, in C.H. TALBERT (ed.), *Perspectives on Luke-Acts* (Perspectives in Religious Studies, 5), Edinburgh-Danville, VA, 1978, pp. 40-61.

166. *Agreements*, p. 251. Contrast his 1971 conclusion: "the hypothesis that Luke was influenced by some early form of the developing Johannine tradition (or perhaps even by an early draft of the original edition of John) *rather than vice versa*" (*St. Luke*, p. 450; = *A Study*, p. 92; italics mine).

tradition"[167], an investigation of the parallels between the two Gospels which led him to the acceptance of a common passion tradition (*Grundschicht* G) behind their respective *Vorlage*, LV and JV. Since Dauer had tried to show that the "parallels" to John (18,1–19,30) in Lk 22,39.40.47.50.52.54.55.58.59.60; 23,2.4.18.19.20.21.22.33.36 are best explained as Lukan redaction ("lukanische Redaktionsarbeit an seiner Mk-Vorlage")[168], one could expect that this part of his work (more | sig-

---

167. *ZNW* 67 (1976) 155-186; = M. LIMBECK (ed.), *Redaktion und Theologie des Passionsberichtes nach den Synoptikern* (Wege der Forschung, 481), Darmstadt, 1981, pp. 366-403.

168. *Die Passionsgeschichte*, pp. 53-60 (Jn 18,1-11), 97-99 (Jn 18,12-27), 155-164 (Jn 18,28–19,16a), 222-225 (Jn 19,16b-30). Compare above, n. 69 (contacts with Mt). Dauer's references to earlier studies (particularly J. Schniewind, 1914, [2]1958, and J.A. Bailey, 1963) are also indicated here (e.g., Jn 18,1: cf. p. 22[6] = note 6, references to Schniewind, Bailey, Léon-Dufour, Osty). On the references to B-L and B-B, cf. below, n. 186.

18,1a   σὺν τοῖς μαθηταῖς αὐτοῦ
        Lk 22,39 ἠκολούθησαν δὲ αὐτῷ καὶ οἱ μαθηταί
        [p. 53, cf. 22[6]] B-L (404a)

18,1b   om. Gethsemane
        Lk 22,40 om.
        [p. 54, cf. 24[15.16]] B-L (404a)

18,2   ὅτι πολλάκις συνήχθη Ἰησοῦς ἐκεῖ μετὰ τῶν μαθητῶν αὐτοῦ
        Lk 22,39 κατὰ τὸ ἔθος
        [p. 55, cf. 26[29]] B-L 405b

18,3   ὁ οὖν Ἰούδας λαβὼν τὴν σπεῖραν ... ἔρχεται ἐκεῖ
        Lk 22,47 ὁ λ. Ἰούδας ... προήρχετο αὐτούς
        [p. 56, cf. 26[32]]

18,4   no sign given by Judas
        Lk 22,47 om. Mk 14,44
        [p. 59, cf. 29[50.51]] B-L (404a)

18,10   αὐτοῦ τὸ ὠτάριον τὸ δεξιόν
        Lk 22,50 τὸ οὖς αὐτοῦ *τὸ δεξιόν*
        [p. 57, cf. 46[135]] Borgen 250(!), B-L 404a(!)

18,10-11   before the arrest (v. 12)
        Lk 22,49-53 before the arrest (v. 54a)
        [p. 58, cf. 46[137]] B-L (404a)

18,11   no flight of the disciples
        Lk 22,53 om. Mk 15,50
        [p. 60, cf. 48[151]]

18,12a   ἡ σπεῖρα (cf. v. 3), ὁ χιλίαρχος (in source: Jews?)
        Lk 22,52 στρατηγοὺς τοῦ ἱεροῦ
        [p. 59, cf. 28]

18,12b   συνέλαβον τὸν Ἰησοῦν ... ἤγαγον
        Lk 22,54 *συλλαβόντες δὲ αὐτὸν ἤγαγον*
        [p. 97, cf. 66[18]] Borgen 256, B-L (409b)

18,18   ἀνθρακιὰν πεποιηκότες
        Lk 22,55 περιαψάντων δὲ πῦρ
        [p. 98, n. 77[82]] B-L (409b)

18,25   μὴ καὶ σύ ἐκ τῶν μαθητῶν αὐτοῦ εἶ; ... οὐκ εἰμί (cf. 17)
        Lk 22,58 *καὶ σύ ἐξ αὐτῶν εἶ*. ... οὐκ εἰμί
        [p. 97, cf. 77] Borgen 256, B-L (411a)

nificant for Luke than for Matthew) would not remain unnoticed in the commentaries on Luke. But most commentators seem to follow the

18,26 εἷς ἐκ τῶν δούλων τοῦ ἀρχιερέως (sing.)
Lk 22,59 ἄλλος τις
[p. 98, cf. 89]

18,27 om. ἀναθεματίζειν καὶ ὀμνύναι (Mk 14,71)
Lk 22,60 om.
[p. 98, cf. 90¹⁸⁰]

18,28 ἄγουσιν τὸν Ἰησοῦν ... εἰς τὸ πραιτώριον
Lk 23,1 ἤγαγον αὐτὸν ἐπὶ τὸν Πιλᾶτον
[cf. p. 121¹²⁵] B-B 200 (?)

18,30 εἰ μὴ ἦν οὗτος κακὸν ποιῶν
Lk 23,22 τί γὰρ κακὸν ἐποίησεν οὗτος·
[p. 147] B-L (417b) B-B 207 (Syn)

18,38b ἐγὼ οὐδεμίαν εὑρίσκω ἐν αὐτῷ αἰτίαν (19,4.6)
Lk 23,4 οὐδὲν εὑρίσκω αἴτιον ἐν τῷ ἀνθρώπῳ τούτῳ
[p. 156, cf. 123¹³³] Borgen 254, B-L 417a B-B 198(?)

18,39 ἀπολύσω ὑμῖν τὸν...
Lk 23,16 αὐτὸν ἀπολύσω
[cf. pp. 124-125¹⁴⁴]

18,40 ἐκραύγασαν λέγοντες· μὴ τοῦτον ἀλλὰ τὸν Βαραββᾶν. ἦν δὲ ὁ Βαραββᾶς...
Lk 23,18-19 ἀνέκραγον ... λέγοντες· αἶρε τοῦτον, ἀπόλυσον δὲ ἡμῖν τον Βαραββᾶν· ¹⁹ ὅστις ἦν...
[p. 157, cf. 125¹⁴⁶] B-L 417b(!) B-B 191

19,4 οὐδεμίαν αἰτίαν εὑρίσκω ἐν αὐτῷ (18,38; 19,6)
Lk 23,22 οὐδὲν αἴτιον θανάτου εὗρον ἐν αὐτῷ
[pp. 158-160, cf. 156³¹⁸] B-L (423b)

19,6a λέγοντες· σταύρωσον σταύρωσον
Lk 23,21 λέγοντες· σταύρου σταύρου αὐτόν
[p. 160, cf. 128¹⁶⁹.¹⁷⁰] B-L (418a, 425b) B-B 196

19,6b ἐγὼ γὰρ οὐχ εὑρίσκω ἐν αὐτῷ αἰτίαν (18,38; 19,4)
Lk 23,22 οὐδὲν αἴτιον θανάτου εὗρον ἐν αὐτῷ
[p. 160; cf. 128] B-L (418a, 423b)

19,12a ἐκ τούτου ὁ Πιλᾶτος ... ἐζήτει ἀπολῦσαι αὐτόν
Lk 23,20 ὁ Πιλᾶτος ... θέλων ἀπολῦσαι τὸν Ἰησοῦν
[p. 162, cf. 128¹⁷⁵] B-L (418a) B-B 212

19,12c ὁ βασιλέα ἑαυτὸν ποιῶν
Lk 23,2 λέγοντα ἑαυτὸν χριστὸν βασιλέα εἶναι
[p. 162, cf. 129¹⁷⁶] B-L 417b, but 425a: Acts 17,7 B-B 213(?)

19,15 ἐκραύγασαν ...· ἆρον ἆρον
Lk 23,18 ἀνέκραγον ...· αἶρε τοῦτον
[p. 163, cf. 130¹⁹⁵] B-B 215

19,18 ὅπου αὐτὸν ἐσταύρωσαν, καὶ μετ᾽ αὐτοῦ ἄλλους δύο
Lk 23,33 ἐκεῖ ἐσταύρωσαν αὐτὸν καὶ τοὺς κακούργους
[p. 222, cf. 171³⁶.³⁸⁻⁴⁰] Borgen 253, B-L (437a.b)

19,18 om. Mk 15,23 (the drink)
Lk 23,33 om.
[p. 223, cf. 174⁶²] B-L (437a)

19,25 εἱστήκεισαν δέ
Lk 23,49 εἱστήκεισαν δέ
[p. 220] B-L (438a)

general trend of the commentaries on the Gospel of John without really reconsidering the question. To quote one of them: "I tend to agree with Brown that nothing suggests that the fourth evangelist knew Luke's Gospel"[169], and: "the impressive list of contacts between the Lucan and Johannine passion narratives ... establishes only that 'Luke knew an early form of the developing Johannine tradition' (Brown) or, as I should prefer to put it, 'early forms' of that tradition"[170].

The most explicit treatment in recent commentaries is that of E. Schweizer (1982). He raises the question about the Lukan *Sonderquelle* and inclines to accept a written source: "Dafür sprechen auch die Parallelen mit Johannes" (21,37-38; 22,3.14.23.27.31.32.47-53.54-71; 23,4.13.18-25; 24,12.40.41)[171]. With less reserve, J.B. Green (1988) has proposed a reconstruction of the *Sonderquelle*[172]. For Green, too, the

---

19,29   σπόγγον ... ὄξους ... προσήνεγκαν αὐτοῦ τῷ στόματι
         Lk 23,36 ὄξος *προσφέροντες αὐτῷ*
         [p. 224, cf. 209[280]] B-L (438a, 440a)

169. J.A. FITZMYER, *Luke*, I, 1981, p. 88 (he cites Brown's list of parallels, with supplements).

170. *Luke*, II, 1985, p. 1366 (with reference to listings by E. Osty, 1951; J.A. Bailey, 1963; F.L. Cribbs, 1971; no mention of Dauer).

Cf. J. ERNST, 1977, p. 34: "Die Vielzahl der Übereinstimmungen deutet darauf hin, daß die lk/joh Passionstradition eine feste sprachliche Gestalt besaß, die sich freilich unterschiedlich weiterentwickelt hat"; G. SCHNEIDER, 1977, p. 637: "Da es sich kaum um Kontakte handelt, die durch direkte Benutzung zustande gekommen sind, kann hier ebenfalls an eine neben dem schriftlichen Markus-Evangelium weitergehende vielfältige Tradition gedacht werden"; E. SCHWEIZER, 1982, p. 2: "eine Überlieferung, die viele Berührungen mit dem vierten Evangelium zeigt, ohne daß an direkte Abhängigkeit des einen vom andern zu denken wäre"; W. WIEFEL, 1988, p. 12: "Berührungen, die sich jedoch kaum zu einer literarischen Abhängigkeit des einen vom anderen oder von einer gemeinsamen Quelle verdichten" (with reference to more explicit treatment by F. Hauck, 1934, pp. 6-7, and W. Grundmann, 1961, pp. 17-22).

171. *Lukas*, pp. 235-237: "Sonderquelle (S) in der Passionsgeschichte?", esp. p. 236 (see also p. 222: Lk 22,31-34). Cf. *Zur Frage der Quellenbenutzung durch Lukas*, in ID., *Neues Testament und Christologie im Werden. Aufsätze*, Göttingen, 1982, pp. 32-85, esp. 84: "*Beweisen* läßt sich also die Sonderquelle nicht. Es scheint mir aber vieles dafür zu sprechen: ... 6. Übereinstimmungen mit Joh..., besonders in der Passions- und Ostergeschichte" (see also p. 55: more hesitant).

Compare now F. BOVON, *Lukas*, I, 1989, p. 21: "Lukas hat hier [in der Passionsgeschichte] entweder Markus stärker adaptiert als sonst bei ihm üblich oder eine konkurrierende Erzählung aufgenommen. Die Übereinstimmungen von Lk 22–23 mit dem johanneischen Passionsbericht deuten eher auf letzteres".

172. J.B. GREEN, *The Death of Jesus. Tradition and Interpretation in the Passion Narrative* (WUNT, 2/33), Tübingen, 1988 (Diss., Aberdeen, under I.H. Marshall, 1987), esp. pp. 24-104 ("The Gospel of Luke") and 324-330 ("Appendix: Sources in Luke's Passion Narrative"): Lk 22,3.14-20.21-23*.24-27.28-30.31-33.35-38.39-42*.43-44.45*.48.50c-51*.52b.53b.54b-62*.63-64.66-71;   23,2.4-5.6-7.8-12.13-16.18-25*.26c-31.34ab.35-37.39-43.44b.48 (combined with Mark, and in some sections [*] conflated with the text of Mark).

I evidence of the John-Luke agreements is of great importance: "These correspondences strongly suggest a common, non-Markan source behind the Lukan and Johannine accounts"[173]. He examines more particularly "three 'test cases' for a Johannine-Synoptic literary relationship": Jn 12,1-8 (the anointing); 13,1-30 (the last supper); 18,13-27 (the interwoven stories of Jesus' trial and Peter's denial), and comes to the conclusion that "in each case the evidence did not support a direct literary relationship": "the passion narrative of the Gospel of John is related to, but not directly dependent on, the passion stories in the Gospels of Matthew, Mark, and Luke"[174].

A more modest, but methodologically more agreeable, work has been published in 1987 by M.L. Soards on "the special material of Luke 22". As a result of his analysis, he presents a list of the non-Markan elements in Lk 22[175]: "Isolated from the other portions of Lk 22, *this is not a continuous narrative*"[176]. Ten passages are marked as "oral tradition drawn on by Luke". This list includes[177] five instances of minor agreement between Matthew and Luke against Mark: "too significant to be reasonably attributed to chance", "probably the result of oral tradition, because there remain striking differences — scarcely the sign of a written common tradition" (22,42.48.51.62.64)[178]. This same solution is applied to two instances of agreement between John and Luke: 22,3a εἰσῆλθεν δὲ σατανᾶς εἰς Ἰούδαν, cf. Jn 13,27 ("both Luke and John derive this detail from an independent tradition that was available to them")[179] and 22,67b-e [λέγοντες· εἰ σὺ εἶ ὁ χριστός,] εἰπὸν ἡμῖν. εἶπεν δὲ αὐτοῖς· ἐὰν ὑμῖν εἴπω, οὐ μὴ πιστεύσητε ("67a-e is I Luke's redacted version of Mark 14.61 based upon an oral tradition that is also reflected

173. Quoted from p. 79 (on Lk 23,4; cf. p. 78: "points to a non-Markan tradition underlying the Johannine and Lukan texts"). See also p. 27 (Lk 22,3).
174. "Three 'Test Cases' for a Johannine-Synoptic Literary Relationship within the Passion Narrative": A. John 12,1-8 (pp. 106-111); B. John 13,1-30 (pp. 111-125); C. John 18,13-27 (pp. 125-127); D. Conclusion (p. 128: text quoted above).
175. M.L. SOARDS, *The Passion according to Luke. The Special Material of Luke 22* (JSNT SS, 14), Sheffield, 1987 (Diss., Union Theol. Sem., New York, 1984). Non-Markan elements (including Lukan composition) are: Lk 22,3a.15a-16c.19a-20c.24a-b.27a-32d.35a-38d.39b.40b.42a-d.48a-49b.51a-c.52b.53c-d.61a.62a-b.64d.66a-68b.
176. *Ibid.*, p. 120 (Soards's emphasis). "Moreover, this material seems to fall naturally into many independent units" (listed on p. 121; text, in English, on pp. 119-120).
177. Besides 22,19-20 (cf. 1 Cor 11,24); 22,28.30 (cf. Mt 19,28 Q) and 22,36 (saying). Cf. *ibid.*, pp. 116-118 (underlined text). Note the case of Lk 22,21: "it is probably best to see this minor agreement on 'hand' between Luke and Matthew as evidence of the continued existence and influence of oral tradition alongside the written Gospel" (p. 35); but marked as (21?) on p. 38 and neglected on p. 116 (unemphasized text).
178. Quotations from pp. 101 (Lk 22,62) and 98 (Lk 22,42).
179. *Ibid.*, p. 49 (see also pp. 32, 44, and 116).

in John 10.24-26")[180]. In both cases, and also in the instances of agreement with Matthew, it can be asked whether Soards did not stop too soon his examination of Lukan redaction on the basis of Mark[181]. In a number of other cases he has shown that the agreement is "not significant", "does not offer much support for (an) alleged point of contact between the two Gospels"[182].

More than any other scholar, M.-É. Boismard has puzzled over the John-Luke agreements: common traditions behind John and Luke (cf. E. Osty), Luke as the "redactor" of the Fourth Gospel (1962), the common source Proto-Luke (1972) and finally dependence of the evangelist (Jn II-B) on the Gospel of Luke (1977)[183]: "les écrits lucaniens, évangile et Actes, ont exercé une influence prépondérante sur certaines parties de l'évangile de Jean II-B"[184]; "Pour composer son évangile, Jean II-B a

180. *Ibid.*, p. 106 (see also pp. 80-81, 104-105, and 118). Compare the text on p. 118: (67a) *saying, "If you are the Christ,"* (italics = "Markan material that Luke has combined with oral tradition"); the underlining of 67b-e continues in: (68a) *and if I ask you,* (b) *you will not answer* (underlined = oral tradition...). But see p. 104: "Luke composed 68a-b to provide a balancing statement for 67d-e" (see also pp. 105 and 106: "a Lukan composition").

181. Soards refers to my discussion of Lk 22,3 in *La matière marcienne dans l'évangile de Luc*, in F. NEIRYNCK (ed.), *L'Évangile de Luc* (BETL, 32), 1973, pp. 157-201, esp. 169-170 (²1989, pp. 79-80; *Evangelica*, pp. 49-50). Soards seems to agree: "Neirynck demonstrates that the mention of Satan entering into Judas at 3a could be the result of Luke's editorial tendencies" (p. 49; cf. 44). Contrast Green's unsatisfactory treatment of Luke's σατανᾶς (p. 27). Soards rightly observes that "John uses the name *Satan* only at 13.27 instead of his usual *the devil* (three times)".
On the Lukan redaction in 22,67-68, see my observations in *ETL* 48 (1972), p. 571 (review of G. Schneider's *Verleugnung*). See also F.J. MATERA, *Jesus before Annas: John 18,13-14.19-24*, in *ETL* 65 (1989) 28-55, pp. 51-52, and W. RADL, *Sonderüberlieferungen bei Lukas? Traditionsgeschichtliche Fragen zu Lk 22,67f; 23,2 und 23,6-12*, in K. KERTELGE (ed.), in *Der Prozess gegen Jesus* (Quaestiones Disputatae, 112), Freiburg, 1988, pp. 131-147, p. 147: "der literarische Bezug zu Lk 20,1-8 als ernst zu nehmende lukanische Alternative, die der ... Annahme eines traditionellen 'johanneischen' Logions, vielleicht sogar vorzuziehen ist" (in reply to G. SCHNEIDER, *ibid.*, p. 117: (V. 67c) wie Joh 10,24f zeigt, 'johanneisch' formuliert und somit wahrscheinlich traditionell). For fuller treatment I refer to A. DAUER, *Spuren der (synoptischen) Synedriumsverhandlung im 4. Evangelium - Das Verhältnis zu den Synoptikern*, in this volume, pp. 307-339; and M. SABBE, *John 10 and Its Relationship to the Synoptic Gospels*, in J. BEUTLER - R.T. FORTNA (eds.), *The Shepherd Discourse of John 10 and Its Context* (SNTS MS, 67), Cambridge, 1991, pp. 75-93, esp. 75-85 (= *Studia Neotestamentica*, n. 2 above, pp. 443-466).

182. The latest study he mentioned in his bibliographical note on the contacts between Luke and John (pp. 134-135, n. 18) is H. Klein's article, *Passionstradition*, 1976: there is no reference to Dauer, 1972! [Note that the same can be said of Fitzmyer's bibliography, 1985, p. 1372.] Soards takes exception to Klein's interpretation explicitly at Lk 22,23 / Jn 13,22 (p. 35, n. 37); Lk 22,33 / Jn 13,36-38 (p. 37, n. 46); Lk 22,53b / Jn 16,2.4; 13,30 (p. 75, nn. 49, 51); Lk 22,54 / Jn 18,12-13 (p. 76, n. 56); and tacitly at Lk 22,27.39.50.58.

183. On this evolution, see my *JeanSyn*, pp. 3-21, esp. 19-20 (on Proto-Luke).

184. B-L, p. 47 (*4y*); with a list of parallel passages.

utilisé dans une très large mesure les écrits | lucaniens; il s'est donc
familiarisé avec le style de Lc-Ac, et il ne faut pas s'étonner si ce style
a quelque peu déteint sur le sien"[185]. It is less clear for me how then he
can still isolate, in the passion narrative[186] and elsewhere, Jn I = Document C, common source of John and Luke, but there is no debate, at
least among us, about the presence of a significant Lukan element in
John.

An important contribution to the study of John and Luke came, once
more, from A. Dauer. His *Johannes und Lukas* (1984)[187] is a collection
of three individual investigations: Jn 4,46-54; 12,1-8; 20,19-29. The
first of these studies has already been mentioned in connection with the
parallel in Matthew. The anointing story is the classic example of dependence on Luke: the anointing of Jesus' head by a woman (Mk/Mt) combined with the story in which a sinful woman wets Jesus' feet with her
tears and dries them with her hair (Lk 7): ἤλειψεν τοὺς πόδας τοῦ
Ἰησοῦ καὶ ἐξέμαξεν ταῖς θριξὶν αὐτῆς τοὺς πόδας αὐτοῦ (Jn 12,3).
Dauer considers two possibilities: either, "auf der Stufe der mündlichen
Tradition", the developing pre-Johannine form of the story is influenced
by the pre-Lukan story, or the pre-Johannine anointing story "ist durch
Ineinanderfließen von *mk* Bethanienerzählung und *lk* (nicht: *vor*-lk!)
Sünderinerzählung entstanden". This last hypothesis of a post-Synoptic
oral tradition at the origin of Jn 12,1-8 finally has Dauer's preference in
light of his findings regarding the Johannine parallels to Lk 7,1-10 and
24,36-49[188].

Dauer's hesitation (contrast M.D. Goulder's *Luke*) is typical of the
present state of scholarly opinion in this question of the relationship
between John and Luke. There is no need, I think, of further collection of similarities. We have to look for "test cases" of Johannine

185. *Ibid.*, p. 65 (*8c*); with a list of similarities in style and vocabulary (pp. 65-66).
Note that "ces rapprochements avec le vocabulaire et le style de Lc/Ac ... n'existent pas
aux niveaux du Document C et de Jean II-A" (p. 66). See my *JeanSyn*, pp. 71-91 ("Le
Document C et les Synoptiques").
186. Cf. above, n. 168 (Dauer's list): the (numerous) references to B-L enclosed
within parentheses indicate Jn-Lk contacts assigned to Document C (but see Jn 18,10;
18,40; 19,12b: Jn II-B). Contrast Baum-Bodenbender (n. 26): see the references to B-B
added to Dauer's list (n. 168). See also *Hoheit*, pp. 193 (Jn 19,2b / Lk 23,11); 206 (Jn
18,29b / Lk 23,2); 216 (Jn 19,16a / Lk 23,25).
187. Cf. n. 13.
188. *Johannes und Lukas*, pp. 204-206. Dauer's study is apparently unknown to
J.F. COAKLEY, *The Anointing at Bethany and the Priority of John*, in *JBL* 107 (1988) 241-
256: "That John's account is independent of both the others was argued by P. Gardner-
Smith and C.H. Dodd and is now the position of most commentators" (p. 241).

dependence. We can mention here Dauer's third example, Jn 20,19-20, which has its *Grundlage* in an editorial composition of Luke[189]:

	Jn 20,19-20	Lk 24,36-43
I	Jn 20,19-20	
19	ἔστη εἰς τὸ μέσον	36 ἔστη ἐν μέσῳ αὐτῶν
	καὶ λέγει αὐτοῖς·	καὶ λέγει αὐτοῖς·
	εἰρήνη ὑμῖν.	εἰρήνη ὑμῖν.
20	καὶ τοῦτο εἰπὼν	40 καὶ τοῦτο εἰπὼν
	ἔδειξεν τὰς χεῖρας	ἔδειξεν αὐτοῖς τὰς χεῖρας
	καὶ τὴν πλευρὰν αὐτοῖς.	καὶ τοὺς πόδας.
	ἐχάρησαν οὖν οἱ μαθηταὶ	41 ἔτι δὲ ... ἀπὸ τῆς χαρᾶς ...
	ἰδόντες τὸν κύριον.	(39 ἐγώ εἰμι αὐτός· ... ἴδετε...)

If, in the text of Luke, we receive v. 36b (the greetings of peace) and v. 40[190], it is scarcely enough to say that John and Luke reflect a parallel but independent tradition[191].

The most impressive test case, however, remains the account of Peter's visit to the tomb[192]:

Jn 20,3-10	Lk 24,12
3 ἐξῆλθεν οὖν ὁ Πέτρος...	ὁ δὲ Πέτρος ἀναστὰς
4 ... προέδραμεν	ἔδραμεν
... ἦλθεν ... εἰς τὸ μνημεῖον	ἐπὶ τὸ μνημεῖον
5 καὶ παρακύψας βλέπει	καὶ παρακύψας βλέπει
κείμενα τὰ ὀθόνια	τὰ ὀθόνια
7 ... οὐ μετὰ ... ἀλλὰ χωρὶς	μόνα,
8 ... ἐπίστευσεν·	
9 οὐδέπω γὰρ ᾔδεισαν ...	
10 ἀπῆλθον ... πρὸς ἑαυτοὺς	καὶ ἀπῆλθεν πρὸς ἑαυτόν
8	θαυμάζων τὸ γεγονός.

The reconstruction of a pre-Johannine source behind Jn 20,3-10 is usually so similar to the text of Lk 24,12 that it is difficult to recognize its *raison d'être*[193]. The textual inauthenticity of the Lukan verse still has

189. See my essay on *Lc 24,36-43: Un récit lucanien*, 1985 (n. 13).

190. On the textual authenticity, see my *JeanSyn*, pp. 126-130 (ctr. B-L, Greeven, *et al.*).

191. This is a paraphrase of Fortna's "independent but parallel tradition" (*The Fourth Gospel*, p. 199; see also p. 200, n. 467).

192. See *NTS* 30 (1984): *John and the Synoptics: The Empty Tomb Stories* (n. 36), esp. pp. 172-178 (= 592-596): "Jn. 20.1-10 and Lk. 24.12" (further bibliographical references in n. 97; see esp. *Evangelica*, 1982, pp. 297-455).

193. See, e.g., Fortna's reconstruction in *The Gospel of Signs*, 1970, p. 144, and more recently in *The Fourth Gospel*, 1988, pp. 188 and 196-197. In his revised version, v. 7 is now a Johannine insertion (p. 197), and v. 5a (καὶ παρακύψας βλέπει κείμενα τὰ ὀθόνια) is replaced by v. 6b (καὶ θεωρεῖ τὰ ὀθόνια κείμενα). The (intended?) result is that the main similarity with Lk 24,12 (καὶ παρακύψας βλέπει τὰ ὀθόνια μόνα) disappears from the source. Fortna still notes similarities in v. 3 (without "the other disciple"), v. 8 (the conjectural "he wondered"), v. 10.

some defenders[194], and it will remain, I think, a last refuge for those who deny the evidence of Johannine dependence.

I Dauer, who in 1984 strongly defends the authenticity of Lk 24,36b and 40[195], in the same volume declares that Jn 20,3-10 / Lk 24,12 "keine echte Parallele ist, sondern bei Lk auf eine spätere Interpolation zurückgeht"[196]. More recently, he published an investigation of "Nachträge" and "Ergänzungen" in Luke-Acts with the intention to show that "mit solchen Redenelementen [= Lk 24,24] nicht die Authentizität einer

---

194. The arguments for inauthenticity are developed, e.g., in C.F. EVANS, *Resurrection and the New Testament* (SBT, 2/12), London, 1970, p. 97, and repeated in his recent commentary, *Saint Luke* (TPI), London-Philadelphia, 1990, pp. 899-900. Contrast my 1984 observation: "For all recent commentators the verse is a genuine part of the text" (p. 164; = *Evangelica II*, p. 577). For a reply to R. Mahoney, who in 1974 at some length argued against the authenticity of Lk 24,12, cf. *JohnSyn*, pp. 99-100 (= 391-392); see now also W.L. CRAIG, *The Disciples' Inspection of the Empty Tomb (Lk 24,12.14; Jn 20,2-10)*, in this volume, pp. 614-619 (esp. 614-615).

In the second part of his study, Craig raises a number of objections against the Lukan origin of Lk 24,12. My arguments are summarily listed with short comments such as "extremely unpersuasive", "fanciful", "pure speculation", "inconclusive". For a reply, I may refer the reader to my earlier essays. The topic was apparently too broad to be properly treated in one short paper. In his brief discussion of the "pattern" (Lk 24,12 compared with 24,1.3.9), Craig does not even mention Lk 24,22-23.24 (cf. n. 200 below). Curiously enough, his final objection is borrowed from Mahoney: "the awkwardness of the insertion of v. 12 into the narrative" (cf. n. 5: "The passage in Luke seems much less an integral part of the whole story than it does in John").

195. *Johannes und Lukas*, pp. 209-216 (and 412-419). See also *JeanSyn*, pp. 126-130 ("L'authenticité de Lc 24,36b et 40").

196. *Ibid.* p. 38. See also p. 216, on his "unterschiedliche Entscheidung für Lk 24,12 und 24,36b.40". Contrast H. Greeven (1981) and Boismard-Lamouille (*Synopsis*, 1986): 24,12 in the text but 24,36b.40 printed in the apparatus.

In his justification, Dauer refers to B.M. Metzger's "Note on Western Non-Interpolations" (*A Textual Commentary*, pp. 191-193) and the Committee's decision "to evaluate each one separately on its own merits" rather than "to make ... a mechanical or doctrinaire judgment" (p. 193). But see now again a global evaluation of Lk 24,3.6.12.36.40.51.52 in M.C. PARSONS, *A Christological Tendency in P*[75], in *JBL* 105 (1986) 463-479; esp. p. 477, on the subunit Lk 24,12.36.40: "Here the common denominator is a dependence on John. ... it is much simpler to understand a similartiy as being due to a scribal harmonization for doctrinal reasons". A more imaginative theory is proposed by C.-B. AMPHOUX, *Le chapitre 24 de Luc et l'origine de la tradition textuelle du Codex de Bèze (D.05) du NT*, in *Filología Neotestamentaria* 4 (1991) 21-50, p. 41: "Marcion révise la tradition de D, non celle de P[75]-B: cette dernière a profité du travail de Marcion". With respect to Lk 24,12: "le v. 12 a comme rôle d'ajouter au récit précédent un groupe de témoins du tombeau vide, en la personne de Pierre. ... Le vocabulaire du v. montre qu'il s'agit d'un résumé du premier épisode de Jn 20" (p. 29). Amphoux ignores all literature on this topic. Regarding the witness of Marcion, cf. *Lc. xxiv 12: Les témoins du texte occidental* (1978), in *Evangelica*, 1982, pp. 313-328, esp. 320-321: "Sur Lc. xxiv 12 le silence de Tertullien et Épiphane est complet, et lorsque Harnack a proposé l'omission marcionite, il l'a fait sans donner la moindre justification" (p. 321).

anderen Stelle [= Lk 24,12] bewiesen werden kann"[197]. Of course, this is only a first (and partial) treatment of the | problem[198] and my answer can only be a provisional one.

Dauer's illustrations of the composition technique of *Nachträge* in which Luke "noch nicht Erzähltes nachträgt" should be taken into consideration by those who argue on the basis of Lk 24,24 for the authenticity of 24,12[199]. But already in 1972[200] it was my point that Lk 24,24 cannot be used *against* the authenticity of 24,12, and this seems to be Dauer's own presupposition: "Diese Argumentation setzt natürlich voraus, daß Lukas in Reden/Gesprächen, die früher Erzähltes rekapitulieren oder wiederaufnehmen, dort erwähnte Einzelheiten *mehr oder weniger exakt wiederholt*. Hierfür gibt es tatsächlich viele Beispiele in den lk Schriften"[201].

M. Myllykoski has recently reexamined "the material common to Luke and John"[202], and at the end of his investigation he presents the

197. *"Ergänzungen" und "Variationen" in den Reden der Apostelgeschichte gegenüber vorausgegangenen Erzählungen. Beobachtungen zur literarischen Arbeitsweise des Lukas*, in H. FRANKEMÖLLE & K. KERTELGE (eds.), *Vom Urchristentum zu Jesus*. FS J. Gnilka, Freiburg, 1989, pp. 307-324 (on Lk 24,12, cf. pp. 307-308: "Anlaß der Untersuchung"); *Beobachtungen zur literarischen Arbeitstechnik des Lukas* (Athenäums Monografien; Bonner Biblische Beiträge, 79), Frankfurt, 1990. The new list of examples includes the instances from Acts he mentioned in 1989 (marked with *): Lk 1,13; 4,23; 7,24.33.44b-46; 9,9.40.49; 13,1.4.31.34; 15,30; 22,31.32; 24,34; Acts 1,18-19*; 5,23; 6,2b.13-14*; 8,36b; 9,27b; 10,1–11,18*; 13,25-29; 19,4; 20,18-35*; 21,21; 23,27.30b; 21,17*; 25,16.18-19; 27,23-24; 28,17b-19a; 22,3-21; 26,1-29.

198. Cf. *Johannes und Lukas* (1984): "wie ich in einem bald zu veröffentlichen Aufsatz zeigen möchte".

199. See the references in *Beobachtungen*, pp. 9-10 (= *"Ergänzungen"*, pp. 307-308).

200. Cf. *ETL* 48 (1972) 548-553 (in conjunction with J. Muddiman's note, pp. 542-548, in reply to K.P.G. Curtis, 1971). But see p. 550: "This Lukan understanding of the double visit [24,22-23.24] may provide the key for the interpretation of v. 12"; see also *JohSyn*, p. 100 (= *Evangelica*, pp. 331 and 392).

201. *"Ergänzungen"*, p. 308 (my emphasis); *Beobachtungen*, p. 11 ("z.T. recht genau, z.T. wenigstens annähernd"; "zahlreiche Beispiele").

202. Cf. above, n. 62. His general conclusion: "John wrote his Gospel without direct literary dependence on Lk"; the similarities can be explained through independent redactions and the use of similar oral traditions (p. 152). First, he eliminates as "useless" the similarities that are "too general and vague" (pp. 119-125). Then, he proposes his solution in cases of "concrete minor agreements conflicting with Mk and Mt": Jn 1,19-20 (Lk 3,15); 1,32-34 (Lk 3,22); 12,13 (Lk 19,38); 12,19 (Lk 19,39-40); 13,2.27 (Lk 22,3); 13,38 (Lk 22,34); 18,2.10.18.25.38 (cf. Dauer's list, n. 168 above); 19,41b (Lk 23,53b) (pp. 125-136). Finally, he deals with "parallel pericopes in Lk and Jn": (21,1-14; 4,46-54; 12,1-11; 10,24b-25a; 20,3-10 and 19-23 (pp. 136-151). Myllykoski rightly observes that "only detailed literary analysis can show whether [John's sources] are to be identified with the synoptic Gospels or not" (p. 119). Unfortunately, his view on John's use of the Synoptics is that of an evangelist who "had two or three Gospel scrolls on his desk" (cf. above, n. 62). Therefore, he tries to show that this "artificial" assumption is unnecessary. See, for instance, his discussion of Jesus' anointing (with the "strikingly similar feature" in Lk 7,38 / Jn 12,3): "It is again unnecessary to assume that John used Lk. *It is a possibility that cannot be totally excluded*; in the case of one single detail it is, however,

two pericopes in the resurrection narratives, Jn 20,3-10 / Lk 24,12 and Jn 20,19-23 / Lk 24,36-43, which are "remarkably closer to each other than the parallels treated above". The source of Jn 20,3-10 is "a tradition strikingly similar to Lk 24,12": the traditional account told first of the appearance of two angels to the women; they went to the disciples, and this motivated Peter to visit the tomb[203]. Is it then | amazing that "Neirynck ... uses this result as evidence for the theory that John used Lk as his source"[204]?

In the case of Jn 20,19-23 Myllykoski proposes the following reconstruction of a common tradition[205].

Lk 24		Jn 20
36a* (33b*)	The disciples are gathered together	19a
36b	Jesus stands in their mids and says to them:	
	"Peace be with you."	19c
37a	The disciples' reaction	–
40	Jesus shows his hands and his feet	20a
41	*The disciples rejoice	20b
–	Jesus gives them the Spirit and authorizes them to forgive	
	and retain sins	22-23*

The main weakness of Myllykoski's reconstruction is his neglect of the theme of doubt. "The theme of doubt forms a redactional addition to the original appearance tradition. When it is removed [from Lk 24,36-43], one is able to work out a coherent and well-motivated account"; "John treats the motif of doubt in vv. 24-29" and this pericope is a creation of the evangelist, "totally dependent on vv. 19-23"[206]. This is quite a contrast to Dauer's hypothesis[207]. Myllykoski was not acquainted with my own treatment of this passage (1985), from which I quote a few sentences[208]:

much easier to assume the use of a traditional pericope than of the Gospel text" (p. 141, my emphasis). On the "possibility" that John used Lk, see also pp. 134 (the threefold statement of Jesus' innocence), 140 (Jn 4,46-54), 142 (Jn 10,24b-25a).

203. Pp. 143-151, esp. 143, 144, 150-151.

204. Cf. p. 144, n. 81.

205. Pp. 144-149, esp. 149.

206. Pp. 146 and 148.

207. *Johannes und Lukas*, pp. 256-259. For many others, too, the theme of doubt was part of the original narrative of the appearance to the disciples (*ibid.*, p. 527).

208. *Lc 24,36-43* (n. 13), pp. 660-661 (= 209-210). On the contacts between Jn 20,21-23 and Lk 24,44-49 (*ib.*, n. 7), cf. M.-A. CHEVALLIER, *Apparentements* (n. 209 below), p. 388: "Le Crucifié annonce/opère le don de l'Esprit pour la mission qui consiste à proclamer le pardon des péchés".

On concédera volontiers que Jn 20,24-29 ne peut avoir existé indépendamment de Jn 20,19-23, mais cela n'exclut nullement une composition parallèle des deux récits à partir d'une tradition préexistante qui ne serait autre que Lc 24,36ss. La dualité des deux apparitions en Jn 20,19-23.24-29 peut s'inspirer directement de la double démonstration en Lc 24,37-40 et 41-43 (v. 41 ἔτι δὲ ἀπιστούντων αὐτῶν...). Par ailleurs, le double emploi du motif de "ses mains et ses pieds" en Lc 24,39 et 40 peut expliquer la répétition du motif de "ses mains et son côté" en Jn 20,20 et 27 (cf. 25). ... Les disciples ... restent néanmoins incrédules (Lc 24,41). Dans le texte actuel de Jean, l'apparition aux disciples est également suivie par une réaction d'incrédulité (dans la personne de Thomas) et, comme dans Lc 24,41-43, une nouvelle démonstration est nécessaire (dans une deuxième apparition).

| To conclude, I mention the study on pneumatology by the late M.-A. Chevallier[209], one of the too rare investigations of the theological connections between John and Luke[210].

---

209. M.-A. CHEVALLIER, *Apparentements entre Luc et Jean en matière de pneumatologie*, in *À cause de l'évangile*. FS J. Dupont (Lectio Divina, 123), Paris, 1985, pp. 377-408 (see also *RSR* 69, 1981, 301-314: *"Pentecôtes" lucaniennes et "Pentecôtes" johanniques*). Cf. p. 406, n. 78: "Il y a trois passages où le contact Luc-Jean en matière de pneumatologie peut être confronté avec précision à des parallèles de Marc et Matthieu" (Lk 3,15-16 / Jn 1,25-27; Lk 3,21-22 / Jn 1,31-34; Lk 23,46 / Jn 19,30). In the first case there are "des indices *littéraires* d'un rapport particulier": Lk 3,15 μήποτε αὐτὸς εἴη ὁ χριστός / Jn 1,25 εἰ σὺ οὐκ εἶ ὁ χριστός and Lk 3,16a ἀπεκρίνατο λέγων πᾶσιν ὁ Ἰωάννης / Jn 1,26a ἀπεκρίθη αὐτοῖς ὁ Ἰωάννης λέγων (*ibid.*). He also notes "des contacts verbaux impressionnants" between Lk 12,12 τὸ γὰρ ἅγιον πνεῦμα διδάξει ὑμᾶς ... ἃ δεῖ εἰπεῖν and Jn 14,26 τὸ πνεῦμα τὸ ἅγιον ... ὑμᾶς διδάξει πάντα ... ἃ εἶπον ὑμῖν ἐγώ (p. 395).
210. There is a third study on John-Luke in FS J. Dupont (1985; cf. nn. 208, 209 above): J. KREMER, *Der arme Lazarus. Lazarus, der Freund Jesu. Beobachtungen zur Beziehung zwischen Lk 16,19-31 und Joh 11,1-46* (pp. 571-584). Cf. by the same author: *Lazarus. Die Geschichte einer Auferstehung. Text, Wirkungsgeschichte und Botschaft von Joh 11,1-46*, Stuttgart, 1985, pp. 82-109 ("Hypothesen zur Entstehungsgeschichte von Joh 11,1-46"). On this topic, see now in this volume: U. BUSSE, *Johannes und Lukas: Die Lazarusperikope Frucht eines Kommunikationsprozesses*, pp. 281-306, esp. 304: "Die lukanische Parabel ... liefert ihm das Erzählgerüst", "Maria und Martha, aus einer weiteren Sondertradition des Lukas"; and this general conclusion: "das Evangelium insgesamt setzt die Synoptiker voraus und rekuriert auf sie, wann immer es dem Autor in seinem angestrebten Dialog mit dem Leser passend erscheint" (p. 305).
One of the privileged themes of study is the footwashing in Jn 13 and its relation to Lk 22,27: cf. above, nn. 19-21 (M. Sabbe, K.T. Kleinknecht, P. Stuhlmacher); see also O. BETZ, *Jesus. Der Herr der Kirche* (WUNT, 52), Tübingen, 1990, pp. 453-457: "Mit der Fußwaschung in Joh 13 wird das Wort Lk 22,27 in die Tat umgesetzt" (p. 453); "Lk 22,27b (wird) in Joh 13 aktualisiert, als wirkliche Handlung berichtet. ... Aber auch die Frage Jesu in Lk 22,27a wird m.E. in Joh 13 aufgenommen und mit der Tat beantwortet" (p. 456). Betz's identification of the Beloved Disciple "durch solch ein syllogistisches Verfahren", Jn 13,23 (ἦν ἀνακείμενος ...) → Lk 22,27 (ὁ ἀνακείμενος) → Mk 10,37 (James and John, the sons of Zebedee), is less convincing indeed: "Freilich mag mancher zögern ..." (p. 456).

IV

John and Mark

It is quite natural that, in the study of "John and the Synoptics"[211], attention is directed to the Gospel of Mark, the originator of the Gospel form and the source of Matthew and Luke. There are a number of detailed parallels and verbatim agreements between John and Mark and there is an undeniable similarity in the basic structure of the | Gospel. For an inventory of all that, I can refer to the paper on "John and Mark" by R. Kieffer[212]; and the important ch. 6 of John is studied by F. Vouga[213].

In the debate on dependence or independence, it seems to be difficult to come to a consensus about what is editorial and what is traditional (oral tradition, pre-Markan source) on the side of Mark. As noted in 1975: "The question whether John depends upon Mark or upon the sources of Mark is primarily a problem of Synoptic criticism"[214]; thus, for instance, the case of the intercalation of the hearing Jn 18,19-23 into the Peter story, with the repetition in vv. 18b and 25a, and the parallel in Mk 14,54.66-67a. This is R.T. Fortna's "Test Case" (1978)[215]. He declares that "the connection between the stories [in Mark] seems to be earlier than a redactional combining on Mark's part", and that the repetition in Mark "appears to be older and better assimilated into the story – a more natural reminder – than in John"[216]. In his more recent work

---

211. For bibliographical references (up to 1985), cf. G. Van Belle, *Johannine Bibliography 1966-1985* (BETL, 82), Leuven, 1988, pp. 140-144: "John and the Synoptics" (esp. 142-143: "The Gospel of Mark").

212. In this volume, pp. 109-125: *Jean et Marc: Convergences dans la structure et dans les détails*. See also M.E. Glasswell, *The Relationship between John and Mark*, in *JSNT* 23 (1985) 99-115: "a defence of the possibility that John knew Mark notwithstanding the divergences between them" (p. 104).

213. In this volume, pp. 261-279: *Le quatrième évangile comme interprète de la tradition synoptique: Jean 6*. On Jn 6 and Mark, cf. above, nn. 23-25 (U. Schnelle; cf. below, n. 227) and 28 (L. Schenke, J.-M. Sevrin). For differing views, see P.W. Barnett, *The Feeding of the Multitude in Mark 6 / John 6*, in D. Wenham - C. Blomberg (eds.), *The Miracles of Jesus* (Gospel Perspectives, 6), Sheffield, 1986, pp. 273-293 ("independent eyewitness recollection"!); J. Painter, *Tradition and Interpretation in John 6*, in *NTS* 35 (1989) 421-450, esp. pp. 422-426: "John 6 and the Synoptics" (cf. below, n. 233); C. Riniker, *Jean 6,1-21 et les évangiles synoptiques*, in J.-D. Kaestli, et al. (eds.), *La communauté johannique* (n. 16), 1990, pp. 41-67 (p. 59: "la tradition johannique est ... plus tardive que la tradition synoptique", "sous une forme écrite", "indépendante des évangiles synoptiques"; cf. below, n. 234). See also n. 236.

214. Cf. *JohnSyn*, p. 87.

215. *Jesus and Peter* (n. 10), presented to the SNTS Seminar on the Synoptic Problem, Tübingen, 1977. Fortna's essay is often cited as the response to the Donahue-Perrin-Dewey thesis. See, e.g., D.M. Smith, *Johannine Christianity*, p. 161, n. 26.

216. *Ibid.*, pp. 373, 379, n. 2.

(1988), he maintains his reconstruction of the sequence in the pre-Johannine source (18,13.**24**.15-16a.19-22.**16b-18**.25b-27) and the attribution of v. 25a to the Johannine redaction ("the mechanical repetition of v. 18b"). The John-Mark parallel is only "tenuous": he believes that it is "really only coincidence"[217]. In the studies on Mark, I the combination of the stories of Jesus' trial and Peter's denial, with the resumptive device in 14,66-67a, is usually discussed in connection with the use of sandwich arrangement elsewhere in the Gospel of Mark[218]. Fortna simply declares that it seems predictable that "the two [traditions] would have been joined together [much earlier] because of their common locale"[219]. He does not consider the specific device of intercalation, and this is all the more amazing because, in his own hypothesis, he suggests a similar redactional intercalation (18,19-22) and resumption (v. 25a) in

---

217. *The Fourth Gospel*, p. 161, and n. 358: "The parallel is more tenuous than Evans supposes". Cf. C.A. EVANS, *"Peter Warming Himself" : The Problem of an Editorial "Seam"*, in *JBL* 101 (1982) 245-249. For Evans, such "a story-telling device of digression and resumption" is best explained as "part of the (somewhat) fixed oral tradition" (pp. 248-249). Note also: "if explained in terms of literary dependence one way or another, [the seam] is better explained as a Marcan improvement upon a very wooden and obvious seam in John rather than as an instance where John betrays his dependence on Mark" (p. 247). Cf. *NT* 24 (1982), pp. 124-126; *Biblica* 64 (1983), p. 158, n. 22: with reference to his short study in *JBL* (1982), Evans repeats his assumption of Johannine independence (cf. J.M. Robinson's 'trajectory' approach) against knowledge of and dependence upon Mark (J.R. Donahue, *et al.*) and the use of a common source advocated by A.B. Kolenkow (*JBL* 95, 1976, 623-638) and R.T. Fortna.

218. See, e.g., J. GNILKA, *Der Prozeß Jesu nach den Berichten des Markus und Matthäus mit einer Rekonstruktion des historischen Verlaufs*, in K. KERTELGE (ed.), *Der Prozeß gegen Jesu* (Quaestiones Disputatae, 112), Freiburg, 1988, pp. 11-40: "Mk hat die Verschachtelung des Synedrialberichtes mit der Verleugnung des Petrus geschaffen. Er greift den in V. 54 fallengelassenen Faden erst in V. 66 wieder auf und umkreist somit mit der Petrus- die Jesus-Geschichte. Zu dieser Vermutung gibt die Beobachtung Anlaß, daß dasselbe, redaktionelle veranlaßte sandwich-agreement [sic] in 3,20-35 und 5,21-43 vorliegt" (pp. 15-16). See my *Evangelica*, 1982, pp. 552-553 (= *ETL* 55, 1979, pp. 33-34); T.A. MOHR, *Markus- und Johannespassion*, 1982, pp. 278-279 ("mit Hilfe des für ihn typischen literarischen Mittels der Perikopenverschränkung"); *et alii*.

It is hardly convincing to accept the device of sandwiching as a Markan redactional technique in other instances and to argue for pre-Markan tradition in the case of Mk 14,53-72 because of the parallel in Jn 18. Cf. D. LÜHRMANN, *Das Markusevangelium* (HNT, 3), Tübingen, 1987, p. 248: "Schon in der Mk vorgegebenen Passionsgeschichte waren die beiden Szenen ineinander verschränkt, wie der Vergleich mit Joh 18,13-27 erkennen läßt" (with no other justification than a reference to Fortna's essay). Compare pp. 74 (3,20-25), 103 (5,21-43), 119 (6,6b-30), 194 (11,12-25). In the case of Mk 14,1-11 (p. 233: "10f greift über 3-9 hinweg den in 2 verlassenen Faden wieder auf"), the anointing story "ist wohl erst sekundär in dem Kontext der Passionsthematik gestellt worden, und zwar schon in dem Grundstock der Mk und Joh vorgegebenen Passionsgeschichte" (p. 232), but it remains unclear whether he regards the intercalation as pre-Markan (cf. p. 230: "bei Joh in anderem Kontext").

219. *Jesus and Peter*, p. 373.

John, and acknowledges that "the Synoptic evidence is useful to us as analogy"[220].

Dauer's work on the passion narrative in the Gospel of John, which can serve as a starting-point for the study of the parallels in Matthew and Luke, is much less explicit regarding specific contacts with Mark. The insertion of 18,19-23(24) in the denial story and the composition of 18,18b.25a are attributed to the evangelist, who is not directly dependent on the Synoptics[221]. Dauer's listing of verbal correspondences nonetheless includes Jn 18,18b / Mk 14,54: μετ' αὐτῶν / μετὰ τῶν ὑπηρέτων (= Mt) and θερμαινόμενος[222]. A more accurate description I could show a more striking similarity: ἦν + ἑστώς/συγκαθήμενος + καὶ θερμαινόμενος (double participle) and the repetition of θερμαινόμενος/-ον in Jn 18,25a / Mk 14,(66-)67 (diff. Mt and Lk):

Jn 18,18b	ἦν δὲ καὶ ὁ Πέτρος μετ' αὐτῶν ἑστὼς καὶ θερμαινόμενος
25a	ἦν δὲ Σίμων Πέτρος ἑστὼς καὶ θερμαινόμενος
Mc 14,54	καὶ ὁ Πέτρος ... καὶ ἦν συγκαθήμενος μετὰ τῶν ὑπηρέτων καὶ θερμαινόμενος πρὸς τὸ φῶς
66	καὶ ὄντος τοῦ Πέτρου κάτω ...
67	καὶ ἰδοῦσα τὸν Πέτρον θερμαινόμενον.

In Dauer's proposal (1972), Jn 18,24 is the remainder of a synoptic-like trial before Caiaphas, located there in the source and deleted by the evangelist. Now, in his paper at this Conference, Dauer tends to take the hearing before Annas (18,19-23) as the Johannine substitute for the Synoptic Sanhedrin trial[223]. This should allow him to reconsider the John-Mark parallel in the structure of this section:

	Mk	Jn
Peter enters the courtyard	14,54a	18,15-16
(First denial)	—	17
Peter warms himself	54b	18
	Trial	Hearing
Resumption of the Peter story	66a	25a
(First denial)	66b-68	—
Second and third denial	69-72	25b-27

I quote from my earlier comment (1975): "It is an inadequate expression – and a somewhat misleading presentation of the evidence – to say that 18,19-24 is inserted in between the first and the second denial. The

220. *The Fourth Gospel*, p. 161, n. 360.
221. *Die Passionsgeschichte*, p. 78.
222. *Ibid.*, p. 93. On Jn 18,18 / Mk 14,54 (ὁ Πέτρος ... θερμαινόμενος), cf. R. KIEFFER, *Jean et Marc* (in this volume), p. 233: "*Trois* mots sont communs. La structure générale de la phrase chez Jean et Marc est semblable et s'écarte nettement de celle de Matthieu et Luc. Seuls Jean et Marc insistent que c'est Pierre qui se chauffe".
223. In this volume, pp. 307-339, esp. p. 316, n. 42.

(Markan) interweaving of the stories is one thing, the transposition of the first denial *within* the Peter story (diff. Mk) is another"[224].

| A similar problem arises with respect to the sequence of the Feeding miracle and the Walking on the Water in Jn 6,1-21 and Mk 6,31-52. "The possibility, that the two writers stumbled by sheer accident upon the same sequence, need not be seriously entertained" (Dodd)[225], and scholars who assume (correctly, I think) that the connection of the two narratives is the result of Mark's editing usually accept the conclusion that in this case John was dependent on Mark. In addition to those listed in 1975[226], special mention should now be made of U. Schnelle (1987)[227]. Not a few commentators, however, continue to argue for a traditional combination in a pre-Markan source, and their main reason is the parallel in Jn 6[228].

---

224. See my essay, *The 'Other Disciple' in Jn 18,15-16*, in *ETL* 55 (1975), 113-141, esp. pp. 130-132 (= *Evangelica*, pp. 335-364, esp. 352-354); quotation from p. 131 (= 353). See now also F.J. MATERA, *Jesus before Annas*, 1989 (n. 181 above): "There is no need to appeal to a non-Markan Passion source. The arrangement of John's narrative reflects the basic structure of Mark's account, and the transposition of the first denial can be explained in light of the Evangelist's redactional activity" (p. 51).
   In his recent study of this passage, M. Myllykoski proposes a reconstruction of the sequence in the pre-Johannine source as follows: 18,15a.c.18.(19-24)*.17.25 (*Die letzten Tage Jesu*, n. 157 above, p. 106). He also observes that the resumption of v. 18b in 18,25a "schon zum traditionellen Stück gehört haben (kann)" (p. 135, n. 60). The pre-Markan origin of the intercalation is his presupposition: "Obwohl die Petrusverleugnung oft als Beispiel für die markinische Technik der Perikopenverschachtelung dargestellt wird, muß die folgende Analyse davon ausgehen, daß ..." (p. 101), and his conclusion: "Ihre Verschachtelung mit der Verhörperikope ist ursprünglich" (p. 111). The common *Vorlage* of Mk and Jn includes (*ibid.*):

Mk 14,53a		54a	54b	66-68a	70b-71	72a
Jn 18,12-14*	15ac	18	17	25bc	27b.	

But see p. 103: "Die Zustimmung zu diesen Ergebnissen hängt entscheidend davon ab, ob die Kenntnis und der Gebrauch des Mk bei Johannes vorausgesetzt wird oder nicht. Eine bejahende Antwort auf diese Frage würde die Übereinstimmungen zwischen den Verleugnungsperikopen sehr einfach erklären ...".
   225. *Historical Tradition*, p. 211. Cf. C.K. BARRETT, *John*, 1978, p. 279: "The fact that in Mark as in John the two events stand side by side increases the probability of literary dependence" (1955, p. 232).
   226. *JohnSyn*, p. 89 (= 381), n. 65. On Jn 6,1-15, cf. *JeanSyn*, pp. 182-187.
   227. *Antidoketische Christologie* (n. 23 above), pp. 119-122: "Joh 6,1-15 im Verhältnis zu Mk 6,32-44 par"; 126-130: "Joh 6,16-21 im Verhältnis zu Mk 6,45-52", esp. p. 129, his investigation of Mark's "redaktionelle Eingriffe", with the conclusion that "die Einheit von Speisungsgeschichte und Seewadel künstlich ist und auf Markus zurückgeht". See already T. SNOY, in *ETL* 44 (1968), esp. pp. 222-234.
   228. J. GNILKA, 1978, p. 266: "schon vormarkinisch verbunden .... Dies wird durch Joh 6,1-21 nahegelegt, wo dieselbe Verknüpfung vorliegt"; D. LÜHRMANN, 1987, p. 121: "Wie in Joh 6,16-21 ..."; he concludes that "Mk und Joh unabhängig voneinander auf gemeinsame Überlieferung zurückgreifen, Joh dabei auf die σημεῖα-Quelle" (cf. above, n. 218); R.A. GUELICH, 1989, p. 347: "two originally independent stories, but the combination of a Feeding and a Crossing in 8:1-10 and John 6:1-21 argues for Mark having

In this discussion, the role of the doublet in Mk 8,1-10 is noteworthy. For C.H. Dodd, "it is scarcely doubtful that in each of the underlying forms of tradition the incident ended with a departure from the scene by boat. The hypothesis is by no means unreasonable, that a third form of tradition also contained the same sequence"[229]. But such an understanding of Mk 8,10 as "almost certainly the conclusion of the [pre-Markan] *pericopé*" is now generally rejected[230]: "Vers 10a ist eine vom Evangelisten geschaffene Überleitung, in der er erneut das bei ihm beliebte Bootsmotiv einbringt" (J. Gnilka); "10 stellt mit dem Motiv des Bootes redaktionell den Zusammenhang zum Kontext her" (D. Lührmann)[231]. "The

found these two combined in his tradition. ... If John 6:1-21 is related in any way to Mark or the tradition underlying 6:45-52, the combination may well have been made by the redactor of the miracle collection in view of the thematic relationship between 6:45-51, the last miracle in the cycle, and 4:35-41, the first miracle in the cycle". Cf. H.-W. Kuhn, 1971; see *JohnSyn*, p. 88 (= 380), n. 63. Compare the reply by L. Schenke, 1974: "Auch ein Hinweis auf Jo 6,1-21 hilft nicht weiter, bevor nicht die eigene literarkritische Problematik des Joh-Ev gelöst ist" (*ibid.*, n. 65), and now by U. Schnelle: "Was bei Markus nicht nachzuweisen ist, kann nicht Johannes belegen!" (p. 130, n. 225).

On the hypothesis of a pre-Markan cycle of miracle stories, see my critical observations in *Evangelica*, 1982, pp. 502-507 (= *ETL* 53, 1977, pp. 164-169). P. Achtemeier (1970) proposes two miracle catenae, the first beginning with 4,35-41 and ending with 6,34-44.53, the second with 6,45-51 and 8,1-10 (the combination of the Feeding and the Crossing is not pre-Markan). A rather curious sequel to Achtemeier's theory is found in B.L. MACK, *A Myth of Innocence. Mark and Christian Origins*, Philadelphia, 1988, pp. 216-222: the two miracle chains in Mk consisted of five stories and the same pattern appears in the Johannine signs source (a set of five miracle stories: Jn 4,46-54; 5,1-9; 6,1-14; 6,16-21; 9,1-34; two stories, "differing from the others", are deleted: 2,1-11; 11,1-44). In my view, the classic hypothesis of the signs source "is open to several objections" (cf. *Evangelica II*, 1991, pp. 651-678), but a theory of a signs source without including 2,1-11 is self-destructive. Compare also Crossan's more recent suggestion of an early miracles collection embedded within Mark and John, with a fivefold sequence: Jn 5,1-18; 6,1-15.16-21; 9,1-7; 11,1-57; cf. Mk 2,1-12; 6,33-44.45-52; 8,22-26; *Sicut Mark*. Cf. J.D. CROSSAN, *The Historical Jesus. The Life of a Mediterranean Jewish Peasant*, San Francisco, 1992, pp. 310-313 and 429 (references to the uncorrected proof, 1991). Regarding Jn 6,1-15.16-21 (Mk 6,33-44.45-52), cf. p. 407: "the order of meal and sea in the *Miracles Source* used by Mark and John may have been reversed ...".

229. *Historical Tradition*, p. 212. Note that for Dodd the reference to another voyage εἰς τὸ πέραν in Mk 8,13 is editorial (*ibid.*).

230. Cf. R.M. FOWLER, *Loaves and Fishes. The Function of the Feeding Stories in the Gospel of Mark* (SBL DS, 54), Chico, CA, 1981, pp. 51-52: "Only two stories in Mark, the Stilling of the Storm (4:35-41) and the Walking on the Water (6:45-52), actually involve a boat in the course of their telling. In all other cases the boat serves merely to transport the characters of the story from one scene to another" (p. 51). On the two sea stories in Mark, see now R.M. FOWLER, *Let the Reader Understand. Reader-response Criticism and the Gospel of Mark*, Minneapolis, MN, 1991, pp. 67-69. — Note also p. 229: "I suspect that John knew all three Synoptic Gospels and is responding to them in his own Gospel, just as Matthew and Luke respond to Mark in theirs".

231. For Gnilka and Lührmann, the boat motif is a Markan redactional link in 8,10 and 13 but also in 5,1-2.18a.21. Contrast R. Pesch who ascribes 8,10a.13 to Markan redaction but not the *Seefahrtnotizen* in 4,35–5,43; cf. *Evangelica*, 1982, p. 505:

similarity [with Jn 6] is more apparent than real and comes from Mark's redactional arrangement. It may reflect the evangelist's desire to coordinate the events after the Feeding here with the order of events after the previous Feeding" (R.A. Guelich)[232].

On the other hand, the similarities with the Feeding story in Luke have been adduced in support of a non-Markan tradition in Jn 6. The Feeding in Lk 9,10-17 is not followed by a sea-crossing and the mention of the boat in Mk 6,32 has no parallel in Lk 9,10. I quote J. Painter: "Neither John nor Luke mentions a boat at this point [Jn 6,1]. While Luke does not recount the return sea-crossing John does and has to introduce the boat at that point, suggesting that the two stories were once separate but had become joined in the tradition used by John yet without introducing the first sea-crossing as do Mark and Matthew"[233]. But the sea-crossing is not absent in Jn 6,1 (ἀπῆλθον ... | πέραν τῆς θαλάσσης, cf. Mk 6,32 ἀπῆλθον ἐν τῷ πλοίῳ), and the boat motif in Jn 6,16-17 (οἱ μαθηταὶ αὐτοῦ ... ἐμβάντες εἰς πλοῖον) resembles Mk 6,45 (τοὺς μαθητὰς αὐτοῦ ἐμβῆναι εἰς τὸ πλοῖον)[234]. Both Painter and C. Riniker draw attention to the "minor agreement" in Mt 14,13 / Lk 9,11, οἱ (δὲ) ὄχλοι ἠκολούθησαν αὐτῷ, par. Jn 6,2 ἠκολούθει δὲ αὐτῷ ὄχλος πολύς. "It might derive from a variant tradition" (Painter), "une *Sondertradition* propre à Jean et à Luc, mais inconnue de l'évangile de Marc" (Riniker)[235]. More careful synoptic investigation may reveal that there is no justification for the statement that the Mt/Lk agreements "suggest that they knew yet another version of the feeding story"[236].

"Puisque Pesch attribue le même motif dans 8,10.13 à la rédaction marcienne (pp. 405-406), on est en droit de lui demander sur quoi il se base pour conclure autrement dans 3,7–6,56".

232. *Mark*, p. 347. It is less clear, however, how then Mk 8,1-10 "argues" for a pre-Markan combination in Mk 6 (cf. n. 228 above).

233. J. PAINTER, *Tradition and Interpretation in John 6* (n. 213 above), p. 424, n. 4.

234. C. Riniker does not hesitate to make a link between Bethsaida in Lk 9,10 and Philip and Andrew in Jn 6,5-9: "originaires de Bethsaïda (Jn 1,44; 12,21), c'est-à-dire du lieu même où Luc situe l'épisode des pains. Cette observation pourrait renforcer la possibilité d'une 'Bethsaïda-tradition' de la MP, que Lc et Jn auraient eue en commun (remarque de F. Bovon)". Cf. C. RINIKER, *Jean 6,1-21 et les évangiles synoptiques* (n. 213 above), p. 54, n. 37. This last sentence is quoted from the unpublished version (p. 49, n. 91); with my thanks to C. Riniker who graciously sent me a copy of his "Mémoire de recherche" (under D. Marguerat), Lausanne, 1988, 70 p. Compare in this volume, pp. 523-534, J. KONINGS, *The Dialogue of Jesus, Philip and Andrew in John 6,5-9*.

235. Painter also indicates an alternative: "It could be argued that John's ὄχλος πολύς is a combination of Mark's πολλοί and Matthew's and Luke's ὄχλοι" (p. 424, n. 3).

236. Cf. *Evangelica II*, 1991, pp. 31-32, 78-81, 85-88. See now also W.D. DAVIES - D.C. ALLISON, *Matthew*, vol. II, 1991, pp. 478-480.

Jn 5,1-18 is my third example of a passage in John with parallels in Mark in which the order of Markan pericopes is involved. All lists of parallels contain the verbatim agreement between Jn 5,8 (ἔγειρε ἆρον τὸν κράβαττόν σου καὶ περιπάτει) and Mk 2,9 (ἔγειρε καὶ ἆρον τὸν κράβαττόν σου καὶ περιπάτει, v. 11 ἔγειρε ἆρον ...). One can hardly play down this parallel as "a stereotyped phrase (which) could occur in various contexts in stories which are independent of each other"[237]. In this case D. Marguerat, who shows much reserve with respect to synop-

— Additional note: For further study of John 6 and the Synoptics I can refer to other contributions in this volume (R. Kieffer, F. Vouga, J. Konings). A few words should be added on C. Riniker's paper (cf. above, nn. 213, 234). His conclusion is unambiguous: "Jn 6, 'lieu classique' pour démontrer la dépendance de l'évangile de Jean par rapport aux évangiles synoptiques dans leur forme finale, ne permet pas de confirmer cette thèse" (p. 58). R. is apparently not impressed by the overall agreement of order between Jn 6 and Mk 6–8, but he suggests that there is a "tradition" behind the sequence in Lk 9,10-17.18-21 and "cette même tradition" might explain the placement of Jn 6,68-69 (p. 54). Verbal parallels are listed but classified as "parallèles non probants" and "réminiscences peu vraisemblables", with one exception in Mk, 6,37 δηναρίων διακοσίων ἄρτους, cf. Jn 6,7 (p. 58: "possible"), and one in Mt, 14,24 σταδίους πολλούς, cf. Jn 6,19 (p. 55: "une influence semble ici quand même possible"). But see also p. 52: Mt 15,29 (ἀναβὰς) εἰς τὸ ὄρος ἐκάθητο ἐκεῖ, cf. Jn 6,3, "mérite vraiment d'être prise au sérieux". There can be no mistake about the purpose of R.'s paper: "J'aimerais mettre en évidence deux ... difficultés majeures de la thèse de Neirynck" (p. 47; cf. p. 49: "ce constat ruine la thèse de Neirynck"). In fact, R. presents an analysis of the vocabulary in Jn 6,1-21; he concludes first, that "l'origine rédactionnelle de l'*ensemble* des parties exclusivement johanniques est invraisemblable", and secondly, "pour composer le récit actuel, Jean aurait dû 'combiner' les éléments synoptiques d'une manière qui semble inconcevable. ... Dans l'hypothèse de Neirynck, Jean aurait dû exploiter les cinq récits synoptiques, puisque tous ont laissé des traces *significatives* dans son texte" (p. 48). Compare Painter's remark: "*if John is to be understood on the basis of dependence on the Synoptics*, it must be dependent on the three of them" (p. 424; cf. p. 425: "a patchwork from all that is now found in Matthew, Mark and Luke"). A first correction is indicated by Painter, "some of these points of contact might be a result of coincidental editing" (p. 424). Second, by concentrating on distinctive contacts with each of the synoptic stories and neglecting common elements (p. 57, n. 42: "les éléments ... sans lesquels on ne pourrait pas raconter les événements en question"), R. gives a somewhat distorted presentation of the dependence hypothesis. Third, R.'s observation on hapaxlegomena and rare words ("très difficile d'attribuer à l'auteur de l'évangile") shows too narrow of a view on John's redactional capacities. Of course, words should be listed *and* studied. On παιδάριον and κρίθινος, cf. *Jean et les Synoptiques*, p. 186.

237. P. BORGEN, *John and the Synoptics*, in *The Interrelations* (n. 57 above), p. 429. See my response in *John 5,1-18 and the Gospel of Mark* (n. 57). See also *JeanSyn*, pp. 175-182. In his analysis of Jn 5,1-18 Borgen uses the model of 1 Cor 11,23b-25(26).27-34 (*Can Paul Offer Help?*) and applies the pattern "text and commentary" to Jn 5,1-9.10-18. In Borgen's hypothesis, however, both the traditional story (5,1-9) and the paraphrasing commentary (5,10-18) are pre-Johannine, in contrast to 1 Cor 11 where the quotation of a pre-Pauline tradition is followed by Paul's own exposition. "Borgen's use of 1 Cor 11,23-34 as a model ... is almost contradictory". On Borgen's second example, Jn 2,13-16.17-22, see my response, pp. 447-450 (= 708-711), esp. 449 (= 710): "John shows here a correct understanding of the Markan intercalation" (Jn 2,18; Mk 11,28).

tic parallels, concedes that "la proximité du v. 8 avec Mc 2,9.11 dénote un contact avec la tradition synoptique"[238]. U. Schnelle rightly ascribes 5,9c-18 to the evangelist. He accepts some intervention of the evangelist in vv. 5 ("die jetzige Formulierung") and 6 but not in v. 8[239]. It seems to me that the recognition of the contact with Mk 2,9 may contribute to our understanding of John's composition in 5,1-18[240].

In the Gospel of Mark the sabbath pericopes are closely connected (Mk 2,23-28; 3,1-6) and form the conclusion of the section 2,1–3,6 beginning with 2,1-12. This context of Mk 2,11 shows a striking parallelism with Jn 5,1-18:

	John		Mark	
5,1-9b	the healing	2,1-12	the healing	
8	... ἆρον τὸν κράβαττόν σου	11	... ἆρον τὸν κράβαττόν σου	
9	... ἦρεν τὸν κράβαττον αὐτοῦ	12	... ἄρας τὸν κράβαττον	
9c	ἦν δὲ σάββατον ἐν ...	2,23	ἐν τοῖς σάββασιν	
10	ἔλεγον οὖν οἱ Ἰουδαῖοι ...·	24	καὶ οἱ Φαρισαῖοι ἔλεγον ...·	
	σάββατόν ἐστιν,		... ποιοῦσιν τοῖς σάββασιν	
	καὶ οὐκ ἔξεστίν σοι		ὃ οὐκ ἔξεστιν.	
	ἆραι τὸν κράβαττόν σου.			
	(the *man* carrying his bed)		(the *disciples* plucking grain)	
11-16	*Jesus* ὁ ποιήσας αὐτὸν ὑγιῆ	3,1-6	*Jesus* εἰ ... θεραπεύσει αὐτόν	
	... ἐν σαββάτῳ (cf. 7,23)	2	τοῖς σάββασιν	
		4	ἔξεστιν τοῖς σάββασιν	
17	... ἐργάζομαι		ἀγαθὸν ποιῆσαι ...	
			ἢ ἀποκτεῖναι;	
18	ἐζήτουν	6	συμβούλιον ἐδίδουν κατ' αὐτοῦ	
	αὐτὸν ... ἀποκτεῖναι		ὅπως αὐτὸν ἀπολέσωσιν.	
			cf. 11,18; 12,12; 14,1: ἐζήτουν ...	
			πῶς αὐτὸν ... ἀποκτείνωσιν.	

In both gospels the motif to kill Jesus appears for the *first* time (Jn 5,18; Mk 3,6) and is connected with the violation of the sabbath. In both gospels too it is found at the conclusion of the same pattern: first the healing, then a controversial sabbath case (in the action of people who

238. D. MARGUERAT, La "source des signes" existe-t-elle? Réception des récits de miracle dans l'évangile de Jean, in J.-D. KAESTLI, La communauté johannique (n. 16 above), pp. 69-93, esp. 86 (on Jn 5, see pp. 72-75 and 89-91). I agree with Marguerat's rejection of the signs source (cf. n. 58 above). He is less convincing when he ascribes vv. 9c-16 to pre-Johannine tradition (p. 75; cf. Bultmann, Becker). On Jn 5, see also in the same volume, pp. 135-151: R.A. CULPEPPER, Un exemple de commentaire fondé sur la critique narrative: Jean 5,1-18.

239. Antidoketische Christologie (n. 23 above), pp. 108-114 ("Joh 5,1-9ab"), esp. 111. His definition of Jesus' command as "Einzellogion" (ibid.) is less appropriate.

240. On John's composition, cf. L.T. WITKAMP, The Use of Traditions in John 5,1-18, in JSNT 25 (1985) 19-47 (= Jesus van Nazareth in de gemeente van Johannes. Over de interaktie van traditie en ervaring, Kampen, 1986, pp. 114-138). He accepts "a tradition-historical connection between the formulation of Jesus' words in Jn 5:8 and Mk 2:9,11".

are related to Jesus: the healed man and the disciples), and finally Jesus' healing activity as a violation of the sabbath.

Three other features in Jn 5,10-18 can be seen in connection with Mk 2,1-12:

1. In the healing stories of Jn 5 and Mk 2 special emphasis is given to the command of Jesus (Jn 5,8; Mk 2,11). Both John and Mark repeat the phrase in the description of the healing as an immediate execution of Jesus' order (Jn 5,9; Mk 2,12) and, more significantly, use the phrase in the debate, John in the sabbath discussion (5,12 τίς ἐστιν ... ὁ εἰπών σοι· cf. 11), and Mark in the debate about forgiveness of sin (2,9 τί ἐστιν εὐκοπώτερον ... ἢ εἰπεῖν·).

2. Jn 5,14 ἴδε ὑγιὴς γέγονας, μηκέτι ἁμάρτανε ... Healing and forgiveness of sin are closely connected in the story of Mk 2,1-12 (vv. 9 and 5b.10b-11). In the light of the parallel in Mark, the healed paralytic is a man to whom Jesus has said: your sins are forgiven.

3. The motive for the Jews seeking to kill Jesus is not only the violation of the sabbath: Jn 5,18 ὅτι οὐ μόνον ἔλυεν τὸ σάββατον, ἀλλὰ καὶ πατέρα ἴδιον ἔλεγεν τὸν θεόν, ἴσον ἑαυτὸν ποιῶν τῷ θεῷ (cf. v. 17 "My Father is working still and I am working")[241]. One can compare I once more with Mk 3,6 (and 2,7: βλασφημεῖ· τίς δύναται ἀφιέναι ἁμαρτίας εἰ μὴ εἷς ὁ θεός;)[242].

It is now a widely accepted view that Mk 2,1–3,6 including 2,1-12 and 3,1-5.6 is Mark's own redactional composition. This section is broken up by Matthew into two segments (9,1-17; 12,1-14) and its climax in 3,6 has only a weak parallel in Lk 6,11 (followed by 6,12ff.). Jn 5,1-18 may reveal a more correct understanding of the Markan text, and could a modern interpreter of Mark blame the Fourth Evangelist for having made the link between Mk 2,1-12 and 3,1-6[243]?

---

241. Cf. R. SCHNACKENBURG, *Das Johannesevangelium*, vol. II, p. 123: "Dem Mann ist mit der Heilung zugleich seine Sünde von Gott vergeben worden; das ist es, was Jesus mit dem Satz meint: 'Mein Vater arbeitet bis jetzt'".

242. Cf. J. GNILKA, *Markus*, vol. I, p. 126: "Die Tötungsabsicht der Gegner erscheint am Ende der Perikope nicht besonders angemessen, wohl nach 2,1–3,5!"; p. 102: "Der Vorwurf der Lästerung [2,7] muß ... mit 3,6 in Verbindung gesehen werden". Cf. Jn 10,33: περὶ βλασφημίας, καὶ ὅτι σὺ ἄνθρωπος ὢν ποιεῖς σεαυτὸν θεόν.

243. This brief presentation of Jn 5,1-18 and Mk 2,1–3,6 (with updating notes) is an excerpt from my 1984 response to P. Borgen, which circulated as an Appendix to my main paper at the Colloquium (1990); now in *Evangelica II* (n. 57 above). On Jn 5,8 and Mk 2,9.11, see also R. KIEFFER, in this volume, pp. 118-119.

On Jn 5,1-18 and Mk 2,1-12; 3,1-6, cf. J. KIILUNEN, *Die Vollmacht im Widerstreit. Untersuchungen zum Werdegang von Mk 2,1–3,6* (AASF, 40), Helsinki, 1985, p. 107, n. 40: "Am wahrscheinlichsten bleibt die Hypothese, dass die Gemeinsamkeiten von einem mehr oder weniger direkten Kontakten mit dem Mk-Ev herrühren".

V

Synoptic Gospels and Oral Tradition

"More to the point is Dodd's finding again and again that the overlap or parallel cannot be satisfactorily explained by Johannine dependence on one or other of the Gospels, and is better explained by John's knowledge of Synoptic-like tradition but not of the Synoptic version of it"[244]. With these words, J.D.G. Dunn concludes his presentation of Dodd's *Historical Tradition* (1963), which he takes as his starting point in an essay on John and Oral Tradition. The author's own conclusion remains very much in the same line: "Most of the earliest historical tradition within John reveals a degree of variation which makes John's direct dependence on one or more of the Synoptics as such highly unlikely"[245]. Written by Barrett's successor at Durham, Dunn's essay cannot simply be dismissed as a nostalgic return to the 1960's.

My first observation concerns the results of Dodd's analysis summarized by Dunn in a double list of narratives and sayings[246]. It includes | the following sayings with Synoptic parallel: 1,*26.27.33*.40-42.51;   2,10.*18.19*;   3,2.*3*.5.8.*29*.35;   4,*35-38.44*;   5,*19-20a*.23.30; 6,*20.26.30*.33.38;   7,4;   8,31-35;   10,*1-5*.15;   12,7-*8*.*25*.26.27(-28).47; 13,*13-16*.17.*20.21.38*;   15,18.20.21;   16,2.23-24.33;   17,2.11.15.25; 18,20; 20,*23*.29. Five narratives (4,46-54; 6,1-15.16-21; 12,1-8.12-19) and a number of sayings (marked by italics in the list above) are briefly discussed by Dunn. In his opinion, they are all rooted in earlier tradition, but it is not unimportant to note that for Dodd (and Dunn) a

---

244. J.D.G. DUNN, *John and the Oral Gospel Tradition*, in H. WANSBROUGH (ed.), *Jesus and the Oral Gospel Tradition* (JSNT SS, 64), Sheffield, 1991, pp. 351-379, esp. 358.

245. *Ibid.*, p. 378.

246. *Ibid.*, pp. 353-359. The passages are listed in the sequence of the Gospel, with page references in brackets. In the list of Narratives, some references to J.A. Bailey (1963) are added: Jn 1,19-21; 12,1-8.12-15; 13,17-20 (pp. 355-356). The list of Sayings (pp. 356-357) includes a few references to B. Lindars (*Traditions*, n. 133 above: Jn 2,10; 5,23; 6,26), J.A.T. Robinson (*Priority*: Jn 1,51; 3,35; 17,25), and to two other contributions in the same volume by D.E. Aune (Jn 3,8.29; 4,35-38; 5,19-20a; 8,31-35; cf. below) and R. Riesner (Jn 18,20). Sayings without indication of Synoptic parallel are Jn 1,15.29.30.36; 4,31-34; 6,51.67-70; 9,2-5.38-41; 14,13-14 (Dodd); 11,9-10; 12,24; 16,21 (Aune). Cf. D.E. AUNE, *Oral Tradition and the Aphorisms of Jesus*, pp. 211-265, with Appendix: "Inventory of Aphorisms of Jesus" (pp. 242-258, esp. nos. 148-155, in Jn alone: 3,8.29; 4,37; 5,19-20a; 8,35; 11,9-10; 12,24; 16,21; see also nos. 16, 20, 112: Jn 4,44; 12,25; 13,16 and 15,20)); R. RIESNER, *Jesus as Preacher and Teacher*, pp. 185-210 (esp. p. 189: Jn 18,20, "genuine in substance").

substantial portion of individual sayings are "Synoptic-like"[247]. I quote Dunn's conclusion on historical tradition in John: "we cannot exclude the possibility that material lacking actual Synoptic parallel was also rooted in historical tradition neglected by the Synoptics" but "our methodology inevitably depends on demonstration of Synoptic or Synoptic-like parallels"[248].

Secondly, Dunn does not deny that "the whole ... is held within the framework of the Gospel structure, as provided probably first for the Jesus tradition as a whole by Mark (driving forward to the climax of the Passion tradition)"[249].

Thirdly, the Fourth Gospel was written in the late first century and traditional elements received a much elaborated treatment in dialogues and discourses "which are both characteristically and distinctively Johannine, and markedly different from the characteristic teaching style of the Synoptics, and which therefore have to be attributed almost entirely to the evangelist rather than to his tradition"[250]. Dunn emphasizes, more than most commentators do, John's "tremendous creativity", "John's freedom in developing earlier tradition", "extensive reworking | and elaboration of the tradition", "a thorough-going editorial job in reworking the traditions", "extensive manipulation", etc. With such a degree of Johannine creativity, it becomes extremely hazardous to argue for independent tradition, since it is "the overlap with and echo of Synoptic tradition" which "must indicate a dependence on early tradition"[251]. The argument is threefold: a certain variation in the saying, a lack of reworking so that the parallel is still visible, and the supposed fixity in oral tradition.

Jn 3,3.5 is one example of how sayings of Jesus "could be elaborated in subsequent usage in an extensive way"[252]. Jn 3,3.5 is a radicalized

---

247. Dunn could have added a reference to R. Schnackenburg's more careful sifting of the evidence (n. 93 above), with differentiation between "Synoptische Logien" (including Jn 1,34; 6,42.69; 16,32; 18,11b: not in Dunn's list) and "Logien mit Anlehnung an synoptische Tradition". — Compare also Dunn's earlier study, *Let John be John: A Gospel for its Time*, in P. STUHLMACHER (ed.), *Das Evangelium und die Evangelien* (WUNT, 28), Tübingen, 1983, pp. 309-339 (ET, Grand Rapids, 1991, pp. 293-322), esp. p. 315; a short selection of sayings with Synoptic parallel includes Jn 3,3.5; 5,19; 10,1-5.15; 13,20; and also "Jn 6,53 drawing on the tradition of the Last Supper". On "recent restatements of the view that John knew and used one or more of the Synoptics", cf. n. 13: "I find the evidence not wholly persuasive".

248. *John*, p. 377.

249. *Ibid.*, p. 378. Cf. *Let John be John*, p. 339: "he (the Fourth Evangelist) chose, and chose deliberately, to retain the developed discourse material within the framework of a Gospel as laid down by Mark".

250. *John*, p. 352.

251. *Ibid.*, p. 358.

252. *Ibid.*, p. 376. The quotations in the text are from pp. 370 (4e) and 375. On Jn 3,3.5, cf. above, Section II,3.

form of Mt 18,3 (from "become a child" to "be born again"), which "probably provided the source for the new birth dialogue of 3.1-10". For Dunn, "such a radicalizing ... simply serves to reinforce and not at all to alter the point of the saying" and "may be regarded as a legitimate (responsible and effective) teaching device". We can agree that Jn 3,3.5 "is certainly plausible as a variant of Mt. 18.3, particularly as it is the *only* passage in John which echoes the normal kingdom language of the Synoptics", but it remains an unprovable suggestion that this variation of the saying is one of "the fixed points of the earlier tradition".

The first saying in Dunn's list is Jn 1,27: "The second clause has just the variations, as between a united Synoptic witness and John, which we would expect in two different translations or Greek versions of a common Aramaic original: different synonyms for 'worthy', different constructions for the subordinate clause, singular/plural sandal(s)"[253]. Contrast Barrett's comment: "John's words are probably dependent upon Mark's. He substitutes the more appropriate ἄξιος for Mark's ἱκανός, drops the vivid but unnecessary κύψας, and, as often, has ἵνα and the subjunctive for the infinitive. The repetition of αὐτοῦ after the relative οὗ ... has been taken over by John from Mark"[254]. It should be noted that Dunn rightly reminds us of John's thorough reworking of the traditions regarding the Baptist[255].

In search of fixed points in the earlier tradition, Dunn emphasizes the close verbal parallels (rather than the variation) in Jn 6,20; 12,7-8; 13,21; 13,28[256]. But it is not at all unlikely that John, if he uses I Mark[257], would preserve more faithfully the wording of these utterances of Jesus within his own account. Dunn notes a clustering of earlier sayings material in Jn 13,13-16.17.20.21. Jn 13,16 is treated in D.E. Aune's study of the aphorisms: "the tendency to expand single line aphorisms by pairing them with analogous sayings in synonymous parallelism suggests the literary character of the transformation"[258]. Both Mt 10,24-25a, pupil/teacher paired with slave/master, and Jn 13,16, slave/master

253. *Ibid.*, p. 369.
254. BARRETT, *John*, ²1978, p. 175. Compare also Lk 3,16 (par. Mk) and Acts 13,25: ἄξιος for ἱκανός (cf. Lk 7,4 ἄξιος, v. 6 ἱκανός Q) and the singular τὸ ὑπόδημα (τῶν ποδῶν).
255. DUNN, *John*, pp. 373-374.
256. *Ibid.*, pp. 364, 365, 372 (4k).
257. Cf. BARRETT, Jn 6,20: "In Mark 6.50 the same words, with θαρσεῖτε prefixed. ... John is probably following Mark" (p. 281); Jn 12,7: "The confusion ... is best explained as due to John's continuing to follow his Marcan source, and thus proves to be a strong argument for his use of Mark" (p. 414; added in ²1978); Jn 13,21: "It seems probable that he is here dependent upon Mark" (p. 446).
258. *Oral Tradition* (n. 246 above), pp. 230-231. See also pp. 248-249 (no. 57) and 254 (no. 112).

expanded with sender/emissary, "which is probably simply a Johannine expansion (absent from Jn 15.20a)", are cited as examples of *literary* formulation. The possibility of John's contact with Mt 10[259] receives no consideration. Another cluster of sayings in Jn 12,25-28 (Dunn) is examined in the same volume by M.L. Soards[260]. Following R. Schnackenburg, he compares Jn 12,27-28 (and 18,11b) with the Synoptic Gethsemane scene: "in both the Synoptics and John one observes a striking cluster of ideas and words"[261], but the scenes are "remarkably different" and this diversity "suggests the existence of an oral tradition behind the accounts"[262]. He could have quoted from another commentary: "The differences are real, but most of them can be explained in terms of Johannine usage and interest"[263], but no effort is made by Soards in this direction.

Dunn is convinced that Jn 2,19 and Mk 14,58 stem from a common original. When he says that "John has been prepared to affirm and interpret appropriately what he heard as attributed to Jesus"[264], this could mean that the saying in Jn 2,19 is an adaptation from Mk I 14,58[265]. Regarding the request for a sign in Jn 2,18 (cf. Mk 11,28), Dunn speaks quite fittingly of "freedom of editorial usage"[266].

With respect to Synoptic-like narratives (Jn 4,46-54; 6,1-21; 12,1-8.12-19), Dunn finds there "the sort of diverse elaboration" that is allowable in oral story-telling: they are "so different in detail that a literary interdependence cannot be demonstrated (though, of course, it also cannot be entirely ruled out)"[267]. This last concession[268] is not untypical in the volume on Oral Tradition which was set up as an attempt to draw

---

259. Cf. above, Section II,1. Aune's other examples of synonymous couplets (p. 231) are from Mk (2,21-22; 3,24-25; 4,22); Q (Lk 6,43; 6,44; 11,23; 12,23) and Mt (10,41).

260. M.L. SOARDS, *Oral Tradition Before, In, and Outside the Canonical Passion Narratives*, pp. 334-350, esp. 340-343. See also pp. 344-345, on Jn 18,11a and Mt 26,52; cf. above, Section II,4. Notes 259 and 260: see pp. 21-26 and 31-33.

261. *Ibid.*, p. 343: "(1) Jesus' soul is distressed; (2) he faced 'the hour'; (3) he prays to his/the Father, asking — or, not asking — to be saved; (4) he calls for God's will to be done; (5) he directs his disciples to prayer that they may avoid temptation; (6) there is an association of an angel or angels with Jesus' facing his hour and his praying; and (7) there is the reference to Jesus' death as his cup".

262. *Ibid.*, p. 343. See also above, nn. 179-180, on John and Luke.

263. BARRETT, *John*, p. 425 (added in ²1978, in answer to Dodd).

264. DUNN, *John*, p. 370.

265. Cf. BARRETT, *John*, pp. 199-200: ναός only in this context in Jn (2,19.20.21); ἐν τρισὶν ἡμέραις only in Mk 15,29 (par. Mt): "probably shows contact with the taunt in Mark". On λύσατε - ἐγερῶ, cf. *ibid.*, and *Evangelica II*, p. 710.

266. DUNN, *John*, p. 369. Cf. BARRETT, p. 199: "These words [Mk 11,28] were probably in John's mind, and he has combined them with the request of Mark 8.11".

267. DUNN, *John*, pp. 359-368, esp. 368.

268. Compare also Dunn's general conclusion: "The extent of the freedom demonstrated by John appears somewhat alarming" (p. 378).

clear distinctions between literary interdependence and oral traditioning process. One of the "accepted findings" is now that "we have been unable to deduce or derive any marks which distinguish clearly between an oral and a written transmission process. Each can show a similar degree of fixity and variability"[269]. The Borgen-Dauer suggestion of a mediate contact with the Synoptics, some elements of the written Synoptic Gospels being fused together with the pre-Johannine oral tradition[270], is curiously absent in this book on Oral Gospel Tradition. It goes without saying that orality understood as transmission of written texts by oral means[271] has its place in the study of John and the Synoptics.

CONCLUSION

At the Colloquium (1990) I concluded my lecture with "a clarification on my own position". In the printed text of my paper this passage is relocated at the end of the Introduction (with notes 57-64).

Recent surveys of Johannine studies make a distinction between synchronic reading and diachronic approach, and in this last section the I Synoptic Gospels and the Signs Source (or Signs Gospel) are treated as the two main alternatives[272] Such an association can be misleading, and H. Thyen's paper has made clear that John's "use" of the Synoptics can be quite different from Fortna's Johannine redactor endorsing his (hypothetical) predecessor's writing[273]. In fact, my understanding of Johan-

---

269. *Jesus and the Oral Gospel Tradition*, pp. 9-15 (Introduction), esp. p. 12. See also D.E. Aune's conclusion (cf. above, n. 246): "the notion that oral tradition is flexible and written tradition is fixed ... is a thoroughly modern assumption which is not supported by the evidence. The analysis of the written evidence for the aphorisms of Jesus suggests that it was as flexible and variable as one might suppose oral tradition to be" (p. 240).

270. Cf. *Evangelica II*, pp. 700-701 ("The Borgen-Dauer Thesis"), in a contribution to the Jerusalem Symposium, 1984 (*The Interrelations*, pp. 439-440; cf. n. 57 above).

271. Cf. P.A. ALEXANDER, *Orality in Pharisaic-rabbinic Judaism at the Turn of the Eras* (in the same volume), pp. 159-184, esp. 159, for the two senses of orality, creation and transmission (n. 1). See also *Evangelica II*, p. 25, on post-Markan oral tradition with respect to the minor agreements (n. 128).

272. See, e.g., the volume *La communauté johannique*, 1990 (n. 16 above), Part II, "Préhistoire de l'évangile" (i.e., C. Riniker on the Synoptic Gospels and D. Marguerat on the Signs Source; cf. p. 70: "la question du rapport entre Jean et les synoptiques" and "la seconde filiation postulée dans la recherche"); cf. J. Beutler's survey in Part I: "1. Approches diachroniques. 2. Approches synchroniques" (note: "diachroniques" in the title on p. 29 is a printing mistake). See also X. LÉON-DUFOUR, *Où en est la recherche johannique? Bilan et ouvertures*, in A. MARCHADOUR (ed.), *Origine et postérité de l'Évangile de Jean* (Lectio Divina, 143), Paris, 1990, pp. 17-41 (1. Approche diachronique; 2. Approche synchronique); for his sentence on "l'unique critique qui ose déclarer que Jean n'a été établi qu'à partir des Synoptiques", cf. above, n. 57.

273. In this volume, pp. 81-107, esp. 85-93.

nine redaction comes closer to a so-called "literary perspective"[274]. One can welcome insights of a new "literary-critical" reading of the text in itself and at the same time recommend not neglecting John's relationship to the Synoptics. I return for a while to my last example, Jn 5,1-18. On this section, R.A. Culpepper has written a commentary "fondé sur la critique narrative", in which he compares the narrative structure of the miracle story with Jn 4,46-54: "La comparaison est éclairante. Elle nous montre comment l'évangéliste joue avec la forme du récit de signe"[275]. This variation in the form of the miracle stories is probably not unrelated to the active intervention and faith of the centurion in Lk 7,1-10 (par. Mt) and the passive role of the paralytic in Mk 2,1-12.

At the 1975 Colloquium the discussion of John and the Synoptics concentrated on the passion and resurrection narratives, and in later studies the dependence hypothesis has received further elaboration with respect to that part of the Gospel. J.D. Crossan has even suggested a double hypothesis: "in the case of John and the synoptics, we must imagine a complicated, double relationship of independence for its sayings and miracles tradition but of dependence for its passion and resurrection narratives"[276]. In subsequent years, however, due I consideration was given to parallel passages in the prepassion part of the Gospel, in full commentaries and in special monographs. In this connection it is typical to mention that A. Dauer's *Passionsgeschichte* was followed by his *Johannes und Lukas*. I would not contest D.M. Smith's statement that with respect to the resurrection narratives there is "a more striking

---

274. Cf. R.A. CULPEPPER - F.F. SEGOVIA (eds.), *The Fourth Gospel from a Literary Perspective* (Semeia, 53), Atlanta, GA, 1991. — For one aspect, see, by one of my students, G. VAN BELLE, *Les parenthèses dans l'Évangile de Jean* (SNTA), 11), Leuven, 1985, and the reactions by E. RUCKSTUHL, *Zur Antithese Idiolekt-Soziolekt im Johanneischen Schriftum*, in *SNTU* 12 (1987) 141-181; C.W. HEDRICK, *Authorial Presence and Narrator in John: Commentary and Story*, in J.E. GOEHRING, et al. (eds.), *Gospel Origins & Christian Beginnings*, FS J.M. Robinson, Sonoma, CA, 1990, pp. 74-93. Cf. *Evangelica II*, pp. 693-698.

275. Cf. R.A. CULPEPPER - F.F. SEGOVIA (eds.), *The Fourth Gospel from a Literary Perspective* (Semeia, 53), Atlanta, GA, 1991. — For one aspect, see, by one of my students, G. VAN BELLE, *Les parenthèses dans l'Évangile de Jean* (SNTA, 11), Leuven, 1985, and the reactions by E. RUCKSTUHL, *Zur Antithese Idiolekt-Soziolekt im Johanneischen Schrifttum*, in *SNTU* 12 (1987) 141-181; C.W. HEDRICK, *Authorial Presence and Narrator in John: Commentary and Story*, in J.E. GOEHRING, et al. (eds.), *Gospel Origins & Christian Beginnings*, FS J.M. Robinson, Sonoma, CA, 1990, pp. 74-93. Cf. *Evangelica II*, pp. 693-698.

275. *Un exemple* (n. 238 above), pp. 141-145 ("La structure narrative"), esp. p. 143. Cf. p. 142: "une variation délibérée de la forme".

276. *The Cross That Spoke*, 1988 (n. 36 above), p. xiii. See now also *The Historical Jesus* (n. 228 above), p. 431: John I is "dependent, but very creatively so, on the *Cross Gospel* and the Synoptic Gospels for its passion and resurrection account".

phenomenon"[277], but in general we can say that scholars who accept dependence in the passion and resurrection narratives are open to this hypothesis in other parts of the Gospels[278].

POSTSCRIPT

After the foregoing material went to the press I received a copy of D. Moody Smith's important new publication: *John among the Gospels: The Relationship in Twentieth-Century Research* (Minneapolis, MN, Fortress, 1992, XIII-210 pages). Compare Smith's earlier works mentioned above, pp. 5 n. 15; 12-13 nn. 48-56; 15 n. 64 (and 26 n. 116). The first part of the book traces the history of the problem up to the 1960s and the early 1970s. The more recent developments are treated in Chapter 5 (The Renaissance of the Problem: Passion Narratives, 111-135) and Chapter 6 (The Dissolution of a Consensus, 139-170). Cf. p. 139: "Yet Neirynck went on to indicate his own dissent from that consensus, and in his 1990 Louvain Colloquium *Forschungsbericht*, he could point to a growing body of exegetical opinion that was challenging the once prevailing critical orthodoxy". Other references to my 1990 Colloquium paper are given on pp. 10 n. 8; 103 n. 39, 152 n. 26, 190. Cf. p. XII: "The renewed interest in John and the Synoptics was indicated by the nearly 150 scholars who attended the 1990 Louvain Biblical Colloquium, which I was devoted entirely to that subject". See also p. 158 n. 33, and his note on H. Thyen, pp. 167-169. "The English commentators" (in Thyen's 1990 paper) are correctly identified as

---

277. Cf. above, n. 56.

278. SUPPLEMENTARY NOTE. Additional material that appeared in the course of 1990 is included in the published text of my paper (delivered at the Colloquium, August 7, 1990). In addition, the editor of this volume gave me the opportunity to insert some references to relevant studies published in 1991: J. Ashton (n. 41), D.A. Carson (n. 43), J.D. Crossan (n. 228), W.D. Davies – D.C. Allison (n. 99), J.D.G. Dunn (n. 244), R.M. Fowler (n. 230), P. Hofrichter (n. 38), H.-J. Klauck (n. 158a), J.P. Meier (n. 62), M. Myllykoski (n. 62: Lk; n. 157: Mk), J.W. Pryor (n. 144), E. Ruckstuhl – P. Dschulnigg (n. 33), M. Sabbe (n. 181), my *Evangelica II* (passim).

See also nn. 196, 246, 260, 271, 274. J. Painter's study of Jn 6 (n. 233) is now reprinted in his *The Quest for the Messiah. The History, Literature and Theology of the Johannine Community*, Edinburgh, 1991, pp. 215-244 (ch. 6: "The Messiah and the Bread of Life"), esp. 217-220: "John 6 and the Synoptics" (quotation from p. 218, n. 10). See also his ch. 2, esp. 74-80: "The Synoptic Tradition".

One more recent contribution can be added here: W. SCHMITHALS, *Johannesevangelium und Johannesbriefe. Forschungsberichte und Analyse* (BZNW, 64), Berlin - New York, 1992, esp. pp. 318-319: "Benutzung der synoptischen Überlieferung". See my review in *ETL* 68 (1992), pp. 166-168.

C.K. Barrett, R.H. Lightfoot and E. Hoskyns (p. 184): cf. Thyen's published text in this volume, p. 95.

I quote one more sentence: "Neirynck offers a succinct redaction-critical rationale to account for how John dealt with his synoptic sources. Increasingly, Neirynck and those who follow him in speaking of John's dependence upon and redaction of the Synoptic Gospels will find it incumbent upon themselves to offer such explanations" (p. 158); and again, in reference to my synoptic studies: "The case for Matthew's and Luke's independent use of Mark is often confirmed by redaction-critical analysis based on that premise. Will it be possible to say the same for John's use of Mark, or of either of the other Synoptics?" (p. 159 n. 33). But see my remark in the text above, p. 15.

For a continuation of the discussion on "John and the Synoptics", see the contributions in *The Four Gospels 1992. Festschrift Frans Neirynck* (BETL, 100), 1992, Part VI: "The Gospel of John" (pp. 1721-2221): by R. Schnackenburg, G. Schneider, D.M. Smith, U. Schnelle, P. Borgen, M. de Jonge, G.R. Beasley-Murray, J. Painter, S. Freyne, G. Van Belle, É. Trocmé, E.D. Freed, D.-A. Koch, B. Lindars, E. Ruckstuhl, H. Thyen, M. Sabbe, U. Busse, J. Zumstein, J. Smit Sibinga, J. Kremer, P.J. Judge, W.S. Vorster.

On John's dependence on the Synoptics, see the more recent commentaries by U. Wilckens and U. Schnelle. Cf. below, 601-615.

BETL 110 (1993) 11-38

2

LITERARY CRITICISM, OLD AND NEW

The previous Colloquium on the New Testament in 1990 was devoted to the Gospel of John and its relationship to the Synoptic Gospels, and on that occasion I had the opportunity to present a survey of the studies on John and the Synoptics. I could observe that this issue had become again a lively debated question and that Johannine dependence is no longer the provocative and isolated thesis it might have seemed to be in 1975[1]. Although the phrase: "How my mind has changed" is now a fashionable title for retrospective essays, such a title would have been inappropriate with regard to the problem of John's relation to the Synoptics. But, and this is my question today, is that also the case regarding the study of the Synoptic Gospels themselves?

I begin with a personal recollection. There is a great variety of scholarly opinion in introductory questions such as the date and the place of origin of each of the Synoptic Gospels, and therefore I am delighted that I can start my own story with a precise date and location: my personal interest in the Synoptic Gospels and the Synoptic Problem began in the year 1953-54 when, as one of the STB students, I attended for the first time Professor L. Cerfaux's course on the Synoptics. With the galley proofs of L. Vaganay's *Le problème synoptique* on his desk, Cerfaux initiated his audience in the primitive-gospel hypothesis, a Proto-Matthew, source of Matthew, Mark and Luke, and much closer to canonical Matthew than Vaganay's *Matthieu grec*. The effect of Cerfaux's course was double. On the one hand, I found his exemplary analytical work of synoptic comparison most stimulating. On the other hand, although like other Cerfaux students at that time I may have professed lip service to Proto-Matthew, I found myself much more attracted to the alternative theory of Markan priority, and I retained the strong conviction that there was some need of refinement in the current argument. The year 1954 was also important for another reason: Hans

---

1. *John and the Synoptics: 1975-1990*, in A. DENAUX (ed.), *John and the Synoptics* (BETL, 101), Leuven, 1992, pp. 3-62. Compare my *John and the Synoptics*, lecture delivered at the Colloquium on John in 1975 (in *Evangelica*, pp. 365-400).

For more complete bibliographical data, up to August 1992, I refer to the Bibliography compiled by G. Van Belle in *The Four Gospels 1992. Festschrift Frans Neirynck* (BETL, 100), Leuven, 1992, pp. 3-24. The two volumes of Collected Essays published in 1982 (BETL, 60) and in 1991 (BETL, 99) are here referred to as *Evangelica* and *Evangelica II*.

Conzelmann's *Die Mitte der Zeit* made a great impression. It meant for me the introduction into Synoptic redaction criticism. My subsequent doctoral work on Luke, under A. Descamps, was partially written in dialogue with Conzelmann (1957). And all my later | research and publications on the Synoptics can be characterized in general as redaction-critical.

Redaction criticism and the study of the Synoptic Problem are interconnected, and it is our custom to use the term "literary criticism" in a broad sense, combining the source-critical and redaction-critical dimensions. Thus, I was not unhappy to observe that also in the Old Testament field the pendulum is now swinging back[2]. On the other hand, we all know that in recent years the methods and the name of secular "literary criticism" have won acceptance in biblical studies[3]. The author of a recent Dictionary article on "Literary Criticism" simply dismisses a scholarship that is "interested in questions of history, reaching behind the texts to their sources, and the events which gave rise to them. This type of scholarship has often been referred to as 'literary criticism', but is more appropriately described as 'source criticism', and will not be further discussed here"[4]. Such a narrow circumscription, degrading the *old* literary criticism to historical criticism in contrast to the interpretation of the Bible as literature in the *new* literary criticism needs correction. It also raises a terminological problem: "Literary Criticism" is no longer the translation of "Literarkritik"[5]. My personal practical solution is to use more specific descriptions, such as narrative criticism, rhetorical criticism, the study of "narrative rhetoric", and to maintain the comprehensive term *Literarkritik* in its traditional acceptance.

2. Cf. L. SCHMIDT, *Literarkritik, I. Altes Testament*, in *TRE* 21 (1991) 211-222: "Eine Trennung von Literarkritik und Redaktionsgeschichte ist (aber) schon forschungsgeschichtlich problematisch. ... Zudem läßt sich sachlich nur schwer zwischen Literarkritik und Redaktionsgeschichte differenzieren. ... M.E. (sind) Analyse und Synthese Gegenstand der Literarkritik" (p. 211).

3. M.A. POWELL, *The Bible and Modern Literary Criticism. A Critical Assessment and Annotated Bibliography* (Bibliographies and Indexes in Religious Studies, 22), New York - Westport, CT - London, 1992, esp. pp. 257-338: "The Gospels" (nos. 1054-1428); M. MINOR, *Literary-Critical Approaches to the Bible. An Annotated Bibliography*, West Cornwall, CT, 1992, esp. pp. 348-450: "The Gospels" (nos. 1565-2035). Cf. my review in *ETL* 68 (1992) 432-433. See also S.D. MOORE, *Literary Criticism and the Gospels. The Theoretical Challenge*, New Haven, CT - London, 1989.

4. M. DAVIES, *Literary Criticism*, in R.J. COGGINS & J.L. HOULDEN (eds.), *A Dictionary of Biblical Interpretation*, London - Philadelphia, PA, 1990, pp. 402-405, esp. 402.

5. The theme of this Colloquium "Source Criticism and the New Literary Criticism" was first announced as: "Literarkritik" and/or Literary Criticism. Compare C. FOCANT, *Mc 7,24-31 par. Mt 15,21-29: critique des sources et/ou étude narrative*, pp. 39-75.

Practitioners of the new literary criticism already made the announcement that the age of redaction criticism has come to its end[6]. In redaction criticism, they say, the evangelists were treated as redactors, editors of traditional texts, and not really as the authors of the gospels. I Interpreters now move to holistic readings, to the study of each gospel as a whole; and what they call an excessive allegiance to diachrony is now being replaced by the primacy of synchrony. The shortcomings of the redaction-critical method are listed, and its first weakness is "reliance on the two-source hypothesis"[7]: "with a requestioning of the priority of Mark, the Markan anchor of control for the distinctive divergences of both Matthew and Luke has become precarious. ... The whole edifice of redaction criticism may be resting on a cracked foundation"[8]. Many more quotations of this sort can be given: the two-source theory is "at an impasse", and one of the advantages of the new discipline of literary criticism is its focus on the final form of the gospel text.

At this point, two observations can be made. My first remark concerns the description of the redaction-critical method. The distinction between redaction and tradition is an important aspect, of course, but it is hardly acceptable that the redaction criticism of the past three decades be reduced to a study of "the redactors' alterations of their sources". For most scholars, redaction criticism and composition criticism are synonymous, and their redactional investigations are not exclusive of respect for the final work of the evangelist as a whole. My second remark regards the recommendation of literary criticism because of the lack of source-critical consensus. This reminds me of a recommendation of form-critical study I could hear here in Leuven in the 1950s: "essayer de contourner le problème synoptique", avoid discussion of the synoptic problem by concentrating directly upon individual sayings and small gospel units. The proposal is now to focus on the final gospel text irrespective of the problem of sources. I agree, this can be a refuge for gospel students who are irremediably skeptical in the question of sources. Those who are not (and I am one of them) should have the right to ask what can be gained by not taking into consideration part of the evidence.

---

6. The title is used by J.B. Muddiman in a review article: *The End of Markan Redaction Criticism?*, in *ExpT* 101 (1989-90) 307-309. Compare the title of Chapter Two in G.N. STANTON, *A Gospel for a New People. Studies in Matthew*, Edinburgh, 1992: "Redaction Criticism: The End of an Era?" (p. 23).

7. E.P. SANDERS & M. DAVIES, *Studying the Synoptic Gospels*, London - Philadelphia, PA, 1989, pp. 201-223, esp. 221.

8. D.P. MOESSNER, *Lord of the Banquet. The Literary and Theological Significance of the Lukan Travel Narrative*, Minneapolis, MN, 1989, p. 5.

I. MATTHEW AND MARK

In the discussion of the synoptic problem, the central issue is, in one form or another, the question of originality of Matthew or priority of Mark. The data of agreement and disagreement in the relative order of pericopes is rightly seen as essential, in particular the divergences I between Mk 1,21–6,13 and the parallel sections in Matthew (at 4,22 / 14,1). This was the main topic of my contribution to the 1965 Colloquium[9]. It was a special satisfaction to me that, following this paper, Cerfaux in his old age decided to rethink his synoptic solution. The effect of the paper was not only immediate and local. In his 1992 book on Matthew, G.N. Stanton has a section on Markan priority[10]:

> in the second half [of Mt] Mark's order is followed most carefully, but in the first half of the gospel Matthew alters the Marcan order very considerably. Is it possible to offer a plausible explanation of Matthew's inconsistency? If not, Matthew's dependence on Mark would seem to be called in question. F. Neirynck [1967] has faced the problem squarely and has examined carefully Matthew's rearrangements of Mark's order. He shows that it is only in Matt. 4.12–11.1 that a problem is posed by a departure from Mark; ... Within the section 4.23–11.1 Matthew's liberty of order is only relative, for Mark's order can still frequently be traced; where the Marcan order is changed by Matthew, he can be shown to have been inspired by his sources. In short, on the hypothesis of Matthean use of Mark, the evangelist's changes to Mark's order are not arbitrary but consistent and coherent.

I came back to this question at the conclusion of a more recent article on the structure of Matthew[11], with the observation that in "literary-critical" studies no distinction is made "between the original Matthean composition in 4,23–11,1 and the other parts of the Gospel where Matthew faithfully follows the story line of Mk 1,1-20 and 6,14–16,8. The whole extant text is, of course, in all its parts the text of the author of the Gospel, but we can learn from redaction criticism that some parts of this text are more Matthean than some other parts. A 'holistic' approach, when separated from redaction criticism, is unable to tell us the whole truth of the Gospel text"[12].

---

9. *La rédaction matthéenne et la structure du premier évangile*, in *ETL* 43 (1967) 41-73; = *Evangelica*, pp. 3-36. See also *ibid.*, 691-723, 729-736, and more recently, *Matthew 4:23–5:1 and the Matthean Composition of 4:23–11:1*, in D.L. DUNGAN (ed.), *The Interrelations of the Gospels* (BETL, 95), Leuven, 1992, pp. 23-46; *Synoptic Problem*, in *NJBC*, 1990, pp. 587-595.

10. *A Gospel for a New People* (n. 5 above), p. 31.

11. ΑΠΟ ΤΟΤΕ ΗΡΞΑΤΟ *and the Structure of Matthew*, in *ETL* 64 (1988) 21-59; = *Evangelica II*, pp. 141-179.

12. *Ibid.*, p. 179. In *Das Matthäus-Evangelium* (Erträge der Forschung, 275), Darmstadt, 1991, A. Sand quotes this conclusion: "Damit ist Neirynck recht zu geben" (p. 42);

One can only express approval when it is said that "three questions (are) essential to the literary critical analysis of Matthew's Gospel: (1) the role of the narrator in telling the story; (2) the content of the story (i.e., the characters, plot, and setting); and (3) the effect of the narraltive, or in other words, that which the implied author communicates to the implied reader"; and in addition, that the passage under examination should be treated as "one piece of a larger whole, one single segment within the 'sequential composite' of events which constitutes Matthew's overall narrative"[13]. But can the writer of a dissertation on Matthew's Missionary Discourse assume "the storyteller's freedom to tell his story in whatever way and by whatever means he chooses"[14] without even mentioning the question of Matthew's sources? And can he/she propose an outline of Matthew's Gospel without considering its possible basis in Mark[15]?

curiously enough, the phrase "a 'holistic' approach" is translated in German as "eine 'polemische' Behandlung"!

13. D.J. WEAVER, *Matthew's Missionary Discourse. A Literary Critical Analysis* (JSNT SS, 38), Sheffield, 1990, p. 28.

14. *Ibid.*, p. 35.

15. Some literary critics, with reference to J.D. Kingsbury, prefer a tripartite structure of Matthew, with the superscription at 1,1; 4,17; 16,21. Cf. U. LUZ, *Matthäus*, vol. II, 1990, p. 485: "das heute am verbreitesten 'narrative' Gliederungsmodell des Mt-Ev". But the argumentation developed by Kingsbury is, if I may say, a pre-'literary' one (1973). The division at 4,17 and 16,21 is much older (cf. Westcott-Hort). In my view, it is based on a misunderstanding of the phrase ἀπὸ τότε ἤρξατο and its relation to the preceding 4,12-16, resp. 16,13-20. Here, too, Matthew's division at 4,12 and 16,13 is parallel to (and dependent upon) Mk 1,14 and 8,27. Cf. *Evangelica II*, pp. 141-179 (n. 11 above), with additional note, pp. 180-182; see already *Evangelica*, pp. 18-20 (n. 9 above). See also B. STANDAERT, *L'évangile selon Matthieu. Composition et genre littéraire*, in *The Four Gospels 1992*, pp. 1223-1250, esp. 1240-1245 ("Les trois ἀπὸ τότε»).

The additional note in *Evangelica II* (on D.R. Bauer 1988, U. Luz 1990, *et al.*) can be supplemented with a reference to J.D. Kingsbury's response, in the new Preface to his *Matthew: Structure, Christology, Kingdom*, Minneapolis, MN, ²1989, pp. IX-XXIV, esp. XV-XX. Kingsbury restates his position: "Asyndetic *apo tote* signals that 4:17 and 16:21 stand apart from the preceding pericopes 4:12-16 and 16:13-20" (p. XX). Contrast A. SAND, *Das Matthäus-Evangelium* (n. 12 above), 1991, pp. 41-42 (on *apo tote* in 4,17 and 16,21): "Daß sie sich auch auf das unmittelbar Vorausgehende beziehen, ist unbestritten (im Sinne von: 'nach diesem Geschehen')" (p. 42, cf. *Evangelica II*, p. 178, n. 203; less consistently, he maintains the caesurae at 4,17 and 16,21). Kingsbury concludes: "The only basis [sic] for Neirynck's assertion of linkage instead of separation as regards 4:17 and 16:21 is his contention that one must revert to Mark if one is to ascertain the structure of Matthew. Since I disagree with this contention, I see no reason to change my position" (p. XX). See, however, also his note 36: "Neirynck establishes the unity of this pericope [16,13-23] not only by reading Matthew in terms of Mark..." (p. XIX). His reply to my observations on the contrast *in Matthew* between the blessing of Peter in 16,17 and the rebuke in 16,23 is rather brief and evasive (*ibid.*). Kingsbury regards it as "one of the great strengths" of his approach not to introduce "all the uncertainties of the synoptic problem into the already complex task of ascertaining the structure of Matthew" (p. XVII,

An extreme example of "narrative-critical reading" is J.P. Heil's essay on Mt 26–28[16]. He divides the text into three major sections |(26,1-56; 26,57–27,54; 27,55–28,20), "each composed of nine scenes that function together as a dynamic progression of seven narrative intercalations or 'sandwiches'"[17]. There is not even one mention of Mark in Heil's book on Matthew. But the same author separately published, the year before, an article on the "narrative structure" of Mk 14,1-52, of which Mt 26,1-56 appears to be the perfect replica[18]. I hope, you will understand when I say that the reading of this sort of literary criticism makes me nostalgic: I remember the good time I had in the early 1970's when D.P. Senior was preparing here his doctoral work, a "redactional" study of the passion narrative according to Matthew[19].

II. THE MINOR AGREEMENTS AND LUKAN REDACTION

Literary critics proclaim freedom from priority assumptions as an advantage of their method "given the uncertainties surrounding competing hypotheses in gospel studies today"[20]. In the current situation, however, if we set aside the neo-Griesbachians and their allies, almost all competing theories are variations of the same basic assumption of Markan priority. The priority of Mark can be mitigated by the acceptance of some form of Proto-Mark, Deutero-Mark, or Deutero-Markan recension; or by subsidiary hypotheses, the influence of tradition variants, or dependence of Luke upon Matthew. There is one main stumbling-block at the origin of all these hypotheses: the phenomenon of the minor agreements of Matthew and Luke against Mark in the triple tradition.

---

n. 26). But when the literary critic reading the Gospel "in terms of Matthew" finds three key summary-passages in 4,[12-]17–11,1 and three passion-predictions in 16,[13-]21–20,34 (pp. X-XI), can it be indifferent for him to know that the three passion predictions are adopted from the parallel text in Mk 8,27–10,52, whereas the three summaries are the product of a specific Matthean arrangement (Mt 4,23–11,1)?

16. J.P. HEIL, *The Death and Resurrection of Jesus. A Narrative-Critical Reading of Matthew 26–28*, Minneapolis, MN, 1991. See also *The Narrative Structure of Matthew 27:55–28:20*, in *JBL* 110 (1991) 419-438 (compare *The Death*, pp. 91-110). On this last essay, cf. D.P. SENIOR, *Matthew's Account* (n. 36), pp. 1435-1437.

17. *The Death*, p. 2.

18. *Mark 14,1-52: Narrative Structure and Reader-Response*, in *Biblica* 71 (1990) 305-332.

19. Cf. below, n. 36.

20. D.B. HOWELL, *Matthew's Inclusive Story. A Study in the Narrative Rhetoric of the First Gospel* (JSNT SS, 42), Sheffield, 1990, p. 35.

Ten years before W.R. Farmer's book on *The Synoptic Problem* we were faced with this phenomenon in Vaganay's *Le problème synoptique*[21], and it is undeniable that his argument, if not convincing, was not devoid of some force of seduction, as can be seen for instance from a late witness by F. Bovon[22]. The minor agreements were studied here I in doctoral dissertations by S. McLoughlin[23] and T. Hansen[24], in our volume published in 1974[25] and in a number of special studies[26], and now recently in the dissertation of T.A. Friedrichsen who surveys and evaluates new developments of the discussion in the years 1974-1991[27]. The minor agreements now receive much consideration in two alternative theories, Deutero-Mark[28] and Lukan dependence on Matthew[29]. It is not

21. L. VAGANAY, *Le problème synoptique*, Tournai, 1954, pp. 69-74 (esp. the negative agreements diff. Mk 6,31-44; 4,35-41) and 405-425 (Excursus on the negative agreements diff. Mk 9,14-29).

22. F. BOVON, *L'Évangile selon saint Luc (1,1–9,50)* (CNT, IIIa), Genève, 1991, p. 495, n. 18 (regarding Lk 9,37-43a, diff. Mk 9,14-29): "j'admire son analyse conduite de main de maître"; in the German edition, *Das Evangelium nach Lukas (Lk 1,1–9,50)* (EKK 3/1), Zürich - Neukirchen-Vluyn, 1989, p. 508, n. 18: "dessen meisterhafte Analyse (mich) überzeugt (hat)".

23. S. McLOUGHLIN, *The Synoptic Theory of Xavier Léon-Dufour. An Analysis and Evaluation*, 1965, esp. pp. 236-291, 507-510; *Les accords mineurs Mt-Lc contre Mc et le problème synoptique. Vers la théorie des deux sources*, in *ETL* 63 (1967) 17-40 (= BETL, 25).

24. T. HANSEN, *De overeenkomsten Mattheus-Lucas tegen Marcus in de drievoudige traditie*, 1969. Cf. n. 25 below.

25. F. NEIRYNCK, *The Minor Agreements of Matthew and Luke against Mark. With a Cumulative List* (BETL, 37), Leuven, 1974 (with the collaboration of T. Hansen and F. Van Segbroeck). Cf. n. 30 below.

26. *Evangelica*, esp. pp. 637-680 (Mk 2,27); 737-768 (order); 769-780 (Dmk); 781-796 (Mk 2,1-4); 797-809 (Mk 9,2-10); 809-810; *Evangelica II*, pp. 3-42 (cf. n. 30 below); 43-48 (Mk 8,31); 49-58 (πάλιν in Mk); 59-73 (Proto-Mk); 75-94 (Mk 6,30-34); 95-138 (Mk 14,65); 187-190 (Mk 3,1-6); 293-320 (duplicate expressions); 321-322 (Mk 1,12-13a); 481-492 (Mt 12,25a / Lc 11,17a); 773-784 (Mk 1,40-45).

27. T.A. FRIEDRICHSEN, *The Matthew-Luke Agreements against Mark: 1974-1991*, 1992. Cf. *'Minor' and 'Major' Matthew-Luke Agreements against Mk 4,30-32*, in *The Four Gospels 1992*, pp. 649-676; *Alternative Synoptic Theories on Mk 4,30-32*, in this volume, pp. 427-450. See also his 1974-1989 survey in F. NEIRYNCK (ed.), *L'Évangile de Luc - The Gospel of Luke* (BETL, 32), Leuven, ²1989, pp. 335-392; and his critical reviews in *ETL* 65 (1989) 390-394 (M.D. Goulder), 395-408 (R.B. Vinson); 66 (1990) 410-413 (H. Riley); 67 (1991) 373-394 (A. Ennulat, J. Rauscher).

28. In its radical form propounded by A. Fuchs and his school, or in the mitigated form of a Deutero-Markan recension (U. Luz, A. Ennulat).

29. With rejection of the Q source (M.D. Goulder) or in combination with Luke's use of Q (R.H. Gundry). Cf. R.H. GUNDRY, *Matthean Foreign Bodies in Agreements of Luke with Matthew against Mark Evidence that Luke Used Matthew*, in *The Four Gospels 1992* (n. 1), pp. 1467-1495, including on pp. 1475-1479 a reply to my "Note on Lk 9,22"; (cf. p. 1468, n. 4: with thanks to Goulder for corrections and suggestions). The instances of agreement with Matthew discussed by Gundry are: Lk 6,13.14; 8,10.12.20.25; 9,1.3.11.22.27.47; 10,25; 11,17; 18,22.31; 20,3.14.18; 22,41-42.70; 23,47.52; 24,5.6.9. On Lk 24,9, cf. below n. 38.

unimportant to observe that on three points they agree with our redactional approach. First, the minor agreements are post-Markan in nature; second, at least some of the minor agreements can be explained by independent (Matthean and Lukan) redaction; third, in some other instances, Matthean redaction is likely and, in their opinion, the problem is on the side of Luke.

The question to be debated mainly concerns Lukan redaction, and it is not by abstract speculation on the acceptable number of agreements that this question can be solved. Neither is it enough, as indicated in I my paper at the Göttingen Conference (1991)[30], to list the verbal agreements with Matthew. When each agreement is carefully examined in its specific context, and in relation to the parallel text in Mark, similarities *and* dissimilarities may appear, and what at first is supposed to be un-Lukan may become quite acceptable Lukan redaction once it is seen in the macro-context of the entire Lukan work. The conclusion I wrote last year can be repeated here[31]:

> In theory I can have no objection against some influence of oral-tradition variants, some occasional dependence on a revised text of Mark, or some subsidiary Lukan dependence on Matthew. But a modification of the Markan hypothesis suggested on the basis of the minor agreements can only be a minor modification, and it is my impression that no such modification is needed after serious examination of the Matthean *and Lukan* redactions.
>
> There is still one dimension of the study of the minor agreements which should be mentioned. Many times the minor agreement works like a signal: the coincidence of Matthew and Luke draws attention to Matthean and Lukan non-coincidental parallels, and without those cases of agreement some aspects of Matthean and Lukan usage would have remained partially unexplored. The minor agreements force us again and again to study each passage in light of the whole Gospel, and this has been, it seems to me, most profitable to our comprehension of the three Synoptic Gospels.

Special mention should be made of the two famous minor agreements in the passion narrative. The suggestion of a textual solution in the case of Lk 22,62 (diff. Mk 14,72) and in the more difficult case of Mt 26,68 (diff. Mk 14,65) gave rise to theoretical discussion about conjectural

---

30. *The Minor Agreements and the Two-Source Theory*, in *Evangelica II*, pp. 3-42 (including examination of significant agreements diff. Mk 5,27; 9,19; 4,11; 14,65; 6,30-34; 9,2-10). Cf. *ETL* 67 (1991) 361-372: *A Symposium on the Minor Agreements*. An adaptation of the Cumulative List (1974, pp. 49-195) has been prepared for the Göttingen Conference: *The Minor Agreements in a Horizontal-line Synopsis* (SNTA, 15), Leuven, 1991. [Cf. below, p. 331 n. 5.]

31. *Evangelica II*, p. 41.

emendation[32]. The debate is not closed, but I see a growing number of scholars for whom an exceptional instance of conjectural reading is no longer methodologically unacceptable[33].

III. THE PASSION AND RESURRECTION NARRATIVES

I D.P. Senior presented in 1972 his dissertation on the passion narrative in Matthew, at the conclusion of four years of research in Leuven. His work is a verse by verse examination of Mt 26,1–27,56 "comparing every single word to Mark's account to see how much one can explain in terms of Matthean use and adaptation of Mark". I quote R.E. Brown: "This dissertation, written under Neirynck's direction in 1972, comes as close as one can to giving a coup-de-grace to any theory positing a major independent source for the Matthean passion narrative"[34]. Similar observations were made by other reviewers[35]. It is Senior's contention that the

32. ΤΙΣ ΕΣΤΙΝ Ο ΠΑΙΣΑΣ ΣΕ, in *ETL* 63 (1987) 5-47; = *Evangelica II*, pp. 95-137 (with additional note, p. 138); see also pp. 27-28. Cf. C.M. TUCKETT, *Reading the New Testament. Methods of Interpretation*, London, 1987, p. 34; *The Minor Agreements and Textual Criticism* (paper read at the Göttingen Conference, 1991). [Cf. below, p. 333 n. 9.]

33. B. Aland mentions the case of Mt 26,68 as "eine seltene Ausnahme ... möglicherweise" (n. 1), and rightly urges: "Beantwortet kann [die Frage nach den Konjekturen] stets nur aufgrund genauer Erörterung der einzelnen Stelle in ihrem Kontext werden". Cf. *Das Zeugnis der frühen Papyri für den Text der Evangelien diskutiert am Matthäusevangelium*, in *The Four Gospels 1992*, pp. 326-335, esp. 326. Cf. A. VANHOYE, *L'intérêt de Luc pour la prophétie en Lc 1,76; 4,16-30 et 22,60-65*, *ibid.*, pp. 1529-1548, esp. 1544-1547 (Lk 22,62) and 1547-1548 (Mt 26,68): "L'hypothèse du Prof. F. Neirynck trouve donc là un appui très ferme" (p. 1548).

See also, in *The Four Gospels 1992*, further discussion of the minor agreements by T.A. Friedrichsen (n. 27), R.H. Gundry (n. 29), and M.E. BORING, *The Synoptic Problem, "Minor" Agreements and the Beelzebul Pericope*, pp. 587-619: extensive treatment of Mt/Lk diff. Mk 3,22-30, with evaluation of the major theories (Griesbach, Farrer-Goulder, Deutero-Mark, and the classical two-source hypothesis); conclusion: "Matthew and Luke used canonical Mark, probably in a slightly revised form, and Q, which contained an independent version of this story" (p. 619).

34. R.E. Brown's review in *CBQ* 38 (1976) 259-260, p. 259. See there also the retraction of his earlier statement (in treating the passion narrative in *John* II, 1970, p. 790) that "The French and the Belgians think that Matthew had a more primitive source than Mark".

35. See, e.g., G. SELLIN, in *TLZ* 102 (1977) 437-439: "Es ist das Hauptverdienst dieser Arbeit, daß die Abweichungen von Mk überzeugend als durchgehende matthäische Redaktion erklärt werden können. Dabei vertritt Senior in lobenswerter methodischer Strenge den asketischen Standpunkt konsequenter redaktionsgeschichtlicher Exegese, wie er in Leuven (F. Neirynck) praktiziert wird, und steht damit auf solidem methodischen Fundament in einer Zeit, wo neutestamentliche Forschung wieder ins Stadium des Wagnisses hypothetischer Rekonstruktionen von Quellen und Traditionen zu treten scheint" (col. 438). "Die Hypothese vom Fehlen jeglicher Sonderquellen und -traditionen in der matthäischen Passionsgeschichte ist damit ein gutes Stück weiter bewiesen" (col. 439).

Matthean *Sondergut* passages, firmly embedded in the Markan context, can be explained as the result of Matthew's theological and literary reflection on his Markan source[36]. My own essay on Mt 28,1-10, first presented in 1967, and in particular I the redactional interpretation of 28,9-10, has played a noticeable role in the debate on John and the Synoptics[37]. The direction of the argument is well sketched by D.M. Smith[38]:

> In an earlier article, Neirynck had shown how Matthew 28:9-10, the story of Jesus' encounter with the women outside the tomb, can be understood as a Matthean editorial composition. The principal argument against this view always refers to the existence of John 20:11-18, the appearance to Mary Magdalene, said to be based on a similar and related tradition. Now Neirynck seeks to show that the Johannine account can be read more intelligibly as an elaboration and retelling of the Matthean story. The logic of his argument is impeccable: if Matthew composed 28:9-10 on no

36. D.P. SENIOR, *The Passion Narrative according to Matthew. A Redactional Study* (BETL, 39), Leuven, 1975 (diss. 1972, with additional notes on recent studies); [2]1982. Other publications on Matthew's special material (in chronological order): *The Fate of the Betrayer. A Redactional Study of Matthew XXVII,3-10*, in *ETL* 48 (1972) 372-426 (= 1975, pp. 343-397); *The Death of Jesus and the Resurrection of the Holy Ones, Matthew 27:51-53*, in *CBQ* 38 (1976) 312-329; *Matthew's Special Material in the Passion Story: Implications for the Evangelist's Redactional Technique and Theological Perspective*, in *ETL* 63 (1987) 272-294 (updating his dissertation, with special attention to Mt 27,3-10.24-25.51b-53); *Matthew's Account of the Burial of Jesus: Mt 27,57-61*, in *The Four Gospels 1992* (n. 1), pp. 1433-1448. See also *The Passion of Jesus in the Gospel of Matthew* (Passion Series, 1), Wilmington, DE, 1985.

37. F. NEIRYNCK, *Les femmes au tombeau. Étude de la rédaction matthéenne (Matt. XXVIII.1-10)*, in *NTS* 15 (1968-69) 168-190 (paper read at the SNTS meeting in Gwatt, 1967), reprinted in *Evangelica*, 1982, pp. 273-295 (with additional note, p. 296); updated and supplemented in *John and the Synoptics* (BETL 44, 1977), in *Evangelica*, pp. 365-398 (388-390: "Mt 28,9-10"); *John and the Synoptics: The Empty Tomb Stories* (*NTS* 30, 1984), in *Evangelica II*, pp. 571-600 (579-588: "Jn 20,11-18 and Mt 28,9-10"; with additional note, p. 600); *John and the Synoptics: 1975-1990* (n. 1 above), 1992, pp. 16-35: "John and Matthew" (esp. pp. 33-35, on Mt 28,9-10).

38. D.M. SMITH, *John among the Gospels. The Relationship in Twentieth-Century Research*, Minneapolis, MN, 1992, p. 157 (with reference to *NTS* 1969 and 1984). Some critics continue to envisage the possibility that "Matt 28:9-10 is a compression of the appearance to Mary Magdalene in John 20:11-18" (D.J. HARRINGTON, *The Gospel of Matthew*, Collegeville, MN, 1991, p. 411) or imagine that Mt 28,9-10.16-20 is Matthew's editing of the lost ending of Mark (R.H. GUNDRY, *Mark. A Commentary on His Apology for the Cross*, Grand Rapids, MI, 1992, pp. 1045-1046), but no new arguments are brought forward. The same can be said of R. Kühschelm's short paper at this Conference. It is not the formulation of ten questions (which are not unanswerable!) which allows to conclude that "die Annahme einer alten Tradition ... *gewichtige Gründe* auf ihrer Seite hat" (p. 563; italics mine). Cf. *Angelophanie - Christophanie in den synoptischen Grabesgeschichten. Mk 16,1-8par unter Berücksichtigung von Joh 20,11-18*, in this volume, pp. 556-565. Kühschelm recognizes in Mt 28,9-10 "viel Matthäisches in Sprache und Konzeption", "redaktionelle Gestaltung", "redaktionelle Formung" (*ibid.*). See also GUNDRY, *Matthew*, 1982, p. 591. On the Mt/Lk agreement ἀπαγγέλλειν (*Mark*, p. 1045), cf. *Evangelica*, pp. 261-263.

traditional basis, and if John can best be understood against that background, John must have known Matthew's Gospel, and other putative sources become superfluous. John has carried forward what was already occurring in Matthew, the displacement of the angelophany (John 20:11-13) by the appearance of Jesus himself. ... Essential elements of Matthew's brief narrative recur in that of John, albeit mostly in different forms. It is, of course, scarcely possible that Matthew redacted and compressed John; on the other hand, that John created his dramatic narrative and gave to Mary Magdalene the central role is easily imaginable.

It is now widely accepted, even by J.B. Green, that "no reason exists to postulate a second, non-Markan, written narrative source for Matthew's passion narrative"[39]. But Green directly adds that the source-|critical problem is more complex with regard to the Lukan passion story. In 1968, when I had to deliver a presidential address for the Colloquium on the Gospel of Luke, I chose to treat the question of Luke's use of Mark, in the form of a critical evaluation of T. Schramm's dissertation on this topic (1966). I was confronted there with the theory that "die Sonderquelle in Lk 22,14ff die Grundlage des Berichtes bildet und Primärquelle ist..."[40]. I replied to this thesis with an examination of the transpositions in Luke[41]:

> C'est sur l'argument des transpositions que beaucoup d'auteurs se décident pour une source non-marcienne en Lc 22–24. ... Il me semble plutôt que l'évangile de Marc n'est pas abandonné en Lc 22,14 (ou 15), mais qu'il continue de guider l'évangéliste jusqu'en 24,12. Je le sais, je ne puis me contenter d'exprimer cette opinion: elle est contestée et doit donc devenir un programme d'études ultérieures[42].

39. J.B. GREEN, *The Death of Jesus. Tradition and Interpretation in the Passion Narrative* (WUNT, 2/33), Tübingen, 1988 (Diss. Aberdeen, 1985, under I.H. Marshall), p. 23 (at the conclusion of his brief treatment of Matthew, pp. 20-23). Cf. below, n. 43.

40. T. SCHRAMM, *Der Markus-Stoff bei Lukas. Eine literarkritische und redaktionsgeschichtliche Untersuchung* (SNTS MS, 14), Cambridge, 1971 (diss. Hamburg, 1966), pp. 50-51, esp. 51 (diss. p. 37).

41. *La matière marcienne dans l'évangile de Luc*, in F. NEIRYNCK (ed.), *L'Évangile de Luc. Problèmes littéraires et théologiques. Mémorial L. Cerfaux* (BETL, 32), Gembloux, 1973, pp. 157-201, esp. 195-199 (= *Evangelica*, pp. 37-81, esp. 75-79); reprinted in ID. (ed.), *L'Évangile de Luc - The Gospel of Luke*, Leuven, ²1989, pp. 67-111, esp. 105-109. See also *The Argument from Order and St. Luke's Transpositions*, in *ETL* 49 (1973) 784-815, esp. pp. 804-814: "The Transpositions in Luke"; = *Evangelica*, pp. 737-768, esp. 757-767, on Lk 6,17-19 and 8,19-21 (on the passion narrative: pp. 759-761).

Cf. J.A. FITZMYER, *The Gospel according to Luke*, vol. I (AB, 28), Garden City, NY, 1981, p. 71 (with reference to my analysis of the transpositions): "I am basically in agreement with his approach both to the transpositions and the Lucan passion narrative". Contrast J.B. GREEN, *The Death of Jesus* (n. 39), pp. 29-30: "Neirynck's essay has not dealt the death-blow to the 'argument from transposition' that he (and Fitzmyer) might have us think" (p. 30).

42. *La matière marcienne*, p. 199 (*Evangelica*, p. 79; ²1989, p. 109). "Zu derselben Meinung sind wir für Lk 23,26-49 aufgrund der literarkritischen Untersuchungen gelangt": F.G. UNTERGASSMAIR, *Kreuzweg und Kreuzigung. Ein Beitrag zur lukanischen*

J.B. Green's book on *The Death of Jesus*[43] and now also the Seminar at this Colloquium conducted by F. Bovon[44] call to mind that this question is still controversial. In the 1960s, when Schramm wrote his dissertation, he could rely on the works of Taylor, Schürmann, Jeremias and Rehkopf[45], but it is not in that direction that the study of Luke's passion narrative has developed in the last 25 years. It may be instructive to study the evolution in the position of a Lukan scholar like G. Schneider[46], or to compare the Anchor Bible commentary of J.A. Fitzmyer (1985) with the commentary on John in the same series by R.E. Brown (1970)[47]. The latest commentary on Luke has only one sentence on this

---

Redaktionsgeschichte und zur Frage nach der lukanischen "Kreuzestheologie" (Paderborner Theologische Studien, 10), Paderborn, 1980, p. 112. Cf. p. 154: "Die innerlukanische Verankerung des nicht-markinischen Passionsstoffes macht es schwer, wenn nicht unmöglich, für die Lk-Passion eine von Mk unabhängige und dem Endverfasser des Lk vorgegebene schriftliche Passions-Sonderquelle zu vermuten. [n. 172:] Auch gegen T. Schramm".

43. Cf. n. 39 above. At the end of his analysis of Lk 22–23, par. Mk (pp. 24-104), he concludes that "we can reasonably propose that Luke knew a second, unified narrative" (p. 104; with a reference to "the programmatic statement by Schramm", n. 365). In Appendix (pp. 324-330) the following verses are marked as Lukan redaction of *Sonderquelle* probable (bold), possible (normal print), conflated with Mk (italic): Lk 22,**3a**.b.14-15a.**15b**.16-18.**19-20**.*21-23*.**24-27**.**28-30**.**31-33**.**35-38**.*39-42*.**43-44**.*45*.**48**.**50c**.**51**.52b.**53b**.*54b-62*.**63-64**.66.**67-68**.69.**70-71**; 23,2.**4-5**.**6-12**.**13-16**.*18-23*.24-25.26c.**27-31**.**34ab**.35.37.**39-43**.**46b**.48.

44. F. BOVON, *Le récit lucanien de la passion de Jésus (Lc 22–23)*, in this volume, pp. 393-423, esp. 406-421: Markan sections (Lk 22,1-14; 22,47–23,5; 23,44–24,11) alternate with sections from the Lukan source: Lk 22,15-46 and 23,6-43.

45. *Der Markus-Stoff*, p. 50, n. 2; in the text: "Durch umfangreiche, gründliche Arbeiten ist, so scheint es, mit ziemlicher Sicherheit erwiesen..." (sic). In the published text of *La matière marcienne* (²1989, pp. 105, 304) I could include two posthumous publications: V. TAYLOR, *The Passion Narrative in Luke*, 1972, and J. JEREMIAS, *Die Sprache des Lukasevangeliums*, 1980.

46. G. SCHNEIDER, *Verleugnung, Verspottung und Verhör Jesu nach Lukas 22,54-71* (SANT, 22), München, 1969, p. 139: "Als Hauptvorlage von Lk 22,54-71 hat der Evangelist die nicht-mk Quelle benutzt"; p. 143: "eine nicht-mk Langform der P, die Lk neben Mk benutzt hat", "die mit dem Einzug Jesu in Jerusalem beginnt", and "die auch Ostergeschichten enthielt". Compare, *Das Verfahren gegen Jesus in der Sicht des dritten Evangeliums (Lk 22,54–23,25). Redaktionskritik und historische Rückfrage*, in K. KERTELGE (ed.), *Der Prozess gegen Jesus* (QD, 112), Freiburg, 1988, pp. 111-130, esp. 113: "[in *Die Passion Jesu*, 1973] kam ich zu der Auffassung, daß Lukas in seinem Kapitel 23 keine Nicht-Mk-Quelle der Passion benutzte, sondern die Mk-Passion bearbeitete und mit Sonderüberlieferungen auffüllte. Dies gilt entsprechend auch für die Inhaftierungsperikope". See also *Das Evangelium nach Lukas* (ÖTK, 3), Gütersloh-Würzburg, 1977, pp. 28; 435-437; 444: Lk 22,15-18 (ctr. *Verleugnung*, p. 149); 469-470: Lk 22,69 (ctr. *Verleugnung*, pp. 118-120). On Lk 22,67-68, cf. below, n. 54.

47. BROWN, *John* II, p. 790: "we think that a solid defense can be made for the thesis that Luke drew on a truly independent, non-Marcan source". Cf. FITZMYER, *Luke* II, pp. 1365-1368 ("The Lucan Passion Narrative"), p. 1366: "Luke has only modified the passion narrative in 'Mk' by adding separate stories or sayings from 'L' (or in one instance from 'Q'), by redacting 'Mk' and by freely composing some material... This

question: "Attempts to locate a separate written Lukan source for the passion have not proven successful"[48].

Fitzmyer retains nevertheless a long list of L passages in Lk 22–23. I One of the texts he ascribes to L is 22,63-65.66-71, the mistreatment and the interrogation of Jesus by the Jewish authorities[49]. For both episodes I can refer to more recent studies, my own analysis of the Lukan redaction in 22,63-65 (1987)[50] and the essays on the "trial" by W. Radl (1988)[51], F.J. Matera (1989)[52] and A. Dauer (1992)[53]. With regard to the special problem of 22,67-68 (cf. Jn 10,24-26) the point I made in a 1972 book review seems to have found its way: "G. Schneider a sans doute raison de rapprocher 22,67d-68b et 20,1-8. Mais il me semble que ce rapprochement devrait permettre d'expliquer le logion comme une création rédactionnelle de Luc"[54].

seems to me to be the better solution. The heavy use of 'L' material in the passion narrative does not argue immediately for a *connected written source* independent of 'Mk'". See also, e.g., F.J. MATERA, *Passion Narratives and Gospel Theologies*, New York - Mahwah, NJ, 1986, p. 155 (and p. 239, n. 7, with reference to Fitzmyer); M.L. SOARDS, *The Passion according to Luke. The Special Material of Luke 22* (JSNT SS, 14), Sheffield, 1987, pp. 120-123 (and p. 126, on Lk 23); R.J. KARRIS, *The Gospel according to Luke*, in *NJBC*, 1990, p. 714.

48. L.T. JOHNSON, *The Gospel of Luke* (Sacra Pagina, 3), Collegeville, MN, 1991, p. 334. Cf. G.W.E. NICKELSBURG, *Passion Narratives*, in *ABD*, 1992, V, 174-175: "While Luke's narrative may well retain unique traditional material, most of the differences from Mark are understandable as expressions of Luke's literary and theological interests, and an independent passion narrative seems an unnecessary hypothesis".

49. *Luke* I, p. 84, with question mark; but see II, p. 1458: "almost certainly". Compare M.L. SOARDS, *The Passion* (n. 47), p. 103: "Verse 64d comes from oral tradition" (cf. Mt); p. 105: "Luke knew an independent oral tradition that lies behind 64a-e" (cf. Jn 10,24-26).

50. ΤΙΣ ΕΣΤΙΝ (n. 32), esp. pp. 14-28 (= *Evangelica II*, pp. 104-118, with additional note, p. 138, on M.L. Soards and J.B. Green).

51. *Sonderüberlieferungen bei Lukas? Traditionsgeschichtliche Fragen zu Lk 22,67f; 23,2 und 23,6-12*, in *Der Prozess gegen Jesus* (n. 46), pp. 131-147, esp. 140-147 (reply to G. Schneider 1969, D.R. Catchpole 1971, A. Strobel 1980).

52. *Luke 22,66-71: Jesus before the* ΠΡΕΣΒΥΤΕΡΙΟΝ?, in *ETL* 65 (1989) 43-59; reprinted in F. NEIRYNCK (ed.), *L'Évangile de Luc – The Gospel of Luke* (n. 41), pp. 517-533: "Luke's version ... does not preserve an independent tradition" (p. 532).

53. *Spuren der (synoptischen) Synedriumsverhandlung im 4. Evangelium. Das Verhältnis zu den Synoptikern*, in A. DENAUX (ed.), *John and the Synoptics* (n. 1), pp. 307-339, esp. 320-336 ("Lk 22,54a.66-71"): "dürfte im wesentlichen auf Mk zurückgehen, die Änderungen gegenüber Mk sind wohl durchweg redaktionell" (p. 336).

54. *ETL* 48 (1972) 570-573 (review of G. Schneider, *Verleugnung*), esp. p. 572. Cf. R. PESCH, *Das Markusevangelium* II, 1977, p. 408; RADL (n. 51), pp. 146-147; MATERA (n. 52), p. 152 (= 526); DAUER (n. 53), pp. 332-333. The remarkable similarity between Jn 10,24-26 and Lk 22,67-68 can be explained by Johannine dependence on Luke's redactional text, indirectly through a pre-Johannine source (Dauer) or, more likely, by John's use of Luke. See, e.g., M. SABBE, *John 10 and Its Relationship to the Synoptic Gospels*, in J. BEUTLER - R.T. FORTNA (eds.), *The Shepherd Discourse of John 10 and Its Context* (SNTS MS, 67), Cambridge, 1991, pp. 75-93, esp. 75-85 ("A Trial of Jesus by

Fitzmyer's other instances of L passages in Lk 22 are vv. 15-18.19c-20.27.31-32.33.35-38[55] (all in the S^{Lk} block delineated by Bovon: 22,15-46)[56]. M.L. Soards, more attentive to Lukan redaction and I composition, has reduced this list to Lk 22,19-20, a tradition similar to that found in 1 Cor 11,23-25, and an independent saying of Jesus incorporated in 22,36[57]. In Lk 23 the following passages are ascribed to L: vv. 6-12.13-16.27-32.35a.36-37.39b-43[58]. The reader of Fitzmyer's notes on tradition history in Lk 23 (with bibliographical references up to 1982) may get the impression that this chapter of the commentary needs updating. With regard to 23,27-31, and the entire section 23,26-49, F.G. Untergassmair's careful analysis (1980) should be considered[59]. G. Schneider

the Jews: John 10,22-39"); = M. SABBE, *Studia Neotestamentica. Collected Essays* (BETL, 98), Leuven, 1991, pp. 443-466, esp. 443-455: "the hypothesis of a direct dependence ... is also valid for this pericope" (p. 455).

55. Fitzmyer's list (I, p. 84), corrected in accordance with the commentary in vol. II (pp. 1386, 1412, 1421, 1429).

56. And, of course, ascribed to the *Sonderquelle* by Green (n. 43 above). For Lk 22,43-44 (pp. 56-57: Sonderquelle probable), the textual authenticity is rejected by Fitzmyer (II, pp. 1443-1444). On Lukan authorship, cf. G. SCHNEIDER, *Engel und Blutschweiz (Lk 22,43-44)*, in *BZ* 20 (1976) 112-116 (ctr. *Verleugnung*, p. 159: Sonderquelle). See now also R.E. BROWN, *The Lukan Authorship of Luke 22:43-44*, in *SBL Seminar Papers 1992*, pp. 154-164. Brown convincingly argues for the authenticity. His thesis on the existence of a pre-Gospel tradition "associating an angelic response with the prayer that Jesus made to the Father concerning the hour/cup" (p. 160, cf. 155) is more questionable. Mt 26,53: "the immediate source of the phrase can best be sought within Matthew's own gospel" (Senior). Jn 12,(28-)29: possibly a recollection of Lk 22,43 (Barrett, Boismard). Justin, *Dial.* 103,8: "Justin reprend l'expression bien caractéristique de *Lc.*: ἱδρὼς ὡσεὶ θρόμβοι» (Massaux). *Historia passionis Domini*: "Sequitur Luc. 22. Apparuit autem ei angelus de celo confortans eum. Qualiter autem angelus Christum in agonia sue oracionis confortaverit dicitur in Evangelio Nazareorum". This is hardly a witness for a pre-Lukan tradition. If it has any value, it seems to refer to an apocryphal expansion of Lk 22,43 in which words of the angel were quoted.

57. *The Passion* (n. 47), p. 54.

58. *Luke* I, p. 84; II, pp. 1479, 1483, 1494, 1500, 1507 (all in Bovon's second S^{Lk} block). For Fitzmyer the only L elements in Lk 23,44–24,11 (cf. Bovon: Markan block) are 23,53c (pp. 1523, 1525: cf. Jn 19,41), 56a (pp. 1523, 1526), 56b (p. 1541). Contrast GREEN, *The Death of Jesus*, pp. 101-102 (Lk 23,50-56a is "best explained as a redaction of his Markan source"). On 23,56a.b, cf. *Evangelica*, pp. 299-301. In Fitzmyer's list (I, p. 84), delete 23,46.47b-49 (p. 1513).

59. *Kreuzweg und Kreuzigung* (n. 42). See now also his essay, *Der Spruch vom "grünen und dürren Holz" (Lk 23,31)*, in *SNTU* 16 (1991) 55-87. Cf. J.H. NEYREY, *Jesus' Address to the Women of Jerusalem (Lk. 23.27-31) - A Prophetic Judgment Oracle*, in *NTS* 29 (1983) 74-86; reprinted in his *The Passion according to Luke. A Redaction Study of Luke Soteriology*, New York - Mahwah, NJ, 1985, pp. 108-121 (p. 121: "... the creation of Luke himself and does not come from the pre-Luke source"; 1983, p. 84: "does not come from a pre-Lucan passage, tradition or source"); C.H. GIBLIN, *The Destruction of Jerusalem according to Luke's Gospel: A Historical-Typological Moral* (AnBib, 107), Rome, 1985, pp. 93-104 (with reference to Neyrey). In the new interpretation of 23,31 suggested by Untergassmair (1991) "the green wood" refers to the judgment of Jerusalem and "the dry wood" to the *Endgericht*.

can no longer be cited among those who ascribe to L the episode of the appearance of Jesus before Herod (23,6-12)[60]. Personally I would agree with the position that "all the differences between Luke and Mark in 23,1-25 should be attributed to Luke's redactional | activity"[61]. Fitzmyer draws attention to the striking resemblance between Lk 23,4b and Jn 18,38c and suggests that "Luke may well have derived from 'L' the tradition of Pilate's triple declaration of Jesus' innocence" (Lk 23,4.14-15.22; cf. Jn 18,38; 19,4.6)[62]. In his commentary the possibility of Lukan redaction and Johannine dependence on Luke is not really taken into consideration[63]. The most famous contacts with John are found in the resurrection narratives: Lk 24,12 (cf. Jn 20,3-10)[64] and Lk 24,36b.40 (cf. Jn 20,19-20)[65]. The common tradition hypothesis may seem to provide here a ready answer to the radical thesis of post-Lukan interpolation. Closer

60. Cf. G. SCHNEIDER, *Das Verfahren* (n. 46), pp. 126-128; and, in the same volume, W. RADL, *Sonderüberlieferungen* (n. 51), pp. 134-140: "Jesus vor Herodes (23,6-12)". Cf. K. MÜLLER, *Jesus vor Herodes. Eine redaktionsgeschichtliche Untersuchung zu Lk 23,6-12*, in G. DAUTZENBERG, et al. (eds.), *Zur Geschichte des Urchristentums* (QD, 87), Freiburg, 1979, pp. 111-141, p. 141: "ohne Abstriche eine Komposition des Lukas" (not mentioned by Fitzmyer); M.L. SOARDS, *Tradition, Composition, and Theology in Luke's Account of Jesus before Herodes Antipas*, in *Bib* 66 (1985) 344-364 (p. 358: a Lukan composition, but a tradition seems to underlie vv. 9a, 12b, and perhaps 7b and 11c); F.J. MATERA, *Luke 23,1-25* (n. 61 below), pp. 541-546.
   Fitzmyer rightly observes that 23,13-16 is "a logical sequence to vv. 6-12 and difficult to separate from them" (p. 1484). Cf. SCHNEIDER, *Lukas*, p. 476: "Es dürfte insgesamt eine lukanische Bildung sein, nicht zuletzt auch deswegen, weil es zur Barabbasszene (23,18-25) überleitet".
61. F.J. MATERA, *Luke 23,1-25: Jesus before Pilate, Herod, and Israel*, in F. NEIRYNCK (ed.), *L'Évangile de Luc - The Gospel of Luke* (n. 41), pp. 535-551, esp. p. 535. By the same author: *Luke 22,66-71* (n. 52); *Passion Narratives* (n. 47); *The Death of Jesus according to Luke. A Question of Sources*, in *CBQ* 47 (1985) 469-485.
62. *Luke* II, pp. 1471-1472, 1488 (cf. I, p. 88).
63. See my *John and the Synoptics: 1975-1990* (n. 1), pp. 35-46: "John and Luke", where I noted this lacuna in Fitzmyer's commentary (p. 38). On Lk 23,4.14.22, cf. A. DAUER, *Die Passionsgeschichte im Johannesevangelium* (SANT, 30), München, 1972, pp. 156, 158, 160 (Lukan redaction); M. SABBE, *The Trial of Jesus before Pilate in John and Its Relation to the Synoptic Gospels*, in A. DENAUX (ed.), *John and the Synoptics* (n. 1), pp. 341-385, esp. 356 (and n. 28); = *Studia Neotestamentica* (n. 54), pp. 467-513, esp. 483.
64. See my contributions on Lk 24,12 in *Evangelica*, pp. 297-455, esp. 329-334 (*ETL* 1972), 390-396 (*BETL* 45); *Evangelica II*, pp. 588-596 (*NTS* 1984); *John and the Synoptics: 1975-1990*, pp. 42-44. For exposition and evaluation of this approach, cf. H. THYEN, *Johannes und die Synoptiker. Auf der Suche nach einem neuen Paradigma zur Beschreibung ihrer Beziehungen anhand von Beobachtungen an Passions- und Ostererzählungen*, in A. DENAUX (ed.), *John and the Synoptics* (n. 1), pp. 81-107, esp. 105-106.
65. On Lk 24,36b.40, cf. *Jean et les Synoptiques* (BETL, 49), 1979, pp. 126-136; *Evangelica II*, pp. 205-226 (*Luc 24,36-43: Un récit lucanien*, in FS J. Dupont, 1985); *John and the Synoptics: 1975-1990*, pp. 41-42, 44-45.

examination, however, led me to conclude that in these cases a more creative Lukan intervention is involved[66].

Some more general trends in the study of the gospels may seem to influence exegetical positions regarding the Sondergut in Luke: Lukan redaction or pre-Lukan tradition. The re-evaluation of the apocryphal gospels is now on the program in some schools, and the Gospel of Peter, for instance, is supposed to preserve a pre-canonical passion and resurrection narrative. Thus, for J.D. Crossan, the mourning in Lk I 23,48, unique to Luke, is "Luke's acceptance of *Gospel of Peter* 7:25 and 8:28"; the story of the two criminals in Lk 23,39-43 is Luke's redactional creation, "but based on elements of the *Cross Gospel*" (GP 4:10.13-14); the "process" before Herod in Lk 23,6-12 is "an attempt to integrate the tradition about Antipas from the *Cross Gospel*" (in GP 1:1-2; 2:5b Herod is in charge of the proceedings)[67]. In each case I agree that there is a certain relationship but I would argue for the inverted direction of influence[68]. M.L. Soards suggests that Lk 23,26-32 is a Lukan composition (vv. 28.32, cf. Mk 15,21.27), but the comparison with the Gospel of Thomas brings him to conclude that Luke (11,27-28; 23,29) and Thomas (logion 79) independently preserve the same tradition[69]. However, the original unity of Lk 11,27-28 and 23,29 (already

---

66. For criticism, cf. W.L. CRAIG, *The Disciples' Inspection of the Empty Tomb (Lk 24,12.24; Jn 20,2-10)*, in A. DENAUX (ed.), *John and the Synoptics* (n. 1), pp. 614-619; A. DAUER, *Lk 24,12 – Ein Produkt lukanischer Redaktion?*, in *The Four Gospels 1992*, pp. 1697-1716. Dauer formulates nine critical observations. Since Dauer himself holds the now exceptional thesis of textual inauthenticity (see my *John and the Synoptics: 1975-1990*, pp. 42-44), one should perhaps not give too much weight to his last difficulty: "widerspricht der Ansicht der meisten Exegeten" (p. 1712). There is no space here for a detailed rejoinder. I just mention his "grundsätzliches Bedenken" against editorial composition of Lk 24,12 (after 24,1-9): Luke's *Dublettenscheu* (pp. 1707-1708: with reference to the omission of Mk 8,1-9 and 14,3-9; see also p. 1709). It would be more to the point to refer to the key passage for my interpretation: Lk 22,22-24, with a different kind of "doublet" in vv. 22-23 (cf. 24,1-9) and v. 24 (cf. 24,12).

67. J.D. CROSSAN, *The Cross that Spoke. The Origins of the Passion Narrative*, San Francisco, 1988, pp. 260, 169-174, 43-45. Crossan's view is, of course, quite different from the classic hypothesis of a pre-Lukan passion source (cf. Bovon): Lk 23,6-12 is "a pure Lukan creation"; the comment on the friendship of Herod and Pilate in v. 12 is the only possibly pre-Lukan element in the entire incident (p. 44; cf. p. 64).

68. With regard to the episode of the two thieves ("a magnificent tableau" in Lk), Crossan cannot accept that the influence goes from Lk to the Gospel of Peter: "I can see no reason for such textual dismemberment" (p. 173). Note, however, that the same Crossan can accept that "Mark had deliberately dismembered the story of the resurrected youth in the *Secret Gospel* and scattered its literary debris throughout his own Gospel" (p. 283). See my *The Apocryphal Gospels and the Gospel of Mark* (1989), in *Evangelica II*, pp. 715-767 (with additional note, pp. 768-772).

69. M.L. SOARDS, *Tradition, Composition, and Theology in Jesus' Speech to the "Daughters of Jerusalem" (Luke 23,26-32)*, in *Bib* 68 (1987) 221-244, esp. pp. 232-237.

suggested by R. McL. Wilson in 1960[70]) is much less likely than a secondary combination in Th 79[71]. In his study of the Lukan redaction in 23,27-31 Soards apparently neglects the link of v. 29 with Lk 21,23a (Mk 13,17)[72].

| In the opposite sense, the new literary-critical approaches emphasize the literary unity of Luke-Acts and this appears to be beneficial for the redactional interpretation of Luke's special material[73].

IV. THE SAYINGS SOURCE Q

In an assessment of the studies on Q at the 1981 Colloquium[74] I could note to my satisfaction:

> Although there is some hesitation about one or another isolated saying, a rather general tendency can be observed to include [in the reconstruction of Q] only passages attested by both Matthew and Luke and to include all of them[75].

70. *Studies in the Gospel of Thomas*, London, 1960, p. 81. In *Ancient Christian Gospels* (London - Philadelphia, PA, 1990) H. Koester compares Th 79a with Lk 11,27-28 (which he ascribes to Q: pp. 88, 141, 144) and Th 79b with Mk 13,17 (p. 108). Although he notices the contrast with Mk 13,17 (n. 2: "formulated as a woe over those who are pregnant and nursing. Thomas, however, is formulated as a beatitude for those who have not conceived and the breasts which have not given milk"), there is no mention of the much closer parallel in Lk 23,29.

71. Compare the reply to Wilson by H.E.W. TURNER, in ID. – H. MONTEFIORE, *Thomas and the Evangelists* (SBT, 35), London, 1962, pp. 35, 38, 96; H. SCHÜRMANN, *Das Thomasevangelium und das lukanische Sondergut*, in *BZ* 7 (1963) 236-260; = *Traditionsgeschichtliche Untersuchungen zu den synoptischen Evangelien*, Düsseldorf, 1968, pp. 228-247; and independently, W. SCHRAGE, *Das Verhältnis des Thomas-Evangeliums zur synoptischen Tradition und zu den koptischen Evangelienübersetzungen* (BZNW, 29), Berlin, 1964, pp. 164-168. Cf. G. SCHNEIDER, *Lukas*, p. 268; J.A. FITZMYER, *Luke*, p. 1494; and now also M. FIEGER, *Das Thomasevangelium. Einleitung, Kommentar und Systematik* (NeutAbh, NF 22), Münster, 1991, pp. 218-219.

72. On another "tradition" related to Lukan Sondergut (24,39), see my *Luc 24,36-43: un récit lucanien* (1985), in *Evangelica II*, esp. pp. 219-223 ("Le témoignage d'Ignace d'Antioche").

73. Cf. D. SENIOR, *The Passion of Jesus in the Gospel of Luke* (The Passion Series, 3), Wilmington, DE, 1989, p. 8 (see the references to recent studies, nn. 2-5). Cf. p. 10: "my own opinion is that the special character of Luke's Passion narrative is due to his creative reinterpretation of Mark's account".

74. *Recent Developments in the Study of Q*, in J. DELOBEL (ed.), *Logia. Les paroles de Jésus - The Sayings of Jesus* (BETL, 59), Leuven, 1982, pp. 29-75; = *Evangelica II*, pp. 409-455 (Supplement, pp. 456-464), esp. pp. 415-421 ("The Reconstruction of Q").

75. *Ibid.*, p. 417. The text continues: "The possibility that a *Sondergut* passage may stem from Q is not denied but it is seen as too uncertain to be reckoned with". See the Table on p. 416. – For a more precise and slightly corrected description (12,54-56 is included), cf. my *Q-Synopsis. The Double Tradition Passages in Greek* (SNTA, 13),

If I had to rewrite my survey in 1992, I would mention that some scholars now tend to include again minor agreements (from the triple tradition)[76] and Sondergut passages[77]. On the other hand, M. Sato (in I the line of his adviser, U. Luz) and D. Kosch reckon with the possibility of an intermediate stage of pre-Matthean and pre-Lukan recensions of Q^{78},

Leuven, 1988: bold face type is used for words and parts of words that are identical in Mt and Lk; special signs indicate omissions (□), inversions (/), synonyms and substitutes (*).

76. See my *The Minor Agreements and Q*, in R.A. PIPER (ed.), *The Gospel*, below, pp. [245-266]. Conclusion: "Q 3,2-4; 3,21-22; 6,12-16; 10,25-28; 12,1b; 17,2; 17,31 are proposed in some recent studies as candidates for inclusion in the double-tradition source Q. In none of them, however, the Matthew-Luke agreements against Mark seem to provide conclusive evidence". See especially Section II, on "The Beginning of Q", with reference to D. Catchpole (n. 93 below), J. Lambrecht (n. 91 below), and J.S. KLOPPENBORG, *City and Wasteland: Narrative World and the Beginning of the Sayings Gospel (Q)*, in *Semeia* 52 (1991) 145-160. On Ναζαρά (Mt 4,13 / Lk 4,16) in the Q source, see now J.M. ROBINSON, *The Sayings Gospel Q*, in *The Four Gospels 1992*, pp. 361-388, esp. 373-380; and my *NAZAPA*, below, pp. [451-461].
  The misuse of the minor agreements by scholars who change the nature of Q by including narratives such as the feeding story (E. Bammel; cf. E.E. Ellis: "a dozen triple-tradition episodes") is not considered here. On the minor agreements as argument against the Q hypothesis (M.D. Goulder), cf. *Evangelica II*, pp. 413-414 (and 463).
  77. Cf. J.S. KLOPPENBORG, *Q Parallels. Synopsis, Critical Notes & Concordance*, Sonoma, CA, 1988. In this handbook for the study of Q (cf. *Evangelica II*, pp. 465-473), the generally accepted extent of Q is printed as unbracketed text, and a number of Sondergut passages appear in parentheses as "probable" extent of Q: Mt 5,41; 7,2a; 11,23b-24; Lk 6,24-26; 6,34-35b; 6,37c-38b; 7,3-5; 7,20; 9,61-62*; 11,21-22*; 11,27-28; 11,36; 12,13-14.16-21*; 12,49*; 13,25(*); 15,8-10; 17,28-29*. The name H. Schürmann (cf. *Evangelica II*, pp. 418-419) occurs without fail in the critical notes. Only in a few instances, marked here with an asterisk, Kloppenborg refers to his own *The Formation of Q*, Philadelphia, PA, 1987. See his comment on Lk 9,61-62: "Of all the Lukan *Sondergut* this has the strongest probability of deriving from Q" (p. 64), but on the other hand Lk 13,25 is "not in Q" (p. 154). Contrast my *Q-Synopsis*, pp. 11 (9,61-62 in small print) and 49 (13,25, cf. Mt 25,10-12). Cf. below, n. 88.
  Other Sondergut passages (cf. Schürmann) are printed in square brackets as "Q origin unlikely", e.g. Mt 10,5b-6.23 (Sato 1984: possibly in Q); Lk 11,5-8 (D.R. Catchpole 1983); Lk 12,35-38 (C.-P. März 1985). On 12,35-38, see now C.-P. MÄRZ, *Zur Vorgeschichte von Lk 12,35-48. Beobachtungen zur Komposition der Logientradition in der Redequelle*, in K. KERTELGE – T. HOLTZ – C.P. MÄRZ (eds.), *Christus bezeugen. FS W. Trilling* (Erfurter Theologische Studien, 59), Leipzig, 1989, pp. 166-178; = C.P. MÄRZ, *"... laßt eure Lampen brennen!" Studien zur Q-Vorlage von Lk 12,35–14,24* (Erfurter Theologische Schriften, 20), Leipzig, 1991, pp. 58-71. See also ID., *Das Gleichnis vom Dieb. Überlegungen zur Verbindung von Lk 12,39 par Mt 24,43 und 1 Thess 5,2-4*, in *The Four Gospels 1992*, pp. 633-648, esp. 639-644; and in this volume, pp. 177-208.
  78. See my *Q^{Mt} and Q^{Lk} and the Reconstruction of Q*, in *ETL* 66 (1990) 385-390; = *Evangelica II*, pp. 475-480. Cf. M. SATO, *Q und Prophetie. Studien zur Gattungs- und Theologiegeschichte der Quelle Q* (WUNT, 2/29), Tübingen, 1988 (diss. Bern, 1984); D. KOSCH, *Die eschatologische Tora des Menschensohnes. Untersuchungen zur Rezeption der Stellung Jesu zur Tora in Q* (NTOA, 12), Freiburg/Schw-Göttingen, 1989 (diss. Freiburg/Schw, 1988).

in parallel to the Deutero-Markan intermediate between Mark and the Gospels of Matthew and Luke[79]. Sato's Q^{Mt} includes the following Sondergut: Mt 5,5.7-9^K; 6,34; (7,2a); 7,6; 10,5b-6(Q?); 10,23(Q?); 11,28-30; (23,15-19); (23,24); 25,1-12[80]; Q^{Lk} includes Lk 3,10-14^K; (4,16-30); 6,24-26^K; 6,37b-38b^K; 7,3-6a^K; 7,29-30 (not in Q); 9,61-62^K; 10,18-19; 11,5-8^K; 11,36; 12,16-21^K; 12,32; 12,35-38; 12,47-48; (12,54-56: not in Q); (13,1-5); (13,6-9); 17,28-29; (18,2-8)[81]. In addition to the passages marked with K, Kosch ascribes to Q^{Lk} the parable of the rich man and the poor Lazarus (16,19-31)[82]. He disagrees with Sato regarding the scattered | double-tradition sayings in Lk 14,26–17,6[83], and the reconstruction of Q he proposes contains all double-tradition passages, in the Lukan order[84], with a number of uncertain texts in parentheses[85].

79. Cf. D. Kosch, *Q: Rekonstruktion und Interpretation. Eine methodenkritische Hinführung mit einem Exkurs zur Q-Vorlage des Lk*, in *FZPT* 36 (1989) 409-425: see the diagram on p. 414 (and n. 18). Compare also U. Luz, *Das Evangelium nach Matthäus*. I. *Mt 1–7*; II. *Mt 8–17* (EKK, I/1-2), Zürich - Neukirchen-Vluyn, 1985, 1990; vol. I, p. 29 (with reference to Sato): "QMt ist eine nur unwesentlich veränderte und erweiterte Fassung von Q", in contrast to "die vermutlich wesentlich erweiterte Fassung der Logienquelle, die Lukas benutzte"; p. 30: "M. E. benutzten Mt und Lk eine Mk-Rezension, die an manchen Punkten gegenüber unserem Mk sekundär ist" (and vol. II, passim, with reference to A. Ennulat). See my review in *ETL* 63 (1987) 410-413; 67 (1991) 169-171; and *Evangelica II*, pp. 477-480 (and pp. 7-8, on DtMk).

80. *Q* (n. 78), pp. 18-19 (Table), 47-50 (Mt 5,3-12), 51-52 (Q^{Mt}). The parentheses indicate some hesitation: "Unsichere Stellen". See also p. 53: 5,19 and 18,16-17.18 possibly Q^{Mt}.

81. *Q*, pp. 54-59. See also p. 60: 14,28-33; 15,8-10; 17,7-10 possibly Q^{Lk}.

82. *Q: Rekonstruktion* (n. 79), pp. 416-420 ("Zum Profil von Q^{Lk}"), esp. p. 417: the theme of reversal of social conditions. See also pp. 418-419: Q^{Lk} 6,27c-28a; 6,27-28/29-30.31 (inversion); 6,29c.d (inversion).

83. Sato, *Q*, pp. 23-24, 52-53, 59-60: the Q origin is doubtful for Lk 14,26.27.34-35; 15,4-7; 16,16.17.18; 17,1.3-4.6 (and the parables 14,16-24; 19,12-27); possibly Q^{Lk} and Q^{Mt}. Kosch has opted for a "Proto-Lukan" fusion of Q and Sondergut: thus, Q 16,13.16-18; S 16,19-26(31); Q 17,1.3-4.6 was one pre-Lukan block of sayings material (*Q: Rekonstruktion*, pp. 415, 417).

84. See, most recently, Kosch, *Q und Jesus*, in *BZ* 36 (1992) 30-58, esp. pp. 33-34. The only dislocations are Lk 11,16 (at 11,29) and 17,33 (after 14,26-27); cf. *Q Parallels*. On the placement of Lk 16,16 / Mt 11,12-13 and Lk 13,34-35 / Mt 23,37-39, see *Q Parallels*, S18 and S52. On Lk 16,13 / Mt 6,24, cf. Sato, *Q*, p. 24: the location of the saying is uncertain ("ganz unsicher") but the Q context in Mt indicates its Q origin. See R.A. Piper, *Wisdom in the Q-Tradition. The Aphoristic Teaching of Jesus* (SNTS MS, 61), Cambridge, 1988, pp. 86-99: Lk 16,13 is part of a previously existent collection, vv. 9-13, probably known to Matthew (p. 96).

85. They are listed here in a comparative table with Kloppenborg (*Q Parallels*) and Sato (1988, pp. 18-19):

3,2-4	[Kl]	(S)	7,29-30	[Kl]	[S]	14,16-24	Kl	[S]	
3,21-22	[Kl]	(S)	12,1	[Kl]	–	14,34-35	Kl	[S]	
4,16	–	(S)	12,49-50	(Kl)	(S)	19,12-27	Kl	[S]	
6,20a	<Kl>	(S)	12,54-56	Kl	[S]	Not in Q:			
7,1a	<Kl>	–	14,5	[Kl]	[S]	14,11/18,14b	Kl	[S]	

In contrast to the new "literary" approach in gospel studies, with its concentration on the gospel as a whole and the typical "literary-critical" aversion to distinctions between tradition and redaction, source criticism and redaction criticism are flourishing in the study of Q. The International Q Project[86] has done intensive research on the reconstruction of the Q text. Phrase by phrase, word by word, the options for the source or for the evangelists' redaction were inventoried with pro's and contra's. The establishment of a critical text of Q is in progress[87] and will be completed in 1994. Here too we can observe I a certain shift of attention from double-tradition texts towards the periphery of Q in minor agreements and Sondergut[88]. The reconstructions already published of Q

Note: Lk 12,1 and 49-50 have no parallel in Mt. In Kosch's reconstruction Q12,1 includes ἤρξατο λέγειν τοῖς μαθηταῖς αὐτοῦ, cf. Lk v. 1a πρὸς ... (Tora, p. 83). Kloppenborg rightly distinguishes between Lk 12,(49) and [50].

86. The project on "Q: A Lost Collection of Jesus' Sayings" was launched in October 1983 at the Institute for Antiquity and Christianity in Claremont, CA (director: J.M. Robinson), in coordination with the Society of Biblical Literature (Annual Meeting, 1983-1985: Consultation; 1985-1989: Q Seminar); from 1989 on: The International Q Project. Reports of the work sessions (and lists of the participants) are published regularly by J.M. Robinson in JBL: see 109 (1990) 499-501; 110 (1991) 494-498; 111 (1992) 500-508.

On the more issue-oriented work of the Q Seminar, cf. J.S. KLOPPENBORG – L.E. VAAGE (eds.), Early Christianity, Q and Jesus (Semeia, 55), 1992. The Seminar considered a series of topics: orality, textuality and the generation of sayings collections (1983), wisdom materials in Q (1984), Mark and Q (1985), apocalypticism and the Son of man (1986), redactional stratigraphy (1987), the social history of the Q people (1988), early pre-Q collections and their settings (1989). See Preface, p. VII. Continuation in Q Section, J.S. Kloppenborg presiding, 1990-1992.

87. The reconstructions of the Q text are published in the annual reports. See the cumulative list of the decisions 1989-1991 in JBL 111 (1992), p. 508. A few observations can be made regarding the extent of Q. After examination, some verses are excluded from Q; other sayings are accepted as belonging to Q with a probability of only C and included [[ ]]: 3,1-4, v. 2 Ἰωάννη (cf. Mt -ς, Lk -v), v. 3 πᾶσα .. η .. περίχωρο .. τοῦ Ἰορδάνου (excluded: vv. 1 and 4), but see n. 76 above; 4,16 [[Ναζαρά]], cf. above, n. 76; — 11,[[16]] "does belong between Q 11:15 and Q 11:17" (p. 503), but see Evangelica II, p. 489 (conclusion: "c'est bien Luc le responsable de la rédaction de Lc 11,16 et sans doute aussi de la place donnée au verset dans l'ensemble de Lc 11,14-36"). — 11,[[36]]: text cannot be reconstructed. — 14,[[5]]: cf. Evangelica II, pp. 186, 193-203. — 14,[[16-23]]: vv. 18-20 cannot be reconstructed, vv. 15.22.24 are excluded from Q. — 17,2 Q = Lk, but see n. 76 above. — 17,24.37.26-27.30.34-35 (vv. 28-29 excluded from Q).

88. The 1992 Meeting Program includes among the passages submitted for approval: Q 3,21-22; 9,61-62; 11,27-28; and among the texts ready to be discussed: Lk 9,1 and 10,1; Mt 10,5b-6.23 (pp. 36-38). This acceptance of minor agreements of Mt/Lk against Mk (Lk 3,21-22; 9,1; cf. n. 87 above: Lk 3,3) and Sondergut passages shows some development in the Project. The original proposal concentrated on "the minimal text of Q to emphasize the strict divergence of the method of our reconstruction of Q from earlier reconstructions which could be characterized as 'only what you make it'" (L.E. VAAGE, "The Reconstruction of Q", Seminar paper 1986, p. 11). On Lk 9,61-62, cf. L.E. VAAGE, The Son of Man Sayings in Q: Stratigraphical Location and Significance, in Semeia 55 (1992) 103-129, p. 114: "It is, however, hardly certain that 9:61-62 ever belonged to Q,

11,16; 13,18; 17,2 show that in these cases no serious consideration has been given to the influence of Mark on the Lukan redaction[89].

In Section III of my 1981 survey I treated the problem of "Mark and Q"[90]. Now, in the course of the current year, there seems to be a reemergence of the thesis of Mark's use of Q. New contributions by the old protagonists have been announced, by J. Lambrecht on Mk 1,1-15[91] and by W. Schenk on Mk 6,6b-13[92], and more significantly, D.R. Catchpole, well known and appreciated researcher on Q, has adopted this thesis in two essays on the same sections: The Beginning of Q and I The Mission Charge[93]. The Mark/Q overlaps, which in passages such as Q 10,2-12 are used by others as evidence of an earlier pre-Q tradition, are here proposed as Markan redaction of the Q text.

Q 10,2-16 and Mark

In his reconstruction of the Q text behind Lk 10,2-16 Catchpole can attribute to Luke a number of editorial additions[94]. He accepts that Q probably contained the prohibition of greetings on the way, singly attested in Lk 10,4b[95]. He also argues that Q contained, along with other prohibitions, the Gentiles/Samaritans saying (Mt 10,5b)[96], and he

at least not if the total absence of any parallel to it in Matthew is taken as significant" (ctr. J.S. Kloppenborg, M.S. Steinhauser); H.T. FLEDDERMANN, *The Demands of Discipleship. Matt 8,19-22 par. Luke 9,57-62*, in *The Four Gospels 1992*, pp. 540-561, esp. 548-552: "both the theme and the vocabulary of Luke 9,61-62 point to Lucan redaction. Q contained only the first two dialogues (Q 9,57-60)" (p. 552).

89. See the references above, n. 76 (Lk 17,2) and n. 87 (Lk 11,16). On Lk 13,18, cf. T.A. Friedrichsen's essay in *The Four Gospels 1992* (n. 27), pp. 662-675 ("The Double Question: Mk 4,30 / Lk 13,18".

90. *Recent Developments* (n. 74), pp. 41-53; = *Evangelica II*, pp. 421-433. See also Additional Notes (*ibid.*, p. 464), with references to J. Schüling 1987 (= 1991), R.A. Piper 1988, D. Lührmann 1989, H. Koester 1990.

91. J. LAMBRECHT, *John the Baptist and Jesus in Mark 1.1-15: Markan Redaction of Q?*, in *NTS* 38 (1992) 357-384. On his earlier work, see my *Recent Developments*, esp. pp. 43-45 (= 423-425).

92. W. SCHENK, *Mk 6,6b-13(30) und sein Verhältnis zu Q*, Seminar paper, SNTS Meeting 1992 (as yet unpublished). On his essay, *Der Einfluss der Logienquelle auf das Markusevangelium*, in *ZNW* 70 (1979) 141-165, see my *Recent Developments*, pp. 42-43 (= 422-423).

93. D.R. CATCHPOLE, *The Beginning of Q: A Proposal*, in *NTS* 38 (1992) 205-221; *The Mission Charge in Q*, in *Semeia* 55 (1992) 147-174. See also his book, *The Quest for Q*, Edinburgh, 1993, pp. 60-78 and 151-188.

94. *The Mission Charge*, passim, esp. pp. 151, 156, 163, 164-166, 170-171: Lk 10,7d μὴ μεταβαίνετε ἐξ οἰκίας εἰς οἰκίαν, 8a καὶ δέχωνται ὑμᾶς, 8b ἐσθίετε τὰ παρατιθέμενα ὑμῖν, 9b ἐφ᾽ ὑμᾶς, 10a εἰς ἣν δ᾽ ἂν πόλιν εἰσέλθητε, 10b εἰς τὰς πλατείας αὐτῆς, 11b πλὴν τοῦτο γινώσκετε ὅτι ἤγγικεν ἡ βασιλεία τοῦ θεοῦ.

95. *Ibid.*, pp. 151, 168.

96. *Ibid.*, pp. 157-161, esp. 160: "There are very good reasons for thinking that Matt 10:5b could fit into Q and that it would be dropped by Luke". Mt 10,6 (and 15,24) is

assumes that the prohibition of carrying a staff was part of the equipment rule (Q 10,4a)[97]. Catchpole then isolates the original pre-Q tradition consisting of the sheep/wolves saying, the equipment rule, and the instructions on conduct in houses and in towns: Q 10,3.4.5-7.8-12. Internal analysis suggests that one single stratum was later superimposed upon it: Q 10,2.13-15.16 (and Mt 10,5b)[98].

The most problematic verses in this repartition between tradition and redaction are the two conclusions, vv. 12 and 16. The "sending" saying, Q 10,16: "As a saying located at the end of this mission charge it is particularly fitting. It matches the recurrent pattern of positive and negative elements in Q 10:5-7,8-12. It overlaps with the explicit 'sending' saying, Q 10:3, at the start of the pre-Q tradition"[99]. All that is | true, and it seems to suggest that Q 10,16 is well fitting at the conclusion of the pre-Q tradition 10,3-11a. The Sodom saying, Q 10,12: "the latter has often been regarded as a Q-redactional anticipation of the woes on the towns (Q 10:13-15). On this very attractive hypothesis, the pre-editorial tradition ended with the dust-shaking (10:11), while the Sodom saying echoes the Tyre and Sidon saying (10:14) with which it is 'astonishingly parallel'"[100]. But Catchpole concludes his discussion of 10,12 by noting

MtR; cf. 9,36: "very probably dependent upon the same source, namely Mark 6:34" (p. 159).

97. Mt 10,10; cf. Lk 9,3: one of the "LukeR reminiscences of Q even when Mark is the primary source" (p. 151).

98. *Ibid.*, pp. 152-156 (Q 10,2); 162-163 (Q 10,13-15); 166-167 (Q 10,16). On Mt 10,5b, cf. n. 96 above. Schürmann *et al.* who assign Mt 10,5b-6 to Q take vv. 5b and 6 as the two halves of one traditional logion. See, e.g., W.D. DAVIES – D.C. ALLISON, *Matthew*, II, 1991, pp. 164, 169; M. SATO, *Q*, 1988, p. 26 (possibly Q, or Q^Mt); U. LUZ, *Matthäus*, II, 1990, p. 88 (Sondergut or Q^Mt); cf. D.J. HARRINGTON, *Matthew*, 1991, p. 141 (special tradition M). Catchpole's proposal, v. 5b Q and v. 6 MtR, is a reversal and correction of the two stages suggested by M. Trautmann (pp. 159-160). However, Catchpole recognizes that Mt 10,5b-6 exhibits "a nicely balanced symmetry" and he knows "Matthew's fondness for creating antithetical sayings" (*ibid.*). Is it then possible to treat v. 5b "by itself and in its own right"? On "The evangelist's hand" in Mt 10,5b-6, see G.N. STANTON, *A Gospel for a New People* (n. 6 above), pp. 330-391 (cf. 139-140).

99. From *The Mission Charge*, pp. 166-167 (in inverted order).

100. *Ibid.*, p. 163. See my *Recent Developments*, p. 65 (= 445): "Lk 10,12 has a compositional function in Q as the conclusion of 10,2-12 and the linkage with 10,13-15. Λέγω ὑμῖν replaces here, in a redactional adaptation, the introductory πλήν of the traditional saying in 10,14"; p. 54 (= 434), on 10,12 as one of "the few verses which were accepted as redactional by D. Lührmann" (with references to P. Hoffmann 1972; R. Laufen 1980; W. Schenk 1981; A.D. Jacobson 1982). New references can be added: J.S. Kloppenborg 1987 (*Formation*, p. 196); M. Sato 1988 (*Q*, p. 38); U. Luz 1990 (*Matthäus*, II, p. 89). Apart from Catchpole's dissenting opinion one could speak of a growing consensus on the Q-redaction of this one verse – at least among those who adopt the Lukan order in their reconstruction of Q 10,12.13-15.16. Contrast W.D. Davies – D.C. Allison (p. 164: placement of 10,13-15 LkR or Q^Lk); D. Zeller (in *Logia*, p. 404: 10,12 secondary but not Q-redaction).

that "it seems fair to register *some hesitation* about the assessment of Q 10:12 as redactional", and in the general conclusion he repeats his suggestion without hesitation[101]. One can agree with a description of 10,12 as the continuation of vv. 10-11a, but is it therefore "*more* a natural development of what precedes it than an anticipation of what follows it"[102]? And is it fair to discuss the radicalism of the saying without further mention of the "parallel" in 10,14? It is not my intention here to contest the value of Catchpole's observations on the traditional mission charge and the superimposition of a single redactional stratum. I simply suggest to correct the repartition of tradition (10,3.4.5-7.8-11a.**16**)[103] and redaction (10,2.**12**.13-15)[104] in the composition of Q 10,2-16.

With regard to the question of Mark's dependence upon Q (the initial suggestion in Catchpole's essay) I may recall the canon I formulated in 1981[105]:

> How do we prove Mark's dependence on Q, and not on a traditional saying or on some pre-Q collection of sayings? This can only be done by | showing a specific dependence on the redaction of Q, dependence on sayings of which the creation or at least the formulation can be attributed to the Q redactor, or dependence on the order of the sayings as found in a redactional Q arrangement. It is not enough to observe that Mark's version of the saying is secondary.

Thus, the less rigorous Mk 6,8-9 may be secondary vis-à-vis the equipment rule in Q 10,4a[106], but this is not necessarily evidence of Mark's use of the Q document. If, with Catchpole, we accept traditional pre-Q material in Q 10,3-11, there may be some correspondence between its fourfold division and the contents of Mk 6,7-11: sending (7), equipment

---

101. *Ibid*, pp. 164 (my emphasis) and 167.

102. *Ibid*, p. 164 (my emphasis).

103. Cf. A.D. JACOBSON, *The Literary Unity of Q. Lc 10,2-16 and Parallels as a Test Case*, in J. DELOBEL (ed.), *Logia* (n. 74), 1982, pp. 419-423. See also J.S. KLOPPENBORG, *Formation*, pp. 192-197; M. SATO, *Q*, pp. 309-313 (Q 10,3-11a); on 10,16 as *Schlußwort* before the insertion of 10,13-15, see pp. 38, 77.

104. The ἐργάτης saying in v. 7b (cf. v. 2) probably belongs to this same stage of redaction: cf. Catchpole (p. 153), *et al.*; in *Logia*: pp. 404 (D. Zeller) en 421 (A.D. Jacobson).

105. *Recent Developments*, p. 45 (= 425).

106. Note, however, that the inclusion of "no staff" in the text of Q 10,4a (Catchpole, p. 169; cf. F. Bovon, *et al.*) is far from certain. Μηδὲ/μήτε ῥάβδον in Mt 10,10 and Lk 9,3 (for Mk 6,8 εἰ μὴ ῥάβδον μόνον) can be the result of assimilation to the other prohibitions. The text of Lk 10,4a (and 22,35) remains a more secure basis for the reconstruction of Q (Polag, Laufen, *et al.*). – For R.H. Gundry (1982, 1992) and M. Goulder (1989) Lk 9,3 is influenced by Mt 10,10 (Matthean rigorism). More specific reasons for LkR are suggested in the commentaries on Luke by H. Schürmann (p. 501, n. 19; p. 502, n. 24); J.A. Fitzmyer (p. 754), W. Wiefel (p. 170).

(8-9), acceptance (10), rejection (11), but this cannot be used as evidence of Mark's dependence on Q. On the other hand, because Q 10,2.12 are without parallel in Mk 6, one could argue that this Q-redactional frame was unknown to Mark. For Catchpole, Q 10,10-11a is incomplete without v. 12 (judgment theme) and he conjectures that "a sense of this incompleteness underlies the MarkR addition of εἰς μαρτύριον αὐτοῖς»[107]. But Mk 6,11 is scarcely more "complete" than the direct speech in Q 10,11a ending with ὑμῖν = "against you"[108]. The evidence Catchpole adduces against Markan independence of Q finally goes not beyond W. Schenk's 1979 argument[109], particularly the dubious reminiscences of Q 10,13-15 in Mk 6,1-6a[110].

For further discussion of "Mark and Q" I can refer to the contribution by C.M. Tuckett[111]. As a two-source theorist, I am used to | recalling that our first hypothesis is the priority of Mark. The Q source is a second and in fact secondary hypothesis, designed to explain the Matthew-Luke agreements in the double-tradition passages. Personally I am not inclined to exclude from Q dispersed sayings common to Matthew and Luke[112]. On the other hand, I recommend much prudence and reserve with regard

107. *The Mission Charge*, p. 173, n. 29.

108. RSV: "against you"; Fitzmyer: "in protest against you". On the direct speech in 10,11a (compare λέγετε in 10,5 and 9): "Die direkte Rede in V 11 ist ursprünglicher als die bloße Anweisung bei Mk/Mt" (SCHULZ, *Q*, p. 407; cf. MARSHALL, *Luke*, p. 423). – The possibility that 10,11a was followed by 10,16 (cf. above) is not taken into consideration by Catchpole (cf. p. 163: "only a weak climax without v. 12, unless v. 16 be drawn in to provide a final comment on the implications of rejection").

109. Cf. above, n. 92.

110. *The Mission Charge*, pp. 150-151: Mk 6,1 his πατρίς = Capernaum (sic), cf. Q 10,15; Mk 6,2 αἱ δυνάμεις ... γινόμεναι, cf. Q 10,13; Mk 6,3.6 their unbelief and being scandalized, cf. the woes pronounced in Q 10,13-15. Other "Q-reminiscences" noted by Catchpole are: kingdom + repentance in Mk 1,14-15, cf. Q 10,9.13; the Eliah-type call associated with kingdom-centered mission in Mk 1,16-20 and 1,14-15, cf. Q 9,57-60 before 10,2-16; μηδὲ ἀκούσωσιν ὑμῶν in Mk 6,11, cf. Q 10,16.

111. In this volume, pp. 149-175. Less helpful is B.L. MACK, *Q and the Gospel of Mark: Revising Christian Origins*, in *Semeia* 55 (1992) 15-39, esp. pp. 25-30: "Mark and Q: An Intertextual Hypothesis". Mack's distinction between the documentary hypothesis and his intertextual model is confusing. Does it mean that creative borrowing and resignification is excluded in a documentary relation? Mack presupposes that Mark used Q. I quote his view on the selection of Q material: "Since Mark was not al all interested in depicting Jesus as a teacher whose teachings were understood and accepted by those who heard him, he 'deleted' the Q¹ material [6,20-21.27-49; 11,2-4.9-13; 12,13-31.33-34.57-59; 16,13]. From Q² the material deleted is similar [3,7-9; 7,1-10.18-35; 10,12-15.16; 13,23-24; 14,16-24; 15,4-7; 16,17; 17,3-4; 19,12-13.15-26]" (p. 26). "As for the mission instructions, Mark deleted the references to 'laborers in the harvest,' the message about the kingdom of God being near, and the peace greeting resting on the children of peace who receive those sent" (p. 28).

112. See, e.g., my *Luke 14,1-6. Lukan Composition and Q Saying* (1991), in *Evangelica II*, pp. 183-203, esp. 202: Q 14,5 among "those sayings whose position in Q cannot be determined with certainty".

to singly attested sayings[113] and, of course, to minor agreements in the triple tradition. In this last case it is not enough to count the Mt-Lk agreements, and no conclusion can be drawn without having seriously examined the possibility of Matthean and Lukan redaction.

J.S. Kloppenborg's work on *The Formation of Q* (1987)[114] has drawn attention to the genre of Q and the history of its composition. Kloppenborg proposes three stages in the development of Q: a first stratum of sapiential instructions, a secondary expansion with interpolated sayings and chriae collections, and a final stage in the direction of a biography (the temptation story)[115]. For F.G. Downing, Q resembles the bios of a Cynic philosopher[116]. In his dissertation, *Q und Prophetie*, M. Sato suggests an alternative proposal and compares the Q source with the prophetic books. The exclusive, eschatological position of *the* prophet makes it different from the Old Testament books: "Mithin scheint Q letzten Endes eine einmalige Grösse zu sein"[117]. In 1976 I used the | phrase "a genre *sui generis*"[118]. It was resumed by Schürmann in 1981: "eine eigene literarische Gattung"[119] and is now corrected and reformulated: "In ihrer Art ist diese Schrift wohl analogielos"[120]. For Kloppenborg, however, Q in each of its compositional stages can be located within the context of ancient sayings collections. The stratigraphy proposed by

113. Cf. above, n. 98, on Mt 10,5b-6.

114. Cf. above, n. 77: *The Formation of Q. Trajectories in Ancient Wisdom Collections*. Compare the original title of Kloppenborg's dissertation: *The Literary Genre of the Synoptic Sayings Source* (Toronto, 1984, under H.O. Guenther).

115. Cf. B.L. MACK, in *Semeia* 55 (1992), p. 16: "Kloppenborg's demonstration [his identification of three major layers in Q's composition] has become the working hypothesis for the [SBL] Q Seminar". For critical remarks, see C.M. TUCKETT, *On the Stratification of Q. A Response*, in the same volume, pp. 213-222; ID., *The Temptation Story in Q*, in *The Four Gospels 1992*, pp. 479-507.

116. F.G. DOWNING, *Quite Like Q. A Genre for 'Q': The 'Lives' of Cynic Philosophers*, in *Bib* 69 (1988) 196-225. But see C.M. TUCKETT, *A Cynic Q?*, in *Bib* 70 (1989) 349-376.

117. *Q und Prophetie* (cf. above, n. 78), p. 95 (1984, p. 110: "In diesem Sinne..."). See also p. 77: "eine Analogie zum Prophetenbuch", but "Gerade diese *exklusive* Position hat kein Prophetenbuch für sich in Anspruch genommen. Hierdurch scheint die Q-Quelle die Gattung 'Prophetenbuch' zu sprengen"; p. 411: "Die Q-Prophetie ... in der bisherigen Geschichte der Prophetie ... ein Unikum".

118. Art. *Q*, in *IDBSup*, 1976, 715-716, p. 716: "The Q source may represent a primitive Christian genre *sui generis*". See below, n. 121 (D. Zeller).

119. H. SCHÜRMANN, *Das Zeugnis der Redenquelle für die Basileia-Verkündigung Jesu*, in J. DELOBEL (ed.), *Logia*, 1982, pp. 121-200, esp. 121, n. 2; see also p. 131: "eine spezifische, neuartig redigierende Gattung"; = *Gottes Reich – Jesu Geschick*, Freiburg, 1983, pp. 65-152, esp. 65 (n. 1!), 77.

120. ID., *Zur Kompositionsgeschichte der Redenquelle. Beobachtungen an der lukanischen Q-Vorlage*, in C. BUSSMANN – W. RADL (eds.), *Der Treue Gottes trauen*. FS G. Schneider, Freiburg, 1991, pp. 325-342, esp. 328 (in answer to Sato's critique; cf. *Q*, pp. 1-2).

Kloppenborg and in particular the separation of a collection of "wisdom speeches" as the formative element in Q will remain on the agenda of our Q-research in the 1990's[121].

V. THE GOSPEL OF MARK

The reorientation of Markan studies from redaction criticism to "literary criticism" began in the early 1970's with the work of N. Perrin[122]. Perrin was present at our Colloquium on Mark in 1971 when I gave my lecture on "Duality in Mark and the Limits of Source Criticism". After an analysis of the so-called duplicate expressions and the double-step progression I could make the observation that "there is a sort of homogeneity in Mark, from the wording of sentences to the | composition of the gospel. After the study of these data one has a strong impression of the unity of the gospel of Mark"[123]. Through Perrin my work on *Duality* became immediately known in Chicago, and appreciated, as can be seen from this hyperbolic statement by W.H. Kelber: "After Neirynck, all source and decomposition theories have to pass the test of his studies"[124]. The book *Duality in Mark* was published with the subtitle: "Contributions to the Study of the Markan Redaction" and in later writings I continued to use the term "redaction-critical" for this kind of study.

121. With regard to the role that has been given to the Gospel of Thomas in this discussion, I can refer to C.M. TUCKETT, *Q and Thomas: Evidence of a Primitive "Wisdom Gospel"? A Response to H. Koester*, in *ETL* 67 (1991) 346-360. See now also D. ZELLER, *Eine weisheitliche Grundschrift in der Logienquelle?*, in *The Four Gospels 1992*, pp. 389-401. I quote his conclusion on the composition of Q: "Das so entstandene Gemisch ist formgeschichtlich ein Unicum, wie F. Neirynck gesehen hat, und nur schwer mit Schriften der Umwelt zu vergleichen. Man kann sich höchstens auf einen sehr allgemeinen Nenner 'Sammlung von Worten eines bedeutenden Mannes mit Nachwirkung' verständigen, wobei in Q zu den Worten Jesu noch die des Täufers kommen, ein Indiz dafür, daß nicht formale Maßstäbe, sondern inhaltliche bei der Komposition leitend waren. Jesus als Weisheitslehrer – das ist in der Logienquelle nur ein Aspekt. Als ganze betrachtet stellt sie fast noch eindrucksvoller seine eschatologische Rolle heraus. Unter diesen Vorzeichen wollen auch die weisheitlichen Teile gelesen werden".

122. Cf. F. NEIRYNCK – J. VERHEYDEN – F. VAN SEGBROECK – G. VAN OYEN – R. CORSTJENS, *The Gospel of Mark. A Cumulative Bibliography 1950-1990* (BETL, 102), Leuven, 1992 (esp. pp. 387-389: N. Perrin's works in chronological order); G. VAN OYEN, *De studie van het Marcusevangelie in de twintigste eeuw* (SNTA, 18), Leuven / (Verhandelingen Kon. Academie, 147) Brussel, 1993, pp. 272-280.

123. *ETL* 48 (1972), p. 174; in *Duality in Mark* (BETL, 31), Leuven, 1972, ²1988, p. 37. On "The Acceptance of 'Duality in Mark'", see the Supplementary Notes, in *Duality*, ²1988, pp. 217-252.

124. W.H. KELBER (ed.), *The Passion in Mark. Studies on Mark 14–16*, Philadelphia, PA, 1976, p. 42, n. 3. Cf. *ibid.*, p. 15 (J.R. Donahue). See also W.H. KELBER, *The Oral and the Written Gospel*, Philadelphia, PA, 1983, pp. 66-67, with my reaction in *Duality*, ²1988, pp. 226-227.

Redaction criticism of the Gospel of Mark has been surveyed and evaluated in a dissertation by C. Clifton Black (1989)[125]. The title of the book, "The Disciples according to Mark" is somewhat misleading. The theme of "the disciples" serves as a test case for the confrontation of three types of redaction criticism[126]. His real topic is the redaction-critical method. At the end of the book, Black briefly sketches his own "synthetic" model of interpretation, and there he acknowledges "the many virtues of the redaction-critical perspective"[127]. The core of the book is a severe critique of the redaction-critical method applied to Mark. Black heavily stresses the lack of consensus. His main objection is "the inherent circularity of Markan redaction criticism": "the rationale and procedure ... is fundamentally circular", "the circularity of the method (is) embarrassing, (and) vicious"; "redaction criticism does not work when applied to the Second Gospel"[128]. In fact, if redaction is understood as the editing of recognizable sources, there is, in contrast to Matthew and Luke, an inherent difficulty in that we have no access to the sources of Mark. In this sense Black may be right: "when dealing with a Synoptic whose priority is assumed, I see no way of escaping this hermeneutical circle"[129]. But is it necessarily a vicious circle? And is he | not arguing with a too narrow definition of redaction criticism, as others are doing in defense of a "literary" approach[130]?

The sources of Mark remains a hotly debated question. The mirage of the primitive-gospel hypothesis comes back again and again, in the form of an original Matthew, Urmarkus, the gospel Q, an extended passion narrative, or in the more attractive form of pre-Markan collections. With

---

125. C.C. BLACK, *The Disciples according to Mark. Markan Redaction in Current Debate* (JSNT SS, 27), Sheffield, 1989 (Diss. Duke University, 1986, under D.M. Smith). Cf. *The Gospel of Mark* (n. 122), p. 43 (with list of reviews).

126. *Ibid.*, pp. 39-181: R.P. MEYE, *Jesus and the Twelve*, 1968 (the 'conservative' position); E. BEST, *Following Jesus*, 1981 (the 'mediate' position); T.J. WEEDEN, *Mark – Traditions in Conflict*, 1971 (the 'liberal' position).

127. *Ibid.*, pp. 223-248 ("Method in Markan Study"), esp. p. 247: "its emphasis on authors as theological thinkers, its desire to read texts holistically, and its recognition of the importance of interpreting texts in traditio-historical context". See also, with some variation, p. 237, including emphasis on "the Evangelists as creative authors in their own right" and concern for "the literary character of the Gospels".

128. *Ibid.*, pp. 119, 222, 249.

129. *Ibid.*, p. 119.

130. Cf. N.R. PETERSEN, *Literary Criticism for New Testament Critics*, Philadelphia, PA, 1978, pp. 18-19: "redaction critics assume that our texts are composed out of sources", "their method (is based) on the distinction between redaction and tradition"; and thus "redaction criticism cannot answer the questions it has raised without becoming something else, namely literary criticism". Cf. ID., *"Literarkritik", the New Literary Criticism and the Gospel according to Mark*, in *The Four Gospels 1992*, pp. 935-948.

regard to all of them, I tried to exorcise where I could[131]. In my opinion, the form-critical supposition of discrete units remains a more secure starting point in our study of the pre-Markan tradition. P. Dschulnigg has confirmed my conclusion on the unity of style in Mark: "Das ganze Evangelium ist von ihm [dem Verfasser] sprachlich mitgeprägt und zwar bis in die einzelnen Perikopen hinein"[132]. This does not mean that seams, insertions, summaries, and other formal categories of R.H. Stein's methodology[133] become simply useless, but it should definitely prevent us of producing the printout of pre-Markan traditions. Nor should we deny the possibility that some pericopae may be Mark's own composition. And without making Mark dependent on the Q document, we can learn from the parallels in Q how sayings material has developed in the Markan redaction[134].

For a more general review and evaluation of recent literary | approaches to the Gospel of Mark, I can now refer to the critical surveys by C. Breytenbach[135] and W.R. Telford[136] and several other papers presented at the Colloquium[137] and in *The Four Gospels 1992*[138].

131. Bibliographical references in *The Gospel of Mark* (n. 122), pp. 360-366. See also W.R. TELFORD, *The Pre-Markan Tradition* (n. 136 below), passim.

132. P. DSCHULNIGG, *Sprache, Redaktion und Intention des Markus-Evangeliums* (SBB, 11), Stuttgart, 1984, ²1986, p. 269; cf. p. 297.

133. *Duality*, p. 13, n. 2. Cf. R.H. STEIN, *Gospels and Tradition. Studies on Redaction Criticism of the Synoptic Gospels*, Grand Rapids, MI, 1991 (reprinted articles). See my review in *ETL* 68 (1992) 435-436.

134. Cf. C. BREYTENBACH, *Vormarkinische Logientradition. Parallelen in der urchristlichen Briefliteratur*, in *The Four Gospels 1992*, pp. 725-749. This paper was first presented at the SNTS Seminar on Pre-Synoptic Tradition (1991). It is the first part of a larger project that will include the comparative study of all Mark-Q parallels (cf. pp. 726 n. 8, 746, 748). His first list of sayings already includes three Q-parallels: Mk 2,16-17a; 2,17b; 4,9.23; 4,24c (Q 6,38c); 7,15; 9,42 (Q 17,1b-2); 9,50c; 10,11-12 (Q 16,18); 12,17; 14,21; 14,22-24. – On Lk 17,2 (pp. 743-745), see my *The Minor Agreements and Q* (n. 76), [pp. 252-254]: the use of Mk 9,42 can explain both Mt 18,6 and Lk 17,2 (not in Q). The combination of Mk 14,21 and 9,42 (Mt 18,6; Lk 17,2) in 1 Clem 46,8 is scarcely an independent oral-tradition variant. Cf. A. LINDEMANN, *Die Clemensbriefe* (HNT, 17/1), Tübingen, 1992, p. 137: the possibility that "er [der Verfasser] die Logien frei zitiert und dabei die Kombination selbst hergestellt hat" is "m.E. wahrscheinlicher". More references in W.-D. KÖHLER, *Die Rezeption des Matthäusevangeliums in der Zeit vor Irenäus* (WUNT, 2/24), Tübingen, 1987, pp. 63-64.

135. C. BREYTENBACH, *Das Markusevangelium als traditionsgebundene Erzählung? Anfragen an die Markusforschung der achtziger Jahre*, in this volume, pp. 77-110; ID., *Vormarkinische Logientradition* (n. 134 above).

136. W.R. TELFORD, *The Pre-Markan Tradition in Recent Research (1980-1990)*, in *The Four Gospels 1992*, pp. 693-723; ID., *Mark and the Historical-Critical Method: The Challenge of Recent Literary Approaches to the Gospels*, in this volume, pp. 491-502.

137. Partially in continuation of the 1991 and 1992 sessions of the SNTS Seminar on Pre-Synoptic Tradition (C. Breytenbach, H. Klein, V.K. Robbins, W.R. Telford).

138. Vol. II, pp. 691-1183: "The Gospel of Mark" (25 essays).

BETL 125 (1996) 141-176

3

THE SAYINGS OF JESUS IN 1 CORINTHIANS

I

When the president-elect of this Colloquium invited me to read a paper in 1994, it was easily agreed that the topic would be: The Sayings of Jesus in 1 Corinthians. In 1992 I was in the retrospective mood of a just retired professor and the recollection of the lecture I delivered at the Colloquium on the Apostle Paul (1984)[1] may, at least partially, explain the choice of the subject: Paul and the Sayings of Jesus, ten years later. It is well known that scholarly opinion is divided on this topic, and so also were the reactions to my paper. On the one hand it marked me with the stigma of a minimalist in this question[2], but on the other hand the

---

1. F. Neirynck, *Paul and the Sayings of Jesus*, in A. Vanhoye (ed.), *L'Apôtre Paul. Personnalité, style et conception du ministère* (BETL, 73), Leuven, University Press – Peeters, 1986, 265-321; = Id., *Evangelica II*, 1991, 511-567 (Additional note, 567-568). Referred to as *Paul*.

My 1984 paper was written in reference to D.C. Allison, Jr., *The Pauline Epistles and the Synoptic Gospels: The Pattern of the Parallels*, in *NTS* 28 (1982) 1-32. See also C.M. Tuckett, *Paul and the Synoptic Mission Discourse?*, in *ETL* 60 (1984) 376-381 (cf. Allison's reply in *ETL* 61, 1985, 369-375); by the same author, *1 Corinthians and Q*, in *JBL* 102 (1983) 607-619; *Synoptic Tradition in 1 Thessalonians?*, in R.F. Collins (ed.), *The Thessalonian Correspondence* (BETL, 87), Leuven, University Press – Peeters, 1990, 160-182.

2. M.B. Thompson, *Clothed with Christ. The Example and Teaching of Jesus in Romans 12.1–15.13* (JSNT SS, 59), Sheffield, JSOT, 1991, p. 16 n. 6: "the minimalist case of Neirynck"; p. 20 n. 3: "the most recent (and thorough) analysis of the parallels is by Neirynck ('Sayings'); the method and conclusions here differ considerably from his"; T. Holtz, *Paul and the Oral Gospel Tradition*, in H. Wansbrough (ed.), *Jesus and the Oral Gospel Tradition* (JSNT SS, 64), Sheffield, JSOT, 1991, 380-393, p. 390 n. 1: "Cf. most recently the thorough analysis of F. Neirynck, although his methodological principles lead him to minimize Paul's reliance on the Jesus tradition"; S. Kim, art. *Jesus, Sayings of*, in G.F. Hawthorne – R.P. Martin (eds.), *Dictionary of Paul and His Letters*, Downers Grove, IL – Leicester, Intervarsity, 1993, 474-492, p. 474: "the 'minimalists' like F. Neirynck and N. Walter"; J.D.G. Dunn, *Jesus Tradition in Paul*, 1994 (below n. 16), p. 173 (and p. 161 n. 18: "Neirynck is one of the most sceptical"); D. Wenham, *The Story of Jesus Known to Paul*, in J.B. Green – M. Turner (eds.), *Jesus of Nazareth: Lord and Christ. Essays on the Historical Jesus and New Testament Christology*, Grand Rapids, MI, Eerdmans; Carlisle, Paternoster, 1994, 297-311, p. 297 n. 1; Id., *Paul: Follower of Jesus or Founder of Christianity?*, Grand Rapids, MI, Eerdmans, 1995, p. 19 n. 57: "Notable skeptics with regard to the quest for allusions include Tuckett [and] Neirynck".

Note Thompson's militarization of the debate: "After a century and a half of dispute, firmly entrenched 'minimalists' and 'maximalists' continue to lob shells into the other's camp with little apparent effect, and the battle shows no sign of abating, although some seek shelter in an agnostic 'no-man's land' between the two extremes" (p. 16).

study was referred to by others as convincing[3] and its general conclusions were cited with approval[4]:

> In the Pauline epistles there are two instances of an explicit reference to a command of the Lord, in 1 Cor 7,10-11 and 9,14, but there is no 'quotation' of the saying. Paul produces in his own formulation 'a halakah based on such a saying'.
>
> Elsewhere in the Pauline letters there is no certain trace of a conscious use of sayings of Jesus. Possible allusions to gospel sayings can be noted on the basis of similarity of form and content but a direct use of a gospel saying in the form it has been preserved in the synoptic gospels is hardly provable. ... Because of the paucity and the anonymity of the possible allusions and reminiscences, and because of their appearance together with other ethical teaching in the paraenetic sections, it remains doubtful whether Paul was using them as sayings of Jesus.

Nikolaus Walter and Alexander J.M. Wedderburn were among the participants at the Colloquium. A few days earlier, at the SNTS meeting in Basel, Walter had delivered a seminar paper on "Paulus und die urchristliche Jesustradition" and in his published text (NTS 1985)[5] he could note that my conclusions and his own assumptions were broadly in agreement[6]. I quote one of his observations on possible allusions to sayings of Jesus[7]:

3. A. LINDEMANN, *Die Funktion der Herrenworte in der ethischen Argumentation des Paulus im ersten Korintherbrief*, in F. VAN SEGBROECK – C.M. TUCKETT – G. VAN BELLE – J. VERHEYDEN (eds.), *The Four Gospels 1992*. FS F. Neirynck (BETL, 100), Leuven, University Press – Peeters, 1992, 677-688, p. 677: "hat in einer m.E. überzeugenden Studie gezeigt, daß sich über die wenigen von Paulus ausdrücklich markierten Jesus-Zitate hinaus keine weitere Benutzung von Jesus-Tradition in den Paulusbriefen identifizieren läßt". Cf. H. VON LIPS, *Paulus und die Tradition. Zitierung von Schriftworten, Herrenworten und urchristlichen Traditionen*, in *Verkündigung und Forschung* 36 (1991) 27-49, pp. 37-43: "Herrenworte" (esp. pp. 31-32); W. SCHMITHALS, *Theologiegeschichte des Urchristentums*, Stuttgart, Kohlhammer, 1994, p. 244. Cf. below n. 6.

4. Quoted from "Conclusion", in *Paul* (n. 1), p. 320 (= 566). See, e.g., W.T. WILSON, *Love without Pretense. Romans 12.9-21 and Hellenistic-Jewish Wisdom Literature* (WUNT, 2/46), Tübingen, Mohr, 1991 (diss. Chicago, under H.D. Betz), 165-171 ("Romans 12.14 and its Relationship with the Synoptic Gospels"), passim (cf. p. 165 n. 54: "most important is the recent study..., whose results are followed rather closely here"; and p. 171 n. 70). Cf. H.D. BETZ, *The Sermon on the Mount*, Minneapolis, MN, Fortress, 1995, p. 6 n. 12. See below n. 25.

5. N. WALTER, *Paulus und die urchristliche Jesustradition*, in *NTS* 31 (1985) 498-522; ET, *Paul and the Early Christian Jesus-Tradition*, in A.J.M. WEDDERBURN (ed.), *Paul and Jesus. Collected Essays* (JSNT SS, 37), Sheffield, JSOT, 1989, 51-80.

6. *Ibid.*, p. 522 n. 60 (= 80 n. 60). Cf. W. SCHMITHALS, *Die Bedeutung der Evangelien in der Theologiegeschichte bis zur Kanonbildung*, in *The Four Gospels 1992* (n. 3), 129-157, p. 129: "Hinsichtlich der Briefe des Apostels Paulus hat F. Neirynck kürzlich ... das einschlägige Material und die neuere Literatur kritisch gesichtet. Sein Ergebnis trifft sich mit dem von N. Walter und mit meinem eigenen Urteil"; with reference to his *Einleitung in die drei ersten Evangelien*, Berlin – New York, de Gruyter, 1985, 99-110 (see esp. pp. 102-106: "Herrenworte").

7. *Paulus*, p. 516 (= 78, slightly adapted). See also p. 501 (= 56), and note 10 (= 9), where he quotes as "eine bedenkenswerte Möglichkeit" the reservation expressed by H.

We cannot be sure whether the passages in which we detect echoes of the Jesus-tradition (*Anklänge an die Jesustradition*) were written by Paul in the consciousness that he was referring to sayings of Jesus.

Wedderburn has written three important articles on the Jesus-Paul issue, and we are all indebted to him because, as co-chairman of the SNTS seminar, he published a fine volume of collected essays on *Paul and Jesus* (1989)[8]. In his postscript to the volume Wedderburn observed that these essays seemed to have left more questions unanswered than they had solved; but he could also add[9]:

> Yet at least some questions have, to my mind, received fairly unequivocal answers: N. Walter has made out a strong case for considerable caution in assessing the amount of Jesus-tradition which Paul knew *as Jesus-tradition*, and the amount which we can say with confidence that he knew is small indeed.

Romans

At about the same time (1988) Michael B. Thompson was writing his Ph.D. dissertation in Cambridge and the opening sentence of his Introduction runs as follows: "One of the unsolved questions in New Testament research is Paul's use of Jesus tradition in his Epistles"[10]. Thompson examined Rom 12,1–15,13 as a test case (*Clothed with Christ*, 1991) and stated in his conclusion that there are three virtually certain echoes of Jesus' teaching (12,14; 13,8-10; 14,14), one highly probable (14,13a) and six less certain but still probable echoes (12,9.17-19; 13,7.11-12; 14,13b.17)[11]. In his Chapter 1 he made a clear distinction between

Schürmann in his 1974 essay on this topic: "An manchen dieser Stellen müßte freilich kritisch eindringlicher gefragt werden, ob die Gemeinsamkeiten zwischen Paulus und den synoptischen Logien nicht in beiden vorausliegenden paränetischen Traditionen des Judentums ihre Erklärung finden".

8. Cf. above n. 5. Wedderburn's three essays are: *Paul and Jesus: The Problem of Continuity* (1985), 99-115; *Paul and Jesus: Similarity and Continuity* (1988), 117-143; *Paul and the Story of Jesus*, 161-189. With regard to the problem of the paucity of references to Jesus' teaching, he proposes "the suggestion that the teaching of Jesus was largely, at that time and in Paul's eyes, 'in enemy hands' in the sense that it was being used in a legalistic way by his Judaizing opponents" (1985, here p. 100). On this problem, see also p. 117(-118) n. 1 (= *NTS* 34, 1988, p. 175 n. 2).

9. *Paul and Jesus*, p. 191.

10. *The Example and Teaching of Jesus in Romans 12.1–15.13* (under J. Sweet); in the published text, *Clothed with Christ* (above n. 2), 1991, p. 15.

11. *Ibid.*, p. 237. In addition: "The influence of Jesus' sayings may appear in Paul's themes of responsibility for the use of varied gifts (12.3-8), brotherly love (12.10), putting the honour of another first (12.10), peace (12.18; 14.19), and service (14.18; cf. 12.11)" (p. 237).

echoes (or reminiscences) used for "cases where the influence of a dominical tradition seems evident, but where it remains uncertain whether he [Paul] was conscious of the influence at the time of dictating" and *allusions* used for "statements which are *intended* to remind an audience of a tradition they are presumed to know as dominical"[12]. By his definition 1 Cor 7,10 and 9,14 are "clear examples" of "allusion". His conclusions, however, show some fluctuation between "virtually certain echoes" and "allusions", although his final conclusion seems to be that in Rom 12–15 "there is at most only one probable allusion to a dominical logion" (12,14)[13]. To his great satisfaction[14] Thompson has found support ("to a number of my conclusions", he says) in James D.G. Dunn's commentary on Romans (1988)[15]; to which we can add Dunn's contribution to the W. Trilling Festschrift, "Paul's Knowledge of the Jesus Tradition: The Evidence of Romans" (1989), now also published in a more elaborate new version (1994)[16]. The passages he retains in Rom 12–15[17] are 12,14.17(21).18; 13,7.9;

---

12. *Ibid.*, p. 30. He uses "quotation" only to refer to "instances in which the writer uses direct quotation with an explicit citation formula" (*ibid.*). — Criteria for evaluating allusions and echoes are presented on pp. 30-36. Compare D. Wenham's adaptation: formal "tradition indicators", verbal and formal similarity, similarity of thought (*Paul*, pp. 26-28), but: "identifying Jesus-tradition in Paul is a complex task. There are a very few cases, such as 1 Cor 7,10-11, where all three of the clues ... come together" (p. 28).

For a series of criteria for identification and interpretation of intertextual echoes, see R.B. HAYS, *Echoes of Scripture in the Letters of Paul*, New Haven, CT – London, Yale University, 1989, pp. 29-32. Hays uses *allusion* of obvious intertextual references, *echo* of subtler ones (p. 29).

13. *Clothed with Christ*, p. 237. But see p. 105: 12,14 "a virtually certain echo, but only possibly an allusion"; p. 199: 14,14 "a probable allusion; a dominical echo is virtually certain". Wenham's list of "highly probable connections" (*Paul*, p. 383) includes Paul's teaching about nonretaliation "strongly reminiscent of Jesus' teaching in the sermon on the mount" (cf. p. 251: Rom 12,14) and Paul's statement in Rom 14,14 "despite some scholarly doubts" (cf. pp. 92-95). With regard to Rom 12–15, Wenham refers to "the authoritative and detailed study by Thompson, *Clothed with Christ*" (p. 250 n. 87; cf. p. 282: "a whole variety of sayings of Jesus are echoed" in Rom 12–15).

14. *Ibid.*, p. 9 (Preface): "It has been particularly heartening to see...".

15. J.D.G. DUNN, *Romans 1–8; Romans 9–16* (WBC, 38A/B), Dallas, TX, Word Books, 1988, esp. pp. 706 (Introduction to 12,1–15,13) and 745 (at 12,14).

16. *Paul's Knowledge of the Jesus Tradition: The Evidence of Romans*, in K. KERTELGE – T. HOLTZ – C.-P. MÄRZ (eds.), *Christus bezeugen*. FS W. Trilling (ETS, 59), Leipzig, St. Benno-Verlag, 1989, 193-207, esp. pp. 200-205: "Paul's use of Jesus tradition"; now, *Jesus Tradition in Paul*, in B. CHILTON – C.A. EVANS (eds.), *Studying the Historical Jesus: Evaluations of the State of Current Research* (NTTS, 19), Leiden, Brill, 1994, 155-178. See also *Prolegomena to a Theology of Paul*, in *NTS* 40 (1994) 407-432, pp. 421-423: "Allusions to Jesus tradition".

17. *Paul's Knowledge*, pp. 200-205; *Jesus Tradition in Paul*, p. 167 (and notes 31-34); and the lists in *Romans*, pp. 706, 745 (Rom 12,17.21 is not included in these lists; but see pp. 747, 752). On Rom 15,3 (added p. 745), see the comment (p. 838).

14,13.14.17.18; 15,1.2[18]. The five "most widely agreed" instances are 12,14.17; 13,7; 14,13.14; the two "strongest" candidates are 12,14 and 14,14[19]. For Dunn, the fact that Paul nowhere cites Jesus as his authority for any of the sayings "is precisely the way in which the Jesus tradition was retained and used"; and the variation between the language of Paul and the Jesus tradition as we have it in the Synoptics "indicates that the Jesus tradition was not yet set in fixed and unyielding forms. Rather it was *living* tradition"[20].

Other commentators on Romans are less assertive. I quote Joseph A. Fitzmyer (1993): "Although there are a few echoes of Jesus' sayings in some letters (1 Cor 7:10-11; 9:14; 11:23-26; 14:37; 1 Thess 4:15-17), Paul passes on nothing in Romans about what the Jesus of history did or said in his earthly life and ministry"[21]. His comments on 12,14.17.18; 13,7.9; 14,14 are rather neutral: "Paul may be echoing a saying of Jesus..."; "Some commentators would see an echo here..."[22]. Victor P. Furnish, in *Jesus According to Paul* (1993)[23], after a new sifting of

18. Other passages outside chs. 12–15 "where some influence of Jesus tradition is at least arguable" (*Paul's Knowledge*, p. 205 n. 32) are: Rom 1,16 (Mk 8,38 / Lk 9,26); 2,1 (Mt 7,1); 2,27 (Mt 12,31-32 / Lk 11,32-33); 6,16 (Mt 6,24); 11,25 (Mk 10,15.23-25); 16,19 (Mt 10,16).

19. The list of five instances in Rom together with 1 Cor 13,2 and 1 Thess 5,2.13.15 is given in his recent *Prolegomena* (p. 422; with reference to Furnish and Allison). A scale of probability is noted in *Jesus Tradition in Paul*: a first group of two instances, 12,14 "one of the most convincing examples, by general consent" and 14,14 "a second widely accepted example" (pp. 161-162, 162-163; = *Paul's Knowledge*, pp. 200-201, 203); second, "also frequently cited (examples), but which are slightly more problematic": 1 Cor 13,2; 1 Thess 5,2; 5,13; third, Rom 13,9; 14,17; 16,19 (here "the echo ... is becoming almost inaudible"); fourth, 1 Thess 5,6; 5,16 ("the echo is still fainter").

20. *Paul's Knowledge*, p. 206 (= *Jesus Tradition in Paul*, p. 174). Cf. *Romans*, p. 745: "a living tradition where the expression of the sense was more important than a particular form of the words". Cf. *The Living Word*, London, SCM, 1987, pp. 25-43 ("The Gospels as Oral Tradition"), esp. p. 39.

21. J.A. FITZMYER, *Romans* (AB, 33), New York, Doubleday, 1993, p. 111. Cf. *Pauline Theology*, in *NJBC*, 1990, 1382-1416, p. 1387: in addition to 1 Thess 4,15; 1 Cor 7,10-11; 9,14; 11,23-25, his list of "allusions or quotations" here includes 1 Thess 4,2*; 5,2.13.15; 1 Cor 13,2* (but not 14,37); Rom 12,14*.17; 13,7; 14,13.14; 16,19* (= *Paul and His Theology. A Brief Sketch*, Englewood Cliffs, NJ, Prentice Hall, 1989, 24-107, p. 33). Compare his *Pauline Theology*, in *JBC*, 1968, 799-827, p. 804: the references marked with asterisk, plus Rom 13,9.

22. Rom 12,14 (Mt 5,44; Lk 6,27-28): "Perhaps an echo of Jesus' words" (*JBC*); "This counsel echoes Jesus' words" (*NJBC*); "... but the wording is not the same" (*AB*, 655). — Rom 14,14: "Most likely it echoes Christ's saying (Mt 15:11)" (*JBC*); "It may echo Jesus' saying ..." (*NJBC*; *AB*, 696). — Rom 12,17: "may echo the words of Jesus" (656); 12,18: "Some commentators ..." (657); "Some commentators ... but there is no real indication that Paul was aware of it [Mk 12,13-17] or that it has any bearing on this passage" (664); 13,9: "Paul may be echoing a saying of Jesus ..." (679).

23. V.P. FURNISH, *Jesus According to Paul* (Understanding Jesus Today), Cambridge, University Press, 1993, ch. 3: "Sayings of Jesus in Paul's Letters", pp. 40-65, esp. 51-61

possible echoes in chs. 12–15, considers the two clearest instances, 12,14 (cf. Mt 5,44; Lk 6,27-28) and 14,14 (cf. Mt 15,11; Mk 7,15). In 14,14, "nothing is unclean in itself" is similar to Mk 7,19b but it is unlikely that the radical Markan form of this saying was part of the pre-Synoptic tradition. The likeliest echo is the admonition in 12,14, "bless those who persecute you, bless and do not curse them". Perhaps Paul knew this saying from the church's moral catechisms: "In that case, he himself might have had no reason to think of it as a saying of Jesus"[24].

Subsequent to Thompson's study, Dunn's commentary and his repeated interventions, the debate on possible allusions or echoes in Romans continues, and even with regard to so-called clusters of allusions in chs. 12–15 it is not very likely that the maximalist thesis will soon become the new consensus[25].

("Echoes of the Sayings Tradition?"). Compare his *Theology and Ethics in Paul*, Nashville TN, Abingdon, 1968, pp. 51-65: five parallels in Rom accepted as convincing (12,14.17; 13,7; 14,13.14) and three in 1 Thess (5,2.13.15). He now eliminates Rom 13,7 (cf. Mk 12,17): "the echo is very faint" (pp. 58-59; see my *Paul*, 286-291 = 532-537) and Rom 14,13 (cf. Mk 9,42): "the similarities [in 13,8-10; 14,13; 15,1-2] ... are so general as to be outweighed by the differences" (p. 52; see my *Paul*, 285-286 = 531-532). He has no comment on Rom 12,17 and 1 Thess 5,2.15. On 1 Thess 5,13, see below, n. 39.

A slightly revised version of Furnish's earlier essay, *The Jesus-Paul Debate: From Baur to Bultmann* (in *BJRL*, 1964-65), is now reproduced in WEDDERBURN (ed.), *Paul and Jesus* (n. 5), 17-50. Cf. p. 44, on Pauline allusions to Jesus' teachings: the most probable instances are Rom 12,14 (1 Cor 4,12) and 14,14; possible instances: Rom 13,8-10 (Gal 5,13-14); much less likely, but worth noting: 1 Cor 13,2; Rom 13,7. — On Rom 13,8-10, see my *Paul*, 291-294 (= 537-540). On 1 Cor 13,2, see below, n. 43.

24. *Jesus*, p. 55. Contrast T. HOLTZ, *Paul* (n. 2), p. 392: "thoroughly probable that in Rom. 12.14 ... Paul was conscious that he was adopting sayings of Jesus into his own speech". This is less certain in other instances: "certainty as a rule eludes us" (p. 390). See my *Paul*, pp. 295-303 (= 541-549), on Rom 12,14 and 12,17.21; pp. 306-308 (= 552-554), on Rom 14,14.

25. See, e.g., W. SCHMITHALS, *Einleitung* (n. 6), p. 106: "Da Paulus in Röm 12,9-21 durchgehend hellenistisch-synagogale Paränese in vorgeprägter Gestalt aufnimmt, besteht kein Anlaß, das Motiv von 12,14 aus diesem Kontext zu isolieren"; J. BECKER, *Paulus. Der Apostel der Völker*, Tübingen, Mohr, 1989, pp. 119-131: "Paulus und Jesus", esp. 123, 129-131: "(im Einzelfall) kann sich natürlich ein Wort wie z.B. Röm 12,14 der in Lk 6,28 erhaltenen Jesustradition verdanken. Aber 1. Kor 4,12; 1. Thess 5,15 warnen davor, bei solcher These zu schnell vorzugehen. Kann nicht vielleicht auch Lk 6,28 jünger sein als die paulinische Paränese? Ein Blick auf die thematisch verwandte Aufforderung im Kontext (Röm 12,17) hilft vielleicht weiter. Sie hat respektable Varianten in der hellenistisch-jüdischen Weisheit. Sollte sich in Röm 12 überhaupt diese anonyme Weisheitslehre wiederfinden, weil sie das Urbild Christi in diesem Fall so gut beschreiben konnte? Dann hätte Paulus auch nicht indirekt in Röm 12 an Jesu Worte gedacht" (pp. 130-131).

See now also H.D. Betz's commentary on the Sermon on the Mount (1995; above n. 4), with regard to Rom 12,14.17.21; 13,8-10; 14,10 (and 2,1-2): "None of these and other passages leads me to assume that Paul was familiar with either the SM or the SP in regard to their entirety or in regard to single sayings contained in them. Rather, he seems to have received them from other sources" (p. 6 n. 12). Cf. W.T. WILSON, *Love without Pretense* (above n. 4), on Rom 12,14 ("the strongest candidate"): "it seems unlikely... A

1 Thessalonians

Although the discussion in recent years more and more concentrates on Romans, I should mention that 1 Thess 5,2.13.15 are cited among "the most widely agreed" instances of allusion. For fuller treatment of the question I can refer to C.M. Tuckett's paper at the 1988 Colloquium on *The Thessalonian Correspondence* ("Synoptic Tradition in 1 Thessalonians?", published in 1990)[26]. I will make here just a few remarks on one of these instances: 1 Thess 5,13b εἰρηνεύετε ἐν ἑαυτοῖς – Mk 9,50b[β] καὶ εἰρηνεύετε ἐν ἀλλήλοις.

Dunn says that "Paul echoes the same exhortation in Rom 12:18 (μετὰ πάντων ἀνθρώπων εἰρηνεύοντες); and to some degree in 2 Cor 13:11 (εἰρηνεύετε)"[27]. He seems to regret that Allison did not accept this case in his list of parallels: "Oddly enough, although Allison makes a good case for the thesis that Paul knew the pre-Markan collection of logia incorporated by Mark at 9:33-50, he makes no mention of the possible link here with Mark 9:50, which would add further strength to his thesis"[28]. This note, first printed in 1989 and repeated in 1994, is not uninteresting in connection with Dunn's reply to my earlier essay. He cites a clause taken from its conclusion ("a direct use of a gospel saying in the form it has been preserved in the synoptic gospels is hardly provable") and then adds the following comment[29]:

> The final clause of this quotation ... is a reminder that Neirynck's real concern is whether the Pauline letters provide evidence of a pre-synoptic gospel or of Q or pre-Q collections. In such a discussion the degree of similarity to the actual wording of the Synoptic parallels must be a decisive consideration. Whereas for us the more productive question is whether such "allusions" within Paul, together with the Synoptic parallels, constitute evidence of a Jesus tradition which was remembered and reused in different forms.

feasible explanation is that Paul drew this saying, or some version of it, from the fund of traditional, anonymous, and probably oral Jewish and Jewish-Christian wisdom available to him" (p. 171); on Rom 12,17a (and 1 Thess 5,15a): "The presence of numerous commands in the Jewish paraenetic tradition with only slightly different permutations indicates that Paul here cites some variation of a proverb" (p. 187); on Rom 12,21: the "structural counterpart" of v. 14 (p. 198).

26. See above, n. 1. — Compare Dunn's list, above n. 19.

27. DUNN, *Jesus Tradition in Paul*, p. 164. Cf. *Paul's Knowledge*, pp. 201-202; see also *Romans*, p. 748 (and pp. 706, 745): Rom 12,18. Cf., e.g., T. HOLTZ, 1986 (below n. 40), p. 246: 1 Thess 5,13 "vermutlich ein Echo auf die Jesus-Überlieferung Mk 9,50"; H. KOESTER, *Ancient Christian Gospels* (below n. 62), who adds Rom 12,18 to Furnish's 1968 list (cf. C.H. Talbert 1969) (p. 53).

28. *Paul's Knowledge*, p. 202 n. 25, reprinted in *Jesus Tradition in Paul*, p. 164 n. 23 (see also p. 160 n. 13; = *NTS*, p. 422 n. 34).

29. *Jesus Tradition in Paul*, p. 173.

In *Paul and the Sayings of Jesus* my ("real") concern was to study the sayings and allusions to sayings in Paul in dialogue with the then latest presentation and "theory", which happened to be D.C. Allison's article, "The Pattern of the Parallels" (NTS 1982), in which he proposes clusters of allusions in the Pauline Epistles and concentration of the parallels in mainly three (pre-Synoptic) collections of sayings in the Gospels. But is it not rather a strange contrast in Dunn's text, on the one hand "similarity" for Synoptic parallels and on the other reuse "in different forms" in Paul? In the same article Dunn refers to Thompson who has attempted (what he calls) a more scientific analysis[30]. As a matter of fact Thompson's first principle runs like this: "Sound method requires (1) discerning whether a significant parallel exists between the two texts...", and the first criterion he develops is "verbal agreement"[31]. In order to be really "productive" the study of the parallels should consider both sides, the Pauline text and the Synoptic text. And I am inclined to follow Tuckett's recommendation[32]:

> In the case of possible implicit allusions to Jesus traditions in Paul, one should perhaps first of all seek to analyse the synoptic parallels in their own right and only bring the Pauline evidence into the discussion secondarily.

In essence one can agree with Dunn's emphasis on "*living* tradition" (adaptable to different needs and diverse contexts) and on "earlier forms" of the material used by the Evangelists. But it needs qualification when we read that the variations between the three Synoptics indicate that "there must have been different versions of much if not all of the Markan material"[33], and that, for instance, "Matthew was able therefore to choose a different version of the tradition in a significant number of occasions"[34]. This was not, I admit, my presupposition in studying possible allusions in Paul. Neither could I take for granted that a pre-Markan collection of logia was incorporated by Mark at 9,33-50 (including v. 50b). By the way, the impression that Allison made no mention of the possible link of 1 Thess 5,13 with Mark is apparently based on a misreading of Allison's article[35] and of my own reply[36]. In his commentary

30. *Ibid.*, p. 160.
31. *Clothed with Christ*, pp. 30-31.
32. *Synoptic Tradition* (n. 1), p. 162. See also p. 164, on 1 Thess 5,13.
33. *Jesus Tradition in Paul*, p. 159.
34. *Matthew's Awareness of Markan Redaction*, in *The Four Gospels 1992* (n. 3), 1349-1359, p. 1350.
35. Cf. *The Pauline Epistles*, p. 14, on 1 Thess 5,13 (in accord with Furnish: "a genuine allusion to tradition"). Allison continues: "Rom. 14,13 *likewise* probably derives from the same compilation" (my emphasis). See also his survey of parallels, p. 20.
36. *Paul*, pp. 282-284, esp. 283 (= 528-530, esp. 529), n. 100.

on Rom 12,18 Dunn suggests that, in addition to Mk 9,50, there may be influence from εἰρηνοποιοί in Mt 5,9, without warning his readers that this would imply that Matthew's seventh beatitude is pre-Matthean and even pre-Pauline Jesus tradition.

Dunn knows, of course, that the link with Mk 9,50 is not unproblematic: "The ideal itself [live in peace] is a widely cherished one (e.g. Sir 6:6; *Epictetus* 4.5.24), and that inevitably raises a suspicion as to the source of Paul's exhortations"[37]. Thompson clearly states that in this case "the criterion of dissimilarity cannot be invoked to support an echo". The parallel in Rom 14,19 τὰ τῆς εἰρήνης διώκωμεν (to pursue peace) "almost certainly reflects the influence of Ps. 33[34].15 (ζήτησον εἰρήνην καὶ δίωξον αὐτήν) on the paraenetic tradition, as indicated by the quotations in 1 Pet. 3,10-12; *1 Clem.* 22.1-7"[38]. V. Furnish, who in 1968 supported the allusion, has now retracted: "Unlike the commandment to 'bless those who curse you,' there is nothing radical, or even distinctively Christian, about the counsel to 'be at peace'"[39].

Before turning to 1 Corinthians I may mention here that, in my understanding, ὑμῖν λέγομεν ἐν λόγῳ κυρίου in 1 Thess 4,15 is not the designation of a saying of Jesus[40], nor is it a dictum of some early Christian prophet[41]: "Because of the Old Testament use of ἐν λόγῳ κυρίου ... it

37. *Jesus Tradition in Paul*, p. 164. Cf. WILSON, *Love* (n. 4), p. 191. — Compare C. BREYTENBACH, *Vormarkinische Logientradition. Parallelen in der urchristlichen Briefliteratur*, in *The Four Gospels 1992* (n. 3), pp. 725-749, esp. 735. His conclusion that Mk 9,50c "Vormarkinisches reflektiert" is based on a comparison with 1 Thess 5,13b (and Rom 12,18); with regard to Mk 9,33-50, cf. p. 733 n. 42 ("berechtigte Kritik"). His survey also includes Rom 13,7 (Mk 12,17); 14,14 (Mk 7,15); 1 Cor 11,23-25 (pp. 731-733); 7,10-11 (pp. 736-739).

38. *Clothed with Christ*, p. 108.

39. *Jesus*, p. 55.

40. See HOLTZ, *Paul* (n. 2), p. 385: "Despite currently widespread objection (n. 5: Neirynck, Walter), the most probable interpretation must be to understand λόγος κυρίου as a designation of a received saying of Jesus". For Holtz, the consequences of this interpretation are considerable: "1 Thess. 4.15 shows that we no longer have at our disposal the whole extent of the Jesus tradition which was available to Paul. Consequently we must assume that a whole series of uses of the Jesus tradition in particular contexts in Paul remains unrecognizable to us" (pp. 389-390). Cf. ID., *Der erste Brief an die Thessalonicher* (EKK, 13), Neukirchen-Vluyn, 1986, pp. 184-185; *Traditionen im 1. Thessalonicherbrief* (1983) and *Jesus-Überlieferung und Briefliteratur* (1985), now reprinted in *Geschichte und Theologie des Urchristentums. Gesammelte Aufsätze*, eds. E. REINMUTH – C. WOLFF (WUNT, 57), Tübingen, Mohr, 1991, pp. 246-269 (esp. 255) and 17-30 (esp. 28).

41. See R.F. COLLINS, in *NJBC*, 1990, p. 778. Cf. TUCKETT, *Synoptic Tradition* (n. 1), pp. 179 (n. 93: "Probably the most popular view") and 182: "(more probably) he is citing a tradition of a prophetic saying claimed to have been received by (another) prophet". See also DUNN, *Jesus Tradition in Paul*, p. 161 n. 17: "better understood as a prophetic utterance than a dominical saying" (= *Paul's Knowledge*, p. 193 n. 1); cf. *Jesus and the Spirit*, London, SCM, 1975, p. 230.

seems preferable to understand Paul's declaration 'by the word of the Lord' as referring to an oracle originating with Paul himself"[42]. In the letters of Paul, explicit references to sayings of Jesus are found only in 1 Corinthians.

1 Corinthians

1 Cor 13,2: ... καὶ ἐὰν ἔχω πᾶσαν τὴν πίστιν ὥστε ὄρη μεθιστάναι

The most frequently cited echo of a Jesus saying in 1 Corinthians is the saying about mountain-moving in 13,2[43]. In 1982 Allison compared 1 Cor 13,2 with Mk 11,23 and did not even mention the parallel in Q[44]. In his commentary on Mt 17,20 he now proposes the Q-variant in Lk 17,6 (the "sycamine" tree) as the original formulation which was secondarily changed to "this mountain" (Mt): "our conclusion entails that Paul already knew the saying in a secondary form"[45]. For his view on

---

42. *Paul*, p. 311 (= 557). Cf. B. HENNEKEN, *Verkündigung und Prophetie im 1. Thessalonicherbrief. Ein Beitrag zur Theologie des Wortes Gottes* (SBS, 29), Stuttgart, KBW, 1969, pp. 73-98, esp. 92-98 (p. 98: "ein Wort des erhöhten Herrn, das in einer besonderen Offenbarung an Paulus erging"); followed by O. HOFIUS, *"Unbekannte Jesusworte"*, in P. STUHLMACHER (ed.), *Das Evangelium und die Evangelien* (WUNT, 28), Tübingen, Mohr, 1983, pp. 355-382, esp. 357-360 (p. 360: "ihnen [the OT parallels] zufolge redet *der ἐν λόγῳ κυρίου*, der *selbst* und *ganz unmittelbar* das 'Wort des Herrn' von Gott empfangen hat"). Hofius now rightly prefers this interpretation ("ein an ihn selbst ergangenes Offenbarungswort des erhöhten Herrn"). Contrast art. *Agrapha*, in *TRE* 2 (1978) 103-110, where he proposed the alternative: "die Wendung ... gibt an, in wessen Auftrag und Autorität er redet" (p. 114). But see now p. 360: "nach meinem Urteil (verdient) der erstgenannte Lösungsvorschlag den Vorzug" (ET, *The Gospel and the Gospels*, Grand Rapids, MI, Eerdmans, 1991, 336-360, p. 340). See now also H. MERKLEIN, *Der Theologe als Prophet. Zur Funktion prophetisches Redens im theologischen Diskurs des Paulus*, in *NTS* 38 (1992) 402-429, p. 413: "man (wird) die Alternative 'Herrenwort oder Prophetenwort' zugunsten des letzteren entscheiden, allerdings mit der präzisierenden Maßgabe, daß Paulus nich (fremdes) Prophetenwort *zitieren*, sondern *selbst prophetisch reden* will".

43. See the references in my *Paul*, pp. 274-275 (= 520-521). See now also, e.g., F. HAHN, *Jesu Wort vom bergeversetzenden Glauben*, in *ZNW* 76 (1985) 149-169, p. 152: "Daß Jesu Wort ... in urchristlicher Zeit bekannt und verbreitet war, zeigt der Apostel *Paulus*"; G.D. FEE, *The First Epistle to the Corinthians* (NICNT), Grand Rapids, MI, Eerdmans, 1987, p. 632 n. 32: "sure evidence of Paul's acquaintance with the teaching of Jesus"; J.H. PETZER, *Contextual Evidence in Favour of καυχήσωμαι in 1 Corinthians 13.3*, in *NTS* 35 (1989) 229-253, p. 240 n. 1: "probably an allusion to Jesus' words"; DUNN, *Jesus Tradition in Paul*, p. 163; also p. 160 n. 13 (= *NTS* 40, 1994, p. 422 n. 34: cf. Allison 1982). Contrast FURNISH, *Jesus*, pp. 60-61.

44. *The Pauline Epistles* (n. 1), p. 20; see also p. 17 (and n. 100). — Allison's list of allusions includes two more instances, 1 Cor 4,12 (cf. Rom 12,14) and Q 6,28: cf. below nn. 70-77; and 1 Cor 8,13 (cf. Rom 14,13) and Mk 9,42: see my *Paul*, pp. 282, 285 (= 528, 531).

45. W.D. DAVIES – D.C. ALLISON, *The Gospel according to Saint Matthew* (ICC), Edinburgh, Clark, vol. 2, 1991, p. 727, esp. n. 35.

the original Q-saying he can refer to "most modern exegetes". With only a few notable exceptions (F. Hahn, D. Lührmann), recent reconstructions of Q reproduce the text of Lk 17,6, occasionally with minor variations from Mt 17,20[46], but mostly in a strictly literal quotation[47]. In my opinion, more serious consideration should be given to Lukan redaction and to the possibility that Luke's reference to the sea may be influenced by the mountain-moving saying of Mark[48]:

Mk 11,23 ἄρθητι   καὶ βλήθητι   εἰς τὴν θάλασσαν
Lk 17,6 ἐκριζώθητι (καὶ φυτεύθητι ἐν τῇ θαλάσσῃ).

A more radical assimilation to Mk 11,23 has taken place in Mt 17,20: "Matthew has taken from Mark the introductory phrase with 'amen' and 'this mountain'" (Allison). Therefore, the existence of "a secondary form" of the Q-saying that was known by Paul is far from evident: "it is in Luke that we come closest to a *pre*-Synoptic saying that Paul might have known. But instead of a mountain, the Lucan version refers to a mulberry tree!"[49].

---

46. See, e.g., J. ZMIJEWSKI, *Der Glaube und seine Macht. Eine traditionsgeschichtliche Untersuchung zu Mt 17,20; 21,21; Mk 11,23; Lk 17,6*, in ID. – E. NELLESSEN (eds.), *Begegnung mit dem Wort*. FS H. Zimmermann (BBB, 53), Bonn, Hanstein, 1980, 81-101, esp. pp. 86-89 (= ID., *Das Neue Testament*, Stuttgart, KBW, 1986, 265-292): ἐὰν ἔχητε (Schulz, Polag, Catchpole), ἐρεῖτε (Schulz), ὑπακούσει (future, cf. Mt). For J. Gnilka (*Mt* II, 1988, p. 106) the introduction ἀμὴν λέγω ὑμῖν may be original (cf. F. HAHN, p. 154).
47. IQP, in *JBL* 110 (1991), p. 498. Cf. H.T. FLEDDERMANN, *Mark and Q. A Study of the Overlap Texts* (BETL, 122), Leuven, University Press – Peeters, 1995, pp. 178-180.
48. Cf. my *Assessment*, in Fleddermann's *Mark and Q*, p. 290. See the original wording of the saying according to Catchpole: "bringing together in a single saying the proverbially tiny mustard seed and the extremely deep rooted sycamine tree". Cf. D. CATCHPOLE, *The Centurion's Faith and its Function in Q*, in *The Four Gospels 1992* (n. 3), 517-540, esp. p. 517 (= ID., *The Quest for Q*, Edinburgh, Clark, 1993, p. 280). Compare, on the one hand, I.H. Marshall's supposition that "Luke's reference to the sea (could be) due to assimilation to Mk" (*Luke*, 1978, p. 645), and on the other F. Hahn's observation: "So gut das Motiv vom 'Sich-Werfen (bzw. Geworfenwerden) ins Meer' zu ὄρος paßt, so wenig paßt die Anschauung vom 'Sich-Einpflanzen ins Meer' zu συκάμινος. Hier liegt offensichtlich eine Parallelbildung zu ἄρθητι καὶ βλήθητι εἰς τὴν θάλασσαν vor, was als Argument gegen die Ursprünglichkeit der Lukasfassung gar nicht genügend beachtet wird" (p. 158). Without good reason, Hahn's own approach disvalues the contrast between the mustard seed and the sycamine tree (cf. Catchpole). On the oddity of Luke's version, see also Fitzmyer's comment: "In the earlier tradition it was probably a mountain that was thrown into a sea, which would be intelligible. But now a mulberry tree being 'planted' in the sea is strange, to say the least" (*Luke*, p. 1144; but see p. 1142: "Luke has here preserved the more original form of 'Q'").
Since Lk 17,2 is probably due to Lukan redaction (cf. *Assessment*, p. 287), one can hardly argue for a catchword connection with "thrown into the sea" within the unit of Q 17,1-6.
49. V. FURNISH, *Jesus* (n. 23), p. 61.

Two sayings of the Gospel of Thomas[50], without referring to faith, seem to be reminiscent of Mt 17,20 (ἐὰν..., ἐρεῖτε τῷ ὄρει τούτῳ· μετάβα ἔνθεν ἐκεῖ, καὶ μεταβήσεται):

Th 48: If two make peace with each other in a single house, they will say to the mountain, "Move from here," and it will move.

Th 106: When you make the two into one, you will become children of humanity, and when you say, "Mountain, move from here," it will move.

1 Cor 13,2 has not such a close similarity with the synoptic sayings, and since removing mountains is a proverbial expression[51] it could have been used by Paul independently. But only in 1 Cor 13,2 and in Mt/Mk is mountain-moving related to faith (faith that does the impossible) and therefore it is tempting to conclude that 1 Cor 13,2 "reflects the force of a well known saying of Jesus about the efficacy of faith"[52]. 1 Cor 13,2 has been cited in support of Mt 17,20 either as the original wording of Q[53] or as the early pre-Matthean development of the Q saying: "When 1 Cor 13:2 is compared with the synoptic evidence, it is clear that Paul's wording is closest to Matt 17:20"[54]. It is true, in 1 Cor 13,2 there is no mulberry tree as in Lk 17,6, and there is no reference to the sea as in Mk 11,23 / Mt 21,21 (and Lk 17,6), but neither is πᾶσαν τὴν πίστιν Mt's "faith like a mustard seed", and ὥστε μεθιστάναι significantly differs from the Matthean formulation of the mountain-moving motif (cf. Th 48 and 106). R.H. Gundry recognizes that the saying known to Paul cannot be this redactional conflation of Mk and Q in Mt 17,20, but what about Mk 11,23?

> 1 Cor 13:2 relates "all faith" to removing mountains and seems to depend on a pre-Marcan version of Mark 11:23. Since "all faith" easily summarizes "and does not doubt in his heart but believes that what he says is happening," but stands opposed to faith *as small as a grain of mustard*, the comparatively very early date of 1 Cor 13:2 favors the originality of the middle part of Mark 11:23.[55]

50. All quotations of Thomas are from M. Meyer's new translation in *The Gospel of Thomas. The Hidden Sayings of Jesus*, San Francisco, Harper, 1992.

51. Dunn's observation that the "attestation (of the proverb) is all a good deal later than Paul" (p. 163) may surprise. Isa 54,10 (τὰ ὄρη μεταστήσεσθαι ...) is a current reference in lexicons and commentaries.

52. Dunn (*ibid.*). See also J.-M. VAN CANGH, *Évolution du motif de la foi dans les miracles synoptiques, johanniques et apocryphes*, in *The Four Gospels 1992* (n. 3), pp. 566-578, esp. 571 (with reference to J. Duplacy and J. Jeremias).

53. W.R. TELFORD, *The Barren Temple and the Withered Tree* (JSNT SS, 1), Sheffield, 1980, p. 103: "supported by Paul". Cf. R. BULTMANN, *Geschichte*, p. 78: "das ὄρος bei Mt wird gegenüber der συκάμινος des Lk durch Mk und 1. Kor 13,2 bestätigt".

54. TUCKETT, *I Corinthians and Q* (n. 1), 1983, p. 614

55. R.H. GUNDRY, *Mark*, Grand Rapids, MI, Eerdmans, 1993, p. 652. This is only one aspect of a series of oppositions Gundry sees between Q 17,6 and Mk 11,23; two different sayings on two different occasions, one about a beneficial use of faith (planting a tree) and one about a destructive use of faith (a mountain lifted up and thrown).

This observation assigns to tradition what is Pauline usage in 1 Cor 13,2: πάντα, πᾶσαν τὴν γνῶσιν, πᾶσαν τὴν πίστιν and ὥστε «eine Art Superlativ einführend"[56]. "In the protases of the three parallel periods he blows up the charismata enormously by, among other things, repeatedly using the word 'all'"[57]. By the way, I do not see how Paul's hyperbolic language in 1 Cor 13,2 could be a valid reason for the suggestion that a Jesus saying on faith has been used and misused by the Corinthians[58].

To conclude, I may quote V. Furnish's final statement on 1 Cor 13,2[59].

> Despite this complicated situation, one point can be made with confidence. If a saying from the Jesus tradition does lie behind 1 Cor 13:2, the apostle has felt quite free to employ it in his own way. The saying had called for faith and had emphasized its astounding power. But Paul is appealing for love, and insists that nothing exceeds it in importance.

Thomas and 1 Cor

For J.M. Robinson, Paul in 1 Cor 13,2 is critical of the Corinthians' use of Jesus' saying on faith, and in this connection he draws attention to Th 48 and 106: "this saying was capable of gnostic interpretation... In *Thomas* 'faith' has been replaced by the more gnostic category of overcoming duality and returning to primordial unity"[60]. Likewise, 1 Cor 4,8 is understood as "Paul's response to a distorting use of the beatitudes": "Paul's critical description of his opponents (ἤδη κεκορεσμένοι ἐστέ, ἤδη ἐπλουτήσατε, χωρὶς ἡμῶν ἐβασιλεύσατε) suggests the woes of the Sermon on the Plain". Here too he refers to a saying of Thomas, Th 2, with its concept of reigning or being king as "a gnostic equivalent"[61]. H. Koester adds further precision: the woes (Lk) would only explain

---

56. J. WEISS, *Der erste Korintherbrief*, 1910, p. 314: "in Anklang an ein Herrenwort und zwar nicht in der Form von Q, sondern in der des Mk 11,23" (cf. Gundry).

57. J.F.M. SMIT, *Two Puzzles: 1 Corinthians 12.31 and 13.3: A Rhetorical Solution*, in *NTS* 39 (1993) 246-264, p. 253.

58. Ctr. D. WENHAM, *Paul*, p. 85 (cf. pp. 82-83: J.M. Robinson): "He may be criticizing the Corinthians' use of that teaching", with reference to Tuckett, "cited favorably by Neirynck" (n. 103). Tuckett's view, "1 Cor 4:8 and 13:2 seem to provide the strongest evidence that Jesus-traditions were being used by the Corinthians" (p. 619), is quoted in my overview (p. 275 = 521). But, in this case, "cited favorably" is not the right word. Cf. below nn. 60-64.

59. *Jesus*, p. 61. See also J.A. FITZMYER, *Luke*, p. 1142: "Paul speaks ... of a charismatic faith... Luke [17,6] does not speak of that sort of faith".

60. J.M. ROBINSON – H. KOESTER, *Trajectories through Early Christianity*, Philadelphia, PA, Fortress, 1971, p. 41 (and n. 30). Cf. above n. 58; see the texts quoted on p. 152. — It is noteworthy that 1 Cor 13,2 is not mentioned in H. Koester's *Ancient Christian Gospels* (below n. 62).

61. *Ibid.*, pp. 43-44.

ἐπλουτήσατε, not ἐβασιλεύσατε⁶². "This (last) characterization of the Corinthians is most likely an ironic rendering of a phrase from the saying in *Gos. Thom* § 2"⁶³:

¹ Let one who seeks not stop seeking until one finds.
² When one finds, one will be troubled.
³ When one is troubled, one *will marvel and* will rule over all.
   P. Oxy. 654,5-9:
¹ μὴ παυσάσθω ὁ ζη[τῶν τοῦ ζητεῖν ἕως ἂν] εὕρῃ,
² καὶ ὅταν εὕρῃ, [θαμβηθήσεται
³ καὶ θαμ]βηθεὶς βασιλεύσῃ (= -ει)   ... one will rule,
⁴ κα[ὶ βασιλεύσας ἀναπα]ήσεται.   and [having ruled], one will [rest].

The seek-and-find saying may rely on a traditional Jesus saying (although it is a widespread motif)⁶⁴, but I see no justification for assigning an early (pre-Pauline) origin to its gnostic expansion (lines 2-4).

The saying cited by Paul in 1 Cor 2,9 with the formula καθὼς γέγραπται (cf. Isa 64,3?) has a parallel in Th 17, where it is quoted as a saying of Jesus ("Jesus said"):

I shall give you what no eye has seen,
and what no ear has heard,
and what no hand has touched,
what has not arisen in the human heart.

This saying has played an important role in Koester's theory about a collection of wisdom sayings which was known to Paul and to the Corinthians: "at least one saying which Paul quotes in the context of his refutation is indeed found in the *Gospel of Thomas* 17"⁶⁵. Starting from

---

62. H. KOESTER, *Ancient Christian Gospels*, London, SCM; Philadelphia, PA, TPI, 1990, p. 60, n. 2. But "reigning" has its counterpart in the βασιλεία of the beatitudes (TUCKETT, p. 609 n. 16).

63. *Ibid.*, p. 60; his translation (on the basis of the Coptic text, the Greek fragment and quotations in Clement of Alexandria, *Stromata* 2,9,45; 5,14,96): "³... he will be king, ⁴and when he has become king, he will find rest". For the Greek fragment, cf. J.A. FITZMYER, *The Oxyrhynchus Logoi of Jesus and the Coptic Gospel according to Thomas* (1959), in *Essays on the Semitic Background of the New Testament*, London, Chapman, 1971, 355-433, pp. 370-373; H.W. ATTRIDGE, *The Greek Fragments*, in B. LAYTON (ed.), *Nag Hammadi Codex II, 2-7* (NHS, 20), Leiden, Brill, 1989, 95-128, p. 113.

64. Note that Th 94 has a second pair like Mt 7,8 = Lk 11,10bc: "One who seeks will find; for [one who knocks] it will be opened". Cf. H.T. FLEDDERMANN, *Mark and Q* (n. 47), pp. 185-186.

65. *Trajectories* (n. 60), p. 186 (= *HTR* 61, 1968, p. 230). Cf. p. 227 n. 47: "Only once does Paul quote a wisdom saying that belongs to the tradition of wisdom sayings of Jesus". See also his more recent *Ancient Christian Gospels* (n. 62), pp. 58-59, 152, on Q 10,23(-24) and its "closest parallel" in Th 17 (1 Cor 2,9). But see TUCKETT, 1983, p. 616, on the "important differences in content" between Q 10,23-24 and 1 Cor 2,9.
   Cf. R. TREVIJANO, *La valoración de los dichos no canónicos: el caso de 1 Cor. 2.9 y Ev. Tom log. 17*, in *Studia Patristica* 24 (1993) 406-414. See also J. VERHEYDEN's paper

1 Cor 2,9 and its parallel in Thomas, Stephen J. Patterson has written a programmatic essay on "Paul and the Jesus Tradition"[66]. The problem, he says, is not simply that of Paul's relative silence on the Jesus tradition. The relationship between Jesus and Paul has been discussed primarily in terms of Paul's use of material directly traceable to the synoptic tradition. By using the new data of the Gospel of Thomas we can broaden our knowledge of the early Christian sayings tradition. New information is provided in Thomas regarding Paul's position on circumcision (Th 53); on food, another aspect of Jewish-Gentile relations (Th 14); on women disciples and the abrogation of the boundary between men and women (Th 114): "Certain sayings in Thomas suggest how Paul may have arrived at some of his classic positions"[67]. In Patterson's opinion, a majority (!) of scholars has come to believe that the Gospel of Thomas represents a trajectory that is for the most part autonomous and not dependent upon the canonical gospels. That makes him predisposed to write for instance in his comment on Th 53: "There is no reason why such a saying [on "true circumcision in spirit"] might not have been attributed to Jesus very early indeed"[68]. By making use of Thomas, "it is possible to arrive at a very early stratum in the sayings tradition". The Thomas tradition "provides us with a crucial and indispensable tool for gaining critical distance on the synoptic tradition, which has so long dominated the Jesus discussion"[69]. For the time being,

---

in this volume: *Origen on the Origin of 1 Cor 2,9*, pp. 491-511, esp. 495 n. 17. On the parallel in the *Prayer of the Apostle Paul* (Koester, p. 59 n. 1), cf. J.-D. DUBOIS, *L'utilisation gnostique du centon biblique cité en* 1 Corinthiens 2,9, in G. DORIVAL – O. MUNNICH (eds.), *ΚΑΤΑ ΤΟΥΣ Ο΄. Selon les Septante*. FS M. Harl, Paris, Cerf, 1995, 371-379.

66. S.J. PATTERSON, *Paul and the Jesus Tradition: It Is Time for Another Look*, in *HTR* 84 (1991) 23-41. On 1 Thess 4,15-17 and "the limited picture of the Jesus tradition" (p. 30), compare Holtz's observation (above n. 40).
On 1 Cor 2,9, which Paul "has drawn from the repertoire of his opponents", see pp. 36-37. Cf. ID., *The Gospel of Thomas and Jesus*, Sonoma, CA, Polebridge Press, 1993 (revised version of his Ph.D. dissertation, Claremont 1988), pp. 85, 108 (summarizing *Trajectories*, 186-187), 205, 233 ("Thom 17, a saying whose antiquity is assured by its independent multiple attestation in Q [Matt 13:16-17 // Luke 10:23-24], 1 Cor 2:9, Dial-Sav 140.1-4, as well as in many other sources of later date").
67. *Paul*, p. 41. Compare C.L. MEARNS, *Early Eschatological Development in Paul: The Evidence of 1 Corinthians*, in *JSNT* 22 (1984) 19-35, p. 31; reprinted in S.E. PORTER – C.A. EVANS (eds.), *The Pauline Writings* (The Biblical Seminar, 34), Sheffield, Academic Press, 1995, 202-219, p. 207 (n. 7, on the sayings of Jesus): "Paul could have derived Rom. 14.14 from the *Gos. Thom.* 14, which is a more primitive version of the saying in Mk 7.15 and Mt. 14.14. This suggestion receives some support because in 1 Cor. 2.9 Paul cites the *Gos. Thom.* 17, showing he could have known this sayings-source as well as Q" (sic).
68. *The Gospel of Thomas and Jesus*, p. 88.
69. *Ibid.*, p. 241 ("Summary").

and particularly in a discussion on "Paul and the sayings of Jesus", I am afraid I will continue to be one of those people living under the dominance of the Synoptic tradition.

1 Cor 4,12

Another possible echo of a *Synoptic* saying in 1 Corinthians is λοιδορούμενοι εὐλογοῦμεν in 4,12. In the exegetical literature, it appears almost as a satellite echo, always cited together with, and in confirmation of, Rom 12,14, which (as indicated above) is the most largely agreed Pauline allusion:

εὐλογεῖτε τοὺς διώκοντας ὑμᾶς,

εὐλογεῖτε καὶ μὴ καταρᾶσθε.

Again and again, after comparing Rom 12,14 with Lk 6,27-28, it is added that it also has parallels in 1 Cor 4,12; 1 Peter 3,9; Didache 1,3[70]. This association of 1 Cor with 1 Peter and Didache in one three-some is somewhat misleading. Both 1 Peter and Didache are post-Synoptic and possibly dependent on the Synoptic Gospels[71] and therefore should be treated apart from the parallel in 1 Cor. In this connection, Thompson objects that I attribute to the author of Didache the same freedom that I implicitly deny Paul[72]. Thompson seems to neglect that Did 1,3 is part of the *sectio evangelica*, 1,3-5, where "the sayings are certainly drawn from written gospels ... in a compilation ... with distinct features of harmonization of the texts of Matthew and Luke" (H. Koester)[73]. If it was

---

70. DUNN, *Paul's Knowledge*, p. 201; *Jesus Tradition in Paul*, p. 162 ("has echoes elsewhere ..."); THOMPSON, *Clothed with Christ*, pp. 97 (1 Cor 4,12; 1 Pet 3,9) and 99 (Did 1,3). Compare HOLTZ, *Paul*, p. 391 (Did.); D. WENHAM, *Paul's Use* (n. 120), pp. 15-16 (Pet).

71. See, e.g., U. LUZ, *Matthäus* I, 1985, pp. 75-76: "In der *Didache* wird die Mt-Redaktion zweifellos vorausgesetzt"; "Man muß m.E. ernsthaft damit rechnen, daß 1 Petr Mt voraussetzt". — On Did 1,3, see my *Paul*, pp. 298-299 (= 544-545); C.M. TUCK-ETT, *Synoptic Tradition in the Didache*, in J.-M. SEVRIN (ed.), *The New Testament in Early Christianity* (BETL, 86), Leuven, 1989, pp. 197-230, esp. 217-224. — For a (rather unconvincing) reply to Tuckett, cf. W. RORDORF, *Does the Didache Contain Jesus Tradition Independently of the Synoptic Gospels?*, in H. WANSBROUGH (ed.), *Jesus and the Oral Gospel Tradition* (n. 2), pp. 394-423 esp. 401-402; A. TUILIER, *La* Didachè *et le problème synoptique*, in C.N. JEFFORD (ed.), *The* Didache *in Context* (NTSupp, 77), Leiden, Brill, 1995, pp. 110-130, esp. 112, 127.

72. *Clothed with Christ*, p. 99. Contrast Wilson's reading of the same passage (*Paul*, p. 299 = 545): "Comparison with 1 Corinthians 4.12b, where the ideas of cursing, blessing, and persecution are combined in a very different literary permutation, is one clue to Paul's compositional freedom". Cf. *Love* (n. 4), p. 170.

73. See my *Paul*, p. 298 (= 544), n. 175 (reference to B. Layton, 1968, *et al.*). Koester's 1957 position is now repeated *ad litteram* in his *Ancient Christian Gospels*, p. 17.

Luke who in Lk 6,27-28 added two clauses to the two-fold command of the Q-tradition[74],

Q 27b ἀγαπᾶτε   τοὺς ἐχθροὺς ὑμῶν,   A
27c καλῶς ποιεῖτε   τοῖς μισοῦσιν ὑμᾶς   (A)
28a εὐλογεῖτε   τοὺς καταρωμένους ὑμᾶς, (B)
Q 28b προσεύχεσθε περὶ τῶν ἐπηρεαζόντων ὑμᾶς   B

there is little doubt that the same clause εὐλογεῖτε τοὺς καταρωμένους ὑμῖν[75] in Did 1,3 is in one way or another dependent on the Gospel of Luke. The parallel to this εὐλογεῖτε in 1 Cor 4,12 is significantly different. In a list of tribulations Paul expresses his response to ill-treatment in three antitheses:

12 b λοιδορούμενοι εὐλογοῦμεν,   A
c   διωκόμενοι ἀνεχόμεθα,   B
13 a δυσφημούμενοι παρακαλοῦμεν.   A

It is quite irrelevant to declare here that "the variation between the Pauline and Gospel forms is no greater than the variation between the Lukan and Matthean forms"[76]. There is no Matthean form of the εὐλογεῖτε clause and the Pauline parallels (Rom 12,14; and subsidiarily 1 Cor 4,12) ought to be studied not as "echoes" of Lk 6,28a but as possible antecedents in Christian paraenesis of this Lukan clause[77].

---

74. See *Paul*, p. 297 (= 543). See now also F. BOVON, *Lukas*, 1989, p. 315: "Chiastisch hat Lukas beide Imperative aus Q paraphrasiert". — On Lk 6,27c, note Tuckett's reaction: "the strongest argument for the activity of LkR concerns the use of καλῶς ποιεῖτε», whereas "Luke's use of μισέω here may well reflect the use of his source" (p. 218, and n. 95). But see now also P. HOFFMANN, *Q 6,22 in der Rezeption durch Lukas*, in C. MAYER, *et al.* (eds.), *Nach den Anfängen fragen*. FS G. Dautzenberg, Gießen, 1994, 293-326, p. 296 (= ID., *Tradition und Situation*, 1995, p. 165): "In Lk 6,27c steht das Verb in Verdacht, lukanisch zu sein. Insofern stellt die beliebte Argumentation für Q mit einem Stichwortzusammenhang zwischen Lk 6,22a und Lk 6,27c einen Zirkelschluß dar".
75. And the phrase τοῖς μισοῦσιν ὑμᾶς (Lk 6,27c: cf. n. 74) switched to ἀγαπᾶτε (φιλεῖτε) τοὺς μισοῦντας ὑμᾶς in Did 1,3.
76. DUNN, *Jesus Tradition in Paul*, p. 162.
77. On Rom 12,14, cf. *Paul*, p. 296 (= 542); and Thompson's reply, *Clothed with Christ*, pp. 97-98. Is it really "a *non-sequitur*" when I said: "In that hypothesis (viz. διωκόντων MtR) Paul could not have taken διώκοντας from the synoptic saying" (p. 98)? He notes that "the similarity with Matthew's version is less clear. ... Nevertheless, ... we should not make much of the difference" (*ibid.*). On the similarities with Luke: "καταρᾶσθε corresponds to τοὺς καταρωμένους, although Luke has the enemies cursing whereas Paul prohibits Christians from cursing" (p. 97); "The exact formal agreement in Luke and Paul (εὐλογεῖτε) proves nothing, since in both passages this is the form we should expect" (p. 98). — If someone explains Lk 6,28a as "derived from Christian paraenesis (1 Cor. 4,12; Rom. 12.14)" (see now also J. BECKER, above n. 25), is it then correct to say that "this begs the question at issue"? Cf. THOMPSON, p. 99.

Beside 1 Cor 13,2 and 4,12, some lists of allusions also include 14,37:
ἐπιγινωσκέτω ἃ γράφω ὑμῖν ὅτι κυρίου ἐστὶν ἐντολή, but this is
rather a reference to Paul's apostolic authority[78].

II

1 Corinthians 7,10-11

10 a   τοῖς δὲ γεγαμηκόσιν παραγγέλλω,
              οὐκ ἐγὼ ἀλλὰ ὁ κύριος,
   b   γυναῖκα ἀπὸ ἀνδρὸς μὴ χωρισθῆναι,
11 a   — ἐὰν δὲ καὶ χωρισθῇ,
              μενέτω ἄγαμος ἢ τῷ ἀνδρὶ καταλλαγήτω, —
   b   καὶ ἄνδρα γυναῖκα μὴ ἀφιέναι.

There are good reasons for devoting the second part of my paper to
the divorce saying in 1 Cor 7,10-11. In this case at least there is something like a scholarly consensus. It is now extremely rare that arguments
such as the use of ὁ κύριος or the present tense of the verb παραγγέλλω are cited against the view that Paul is referring to a saying of the
earthly Jesus[79]. However encouraging this consensus may be, there is a

78. Cf. Furnish, *Jesus*, p. 62. Ctr. the lists in Koester, *Ancient Christian Gospels*,
p. 53; Fitzmyer (above n. 21); *et al*. Antoinette C. Wire treats 14,37 together with 7,10-
11 and 9,14 as "argument from the Lord's command", but here "Paul is not referring to
some unattested saying of Jesus but to a command he has received spiritually". Cf. A.C.
Wire, *The Corinthian Women Prophets. A Reconstruction through Paul's Rhetoric*, Minneapolis, MN, Fortress, 1990, pp. 33-35, esp. 34. Cf. P. Richardson – P. Gooch, *Logia
of Jesus in 1 Corinthians*, in D. Wenham (ed.), *The Jesus Tradition Outside the Gospels*
(Gospel Perspectives, 5), Sheffield, JSOT, 1985, 39-42, pp. 42-44: 1 Cor 7,10-11; 9,14
(Jesus' teaching) and 14,37 (p. 44: "a command from the risen Lord"); Kertelge (below
n. 111), p. 107: "V. 37 (ist) als Ausdruck für einen höchst autoritativen Anspruch des
Apostels zu lesen", with reference to J.D.G. Dunn, *The Responsible Congregation (1 Cor
14,26-40)*, in L. de Lorenzi (ed.), *Charisma und Agape (1 Kor 12–14)* (Benedictina, 7),
Rome, Benedictina, 1983, pp. 201-236, esp. 233: "We gain from these verses a valuable
insight into Paul's conception of his own authority". — On 1 Cor, see the references to
B. Fjärstedt (1973), C.M. Tuckett (1983), P. Richardson (1984), *et al*. in *Paul*, p. 272-277
(= 518-523).
   79. P. Richardson, *'I Say, not the Lord': Personal Opinion, Apostolic Authority and
the Development of Early Christian Halakah*, in *Tyndale Bulletin* 31 (1980) 65-86, p. 71:
"though it flies in the face of the majority opinion, I am attracted to the view of Oscar
Cullmann...". Contrast P. Richardson – P. Gooch, *Logia of Jesus* (n. 78), p. 59: the ref-
erence to Cullmann is now relegated to a footnote and followed by "per contra W.D.
Davies..." (p. 59 n. 59).
   For a divergent opinion, cf. M.R. D'Angelo, *Remarriage and the Divorce Sayings
Attributed to Jesus*, in W.P. Roberts (ed.), *Divorce and Remarriage*, Kansas City, MO,
Sheed and Ward, 1990, pp. 78-106, esp. 87-88: a prophetic saying, attributed to a prophet

great divergence of opinion on further questions about the function of this text in Paul's letter to the Corinthians and its relationship to the Synoptic divorce sayings. Jerome Murphy-O'Connor's interpretation of the passage (1981)[80], which I briefly discussed in 1984[81], has received a new summary presentation in his commentary in *NJBC*[82]. Raymond F. Collins, my former colleague, begins his book on *Divorce in the New Testament* (1992) with "A Problem at Corinth"[83] and the title most frequently cited in his first chapter is "The Divorced Woman in 1 Cor 7:10-11". Andreas Lindemann (*Die Funktion der Herrenworte*, 1992) notes explicitly: "Am stärksten berühren sich meine Überlegungen mit den Ausführungen bei J. Murphy-O'Connor"[84]. M.-O'C. is a reputed specialist in the study of *St. Paul's Corinth*[85]. These data, taken together, were for me a strong incentive to reconsider in this paper his view on 1 Cor 7,10-11. It can be summarized as follows.

When Paul addresses the married (v. 10a τοῖς γεγαμηκόσιν) he has in mind a very specific case. He first intended to make a personal statement (παραγγέλλω) but "then it suddenly struck him that the authority of a dominical logion would reinforce his position". Hence the awkward formulation, οὐκ ἐγὼ ἀλλὰ ὁ κύριος: "The invocation of the dominical directive is an afterthought". The wife is mentioned first: γυναῖκα ἀπὸ ἀνδρὸς μὴ χωρισθῆναι. This passive voice should be taken seriously ("to be separated"): "7,10b reflects a Jewish milieu in which the right to divorce belonged exclusively to the husband". One should expect the husband to be mentioned first, but Paul changed the order and this reverse order has to do with the application to a particular case. The parenthetical clause makes it clear. Ἐὰν δὲ καὶ χωρισθῇ is a reference

other than the apostle himself; reported with reply by R.F. Collins, *Divorce* (below n. 83), pp. 30-31. Less convincing is "the implication" Collins proposes in the use of παραγγέλλω: "Paul's use of the word suggests that he is not appealing to his own authority; rather, he seems to be appealing to the authority of another" (p. 30; cf. p. 242 n. 106: "the root connotation of the verb is to transmit a message"). It is preferable not to anticipate Paul's οὐκ ἐγώ in the use of the verb.

80. J. MURPHY-O'CONNOR, *The Divorced Woman in 1 Cor 7:10-11*, in *JBL* 100 (1981) 601-606.

81. *Paul*, pp. 316-318 (= 562-564).

82. *The First Letter to the Corinthians*, in *NJBC*, 1990, 798-815, p. 804.

83. R.F. COLLINS, *Divorce in the New Testament* (Good News Studies, 38), Collegeville, MN, Glazier, 1992, pp. 9-39 and 233-246 (notes).

84. *Funktion* (n. 3), p. 678 n. 8.

85. Cf. J. TAYLOR, *Jerome Murphy-O'Connor, O.P.*, in J. MURPHY-O'CONNOR, *The École Biblique and the New Testament: A Century of Scholarship (1890-1990)* (NTOA, 13), Freiburg/Schw., Universitätsverlag; Göttingen, Vandenhoeck & Ruprecht, 1990, pp. 103-125, esp. 114-117: "The Corinthian Correspondence" (with bibliographical note, p. 114 n. 17). See also pp. 186-190 (Bibliography); add: *What Paul Knew of Jesus*, in *Scripture Bulletin* 12 (1981) 35-40.

to a specific incident at Corinth: a divorce was about to take place when Paul's informants left the city and this pending divorce could have been finalized by the time the letter reached Corinth. We should imagine a husband preparing to divorce for ascetic reasons and his wife naturally thinking of remarriage. This is suggested as "a new interpretation designed to do justice to all aspects of the text". But how new is this interpretation, and does it really do justice to all aspects of the text?

In the paper I read at the Colloquium (August 10, 1994) I tried to answer these questions by proposing an alternative reading of 1 Cor 7,10-11 (and 12-16). For the "Synoptic Parallels" I could refer to my "Paul and the Sayings of Jesus" (1986)[86], now updated in two more recent contributions[87]. In the course of 1995 new essays on the divorce sayings in the Gospels and Paul were published. In particular, the well balanced treatment of 1 Cor 7,10-11 in the EKK commentary by Wolfgang Schrage deserves special mention. References to these recent studies are added here in the footnotes[88].

Μὴ χωρισθῆναι

Regarding the passive χωρισθῆναι translated as "to be separated" and the Jewish situation of this terminology, M.-O'C. relies on

---

86. *Paul*, pp. 312-315 (= 558-561).

87. F. NEIRYNCK, *The Divorce Saying in Q 16:18*, in *Louvain Studies* 20 (1995) 201-218; *De echtscheidingslogia in de evangeliën* (Mededeling, Klasse der Letteren, 21 januari 1995), in *Academiae Analecta* 58 (1996) 21-42.

88. W. SCHRAGE, *Der erste Brief an die Korinther. 2. Teilband: 1 Kor 6,12–11,16* (EKK, 7/2), Solothurn-Düsseldorf, Benziger; Neukirchen-Vluyn, Neukirchener, 1995, esp. pp. 97-103 (and 92-93, 116-121). Referred to here by the author's name.

For exegetical study combined with references to pastoral problems of divorce and remarriage, see N. BAUMERT, *Antifeminismus bei Paulus? Einzelstudien* (FzB, 68), Würzburg, Echter, 1992, 207-260: "VI. Die Freiheit der/des unschuldig Geschiedenen: 1 Kor 7,10f"; ID., *Frau und Mann bei Paulus. Überwindung eines Mißverständnisses*, Würzburg, Echter, 1992, ²1993; cf. ID., *Ehelosigkeit und Ehe im Herrn: Eine Neuinterpretation von 1 Kor 7* (FzB, 47), Würzburg, Echter, 1984; and more recently, H. FRANKEMÖLLE, *Ehescheidung und Wiederverheiratung von Geschiedenen im Neuen Testament*, in T. SCHNEIDER (ed.), *Geschieden, wiederverheiratet, abgewiesen? Antworten der Theologie* (QD, 157), Freiburg, Herder, 1995, 28-50; J. KREMER, *Jesu Wort zur Ehescheidung. Bibeltheologische Überlegungen zum Schreiben der Päpstlichen Glaubenskongregation von 14.9.1994*, in *Stimmen der Zeit* 213 (1995) 89-105; reprinted in T. SCHNEIDER (ed.), *Geschieden*, 51-67; M. THEOBALD, *Jesu Wort von der Ehescheidung. Gesetz oder Evangelium?*, in *Theologische Quartalschrift* 175 (1995) 109-124. — See also: J. NOLLAND, *The Gospel Prohibition of Divorce: Tradition History and Meaning*, in *JSNT* 58 (1995) 19-35; cf. ID., *Luke 9:21–18:34* (WBC, 35B), Dallas TX, Word Books, 1993, 816-821 (Lk 16,18).

Fitzmyer's article on the divorce texts (1976)[89]. But a more recent state-ment by Fitzmyer is quite unambiguous: "in saying that 'the wife should not separate from her husband,' Paul's formulation is already adapted to a Greco-Roman setting, where divorce instituted by a woman was possible (cf. the Palestinian setting in the formulation of Luke 16:18)"[90]. In the light of Paul's use of ἀφιέναι for the husband and the wife alike in vv. 12 (μὴ ἀφιέτω αὐτήν) and 13 (μὴ ἀφιέτω τὸν ἄνδρα) and of χωρίζεσθαι for both in v. 15 (εἰ δὲ ὁ ἄπιστος χωρίζεται, χωριζέσθω) one can argue, not for an opposition between "a Greco-Roman cultural setting" in v. 13 and "a Jewish milieu" reflected in v. 10b[91], but for the correspondence in Paul's own formulation of the Jesus tradition between μὴ χωρισθῆναι and μὴ ἀφιέναι precisely not in the sense of a passive "be divorced" and an active "divorce"[92] (not even, I think, in the sense of "sich scheiden lassen", "to allow herself to be separated")[93]: "Das χωρισθῆναι muß parallel dem ἀφιέναι v. 11 die aktive Handlung der Scheidung bedeuten" (Lietzmann)[94].

89. J.A. Fitzmyer, *The Matthean Divorce Texts and Some New Palestinian Evidence*, in *Theological Studies* 37 (1976) 197-226, pp. 198-200 and 211; = Id., *To Advance the Gospel: New Testament Essays*, New York, Crossroad, 1981, 79-111, pp. 81 and 89-90. Compare P.J. Tomson's observation: "This terminology corresponds to the distinct legal position of man and woman in Jewish law" (with reference to Fitzmyer). Cf. P.J. Tomson, *Paul and the Jew-ish Law: Halakha in the Letters of the Apostle to the Gentiles* (CRINT, 3/1), Assen – Maas-tricht, Van Gorcum; Minneapolis, MN, Fortress, 1990, pp. 97-149 ("The Halakha in First Corinthians"), here p. 118; see also his *Paulus und das Gesetz: die konkreten Halachot über Ehe und Scheidung 1. Kor 7*, in K. Ebert (ed.), *Alltagswelt und Ethik. FS A. Weyer*, Wup-pertal, 1988, 157-175. Tomson's clause is quoted by Brian S. Rosner in (less evident) con-nection with his own statement that "Paul may well have thought of the words of Jesus to which he refers as having some basis in Scripture". Cf. B.S. Rosner, *Paul, Scripture and Ethics. A Study of 1 Corinthians 5–7* (AGJU, 22), Leiden, Brill, 1994, p. 168.
90. *Pauline Theology* (n. 21), 1990, p. 1415 (= 1989, p. 104). See also his *Luke*, vol. 2, 1985, p. 1120.
91. Cf. *The Divorced Woman*, p. 602. In Tomson's (less convincing) opinion, "the others" who were called neither "unmarried" nor "married" presented a category in between: "they were married informally" and in their case Paul "did not consider a for-mal marriage terminated" (*Paul* [n. 89], p. 118).
92. *Ibid.*, p. 605 (cf. Fitzmyer, 1976, p. 211).
93. *Ibid.*, p. 602. On this causative sense of the passive, cf. BDR § 314.
94. *Paul*, p. 318 (= 564). Cf. Lindemann, *Funktion* (n. 3), p. 681 n. 21. See also Baumert, *Antifeminismus* (n. 88), p. 256 n. 579: "Andernfalls wäre inhaltlich V 10b [!] gleich 11b: Die Frau soll nicht getrennt werden (durch den Mann) und der Mann soll sie nicht fortschicken" (in reply to Fitzmyer and Murphy-O'Connor); Schrage, p. 99: "das Passiv (steht) oft im Sinne von 'sich lassen', aber auch im Sinne des 'sich Scheiden', setzt also nicht voraus, daß die Initiative vom Mann ausgeht"; and n. 265, with reference to my *Paul* (p. 318 = 564: "Paul's injunction to reconciliation implies an active part of the wife: τῷ ἀνδρὶ καταλλαγήτω"). Compare the use of καταλλάσσω in P. Oxy. I, 104 (A.D. 96): ἐὰν ἀπαλλαγῇ τοῦ ἀνδρὸς μέχρι οὗ ... καταλλαγῇ. Cf. S.E. Porter, *Καταλλάσσω in Ancient Greek Literature, with Reference to the Pauline Writings* (Estudios de Filología Neotestamentaria, 5), Córdoba, El Almendro, 1994, p. 67 (and pp. 119-121: 1 Cor 7,11).

Ἐὰν δὲ καὶ χωρισθῇ...

The most distinctive trait in M.-O'C.'s "new" interpretation concerns the parenthetical clause: ἐὰν δὲ καὶ χωρισθῇ... As far as I see, the reading he proposes was suggested for the first time by Leopold J. Rückert in 1836: Paul writes "mit Rücksicht auf einem bestimmten Falle", "*Wenn sie sich aber etwa schon getrennt haben sollte*, nehmlich vor Empfang dieser jetzigen Anordnung"[95]. The first reactions were rather negative (Meyer 1839, de Wette 1841, Winer [6]1855, Godet 1886, Schmiedel 1891). A more positive response came from Hoffmann (1866), Heinrici (1881) and Bachmann (1909): "if such a separation has already taken place". For J. Weiss (1910) this is a possible explanation, although he finally decided to follow C. Holsten (1880) and considered v. 11a a later casuistic interpolation. The possibility that ἐὰν δὲ καὶ χωρισθῇ may refer to the past is also mentioned by É.-B. Allo (1934: "ἐάν est bien la particule d'éventualité la plus générale, mais le καί pourrait marquer un fait déjà posé, connu"). Allo himself was rather undecided[96], but his formulation was taken up and further developed first by D.L. Dungan (1971: "The divorce was about to happen when the letter bearers left Corinth to come to Paul. Thus it could have become a completed act by the time they had returned with Paul's answer and so he writes as if it were...")[97] and then, following Dungan, by M.-O'C.[98].

Other commentators who consider ἐὰν δὲ καὶ χωρισθῇ to be a reference to the past prefer this explanation in order to avoid the intolerable

95. L.J. RÜCKERT, *Der erste Brief Pauli an die Korinther*, Leipzig, K.F. Köhler, 1836, p. 189. For the reactions, see the commentaries on 1 Cor, *ad locum*; and Winer's *Grammatik*, [8]1855, p. 262 ("ist unwahr"; ET 1870: "is incorrect").

96. "On ne peut guère décider si les mots ἐὰν δὲ καὶ χωρισθῇ se rapportent au passé, au futur, ou envisagent la séparation en général, sans rapport à un temps déterminé"; "aussi notre traduction reste imprécise à dessein" (p. 163: "au cas même d'une séparation"). Cf. p. 164: "on peut se trouver en face de cas de séparations. ... il peut même y en avoir dans l'avenir (contre *Bachmann*)".

97. D.L. DUNGAN, *The Sayings of Jesus in the Churches of Paul: The Use of the Synoptic Tradition in the Regulation of Early Church Life*, Oxford, Blackwell; Philadelphia, PA, Fortress, 1971, p. 90 n. 1: "Perhaps the best solution to the time-question of the opening phrase has been given by Allo, following J. Weiss". For Dungan it is "a potential case of divorce, which was being instigated by the wife", either "she wanted a divorce for ascetic reasons" (what he calls the 'usual' view) or "she wanted a divorce in order to marry someone else" (what he calls 'normal' divorce; p. 92). See now also SCHRAGE, p. 101: "die Beziehung auf eine bereits vollzogene Trennung" is possible; "Diese Deutung macht sachlich weniger Schwierigkeiten" (n. 279: Rückert, *et al.*). Murphy-O'Connor can be added to this n. 279; Allo is rather uncertain (cf. n. 96).

98. But now (and that is new) in connection with the "true value" given to the *passive* χωρισθῆναι (*The Divorced Woman*, p. 603 n. 7).

impression that Paul would seem to permit (future) exceptions to the dominical command. Too easily, however, they presuppose that the prohibition of divorce is made known by Paul for the first time in this letter, so that in the past violations of the command could have taken place unwittingly (*unwissentlich*: H. Lietzmann, H. Conzelmann)[99]. Dungan's solution is quite different: Paul permits the divorce if it has taken place, and this is in contradiction to the brief formulation in v. 10b (μὴ χωρισθῆναι) but corresponds to "the central thrust of Jesus' original statements" forbidding remarriage but not divorce[100]. In 7,11a and also in the case of mixed marriages (7,15) "divorce is allowed (reluctantly). Remarriage, on the other hand, is not. Rather, in both cases, eventual reconciliation is held out as the alternative"[101]. M.-O'C. replies to Dungan by saying that "an injunction directed to a particular case in 7:11a cannot be applied to a very different type of situation and so 7:15 must be interpreted in terms of the right to remarriage implicit in a legal divorce". This contrast between 7,11a and 15a brings M.-O'C. to his much quoted concluding statements[102]:

> The truth of the matter is that Paul is not consistent, and recognition of this point is of crucial importance for a correct understanding of Paul's attitude towards the dominical logion...
> The dominical logion does not control Paul's thought in 7:1-11, it is brought in as an afterthought because of its pastoral utility. Nor does the logion constrain him in 7:15; he does precisely what the logion forbids.

Thus, for M.-O'C., Paul refuses a divorce in 7,10-11, and permits a divorce in 7,15 "in flat opposition to Jesus' prohibition"[103].

That the parenthesis in 1 Cor 7,11a refers to a divorce that has taken place, or at least has been initiated, is far from obvious. Ἐὰν χωρισθῇ

---

99. LIETZMANN, p. 31. Cf. CONZELMANN, p. 145: "Jedenfalls klingt der Ausdruck so, als teile ihn Paulus zum erstenmal mit". With an echo in COLLINS, *Divorce*, p. 35: "Paul's tone seems to suggest that the Corinthians had not been aware of the Lord's teaching on divorce". Cf. BAUMERT, *Ehelosigkeit* (n. 88), p. 64 n. 131: "Ich kann diesen 'Klang' nicht heraushören". Following W. Meeks, J.M. Gundry-Volf (in this volume, p. 527) assumes that Jesus' divorce saying was known to the Corinthians. Cf. W.A. MEEKS, *The First Urban Christians. The Social World of the Apostle Paul*, New Haven, CT – London, Yale University, 1983, p. 101.

100. *Sayings* (n. 97), p. 140.

101. *Ibid.*, p. 28.

102. *The Divorced Woman*, p. 606. M.-O'C.'s conclusion is quoted by LINDEMANN, *Funktion* (n. 3), p. 687 n. 50; R.W. WALL, art. *Divorce*, in *ABD* 2 (1992) 217-219, p. 218: "Jesus' prohibition (qualified) as an 'afterthought because of its pastoral utility' rather than as a normative principle"; COLLINS, *Divorce*, p. 34: "the ... dominical logion does not, per se, control Paul's thought". But see BAUMERT, *Antifeminismus*, p. 257 n. 580: "zeigt nur die ganze Problematik seiner Interpretation".

103. *NJBC*, p. 805.

normally represents an event as a future possibility (of course, "conceived as taking place before the time of the action of the main verb") and I do not see how an added καί would imply that the divorce is conceived as prior to Paul's writing (or to the Corinthians' reading of the letter)[104]. Ἐὰν δὲ καὶ (γαμήσῃς) is used in 7,28 to introduce a generic condition, but for M.-O'C. this cannot be the sense of 7,11a: "this view loses all plausibility when the passive chōristhēnai is given its true value because it is the one initiating the divorce who is suspected of an interest in remarrying"[105]. But in his own description of the case in Corinth the one initiating the divorce is a husband who had renounced sexual relations: "Should the divorce go through, even against the opposition of the wife, it seems inevitable that she ... should think very seriously of remarriage"[106]. On which side, then, is the loss of plausibility?

Dungan and M.-O'C. rightly keep the topics of 7,10-11 and 7,12-16 separate: in their view the case of the woman in v. 11a is not a kind of mixed-marriage case of a woman separated before becoming a christian[107].

104. *Paul*, p. 319 (= 565) n. 297; BAUMERT, *Ehelosigkeit* (n. 88), p. 66 n. 135. On ἐὰν καί, see E.D. BURTON, *Galatians* (ICC), Edinburgh, Clark, 1921, p. 326: "in 1 Cor 7,11.28 it stands in a protasis referring to a condition which the apostle has in a preceding sentence said ought never to occur; its force may be reproduced in English by an emphatic form (if she *do* depart, 1 Cor 7,11; if thou *dost* marry, 7,28)". Cf. SCHRAGE, p. 101: "Sprachlich das Normale wäre zweifellos, wenn Paulus mit dem ἐάν-Satz einen künftigen Eventualfall ins Auge faßte ('falls sie sich aber scheiden läßt'), und diese Deutung ist auch hier nicht auszuschließen"; LINDEMANN, *Funktion*, p. 684: "(er) kommentiert in V. 11a *möglicherweise eintretende* (oder bereits eingetretene) *besondere Fälle*" (my emphasis; cf. p. 682). The presentation of a "fait accompli" as the *opinio communis* in COLLINS, *Divorce* (p. 25) could be more nuanced.

Baumert now considers the possibility that "Paulus zwar allgemein spricht, aber einen konkreten Fall im Auge hat" (*Antifeminismus*, p. 258 n. 582, with reference to M.-O'C.); "Vielleicht denkt Paulus dabei an einen aktuellen Fall in Korinth" (*Frau und Mann*, p. 54, again with reference to M.-O'C.). But still now he notes: "Der griechische Aorist ist zwar mit einer relativen Vorzeitigkeit (wenn eine Lösung vollzogen ist) genügend erklärt und besagt dann Allgemeingültigkeit" (n. 89, with reference to *Ehelosigkeit*, pp. 65-66). Some commentators tend to avoid discussion of the grammatical difficulty: see COLLINS, *Divorce*, p. 241 n. 96. It is not quite clear to me how, on the one hand, "the separation belongs to the relative past, rather than to the absolute past" (*ibid.*, p. 25) and, on the other, the use of ἐάν + subjunctive "constitutes a grammatical argument in favor of the idea that Paul is writing about a real case". Cf. LINDEMANN, *Funktion*, p. 682 n. 26: "das grammatische Problem kann jedenfalls nicht von modernen theologisch-hermeneutischen Voraussetzungen her gelöst werden".

105. *The Divorced Woman*, p. 603 n. 7.
106. *Ibid.*, p. 604.
107. On R. Pesch, *et al.*, cf. my *Paul*, pp. 316, 318-319 (= 562, 564-565); echoed in COLLINS, *Divorce*, p. 28 and nn. 93-94. See now also S. SCHULZ, *Neutestamentliche Ethik*, Zürich, Theologischer Verlag, 1987, p. 430. Moiser argues, without good reason, that "the married" in 7,10-11 are those who were already married at the time of their conversion, and not simply the married in general as in vv. 2-6. Cf. J. MOISER, *A Reassessment of Paul's View of Marriage with Reference to 1 Cor 7*, in *JSNT* 18 (1983) 103-122.

What more can be said? "Since Paul seems to imply that it was the wife who actively sought the divorce, it is hardly likely that he was thinking of a woman who had been put aside by an ascetical husband". Can we be more specific? Was it a divorce on ascetic grounds? But why then Paul's warning against remarriage (μενέτω ἄγαμος)? Or was it for some other reason? With the intention of remarrying? "The data provided by Paul are not sufficient to allow for an accurate reconstruction of the situation which he has in mind"[108].

Moreover, it remains questionable whether Paul in v. 11a envisages the real situation of a particular case in Corinth. The command that "the wife should not separate from her husband; but if she does..." can be translated *ad sensum* in the plural: "wives should not separate from their husbands; but if they do...". The presentation of "the divorced woman" (in singular) is an exegetical dramatization of Paul's parenthetical remark. (1) Ἐάν with subjunctive is the appropriate grammatical form for expressing a general condition[109]. (2) From ch. 7 one retains the impression of a systematic treatment of all possible questions (thus in 7,12-16 "jeden in Frage kommenden Einzelfall berücksichtigend")[110], which justifies some doubt whether every possibility Paul formulates is meant to be concrete reality in Corinth. (3) The suggestion that the case

108. Quotations from COLLINS, *Divorce*, pp. 28-29. Cf. Baumert's reconstruction: "so macht er hier der Frau, die *aus einem Wunsch nach Enthaltsamkeit* von ihrem Mann weggeht (gegangen ist), bewußt, daß sie später nicht mehr einen anderen heiraten darf, sondern dann auch *ihrem Vorsatz treu bleiben soll*, falls sie nicht wieder mit ihrem Mann zusammenzieht"; "Paulus sieht ... sehr nüchtern die Grenzen und Gefährdungen des Menschen" (*Frau und Mann*, p. 55; emphasis mine).

109. Cf. above, n. 104. See now also G.D. FEE (n. 43), 1987, p. 295 n. 23: "the present general condition ... represents for him [Paul] a hypothetical 'if ever such a condition exists'"; with reference to the review of Dungan's *Sayings* by B.A. PEARSON, in *Interpretation* 26 (1972) 348-351: "only the most boorish writer of Greek would use the subjunctive with the particle *ean* to indicate past action, and one would be hard pressed to find an example of such usage in the New Testament"; on the addition of καί (Allo): "that this, too, is wrong can be seen from the use of *ean de kai* + subjunctive in verse 28 of the very same chapter!" (p. 350; cf. above, p. 164).

A.C. WIRE, in *The Corinthian Women Prophets* (above n. 78) notes that ἐάν + aorist subjunctive can occasionally refer to "a condition impending in the past" (cf. BDF § 373,3), "but this occurs in sentences using past tenses in the main clause" (p. 276 n. 8). In 1 Cor 7,11a it "does not refer to past events but to the present and the future, so it cannot be explained as Paul's advice to an already separated woman. Apparently he thinks that some women will leave their husbands even after being instructed by the Lord's word. The lack of a similar aside to the men ... suggest that the men are not the problem to Paul on this front" (p. 84).

110. LINDEMANN, *Funktion*, p. 682. Compare his paper in this volume, *Die paulinische Ekklesiologie angesichts der Lebenswirklichkeit der christlichen Gemeinde in Korinth*, p. 77: "in erstaunlicher Ausführlichkeit", "die detaillierte kasuistische Argumentation". Cf. A. STROBEL (ZBK, 6/1, 1989): "Das 'die übrigen' bezieht sich auf einen jeden weiteren möglichen Fall" (p. 121).

of a divorced woman (v. 11a) was the occasion for Paul's citing the command of the Lord (vv. 10b.11b) may be reversible. For Paul, in his chapter on marriage questions, the traditional logion on divorce is a "must", and the absolute prohibition of divorce may have led to an "interpretierende Abwandlung"[111]. In a case of divorce two options are possible: μενέτω ἄγαμος ἢ τῷ ἀνδρὶ καταλλαγήτω (v. 11a). Yet, the disjunctive ἢ should not prevent us from understanding the first (remain unmarried) as the prerequisite for the second (reconciliation), and thus, in this less than ideal situation, Paul's advice rejoins the inspiration of the Jesus logion[112].

The Jesus Tradition

Since the reference to a command of the Lord in 1 Cor 7,10-11 is not a "quotation" of the Jesus saying, the discussion of a textual *Vorlage* could be set aside as a moot question[113]. Yet, the very form of the double phrase in vv. 10b.11b gives occasion for reconstruction, and under that aspect it is quite different from 9,14 (διέταξεν) ἐκ τοῦ εὐαγγελίου ζῆν. Furthermore, the prohibition of divorce, in some sense unique in Paul, has been described as "the best-attested tradition in the gospels"[114].

111. The expression is used by K. Kertelge with reference to 1 Cor 7,12-16 (no comment on 7,11a) in *Autorität des Gesetzes und Autorität Jesu bei Paulus*, in H. FRANKEMÖLLE – K. KERTELGE (eds.), *Vom Urchristentum zu Jesus*. FS J. Gnilka, Freiburg, Herder, 1989, 358-376 (pp. 367-374: "Die Lehrautorität Jesu im Lehrwort des Paulus", 1 Cor 7,10; 9,14; 1 Thess 4,15; 1 Cor 14,37), here 369. He avoids to call it "ein Widerspruch": in the apostle's interpretation "kommt der Sinn des vorgegebenen Herrenwortes zu seiner Geltung" (p. 370). Reprinted in *Grundthemen paulinischer Theologie*, Freiburg, Herder, 1991, 92-110 (pp. 101-108; here 103).

112. *Paul*, p. 319 (= 565) n. 296. Cf. H. MERKLEIN, *Die Gottesherrschaft als Handlungsprinzip. Untersuchung zur Ethik Jesu* (FzB, 34), Würzburg, Echter, 1978, ³1984, p. 288: "Insofern würde es genau mit dem Anliegen der Weisung Jesu übereinstimmen, nur daß es dieses Anliegen nun auch über die Trennung hinweg aufrechterhält". See also *"Es ist gut für den Menschen, eine Frau nicht anzufassen". Paulus und die Sexualität nach 1 Kor 7*, in G. DAUTZENBERG (ed.), *Die Frau im Urchristentum* (QD, 95), Freiburg, Herder, 1983, 225-253, p. 236; ID., *Studien zu Jesus und Paulus* (WUNT, 43), Tübingen, 1987, 385-408, p. 394. Cf. SCHRAGE, p. 103 n. 285: "Der Rat zum ἄγαμος-Bleiben hängt ... vermutlich einfach mit der Bevorzugung des μένειν zusammen, allenfalls mit dem Offenhalten einer Versöhnung (so Neirynck im Anschluß an Merklein, weil dadurch der Kontrast zum Scheidungsverbot geringer werde)". Baumert thinks that the text can be clarified by adding (Paul's?) "unausgesprochene Voraussetzung(en)": μενέτω ἄγαμος «falls der Mann wieder geheiratet hat" ἢ τῷ ἀνδρὶ καταλλαγήτω «falls er noch frei ist" (*Frau und Mann*, p. 54; *Antifeminismus*, p. 257).

113. Cf. LINDEMANN, *Funktion*, p. 678.

114. Cf. E.P. SANDERS, *The Historical Figure of Jesus*, London, Allen Lane (Penguin), 1993, pp. 198-200 (p. 198). But see p. 200: "It is typical of the material about Jesus that his precise meaning is uncertain even on this topic".

D.R. Catchpole (1974) wrote a critical response to Dungan's thesis of Matthean originality and to his position on the divorce sayings in the Synoptics[115]. Catchpole himself proposed a double suggestion on tradition(s) behind 1 Cor 7,10-11. First, vv. 10b.11b is one bipartite saying of which the original form may have been a splitting of the statement in Mk 10,9 (second half):

ὃ ὁ θεὸς συνέζευξεν

ἄνθρωπος μὴ χωριζέτω: ἀνὴρ γυναῖκα μὴ ἀφιέτω

γυνὴ ἀπὸ ἀνδρὸς μὴ χωριζέτω.

Like Mk 10,9, this pre-Pauline saying is concerned with divorce alone, not with subsequent remarriage[116]. Second, the parenthesis in v. 11a, which is not simply a Pauline gloss, was based on a traditional saying prohibiting the remarriage of a divorced woman, in Paul's view also a dominical saying (compare the Synoptic divorce sayings)[117]. For Catchpole, both sayings were unrelated primary traditions. Others, like D. Wenham, have tried to show that the sequence of vv. 10b (μὴ χωρισθῆναι) and 11a (ἐὰν..., μενέτω ἄγαμος) has particular links with Mk 10,9 (μὴ χωριζέτω) and 11 (ὃς ἂν ... γαμήσῃ ἄλλην), switching from divorce to remarriage[118]. H. Merklein, now followed by Wolfgang Weiss (1989)[119], has given special emphasis to the parallelism between 1 Cor 7,10b.11b / 11a and Mk 10,9 / 11, "theologischer Grundsatz" in the apodictic prohibition of v. 9 and "praktische Regel" in v. 11[120]:

> ... die Parenthese von 1 Kor 7,11a (bestätigt), daß der Zusatz καὶ γαμήσῃ ἄλλην in Mk 10,11 tatsächlich als eine "Konzession" der Praxis gegenüber dem theologischen Grundsatz Mk 10,9 zu interpretieren ist.
> Der Sache nach dürfte Paulus eine Regel wiedergeben, wie sie ihm aus der Tradition bekannt ist und deren Entstehungsgeschichte man sich ähnlich wie Mk 10,11(f) mit dem Zusatz καὶ γαμήσῃ ἄλλην wird vorzustellen haben.

115. D.R. CATCHPOLE, *The Synoptic Divorce Material as a Tradition-historical Problem*, in *BJRL* 57 (1974-75) 92-127.

116. *Ibid.*, pp. 107, 118. On the two verbs "in marked contrast with Paul's own usage" (sic; p. 107 n. 2), see also B. WITHERINGTON III, *Women in the Earliest Churches* (SNTS MS, 59), Cambridge, University Press, 1988, p. 42: "may indicate something about his source".

117. *Divorce Material*, pp. 106-107. No precise reconstruction is proposed by Catchpole.

118. D. WENHAM, *Paul's Use of the Jesus Tradition: Three Samples*, in ID. (ed.), *The Jesus Tradition* (n. 78), 1985, 7-37, pp. 7-15: "1 Corinthians 7:10,11", esp. p. 8. See now his *Paul* (n. 2), 1995, pp. 242-244, 282-284.

119. Cf. W. WEISS, *"Eine neue Lehre in Vollmacht". Die Streit- und Schulgespräche des Markus-Evangelium* (BZNW, 52), Berlin – New York, de Gruyter, 1989, pp. 177-202 (Mk 10,2-12), esp. p. 196: "Im Hinblick auf Mk 10,2-9.11f erhellt der Vergleich mit 1 Kor 7,10f, daß die Zusammenordnung von Verbot der Ehescheidung und Verbot der Wiederheirat einem vorgegebenem Schema entspricht".

120. *Die Gottesherrschaft* (n. 112), pp. 280, 281. See also R. BUSEMANN, *Die Jüngergemeinde nach Markus 10* (BBB, 57), Bonn, Hanstein, 1983, p. 117.

However, the connection between Mk 10,9 and 11 is redactionally created by Mark, who added the transitional verse 10, and it is far from evident that the Markan pattern of interpretation can be transferred to pre-Pauline tradition[121]. But, apart from questionable traditio-historical linkage[122], is it possible to recognize a comparable praxis behind 1 Cor 7,11a and Mk 10,11?

1. I can quote here a recent statement by M. Theobald[123]:

> Da Mk 10,12 (über Jesus hinaus) die Situation nach dem griechischen und römischen Scheidungsrecht wie 1 Kor 7,10b mit einbezieht, legt sich die Annahme nahe, daß auch jene die Wiederheirat betreffende Wendung mit *der von Paulus in seinen Gemeinden propagierten Praxis* im Zusammenhang steht: *der Tolerierung der Scheidung bei gleichzeitigem Verbot einer Wiederheirat* für den Eheteil, der die Entlassung des Partners zu verantworten hat. Dies dürfte sich in den hellenistischen Gemeinden eingebürgert haben und so auch zu Markus gelangt sein. Daß dieser eine aufgrund von Erfahrung bewährte Praxis in das Jesus-Wort selbst redaktionell eingezeichnet hat, ist, hermeneutisch gesehen, ein bemerkenswerter Vorgang.

Like many other German scholars[124], Theobald proposes a reconstruction of the Q-version of the saying on the basis of Mt 5,32: πᾶς ὁ ἀπολύων τὴν γυναῖκα αὐτοῦ ποιεῖ αὐτὴν μοιχευθῆναι[125]. The phrase on remarriage, "and marries another" (Lk καὶ γαμῶν ἑτέραν, Mk καὶ γαμήσῃ ἄλλην), is understood as a secondary adaptation and mitigation of the radical prohibition of divorce: "das Böse bestehe ... erst in der Wiederheirat"[126]. As indicated elsewhere[127], I am not

---

121. Note Weiss's warning against pre-Markan connection: "Grundsatz und praktische Anwendung nach einem verbreiteten Schema zusammenzuordnen, war auch für Markus naheliegend" (p. 196; contrast MERKLEIN, p. 280: "der Zusammenhang ... war bereits vor Mk bekannt").

122. Even the order woman – man in 1 Cor 7,10-11 has been connected with Mk 10,11-12 in the reading of W 1 *pc* sy^s: "Paul appears to have in mind a dominical saying in which the same order was found, since he gives the woman precedence...". Cf. J.N. BIRDSALL, *The Western Text in the Second Century*, in W.L. PETERSEN (ed.), *Gospel Traditions in the Second Century*, Notre Dame, IN – London, 1989, 3-17, p. 15. For a reply, see R.H. GUNDRY, *Mark* (n. 55), p. 543.

123. *Jesu Wort* (n. 88), p. 114 (emphasis mine).

124. See the references in my *The Divorce Saying in Q 16:18* (n. 87), pp. 206-207 (and 216-217).

125. *Jesu Verbot*, p. 118: "Auf das Konto sekundärer rechtlicher Applikation (geht) auf der griechisch-römischen 'Schiene' (Pl-Mk-Lk) ... die Einführung des Verbots der Wiederheirat; letzteres fehlt in der darin ursprünglicheren Q-Fassung (Mt 5,32)" .

126. Cf. J. KREMER, *Jesu Verbot* (n. 88), p. 57: "Nach Ansicht mancher Ausleger...". Kremer himself regards it as an addition to the original saying (p. 56: "die meisten Exegeten"), but: "Näher liegt es jedoch, in diesem Zusatz ... einfach eine Verdeutlichung der Zurückweisung jeglicher Ehescheidung durch Jesus zu sehen".

127. *Huwelijk en echtscheiding in het evangelie*, in *CBG* 6 (1960) 123-130, pp. 128-129 (response to J. Dupont); *De Jezuswoorden over echtscheiding* (1972), in *Evangelica*

convinced that this is a correct understanding of the remarriage phrase; neither is it a valid reason for eliminating it from the traditional saying. The style of the saying is "casuistic" in the sense that it describes the concrete case of someone who divorces and remarries, without implying that only remarrying is stigmatized in the apodosis[128]. Some of N. Baumert's comments now show the same line of thinking[129]:

> ... (es) handelt es sich bezeichnenderweise immer um Tateinheit von zwei Vergehen: 'seine Frau/ihren Mann entlassen *und* einen anderen Partner heiraten'. ... man (darf) nicht einen Partner entlassen, und (*um*) einen anderen (zu) heiraten.
>
> ... "und heiratet eine andere" gehört wesentlich dazu, damit der Tatbestand des μοιχεύειν gegeben ist; es ist nicht etwa ein "Zusatz", sondern "certainly part of the original prohibition".

Also J. Nolland's divorce-for-the-sake-of-remarriage understanding of the earliest recoverable form of the tradition goes in that line[130], though I am less happy with his sentence on divorce "no more than the logically necessary antecedent of the remarriage". *Tateinheit* is a better word: the unified action of divorce-and-remarriage, which scarcely can be cited in confirmation of the Pauline praxis defined by Theobald as "*Tolerierung der Scheidung* bei gleichzeitigen Verbot einer Wiederheirat".

2. The title of N. Baumert's study, "Die Freiheit der/des unschuldig Geschiedenen"[131], formulates his thesis:

> Das Gebot Jesu, "was Gott verbunden hat, soll der Mensch nicht trennen/scheiden", besagt nur, daß niemand eine Scheidung *betreiben* darf; wenn es eine/r dennoch tut, bleibt die/der unschuldig Geschiedene frei für eine weitere Ehe.[132]
>
> V. 11a [in 1 Cor 7] stimmt mit unserer Deutung der synoptischen Texte überein, insofern immer von dem aktiven Teil formuliert und nur *diesem* eine neue Ehe verwehrt wird.[133]

I, 1982, 821-833, pp. 827-829 (reply to B. Schaller); *The Divorce Saying in Q 16:18*, 1995, p. 217: "the phrase 'and marries another' was most probably found in Q" (cf. *Evangelica II*, 1991, pp. 432, 560).

128. *The Divorce Saying*, p. 218. Compare Gundry's comment on Mk 10,11: "Why would remarriage count as adultery if divorce is not wrong in and of itself, as in v 9". *Mark* (n. 55), p. 541; in reply to D.O. VIA, *The Ethics of Mark's Gospel – in the Middle Time*, Philadelphia, PA, Fortress, 1985, pp. 111-115 (on the "conceivability" of divorce).

129. *Antifeminismus*, p. 249; and pp. 233-234 (with reference to Fitzmyer's comment on Lk 16,18). See also p. 228: the *Tateinheit* is in Mk 10,11 (καί!) "nicht so deutlich wie in V 12" (ἀπολύσασα ... γαμήσῃ).

130. *The Gospel Prohibition of Divorce* (n. 88), p. 33.

131. Cf. above n. 88.

132. *Frau und Mann*, p. 54. Text quoted by H. Frankemölle (*Ehescheidung*, p. 38); see his references to Baumert in nn. 29-34.

133. *Antifeminismus*, p. 257.

The most difficult text for his thesis is undeniably the second half of the Q-saying: καὶ ὁ ἀπολελυμένην γαμῶν μοιχεύει (cf. Mt 5,32b / Lk 16,18b). Theobald, who supports Baumert's approach to 1 Cor 7,11a[134], notes here: "jetzt (fällt) auch auf den *geschiedenen* Teil, wenn er wiederheiratet, der Schatten des Ehebruchs"[135]. Against this traditional interpretation of ἀπολελυμένη, Baumert reads Lk 16,18b as a parallel to Mk 10,12 and explains ἀπολελυμένη as a reflexive middle: "eine, die *sich* getrennt hat, aktiv, aufgrund eigener Initiative"[136]; in Mt 5,32b "(ist) das Medium im gleichen Sinn aktivisch aufzufassen"[137]. Compare again J. Nolland's suggestion that "the second half envisages a situation in which the initiative for the divorce has come from the woman... The sense of ἀπολελυμένην would then be 'a woman who has gained a divorce from' (rather than 'been divorced by') her husband"[138].

In handbooks for translators one can read that the translation "*from* her husband" is preferable "though no presumption is implied as to the initiative in bringing about the divorce"[139]. "A woman divorced from her husband" is now the common translation in English[140], with ἀπολελυμένη understood as a passive. The man who marries a divorcee "commits adultery" because he marries the wife of another man: not even divorce can change the permanent character of marriage.

Baumert justifies his interpretation of ἀπολελυμένη by referring to the "parallel" in Mk 10,12, "the woman who divorces...". But, first, the source of Lk 16,18b is the saying in Q (probably without ἀπὸ ἀνδρός).

134. *Jesu Wort*, p. 111 n. 10 ("mit Recht").

135. *Ibid.*, p. 117: "So kann man hier in der Tat von einem Verbot der 'Wiederheirat Geschiedener' sprechen". Baumert's interpretation of ἀπολελυμένη is not even mentioned.

136. *Antifeminismus*, p. 232.

137. *Ibid.*, p. 235.

138. *The Gospel Prohibition of Divorce*, p. 31; see already his *Luke* (n. 88), 1993, p. 819. It is noteworthy that Baumert and Nolland are mutually independent (cf. p. xii: "the manuscript left my hands in January 1989"; there is no reference to Baumert in his Bibliography, p. 812).

139. J. REILING – J.L. SWELLENGREBEL, *A Translator's Handbook on the Gospel of Luke*, Leiden, Brill, 1971, p. 569 ("The perfect tense of the participle *apolelumenēn* points to a situation in which a woman finds herself after having been divorced from her husband"). Baumert pushes his grammatical argument too far by saying that "bei einem Passiv" Luke should have used ὑπό (*Antifeminismus*, p. 232). Cf. my *The Divorce Saying in Q 16:18*, pp. 212-213: ἀπὸ ἀνδρός probably added by Luke.

140. NRSV, REB, NAB, SV, Fitzmyer, *et al.* NJB: "a woman divorced by her husband" apparently depends on the French version ("une femme répudiée par son mari"). Contrast Nolland: "someone who has gained dismissal from a husband". — On ways in Jewish law in which a woman could manipulate a situation to guarantee the granting of a divorce", see the references above in n. 138; see also H. FRANKEMÖLLE, *Ehescheidung*, pp. 31-33. For a more reserved approach, see my *Echtscheidingslogia* (n. 87).

Second, what is said explicitly in Mk is in any case only implicit in Lk. Baumert's real argument is that, in the woman's case, exclusion from remarriage would be unthinkable without her being personally responsible. The problem, however, is that the man is the one who divorces-and-remarries in the first half of the saying and the one who marries a divorcee in the second half. The woman's responsibility is apparently not the theme of this saying.

1 Cor 7,11a has its own theme: the initiative for the divorce comes from the woman and she should remain unmarried. Can we then conclude: "die/der unschuldig Geschiedene bleibt frei für eine weitere Ehe"? Is it justified that Paul's τῷ ἀνδρὶ καταλλαγήτω be supplemented with our own explanatory "sofern dieser noch frei ist"[141]?

3. Mutual confirmation of 1 Cor 7,11a and the divorce sayings in the gospels is most evident in the traditional view on the πορνεία clauses in Mt: unchastity on the part of the wife is accepted as a legitimate ground for divorce but subsequent remarriage is not allowed[142]. Although such a reading of Mt 19,9 (in the light of 19,10-12) has now gained some new adherents, this sense of divorce (separation – no remarriage) remains, it seems to me, hardly defendable in the context of Mt 19,3-9[143]. And here can then appear in a new form the association of Matthew and Paul[144]:

> Sie haben ... das Wort Jesu von der unbedingten Gültigkeit der Ehe als Norm festgehalten und zugleich anerkannt, daß es Situationen gibt, die eine Scheidung der Ehe ermöglichen – mit der Folge, unverheiratet zu bleiben (1 Kor 7,11) oder neu zu heiraten (Mt 5,32; 19,9).

"I say, not the Lord"

For M.-O'C., Paul in 1 Cor 7,15 permits a full divorce, "essentially the right of remarriage"; Jesus' prohibition of divorce is inappropriate in this case, without relevance to this particular situation. Lindemann's

---

141. *Antifeminismus*, p. 257; *Frau und Mann*, p. 54.

142. J. DUPONT, *Mariage et divorce dans l'Évangile. Matthieu 19,3-12 et parallèles*, Bruges, Desclée De Brouwer, 1959, esp. pp. 69-73 (on 1 Cor 7,11a). See now R.H. GUNDRY, *Matthew*, Grand Rapids MI, Eerdmans, 1982, ²1994, pp. 380-383; W. WEREN, *Matteüs*, 's-Hertogenbosch, KBS; Brugge, Tabor, 1994, pp. 178-179; S.C. BARTON, *Discipleship and Family Ties in Mark and Matthew* (SNTS MS, 80), Cambridge, University Press, 1994, pp. 191-204, esp. 198 (see my review in *ETL* 72, 1996, 238-239).

143. See already *Het evangelisch echtscheidingsverbod*, in *CBG* 4 (1958) 25-46. On the divorce-separation theory (and on the πορνεία – incestuous marriage interpretation), see now *Echtscheidingslogia* (n. 87).

144. H. FRANKEMÖLLE, *Ehescheidung*, p. 47.

comment goes in the same direction: Paul presents "praktikable Alternativen", and: "eben das tut der Apostel — unter ausdrücklichen Hinweis darauf, daß er damit im Widerspruch steht zur Weisung des κύριος". This is apparently meant to be the echo of Paul's introductory phrase: λέγω ἐγὼ οὐχ ὁ κύριος (v. 12)[145]. Furnish is quite explicit on this point[146]:

> In distinction from the way he introduces his later counsel to virgins (v. 25), Paul does not say, in verse 12, that he has no instruction from the Lord. He only indicates that the directives about mixed marriages are his own, *not* the Lord's. Thus the apostle could mean that on this subject he is *departing* from the Lord's instruction. In fact, he does exactly that in verse 15. There he counsels that in one particular circumstance divorce is permissible: "If [in the case of a believer married to an unbeliever] the unbelieving partner separates, let it be so; *in such a case the brother or sister is not bound*. It is to peace that God has called you".

Furnish, however, recognizes that another (more usual) interpretation can be suggested by the parallel in v. 25, "I have no rule from the Lord, but I give my opinion". Verse 12a, on the topic of mixed marriages, can be interpreted accordingly: "since there is no instruction from the Lord, λέγω ἐγώ, I am offering my own advice". Nothing in these words implies the introduction of a *Widerspruch*, and Paul begins, in verses 12-14, by giving instructions "in full accord with the saying of Jesus that he has just cited". The words ἐγὼ οὐχ ὁ κύριος (v. 12) are related to οὐκ ἐγὼ ἀλλὰ ὁ κύριος in v. 10 and add emphasis to that (unique) reference to a command of the Lord. An emphatic phrase is not necessarily an awkward phrase, nor can it be said that the dominical directive is simply brought in as an afterthought[147]. M.-O'C. maintains this idea in his commentary (1990), but now seems to correct it implicitly in a new comment on v. 14: "the simplest interpretation (of ἡγίασται) is that Paul considered the unbeliever holy because by deciding to maintain the

---

145. *Funktion* (n. 3), p. 687. See also, more correctly, p. 682 n. 27: "Die Wendung ἐγὼ οὐχ ὁ κύριος ist lediglich das Pendant zu οὐκ ἐγὼ ... in V. 10a" (in reply to Walter's suggestion; cf. n. 146).

146. *Jesus* (n. 23), p. 46. — Compare N. Walter's emphasis on the difference between 7,25 (no word of the Lord available) and 7,12a, where the formulation could mean: "sage ich, abweichend von einem bekannten Wort des Herrn" (p. 510 = 70). Curiously enough, Walter does not mention 7,15 but 7,12-13 ("nicht an Ehescheidung denken") in contrast to the Jesus saying in Lk 14,26!

147. Cf. above, n. 102. Note, however, Lindemann's reservation: "nicht ... nur beiläufig", neither "erst während des Briefdiktats" (p. 680). Cf. P. RICHARDSON – P. GOOCH, *Logia of Jesus* (n. 78), p. 44: "The Lord's command is not precisely an afterthought, but neither is it foremost in Paul's mind as he writes". They refer to the first person singular verb in 7,6.7-8.10.12.17, but one could argue that precisely this use makes "not I but the Lord" so significant.

marriage, he or she is acting in conformity with the divine plan ... and the dominical directive in 7:10-11"[148]. If this is correct, and in 7,12-14 Paul still has in mind the dominical logion, one can hardly call it a mere afterthought.

And is it then likely that in the following verse 15 Paul "does precisely what the logion forbids"? The fact that in 7,15 there is no mention of remarriage makes us suspicious. Of course, some will argue that precisely the lack of an injunction like μενέτω ἄγαμος (v. 11a) indicates that Paul does not disallow remarriage in the case of v. 15[149]. But those who are more hesitant about Pauline inconsistency can reply that "Paul seems to be faithfully following the guidelines laid down in the preceding case (v. 11a)" if here divorce is allowed but not remarriage[150]. Dungan is not alone in making this point[151]. In any case I see no justification in v. 15 for unrestricted comments like Conzelmann's "Er kann wieder heiraten"[152]. Paul has no other instruction on second marriages than his final word of ch. 7 on marriage that is for life: a wife is accorded freedom to marry again after the death of her husband

---

148. *NJBC* (n. 82), pp. 804-805. Cf. H. MERKLEIN, *Es ist gut* (n. 112), p. 236: "Paulus plädiert auch hier *im Sinne des Herrenwortes* für die Aufrechterhaltung der Ehe" (my emphasis).

149. Thus LINDEMANN, *Funktion* (n. 3), p. 683: "angesichts von V. 11a ist es ... wahrscheinlich, daß er ein Verbot der Wiederverheiratung gegebenenfalls ausdrücklich ausgesprochen hätte".

150. D.L. DUNGAN, *Sayings*, p. 98.

151. See, e.g., B. SCHALLER, *Die Sprüche über Ehescheidung und Wiederheirat in der synoptischen Überlieferung*, in E. LOHSE (ed.), *Der Ruf Jesu und die Antwort der Gemeinde*. FS J. Jeremias, Göttingen, Vandenhoeck & Ruprecht, 1970, pp. 226-246, esp. 244: "(er betont) für den christlichen Partner einer solchen geschiedenen Ehe, er solle sich nicht wieder verheiraten. (n. 77:) Deutlich ausgesprochen in V. 11. Aber auch für die Christen in einer Mischehe dürfte dies gelten". Cf. C.F.G. HEINRICI, 81896, p. 226: "Sicherer erscheint im Hinblick auf V. 11 der Schluss, dass er unverheiratet bleiben soll"; R.L. ROBERTS, JR., *The Meaning of* Chōrizō *and* Douloō *in I Corinthians 7:10-17*, in *Restoration Quarterly* 8 (1965) 179-184: "The problem of this passage is not that of remarriage" (p. 184); "If Paul had been wanting to express such an idea, he could easily have used a more natural expression such as that which he did use in verse 39: *eleuthera ... gamēthēnai*" (p. 183). On G.D. Fee, see below n. 153.

Less convincingly, J.K. Elliott defends a differentiation between ἀφίημι and χωρίζομαι and proposes that "as in *v.* 10 Paul in *v.* 15 is speaking of separation". Cf. *Paul's Teaching on Marriage in I Corinthians: Some Problems Considered*, in *NTS* 19 (1972-73) 219-225, pp. 224-225.

152. 1969, p. 149. Cf. MURPHY-O'CONNOR, *The Divorced Woman*, p. 606: "7:15 must be interpreted in terms of the right to remarriage implicit in a legal divorce". More hesitant: COLLINS, *Divorce*, p. 64: "Paul does not explicitly forbid remarriage", but "arguments from silence are always weak"; LINDEMANN, *Funktion*, p. 683: "Ob Paulus in diesem Fall analog zu V. 39 eine neue Ehe für erlaubt hält, läßt sich nicht sicher sagen". Cf. SCHRAGE, p. 110, n. 329 (and n. 332: "Das [Nicht-Gebundensein] impliziert aber nicht eo ipso Freigabe einer Wiederheirat").

(7,39-40, cf. vv. 8-9; Rom 7,2)[153]. Remarriage is not mentioned in v. 15, and, with G.D. Fee, we can say: remarriage is not the issue there. Fee, too, refers to v. 11 where "even though there is a similar exception regarding divorce, he [Paul] explicitly disallows remarriage"[154].

If J. Jeremias's interpretation of v. 16 is correct and the questions τί οἶδας, γύναι and τί οἶδας, ἄνερ can be read as a missionary statement in continuation of v. 14 (and of its ἀνήρ-γυνή language)[155], verse 15ab appears to be a parenthesis in Paul's exposition on mixed marriages (vv. 12-14.15c-16). The style of this section differs from 7,10-11, but in both the exception "functions as a parenthesis within its paragraph"[156]. Taking into account this similarity in the form of the section and the thematic unity of 7,10-11.12-16 (injunctions against dissolving the marriage), it is tempting indeed to read 7,15 in the light of 7,11a.

1 Cor 7,10 and 9,14

In his comment on 1 Cor 9,14 (ὁ κύριος διέταξεν τοῖς τὸ εὐαγγέλιον καταγγέλλουσιν ἐκ τοῦ εὐαγγελίου ζῆν) Murphy-O'Connor has made the link with the Jesus saying in ch. 7[157]:

153. The verb used in 1 Cor 7,39 and Rom 7,2 is (γυνὴ) δέδεται; contrast οὐ δεδούλωται in 7,15. Cf. G.D. FEE, 1987, p. 303, on 7,15: "Paul does *not* intend to say one is not 'bound to the marriage'. One is simply not under bondage to maintain the marriage, which the other person wishes to dissolve".

154. *Ibid.*, p. 303. Regarding 7,15, his conclusion is extremely prudent: "All of this is not to say that Paul *disallows* remarriage in such cases; he simply does not speak to it at all". Cf. W. DEMING, *Paul on Marriage and Celibacy: The Hellenistic Background of 1 Corinthians* (SNTS MS, 83), Cambridge, University Press, 1995, p. 215: "Paul's treatment of marriage in 1 Corinthians is not designed to cover everything. He gives no ruling, for example, regarding remarriage for Christians whose non-Christian husbands or wives have left them".

On the position of Roman Catholicism (FEE, p. 302 n. 34), cf. R. SCHNACKENBURG, *The Moral Teaching of the New Testament*, London, 1965, pp. 249-250: "there is no mention of remarriage. The general tendency of the passage (cf. verses 10ff.) would not seem to point in that direction either... The Pauline privilege, therefore, is an extension of the Pauline concession of separation...". See now his *Die sittliche Botschaft des Neuen Testaments* (HTKNT, Suppl. 1-2), Freiburg, Herder, 1986, vol. 1, p. 243: "weniger deutlich ist, ob er damit auch den Weg freigeben will, daß der christliche Teil eine neue Ehe eingeht... Unmittelbar gesagt ist das nicht".

155. Cf. MURPHY-O'CONNOR, in *NJBC*: "*Perhaps you will save*. The intention of the phrase is positive" (p. 805). See, e.g., COLLINS, *Divorce*, pp. 60-62; on 7,15c, see pp. 54-55. Cf. SCHRAGE, p. 111: "Wahrscheinlicher ... kehrt Paulus [in 7,15c] zur Aussage von V 12-14 zurück... Mit dem adversativen δέ aber wird die unter den genannten Umständen freigestellte Trennung sofort wieder eingeschränkt und der Normalfall angesteuert".

156. Cf. CATCHPOLE, *The Synoptic Divorce Material* (n. 115), p. 108 n. 2 (cf. p. 106).

157. *NJBC*, p. 806. Cf. *What Paul Knew of Jesus* (n. 85), p. 40.

The arguments in vv 7, 8, and 13 gave Paul a privilege that he was free to waive, but the dominical directive imposed an obligation. The fact that he did not obey indicates that for him even commands of the Lord were not binding precepts.

Lindemann is even more explicit[158]:

> Paulus betont in 9,15-18 mit großen Nachdruck, daß die Nichteinhaltung der Weisung Jesu geradezu ein integrierender Bestandteil seines apostolischen Selbstverständnisses ist. ... Von daher ist dann auch die paulinische Argumentation in 1 Kor 7,10f zu erklären.

For Lindemann, it is not enough to say that "in 9,14 the Lord's command is understood as a right given to those who proclaim the gospel and Paul feels himself free not to make use of this right": "er weigert sich, die Weisung des κύριος ... für sich selbst anzuwenden"[159]. However, not to make use of his rights is Paul's own expression: 15a ἐγὼ δὲ οὐ κέχρημαι οὐδενὶ τούτων, 18b ... εἰς τὸ μὴ καταχρήσασθαι τῇ ἐξουσίᾳ μου ἐν τῷ εὐαγγελίῳ, cf. 12b ἀλλ' οὐκ ἐχρησάμεθα τῇ ἐξουσίᾳ ταύτῃ. The problematic word is of course διέταξεν referring to a saying of Jesus which itself is not a command or obligation laid upon the missionaries[160]. A solution has been sought in two directions. (1) The word of Jesus is not a command given *to* the missionaries but *for* their benefit, an obligation laid upon the congregations, and as such it can probably be described in the early church as a command of the Lord[161]. (2) The saying, "the laborer deserves to be paid", in Q and probably already in some pre-Q collection, has its place in Jesus' instructions to those to be sent out, and thus can be part of "the Lord's

---

158. *Funktion*, pp. 684-687, esp. 686, 687. — Contrast Dunn's *Jesus Traditon in Paul* (1994), which has only one line on 1 Cor 7,10-11; 9,14 (p. 160: "All are agreed that Paul does cite or refer to dominical tradition at two points") and one footnote: "In fact, however, in the two most cited cases, Paul quotes a word from the Lord in order to *qualify* it!" (p. 178 n. 72). Cf. LINDEMANN, p. 686: "es genügt nicht, diesen Befund lediglich zu konstatieren, sondern es muß versucht werden ihn auch zu erklären".

159. *Funktion*, p. 685: in reply to my presentation (quoted in the text above): "scheint mir zu problematisch" (n. 40). Cf. *Paul*, p. 320 (= 566).

160. Cf. Q 10,7b ἄξιος γὰρ ὁ ἐργάτης τοῦ μισθοῦ αὐτοῦ (Mt τῆς τροφῆς). Note that the first half of Dungan's book is a study of 1 Cor 9,14 (*Sayings*, pp. 1-80; cf. above n. 97). His main theme is "Paul's apparent unconcern at setting aside a command of the Lord explicitly ordering him as well as the other apostles to accept financial support" (p. 20). Cf. SCHRAGE, p. 310: "von 'unconcern' o.ä. (kann) kaum die Rede sein" (n. 192). Schrage is also rightly critical of the hypothesis that "man Paulus in Korinth die Übertretung eines Herrengebotes vorgeworfen habe" (p. 282 n. 26: Dungan; p. 310 n. 193: H.-J. Klauck).

161. FEE, p. 413. Cf. SCHRAGE, p. 309: "διατάσσω ... sonst für das autoritative Gebieten", but: "In der *Sache* ist es allerdings zutreffend ..., daß eher eine Konzession als eine Forderung vorliegt" (n. 182).

decree". In any case, "Paul's response is to re-interpret that decree as a 'right' which, for the sake of the gospel, he is free to give up"[162].

The case of 9,14, and in particular the use of the verb διέταξεν, deserves closer examination than it was possible to do in this paper. I only observe here that amalgamation should be avoided and 1 Cor 7,10 and 9,14 ought to be studied on their own right.

CONCLUSION

Scholars who defend a high number of allusions in the Pauline Letters have to cope with the very fact that there are only two explicit references. The analogy of Paul's use of the Old Testament in echoes and allusions is not very helpful given the proportion of explicit scriptural citations[163]. It is curious that the same scholars who magnify the presence of allusions and echoes seem to have no difficulty in noting that "the only two explicit attributions are to be found in cases where Paul cited the authorization of Jesus only to qualify it": this "should occasion no surprise"[164]. Is that then a case of Pauline inconsistency, or is it inconsistency in the mind of Paul's interpreters, maximalists in counting possible echoes of the Jesus tradition who become minimalist in evaluating Paul's explicit references?

It is with special emphasis that Paul in 1 Cor 7,10 refers to Jesus' prohibition of divorce, and I have tried to show that this command of the Lord is still on Paul's mind when he formulates his own instructions on mixed marriages. The possibility of divorce is envisaged by Paul (v. 11a) without giving up the inspiration of the dominical logion. This involves a notion of divorce-separation, unattested I think in the gospel sayings and probably unkown in the pre-Pauline Jesus tradition.

---

162. FURNISH, *Jesus*, p. 51.
163. Cf. P. RICHARDSON – P. GOOCH, *Logia of Jesus* (n. 78), pp. 52-53.
164. DUNN, *Prolegomena* (n. 16), p. 422.
— Additional note: M. and R. ZIMMERMANN, *Zitation, Kontradiktion oder Applikation? Die Jesuslogien in 1 Kor 7,10f. und 9,14: Traditionsgeschichtliche Verankerung und paulinische Interpretation*, in ZNW 87 (1996) 83-100, esp. pp. 88-90, 94-96, 97-99 (1 Cor 7,10-11).

BETL 131 (1997) 27-64

4

Q 6,20b-21; 7,22 AND ISAIAH 61

When, in 1994, I submitted to our president-elect the title of my lecture, *Scriptural Quotations and Interrelationship of the Gospels*, my choice was influenced by reading a dissertation entitled *Old Testament Quotations in the Synoptic Gospels, and the Two-Document Hypothesis*, written by David S. New and published in the SBL series "Septuagint and Cognate Studies" (1993)[1]. This study was limited to the explicit Old Testament quotations, and the examination of their appearance and of their text-type led the author to conclude that (I summarize) the pattern of the quotations in the Synoptic Gospels favours the two-document hypothesis and offers "embarrassing" difficulties for advocates of the Griesbach theory. The priority of Mark versus originality of Matthew remains of course the basic question of interrelationship of the Gospels, though one can hardly say that it constitutes the central discussion in present-day gospel studies. D. New's treatment also includes quotations in Q material (Mt 4,4.6.7.10 / Lk 4,4.10-11.12.8; Mt 11,10 / Lk 7,27)[2], and it is fair to say, I think, that the second source Q is one of the Gospel issues which now appear to inspire NT scholarship more particularly. In recent years, there is an extraordinary proliferation of studies on Q[3]. In the programme of lectures and seminars at our Colloquium on Scriptures in the (Four) Gospels there was no explicit reference to Q[4], and it struck me that the article "Old Testament in the Gospels" in a Dictionary of the Gospels treats Jesus, Mk, Mt, Lk, Jn, but has nothing on Q[5]. Therefore,

---

1. D.S. NEW, *Old Testament Quotations in the Synoptic Gospels, and the Two-Document Hypothesis* (Septuagint and Cognate Studies, 37), Atlanta, GA, Scholars Press, 1993. Doctoral dissertation at McMaster University, under S.R. Westerholm, 1990. See my review in *ETL* 70 (1994) 167-168.

2. *Ibid.*, pp. 54-64.

3. It can suffice, for the moment, to refer to one of the latest published volumes on Q: C.M. TUCKETT, *Q and the History of Early Christianity: Studies on Q*, Edinburgh, Clark, 1996. See now also the first volume of *The Database of the International Q Project* (Documenta Q), *Q 11:2b-4*, by S. Carruth, A. Garsky, and S.D. Anderson, Leuven, Peeters, 1996; cf. my review in *ETL* 72 (1996) 418-424.

4. I refer here to the programme as it was announced in December 1995 with unspecified mention of the "Presidential Address". In fact, at the Colloquium, C.M. Tuckett's opening paper was devoted to "Scripture and Q" (in this volume, pp. 3-26) and Q texts were treated in offered papers by T.L. Brodie, M. Hasitschka, C. Heil, and J. Schröter.

5. C.A. EVANS, *Old Testament in the Gospels*, in J.B. GREEN – S. McKNIGHT (eds.), *Dictionary of Jesus and the Gospels*, Downers Grove, IL – Leicester, Intervarsity, 1992, pp. 579-590. The quotations in Q 4,1-13; 7,27; 10,15; 12,53; 13,27.35 are mentioned (with reference to Mt) in the section on "Jesus' Use of the OT" (pp. 579-583).

I decided to concentrate in this last lecture on scriptural quotations in Q (or, as some would now prefer to call it, the Sayings Gospel Q).

I begin with a preliminary observation on the extent of Q[6]. I think we can exclude from Q triple-tradition texts such as the quotation of Isa 40,3 in Lk 3,4 / Mt 3,3 (par. Mk 1,2-3)[7], and the quotation of Deut 6,5; Lev 19,18 in the pericope of the great commandment (Lk 10,27 / Mt 22,37.39, par. Mk 12,30.31 and 33)[8], and also the Lukan Sondergut in Lk 4,18-19[9]. As a provisional list of quotations and allusions (*) in Q[10] I refer to the "quotations" printed in italics in the N-A text at Lk 4,4.8.10-11.12; 7,22*.27; 12,53*; 13,19*.27*.35ᶜ; and in addition four phrases in Lk 10,15; 13,29.35ᵃ; 17,27, marked in N (= H) but now printed in normal type in N-A (1979[26], 1993[27])[11]. Apart from a few minor differences else-

---

6. Cf. *Recent Developments in the Study of Q* (1982), in *Evangelica II: 1982-1991* (BETL, 99), Leuven, 1991, esp. pp. 415-419; *Q-Synopsis* (SNTA, 13), Leuven, ²1995.

7. *The First Synoptic Pericope: The Appearance of John the Baptist?*, in *ETL* 72 (1996) 41-74. Cf. below, pp. [207-240].

8. *Luke 10:25-28: A Foreign Body in Luke?*, in S.E. PORTER – P. JOYCE – D.E. ORTON (eds.), *Crossing the Boundaries. Essays in Biblical Interpretation*. FS M.D. Goulder (Biblical Interpretation Series, 8), Leiden, Brill, 1994, pp. 149-165; *The Minor Agreements and Lk 10,25-28*, in *ETL* 71 (1995) 151-160. See also in this volume, F. NOËL, *The Double Command of Love in Lk 10,27*, pp. 559-570. Contrast C.M. TUCKETT, *Q and the History* (n. 3), pp. 416-418 (cf. *Revival*, 1983, pp. 125-133: Mk and Q two forms of this pericope in the tradition).

9. On this case, see C.J. SCHRECK, *The Nazareth Pericope: Luke 4,16-30 in Recent Study*, in F. NEIRYNCK (ed.), *L'évangile de Luc – The Gospel of Luke* (BETL, 32), Leuven, ²1989, pp. 399-471, esp. 414-417: "Tuckett's Proposal: Q" (cf. below, n. 17). R. Hodgson includes Lk 4,18-19 (and 6,27c-28a; 9,61; 17,32 as well) in his list of twenty-two OT citations and allusions. Cf. R. HODGSON, *On the* Gattung *of Q: A Dialogue with James M. Robinson*, in *Bib* 66 (1985) 73-95, esp. pp. 77-85 ("Q and the Old Testament").

10. On quotations in Q, cf. S. SCHULZ, *Q: Die Spruchquelle der Evangelisten*, Zürich, Theologischer Verlag, 1972, pp. 27-28 ("Die Septuaginta-Benutzung"), with references to P. Wernle (1899), S.E. Johnson (1943), K. Stendahl (1954). See also A.W. ARGYLE, *The Accounts of the Temptations of Jesus in Relation to the Q Hypothesis*, in *ExpT* 64 (1952-53) 382; ID., *Scriptural Quotations in Q Material*, in *ExpT* 65 (1953-54) 285-286; H.T. FLEDDERMANN, *Mark and Q* (BETL, 122), Leuven, 1995, p. 27 n. 10 (and my comment: p. 269 nn. 26-30). – For a full discussion of OT quotations and allusions in Q see now J. SCHLOSSER, *L'utilisation des Écritures dans la source Q*, in *L'Évangile exploré*. *Mélanges offerts à Simon Légasse* (LD, 166), Paris, Cerf, 1966, pp. 126-146.

11. "Allusions" (here marked *) are printed in normal type in GNT³·⁴. For a list of OT allusions on the basis of N-A, see J.J. O'ROURKE, *Possible Uses of the Old Testament in the Gospels: An Overview*, in C.A. EVANS – W.R. STEGNER, *The Gospels and the Scriptures of Israel* (JSNT SS, 104), Sheffield, Academic, 1994, pp. 15-25; C.A. KIMBALL, *Jesus' Exposition of the Old Testament in Luke's Gospel* (JSNT SS, 94), Sheffield, Academic, 1994, pp. 204-205 (quotations in Lk), 206-212 (allusions in Lk). For a more complete (over-complete?) list of "Biblische Zitate, Anspielungen und Motive im Matthäusevangelium", see H. FRANKEMÖLLE, *Die matthäische Kirche als Gemeinschaft des Glaubens*, in R. KAMPLING – T. SÖDING (eds.), *Ekklesiologie des Neuen Testaments*. FS K. Kertelge, Freiburg, Herder, 1996, pp. 85-132, esp. 127-132. The following verses with Q-material can be selected from his list: Mt 3,11;

where[12], there seems to be some confusion in the presentation of Q 7,22: in Mt 11,5 and in Lk κωφοὶ ἀκούουσιν and νεκροὶ ἐγείρονται are now printed in italics, but πτωχοὶ εὐαγγελίζονται is printed in normal type, and such is the case also with οἱ πτωχοί in Mt 5,3 and Lk 6,20 and πενθοῦν-τες, παρακληθήσονται in Mt 5,4 (diff. Lk 6,21b), in contrast to N (= H)[13].

I

It cannot be a surprise that I start with the first three Beatitudes (Q 6,20b.21a.b). Here in Leuven, and elsewhere, we are all familiar with Jacques Dupont's essential studies on this topic[14] and with his special emphasis on the significance of Isa 61. Those who were not acquainted with Dupont's work are now reminded of it by the *DBS* article on the Sermon on the Mount[15] and by numerous references in H.D. Betz's massive commentary[16]. Most recently, C.M. Tuckett's book on Q has a section on "Isa 61 and Q", in which he recapitulates and updates the two

4,2.3.4.5.6.7.8.10.11; 5,3.4.6.11.12.18.39.42.44.48; 6,9.10.11.12.13.19.20.22.23.26.27.28. 29.33; 7,1.7.8.12.20.21.22.23.24.25.27; 8,11.12.20.21; 9,38; 10,8.10-11.15.16.19.30.32. 35.37; 11,3.5.10.11.17.19.21.22.23.25.27; 12,39.40.41.42; 13,32.33; 18,12.15; 19,28; 22,3.4; 23,12.13.34.36.38.39; 24,28.37.38. For allusions to OT figures in Q, see D. LÜHRMANN, *Die Redaktion der Logienquelle* (WMANT, 33), Neukirchen, Neukirchener, 1969, p. 98. See now also J. SCHLOSSER (n. 10), pp. 127-132.

12. Words printed in normal type in N: Lk 4,8 μόνῳ, 7,27 σου[2]; but 12,53 ἐπὶ (ante πατρί).

13. With the exception of οἱ πτωχοί in Lk 6,20 (normal type in H).

14. J. DUPONT, *Les Béatitudes*, first edition, Bruges, 1954; new edition in three volumes: I. *Le problème littéraire*, 1958; II. *La Bonne Nouvelle*, 1969; III. *Les évangélistes* (Études Bibliques), Paris, Gabalda, 1973. Cf. *Introduction aux Béatitudes*, in NRT 108 (1976) 97-108. See also ID., *L'ambassade de Jean-Baptiste (Matthieu 11,2-6; Luc 7,18-23)*, in NRT 83 (1961) 805-821, 943-959; *Jésus annonce la bonne nouvelle aux pauvres*, in Evangelizare pauperibus. Atti della XXIV Settimana biblica, Brescia, Paideia, 1978, pp. 127-189; = ID., *Études sur les évangiles synoptiques* (BETL, 70-A), Leuven, 1985, pp. 23-85.

15. M. DUMAIS, *Sermon sur la montagne*, in DBS fasc. 68-69 (1993-1994) 699-938, esp. cc. 776-817 ("Les Béatitudes"). Cf. c. 778: "Parmi tous ceux qui ont écrit sur le sujet, l'exégète belge J. Dupont demeure le maître par excellence... De nombreux commentateurs des béatitudes puisent largement dans ces études de J. Dupont". Dumais's article now appeared in a revised format: *Le Sermon sur la montagne. État de la recherche, interprétation, bibliographie*, Paris, Letouzey et Ané, 1995, 331 p.

16. H.D. BETZ, *The Sermon on the Mount* (Hermeneia), Minneapolis, MN, Fortress, 1995, pp. 91-153 (Mt 5,3-12), 571-589 (Lk 6,20b-26). See the references to J. Dupont (mostly vol. III) in the section on Mt: nn. 135, 147, 154, 169, 174, 178, 179, 207, 209, 271, 273, 286, 289, 290, 292, 293, 294, 298, 304, 311, 331, 332, 334, 360, 402, 403, 406, 426, 440, 446, 453, 496, 498, 514; less frequent, and only to vol. I, in the section on Lk (nn. 6, 55, 118).

Contrast H. FRANKEMÖLLE, *Die Makarismen (Mt 5,1-12; Lk 6,20-23): Motive und Umfang der redaktionellen Komposition*, in BZ 15 (1971) 52-75; cf. Dupont's reaction: "l'information... est exclusivement limitée aux publications de langue allemande; un pareil isolationnisme interdit évidemment toute discussion scientifique sérieuse" (*Béatitudes* III, p. 41 n. 2; but on Frankemölle's view on the evangelist's redaction, see p. 13 n. 1: "fon-

papers on this topic he delivered in the early 1980's[17]. The clause πτωχοὶ εὐαγγελίζονται is at the centre of J.M. Robinson's attempt to justify the designation "Gospel" in the text of Q itself[18]. I wrote a short reply[19], calling for a more cautious reading of Q 7,22; a too short statement, which needs further elaboration.

Q 6,20b-21

J. Dupont[20]

[3]μακάριοι οἱ πτωχοί,
ὅτι αὐτῶν ἐστιν ἡ βασιλεία τοῦ θεοῦ[22].
[4]μακάριοι οἱ πενθοῦντες,
ὅτι αὐτοὶ παρακληθήσονται.
[6]μακάριοι οἱ πεινῶντες (καὶ διψῶντες)[22],
ὅτι αὐτοὶ χορτασθήσονται.

H. Schürmann[21]

[20b]μακάριοι οἱ πτωχοί,
ὅτι ὑμῶν* ἐστιν ἡ βασιλεία τοῦ θεοῦ.
[21a]μακάριοι οἱ πεινῶντες,
ὅτι χορτασθήσεσθε.
[21b]μακάριοι οἱ κλαίοντες,
ὅτι γελάσετε.

cièrement saine"; p. 308 n. 5: "quelques remarques justes"). For a discussion of the Beatitudes in constant dialogue with "dem Autor des dreibändigen Werkes über die Seligpreisungen" (p. 18), see I. BROER, *Die Seligpreisungen der Bergpredigt. Studien zu ihrer Überlieferung und Interpretation* (BBB, 61), Königstein/Ts.–Bonn, Hanstein, 1986. For an earlier survey of studies "published since Dupont's magisterial work appeared", cf. N.J. MCELENEY, *The Beatitudes of the Sermon on the Mount/Plain*, in *CBQ* 43 (1981) 1-13; with critique of conjectural reconstructions by G. Schwarz, D. Flusser, and S. Lachs (pp. 6, 8, 11).

17. C.M. TUCKETT, *Q and the History* (n. 3), pp. 221-237: "Isa 61 and Q" (Q 7,22; 6,20-21; Lk 4,16ff.). Cf. *The Beatitudes: A Source-Critical Study*, in *NT* 25 (1983) 193-207 (with "A Reply" by M. Goulder, pp. 207-216), a paper read at the SNTS Seminar on the Synoptic Problem (Toronto, 1980); *Luke 4,16-30, Isaiah and Q*, in J. DELOBEL (ed.), *Logia. Les paroles de Jésus – The Sayings of Jesus* (BETL, 59), Leuven, 1982, pp. 343-354 (paper read at the Colloquium Biblicum Lovaniense, 1981). Cf. below, n. 79. See now his *Scripture and Q* in this volume, pp. 3-26, esp. 20-26 ("Isaiah 61 and Q").

18. J.M. ROBINSON, *The Sayings Gospel Q*, in *The Four Gospels 1992*. FS F. Neirynck (BETL, 100), Leuven, 1992, pp. 361-388, esp. 368-372; *The Incipit of the Sayings Gospel Q*, in *RHPR* 75 (1995) 9-33, esp. pp. 31-33.

19. Cf. *Q: From Source to Gospel*, in *ETL* 71 (1995) 421-430, pp. 425-427.

20. *Béatitudes* I, p. 343 (= 1954, p. 127). Compare (without καὶ διψῶντες): A. HARNACK, 1907, p. 89; K. KOCH, *Was ist Formgeschichte?*, Neukirchen, Neukirchener, 1964, p. 247 (cf. pp. 46-47); J. SCHLOSSER, *Le règne de Dieu dans les dits de Jésus* (Études Bibliques), Paris, Gabalda, 1980, II, pp. 423-450 ("La béatitude des pauvres [Lc 6,20 par. Mt 5,3]"), esp. 425-430; D.R. CATCHPOLE, *The Quest for Q*, Edinburgh, Clark, 1993, pp. 81-94 ("The Beatitudes and Woes. Q 6:20b-23,24-26"), here 86; *et al.* Cf. M. DUMAIS, *Sermon* (n. 16), p. 784: "le texte de base des béatitudes dans la source Q... à partir de la reconstruction proposée par J. Dupont et reprise presque textuellement par J. Lambrecht" (but see below, n. 51).

21. H. SCHÜRMANN, *Die Warnung des Lukas vor der Falschlehre in der "Predigt am Berge" Lk 6,20-49*, in *BZ* 10 (1966) 59-81, esp. pp. 74-78 ("Lk 6,20-26"); = *Traditionsgeschichtliche Untersuchungen zu den synoptischen Evangelien*, Düsseldorf, Patmos, 1968, pp. 290-309, esp. 303-307; *Das Lukasevangelium* I (HTK, 3/1), Freiburg, Herder, 1969, pp. 325-341, esp. 329-330. Lk's ὑμετέρα "hat vielleicht ein ὑμῶν verdrängt" (p. 329 n. 24). The second person (= Q) is possibly not the original form and the change to the third person in Mt would be "eine Wiederherstellung des Ursprünglichen" (p. 328).

22. Τῶν οὐρανῶν (1954, p. 80); cf. I, pp. 209-210: "question ouverte". Καὶ διψῶντες: "Pas de raison suffisante pour écarter les 'assoiffés'" (I, p. 223); G.

With regard to the original three beatitudes, J. Dupont and H. Schürmann represent two different types of reconstruction of the Q text: in the third person (*Aussage*) for Dupont and in the second person (*Anrede*) for Schürmann. Dupont's Matthean type of reconstruction has Mt 5,4 in the order of Mt as the second beatitude and in the wording of Mt: πενθοῦντες and παρακληθήσονται. Schürmann has the Lukan type of reconstruction: Lk 6,21b as the third beatitude and in the vocabulary of Lk: κλαίοντες and γελάσετε. This is now also the IQP text, printed here in contrast to A. Polag's compromise (Polag has Mt's third person but the Lukan order; and, in the third beatitude, Mt's παρακληθήσονται but Lk's κλαίοντες):

A. Polag[23]	IQP (1992)[24]
μακάριοι οἱ πτωχοί,	20b μακάριοι οἱ πτωχοί,
ὅτι αὐτῶν ἐστιν ἡ βασιλεία τοῦ θεοῦ.	ὅτι [[ὑμετέρα]] ἐστὶν ἡ βασιλεία τοῦ θεοῦ.
μακάριοι οἱ πεινῶντες νῦν,	21a μακάριοι οἱ πεινῶντες,
ὅτι χορτασθήσονται.	ὅτι χορτασθήσεσθε.
μακάριοι οἱ κλαίοντες νῦν,	21b μακάριοι οἱ [[κλαί]]οντες,
ὅτι παρακληθήσονται.	ὅτι γελάσετε.

There is almost a consensus on the Lukan addition of the adverb νῦν in 6,21a.b (but see Polag), on the substitution of τῶν οὐρανῶν (for τοῦ θεοῦ) in Mt 5,3 and the Matthean additions τῷ πνεύματι in v. 3 and (καὶ διψῶντες) τὴν δικαιοσύνην in v. 6. It is widely agreed that the fourth beatitude (Lk 6,22-23 / Mt 5,11-12, on persecution) was already

STRECKER, *Makarismen* (n. 25), p. 264: "zweifelhaft"; J.A. FITZMYER, *Luke* I, 1981, p. 634: "'and thirst'... comes to Matthew from 'Q'". But see above, n. 20. Note that διψῶντες in Mt has no matching term besides χορτασθήσονται.

23. A. POLAG, *Fragmenta Q. Textheft zur Logienquelle*, Neukirchen, Neukirchener, 1979, ²1982, p. 32. For the combination of κλαίοντες (Lk) and παρακληθήσονται (Mt), see W. Grimm (1976), I.H. Marshall (*Lk*, 1978), and M.E. BORING, *Criteria of Authenticity: The Lucan Beatitudes as a Test Case*, in *Forum* 1/4 (1985) 3-38, here p. 20 (contrast IQP!); ID., *The Continuing Voice of Jesus*, St. Louis, KY, Westminster/John Knox, 1991, pp. 192-206 ("Q 6:20b-23"). For the Lukan order combined with the third person (Mt), see S. Schulz (1972), H. Merklein (1978), W. Schenk (1981), J. Lambrecht (1983), M.E. Boring (1985), *et al.* Cf. Dupont's "base commune" in *Introduction* (n. 14), p. 99! Undecided: J. SCHLOSSER (n. 20), p. 424: "il paraît préférable... de laisser la question ouverte"; W.D. DAVIES & D.C. ALLISON, *The Gospel according to Saint Matthew*, Edinburgh, Clark, vol. I, 1988, pp. 445-446: "No agreement has been reached... we still await a decisive observation".

24. Cf. *JBL* 111 (1992), pp. 501-502. Cf. U. LUZ, *Das Evangelium nach Matthäus* I (EKK, 1/1), Zürich, Benziger – Neukirchen, Neukirchener, 1985, p. 200 (and 201); ET, 1989, p. 227; M. SATO, *Q und Prophetie. Studien zur Gattungs- und Traditionsgeschichte der Quelle Q* (WUNT, 2/29), Tübingen, Mohr, 1988, p. 254 (= 1984, p. 297); J.S. KLOPPENBORG, *Q Thomas Reader*, Sonoma, CA, Polebridge, 1990, p. 38; E. SEVENICH-BAX, *Israels Konfrontation mit den letzten Boten der Weisheit. Form, Funktion und Interdependenz der Weisheitselemente in der Logienquelle* (MThA, 21), Altenberge, Oros, 1993, pp. 95-98, 103.

added to the original three in the common source Q and that the additional beatitudes in Mt 5,5.7-9.10 are later insertions (Q^{mt} or, more likely, MtR)[25].

There are of course opponents to the Q hypothesis. Thus, D.A. Hagner writes in his *Matthew* (1993), "It may well be that each evangelist follows an independent, though overlapping, oral tradition" (cf. I.H. Marshall: "two different forms of the tradition; an original bifurcation in the tradition")[26]. For H.D. Betz, the SM and the SP existed first apart from Q and, in the beatitudes, the differences "seem to be original to the (presynoptic) compositions and reflect fundamentally different presuppositions"[27]. Redactional interventions of the evangelists are radically excluded: "there is nothing within the SM that has the specific character of Matthew's redaction"; and even: "I do not see any place within the SM where I would be able to recognize sufficient reasons for assuming the interferring hand of the Gospel writer Matthew"[28]. Quite opposite to Betz, but in his own way also emphasizing the unitary composition of the beatitudes, M.D. Goulder proposes that Matthew is responsible for the creation of the beatitudes and Mt 5,3-12 was the

25. For most authors Mt 5,10 is due to MtR. In defence of the Q^{mt} hypothesis (Mt 5,5.7-9: R.A. Guelich [n. 56], 1976; U. Luz, 1985; M. Sato, 1984=1988; *et al.*), G. Strecker's lecture at our 1970 Colloquium has been most influential: *Die Makarismen der Bergpredigt*, in *NTS* 17 (1970-71) 255-275, p. 259; = *Les macarismes du Discours sur la montagne*, in M. DIDIER (ed.), *L'évangile selon Matthieu* (BETL, 29), 1972, pp. 185-208, esp. 190. See also *Die Bergpredigt*, Göttingen, Vandenhoeck & Ruprecht, 1984; ET: *The Sermon on the Mount: An Exegetical Commentary*, Edinburgh, Clark, 1988, p. 30. But see, e.g., D.R. CATCHPOLE, *Quest* (n. 20), pp. 81-83, for the attribution to the evangelist.

26. D.A. HAGNER, *Matthew 1–13* (WBC, 33A), Dallas, TX, Word, 1993, p. 89; I.H. MARSHALL, *The Gospel of Luke*, Exeter, Paternoster, 1978, p. 247; D.L. BOCK, *Luke I*, Grand Rapids, MI, Baker, 1994, p. 550. Cf. H.-T. WREGE, *Die Überlieferungsgeschichte der Bergpredigt*, Tübingen, Mohr, 1968.

27. *The Sermon on the Mount* (n. 16), esp. p. 571. On the "relationship" between SM and SP, see also pp. 109-110: "the Sermons operate with different views about what these beatitudes mean" (p. 109). Betz is extremely critical of redaction criticism; see p. 94, on the second- and third-person form (n. 13); pp. 577-578, on Lk 6,21b / Mt 5,4: "Scholars have done their best to show how Matthew may have reformulated the Q-version found in Luke, but with little success. If Matthew had the Lukan version or something similar in front of him, no convincing reason has been presented for changing the wording to what is Matthew's second beatitude". Cf. below, n. 69.

28. BETZ, *The Sermon on the Mount in Matthew's Interpretation*, in B.A. PEARSON (ed.), *The Future of Early Christianity*. FS H. Koester, Minneapolis, MN, Fortress, 1991, pp. 258-275, here 260 (referring to his forthcoming commentary). See, e.g., *Sermon*, 1995, p. 131: "This interpretation of the notion of righteousness, central as it is for the SM, differs from that of the evangelist Matthew"; p. 127: on πραεῖς (5,5) and Jesus' meekness in Mt "different from the SM". For critical reactions to Betz's hypothesis, see J.S. KLOPPENBORG (ed.), *Conflict and Invention*, 1995, pp. 7-8 (cf. *ETL* 72, 1996, p. 442); P. HOFFMANN, in *AAR/SBL Abstracts 1996*, pp. 246-247: "One may ask whether Betz does not underestimate the work of the evangelists" (p. 247).

unique source of Lk 6,20-26[29]. With É. Puech the restoration of the traditional Matthean hypothesis comes to completion: the source-text of Mt includes τῷ πνεύματι, τῶν οὐρανῶν, τὴν δικαιοσύνην, in an original composition of the beatitudes, (4+4)+1: "Le nombre primitif de cette composition n'est pas de 3 ou 4 (= 3+1) béatitudes comme en Luc ou le prétendu document Q(uelle), mais de 8"[30].

There is one element that opponents of Q have in common with its defenders: in their comments on the Beatitudes, at some stage, traditional or redactional, they all refer to Isa 61. The reference is usually connected with the theme of the πτωχοί in the first beatitude (Isa 61,1 εὐαγγελίσασθαι πτωχοῖς)[31], but can be extended to the second beatitude in Mt 5,4 with πενθοῦντες and παρακληθήσονται, diff. Lk 6,21b (Isa 61,2 παρακαλέσαι πάντας τοὺς πενθοῦντας). For Dupont and many others Mt 5,3-4 clearly alludes to Isa 61,1-2 and this is one of the reasons for considering the pairing of πενθεῖν (mourn) and παρακαλεῖσθαι (being comforted) the original wording of the beatitude. Those who, like Dupont, argue that the woe-sayings in Lk 6,24-26

29. M.D. GOULDER, *Midrash and Lection in Matthew*, London, SPCK, 1974, esp. pp. 252-254: "The simplest explanation must be that Matthew wrote the Beatitudes, and that Luke rewrote them" (p. 254); *Luke: A New Paradigm* (JSNT SS, 20), Sheffield, Academic, 1989, pp. 346-360, esp. 356-358. Cf. above, n. 17, Goulder's "Reply" to Tuckett (1983). See D.R. Catchpole's response in *Quest* (n. 20), ch. 1: "Did Q Exist?", pp. 1-59, esp. 16-23 ("The Beatitudes"); 43-45 ("The Baptist's Question"). See also C.M. TUCKETT, *Q and the History* (n. 3), pp. 1-39, ch. 1: "The Existence of Q".

30. É. PUECH, *Un hymne essénien en partie retrouvé et les Béatitudes. 1QH V 12 – VI 18 (= col. XIII-XIV 7) et 4QBéat*, in *RQ* 13 (1988) 59-88, esp. p. 87; *4Q525 et les péricopes des Béatitudes en Ben Sira et Matthieu*, in *RB* 98 (1991) 80-106 (here p. 97). For a reaction with reservations, see J.A. FITZMYER, *A Palestinian Collection of Beatitudes*, in *The Four Gospels 1992*. FS F. Neirynck (BETL, 100), 1992, pp. 509-515. Puech adopts the structure suggested by A. Di Lella on the basis of the number of words: the original group of eight Beatitudes in Mt 5,3-10 with two sections of exactly thirty-six words (vv. 3.5.4.6 and 7-10). Cf. A.A. DI LELLA, *The Structure and Composition of the Matthean Beatitudes*, in M.P. HORGAN – P.J. KOBELSKI (eds.), *To Touch the Text*. FS J.A. Fitzmyer, New York, Crossroad, 1989, pp. 237-242. I cite here a few examples of this author's argument of the word counts: "one of the reasons for the addition of the phrase τῷ πνεύματι was to give v. 3 the twelve words it would need in order to correspond to the twelve words in v. 10" (p. 239); one of the reasons for the inclusion of the πραεῖς beatitude: "its eight words were required for the sum of thirty-six words that comprise the first strophe" (p. 240). Note that Di Lella's article is written to help scholars avoid "subjectivity and circular arguments" (p. 242)! Compare M. Dumais's comment on Puech's hypothesis: "l'argument principal qui la fonde n'évite pas le cercle vicieux: en effet, la séquence de huit macarismes du fragment incomplet 4Q525 est établie à partir de Mt v,3-10, vu comme parallèle. De plus, l'A. ne considère pas les autres arguments qui militent en faveur d'une activité rédactionnelle de Mt en v,3-10" (*Sermon* [n. 15], c. 785). Cf. B.T. VIVIANO, *Eight Beatitudes at Qumran and in Matthew? A New Publication from Cave Four*, in *SEÅ* 58 (1993) 71-84; *BAR* 18/6 (1992) 53-55.66.

31. DUPONT, *Introduction* (n. 14), p. 100: "La première béatitude donne le ton. C'est aussi celle qui rappelle le mieux la prophétie d'Isaïe".

were not part of Q but are due to LkR (or Q[lk])[32], can explain the Lukan parallel(s) without too much difficulty: the verbs κλαίειν and γελᾶν are Luke's substitutes for πενθεῖν and παρακαλεῖσθαι (Q), in the beatitude (6,21b κλαίοντες – γελάσετε) and in the corresponding woe (6,25b γελῶντες – κλαύσετε), and πενθήσετε in the double phrase πενθήσετε καὶ κλαύσετε is regarded as a reminiscence of the original wording of the beatitude in Q. Likewise, τὴν παράκλησιν ὑμῶν (6,24) is supposed to be a reminiscence of παρακληθήσονται in the Q-beatitude.

Defenders of the pre-Lukan origin of the woes can reverse the argument of the reminiscences and assign the use of the verbs πενθεῖν and παρακαλεῖσθαι in Mt 5,4 to Matthean redaction influenced by the tradition of the woes. In reply to H. Schürmann[33] (followed by H. Frankemölle, R.H. Gundry, et al.)[34] it has been observed that, if Matthew picked up his two verbs in the woes, then the "allusion" to Isa 61 was mere coincidence ("rein zufällig entstanden")[35]. It can be asked, however, whether it is likely that πενθοῦντες in the beatitude would come from the corresponding woe-saying in Lk 6,25b and παρακληθήσονται, in the same beatitude, would derive from a different woe-saying (6,24, on the rich) and from a quite different phrase: ὅτι ἀπέχετε τὴν παράκλησιν ὑμῶν. Moreover, the question of Lukan authorship can be raised, if not (as I think it should) for the whole complex of the four woes (Lk 6,24-26), at least for the terms παράκλησιν and πενθήσετε (6,24.25b). For Schürmann, the pre-Lukan origin of πενθήσετε (in combination with καὶ κλαύσετε) can be explained as stereotyped usage, and J.A. Fitzmyer who argues for Lukan composition

32. Cf. U. Luz, *Matthäus* (n. 24), pp. 200-201: "Die von Jes 61,2 her erfolgte Neuformulierung der zweiten Seligpreisung ist... eindeutig vormatthäisch. [n. 9] Die Weherufe Lk 6,24.25b setzen V4 in der mt Fassung wohl bereits voraus" (p. 200). Compare G. Strecker, *Makarismen* (n. 25), p. 263 n. 1; reprinted in Id., *Eschaton und Historie*, Göttingen, Vandenhoeck & Ruprecht, 1979, pp. 108-131, here 117, n. 27 (= *Macarismes*, p. 195 n. 27); cf. *Sermon*, pp. 34-35.

33. *Warnung* (n. 21), 1966, p. 77 (= *TrU*, p. 305); *Lukasevangelium*, p. 339: "Das πενθήσετε Lk 6,25 wird Matth mitbestimmt haben, Mt 5,4 die κλαίοντες in die πενθοῦντες zu ändern [p. 331 n. 42]. Wahrscheinlich hat Mt in 5,4 auch entsprechend das γελάσετε in παρακληθήσονται geglättet, wobei ihm eine Vorlage wie 6,24 (παράκλησις) half [pp. 332 n. 45; 336 n. 84]".

34. H. Frankemölle, *Makarismen* (n. 16), p. 64; R.H. Gundry, *Matthew*, Grand Rapids, MI, Eerdmans, 1982, ²1994, p. 68. Cf. J. Nolland, *Luke 1–9:20* (WBC, 35A), Dallas, TX, Word, 1989, pp. 287, and 280: "Matthew will have the verb he uses here ('mourn') from the corresponding Lukan woe".

35. E. Schweizer, *Formgeschichtliches zu den Seligpreisungen Jesu*, in *NTS* 19 (1972-73) 121-126, p. 122 n. 4; = *Matthäus und seine Gemeinde* (SBS, 71), Stuttgart, KBW, 1974, pp. 69-76, esp. 71 n. 9.

can repeat this same explanation[36]. One may add that the emphatic pleonasm is used quite fittingly in this third woe-saying[37]. Fitzmyer's comment is even more explicit on παράκλησις in 6,24: "*Paraklesis* is used by Luke alone among the evangelists... This is a sign that the woes were not part of 'Q'"[38]. More recently, D.R. Catchpole, in *The Quest for Q*, has inserted an analysis and reconstruction of the first three woes, which he considers to be pre-Lukan:

Lk 6,24-25	Catchpole
[24]πλὴν οὐαὶ ὑμῖν τοῖς πλουσίοις,	οὐαὶ τοῖς πλουσίοις,
ὅτι ἀπέχετε τὴν **παράκλησιν** ὑμῶν.	ὅτι ἀπέχουσιν τὸν **μισϑὸν** αὐτῶν.
[25a]οὐαὶ ὑμῖν, οἱ ἐμπεπλησμένοι νῦν,	οὐαὶ τοῖς (?γελῶσιν/**χαίρουσιν**),
ὅτι πεινάσετε	ὅτι πενϑήσουσιν.
[25b]οὐαί, οἱ γελῶντες νῦν,	οὐαὶ τοῖς ἐμπεπλησμένοις,
ὅτι **πενϑήσετε** καὶ κλαύσετε.	ὅτι πεινάσουσιν.

I quote: "The one difficulty is the woe on the rich which ought to function as a heading for the other two woes and which is unlikely to have

36. SCHÜRMANN, *Lukasevangelium*, p. 331 n. 42: "Es ist Lk 6,25 wohl durch das stereotyp-gewohnheitsmäßige Nebeneinander der beiden Verben... vorluk in den Weheruf geraten und von dort in die matth Seligpreisung"; cf. *Warnung*, p. 75 n. 65. FITZMYER, *Luke* I, 1981, p. 637 (cf. 627): "The pair, 'weep and mourn' (*penthein* and *klaiein*), is found in Greek papyri (MM, 502-503 [POxy 528,9]) and in the LXX (2 Sam 19:2; 2 Esdr 18:19). See further Mark 16:10; Jas 4:9; Rev 18:11,15,19". Cf. J. GNILKA, *Matthäusevangelium* I, 1986, p. 122: "eine manchmal fast floskelhafte Verbindung"; H.-D. BETZ, *Sermon* (n. 16), p. 588: "The combination of the two verbs is traditional, so that one should rule out redactional operations on this point". See also H.-T. WREGE, *Bergpredigt* (n. 26), p. 16, with reference to TJud 25,5; TJos 3,9 (ἐπένϑησα, A[ab] add καὶ ἔκλαυσα); add: TZeb 4,8 μὴ κλαίε μηδὲ πένϑει (*v.l.* λυποῦ). In reply to Wrege, Dupont observes that πενϑεῖν καὶ κλαίειν in this order occurs only once in the LXX (Neh 8,9 = 2 Esdr 18,19), and in the NT: Jas 4,9; Mk 16,10; in inverted order: Rev 18,11.15.19. It may suffice to note here: "on les [les deux verbes] rencontre plus souvent en parallélisme synonymique (Gen 37,35; 2 S 19,1 [= 2]; Neh 1,4 [2 Esdr 11,4]; Ps 77,63-64; Is 16,8-9; Si 7,34)... probable en *Hen* 96,2" (*Béatitudes* III, p. 75 n. 2).
For Tuckett, "Luke's πενϑήσετε καὶ κλαύσετε... looks overloaded, and if κλαίω is redactional, this would confirm the use of πενϑέω in Luke's tradition here" (*Q and the History*, p. 225). If overloaded, πενϑεῖν may have been added redactionally to the traditional κλαίειν (cf. 6,21b οἱ κλαίοντες). In *Beatitudes* (n. 17) Tuckett replies to Schürmann and Wrege: "the coupling is not that common and relatively rare in the LXX", and "if πενϑέω is an addition to an original κλαίω, one would expect πενϑέω to come second" (p. 199 n. 24). But since "there is no fixed order to the coupling" (*ibid.*), the argument "from order" is at least reversible in the light of the first member of the woe-saying (οἱ γελῶντες): "Luke's use of κλαίω may also be partly occasioned by the presence of γελάω, since 'weeping' might be seen as a natural antithesis to 'laughing'" (p. 199).
37. P. KLEIN, *Die lukanischen Weherufe Lk 6,24-26*, in *ZNW* 71 (1980) 150-159 (on Lukan redaction), here p. 156: "die stärkere Betonung des bejammernswerten Zustandes der jetzt Privilegierten in der Zukunft durch die pleonastische Ausdrucksweise".
38. *Luke*, p. 636. Cf. Lk 2,25; Acts 4,36; 9,31; 13,15; 15,31. Cf. H. KLEIN, in *NTS* 42 (1996), p. 422: "die Weherufe (standen) nicht in der Logienquelle". On Luke's use of παράκλησις in 6,24 in the light of Lk 2,25, cf. P. KLEIN, *Weherufe*, p. 155.

included the very Lukan word παράκλησις"[39] (compare Goulder: "a perfectly Lukan word"[40]). Therefore, in the *pre-Q* tradition of the woes, he proposes to read τὸν μισθόν instead of τὴν παράκλησιν[41].

If, in the woes, we can explain παράκλησιν (6,24) and πενθήσετε (6,25b) as redactional without necessarily referring to Mt 5,4, there remains in Lk no positive evidence for a Q (or Q^{mt}) origin of Mt's verbs πενθεῖν and παρακαλεῖν. Lukan redaction of κλαίειν and γελᾶν is Catchpole's second argument. But the statistics are rather confusing: apart from Lk 6,21b.25b there are in Lk-Acts ten (or eleven)[42] occurrences of κλαίειν and none of γελᾶν. For Catchpole, this can be "no problem in view of the profusion of *hapax legomena* in Luke-Acts"[43], though for οἱ γελῶντες in the woe (Lk 6,25b) the possibility of tradition is left open in his reconstruction: οὐαὶ τοῖς (?γελῶσιν/χαίρουσιν)[44]. Tuckett's option for tradition is less ambiguous. Because of the pejorative use of γελᾶν (derision) in the LXX, he concludes that "the usage in the woe is more original and that [less appropriate] in the beatitude is due to LkR"[45]. However, the whole argument is very much relativized by Tuckett's final observation that Luke "may have been unaware of the slightly specialised use of the verb in the OT"[46]. In this connection,

---

39. *Quest* (n. 20), p. 90. Catchpole seems to correct his argument when he notes that Luke's παρακαλεῖν/παράκλησις "never (represents) the original prosperity of the rich as such" and "the contrivedness of the παράκλησις usage in Luke 6:24" can be an echo of the "natural" usage in Mt 5,4 (p. 85 n. 17). But see n. 38.

40. "Reply" (n. 17), p. 215.

41. *Quest*, p. 90. Cf. Mt 6,2.5.16: "Matthew appears to know Luke 6:24" (p. 89), which is an inversion of Dupont's suggestion (I, p. 163 n. 1). Compare the theme in Lk 16,25 ἀπέλαβες τὰ ἀγαθά σου ἐν τῇ ζωῇ σου. The verb ἀπέχετε can be Lk's variation for the other commercial term ἀπολαμβάνειν. There is no need for a source-text with μισθός (for the Lukan παράκλησις).

42. If Lk 22,62 (par. Mk 14,72) is included; on the textual problem, cf. *Evangelica* II, pp. 109 n. 85, 135. Cf. TUCKETT, *Beatitudes* (n. 17), p. 198: 2–4–10+3 (correction: Acts 9,39; 21,13). The occurrences in Mk are: 5,38.39 (diff. Mt); 14,72 (= Mt); [16,10]; in Mt 2,18 (quotation); 26,75 (= Mk). On Luke's use of κλαίειν, cf. DUPONT, *Béatitudes* III, pp. 69-74.

43. *Quest*, p. 85.

44. *Ibid.*, p. 90.

45. Cf. above, n. 17: *Luke 4,16-30*, p. 343 n. 1; *Beatitudes*, p. 198; *Q*, pp. 224-225. Compare J. SCHLOSSER (n. 20), 1980, p. 428: "De la malédiction (Lc 6,25b), dans laquelle ils sont bien en situation, les vocables [κλαίω, γελάω] auront passé dans la béatitude correspondante (Lc 6,21b), où ils conviennent beaucoup moins".

46. *Ibid.* Cf. *Scripture and Q*, p. 19, n. 71: "The reference to laughter here in Luke [6:25] seems to have been misunderstood by Luke himself... Luke perhaps is unaware of this...". But see DUPONT, *Béatitudes* III, p. 69: "Il reste donc à prendre le 'rire' dans le sens du vocabulaire grec courant"; in the beatitude, and in the woe-saying: "Inutile d'y chercher une attitude hostile à l'égard de ceux dont ils se moqueraient. On s'en prend à leur bonheur satisfait et sûr de lui-même".

Goulder refers to Ecclesiastes 3,4a (καιρὸς τοῦ κλαῦσαι καὶ καιρὸς τοῦ γελάσαι): "Luke takes the word [γελᾶν] as an obvious converse to κλαίειν in the light of Eccl. 3.4"[47]. Tuckett reverses this observation: "given the slightly more unusual idea of laughter [γελᾶν], one can see how 'weeping' (κλαίειν) might arise as an antithesis on the basis of Eccles. 3"[48]. But do we really need to think, in one sense or another, of dependence on Qohelet in the case of οἱ κλαίοντες and the antithetic γελᾶν, preceded here by οἱ πεινῶντες and its antithesis χορτασθῆναι? There can be no dispute that this last pair comes from Q (Lk 6,21a; Mt 5,6).

By saying "preceded by the πεινῶντες" I am expressing a provisional option for the order of Lk 6,21a.b as the order of Q. Of course, the possibility of a Lukan reordering of the second and third beatitudes can be envisaged. It has been suggested by Dupont that Luke moved the πεινῶντες from the third place to the second (after πτωχοί) because he associated hunger with poverty[49]. But this association can be traditional and there is an elementary logic in the order of πτωχοί and πεινῶντες – κλαίοντες which Luke may have found in the original three beatitudes. Catchpole proposes that the beatitude on the κλαίοντες is placed last by Luke as a transition to the fourth beatitude on persecution[50]. But if it is agreed that the combination of the fourth beatitude with the first three already took place in Q, it is less evident that we can still speak of a specific Lukan interest. The integration of the final beatitude with those preceding is clearly Matthew's concern, as appears from the creation of the bridge saying on the persecuted in Mt 5,10, without parallel in Lk. Mt 5,10 forms an *inclusio* with 5,3 (second line: ὅτι αὐτῶν ἐστιν ἡ βασιλεία τῶν οὐρανῶν), and its phrase ἕνεκεν δικαιοσύνης in the first line echoes the theme of Matthew's reformulation of the πεινῶντες beatitude in 5,6. Matthew added (καὶ διψῶντες) τὴν

47. *Luke*, p. 359. Cf. SCHULZ, p. 78: "entspricht genau κλαίειν".

48. *Beatitudes*, p. 199 n. 25. Cf. above, n. 36. Note that for Tuckett (in contrast to Strecker) the acceptance of a traditional γελᾶν in 6,25 does not imply that κλαίειν in the same woe is also traditional. Compare G. STRECKER, *Sermon*, p. 34: "The opposition of laughing and weeping occurs also in the woe of Luke 6:25, and it is conceivable that Luke found it present in his copy of Q (Q^Luke) and on that basis changed the language of the second beatitude".

49. *Béatitudes* I, pp. 271-272: "Un lien étroit s'établit dans la pensée de l'évangéliste entre la pauvreté et la privation de nourriture". But see III, p. 46: "Les 'affamés' sont traditionnellement mentionnés en parallélisme synonymique avec les pauvres (voir Is 58,7...). ... ce sont ces mêmes pauvres considérés dans la réalité concrète de leur détresse".

50. Cf. D. CATCHPOLE, *Quest*, p. 85; ID., *Beatitudes*, in R.J. COGGINS – J.L. HOULDEN (eds.), *A Dictionary of Biblical Interpretation*, London, SCM – Philadelphia, TPI, 1990, pp. 79-82, here 81.

δικαιοσύνην and, very probably, relocated this beatitude at the end of the first set of four[51].

The question of the order in Mt is complicated by the textual problem concerning the inversion of 5,5 πραεῖς and 5,4 πενθοῦντες (D 33 lat sy^c bo^ms; Or Eus). It is now less usual that Mt 5,5 is treated as a later gloss (μακάριοι **οἱ πραεῖς**, ὅτι αὐτοὶ **κληρονομήσουσιν** τὴν γῆν, cf. Ps 36,11a LXX)[52], though N.J. McEleney (1981) still invented a post-Matthean redactor in charge of v. 5[53]. J. Dupont in 1958 defended the originality of the order 5,3.5.4 (πτωχοί immediately followed by πραεῖς) in the text of Mt[54]. For others, this order is pre-Matthean and the evangelist is responsible for the relocation of πενθοῦντες (v. 4) before πραεῖς (v. 5). Thus, for Davies & Allison, Mt 5,5 was originally "added by an editor of Q^mt in order to explicate the first beatitude (which it at some time immediately followed)"[55]. Compare R.A. Guelich's statement: "The two Beatitudes would then have been trans-mitted together in the tradition until Matthew... rearranged them"[56]. The influence of Dupont, which is undeniable, goes here far beyond his own intention by positing a pre-Matthean origin of Mt 5,5 and by using in this regard the text-critical evidence[57]. In this case one may regret that

---

51. Compare J. Lambrecht's reconstruction of the beatitude in Q: the wording of Mt 5,4 but in the Lukan order. See *Maar ik zeg u. De programmatische rede van Jezus (Mt. 5–7; Lc. 6,20-49)*, Leuven, VBS-Acco, 1983, p. 53 (GT, 1984, p. 46; ET, 1985, p. 43; FT, 1986, p. 44). Cf. above, n. 23. Less convincing is S. Schulz's distinction between Mt 5,3-4 ("menschliche Notlage") and 5,5-10 ("christliche Tugenden"), including v. 6 (p. 76).
52. J. Wellhausen (1904), followed by A. Harnack (1907), E. Klostermann (1909), R. Bultmann (1921), C.H. Dodd (1955). More recently, and now rather exceptionally, M.-É. BOISMARD, *Synopse* II, 1972, p. 127; K.C. HANSON, *"How Honorable! How Shameful!" A Cultural Analysis of Matthew's Makarisms and Reproaches*, in *Semeia* 68 (1996) 81-111, here p. 99. See also the footnote that appears in all editions of the Jerusalem Bible: "Le v. 4 [*les doux*] pourrait n'être qu'une glose du v. 3; son omission ramènerait le nombre des béatitudes à sept" (1955, p. 1294; 1973, p. 1420, n. *i*; cf. P. Benoit, 1950, p. 51, note).
53. *Beatitudes* (n. 16), p. 12; see also p. 13: addition of τὴν δικαιοσύνην in v. 6.
54. *Béatitudes* I, pp. 251-257, esp. 253: "les hésitations de la tradition textuelle s'ex-pliquent à partir d'une rédaction primitive plaçant les 'doux' en deuxième rang". The strength (and the weakness!) of Dupont's argument lies in the concentration on πτωχοί/πραεῖς (= *ănāwîm*) as the link between the two beatitudes: "un copiste grec ne pouvait plus le percevoir" (p. 253). See also III, pp. 473-474 ("cette question reste dis-cutée...").
55. *Matthew* I, p. 449. But see p. 447 n. 30, on the textual witnesses.
56. R.A. GUELICH, *The Sermon on the Mount*, Dallas, TX, Word, 1982, p. 82. Cf. ID., *The Matthean Beatitudes: 'Entrance-Requirements' or Eschatological Blessings?*, in *JBL* 95 (1976) 415-434, p. 426.
57. Cf. GUELICH, *Beatitudes* (n. 56), p. 426: "Text-critically, however, there is ample witness to indicate that originally there was no intervening Beatitude [between 5,3 and 5]". "Originally" here means in the pre-Mt tradition different from the text of Mt.

the readers of Dupont's *Béatitudes* almost never refer to its first edition. I quote from the 1954 volume[58]:

> Inspirée du psaume 36, elle [la béatitude des doux] a été insérée par l'éditeur du premier évangile après la béatitude des affligés.
> Nous préférons nous en remettre au témoignage de la tradition manuscrite et laisser la béatitude des doux en troisième place.

With only a few exceptions[59] modern text editions prefer this more common reading of the Greek manuscripts (with good reason, I think)[60]. Nevertheless we can retain from Guelich's approach at least one valid observation: the order of the beatitudes πτωχοί – πενθοῦντες in Mt 5,3.4 is due to MtR, more particularly, to Matthew's "desire to align the initial Beatitudes more closely to the language and order of Isa 61:1-2"[61]. In addition to the arrangement of the πεινῶντες beatitude in Mt 5,6 (mentioned above) this alignment to Isa 61,1-2 can be another, and perhaps more important, reason for Matthew's reordering of the second and third Q-beatitudes.

The influence of Isa 61,1-2 on Matthew's relocation of Mt 5,4 (cf. Lk 6,21b) is accepted by Schürmann and even extended by him to the influence of Isa 61 on Mt 5,6: χορτασθήσονται has a parallel in Isa 61,6

58. *Béatitudes*, 1954, pp. 292 and 87-90 (here, p. 89 n. 2). Contrast vol. I, 1958, pp. 252-253.

59. Lachmann, Tischendorf, Lagrange, Bover. See also the French translations in the Jerusalem Bible (ET: NJB, 1990) and TOB. Cf. P. Benoit's commentary (1950), with a famous lapsus in the note on "les doux": "Rejeté après le v. 5 par D 33..." (³1961, p. 54).

60. "If verses 3 and 5 had originally stood together, with their rhetorical antithesis of heaven and earth, it is unlikely that any scribe would have thrust ver. 4 between them" (B.M. METZGER, *Textual Commentary*, ²1994, p. 10). Cf. H. FRANKEMÖLLE, *Makarismen* (n. 16), p. 70 n. 71: "nicht nur die handschriftliche Überlieferung, sondern auch der enge Bezug in V 3f auf Js 61,1f". See also U. LUZ, *Matthäus* I, p. 199 n. 1: "V 4 und 5 sind in westlichen Textzeugen umgestellt, vermutlich um der so entstehenden Parallelität in der Apodosis willen" (3/5: οὐρανοί – γῆ; 4/6 Schluß auf -θήσονται)". On this last parallel, see also J. GNILKA, *Matthäusevangelium* I, p. 119 n. 17. – A.A. Di Lella (n. 30) strangely argues for the originality of Mt 5,3.5 by referring to the phrase τὸν οὐρανὸν καὶ τὴν γῆν in Gen 1,1 and 2,4a (p. 242; followed by É. Puech, p. 98). No more convincing is their argument based on the number of words (Di Lella, p. 241; Puech, p. 97). M. Dumais (n. 15) presents the "Béatitudes matthéennes" (cc. 797-817) in the order: "a) Les 'pauvres en esprit' (v,3); b) Les 'doux' (v,4); c) Les 'affligés' (v,5)...", without really discussing the location of πραεῖς. He notes that "la béatitude des 'doux' [his 5,4] a essentiellement le même sens que celle des 'pauvres en esprit'" and seems to rely on J. Dupont (c. 800).

61. GUELICH, *Sermon*, p. 82. See also W. GRUNDMANN, *Das Evangelium nach Matthäus* (THKNT, 1), Berlin, Evangelische Verlagsanstalt, 1968, p. 123: "Die dritte lukanische Seligpreisung rückt bei Matthäus an die zweite Stelle; diese Stellung ist bestimmt durch Jes. 61,1-3".

κατέδεσθε (you shall *eat...*); "Die Sättigung der Hungernden mußte umgestellt werden, wenn Is 61,6 κατέδεσθε anklingen sollte"[62]. My comment can be brief. I subscribe to Tuckett's statement saying that "the verbal agreement is not at all close and one should probably not lay any great value [or any value at all] on such a possible parallel"[63]. Unlike the parallel with Mt 5,4 in Isa 61,2, the Greek word in 61,6 is not the same and the theme is different: "you shall eat the wealth of the nations". Moreover, Schürmann also considers the following v. 7: κληρονομήσουσιν τὴν γῆν, par. Mt 5,5; this would imply that Mt 5,6 is once more "umgestellt", now with reference to the parallels in Isa 61,6.7 (Mt 5,6.5).

Mt 5,5 has a much closer parallel in Ps 36(LXX),11a, with the subject οἱ πραεῖς[64]. For M. Hengel one may find there the key for understanding the relocation of Mt 5,6: the Q-beatitudes "werden von ihm [Mt] umgestellt... dem Tenor von Jes 61 und Ps 37 entsprechend. Mt 5,3 und 4 läßt deutlich Jes 61,1-3 anklingen, Mt 5,5 und 6 Ps 37,11 und [19]"[65].

---

62. *Lukasevangelium*, p. 336 n. 84. Cf. p. 330 n. 30: "unter Einfluß von Is 61,1ff.6f[!]". Quoted by Schulz (p. 76 n. 124).

63. *Q and the History*, p. 226. The conjunction with Ps 146,7b, "the Lord gives food to the hungry", in *Scripture and Q* (p. 24) illustrates anew that for Tuckett the parallel in Isa 61,6 has no great value. Contrast J. DUPONT, *Béatitudes* II, p. 94.

64. Cf. above, n. 52. See also DAVIES & ALLISON, *Matthew* I, p. 451: "Given the other allusions to Isa 61 in the other beatitudes, perhaps 5.5 should recall Isa 61.7 even though 5.5 clearly quotes Ps 37.11 – especially since both Matthew and Isaiah agree, against the psalm, in having the definite article before γῆν". Contrast I. BROER (n. 16), p. 67 n. 16: "Da Mt 5,5 auf Ps 36,11 LXX basiert, ist eine doppelte Vermittlung unwahrscheinlich und auch unnötig" (cf. below, n. 74); here in reply to D. Flusser.
In Flusser's theory the original saying (in Hebrew) is preserved in Mt 5,3-5. He prefers the order 3-5-4 because in his view v. 3 (on the poor "endowed with the Holy Spirit": theirs is the kingdom of heaven) is an explanation (*pesher*) of v. 5 (= Ps 37,11: the meek shall inherit the earth); at the same time it is "the explanation of עניים in Isa. 61,1" (nn. 5 and 9). This order is also closer to a parallel passage in 1QH. Since Mt 5,3-5-4 and 1QH 23(18),14-15 are based on the same combination of Isa 61,1-2 and 66,2, there is "some literary connection" between the two passages and "the source of the three first Beatitudes (probably) originated in the Dead Sea Sect or in some milieu close to it". Cf. *Blessed are the Poor in Spirit...*, in *Israel Exploration Journal* 10 (1960) 1-13; reprinted in his *Judaism and the Origins of Christianity*, Jerusalem, Magnes, 1988, pp. 102-114 (passim). Note that for Flusser Luke has no parallel to Mt 5,4: Lk 6,21b is a different beatitude, which is omitted by Matthew. The original number of beatitudes was probably ten (9 + 1) and they all had their counterpart in the woes (pp. 11-12 = 112-113). For criticism see e.g. J. DUPONT, *Béatitudes* II, p. 98 n. 3. In particular, Dupont rejects the influence of Isa 66,2 on Matthew's addition of τῷ πνεύματι in 5,3: "Cet appel à *Is* 66 nous paraît parfaitement inutile". Contrast GUNDRY, *Matthew*, p. 67: "Matthew adds 'in spirit' from Isa 66:2 ('poor and contrite of spirit')". Flusser has further developed his construction in *Some Notes to the Beatitudes*, in *Immanuel* 8 (1978) 37-47 (= *Judaism*, pp. 115-125, esp. pp. 42-44 (= 120-122) on Mt 5,6.

65. M. HENGEL, *Zur matthäischen Bergpredigt und ihrem jüdischen Hintergrund*, in *TR* 52 (1987) 327-400, esp. pp. 348-357 (on the beatitudes), here p. 354. Hengel refers to

Hengel seems to neglect that the case of Mt 5,6 is quite different from Mt 5,4. Without discussing here the parallel in Ps 36,19b (καὶ ἐν ἡμέραις λιμοῦ χορτασθήσονται)[66], one should note that the refrain κληρονομήσουσιν γῆν is repeated throughout the psalm (vv. 9.11.22.29; cf. 34), before and after v. 19; this is of course an unsuitable basis for an argument "from order".

The influence of Isa 61,2 on the wording and location of Mt 5,4 can be acknowledged without reserve and, in accord with Hengel, can be assigned to MtR (and not to Q or Q^mt)[67]. Word statistics of the Synoptics alone (as practiced by T. Bergemann)[68] can hardly demonstrate redactional usage in Mt 5,4 (diff. Q 6,21b), though the occurrence of πενθεῖν in 9,15 (Mk νηστεύειν) and the use of παρακληθῆναι in the sense "be comforted" in 2,18 (Jer 31[38],15) should not be neglected in a statistical analysis. As indicated above, Matthew's dependence on the woe-say-

Ps 37,11 and "17-18" (my correction: "19"). Cf. pp. 351-353: "Das Problem des Einflusses von Jes 61", esp. 352: "in 5,3-6 (werden) Textstücke, Begriffe und Motive aus Jes 61,1-8 und Ps 37 (vor allem V. 11.14.19) miteinander 'verwoben'"; and "Die Verheißung κληρονομήσουσιν τὴν γῆν nimmt Jes 61,7 zusammen mit Ps 37,11 in 5,5 auf".
    Compare G.W. Buchanan's "midrashic" analysis: *Matthean Beatitudes and Traditional Promises*, in W.R. FARMER (ed.), *New Synoptic Studies*, Macon, GA, Mercer, 1983, pp. 161-184; on parallels in Ps 37(36), see esp. 166-168. Cf. DAVIES & ALLISON, p. 438 n. 16: "Most of these [parallels] must..., *pace* Buchanan, be regarded as insignificant".
    66. Cf. M.-É. BOISMARD, *Synopse* II, 1972, p. 128; D.A. HAGNER, *Matthew* I, p. 93: Mt 5,6 may reflect the language of Ps 106(LXX),5a πεινῶντες καὶ διψῶντες, 9 ὅτι ἐχόρτασεν ψυχὴν κενὴν καὶ ψυχὴν πεινῶσαν ἐνέπλησεν ἀγαθῶν. See also Isa 49,10 οὐ πεινάσουσιν οὐδὲ διψήσουσιν.
    67. Contrast DAVIES & ALLISON, *Matthew* I, p. 438: "the strongest links with Isa 61 [in Mt 5,3-4] are to be assigned not to Q^mt but to an earlier stage of Q"; "the farther back we go, the greater the impact of Isa 61 seems to be... Matthew has not done much if anything to accentuate the connexions between Isa 61 and Mt 5.3-12"; "the connexion with Isa 61... gradually weakened over time" (p. 437; cf. W. Grimm); J. DUPONT, *Jésus, messie des pauvres, messie pauvre* (1984), in *Études* (n. 14), pp. 86-130: "Ce n'est pas au niveau de la rédaction des deux évangélistes (que le texte d'Is 61,1 a exercé son influence sur la formulation de la première béatitude): ni l'un ni l'autre n'ont perçu la référence, et les retouches que chacun d'eux a apportées au texte de base ont éloigné la béatitude de l'oracle qui l'inspirait" (p. 99). – On Q^mt, cf. above, nn. 25 and 32. See also M. SATO, *Q*, p. 47 (1984, p. 54). The π-alliteration in Mt 5,3-6 (Luz, Sato: cf. C. Michaelis) can be coincidental: πτωχοί (from Q), πενθοῦντες (from Isa 61,2), πραεῖς (from Ps 36,11), πεινῶντες (from Q) + καὶ διψῶντες (MtR).
    68. T. BERGEMANN, *Q auf dem Prüfstand. Die Zuordnung des Mt/Lk-Stoffes zu Q am Beispiel der Bergpredigt* (FRLANT, 158), Göttingen, Vandenhoeck & Ruprecht, 1993. For critique, cf. A. DENAUX, *Criteria for Identifying Q-Passages*, in *NT* 37 (1995) 105-129. On πενθέω Bergemann expresses "eine gewisse Unsicherheit" (p. 76); with quotation of Sato's remark on Mt 9,15: "damit *muss* dasselbe Wort in Mt 5,4 nicht redaktionell sein" (n. 7), but no reference to Isa 61,2! On παρακαλέω (pp. 79-80), n. 43: "Schulz... vermutet... eine matthäische Formulierung in Anlehnung an Jes 61,2, ohne dies wahrscheinlich machen zu können"; without further discussion.

ings (6,24 παράκλησιν; 6,25 πενθήσετε) is doubtful, for more than one reason. On the contrary, Isa 61,2 παρακαλέσαι πάντας τοὺς πενθοῦντας (together with the reference to πτωχοί in v. 1) provides a satisfactory explanation of Matthew's changing κλαίοντες – γελάσετε to πενθοῦντες – παρακληθήσονται. The influence of Isa 61,2 can be the "convincing reason" H.D. Betz is looking for[69].

However, with the allusion to Isa 61,2 in Mt 5,4 new problems arise. Our discussion of possible influences on the location of Mt 5,6 has shown that for Schürmann and Hengel the parallels to the Matthean beatitudes are not restricted to Isa 61,1-2. Hengel emphasizes that "ein Zitat den ganzen Kontext, aus dem er stammt, miteinbringen kann", and: "Man darf bei Mt nicht nur 'platte' Zitate erwarten, vielmehr wird aus wenigen Zitate und mancherlei Anspielungen ein bunter Teppich geflochten, der den Schriftkundigen erfreut"[70]. All sorts of parallels from Isa 61 (or at least 61,1-8), "Textstücke, Begriffe, Motive", are recorded by both Schürmann (1969)[71] and Hengel[72]:

Isa 61 LXX	Mt 5,3-12
1 πνεῦμα κυρίου ἐπ' ἐμέ, οὗ εἵνεκεν ἔχρισέν με·	
εὐαγγελίσασθαι πτωχοῖς ἀπέσταλκέν με,	3
ἰάσασθαι τοὺς συντετριμμένους τῇ καρδίᾳ,	(3a)8a
· κηρύξαι αἰχμαλώτοις ἄφεσιν καὶ τυφλοῖς ἀνάβλεψιν,	
2 καλέσαι ἐνιαυτὸν κυρίου δεκτὸν καὶ ἡμέραν ἀνταποδόσεως,	(3b)
παρακαλέσαι πάντας τοὺς πενθοῦντας[a],	4
3 δοθῆναι τοῖς πενθοῦσιν[b] Σιων	
δόξαν[a] ἀντὶ σποδοῦ,	(8b.9b)
ἄλειμμα εὐφροσύνης ῾τοῖς πενθοῦσιν[c],	῾ἀντὶ πένθους (Ziegler)

69. Cf. above, n. 27.
70. *Bergpredigt* (n. 65), p. 351.
71. List of parallels in *Lukasevangelium*, p. 336 n. 84. See also Davies & Allison's list (pp. 436-437), with reference to W. Grimm: "some less certain than others". Cf. W. GRIMM, *Die Verkündigung Jesu und Deuterojesaja* (ANTJ, 1), Frankfurt, P. Lang, 1976 (first title: *Weil Ich dich liebe*), pp. 68-77; [2]1981, pp. 68-77 (revised). See also K. KOCH, *Formgeschichte* (n. 20), p. 247: Mt 5,3.4 (Isa 61,1.2), and "weitere Bezugnahme auf Jes. 61" in Mt 5,5 (Isa 61,7); 5,6 (Isa 61,6); same references in GUNDRY, *Matthew*, at Mt 5,3.4.5.6.
72. *Bergpredigt*, p. 352: "die Umformung von Lk 6,21 (Q) unter dem Einfluß von Jes 61,2f. in 5,4 und außerdem... weitere Anspielungen... In dem πτωχοὶ τῷ πνεύματι klingt das συντετριμμένους τῇ καρδίᾳ von Jes 61,1 mit an (vgl. auch 5,8). Die Verheißung κληρονομήσουσιν τὴν γῆν nimmt Jes 61,7 zusammen mit Ps 37,11 in 5,5 auf, das Stichwort 'Gerechtigkeit' von Jes 61,3 und 8 findet sich wieder in 5,6.10. Jes 61,6: ὑμεῖς δὲ ἱερεῖς κυρίου κληθήσεσθε, λειτουργοὶ θεοῦ klingt in 5,9 ὅτι αὐτοὶ υἱοὶ θεοῦ κληθήσονται an... Sachlich ist 'das angenehme Jahr des Herrn' und 'der Tag der Vergeltung' (61,2) identisch mit dem Anbruch der Gottesherrschaft, und die dreimalige Nennung der δόξα in 61,3, das dann ausklingt in dem φύτευμα κυρίου εἰς δόξαν, mit der eschatologischen Gottesschau und Gottessohnschaft".

καταστολὴν **δόξης**[b] ἀντὶ **πνεύματος** ἀκηδίας·   3a
καὶ **κληθήσονται**[a] γενεαὶ **δικαιοσύνης**[a], φύτευμα κυρίου εἰς **δόξαν**[c].   6.10
9b.6a=10a
6 ὑμεῖς δὲ ἱερεῖς κυρίου **κληθήσεσθε**[b], λειτουργοὶ θεοῦ·   9b
   ἰσχὺν ἐθνῶν **κατέδεσθε**   6b
   καὶ ἐν τῷ πλούτῳ αὐτῶν θαυμασθήσεσθε.
7 οὕτως ἐκ δευτέρας **κληρονομήσουσιν τὴν γῆν**,   5
   καὶ εὐφροσύνη αἰώνιος ὑπὲρ κεφαλῆς αὐτῶν.
8 ἐγὼ γάρ εἰμι κύριος ὁ ἀγαπῶν **δικαιοσύνην**[b]
   καὶ μισῶν ἁρπάγματα ἐξ ἀδικίας·...
10 ... **ἀγαλλιάσθω**[a] ἡ ψυχή μου ἐπὶ τῷ κυρίῳ·...   12
11 ... οὕτως ἀνατελεῖ κύριος **δικαιοσύνην**[c]
   καὶ **ἀγαλλίαμα**[b] ἐναντίον πάντων τῶν ἐθνῶν.

The section on Isa 61 in Hengel's survey article (*TR*, 1987) was written in response to I. Broer (*Seligpreisungen*, 1986). Broer's thesis is the extreme opposite to Hengel's approach: "der Einfluß von Jes 61 beschränkt sich auf Mt 5,4"; "über Mt 5,4 hinaus sind in der matthäischen Makarismenreihe keine zusätzliche Elemente zu finden, die auf Jes 61 hinweisen"[73]. Broer defends, in the line of Schürmann and Frankemölle, the pre-Lukan origin of the woe-sayings, but he is critical of what he calls "eine doppelte Vermittlung", i.e., the acceptance of a double dependence in Mt 5,4 on both the Isaiah prophecy (61,2) and the woe-sayings (Lk 6,24.25b): "eine Ableitung aus Jes 61,2 (ist) völlig ausreichend"[74]. His method of neutralizing the parallels in the woes, παράκλησιν and πενθήσετε, is not completely my way of arguing but it leads to the same result.

Broer shows the contingency of parallels (other than with Mt 5,4 in Isa 61,2) such as τῇ καρδίᾳ in 61,1 (Mt 5,8: cf. Ps 23 LXX,4), the word πνεύματος in 61,3 (Mt 5,3), κληθήσονται in 61,3 (Mt 5,9), κατέδεσθε in 61,6 (Mt 5,6), κληρονομήσουσιν τὴν γῆν in 61,7 (Mt 5,5; cf. Ps 36 LXX,11: another "doppelte Vermittlung")[75]. With regard to the beatitudes in Q, Broer cites with approval the much-quoted passage in Frankemölle's 1971 article[76]:

73. *Seligpreisungen* (n. 16), pp. 64-67 ("Der Zusammenhang der Makarismen mit Jes 61"), here 67 and 65.
74. *Ibid.*, p. 20. See also U. LUZ, *Matthäus*, p. 200 n. 9; E. SEVENICH-BAX, *Konfrontation* (n. 24), p. 76 (ctr. SCHÜRMANN, *Lukasevangelium*, p. 336 n. 84).
75. *Ibid.*, pp. 65-66. Frankemölle prefers to retain this last parallel (61,7: Mt 5,5), as well as δικαιοσύνη (61,5.6.8: Mt 5,6.10): *Makarismen*, p. 69; ID., *Matthäus Kommentar I*, Düsseldorf, Patmos, 1994, pp. 210-211. See also R.A. GUELICH, *Matthean Beatitudes*, pp. 427-428; J.M. ROBINSON, *The Sayings Gospel Q* (n. 18), p. 369: Mt 5,5 and Isa 61,6 (= 7); 60,21 (no mention of Ps 36 LXX); Mt 5,10 and Isa 60,21 ("may have supplied δίκαιος to suggest δικαιοσύνη as an addition...."); on Mt 5,4 and Isa 61,2, *ibid.* (and n. 8: in his view, the woes in Lk 6,24.25 "may reflect also the influence of Isa 61,2").
76. *Makarismen*, p. 60; quoted by Broer (p. 64). Cf. below, n. 81.

Unter der Voraussetzung, daß Lk der Q-Tradition in den VV. 20b-21b ziemlich nahesteht..., darf man die These wagen, daß... kein Bezug zur messianischen Prophezeiung Jes 61,1f. vorlag. Wer wollte dies einzig und allein durch das Wort οἱ πτωχοί (die Armen) als erwiesen ansehen?

Unlike οἱ πτωχοί (τῷ πνεύματι)[77] in Mt 5,3, the word οἱ πτωχοί in Lk is not supported by a further parallel with Isa 61 in the second or third beatitude: "As Luke's Beatitudes now stand they reflect little or no connection with Isa 61:1-3" (Guelich)[78]. For those who argue that the wording of Mt 5,4 comes closer to Q than that of Lk 6,21b, "it may be significant [I quote Tuckett] that Luke may have redacted the beatitudes in such a way that the allusion to Isa 61 is diminished rather than increased"[79]. The alternative solution proposes that Matthew may have seen in οἱ πτωχοί (Q) an allusion to Isa 61,1 and may have increased the parallelism with Isa in the redaction of his second beatitude (5,4). I refer here to a note on Q 6,20b by M. Sato, which goes in the same direction[80]:

> Unser Text ist nicht auf Jes 61,1ff zu beziehen. Das Wort "Arme" reicht dafür nicht aus. Die Anspielung auf Jes 61,1ff geschah in unseren Makarismen erst im Stadium von Q-Matthäus (Mt 5,4: πενθέω/παρακαλέω wie Jes 61,2f).

Οἱ πτωχοί in Q 6,20b (= Lk) is only an incomplete parallel to the phrase in Isa 61,1 (εὐαγγελίσασθαι πτωχοῖς)[81] and the evidence for an allu-

---

77. For an (exceptional) interpretation of ἐν πνεύματι in the light of Isa 61,1 (πνεῦμα κυρίου), see the recent suggestion of an instrumental sense: M. LATTKE, *Glückselig durch den Geist (Matthäus 5,3)*, in C. MAYER, et al. (eds.), *Nach den Anfängen fragen*. FS G. Dautzenberg, Gießen, 1994, pp. 363-382.

78. *Matthean Beatitudes*, p. 424.

79. C.M. TUCKETT, *The Lukan Son of Man*, in ID. (ed.), *Luke's Literary Achievement*. *Collected Essays* (JSNT SS, 116), Sheffield, Academic, 1995, pp. 198-217, p. 217 n. 65. Compare DAVIES & ALLISON and DUPONT (above, n. 67).

80. *Q und Prophetie* (n. 23), 1988, p. 255 n. 449 (1984, p. 530 n. 491). I would say: at the stage of MtR.

81. Cf. H. FRANKEMÖLLE, *Evangelium, Begriff und Gattung. Ein Forschungsbericht* (SBB, 15), Stuttgart, KBW, ²1994, p. 129: "allein das Wort οἱ πτωχοί, das hier wie dort auftaucht (dazu noch in einem anderen Kasus), belegt noch keine Abhängigkeit" (with reference to Broer in n. 156; and again, p. 146 n. 193); ID., *Jesus als deuterojesajanischer Freudenbote? Zur Rezeption von Jes 52,7 und 61,1 im Neuen Testament, durch Jesus und in den Targumim*, in ID. – K. KERTELGE (eds.), *Vom Urchristentum zu Jesus*. FS J. Gnilka, Freiburg, Herder, 1989, pp. 34-67, esp. 49-50: "Mt 5,3 par Lk 6,20" (cf. *Evangelium*, pp. 145-146). See also ID., *Evangelium und Wirkungsgeschichte*, in L. OBERLINNER – P. FIEDLER (eds.), *Salz der Erde – Licht der Welt. Exegetische Studien zum Matthäusevangelium*. FS A. Vögtle. Stuttgart, KBW, 1991, pp. 31-89, here 51-52. Frankemölle kommt closer to Hengel than would be suggested by his rather tendentious assimilation of Hengel's position with the "Konsens der Forscher" [?], i.e., "die These, wonach in Lk 6,21b [Q] bereits auch schon Jes 61,2 rezipiert sei" (p. 52); see also his critique of Broer (p. 52 n. 73; cf. above, n. 75).

By suggesting "more light" from a "broader tradition" of Isa 61 and Ps 146 "taken together", C. Tuckett (*Scripture and Q*, p. 24) seems to recognize that there is a problem with οἱ πτωχοί as reference to Isa 61,1 (see his n. 90).

sion to Isa 61,1 is usually taken from Q 7,22 πτωχοὶ εὐαγγελίζονται (if not from the quotation in Lk 4,18-19)[82]. It is to this factor, external to the beatitudes, that I will turn in the second part of this lecture.

II

Except for the opening phrase, which is probably redactional in both versions[83], Mt 11,2-6 represents the text of the common source Q, possibly with a few minor changes:

---

82. Cf. SCHÜRMANN, *Lukasevangelium*, p. 341: "in Bezugnahme auf Is 61,1 und von Lk 4,18 und 7,22 her" (see also pp. 326, 328). Note however that, in contrast to Davies & Allison, *et al.* (nn. 67, 79), Schürmann stresses that "Matth erkennt und verdeutlicht ergänzend... die Is-Anspielung der Heilrufe Jesu" (p. 336 n. 84).

In his 1981 Leuven paper Schürmann has reformulated his position: *Das Zeugnis der Redenquelle für die Basileia-Verkündigung*, in J. DELOBEL (ed.), *Logia*, 1982, pp. 121-200, esp. 136-140; reprinted in his *Gottes Reich – Jesu Geschick*, Freiburg, 1983, pp. 65-152, esp. 83-88. He still maintains that in the original version (= Lk 6,20b-21) "die Vermeldung an die 'Armen' immerhin an Jes 61,1 anklingen mag", but: "hier wird nicht ein Jesaja-Text zitiert in der Art, wie das Lk 7,22 par Mt, dann auch Lk 4,18f geschieht. Es ist auch nicht in Anspielung auf Jesaja vom εὐαγγελίζεσθαι Jesu die Rede... Hier wird das dem 'Lachen' entsprechende 'Weinen' noch nicht (wie dann Mt 5,4) durch 'Tröstung' der 'Trauernden' (in Wortlaut und Stellung!) von Jes 61,2 gebracht... Wo, wie Lk 7,22 par und 4,18.21, ein deutlicher Rückverweis auf Jes 61,1 vorliegt, wird... die Basileia nicht ins Spiel gebracht" (pp. 138-139 = 85-86).

83. Mt 11,2a ἀκούσας ἐν τῷ δεσμωτηρίῳ τὰ ἔργα τοῦ Χριστοῦ / Lk 7,18a ἀπήγγειλαν Ἰωάννῃ οἱ μαθηταὶ αὐτοῦ περὶ πάντων τούτων. See P. HOFFMANN, *Studien*, pp. 192-193 (undecided: ἐν τῷ δεσμωτηρίῳ); S. SCHULZ, *Q*, pp. 190-191; W. SCHENK, *Synopse*, p. 40; IQP, in *JBL* 113 (1994), pp. 497-498; *et al.* Contrast the combination of both versions in ἀκούσας + περὶ πάντων τούτων: A. POLAG, *Fragmenta Q*, p. 41; E. SEVENICH-BAX, *Konfrontation* (n. 24), p. 195 (and 239); R.L. WEBB, *John the Baptizer*, p. 280; D. CATCHPOLE, *Quest*, p. 239 (πάντων LkR). In reply to M.D. Goulder, Catchpole shows that it would be natural for Luke to retain the phrase τὰ ἔργα τοῦ χριστοῦ if he were using Matthew (pp. 43-45). The preceding context in Q is the Centurion's Son (Q 7,1-10) and, as noted by Catchpole, the alternative responses to Jesus are present in the two adjacent passages: πίστις in 7,9 and σκανδαλίζεσθαι in 7,23 (p. 281).

For recent study of Q 7,18-23, cf. V. SCHÖNLE, *Johannes, Jesus und die Juden. Die theologische Position des Matthäus und des Verfassers der Redenquelle im Lichte von Mt. 11* (BEvT, 17), Frankfurt, Lang, 1982, pp. 38-41, 57-64, 97-100; D. VERSEPUT, *The Rejection of the Humble Messianic King. A Study of the Composition of Matthew 11–12* (EHS, 23/291), Frankfurt, Lang, 1989, esp. pp. 56-76; J. ERNST, *Johannes der Täufer. Interpretation – Geschichte – Wirkungsgeschichte* (BZNW, 53), Berlin – New York, de Gruyter, 1989, pp. 56-60; K. BACKHAUS, *Die "Jüngerkreise" des Täufers Johannes. Eine Studie zu den religionsgeschichtlichen Ursprüngen des Christentums* (Paderborner Theologische Studien, 19), Paderborn, Schöningh, 1991, pp. 116-137; R.L. WEBB, *John the Baptizer and Prophet. A Socio-Historical Study* (JSNT SS, 62), Sheffield, Academic, 1991, pp. 278-282; G. HÄFNER, *Der verheißene Vorläufer. Redaktionskritische Untersuchung zur Darstellung Johannes des Täufers im Matthäusevangelium* (SBB, 27), Stuttgart, KBW, 1994, pp. 159-191.

On the reconstruction of the introduction, see HÄFNER, pp. 166-168: "Eine entsprechende Aussage in der Logienquelle [the common content: 'Kenntnisnahme vom Wirken Jesu'] ist also wahrscheinlich, auch wenn der genaue Wortlaut nicht mehr rekon-

19a ὁ Ἰωάννης... πέμψας διὰ τῶν μαθητῶν αὐτοῦ εἶπεν αὐτῷ·
  b σὺ εἶ ὁ ἐρχόμενος ἢ ἕτερον προσδοκῶμεν;
22a καὶ ἀποκριθεὶς ὁ Ἰησοῦς εἶπεν αὐτοῖς·
  b πορευθέντες ἀπαγγείλατε Ἰωάννῃ ἃ ἀκούετε καὶ βλέπετε·
  c τυφλοὶ ἀναβλέπουσιν καὶ χωλοὶ περιπατοῦσιν,   (1) (2)
  d λεπροὶ καθαρίζονται καὶ κωφοὶ ἀκούουσιν   (3) (4)
  e καὶ νεκροὶ ἐγείρονται καὶ πρωχοὶ εὐαγγελίζονται·   (5) (6)
23 καὶ μακάριός ἐστιν ὃς ἐὰν μὴ σκανδαλισθῇ ἐν ἐμοί[84].

It is undisputed that several phrases in Jesus' answer to John (Q 7,22cde) allude to Isaianic passages. The primary parallels are Isa 35,5-6 and 61,1 but the recent literature on Q 7,22 from J. Dupont (1961) to G. Häfner (1994)[85] also refers to a number of secondary parallels:

Isa 26,19   ἀναστήσονται οἱ **νεκροί**,   (5)
           καὶ **ἐγερθήσονται** οἱ ἐν τοῖς μνημείοις,
           καὶ εὐφρανθήσονται οἱ ἐν τῇ γῇ

    29,18   καὶ **ἀκούσονται**... **κωφοὶ** λόγους βιβλίου,   (4)
           καὶ οἱ ἐν τῷ σκότει... ὀφθαλμοὶ **τυφλῶν** βλέψονται.   (1)
     19   καὶ ἀγαλλιάσονται **πτωχοὶ** διὰ κύριον ἐν εὐφροσύνῃ   (6)
           καὶ οἱ ἀπηλπισμένοι τ. ἀ. ἐμπλησθήσονται εὐφροσύνης.

    35,5   τότε ἀνοιχθήσονται ὀφθαλμοὶ **τυφλῶν**,   (1)
           καὶ ὦτα **κωφῶν ἀκούσονται**.   (4)
     6   τότε ἁλεῖται ὡς ἔλαφος ὁ **χωλός**,   (2)
           καὶ τρανὴ ἔσται γλῶσσα μογιλάλων,...

     8   ἐκεῖ ἔσται ὁδὸς καθαρὰ καὶ ὁδὸς ἁγία κληθήσεται,   (3)
           καὶ οὐ μὴ παρέλθῃ ἐκεῖ ἀκάθαρτος, οὐδὲ ἔσται ἐκεῖ ὁδὸς ἀκάθαρτος

    42,7   ἀνοῖξαι ὀφθαλμοὺς **τυφλῶν**,   (1)
           ἐξαγαγεῖν ἐκ δεσμῶν δεδεμένους
           καὶ ἐξ οἴκου φυλακῆς καθημένους ἐν σκοτεῖ

---

struiert werden kann" (p. 168). On ἐν τῷ δεσμωτηρίῳ in Q (Webb, *et al.*), see *ibid.*: "... wahrscheinlicher, daß Mt an eine prinzipiell vorausgesetzte Situation noch einmal ausdrücklich erinnert" (pp. 167-168); undecided: Hoffmann, Polag ("possible"), Ernst (p. 57), Backhaus (p. 117; cf. p. 130: "zumindest... implizite"). But Schürmann rightly observes: "Lk 7,18 dürfte darauf hinweisen, daß die Redequelle die Gefangensetzung des Johannes noch nicht erzählt hatte" (*Lukasevangelium*, p. 184). See also Schönle, p. 40: not in Q.

84. Words in verbatim agreement with Lk appear in bold type in the text above. The differences (in normal type) are: πέμψας... εἶπεν αὐτῷ / ἔπεμψεν... λέγων, διὰ / δύο (v. 18b), ἕτερον / ἄλλον, ὁ Ἰησοῦς / om., ἀκούετε κ. βλέπετε / εἴδετε κ. ἠκούσατε (but see p. 62) καὶ ter / om. (cf. below, n. 88 on καί in Q 7,22). The pluses in Lk 7,20.21 (and v. 18b: calling two of his disciples) can be assigned to the evangelist (ctr. Gundry, Hagner, *et al.*: Mt's characteristic abbreviation). On Lk 7,20, cf. Kloppenborg, *Q Parallels*, p. 52; Häfner, *Vorläufer*, pp. 165-166.

85. Dupont, *L'ambassade* (n. 14), pp. 948-950; *Jésus annonce*, pp. 177-178 (= 73-74): "Attaches dans le Livre d'Isaïe"; Häfner, *Vorläufer*, pp. 179-180 (with references).

18   οἱ **κωφοί**, ἀκούσατε,   (4)
     καὶ οἱ **τυφλοί**, ἀναβλέψατε ἰδεῖν   (1)

61,1   εὐαγγελίσασθαι πτωχοῖς ἀπέσταλκέν με,   (6)
           ἰάσασθαι τοὺς συντετριμμένους τῇ καρδίᾳ,
           κηρύξαι αἰχμαλώτοις ἄφεσιν
           καὶ **τυφλοῖς** ἀνάβλεψιν   (1)

It has been observed that the allusion to Isa 61,1 has a climactic position at the conclusion of the sixfold series in Q 7,22. But is it correct to
say that both the first item in the list (τυφλοὶ ἀναβλέπουσιν) and the
last item (πτωχοὶ εὐαγγελίζονται) come from Isa 61,1[86]? Isa 61,1 LXX
reads τυφλοῖς ἀνάβλεψιν (text cited in Lk 4,18)[87], but the association
of τυφλοί with κωφοί that appears in other passages is perhaps a more
notable parallel: Isa 35,5; 42,18 (with the verb ἀναβλέπειν); 29,18. If
the καί's in Mt 11,5 (diff. Lk) stem from Q, including the καί before
νεκροί[88], then the healing miracles in Q 7,22 form one group of four
specific classes of sufferers, in two pairs, beginning with τυφλοί and
ending with κωφοί[89].

86. Cf. below, n. 92. See also J.M. ROBINSON, *The Sayings Gospel Q* (n. 18), pp. 363-
364: the first and last items "in chiastic order" in Q 7,22 and even the healings "perhaps
triggered by an intervening phrase in Isa 61,1: ἰάσασθαι...". J.S. KLOPPENBORG, *The
Formation of Q*, Philadelphia, Fortress, 1987, p. 108 n. 24: "The phrase τυφλοὶ
ἀναβλέπουσιν reveals dependence on the LXX of Isa 61:1-2". See however TUCKETT, *Q
and the History*, p. 129 n. 77: "The reference to the 'blind seeing' could derive from Isa
35:5 rather than Isa 61 LXX" (cf. n. 75); see also p. 232 n. 81: "more likely".
   On E. Hirsch's reconstruction of the original saying (τυφλοί, πτωχοί), see A. Strobel's comment in his *Untersuchungen zum eschatologischen Verzögerungsproblem*
(NTSup, 2), Leiden, Brill, 1961, p. 274 n. 2: "So hypothetisch dieser Vorschlag auch sein
mag, die Bedeutung von Jes 61 wird mit ihm besonders augenfällig unterstrichen".
87. On the Hebrew text, פְּקַח-קוֹחַ וְלַאֲסוּרִים "and to those who are bound opening"
(liberation of prisoners), cf. W.A.M. BEUKEN, *Servant and Herald of Good Things. Isaiah
61 as an Interpretation of Isaiah 40-55*, in J. VERMEYLEN (ed.), *The Book of Isaiah – Le
Livre d'Isaïe* (BETL, 81), Leuven, 1989, pp. 410-442, esp. 419-420; W. LAU, *Schriftgelehrte Prophetie in Jes 56-66* (BZAW, 225), Berlin – New York, de Gruyter, 1994,
p. 74 n. 232.
88. Most authors assign Mt's four καί's to Q and regard Lk's one καί and the two
groups of three asyndetic clauses joined by this καὶ before κωφοί as stylistic improvement. Exceptions are (besides Polag who deletes the καί before νεκροί in his Q text)
Schenk (p. 40), Gundry (p. 206) and Kloppenborg (*Q – Thomas* [n. 24], p. 44), who opt
for Lk's single καί before κωφοί. The καί in Lk is omitted in the Majority text (TR T S
V B Greeven).
89. Cf. J. GNILKA, *Matthäusevangelium* I, p. 405: "In formaler Hinsicht werden die
ersten 4 Tätigkeiten paarweise zusammengeschlossen. Tätigkeit 5 und 6 erscheinen dann
(mit καὶ angefügt) wie eine Steigerung". It is less clear whether items 5 and 6 in Q are
taken individually (VERSEPUT, pp. 67-68 and 71: "After listing in pairs the healing miracles Jesus builds to a polysyndetic climax"; SEVENICH-BAX, pp. 201, 239; cf. GUNDRY,
p. 206: MtR) or form a third and last pair introduced with καί (DAVIES & ALLISON, II,
p. 242 n. 29).

In his comment on τυφλοὶ ἀναβλέπουσιν in Lk 7,22 Fitzmyer notes that "interpreters debate whether Jesus' words allude to Isa 61:1 or 35:5". He then refers to the quotation of Isa 61,1 in Lk 4,18 and concludes: "it should be so understood here"[90]. This is a valuable observation in a commentary on Lk, though the argument is less serviceable with regard to Q if, as he maintains, Lk 4,17-21 is "better ascribed to Luke's own pen"[91]. It is not uncommon that the use of Isa 35,5-6 in Q 7,22 is seen as an extension of the allusion to Isa 61,1[92]:

> *Is.* 61,1 fournit le premier et le dernier terme de la liste évangélique; mais la mention initiale des 'aveugles' permet un rapprochement avec *Is.* 35,5, qui rend compte de la mention des 'sourds' en quatrième place, et aussi de celle des 'impotents' en deuxième place.

Dupont can hardly be blamed for minimizing the importance of Isa 35,5-6. Not only, like many others, he refers to this passage for parallels to χωλοί ("la mention peut être suggérée par *Is.* 35,6")[93] and κωφοί ("Le parallèle le plus intéressant est *Is.* 35,5"), he even attempts to explain λεπροὶ καθαρίζονται in reference to the context of this same passage (35,8)[94]. But does he not show too much reserve in the case of τυφλοί? If "the most interesting parallel" to κωφοὶ ἀκούουσιν is found in Isa

---

90. *Luke* I, p. 668. Cf. p. 664: "Luke 7:22 is to be understood as an echo of the quotation of Isa 61:1, as presented by Luke in 4:18".

91. *Ibid.*, p. 527.

92. DUPONT, *Jésus annonce*, p. 178 (= 74). Cf. p. 177 (= 73): "Le premier terme... semble donc emprunté au dernier terme d'*Is.* 61,1, le verset dont le premier terme fournit le dernier de la liste évangélique. Celle-ci doit donc son cadre à *Is.* 61,1". See also SCHÜRMANN, *Lukasevangelium* I, p. 411: "isaianische Prophetien – rahmend Is 61,1 [*n. 26*: Aber in umgekehrter Folge], formiert durch Is 35,5f"; R. PESCH, *Jesu ureigene Taten? Ein Beitrag zur Wunderfrage* (QD, 52), Freiburg, Herder, 1970, pp. 36-44, esp. 42: "Jes 61,1 (scheint) den Rahmen, Jes 35,5-6 die Reihenfolge der Aufzählung zu bestimmen"; A. VÖGTLE, *Wunder und Wort in urchristlicher Glaubenswerbung (Mt 11,2-5 / Lk 7,18-23)*, in ID., *Das Evangelium und die Evangelien*, Düsseldorf, Patmos, 1971, pp. 219-242, esp. 232: "Den eigentlichen Basistext dürfte Jes 61,1 stellen", with reference to K. Stendahl (1962: "The quotation is basically from Isa 61:1") and P. Stuhlmacher (1968: " Jes. 61,1 ist tatsächlich das Oberthema").

93. The allusion to Isa 35,6 (ὁ χωλός) is accepted by most commentators. Contrast Fitzmyer's statement: not related to any promise of the OT (*Luke*, p. 668). The verb used in Q 7,22 is περιπατοῦσιν (cf. Mk 2,9 par. Mt, Lk, Jn). The verbs ἅλλεσθαι and περιπατεῖν are combined in Acts 3,8 and 14,10.

94. *L'ambassade*, p. 950; *Jésus annonce*, p. 178 (= 74). Dupont's suggestion is now mentioned, after R. Pesch (p. 42: "vielleicht") and D. Verseput (p. 69), by Häfner: "Wenn ich recht sehe, hat auf diesen möglichen Bezugspunkt erstmals J. *Dupont* hingewiesen. Sein Vorschlag ist aber kaum beachtet worden" (*Vorläufer*, p. 180 n. 4, with reference to *L'ambassade* only). But see already B. WEISS, *Das Matthäus-Evangelium* (KEK, 1/1), Göttingen, ⁸1890, p. 210 n. 1: "dass nach V. 8 kein Unreiner auf dem heiligen Wege gehen wird, hat mit der Reinigung der Aussätzigen nichts zu thun". See also E. SEVENICH-BAX, *Konfrontation* (n. 24), p. 328: "eine entfernte Analogie".

35,5b (the ears of the deaf), how can he be critical with regard to the parallel in Isa 35,5a (the eyes of the blind), where "the blind" comes first in the list like τυφλοὶ ἀναβλέπουσιν comes first in Q 7,22? The same form is adopted in all six clauses of the gospel saying (in the third person plural: anarthrous subject and verb) and none of the supposed Isaianic parallels is strictly identical. Assertions that τυφλοὶ ἀναβλέπουσιν draws on Is 61,1 "in the use of ἀναβλέπειν"[95] seem to neglect that the verb is not used in Isa 61,1 (τυφλοῖς ἀνάβλεψιν) and restrict the Isaianic background to Isa 61,1 and 35,5-6. Parallels such as 29,18-19; 42,7; and 42,18 (οἱ τυφλοί, ἀναβλέψατε ἰδεῖν) are explicitly refused by J. Gnilka "weil an diesen Stellen das Blind- und Taubsein metaphorisch gemeint ist"[96]. But there is at least some truth in G. Häfner's reply: "Der ursprüngliche Sinn einer atl Stelle war kein Kriterium für die urchristliche Bezugnahme auf das AT"[97].

The 19th-century consensus, still represented in some later commentaries[98], combines allusions to Isa 35,5-6 (the blind, the deaf, the lame) and Isa 61,1 (the poor), together with the two additional clauses, "lepers are cleansed" and "dead are raised". More recent studies generally include the parallels Isa 29,18-19 (cf. 35,5-6) and Isa 26,19 (the raising of the dead)[99]. Only the cleansing of the lepers is not related to an Isaianic parallel and the traditional solution that the raising of the dead and the cleansing of the lepers were added in reference to the miracles of the historical Jesus[100] is now applied to the cleansing of the lepers

95. R.H. GUNDRY, *The Use of the Old Testament in St. Matthew's Gospel* (NTSup, 18), Leiden, Brill, 1967, p. 79.

96. J. GNILKA, *Matthäusevangelium* I, p. 408. See also H. GIESEN, *Jesu Krankenheilungen im Verständnis des Matthäusevangeliums*, in L. SCHENKE (ed.), *Studien zum Matthäusevangelium*. FS W. Pesch, Stuttgart, KBW, 1988, pp. 79-106, esp. 100 n. 72 (with reference to Gnilka: "mit Recht"). See also P. BONNARD, *L'évangile selon saint Matthieu* (CNT, 1), Neuchâtel, 1963, p. 161: Isa 29,18 rejected because of its "sens figuré".

97. *Vorläufer*, p. 180 n. 2.

98. See the commentaries on Mt 11,5: W.M.L. de Wette ("bezieht sich offenbar auf Jes. 35,5f. 61,1"), B. Weiss, P. Schanz, *et al*. See also J. Knabenbauer, J. Weiss, E. Klostermann, P. Gaechter, P. Bonnard, W. Trilling, D. Hill, H.B. Green, F.W. Beare, M. Davies.

99. Isa 26,19 and 29,18-19 are included in commentaries (besides special studies: J. Dupont, R. Pesch, A. Vögtle; P. Hoffmann, *Studien*, p. 204): P. Benoit, H. Schürmann, F.W. Danker, I.H. Marshall, R.H. Gundry, W.D. Davies – D.C. Allison, F. Bovon, R. Schnackenburg, D.A. Hagner; Isa 26,19 only: J.A. Fitzmyer, J. Gnilka; Isa 29,18-19 only: B.W. Bacon, J.C. Fenton, M.-É. Boismard, U. Luz.

This development can be seen in the marginal annotations of the Nestle editions at Mt 11,5: Isa 35,5-6; 61,1; 1927[13]: + 29,18-19; 1979[26]: + 26,19 and 42,7.18.

100. Cf. P. SCHANZ, *Matthäus*, 1879, p. 306: "nimmt auf Jes. 35,5; 61,1 Rücksicht, erweitert aber die Prophetie nach der Erfüllung"; J. JEREMIAS, *Die Gleichnisse Jesu*, Göttingen, Vandenhoeck & Ruprecht, [4]1956, p. 99 (= [8]1970, p. 116): "Wenn dabei die Nen-

alone[101]. Others prefer the alternative explanation that the cleansing of the lepers was added to the list because of the impact of leprosy in the environment of the gospel tradition[102]. Still others think that the cleansing of the lepers has a link with the OT, not with Isa 35,8 (Dupont) but with 2 Kgs 5 as an Elisha typology[103]. Finally some do not mention Isa 26,19 and join again raising the dead and cleansing the lepers by extending the OT background to the stories of Elijah and Elisha in 1 Kgs 17,17-24; 2 Kgs 4,18-37 (raising the dead) and 2 Kgs 5,1-27 (cure of Naaman's leprosy)[104].

---

nung der Aussätzigen und der Toten über Jes. 35,5f. hinausgeht, so heißt das: die Erfüllung transzendiert alle Hoffnungen, Erwartungen, Verheißungen" (*Theologie*, below n. 106, p. 107: "... weit übersteigt"); GUNDRY, *The Use* (n. 95), p. 80: "Jesus adds references to his cleansing the lepers and raising the dead to show that his ministry *surpasses the prophetic expectation*" (but see below, n. 101); P. STUHLMACHER, *Das paulinische Evangelium*, I (FRLANT, 95), Göttingen, Vandenhoeck & Ruprecht, 1968, p. 221: "dem irdischen Jesus (war) die Heilung Aussätziger und die Erweckung Toter nachzurühmen".

See also, on this basis, the conclusion on the tradition history of Q 7,22: A. VÖGTLE, *Wunder und Wort* (n. 92), p. 242: "nicht alle der jetzt aufgezählten Wunder (wie etwa Totenerweckungen und Aussätzigenheilungen) mußten schon von Anfang an genannt worden sein"; cf. p. 233: "könnten später zur Vervollständigung des Wunderkatalogs hinzugefügt worden sein"; A. STROBEL, *Verzögerungsproblem* (n. 86), p. 274 n. 1: "womöglich hinzugesetzte Elemente"; D. FLUSSER, *Jesus in Selbstzeugnissen und Bilddokumenten*, Hamburg, 1968, Rowohlt, p. 36; E. SCHWEIZER, *Matthäus*, 1973, p. 165: "Die bei Jesaja fehlenden Wunder... sind vielleicht in Q im Blick auf die von Jesus berichteten Taten zugefügt worden"; CATCHPOLE, *Quest*, p. 239 n. 30: "Of course, we cannot rule out the further possibility, even probability, that some of the actions listed are additions to the original list. This applies particularly to 'lepers are cleansed' and 'the dead are raised up'".

101. P. HOFFMANN, *Studien*, pp. 208-209: "möglicherweise... eine Reminiszenz an Jesu Tätigkeit", and: "Die Totenerweckungen sind aber hier eher durch Jes 26,19 angeregt worden"; GUNDRY, *Matthew*, p. 206: "Raising the dead... does appear in Isa 26:19. Cleansing lepers does not appear in any of these passages or others of similar kind. This surplus shows that Jesus' deeds exceed the demands of John's question..."; DAVIES & ALLISON, *Matthew* II, p. 243: "Perhaps one is to infer that Jesus' works go even beyond what the OT anticipates" (cf. SCHÜRMANN, *Lukasevangelium*, p. 412).

The case of the cleansing of the lepers leads to a more general conclusion, "Die Formulierungen scheinen daher mehr von den Ereignissen des Auftretens Jesu geprägt zu sein als vom Wortlaut der Schrift": A. POLAG, *Die Christologie der Logienquelle* (WMANT, 45), Neukirchen, Neukirchener, 1977, p. 36 n. 100; A. SAND, *Das Evangelium nach Matthäus* (RNT), Regensburg, Pustet, 1986, p. 238.

102. H.-W. KUHN, *Enderwartung und gegenwärtiges Heil* (SUNT, 4), Göttingen, Vandenhoeck & Ruprecht, 1966, p. 196 n. 4: "eine häufige Krankheit im Palästina der Zeit Jesu"; P. HOFFMANN, *Studien*, p. 209 (as a possibility); J. GNILKA, *Matthäusevangelium* I, p. 408: "Die nicht schriftgemäße Erwähnung der Reinigung der Aussätzigen erklärt sich am besten daraus, daß der Aussatz eine häufig auftretende Krankheit gewesen ist".

103. As a possibility ("perhaps"): I.H. MARSHALL, *Luke*, p. 292; DAVIES & ALLISON, *Matthew* II, p. 243.

104. LUZ, *Matthäus* II, p. 169 (no mention of Isa 26,19; see n. 37: "die 'unbiblische' Aufnahme von Aussätzigenheilung und Totenerweckung"); M. SATO, *Q und Prophetie*, p. 142 (= 167). Cf. TUCKETT, *Luke 4,16-30* (n. 17), p. 353: "part of the significance of

The inclusion of Isa 29,18-19 among the parallels may also have some consequences. Isa 61,1 and 29,18-19 are cited at the top of U. Luz's list of Isaianic parallels (before 35,5-6 and 42,18) with the following comment: "Beide Stellen bilden so den Rahmen für Mt 11,5. Es ist also voreilig, einseitig Jes 61,1 zum 'Oberthema' der Antwort Jesu zu machen"[105]. The specific role of Isa 29,18-19 probably receives a more satisfactory presentation in J. Jeremias's approach[106]:

> Jesus zitiert in freier Wiedergabe die prophetische Verheißung Jes. 35,5f. (Blinde, Taube, Lahme) und fügt (*wohl unter dem Einfluß von Jes. 29,18f.*: Taube, Blinde, *Arme* und Elende) Jes. 61,1 hinzu: 'Den Armen wird die Frohbotschaft verkündigt'.

The implication of Jeremias's reading seems to be that Isa 61,1 is not to be regarded as the *Rahmen* of the list in Q 7,22. But before we reach any conclusion we have to consider the new parallel to Q 7,22 in a Dead Sea fragment.

The manuscript 4Q521 (seventeen fragments) was published in 1992 by É. Puech and is known under the title Messianic Apocalypse[107]. The

---

these extra activities [not in Isa 29,18-19; 35,5-6] may be that they show Jesus continuing in the line of Elijah and Elisha"; *Q and the History*, p. 222 (though influence of Isa 26,19 is "not quite impossible").

105. LUZ, *ibid.*, n. 38 (in reply to P. Stuhlmacher).

106. *Jesu Verheißung an die Völker*, Stuttgart, 1956, p. 39 (emphasis mine). See also his *Neutestamentliche Theologie. I. Die Verkündigung Jesu*, Gütersloh, Mohn, 1971, p. 106: "eine freie Zitatkombination von Jes 35,5ff. und 29,18f. mit 61,1f."; p. 107: "Mit allen drei Jesajastellen teilt Lk 7,22f. par. in formaler Hinsicht den Listencharakter" (n. 29: "Auch Jes 26,19 spielt herein"). – J. Dupont has drawn attention to Isa 29,18-19, in *Jésus annonce*, p. 177 (= 73) n. 9: "mérite une attention particulière, parce qu'il y est question successivement de sourds, d'aveugles et de pauvres". Dupont's conclusion is extremely brief: "Les contacts littéraires ne s'imposent cependant pas" (*ibid.*). Looking for "literary contacts" was he expecting too much from this parallel? Compare P. GRELOT, *"Celui qui vient" (Mt 11,3 et Lc 7,19)*, in *Mélanges B. Renaud* (cf. below, n. 111), 1995, pp. 275-290, esp. 282, on the parallel in Isa 29,18-19: "La chose est d'autant plus remarquable que la suite [au v. 19] mentionne explicitement 'les pauvres', qu'on retrouve dans l'énumération analysée ici: il y a une affinité entre le fait qu'ils 'se réjouiront en YHWH' et le fait qu'ils 'soient évangélisés'".

I noted however some confusion in Grelot's description of the Isaianic parallels (pp. 280-283). Cf. p. 282 n. 7: "pour les aveugles mentionnés dans Is 35,5..., le texte évangélique semble renvoyer au texte de la Bible grecque plutôt qu'à l'hébreu", and p. 281: "La Septante porte ἀνοιχθήσονται, où le préfixe verbal rappelle celui de ἀναβλέπουσιν" (sic). But see p. 282, on κωφοί in Isa 35,5: "mais on n'a pas le verbe entendre en cet endroit"; contrast Isa 35,5b καὶ ὦτα κωφῶν ἀκούσονται! On the other hand Grelot is perhaps too certain about the parallel to τυφλοί in Isa 61,1: "L'allusion à Is 60,1 [read 61,1] est donc certaine" (p. 281).

107. É. PUECH, *Une apocalypse messianique (4Q521)*, in *RQ* 15/60 (1992) 475-522; ID., *La croyance des Esséniens en la vie future* (Études Bibliques, NS 22), Paris, Gabalda, 1993, vol. II, pp. 627-669: "Une apocalypse messianique (4Q521)" (followed by "Com-

longest and most important fragment (frags. 2 col. ii + 4) runs as follows (English translation by J.A. Fitzmyer)[108]:

1 [the hea]vens and the earth will listen to His Messiah,

2 [and all th]at is in them will not swerve from the commandments of holy ones.

3 Be strengthened in his service, all you who seek the Lord!

4 Shall you not find the Lord in this, all those who hope in their hearts?

5 For the Lord will visit pious ones, and righteous ones he will call by name.

6 Over lowly ones will His Spirit hover, and faithful ones will He restore with His power.

7 He will honor (the) pious ones on a throne of eternal kingship,

8 as He frees prisoners, gives sight to the blind, straightens up those be[nt over].

9 For[ev]er shall I cling [to tho]se who hope, and in His steadfast love He will recompense;

10 and the frui[t of a] good [dee]d will be delayed for no one.

11 Wond<r>ous things, such as have never been, the Lord will do, as He s[aid].

12 For He will heal (the) wounded, revive the dead, (and) announce good news to lowly ones;

13 (the) [po]or He will satisfy, (the) uprooted He will guide, and on (the) hungry He will bestow riches;

14 and (the) intel[ligent], and all of them (shall be) like hol[y ones].

mentaire général", pp. 669-692); Hebrew text and translation, pp. 485-486 (= 632-633). See also ID., *Messianism, Resurrection, and Eschatology at Qumran and in the New Testament*, in E. ULRICH – J. VANDERKAM (eds.), *The Community of the Renewed Covenant. The Notre Dame Symposium on the Dead Sea Scrolls* (CJAS, 10), Notre Dame, IN, 1994, pp. 235-256, esp. 243-246.

Previously to Puech's edition the fragment was entitled "On Resurrection" because of its reference to revivifying in line 12. Cf. TABOR & WISE (below n. 109), p. 149 n. 1. For Fitzmyer (n. 108), "this is a misuse of the term, especially with its Christian connotation" (p. 315). On the use of the term "apocalypse", cf. PUECH, p. 515 n. 63 (= 664 n. 71); *Messianism*, p. 241 n. 20: "I use 'apocalypse' in its broad sense". But see COLLINS, *Works* (below n. 114), p. 98: "The extant fragments show none of the formal marks of apocalyptic revelation". The term "messianic" refers to the mention of "his messiah" (or anointed ones?) in line 1: cf. below. A more acceptable designation of the genre would be to call it an eschatological psalm. Cf. R. BERGMEIER, *Beobachtungen* (below n. 120): "Sprechen wir also lieber von einem Psalm eschatologischen Inhalts!" (p. 41). See now also K.-W. Niebuhr, in this volume pp. 637-646.

108. J.A. FITZMYER, *The Dead Sea Scrolls and Early Christianity*, in *Theology Digest* 42 (1995) 303-319, esp. p. 314. – F. GARCÍA MARTÍNEZ, *The Dead Sea Scrolls Translated. The Qumran Text in English* (ET: W.G.E. Watson), Leiden, Brill, 1994, p. 394; ID. – A.S. VAN DER WOUDE, *De rollen van de Dode Zee ingeleid en in het Nederlands vertaald*, I, Kampen, Kok – Tielt, Lannoo, 1994, pp. 420-424 ("Over de Opstanding"). Cf. F. GARCÍA MARTÍNEZ, *Los Mesías de Qumrân. Problemas de un traductor*, in *Sefarad* 53 (1993) 345-360; ID., *Messianische Erwartungen in den Qumranschriften*, in *Jahrbuch für Biblische Theologie* 8 (1993) 171-208, esp. pp. 180-185 (GT: G. Stemberger); = *Messianic Hopes in the Qumran Writings* (ET: W.G.E. Watson), in ID. – J. TREBOLLE BARRERA, *The People of the Dead Scrolls*, Leiden, Brill, 1995, pp. 159-189, esp. 168-170 (original: *Los Hombres de Qumrân*, Madrid, 1993). – J. MAIER, *Die Qumran-Essener: Die Texte vom Toten Meer, II: Die Texte der Höhle 4* (UTB, 1863), München-Basel, Reinhardt, 1995, pp. 683-687 (…"On Resurrection").

Already before Puech's *editio princeps* R.H. Eisenman had published in 1991 a photograph and translation of the text, and preliminary studies by M.O. Wise and J.D. Tabor had appeared in 1992[109]. In "The Messiah at Qumran" the lines 1 and 12 of this "extremely important text" are excerpted and printed in boldface: *The heavens and the earth will obey His Messiah... He will heal the sick, resurrect the dead, and to the poor announce glad things.* By combining lines 1 and 12 Wise & Tabor suggest that the author of 4Q521 intends to say that it is the Messiah who will raise the dead. I summarize here their argument: Jews who believed in resurrection apparently thought that it was something God, not the Messiah, would do. But in this text the last phrase of line 12 "to the poor announce glad things" is a direct quotation of Isa 61,1 which tells of an anointed one (i.e. Messiah) who will work various signs before the Day of the Lord. Although in the entire Hebrew Bible there is nothing at all about a messianic figure raising the dead, in 4Q521 "raising the dead" is linked to glad tidings for the poor: the two phrases are linked as "signs of the Messiah". This language is "virtually identical" to that of Q 7,22: healing the sick and, in identical order, νεκροὶ ἐγείρονται and πτωχοὶ εὐαγγελίζονται. Q 7,22 and 4Q521 share "the same technical list of criteria for identification of the Messiah".

The problem is however that the Messiah is mentioned only in the first line ("His Messiah"). Lines 3ff. explicitly refer to God (אדני, the Lord) and the works described in line 8 are works of God. Therefore it was suggested that the text returns to the messianic figure with an explicit mention prior to line 12: *10... His] holy [Messiah] will not be slow [in coming.] 11 And as for the wonders that are not the work of the Lord, when he* (i.e. the Messiah) *[come]s*[110]. Critical misfortune awaited this conjecture "His Messiah" (line 10) and the notion "not the work of the Lord" (line 11): "paleographically impossible" and "an idea which

---

109. R.H. EISENMAN, *A Messianic Vision*, in *BAR* 17/6 (1991), p. 65; ID. – M.O. WISE, *The Dead Sea Scrolls Uncovered*, Shaftesbury – Rockport, MA – Brisbane, Element, 1992, pp. 19-23: "The Messiah of Heaven and Earth" (GT: *Jesus und die Urchristen: Die Qumran-Rollen entschlüsselt*, München, 1992); M.O. WISE – J.D. TABOR, *The Messiah at Qumran*, in *BAR* 18/6 (1992) 60-65; TABOR & WISE, *4Q521 'On Resurrection' and the Synoptic Gospel Tradition: A Preliminary Study*, in *Journal for the Study of Pseudepigrapha* 10 (1992) 149-162, esp. pp. 158-162; reprinted in J.H. CHARLESWORTH (ed.), *Qumran Questions* (The Biblical Seminar, 36), Sheffield, Academic, 1995, pp. 151-163.

110. Cf. *BAR*, p. 62; *JSP*, p. 151 (= 1995, p. 153). See also EISENMAN & WISE, *The Dead Sea Scrolls Uncovered*, p. 23: same text in line 11, but more hesitant regarding line 10: "...] of Holiness will not delay..."; cf. p. 20: "in Lines 11-13, it is possible that a shift occurs, and the reference could be to 'His Messiah'. The editors were unable to agree on the reconstruction here".

does not appear in the text if read correctly" (F. García Martínez)[111]. For J.J. Collins, "To suggest that the works of the messiah are 'not the works of the Lord' makes no sense"[112]. Puech's quite different text of lines 10-11 is now accepted by almost all translators[113].

Apart from his critique of the Wise & Tabor reading of lines 10 and 11, Collins proposes an interpretation of line 12 that can be seen as a corrected version of their approach[114]:

111. *Messianic Hopes*, pp. 169, 170 (= *Messianische Erwartungen*, pp. 184-185). *Ibid.*, p. 170: "all these speculations are unnecessary if the text is read correctly. In it, the Messiah does not raise up the dead, nor are there wonderful deeds which are not the work of God". See also, with reference to García Martínez, J. DUHAIME, *Le messie et les saints dans un fragment apocalyptique de Qumrân (4Q521 2)*, in R. KUNTZMANN (ed.), *Ce Dieu qui vient*. FS B. Renaud (Lectio Divina, 159), Paris, Cerf, 1995, pp. 265-274, esp. 273, on the mention of Messiah in line 10: "il s'agit là d'une pure spéculation".

112. On Collins's contribution see below n. 114; here, *Works*, p. 100 n. 6; *Scepter*, p. 132 n. 83.

113. In line 11 Puech reads יעשה (the Lord *will do*), and not מעשה (the *work* of the Lord). Cf. above, Fitzmyer's translation. Compare, e.g., the translations by Puech, García Martínez, and J. Maier (see also below, n. 160):

¹⁰ et le fru[it d'une] bonne [œuvr]e ne sera différé pour personne,
  ¹¹ et des actions glorieuses qui n'ont jamais eu lieu, le Seigneur réalisera comme il l'a d[it].

¹⁰ and from no-one shall the fruit [of] good [deeds] be delayed,
  ¹¹ and the Lord will perform marvellous acts such as have not existed, just as he sa[id].

¹⁰ und die Fruch[t guter Ta]t wird sich einem Mann nicht verzögern,
  ¹¹ und die glorreiche Dinge, die (so noch) nicht gewesen, wird der Herr tun, wie Er ges[agt hat].

114. J.J. COLLINS, *The Works of the Messiah*, in *Dead Sea Discoveries* 1 (1994) 98-112 (here p. 100); slightly revised in ID., *The Scepter and the Star: The Messiahs of the Dead Sea Scrolls and Other Ancient Literature*, New York, Doubleday, 1995, pp. 117-122 ("Q4521"), here pp. 118, 132 n. 85 ("not... as mutually exclusive"). Compare however TABOR & WISE, p. 158: "The Messiah resurrects the dead as God's agent" and COLLINS, *Works*, p. 101, on the possibility that "God should use an agent in the resurrection". Compare É. PUECH, in *Messianism* (n. 107), pp. 245-246: "In 4Q521, God himself accomplishes these signs (probably in the days of the Messiah and through his messenger)... In the gospels, by contrast, Jesus ... acts by himself as the Elect, the Son of God". The first sentence is now quoted by Collins in *Jesus* (cf. below), p. 297 n. 52.

See also COLLINS, *"He shall not judge by what his eyes see" : Messianic Authority in the Dead Sea Scrolls*, in *Dead Sea Discoveries* 2 (1995) 145-164, esp. pp. 161-163; *Jesus and the Messiahs of Israel*, in H. LICHTENBERGER (ed.), *Geschichte – Tradition – Reflexion*. FS M. Hengel, III. *Frühes Christentum*, Tübingen, Mohr, 1996, pp. 287-302, esp. 296-298. Collins's first essay in *Dead Sea Discoveries* originally circulated as a Sample Issue (1994), pp. 1-15. It was written in dialogue with Wise & Tabor (see p. 98 n. 1: "The text is discussed..."); compare: "an exceptionally interesting text" (an extremely important text); "Three aspects of the text are especially interesting" (Three striking features of this text are significant), i.e., mention of a messiah, reference to resurrection, and close parallel in Q 7,22.

Several other contributions on 4Q521 were written in reference to Wise & Tabor. Cf. F. GARCÍA MARTÍNEZ, *Messianic Hopes* (n. 108), pp. 169-170 ("The only study of this manuscript which has appeared so far"); with reference to Eisenman & Wise: K.

In view of the introduction of a 'messiah' in the first line of the fragment, it is likely that God acts through the agency of a prophetic messiah in line 12. [n. 9:] My position here differs from that of Wise and Tabor in so far as I do not see the agency of God and of the messiah as alternatives to each other.

But how certain is their common starting point: the mention of "His Messiah" in line 1? First, although משיחו is read by Puech as a singular ("très probablement"), his translation indicates the possibility of a plural: "Son (/Ses?) Messie(s)"[115]. For M.G. Abegg, Jr., there is a need for further reflection because "the word is situated on the left margin of the fragment; the right margin having been eroded. Given Qumran paleography and orthography, the text could also be read 'his messiahs' (משיחיו), or perhaps more likely, 'the anointed of...' (משיחי)"[116]. Second, the word occurs in the plural in 4Q521 frag. 8: "and all her [Zion's?] anointed ones" (line 9: וכל משיחיה)[117]. This plural, probably referring to the priests (cf. line 8: "holy vessels")[118], has been used against reading the plural in frag. 2 (Puech, García Martínez, Duhaime) but also as a confirmation of the plural in frag. 2 (Abegg, Maier). Third, the parallelism of lines 1 and 2 should not be neglected:

¹ *the heavens and the earth will listen to* משיחו
² *and all that is in them will not turn away from the commandment(s) of* קדושים.

Fitzmyer's translation: *His Messiah and holy ones*[119] is accompanied with the following comment: "Because the text is fragmentary it is not

---

BERGER, *Qumran und Jesus. Wahrheit unter Verschluß?* Stuttgart, Quell, 1993, esp. pp. 99-100 (cf. below, n. 134); O. BETZ, in ID. – R. RIESNER, *Jesus, Qumran und der Vatikan. Klarstellungen*, Gießen/Basel, Brunnen – Freiburg, Herder, 1993, pp. 111-115: "Gott und der helfende Messias (4Q521)". Cf. below, n. 119.

115. *RQ*, p. 486; see p. 487 n. 14 (= *Croyance*, pp. 633, 634): "Une orthographe MŠYḤW peut être lue au pluriel, 'ses messies'; pour une trentaine de cas dans les textes déjà publiés, voir E. QIMRON, *The Hebrew of the Dead Sea Scrolls* (HSS, 29), 1986, p. 59".

116. M.G. ABEGG, JR., *The Messiah at Qumran: Are We Still Seeing Double?*, in *Dead Sea Discoveries* 2 (1995) 125-144, esp. pp. 141-143 (here 142).

117. PUECH, p. 508 (= 659): "et tous ses oints"; MAIER, p. 686: "und alle ihre Gesalbten" (n. 655: the feminine suffix = Jerusalem). – The plural can possibly be read in frag. 9: "you will abandon into the power of (your) messiah (or messiahs?)" (line 3: משׁיח[). Cf. PUECH, p. 509 (= 660): "[son/ses] oint(s)".

118. PUECH, et al.; García Martínez: the prophets. Cf. COLLINS, *Scepter*, p. 118.

119. This is the most usual translation of קדושים: "of (the) holy ones", "des saints", "Heiliger" (sometimes identified as "angels"). Contrast García Martínez: "the holy precepts" ("de heilige geboden").

Note the translation of line 2 by Wise & Tabor (Eisenman & Wise and Tabor & Wise): "[The sea and all th]at is in them. He will not turn aside from the commandment of the Holy Ones" (He = the Messiah). This translation is adopted by O. Betz: "Auch der

possible to be certain about who those are who are called *qĕdôšîm*"[120]. What is important for us here is the synonymous parallelism which may recommend the reading of the plural in line 1: "the anointed ones"[121]. The text is fragmentary indeed and one of our uncertainties concerns the possible connection with a preceding context. Puech proposes the restoration of a two-letter word at the opening of the first line: כי, translated in French: "car(?)" (García Martínez: "for")[122]. This conjecture presupposes a context of which we can only guess that it could explain the reading "His Messiah" or "the anointed ones" in line 1 of the fragment[123]. What we know is the fact that, if "his messiah" is to be read, this "anomalous reference in the adaptation of Psalm 146" (Collins) is never mentioned again in lines 3-14[124].

The second argument Collins has in common with Wise & Tabor is the allusion to Isa 61,1. "In view of the role of the anointed prophet in Isaiah 61" line 12c becomes the key for the messianic interpretation. His basic observation concerns ענוים יבשר: "It is surprising to find God as the subject of preaching good news. This is the work of a herald or messenger. The phrase in question is taken from Isa. 61:1..."[125]. Three

---

Messias wird nicht von den Geboten weichen, an die sich selbst die Engel halten". Cf. *Jesus* (n. 114), p. 115; see also pp. 111, 112 ("d.h. von den Weisungen Gottes, die auch die Engel, die besonderen und himmlischen Diener Gottes, befolgen").

120. *Scrolls* (n. 108), p. 314. See, e.g., J. Duhaime's suggestion "qu'il s'agisse d'un messie royal (angélique?) dont *les fidèles* partageraient le pouvoir". Cf. *Le messie et les saints* (n. 111), pp. 272, 274. A peculiar solution is suggested by R. BERGMEIER, *Beobachtungen zu 4 Q 521 f 2, II, 1-13*, in *ZDMG* 145 (1995) 38-48, here pp. 39 (n. 9), 44. In parallel to the singular in the first line he proposes to read קדושים "als Hoheitsname Gottes (= der Hochheilige)": "seinen Gesalbten" and "den Geboten des Hochheiligen".

121. Cf. J. MAIER, p. 683 n. 651: "Hier scheint ein Parallelismus mit 'Heiligen' (Engeln?) im Sinne von hohen Amtsträgern vorzuliegen". In a short paper delivered at the Colloquium the reading "the anointed ones" (for priestly figures of the end-time) was defended by K.-W. Niebuhr on the basis of the synonymous parallelism. See in this volume: K.-W. NIEBUHR, *Die Werke des eschatologischen Freudenboten: 4Q521 und die Jesusüberlieferung*, pp. 637-646.

122. Cf. *Rollen* (n. 108): "want". See also L.H. SCHIFFMAN, *Reclaiming the Dead Sea Scrolls*, Philadelphia – Jerusalem, Jewish Publication Society, 1994, pp. 347-350 ("The Messianic Apocalypse"), here p. 347: "For...".

123. Cf. J. VANDERKAM, *Messianism in the Scrolls*, in *Community* (n. 107), pp. 211-234, here 215: "the unknown factor is what came before the heavens and the earth – the angels?". The possibility is suggested by R. Bergmeier (n. 120) "daß Z. 1-2 Schlußzeilen eines vorausgehenden Psalms wären" (p. 39 n. 7).

124. Therefore scholars who accept the reading "His Messiah" remain reticent about the subject in line 12. See, e.g., J. VANDERKAM, *Messianism* (n. 123), p. 215: "It remains unclear whether the messiah of the first line or the Lord who is mentioned several times thereafter is the one who does these miracles. The context favors the latter option". – Collins's phrase (in the text) is from *Messianic Authority* (n. 114), p. 162.

125. *Works*, p. 100; repeated in *Scepter*, p. 118; *Messianic Authority*, p. 162. Compare TABOR & WISE, p. 157: "ענוים יבשר is a modified quotation of Isa. 61.1 and a critical phrase

reflections can be made. First, defining by virtue of biblical quotation the identity of the agent of the third activity in line 12 can become problematic if it implies making him (the Messiah) responsible for all activities in line 12 (and 13). In particular, Collins knows quite well that to give life to the dead (12b מתים יחיה) is a function that is usually reserved for God. In 4Q521 frag. 7, "the one who gives life to the dead of this people" (line 6: המחיה את מתי עמו), "the reference is presumably to God"[126]. Second, the fact that in Isa 61,1 the "prophet" who has to announce-good-news is sent by God makes it less difficult to integrate this action in "the works of the Lord"[127]. Third, line 12 cannot be treated in isolation from its context in the fragment. The influence of Psalm 146 is generally recognised. Collins calls it "the base-text"[128], and for Tabor & Wise "this Psalm was very influential on the author's thinking, both verbally and conceptually"[129]. One can observe already in line 1 (and 2) the influence of Ps 146,6: "(his hope is in Yahweh his God) who made *heaven and earth*, the sea *and all that is in them*". The text of line 8, "freeing the prisoners, giving sight to the blind, lifting up those who are bo[wed down", is a quotation of Ps 146,7c.8a.b:

יהוה מתיר אסורים
יהוה פקח עורים
יהוה זקף כפופים

The explicit mention of the subject Yahweh (omitted in line 8)[130] is typical of Ps 146 (vv. 1.2.5.7c.8a.b.c.9a.10). The substitute אדני is used in lines 3, 4, and 5: "The Lord will visit..." governing the following lines 6-8, and is used again in line 11: "the *mirabilia* the Lord will do". Since there is no change of subject the text of line 12 (and 13)[131] should be

in answering the question who is the agent responsible for the actions in l. 12" (p. 158: "Note that the Bible never uses בשר of God"). See also O. BETZ, *Jesus* (n. 114), p. 113.

126. *Works*, p. 101. Cf. PUECH, *Croyance*, p. 687: "La résurrection, un des actes de justice de Dieu (fg 7,7), est clairement l'œuvre de Dieu lui-même, créateur, fg 7,1-3, vivificateur, fg 7,6, qui ouvre (les tombeaux / les livres?), fg 7,8".

127. In this sense J. Duhaime, in *Le messie et les saints* (above, n. 111), can speak of harmonization "faisant de Dieu lui-même le sujet de toutes ces actions" (p. 273).

128. *Works*, p. 100.

129. *4Q521*, p. 151 (= 153). Cf. PUECH, p. 515 (= 664): "une sorte de midrash du *Ps* 146, hymne au Dieu secourable, qui a fourni quelques thèmes centraux, Dieu créateur et sauveur, distinction entre justes et impies". Cf. below, nn. 130-131.

130. Cf. TABOR & WISE, p. 153 (= 155): "This line is a slightly modified quotation of Ps 146,7-8, dropping only the Tetragrammaton"; PUECH, p. 490 (= 637): "citation presque littérale de Ps 146,7b-8a-b, avec omission de YHWH à chaque stique mais le sujet ʾDNY est son équivalent et son *ersatz*". Cf. COLLINS, *Works*, p. 99: "In lines 1-8, this passage is heavily dependent on Psalm 146".

131. Compare the last phrase in line 13 on the רעבים ("the hungry he will enrich") with Ps 146,7b: "he gives food to the hungry". Cf. WISE & TABOR, p. 62: "This psalm

read in the spirit of Ps 146. Interpretations emphasizing the parallel to Isa 61,1 in line 12c seem to read 4Q521 (too much) in light of Q 7,22.

Q 7,22 is no doubt "the most fascinating parallel" to 4Q521: "the parallel... is intriguing since both go beyond Isaiah 61 in referring to the raising of the dead"[132]. On the side of 4Q521, Q 7,22 is adduced as decisive evidence for the messianic interpretation. In itself a remarkable parallel to line 12 (... νεκροὶ ἐγείρονται, πτωχοὶ εὐαγγελίζονται)[133] it has been enlarged with the introduction to John's question including Mt 11,2 τὰ ἔργα τοῦ Χριστοῦ, The Works of the Messiah (title of Collins's essay)[134]. On the side of Q 7,22, the parallel gives rise to suggestions on tradition history: "This can hardly be coincidental. It is quite possible that the author of the Sayings source knew 4Q521; at the least he drew on a common tradition"[135].

It is time now to come back to Q 7,22. We can no longer speak of the uniqueness of its reference to raising the dead followed by evangelizing the poor. It would be too rash a conclusion, however, to suggest that "New Testament writers"[136] may have known 4Q521. But one can

was apparently quite important for the author of our text. Both the psalm and our text reflect a concern for the destitute – the poor and the hungry".

132. COLLINS, *Works*, pp. 106, 107.

133. Recognised as such for instance by García Martínez: "the combination in a single phrase of the resurrection of the dead with the announcement of good news to the ʾanawim, which comes from Is 61:1, was not previously documented outside the New Testament" (*Messianic Hopes*, n. 108, p. 169). Cf. below, n. 135.

134. Compare K. BERGER, *Qumran und Jesus* (n. 114), p. 100: "Überdies bezeichnet Matthäus in Mt 11,2 diese Liste als 'Werke des Christus', dem entspricht vielleicht in Zeile 11 des hier zitierten Dokuments der Ausdruck 'Werke Gottes'" (on line 11, see above n. 113). In the same passage one can read, p. 99: "Totenerweckungen kommen bei Jesaja nicht vor" (no reference to Isa 26,19); and p. 100: "In der gemeinsamen Quelle für Matthäus und Lukas, der sogenannten Logienquelle, wo die Liste vielleicht zuerst stand, hatte es eine Totenerweckung als Tat Jesu auch nicht gegeben" (sic).

135. COLLINS, *Works*, p. 107; with an echo in G. BROOKE, *Luke-Acts and the Qumran Scrolls: The Case of MMT*, in C.M. TUCKETT (ed.), *Luke's Literary Achievement* (n. 79), 1995, pp. 72-90, esp. 75-76 (here 76). Compare TABOR & WISE, *4Q521*, p. 161: "Although it is unlikely that Luke knew the Qumran text directly, it seems that he shares with its author a common set of messianic expectations"; BERGER (n. 134), p. 100: "Hier liegt eine gemeinsame (wohl: mündliche) Auslegungstradition vor" ("eine Form der Jesaja-Interpretation").

136. GARCÍA MARTÍNEZ, *Rollen* (n. 108), p. 421: "Mogelijk kenden de Nieuwtestamentische schrijvers de tekst van 4Q521. Tenminste is een gemeenschappelijke traditie aan te nemen". – I may refer here to his recent essay, *Two Messianic Figures in the Qumran Texts*, in D.W. PARRY – S.D. RICKS (eds.), *Current Research and Technological Developments on the Dead Sea Scrolls* (Studies on the Texts of the Desert of Judah, 20), Leiden, Brill, 1996, pp. 14-40. The text of 4Q521, "one of the most beautiful fragments of the Qumran texts", is quoted on pp. 39-40. Although "the ambiguity of the fragmentary text cannot be resolved", he maintains his identification of the messiah in line 1 as

expect that the comparison with the parallel in 4Q521 will have some effect in judgments on the originality of Q 7,22. The association of νεκροὶ ἐγείρονται with "lepers are cleansed" as non-Isaianic and possibly secondary item in Q 7,22[137] does not, to say the least, receive confirmation in the presence of "reviving the dead" in 4Q521.

As indicated above, the climactic position of πτωχοὶ εὐαγγελίζονται in Q 7,22 is widely acknowledged. The parallel in 4Q521 is found in line 12, in the same order (healing the sick – raising the dead – evangelizing the poor), but the list continues in line 13 and עגוים יבשר does not represent that same climax. The allusion to Isa 61 takes its place among the blessings of salvation. The distinctiveness of the last phrase in Q 7,22 has to do with its content (after the deeds comes the word: preaching-good-news)[138] and with its specific background in Isa 61,1[139]:

> The first two passages [Isa 29,18-19; 35,5-6] provide the general theme of an eschatological time when the deaf will hear, the blind see and the lame walk. But the climax clearly comes with the allusion to Isa. 61:1, πτωχοὶ εὐαγγελίζονται. Only with these words do we have a hint of a more specific answer to John's question about the person of Jesus... For the Q community this was the point of Jesus' reply... There is now clear evidence that at the time of Jesus Isa. 61:1 was being interpreted in a quite specific way as referring to *the* eschatological prophet.

This alludes of course to 11QMelch 2,18 [והמבשר הו[אה מ[שיח הרו[ח], "and the herald [Isa 52,7] is the one anointed with the Spirit [cf. Isa 61,1]"[140]. In his comment on 11QMelch M. de Jonge could refer to Q

---

the Royal Messiah (n. 40) and is "not sure that this messiah should be identified with the expected eschatological Prophet" (p. 39).

137. Cf. above, nn. 100, 104.

138. Possibly in a chiastic correspondence to the introductory phrase ἃ ἀκούετε καὶ βλέπετε (= Mt). Cf. GNILKA, *Matthäusevangelium* I, p. 407: "Hören/Sehen – Wunder/Wort"; HÄFNER, *Vorläufer*, p. 179: "der Bezug auf das Wort Jesu rahmt die Aussagen über die Wundertaten": MtR? (cf. below, p. 62). J.M. ROBINSON (cf. above, n. 86) does not consider this chiastic order; he apparently reads Q 7,22b ἃ εἴδετε καὶ ἠκούσατε (= Lk). Cf. *The Sayings Gospel Q* (n. 18), p. 364. On chiastic arrangement in Q, see *ibid.*, p. 365; *The Incipit*, p. 32:

> Inaugural Sermon ⟍ ⟋ Healings (7,22)
> Centurion ⟋ ⟍ Evangelizing the poor (7,22)

139. Quotation from G.N. STANTON, *On the Christology of Q*, in B. LINDARS, et al. (eds.), *Christ and the Spirit in the New Testament*. FS C.F.D. Moule, Cambridge, University Press, 1973, pp. 27-42, esp. 29-30.

140. "Der Textzusammenhang fordert, daß dies eine endzeitlich-prophetische Figur (der endzeitliche Prophet?) ist": P. STUHLMACHER, *Das paulinische Evangelium*, I (n. 100), 1968, pp. 142-147 (1QH 18,14; 11QMelch), here p. 145; see also pp. 218-225 (Q 7,18-23), esp. p. 219. But see his retraction in *Das paulinische Evangelium*, in ID. (ed.), *Das Evangelium und die Evangelien* (WUNT, 28), Tübingen, Mohr, 1983, pp. 157-182 (ET: *The Gospel and the Gospels*, Grand Rapids, MI, Eerdmans, 1991, pp. 148-172):

7,22: "This passage deals with Jesus' deeds and words; implicitly it is said that he [Jesus] is the εὐαγγελιζόμενος" (1966)[141]. Some twenty years later this statement was supplemented[142]:

> I cannot find any sign that Jesus' preaching of good news to the poor was connected with 'anointing through the Spirit' before Luke. In Jesus' answer to the question of John the Baptist in Q the word χριστός did not occur. [n. 101:] χριστός is never used in Q.

Collins has now replied in "The Works of the Messiah"[143]:

> We now have in 4Q521 a remarkable parallel to Jesus' answer to the Baptist, which also refers to a messiah, whom heaven and earth obey.
> There is good reason to think that actions described in Isaiah 61, with the addition of the raising of the dead, were already viewed as 'works of the messiah' in some Jewish circles before the career of Jesus.

The works-of-the-messiah interpretation goes not uncontested and an alternative reading of 4Q521 may imply a different view on the comparison with Q 7,22. There is first of all the problem of the literary unity of Q 7,18-23[144], which seems to be neglected in the studies on 4Q521.

"J.A. Fitzmyer [*JBL*, 1967], in my opinion very appropriately, points out that in 11QMelch 4ff. both Isa. 61:1f. and Isa. 52:7 must be related to the eschatological appearance of Melchizedek as heavenly redeemer" (p. 173 = 164, n. 37); "The interpretation I proposed... as referring to a (or the) end-time prophet is much less probable" (p. 171 = 162, n. 32); ID., *Biblische Theologie des Neuen Testaments*, I, Göttingen, Vandenhoeck & Ruprecht, 1992, p. 112: "In 11QMelch werden der Freudenbote von Jes 52,7 und der Geistgesalbte von Jes 61,1-2 auf *Melchisedek* als himmlischen Erlöser gedeutet". See also, e.g., J. BECKER, *Johannes der Täufer und Jesus von Nazareth* (BSt, 63), Neukirchen, Neukirchener, 1972, pp. 53-54.

141. M. DE JONGE – A.S. VAN DER WOUDE, *11Q Melchizedek and New Testament*, in *NTS* 12 (1965-66) 301-326, esp. pp. 309-312 ("The Use of Isa. LII.7 and LXI.1f. in the New Testament"), here p. 309. – In the same passage the authors refer to the first beatitude: in Mt 5,3 they find "a clear allusion" to Isa 61,1 and in Lk 6,20 "the connexion is even clearer because this evangelist writes οἱ πτωχοί without the addition τῷ πνεύματι...". But on this question see Part I of my paper.

142. *The Earliest Christian Use of* Christos: *Some Suggestions*, in *NTS* 32 (1986) 321-343; = ID., *Jewish Eschatology, Early Christian Christology and the Testaments of the Twelve Patriarchs. Collected Essays* (NTSup, 63), Leiden, Brill, 1991, pp. 102-124, esp. 116-117.

143. *Works*, pp. 110, 112; *Scepter*, p. 205.

144. Those who are in favour of the historicity of the Baptist's question and Jesus' response defend the unity of Q 7,18-23. See, e.g., W.G. KÜMMEL, *Jesu Antwort an Johannes den Täufer. Ein Beispiel zum Methodenproblem in der Jesusforschung*, Wiesbaden, Steiner, 1974. The unitary composition is also maintained by scholars like A. VÖGTLE, *Wunder und Wort* (n. 92; p. 242: "eine erst urchristliche Bildung", with the missionary purpose "noch abseitsstehende Täuferkreise für den Christusglauben zu gewinnen"); and, more recently, K. BACKHAUS, *Die "Jüngerkreise"* (n. 83), esp. pp. 118-119: "im ganzen (darf) die literarische Einheitlichkeit der Perikope als gesichert gelten; die weitere Analyse ergibt, daß diese Einheit sich im wesentlichen auf die Q-Gemeinde zurückführen läßt" (p. 119). Cf. J.S. KLOPPENBORG, *Formation* (n. 86), pp. 107-108:

Researchers on Q are more readily inclined to separate Q 7,22 (without direct reference to the question σύ εἶ;)[145] from its present framework. I may refer to Tuckett's statement: "The best explanation is that the putting together of Jesus' claims with John's question is a secondary composition by a later editor"[146], and to Catchpole's recent discussion of the secondariness of the framework: "The necessary conclusion seems to be that everything in this tradition apart from the six-fold list in Q 7:22 is Q-editorial"[147]. For Sato too the list in 7,22 is "als eigenständiges Stück isolierbar"[148]. Although there is a scholarly tradition[149] in favour of the authenticity of the Jesus saying Q 7,22+23, I consider here "the list of miracles"[150] in

"It is more likely ... that the entire pronouncement story is a post-Easter creation", and 7,22 "a post-Easter interpretation of Jesus' deeds as evidence of the presence of the kingdom". But see below, n. 151.

145. For a particular analysis of Q 7,18-23 see R. CAMERON, *"What Have You Come Out To See?" Characterizations of John and Jesus in the Gospels*, in *Semeia* 49 (1990) 35-69, esp. pp. 51-55. The original chreia comprised a question (v. 19b) and a response (v. 23): "When asked, 'Are you the one who is to come or should we expect another?' Jesus replied, 'Whoever is not offended by me is blessed'" (p. 52). In a later stage another response to the original question was substituted (v. 22) and John and his disciples were introduced into the narrative (vv. 18-19). Now, "the allusions to Isaiah... permit 'Jesus' to construct an argument that turns not simply on a saying attributed to him, but on a chreia that makes reference to a known, biblical authority" (p. 55); "the references to scripture... fit the developing portraits that are made in the elaboration pattern" in Q 7,18-35 (p. 51). Apart from the characterization of John and Jesus as "Cynic figures" and the construction of an original chreia, one may consider here Cameron's basic observation on linking 7,19b.23 (σύ εἶ...; ... ἐν ἐμοί).

146. *Q and the History*, p. 126. With reference to Bultmann, *et al.*: "According to many, the reply in v. 22 ... can confidently be regarded as an authentic saying of the historical Jesus" (*ibid.*).

147. *Quest*, p. 239. Cf. W. SCHENK, *Synopse*, p. 40.

148. *Q und Prophetie* (n. 24), 1988, pp. 140-144 (1984, pp. 165-169), here 141 (165); "Lk 7,23 par ist erst mit dem Apophthegma entstanden; Lk 7,22 par ist dagegen älter" (*ibid.*). See also J. SCHÜLING, *Studien zum Verhältnis von Logienquelle und Markusevangelium* (FzB, 65), Würzburg, Echter, 1991, p. 80: "Endzeitschilderung und Makarismus waren wahrscheinlich zunächst isoliert überliefert und später sekundär als Antwort auf die Täuferfrage zusammengestellt worden"; M. TILLY, *Johannes der Täufer und die Biographie der Propheten. Die synoptische Täuferüberlieferung und das jüdische Prophetenbild zur Zeit des Täufers* (BWANT, 137), Stuttgart, Kohlhammer, 1994, p. 86 n. 220: "Ursprünglich wurde wohl die zunächst isoliert tradierte Zusammenfassung der eschatologischen Heilszeichen Jesu nicht mit der als sekundäre christliche Bildung anzusehenden Täuferfrage verknüpft".

149. Named after Bultmann, *Geschichte*, ²1931, pp. 22.115; cf. 133.135.136 (= 1921, pp. 11.66; cf. 76-78). See, e.g., H. MERKLEIN, *Die Gottesherrschaft als Handlungsprinzip. Untersuchung zur Ethik Jesu* (FzB, 34), Würzburg, Echter, 1978, pp. 162-163.

150. Though with some reservation about supposed "independence of the miracle-list form in early Christian tradition", I refer here to D.T.M. FRANKFURTER, *The Origin of the Miracle-List Tradition and Its Medium of Circulation*, in *SBL 1990 Seminar Papers*, pp. 344-374, esp. 351-352: the list in Q 7,22 "more likely circulated originally independently of the oral miracle stories"; cf. J.D. CROSSAN, *Lists in Early Christianity*, in *Semeia* 55 (1992) 235-343, esp. pp. 238-240 ("Miracle Lists").

Q 7,22[cde] and its original independence. In defining the genre of the logion itself, the parallel in 4Q521 can be helpful as an example of the *topos* of a description of the time of salvation[151]. The integration of "evangelizing the poor" in the glorious works of the Lord should perhaps prevent from dividing Q 7,22 into "deeds" and "words". As noted already[152], Isa 29,19a ("The ʿanawim shall obtain fresh joy in Jahweh") may withhold from dichotomizing the Isaianic allusions.

I conclude with a corollary on Q 7,22[b]. Mt's ἀκούετε κ. βλέπετε is adopted in the IQP text[153] and in many other reconstructions of Q[154], but the word order of Lk's εἴδετε κ. ἠκούσατε also has its defenders, in the aorist (Gundry) or, with greater probability, in the present tense: βλέπετε κ. ἀκούετε (Vögtle, Polag, Schenk). Those who opt for Mt's order are well aware that the evidence is reversible[155]. Schürmann recognises: "Die Vorordnung des Sehens entspricht besser V 22"[156], and Sevenich-Bax even proposes the dubious argument that the order hearing and seeing is the *lectio difficilior* (and therefore "zu bevorzugen")[157]. For the point I made in my lecture at the Colloquium I was happy to find confirmation in B. Kollmann's study (1996)[158].

---

151. Cf. BULTMANN, *Geschichte*, p. 22: "das Wort (will) eigentlich nur mit den Farben des (Deutero-)Jesajas die selige Endzeit schildern"; J. JEREMIAS, *Die Gleichnisse Jesu* (n. 100), p. 99 (= 116); *Neutestamentliche Theologie* (n. 106), p. 107; ET, p. 104: "all age-old phrases for the time of salvation, when there will be no more sorrow, no more crying and no more grief"; H.-W. KUHN, *Enderwartung* (n. 102), p. 196: "Mit Motiven des Jesajabuches wird die eschatologische Heilszeit geschildert". Cf. H. MERKLEIN, n. 149, p. 163: "es (geht) um eine (allgemeine) Charakterisierung der Heilszeit". Compare now P. GRELOT, *"Celui qui vient"* (n. 106), p. 284: "c'est Dieu qui vient accomplir ici-bas le renversement eschatologique de la situation à laquelle étaient liés tous les maux humains"; J.S. KLOPPENBORG, *The Sayings Gospel Q and the Quest of the Historical Jesus*, in HTR 89 (1996) 307-344, p. 330 n. 101: on the list in 4Q521 which "bears an uncanny resemblance to the deeds of Jesus listed in Q 7:22"; and 331: "One cannot even be sure that the wonders to which Q alludes were meant to be understood as Jesus' own works"; "nothing in Q 7:22; 10:13-14 or 10:23-24 requires that Jesus was the only performer of wonders".

152. Cf. above, n. 106.

153. Cf. *JBL* 113 (1994), p. 498. Contrast KLOPPENBORG, in *Q – Thomas Reader*, p. 44 (cf. p. 34).

154. Harnack, Schürmann, Hoffmann, Schulz, Bovon, Gnilka, Catchpole, Sevenich-Bax, *et al.*

155. See, e.g., HOFFMANN, *Studien*, p. 193 n. 14: "Allerdings zeigt Matthäus umgekehrt ein Interesse am Hören (vgl. z.B. Mt 13,16f); er könnte die Reihenfolge der Verben hier dem Aufbau seines Evangeliums angepaßt haben".

156. *Lukasevangelium* I, p. 410 n. 20.

157. *Konfrontation*, p. 201.

158. B. KOLLMANN, *Jesus und die Christen als Wundertäter. Studien zu Magie, Medizin und Schamanismus in Antike und Christentum* (FRLANT, 170), Göttingen, Vandenhoeck & Ruprecht, 1996, pp. 216-221: "Die Wunder stehen im Vordergrund, bevor mit πτωχοὶ εὐαγγελίζονται im nachhinein die Verkündigung Erwähnung findet... [H]ier

CONCLUSION

The significance of Q 7,18-23 (Mt 11,2-6) for the composition of the Gospel of Matthew is undisputed[159]. In the Gospel of Luke too the insertion of 7,11-17 after 7,1-10 and the creation of 7,21 are rightly connected with the answer of Jesus in 7,22. It is less clear, however, whether similar conclusions can be drawn with regard to the composition of Q. The allusion to Isa 61,1 in Q 7,22 may on the one hand have influenced Matthew's redaction of the beatitudes (Mt 5,3-4) and on the other the quotation in the Nazareth pericope (Lk 4,18-19), both at the post-Q level of the evangelists' redaction.

SUPPLEMENTARY NOTE: J.M. Robinson has now reformulated his view in a recent article, *Building Blocks in the Social History of Q*, in E.A. CASTELLI – H. TAUSSIG (eds.), *Reimagining Christian Origins*. FS B.L. Mack, Valley Forge, PA, Trinity Press International, 1996, pp. 87-112, esp. 92-93: "Indeed there was hardly a time in the Q trajectory when Isaiah 61:1-2 was not in view" (p. 93); "already the formative stage of Q used Isaiah 61:1-2 to compose the Beatitudes" (*ibid.*); "Q 7:22 plays for the Q redaction the decisive role of a summary of, or a *post factum* organizing principle for, the first major section of Q, Q 3–7" (p. 92).

At least on two points Robinson is now more assertive than he was before. First, his position on the question whether the Baptism of Jesus is to be included in Q is well known, but it is new that the minor agreement ἐπ᾽ αὐτόν (for εἰς αὐτόν in Mk) is no longer "notoriously inconclusive" (*The Sayings Gospel Q*, p. 383; referring to Kloppenborg): "It is in fact a very significant agreement. For the point is that the Q redactor was fully aware of Q 3–7 fulfilling Isa. 61:1" (p. 108 n. 20). Second, in my comment on his *The Sayings Gospel Q* I could still note that "Robinson himself does not suggest that πενθοῦντες and παρακληθήσονται in Mt 5,4 are from Q" (*ETL* 71, p. 426), with reference to his phrase "if it originally read κλαίοντες" (p. 369) and the IQP reconstruction ⟦κλαί⟧οντες (Robinson being one of the respondents at the discussion of Q

(erhielt) Jes 29,18f. gegenüber Jes 61,1f. mit der umgekehrten Rangordnung von Wundergeschichten und Verkündigung den Vorzug. Zudem ist auch Lk 7,22 (Q) mit ἃ εἴδετε καὶ ἀκούσατε eine formale Vorordnung der Tat gegenüber dem Wort gegeben" (p. 220).

159. On the Matthean composition of Mt 4,23–11,1, cf. D.L. DUNGAN (ed.), *The Interrelations of the Gospels* (BETL, 95), Leuven, 1990, pp. 23-46. Compare J.M. ROBINSON, *The Incipit*, p. 33. However, Matthew's redactional coordination of the Sermon and Healing in Mt 5–7 and 8–9 (cf. 11,4b: hear and see) hardly justifies retroactive extension to Q 6,20-49 and 7,1-10 (cf. above, n. 138).

6,20-21). Robinson now says that here he diverges from the IQP text but follows "the revision by the General Editors in the forthcoming critical edition" (p. 109 n. 21). Note: the three general editors are Robinson, Kloppenborg (but see above, n. 24) and P. Hoffmann. Hoffmann was undecided in *Bibel und Leben* 10 (1969), p. 114: "die älteste Textgestalt: die Armen, die Hungernden, die Trauernden (Weinenden?)" (in Mt's third person but in the Lukan order).

Luke used Isa 61,1-2 in his new Inaugural Sermon (4,18-19). But the same Luke is supposed to have shifted the Isaianic mourn/comfort language in 6,21b to the weep/laugh of the woe. "Mourn" and "be comforted" in Mt 5,4 stem from Q and Matthew only used the context of Isa 61,1-2 in creating new Beatitudes (p. 93: Isa 61,3 "righteousness"; 61,7 "inherit the earth"). For a different view on Q 6,21b / Mt 5,4 I may refer to Part I of the present paper.

With regard to Q 7,22 Robinson repeats the statement that "Q 7:22, in chiastic order, begins with the conclusion of Isaiah 61:1 (the blind see) and ends with the first item listed in Isaiah 61:1 (the evangelizing of the poor)" (p. 92).

ADDENDUM: Q 6,21b

IQP (1992): [[κλαί]]οντες   CritEd (2000): [[πενθ]]ο[[ῦ]]ντες
γελάσετε   [[παρακληθήσ<εσθε>]]

Cf. J.S. KLOPPENBORG VERBIN, *Excavating Q: The History and Setting of the Sayings Gospel*, Minneapolis, MN, Fortress, 2000, p. 405: "Robinson now even prefers (against the IQP) to reconstruct Q 6:20b-21 with vocabulary from Isa 61:1-2" (n. 72). J.S.K.: [[κλαί]]οντες, [[γελάσετε]]. C.M. Tuckett is a steadfast defender of the Matthean form of the beatitudes in Q (references above, p. 130 n. 17). Contrast DAVIES-ALLISON: "it may also be that neither Matthew nor Luke has preserved the wording of Q" (I, 447). But see now D.C. ALLISON, *The Intertextual Jesus: Scripture in Q*, Harrisburg, PA, TPI, 2000, pp. 105, 112-113 (with references to Tuckett: 1996, 223-226; 1997, 23-25). Allison limits "the strongest contacts" with Isa 61 to those beatitudes that stood in Q (105). The points of contact can be further restricted to Mt 5,4, diff. Lk 6,21b (cf. above, p. 144).

On 4Q521 (in Part II), see K.-W. NIEBUHR, *4Q521,2 II – Ein eschatologischer Psalm* (Qumranica Mogilanensia, 15; ed. Z.J. KAPERA), Kraków, 1998, pp. 151-168. Cf. below, p. 206.

BETL 142 (1999) 357-395

5

LUKE 4,16-30 AND THE UNITY OF LUKE–ACTS

When the president of the Colloquium invited me to give this lecture he referred to the session on the Gospel of Luke I was given to preside in 1968[1]. We are now thirty years later and the president of this year is now at the age I was in 1968. But it soon became clear that he did not intend to speculate on coincidences in the number of years. His point was a more serious one, the unity of Luke–Acts, and what he so kindly suggested was in fact some sort of "amende honorable", the Gospel of Luke this time to be studied as part of Luke–Acts.

There are a number of good reasons to justify the choice of Lk 4,16-30, widely held to be programmatic for Luke–Acts. First, I can refer to the example of a great *alumnus Lovaniensis*: the Nazareth pericope was studied by J. Dupont in his SNTS paper of 1959 ("Le salut des Gentils et la signification théologique du Livre des Actes")[2], and again in 1978 as Part One of his essay "Jésus annonce la bonne nouvelle aux pauvres" (with a special section on "L'épisode de Nazareth dans le cadre de l'ouvrage de Luc")[3]. Secondly, I may refer to the second edition of the volume of the Colloquium on the Gospel of Luke which was published in 1989, enlarged with substantive supplements including a 73-page survey

1. F. NEIRYNCK (ed.), *L'Évangile de Luc. Problèmes littéraires et théologiques.* Mémorial Lucien Cerfaux (BETL, 32), Gembloux, 1973 (²1989, cf. n. 4); 19th Colloquium Biblicum Lovaniense, 1968.
2. J. DUPONT, *Le salut des Gentils et la signification théologique du Livre des Actes,* in *NTS* 6 (1959-60) 132-155, esp. 141-146 ("Discours de Nazareth et discours de la Pentecôte"); = ID., *Études sur les Actes de Apôtres* (LD, 45), Paris, 393-419, esp. 404-409; *The Salvation of the Gentiles. Essays on the Acts of the Apostles* (ET by J. Keating), New York, 1987, 11-33: *The Salvation of the Gentiles and the Theological Significance of Acts* (no footnotes included).
3. J. DUPONT, *Jésus annonce la bonne nouvelle aux pauvres,* in *Evangelizare pauperibus* (Atti della XXIV Settimana Biblica Italiana), Brescia, 1978, 127-189, esp. 129-164 (147-155); = ID., *Études sur les Évangiles synoptiques* (BETL, 70), Leuven, 1985, 23-85, esp. 25-60: "Jésus à Nazareth (*Lc.* 4,16-30)" (43-51: "L'épisode de Nazareth dans le cadre de l'ouvrage de Luc"). See also his *La conclusion des Actes et son rapport à l'ensemble de l'ouvrage de Luc,* in J. KREMER (ed.), *Les Actes des Apôtres: Traditions, rédaction, théologie* (BETL, 48), Gembloux, 1979, 359-404, esp. 396-401; = *Nouvelles études sur les Actes des Apôtres* (LD, 118), Paris, 1984, 457-511, esp. 502-508. Cited here as *Jésus* and *Conclusion*.

J. Dupont (°1915) died on September 10, 1998. Cf. F. NEIRYNCK, *L'exégèse catholique en deuil: R.E. Brown – J. Dupont,* in *ETL* 74 (1998) 506-516. Dupont served as the president of the 24th Colloquium Biblicum Lovaniense in 1973 ("Jésus aux origines de la christologie"). On his life and work, see B. STANDAERT, *"Au carrefour des Écritures" : Le Père Jacques Dupont, moine exégète* (Cahiers de Clerlande, 6), Ottignies, 1998.

by C. Schreck: "The Nazareth Pericope: Luke 4,16-30 in Recent Study"[4]. The third reason is my friendly dispute with C.M. Tuckett on the presence of Q-material in Lk 4,16-30[5], a still ongoing debate, now revived and facilitated by the publication of the *Documenta Q* volume on the alleged Q fragment *Nazara* in Lk 4,16[6]. But it is quite obvious, my decisive reason is the fact that, more than for any other section in the Gospel of Luke, the parallels in Acts and the way these parallels are read play an important role in the interpretation of the Nazareth episode in Lk.

In accord with an almost universal consent today[7], the theory that the Book of Acts was written before the Gospel of Luke will not be consid-

4. C.J. SCHRECK, *The Nazareth Pericope: Luke 4,16-30 in Recent Study*, in F. NEIRYNCK (ed.), *L'Évangile de Luc – The Gospel of Luke* (BETL, 32), Leuven, ²1989, 399-471 (456-471: "Studies on Luke 4,16-30, 1973-1989"); revised and enlarged in Chapter V of his unpublished dissertation, *Luke 4,16-30. The Nazareth Pericope in Modern Exegesis: A History of Interpretation*, Leuven, 1990, 333-421; with supplement on two 1989 dissertations: S.J. NOORDA, *Historia vitae magistra. Een beoordeling van de geschiedenis van de uitleg van Lucas 4,16-30 als bijdrage aan de hermeneutische discussie*, Amsterdam, 1989; G.K.-S. SHIN, *Die Ausrufung des entgültigen Jubeljahres durch Jesus in Nazareth. Eine historisch-kritische Studie zu Lk 4,16-30* (EHS, 23/378), Bern-Frankfurt, 1989 (423-438).

In the same volume (BETL, 32): J. DELOBEL, *La rédaction de Lc. IV, 14-16a et le "Bericht vom Anfang"*, ²1989, 113-133 (= 1973, 203-223), reprinted with additional note, 306-312.

5. C.M. TUCKETT, *Luke 4,16-30: Isaiah and Q*, in J. DELOBEL (ed.), *Logia: Les paroles de Jésus – The Sayings of Jesus*. Mémorial Joseph Coppens (BETL, 59), Leuven, 1982, 343-354 (p. 354: 4,16-21.23.25-27 form a unit in the source used by Luke); *On the Relationship between Matthew and Luke*, in *NTS* 30 (1984) 130-142, p. 131 (Ναζαρά); *The Temptation Narrative in Q*, in F. VAN SEGBROECK, C.M. TUCKETT, G. VAN BELLE, J. VERHEYDEN (eds.), *The Four Gospels 1992*. FS F. Neirynck (BETL, 100), Leuven, 1992, 479-507, p. 501 n. 101; *The Lukan Son of Man*, in ID. (ed.), *Luke's Literary Achievement: Collected Essays* (JSNT SS, 116), Sheffield, 1995, 198-217, p. 217 n. 65; *Q and the History of Early Christianity: Studies on Q*, Edinburgh, 1996, 226-237 ("Luke 4:16ff."; also 124 and 428-431). See p. 227: "I remain persuaded…".

6. *Documenta Q: Q 4:1-13,16. The Temptations of Jesus. Nazara*, Leuven, 1996. The first and main part of the volume (1-389) treats "Q 4:1-4,9-12,5-8,13: The Temptations of Jesus"; cf. F. NEIRYNCK, *Note on Q 4,1-2*, in *ETL* 73 (1997) 94-102. The second part (391-462) is devoted to "Q 4:16,3‡: Nazara"; cf. F. NEIRYNCK, *NAZAPA in Q: Pro and Con*, in *From Quest to Q*. FS J.M. Robinson (BETL, 146), 2000. Cf. below, 451-461.

7. C.M. TUCKETT, *Luke* (New Testament Guides), Sheffield, 1996, 14. Cf. J. JERVELL, *Die Apostelgeschichte* (KEK[17]), Göttingen, 1998, 85 (n. 194: Bowman, read Bouwman); B. WITHERINGTON, *The Acts of the Apostles. A Socio-Rhetorical Commentary*, Grand Rapids, MI / Cambridge, UK – Carlisle, 1998, 60; J.A. FITZMYER, *The Acts of the Apostles* (AB, 31), New York, 1998, 51: "most of the reasons suggested for such a view are highly speculative and unconvincing"; C.K. BARRETT, *The Acts of the Apostles* (ICC), vol. II, Edinburgh, 1998, XIX-CXVIII (Introduction), esp. LI. Cf. ID., *The Third Gospel as a Preface to Acts? Some Reflections*, in *The Four Gospels 1992* (n. 5), 1451-1466. On Lk 4,16-30: "Luke certainly was aware of the fact that the mission to Gentiles would be a major theme in any continuation that he wrote" (1455). — Special attention is given to the four commentaries on Acts that independently appeared in the course of 1998; here in the order: Jervell, Witherington, Fitzmyer, and Barrett (vol. I, 1994). For the commentaries, the abbreviation *Acts* or *Apg* will be used in the footnotes.

ered in this paper. Just one preliminary remark: for scholars who defend the priority of Acts, the parallel to the Nazareth pericope in Paul's first major speech in Ac 13,14-52 is part of their argument[8].

In my investigation Lk 4,16-30 will be treated as a Lukan composition relocating the story of the rejection of Jesus in his hometown (Mk 6,1-6a) and taking from Q 6,20-49 the function of Jesus' inaugural sermon.

I. Lk 4,16-30 AND PAUL'S SYNAGOGUE PREACHING

Acts 9,19b-25

19b Ἐγένετο δὲ μετὰ τῶν ἐν Δαμασκῷ μαθητῶν ἡμέρας τινὰς
20   καὶ εὐθέως ἐν ταῖς συναγωγαῖς ἐκήρυσσεν τὸν Ἰησοῦν ὅτι
     οὗτός ἐστιν ὁ υἱὸς τοῦ θεοῦ.
21   ἐξίσταντο δὲ πάντες οἱ ἀκούοντες καὶ ἔλεγον·
     οὐχ οὗτός ἐστιν ὁ πορθήσας εἰς Ἰερουσαλὴμ τοὺς ἐπικαλουμέ-
     νους τὸ ὄνομα τοῦτο, καὶ ὧδε εἰς τοῦτο ἐληλύθει ἵνα δεδεμένους
     αὐτοὺς ἀγάγῃ ἐπὶ τοὺς ἀρχιερεῖς;
22   Σαῦλος δὲ μᾶλλον ἐνεδυναμοῦτο καὶ συνέχυννεν [τοὺς] Ἰουδαίους
     τοὺς κατοικοῦντας ἐν Δαμασκῷ συμβιβάζων ὅτι
     οὗτός ἐστιν ὁ χριστός.
23   Ὡς δὲ ἐπληροῦντο ἡμέραι ἱκαναί, συνεβουλεύσαντο οἱ Ἰουδαῖοι
     ἀνελεῖν αὐτόν·
24   ἐγνώσθη δὲ τῷ Σαύλῳ ἡ ἐπιβουλὴ αὐτῶν. παρετηροῦντο δὲ καὶ τὰς
     πύλας ἡμέρας τε καὶ νυκτὸς ὅπως αὐτὸν ἀνέλωσιν·
25   λαβόντες δὲ οἱ μαθηταὶ αὐτοῦ νυκτὸς διὰ τοῦ τείχους καθῆκαν αὐτὸν
     χαλάσαντες ἐν σπυρίδι.

To begin with, I cite P.F. Esler's summary presentation of the similarities between Lk 4,16-30 and Paul's preaching at Damascus[9]:

1. both Jesus and Paul enter a synagogue as the first public step in their ministry and deliver a message of salvation; 2. their respective audiences

---

8. See G. BOUWMAN, Le "premier livre" (Act., I,1) et la date des Actes des Apôtres, in L'Évangile de Luc – The Gospel of Luke, 1989 (above n. 4), 553-565, esp. 563; ID., De derde nachtwake. De wordingsgeschiedenis van het evangelie van Lucas, Tielt – Den Haag, 1968, 93-95 (= Das dritte Evangelium. Einübung in die formgeschichtliche Methode, Düsseldorf, 1968). See also among the more recent curiosa: J.L. STALEY, "With the Power of the Spirit" : Plotting the Program and Parallels of Luke 4:14-37 in Luke–Acts, in SBL 1993 Seminar Papers, 281-302, esp. 287-291 (Lk 4,16-30); = Narrative Structure (Self Structure) in Luke 4:14–9:62: The United States of Luke's Story World, in Semeia 72 (1995) 173-213, esp. 187-191 (see also 176 and 201: "it was not until after he had written Acts, that he could finally envision a way to revise Mark. The Lukan author then wrote a prequel to Acts, by putting back into his plot of the Jesus story his idealized, previously composed description of Paul's evangelistic program").

9. P.F. ESLER, Community and Gospel in Luke–Acts (SNTS MS, 57), Cambridge, 1987, 235 n. 39; followed by B. WITHERINGTON, Acts, 1998 (n. 7), 320.

are astonished and also confused by the change of roles they observe in Jesus and Paul, with the Jews in Nazareth asking if this is not the son of Joseph and those in Damascus asking if this is not the man who has hitherto opposed Christianity; 3. there is an attempt to kill Jesus and a plot to kill Paul; 4. both Jesus and Paul escape.

The short story of "Paul at Damascus" (9,19b-25)[10] is the first example and in some sense the proto-type of the well-known pattern for Paul's preaching in Acts: "Luke is already following what he takes to have been Paul's regular plan of starting mission work in the synagogue"[11]. The preaching in the synagogues of the Jews is indeed a constant motif of Paul's missionary journeys: 13,5 (Salamis); 13,14 (Pisidian Antioch); 14,1 (Iconium); 17,1-2 (Thessalonica); 17,10 (Beroea); 17,17 (Athens); 18,4 (Corinth); 18,19 and 19,8 (Ephesus). The peculiarity of his preaching in the synagogues of Damascus is that it comes first[12] after Paul's conversion and hence for Paul, like the Nazareth pericope for Jesus, inaugurates his preaching ministry.

Paul's own parallel accounts exhibit significant differences. First, Gal 1,17... ἀπῆλθον εἰς Ἀραβίαν καὶ πάλιν ὑπέστρεψα εἰς Δαμασκόν. His return to Damascus may imply that he had been in Damascus before going to Arabia (cf. Ac 9,19b). But in Acts there is no mention at all of a trip to Arabia or of any interruption of his stay in Damascus. Second, 2 Cor 11,32-33: ἐν Δαμασκῷ ὁ ἐθνάρχης Ἀρέτα τοῦ βασιλέως ἐφρούρει τὴν πόλιν Δαμασκηνῶν πιάσαι με, [33] καὶ διὰ θυρίδος ἐν σαργάνῃ ἐχαλάσθην διὰ τοῦ τείχους καὶ ἐξέφυγον τὰς χεῖρας αὐτοῦ. The means of Paul's escape are the same in Ac 9,25 (ἐν σαργάνῃ/σπυρίδι ἐχαλάσθην/χαλάσαντες διὰ τοῦ τείχους), though the assistance of (his?)[13] disciples is not mentioned in Paul's own ver-

10. On the segment 9,19b-25 in the text of Ac 9,1-30(31), see Tischendorf, Wikenhauser, Dupont, Dillon, Bossuyt-Radermakers, Jervell, Fitzmyer. Contrast Westcott-Hort, Nestle, Nestle-Aland: three paragraphs (9,19b-22.23-25.26-30), in GNT entitled as: Saul preaches at Damascus, Saul escapes from the Jews, Saul at Jerusalem. Even more problematic is J.D.G. Dunn's proposal (Acts, 1996): The conversion of Paul (9,1-22) and The initial opposition to Paul (9,23-31). See D. MARGUERAT, Saul's Conversion (Acts 9, 22, 26) and the Multiplication of Narrative in Acts, in Luke's Literary Achievement (n. 5), 127-155: "a parallelism of motifs is to be detected between 9.19b-25 and 26-30, which function like twin narratives" (135 n. 23).

11. BARRETT, Acts, 464.

12. And without delay: εὐθέως. Compare εὐθέως after his conversion in Gal 1,16b. On this link between Paul's conversion and his preaching in Damascus, see Barnabas's declaration in 9,27: πῶς ἐν τῇ ὁδῷ ... καὶ πῶς ἐν Δαμασκῷ ἐπαρρησιάσατο ἐν τῷ ὀνόματι τοῦ Ἰησοῦ.

13. "The most satisfactory solution appears to be the conjecture that the oldest extant text arose through scribal inadvertence, when an original αὐτόν was taken as αὐτοῦ" (METZGER, Textual Commentary, 321-322). Cf. Conzelmann, Haenchen, et al. Jervell reads αὐτοῦ: "das zeigt die besondere Stellung des Paulus in der Kirche" (Apg, 286); cf.

sion. Neither the status of the ethnarch (Nabatean governor?)[14] nor the motive of his action (Paul's mission in Arabia?)[15] can be identified; and the incident of the escape is not associated with any particular period of Paul's life (the end of a second stay in Damascus?). In Ac 9 it is linked with Paul's post-conversion preaching: *the Jews* of Damascus were confounded by Paul's powerful preaching (v. 22), and "when some time had passed" *they* plotted to kill him (v. 23) and *they* were watching the gates (v. 24). Since it is hardly provable that the Nabatean king Aretas made common cause with the Jews, or that "Paul wanted to spare his own countrymen by not mentioning their participation in the persecution of Damascus"[16], it is most likely that it was Luke, responsible for the reworking of a tradition like 2 Cor 11,32-33, who introduced here the hostile action of the Jews[17].

"Paul and the Jews" is a major theme of the two- or three-stage theory in the volumes *Les Actes des deux apôtres*[18]:

Paulus in der Apostelgeschichte und die Geschichte des Urchristentums, in NTS 32 (1986) 378-392: "Lukas stellt wiederholt Ähnlichkeiten oder Parallelen zwischen Jesus und Paulus dar... Paulus ist ausser Jesus der einzige in Acta der Jünger hat, 9.25" (383, and 392 n. 29). Fitzmyer shows more reserve: "One can only ask who 'his disciples' might have been" (*Acts*, 436). — For some commentators of 2 Cor the passive voice ἐχαλάσθην indicates that Paul had assistance, "and this in accord with Acts 9:25" (V.P. FURNISH, 522).

14. J. TAYLOR, *The Ethnarch of King Aretas at Damascus: A Note on 2 Cor 11,32-33*, in RB 99 (1992) 719-728.

15. R. RIESNER, *Paul's Early Period: Chronology, Mission Strategy, Theology*, Grand Rapids, MI, 1998, 258-260: "It thus remains a possibility worthy of consideration that for some time... Paul lived in 'Arabia' somewhat reclusively" (260).

16. *Ibid.*, 89. Cf. 86-89: "The Circumstances of Paul's Flight".

17. M. HARDING, *On the Historicity of Acts: Comparing Acts 9.23-25 with 2 Corinthians 11.32-3*, in NTS 39 (1993) 518-538, esp. 536; A. WEISER, *Apg*, 232: "(wahrscheinlich ist) die Nennung der Juden als Gegner des Saulus erst von Lukas eingeführt"; C. BURCHARD: "Zu fragen ist nur, ob erst Lukas 'die Juden' hereingebracht hat. Denkbar ist das; Lukas beschreibt immer wieder eben sie als Paulus' Gegner und hält sie auch eines Mordes durchaus für fähig" (152). See *Der dreizehnte Zeuge. Traditions- und kompositionsgeschichtliche Untersuchungen zu Lukas' Darstellung der Frühzeit des Paulus* (FRLANT, 103), Göttingen, 1970, 136-161 ("Der Beginn der paulinischen Wirksamkeit: Apg. 9,19b-30"): Ac 9,19b-25 is a Lukan composition, only vv. 24b-25 rely on "geformte Tradition" (153). See also L. WEHR, *Petrus und Paulus – Kontrahenten und Partner* (NTAbh, 30), Münster, 1996, 131 n. 25 (with reference to A. LINDEMANN, *Paulus im ältesten Christentum*, 1979, 169 n. 129).

18. In anticipation of the 'Cleopas question' (on the things that have happened in Jerusalem) I mention here the thesis propounded by M.-É. Boismard – A. Lamouille and J. Taylor: Ac 9,20.23.30* are from Proto–Luke (= Act I) and 9,19b.21-22.24-25 are added by Luke (= Act II); on v. 20c, see below n. 22. Cf. *Les Actes des deux apôtres*: M.-É. BOISMARD – A. LAMOUILLE, vol. I-III (ÉB 12, 13, 14), Paris, 1990: vol. I. *Introduction – Textes*, 39, 98; vol. II. *Le sens des récits*, 120-121, 123-134 (Act I); 182, 185-186 (Act II); 211 (Act III); vol. III. *Analyses littéraires*, 133-137; vol. V: J. TAYLOR, *Commentaire historique (Act. 9,1–18,22)* (ÉB 23), 1994, 15-25. Two commentaries on

Pour Act I, Paul est avant tout celui qui, de ville en ville, entre dans les synagogues, y annonce aux Juifs le message chrétien, mais, malgré quelques succès, se heurte à une hostilité de plus en plus marquée, à une volonté de le mettre à mort...[19]
Act II évite de condamner en bloc "les Juifs"... Dans la geste de Paul, ce ne sont plus "les Juifs" (Act I) qui s'en prennent violemment à la prédication de l'évangile, mais seulement certains d'entre eux (17,5 TO; 18,6 TO; cf. 23,12).[20]
Mais dans ces cas, Act III abandonne les textes de Act II pour revenir à ceux de Act I... Cette tendance 'dure' se manifeste à l'égard des Juifs, alors que Act II voulait au contraire les innocenter.[21]

In the case of Ac 9,19b-25 the reconstruction of *Act I* (= Proto-Luke) includes nothing more than the two verses 9,20.23 (and 30ac). The hostility of the Jews is evident in v. 23: they conspired to murder him. It is less evident that the term οἱ Ἰουδαῖοι can be used as an argument for Proto-Luke. This is the first reference to οἱ Ἰουδαῖοι in *Act I* and without the preceding v. 22 it comes rather unprepared. In the text of *Act II* (= Luke) it resumes [τοὺς] Ἰουδαίους τοὺς κατοικοῦντας ἐν Δαμασκῷ (v. 22), not unlike οἱ μαθηταί in v. 25 (if read, with αὐτόν, as "the disciples") resumes μετὰ τῶν ἐν Δαμασκῷ μαθητῶν (v. 19b). Following the same theory, verses 24–25 were added to the source by Luke, but given the emphasis on the Jews' ἐπιβουλή and their activity (v. 24: παρετηροῦντο ... ὅπως αὐτὸν ἀνέλωσιν) one can hardly say: "Act II voulait les innocenter"[22]. — In Proto-Luke (the still undivided

---

Acts, both published in the second half of 1998 (above, n. 7), contain a summary presentation and brief evaluation of the theory: BARRETT, XXX-XXXI: "incapable of proof or of disproof, and therefore beyond serious discussion" (XXXI); FITZMYER, 84-85: "The major problem with it is the building of hypothesis on hypothesis, for the linking of hypotheses decreases the probability, the more one links them" (85). Fitzmyer prefers P. Benoit's less complicated source analysis. He assigns Ac 9,19b-25 to the Pauline source.

On Luke's direct use of Paul's Letters, in Ac 9,24-25 (cf. 2 Cor 11,32-33): "le propre récit de Paul est probablement la source de celui de Luc" (V, 21; cf. I, 38; II, 186: "L'allusion... est ici transparente"; III, 135; V, 21 n. 5: "les contacts littéraires... sont pourtant évidents"); see also Ac 9,21 ὁ πορθήσας, cf. Gal 1,13.23: "le contact littéraire est quasi certain"; 9,22 ἐνεδυναμοῦτο: "une influence paulinienne... probable" (II, 185). Contrast FITZMYER, 434: "There is no substantial evidence that Luke had ever read any of Paul's letters. Rather, the information that Luke has about Saul and his ministry has come to him from other sources, esp. his Pauline source".

19. *Les Actes*, vol. I, 26-27. Cf. vol. II, 123: "La réaction hostile des Juifs".
20. Vol. I, 33. Cf. II, 187: "Une perspective plus favorable aux Juifs".
21. Vol. I, 48, 49.
22. Note on ὁ υἱὸς τοῦ θεοῦ: added by Act II in 9,20c to replace ὁ χριστός (= Act 1), now in v. 22c (*Les Actes*, vol. III, 133-134; cf. II, 187). On the order in vv. 20 (the Son of God) and 22 (the Christ): "l'on aurait attendu l'inverse (cf. Lk 22,67.70)". No other parallel in Luke–Acts is cited. The decrescendo in Ac 9,20.22 has a parallel in Lk 4,41 (ὁ υἱὸς τοῦ θεοῦ, τὸν χριστόν). The observation on grammatical ambiguity seems to neglect that v. 22 repeats the parallel v. 20 (τὸν Ἰησοῦν ὅτι οὗτός ἐστιν).

L + Act I) the Nazareth section does not include Lk 4,22b-30[23]. The parallel between Jesus and Paul is thus restricted to the christological preaching in Lk 4,16-22a and Ac 9,20, and that is much less than the common pattern assigned to Act I[24]. Not even the question in Lk 4,22b and its parallel in Ac 9,21[25] are assumed to be part of Proto-Luke.
At this point I conclude with a quotation from J. Dupont[26]:

> Dans l'ensemble des Actes, la notice sur la première prédication de Paul dans les synagogues de Damas (9,20-25) n'est encore qu'un prélude. Déjà cependant, elle se déroule en deux temps... Pour saisir le rapport entre cette courte notice et les récits concernant Antioche de Pisidie et Rome, il faudrait tenir compte en même temps de l'épisode de Nazareth en Lc 4,16-30.

Acts 13,5

Paul's mission to Cyprus (13,4-12) is the initial episode of his first missionary journey: Barnabas and Saul sailed to Cyprus and "arriving at Salamis they proclaimed the word of God in the synagogues of the Jews" (κατήγγελλον τὸν λόγον τοῦ θεοῦ ἐν ταῖς συναγωγαῖς τῶν Ἰουδαίων). The reference in 13,5 is extremely brief; the story simply continues in v. 6: "They went through the whole island as far as Paphos". Two comments are in order: (1) The plural ἐν ταῖς συναγωγαῖς

---

23. M.-É. BOISMARD, En quête du proto-Luc (ÉB, 37), Paris, 1997, 190-194; cf. 264-266: Lk 4,14a.16-22a.42-43.15.14b. See my review in ETL 73 (1997) 453-455.

24. TAYLOR, vol. V, 20: "un schéma de récit". Cf. vol. II, 124.

25. See the commentaries: "der an Lk 4,22 erinnernde Vers" (Haenchen); "die Sachparallele Lk 4,22" (Schneider); "vgl. Lk 4,22; Apg 2,7.12" (Weiser). Compare:
Ac 9,21a ἐξίσταντο δὲ πάντες οἱ ἀκούοντες
    b καὶ ἔλεγον· οὐχ οὗτός ἐστιν ὁ πορθήσας;
Lk 4,22a καὶ πάντες ... καὶ ἐθαύμαζον...
    b καὶ ἔλεγον· οὐχὶ υἱός ἐστιν Ἰωσὴφ οὗτος;
Ac 2,7   ἐξίσταντο δὲ καὶ ἐθαύμαζον
    λέγοντες· οὐχ ἰδοὺ ἅπαντες οὗτοί εἰσιν οἱ λαλοῦντες Γαλιλαῖοι;
On Lk 4,22 / Ac 2,7, cf. É. SAMAIN, Le récit de Pentecôte dans l'exégèse actuelle (STL diss.), Leuven, 1964, 55: "un excellent parallèle tant au point de vue du sens que du vocabulaire employé"; cf. ID., Le discours-programme de Jésus à la synagogue de Nazareth. Lc 4,16-30, in CBFV 10 (1971) 25-43, here 41; C. BURCHARD, Der dreizehnte Zeuge (n. 17), 1970, 152: "die Strukturverwandtschaft von V. 20-22 mit Apg 2,7.12 und besonders mit Lk 4,22"; J. DUPONT, Jésus, 130 (= 24): "un excellent parallèle"; F. BOVON, Lukas, 1989, 213 n. 29 (Luc, 1991, 208); T. BERGHOLZ, Der Aufbau des lukanischen Doppelwerkes. Untersuchungen zum formalliterarischen Charakter von Lukas-Evangelium und Apostelgeschichte (EHS, 23/545), Frankfurt, 1995, (diss. Bonn, 1994), 85.

26. Conclusion, 383 (= 487), n. 68. Cf. Le discours de l'Aréopage (Ac 17,22-31), in Bib 60 (1979) 530-546, here 532 (= 382): "chacun (des trois grands discours) avait été annoncé par une première ébauche: le thème de la prédication de Paul aux Juifs (13,16-41) est indiqué dès la notice de 9,20.22 sur son activité dans les synagogues de Damas".

is usually understood as suggesting the presence of a considerable Jewish population in Salamis, with more than one local synagogue (cf. 9,20: Damascus). But G. Schneider considers another possibility: "Oder sollte der Plural 'in den Synagogen' schon auf den Anfang von V 6 bezogen sein?" (i.e., throughout the island)[27]. (2) In contrast to the Damascus story there is here no mention of any reaction[28]. For Boismard this silence can be explained as follows:

> Act I ne mentionne aucune réaction favorable à leur prédication, seul cas dans les Actes... Act I nous fait comprendre, discrètement, que Barnabé et Saul n'eurent guère de succès dans leurs efforts pour implanter le christianisme à Chypre.[29]

Even the reason for their failure can be indicated:

> l'argument apologétique du miracle n'avait plus aucune valeur dans un milieu où les mages prodiguaient eux-mêmes de tels signes et de tels prodiges. D'où l'échec de la prédication de Barnabé et de Saul.[30]

In this solution, however, the continuation of the Cyprus episode in vv. 6-12, with the Jewish magician and the proconsul Sergius Paulus, is left out of consideration. If this story, ending with the conversion of the proconsul (v. 12b in *Act I*: ἐπίστευσεν ἐκπλησσόμενος ἐπὶ τῇ διδαχῇ τοῦ κυρίου)[31], is taken together with v. 5a, one can no longer, with regard to the preaching on Cyprus, employ general qualifications such as *insuccès*, *échec*, and *fiasco*. Contrast Fitzmyer: "... Cyprus, where he and Barnabas have some success... They convert even the proconsul..."[32], and Jervell:

> Nichts wird über den Erfolg der Verkündigung in den Synagogen gesagt, wahrscheinlich weil die grösste Erfolg die Bekehrung des gottesfürchtigen Prokonsul Sergius Paulus, V 12, ist.[33]

27. *Apg*, 120 n. 19. Cf. TAYLOR, vol. V, 134: "Le pluriel indiquerait plutôt que c'est durant leur trajet jusqu'à Paphos (cf. v. 6) qu'ils prêchaient dans les communautés juives réparties dans l'île" (n. 4: ctr. Haenchen). Cf. D.W.J. GILL, *Paul's Travels through Cyprus (Acts 13.4-12)*, in *TyndB* 46 (1995) 219-228.

28. HAENCHEN, 339 (= 381): "Über den Erfolg der Predigt sagt Lukas nichts"; G. SCHILLE, 287: "Er (Lukas) notiert nicht einmal den Erfolg in Salamis!"

29. Vol. II, 233: "Insuccès de la prédication de la Parole". See also TAYLOR: "Il semble que la mission n'eut aucun succès" (vol. V, 135).

30. Vol. II, 233 (slightly adapted).

31. Ἐκπλησσόμενος ἐπὶ τῇ διδαχῇ τοῦ κυρίου (Act I) is replaced with ἰδὼν τὸ γεγονός in Act II (vol. II, 267: "la force apologétique des miracles"), and both are combined in Act III (358: "il obtient ainsi un texte un peu boiteux"). But this combination can be Lukan: see Lk 4,36 and 32 (ἐξεπλήσσοντο ἐπὶ τῇ διδαχῇ αὐτοῦ).

32. *Acts*, 500.

33. *Apg*, 345. On the God-fearer: "Er gehört offenbar zu den Gottesfürchtigen" (346, and n. 422; 374 n. 574), contrast his *Retrospect and Prospect in Luke–Acts Interpretation*, in *SBL 1991 Seminar Papers*, 383-404: "where do we find 'pure' Gentiles without any connection to the synagogue? Perhaps Sergius Paulus is one" (391).

Jervell concludes with a comment on Lukan redaction, "vor allem" their being sent "by the Holy Spirit" (v. 4) and their preaching in the synagogues (v. 5)[34]. L.T. Johnson notes Luke's penchant for parallellism in Ac 13,1-3.4-12 (cf. Lk 3,21-22; 4,1-13): "empowerment by the Holy Spirit followed immediately by a confrontation with demonic powers. Such was the case with Jesus after his baptism with the Spirit"[35].

Acts 13,14-52

Paul and his company continued their journey from Paphos to Perga in Pamphylia and from Perga they came to Antioch of Pisidia. The long section on Pisidian Antioch characteristically articulates the synagogue setting and presents Paul's *first* speech (13,16-41) as a synagogue sermon. The similarities between Ac 13,14-52[36] and Lk 4,16-30 are generally recognized and W. Radl's survey[37] is a steadfast reference in the studies on the Nazareth pericope in Lk.

Ac 13,14-16a

14 Αὐτοὶ δὲ ... παρεγένοντο εἰς Ἀντιόχειαν τὴν Πισιδίαν, καὶ [εἰσ]ελθόντες εἰς τὴν συναγωγὴν τῇ ἡμέρᾳ τῶν σαββάτων ἐκάθισαν.

34. *Apg*, 349. For more detail, see A. WEISER, *Apg*, 1985, 312-314 ("Tradition und Redaktion"), esp. 313.

35. *Acts*, 1992, 226. See also 237 and 243, on "narrative mimesis" in Ac 13,13-41 and 42-52 (cf. Lk 4,22.23-27.28-29). On Johnson's parallel reading of Ac 13, see S. CUNNINGHAM, *'Through Many Tribulations'. The Theology of Persecution in Luke–Acts* (JSNT SS, 142), Sheffield, 1997, 244 n. 194.

36. On the three stages in Ac 13,14-52 according to Boismard-Lamouille-Taylor (n. 18), see *Les Actes*, vol. I, 113-117; vol. II, 237-240, 267-271, 358-359; vol. III, 184-188; vol. V, 150-165: Ac 13,14-16a|16b.17-22a^J.22b.23^J.24-25.26^J.27-31.32-34a.34b-35a.35b. 36-37.38.39.[40-41]|42.43.44-48.49-51.52. The Act I text (including J = Johannite source) is marked by underlining; verses within brackets are from Act III. – Ac 13,43 (= Act I) is replaced by v. 42 in Act II (v. 44: the next sabbath); both are combined in Act III. But see G. SCHILLE: the doublet is only "scheinbar" (*Apg*, 297: "Tatsächlich muß die Bitte um eine weitere Ausführung zum Gegenstand dem, was nach der Versammlung geschieht, vorausgehen").
For an analysis of Ac 13,14-52, see M.F.-J. BUSS, *Die Missionspredigt des Apostels Paulus in Pisidischen Antiochien. Analyse von Apg 13,16-41 im Hinblick auf die literarische und thematische Einheit der Paulusrede* (FzB, 38), Stuttgart, 1980; J. PICHLER, *Paulusrezeption in der Apostelgeschichte. Untersuchungen zur Rede im pisidischen Antiochien* (Innsbrucker theologische Studien, 50), Innsbruck-Wien, 1997 (88-92: "Apg 13 und Lk 4").

37. W. RADL, *Paulus und Jesus im lukanischen Doppelwerk. Untersuchungen zu Parallelmotiven im Lukasevangelium und in der Apostelgeschichte* (EHS, 23/49), Bern-Frankfurt, 1975, 82-100 ("Der Anfang: Apg 13,14-52 – Lk 4,16-30"). Cf. M. KORN, *Die Geschichte Jesu in veränderter Zeit. Studien zur bleibenden Bedeutung Jesu im lukanischen Doppelwerk* (WUNT, 2/51), Tübingen, 1993, 56-85: "Jesu Antrittspredigt in Nazareth als Programm des lukanischen Doppelwerks (Lk 4,16-30)", esp. 60. See also A. WEISER, *Apg*, 339-340.

15 μετὰ δὲ τὴν ἀνάγνωσιν τοῦ νόμου καὶ τῶν προφητῶν ἀπέστειλαν οἱ ἀρχισυνάγωγοι πρὸς αὐτοὺς λέγοντες· ἄνδρες ἀδελφοί, εἴ τίς ἐστιν ἐν ὑμῖν λόγος παρακλήσεως πρὸς τὸν λαόν, λέγετε. 16a ἀναστὰς δὲ Παῦλος καὶ κατασείσας τῇ χειρὶ εἶπεν·

The mise-en-scene in Ac 13,14-16a can be compared with Lk 4,16: Καὶ ἦλθεν εἰς Ναζαρά, οὗ ἦν τεθραμμένος, καὶ εἰσῆλθεν κατὰ τὸ εἰωθὸς αὐτῷ ἐν τῇ ἡμέρᾳ τῶν σαββάτων εἰς τὴν συναγωγὴν καὶ ἀνέστη ἀναγνῶναι. The phrase εἰσελθεῖν εἰς τὴν συναγωγήν (Lk 4,16, cf. Mk 1,21; Lk 6,6 = Mk 3,1) is a standard formula in Acts (13,14; 14,1; 18,19; 19,8)[38]. The closest parallel is Ac 13,14, where it is used in combination with the phrase ἐν τῇ ἡμέρᾳ τῶν σαββάτων (om. ἐν)[39]. It is less likely that we can infer from Ac 13,15 that "Jesus was invited by the president of the synagogue assembly to read and expound a Scripture text"[40]. In Ac 13,15 Paul and Barnabas are present as visitors at the sabbath service in Antioch (v. 14 ἐκάθισαν) and it is *after* the reading of the Law and the Prophets[41] that they were invited to address the congregation. Then Paul stood up (ctr. Lk 4,20 ἐκάθισεν, after the reading) and with the gesture of an orator[42] he began to speak. Here too some commentators think that "we must assume some previous conversation with the synagogue rulers"[43]. Lk 4,16c has καὶ ἀνέστη ἀναγνῶναι and the Scripture text from Isaiah is quoted sur-

---

38. Cf. Ac 17,2 εἰσῆλθεν πρὸς αὐτούς (v. 1 συναγωγὴ τῶν Ἰουδαίων); 17,10 εἰς τὴν συναγωγὴν τῶν Ἰουδαίων ἀπήεσαν.

39. See also Ac 16,13 τῇ τε ἡμέρᾳ τῶν σαββάτων ... (οὗ ἐνομίζομεν προσευχὴν εἶναι). Cf. 20,7 ἐν δὲ τῇ μιᾷ τῶν σαββάτων. Lk 13,14.16 τῇ ἡμέρᾳ τοῦ σαββάτου (in contrast to the ἓξ ἡμέραι in v. 14); 14,5 ἐν ἡμέρᾳ τοῦ σαββάτου. — Busse's emphasis on the plural τῶν σαββάτων: "betont die Modelhaftigkeit des Ereignisses durch den Plural 'am Tage *der Sabbate'*" is less convincing. See U. BUSSE, *Das Nazareth-Manifest Jesu. Eine Einführung in das lukanische Jesusbild nach Lk 4,16-30* (SBS, 91), Stuttgart, 1978, 31. Cf. J. JEREMIAS, *Sprache*, 121: "formelhafte Septuagintawendung..., die Lukas unbedenklich übernehmen konnte (Lk 4,16; Apg 13,14; 16,13), weil durch das vorangestellte τῇ ἡμέρᾳ die singularische Bedeutung von τὰ σάββατα klargestellt war".

40. FITZMYER, *Luke*, 531. Cf. J.D. KINGSBURY, *Conflict in Luke: Jesus, Authorities, Disciples*, Minneapolis, MN, 1991, 44: "Invited by the leader of the synagogue to read from scripture"; BOVON, *Lk*, 210: "sonst hätte er (Lukas) sicher die ungewöhnliche Initiative Jesu als solche signalisiert". Compare MARSHALL, *Luke*, 182: "Possibly Jesus had informally requested permission to read before the service began, and Luke has not gone into the details of the arrangement" (sic). Cf. below, n. 43.

41. Cf. 13,27 τὰς φωνὰς τῶν προφητῶν τὰς κατὰ πᾶν σάββατον ἀναγινωσκομένας and 15,21 Μωϋσῆς ... ἐν ταῖς συναγωγαῖς κατὰ πᾶν σάββατον ἀναγινωσκόμενος. It is of course not so that "he [Paul] reads from the Law and Prophets" (JOHNSON, 237).

42. Haenchen, Conzelmann, Schneider, Weiser, *et al.* Cf. WITHERINGTON, 407: "it is probable that Luke intends to portray Paul in his first major discourse in Acts as a great orator". Contrast Jervell: "zeigt nur, dass er zum Reden bereit ist" (353).

43. B. WITHERINGTON, 406. Cf. above, n. 40.

rounded with an artful chiastic structure from v. 16c (ἀνέστη) to v. 20a (ἐκάθισεν)[44]:

A ἀνέστη ἀναγνῶναι.
B   καὶ ἐπεδόθη αὐτῷ βιβλίον τοῦ προφήτου Ἠσαΐου
C   καὶ ἀναπτύξας τὸ βιβλίον
D   εὗρεν τὸν τόπον οὗ ἦν γεγραμμένον· [ ]
C'   καὶ πτύξας τὸ βιβλίον
B'   ἀποδοὺς τῷ ὑπηρέτῃ
A' ἐκάθισεν.

One may observe that Luke's account is elliptical and presupposes an intervention of the ruler of the synagogue, the lection of the Torah, and other elements of the synagogue worship, but the point Luke is making concerns the prophetic text he quotes from Isaiah.

In this connection mention should be made of the phrase (εἰσῆλθεν) κατὰ τὸ εἰωθὸς αὐτῷ in Lk 4,16 and its parallel in Ac 17,2: κατὰ δὲ τὸ εἰωθὸς τῷ Παύλῳ (εἰσῆλθεν). A few comments on Lk 4,16: "the parallel expression in Acts 17:2 suggests that here the reference is rather to his regular use of the synagogue for teaching (4:15)" (Marshall); "Luke's presentation indicates… that it was his habit to take the role of the one who read and expounded the Scriptures (cf. Acts 17:2)" (Green)[45]. Instead of reading Lk 4,16 in the light of Ac 17,2, as these commentators do, Boismard-Lamouille-Taylor propose a reverse relationship: "le texte de Act I renvoie implicitement à Lc 4,16"; "le récit est calqué sur celui de Jésus dans la synagogue de Nazareth"[46].

44. See, e.g., J.-N. ALETTI, L'art de raconter Jésus-Christ. L'écriture narrative de l'é-vangile de Luc, Paris, 1989, 39-61: "Récit et révélation. Lc 4,16-30" (esp. 41: "la disposition concentrique"); J.S. SIKER, "First to the Gentiles" : A Literary Analysis of Luke 4:16-30, in JBL 111 (1992) 73-90, esp. 77: "showing Luke's intention to highlight the Isaiah reading"; U. BUSSE, Nazareth-Manifest (n. 39), 32: "eine Ringkomposition, die… stilistisch die Bedeutung des Mischzitats unterstreichen soll". It is less appropriate to include, as does Siker (et al.: see below, n. 144; cf. N.W. Lund), vv. 16b καὶ εἰσῆλθεν … εἰς τὴν συναγωγήν and 20b καὶ … ἐν τῇ συναγωγῇ, or, as does Busse (esp. 49: Ringkomposition 4,17-20), to include v. 20b and not v. 16c. For a correct presentation of Luke's procédé d'inclusion, see J. DUPONT, Jésus, 130 (= 24); Conclusion, 398 (= 504). See also ibid. his description of this procédé d'encadrement in v. 4,20b-22:
    20b καὶ πάντων οἱ ὀφθαλμοὶ ἐν τῇ συναγωγῇ…
    21 Jesus' saying
    22 καὶ πάντες ἐμαρτύρουν αὐτῷ…
45. MARSHALL, Luke, 181; GREEN, Luke, 209. Cf. NOLLAND, 195: "It refers to Jesus' synagogue teaching habits".
46. Les Actes, I, 130; II, 243-244, 293, 365; III, 224; V, 269. See esp. II, 244 (Lc 4,16 / Ac 17,1b-2a): "La suite des deux récits offre des analogies évidentes: Jésus et Paul partent des Écritures pour montrer la légitimité de la mission de Jésus (Lc 4,17-21; Act 17,2b-3). La réaction des auditeurs est analogue; les uns sont favorables (Lc 4,22; Act 17,4) tandis que d'autres veulent lapider Jésus (Lc 4,29) ou suscitent une émeute contre Paul et son compagnon (Act 17,5). Mais Jésus (Lc 4,30) comme Paul et son compagnon

Lk 4,16	Ac 17,1b-2a
καὶ ἦλθεν εἰς Ναζαρά,	ἦλθον εἰς Θεσσαλονίκην
οὗ ἦν τεθραμμένος,	ὅπου ἦν συναγωγὴ τῶν Ἰουδαίων.
καὶ εἰσῆλθεν	
κατὰ τὸ εἰωθὸς αὐτῷ	κατὰ δὲ τὸ εἰωθὸς τῷ Παύλῳ
	εἰσῆλθεν πρὸς αὐτοὺς
ἐν τῇ ἡμέρᾳ τῶν σαββάτων	καὶ ἐπὶ σάββατα τρία...
εἰς τὴν συναγωγήν	

Taken by itself, Lk 4,16 allows us to read the phrase "as was his custom" not about Jesus' habitual synagogue teaching in Galilee (as exemplification of 4,15) but as referring to his regular synagogue attendance in Nazareth[47], and ἀνέστη ἀναγνῶναι as *erstmalig* in Nazareth and as Jesus' own initiative[48].

Ac 13,43: Jews and proselytes

The synagogue sermon in Ac 13 concludes with the positive reaction of πολλοὶ τῶν Ἰουδαίων καὶ τῶν σεβομένων προσηλύτων. Together with the addresses in vv. 16 (ἄνδρες Ἰσραηλῖται καὶ οἱ φοβούμενοι τὸν θεόν) and 26 (ἄνδρες ἀδελφοί, υἱοὶ γένους Ἀβραὰμ καὶ οἱ ἐν ὑμῖν φοβούμενοι τὸν θεόν), the phrase in v. 43, with a shift in the terminology from φοβούμενοι to σεβόμενοι[49], is one of the central data in the debate on the God-fearers in Acts[50]. It is now almost a common

(Act 17,10) échappent au danger qui les menace". Note however that the distinction "les uns... d'autres" (Ac 17,4.5) is not applicable in the case of Lk 4,22.29. — On Lk 4,22b-30 excluded from Boismard's reconstruction of Proto-Lk (L+Act I), see above, n. 23.

47. In connection with 4,16a Ναζαρά, οὗ ἦν τεθραμμένος. See E. KLOSTERMANN, 1919, 425 (²1929, 62): "die Gewohnheit scheint nur von dem sabbatlichen Synagogen-*besuch* ausgesagt zu sein, nicht von dem Lehren bei solcher Gelegenheit"; FITZMYER, 530: "stresses Jesus' habitual frequenting of the synagogue". Cf. J. ERNST, 169: "eine biographische Reminiszenz aus der Jugendzeit Jesu"; Bengel, Meyer, Godet, *et al.*

48. SCHÜRMANN, 227: "Jesus wird hier (anders als Apg 13,15) betont in Eigeninitiative geschildert". Cf. GRUNDMANN, 120: "Jesus ... der die Initiative ergreift"; REILING-SWELLENGREBEL, 198: "the fact that there is no hint at such an invitation seems to suggest that Jesus himself wanted to address the Nazarenes". See U. BUSSE, *Nazareth-Manifest* (n. 39), 33: "eine selbständige, auf die Sitte wenig Rücksicht nehmende Initiative (vgl. dagegen Apg 13,15)"; 50: "ohne Einladung ergreift er im Synagogengottesdienst die Initiative und liest die Haphthara".

49. Note οἱ φοβούμενοι τὸν θεόν in 13,16.26 (cf. 10,2.22.35) and σεβόμενοι in 13,43 (cf. 13,50; 16,14; 17,4.17; 18,7).
In the new Dutch translation (NBV, 1998): "die *de* God *van Israël* vereert" (italics F.N.). Cf. NBG: "vereerder van God / die God vereert"; NWV: "godvrezende". Note Ac 13,43: "vrome bekeerlingen"; compare RSV: "devout converts to Judaism". Why not "proselieten" (= 2,11; 6,5), and why the first addition ("van Israël") and not this last addition ("to Judaism")?

50. See the bibliography in FITZMYER, *Acts*, 450, including I. LEVINSKAYA, *The Book of Acts in Its Diaspora Setting* (BAFCS, 5), Grand Rapids, MI, 1996, ch. 7: "God-fearers: The Literary Evidence", 117-126 (for critical review, cf. R.S. ASCOUGH, in *Toronto*

assumption that the word προσηλύτων either can be dropped from the text as "eine alte Glosse" (Haenchen)[51] or as "sorglose Ausdrucksweise" (Conzelmann)[52]. For K. Lake the meaning is "many of the Jews and the proselytes who were worshipping"[53]. At least one commentator of the post-Haenchen era reads τῶν σεβομένων προσηλύτων in v. 43 ("fromme Proselyten") and raises the further question: "Sind also die 'Gottesfürchtigen' von V 16b als Proselyten zu verstehen?"[54]. Barrett answers positively: "In the present verse [16], Paul (as represented by Luke) is probably addressing Jews and proselytes... It would be strange if, in v. 16, Paul ... ignored the proselytes completely. In fact we know that he did not ignore the proselytes for they are mentioned in v. 43... [In v. 26] it seems best to take οἱ φοβούμενοι to be not uncircumcised 'God-fearers' but proselytes. They are ἐν ὑμῖν, *among you*... they have joined your ranks. [And in v. 43] *Jews* will mean Jews by birth, *proselytes* Jews by conversion and adoption... *devout proselytes*, perhaps *worshipping proselytes*, that is, proselytes who had duly attended the Sabbath service in the synagogue". See also his comment on the 'God-fearer' term at Ac 10,2: "not so fully and universally technical in the description of Gentile adherents that they could not be used of Jews and

---

Journal of Theology 44, 1998, 268-169). Add the survey article M.C. DE BOER, *God-fearers in Luke–Acts*, in *Luke's Literary Achievement* (n. 5), 1995, 50-71 (esp. 53, for the 'consensus' on the God-fearers in Ac 13,16.26 as "Gentile sympathizers, such as Cornelius"; cf. Fitzmyer); B. WANDER, *Trennungsprozesse zwischen Frühem Christentum und Judentum im 1. Jahrhundert n. Chr.* (TANZ, 16), Tübingen-Basel, 1994, 173-185 ("Exkurz: 'Gottesfürchtig'"); ID., *Gottesfürchtige und Symphatisanten. Studien zum heidnischen Umfeld von Diasporasynagogen* (WUNT, 2/104), Tübingen, 1998; M. REISER, *Hat Paulus Heiden bekehrt?*, in *BZ* 39 (1995) 76-91; H.-J. KLAUCK, *Gottesfürchtige im Magnificat?*, in *NTS* 43 (1997) 134-139. See also B. Witherington's excursus "Gentile God-fearers – The Case of Cornelius" (*Acts*, 1998, 341-344), esp. 343: "we can't be sure Luke isn't simply equating proselytes with God-fearers";

51. *Apg*, at 13,43. See also J. ROLOFF ("vielleicht"); K.G. KUHN, in *TWNT* 6, 743: "eine Ungenauigkeit des Lukas oder eine alte Glosse"; H. KUHLI, in *EWNT* 3, 413; CAMERLYNCK – VANDER HEEREN, [7]1923, 255: "Non immerito forte supponeres textum primitivum de solis *colentibus* Deum egisse".

52. *Apg*, at 13,43. See also n. 51. G. SCHILLE: "ungenaue Redeweise"; A. WEISER: "Der Ausdruck 'Proselyten' ist hier ungenau"; R. DILLON: "Does this not commingle separate groups: converts and nonconverts?" (*NJBC*, 750). Cf. BAUER-ALAND: "eine Vermischung beider Arten"; BAG: "a mixed expression". See TAYLOR, *Les Actes*, vol. V, 158-162 ("Les 'craignant-Dieu' à Antioche"), 159 n. 1: "plusieurs justifications". Cf. below, n. 55.

53. K. LAKE, *Proselytes and God-fearers*, in *Beginnings*, vol. V, 1933, 74-96, 88. Cf. 86: "It should be noted... that a proselyte is in Jewish thought quite as much an Israelite as a born Jew". Compare G. WASSERBERG (cf. below, n. 55), 49: "ein Proselyt war Juden rechtlich gleichgestellt und verhielt sich kultisch-religiös wie ein geborener Jude".

54. G. SCHNEIDER, *Apg* II, 131; see also 142 n. 141: "Doch ist auch denkbar, daß Lukas mit Hinblick auf 13,46f deutlich machen will, am ersterwähnten Sabbat habe es sich nur um geborene Juden und zum Judentum voll Übergetretene gehandelt".

full proselytes"[55]. In his speech at Antioch Paul speaks as a Jew to a Jewish audience, referring to "our fathers" in treating the history of "this people Israel" (13,17), and it would not be correct to call it simply a mixed audience of two groups, Jews and Gentiles[56]. On the following sabbath, Paul and Barnabas can declare to the Jews: "it was necessary that the word of God should be spoken *first* to you" (13,46).

The reaction of Jews-and-proselytes in v. 43 has been seen as comparable to the initial attitude of the people in the synagogue of Nazareth in Lk 4,22. Both will be followed by comparable reactions of hostility: ἐπλήσθησαν ζήλου... (the Jews in Ac 13,45) and ἐπλήσθησαν πάντες θυμοῦ... (in Lk 4,28). For not a few interpreters, however, there is a significant difference: in Ac 13,43 these πολλοί "have become Christians" and should not be included among those Jews filled with jealousy on the following sabbath. I quote J. Dupont: "Il est clair que ces convertis, qu'on invite à se montrer fidèles à la grâce de Dieu, ne sont pas inclus dans ce que le v. 45 dit de l'hostilité des 'Juifs'"[57]. Some commentators attenuate their expression: "οἱ Ἰουδαῖοι (in v. 45) can hardly refer to all the Jews, since some of them seem to have been *favourably*

---

55. *Acts*, 631, 630, 639, 654. See now also G. WASSERBERG, *Aus Israels Mitte – Heil für die Welt. Eine narrativ-exegetische Studie zur Theologie des Lukas* (BZNW, 92), Berlin – New York, 1998, 48-51: "Zur Crux interpretum οἱ σεβόμενοι προσήλυτοι (Act 13,43)". There is no mention of Barrett, *Acts* I (1994). He refers to Schneider (142 n. 141), though not to his text at 13,16b (131, quoted above), and so he states incorrectly that Schneider did not consider "die Konsequenzen, die sich daraus für die Deutung der 'Gott Fürchtenden' Act 13,16.26 ergeben müßten" (51 n. 59). — Wasserberg's own argument: "Da Lukas sowohl Juden (Lk 1,50) wie auch ἔθνη (Act 10,2.22) mit dem Etikett der Gottesfurcht behaften kann, muß folglich am Einzelfall entschieden werden, welcher ethnischen Herkunft die jeweils 'Gott Fürchtenden' sind. Wenn einmal das 'Vor-Urteil' beiseite gelassen wird, die von Lukas gekennzeichneten 'Gott Fürchtenden' seien selbstredend nichtjüdische Sympathisanten, so eröffnet sich auch ein neuer Zugang zur Deutung der Gottesfürchtigen in Act 13,16.26. Sie hat von Act 13,43 her zu erfolgen" (50); "Folglich besteht der Adressatenkreis ... für Lukas aus Juden und Proselyten (Act 13,43), nicht auch aus vermeintlichen 'Gottesfürchtigen'" (51).

Cf. J. MURPHY-O'CONNOR, *Lot of God-fearers? Theosebeis in the Aphrodisias Inscription*, in *RB* 99 (1992) 418-424. The second list contains 52 names introduced as *kai hosoi theosebis*, but the Jewish group in the first list includes three names identified as proselytes and two others identified as *theosebeis* (Emmonios and Antoninos). Note therefore Murphy-O'Connor's conclusion: "the fact that here it is used in two consciously differentiated senses in the same document makes it clear that the meaning of the term *must be determined in each instance from the context*" (424, italics F.N.).

56. BUSS, *Missionspredigt* (n. 36), 34-35, although he emphasizes "die gemeinsame Anrede von Israeliten und Proselyten" (35) and also notes that Paul "in Antiochien vor Juden situationsgerecht zunächst vom Schöpfer und Erhalter Israels (spricht)" (37). Cf. JERVELL, on Ac 13,16.26: "es (gibt) in der Synagoge zwei Gruppen, die voneinander getrennt sind" (353; cf. 357).

57. *Conclusion*, 384 (= 488). Cf. below, n. 140.

impressed by what Paul had said" (Barrett)[58]. Others, like Jervell, stress the notion of conversion (*Bekehrung*) and include Ac 13,43 in the list of Luke's characteristic reports of "mass conversions of God-fearers"[59]. But it has been rightly observed: v. 43 "spricht noch nicht von Bekehrungen"[60]. Ἀκολουθεῖν has its literal meaning: they 'followed' Paul and Barnabas[61]. The phrase προσμένειν τῇ χάριτι τοῦ θεοῦ has been compared to 11,23 (τὴν χάριν [τὴν] τοῦ θεοῦ ... προσμένειν τῷ κυρίῳ) and 14,22 (ἐμμένειν τῇ πίστει), but in both cases the context clearly indicates that the exhortation to remain faithful is addressed to Christians (cf. 11,21; 14,22a), whereas in ch. 13 an act of believing is not mentioned before v. 48 (ἐπίστευσαν).

The conclusion in Ac 13,43 (λυθείσης δὲ τῆς συναγωγῆς...) is preceded by an immediate reaction to Paul's speech: ἐξιόντων δὲ αὐτῶν παρεκάλουν εἰς τὸ μεταξὺ σάββατον λαληθῆναι αὐτοῖς τὰ ῥήματα ταῦτα (13,42)[62]. The verb παρεκάλουν has no expressed subject and can be translated: *"the people* urged them" (NRSV; Luther: *"die Leute"*). Some translators prefer to keep the indefinite "they" (*"man"*). In J. Roloff's understanding it refers to the synagogue officials (cf. 13,15) who invite Paul and Barnabas to speak again on the following sabbath. In v. 45 "die anfänglich freundliche Zurückhaltung der

---

58. *Acts*, 655 (italics mine). Moreover, see 624: "does Luke imply that those who at first were favourably impressed changed their minds?".

59. *Apg*, 362 (cf. 151, 524): "auch hier: *Einige* glauben" (italics F.N.). — Jervell's list (* = conversions of 'God-fearers'): Ac 2,41; 4,4; 5,14; 6,7; 9,42; 11,21*.24*.26; 12,24; 13,43*; 14,1*; 17,4*.12*; 18,8*.10; 21,20 (cf. 151, 297, 524; *Retrospect* [n. 33], 390-391). With regard to "God-fearers" and proselytes, Jervell (here, 362 n. 505, and again 389 n. 647) refers to M. KLINGHARDT, *Gesetz und Volk Gottes. Das lukanische Verständnis des Gesetzes nach Herkunft, Funktion und seinem Ort in der Geschichte des Urchristentums* (WUNT, 2/32), Tübingen, 1988, 183-184: "Die Verwendung der Bezeichnung Proselyt für den beschnittenen Konvertiten ist mE. keineswegs so eindeutig, wie dies aus den neueren Untersuchungen hervorzugehen scheint. Es ist denkbar, daß man – obwohl in aller Regel ein eindeutiger, technischer Sprachgebrauch vorliegt – bewußt oder unbewußt die Grenze zwischen beschnittenen Konvertiten und unbeschnittenen Gottesfürchtigen nicht so streng gezogen hat, zumal die Gottesfürchtigen sehr häufig Frauen waren, bei denen der Übertritt zum Judentum nicht so eindeutig war, da die Beschneidung fehlte". Klinghardt reads "proselytes" in Ac 13,43 as "eine Gruppe von Gottesfürchtigen, frommen Heiden also, die sich eng zur Synagoge hält"; he uses the term God-fearer without discussing its meaning, technical or descriptive.

60. BUSS, *Missionspredigt* (n. 36), 134. Cf. SCHNEIDER: "Daß sie gläubig geworden seien, sagt der Bericht nicht" (142). Ctr. G. Stählin, F. Mussner, A. Weiser, J. Jervell, B.J. Koet, *et al.*

61. Cf. WASSERBERG, *Aus Israels Mitte* (n. 55), 314. Ctr. MUSSNER, 82: "schließen sich... an, d.h. sie werden Christen"; WEISER, 337: "'Nachfolgen': Anschluß an den christlichen Glauben".

62. Cf. above, n. 36.

maßgeblichen jüdischen Kreise (schlägt um) in unverhohlene Ablehnung"[63]. Compare again Lk 4,22 and 28.

Ac 13,45: The jealousy of the Jews

The story of the second sabbath at Pisidian Antioch begins with the gathering of "almost the whole city" (v. 44) and the reaction of the Jews: ἰδόντες δὲ οἱ Ἰουδαῖοι τοὺς ὄχλους ἐπλήσθησαν ζήλου... (v. 45). The same phrase is used in the conflict of the high priest and the Sadducees with the apostles (5,17) and is usually translated: "they were filled with jealousy"[64]. The participle ζηλώσαντες, in the same meaning, occurs at 7,9 and 17,5. This motif in Ac 13,45 is not irrelevant in a study of the Nazareth pericope because of the parallel expression in Lk 4,28: ἐπλήσθησαν πάντες θυμοῦ (in reaction to 4,25-27)[65]. Moreover, jealousy is implied in the demand attributed to the people of Nazareth: "the things that we have heard you did at Capernaum do also here ἐν τῇ πατρίδι σου" (Lk 4,23)[66].

B. Koet has devoted a special study to Ac 13,45. I quote here his conclusion: "We cannot interpret the reaction of the Jews to what Paul has said as jealousy. Their attitude is based on zeal for their interpretation of the Law"[67]. The Jews in 13,45 react to Paul's pronouncement on the Law. They are not jealous but they show a certain zealousness and especially a zeal against the interpretation of the *Torah* as presented in Paul's speech, 13,38-41. Koet has to note that the use of ζῆλος in 5,17 "is not clearly related to zeal for the Law", but he stresses the parallel in 17,5, ζηλώσαντες δὲ οἱ Ἰουδαῖοι: the Jews in Thessalonica "are not jealous but they disagree with zeal against Paul's preaching of the Word of God to the Gentiles"[68].

---

63. *Apg*, 209.

64. EÜ: wurden eifersüchtig; BJ: furent remplis de jalousie; NWV: werden met jaloezie vervuld. — Compare the variation in NBG: naijver (5,17; 7,9), nijd (13,45), afgunst (17,5). See now NBV (1998): 5,17 vervuld van jaloezie; 7,9 (waren) jaloers; 13,45 werden jaloers; 17,5 werden vervuld van jaloezie. The inversion of 13,45 and 17,5 would be closer to the Greek: ἐπλήσθησαν ζήλου, and ζηλώσαντες (cf. NWV).

65. BJ: furent remplis de fureur; TOB: remplis de colère. — Note the TOB translation of ζῆλος in Ac 13,45: "furent pris de fureur" (5,17: remplis de fureur; 17,5: furieux)!

66. J. DUPONT, *Jésus*, 149 (= 45): "On peut se demander ici si le récit des Actes ne manifeste pas le sous-entendu de *Lc.* 4,23: les Nazaréens sont jaloux". Cf. R.C. TANNEHILL, *The Narrative Unity* (below, n. 74), 70: "the jealous possessiveness which is indicated by v. 23 and underscored by the angry reaction to vv. 25-27".

67. B.J. KOET, *Paul and Barnabas in Pisidian Antioch: A Disagreement over the Interpretation of the Scriptures (Acts 13,42-52)*, in ID., *Five Studies on Interpretation of Scripture in Luke–Acts* (SNTA, 14), Leuven, 1989, 97-118, 117.

68. *Ibid.*, 101, 105 n. 28, 104.

In 13,45 it is said that the Jews contradicted "what was spoken by Paul", ἀντέλεγον τοῖς ὑπὸ Παύλου λαλουμένοις. Does it mean that they particularly object to "Paul's pronouncement on the Law"? What Paul said in his synagogue preachings is time and again summarized by Luke: that Jesus is the χριστός (9,22)[69]. Thus, in 17,3 ὅτι οὗτός ἐστιν ὁ χριστὸς [ὁ] Ἰησοῦς and 18,5b διαμαρτυρόμενος τοῖς Ἰουδαίοις εἶναι τὸν χριστὸν Ἰησοῦν (cf. 18,28 Apollos), in each instance followed by the Jews' opposition. The christological theme is of course not absent in 13,38 on forgiveness of sins (διὰ τούτου) and in v. 39 on justification (ἐν τούτῳ). Is it not thinkable[70] that the λαλούμενα in 13,45 refer to a preaching of Paul on the second sabbath, not quoted but implied in the intention of the people of Antioch "to hear the word of the Lord"? Anyway in the text of Ac 13,45 "the immediate cause of the reaction of the Jews is their 'seeing the multitudes'" (Koet) and I see no urgent reason for changing here the usual translation of ζῆλος (and of ζηλώσαντες in 17,5)[71].

J.B. Tyson[72] has repeatedly studied the pattern of initial acceptance and final rejection:

> The narrative about Paul in Pisidian Antioch expresses this literary pattern in fullest fashion... In Acts 13 ... Paul speaks on two Sabbaths. After the first, many Jews and proselytes join with Paul and Barnabas, and Paul is invited to speak again. But on the second Sabbath there is nothing but opposition. 'But when the Jews saw the crowds, they were filled with jealousy; and blaspheming, they contradicted what was spoken by Paul' (13,45). As was the case with the sermon of Jesus in Luke 4, so here with Paul initial acceptance is followed by rejection, in a pattern that is familiar to readers of Luke–Acts.

> In terms of public response the pattern is clear: initial acceptance followed by rejection. Luke 4:16-30 anticipates the Jewish public response to Jesus

---

69. Cf. P. POKORNÝ, *Theologie der lukanischen Schriften* (FRLANT, 174), Göttingen, 1998, 112: "Der Satz, wonach 'dieser' (d.h. Jesus) der Sohn Gottes (d.h. auch Messias – Act 9,22) sei, ist nach Lukas die Zusammenfassung dessen, was Paulus in den Synagogen predigte (Act 9,20; 13,33)".

70. See E. PLÜMACHER, *Die Missionsreden der Apostelgeschichte und Dionys von Halikarnass*, in *NTS* 39 (1993) 161-177: "Da Lukas den Paulus das Missionskerygma wenige Verse zuvor schon ausführlich hat vortragen lassen und man aus V. 42 weiß, daß er es jetzt lediglich wiederholen wird, braucht Lukas es nicht abermals *verbaliter* zu präsentieren; der schlichte Hinweis auf die Tatsache, daß Paulus predigt, auf τὰ ὑπὸ Παύλου λαλούμενα, genügt" (165).

71. On Ac 13,45, see also WASSERBERG, *Aus Israels Mitte* (n. 55), 315-316. On Ac 17,5, cf. below, text at n. 80.

72. Cf. J.B. TYSON, *The Jewish Public in Luke–Acts*, in *NTS* 30 (1984) 574-583; = *The Death of Jesus in Luke–Acts*, Columbia, SC, 1986, 29-47 ("Acceptance and Rejection: Jesus and the Jewish Public"); *The Gentile Mission and the Authority of Scripture in Acts*, in *NTS* 33 (1987) 619-631 (esp. 622-624); *Jews and Judaism in Luke–Acts: Reading as a Godfearer*, in *NTS* 41 (1995) 19-38 (esp. 29-37).

that will be worked out in the rest of the Gospel (and Acts). It is significant that the rejection is associated with favourable treatment of Gentiles.[73]

Ac 13,46: Turning to the Gentiles

ὑμῖν ἦν ἀναγκαῖον πρῶτον λαληθῆναι τὸν λόγον τοῦ θεοῦ·
ἐπειδὴ ἀπωθεῖσθε αὐτὸν καὶ οὐκ ἀξίους κρίνετε ἑαυτοὺς τῆς αἰωνίου ζωῆς,
ἰδοὺ στρεφόμεθα εἰς τὰ ἔθνη.

Ac 13,46 is the first of three announcements that Paul is turning to the Gentiles (cf. 18,6; 28,28): "Rejection by Jews and turning to Gentiles, the pattern of Paul's mission in Acts"[74]. For those who accept the allusion to the Gentiles in Lk 4,25-27 (the Elijah and Elisha material) it is easy to make the link with Nazareth. Thus, for J. Dupont,

> Le récit d'Antioche de Pisidie nous est précieux, car c'est lui qui assure le pont entre l'épisode de Nazareth et celui de Rome... Les déclarations faites par Paul aux Juifs d'Antioche de Pisidie (13,46-47) et de Corinthe (18,6) [sont des] déclarations préparées de longue main par les précédents prophétiques auxquels Jésus se réfère à Nazareth, en Lc 4,25-27. Nazareth, Antioche de Pisidie, Rome: trois jalons d'une même histoire, trois situations permettant des variations sur le même thème: le salut passe des Juifs aux Gentils.[75]

The solemn announcement in 13,46(-47)[76] is followed by the joyful reaction of the Gentiles and, in v. 50, the final, and now more than verbal, aggression by the Jews of Antioch. Notice the phrase ἐξέβαλον αὐτοὺς ἀπὸ τῶν ὁρίων αὐτῶν and Lk 4,29 ἐξέβαλον αὐτὸν ἔξω τῆς πόλεως[77]. Note also 13,51...ἦλθον εἰς Ἰκόνιον, followed by a new synagogue scene in 14,1-7 (cf. Lk 4,30... ἐπορεύετο. 31 καὶ κατῆλθεν εἰς Καφαρναοὺμ...). The opening sentence in 14,1 makes clear that,

---

73. Quotations: 1995, 29-30; 1984, 578 (1986, 33: "and Acts", "connected").

74. R.C. TANNEHILL, *Rejection by Jews and Turning to the Gentiles*, in *SBL 1986 Seminar Papers*, 130-141 (= J.B. TYSON, ed., *Luke–Acts and the Jewish People*, Minneapolis, MN, 1988, 83-101); *The Narrative Unity of Luke–Acts: A Literary Interpretation*. I. *The Gospel according to Luke*, Minneapolis, MN, 1986 (esp. 60-73); II. *The Acts of the Apostles*, 1990 (esp. 164-175). Cf. *The Mission of Jesus according to Luke* IV 16-30, in W. ELTESTER (ed.), *Jesus in Nazareth* (BZNW, 40), Berlin – New York, 1972, 51-75.

75. *Conclusion*, 400-401 (= 507-508).

76. On the citation of Isa 49,6, interpreted as a direct command of the Lord (v. 47 οὕτως γὰρ ἐντέταλται ἡμῖν ὁ κύριος· τέθεικά σε εἰς φῶς ἐθνῶν τοῦ εἶναί σε εἰς σωτηρίαν ἕως ἐσχάτου τῆς γῆς), see B.J. KOET, *Paul and Barnabas* (n. 67), 106-114; H. VAN DE SANDT, *The Quotations in Acts 13,32-52 as a Reflection of Luke's LXX Interpretation*, in *Bib* 75 (1994) 26-58, esp. 50-54; G.J. STEYN, *Septuaginta Quotations in the Context of the Petrine and Pauline Speeches of the Acta Apostolorum* (CBET, 12), Kampen, 1995, 159-202 (Ac 13), esp. 196-201.

77. This parallel is heavily stressed by G. Muhlack, *Parallelen* (below, n. 83), 124 ("Die Parallele... reicht bis in die Ausdrucksweise"), 139. See also n. 80.

despite their turning to the Gentiles (v. 46), "they entered into the synagogue of the Jews κατὰ τὸ αὐτό"[78], i.e., *in the same way* as in Antioch (emphasized in NRSV: "The same thing occurred in Iconium...">"):

> The scene is almost a replay of that in Antioch, and its literary function is much the same. Luke is at great pains to show that the turn to the Gentiles was not because God rejected the Jews, but because some Jews rejected the gospel and prevented its being spread among them. Nothing will make the point more forcibly than such repetition of patterns.[79]

The three stations of Antioch, Iconium, and Lystra are marked by growing Jewish opposition. In Antioch Paul and Barnabas are persecuted and expelled from the district (13,50), in Iconium there is an attempt to stone them (14,5), and in Lystra "Jews came there from Antioch and Iconium; and having persuaded the people, they stoned Paul and dragged him out of the city" (14,19). Compare the repetition of the pattern in Ac 17: Paul's successful preaching in Thessalonica (vv. 1-4) is followed by opposition of "the Jews" who became jealous (v. 5) and in Beroea "the Jews of Thessalonica... came there too, to stir up and incite the crowds" (v. 13)[80].

II. Lk 4,16-30 and Peter's Mission Speeches

The sermon in the synagogue of Pisidian Antioch is Paul's inaugural speech, the first of his three major speeches in Acts: 13,16-41

---

78. Κατὰ τὸ αὐτό = in the same way, *ebenso*: compare the plural κατὰ τὰ αὐτά in Lk 6,23.26; 17,30 (cf. κατὰ τὸ εἰωθὸς τῷ Παύλῳ in Ac 17,2). The alternative translation: together, *zusammen* (Vulg. *simul*) reads the singular as a variant of ἐπὶ τὸ αὐτό (Lake-Cadbury, Bauer *Wb*, REB, NAB; undecided: Conzelmann, Fitzmyer). More exceptional, and less convincing: "vers la même époque" (Delebecque, Bossuyt-Radermakers).

79. L.T. Johnson, *Acts*, 250. For a stylistic analysis of Ac 13,44-52 / 14,1-7, see C. Breytenbach, *Paulus und Barnabas in der Provinz Galatien. Studien zu Apostelgeschichte 13f.; 16,6; 18,23 und den Adressaten des Galaterbriefes* (AGAJU, 38), Leiden, 1996, 24:

Interessierte Heiden	13,44	14,1d
Hindernis durch Juden	45	2
Rede	46-47	3
Überwindung	48-49	—
Steigerung des Konfliktes	50	4-5
Jüngerflucht	51	6-7
Missionserfolg	52	—

80. In connection with Ac 13,50 (n. 77) I note here the parallels between Lk 4,28-29 and the account of Stephen's death: Lk 4,28 ἀκούοντες ταῦτα, 29 καὶ ... ἐξέβαλον αὐτὸν ἔξω τῆς πόλεως and Ac 7,54 ἀκούοντες δὲ ταῦτα, 58 καὶ ἐκβαλόντες ἔξω τῆς πόλεως ἐλιθοβόλουν (cf. Ac 14,5 λιθοβολῆσαι). See also J. Nolland, *Luke*, 201: "Both Stephen and Jesus accuse their hearers of rejecting God's prophets (Acts 7:52; Luke 4:24) and identify them as outsiders to what God is presently doing (Acts 7:51; Luke 4:25-27)".

(addressed to a Jewish audience); 17,22-31 (to Gentiles in Athens); 20,18-35 (to Christians in Miletus). In this second part I turn to Peter's three major mission speeches (2,17-40; 3,12-26; 10,34-43), beginning with his Pentecost sermon, the inaugural discourse in the Book of Acts.

Acts 2,17-40

C.H. Talbert describes the parallel with Lk 4,16-30 as follows: "each speech (1) opens a period of public ministry (Jesus' resp. the church's) and (2) gives the theme for what follows in that ministry, namely, fulfillment of prophecy and rejection of Jesus by many of the Jewish people"[81]. Compare D.L. Tiede: "Thus as the Isaiah prophecy in Luke 4 serves to articulate the program of the Spirit-anointed Jesus, so the direct citation of the Book of Joel identifies the new phase of the eschatological activity of God's Spirit which is being disclosed at Pentecost"[82]. The "Antrittspredigten" in Lk 4, Ac 2 (and Ac 13) are included in G. Muhlack's survey of *Parallelen*[83]. The parallelism between Lk 4,16-30 and Ac 2,14-40 is now examined anew in A. Lindemann's seminar paper[84]. At first glance his conclusion goes in the traditional line of previous studies[85]:

> Die beiden Redeszenen in Lk und in Apg 2 ... leiten das öffentliche Auftreten der im folgenden dargestellten Hauptpersonen ein; in beiden Reden geht es darum, das geschilderte Geschehen und die damit verbundenen Personen umfassend zu deuten; beide Reden beziehen sich auf das Wirken des göttlichen Geistes.

81. C.H. TALBERT, *Literary Patterns, Theological Themes, and the Genre of Luke–Acts*, Missoula, MT, 1974, 18-19, esp. 16.

82. D.L. TIEDE, *Acts 2:1-47*, in *Interpretation* 33 (1979) 62-67, here 63. Cf. J.-N. ALETTI, *Quand Luc raconte. Le récit comme théologie* (Lire la Bible, 114), Paris, 1998, 81: "Discours inaugural (insistant sur l'Esprit de prophétie)". See also in this volume: H. BAARLINK, *Die Bedeutung der Prophetenzitate in Lk 4,18f. und Apg 2,17-21 für das Doppelwerk des Lukas*, 483-491. His thesis: "die theologischen Eckdaten der Apostelgeschichte (haben) die Strukturierung und Darstellung in seinem Evangelium maßgeblich mitbestimmt" (491). Yet, the evidence he provides, the influence of Ac 2,17-21 (= Joel) upon Lk 8,1-3 and the man-woman pairs in Lk, is hardly convincing.

83. G. MUHLACK, *Die Parallelen von Lukas-Evangelium und Apostelgeschichte* (Theologie und Wirklichkeit, 8), Frankfurt, 1979, 117-139 ("Die Antrittspredigt in Lukas-Evangelium und Apostelgeschichte"), esp. 118, 125-131, 138 ("Die Pfingstpredigt des Petrus").

84. "Zu Form und Funktion von Reden und Wundererzählungen im Lukasevangelium und in der Apostelgeschichte. A. Reden im lukanischen Doppelwerk" (pp. 1-5; discussion paper available at the Colloquium). See now the slightly revised text, supplemented with footnotes, in this volume: *Einheit und Vielfalt im lukanischen Doppelwerk. Beobachtungen zu Reden, Wundererzählungen und Mahlberichten*, 225-253, esp. 225-237 ("I. Jesu Antrittsrede in Nazareth und die Pfingstpredigt des Petrus in Jerusalem").

85. *Ibid.*, 234 ("Ergebnis des Vergleichs"). Cf. BAARLINK (n. 82), 485.

Yet the words omitted in this quotation need further explication: "Beide sind von Lukas offensichtlich bewußt parallel gestaltet worden". Lindemann emphasizes the presence of structural analogies in the text and context of Lk 4,16-30 and Ac 2,14-41. Both speeches are followed by a narrative summary, Lk 4,31-32 and Ac 2,42.43-47. In both scenes he notes a two-part division: an opening section (*Eröffnung*), Lk 4,16-21 and Ac 2,14-36, and in a second part the reaction of the audience (*Reaktion der Hörer*), Lk 4,22-30 and Ac 2,37-41, both in the form of a question to the speaker. However, in his own interpretation, the question in Lk 4,22 is an expression of "ungläubige Skepsis"[86], while Peter's listeners were "cut to the heart" and they inquired, "What are we to do?" (Ac 2,37). The Nazareth scene ends with Jesus' failure (*Fehlschlag, Niederlage, Katastrophe*) in contrast to the success of Peter's speech ("endet mit einem grandiosen Triumph des Redners"). In Lk 4,30 a change of location forms the transition to the summary (4,31-32), while in Ac 2 there is no such *Ortswechsel*. The differences are even more striking in the so-called first part. Ac 2,14-36 is one continuous uninterrupted speech of Peter, with no other parallel than Jesus' *Predigt* in Lk 4,21b. The presentation of correspondences in a synoptic table[87] creates a misleading impression. The *Orts- und Situationsangabe* Lk 4,16 / Ac 2,1-13(15) as well as the *Einleitung* Lk 4,17 / Ac 2,16 are in reality hardly comparable parallels. The quotations in Lk 4,18-19 / Ac 2,17-21 are presented as parallels, but Lindemann's comment shows that there is "ein wesentlicher Unterschied" between Jesus' reading of the Isaiah text and Peter's use of Joel 3,1-5 as the correct interpretation of "ein bereits geschehenes Ereignis"[88].

Since Lindemann understands Lk 4,25-27 as "Vorausverweis auf die Apg"[89], it is rather amazing that he has no comment on Ac 2,39: ὑμῖν γάρ ἐστιν ἡ ἐπαγγελία καὶ τοῖς τέκνοις ὑμῶν καὶ πᾶσιν τοῖς εἰς μακράν, ὅσους ἂν προσκαλέσηται κύριος ὁ θεὸς ὑμῶν[90]. Cf. Dupont's *Le salut des Gentils*:

---

86. *Ibid.*, 233 (in confrontation with U. Busse, *Nazareth-Manifest*). Cf. below, n. 156.

87. *Ibid.*, 228.

88. *Ibid.*, 231.

89. In the revised text: "ein gezielter Vorausverweis auf die erst in der Apostelgeschichte dargestellte Entwicklung" (237), here too in dialogue with Busse (n. 53).

90. Two OT passages are alluded to: Joel 3,5d καὶ εὐαγγελιζόμενοι οὓς κύριος προσκέκληται (cf. 3,1-5a LXX, quoted in Ac 2,17-21) and Isa 57,19a εἰρήνην ἐπ' εἰρήνην τοῖς *μακρὰν* καὶ τοῖς ἐγγὺς οὖσιν (cf. Eph 2,17; Ac 22,21, the commission conferred on Paul: πορεύου, ὅτι ἐγὼ εἰς ἔθνη μακρὰν ἐξαποστελῶ σε). – "Per eos hic nonnulli intelligunt Gentes, tamquam quae Judaeis ut τοῖς ἐγγὺς opponi soleant. Ita olim Theophylactus..." (J.C. WOLFIUS, 1725, at Ac 2,39). H.H. Wendt calls it "die gewöhnliche Erklärung" (⁹1913, 96). Wendt himself opted for Diaspora Jews; see also Zahn, Roloff, Mussner, Witherington. Less likely: of time, "future generations" (BAUER, *Wb*, art. μακράν 1.b).

La conclusion du discours permet un rapprochement avec la conclusion de la prédication de Jésus à Nazareth... L'expression d'Ac 2,39 "tous ceux qui sont au loin", formant antithèse avec "vous et vos enfants", s'entend assez naturellement des Gentils, ou plus exactement de ceux qu'en grand nombre, parmi les Gentils, le Seigneur appellera.[91]

The promise is "even to 'those still far off'. So Luke foreshadows the carrying of Christian testimony to Gentiles, which will become the burden of his narrative in the later chapters of Acts" (Fitzmyer)[92]. One can agree with Lindemann's statement in reference to Lk 4,25-27: "wird erst in der Apostelgeschichte verwirklicht werden"[93], but it is still in the form of *Vorausverweis* that Peter alludes to the Gentiles in his Pentecost speech (Ac 2,39): "Luc ne pouvait pas prêter à Pierre au jour de la Pentecôte un universalisme explicite, qui aurait été anachronique"[94].

Acts 3,11-26

Peter's Temple discourse is mentioned here for two reasons. First, the contrast between the end of Lk 4,16-30 and the response to Peter's speech in Ac 2 ("in höchstem Maße erfolgreich")[95] can in some sense be mitigated if the reaction to Ac 3,11-26 in 4,1-3.5ff. is taken into consideration. Second, the allusion to the Gentiles in Ac 2,39 receives here confirmation: "die Analogie von 3,26 πρῶτον (spricht) für die gewöhnliche Beziehung auf die Heiden" (Holtzmann)[96]. I can refer again to J. Dupont:

Ce "d'abord" suppose un "ensuite"; le contexte indique clairement le sens: La bénédiction est d'abord pour Israël, ensuite pour toutes les nations de la terre... Les deux premiers discours missionnaires de Pierre se terminent donc par un élargissement des perspectives, élargissement qui fait prévoir l'évangélisation des Gentils.[97]

91. *Le salut des Gentils* (n. 2), 145 (= 408). Cf. *Jésus*, 148 (= 44); *Conclusion*, 392 (= 497). See also BOISMARD-LAMOUILLE, *Les Actes*, vol. II (n. 18), 1990, 148-150 ("L'universalisme"; Act II); H. VAN DE SANDT, *The Fate of the Gentiles in Joel and Acts 2: An Intertextual Study*, in ETL 66 (1990) 56-77, esp. 72-74 ("The Intertextual Functions of Isa 57,19a and Joel 3,5b.d in Act 2,39").

92. *Acts*, 265 (and 267). Cf. note on 22,21: "'Far away' is an allusion to Isa 57:19 and echoes Acts 2:39" (709). On "Lucan foreshadowing" at work in Acts, cf. his *Luke the Theologian: Aspects of His Teaching*, New York – Mahwah, NJ, 1989, 192.

93. *Einheit und Vielfalt*, 237.

94. DUPONT, *Conclusion*, 392 (= 497). See also 395 (= 500), on πᾶσαι αἱ πατριαὶ τῆς γῆς in Ac 3,25: "La citation parle de toutes les 'familles' de la terre...: est-ce parce qu'il serait prématuré de parler déjà des ἔθνη, dans leur opposition au peuple juif?". On this possibility, see also G.J. STEYN, *Quotations* (n. 76), 157: "because Luke could not refer explicitly to the Gentiles without a clear reference to the gentile mission, which at this stage in the story still lies in the future" (cf. Haenchen).

95. See Lindemann's conclusion (237).

96. *Apg*, 1889, 335.

97. *Le salut des Gentils* (n. 2), 146 (= 409).

Ac 3,26 ὑμῖν πρῶτον ἀναστήσας ὁ θεὸς τὸν παῖδα αὐτοῦ... The ὑμῖν are the Jewish people Peter is addressing in this call to conversion (εὐλογοῦντα ὑμᾶς ἐν τῷ ἀποστρέφειν ἕκαστον ἀπὸ τῶν πονηριῶν ὑμῶν). Apart from the debate on ἀναστήσας either referring to the earthly mission of Jesus or (more likely) to the resurrection, πρῶτον is qualifying ὑμῖν and "wird durch 13,46 erklärt" (Conzelmann)[98].

Acts 10,34-43

If already in the speeches to the Jews in Jerusalem Luke alludes to the Gentiles (2,39; 3,25-26), the turning point in Acts comes much later in the Cornelius episode with Peter's speech in Cornelius's house: 10,34-43. "After the speech, the narrative is resumed, and Peter's listeners are baptized and receive the Spirit. In effect, it recounts a 'Pentecost of the Gentiles'"[99].

Peter begins his speech in vv. 34-35 with a reference to God's impartiality and the statement that "in every nation (ἐν παντὶ ἔθνει) anyone who fears him and does what is right is acceptable to him" (v. 35), in correspondence to Peter's last words in v. 43: πάντα τὸν πιστεύοντα εἰς αὐτόν. Note also the universalistic πάντων in the parenthetical clause οὗτός ἐστιν πάντων κύριος (v. 36b) and οὗτός ἐστιν ... κριτὴς ζώντων καὶ νεκρῶν (v. 42).

Ac 10,42-43 shows a striking resemblance to Lk 24,47: καὶ κηρυχθῆναι ἐπὶ τῷ ὀνόματι αὐτοῦ μετάνοιαν εἰς ἄφεσιν ἁμαρτιῶν εἰς πάντα τὰ ἔθνη.... 48a ὑμεῖς μάρτυρες τούτων. Compare Ac 10,42 καὶ παρήγγειλεν ἡμῖν κηρύξαι... 43... μαρτυροῦσιν ἄφεσιν ἁμαρτιῶν λαβεῖν διὰ τοῦ ὀνόματος αὐτοῦ... G. Schneider's comment on this parallel is noteworthy[100]:

> Die Diskrepanz zwischen Lk 24,47 und Apg 10,34-43 hat Lukas wohl empfunden: Petrus hätte von der Ostererscheinung Jesu den Auftrag zur Heidenmission kennen müssen. Dennoch wird er Apg 10 erst von Gott zu den Heiden gewiesen.
>
> Möglicherweise hatte er [Lukas] beabsichtigt, daß man die beiden Schriften seines Doppelwerks auch unabhängig voneinander lesen konnte. Vielleicht hängt damit zusammen, daß Lk 24,47 die Heidenmission schon am Ostertag von Jesus angeordnet sein läßt.

---

98. A few more recent comments: "Nur mit einem Wort eröffnet Lukas vorsichtig eine weitere Perspektive. Israel wird zuerst gesegnet, später kommen aber auch andere hinzu, die Heiden" (JERVELL, *Apg*, 171); "Here (v. 25) and in v. 26 the blessing of the Gentiles is clearly alluded to, but only in connection with Jews or after the Jews. Luke is masterfully preparing for later developments in his narrative" (WITHERINGTON, *Acts*, 188).

99. FITZMYER, *Acts*, 460.

100. *Petrusrede*, 1985 (below, n. 120), 278 n. 159, 279 and n. 161.

Thus the hints at Ac 2,39; 3,25-26 and the solemn inauguration of the Gentile mission in Ac 10 appear to be strangely parallel to the indirect allusion in Lk 4,25-27 on the one hand and the explicit command of the risen Christ in Lk 24 (and Ac 1,8) on the other.

More directly relevant for our study of the Nazareth pericope is the reminiscence of Lk 4,18 in Ac 10,38:

a Ἰησοῦν τὸν ἀπὸ Ναζαρέθ,
   ὡς ἔχρισεν αὐτὸν ὁ θεὸς πνεύματι ἁγίῳ καὶ δυνάμει,
b ὃς διῆλθεν εὐεργετῶν
   καὶ ἰώμενος πάντας τοὺς καταδυναστευομένους ὑπὸ τοῦ διαβόλου,
c ὅτι ὁ θεὸς ἦν μετ' αὐτοῦ.

Once more I can refer to J. Dupont's 1978 essay[101]:

> Dans l'état actuel de nos connaissances, *Act.* 10,38 et son exégèse d'*Is.* 61,1 doivent être lus comme une composition de Luc, relevant du même niveau littéraire que *Lc.* 4,16-22.

Lk 4,18-19

The Isaiah text quoted in Lk 4,18-19 corresponds to Isa 61,1-2a LXX:

18a πνεῦμα κυρίου ἐπ' ἐμέ, οὗ εἵνεκεν ἔχρισέν με·
  b εὐαγγελίσασθαι πτωχοῖς ἀπέσταλκέν με,
  c κηρύξαι αἰχμαλώτοις ἄφεσιν καὶ τυφλοῖς ἀνάβλεψιν,
  d ἀποστεῖλαι τεθραυσμένους ἐν ἀφέσει,
19 κηρύξαι ἐνιαυτὸν κυρίου δεκτόν.

Three differences (besides the omission of καὶ ἡμέραν ἀνταποδόσεως) are to be noted: the omission of ἰάσασθαι τοὺς συντετριμμένους τῇ καρδίᾳ / τὴν καρδίαν (before 18c); the insertion of 18d ἀποστεῖλαι τεθραυσμένους ἐν ἀφέσει from Isa 58,6d (ἀπόστελλε...); and in v. 19 κηρύξαι (for καλέσαι in Isa 61,2a). These divergences from the Septuagint are occasionally cited as an argument for dependence on a pre-Lukan source, either Q[102] or Proto-Luke[103] or some undefined source of Lk[104].

---

101. *Jésus*, 155 (= 51).

102. Cf. above, n. 5: TUCKETT, *Luke 4,16-30*, 1982, esp. 346-351; *Q*, 1996, esp. 229-236. For Tuckett, "the reference to Ναζαρά in v. 16a and the Isaiah quotation belong together. Thus if Ναζαρά derives from Q, the Isa 61 citation *may* also derive from Q" (1996, 229); cf. 1982, 345: "... *must* also derive from Q" (italics F.N.). On Ναζαρά in Q, cf. above, n. 6.

103. On Lk 4,16-22a in Proto-Luke, cf. above, n. 23 (M.-É. Boismard, 1997). See now also T.L. Brodie in this volume (627 n. 3): 4,16-22a (compare 1993: 4,16-30; 1997: 4,16-27).

104. See, e.g., M. TURNER, *Power from on High. The Spirit in Israel's Restoration and Witness in Luke–Acts* (Journal of Pentecostal Theology SS, 9), Sheffield, 1996, 220-

As indicated in an earlier paper, the allusion to Isa 61 in Q 7,22 (with πτωχοὶ εὐαγγελίζονται in final position) may have called forth the Isaiah text for quotation by Luke in his inaugural Nazareth section[105]. The redactional composition of Lk 7,21 in preparation of Q 7,22 clearly indicates that physical healing is regarded by Luke as the fulfilment of Isa 61,1:... καὶ τυφλοῖς πολλοῖς ἐχαρίσατο βλέπειν (in reference to τυφλοὶ ἀναβλέπουσιν which comes first in 7,22). In the light of this clause in 7,21 the objection that "curing blindness is not prominent among Luke's miracle stories"[106] has little force. Physical healing is so "prominent" in Lk's summaries (7,21 ἐθεράπευσεν πολλοὺς ἀπὸ νόσων καὶ μαστίγων καὶ πνευμάτων πονηρῶν, cf. 6,18 ... ἰαθῆναι ἀπὸ τῶν νόσων αὐτῶν· καὶ οἱ ἐνοχλούμενοι ἀπὸ πνευμάτων ἀκαθάρτων ἐθεραπεύοντο) that it can be assumed to explain Luke's deletion of ἰάσασθαι τοὺς συντετριμμένους τῇ καρδίᾳ / τὴν καρδίαν. In Luke–Acts, except Ac 28,27 (= Isa 6,10 ἰάσομαι αὐτούς), the verb ἰᾶσθαι is never used metaphorically, as it clearly is in Isa 61,1: "to 'heal' the broken-hearted"[107].

Lk 4,18d ἀποστεῖλαι τεθραυσμένους ἐν ἀφέσει (from Isa 58,6) is usually translated in English: "to let the oppressed go free" (NRSV).

226 (226: "The citation form in Lk. 4.18-19 belongs fundamentally to Luke's source, not to his own redactional activity"). This source of Luke is not Q (219: ctr. Tuckett). Cf. *The Spirit and the Power of Jesus' Miracles in the Lucan Conception*, in *NT* 33 (1991) 124-152, esp. 150-152; *The Spirit of Prophecy and the Power of Authoritative Preaching in Luke–Acts: A Question of Origins*, in *NTS* 38 (1992) 66-88.

105. *Q 6,20b-21; 7,22 and Isaiah 61*, in C.M. TUCKETT (ed.), *The Scriptures in the Gospels* (BETL, 131), Leuven, 1997, 27-64, esp. 63. On Q 6,20b, see *ibid.*, 44. On Lk 4,18-19 and 7,18-23, see M.D. HOOKER, *'Beginning with Moses and from all the Prophets'*, in M.C. DE BOER (ed.), *From Jesus to John*. FS M. de Jonge (JSNT SS, 84), Sheffield, 1993, 216-230, esp. 223.

106. TUCKETT, *Q*, 232 (= 1982, 348). Tuckett tries to minimize the evidence of Lk 7,21 (LkR): "the clause in 7:21 prepares for 7:22 which is more likely to be an allusion to Isa 35:5 (and in any case this is already in Q, not LkR)" (*ibid.*, n. 81). One can agree about the influence of Isa 35,5 on the Q-saying (cf. my *Q 6,20b-21; 7,22 and Isaiah 61*, 46-49), but the point is that Lk 7,21 testifies for Luke's redactional understanding of τυφλοὶ ἀναβλέπουσιν in Q.

107. Cf. J. DUPONT, *Les Béatitudes*, vol. II, Paris, 1969, 132 n. 1: "Luc entend le verbe 'guérir' au sens propre; cela le porte à omettre l'expression 'guérir les cœurs brisés' en *Lc* 4,18". See also D.R. CATCHPOLE, *The Anointed One in Nazareth*, in M.C. DE BOER (ed.), *From Jesus to John* (n. 105), 231-251, here 237: "the absence of the one element of the Isa. 58.6 text [read: 61.1] which has no counterpart in Isa. 61.1 [read 58.6], that is, τὴν καρδίαν ... serves to highlight the achievement of *physical* healing within the programme"; see 236: "The omission... is only partial"; συντρίβειν, cf. θραύειν in v. 18d; ἰάσασθαι, cf. the ἰατρός proverb in v. 23. — See also Catchpole's reply to Tuckett ("There is no good reason why Luke should omit the healing clause from Isaiah 61"): "the heavy emphasis on healings within vv. 18-19... makes the address ἰατρέ [v. 23a] appropriate and the omission of the healing clause from Isaiah 61 a mark of sophistication rather than a cause of surprise" (252, and n. 1).

Άπόστελλε (LXX) is changed to the syntax of Isa 61,1, the infinitive
άποστεῖλαι, possibly in assimilation to κηρύξαι in v. 18c. Ἄφεσις
may have been the link word: "release" for the prisoners and "release"
for the oppressed. In M. Turner's opinion Isa 58,6 was possibly incorporated "to clarify that he [Jesus] does not merely announce messianic
liberty (as the use of Isa. 61.1-2 alone might suggest) but also *effects* it.
Luke ... has an interest in such a theme"[108].

One could argue that, in contrast to "the important Lukan theme"
ἄφεσις ἁμαρτιῶν (Lk 1,77; 3,3 [= Mk]; 24,47; and five occurrences in
Acts), the word ἄφεσις alone is "highly unusual in Luke"[109]. But the
word is there, in the Isaiah text, following on εὐαγγελίσασθαι πτωχοῖς
(which is accepted as congenial to Luke) and in parallel to τυφλοῖς
ἀνάβλεψιν (the healing of the blind, stressed by Luke in 7,21). Such a
context is not at all un-Lukan, and in this context the literal meaning of
ἄφεσις (used with αἰχμαλώτοις), though unique in Luke–Acts, is
hardly refutable. – It is amazing how word statistics are sometimes mis-
interpreted: the meaning "forgiveness of sins" of the stereotyped ἄφεσις ἁμαρτιῶν (eight times in Luke–Acts) is applied again and again in
comments on the two instances of ἄφεσις (4,18c and d)[110].

108. *Power from on High*, 224 (= *Spirit*, 1991, 148). See also G.R. BEASLEY-MURRAY,
in *Mélanges Bibliques*. FS B. Rigaux, Gembloux, 1970, 473. Cf. R. ALBERTZ, *Die
"Antrittspredigt" Jesu im Lukasevangelium auf ihrem alttestamentlichen Hintergrund*, in
ZNW 74 (1983) 182-206, esp. 198, on Luke's insertion of Isa 58,6: "Damit konkretisiert
er die schwebende, übertragene Sprache von Jes 61,1f. in soziale Richtung"; cf. 197:
"mit den τεθραυσμένοι (sind) eindeutig die wirtschaftlich Ruinierten gemeint".
On the catchword ἄφεσις: "The link appears to have been made via the Greek word
ἄφεσις in both Isaianic texts and hence seems to depend on the LXX version of the two
texts concerned (the MT has חפשׁים in Isa 58:6 and דרור in Isa 61:1)" (TUCKETT, *Q*, 232).
Cf. B.J. KOET, *Five Studies* (n. 67), 29-30 (= 1986, 372-373), on the later rabbinic
midrashic technique *gezerah shawah*. See now C.A. KIMBALL, *Jesus' Exposition of the
Old Testament in Luke's Gospel* (JSNT SS, 94), Sheffield, 1994, 97-119 ("The Nazareth
Sermon"): "In Jesus' day the *gezerah shawah* technique ... was frequently used" (107);
"the unique text form caused by the insertion ... is evidence for the authenticity of the
citation on the lips of Jesus" (109), though "the joining of these two texts was only possible on the basis of a Greek text" (107)!
109. TUCKETT, *Q*, 233, 234 n. 86 (= 1982, 348). Cf. TURNER, *Power from on High*,
223. On the use of Isa 61,1 (ἄφεσις) in Ac 10,43 (ἄφεσις ἁμαρτιῶν), suggested by
Dupont, see my reply in *Ac 10,34-43* (below, n. 120), 113 (= 231): "La suggestion... n'a
pas été faite à propos des autres discours (ἄφεσις ἁμαρτιῶν: Ac 2,38; 5,31; 10,43;
13,38; 26,18; cf. Lc 24,47)".
110. See, e.g., M. KORN, *Geschichte* (n. 37), esp. 75-78 (with reference to M. Rese,
1969; contrast U. Busse, 1978). See also B.J. KOET, *Five Studies* (n. 67), 24-55 ("Luke
4,16-30"), esp. 34 (with reference to J.J.A. Kahmann, 1975); and more recently, R.
O'TOOLE, *Does Luke also Portray Jesus as the Christ in Luke 4,16-30?*, in Bib 76 (1995)
498-522, esp. 511-512 (cf. 511, on the metaphorical use of "open the eyes"); R.I. DEN-
OVA, *The Things Accomplished Among Us: Prophetic Tradition in the Structural Pattern
of Luke–Acts* (JSNT SS, 141), Sheffield, 1997, 133-138: ἄφεσις = forgiveness of sins in

The insertion of 4,18d from Isa 58,6d is part of the evidence mounted against assigning the Isaiah quotation in Lk 4,18-19 to Luke: "There is no other example of a similarly mixed citation in Luke–Acts"[111]. One may have some doubt about the relevance of this observation with regard to the Scripture text chosen by Luke for the opening of Jesus' public ministry. What is meant by "mixed" or "composite" citation, said to be unique in Luke–Acts, is not entirely clear. In Ac 1,20 there is a quotation from "the book of the Psalms" combining simply with καί Ps 68,26 and 108,8b LXX[112]. Another example, Ac 3,22-23 introduced with "Moses said": "ein Zitat von Dtn 18,15, das ergänzt ist durch ein Mischzitat aus Dtn 18,19 und Lev 23,29"[113]. Thus it is apparently not without certain analogies in Acts that the combination of Isa 61,1-2a and 58,6d in Lk 4,18-19 is introduced as one quotation taken from "the book of Isaiah" (v. 17).

There is still the change of καλέσαι (LXX) to κηρύξαι in Lk 4,19, which can be seen as an attempt "Jesu Verkündigung in das Jesajazitat einzutragen"[114].

The discussion of the divergences from the Septuagint should not obnubilate the basic conformity of Lk 4,18-19 to the Isaian text[115]. To a

---

4,18g (the oppressed) but not in 4,18e (the captives) (136-137); "sight to the blind": both metaphorical and literal (135). For emphasis on literalness and physicality of Jesus' announcements in Lk 4,18-19, see P.F. ESLER, *Community* (n. 9), 179-183.

111. TUCKETT, *Q*, 232 (= 1982, 347). Tuckett calls it "this *mixed* citation" (232 n. 79) or "the specific *composite* citation of Isa 61 + 58" (431). See also TURNER, *Power from on High*, 216: "Luke–Acts never elsewhere *sandwiches* one Old Testament quotation within another in this way" (cf. *Spirit*, 146; italics F.N.); C.A. KIMBALL, *Jesus' Exposition* (n. 108), 109: "The insertion of one text between another is not paralleled elsewhere in the Gospels or Acts"; D.R. CATCHPOLE, *Anointed One* (n. 107), 239: "the interpenetration of OT texts ... is not atypical of the writer of the Gospel (though, one might add, less untypical of the writer of Acts)".

112. The two quotations are introduced with a single formula (v. 20a) and are linked together with καί· (cf. text editions). However, this καί can be part of the second quotation text itself (LXX: καὶ τὴν...): see G.D. KILPATRICK, *Some Quotations in Acts*, in J. KREMER (ed.), *Les Actes des Apôtres*, 1979, 81-97, esp. 87; HAENCHEN, *Apg*, 124 n. 6 (= 163 n. 6). In G.J. Steyn's opinion both can be combined: καί part of the quoted text and connecting word. Cf. *Septuagint Quotations* (n. 76), 58. In any case, the two quoted texts "are presented as one single explicit quotation" (62).

113. SCHNEIDER, *Apg*, I, 328. See KILPATRICK, *Some Quotations*, 86: "Like Acts 15,16-18, Acts 3,22f is a composite quotation". Cf. FITZMYER, *The Use of the Old Testament in Luke–Acts*, in *SBL 1992 Seminar Papers*, 524-238: "In three instances (Luke 4:18-19; 19:46 [par. Mk]; Acts 3:22-23) he [Luke] combines two quotations" (526 n. 5).

114. M. KORN, *Geschichte* (n. 37), 74: Lk 4,19 "als Umschreibung der Verkündigung der Gegenwart des Reiches Gottes".

115. The "mixed" form of the citation does not allow to treat Lk 4,18-19 as "a free composition" which because of the centrality of ἄφεσις (supposed to be "*un*characteristic for Luke") cannot be due to LkR. Cf. TUCKETT, *Q*, 235 n. 86. See n. 87 (and 229 n. 68): "It is of course pre-Lukan in the sense of being words from Isaiah"!

certain degree it can be called conflation or composite citation, but *text* citation it certainly is, and, in my view, not so close to conflational compositions like 4Q521 as some now seem to suggest[116].

Ac 10,38

Lk 4,18 πνεῦμα κυρίου ἐπ' ἐμὲ οὗ εἵνεκεν ἔχρισέν με. The Spirit of the Lord is upon Jesus by reason of his anointing. Fitzmyer's comment is concise: "In the baptism (3:22; cf. Acts 10:38)". In Lk 4 it is not said that the 'anointing' occurred at his baptism, and it is hard to maintain that, in the account of Jesus' baptism and the descent of the Spirit upon him (Lk 3,22), Luke changed Mk's εἰς αὐτόν to ἐπ' αὐτόν precisely in view of ἐπ' ἐμέ in 4,18 (Isa 61,1)[117]. In the prayer of the Christians at Ac 4,27-30, συνήχθησαν ... ἐπὶ τὸν ἅγιον παῖδά σου Ἰησοῦν ὃν ἔχρισας (4,27) is a word-for-word paraphrase of Ps 2,2 συνήχθησαν ... κατὰ τοῦ κυρίου καὶ κατὰ τοῦ χριστοῦ αὐτοῦ (quoted in v. 26)[118]. Nothing in this etymology of the χριστός title refers to the baptism of Jesus[119].

116. K.-W. NIEBUHR, *Die Werke des eschatologischen Freudenboten (4Q521) und die Jesusüberlieferung*, in C.M. TUCKETT (ed.), *The Scriptures in the Gospels* (n. 105), 637-646. He refers to "die freie, mosaikartige Rezeption biblischer Wendungen in frühjüdischen Texten" (644). It is noteworthy that 4Q521 connects Isa 61,1 with the Messiah. On the similarities with Q 7,22 (not a citation!), cf. above, n. 105.

117. Ctr. J. NOLLAND, *Lk*, 161: "The change ... anticipates Luke 4:18" (R.F. Collins, *TBT* 84 [1976] 824)"; KORN, *Geschichte* (n. 37), 65 n. 47 ("Daß Lukas die Beziehung des Taufberichts zu Lk 4,18a bewußt war,..."). J.M. Robinson's view on ἐπ' αὐτόν shows a noteworthy 'trajectory' from LkR to Q. See his *The Sayings Gospel Q*, in *The Four Gospels 1992* (n. 5), 361-388, here 383, on the minor agreements diff. Mk 1,10: "notoriously inconclusive", with reference to J. Kloppenborg in n. 30: the use of ἐπί is preferred by Luke "in dependence on Isa 61,1-2 (quoted Lk 4,18)"; now in *The Matthean Trajectory from Q to Mark*, in A.Y. COLLINS (ed.), *Ancient and Modern Perspectives on the Bible and Culture*. FS H.D. Betz, Atlanta, GA, 1999, 122-154, here 131-132: Jesus' baptism is ascribed to Q, "where the minor agreements of Q using the Isa 61:1 LXX preposition ἐπ' rather than Mark's εἰς for 'upon' is a tell-tale sign" (131 n. 13); contrast Lk 4,18 (not Q): "The ἔχρισέν με of Isa 61:1 is a christological point of departure not picked up explicitly either by Q or by Matthew" (132). But see Kloppenborg's argument in *The Formation of Q*, 1987, 85 n. 157: "assimilation to Isa 61:1-2 (= Luke 4:18) *and* [!] general Lucan usage (Acts 1:8; 2:17,18; 10:44,45; 11:15; 19:16)". Cf. my *The Minor Agreements and Q*, in R. PIPER (ed.), *The Gospel Behind the Gospels* (NTSup, 75), Leiden, 1995, 49-72, here 65.

On the relation between Lk 4,18-19 and Ac 10,38, see U. BUSSE, *Wunder* (below, n. 128), 369: "Lk 4,18f steht... zu Apg 10,38 wie die erste Verkündigung zur abschließenden Zusammenfassung, in der die Realisierung des angekündigten Auftrages bestätigt wird".

118. On ἐπί + acc. in hostile sense (for κατά + gen.), cf. J.A. WEATHERLY, *Jewish Responsibility for the Death of Jesus in Luke–Acts* (JSNT SS, 106), Sheffield, 1994, 92 (ctr. J.T. Sanders).

119. Ctr. JERVELL, *Apg*, 187: "ὃν ἔχρισας, d.h. er wurde bei der Taufe in das messianische Amt eingesetzt". Cf. WENDT, *Apg*, 116 ("Wahrscheinlich"); more hesitant: LAKE-CADBURY, *Acts*, 47; SCHILLE, *Apg*, 141.

An explicit reference to anointing and baptism is provided in Ac 10,38. Verse 38a is to be read, I think, in parallel with v. 37b:

37a   ὑμεῖς οἴδατε τὸ γενόμενον ῥῆμα καθ' ὅλης τῆς Ἰουδαίας,
37bᵃ   ἀρξάμενος ἀπὸ τῆς Γαλιλαίας
37bᵝ   μετὰ τὸ βάπτισμα ὃ ἐκήρυξεν Ἰωάννης,
38aᵃ   Ἰησοῦν τὸν ἀπὸ Ναζαρέθ,
38aᵝ   ὡς ἔχρισεν αὐτὸν ὁ θεὸς πνεύματι ἁγίῳ καὶ δυνάμει.

The beginning of Jesus' public ministry throughout Judea (cf. Lk 23,5) is described as starting from Galilee (par. Nazareth) after the baptism (par. anointing)[120]. Luke never uses the identification Ἰησοῦς ὁ ἀπὸ Ναζαρέθ for "Jesus of Nazareth"[121], and here in parallel to ἀπὸ τῆς Γαλιλαίας the preposition ἀπό may indicate "the point from where" Jesus' ministry began.

The first principle C.M. Tuckett applies in his approach to Lk 4,18-19 is his statement that "in Luke–Acts the Spirit is never the agent by which miracles occur"[122]. This leads to a rather strange comment on Ac 10,38. He admits that it is "probably referring explicitly to Luke 4:18-19", but:

Acts 10:38 appears to avoid attributing this aspect of Jesus' work to the Spirit. Luke here says that Jesus was anointed with the Spirit 'and power'

120. On symmetric composition, parallel ἀπό (= from), and temporal ὡς (= when, after), see É. SAMAIN, *La notion de* ΑΡΧΗ *dans l'œuvre lucanienne*, in F. NEIRYNCK (ed.), *L'Évangile de Luc*, 1973 (n. 1), 299-328; = ²1989, 209-238, esp. 218-220; with my additional note (327) on É. Samain (diss. 1965), J. Dupont, and G. Schneider. Cf. DUPONT, *Jésus*, 150-155 (= 46-51): "Is. 61,1-2 dans le discours de Césarée (Act. 10,34-43)". — On the Lukan composition of Ac 10,34-43, see my *Ac 10,36-43 et l'évangile*, in *ETL* 60 (1984) 109-117 (= *Evangelica II*, 227-235), and the additional note on A. Weiser and G. Schneider in *ETL* 62 (1986) 194-196 (= *Evangelica II*, 235-236). Cf. A. WEISER, *Tradition und lukanische Komposition in Apg 10,36-43*, in *À cause de l'évangile*. FS J. Dupont (LD, 123), Paris, 1985, 757-767; G. SCHNEIDER, *Die Petrusrede vor Kornelius. Das Verhältnis von Tradition und Komposition in Apg 10,34-43*, in ID., *Lukas, Theologe der Heilsgeschichte. Aufsätze zum lukanischen Doppelwerk* (BBB, 59), Königstein-Bonn, 1985, 253-279.

121. Ἰησοῦς ὁ Ναζαρηνός (Lk 4,34; 24,19); Ἰησοῦς ὁ Ναζωραῖος (Lk 18,37; Ac 2,22; 3,6; 4,10; 6,14; 22,8; 16,9). On Mt 21,11; Jn 1,45, cf. J.M. ROBINSON, in *The Four Gospels 1992* (n. 117), 377.

122. *Q*, 230 (= 1982, 347). Cf. 231: "miracles do not generally seem to be the work of the Spirit" (with reference to E. SCHWEIZER, art. πνεῦμα, in *TWNT* 6, 405; *TDNT* 6, 407). Tuckett interprets πνεῦμα in Luke–Acts in the line of E. Schweizer (the Spirit of prophecy), against those who, on the basis of "occurrences where πνεῦμα and δύναμις occur together, or possibly interchangeably", argue "that πνεῦμα for Luke can be the agency by which miracles occur" (230 n. 73; cf. 231 n. 74: Conzelmann, Busse, Neirynck, Turner). J. Jervell's recent commentary can be added to the list: "Er hat Jesus mit heiligem Geist und Kraft gesalbt. Das sind kaum zwei verschiedene Grössen, denn für Lukas ist der Geist vor allem mirakulöse Wunderkraft. Nicht nur Kraft, denn der Geist ist viel mehr…".

(δύναμις being often used by Luke to describe the agency by which miracles occur), and that Jesus heals 'because God was with him'.[123]

The addition (by Luke?) of the clause ὅτι ὁ θεὸς ἦν μετ' αὐτοῦ is indicated without further comment (cf. Ac 7,9 Joseph). With regard to καὶ δυνάμει, it is noted that "Luke's tendency is always to use δύναμις language when referring to miracles" (Lk 4,36; 5,17; 6,19; 9,1; Ac 6,8; 10,38)[124]. In a separate list he cites the instances where δύναμις and πνεῦμα appear together or in parallel (Lk 1,35; 4,14; Ac 1,8; cf. too Lk 1,17; 24,49). Tuckett wishes not to argue for a rigid distinction: "δύναμις for Luke is clearly broader than that, as texts like Luke 4:14 show"[125]. However, his illustration is one-directional: "the immediate context in v. 15 speaks exclusively of Jesus' 'teaching' only"[126]. The context of Lk 4,14a deserves closer examination. In the broader context of Lk 3–4, the Lukan phrases in 4,1a πλήρης πνεύματος ἁγίου and 4,14a ἐν τῇ δυνάμει τοῦ πνεύματος (before and after the temptation ὑπὸ τοῦ διαβόλου) appear as stepping-stones from 3,22 to 4,18. The most immediate context of 4,14a, v. 14b καὶ φήμη ἐξῆλθεν καθ' ὅλης τῆς περιχώρου περὶ αὐτοῦ, corresponds to 4,37 καὶ ἐξεπορεύετο ἦχος περὶ αὐτοῦ εἰς πάντα τόπον τῆς περιχώρου, both parallel to Mk 1,28. Like Lk 4,37 follows on the reaction to the exorcism in v. 36: ἐν ἐξουσίᾳ καὶ δυνάμει ('power' LkR), so Lk 4,14b follows on v. 14a, ἐν τῇ δυνάμει τοῦ πνεύματος. That Lk 4,15 mentions Jesus' teaching in their synagogues (generalizing Mk 1,21-22, cf. v. 39) is not a valid reason for making it the exclusive theme in 4,14. In v. 14a "the thought of power to do mighty works may be present" (Marshall: cf. 4,23). If in Lukan usage there is no disjunction between 'power' and 'Spirit', we can read πνεύματι ἁγίῳ and καὶ δυνάμει in Ac 10,38 without assigning them to separate levels, pre-Lukan tradition and Lukan redaction[127].

Tuckett's discussion with U. Busse on Ac 10,38 and Lk (1982, reprinted in 1996)[128] concentrates upon "healing all those oppressed by

123. *Q*, 234 (= 1982, 349).

124. *Q*, 231 n. 77 (and 230). I note here a corrigendum on Ac 6,8.10 ("Neirynck runs the two together…"). In fact my observation did concern the two "full of" phrases in Ac 6,5 πλήρης πίστεως καὶ πνεύματος ἁγίου, 8 πλήρης χάριτος καὶ δυνάμεως.

125. *Q*, 231 v. 77.

126. *Ibid.*, n. 75.

127. This is, I think, what was suggested by Tuckett, although his description of "the earlier passage" (or "original passage") and "Luke's interpretation" (or "slight modification") could be understood as a distinction between 'Q' 4,18-19 (source) and Ac 10,38 (Luke).

128. *Q*, 230 n. 73; 235-236 n. 90 (= 1982, 347 n. 23; 349-350 n. 36). Cf. U. Busse, *Die Wunder des Propheten Jesus. Die Rezeption, Komposition und Interpretation der Wundertradition im Evangelium des Lukas* (FzB, 24), Stuttgart, 1977, 59-60; Id., *Nazareth-Manifest* (n. 39).

the devil". One can agree with Tuckett that in Lk not all healings are regarded as exorcisms and that the neutral words θεραπεύειν and ἰᾶσθαι are used for both, but Busse's reading of Ac 10,38 in the light of Lk 4 cannot be dismissed by stating that "there are no extra exorcism stories in the gospel"[129]. Lk 4,31-43 is a Markan sequence, but the "arrangement" is Lukan: the exorcism in 4,33-37 is distinguished from 4,31-32, in 4,38-39 Jesus rebukes the fever as one rebukes a demon, and in 4,40-41 demon possessions are treated as a higher or stronger form of illness.

Since it is undisputed that in Lk the use of ἰᾶσθαι in combination with δύναμις is redactional (5,17 καὶ δύναμις κυρίου ἦν εἰς τὸ ἰᾶσθαι αὐτόν, cf. 6,19; 8,46.47; 9,1.2), it is less certain that ἰώμενος in Ac 10,38 should be seen as part of the allusion to Isa 61,1 (ἰάσασθαι... omitted in Lk 4,18)[130]. As Tuckett wrote, "It may be that the 'oppressed' of Isa 58:6 in Luke 4:18 is seen by Luke as referring to oppression by Satan"[131].

Turning back to the text of Lk 4,18-19, the parallel in Ac 10,38a indicates that the punctuation of N-A, et al. (ἔχρισέν με εὐαγγελίσασθαι πτωχοῖς,) should be corrected by placing a stop after ἔχρισέν με (and not after πτωχοῖς)[132].

III. Lk 4,16-30 and the End of Acts

J. Dupont's essay *La conclusion des Actes* (which was delivered here at the Colloquium in 1977) is completed with a corollary on Lk 4,16-30:

> Pour montrer que la double rencontre de Paul avec les Juifs de Rome constitue bien la conclusion de l'ensemble de l'ouvrage de Luc, il semble que

129. *Q*, 235 (= 349).
130. The influence of Ps 106,20 LXX καὶ ἰάσατο αὐτούς (G.N. Stanton, P. Stuhlmacher, *et al.*) is even more doubtful: see my *Ac 10,36-43*, 115 (= 233); SCHNEIDER, *Petrusrede*, 275 n. 137; WEISER, *Tradition*, 762 n. 29; 764 n. 38: "Die relativ häufige Verwendung von *iasthai* im Werk des Lukas empfiehlt nicht die Annahme, daß Apg 10,38 von Ps 106,20 LXX beeinflußt ist". The case of Isa 61,1 is different because of the allusion to ἔχρισέν με in v. 38a. But given the indeed relatively frequent use of the verb in Luke–Acts, the influence of ἰάσασθαι remains uncertain because of its lacking in Lk 4,18 and the change of the complement of the verb from "the brokenhearted" to "all the oppressed by the devil". See my *Ac 10,36-43*, 115 (= 233): "si on continue de donner à ἄφεσις en Lc 4,18 son sens propre de délivrance des captifs et des opprimés (la bonne nouvelle aux pauvres), on peut y rattacher l'idée de 'guérir ceux qui sont au pouvoir du diable' (Ac 10,38)".
131. *Q*, 233 (= 349). On his objections, see above.
132. NOORDA, *Historia* (n. 4), 226; DUPONT, *Jésus*, 133 (= 27): "Il me paraît certain, quant à moi, que seule la seconde (ponctuation) correspond à la manière dont Luc a lu le texte"; cf. Lc 4,43; Ac 10,38. See Greeven's text, the commentaries by Marshall, Fitzmyer, Nolland, Johnson, Green and the translations REB (English), EÜ (German), Osty (French), NWV (Dutch).

nous pouvons concentrer notre attention sur un texte principal: celui par lequel Luc a voulu introduire toute l'histoire du ministère de Jésus... En esquissant le programme du ministère public de Jésus, cette page fait en même temps pressentir toute la suite du récit jusqu'à la conclusion que lui donne l'épisode de Rome.[133]

I may cite here one of R. Maddox's 1982 statements on the unity of Luke–Acts:

> More significant is the fact that the mission of Jesus begins with a scene in which the rejection of the message of salvation by the Jews and its acceptance by the Gentiles is anticipated, and the mission of Paul ends with a scene in which this is declared to be an established fact (Luke 4:16-30; Acts 28:17-28). This looks like a deliberate, structural element.[134]

Other authors like D.R. Miesner[135], A. Weiser[136], and J.T. Sanders[137] have provided more detailed descriptions of the parallels between Lk 4,16-30 and Ac 28,17-31. I quote here a passage taken from Sanders:

> This final scene of Paul's ministry is therefore a reprise of the first scene of Jesus. Do we have a synagogue sermon there? So we have here, with the adjustment for verisimilitude that Paul is a prisoner. Is the Book of Isaiah quoted there? So it is here. Is there at first a favorable and then a hostile response there? Similarly here the one response is mixed, part favorable and part unfavorable. And does Jesus there make it clear to his audience that they were never the intended recipients of God's salvation, which is a salvation for the Gentiles? So here as well. The issue was never in doubt.[138]

Ac 28,17-31

The section "Paul at Rome" in Ac 28,17-31 comprises two meetings with the leaders of the Jews in Rome (vv. 17-22 and 23-28) and a concluding summary (vv. 30-31). The double encounter shows striking similarities with Ac 13,14-43.44-52[139]. The first meeting upon invitation by

133. "La prédication de Jésus dans la synagogue de Nazareth", in *Conclusion*, 396-402 (= 502-508), here 396 (= 502).

134. R. Maddox, *The Purpose of Luke–Acts* (FRLANT, 126), Göttingen, 1982, 2-6: "The Unity of Luke–Acts", here 5.

135. D.R. Miesner, *The Circumferential Speeches of Luke–Acts: Patterns and Purpose*, in *SBL 1978 Seminar Papers*, 223-237, esp. 234 (table of twelve "Parallels at the Circumference", Lk 4,14-30 and Ac 28,17-31).

136. A. Weiser, *Apg* II, 1985, 678 ("enge Beziehungen zur *Nazaret-Perikope* Lk 4,16-30").

137. J.T. Sanders, *The Jewish People in Luke–Acts*, in *SBL 1986 Seminar Papers*, 110-129, esp. 127 (with reference to Dupont's remark on "the three landmarks of the same history": see above, n. 75).

138. *Ibid.* This last issue, as stated by Sanders ("never ... intended"), is not undisputed. On the mixed response, cf. below, n. 140.

139. Cf. Weiser, 678: "hat inhaltlich und formal große Ähnlichkeiten mit der *Doppelszene am Anfang der ersten Missionsreise*" (cf. 679 on 28,17-31: "erst Lukas selbst

Paul is followed by a second meeting on a fixed day (28,23a; cf. 13,42: on the following sabbath); the Jews are present in larger numbers (πλείονες, cf. 13,44); Paul testifies to the kingdom of God and tries to convince them about Jesus; the reactions of the Jews are mixed: καὶ οἱ μὲν ἐπείθοντο τοῖς λεγομένοις, οἱ δὲ ἠπίστουν (28,24; cf. 13,43); but Paul's last speech is a quotation of Isa 6,9-10 with a concluding word on the salvation of the Gentiles: γνωστὸν οὖν ἔστω ὑμῖν ὅτι τοῖς ἔθνεσιν ἀπεστάλη τοῦτο τὸ σωτήριον τοῦ θεοῦ· αὐτοὶ καὶ ἀκούσονται (28,28; cf. 13,46.48).

> La seconde scène d'Antioche peut être considérée comme un développement de ce que la déclaration de 28,28 condense en quelques mots. L'essentiel est dit en 13,46... Il faut noter d'ailleurs que, pas plus que la déclaration de Rome, celle d'Antioche ne tient compte du fait que la prédication de Paul a convaincu un certain nombre de ses auditeurs juifs.[140]

Paul's speech at the first meeting in Ac 28,17b-20 is a more personal defense in view of his approaching trial: "he delivers an apologetical exposition in which the content of the preceding chapters in Acts is summed up and his innocence is affirmed"[141]. Likewise, within the lit-

---

hat diesen Abschluß geschaffen"). Contrast BARRETT, 1236-1237: "There seems little point however in an artificial repetition of this double scene; it would have been easy to compress the substance of vv. 17-28 into one event, and there is therefore some probability that there is some distinct traditional recollection of what took place". But the point is that Luke did not compress this substance into a one-day meeting. Cf. Ac 28,23: "Paul's (second) interview with the Jewish representatives lasted all day" (BARRETT, 1243). Moreover the content is different (see text).

140. DUPONT, *Conclusion*, 384 (= 488); cf. above, n. 57. See also 386 (= 490), in Corinth: "Le fait que certains parmi les Juifs se soient convertis ne change rien à la manière dont le tournant se prend" (Ac 18,6 ἀπὸ τοῦ νῦν εἰς τὰ ἔθνη πορεύσομαι). Notwithstanding their "part favorable and part unfavorable" reactions, the Jews in Ac 13,45 (οἱ Ἰουδαῖοι); 18,6 (αὐτῶν, cf. v. 5); 28,28 (ὑμῖν) are taken as one whole of unconverted Jews (compare Lk 4,28-29). "Jewish acceptance of Jesus and the early Christians has been either neglected or suppressed" (J.B. TYSON, *The Jewish Public*, 582; cf. n. 72). This is one of the "inconsistencies" in Acts. But is it a reason to conclude that "das für Lk 4,22-30 gültige Schema in Apg nicht in gleicher Weise wiederkehrt"? Cf. M. MEISER, *Die Reaktion des Volkes auf Jesus. Eine redaktionskritische Untersuchung zu den synoptischen Evangelien* (BZNW, 96), Berlin – New York, 1998, 277 n. 74 (and 285 n. 115); with reference to R.S. ASCOUGH, *Rejection and Repentance: Peter and the People in Luke's Passion Narrative*, in *Bib* 74 (1993) 349-365, here 349. It is another "inconsistency" that, after the statements on turning to the Gentiles in 13,46 and 18,6, Paul returns to speak in Jewish synagogues. Neither is it consistent that Paul and Barnabas after the symbolic gesture in 13,51 return to Pisidian Antioch as if it were already evangelized (14,22-23).

141. H. VAN DE SANDT, *Acts 28,28: No Salvation for the People of Israel? An Answer in the Perspective of the LXX*, in *ETL* 70 (1994) 341-358, here 341. The author's conclusion: "the charge with obduracy of Isa 6,9-10 is extended and sharpened in Acts 28,25c-28 under the influence of Ezek 2,3-5 and 3,4-7" (357). On rephrasing of Ezek 3,6b in Ac 28,28 (*ibid.*), see now also FITZMYER, *Acts*, 796.

erary unit of Lk 4,16-30, one can distinguish two parts (4,16-22 and 23-30)[142], each with a speech of Jesus: first his personal self-presentation in vv. 18-19 and 21 and then the more polemic vv. 23-27, ending with a reference to Elijah and Elisha and to the benefits of their healing ministry outside Israel (vv. 25-27). Cf. Dupont's remark on the two-part division:

> Remarquons simplement le rapprochement qui peut être fait entre l'épisode de Nazareth et celui de Rome en raison de ce qu'ils sont divisés en deux temps l'un et l'autre, en raison aussi de ce que le premier temps doit permettre au personnage principal, Jésus ou Paul, de se présenter lui-même à ses compatriotes.[143]

More structural resemblances can be added. The Isaiah text quoted in Lk 4,18-19 is followed in v. 21 by the one-line commentary: σήμερον πεπλήρωται ἡ γραφὴ αὕτη ἐν τοῖς ὠσὶν ὑμῶν. Some analogy has been seen in Paul's quotation of Isa 6,9-10 in Ac 28,25-27 and the brief explicatory comment in v. 28[144].

Lk 4,30 αὐτὸς δὲ ... ἐπορεύετο concludes the Nazareth pericope (cf. 16a καὶ ἦλθεν εἰς Ναζαρά). It is clearly to be read in connection with v. 29 (διελθὼν διὰ μέσου αὐτῶν) and not a few interpreters refer to Johannine parallels (Jn 7,30.44; 8,59; 10,39)[145]. Some call it "a fitting prelude to the story which is to follow in Acts"[146]. J. Dupont compares

---

142. On the interpretation of Lk 4,22b, cf. below, 393-394.

143. *Conclusion*, 398 (= 504). See also *Jésus*, 148 (= 44): "Comme la scène de Nazareth, celle de Rome se divise en deux temps, caractérisés par deux attitudes différentes de la part des auditeurs juifs de Paul". Cf. above, n. 140.

144. DUPONT, *ibid*. On the parallel "quotation from Isaiah", see D.R. MIESNER, *Circumferential Speeches* (n. 135), 234. Miesner proposes for both Lk 4,18-19 and Ac 28,25-29 (v. 29 included!) a chiastic structure turning around "to give sight to the blind" and "blindness confirmed" (224, 230). — On Lk 4,18-19, see K.E. BAILEY, *Poet & Peasant*, Grand Rapids, MI, 1976 (= 1985), 68; D.L. TIEDE, *Prophecy and History in Luke–Acts*, Philadelphia, PA, 1980, 35. But see J.S. SIKER, *"First to the Gentiles"* (above, n. 44), 77 n. 13: "By structuring even the Isaiah citation chiastically, Tiede stretches the structure a bit further than it really goes". The same remark applies to J.-N. Aletti's suggestion. For criticism of R. Meynet (1979), cf. NOORDA, *Historia* (n. 4), 226-227. Cf. J.-N. Aletti's *L'art de raconter* (n. 44), 60 n. 28; *Jésus à Nazareth (Lc 4,16-30). Prophétie, Écriture et typologie*, in R. GANTOY (ed.), *À cause de l'Évangile*. FS J. Dupont (LD, 123), Paris, 1985, 431-451, esp. 439 n. 15: "Tous les commentateurs..." (sic). Lk 4,18b is not included: κυρίου κηρύξαι ἄφεσιν τυφλοῖς ἀφέσει κηρύξαι κυρίου. Cf. R.C. Tannehill: τυφλοῖς between the lines which refer to ἄφεσις.

145. See the commentaries on Lk by E. Klostermann, F. Hauck, W. Grundmann, W. Wiefel (Jn 10,39!), E.E. Ellis, *et al*.

146. J.M. Creed; cf. A. Loisy. See G. SCHNEIDER, 111: "Die Verfolgung von seiten der Israeliten behindert nicht nur nicht das Fortschreiten der Botschaft Jesu, es fördert dieses sogar (vgl. Apg 13,46; 18,6; 19,9; 28,24-28). Das ist ein feststehendes Schema zum Ausdruck der lukanischen Auffassung" (see also J.A. Fitzmyer). F. HAUCK: "Das Heil geht seinen Weg weiter (AG 28,28)" (65).

Lk 4,30 with the concluding summary in Ac 28,30-31 and notes "sa parenté profonde avec l'adverbe ἀκωλύτως qui termine les Actes"[147].

Lk 4,25-27

The salvation for the Gentiles is the prevailing theme in Ac 28 (v. 28c αὐτοὶ καὶ ἀκούσονται). Though not undisputed[148], it is widely held that the Gentile mission is foreshadowed in the references to Elijah and Elisha in Lk 4,25-27[149]:

25 ἐπ᾽ ἀληθείας δὲ λέγω ὑμῖν,
   πολλαὶ χῆραι ἦσαν ἐν ταῖς ἡμέραις Ἠλίου ἐν τῷ Ἰσραήλ,
      ὅτε ἐκλείσθη ὁ οὐρανὸς ἐπὶ ἔτη τρία καὶ μῆνας ἕξ,
      ὡς ἐγένετο λιμὸς μέγας ἐπὶ πᾶσαν τὴν γῆν,
26 καὶ πρὸς οὐδεμίαν αὐτῶν ἐπέμφθη Ἠλίας
   εἰ μὴ εἰς Σάρεπτα τῆς Σιδωνίας πρὸς γυναῖκα χήραν.
27 καὶ πολλοὶ λεπροὶ ἦσαν ἐν τῷ Ἰσραὴλ ἐπὶ Ἐλισαίου τοῦ προφήτου,
   καὶ οὐδεὶς αὐτῶν ἐκαθαρίσθη
      εἰ μὴ Νααμὰν ὁ Σύρος.

In D. Catchpole's opinion, however, "the function of vv. 25-27 is more limited than some commentators suppose... Not even a sidelong glance is cast at any mission among Gentiles"[150]; and: "The principle is

147. *Conclusion*, 397 (= 503). See also M. KORN, *Geschichte* (n. 37), 84.
148. C.J. SCHRECK, *The Nazareth Pericope* (n. 4), 445-449: "vigorously challenged by B. Koet (1986), R.L. Brawley (1987), R.J. Miller (1988), and W. Wiefel (1988), respectively" (445). See now also D.R. CATCHPOLE, *Anointed One*, 1993 (n. 107), 244-250; J.A. WEATHERLY, *Jewish Responsibility* (n. 118), 127-128.
149. See Schreck's list, from 1973 (S.G. Wilson) to 1989 (G.N. Stanton), supplemented in his dissertation (402-404, and passim). See now also M. ÖHLER, *Elia im Neuen Testament. Untersuchungen zur Bedeutung des alttestamentlichen Propheten im frühen Christentum* (BZNW, 88), Berlin – New York, 1997, 175-184 ("Jesus in Nazareth: Lk 4,25-27"), here 182 n. 369 ("das Ziel des Lk (ist) hier die Heidenmission": some 30 scholars). His list of the opposite position ("... keinen Hinweis auf Mission") includes Brawley and Catchpole (but not Koet) and, more contestably, Tuckett and Nolland. Cf. Nolland's distinction between Lk 4,25-27 "in the immediate context" and "the wider Lukan context" in which "the blessed Gentiles adumbrate the universalism which is to be the basis of the Gentile mission (see already 2:32; 3:6)" (*Luke* I, 201 and 203); ID., *Salvation-History and Eschatology*, in I.H. MARSHALL – D. PETERSON (eds.), *Witness to the Gospel. The Theology of Acts*, Grand Rapids, MI – Cambridge, U.K., 1998, 63-81, here 77 ("in a later reading and in the context of the whole story of Luke–Acts..."). Compare Tuckett's distinction between Lk 4,25-27 in Q (1982, 352-353) and the Lukan redaction: cf. *Luke* (above, n. 7), 52 (and 54); *Q*, 277; and now his *Christology* (in this volume, 152 n. 70): "I remain convinced that Lk 4,25-27 does function within the Lukan narrative, at least for Luke, to prefigure the Gentile mission" (*contra* B.J. Koet and D.R. Catchpole). See also above, 377, n. 89 (A. Lindemann).
150. *Anointed One* (n. 107), 245, 249 (ctr. L.C. Crockett and P.F. Esler: neither Jew/Gentile table-fellowship nor the inclusion of God-fearers).
Cf. L.C. CROCKETT, *Luke 4,25-27 and Jewish-Gentile Relations in Luke–Acts*, in *JBL* 88 (1969) 177-183. Starting from v. 25bc (without counterpart in v. 27) he compares the

not that of 'Gentiles as well as Jews', which is the missionary programme of Acts, but 'Gentiles instead of Jews' in a very limited and
well defined context"[151]. Though not mentioned in Catchpole's essay
B.J. Koet and R.L. Brawley are not far away. The same volume includes
an article by M.D. Hooker on Luke's use of Old Testament quotations
and allusions. The Gospel of Luke, she writes, "contains very little
about salvation for the Gentiles", but "there are hints of that theme":
"The references to Elijah and Elisha... point forward to the mission to
the Gentiles which lies beyond Jesus' rejection, death and resurrection"
and "it is the promise of salvation for the Gentiles which stirs up his
countrymen's hostility"[152].

Like Catchpole, A. Vanhoye refers to C. Schreck's critical survey as
a challenge inciting him to a renewed study of Lk 4,16-30. He proposes
a two-stage reading ("il importe de bien distinguer les deux temps de
lecture"), comparable to that in Nolland's commentary. The possessive
attitude of the people of Nazareth is the theme of the first stage, in which
"l'épisode ne préfigure pas l'évangélisation des païens". But this first
stage seems to be only a theoretical possibility[153]:

clause on the famine in Elijah's time with Agabus' prediction in Ac 11,28 and regards the
Elijah-widow and Elisha-Naaman narratives, joined in Lk 4,25-27, as "models" for the
events narrated in Ac 10–11, "as a prolepsis ... of Jewish-gentile *reconciliation*" (183).
Catchpole's reply: the fact that the language in Lk 4,25c is traditional biblical "does not
help the suggestion that Luke intends to foreshadow Acts 11.28" (245). In addition, it is
not said in Lk 4,25-26 that Elijah is sent to the widow "in order to be fed there" and that
"the result is beneficial to both" (cf. Crockett, 179). Anyway the emphasis is not on
"reconciliation". — For P.F. Esler the reference in Lk 4,25-27 is "undoubtedly meant to
foreshadow a mission among non-Jews in the Christian period" (*Community*, 34; cf.
above, n. 9). It is less apparent that the poor widow and the army commander in Lk 4,25-
27 "pointed to the presence in Luke's community of representatives from either extreme
of the socio-economic spectrum" (183). On (Naaman and) the God-fearers in Luke–Acts
(33-45, esp. 37), see also R.I. DENOVA, *Things Accomplished* (n. 110), 149: "in Lk 4,25-
27, we have the origins of Luke's conception of God-fearers". Cf. above, n. 50.
    151. *Ibid.*, 248. These statements are extracted from an overall analysis of Lk 4,16-30.
Catchpole shows convincingly the exclusively Markan derivation of vv. 16, 22b, and 24;
he stresses the careful construction of the quotation in 4,18-19 ("a literary product", "the
creation of Luke") and the significance of physical healing (above, n. 107); he proposes
Lk 4,14 as "wholly adequate preparation" for v. 23b (243: the Capernaum crux). I discussed elsewhere his position on Mark's use of Q (234) and the Q-origin of Ναζαρά
(235; cf. above, n. 6).
    On the alleged Q-origin of 4,25-27 (Tuckett): "the extent to which this pair of Old
Testament-based arguments reflects the concerns of the Lucan gospel and connects up
with LukeR activity in 4,23, suggests that the evangelist is responsible for an imitation of
the approach of Q" (249). Compare BUSSE, *Nazareth-Manifest* (n. 39), 41-45 ("Lukas als
Verfasser des Doppelspruchs"); 43: "mit Hilfe von Lk 11,31f" (= Q). Lk 4,25-26.27 can
be added to H. Baarlink's list of man-woman pairs in Luke–Acts (in this volume, 489).
    152. M.D. HOOKER, *'Beginning with Moses and from all the Prophets'* (n. 105), here
218, 224 (n. 1: in reply to Koet).
    153. A. VANHOYE, *L'intérêt de Luc pour la prophétie en Lc 1,73; 4,16-30 et 22,60-65,*

... la portée prophétique de cet épisode inaugural s'étend beaucoup plus loin. Il préfigure, en effet, le sort de la prédication chrétienne, telle qu'elle est décrite dans les Actes.[154]

The important element in Vanhoye's approach remains that

> l'attitude possessive des Nazaréens, qui *rend ambigu leur accueil favorable*, provoque donc une mise au point de la part de Jésus et ensuite, pour ce motif, un retournement complet de leur part. Ce schéma complexe se retrouve en Ac 13,43-45.50; 17,1-5; 22,17-22.... Comme dans le récit de Lc 4, ... *ils veulent garder leur Messie pour eux.*[155]

'Jealous possessiveness' (Tannehill) is suggested by Vanhoye as the factor of coherence in Lk 4,16-30, explaining the turn from initial acceptance to final rejection: following the reference to Elijah and Elisha's ministry among the Gentiles, "la tendance possessive provoque une amère déception et se mue en agressivité (Lc 4,28-29)"[156].

A more radical option for coherence is to eliminate from v. 22 all connotation of acceptance or approval and to read the entire verse in a hostile sense as witnessing against Jesus (J. Jeremias, H. Baarlink, *et al.*)[157]. In a more nuanced approach F. Ó Fearghail interprets ἐμαρτύρουν in a neutral sense but argues that ἐθαύμαζον indicates "astonishment coupled with criticism and rejection" and takes καὶ ἔλεγον as an explicative phrase: "And they all witnessed to him, and (= *but*) were astonished, and (= *for*) they said: Is not this Joseph's son?"[158]. Many others take (ἐμαρτύρουν and) ἐθαύμαζον in a positive sense while seeing the question in v. 22b as negative, (merely) Joseph's son: "der Einwand der Leute bereitet den *Umschwung* des Urteils vor (28)" (F. Hauck), and

---

in *The Four Gospels 1992* (n. 5), 1529-1548, esp. 1535-1543 ("Jésus prophète dans sa patrie. Lc 4,16-30"), here 1542 n. 43: "... pour un lecteur qui suit pas à pas le récit de Luc. Mais s'il s'agit d'un lecteur déjà catéchisé (Lc 1,4), ce premier stade n'est guère possible. Le lecteur voit tout de suite plus loin".

154. *Ibid.*, 1541; with reference to J. DUPONT, *Jésus*, 148-150 (= 44-46), on Ac 13,34-52.

155. *Ibid.*, 1541-1542 (italics F.N.). As for Ac 22,17-22, cf. J.-N. ALETTI, *Quand Luc raconte* (n. 82), 149-150: "Jésus à Nazareth (Lk 4,24.26) et Paul à Jérusalem (Ac 22,18.21), les deux discours finissent pratiquement de la même façon, sur l'envoi aux étrangers et sur le refus de croire des concitoyens" (150). Note, however, that the positive reaction (the initial acceptance in Lk 4,22) has no parallel in Ac 22. There is no mention of Ac 22 in A. VANHOYE, *Les Juifs selon les Actes des Apôtres et les Épîtres du Nouveau Testament*, in *Bib* 72 (1991) 70-89, esp. 75: the pattern in Ac 13,14-52 (complete: nos. 1-6); 14,1-7; 17,1-10; 17,10-15; 18,4-11; 19,8-10 (and 28,22.28).

156. *L'intérêt de Luc*, 1540.

157. Cf. SCHRECK, 427-436 ("Internal Coherence"); NOORDA, *Historia*, 155-160. See also above, n. 86 (A. Lindemann).

158. F. Ó FEARGHAIL, *Rejection in Nazareth: Lk 4,22*, in *ZNW* 75 (1984) 60-72; ID., *The Introduction to Luke–Acts: A Study of the Role of Lk 1,1–4,44 in the Composition of Luke's Two-Volume Work* (AnBib, 126), Rome, 1991, 31 n. 128.

less reservedly: "Die Stimmung der Zuhörer schlägt jedoch mit der Rückfrage V. 22 Ende um" (G. Petzke)[159]. Catchpole defends a quite different view on Lk 4,22: "the evangelist wants to underline with all possible firmness the positive reaction which is forthcoming from the audience in Nazareth". The witnessing (ἐμαρτύρουν αὐτῷ) is positive. The astonishment (ἐθαύμαζον ἐπί) is also positive. "And even the question (οὐχὶ υἱός ἐστιν Ἰωσὴφ οὗτος) is positive – just as positive as the questions which erupt in Lk. 4.36; 8.25"[160]. It is a more problematic suggestion that "the tone of the hypothetical request in v. 23 must be adjudged entirely positive"[161].

The discussion of the Nazarenes' initial reaction to Jesus concentrates on v. 22b, the question of Jesus' identity. Mark's "the son of Mary" (6,3 οὐχ οὗτός ἐστιν ... ὁ υἱὸς τῆς Μαρίας) is changed by Luke to "son of Joseph" in accordance with Lk 3,23 (ὢν υἱός, ὡς ἐνομίζετο Ἰωσήφ). I quote here Green's recent commentary:

> Luke has already informed us that people assumed that Jesus was son of Joseph (3:23) ... In this way, ... they respond to Jesus according to their own parochial understanding ... They claim Jesus as 'the son of one of our own' – indeed, as 'one of us'. Reading their response from within the narrative, we can understand that their response is positive, even expectant ... *We* (Luke's readers outside the narrative) know that their understanding of Jesus is erroneous, for we know that Jesus is Son of God, not son of Joseph.[162]
> [In 4,23] Jesus addresses the parochial version of his townspeople directly, countering their assumptions that, as Joseph's son, he will be especially for them a source of God's favor.[163]

The articulation of their unspoken thoughts in the words of Luke's Jesus in 4,23 may indicate the inadequacy of their understanding[164]; it does not imply that their reaction is not presented positively in v. 22[165]. "Der

---

159. G. PETZKE, *Das Sondergut des Evangeliums nach Lukas*, Zürich, 1990, 79. Cf. F. HAUCK, *Lk*, 64 (62: "sich an seiner geringen Herkunft stoßend"). Note Hauck's division of the pericope: a) *Die Bewunderung 16-22ᵃ*, b) *Das Ärgernis 22ᵇ-30*.
160. *Anointed One*, 239.
161. *Ibid.*, 240. Cf. 239: "the eminent reasonableness of the request 'physician, heal yourself'".
162. J.B. GREEN, *Luke*, 1997, 215.
163. *Ibid.*, 217.
164. G. WASSERBERG, *Aus Israels Mitte* (n. 55), 160: "ohne in ihm den Sohn Gottes zu sehen"; in that sense "(ist) der Satz 'Ist das nicht Josefs Sohn?' der Schlüssel zum Verständnis der lk Nazaretperikope" (*ibid.*). Cf. W. WIATER, *Komposition als Mittel der Interpretation im lukanischen Doppelwerk* (diss.), Bonn, 1972, 90-105 (Lk 4,16-30), here 101: "der Angelpunkt" in the composition of Lk 4,16-30.
165. See R.C. TANNEHILL, *Mission*, 1972, 53: "So the question of the Nazarenes indicates their failure to understand who Jesus is, ... but it is not an indication of hostility"; ID., *Narrative Unity*, 1984, 68 (cf. above, n. 74). Ctr. J.A. WEATHERLY, *Jewish Responsibility* (n. 118), 122-124.

Umschlag der Stimmung erfolgt erst in 4,28" (Wellhausen). The shift comes after 4,25-27 (v. 28 ἀκούοντες ταῦτα). R.L. Brawley stresses the parallellism between 4,25-27 and v. 24: "The function of the allusions to Elijah and Elisha is to demonstrate that a prophet is not acceptable ἐν τῇ πατρίδι αὐτοῦ"[166]. But nothing in the text of Luke(!)[167] alludes to inacceptability of both prophets. The change from ἐν τῇ πατρίδι αὐτοῦ (v. 24) to ἐν τῷ Ἰσραήλ indicates that more is involved than an analogy to the Nazareth-Capernaum antithesis. Catchpole's comment stresses God's freedom of choice (cf. the divine passives ἐπέμφθη and ἐκαθαρίσθη) and a *Sitz im Leben* of Lk 4,25-27 which is "quite unmistakably mission in Israel"[168]. But the emphasis in Lk 4,25-27 is laid on Elijah and Elisha's work among non-Israelites in contrast to the πολλαὶ/πολλοὶ ἐν τῷ Ἰσραήλ and οὐδεμίαν/οὐδεὶς αὐτῶν:

> The emphasis on Elijah and Elisha's ministry among Gentiles rather than Jews foreshadows the development of the Gentile mission in Acts... This reference (to Gentiles) is not out of place when we view the scene from the larger Lukan perspective.[169]

Defenders of a proleptic allusion to Gentile mission in Lk 4,25-27 may refer to Simeon's announcement of universal salvation: φῶς εἰς ἀποκάλυψιν ἐθνῶν καὶ δόξαν λαοῦ σου Ἰσραήλ (2,32)[170]. Cf. Ac 13,47: τέθεικά σε εἰς φῶς ἐθνῶν (Isa 49,6). Although some commentators hesitate about the meaning of πάντες οἱ λαοί in v. 31[171], ὅτι εἶδον οἱ ὀφθαλμοί μου τὸ σωτήριόν σου (2,30) can be read in the light of 3,6: καὶ ὄψεται πᾶσα σάρξ τὸ σωτήριον τοῦ θεοῦ (Isa 40,5) and of Luke's third use of σωτήριον in Ac 28,28: γνωστὸν οὖν ἔστω ὑμῖν ὅτι τοῖς ἔθνεσιν ἀπεστάλη τοῦτο τὸ σωτήριον τοῦ θεοῦ· αὐτοὶ καὶ ἀκούσονται[172].

---

166. *Luke–Acts and the Jews: Conflict, Apology, and Conciliation* (SBL MS, 33), Atlanta, GA, 1987, 11 (and passim: cf. 9, 16).

167. B.J. KOET notes that "Luke enlarges the contrast between the inhabitants of Israel and the Gentiles", but he reads Lk 4,25-27 in the light of 1-2 Kings as the prophet's task to incite people to conversion (*Five Studies*, 50).

168. *Anointed One* (n. 107), 248-249.

169. R.C. TANNEHILL, *Narrative Unity* (n. 74), 71.

170. Cf. B.J. KOET, *Simeons Worte (Lk 2,29-32.34c-35) und Israels Geschick*, in *The Four Gospels 1992* (above, n. 5), 1551-1569; on δόξαν in parallel with ἀποκάλυψιν, see 1551-1552 n. 12. See also G. WASSERBERG, *Aus Israels Mitte* (n. 55), 134-147 («Lk 2,29-35»), here 138 (note 13: read «1552, Anm. 12»).

171. Cf. G.D. KILPATRICK, *Λαοί at Luke ii.31 and Acts iv.25,27* (1965), in his Collected Essays (BETL, 96), Leuven, 1990, 312. See G. WASSERBERG, 139-140.

172. Cf. above, 389.

NOTE

In these essays of Part One the phrase "in the present volume" refers to the respective CBL volume (page and note). Cf. First Publication, p. XIII.

I.   **John and the Synoptics 1975-1990**

C.P. BAMMEL, *The First Resurrection Appearance to Peter: John 21 and the Synoptics*, 620-631 [11[39]]. M.-É. BOISMARD, *Jean 4,46-54 et les parallèles synoptiques*, 239-259 [20[80]]. C. BREYTENBACH, *MNHMONEYEIN. Das "Sich-Erinnern" in der urchristlichen Überlieferung: Die Bethanienepisode (Mk 14,3-9 / Jn 12,1-8) als Beispiel*, 548-557 [5[13]]. U. BUSSE, *Johannes und Lukas: Die Lazarusperikope, Frucht eines Kommunikationsprozesses*, 281-306 [47[210]]. W.L. CRAIG, *The Disciples' Inspection of the Empty Tomb (Lk 24,12.24; Jn 20,2-10)*, 614-619 [44[194]]. A. DAUER, *Spuren der (synoptischen) Synedriumsverhandlung im 4. Evangelium: Das Verhältnis zu den Synoptikern*, 307-339 [41[181] 50[223]]. I. DUNDERBERG, *Zur Literarkritik von Joh 12,1-11*, 558-570 [5[13]]. R.T. FORTNA, *Diachronic/Synchronic: Reading John 21 and Luke 5*, 387-399 [11[39]]. R. KIEFFER, *Jean et Marc: Convergences dans la structure et dans les détails*, 109-125 [48[212] 54[236] 56[243]]. J. KONINGS, *The Dialogue of Jesus, Philip and Andrew in John 6,5-9*, 523-534 [53[234] [236]]. M. MENKEN, *The Quotations from Zech 9,9 in Mt 21,5 and in Jn 12,13*, 571-578 [26[118]]. M. MORGEN, *Jean 3 et les Synoptiques*, 514-522 [31[143]]. M. SABBE, *The Trial of Jesus before Pilate in John and Its Relation to the Synoptists*, 341-385 [18[70]]. W. SCHENK, *Die Um-codierungen der matthäischen Unser-Vater-Redaktion in Joh 17*, 587-607 [34[159]]. B. STANDAERT, *Jean 21 et les Synoptiques: L'enjeu interecclésial de la dernière rédaction de l'évangile*, 632-643 [11[39]]. H. THYEN, *Johannes und die Synoptiker: Auf der Suche nach einem neuen Paradigma zur Beschreibung ihrer Beziehungen anhand von Beobachtungen an Passions- und Ostererzählungen*, 81-107 [61[273]]. F. VOUGA, *Le quatrième évangile comme témoin interprète de la tradition synoptique: Jean 6*, 261-279 [48[213] 54[236]]

II. **Literary Criticism, Old and New**

F. BOVON, *Le récit lucanien de la passion de Jésus (Lc 22–23)*, 393-423 [76[44]]. C. BREYTENBACH, *Das Markusevangelium als traditionsgebundene Erzählung? Anfragen an die Markusforschung der achtziger Jahre*, 77-110 [92[135]]. T.A. FRIEDRICHSEN, *Alternative Synoptic Theories on Mk 4,30-32*, 427-450 [71[27]]. R. KÜHSCHELM, *Angelophanie-Christophanie in den synoptischen Grabesgeschichten Mk 16,1-8 par. (unter Berücksichtigung von Joh 20,11-18)*, 556-565 [74[38]]. C.P. MÄRZ, *Zur Q-Rezeption in Lk 12,35–13,35 (14,1-24). Die Q-Hypothese und ihre Bedeutung für die Interpretation des lukanischen Reiseberichtes*, 177-208 [82[77]]. W.R. TELFORD, *Mark and the Historical-Critical Method: The Challenge of Recent Literary Approaches to the Gospel*, 491-502 [92[136]]. C.M. TUCKETT, *Mark and Q*, 149-175 [88[111]]. Cf. C. FOCANT, [66[5]]

III. **The Sayings of Jesus in 1 Corinthians**

J. GUNDRY-VOLF, *Controlling the Bodies. A Theological Profile of the Corinthian Sexual Ascetics (1 Cor 7)*, 519-541 [115[99]]. A. LINDEMANN, *Die paulinische Ekklesiologie angesichts der Lebenswirklichkeit der christlichen Gemeinde in Korinth*, 63-66 [117[110]]. J. VERHEYDEN, *Origen on the Origin of 1 Cor 2,9*, 491-511 [107[65]]

IV. **Q 6,20b-21; 7,22 and Isaiah 61**

T.L. BRODIE, *Intertextuality and Its Use in Tracing Q and Proto-Luke*, 469-477 [129[4]]. M. HASITSCHKA, *Die Verwendung der Schrift in Mt 4,1-11*, 487-490 [129[4]]. K.-W. NIEBUHR, *Die Werke des eschatologischen Freudenboten: 4Q521 und die Jesusüberlieferung*, 637-646 [154[107]]. F. NOEL, *The Double Commandment of Love in Lk 10,27*, 559-570 [130[8]]. J. SCHRÖTER, *Erwägungen zum Gesetzverständnis anhand von Q 16,16-18*, 441-458 [129[4]]. C.M. TUCKETT, *Scripture and Q*, 3-26 [129[4] 132[17] 142[63] 146[81]]

V.   **Luke 4,16 and the Unity of Luke-Acts**

H. BAARLINK, *Die Bedeutung der Prophetenzitate in Lk 4,18-19 und Apg 2,17-21 für das Doppelwerk des Lukas*, 483-491 [186[82] 202[151]]. A. LINDEMANN, *Einheit und Vielfalt im lukanischen Doppelwerk: Beobachtungen zu Reden, Wundererzählungen und Mahlberichten*, 225-253 [186[84]]. C.M. TUCKETT, *The Christology of Luke-Acts*, 133-164 [201[149]]

II

THE MINOR AGREEMENTS

ETL 72 (1996) 41-74

6

THE FIRST SYNOPTIC PERICOPE
THE APPEARANCE OF JOHN THE BAPTIST IN Q?

I. A SYNOPTIC SOURCE DIFF. MK 1,1-6

Some forty years ago I received my first training in the study of the Synoptics with the Louvain professor L. Cerfaux. His lectures on "La préhistoire des évangiles" in 1952-1954 were in fact a reading of the Synoptic Gospels in which he developed his argument for the common-source hypothesis. It began straightaway with the first Synoptic pericope[1]:

> Il y a deux possibilités: Mc ou Mg. Ici Lc s'entend plutôt avec Mg, en tant qu'à travers Mt on retrouve Mg par comparaison avec Lc. En effet ils ne commencent pas cette section (et l'évangile) comme Mc en citant d'abord le texte de l'Écriture. Dans Mt et Lc nous avons d'abord la présentation du Baptiste puis la citation de l'Écriture... Lc et Mt citent exactement et uniquement Isaïe... Nous avons donc accord de Lc et Mt contre Mc, ce qui nous fait arriver à Mg.

L. Vaganay's book on *Le problème synoptique*, published in 1954 with a Preface by L. Cerfaux, includes an Excursus on Mk 1,1-6 and parallels[2]:

> ... nous avons cherché à établir que les récits et les discours synoptiques postulent l'existence d'une source commune à Mt.-Mc.-Lc. et antérieure à Mc. ... À ce sujet nous avons montré que les accords positifs de Mt.-Lc. contre Mc. constituaient un des plus forts arguments. Il convient de vérifier la justesse de ce point de vue dans une application pratique.

The main conclusion of his analysis of "the first Synoptic pericope" concerns the presence of three significant Matthew-Luke agreements against Mark[3].

---

1. I quote from unpublished student notes. Compare L. CERFAUX, *À propos des sources du troisième Évangile: proto-Luc ou proto-Matthieu?*, in *ETL* 12 (1935) 5-27, esp. p. 14: "*Lc.* s'accorde avec *Mt.* contre Mc. pour la place donnée à la citation prophétique et pour l'omission, dans celle-ci, du texte de Malachie. ... Une rencontre verbale au moins entre *Mt.* et *Lc.* est significative: πᾶσαν τὴν περίχωρον τοῦ Ἰορδάνου (*Lc.*, III,3 = *Mt.*, III,5)" (= *Recueil L. Cerfaux*, I, 399-400).

2. L. VAGANAY, *Le problème synoptique. Une hypothèse de travail*, Paris-Tournai, 1954: "Les traits rédactionnels de Marc dans la première péricope synoptique (Mt. 3,1-6; Mc. 1,1-6; Lc. 3,1-6)" (Excursus III; pp. 344-360). The quotation is taken from the opening paragraph (p. 344).

3. Besides the temporal indication at the beginning (p. 345: "un certain accord"), the three Mt-Lk agreements are: 1. the order of the section (p. 347: "la disposition de Mc. doit être secondaire"); 2. the quotation of Mal 3,1 in Mt 11,10 / Lk 7,27 (p. 354: "au même endroit, différent de celui de Mc. et bien meilleur que celui de Mc."); 3. Mt 3,5

Vaganay's theory of Proto-Matthew as the Synoptic source behind Mk 1,1-6 is now generally abandoned[4]. Yet the reconstruction of Proto-Mk (= Mk[1]) that was recently proposed by N. Walter (1992)[5] has reminded me of Mg. The starting point is his assumption that "der ursprüngliche Markustext [Mk 1,2-6] in etwa so aussah, wie er mit Hilfe der Übereinstimmungen von Mt und Lk zu erschließen ist", and that "die major agreements, die normalerweise auf Q deuten [Q 3,7-9.16-17], im Zusammenhang mit den minor agreements ... zu sehen (sind)"[6]. It looks like an echo of Vaganay's Mg theory. He arrives at an almost identical reconstruction of Mark's source: Mk 1,4.2a.3.6.5(+ πᾶσα ἡ περίχωρος τοῦ Ἰορδάνου)[7] and the same identification of Markan redaction: addition of v. 1; inverted order of vv. 2a.3 (Isa 40,3) and 4; addition of v. 2b (Mal 3,1); inverted order of vv. 5 and 6; and omission of πᾶσα ἡ περίχωρος τοῦ Ἰορδάνου in v. 5. Walter's combination in Mk[1] of the minor agreements diff. Mk 1,1-6 with the major agreements of Mt 3,7-12 / Lk 3,7-9.16-17 has been welcomed by A. Fuchs: "Walter hat das Plus, daß er minor und major agreements (vgl. Mt 3,7-10.12) auf gleicher Ebene sieht und demselben Redaktor zuschreibt"[8]. For both

---

πᾶσα ἡ περίχωρος τοῦ Ἰορδάνου (p. 359: "Lc. anticipe la même donnée"): "un accord positif d'un très grand poids" (p. 360). I quote here his conclusion: "par trois fois, Mt.-Lc. s'accordent contre Mc. Qu'on poursuive ce travail pour toutes les péricopes de la triple tradition, on arrivera à former un bloc imposant d'arguments littéraires qui, dans la solution du problème synoptique, emporteront la conviction sur un point important, à savoir: l'existence du Matthieu araméen (M), traduit en grec (Mg), qui doit être placé à la source de Mt.-Mc.-Lc." (p. 360).

4. See for instance Boismard's latest reconstruction of Proto-Mk, without the characteristic Mt/Lk agreements and quite different from Mg: v. 4a (ἐγένετο Ἰωάννης ὁ βαπτίζων ἐν τῇ ἐρήμῳ) and vv. 5-6. Cf. M.-É. BOISMARD, L'évangile de Marc. Sa préhistoire (ÉB n.s., 26), Paris, 1994, p. 243 (pp. 22-24, 51-54). See my review in ETL 71 (1995) 166-175.

5. N. WALTER, Mk 1,1-8 und die "Agreements" von Mt 3 und Lk 3. Stand die Predigt Johannes des Täufers in Q?, in F. VAN SEGBROECK, C.M. TUCKETT, G. VAN BELLE, J. VERHEYDEN (eds.), The Four Gospels 1992. FS F. Neirynck (BETL, 100), Leuven, 1992, pp. 457-478, esp. 467-470 (and 473-475, on Mk 1,1). See already his Das Markus-Evangelium und Rom. Das kanonische Markus-Evangelium als überarbeitete Fassung des ursprünglichen Textes, in Helikon 18-19 (1978-79) 22-40, esp. p. 33.

Walter now uses the siglum Mk[1] for Proto-Mark and Mk[2] for Mark. Like H. Koester, he avoids the term Urmarkus (p. 492); cf. The Minor Agreements and Proto-Mark. A Response to H. Koester, in ETL 67 (1991) 82-94, p. 82 (= Evangelica II, 59).

6. Mk 1,1-8, pp. 470, 476.

7. Vaganay's Proto-Matthew (Mg) also includes ἐν ταῖς ἡμέραις ἐκείναις, τῆς Ἰουδαίας (Mt 3,1), and καὶ λέγων· μετανοεῖτε· ἤγγικεν γὰρ ἡ βασιλεία τῶν οὐρανῶν (Mt 3,2). With regard to the double-tradition passages in Lk 3–7, all assigned to Mg, cf. below, II.2. Up to now, Walter's Mk[1] theory concerning the Q texts is restricted to the Baptist section in Q 3,7-9.16-17. Cf. below, n. 89.

8. A. FUCHS, Exegese im elfenbeinernen Turm. Das quellenkritische Problem von Mk 1,2-8 par Mt 3,1-12 par Lk 3,1-17 in der Sicht der Zweiquellentheorie und von Deutero-

Fuchs and Walter the minor agreements against Mark are the main reason why the "Synoptic" Mark (i.e. the source of Mt and Lk) cannot be
our "canonical" Mark. Whereas Fuchs has opted for Deutero-Mark
(rejected by Walter as "äußerst unwahrscheinlich")[9], Walter proposes a
Proto-Mark theory (cf. Fuchs's comment: "Sie erklärt bei den agreements den kanonischen Text des Mk für sekundär und die agreements
selbst für alt, was die Sache auf den Kopf stellt")[10]. They join together
in their refusal of Q by extending their Proto-Markan or Deutero-
Markan source to Mt 3,7-12 / Lk 3,7-9.16-17. Once again, this may
remind us of Vaganay's Mg.

It is more common, at least in the two-source theory, to regard Q 3,7-
9 as the first section of Q, and it is usually in connection with "the
beginning of Q" that the existence of a non-Markan source behind Mt
3,1-6 / Lk 3,1-6 is being discussed. In his 1978 dissertation (published in
1992) A.D. Jacobson has proposed a tentative reconstruction as follows[11]:

> [1]In those days, [2]John came preaching [3]in all the region of the Jor-
> dan,
> [4]as it is written in the book of the words of Isaiah the prophet,
> 　A voice crying in the wilderness,
> 　prepare the way of the Lord,
> 　make his paths straight.

Compare A. Polag's reconstruction in *Fragmenta Q* (1979)[12]:

markus, in *SNTU* 20 (1995) 23-149, esp. pp. 63-74 ("N. Walter, 1978/79 und 1992"). See
p. 67 (the quoted passage), and again on p. 69: "Er betont zu Recht..., daß die minor
zusammen mit den major agreements zu betrachten und auf *ein und derselben* Ebene zu
behandeln sind, wie es von der Dmk-These von Anfang an vertreten wird"; and p. 141
("bedeutsam"). Cf. below, n. 23.

　9. *Mk 1,1-8*, p. 462.

　10. *Exegese* (n. 8), p. 72. In this essay A. Fuchs presents a survey of studies on Mk
1,2-8 and par. from 1969 (H. Schürmann) to 1995. He can refer to his own Dmk theory
in *Die Überschneidungen von Mk und "Q" nach B.H. Streeter und E.P. Sanders und ihre
wahre Bedeutung (Mk 1,1-8 par.)*, in W. HAUBECK – M. BACHMANN (eds.), *Wort in der
Zeit. Neutestamentliche Studien*. FS K.H. Rengstorf, Leiden, 1980, pp. 28-81, esp. 57-78
(Part II). The "umfangreichere Studie" he had announced there (pp. 57, 75) is still unpublished. See occasional references in *SNTU* 8 (1983), 13-14; 17 (1992), 73-74; 18 (1993),
190-196; 19 (1994), 88; *Exegese*, p. 33, and passim.

　11. A.D. JACOBSON, *Wisdom Christology in Q*, Ph.D. Diss. Claremont (dir. J.M.
Robinson), 1978, p. 29; slightly adapted in *The First Gospel. An Introduction to Q*,
Sonoma, CA, 1992, p. 80: "The Q account presumably contained (a) a general indication
of time, (b) a reference to John's 'coming', (c) a reference to the location of John's activity, and (d) the quotation of Isa 40:3 LXX with a citation formula". With regard to (a),
he adds: "possibly a reference to Herod" (cf. the Gospel of the Ebionites).

　12. A. POLAG, *Fragmenta Q. Textheft zur Logienquelle*, Neukirchen-Vluyn, 1979,
[2]1982, p. 28 (Greek text). In English translation: I. HAVENER, *Q. The Sayings of Jesus*,

1 ['Εν ταῖς ἡμέραις ἐκείναις παραγίνεται 'Ιωάννης
2 κηρύσσων ἐν τῇ ἐρήμῳ <βάπτισμα μετανοίας>
3 ὡς γέγραπται (διὰ 'Ησαΐου τοῦ προφήτου)
4 φωνὴ βοῶντος ἐν τῇ ἐρήμῳ·
5 ἑτοιμάσατε τὴν ὁδὸν κυρίου,
6 εὐθείας ποιεῖτε τὰς τρίβους αὐτοῦ.
7 Καὶ ἦλθεν εἰς πᾶσαν τὴν περίχωρον τοῦ 'Ιορδάνου.]

In Polag's first study on the extent of Q (1966), the quotation of Isa 40,3 (lines 3-6) is not mentioned[13]. In his later work on the christology of Q (1968, 1977) he apparently intends to include the quotation, possibly even in its longer Lukan form: "Das Zitat Jes 40,3-5[!] ... könnte durchaus in Q gestanden haben. ... Doch kommt man auch bei diesem Zitat über die Feststellung der Möglichkeit einer Zugehörigkeit zu Q nicht hinaus"[14].

In recent years there is clearly a revival of interest in this question, mainly for two reasons. First, the International Q Project has drawn attention to the problem of the beginning of Q. The critical text proposed by IQP includes Q 3,2 . . . 'Ιωάννη . . . and 3,3 . . . πᾶσα . . η . . περίχωρο . . . τοῦ 'Ιορδάνου . . ., and its publication (1992)[15] has been accompanied with special studies by J.S. Kloppenborg[16] and J.M. Robinson[17]. Second, two essays on Mk 1,1-6 and Q published in *NTS* 1992, by

Wilmington, DE, 1987, Part Two: "The Text of Q by *Athanasius Polag*", pp. 109-165 (p. 123). The brackets indicate the degree of probability: (*wahrscheinlich*), [*vermutlich*], <*möglich*>. For the square brackets added here at the beginning and at the end of the section (ctr. Polag and Havener), see the Table of Q Contents (p. 23; Havener, p. 117). Differences beween Mt and Lk are in small print: ταῖς ἡμέραις ἐκείναις, παραγίνεται, διά (Mt only); βάπτισμα, ὡς, ἦλθεν εἰς (Lk only). Differences in Mt-Lk words (normal print) are not marked by Polag: line 1, 'Ιωάννης (Mt 3,1) and 'Ιωάννην (Lk 3,2); line 2, μετανοίας (Lk 3,3) and μετανοεῖτε (Mt 3,2); line 3, γέγραπται (Lk 3,4) and οὗτος γὰρ ἐστιν ὁ ῥηθείς (Mt 3,3); line 4, πᾶσαν τὴν περίχωρον (Lk 3,3) and πᾶσα ἡ περίχωρος (Mt 3,5). The difference in line 3 is more than "one of word-ending or between a word and its compound" (p. 14).

13. *Der Umfang der Logienquelle*, (unpublished) Lic. Diss. Trier, 1966, pp. 108-110 (p. 110). The elements he here assigns to Q are: παραγίνεται – 'Ιωάννης – κηρύσσων – βάπτισμα μετανοίας – [ἐν τῇ ἐρήμῳ τῆς 'Ιουδαίας] – πᾶσα ἡ περίχωρος τοῦ 'Ιορδάνου.

14. *Die Christologie der Logienquelle* (WMANT, 45), Neukirchen-Vluyn, 1977, p. 157 (Diss. Trier, 1968, p. 144).

15. Cf. *JBL* 111 (1992), p. 501. On IQP, see *ETL* 69 (1993) 221-225; 71 (1995), p. 430.

16. J.S. KLOPPENBORG, *City and Wasteland: Narrative World and the Beginning of the Sayings Gospel (Q)*, in *Semeia* 52 (1991) 145-160. See also his translation of Q in *Q–Thomas Reader*, Sonoma, CA, 1990, p. 35: "Introduction: <**John** came into **all the region about the Jordan**...>".

17. J.M. ROBINSON, *The Sayings Gospel Q*, in *The Four Gospels 1992* (n. 5), pp. 361-388; *The Incipit of the Sayings Gospel Q*, in *RHPR* 75 (1995) 9-33 (esp. pp. 12-14).

D.R. Catchpole[18] and by J. Lambrecht[19], have developed the thesis of Mark's use of Q[20] and were already followed by a number of critical reactions in the course of 1995[21].

| "The main argument for the existence of Q in this pericope rests on the order of the Q material" (Jacobson). The common scheme in the reconstructions of Q proposed by Catchpole and Lambrecht is this Mt-Lk agreement of order: the coming of John followed by the quotation of Isa 40,3. The phrase "all the region about the Jordan" is applied differently, according to Lk 3,3 (Catchpole) or according to Mt 3,5 (Lambrecht). These and other differences are marked here by underlining[22]:

Catchpole's proposal:

Ἰωάννης <u>ὁ βαπτίζων</u>
  <u>ἦλθεν εἰς πᾶσαν τὴν περίχωρον τοῦ Ἰορδάνου</u>
κηρύσσων βάπτισμα μετανοίας <u>εἰς ἄφεσιν ἁμαρτιῶν</u>,
καθὼς γέγραπται ἐν τῷ Ἠσαΐᾳ τῷ προφήτῃ·
  φωνὴ βοῶντος ἐν τῇ ἐρήμῳ·
  ἑτοιμάσατε τὴν ὁδὸν κυρίου,
  εὐθείας ποιεῖτε τὰς τρίβους αὐτοῦ.

Lambrecht's reconstruction:

Q3. 2 John came <u>in the wilderness,</u>
     3 preaching the baptism of repentance,
     4a as it is written in Isaiah the prophet:
      b   The voice of one crying in the wilderness:
      c   Prepare the way of the Lord,
      d   make his paths straight.
     6b <u>All the region about the Jordan</u> <u>went out to him,</u>
      c <u>and they were baptized by him in the river Jordan.</u>

18. D.R. CATCHPOLE, *The Beginning of Q: A Proposal*, in *NTS* 38 (1992) 205-221; reprinted in his *The Quest for Q*, Edinburgh, 1993, pp. 60-78 ("The Beginning of Q").
19. J. LAMBRECHT, *John the Baptist and Jesus in Mark 1.1-15: Markan Redaction of Q?*, in *NTS* 38 (1992) 357-384 (on Mk 1,1-6, pp. 363-364, 372-373).
20. See also J. MARCUS, *The Way of the Lord. Christological Exegesis of the Old Testament in the Gospel of Mark*, Louisville, KY, 1992; Edinburgh, 1993, pp. 12-47 ("Mark 1:2-3"), esp. p. 15: because of the Mt-Lk agreements "it seems likely that Matthew and Luke are following Q rather than Mark in their parallels to Mark 1:2-6" (with reference to H. Schürmann, 1969; cf. below, n. 54); no verbal reconstruction of Q is provided.
21. In order of appearance: F. NEIRYNCK, *The Minor Agreements and Q*, in R.A PIPER (ed.), *The Gospel Behind the Gospels* (NTSup, 75), Leiden, 1995, pp. 49-72 (esp. 65-72: "The Beginning of Q"); J.M. ROBINSON, *The* Incipit (n. 17), esp. pp. 14-19 ("Mark 1:2a,4,3?"); I. DUNDERBERG, *Q and the Beginning of Mark*, in *NTS* 41 (1995) 501-511; H.T. FLEDDERMANN, *Mark and Q. A Study of the Overlap Texts* (BETL, 122), Leuven, 1995, p. 31 n. 24 (see also p. 265 n. 14); A. FUCHS, *Exegese* (n. 8), esp. pp. 108-119.
22. Cf. JACOBSON, *Gospel* (n. 11), p. 80; CATCHPOLE, p. 218 (= 75); LAMBRECHT, p. 364.

For both, the Q text continues in Q 3,7-9: ἔλεγεν δὲ τοῖς ὄχλοις ἐρχ-ομένοις ἐπὶ τὸ βάπτισμα... (He said to the people that were coming to the baptism...). And again A. Fuchs can express approval. He finds here a new application of the principle of *Kohärenz* of all agreements against Mk: minor agreements and major agreements are treated *einheitlich*[23]. I However, one should not neglect the reverse direction of this association. Contrary to what happens in a (Proto-Mk or) Deutero-Mk hypothesis, it is the nature of the major agreement Q 3,7-9 which is projected on the minor-agreements source diff. Mk 1,1-6.

The acceptance of Mark's use of Q in Mk 1,1-6 would lead us back to the common-source hypothesis of the early 1950's. Is there evidence strong enough to force us to this step? The Mt-Lk agreements against Mk are the common basis in all theories of the existence of Q (or Mg), Proto-Mk, or Deutero-Mk in this first Synoptic pericope. These minor agreements are even more important, at least on the side of Lk, for theories of Luke's use of Mt, either in the hypothesis of Matthean originality[24] or in the paradigm of Q=Matthew (Luke's second source besides Mk)[25].

23. *Exegese* (above, n. 8), p. 141; see also pp. 69 and 132 ("*eine* gestaltende Hand"). With regard to Fuchs's constant theme of "atomization" in the study of the minor agreements, I may quote F. Fendler: "es ist ... unsachgemäß, eine systematische Behandlung der minor agreements als 'isolierendes' Verfahren abzutun" (*Studien* [below, n. 71], p. 174 n. 133). How indeed can the possibility of Matthean and Lukan redaction be tested without studying (all) the agreements one by one, in their immediate context and in the broader context of the respective gospel redactions? The comment I made earlier on the high number of minor agreements in general, can be applied to the case of Mk 1,1-6 par.: "it is hardly conceivable that the total number of *explained* agreements could become unexplainable" (*Evangelica II*, 40).

24. Cf. L. COPE, et al., *Narrative Outline of the Composition of Luke according to the Two Gospel Hypothesis*, in *SBL Seminar Papers* (1992) 98-120, p. 100, on Lk 3,1-6 (Mt 3,1a.3.5); D.L. DUNGAN, *Response to the Two-Source Hypothesis*, in ID. (ed.), *The Interrelations of the Gospels* (BETL, 95), Leuven, 1990, pp. 200-216, esp. 208 ("Mk conflates Mal 3:1 with the Isa 40:3 quote in his sources, creating a minor agreement against him").

25. Cf. M.D. GOULDER, *Luke. A New Paradigm* (JSNT SS, 20), Sheffield, 1989, pp. 270-273. On Mt 3,1-6: "It has not normally occurred to commentators on Matthew that there is any necessity for a Q-*Vorlage* to explain Mt. 3.1-6: W.C. Allen (1907), A.H. McNeile (1915), J. Schniewind (1936), E. Lohmeyer – W. Schmauch (1962), P. Bonnard (1963), J.C. Fenton (1963), E. Schweizer (1973), H.B. Green (1975) explain the wording as a straightforward Matthaean relation to Mark" (p. 271). Note, however, some of their comments on Mt 3,5: "Mt. and Lk. must have derived πᾶσα ἡ περίχωρος τοῦ Ἰορδά-νου either from a non-Marcan source or from a recension of Mk. different from that which we possess" (McNEILE, p. 26); "der Zusatz..., der bei Mt und Lk nur in diesem Stück begegnet und darum wohl schon einer Überlieferung entstammt" (LOHMEYER, 1956, p. 36); "Auf sie [die Redequelle Q] geht vielleicht auch die Angabe von der Täuferpredigt in der 'Umgebung des Jordans' (Mt. 3,5 = Lk. 3,3) zurück" (SCHWEIZER, p. 24).

II. RETROSPECT

1. In contrast to the older debate on the text of Mk, text-critical problems on Mk 1,1-4 now tend to disappear from the discussion of the Mt-Lk agreements against Mk. The Nestle-Aland editions N[17] through N[27] maintain in their apparatus the reference to Lachmann's conjectural omission of Mk 1,2-3, but it is extremely rare in recent studies to find an echo of J. Wellhausen's comment on these verses[26]:

> Mc führt sonst niemals von sich aus eine Alttestamentliche Weissagung an, und hier würde er noch über Matthäus und Lucas hinausgehn... Man wird mit Lachmann ... die zwei Verse als zugesetzt betrachten müssen, obwohl sie ganz fest bezeugt und alt sind.

The verdict on Mk 1,2b has received a much wider acceptance: "ein Einschiebsel eines Späteren aus Mt. 11,10 = Lc. 7,27", "eine früh in den Text eingedrungene Glosse" (Simons); "c'est un glossateur qui lisant le passage dans Lc. ou dans Mt. l'a transposé dans Mc." (Lagrange); "it is best to regard the quotation ... as a later insertion, despite the fact that there is no textual evidence against it" (Taylor)[27]. By dropping 1,2b from the text of Mk the interpolation theory eliminates the negative agreement of Mt 3,3 and Lk 3,4 against Mk. This case is different from the other Mt/Lk agreements in this section: in Mk because of the anomaly of the quotation of Mal 3,1 within the Isaiah quotation, and in Mt/Lk because of the doublet in Mt 11,10 / Lk 7,27 (Q). However tempting it may have been therefore to concur with "the widespread belief" that v.

On Luke's use of Mt as an overlay, without denying the existence of Q, cf. E. SIMONS, *Hat der dritte Evangelist den kanonischen Matthäus benutzt?*, Bonn, 1880. See now R.H. GUNDRY, *Matthew*, Grand Rapids, MI, 1982, ²1994, pp. 41-46; on the περίχωρος phrase: "Luke seems to have borrowed it from Matthew" (p. 46). But note his comment on the omission of Mk 1,2b (cf. Mt 11,10; Lk 7,27): "suggest that these evangelists are following a source different from Mark" (p. 44).

The more exceptional thesis of Matthew's dependence on Lk can be neglected here. Ctr. E. LUPIERI, *Giovanni Battista nelle tradizioni sinottiche* (Studi Biblici, 82), Brescia, 1988. See p. 104, on the περίχωρος phrase in Lk 3,3 (Gen 13,10).

26. *Mc*, 1903, pp. 3-4. For a reply, see E. WENDLING, *Die Entstehung des Marcus-Evangeliums*, Tübingen, 1908, p. 2. The possibility of an interpolation is mentioned by E. Klostermann (*Mk*, 1907, 5; dropped in the later editions); R. Bultmann (*Geschichte*, 1921, 151; ²1931, 261); F. Hauck (*Mk*, 1931, 11: "jedenfalls alter Zuwachs").

27. E. Simons (1880, 22-23), M.-J. Lagrange (*Mc*, 1911, 3), V. Taylor (*Mk*, 1952, 153): all three refer to Holtzmann. In fact, Holtzmann calls it "ein missglückter Einschub aus Mt 11,10, Lc 7,27" (³1901, 112), but in 1863 (*Die synoptischen Evangelien*, p. 67: "von Marcus hereingebracht") as well as in his later commentary he treats Mk 1,2b as a Markan insertion in Urmarcus (1863, 261, 385; cf. ³1901, 17); see below, n. 38.

2b may be a later gloss in Mk[28], most authors now seem to give up this theory because of the lack of textual support[29].

The variant reading ἐν τοῖς προφήταις in Mk 1,2a (for ἐν τῷ Ἡσαΐᾳ τῷ προφήτῃ)[30] would create a new Mt/Lk agreement against Mk and a secondary harmonization to Mt 3,3a / Lk 3,4a ("Isaiah the prophet") in the text of Mk. However, the formula "in the prophets" introducing the composite quotation (Mal 3,1 and Isa 40,3) is rightly suspected to be one of the many "easier" readings of the Majority text (TR)[31].

The omission of Mk 1,1 is cited by W. Schmithals as a negative agreement of Mt/Lk: "V 1 haben Mt und Lk anscheinend noch nicht gelesen; | er dürfte Mk erst später zugewachsen sein"[32]. More recently H. Koester has adopted Schmithals's suggestion: "It is not impossible that a scribe added the phrase 'Beginning of the gospel of Jesus Christ' in order to indicate the point in his manuscript at which the text of another writing began"[33]. One can refer here to Koester's earlier statement: "Since Matthew begins his gospel with the birth narratives of Jesus, one would, of course, not expect Mk 1:1 to appear in Matthew" (1983)[34]. Yet it may be added that Mk 1,1 is probably not wholly absent: "Mt 1,1 imitiert ihn"[35]. All interlocutors in the debate on the minor agreements I mentioned in the first section of this paper assume the authenticity of Mk 1,1. The son-of-God title (if original, as I think it is)[36] and the term εὐαγγέλιον are undeniably Markan usage indeed.

28. See, e.g., E. Klostermann (1907, 5); T. Stephenson (1920, 133); W. Larfeld (1925, 241); A.E.J. Rawlinson (1925, 6); E. Hirsch (1941, 3); T.W. Manson (1949, 69); K. Stendahl (1954, 51); W.E. Bundy (1955, 43); G. Strecker (1962, 63 n. 1); W. Feneberg (1974, 184; and n. 276). — The position of Lagrange (Mt, 1922, cxx: "transporté par un glossateur très ancien") has been most influential. Even for J. Schmid it was "jedenfalls erwägungswert" (1930, 81 n. 2). But see Lc, 1921, p. LVIII: "Il n'est point étonnant qu'il ait omis Mc. 1,2ᵇ, attribué à Isaïe".

29. Cf. C.M. TUCKETT (1984, 135; 1993, 167); M.D. GOULDER (1978, 225; 1989, 393; 1993, 152): see below, n. 88.

30. See the apparatus in N²⁷ and Metzger's Textual Commentary (²1994, 62).

31. Cf. G.D. FEE, The Majority Text and the Original Text of the New Testament, in E.J. EPP – G.D. FEE, Studies in the Theory and Method of New Testament Textual Criticism, Grand Rapids, MI, 1993, pp. 183-208, esp. 197-198. Defenders of this reading are W. Pickering (1977) and J. van Bruggen (Marcus, Kampen, 1988, p. 30).

32. Mk, 1979, p. 73.

33. NTS 35 (1989), p. 370; Gospels (n. 53), p. 13.

34. Cf. ETL 67 (1991), p. 84 (= Evangelica II, 61).

35. E. WENDLING, Entstehung (n. 26), p. 1 n. 3 (in reply to E. Nestle's suspicion that "der Eingang des Mc erst von der Zusammenstellung der vier Evangelien herrühre"). One may hesitate between two competing interpretations of βίβλος γενέσεως..., understood either as the title of the entire gospel (Davies-Allison, 1988, 156) or as referring to the genealogy in 1,2-17 (Gundry, 1982, 131). In each case Mt's opening verse can be compared with Mk 1,1. See the commentaries.

36. The textual debate on Mk 1,1 that is still going on concerns the words υἱοῦ θεοῦ. Cf. A.Y. COLLINS, Establishing the Text: Mark 1:1, in T. FORNBERG – D. HELLHOLM (eds.),

2. The theories of L. Vaganay (Mg), N. Walter (Mk[1]) and A. Fuchs (Dmk) concern not only the triple-tradition section Mk 1,1-6 but also the double-tradition passage Mt 3,7-10 / Lk 3,7-9. Fuchs has developed his hypothesis in three stages: he has proposed the Deutero-Markan redaction to explain, first, the phenomenon of the minor agreements diff. Mk; second, the location of Q passages in relation with Dmk sections; third, the composition of the double-tradition texts in coherence with Dmk as an overall gospel redaction. For other scholars like U. Luz, A. Ennulat, and F. Fendler, Dmk represents in various degrees a less intense redaction of Mk. In their approach they can propose a Dmk recension for (some of) the minor agreements diff. Mk 1,1-6 and retain Q 3,7-9 as the beginning of the independent second source Q. Fuchs himself is (or once was) not unfamiliar with such a view[37]:

> Es ist nicht zu übersehen, daß Mt und Lk hier weit enger miteinander übereinstimmen als im vorausgehenden Täuferabschnitt. Man kann deshalb kaum bezweifeln, daß für diese Perikope in beiden Evangelien die gleiche Quelle benützt wurde, und zwar, wie die Verwandtschaft mit ähnlichen Stücken schließen läßt, ganz unzweifelhaft Q.

Q 3,7-9 is the first double-tradition section and, in the two-source theory, the first Q passage; at least according to the widely accepted description of the contents of the Q source. Vaganay proposes a quite different second source (Sg) including double-tradition material from Lk 9,57–17,37. All double-tradition passages in the earlier chapters, including the Baptist sections in Lk 3 and 7, are assigned to Mg (3,7-9 ... 7,18-35). This is in some sense a variation of Holtzmann's hypothesis of Q 7,18-35 as the beginning of Q and all earlier double-tradition texts assigned to Proto-Mark (A). In this theory, Mk 1,2-3 combines the quotations from the beginnings of each source: Isa 40,3 in 1,2a.3 from

Texts and Contexts. FS L. Hartman, Oslo, 1995, pp. 111-127. Her conclusion: "It is rather unlikely that the words were omitted by accident. But it is quite credible that they were added, either out of piety or to combat too human an understanding of Jesus" (p. 125). Yet, "the weight of the external evidence supports variant (IV), which has these words" (*ibid.*). On internal criticism, "the presence of this theme (in Mark) shows that the words υἱοῦ θεοῦ *may* have stood in the original form of Mark 1:1, not that they in fact did" (p. 121). But can the internal evidence for a reading do more? Accidental scribal error is not the only possible explanation of omission: "erklärt sich aus der ungewöhnlichen Charakterisierung des Evangeliums" (J. Gnilka, 1978, p. 43); "Unter Einfluß des vor allem aus Paulus vertrauten Sprachgebrauchs" (D. Lührmann, 1987, p. 33). See also R.H. GUNDRY, *Mark*, 1993, p. 39.

37. *Intention und Adressaten der Bußpredigt des Täufers bei Mt 3,7-10*, in SNTU 1 (1976) 62-75, here 62. But see now below, n. 89. Compare the development of Fuchs's Dmk with regard to the Markan material: the theory explaining the Mt-Lk agreements against Mk was extended with the assumption that "der gesamte Mk-Stoff nur über Dmk in das Mt- bzw. LkEv Aufnahme fand" (*Exegese*, p. 101 n. 211). Thus, Mk 1,5-6 came to Matthew through Dmk.

A (Mt 3,3; Lk 3,4) and Mal 3,1 in 1,2b from Q (Mt 11,10; Lk 7,27)[38]. For Vaganay, both quotations are from the same source: Mk 1,2a.3 (and par.) is a Mg text and Mk 1,2b is anticipated by Mark from the later context in the same Mg (Mt 11,10; Lk 7,27). Vaganay's Mg can be compared with B. Weiß's Q source[39]. According to Weiß, the Apostolic Source was used by Mark and he argues for the attribution of Isa 40,3 to Q on the basis of Mk 1,2-3: scriptural quotations are exceptional in Mk, and the parallel in Mt 11,10 / Lk 7,27 shows the Q origin of Mk 1,2b (in a different context) and therefore also of Mk 1,2a.3, par. Mt 3,3 / Lk 3,4[40]. The argument will be resumed by B.H. Streeter: "It looks as if Mark's double quotation in this passage is a conflation of the two quotations applied to John in two different contexts of Q"[41].

I conclude this survey with a remark on Weiß's reconstruction of the Q text[42]:

    (Lk 3)
    ἐν ταῖς ἡμέραις ἐκείναις
2b ἐγένετο ῥῆμα θεοῦ ἐπὶ Ἰωάννην τὸν Ζαχαρίου υἱὸν
    ἐν τῇ ἐρήμῳ,
3   καὶ *παραγίνεται* εἰς πᾶσαν τὴν περίχωρον τοῦ Ἰορδάνου.
4   *οὗτός ἐστιν ὁ ῥηθεὶς διὰ Ἡσαΐου τοῦ προφήτου λέγοντος·*
    φωνὴ βοῶντος ἐν τῇ ἐρήμῳ·
    ἑτοιμάσατε τὴν ὁδὸν κυρίου,
    εὐθείας ποιεῖτε τὰς τρίβους αὐτοῦ.
5   πᾶσα φάραγξ πληρωθήσεται
    καὶ πᾶν ὄρος καὶ βουνὸς ταπεινωθήσεται.
    καὶ ἔσται τὰ σκολιὰ εἰς εὐθείας
    καὶ αἱ τραχεῖαι εἰς ὁδοὺς λείας,
6   καὶ ὄψεται πᾶσα σὰρξ τὸ σωτήριον τοῦ θεοῦ.

38. H.J. HOLTZMANN, *Die Synoptiker*, Tübingen, ³1901, p. 17. Cf. above, n. 27.

39. His *Matthäusquelle Q* is in fact a primitive gospel (without a passion narrative). The narrative element in Weiß's reconstruction of Q is not restricted to introductions of double-tradition passages. It includes, besides the presentation of John the Baptist at the beginning (cf. Mt 3,1-3) and the anointing story at the end (Mt 26,6-13), a large amount of Markan material: Mt 8,2-4.24-27.28-34; 9,1-8.18-25; 12,2-8.46-50; 13,3-9; 14,15-21; 15,22-28; 17,2-5.14-20; 21,33-44; 22,35-40.

40. See already in 1861 (p. 61) and 1865 (p. 356). Cf. below, n. 44.

41. *St. Mark's Knowledge and Use of Q*, in *Oxford Studies*, 1911, pp. 165-183, esp. 168.

42. Cf. B. WEISS, *Die Quellen der synoptischen Überlieferung* (TU, 32/3), Leipzig, 1908, pp. 1-74: "Aufstellung der Matthäusquelle (Q)", p. 1. See also *Die Quellen des Lukasevangeliums*, Stuttgart-Berlin, 1907, pp. 189-190. Words from Mt (not in Lk) are printed in italics in the text above.

References to Weiß usually cite this final form of his reconstruction[43]. We may observe here that it differs from his earlier suggestions. It was always his opinion (already in 1861, 1865)[44] that the Source contained a brief presentation of John the Baptist followed by the quotation of Isa 40,3. But, in contrast to 1872 and 1876, the final form assigns to the Source Matthew's παραγίνεται[45] and οὗτός ἐστιν ὁ ῥηθεὶς διά[46]. In 1907, it was also for the first time that he attributed to Q the extension of the quotation in Lk 3,5-6 (= Isa 40,4.5b)[47]. H. Schürmann, in his commentary on Lk (1969), is one of the rare defenders of this full text of Lk 3,4-6 in Q[48]. Practically all later commentators assign the addition

43. Cf. J.M. ROBINSON, *The* Incipit (n. 17), p. 14. See also J.S. KLOPPENBORG, *Q Parallels*, p. 6 ("Weiß 1907").

44. In chronological order: *Zur Entstehungsgeschichte der drei synoptischen Evangelien*, in *TSK* 34 (1861) 29-100, 646-713 (I. "Das kanonische Matthäusevangelium", II. "Das Markusevangelium"), p. 61; *Die Redestücke des apostolischen Matthäus*, in *Jahrbücher für Deutsche Theologie* 9 (1864) 49-140; *Die Erzählungsstücke des apostolischen Matthäus*, ibid., 10 (1865) 319-376, esp. 355-356; *Das Marcusevangelium und seine synoptischen Parallelen*, Berlin, 1872; *Das Matthäusevangelium und seine Lucas-Parallelen*, Halle, 1876; *Die Evangelien des Markus und Lukas* (KEK, I/2), Göttingen, ⁶1878, ⁷1883, ⁸1892 (*Markus*), ⁹1901; *Das Evangelium nach Matthäus* (KEK, I/1), ⁷1883, ⁸1890, ⁹1898, ¹⁰1910.

45. 1908, p. 1 n. 1: "Es ist sehr wahrscheinlich, daß auch das παραγίνεται Mt 3,1 (vgl. Lk 8,19. 11,6 in Q) der Quelle angehört, da sonst nicht abzusehen ist, warum der Aor. Mk 1,4 in das Präsens verwandelt wurde, während das καὶ ἦλθεν Lk 3,3 dem Aor. ἐγένετο v. 2 konformiert ist. Das Präsens entspricht dem folgenden οὗτός ἐστιν». Contrast 1872, p. 42: "Matthäus ... bestimmt das ἐγένετο näher durch παραγίνεται».

46. *Ibid.*, n. 2: "Die ganz eigenartige Zitationsformel, die von der sonst stereotypen bei Matth. abweicht, kann nur als Q sein". Contrast 1876, p. 102, n. 1: "das ῥηθεὶς διά ... verräth die Hand des Evangelisten".

47. 1907, p. 190: "Wenn nun auch die Act. zeigen, daß Lukas ziemlich bewandert im AT. ist, so lag doch hier für ihn nicht der geringste Grund vor, das Zitat nachzuschlagen und zu vervollständigen, da die angebliche Beziehung der πᾶσα σάρξ auf seinen Universalismus, mit dem doch der Ausdruck beim Propheten sicher nichts zu tun hat, immer etwas gesucht ist. Es wird also in Q gestanden haben". Contrast *Lukas*, ⁶1878, p. 314 ("Lukas fügt zu Jes. 40,3 noch V. 4f. hinzu, frei nach den LXX"); ⁹1901, p. 323: "Dagegen ist gar kein Grund, die Erweiterung des Citats dem Lk abzusprechen (vgl. Aufl. 8), der sich in den Act. zweifellos in den LXX bewandert zeigt, da dieselbe offenbar seiner universalistischen Anschauung entspricht" (in reply to J. WEISS, *Lukas*, ⁸1892, p. 350: "Vielleicht schon der zwar judenchristliche, aber doch universalistische Verfasser von LQ").

48. *Lk* (n. 54), p. 161. Contrast J. DUPONT, *Le salut des Gentils et la signification théologique du livre des Actes*, in *NTS* 6 (1959-60) 132-155, pp. 137-138: "il est seul à prolonger la citation d'Isaïe jusqu'au *v*. 5; c'est en cela qu'il fait œuvre personnelle". See also his *Nouvelles études sur les Actes des Apôtres* (LD, 118), Paris, 1984, pp. 38, 131, 346, 348, 509: on Lk 3,5-6 and τὸ σωτήριον τοῦ θεοῦ in Acts 28,28 (cf. Lk 2,30); *Études sur les évangiles synoptiques* (BETL, 70), Leuven, 1985, p. 94: "Il s'était inspiré ... d'une indication fournie par Mc 1,3 (Is 40,3), mais en l'amplifiant pour lui donner les proportions d'un programme; l'importance qu'il attache à cet oracle ressort du fait qu'en Ac 28,28 il termine son ouvrage par un rappel d'Is 40,5".

of Lk 3,5-6 to LkR[49], and we can take it for granted. None of the above-mentioned recent reconstructions of Q (Jacobson, Polag, Catchpole, Lambrecht) includes Lk 3,5-6.

The text of the quotation of Isa 40,3 in Mt 3,3b and Lk 3,4b is strictly identical with Mk 1,3 and there can be no dispute about its wording in Q. On the contrary, the quotation formula allows for several options: the Matthean form (Weiß), the Lukan form (Jacobson), Lk's ὡς... and Mt's διά... combined (Polag), or simply Q = Mk 1,2a (Catchpole; cf. Vaganay: "c'est Mc. qui a le mieux conservé la formule d'introduction")[50]. B.S. Easton's comment forms an excellent transition to our next section on the minor agreements: "Mt's ὁ ῥηθεὶς διά belongs to his own style (1:22, 2:15,17,23, etc), while Lk's ἐν βίβλῳ is 'Lukan' (20:42, Acts 1:20, 7:42, elsewhere in the New Testament only Mk 12:26). So Mk's simple ἐν Ἠσαΐᾳ may be the original form. The Mt-Lk contact of the genitives (Ἠσαΐου τοῦ προφήτου) seems to be accidental"[51].

III. THE MINOR AGREEMENTS

| A. Harnack's reconstruction of Q includes before 3,7ff. nothing more than [. . πᾶσα ἡ περίχωρος τοῦ Ἰορδάνου...][52] and, as noted above, the same reserved position is now adopted in the IQP text. In the years between 1907 and 1992 a considerable list of gospel commentaries and

---

49. Cf. G. Schneider, 1977; J. Ernst, 1977; I.H. Marshall, 1978 ("*Pace* Schürmann"); J. Jeremias, 1980; W. Schmithals, 1980; J.A. Fitzmyer, 1981; J. Kremer, 1988; W. Wiefel, 1988; F. Bovon, 1989; J. Nolland, 1989; L.T. Johnson, 1991; J. Ernst, [2]1993; cf. also T. Schramm (1971, 35); S.G. Wilson (1973, 38-39); R.C. Tannehill (1986, 40). — But see G. HÄFNER, *Der verheißene Vorläufer. Redaktionskritische Untersuchung zur Darstellung Johannes des Täufers im Matthäusevangelium* (SBB, 27), Stuttgart, 1994, p. 6: "nicht ohne weiteres wahrscheinlich zu machen", and the shortening of the quotation in Mt "durchaus denkbar". His observations are admittedly "zu vage" (p. 7).

50. *Le problème synoptique*, p. 351.

51. *Lk* (n. 53), 1926, p. 37. Compare:

Mt 3,3a   οὗτος γάρ ἐστιν ὁ ῥηθεὶς διά   Ἠσαΐου τοῦ προφήτου λέγοντος·
Mk 1,2a   καθὼς   γέγραπται ἐν   Ἠσαΐα τῷ   προφήτῃ·
Lk 3,4a   ὡς   γέγραπται ἐν βίβλῳ λόγων Ἠσαΐου τοῦ προφήτου·

M. Goulder's observation that "'the book λόγων' may ... owe something to Matthew's 'the prophet λέγοντος'" (p. 271) and T. Schramm's suggestion that Mk 1,2 ... ἐν τῷ Ἠσαΐᾳ and Mt 3,3 (= Q) ... διά Ἠσαΐου τοῦ προφήτου λέγοντος are combined in Lk's ἐν βίβλῳ λόγων Ἠσαΐου τοῦ προφήτου (p. 35) are scarcely relevant. On Mt 3,3a, cf. below, pp. 58-59.

52. A. HARNACK, *Sprüche und Reden Jesu. Die zweite Quelle des Matthäus und Lukas* (Beiträge zur Einleitung in das Neue Testament, 2), Leipzig, 1907, pp. 33, 88 (and 109-110: Ἰορδάνης; περίχωρος, ἡ); E.T. (by J.R. Wilkinson): *The Sayings of Jesus. The Second Source of St Matthew and St Luke*, London – New York, 1908, p. 27.

special studies on Mt 3,1-6 / Lk 3,1-6 can be cited in which the existence of Q is accepted without precise indication of its wording other than the περίχωρος phrase[53]. Some authors rather concentrate on the placement

53. Like Harnack, some merely note the περίχωρος phrase as an element of Q: V.H. STANTON, *The Gospels as Historical Documents*, II. *The Synoptic Gospels*, Cambridge, 1909, p. 208: 3a = "due to the influence of the Logian document"; H. CONZELMANN, *Die Mitte der Zeit. Studien zur Theologie des Lukas* (BHT, 17), Tübingen, 1954, p. 11; ³1960, p. 13: "womit zu rechnen ist"; W. GRUNDMANN, *Das Evangelium nach Matthäus* (THNT, 1), Berlin, 1968, p. 90: "wobei ... möglicherweise ein Stück Rahmennotiz der Spruchquelle durchschimmert"; P. HOFFMANN, *Studien zur Theologie der Logienquelle* (NTAbh, 8), Münster, 1972, p. 17: "Vielleicht ... ein Rest der Einleitung von Q; sichere Ergebnisse lassen sich jedoch nicht mehr gewinnnen"; E. SCHWEIZER, *Das Evangelium nach Matthäus* (NTD, 2), Göttingen, 1973, p. 24 (cf. above, n. 25); *Das Evangelium nach Lukas* (NTD, 3), Göttingen, 1982, p. 46: "vielleicht auf Grund von Q"; U. LUZ, *Das Evangelium nach Matthäus*, I (EKKNT, 1/1), Zürich – Neukirchen-Vluyn, 1985, p. 143 n. 1 (cf. below, n. 54); W. SCHENK, *Die Sprache des Matthäus. Die Text-Konstituenten in ihren makro- und mikrostrukturellen Relationen*, Göttingen, 1987, p. 112: περίχωρος "Q-Mt 3,5"; p. 402: πᾶσα 3,5c "(=Q)" (but see p. 85: Ἰορδάνης; and contrast his *Synopse*, 1971: cf. below, n. 155). See also G. HÄFNER, *Vorläufer* (n. 49), 1994, p. 31 (cf. p. 6).

Others suggest an extension of this Q phrase: F. NICOLARDOT, *Les procédés de rédaction des trois premiers évangélistes*, Paris, 1908, pp. 217-218; B.H. STREETER, *The Original Extent of Q*, in *Oxford Studies*, 1911, pp. 185-208, esp. 186: "The agreement ... suggests that Q had also a word or two of narrative introduction" (= *The Four Gospels*, 1924, p. 305); B.S. EASTON, *The Gospel According to St. Luke. A Critical and Exegetical Commentary*, Edinburgh, 1926, pp. 36-37: "points decisively to a non-Markan source; this would have been the preface to the Q section in vv. 7-9"; V. TAYLOR, *Behind the Third Gospel*, Oxford, 1926, pp. 145-146; S. MCLOUGHLIN, *Les accords mineurs Mt-Lc contre Mc et le problème synoptique. Vers la théorie des deux sources*, in *ETL* 43 (1967) 17-40, p. 24 n. 14: "Nous sommes tenté de croire qu'en *Lc.*, III,2b-3a, nous avons l'*incipit* de Q"; T. SCHRAMM, *Der Markus-Stoff bei Lukas* (SNTS MS, 14), Cambridge, 1971, pp. 34-35 (Diss. Hamburg, 1966, pp. 25-26); I.H. MARSHALL, *The Gospel of Luke*, Exeter, 1978, p. 135: "The use of περίχωρος betrays the presence of Q material" (p. 132: "the use of Q ... is highly likely"); W. SCHMITHALS, *Das Evangelium nach Lukas* (Zürcher Bibelkommentare NT, 3/1), Zürich, 1980, p. 49: "Der Anfang des Q-Berichtes kann aus Luk. 3,2bf. und Mat. 3,1f.5 nur mit einigen Unsicherheiten rekonstruiert werden; dann folgte in Q das Zitat (= Luk. 3,4)", but see the following paragraph: "die Fassung und Stellung des Zitats ist sekundär gegenüber Markus"; J.D. CROSSAN, *In Fragments. The Aphorisms of Jesus*, San Francisco, CA, 1983, p. 342; D. ZELLER, *Kommentar zur Logienquelle* (Stuttgarter kleiner Kommentar, NT 21), Stuttgart, 1984, p. 17: "Vielleicht... Doch hier tappen wir ziemlich im Dunkeln"; W.D. DAVIES – D.C. ALLISON, *The Gospel according to Saint Matthew*, I (ICC), Edinburgh, 1988, p. 294 (3,3: "might be explained by the influence of Q") and 297 (3,5: "might be due to Q's account..."); M. SATO, *Q und Prophetie. Studien zur Gattungs- und Traditionsgeschichte der Quelle Q* (WUNT, 2/29), Tübingen, 1988, p. 21 (Diss. Bern, 1984, p. 23): (Q 3,2-4) "der genaue Wortlaut läßt sich nicht rekonstruieren" ("ist völlig unrekonstruierbar"); D. KOSCH, *Die eschatologische Tora des Menschensohnes* (NTOA, 12), Freiburg/Schw. - Göttingen, 1989, p. 217 (and n. 16); F. BOVON, *Das Evangelium des Lukas*, I (EKK 3/1), Zürich - Neukirchen-Vluyn, 1989, p. 166 (and n. 3: "könnten auf Q zurückgehen"); H. KOESTER, *Ancient Christian Gospels*, London - Philadelphia, PA, 1990, p. 135 (cf. below, n. 151). More recently, D.A. HAGNER, *Matthew 1–13* (WBC, 33A), Dallas, TX, 1993, pp. 45 and 49 ("possibly drawn from Q; cf. Luke 3:3"); R. URO, *John the Baptist and the Jesus*

of the quotation (Isa 40,3) after the presentation of John the Baptist[54]. Others are less selective and present three or four of the Mt/Lk agreements listed here below: (1) indication of time, diff. Mk 1,1; (2) order Mk 1,4.2a.3; (3) Mk 1,2b om.; (4) Mk 1,5: Mt 3,5 πᾶσα ἡ περίχωρος τοῦ Ἰορδάνου / Lk 3,3 πᾶσαν τὴν περίχωρον τοῦ Ἰορδάνου[55].

1. Mt 3,1a   ἐν δὲ ταῖς ἡμέραις ἐκείναις
Lk 3,1-2a ἐν ἔτει δὲ πεντεκαιδεκάτῳ τῆς ἡγεμονίας ...
om. Mk

Common source, Q source. WEISS, 1876: "Wir werden also nicht irren, wenn wir annehmen, dass die Quelle mit ἐν ταῖς ἡμέραις ἐκείναις begann" (100). 1908: "Verständlich ist es nur in einer Quelle, die damit begann" (1 n. 1). — VAGANAY, 1954: "Tous deux commencent par une donnée chronologique absente de Mc. ... Matthieu araméen pouvait très bien commencer par le ministère de Jean-Baptiste avec la formule: 'En ces jours-là'" (345). Lk: "au lieu de s'en tenir, comme Mt., à la notation originale, il a préféré la développer à l'aide de nombreux synchronismes" (346). — POLAG, 1979, 28. — JACOBSON, 1992, 80.
I Luke dependent on Mt. SIMONS, 1880: "es scheint ... die chronologische Notiz des Lc. eine Ausführung von ἐν δὲ ταῖς ἡμέραις ἐκείναις Mt. 3,1 zu sein. ... (wir) haben die Erweiterung Lc. 3,1.2 als auf Kenntniss des Mt beruhend zu denken" (22). — GUNDRY, 1982, 41. — GOULDER, 1989: "Matthew began with a loose time-reference, 'In those days'. But to Luke that is quite inadequate... Luke marks the occasion with a seven-fold dating" (270). **Deutero-Mk:** FUCHS, 1980, 63.

Movement: What Does Q Tell Us?, in R.A. PIPER (ed.), *The Gospel Behind the Gospels* (NTSup, 75), Leiden, 1995, pp. 237, 239, 246: "a short narrative description of John's appearance (3:3), although most of it has been covered under the later redactions by Matthew and Luke"; cf. p. 256 (IQP).
    For proponents of Q, see also Kloppenborg's *Q Parallels*, 1988, p. 6. The notation "Not in Q" includes Kloppenborg 1987 (but see now above n. 16); W.L. Knox (but see *The Sources of the Synoptic Gospels*, vol. II, Cambridge, 1957, p. 4 n. 2); Schenk (but see above in this note).
    54. H. SCHÜRMANN, *Das Lukasevangelium*, I (HTKNT, 3/1), Freiburg, 1969, p. 161 ("Lk 3,3-6 folgt Luk Q"): the agreement in order and the omission of Mal 3,1 are mentioned first, and then: "vgl. ferner...". Cf. G. SCHNEIDER, *Das Evangelium nach Lukas* (ÖTKNT, 3/1), Gütersloh-Würzburg, 1977, p. 84 (the περίχωρος phrase is not even mentioned as an agreement); see p. 82: "Q (vgl. VV 3f. mit Mt 3,3)", with no mention of Mt 3,5. Compare J.M. CREED, *The Gospel according to St. Luke*, London, 1930, p. 47: "Luke is following Q" (emphasis on Mk 1,2b om.). — Contrast U. LUZ, *Matthäus* (n. 53), p. 143: "ein Stück der Logienquelle, das vermutlich einen kurzen Bericht über das Auftreten des Täufers mit einem Schriftzitat aus Jes 40,3 ... umfaßte", but see n. 1 (on the περίχωρος phrase): "Ob das Jesajazitat aus Q stammt, muß offenbleiben". See also CATCHPOLE, pp. 217-218 (on περίχωρος) and, almost as an appendix, the agreement of order (p. 218); LAMBRECHT, p. 363 ("most strikingly" the περίχωρος phrase).
    55. For a full description of the minor agreements, see my *The Minor Agreements of Matthew and Luke against Mark with a Cumulative List* (BETL, 37), Leuven, 1974, pp. 55-56 (§ 1: Mc 1,1-6); *The Minor Agreements in a Horizontal-Line Synopsis* (SNTA, 15), Leuven, 1991, p. 11.

The commentaries on Lk, from Schürmann (1969) to Bovon (1989), are almost unanimous: the synchronism in Lk 3,1-2a is clearly Lukan composition ("offensichtlich redaktionell"). It is so characteristically Lukan and so different from "in those days" that we can easily dispense with dependence on Mt or Mt's source. The Proto-Luke hypothesis (Streeter, *et al.*), which is now generally abandoned, seems to have left its vestige[56]:

> ... it seems obvious that 3:1-2 was at one time a formal introduction to the work... Introducing, as it does, the ministry of John the Baptist, it shows that the Lucan Gospel once began at the point at which the Marcan Gospel now begins...
> It again suggests ... that the Lucan infancy narrative was added to the Gospel at a stage later than the rest.

Rather than a two-stage redaction of the Lukan Gospel, Luke's use of Mk from chap. 3 on can explain the composition of Lk 3,1-2a and its place in the structure of Lk (3,1-20; 3,21ff.)[57].

For the phrase "in those days" in Mt 3,1a, I can refer to a comprehensive study recently published by G. Häfner[58]. In the first part of his article the author discusses a variety of interpretations of this "in those days", all unsatisfactory: a loose connecting link, the expression of thematic continuity, a reference to the special time of revelation or to the time of eschatological fulfillment. He then proceeds to a *Neubegründung* of reading "in those days" in connection with 2,23 as a reference to "die Zeit des Wohnens Jesu in Nazaret". Of course, such an interpretation is not new[59], but Häfner's way of arguing and his suggestion concerning the l structure of Mt deserve our attention. He combines a double parallelism, between 2,22-23 and 4,12-16 (settled in Nazareth – settled in

---

56. J.A. FITZMYER, *The Gospel According to Luke*, I (AB, 28), Garden City, NY, 1981, pp. 310, 450. But W. Wiefel rightly replies: "die Rückbeziehung ... auf die Kindheitsgeschichte ('Sohn des Zacharias'; sein Wüstenaufenthalt in 1,80 und 3,2) läßt deren nachträgliche Voranstellung jedoch wenig wahrscheinlich erscheinen" (*Lk*, p. 86). See also G. SCHNEIDER (*Lk*, p. 83).

57. See *ETL* 58 (1982), p. 394; cf. 54 (1978), p. 192. On Lk 3,1-20 and 3,21ff., see now also M. DIEFENBACH, *Die Komposition des Lukasevangeliums unter Berücksichtigung antiker Rhetorikelemente* (FTS, 43), Frankfurt, 1993, pp. 61-65, esp. 62 ("der V. 21 ist wie eine Überschrift zum Leben-Jesu-Erzählzyklus zu verstehen").

58. G. HÄFNER, *"Jene Tage" (Mt 3,1) und der Umfang des matthäischen "Prologs".* *Ein Beitrag zur Frage nach der Struktur des Mt-Ev*, in *BZ* 37 (1993) 43-59. Cf. ID., *Der verheißene Vorläufer* (n. 49), pp. 9, 155-158 ("Johannes der Täufer im matthäischen 'Prolog'").

59. He refers to T. Zahn, T.V. Filson, R.H. Gundry, R.T. France (p. 52 n. 41). One could add that it has been a very common view, from Beza and Maldonatus ("significatur tempus, quo adhuc in Nazareth Christus habitabat") over Bengel and Kuinoel to Meyer, Schanz, *et multi alii*.

Capernaum) and between 3,2 and 4,17 (preaching of John – preaching of Jesus)[60], and regards 2,22-23; 3,1-2 as strongly interconnected in 3,1a: "in those days". Unfortunately, Häfner did not study the "mk Vorlage" and the parallel in Mk 1,9 is not even mentioned[61]. Since Holtzmann (1863), it has been repeated in many commentaries: "Possibly Matthew has taken these words from Mark 1,9" (Fenton), "ἐν ταῖς ἡμέραις ἐκείναις is drawn forward from Mk. 1.9" (Goulder), and Häfner is too well acquainted with Gundry, Luz, Gnilka, Davies and Allison to have missed this comment on "Jene Tage"[62]. Compare Mt 3,1 ἐν δὲ ταῖς ἡμέραις ἐκείναις παραγίνεται Ἰωάννης... with Mk 1,9 καὶ ἐγένετο ἐν ἐκείναις ταῖς ἡμέραις ἦλθεν Ἰησοῦς (par. Mt 3,13 τότε παραγίνεται ὁ Ἰησοῦς). Matthew has assimilated the preaching of John to that of Jesus (3,2 = 4,17)[63] but he has also anticipated aspects of the appearance of Jesus (Mk 1,9; Mt 3,13) in the parallel appearance of John[64]. "In those

60. Häfner thinks that because of these parallelisms Mt 4,12-16.17 should be included in the Prologue of Mt which extends through 4,18-22 (the call of the four disciples). Therefore he rejects the division of Mt 1–2 | 3,1–4,11 | 4,12ff. Cf. *"Jene Tage"*, p. 56; in reaction to my *ΑΠΟ ΤΟΤΕ ΗΡΞΑΤΟ and the Structure of Matthew*, in *ETL* 64 (1988) 21-59 (= *Evangelica II*, 141-182). Some of his references to my essay need to be corrected. Thus, with regard to 2,22-23 and 4,12-16, I had no intention to downgrade their "gegenseitige Bezogenheit" (p. 53 n. 43; *Vorläufer*, p. 157 n. 2). My question was, I quote: "is it justifiable to *separate* the beginning of Jesus' ministry *(4,17)* from its pre-liminaries in *4,12-16* on the basis of similarities with 2,22-23?" (p. 46 = 166, emphasis added). The verbal correspondences between 2,22-23 and 4,12-16 are even more significant if 3,1–4,11 is regarded as Mt's "second prologue", with the double move before: to the land of Israel and from Judea to Galilee (Nazareth), and after: to Galilee and from Nazareth to Capernaum.

61. This is rather strange since elsewhere, with regard to Mt 4,17 (par. Mk 1,15), Häfner rightly observes that "der Verzicht auf die diachrone Betrachtungsweise ... einen Verlust von für die Auslegung wichtigen Hinweisen bedeuten kann" (*Vorläufer*, p. 11 n. 3). This can be true also, I may observe, with regard to Mt 4,12 (par. Mk 1,14).

62. See the commentaries, *ad locum*. Cf. Holtzmann, 1863: "wahrscheinlich aus einem Vorblick auf A Mr. 1,9 zu erklären" (p. 172); Simons, 1880, p. 22. B. Weiss, after a positive comment in 1872 (pp. 42, 49), rejected the dependence on Mk in 1876. The suggestion that Holtzmann retracted his view (T. Zahn, *Matthäus*, [4]1922, p. 121 n. 3: "im Handb. nicht wiederholt") needs to be corrected. Cf. *Die Synoptiker*, [3]1901, p. 147 (at Mt 3,13): "Das ἐν ἐκείναις ταῖς ἡμέραις Mc 9 war schon 3,1 vorweggenommen und wird um so mehr durch das bei Mt so beliebte τότε ersetzt".

63. Of course, this redaction-critical standpoint differs from a reading of the Gospel "in der Perspektive der Leser". Cf. H. Frankemölle, *Matthäus Kommentar*, vol. 1, Düsseldorf, 1994, p. 181.

64. In Mk 1,9 the main character of the Gospel story appears on the scene, and some have taken Mk 1,1-8 as "prologue": see Westcott-Hort, Nestle[1-25], G. Hartmann (cf. *ETL* 55, 1979, p. 347; = *Evangelica*, 915). See now also B.L. Mack (1988, 390). Cf. H. Merklein, in *The Four Gospels 1992* (above, n. 5), p. 231: "Dies würde auch den markanten Neueinsatz mit καὶ ἐγένετο ἐν ἐκείναις ταῖς ἡμέραις in 1,9 gut erklären" (n. 31), and, I may add, explain the advance of the temporal phrase to the beginning at Mt 3,1 as well.

days" in 3,1a | is no doubt a connecting phrase, but its chronological significance is probably less precise than the traditional paraphrase "in diebus *illis*, quibus Jesus Nazarethi habitabat..." (Lucas Brugensis)[65]. Similar phrases in Mt such as ἐν ἐκείνῳ τῷ καιρῷ (11,25; 12,1; 14,1) scarcely allow more to be said.

If Matthew's "in those days" comes from Mk 1,9, the hypothesis of its origin in Q is without foundation. That the indication of time in Q could contain a reference to Herod[66] is an unwarranted suggestion. The phrase ἐγένετο ἐν ταῖς ἡμέραις Ἡρῴδου βασιλέως τῆς Ἰουδαίας in the Gospel of the Ebionites (Panarion 30,13,6) is borrowed from Lk 1,5[67] and can hardly show that "the first Gospel" might begin in this way[68].

2. Diff. Mk 1,2-3.4 where the quotation comes first, Mt 3,1-2.3 and Lk 3,2b-3.4-6 agree in introducing John before the quotation.

"Mt. et Lc. ont conservé sans aucun doute l'ordre original. En effet, c'est l'ordre le plus naturel" (Vaganay)[69]. Yet the "natural" order is an ambiguous argument. A more logical order is not necessarily the more original one and can be the result of redactional improvement. Thus, for Goulder, "Matthew transferred John's preaching 'in the desert' from after the Isaiah quotation ... to its natural place before" and "Luke has followed Matthew's order"[70]. For Fuchs, the transposition is a Deutero-Markan correction, "eine Verbesserung gegenüber Mk", and Dmk is the source used by Matthew and Luke[71]. The Mt/Lk order is secondary to

65. Such an (implicit) emphasis on Nazareth at the beginning of 3,1–4,11 receives no verification in 3,13 where Nazareth is omitted by Matthew (diff. Mk 1,9).

66. Cf. above n. 11 (Jacobson).

67. Note also the clause ὃς ἐλέγετο εἶναι ἐκ γένους Ἀαρὼν τοῦ ἱερέως, παῖς Ζαχαρίου καὶ Ἐλισάβετ (cf. Lk 1,5). Cf. *ETL* 44 (1968), pp. 146-147. On "the general agreement about GEb's dependence on the synoptic gospels", cf. *Evangelica II*, pp. 749-752 (with reference to W.-D. Köhler, 1987).

68. The verbal agreement ἐν δέ / ἐν ἔτει δέ has no source-critical relevance. In Mt 3,1 the reading is uncertain: δέ om. von Soden, Greeven, Gnilka (p. 65 n. 6); cf. McNeile (p. 24: "perhaps"); Davies-Allison (p. 288 n. 2: "one can hardly decide..."). On the use of δέ in Mt 3,1 as a connective (Kingsbury), disjunctive (Hill), or transitional particle (Bauer: "bloße Übergangspartikel"), cf. HÄFNER, *"Jene Tage"*, p. 51 n. 39.

69. *Le problème synoptique*, p. 346.

70. *Luke*, pp. 271, 273.

71. *Überschneidungen* (n. 10), p. 61. Cf. *SNTU* 18 (1993), p. 193; 20 (1995), p. 33: "Weiterentwicklung des Mk-Stoffes". Cf. F. FENDLER, *Studien zum Markusevangelium* (GTA, 49), Göttingen, 1991, pp. 147-190 ("Deuteromarkus"), 173-174: "Die Veränderung stellt eine deutliche und einschneidende Verbesserung des Erzählduktus dar...", and: "So ist auch für diesen Fall mit einer bereits verbesserten Markusvorlage der Seitenreferenten zu rechnen" (contrast p. 160 n. 87, on the omission of Mk 1,2b).

Mk, and in both theories a single editor of Mk (Matthew or Deutero-Mark) is responsible for the change of order. Others assume the existence | of the non-Markan Q source, or of Proto-Mk, for the same reason: "Es ist kaum denkbar, daß Mt und Lk unabhängig voneinander die gleiche Umstellung ... vorgenommen hätten"[72]. But is it really unthinkable? Even if the quotation in Mk 1,2-3 should be taken as a syntactical unit with v. 1 (ἀρχή..., καθὼς γέγραπται...)[73], Matthew and Luke following their disuse of Mk 1,1 will have read vv. 2-3 as syntactically related to v. 4 (καθὼς γέγραπται ... ἐγένετο). The fact that καθὼς γέγραπται usually refers to preceding rather than succeeding material may have stimulated Matthew and Luke to make the same change of order[74].

Matthew not only changed the position of the quotation, he adapted the introduction in partial assimilation to the formula of his *Reflexionszitate*[75]. He also rearranged the second part of the section (without parallel in Lk) by re-ordering Mk 1,5.6 in Mt 3,4.5-6: first the description of John's clothing and diet and then the people coming out to him. In Lk, as a result of the omission of Mk 1,5-6, the presentation of John and the Isaiah quotation are the unique movement in Lk 3,1-6. Through the final position of the quotation and its extension with Isa 40,4.5b (Lk 3,5-6, ending with καὶ ὄψεται πᾶσα σὰρξ τὸ σωτήριον τοῦ θεοῦ)[76], the change of order is so much more than an "agreement" with Mt. Also in the introduction of John, transferred from Mk 1,4, Matthew and Luke go their own way[77].

72. N. WALTER, *Mk 1,1-8*, p. 469 (Proto-Mk). For the Q source, cf. B. Weiß (see above, p. 50), Nicolardot (1908), Easton (1926), Schürmann (1969), Schneider (1977), Polag (1979), Gundry (1982), Davies-Allison (1988), Bovon (1989), Catchpole, Lambrecht, Marcus (1992).

73. D. CATCHPOLE, *Beginning*, p. 219 (= *Quest*, p. 76); J. MARCUS, *The Way* (n. 20), p. 18; I. DUNDERBERG, *Q* (n. 21), p. 511; all with reference to R. Guelich. Cf. M.E. BORING, *Mark 1:1-15 and the Beginning of the Gospel*, in *Semeia* 52 (1991) 43-81, p. 49 (Boring agrees with the majority view that Mk 1,1 is a title).

74. Cf. DUNDERBERG, p. 506. Compare J. NOLLAND, *Luke* I, 1989, p. 138: "The later position of the quotation and the omission of the words from Mal 3:1 are not sufficient to guarantee for Matthew and Luke a common second source here"; L.T. JOHNSON, *Luke*, 1991, p. 66: "Luke's interest in what he thinks is proper sequence is shown by his alteration of Mark's order". — Even F. Fendler (above, n. 71) regards the transposition as a correction which "für unabhängige Redaktoren nicht völlig ausgeschlossen werden kann (der markinische Satzbau wirkt allzu unbeholfen)" (p. 174).

75. Cf. *ETL* 44 (1968), p. 148: "C'est l'ordre normal des *Reflexionszitate* et on doit y voir le travail du même rédacteur. Au chap. XV de *Mt.*, une des rares transpositions dans la seconde partie de l'évangile s'explique de la même façon (XV,3-6.7-9)". See *ETL* 43 (1967), p. 59.

76. Cf. above, nn. 48-49.

77. J.A. FITZMYER, *Luke* I, p. 452, on the move of the phrase ἐν τῇ ἐρήμῳ to Lk 3,2. Cf. below, n. 135. Less understandable is M. Goulder's comment on Lk 3,3: "'... in the

3. Mk 1,2b (om. Mt, Lk)
ἰδοὺ ἀποστέλλω τὸν ἄγγελόν μου πρὸ προσώπου σου,
ὃς κατασκευάσει τὴν ὁδόν σου·
Q 7,27b + ἔμπροσθέν σου

The omission of this quotation of Mal 3,1 (Ex 23,20) in Mt 3,3 and Lk 3,4 can be explained without referring to a common source other than Mk[78]:

> Mark's introduction of his OT quotation(s) as something found in "Isaiah" when the first part of it actually comes from Malachi is something that both later evangelists might have wanted to correct quite incidentally and independently of each other.

It has been objected that Matthew, if he wanted to correct Mk 1,2a, could have changed the introduction to a phrase like διὰ τῶν προφητῶν in 2,23[79]. But Ναζωραῖος is too different, and too enigmatic, to be compared with the explicit scripture quotations in Mt 3,3 par. Mk 1,2-3. Moreover, this objection neglects Matthew's special interest in "Isaiah the prophet"[80]:

4,14   τὸ ῥηθὲν διὰ Ἠσαΐου τοῦ προφήτου λέγοντος
8,17   τὸ ῥηθὲν διὰ Ἠσαΐου τοῦ προφήτου λέγοντος
12,17   τὸ ῥηθὲν διὰ Ἠσαΐου τοῦ προφήτου λέγοντος
13,15   ἡ προφητεία Ἠσαΐου ἡ λέγουσα
13,35   τὸ ῥηθὲν διὰ Ἠσαΐου[81] τοῦ προφήτου λέγοντος.

Because of the presence of the overlap text in Mt 11,10 and Lk 7,27 (Q), one might also think of avoidance of duplication as a possible

---

wilderness/preaching' is in the Matthaean order and wording" (p. 272). Compare the order and the wording of Lk 3,2 ἐν τῇ ἐρήμῳ, 3 κηρύσσων with Mk 1,4 ἐν τῇ ἐρήμῳ καὶ κηρύσσων (ctr. Mt 3,1 κηρύσσων / ἐν τῇ ἐρήμῳ τῆς Ἰουδαίας).

78. FITZMYER, p. 452 (and p. 461). See also, e.g., F.W. BEARE, *The Earliest Records of Jesus*, Oxford, 1962, p. 37: "the error is silently corrected by Matthew and Luke, who cut out the Malachi fragment at this point"; I. DUNDERBERG, *Q* (n. 21), p. 506: "it is hardly surprising...". Cf. above, n. 71 (F. Fendler).

79. G. HÄFNER, *Vorläufer* (n. 49), p. 21. But see his own comment on Mt 11,10: "das Zitat (bot sich) auch nicht dazu, den Fundort näher anzugeben, da es eine Mischung aus Mal 3,1 und Ex 23,20 darstellt, also auch selbst ein zusammenfassender Begriff wie διὰ τῶν προφητῶν (vgl. 2,23) kaum passend war" (pp. 223-224).

80. This is true also with regard to N. Walter who rejects Matthew's "Zitat-Korrektur" in 3,3 by simply referring to Mt 27,9-10 (p. 469). If Matthew's *Vorzugsprophet* (Jeremiah) can be an argument, it applies certainly here in reference to Isaiah.

81. On this reading, cf. F. VAN SEGBROECK, *Le scandale de l'incroyance. La signification de Mt., XIII,35*, in *ETL* 41 (1965) 344-372, pp. 360-364. The reading is adopted in U. LUZ, *Matthäus* II, 1990, p. 336 n. 1.

reason for the omission of Mk 1,2b[82]. More particularly, Matthew's adaptation of the introductory formula of Mk 1,2a (καθὼς γέγραπται...) may indicate that he was conscious of the parallel in 11,10 (οὗτός ἐστιν περὶ οὗ γέγραπται, said by Jesus) when he wrote 3,3a: οὗτος γάρ ἐστιν ὁ ῥηθεὶς... (contrast τὸ ῥηθέν in the introductions to his fulfillment-quotations)[83].

The omission in Lk 3,4 must be seen in connection with the redactional extension of the Isaiah quotation. By extending the text of Isa 40,3 with vv. 4.5b in Lk 3,4-6 Luke shows that he is able to check Mk 1,2-3 "in the book of the words of the prophet Isaiah"[84]. Both Matthew and Luke omit Mk 1,2b, so that the reference to Isaiah is now followed by the text of Isa 40,3: φωνὴ βοῶντος ἐν τῇ ἐρήμῳ...[85]. For Matthew this first line is important after his presentation of John as κηρύσσων ἐν τῇ ἐρήμῳ τῆς Ἰουδαίας (3,1). Luke has a different presentation: the call of John (not his preaching) is located ἐν τῇ ἐρήμῳ (3,2; cf. 1,80) and a different interest in the text of Isaiah: the last line is the important one (Lk 3,6: Isa 40,5b καὶ ὄψεται πᾶσα σὰρξ τὸ σωτήριον τοῦ θεοῦ).

D. Catchpole emphasizes the awkwardness of Mk 1,2b: "This awkwardness is confirmed, of course, by ... the removal of v. 2b by both Matthew and Luke"[86]. If, however, it is agreed that Mk 1,2b has been removed by Matthew and Luke, one may still argue on other grounds for a pre-Markan tradition consisting of vv. 2a.3, but hardly on the basis of the omission of v. 2b in Mt and Lk. B.S. Easton, too, had combined two possibilities: "Lk and Mt have omitted it, partly because it was not in Q, partly because it was not in Isaiah"[87]. I may repeat: if "because it was not in Isaiah" was really a reason for omitting v. 2b, then this common

---

82. G. Häfner, *Vorläufer*, p. 21 (and p. 6 n. 1): omitted in Mt "zwecks Vermeidung einer Dublette" (with reference to S. von Dobbeler, 1988, 161, and J. Ernst, 1989, 157).

83. Οὗτός ἐστιν calls attention to the identity of John: "auf die Person des Johannes gerichtete Aussage". Cf. Häfner, p. 16 (and 22); Gundry, *Matthew*, p. 44: "'This is' anticipates 11:10, where it is traditional (Luke 7:27)". See also *Mark*, p. 42.

84. Cf. I. Dunderberg, *Q* (n. 21), p. 506. This is clearly recognized even by N. Walter: "Lukas hat gewiß in seiner Jesajarolle nachgelesen – und noch ein paar Verse aus Jes 40 angefügt (daß sich darin seine redaktionelle Tätigkeit zeigt, ist allgemein anerkannt). Ihm wäre also die Streichung der 'falschen' Zitatzeilen zuzutrauen" (p. 469). On his view on Mt, cf. above n. 80.

85. The quotation of Isa 40,3 is strictly identical with Mk 1,3, and it cannot be cited as one of the "minor agreements" (and a "significant feature" of the Q quotation of Isa 40,3) that Matthew and Luke "quote that text ... in a form which makes ἐν τῇ ἐρήμῳ define the location of the herald and not that of 'the way of the Lord'". Cf. Catchpole, *Beginning*, pp. 218, 220 (= *Quest*, pp. 75, 77-78).

86. *Beginning*, p. 214 (= *Quest*, p. 71).

87. *Luke* (n. 53), p. 37.

omission cannot be cited as a Lk-Mt contact pointing to the (still unproven) existence of a Q parallel.

The negative agreement between Mt 3,3 and Lk 3,4 and the related problem of the overlap texts in Mk 1,2b and Q 7,27 are intensely debated in recent studies[88]. That Mt 11,10 / Lk 7,27 and the whole of Q 7,24-28 I derive from Q is undisputed among upholders of the two-source theory[89] but there is a lively discussion on stratigraphy[90]. In his recent essay on John the Baptist in Q, L.E. Vaage proposes that there is some sort of consensus on the literary status of Q 7,27[91]: "Virtually all

---

88. M.D. GOULDER, *On Putting Q to the Test*, in *NTS* 24 (1977-78) 218-234, esp. pp. 224-225; *Luke*, 1989, pp. 270-273 (Lk 3,1-6), 392-393 (Lk 7,27); *Luke's Knowledge of Matthew*, in G. STRECKER (ed.), *Minor Agreements. Symposium Göttingen 1991* (GTA, 50), Göttingen, 1993, pp. 143-162, esp. 151-153. — C.M. TUCKETT, *On the Relationship between Matthew and Luke*, in *NTS* 30 (1983-84) 130-142, esp. pp. 134-135; *Mark and Q*, in C. FOCANT (ed.), *The Synoptic Gospels* (BETL, 110), Leuven, 1993, pp. 149-175, esp. 162-168 ("Q 7,27 / Mk 1,2"). — D. CATCHPOLE, *Beginning*, esp. pp. 207-213 (= *Quest*, pp. 63-70: "Jesus' Testimony to John. Q 7:24-28"). — H.T. FLEDDERMANN, *Mark and Q*, 1995 (n. 21), pp. 25-31 (§ 1); cf. F. NEIRYNCK, *Assessment*, esp. pp. 268-270.

89. Defenders of a Proto-Mk without 1,2b (H.J. Holtzmann, ³1901, p. 17; N. Walter, p. 471) can be included. Contrast M.D. Goulder's alternative theory: Matthew has composed the whole passage himself, out of a matrix of Mk 1,2, and Luke copied it (cf. 1993, p. 152). The question remains unclear in A. Fuchs's Dmk theory. See his reply to Tuckett in *Exegese* (1995): "Wie schon zu Beginn dieser Untersuchung erwähnt [p. 30], müßte der Frage tatsächlich nachgegangen werden, ob es sich bei der zitierten Komposition 'ein-fach' um Q handelt oder ob man mit *einer von Dmk aus verschiedenen Traditionen geschaffenen Komposition* rechnen muß. Ohne daß das hier näher behandelt werden kann..." (p. 121; emphasis mine). — A parenthetical remark may be added here in response to Fuchs's complaint that his Dmk hypothesis receives no mention in my *The Minor Agreements and Q* (above, n. 21); he uses the word "verschweigen" (*Exegese*, p. 133; cf. p. 132: "Neirynck verschweigt..."). But see the special paragraph on Dmk in my 1995 article, pp. 52-53. Readers of *ETL* have been regularly informed about the devel-opment of the Dmk hypothesis in Fuchs's work (56, 1980, 397-408; 67, 1991, 366-367; 69, 1993, 429; cf. above nn. 8, 10, 37) and in that of his students (65, 1989, 440-441, 441-442; 67, 1991, 385-390). See also BETL 32, 1989, pp. 360-365 (T.A. Friedrichsen).

90. Cf. J.S. KLOPPENBORG (ed.), *Conflict and Invention. Literary, Rhetorical, and Social Studies on the Sayings Gospel Q*, Valley Forge, PA, 1995, with a presentation of "Recent Studies on Q" by the editor (pp. 1-14) and four essays on "John the Baptist in Q", by W. Cotter, P.J. Hartin, W. Arnal, and L.E. Vaage (pp. 133-202). Cotter's contri-bution (pp. 135-150) presupposes the stratigraphy reconstructed by Kloppenborg (*The Formation of Q*, 1987): the material relating to John in Q 3,7-9.16-17; 7,18-35, belongs to the secondary stage (Q²). Vaage's analysis, here in *More Than a Prophet, and Demon-Possessed: Q and the "Historical" John* (pp. 181-202), and already in his *Galilean Upstarts. Jesus' First Followers According to Q*, Valley Forge, PA, 1994, leads to the conclusion that Q 7,24b-26.28a.33-34 can be assigned to Q's formative stratum (Q¹). Note Kloppenborg's reservation: "there is no good reason to suppose that they already belonged to Q¹" (p. 11).

91. *More Than a Prophet* (n. 90), p. 193. See also *Galilean Upstarts*, p. 184 n. 76: "Most scholars believe..." (with references). More references can be added: e.g., J. ERNST, *Johannes der Täufer. Interpretation – Geschichte – Wirkungsgeschichte*

scholars agree that 7:27 has been secondarily added to 7:24b-26. Many would also agree that 7:27 was inserted at its present location in the Synoptic Sayings Source between 7:26 and 7:28 after 7:28a(b) was first appended to 7,24b-26"[92]. Thus, for J.S. Kloppenborg, for instance, "the best solution is that Q 7:28 was attached to 7:26b first and only later was 7:27 interpolated", whereas for D. Catchpole the secondary editorial elements are I Q 7,27 and 28b. Both recognize the intrusive character of Q 7,27, but they differ considerably in their judgment on Mk 1,2b. While for Kloppenborg the quotation "appears *independently* in a different literary context in Mark 1:2", Catchpole sees in Mk 1,2b "evidence of MarkR based on Q-redaction" and also "evidence of an emergent pre-Marcan tradition consisting of vv. 2a, 3"[93]. Catchpole's reconstruction of the original beginning of Q has here its starting point, in his consideration of the overlap texts in Q 7,27 and Mk 1,2b. H.T. Fleddermann (1995) has resumed the argument, at least as far as Q 7,27 (and not v. 28) and Mk 1,2b (and not vv. 2a.3 = Q) are concerned. His description of the Markan redaction is a more neutral one, in the sense that he avoids speaking of (secondary) insertion in between Mk 1,2a and 3[94]. If one might agree that it could be Mark who brought together Isa 40,3 and Mal 3,1 (Ex 23,20)[95], this would not yet imply the pre-Markan existence of Mk 1,2a.3 in Q. With regard to the consensus of "virtually all scholars", Fleddermann argues that it was indeed "the Q *redactor* (who) assimilated the Malachi quotation to Exodus to fit the context..."[96]. But the preceding context is the (pre-redactional) unit Q

(BZNW, 53), Berlin - New York, 1989, p. 61: "Das Schriftzitat fällt stilistisch und inhaltlich aus dem Rahmen"; M. SATO, in *The Shape of Q* (1994; below n. 102), p. 167: "In all probability, Q 7:27 is a later interpolation" (= *Q und Prophetie*, 1988, p. 35).

92. Vaage continues: " ... at the earliest, 7:27 was first introduced into Q when the two sayings-complexes regarding John in 3:7b-9,16-17 and 7:18-35 were created. In fact, it may have been even later" (*ibid.*), and he adds in n. 44: "7:27 may, in fact, be due to Q's tertiary redaction" (p. 202). Cf. *Galilean Upstarts*, p. 186 n. 10.

93. KLOPPENBORG, *Formation*, pp. 110, 108 (emphasis mine); CATCHPOLE, *Beginning*, pp. 213, 214 (*Quest*, pp. 70, 71).

94. *Mark and Q*, pp. 25-30 (and 31 n. 24): "Mark took over the Q quotation, joined the traditional quotation from Isaiah to it, and then erroneously attributed the whole to Isaiah because he only knew the origin of the last part of the combined quotation" (p. 30).

95. Note, however, that for instance F. Hahn, in his *Christologische Hoheitstitel* (FRLANT, 83), Göttingen, 1963, regards the combination of quotations in Mk 1,2-3 as pre-Markan (p. 378). Cf. p. 379: "(es) ist nicht zu verkennen, daß beide Zitate vom Vorangehen und vom Zurüsten des Weges sprechen, also offensichtlich als Parallelaussagen miteinander verbunden worden sind, wobei dem älteren Schriftbeweis Mal 3,1 später Jes 40,3 an die Seite gestellt wurde".

96. *Mark and Q*, p. 39 (emphasis mine); cf. p. 30.

7,24b-26, and there is a now growing conviction that the statement in 7,26 ("something more than a prophet") needs further explication[97]. C.M. Tuckett has shown that "v. 27 provides a very good conclusion to vv. 24-26 and there is no need to drive too much of a wedge between the two"[98].

The quotation in Q 7,27 in combination with "Q" 3,4 plays a special role in A.D. Jacobson's theory[99]. The first section in Q (from 3,1 to 7,35) | begins and ends with material dealing with John and the introductory and concluding pericopes both cite an Old Testament passage referring to a way being prepared (Q 3,4 and 7,27)[100]. On the one hand, Jacobson tends to assimilate Q 7,27 to "Q" 3,4: the quotation "seems to use Mal 3,1 not as an allusion to an Elijanic messenger but simply to refer to one who prepares the way, as in Q 3:4"[101]. On the other hand, the use of Mal 3,1 in Q differs from Mk 1,2b which subordinates John to Jesus: the quotation occurs later, during Jesus' ministry, so that John's work is not something done before Jesus arrives but still has validity during the ministry of Jesus; John is independent, a prophet in his own right: he prepares the way for the coming of Yahweh in judgment[102]. Jacobson's comments on Q 7,27 ("The ὁδός that is prepared is in Q 7:27 the people's"; "In any case, Mal 3:1 is here used to designate John as forerunner of Yahweh") miss the point. He stresses the first part of the quotation, Ex 23,20 (and 21)[103], unfortunately without noticing

---

97. C.M. TUCKETT, *Mark and Q* (1993), p. 165 n. 58. Cf. J. NOLLAND, *Luke* I, p. 335: "a quotation of Mal 3:1 or, perhaps even an allusion to the verse would seem to be an inalienable part of the unit"; cf. p. 337: "the text does seem to have a more logically coherent development if v 27 is retained in some form". See also K. BACKHAUS, *Die "Jüngerkreise" des Täufers Johannes* (PTS, 19), Paderborn, 1991, p. 56 n. 194: "ein ursprünglicheres Äquivalent (wäre) zu vermuten".

98. Cf. his *Mark and Q*, pp. 165-166. See the quotation (with approval) in my *Assessment* (1995), pp. 268-269.

99. *The First Gospel* (n. 11 above). Leaving aside the dispute on the redactional stage of Q 7,28 (p. 116: "a late creation"; cf. TUCKETT, p. 163) I mention here Jacobson's suggestion that Q 7,24-27 may originally have been joined to Q 6,47-49 (pp. 114, 119, 129). Though one may be skeptical about the evidence of catchword linking, it shows that for Jacobson Q 7,27 is not a late interpolation. Cf. above, nn. 91-92 (and 97).

100. Cf. *The First Gospel*, p. 115: "the idea that John 'prepared the way' (is) a point also made in the citation of Isa 40:3 in Q 3:4". See also p. 128: "both use Old Testament citation formulas which are nearly the same". But γέγραπται is the only common element in his reconstruction of "Q" 3,4 (above n. 11).

101. *Ibid.*, p. 119.

102. *Ibid.*, pp. 69, 81, 115, 119. For the first passage on "John the Baptist" (p. 69), cf. his *The Literary Unity of Q*, in *JBL* 101 (1982) 365-389, esp. pp. 380-381; reprinted in J.S. KLOPPENBORG (ed.), *The Shape of Q*, Minneapolis, MN, 1994, pp. 98-115, esp. 106-107.

103. *The First Gospel*, p. 115.

that the combination with Ex 23,20 (LXX ... τὸν ἄγγελόν μου πρὸ προσώπου σου) contributes to the change of "before me" to "before you" in the quotation of Mal 3,1[104]: in Q 7,27, not unlike Mk 1,2b, John is identified as the precursor of Jesus. The saying in Q 7,24-27 looks back to the "ministry" of John in the past.

4. Mt 3,5b καὶ   **πᾶσα ἡ περίχωρος τοῦ Ἰορδάνου**
    Lk 3,3a   καὶ ἦλθεν εἰς πᾶσαν τὴν περίχωρον τοῦ Ἰορδάνου

I The περίχωρος phrase in Mt 3,5 and Lk 3,3 is one of the significant minor agreements of Mt and Lk against Mk[105]. It can be no surprise that this phrase is found in all reconstructions of Q (Polag, Jacobson, Catchpole, Lambrecht) or other source texts behind Mt 3,5 / Lk 3,3 (B. Weiß, Vaganay, Walter). The verbal agreements of such a five-word phrase are impressive, though, as it is the case in many other minor agreements, here too these striking agreements imply "a certain amount of disagreement"[106]. The definite article τήν in Lk is omitted in Westcott-Hort and bracketed in Nestle-Aland (already in UBS 1966), but its omission (A B L N W Ψ *l*844 *pc*; Or) can be accidental. It is more important that Lk has the accusative, which is governed by ἦλθεν εἰς, and that its location differs from Mt 3,5. The immediate context in Mt is clearly Markan:

Mt 3,5-6	Mk 1,5
[5]τότε ἐξεπορεύετο πρὸς αὐτὸν	καὶ ἐξεπορεύετο πρὸς αὐτὸν
Ἱεροσόλυμα	
καὶ πᾶσα ἡ Ἰουδαία	πᾶσα ἡ Ἰουδαία
καὶ πᾶσα ἡ περίχωρος	χώρα
τοῦ Ἰορδάνου,	καὶ οἱ Ἱεροσολυμῖται πάντες,

104. Q 7,27 τὴν ὁδόν <u>σου</u> ἔμπροσθέν <u>σου</u> (Mal 3,1 LXX ὁδὸν πρὸ προσώπου <u>μου</u>). Τὴν ὁδόν σου may be used to balance τὸν ἄγγελόν σου and ἔμπροσθέν σου to avoid repeating πρὸ προσώπου σου (FLEDDERMANN, p. 27). The omission of ἔμπροσθέν σου in Mk 1,2 is rightly seen in connection with the following v. 3: "Mk 1,2c dürfte ... mit Rücksicht auf die Korrespondenz zu V 3b (τὴν ὁδόν σου – τὴν ὁδὸν κυρίου) gekürzt sein" (R. PESCH, *Mk* I, p. 78; cf. J. LAMBRECHT, *John the Baptist*, p. 372 n. 56).
    In M. Goulder's reversal of Mark's use of (a text like) Q 7,27, the prepositional phrase ἔμπροσθέν σου has been added by Matthew: "This phrase is almost certainly Matthew's own, ἔμπροσθεν being a favourite word of his" (1974, p. 225); "Luke prefers ἐνώπιον» (1993, p. 152). But Q 7,27 is not the only instance of ἔμπροσθεν + gen. in Q (cf. 10,21; 12,8a.b) and Matthew can occasionally have taken this "favourite word" from his source, as in Mt 17,2 (= Mk). Moreover, Goulder (1989, p. 587) agrees that ἔμπροσθεν is used redactionally by Luke in Lk 5,19; 14,2; 19,27; 21,36.
105. See my *The Minor Agreements and the Two-Source Theory*, in *Evangelica II*, 1991, pp. 3-42, esp. 10 ("Significant Agreements"); reprinted in G. STRECKER (ed.), *Minor Agreements* (n. 88), 1993, pp. 25-63, esp. 32.
106. Cf. *ETL* 60 (1984), p. 41 (= *Evangelica II*, p. 91).

⁶καὶ ἐβαπτίζοντο
　ἐν τῷ Ἰορδάνῃ ποταμῷ
　ὑπ' αὐτοῦ
　ἐξομολογούμενοι
　τὰς ἁμαρτίας αὐτῶν.

καὶ ἐβαπτίζοντο
　ὑπ' αὐτοῦ
　ἐν τῷ Ἰορδάνῃ ποταμῷ
　ἐξομολογούμενοι
　τὰς ἁμαρτίας αὐτῶν.

The context of the phrase in Lk is rather Mk 1,4, or at least some elements of it, which in Lk are advanced before the quotation of Isa 40,3:

Lk 3,2b
²ᵇἐγένετο ῥῆμα θεοῦ ἐπὶ Ἰωάννην...
　ἐν τῇ ἐρήμῳ
³καὶ ἦλθεν
　εἰς **πᾶσαν τὴν περίχωρον**
　　τοῦ Ἰορδάνου
κηρύσσων βάπτισμα μετανοίας
　εἰς ἄφεσιν ἁμαρτιῶν.

Mk 1,4
ἐγένετο Ἰωάννης...
　ἐν τῇ ἐρήμῳ
καὶ

κηρύσσων βάπτισμα μετανοίας
　εἰς ἄφεσιν ἁμαρτιῶν.

The differences in the location of the περίχωρος phrase in Mt and Lk have apparently embarrassed the reconstruction of a non-Markan source. I Three options can be observed. While Vaganay (Mg) and Lambrecht (Q) follow the Matthean wording of the phrase and its placement within Mk 1,5 (Mt 3,5-6), Weiß[107], Jacobson and Catchpole have the Lukan ἦλθεν εἰς... before the quotation, as in Lk 3,3; Polag also adopts the Lukan phrase but relocates καὶ ἦλθεν εἰς... after the quotation. A minimal form of reconstruction simply takes the text of Lk 3,3a: "John came into all the region about the Jordan" (Kloppenborg, 1990)[108].

Some efforts were made to include the verb ἦλθεν with the Mt-Lk agreements. B. Weiß's reconstruction replaces ἦλθεν with παραγίνεται from Mt 3,1. T. Zahn separates the περίχωρος phrase from the verb ἦλθεν: "Es wird also ἦλθεν für sich im Sinne von 'er trat auf' zu nehmen und εἰς πᾶσαν τ. π. mit κηρύσσων zu verbinden sein"[109]. M.-J. Lagrange compares παραγίνεται with ἦλθεν: "convient bien ici pour marquer l'entrée en scène de Jean; ici dans le sens de survenir, plutôt que d'être présent. C'est la même nuance que Lc. (ἦλθεν)"[110].

---

107. Weiß's reconstruction is unique in adopting Lk 3,2b (SLk) together with 3,3a (and using Mt's παραγίνεται instead of ἦλθεν). Compare also his use of Lk 3,5-6 (SLk) and Mt's quotation formula.

108. Cf. above, n. 16. On the περίχωρος phrase as Q element (without reconstruction of a Q narrative), see nn. 52-54.

109. *Das Evangelium des Lucas*, Leipzig-Erlangen, 1913, ³⁻⁴1920, p. 190. For criticism, see the commentaries on Lk by E. Klostermann (1919, 11; ²1929, 52); F. Hauck (1934, 49); W. Grundmann (1961, 102); H. Schürmann (1969, 155 n. 51).

110. *Matthieu*, 1922, p. 46.

H. Schürmann thinks that the absolute use of ἦλθεν was found in the Q source: "Er [Luke] wird ein ursprünglich absolutes καὶ ἦλθεν durch Einfügung der Zielbestimmung irritiert haben" (with reference to "das parallel stehende absolute παραγίνεται Mt 3,1")[111]. Since Schürmann does not at all contest Matthew's redactional use of παραγίνεται in 3,1 (par. Mk 1,4 ἐγένετο) and 3,13 (par. Mk 1,9 ἐγένετο ... ἦλθεν)[112], I do not see how this παραγίνεται could suggest the existence of an original absolute ἦλθεν which has left no trace in the Lukan text itself.

The main argument for Q-origin of the περίχωρος phrase seems to be that "both Matthew and Luke use the phrase quite awkwardly"[113]. For Catchpole, "the MattR combination of it with τότε ἐξεπορεύετο πρὸς αὐτὸν Ἱεροσόλυμα καὶ πᾶσα ἡ Ἰουδαία is awkward"[114]. This is an intriguing statement indeed, when confronted with R.H. Gundry's comment that "we can easily see how Matthew developed the phrase from Mark"[115]. Catchpole's problem is that "it hardly makes sense to say that I the surrounding area of Jordan went *out* to the Jordan". If this is a real problem (though the text of Mt = Mk reads: to him, and not: to the Jordan)[116], it would be an objection against Lambrecht's reconstruction of the Q source ("All the region about the Jordan went out to him") but much less against Matthew's redactional addition to the text of Mk 1,5. The subject of ἐξεπορεύετο in Mk is πᾶσα ἡ Ἰουδαία χώρα καὶ οἱ Ἱεροσολυμῖται πάντες. This is one of Mark's typical double expressions with a progression from general (Judea) to special (Jerusalem)[117], first the region and then (the inhabitants of) the city, with πᾶσα and πάντες in a chiastic position. Mark uses ἡ Ἰουδαία again in 3,7; 10,1; 13,14; but never as an adjective with χώρα and never by metonymy for the inhabitants (cf. 13,14 οἱ ἐν τῇ Ἰουδαίᾳ!). The metonymical use of ἡ Ἰουδαία is equally unique in Matthew (3,5)[118]. The change of

111. *Lk*, 1969, pp. 154-155 n. 51. Cf. p. 154: "In ἦλθεν klingt das absolute ἦλθεν der Tradition vielleicht noch leicht nach". On p. 161 it is cited as one of the Mt-Lk agreements: "die verwandte Schilderung des Auftretens des Täufers".
112. *Ibid.*, p. 155 n. 51: "das ... Luk aber kaum vermieden hätte".
113. *City and Wasteland* (n. 16), p. 150.
114. *Beginning*, p. 217 (= *Quest*, p. 74).
115. *Matthew*, p. 46.
116. See my *The Minor Agreements and Q*, p. 71, with a more ad hominem response referring to Lk's ἐκπορευομένοις for ἐρχομένοις in Q 3,7a (Catchpole's reconstruction).
117. Cf. *Duality in Mark*, p. 96 (no. 11). See W.M.L. DE WETTE, *Markus*, ³1845, p. 170, who compares Mk 1,5 "*und* (insbesondere) *die Jerus.*" with Mk 16,7 "*und* (namentlich, insbesondere) *dem Petrus*" (p. 253).
118. Cf. Mt 4,25; 19,1; 24,16: par. Mk; Mt 2,2.5.22; and 3,1 (τῆς Ἰουδαίας, added to ἐν τῇ ἐρήμῳ).

Ἱεροσολυμῖται (unique in Mk, never in Mt)[119] to Ἱεροσόλυμα, in parallel to πᾶσα ἡ Ἰουδαία, can be compared with Mt 2,3 (ἐταράχθη καὶ πᾶσα Ἱεροσόλυμα μετ' αὐτοῦ)[120]. Only in 2,3 and 3,5 does Matthew use the form Ἱεροσόλυμα metonymically, in both occurrences as a singular feminine noun in the nominative[121]. Gundry notes the conformity to 2,3: "Matthew has emphasized Jerusalem as a place full of persecutors by using 'all' with 'Jerusalem' in 2:3. But he will not admit to a Jerusalem full of penitents; therefore he omits 'all' here"[122]. However, Gundry seems to neglect that in 3,5 Ἱεροσόλυμα is followed by καὶ πᾶσα ἡ... καὶ πᾶσα ἡ... The repetition of πᾶσα before περίχωρος is of course parallel to πᾶσα ἡ Ἰουδαία, but is it not also reminiscent of the residual word πάντες, following on πᾶσα ἡ Ἰουδαία, in Mk 1,5? More correctly, Gundry observes that "Mark's χώρα drops out as awkward after the noun Ἰουδαία» and that "Matthew immediately takes up χώρα into περίχωρος». The word περίχωρος is used once more in Mt: 14,35 ὅλην τὴν περίχωρον ἐκείνην (for ὅλην τὴν χώραν ἐκείνην in Mk 6,55)[123]. The addition of the Jordan region in association with Judea may l have been suggested by καὶ πέραν τοῦ Ἰορδάνου in Mk 3,8 (v. 7 ἀπὸ τῆς Ἰουδαίας) and 10,1 (after εἰς τὰ ὅρια τῆς Ἰουδαίας)[124]. The parallel to Mk 3,7-8 in Mt 4,25 is most significant:

119. Jn 7,25 is the only other occurrence of the gentilic in the New Testament.

120. Cf. Mt 21,10 (καὶ εἰσελθόντος αὐτοῦ εἰς Ἱεροσόλυμα) ἐσείσθη πᾶσα ἡ πόλις. See also Mt 8,34 πᾶσα ἡ πόλις (diff. Mk); Mk 1,33 ὅλη ἡ πόλις (om. Mt).

121. Compare Mt 23,37 (Q) the indeclinable form Ἱερουσαλήμ (bis). The nine other occurrences of the Hellenistic form are 2,1; 5,35; 16,21; 20,17.18; 21,1.10: εἰς Ἱεροσόλυμα; 4,25; 15,1: ἀπὸ Ἱεροσολύμων.

122. *Matthew*, p. 45.

123. In Gundry's opinion περίχωρος (for χώρα) in Mt 14,35 may have been influenced by Mark's verb περιέδραμον: "the prefix περι- is a remnant of the replaced verb" (p. 301). It is more important to note how the choice of περίχωρος is consistent with Matthew's general reworking of Mk 6,53-56. Matthew clearly distinguishes between "that place" and "the surrounding district" and replaced Jesus' healing ministry from place to place with a healing activity at this one place where the sick are brought to him. Thus, for Mark's περιέδραμον ὅλην τὴν χώραν ἐκείνην, Matthew has οἱ ἄνδρες τοῦ τόπου ἐκείνου ἀπέστειλαν εἰς ὅλην τὴν περίχωρον ἐκείνην. W. Schenk rightly observes that here, like in 3,5, περίχωρος is used for "die ganze *Bewohnerschaft*" (art. περίχωρος, in *Sprache*, p. 112).

124. Mk 10,1 εἰς τὰ ὅρια τῆς Ἰουδαίας [καὶ] πέραν τοῦ Ἰορδάνου. Cf. V. TAYLOR, *Mark*, 1952, p. 416: "a journey through Peraea to Judaea. ... there is a similar inversion in xi.1, where Jerusalem is the place reached last". The reading without καί (J. Wellhausen, W. Marxsen, J. Gnilka) can be an assimilation to Mt 19,1 (B.M. Metzger). The omission of καί in Mt 19,1 (variant reading in Mk 10,1) seems to take Transjordan as part of Judea. Cf. GUNDRY, p. 375; O. BETZ, art. Ἰουδαία, in *EWNT* II (1981) 468-470, p. 469: "das von Herodes Antipas regierte Peräa wird also hier zu Judäa gerechnet". — Two other interpretations have been suggested. First, πέραν τοῦ Ἰορδάνου is read in connection with ἔρχεται (Mk) or ἦλθεν (Mt) indicating the way through Perea

ἀπὸ τῆς Γαλιλαίας καὶ Δεκαπόλεως
καὶ Ἱεροσολύμων καὶ Ἰουδαίας καὶ πέραν τοῦ Ἰορδάνου.

We note here the same inversion of Mark's Judea-Jerusalem to Jeru-salem-Judea, followed by the Jordan region, ἡ περίχωρος τοῦ Ἰορδά-νου in 3,5 taking the place of πέραν τοῦ Ἰορδάνου. This assimilation in 3,5 and 4,25 of the people's coming to John and to Jesus is only one aspect of the John-Jesus parallelization in the Matthean redaction[125]. Thus, within the "Markan" context of Mt 3,5-6, the mention of the Jor-dan region in v. 5 prepares for the people's baptism in the Jordan in v. 6, | with ἐν τῷ Ἰορδάνῃ ποταμῷ[126] being advanced before ὑπ' αὐτοῦ. Thus, in all its elements, καὶ πᾶσα ἡ περίχωρος τοῦ Ἰορδάνου is explainable as part of Matthew's rewriting of Mk 1,5[127]. It can be added that the word περίχωρος occurs once in Mk: εἰς ὅλην τὴν περίχωρον τῆς Γαλιλαίας (1,28). It is changed to εἰς ὅλην τὴν Σύριαν in Mt 4,24a, but its possible influence on Matthean phraseology is perhaps not to be restricted to this direct parallel[128]. And finally, the full phrase πᾶσα

(Meyer, B. Weiß, Zahn, *et al.*); compare the variant reading διὰ τοῦ in Mk 10,1 (Textus Receptus; G. Wohlenberg). Second, Judea beyond the Jordan in Mt 19,1 is understood from the evangelist's Transjordanian standpoint (F. Delitzsch, 1850; K.R. Köstlin, 1853): H.D. SLINGERLAND, *The Transjordanian Origin of St. Matthew's Gospel*, in *JSNT* 3 (1979) 18-28: origin of Mt in Pella on the basis of 19,1 (pp. 18-22) and 4,15 (πέραν τοῦ Ἰορδάνου said of Galilee in the quotation); G. THEISSEN, *Lokalkoloritforschung in den Evangelien*, in *Evangelische Theologie* 45 (1985) 481-499, pp. 492-493: "Eindeutig ist Mt 19,1, da hier Judäa 'jenseits des Jordan' lokalisiert wird"; see also Mt 4,15.25. Cf. *Lokalkolorit und Zeitgeschichte in den Evangelien* (NTOA, 8), Freiburg/Schw. - Göttin-gen, 1989, p. 261 (= *The Gospels in Context*, Edinburgh, 1992, pp. 249-250). See also W. SCHENK, *Sprache*, 1987, art. πέραν, p. 112: "unmißverständlich" in the *Rahmenstellen* 4,15 and 19,1; less certain in 4,25; possible also in εἰς τὸ πέραν 8,18.28 (Gadara); 14,22; 16,5: Matthew's *Standort* in Damascus or in Gadara? But see the commentaries on Mt 4,24a and the Syrian provenance of the Gospel: this, too, is "no more than a guess" (D.A. HAGNER, *Mt*, p. 80).
125. Compare Gundry's comment on Mt 4,25: "Matthew reverses Mark's order of Judea and Jerusalem to conform to his distinctive order in 3:5. Mark's references to Idumea and Tyre and Sidon drop out, again for conformity to 3:5. But 'Transjordan' remains because of its correspondence to 'the region around the Jordan' in 3:5. Matthew wants to match 3:5 in order to parallel so far as possible the ministries of John and Jesus". W. Schenk (*Sprache*) rightly emphasizes the correspondence between 3,5 and 4,25: pp. 64 (art. Ἱεροσόλυμα), 131 (art. Ἰουδαία), 112 (art. πέραν): 4,25 "in Angle-ichung an 3,5 (Täufer-Jesus-Parallelität)".
126. Ποταμῷ om.: Textus Receptus, von Soden, Greeven, Boismard.
127. Cf. J. GNILKA, *Mt* I, p. 64 n. 2: "Es ist kaum anzunehmen, daß E diese Bemerkung in Q las, da er sich in diesem Abschnitt deutlich an die Mk-Vorlage hält".
128. Cf. GUNDRY, *Mt*, p. 45, on περίχωρος in Mt 3,5: "suggested perhaps by Mark 1:28"; LUZ, *Mt* II, p. 413, on Mt 14,35: "eine nicht gebrauchte Wendung aus Mk 1,28"; SCHENK, art. περίχωρος, p. 113, on 14,35: "wo das mk Simpl. durch das aus Mk 1,28 permutierte Komp. ersetzt wurde". — On the parallel(s) to Mk 1,28 on Lk, see below p. 68.

ἡ περίχωρος τοῦ Ἰορδάνου occurs in the LXX, and those who, with Kloppenborg, are ready to accept that it was used in Q under the influence of Gen 13,10 can hardly deny some possible LXX influence on Matthew's redaction of Mk 1,5[129].

Kloppenborg is not unaware of the parallel between Mt 3,5 and 4,25: "His (Matthew's) intent is probably to anticipate the description of the locales from which Jesus' followers come in Matt 4:25"[130]. Although there is indeed a certain degree of conformity (Jerusalem – Judea – 'Jordan'), this should not be radicalized to an identification with "those who would later follow Jesus". Compare G. Häfner's comment on the parallel between Mt 3,5 and 4,25[131]:

> ...ist ein Beweis dafür, daß sich die beiden gegenläufigen Tendenzen der Angleichung und Unterordnung auch in diesem Punkt treffen können. Denn: Einerseits verbindet Johannes mit Jesus im Zulauf der Menschen die Tatsache eines positiven Echos auf ihr Wirken, andererseits übertrifft Jesus den Täufer in dieser Hinsicht.

| The parallel between Mt 3,5 (John) and 4,25 (Jesus) is a rather unsure basis for the statement that Matthew "is using 'the region of the Jordan' in a much broader sense than normal"[132].

With regard to Lukan redaction there is a common assumption in all sorts of theories on the "Matthean" setting of the περίχωρος phrase (par. Mk 1,5)[133]: Luke transfers the whole phrase to Lk 3,3 (before the

---

129. See my *Une nouvelle théorie synoptique (à propos de Mc., I,2-6 et par.)*, in *ETL* 44 (1968) 141-153; = *Jean et les Synoptiques* (BETL, 49), 1979, pp. 299-311: "on ne voit pas très bien comment la référence à *Gen.*, XIII,10 puisse devenir un argument en faveur d'une rédaction exclusivement lucanienne. L'expression biblique peut s'insérer aussi dans la rédaction d'un *Mt.*!" (p. 150 = 308). See the reference in I. DUNDERBERG, *Q* (n. 21), p. 507 n. 24, with a rather curious comment: "but even here the common source of Matthew and Luke is preferred". My note (in reply to M.-É. Boismard's 1966 theory, cf. below n. 141) was written in defense of "une rédaction matthéenne indépendante". Dunderberg seems to have misread my last sentence: "D'autres, cependant, ..." (*ibid.*).

130. *City and Wasteland*, p. 150.

131. *Vorläufer*, p. 403. See also p. 33: "Zugleich wird ... dieser (Johannes) mit Jesus parallelisiert – und ihm untergeordnet". Cf. H. FRANKEMÖLLE, *Matthäus* (n. 63), p. 179: "Jesus überragt Johannes bei weitem, auch wenn Matthäus sehr groß von Johannes redet"; and, in contrast to "geographical confusion" (Kloppenborg): "die matthäische Partitur ist geographisch stimmig, nicht um der Geographie willen, sondern Orte sind Zeichen für die in ihnen handelnden Personen".

132. KLOPPENBORG, p. 150. He notes, however, that "the exact extent of the region is unclear". Anyway, in an evaluation of the Matthean geography, the "technical connotation" of the term cannot be taken as the unique criterion.

133. This can be Lukan dependence on Mt (SIMONS, 1880, 22; GUNDRY, 1982, 46; GOULDER, 1989, 271); on Dmk (FUCHS, 1980, 65: "ein Text, der von Lk nachträglich vorausgestellt wurde"; in Mk 1,5 "mochte ein späterer Leser oder Redaktor die Erwäh-

quotation) and changes the metonymy to the geographical name of the region, in the accusative, connected with ἦλθεν εἰς. Those who restrict the Q element in Lk 3,2b-3 to the περίχωρος phrase itself, with no context[134], defend in fact the same view on Lukan redaction. In contrast to Mk 1,4, ἐν τῇ ἐρήμῳ is used by Luke to locate John's call and with ἦλθεν εἰς he indicates a distinctive location for John's activity[135]. This may create complications because of the quotation in Lk 3,4 (ἐν τῇ ἐρήμῳ)[136] and Jesus' saying about John in Lk 7,24Q (εἰς τὴν ἔρημον). But the insertion of ὑπέστρεψεν ἀπὸ τοῦ Ἰορδάνου in Lk 4,1, following the baptism of Jesus, shows the same Lukan interest in separating the Jordan region and the ἔρημος[137].

The term περίχωρος is used by Luke three times in dependence on (or in assimilation to) Mk 1,28:

> καὶ ἐξῆλθεν ἡ ἀκοὴ αὐτοῦ εὐθὺς πανταχοῦ
>   εἰς ὅλην τὴν περίχωρον τῆς Γαλιλαίας.
> Lk 4,37 καὶ ἐξεπορεύετο ἦχος περὶ αὐτοῦ
>   εἰς πάντα τόπον τῆς περιχώρου.
> I   4,14b καὶ φήμη ἐξῆλθεν
>   καθ' ὅλης τῆς περιχώρου περὶ αὐτοῦ.
> 7,17 καὶ ἐξῆλθεν ὁ λόγος οὗτος
>   ἐν ὅλῃ τῇ Ἰουδαίᾳ περὶ αὐτοῦ
>   καὶ πάσῃ τῇ περιχώρῳ.

See also Lk 8,37 ἅπαν τὸ πλῆθος τῆς περιχώρου τῶν Γερασηνῶν (cf. 8,26 = Mk 5,1 τὴν χώραν τῶν Γερασηνῶν)[138] and Acts 14,6.

---

nung der näheren Umgebung der Taufstelle und ihrer Bewohner vermissen und diesen Mangel durch den neuen Text beheben"); on Proto-Mt (VAGANAY, 1954, 359); or on "Q" (LAMBRECHT, 1992, 364; cf. p. 373: in Mk 1,5 "Mark ... broadens the success: 'all the region about the Jordan' (Q) becomes 'all the region of Judea and all the people of Jerusalem'. [n. 59:] Of course, the basic text of Q remains somewhat uncertain").

134. Cf. above, n. 15 (IQP) and n. 17. See J.M. ROBINSON, *The Sayings Gospel Q*, p. 387: "the context of this phrase in Q is not clear. Thus it is not necessary that the expression occurred in Q either in the Matthean or in the Lucan narrative framework"; *The Incipit*, p. 19: "the context of 'John' and 'all the region of the Jordan' cannot be recovered".

135. "Zuerst ist er in der Wüste, dann tritt er am Jordan auf" (H. CONZELMANN, *Die Mitte*, p. 12); "Die Wüste ist Ort der Berufung, die Jordangegend Ort der Verkündigung" (F. BOVON, *Lk*, p. 169).

136. But see above, III.3 (p. 59). This is a more serious problem on the level of a Q source with "in all the region of the Jordan" followed by the quotation of Isa 40,3 (Jacobson; cf. Catchpole).

137. Cf. G. THEISSEN, *The Gospels in Conflict* (n. 124), pp. 39-40.

138. The translation of Lk 8,37 "die Gerasener und was um sie her wohnt" (Bauer-Aland) should be corrected: "die Gegend der Gerasener selbst" (Bovon).

The number of occurrences in Lk-Acts (2/1/5+1) has impressed some commentators[139]. It is noticeable that no instance of metonymy (cf. Mt 3,5) is found in Luke's use of περίχωρος. For this reason, too, is Luke's (καὶ ἦλθεν εἰς) πᾶσαν τὴν περίχωρον τοῦ Ἰορδάνου more easily comparable to the LXX use of the phrase: "Une expression toute faite empruntée à l'A.T. (Gen. XIII,10.11; II Chr. IV,17)" (Lagrange)[140]. In 1966 M.-É. Boismard noted this contact with Gen 13,10 and connected it with John's repentance preaching[141]. More recently, J.S. Kloppenborg has developed the theory that πᾶσα ἡ περίχωρος τοῦ Ἰορδάνου was used in the introduction to Q 3,7-9, that Q understood the phrase ("more precisely than did Matthew and Luke") in reference to Gen 13,10-11, and that "John's speech itself contains several images which evoke the story of Lot"[142]. I will not repeat here the critical reactions of R.C. Tannehill[143] | and J.M. Robinson[144]. My question concerns the initial statement: "neither (Matthew nor Luke) seems to have connected the phrase with its principal OT context, the Lot story"[145]. Of Luke's most explicit reference to Lot in Lk 17,28-32, only 17,28-29 is taken into considera-

139. Cf. M.-É. BOISMARD, Synopse II, Paris, 1972, p. 74: "plutôt lucanien" and supposed to be added by the Matthean redactor ("l'ultime Rédacteur matthéo-lucanien"). Compare his 1966 position: "reprise de Lc. III,3" (p. 351; cf. below, n. 141).

H. Sahlin's suggestion, with references to the other occurrences of περίχωρος in Lk-Acts, to cancel τοῦ Ἰορδάνου has no textual basis. Cf. Studien zum dritten Kapitel des Lukasevangeliums, Uppsala-Leipzig, 1949, pp. 11-13.

140. Luc, p. 104. It is true that the context of 2 Chr 4,17 / 3 Kgs 7,33 (= 46) ἐν τῷ περίχωρῳ/περιοίκῳ τοῦ Ἰορδάνου «has nothing to do with Lot" (TANNEHILL; cf. below, n. 143), but, without being unique, "the Jordan region" in the story of Lot can be a significant OT parallel. Cf. F. BOVON, Lk I, 1989, pp. 169-170 ("Der ... Ausdruck ist alttestamentlich"). His question: "Denkt Lukas an Lot und Abraham, wenn er Johannes und Jesus trennt?" (p. 170) is apparently borrowed from H. Schürmann's (critical) reference to Conzelmann's view on the separation between John's territory and that of Jesus' ministry: "wie Lot sich einst von Abraham trennte und sich πᾶσαν τὴν περίχωρον τοῦ Ἰορδάνου (Gn 13,11) wählte?" (Lk I, p. 155 n. 56).

141. Évangile des Ébionites et problème synoptique (Mc., 1,2-6 et par.), in RB 73 (1966) 321-352, p. 326.

142. City and Wasteland, pp. 151-152: "The Beginning of Q and the Story of Lot".

143. Beginning to Study "How Gospels Begin", in Semeia 52 (1991) 185-192, esp. p. 190. See the quotation in my The Minor Agreements and Q, p. 70: "his interpretation of the beginning of Q depends on his assertion that it reflects the Lot and Sodom story in Gen 19. I doubt that there is sufficient evidence to support this connection". But see above, n. 140. Neither can the use of περίχωρος with other geographical names (ibid.) exclude specific contact with the Lot story.

144. The Incipit (n. 17), p. 13 n. 14: "The argumentation ... seems overdrawn in some details". He seems to consider "all this interpretation too subtle to be ascribed to the intention of the Q redactor" (p. 14).

145. City and Wasteland, p. 150. With reference to C.C. MCCOWN, The Scene of John's Ministry and Its Relation to the Purpose and Outcome of his Mission, in JBL 59 (1940) 113-131, p. 117.

tion (and 17,34-35, where "the allusion is to the Lot story"). The ascription to Q of 17,28-29 is doubtful (without parallel in Mt and deleted from Q in IQP); it is followed by 17,30 (from Q, cf. Mt 24,39b), 17,31 (from Mk 13,14-15)[146], and the explicit Lukan reference to Lot in 17,32. Given this demonstration of Luke's interest in the Lot story[147], it may seem unwise to preclude in Lk 3,3a the possibility of Lukan redaction under the influence of Gen 13,10 καὶ Λωτ ... εἶδεν πᾶσαν τὴν περίχωρον τοῦ Ἰορδάνου (ὅτι πᾶσα ἦν ποτιζομένη...) 11 καὶ ἐξελέξατο ἑαυτῷ Λωτ πᾶσαν τὴν περίχωρον τοῦ Ἰορδάνου[148].

IV. How Q Begins

The debate on minor agreements of Matthew and Luke against Mark is almost exclusively a discussion among Markan priorists: Can these agreements in the triple tradition be explained by Matthew's and Luke's independent redaction of the text of Mk? Or do we need to have recourse to a supplementary hypothesis? Four types of alternatives are currently presented in the literature on the Synoptics[149]:

146. See my *The Minor Agreements and Q*, pp. 54-56.

147. Contrast T.W. MANSON, *The Sayings of Jesus*, London, 1949 (= 1937), p. 144: "The conjunction of *vv.* 28-30 and *vv.* 31f. goes back to the time of oral tradition: it is probably older than Q"; J.A. FITZMYER, *Luke*, p. 1165: "*vv.* 28-32 should be regarded as a unit, probably derived from 'L'". The unit is more probably Lukan, the saying about the days of Lot (after "the days of Noach") being inserted by Luke in Q 17,26-27.30. For alternative views on Lk 17,28-29, cf. KLOPPENBORG, *Q Parallels*, pp. 192, 194 (add Sato, 1988: QLk; Catchpole, 1993: Q).

148. The link is made with Gen 19: "This was before the Lord had destroyed Sodom and Gomorrah" (13,10b; cf. Josephus, *AJ* 1.170). Other occurrences of כִּכַּר in the Lot and Sodom story: Gen 13,12 τῶν περιχώρων; 19,17 ἐν πάσῃ τῇ περιχώρῳ, 25 πᾶσαν τὴν περίοικον, 28 τῆς περιχώρου, 29 τῆς περιοίκου.

149. I do not mention Proto-Mt (Mg) because, as a common-source hypothesis, it corresponds to the Proto-Mk type. Q is mentioned here as a second source, without referring to the suggestion of Mark's use of Q (and Q becoming a common source of Mt, Lk, and Mk). The existence of Q par. Mk 1,1-6 is usually combined with Mt's and Lk's dependence on Mk (esp. Mt 3,4-6 = Mk 1,5-6; Lk 3,3b = Mk 1,4b). It is much more hypothetical to extend Q beyond the Mt-Lk agreements and to include SMt and SLk (cf. above, n. 107: B. Weiss), Mt-Mk (Lambrecht: Mt 3,5a.6a), or Lk-Mk (Polag, Catchpole, Lambrecht: Lk 3,3b βάπτισμα μετανοίας; and Catchpole: + εἰς ἄφεσιν ἁμαρτιῶν).

In the two-source theory there is a special reason for the proposal of a Q version in parallel to Mk 1,1-6. It has been described as one of the "minor agreements" that "both (Matthew and Luke) continue John's coming immediately with John's preaching (Matt 3.7-10 and Luke 3.7-9)"[150], and the search for a Q parallel to Mk 1,1-6 has been justified by "the likelihood that the Q preaching of John needs a kind of introduction such as the one present in our gospels"[151]. Q 3,7a is therefore supposed to be the continuation of such a Q introduction: ἔλεγεν δὲ τοῖς ὄχλοις ἐρχομένοις ἐπὶ τὸ βάπτισμα[152].

In the Gospel of Mark the appearance of John the Baptist in 1,4-6 is followed by his saying on the two baptisms (1,7-8), cited in direct discourse and introduced with καὶ ἐκήρυσσεν λέγων (v. 7a). It is quite understandable that both Matthew and Luke have chosen to locate here, at the intersection of Mk 1,5-6 and 7-8, John's preaching from Q 3,7ff.[153] Matthew's inversion of Mk 1,5.6 in Mt 3,4 and 5-6 (τότε ἐξεπορεύετο πρὸς αὐτὸν...) must facilitate the transition to Mt 3,7a (ἰδὼν δὲ...). In a Synopsis that is carefully made with respect to the order of (Mk and) Lk, the text of Lk 3,7a can be placed in parallel to Mk 1,5[154]. Moreover, Lk 3,7a looks like the summary of Mk 1,5: ἐκπορευομένοις (cf. ἐξεπορεύετο), τοῖς ὄχλοις (cf. πᾶσα, πάντες), βαπτισθῆναι ὑπ' αὐτοῦ (cf. ἐβαπτίζοντο ὑπ' αὐτοῦ). With a *Vorlage* of Lk 3,7a reconstructed as suggested by S. Schulz (τοῖς ἐρχομένοις | ἐπὶ τὸ βάπτισμα)[155] the influence of Mk 1,5 on the Lukan redaction is undeniable.

---

150. J. LAMBRECHT, *John the Baptist*, p. 363. This "agreement" is briefly discussed by E. Simons (1880). He refers to B. Weiß's "unsatisfactory" opinion, "nach welcher beide Evangelisten unabhängig von einander bei den gleichen Mr.-Vers (Mr. 1,5) zu Q. übergegangen sein sollen" (1872, p. 43); his reply: "es ist, in dieser Combination von Mr. und Λ, die Abhängigkeit des Lc. von Mt. zu behaupten" (p. 23).

151. LAMBRECHT, p. 363; with reference to H. Schürmann (*Lk*, p. 161: "die allgemeine Überlegung, daß vor Lk 3,7ff = Mt 3,7ff [= Q] schon irgendwie der Täufer eingeführt gewesen sein muß") and H. Koester (*Gospels*, p. 135: "It is reasonable to assume that Q must have introduced the appearance of John in some fashion"). The quotation from B.H. Streeter on the Baptism in Q (in the same note) is not directly to the point.

152. CATCHPOLE, *Beginning*, p. 218 (= *Quest*, p. 76), with reference to S. Schulz's reconstruction (n. 48 = 53: ὄχλοις to be added; cf. below, n. 162).

153. There is no need to minimize "the common order of Matthew and Luke" (cf. I. DUNDERBERG, *Q*, p. 507: "is rather slight"). It is more important to see that *each in his own way* realizes the connection with Mk 1,5.

154. BOISMARD – LAMOUILLE, *Synopsis Graeca*, Leuven, 1986, §16. — On the reading ἐνώπιον (for ὑπ' = Mk) in Lk 3,7, cf. *ETL* 63 (1987), p. 129 (= *Evangelica II*, 399).

155. S. SCHULZ, *Q. Die Spruchquelle der Evangelien*, Zürich, 1972, p. 367 (cf. below, n. 156). See also R. URO, *John the Baptist* (n. 53), p. 256: om. ὄχλοις (deviation from IQP: cf. *JBL* 112, 1993, p. 501).

Schulz's reconstruction and the subsequent variants[156] are based on the observation of parallel components in Mt 3,7a / Lk 3,7a: (here in the order of Lk) ἔλεγεν / εἶπεν, οὖν / δέ, ἐκπορευομένοις / ἐρχομένους, ὄχλοις / πολλούς (αὐτοῖς), βαπτισθῆναι ὑπ' αὐτοῦ / ἐπὶ τὸ βάπτισμα αὐτοῦ[157]. It may be tempting to conclude from these similarities that the core of Mt 3,7a / Lk 3,7a must come from Q[158]. Though there is much hesitation because of the possibility of redaction in each version[159], every l element in the description of the addressees has its defenders of Q-origin: in Lk, τοῖς ὄχλοις (Catchpole 1992), ἐκπορευομένοις (Nolland

156. For comparison I mention here a few examples:
Harnack (1907, 33)   ἰδὼν πολλοὺς ... ἐρχομένους ἐπὶ τὸ βάπτισμα εἶπεν αὐτοῖς
Schulz (1972, 367)   Ἰωάννης εἶπεν τοῖς ἐρχομένοις ἐπὶ τὸ βάπτισμα
Polag (1979, 28)   ἔλεγεν δὲ τοῖς ὄχλοις ἐρχομένοις ἐπὶ τὸ βάπτισμα αὐτοῦ
Schenk (1981, 17)   (Johannes) sagte zu den Leuten, die er zur Taufe kommen sah
Catchpole (1992, 218) ἔλεγεν δὲ τοῖς ὄχλοις ἐρχομένοις ἐπὶ τὸ βάπτισμα
IQP (1993, 501)   ε[[ἶπ]]εν τοῖς ἐ[[ρχ]]ομένο<ι>ς [[ὄχλοις]] [[ἐπὶ τὸ]] βάπτισ[[μα]] αὐτοῦ
Häfner (1994, 40)   (Ἰωάννης) εἶπεν τοῖς ἐρχομένοις ὄχλοις βαπτισθῆναι ὑπ' αὐτοῦ.
See also Harnack's alternative: "ἰδὼν [Ἰωάννης] πολλοὺς [oder τοὺς ὄχλους]..." (p. 80, cf. p. 33 n. 1). On the name "John", cf. SCHULZ, p. 367 n. 294: "Johannes muß als Subjekt genannt gewesen sein da diese Täuferpredigt wohl den Anfang der Logienquelle gebildet hat". In the hypothesis of a preceding unit existing in Q (Polag, Catchpole; fragmentary: IQP), the name appears already there.
Schenk's reconstruction (1981: "die er zur Taufe kommen sah"; cf. Harnack: ἰδὼν Mt) is corrected in *Sprache*, 1987, p. 395 (ἰδών is redactional) and p. 86 (βάπτισμα = "Mk 1,4 permutiert").
157. Note on the reading αὐτοῦ in Mt 3,7 (om. T H N): the word is printed in the UBS text (already in 1966) and in Nestle-Aland, but in B.M. Metzger's *Textual Commentary* (1971) one can read that "the Committee preferred the reading ἐπὶ τὸ βάπτισμα without any addition... If the possessive had been present originally, there seems to be no good reason why it should have been deleted" (p. 9). This rather confusing annotation is now dropped in the new edition (1994, p. 8). Strangely enough, Davies – Allison (1988) refer to Metzger as follows: "Metzger, p. 9, argues that αὐτοῦ was easily passed over as unnecessary or inappropriate" (p. 301 n. 30); compare R.L. Webb (without reference to Davies-Allison): "Metzger, p. 9, observes that αὐτοῦ would be easily dropped from the text as inappropriate or unnecessary": cf. R.L. WEBB, *John the Baptizer and Prophet. A Socio-Historical Study* (JSNT SS, 62), Sheffield, 1991, p. 175 n. 32. Webb rightly stresses the meaning of αὐτοῦ: "to his baptism" (and not: "for baptism"; cf. below, n. 168). On αὐτοῦ, see also W. SCHENK, art. βάπτισμα (*Sprache*, p. 86).
158. A. FUCHS, *Intention und Adressaten* (n. 37), p. 65: "über den Kern selbst kann ... keine Zweifel bestehen"; C.R. KAZMIERSKI, *The Stones of Abraham: John the Baptist and the End of the Torah (Matt 3,7-10 par. Luke 3,7-9*, in *Biblica* 68 (1987) 22-40, p. 28: "While the exact wording of the *Vorlage* is unlikely to be clear, the core of the text unmistakably refers to an audience of great numbers".
159. See, e.g., W. TRILLING, *Die Täufertradition bei Matthäus*, in BZ 3 (1959) 271-289, p. 283: "Daß schon in Q eine Rahmennotiz gestanden haben kann, ist durchaus möglich, jedoch aus Lk nicht zu erschließen, da er Mk 1,5 ausgelassen und in Lk 3,7 zusammengefaßt hat"; P. HOFFMANN, *Studien*, 1972, p. 17 (cf. above, n. 53); H. MERKLEIN, *Die Umkehrpredigt bei Johannes dem Täufer und Jesus von Nazaret*, in BZ 25 (1981) 29-46, p. 31: "Unsicher muß die Rekonstruktion von Mt 3,7a par bleiben"; DAVIES – ALLISON, *Mt* I, p. 303 n. 36: "It may be that neither Matthew nor Luke has the Q introduction".

1989), βαπτισθῆναι ὑπ' αὐτοῦ (Häfner 1994). In the last case, the proposal is that this Q-phrase is transferred by Matthew to Mt 3,13 (diff. Mk 1,9): τοῦ βαπτισθῆναι ὑπ' αὐτοῦ[160]. But is it not a more satisfactory solution that the phrase in Mt 3,13 is simply reminiscent of Mt 3,6 = Mk 1,5? The use of the telic infinitive (compare πειρασθῆναι in the opening of the next pericope, Mt 4,1 diff. Mk 1,12) cannot be separated from the allegedly redactional ὁ δὲ διεκώλυεν... With regard to ἐκπορευομένοις, J. Nolland declares that it is not "Lukan composition", though he admits that "an influence from Mk 1:5 is possible"[161]. That for Matthew "the 'going out' has already occurred in v 5" can be a valid reason for his use of ἔρχεσθαι, but it does not prove that ἐκπορευομένοις in Lk 3,7a is pre-Lukan. The word is used in Lk 4,22 ("Septuagintalism") and 4,37 (where "Luke has almost completely reformulated the Markan text"). Catchpole modifies Schulz's reconstruction by adding ὄχλοις: "Luke's ὄχλοι may be pre-Lucan since it is more typical of Q, cf. 11.14,29, and present in Q 7.24"[162]. But neither the fact that Matthew's "Pharisees and Sadducees" are redactional nor the presence of two occurrences in Q (11,29 is probably LkR) can be decisive in the case of ὄχλοις in Lk 3,7. That Luke may use τοῖς ὄχλοις for Mk's πάντες can be seen in Lk 4,42: οἱ ὄχλοι ἐπεζήτουν αὐτόν (cf. Mk 1,37 πάντες ζητοῦσίν σε)[163]. The function of Lk 3,7a in the Lukan composition is not only to introduce Q 3,7b-9: "Wahrscheinlich betrachtet der Evangelist die VV 7-9 als ersten Kontakt mit der Menge"[164]. In the parenesis on true repentance (3,10-14), the setting of 3,7a will be resumed: v. 10 οἱ ὄχλοι (and v. 12: ἦλθον ... βαπτισθῆναι).

No more than Luke's ἐκπορευομένοις ... βαπτισθῆναι ὑπ' αὐτοῦ presupposes a source text like ἐρχομένοις ἐπὶ τὸ βάπτισμα αὐτοῦ is his τοῖς ὄχλοις to be understood as the generalization of a more original "Pharisees and Sadducees" in Q[165] (or in Mt)[166]. The evidence of Mt 16,1-12 (vv. 1.6.11.12) and the association of Sadducees and Pharisees

---

160. HÄFNER, *Vorläufer*, p. 39. Cf. GUNDRY, *Mt*, p. 50.

161. *Luke* I, p. 146. The quotations in the text refer to Nolland's commentary.

162. See the reference in n. 152. Compare Harnack's alternative: "Doch kann auch ὄχλοι in Q gestanden haben, da sich das Wort auch sonst dort findet" (p. 33 n. 1).

163. On the Lukan use of οἱ ὄχλοι (diff. πολλοί in Mk), see my *The Matthew-Luke Agreements in Mt 14,13-14 / Lk 9,10-11 (par. Mk 6,30-34)*, in *ETL* 60 (1984) 25-43, esp. pp. 36-38 (= *Evangelica II*, 86-88). Cf. J. JEREMIAS, *Sprache*, 1980, p. 104; J.A. FITZMYER, *Luke* I, 1981, p. 467. Häfner's reply (pp. 38-39) neglects both the contact with Mk 1,5 and the broader context in Lk.

164. F. BOVON, *Lukas*, p. 173.

165. J.A. FITZMYER, *Luke*, 1981, p. 467. Cf. E.E. ELLIS, *Luke*, 1966, p. 89: "*Multitudes* is a deliberate generalization".

166. M.D. GOULDER, *Luke*, 1989, p. 273: "Luke ... generalizes the diatribe, a little unhappily". Contrast R.H. GUNDRY, *Mt*, p. 46.

in Mt 22,23-33.34-40 scarcely allow doubt that this is Matthew's own redactional identification of John's audience[167]. The presence of Jesus' opponents already in the story of John as well as the contrast between the people going out to him and being baptized (3,5-6) and these Jewish leaders who come to observe[168] are both characteristically Matthean features.

Mt 3,7a and Lk 3,7a are printed as uncertain Q texts in my *Q-Synopsis*[169], and, to conclude, I am very much inclined to repeat an earlier comment on this first segment of Q: "In this case I prefer to follow the old B. Weiß: 'Es muss in ihr [Q] noch jede Angabe darüber gefehlt haben, an wen die Rede gerichtet war'"[170]. Attempts at reconstruction of Q should have their basis in the texts of Mt and Lk. We can reasonably assume that Q 3,7b-9 was introduced with something like "John said"[171], but the evidence is deficient for reconstructions of Q 3,1-6, or Q 3,2-4, and 3,7a, and a fortiori for a demonstration of Mark's use of Q.

---

167. R.L. Webb's suggestion that "in Q the original audience for this saying was only Sadducees" can hardly convince. Cf. *John the Baptizer* (n. 157), p. 178.

On this «gemeinsame Frontstellung» of John and Jesus «in der Perspektive der Leser» (cf. above, n. 63), see now H. FRANKEMÖLLE, *Johannes der Täufer und Jesus im Matthäusevangelium: Jesus als Nachfolger des Täufers*, in *NTS* 42 (1996) 196-218, p. 213.

168. R.H. GUNDRY, *Mt*, p. 46: "they simply come 'to the baptism,' presumably for critical observation"; W. SCHENK, art. βάπτισμα: "die mt Gegner (kommen) nur zum *Ort der Taufe* (= *zum Täufer*), nicht aber mit der Absicht der Taufe, was auch aus der red. Präp. (= 3,13) hervorgeht" (*Sprache*, p. 86); R.L. WEBB, *John the Baptizer*, p. 175 n. 32 ("coming to *his* baptism"): "αὐτοῦ indicates the baptism is identified with John, and may more subtly suggest that the Pharisees and Sadducees did not wish to be identified with the baptism".

169. *Q-Synopsis* (SNTA, 13), Leuven, 1988, ²1995, pp. 6-7 (in small print; with annotation of the respective synonyms). No Q parallel to Mk 1,1-6 is included.

170. *The Minor Agreements and Q*, p. 71; with reference to B. WEISS (above, n. 44), ⁹1901, p. 324. Weiß retains ἔλεγεν οὖν as "die Art, wie die beiden Evangelien gemeinsame Quelle (Q) ihre Redestücke in der einfachsten Form einleitete" (*ibid.*; see also 1907, p. 64; 1876, p. 103: ἔλεγεν οὖν or ἔλεγεν οὖν τοῖς ὄχλοις).

171. Cf. M. DEVISCH, *De geschiedenis van de Quelle-hypothese*, STD Diss. (unpublished), Leuven, 1975, pp. 491-509 (Q 3,7a): "'Johannes sprak' als oorspronkelijke inleiding" (p. 509); H. FLEDDERMANN, *The Beginning of Q*, in *SBL Seminar Papers* (1985) 153-159, esp. pp. 153-155 (summary of Devisch's analysis): "So the Q introduction was: εἶπεν Ἰωάννης" (p. 155). See now also W. ARNAL, *Redactional Fabrication and Group Legitimation: The Baptist's Preaching in Q 3:7-9,16-17*, in J.S. KLOPPENBORG (ed.), *Conflict and Invention*, 1995 (cf. above, n. 90), pp. 165-180, esp. 167-168: "... it is only necessary for Q to read here 'he said' (*elegen / eipen*). Matthew's and Luke's failure to depart significantly from their Markan source here renders it highly improbable that the Q opening to this chreia provided any more informative a description than this bare indication of speech". On the name of the speaker, cf. above, n. 156.

Novum Testamentum Supplements 75 (1995) 49-72

7

THE MINOR AGREEMENTS AND Q

"Although there is some hesitation about one or another isolated saying, a rather general tendency can be observed to include only passages attested by both Matthew and Luke and to include all of them. The possibility that a *Sondergut* passage may stem from Q is not denied but it is seen as too uncertain to be reckoned with"[1]. This was, it seems to me, a fair description of the situation in the study of Q in 1981. Contributors to the Louvain Colloquium of that year were mainly interested in the composition of Q and pre-Q collections, i.e., the "formation" of Q rather than the expansion of its extent with Sondergut passages. In the past ten years, however, there seems to be a shift of scholarly interest. It is noticeable that J.S. Kloppenborg explicitly included Lk 9,61-62 and 12,13-14.16b-21 in his list of Q pericopae[2]. In his edition of *Q Parallels* (1988) he distinguishes between the generally accepted extent of Q and 'probable' and 'possible' extent of Q printed in parentheses and in square brackets. His first category (Q origin likely) comprises the following pericopae: Mt 5,41; 7,2a; 10,23; 11,23b-24; Lk 6,24-26; 6,34-35b; 6,37c-38b; 7,3-5; 7,20; 9,61-62; 11,21-22; 11,27-28; 11,36; 12,13-14.16-21; 12,49; 13,25; 15,8-10; 17,28-29. For all passages from Luke (and Mt 10,23) Kloppenborg can refer to suggestions made by H. Schürmann (1968, 1969), and although he opposes his own "limited selection" to Schürmann's "substantial expansion of I the extent of Q"[3], one can speak of a return to a more positive attitude toward Sondergut candidates for membership in Q. A more reserved position is shown in my *Q-Synopsis*[4], where Mt 10,23; 11,23b-24; Lk 11,27-28; 11,36; 12,13-14.16-21; 15,8-10 are not retained in the text, and small print (uncertain Q text) is used for all other passages, with the exception of Lk 13,25 / Mt 25,11. M. Sato

---

1. F. Neirynck, *Recent Developments in the Study of Q*, in J. Delobel (ed.), *Logia. Les paroles de Jésus - The Sayings of Jesus* (BETL, 49), Leuven, 1982, pp. 29-75, esp. 35-41: "The Reconstruction of Q" (37); = *Evangelica II* (BETL, 99), 1991, pp. 409-455 (417).

2. *The Formation of Q. Trajectories in Ancient Wisdom Collections*, Philadelphia, PA, 1987, p. 92, n. 5.

3. *Q Parallels. Synopsis, Critical Notes & Concordance*, Sonoma, CA, 1988, xxiv (the name of Schürmann is missing in the list of authors, p. xxvii). Cf. *A Synopsis of Q*, in *ETL* 64 (1988) 441-449 (= *Evangelica II*, 465-473).

4. *Q-Synopsis. The Double-Tradition Passages in Greek* (SNTA, 13), Leuven, 1988; ²1995.

(1984, 1988)[5], followed by D. Kosch (1989)[6], has opted for a middle position ascribing Lk 6,24-26; 6,37c-38b; 7,3-6a; 9,61-62; 11,36; 12,16-21; 17,28-29 not to the common source Q but to the Lukan recension of it. Other Sondergut pericopae, printed in square brackets in *Q Parallels* (Q origin unlikely), are also assigned to Q^{Lk} by Sato: Lk 3,10-14; 7,29-30; 10,18-20; 11,5-8; 12,35-38[7]. All these passages appear in Schürmann's list of Q pericopae, and for some of them the ascription to Q has received new support in recent special studies. D.R. Catchpole's essay on Lk 11,5-8[8] and R.A. Piper's investigation of Lk 16,9-12(13)[9] are among the most notable examples.

The expansion of Q is not limited to Sondergut material with verbal reminiscences in Matthew or Luke and structural similarities in the double tradition. The phenomenon of the minor agreements in triple-tradition passages is also cited as evidence for Q. This argument takes an extreme form in E. Hirsch's suggestion[10] that the Q source contained a passion narrative, on the basis of I *Kleinübereinstimmungen* in Mt 26,50 / Lk 22,48; Mt 26,64 / Lk 22,69; Mt 26,68 / Lk 22,64; Mt 26,75 / Lk 22,62; Mt 28,19 / Lk 24,47[11]. G. Schneider wrote a reply to Hirsch in his dissertation on Lk 22,54-71[12], but he himself, impressed by the Mt-Lk agreements against Mk 11,27-33, hesitantly raised the question: "Vielleicht ergibt sich daraus, daß die Redenquelle (Q) doch eine P[assionsgeschichte] erhalten hat und somit eine Evv-Schrift gewesen ist"[13]. The

5. *Q und Prophetie. Studien zur Gattungs- und Traditionsgeschichte der Quelle Q* (WUNT, 2/29), Tübingen, 1988 (Diss. Bern, 1984).

6. *Die eschatologische Tora des Menschensohnes. Untersuchungen zur Rezeption der Stellung Jesu zur Tora in Q* (NTOA, 12), Freiburg/Schw. - Göttingen, 1989 (Diss. Freiburg, 1988). See also his *Rekonstruktion und Interpretation. Eine methodenkritische Hinführung mit einem Exkurs zur Q-Vorlage des Lk*, in FZPT 36 (1989) 409-425.

7. For more detailed information, cf. Q^{Mt} and Q^{Lk} and the Reconstruction of Q, in ETL 66 (1990) 385-390 (= *Evangelica II*, 475-480).

8. *Q and 'The Friend at Midnight' (Luke xi.5-8/9)*, in JTS 34 (1983) 407-424. But see C.M. TUCKETT, *Q, Prayer, and the Kingdom*, in JTS 40 (1989) 367-376; and *A Rejoinder* by CATCHPOLE, *ibid.*, pp. 377-388.

9. *Wisdom in the Q-tradition. The Aphoristic Teaching of Jesus* (SNTS MS, 61), Cambridge, 1988, pp. 86-99: "Lk 16:9-13".

10. *Frühgeschichte des Evangeliums*, vol. I, Tübingen, 1941, pp. 243-246. Cf. KLOPPENBORG, *Formation*, p. 86.

11. For description of the agreements, cf. F. NEIRYNCK, *The Minor Agreements of Matthew and Luke against Mark, with a Cumulative List* (BETL, 37), Leuven, 1974, pp. 175, 178, 179, 182, 195; *The Minor Agreements in a Horizontal-line Synopsis* (SNTA, 15), Leuven, 1991.

12. *Verleugnung, Verspottung und Verhör Jesu nach Lukas 22,54-71* (StANT, 22), München, 1969, pp. 47-60 (on Mt-Lk agreements).

13. *Ibid.*, p. 117 (cf. 56: Lk 22:68a). For a critique, cf. ETL 58 (1972) 570-573, 572; D.R. CATCHPOLE, *The Trial of Jesus* (SPB, 22), Leiden, 1971, pp. 276-278.

evaluation of the minor agreements, first in Lk 9[14] and then in general, has led E.E. Ellis to another radical conclusion: "When these agreements are given their full weight, Q could well be understood as a (derivative of a) primitive Gospel or Gospels postulated by earlier criticism on which all three Synoptics are in one way or another dependent"[15]. The great B. Weiss cast a long shadow upon 20th-century Gospel studies. His *ältere Quelle* (Q)[16] provides indeed an easy explanation of the Matthew/Luke agreements. It includes sayings material *and* narratives and is used by Matthew and Luke in combination with Mark. I cite three examples[17]:

I   [Lk 9,10-17] Wie in der Einleitung V. 11, so sind die Reminiscenzen an die vielfach noch bei Mt erhaltenen kürzere Erzählungsform (Q) in V. 13. 14. 17 unleugbar.

[Lk 9,37-43] … er kannte noch eine kürzere Erzählungsform dieser Geschichte, die sich im Wesentlichen noch bei Mt 17,14ff. erhalten hat, … Diese Form wird dann aus Q stammen.

[Lk 20,9-19] … es fehlte nicht an Anzeichen, wonach ihm dies Gleichnis noch in einer älteren Gestalt vorlag, und da eine solche auch noch bei Mt durchblickt, so wird dieselbe in Q gestanden haben.

The first example is M.-É. Boismard's test case, and the Synoptic solution he proposes is that of B. Weiss (Proto-Matthew)[18]. For H. Hübner, too, the minor agreements against Mk 2,23-28 can be explained by acceptance of a shorter form of this story (without v. 27) in the second source Q[19].

14. E.E. ELLIS, *The Composition of Lk 9 and the Sources of Christology*, in G.F. HAWTHORNE (ed.), *Current Issues in Biblical and Patristic Interpretation*. FS M.C. Tenney, Grand Rapids, MI, 1975, pp. 121-127; F.T. in J. DUPONT (ed.), *Jésus aux origines de la christologie* (BETL, 40), Leuven, 1975, ²1989, pp. 193-200, esp. 196-197.

15. *Gospels Criticism. A Perspective on the State of the Art*, in P. STUHLMACHER (ed.), *Das Evangelium und die Evangelien* (WUNT, 28), Tübingen, 1984, pp. 27-54, esp. 38 (E.T., *The Gospel and the Gospels*, Grand Rapids, MI, 1991, pp. 26-52, esp. 36).

16. *Note on the Siglum Q*, in *Evangelica II*, p. 474: on the use of 'Q' (with reference to B. Weiss) in E. SIMONS, *Hat der dritte Evangelist den kanonischen Matthäus benutzt?*, Bonn, 1880(!).

17. *Die Evangelien des Markus und Lukas* (KEK, 1/2), Göttingen, ⁹1901, pp. 422, 431 n. 1, 600. In each of these three instances B. Weiss's position is at least indirectly alluded to in J.A. Fitzmyer's commentary on Luke (1981, 1985); p. 763: "not impossible, but can scarcely be proved" (cf. 766); p. 806 ("a shorter 'Q' form … So B. Weiss"); p. 1278 ("but such a position counters the basic understanding of 'Q'"). For more complete references to Weiss's Q hypothesis in Markan sections with 'Lk-Mt contacts', see B.S. EASTON, *The Gospel according to St. Luke*, Edinburgh, 1926. Q influence is assumed by Easton in Lk 9,10-17 (p. 137); 5,17-26 (p. 67); and, with less probability, 5,12-16 (p. 64).

18. *The Two-Source Theory at an Impasse*, in *NTS* 26 (1979-80) 1-17. For a response, cf. *Evangelica II*, pp. 75-94, and 29-34.

19. *Das Gesetz in der synoptischen Tradition*, Witten, 1973; Göttingen, ²1986, pp. 117-119. For a response, cf. my *Jesus and the Sabbath* (1975), p. 270 n. 157 (= *Evangelica*,

The minor agreements also have their bearing on the Q hypothesis in a quite different direction. A. Fuchs and his school[20] emphasize the unitary character of the minor agreements and their relatedness to the text of Mark: they are secondary to Mark and explainable by Matthew's and Luke's common dependence on a hypothetical Deutero-Markan redaction. In a first stage of this theory, dependence on *Deuteromarkus* was suggested for the location of Q material that is found in the same Markan context in Matthew and Luke. In a second stage, the double-tradition pericopae overlapping with Mk 1,7-8 (the preaching of John the Baptist); 1,12-13 (the temptations of Jesus); 3,22-26 (the Beelzebul I controversy); 4,30-32 (the mustard seed parable) are subtracted from Q, and a strict definition of the second Synoptic source is urged by Fuchs: '*Rede*quelle' or '*Logien*schrift' without narrative elements[21].

In a more drastic way the minor agreements are used as an argument against the very existence of Q by M.D. Goulder: "The issue ... is central because if Luke knew Matthew, we should have lost the main reason for believing in the existence of Q"; and: "if there were one significant and clear MA in the Passion story, then we should know that Luke was following Matthew; and Q, and with it the whole structure, would be undermined"[22]. In answer to this 'putting Q to the test', one can observe that "If [*dato non concesso*] Lukan knowledge of Matthew would be the conclusion to be drawn for the minor agreements, then Luke would have used Mark notwithstanding his knowledge of Matthew, and the inference could only be that elsewhere, where Luke is using another source, a similar subsidiary influence of Matthaean reminiscences can be expected"[23].

1982, 680): "a typically B. Weiss solution"; J. KIILUNEN, *Die Vollmacht im Widerstreit* (AASF, 40), Helsinki, 1985, pp. 199-203; H. SARIOLA, *Markus und das Gesetz* (AASF, 56), Helsinki, 1990, pp. 84-86.

20. See esp. A. FUCHS, *Die Entwicklung der Beelzebulkontroverse bei den Synoptikern* (SNTU, B/5), Linz, 1980, and numerous contributions in *SNTU*, from 3 (1978) to 15 (1990); F. KOGLER, *Das Doppelgleichnis vom Senfkorn und vom Sauerteig in seiner traditionsgeschichtlichen Entwicklung* (FzB, 59), Würzburg, 1988. Cf. T.A. FRIEDRICHSEN, *The Matthew-Luke Agreements against Mark. A Survey of Recent Studies: 1974-1989*, in F. NEIRYNCK (ed.), *L'Évangile de Luc - The Gospel of Luke* (BETL, 32), Leuven, 1989, pp. 335-392, esp. 360-365.

21. FUCHS, *Entwicklung*, p. 199; *SNTU* 5 (1980), p. 142; 9 (1984), p. 144. Kogler seems to propose further limitations to the Q source (*Doppelgleichnis*, 219: "nicht ... ohne Einschränkungen").

22. *Luke. A New Paradigm* (JSNT SS, 20), Sheffield, 1989, p. 6. See also pp. 47-50 ("The Arguments against Q: 2. The Minor Agreements"). On Mt 26,68 / Lk 22,64 (6-7), see my response in *Evangelica II*, pp. 27-28 (and 95-138); on Lk 9,22, Goulder's example of "the accumulation of *un*characteristic Lucan changes" (pp. 48-50), see *Evangelica II*, pp. 43-48.

23. *Evangelica II*, p. 144 (= *The Study of Q*, p. 34).

As indicated above, the point of departure of this paper is the list of double-tradition pericopae commonly accepted as the contents of Q. Without espousing B. Weiss's position, a more modest expansion of Q on the basis of the minor agreements is suggested anew in some recent studies[24]. Possible candidates for inclusion I will be examined one by one, in the reversed order, first individual sayings in Luke's central section with a distant parallel in Mark[25], and then sayings material in the Markan order prior to the Sermon Q 6,20-49[26].

The basic assumption of Markan priority will be my guiding methodology in this paper: in triple-tradition passages where Matthew's and Luke's independent redactions provide a satisfactory explanation of their agreements against Mark there is no need to suggest the existence of a second non-Markan source (Q).

24. For Sato (n. 5 above), Lk 3,2-4; 10,25-28 are possibly Q texts; 6,20a: uncertain; 3,21-22: probably (p. 25: "nicht völlig sicher, aber wahrscheinlich"). The mention of "sonstige 'minor agreements' zwischen Matthäus und Lukas" (diss., p. 23: "höchst unwahrscheinlich") is deleted in the published text (p. 21). Kosch (n. 6 above) ascribes to Q: Lk 3,2-4; 3,21-22 (p. 217: probably); 6,12a ("vielleicht").17a.20a (p. 229: ὄχλος and μαθηταί: "vermutlich"), not 6,13-16 (p. 226); 12,1b (p. 83, cf. 79); but not 10,25-28 (p. 93: "kaum nachweisbar"). Lk 3,3-4; 3,21-22a(!); 6,12-16 (and 8,9-10: cf. Pesch-Kratz) are mentioned by J. SCHÜLING, Studien zum Verhältnis von Logienquelle und Markusevangelium, Diss., Giessen, 1987, p. 59 (57-59 and 203-206 are not reprinted in the published text: FzB, 65; Würzburg, 1991).

Compare A. Polag's reconstruction of Q: [3,2b-4]; [3,21-22]; 6,12a.17a.20a; [17,2]; 17,31 (Evangelica II, pp. 417-419; = The Study of Q, pp. 37-39). None of these passages, except 6:20a, is included in my Q-Synopsis. Cf. Kloppenborg's Critical Notes in Q Parallels, pp. 6: (3,2-4), 16 (3,21-22), 22 (6,12a.17a.20a), 118 (12,1), 182 (17,2), 194 (17,31). Q Thomas Reader (Sonoma, CA, 1990) includes <6,20a>, 17,2 (cf. Q Parallels) and also <Q 3,3> (incorrectly cited as 3,2).

25. On the argument of "der markusferne Kontext", cf. Evangelica II, pp. 427-432 (= The Study of Q, pp. 47-52). The placement in Luke's central section by itself is not a valid reason for ascription to a non-Markan source, L or Q.

26. The overlapping of Q and Mark (Mk 1,7-8; 1,12-13; 3,22-26; 4,30-32) is a related problem but neither these "major" agreements nor the influence of the Q-doublet on Lk 8,16.17; 9,1-5; 20,46 (par. Mk) are directly considered here. See now the contributions on Mk 3,22-26 and 4,30-32 in The Four Gospels 1992. FS F. Neirynck (BETL, 100), Leuven, 1992, pp. 587-619: M.E. BORING, The Synoptic Problem, 'Minor' Agreements and the Beelzebul Pericope" (pp. 587-619); T.A. FRIEDRICHSEN, 'Minor' and 'Major' Matthew-Luke Agreements against Mk 4,30-32 (pp. 649-676). On Mk 1,7-8, see C.M. TUCKETT, Mark and Q, in C. FOCANT (ed.), The Synoptic Gospels (BETL, 110), 1993, pp. 149-175, 168-172 (section: Mk 1,7f. / Q 3,16).

I. MARK, NOT Q, IN LUKE'S CENTRAL SECTION

1. Luke 17,31 (Mk 13,15-16 / Mt 24,17-18)[27]

The text of Lk 17,31 is printed in A. Polag's reconstruction of Q, with two omissions (καὶ τὰ σκεύη αὐτοῦ ἐν τῇ οἰκίᾳ and ὁμοίως, both peculiar to Lk) and one conjecture (τὰ ἐν τῇ οἰκίᾳ)[28]:

ἐν ἐκείνῃ τῇ ἡμέρᾳ
ὃς ἔσται ἐπὶ τοῦ δώματος [ ]
μὴ καταβάτω ἆραι (τὰ ἐν τῇ οἰκίᾳ),
καὶ ὁ ἐν ἀγρῷ [ ]
μὴ ἐπιστρεψάτω εἰς τὰ ὀπίσω.

Matthew's and Luke's common use of a plural object of ἆραι (Mt 24,17 τὰ ἐκ τῆς οἰκίας αὐτοῦ and Lk 17,31 αὐτά, resuming τὰ σκεύη αὐτοῦ ἐν τῇ οἰκίᾳ, against Mk 13,15 τι ἐκ τῆς οἰκίας αὐτοῦ) and their common omission of μηδὲ εἰσελθάτω (after μὴ καταβάτω in Mk) are noted by J. Lambrecht as traces of the Q saying which he supposes to be the source of Mk 13,15-16[29]. I.H. Marshall mentions a third agreement: the preposition ἐν (diff. Mk 13,16 εἰς)[30]. Contrary to Polag, he holds that Luke's phrase καὶ τὰ σκεύη αὐτοῦ ἐν τῇ οἰκίᾳ and αὐτά belong to the Q saying[31]. R.H. Gundry (1982) too draws attention to the omission of "neither let him enter" and to the use of the plural τά: "It looks as though Matthew has conflated the two forms of the saying"[32].

For J.A. Fitzmyer, Lk 17,31 is not a parallel to Mk 13,15-16 ("the wording is quite different") and 17,28-31 "should be regarded as a unit,

---

27. On Lk 21,21bc, Luke's substitute for Mk 13,15-16, cf. my *The Eschatological Discourse*, in D.L. DUNGAN (ed.), *The Interrelations of the Gospels* (BETL, 95), Leuven, 1990, pp. 108-124, esp. 116. On the hypothesis of a special source in Lk 21, see the critical remarks by J. VERHEYDEN, *The Source(s) of Luke 21*, in *Luc-Luke* (n. 20 above), pp. 491-516, esp. 510.

28. *Fragmenta Q*, pp. 78-79.

29. *Die Logia-Quellen von Markus 13*, in *Biblica* 47 (1966) 321-360, p. 342; *Die Redaktion der Markus-Apokalypse* (Analecta Biblica, 28), Rome, 1967, pp. 157-159, esp. 157: the Mt/Lk agreements "machen es zugleich unwahrscheinlich, dass Lk 17,31 in Abhängigkeit von Mk 13 redigiert wurde" (incorrectly rendered by J. ZMIJEWSKI, *Die Eschatologiereden* [n. 40], p. 474, n. 43).

30. *Luke*, p. 665: "the correction may be coincidental or due to non-Marcan tradition". Cf. D. WENHAM, *The Rediscovery of Jesus' Eschatological Discourse* (Gospel Perspectives, 4), Sheffield, 1984, pp. 189-192: the three agreements point to "the existence of a pre-synoptic form of the tradition", but ἐν for εἰς "could be coincidental" (p. 190).

31. *Ibid.* See also J. JEREMIAS, *Die Sprache des Lukasevangeliums*, Göttingen, 1980, p. 269: the anacolouthon is pre-Lukan.

32. *Matthew*, p. 483. The omission of δέ and the use of ἐν (for εἰς) are not treated as agreements with Lk. For a full description of the minor agreements, cf. my *The Minor Agreements*, § 84. Mk 13,15 δέ (om. N): TR T h S V B [N²⁶] Greeven.

probably derived from L"[33]. Such a solution, however, seems to neglect the double-tradition parallel Mt 24,39b / Lk 17,30. With regard to Lk 17,31, even Marshall could not deny that "the language, it is true, is close to that of Mk"[34]. The main differences are in the first part. The beginning is distinctively Lukan, in contrast to καὶ ὁ in the second clause (= Mk/Mt). I Lk 17,31 is placed by Luke in a Q context[35], and the wording of the saying may have been influenced by this context:

30 κατὰ τὰ αὐτὰ (Mt οὕτως) ἔσται ᾗ *ἡμέρᾳ*...
31 ἐν ἐκείνῃ τῇ ἡμέρᾳ ὃς ἔσται...
34 ταύτῃ τῇ νυκτὶ *ἔσονται* δύο... 35 *ἔσονται* δύο...

"On that day" refers back to the day when the Son of Man is revealed. In v. 31 Luke speaks of people outside the house, on the roof or in the field, and in vv. 34-35 he speaks of people inside the house, in bed or at the mill. Luke cannot be blamed for writing the relative ὃς ἔσται ... *καὶ τὰ σκεύη αὐτοῦ ἐν τῇ οἰκίᾳ* (= *οὗ τὰ σκεύη*...)[36]. This introduction of the man on the roof "and his goods in the house" was suggested to Luke by Mk's μηδὲ εἰσελθάτω and τι ἐκ τῆς οἰκίας αὐτοῦ[37], which he can simply replace by a resumptive αὐτά. The addition of ὁμοίως and the change of εἰς to ἐν in the second clause[38] are clearly due to Lukan redaction. A more important modification is the omission of ἆραι τὸ ἱμάτιον αὐτοῦ at the end and v. 32, "Remember Lot's wife", directly connected with μὴ ἐπιστρεψάτω εἰς τὰ ὀπίσω.

A quite different, typically Matthean care for parallel structure is at the origin of the minor changes in Mt 24,17-18:

ὁ ἐπὶ τοῦ δώματος μὴ καταβάτω[39] []   ἆραι τὰ ἐκ τῆς οἰκίας αὐτοῦ,
καὶ ὁ *ἐν τῷ ἀγρῷ* μὴ ἐπιστρεψάτω [] ὀπίσω ἆραι τὸ ἱμάτιον αὐτοῦ.

---

33. *Luke*, p. 1165.
34. *Luke*, p. 665.
35. Lk 17,30.34-35; v. 32 is redactional and v. 33 stems from Q=Mt 10,39, or Mk 8,35 (cf. *The Study of Q*, pp. 49-50; = *Evangelica II*, pp. 429-430).
36. For examples of this usage, cf. KÜHNER-GERTH, *Grammatik*, II, pp. 432-433.
37. By treating καὶ τὰ σκεύη αὐτοῦ ἐν τῇ οἰκίᾳ as "clearly a Lucan addition" Kloppenborg seems to neglect this connection (*Formation*, p. 159). Is it not rearrangement rather than addition? In good Lucan style the prohibition is preceded by an appropriate 'setting'.
38. The anarthrous ἐν ἀγρῷ (12,28; 15,25) may be formula-like but is it therefore pre-Lukan (ctr. JEREMIAS, *Sprache*, p. 269; cf. 218)?
39. Greeven: καταβαινέτω (TR S). In Mk 13,15 Greeven reads εἰς τὴν οἰκίαν: TR S V; τι ἆραι (word order): H S V M N (both diff. Mt/Lk).

The agreements with Lk 17,31 are coincidental resemblances in two independent redactions of Mk 13,15-16 and "do not justify positing a Q Vorlage"[40].

2. Luke 17,2 (Mk 9,42 / Mt 18,6)

| The saying on scandals is printed in Polag's reconstruction in square brackets: *vermutlich* in Q. The saying is given in the order of Lk, preceded by Q 17,1b, and the reconstruction is based on the text of Lk, with two exceptions: μύλος ὀνικός (Lk λίθος μυλικός) and ἕνα τῶν μικρῶν τούτων (Lk 2-4,1), both from Mt=Mk[41].

> ἀνάγκη ἐλθεῖν τὰ σκάνδαλα,
> πλὴν οὐαὶ τῷ ἀνθρώπῳ δι' οὗ τὸ σκάνδαλον ἔρχεται.
> [λυσιτελεῖ αὐτῷ,
> εἰ μύλος ὀνικὸς περίκειται περὶ τὸν τράχηλον αὐτοῦ
> καὶ ἔρριπται εἰς τὴν θάλασσαν,
> ἢ ἵνα σκανδαλίσῃ ἕνα τῶν μικρῶν τούτων.]

In a short study on Lk 17,2 J. Schlosser has defended the Q origin of the saying ("*wahrscheinlicher* ... als oft angenommen", "nicht sicher")[42]. He notes that there is at least one minor agreement against Mk: "Mt and Lk ... (haben) nach 'es ist besser' je einen ἵνα-Satz als Subjekt"[43]. To Schlosser's list of defenders of Q 17,2 (up to 1981) we can now add Fitzmyer, Kloppenborg, Davies and Allison[44].

My position is correctly described in Kloppenborg's critical note: "Luke 17:1-2 is a combination of Q (17:1) and Mark 9:42 (17:2)"[45].

---

40. KLOPPENBORG, *Formation*, p. 157, n. 247. See also A. ENNULAT, *Die 'Minor Agreements'*, 1989, pp. 302-303. On Lk 17;31-33, cf. J. ZMIJEWSKI, *Die Eschatologiereden des Lukas-Evangeliums* (BBB, 40), Bonn, 1972, pp. 465-489 (478: "Die Anhaltspunkte für Q [in Lk 17;31] sind ... keineswegs überzeugend").

41. *Fragmenta Q*, pp. 74-75. Like most authors, I accept the Q origin of Q 17,1b. On M. Sato's reserve concerning the scattered sayings between Lk 14,26 and 17,6 (and D. Kosch's reply: sequence Q 17,1.3-4.6; but see *Tora*, p. 147: "unsicher"), cf. *Evangelica II*, pp. 476, 478. W. Schenk's reconstruction of Q 17,1b (*Synopse*, 1981) is identical with Polag's. J. Schlosser (cf. below, n. 42) deletes τὸ σκάνδαλον (p. 77: "plumbe Wiederholung", MtR).

42. *Lk 17,2 und die Logienquelle*, in *SNTU* 8 (1983) 70-78, esp. p. 78.

43. *Ibid.*, pp. 73-74, in reply to R. Laufen's statement: "Übereinstimmungen zwischen Matthäus und Lukas gibt es nicht" (p. 87). This MA is not included in my list, *The Minor Agreements*.

44. FITZMYER, *Luke*, p. 1137; KLOPPENBORG, *Q Parallels*, p. 182; W.D. DAVIES and D.C. ALLISON, *Matthew* II, 1991, p. 761. Cf. Schlosser's list: p. 74, n. 21.

45. Cf. *Evangelica II*, p. 432 (*The Study of Q*, p. 52).

Schlosser refers to a comment I wrote in 1966, from which I quote here a few sentences[46]:

It is hardly strange that Matthew [18,6.7] brought together sayings about scandal from Mk and Q. ... Lk 17:2 shows no specific similarity with Mt 18:6 and negative agreements against Mk (καλόν ἐστιν, βέβληται) only confirm that Mk 9:42 has been handled in two different I ways... For the connection of Mk 9:42 with 17:1b(Q) Luke may have been inspired by the word about the traitor in Mk 14:21. The scheme is identical: it is necessary (as is written) – woe to him who – it would be better for him...

Mt 18,6 is closely parallel to Mk 9,42 and all changes can be redactional: δέ (for καί), συμφέρει (καλόν ἐστιν ... μᾶλλον), ἵνα (εἰ), κρεμασθῇ (περίκειται), καταποντισθῇ ἐν τῷ πελάγει + gen. (βέβληται εἰς + acc.). Quite understandably, none of them is retained in Polag's reconstruction of Q. Polag takes the three verbs from Lk 17,2. He is followed by Schlosser, but with hesitancy: λυσιτελεῖ (for καλόν ἐστιν) could be "ein von Lk ausgesuchtes, gut griechisches Wort"; περίκειται is borrowed from Mk (Schlosser conjectures the verb περιτίθημι in Q, cf. 1 Clem 46,8); ἔρριπται (for βέβληται) is "gut lukanisch" (Lk 4,35, diff. Mk; Acts 22,23; 27,19.29)[47]. On the other hand, Schlosser differs from Polag regarding λίθος μυλικός and the postposition of ἕνα (Lk=Q, against Mt=Mk). The first case is irrelevant for us (though Lukan correction of μύλος ὀνικός is likely). He argues more specifically about εἷς + partitive genitive: there are only two other occurrences of the postposition in the Synoptics, Lk 15,4 and 16,7, which are "allgemein anerkannte Q-Texte"[48]. But the text of Lk 17,2 is not wholly certain: ἕνα τ. μ. τ. (TR) is read by Kilpatrick and Greeven[49], and in the two other instances the word order in Q is scarcely "allgemein anerkannt"[50].

There is one more divergence from Polag in Schlosser's reconstruction of Q, λυσιτελεῖ ... ἵνα[!] ... ἢ ἵνα (cf. Mt συμφέρει ... ἵνα): in place of the first ἵνα Lk wrote εἰ under the influence of Mk's καλόν ἐστιν ... εἰ[51]. The force of this minor agreement is weakened in two

46. *The Tradition of the Sayings of Jesus: Mark 9,33-50*, in *Concilium*, 1966: cf. *Evangelica* (BETL, 60), 1982, p. 817.
47. *Lk 17,2*, pp. 77-78, cf. 71, 72.
48. *Ibid.*, p. 75.
49. See also DAVIES and ALLISON, II, p. 761. Schlosser refers to Aland's *Konkordanz* without noticing the lacuna at Lk 17,2 (no mention of TR).
50. Q 16,17 μία κεραία ... ἀπὸ τοῦ νόμου (= Mt): Polag, cf. Harnack, Schmid. Q 15,4 stresses the contrast: ἑκατὸν πρόβατα, ἐξ αὐτῶν ἕν (diff. Mt), τὰ ἐνενήκοντα ἐννέα (cf. v. 7).
51. *Lk 17,2*, p. 77.

ways. First, the redactional use of συμφέρει + ἵνα (Mt) for καλόν ἐστιν is well attested in Mt 5,29.30 (doublet of 18,8.9, par. Mk 9,43.45.47). Second, the direct parallel is Lk 17,2a (λυσιτελεῖ αὐτῷ εἰ, cf. Mk) and not the second I clause ἤ ἵνα in v. 2b. Schlosser adduces several considerations against the dependence of Lk 17,2b on Mk 9,42a[52]. (1) The *Tobspruch* in Lk 17,2 is more original than the broken form in Mk/Mt. But the 'full form' of καλόν ἐστιν with ἤ and a second clause in the immediate context (Mk 9,43.45.47) may have influenced Luke's reworking of Mk 9,42. (2) The absence of a comparative before ἤ is unusual in Lk. But this is apparently not the case with λυσιτελεῖ in a comparative sense[53]. (3) The normal construction is λυσιτελεῖ with infinitive, and not with εἰ. But the direct parallel (and source) is καλόν ἐστιν + εἰ in Mk[54]. (4) The unclassical use of ἵνα in a non-purpose sense (in Q 4,3; 6,31; 7,6) is not favoured by Luke: he shows "eine deutliche Zurückhaltung" (with reference to Jeremias)[55]. But Jeremias cites Lk 9,45 as an example of redactional use; Lk 8,32 (diff. Mk 5,12) can be added, and other occurrences in the Sondergut may be redactional as well (7,36; 16,27; 21,36)[56]. (5) The main reason is "das Fehlen des Partizips πιστευόντων"[57]. But this is really a strange argument in Schlosser's theory. If omission by Luke is "durchaus unwahrscheinlich", is it then thinkable that the same Luke who depends on Mk 9,42b in 17,2a (εἰ ... περίκειται, for ἵνα + conj. in Q) would be unaware of this parallel in Mk 9,42a when he copies his Q source in v. 2b? The debate on the identity of "the little ones" is not closed[58].

52. *Ibid.*, (1): p. 75; (2), (3): p. 71; (4): p. 75; (5): pp. 73-74. – Schlosser also rejects the (less probable) explanation of Lk 17,2b ἤ ἵνα... (= Mk 9,42a) as added to Q (v. 2a) by Luke. Cf. H. FLEDDERMANN, in *CBQ* 43 (1981), p. 68; DAVIES and ALLISON, II, p. 761: "from Q or Mark?"

53. Cf. Tobias 3,6 BA λυσιτελεῖ μοι ἀποθανεῖν ἤ ζῆν. Andocides, *Or.* 1.125: τεθνάσαι νομίσασα λυσιτελεῖν ἤ ζῆν.

54. On the '*magna vis*' in this use of εἰ + indicative, see M. ZERWICK, *Graecitas Biblica*, § 311. Cf. BDR § 372,3.

55. *Die Sprache*, p. 58. The figure of the omissions in Lk, diff. Mk ("Von den 22 Belegen ... behielt er nur 8 bei und beseitigte er 14") needs correction. Seven instances have a parallel in Lk: Mk 5,18.23.43; 8,30; 15,21 (infinitive); 6,8; 15,11 (oratio recta), but in the seven other instances either the ἵνα clause or the verb + ἵνα or both are lacking in Lk (Mk 6,12; 9,9.30; 11,28; 12,15; 14,35.49).

56. Cf. P. LAMPE, art. ἵνα, in *EWNT* II, pp. 460-466: "Die lk Red. zeigt 4 unklass. Beispiele: 7,36; 8,32; 17,2; 9,45" (p. 463).

57. SCHLOSSER (72, n. 12) prefers the shorter reading against N[26] [εἰς ἐμέ], par. Mt.

58. Cf. D.P. MOESSNER, *Lord of the Banquet*, Minneapolis, MN, 1989, pp. 201-202.

3. Luke 12,1b (Mk 8,15 / Mt 16,6)

I "There is one slight agreement with Mt. 16,6 diff. Mk., which supports the hypothesis that it is derived from Q and not from Mk." (Marshall)[59]. The saying in Lk 12,1b is now assigned to Q in some recent commentaries on Matthew, though with less emphasis on the minor agreement: "the use of προσέχετε ... need not point to a common source"[60]. The location of Mt 16,6 is strictly parallel to Mk 8,15 and the change to "Pharisees *and Sadducees*" is characteristically Matthean. For Mk's ὁρᾶτε, βλέπετε ἀπό Matthew writes first ὁρᾶτε καὶ προσέχετε ἀπό (16,6) and then repeats the saying in v. 11 with προσέχετε (without ὁρᾶτε) and again in his own comment, v. 12 (εἶπεν) προσέχειν. He uses προσέχετε ἀπό in 7,15; 10,17 (diff. Mk 13,9 βλέπετε...) and προσέχετε μή in 6,1.

For Fitzmyer Lk 12,1b is more likely derived from L and not from Mk, "since only five words are common to Mark and Luke"[61]. But in this short saying the five words, ἀπὸ τῆς ζύμης τῶν Φαρισαίων, is rather a high percentage of common words. In 12,1 Luke writes προσέχετε ἑαυτοῖς ἀπό for Mk's double imperative ὁρᾶτε, βλέπετε ἀπό, and again in 20,46 προσέχετε ἀπό for βλέπετε ἀπό: "He substitutes a characteristic verb *prosechein* for the Marcan *blepein*" (Fitzmyer, at 20,46)[62]. Προσέχετε ἑαυτοῖς is Lukan usage: Lk 17,3; 21,34; Acts 5,35; 20,28.

The relation of Lk 12,1b to the preceding Q section (11,39-52) is cited as a second argument for its ascription to Q: Matthew's designation of the Pharisees as "hypocrites" (in the Woes, Mt 23, diff. Lk) is supposed to be a reminiscence of ὑπόκρισις in the Q I saying[63]. Such a position is not irreversible[64], but if the clause ἥτις ἐστιν ὑπόκρισις is a Lukan

59. *Luke*, p. 510 (cf. 511, with reference to Schürmann). The saying is classified with the uncertain texts in Polag's *Fragmenta Q*, p. 86. Cf. *Der Umfang der Logienquelle*, Diss., Trier, 1966, pp. 57, 124a: probably from Q (*Sondervers*, without parallel in Mt; n. 271: "Das προσέχετε in Mt 16,6 genügt nicht").

60. DAVIES and ALLISON, *Matthew* II, 1991, p. 589. See also GNILKA, *Matthäusevangelium* II, 1988, p. 43 ("Ein Einfluß des Q-Logions auf Mt ist nicht feststellbar". Cf. W. WIEFEL, *Lukas*, 1988, p. 232 ("aus Q", but no comparison with Mt).

61. *Luke*, p. 953. "The saying is often ascribed to Q" (*ibid.*, with reference to Marshall and Schneider); contrast KLOPPENBORG, *Q Parallels*, p. 118: "Not in Q: Most authors". But see above, n. 60.

62. *Luke*, p. 1316. It is less evident that the verb in Lk 20,46 "may have been drawn from Luke's source in 12:1" (MARSHALL, p. 749). Nor can the use of βλέπετε μή in Lk 21,8 (par. Mk 13,5) offer evidence for a non-Markan source in Lk 12,1 and 20,46 (ctr. D.M. SWEETLAND, in *Biblica* 65, 1984, p. 65 n. 22).

63. LkR "hypocrites" in MARSHALL, *Luke*, p. 512 (cf. Schürmann).

64. U. WILCKENS (*TWNT* 8, p. 566 n. 45): ὑπόκρισις in Lk 12,1 derived from Q (cf. Mt 23). Compare E. SIMONS (n. 16 above), pp. 72-73: Luke's dependence on Mt 23.

insertion[65], it can suffice to refer to 11,39-44 (Q) and the criticism in v. 44 that "the Pharisees conceal their true nature"[66]. Luke's understanding of their ὑπόκρισις (Mk 12,15) is made clear in Lk 20,20, ὑποκρινομένους ἑαυτοὺς δικαίους εἶναι. "Ein in Lk 12:1 erhaltenes Q-Logion gibt es nicht"[67]. The use of Mk 8,15 in Lk 12,1b is not unique. Compare Luke's framing of the Q sections in Lk 11,16.29 (cf. Mk 8,11); Lk 11,37-38 (cf. Mk 7,1.5); Lk 12,1 (cf. Mk 8,14-15): all from the great omission and all referring to the Pharisees[68].

4. Luke 10,25-28 (Mk 12,28-34 / Mt 22,34-40)

The Great Commandment was not included in my 1981 survey of current reconstructions of Q[69], and ten years later there is not much change in this situation[70]. The combination of Mk and Q in Mt 22,34-40 and Lk 10,25-28 is of course a possible solution for their well-known minor agreements against Mk[71]. Defenders of | this solution now recognize that it is not wholly satisfactory[72], and other scholars prefer for instance the suggestion of a Deutero-Markan recension[73]. But do we really need a

65. "Perhaps" the more likely alternative for Davies and Allison (n. 60 above).

66. Marshall's comment (*Luke*, p. 499). Cf. FITZMYER, *Luke*, p. 954 ("their dissemblance in conduct"): "This explains why Jesus could call some Pharisees 'unmarked graves' (11:44)".

67. U. LUZ, *Matthäus* II, 1990, p. 466, n. 4. Cf. B. WEISS, *Lukas*, [9]1901, p. 484.

68. Cf. D. ZELLER, in *Logia* (n. 1 above), p. 398. On Lk 11,37-39a (LkR), cf. KOSCH, *Tora*, pp. 63-73. Less convincingly, Kosch proposes a pre-Lukan transition in 12,1a (p. 83: ἤρξατο λέγειν τοῖς μαθηταῖς αὐτοῦ).

69. Cf. *The Study of Q*, pp. 36-37, 53 (= *Evangelica II*, 416-417, 433): P. Hoffmann, R. Laufen, D. Lührmann, R. Morgenthaler, A. Polag, W. Schenk, W. Schmithals, P. Vassiliadis.

70. "In der Mehrzahl der modernen Q-Arbeiten (wird) mit einer Q-Parallele nicht gerechnet" (Kiilunen [n. 74 below], p. 17, n. 5, and similar observation by Ennulat [n. 73 below], p. 269, both in 1989). Cf. KLOPPENBORG, *Formation*, 1987; *Q Parallels*, 1988; NEIRYNCK, *Q-Synopsis*, 1988. The possibility of a Q version is mentioned by D. Zeller (1984, p. 70) and by M. Sato: "möglich, aber unsicher" (p. 22) and finally not taken into consideration because of uncertain location in Q (p. 39).

71. Cf. *The Minor Agreements*, § 77.

72. K. KERTELGE, *Das Doppelgebot der Liebe im Markusevangelium*, in À *cause de l'Évangile*. FS J. Dupont (Lectio Divina, 123), Paris, 1985, pp. 303-322, esp. 307-312: "Trotz der bestehenden Schwierigkeiten... Mit den immer noch offenen Teilfragen..." (p. 309). Cf. MARSHALL, *Luke*, p. 441: "although Matthew might then have shown more influence from it [Q]"; SATO, p. 39: "Falls [Lk 10:25-28] wirklich zu Q gehörte, wäre ihre Stellung dort ganz unklar" (see also ENNULAT, p. 271). – Defenders of the Q version are listed, e.g., by KERTELGE (p. 310, n. 17), KIILUNEN (p. 17, n. 5), ENNULAT (p. 269, n. 2), FRIEDRICHSEN (in *Luc-Luke* [n. 20 above], 1989, p. 389). [Cf. 280 n. 8.]

73. A. ENNULAT, *Die 'Minor Agreements'*, Diss., Bern, 1989, pp. 269-278 (brief discussion of all agreements against Mark 12,28-34). See also D. KOSCH, *Tora*, p. 94, n. 142.

source-critical solution other than the priority of Mark? Is the true alternative to Mk+Q not Matthew's and Luke's independent redaction of Mk 12,28-34[74]?

I will concentrate here on Lk 10,25-28 because, as so often with the minor agreements, the problems are mainly on the side of Lk[75]. Mk 12,28-34 is omitted by Luke but the remains of the episode are still there: Lk 20,39 ἀποκριθέντες δέ τινες τῶν γραμματέων (cf. v. 28 εἷς τῶν γραμματέων) εἶπαν· διδάσκαλε, καλῶς εἶπας (cf. v. 32a). 40 οὐκέτι γὰρ ... (v. 34b καὶ οὐδεὶς οὐκέτι...). We cannot simply say that Mk 12,32-34 is "a later addition to Mark's text" and that this 'appendix' is missing in Luke[76]. Lk 20,39-40 at least shows some traces of it. Moreover, it is not completely absent in Lk 10,25-28. The structure of Lk 10,25-28 is more complex than the question-and-answer in Mt 22,34-36.37-40, par. Mk 12,28.29-31:

I	question	Lk 10,25	Mk 12,28	scribe (question)
	counter-question	26	29-31	Jesus (answer)
	answer	27	32-33	scribe
	reply	28	34	Jesus

In contrast to the answer given by Jesus in Mk 12,29-31 (par. Mt), the answer is spoken by the scribe/lawyer himself in Mk 12,32-33 and Lk 10,27 and he receives approval by Jesus: he saw that he answered wisely, νουνεχῶς ἀπεκρίθη (Mk 12,34a), ὀρθῶς ἀπεκρίθης (Lk 10,28). The distinction between first and second commandment: πρώτη ἐστιν and δευτέρα αὕτη (Mk 12,29.31, cf. Mt) is lacking in Lk 10,27 (ἀγαπήσεις ... καὶ...), and this formulation is closer to that of Mk 12,32-33 (τὸ ἀγαπᾶν ... καὶ τὸ ἀγαπᾶν..., in contrast with "sacrifices").

The three main positive agreements are found at the beginning: νομικός, ἐκπειράζων, διδάσκαλε (Lk 10,25)[77]. Νομικός is a customary

74. See esp. J. KIILUNEN, *Das Doppelgebot der Liebe in synoptischer Sicht* (AASF, B-250), Helsinki, 1989, passim (with references to J.-G. Mudiso Mbâ Mundla 1984, J. Gnilka 1988, W. Weiss 1989, *et al.*); review in *ETL* 67 (1991) 432-433.

75. "There is not the least difficulty in expounding Mt. 22.34-40 as a redaction of Mark" (GOULDER, *Luke*, p. 486, with reference to Gundry's commentary). This is apparently also the opinion of Fitzmyer who ascribes the Lukan form of the story to 'L' (*Luke*, p. 877). For both Goulder and Gundry (*Matthew*, 1982) the agreements in Luke can be ascribed to Matthean influence. See now also R.H. GUNDRY, *Matthean Foreign Bodies in Agreements of Luke with Matthew against Mark: Evidence that Luke Used Matthew*, in *The Four Gospels 1992* (n. 26 above), pp. 1468-1495, esp. 1480-1482.

76. H. KOESTER, *Ancient Christian Gospels*, Minneapolis, MN, 1990, pp. 277; 343, n. 3.

77. Mt 22,35: ...[νομικὸς] πειράζων αὐτόν· 36 διδάσκαλε, ("eine dreifache Übereinstimmung ... derart massiv" (ENNULAT, pp. 273, 275).

Lukan term[78], and the opening phrase is undeniably Lukan style: καὶ ἰδοὺ νομικός τις ἀνέστη (for καὶ προσελθὼν εἷς τῶν γραμματέων in Mk 12,28a). The lawyer's question is taken from Mk 10,17, par. Lk 18,18: λέγων· διδάσκαλε (om. ἀγαθέ), τί ποιήσας ζωὴν αἰώνιον κληρονομήσω[79]; the agreement with Mt 22,36 can be no reason for excising διδάσκαλε from this parallel[80]. Ἐκπειράζων (Mt πειράζων) is a more significant agreement: by this addition the school debate turned into a controversy dialogue (Bultmann). In Gundry's opinion, Luke lacks Matthew's reasons for making this change: "Hence, influence from Matthew | seems likely"[81]. But is ἐκπειράζων (for ἐπηρώτησεν in Mk) really a "foreign body" in Luke? Lk 10,25-28 should be read in connection with the "example" in 10,29-37[82]. The introduction of the lawyer's new question in v. 29, ὁ δὲ θέλων δικαιῶσαι ἑαυτόν (cf. 16,15; 18,9.14), seems to confirm the hostile intent of the "testing" question in v. 25. Jesus replies with a counter-question in v. 26, as he did in Mk 10,3 (cf. v. 2 πειράζοντες αὐτόν) and Mk 12,15 (τί με πειράζετε;)[83].

Lk 10,26 contains a fourth[84] minor agreement: ἐν τῷ νόμῳ, in a slightly different context in Mt 22,36, the lawyer's question: μεγάλη ἐν

78. Cf. *Evangelica II*, pp. 190-193 (= *Luke 14,5*, 1991, pp. 249-251). Cf. *Luke 14,1-6. Lukan Composition and Q Saying*, in C. BUSSMANN - W. RADL (eds.), *Der Treue Gottes trauen. Beiträge zum Werk des Lukas*. FS G. Schneider, Freiburg, 1991, pp. 243-263, esp. 249-251 (= *Evangelica II*, 190-193). Schürmann's retraction (*ibid.*, n. 51) is more explicit in *SNTU* 11 (1986), p. 59, n. 77. On the other hand, "Luke's predilection for νομικός" is now discarded by Gundry (1992). However, his word statistics (p. 1480, n. 27) need correction by distinguishing between plural and singular in Luke's use of γραμματεύς (cf. *Evangelica II*, p. 191).

79. Ctr. MARSHALL (*Luke*, p. 442) who suggests influence of the pre-Lukan source (10,25 Q) upon 18,18!

80. Moreover, διδάσκαλε, lacking in the scribe's question in Mk 12,28, appears in his comment in v. 32a (cf. Lk 20,39). Occurrences of διδάσκαλε in Lk (besides 10,25): 9,38; 18,18; 20,21.28.39; 21,7 (cf. Mk 13,1): all par. Mk; 3,12; 7,40; 11,45(!); 12,13; 19,39. In Lk 11,45 (redactional transition) there is a new intervention of τις τῶν νομικῶν, again with διδάσκαλε.

81. *Matthew*, p. 448. See now also his "Matthean Foreign Bodies" (n. 75), p. 1481. Here, too, no consideration is given to the context in Luke, including 10,29-37.

82. The (Lukan) framing of the parable repeats the same structure (question - counter-question - answer - final reply): 10,29.(30-)36.37a.37b. – On the priest and the levite (*Kultpersonen*) in the parable (10,31-32) and a possible link with Mk 12,33b, cf. KIILUNEN, *Doppelgebot*, pp. 76-77; see also M.-É. BOISMARD, *Synopse II*, p. 350.

83. Cf. Lk 20,20 ὑποκρινομένους ἑαυτοὺς δικαίους εἶναι. See also πειράζοντες in Mk 8,11 and Lk 11,16. The use of the compound verb in Lk 10,25 does not necessarily imply the motif of "testing the Lord" (Dt 6,16 in Q 4,12).

84. In Ennulat's classification this is the last of the minor agreements of category I (highest probability for Dmk). He also mentions the omission of Mk 12,29b (Shema‛) as category II (p. 276). Cf. FITZMYER, *Luke*, pp. 877-878: "The use of 'lawyer' instead of 'one of the Scribes' and the omission of the first part of the Shema‛ (Deut 6,4; cf. Mark

τῷ νόμῳ (diff. Mk: πρώτη πάντων). Jesus' counter-question is formulated as a double question: ἐν τῷ νόμῳ τί γέγραπται; πῶς ἀναγινώσκεις[85]; The motif of this reply can be compared with Mk 10,17
followed by τὰς ἐντολὰς οἶδας in v. 19 (Lk 18,18.20)[86]. For ἐν τῷ
νόμῳ + γέγραπται, cf. Lk 2,23 καθὼς γέγραπται ἐν νόμῳ κυρίου and
24,44 πάντα τὰ γεγραμμένα ἐν τῷ νόμῳ Μωϋσέως... Other minor
agreements in Lk 10,25-28 are 'minor' (Ennulat's "neutrale Grauzone")
and less decisive in a debate on Q[87].

II. THE BEGINNING OF Q

I There is a broad consensus about the beginning of Q, at least in its
final form[88], with Jesus' inaugural sermon preceded by John's preaching
and the temptations of Jesus. In each of the three sections, however, the
existence of a prepositive unit has been suggested, and the argument of
the minor agreements against Mark has been advanced in each case:

[3,2b-4]	3,7-9.16-17
[3,21-22]	4,1-13
[6,12a.17a.20a]	6,20b-49

Regarding "The Setting of the Sermon in Q" I can refer to a recent critical note: "All we can possibly retain ... is the assumption that the Q
introduction had the disciples as the audience of the Sermon"[89].

12,29b) could easily be explained by Luke's redactional concern for the predominantly
Gentile audience for whom he was writing".

85. Luke retained a few of Mk's double questions: Lk 4,34; 5,21; 5,22-23; 13,18
(single question in Q?); 20,2; 21,7, and wrote a double question in 7,31 (single question
in Q?) and 13,15-16. Cf. *Evangelica II*, p. 432 (and 495, n. 4). See now also T.A.
Friedrichsen's study of the double question in Lk 13,18 (n. 26), pp. 662-675.

86. KIILUNEN, p. 59.

87. See Kiilunen's study. Cf. K. SALO, *Luke's Treatment of the Law* (AASF, 57),
Helsinki, 1991, pp. 104-111: "In my previous work I favoured the theory of the Q-source
being behind this pericope, but after being introduced to Kiilunen's work I had to change
my mind" (p. 107, n. 18).

88. In Kloppenborg's analysis, 3,7-9.16-17 (Q²); 4,1-13 (Q³); 6,20-49 (Q¹)... Cf. J.M.
ROBINSON, in *Q Thomas Reader* (n. 24 above), p. viii: "The opening line in the original
form of Q was probably the first beatitude, which initiates Jesus' inaugural sermon in Q".
On the temptations as an integral part of Q, see C.M. TUCKETT, *The Temptation Narrative
in Q*, in *The Four Gospels 1992* (n. 26), pp. 479-507.

89. Cf. my *Matthew 4:23–5:2 and the Matthean Composition of 4:23–11:1*, in *The
Interrelations* (n. 27), 1990, pp. 23-46, esp. 36-38 (38), with reference to R.A. Guelich,
1982; T.L. Donaldson, 1985; K. Syreeni, 1987. On Matthean redaction in Mt 4,23–5,2,
see *ibid.*, pp. 26-36; on Lukan redaction in Lk 6,12-19, see *Evangelica*, 1982, pp. 761-
764 (= ETL 49, 1973, 808-811). See now also KOSCH, *Tora*, pp. 223-226, on Lk 6:13-16.

5. Luke 3,21-22 (Mk 1,9-11; Mt 3,13-17)

Mt 3,16 ἠνεῴχθησαν οἱ οὐρανοί: "That Luke has ἀνεῳχθῆναι τὸν οὐρανόν can scarcely be taken as the firm sign of a common source"; ἐπ' αὐτόν: "The coincidental use by both Matthew and Luke of ἐπί is probably just that, coincidental: both have independently corrected Mark" (Davies and Allison). But their first | sentence receives a continuation: "Nevertheless, because Q contained an account of the Baptist preaching shortly followed by a temptation narrative which presupposes Jesus' divine sonship, it is likely that ... there was a notice of the baptism"[90]. The real argument is clearly not that of the agreements against Mark but the fact that the temptations in Q presuppose the Son of God title (Mk 1,11 parr.)[91]. One can reply, with Kloppenborg, that this title "does not require an explanatory narrative any more than does the title 'Son of Man' which is by far the more common title for Q"[92]. C.M. Tuckett, in his essay on Q 4,1-13, proposes a more pertinent suggestion: the Greek in Q 4,3.9 lacks an article with υἱός and, within the context of Q, εἰ υἱὸς εἶ τοῦ θεοῦ can possibly be interpreted in a non-Christological way[93]. The connection with πνεῦμα (Mk 1,10 parr.)[94] is a much weaker argument. The Mt/Lk agreement in the narrative introductions, Mt 4,1 (ἀνήχθη εἰς τὴν ἔρημον ὑπὸ τοῦ πνεύματος) and Lk 4,1 (ἤγετο ἐν τῷ πνεύματι ἐν τῇ ἐρήμῳ), can be the result of independent redaction (cf. Mk 1,12 τὸ πνεῦμα αὐτὸν ἐκβάλλει εἰς τὴν ἔρημον)[95], and is too easily accepted in reconstructions of Q[96]. Together with Jesus'

The correspondence between Lk 6,20a and Mt 5,1-2, μαθητ(αὶ) ... αὐτοῦ ... λέγ(ειν)... is noted by Sato (p. 24), Kosch (p. 229), et al. (cf. Q-Synopsis). For Kosch, the mention of the mountain is "gut denkbar" (pp. 228; 229: "vielleicht"); but both Lk 6,12 and Mt 5,1 depend on Mk 3,13. "Aufgrund von Mt 4,25 ... ist zu vermuten, dass in Q von ὄχλος (πολύς) die Rede war" (229); but Mt 4,25 is "gut mt" and Lk 6,17 ὄχλος πολὺς μαθητῶν αὐτοῦ "LkRed" (ibid.)!

90. Matthew I, pp. 329, 334.

91. See, e.g., Luz, Matthäus I, p. 160; Sato, Q und Prophetie, p. 25: "Hier wird über die vorher proklamierte Gottessohnschaft neu reflektiert".

92. Formation, p. 85. Cf. A. Vögtle, Herkunft und ursprünglicher Sinn der Taufperikope Mk 1,9-11 (1972), in Id., Offenbarungsgeschichte und Wirkungsgeschichte, Freiburg, 1985, pp. 70-108, esp. 72-75: "Zur Erklärung der Anknüpfung des Versuchers an den Gottessohntitel verbleiben auch andere Möglichkeiten" (p. 74, with reference to P. Hoffmann, 1969).

93. The Temptation Narrative in Q (n. 88), pp. 495-496 (cf. 483, 492).

94. Luz, Matthäus I, p. 151, n. 2. Cf. Sato, Q und Prophetie, p. 25 ("nicht völlig sicher").

95. Cf. Evangelica II, pp. 321-322: post-Markan redaction (not Deutero-Markan, ctr. A. Fuchs, SNTU 9, 1984, pp. 101-106).

96. Cf. Schulz, Polag, et al. Cf. Schenk (1981), but see now Die Sprache des Matthäus, 1987: εἰς, ἔρημος, πνεῦμα, = Mk (229, 248, 413); ὑπό "dupl. von V. 1b (= Mk)" (450); ἀνάγω derived from QLk 4,5 (12: "permutiert").

'fasting' and hunger the location in the wilderness can be an appropriate setting for the first temptation in Q, but the link with the account of Jesus' baptism and the motif that "he was led by the Spirit" may derive from Mk 1,12[97].

A full description of the Mt/Lk agreements against Mk 1,9-11 includes besides the verb ἀνοίγω (for σχίζω) and the preposition ἐπί (for εἰς), already mentioned, the participial construction | βαπτισθείς / βαπτισθέντος (for ἐβαπτίσθη), τοῦ θεοῦ / τὸ ἅγιον (added to τὸ πνεῦμα), and an agreement in word order (against ὡς περιστερὰν καταβαῖνον)[98]. There is no need to repeat here the demonstration that these agreements are easily explained as redactional changes of Mark[99].

6. Luke 3,2b-4 (Mk 1,2-6 / Mt 3,1-6)

The problem of the minor agreements already arises in the very first Synoptic pericope. The presence of Q material overlapping with Mk 1,2-6 has been suggested because of (a) the omission of the quotation from Mal 3,1; (b) the inverted order, the introduction of John before the quotation; (c) the verbal agreement between Mt 3,5 and Lk 3,3, πᾶσα ἡ περίχωρος τοῦ Ἰορδάνου / (εἰς) πᾶσαν τὴν περίχωρον τοῦ Ἰορδάνου[100]. It is less difficult to accept that "both Matthew and Luke realized independently that the quotation of the OT as given in Mark was not adequately covered by the introductory formula"[101]. By placing the presence of John before the quotation, Matthew adopts the scheme of his fulfilment quotations; Luke rearranges the order in view of his extended quotation of Isaiah at the conclusion of the section[102]. The striking

97. Cf. VÖGTLE, *Herkunft*, p. 74: "innerhalb der Q-Versuchungsperikope (wird) nicht auf den Geistbesitz Jesu abgehoben".

98. Cf. *The Minor Agreements*, § 3. On Ἰησοῦς / Ἰησοῦ, cf. EASTON, *Luke* (n. 17 above), p. 43.

99. KLOPPENBORG, *Formation*, p. 85, n. 157; FITZMYER, *Luke*, p. 480 (ἀνοίγω). Cf. M. DEVISCH (n. 104 below), 1975, pp. 444-451 (in response to Schürmann and Polag).

100. SATO, *Q und Prophetie*, p. 21. Cf. LUZ, *Matthäus* I, p. 143, n. 1 (Mt 3,5 / Lk 3,3): "Ob das Jesajazitat aus Q stammt, muß offenbleiben".

101. FITZMYER, *Luke*, p. 461. "Of course, the later use of this quotation in 11:10 and Luke's agreement with Matthew in the present omission and later use (Luke 7:27) suggest that these evangelists are following a source different from Mark (see also vv 7-10)" (R.H. GUNDRY, *Matthew*, p. 44). On the overlap Mk 1,2b and Q 7,27, cf. C.M. TUCKETT, *Mark and Q* (n. 26): Q 7,27 is not redactional in Q and provides no evidence for concluding that Mark was dependent on Q (in reply to D.R. Catchpole; cf. n. 121 below).

102. On Mt 1,2-6 and par., cf. *ETL* 44 (1968) 141-153; = *Jean et les Synoptiques* (BETL, 49), Leuven, 1979, pp. 299-311, esp. 306-309.

verbal similarity in the third agreement is more fascinating, or at least, as recently shown by Kloppenborg, it can give rise to fascinating theory[103].

Kloppenborg's essay is written in response to a reconstruction of "The Beginning of Q" by H. Fleddermann: Q 3,7b-9.16b-17, | with a short phrase εἶπεν Ἰωάννης to introduce these sayings of John[104]:

> Fleddermann is undoubtedly correct in concluding that "Pharisees and Sadducees" is Matthean and that ὄχλοι ("crowds") is Lukan, and that Luke's wording of 3:7a has been influenced by Mark 1:5. Nevertheless, John's question "Who warned you to flee?" presupposes precisely what Luke 3:7a envisages: a group of persons coming out to John (cf. Q 7:24). Moreover, John's own clarification of the nature of his baptism in contradistinction to that of the Coming One is intelligible if the audience has come either to participate in or perhaps simply to be spectators at John's baptism[105].

Kloppenborg's personal suggestion concerns more specifically the presence of the phrase πᾶσα ἡ περίχωρος τοῦ Ἰορδάνου in this introduction:

> ... the opening lines of the Sayings Gospel framed John's speech as an address to persons ... seeking out John *in the circuit of the Jordan*. ... The phrase itself is firmly anchored in the Lot narrative ... Q 3:(3a),7-9 raises the specter of Sodom's destruction and seals off the most convenient avenue of escape, offering moral reform as the only route[106].

The acceptance of πᾶσα ἡ περίχωρος τοῦ Ἰορδάνου in the Introduction of Q is a new step in Kloppenborg's Q studies[107]. His basic observation is that "the technical term for the southern Jordan basin" is used "quite awkwardly" by both Matthew and Luke. Is it then no longer "unwise to include it in Q"[108]?

---

103. J.S. KLOPPENBORG, *City and Wasteland: Narrative World and the Beginning of the Sayings Gospel (Q)*, in *Semeia* 52 (1991) 145-160.

104. H. FLEDDERMANN, *The Beginning of Q*, in *SBL 1985 Seminar Papers*, pp. 153-159. Fleddermann relies on the work of a student of mine: "Michel Devisch has shown that the linguistic evidence does not support a Q text behind Luke 3:3-6. ... I will follow Devisch's reconstruction of Q 3:7-9" (153). Cf. M. DEVISCH, *De geschiedenis van de Quelle-hypothese*, Diss., Leuven, 1975, pp. 402-421 (Lk 3,3-6), 491-509 (Lk 3,7a), 509-515 (Lk 3,7b-9). For Fleddermann's reconstruction of Q 3,16b-17, cf. *John and the Coming One (Matt 3:11-12 // Lk 3:16-17)*, in *SBL 1984 Seminar Papers*, pp. 377-384.

105. *City and Wasteland*, p. 149.

106. *Ibid.*, p. 151 (italics mine).

107. Conjectural reconstruction in *Q Thomas Reader*, 1990, p. 35: <*John came into all the region about the Jordan* ...>.

108. *Q Parallels*, p. 6; on Q 3,2-4: "The agreements of Matthew and Luke against Mark are slight and can be explained without recourse to a Q *Vorlage*". Cf. *Formation*, p. 74.

In Mt 3,5 it is part of a threefold subject in parallel to Mk 1,5,

| (a) Ἱεροσόλυμα   (b) καὶ Ἱεροσολυμῖται πάντες
  (b) καὶ πᾶσα ἡ Ἰουδαία   (a) πᾶσα ἡ Ἰουδαία
  (c) καὶ πᾶσα ἡ περίχωρος τ. Ἰ.   χώρα

The phrase looks like a duplication of Mk's Ἰουδαία χώρα, used by metonymy for the inhabitants who went out to John[109]. The term περίχωρος occurs once in Mk, εἰς ὅλην τὴν περίχωρον τῆς Γαλιλαίας (1,28), with a secondary parallel in Mt 4,24, εἰς ὅλην τὴν Συρίαν, i.e., the region around Galilee[110]. There is one other occurrence in Mt: οἱ ἄνδρες τοῦ τόπου ἐκείνου ἀπέστειλαν εἰς ὅλην τὴν περίχωρον ἐκείνην, i.e., the surrounding region (14,35, diff. Mk 6,55 περιέδραμον ὅλην τὴν χώραν ἐκείνην)[111]. Is it so awkward that in 3,5, "Then went out to him (Jerusalem and all Judaea), and were baptized in the Jordan", Matthew added "and all the region about the Jordan"[112]? "His intent is probably to anticipate the description of the locales from which Jesus' followers come in Matt 4:25"[113].

Kloppenborg correctly indicates how Luke "distinguishes between the ἔρημος where John's call occurs and the circuit of the Jordan where he preaches", "suggesting that John is an itinerant in the 'region of the Jordan', a notion which is otherwise unattested, but which parallels the itinerancy of Jesus which Luke elsewhere stresses"[114]. It is less clear for me how then he can conjecture that Lk 3,3a καὶ ἦλθεν εἰς πᾶσαν τὴν περίχωρον τοῦ Ἰορδάνου derives from Q. The phrase itself may be known to Luke | from the LXX (Gen 13,10.11 πᾶσα ἡ περίχωρος τοῦ Ἰορδάνου; 19,17 πᾶσα ἡ περίχωρος). It is less evident, however, that

---

109. On Jerusalem, for Jerusalemites, cf. Mt 2,3 (and 21,10).

110. On περίχωρος in Mt 3,5, "suggested perhaps by Mark 1:28", cf. GUNDRY, *Matthew*, p. 45; in Mt 14,35, "eine nicht gebrauchte Wendung aus Mk 1:28", cf. LUZ, *Matthäus* II, p. 413.

111. There is a notable difference in Mt: the people of that place "sent" to all the region around and (from there) they come to Jesus (*stabilitas loci* in contrast to Jesus' itinerancy in Mk).

112. Cf. SCHENK, *Die Sprache*, art. Ἰορδάνης: "3,6 (= Mk) ... und von daher 3,5 (+Mk) dupliziert zum 'Umkreis des 'I.'" (p. 85) (= *The Gospels in Context*, Edinburgh, 1992, p. 40). – There is no need to conclude with G. Theissen that "sich der Täufer nicht direkt am Jordan befinden (kann)". Cf. *Lokalkolorit und Zeitgeschichte in den Evangelien* (NTOA, 8), Freiburg/Schw. - Göttingen, 1989, pp. 41-42. See above, n. 111.

113. *City and Wasteland*, p. 150. Cf. my *Matthew 4:23–5:2* (n. 89 above), pp. 32-33: Mt 4,25, cf. Mk 3,8: Judaea/Jerusalem (inverted in Mt) and πέραν τ. Ἰ.

114. *City and Wasteland*, p. 150, with references to Lk. Contrast F. BOVON, *Lukas*, p. 170: "das Bild eines Wanderpredigers (aus Q; vgl. Mt 3,1)" (sic).

it directly alludes to the story of Lot[115]. R.C. Tannehill's reserve with respect to Q applies to its use by Luke as well[116]:

> Although Kloppenborg's description of city and wasteland in Q may be valid, his interpretation of the beginning of Q depends on his assertion that it reflects the Lot and Sodom story in Gen 19. I doubt that there is sufficient evidence to support this connection. ... But is this phrase sufficiently distinctive to remind one of the Lot story? "The region of the Jordan" also occurs in 2 Ch 4:17 in a context that has nothing to do with Lot, and περίχωρος is frequently followed by the name of a geographical area or of the people occupying that area in the LXX and NT[117].

Kloppenborg can cite a further allusion to the story of Sodom in Q 10,12, which provides a conclusion to 10,2-11 and a transition to 10,13-15, the woes against the Galilean towns[118]. Q 10,13-15 also shows how sayings without framing introduction are included in Q and such an introduction is secondarily added in Mt 11,20. The motifs of 10,13-15, reproach of impenitence and announcement of judgment, are those of the preaching of John in the first Q segment, Q 3,7-9.16-17. Here the reconstruction of the Q introduction is mere conjecture. One can guess that the name of the speaker was indicated: John said (or used to say). It appears in the saying that the addressees are children of Abraham and that he baptizes (them) with water. In the light of Mk 1,5 both Matthew and Luke can project this data into a narrative introduction of their own. Their agreement in Lk 3,7a and Mt 3,7a is only partial: "crowds" or "Pharisees and Sadducees", coming "to be baptized by him" or "to the baptism" (for critical observation), and "it may be that neither Matthew nor I Luke has the Q introduction"[119]. In this case I prefer to follow the old B. Weiss: "Es muss in ihr [Q] noch jede Angabe darüber gefehlt haben, an wen die Rede gerichtet war"[120].

---

115. Ctr. F. BOVON, *Lukas*, p. 170 ("Denkt Lukas an Lot und Abraham...?"); pp. 365-366 (Lk 7,17). Bovon's interpretation of τῆς περιχώρου τῶν Γερασηνῶν in Lk 8,37 is quite correct: "die Gegend der Gergesener selbst; περι- weist auf die Umgebung hin, nicht auf Nachbargegenden" (p. 438); cf. 8,26 τὴν χώραν τῶν Γερασηνῶν. Compare (par. Mk 1,28 πανταχοῦ εἰς ὅλην τὴν περίχωρον τῆς Γαλιλαίας) Lk 4,37 εἰς πάντα τόπον τῆς περιχώρου (cf. v. 31 τῆς Γαλιλαίας); 4,14b καϑ' ὅλης τῆς περιχώρου (14a Galilee); 7,17 (ἐν ὅλῃ τῇ Ἰουδαίᾳ περὶ αὐτοῦ καὶ πάσῃ τῇ περιχώρῳ: synonymous?); Acts 14,6.

116. *Beginning to Study 'How Gospels Begin'*, in *Semeia* 52 (1990) 185-192, esp. p. 190.

117. His references are: Dt 3,4.13.14; 34,3; 1 Chr 5,16; 2 Chr 16,4; 2 Esdras 13,9.12.14.16.17.18; Mk 1,28; Lk 8,37.

118. *City and Wasteland*, p. 151. Cf. *Formation* pp. 146, 243.

119. DAVIES and ALLISON, *Matthew* I, p. 303 n. 36. Cf. J. ERNST, *Johannes der Täufer* (BZNW, 53), Berlin - New York, 1989, pp. (41-)42: "Der ursprüngliche Wortlaut wird sich kaum noch rekonstruieren lassen".

120. *Markus und Lukas* (n. 17 above), ⁹1901, p. 324; cf. ⁶1878, p. 316.

CONCLUSION

Since the completion of this paper (December 1991) the problem of the beginning of Q has received extensive treatment in two essays published in *NTS* 1992 by D.R. Catchpole and J. Lambrecht[121]. Both propose, on the basis of the Mt/Lk minor agreements against Mk 1,2-6, the reconstruction of a Q text preceding the introduction of John's preaching (Q 3,7a). For Catchpole[122] πᾶσα ἡ περίχωρος τοῦ Ἰορδάνου appears in an awkward combination in Mt 3,5 and "there must be a preference for the Lucan setting of the phrase": [Ἰωάννης ὁ βαπτίζων] ἦλθεν εἰς πᾶσαν τὴν περίχωρον τοῦ Ἰορδάνου κηρύσσων βάπτισμα μετανοίας εἰς ἄφεσιν ἁμαρτιῶν (= Lk 3,3), καθὼς γέγραπται ἐν τῷ Ἡσαΐᾳ τῷ προφήτῃ· φωνὴ ... αὐτοῦ (= Mk 1,2a.3). The possibility of Lukan editorial intervention in Lk 3,2 *and 3a* is not even taken into consideration. On the other hand, the Matthean version in Mt 3,5 is declared to be an awkward combination without making any effort at understanding this "combination" in its relation to Mk 1,5. If the awkwardness is seen in the use of the verb ἐξεπορεύετο (= Mk)[123], is it then less awkward that Luke replaces ἐρχομένοις (Catchpole's reconstruction of Q 3,7a) by Mark's ἐκπορευομένοις, said of "the crowds" without the | connotation of Mark's Judaea and Jerusalem? Lambrecht's reconstruction is significantly different[124]:

> John came in the wilderness,
> preaching a baptism of repentance,
>   as it is written...
> All the region about the Jordan went out to him,
> and they were baptized by him in the river Jordan.

By retaining the coming of John ἐν τῇ ἐρήμῳ and, after the quotation, a parallel to Mk 1,5 (the Matthean setting of the phrase "all the region

121. D.R. CATCHPOLE, *The Beginning of Q: A Proposal*, in *NTS* 38 (1992) 205-221; J. LAMBRECHT, *John the Baptist and Jesus in Mark 1.1-15: Markan Redaction of Q*, ibid., 357-384.

122. See esp. pp. 217-218. It is quite correct that Matthew and Luke agree in introducing John before the quotation (218), but it is rather amazing that obvious redactional explanations are not even mentioned. The form of the quotation "which makes ἐν τῇ ἐρήμῳ define the location of the herald and not that of 'the way of the Lord'" (*ibid.*) is not an agreement against Mark.

123. "It hardly makes sense to say that the surrounding area of Jordan went *out* to the Jordan" (p. 217). But Matthew reads: ἐξεπορεύετο πρὸς αὐτόν (to him, and not: to the Jordan). And is it not a dubious criterion that awkwardness indicates secondary redaction and smoothness is the property of original tradition (cf. 214)?

124. See esp. pp. 363-364. That both continue John's coming immediately with John's preaching (p. 363) is hardly an agreement against Mark.

about the Jordan"), the hypothetical Q text is made more similar to Mark, and ... Mark's redaction of Q more easily arguable. But the existence of minor agreements is the starting point of this reconstruction. Matthean and Lukan redaction can explain each of them taken separately, but: "Will such an explanation do for the four taken together? Hardly"[125]. Without real discussion of these explanations, the argument is once more the (high) number of minor agreements. I may repeat my comment: "In fact, it is hardly conceivable that the total number of *explained* agreements could become *unexplainable*"[126].

Q 3,2-4; 3,21-22; (6,12-16); 10,25-28; 12,1b; 17,2; 17,31 are proposed in some recent studies as candidates for inclusion in the double-tradition source Q. In none of them, however, the Matthew-Luke agreements against Mark seem to provide conclusive evidence.

ADDENDUM

See now my paper in A. LINDEMANN (ed.), *The Sayings Source Q and the Historical Jesus* (BETL, 158), Leuven, 2001, pp. 53-146: *The Reconstruction of Q and IQP/CritEd Parallels*, esp. pp. 71-86 "The Beginnings of Q", including: Q? 3,2-3 (82-85); Q? 3,21-22 (78-82); Q? 6,20a (71-73; note here the conclusion: "his disciples" is probably redactional in both Mt and Lk). See also pp. 89-92 (Lk 17,2). On Lk 10,25-28, cf. below, pp. 267-282, 283-294, and 300-306.

---

125. *Ibid.*, p. 363. On one of the "four" agreements, cf. n. 124 above. Lambrecht presents his own approach as "careful guessing" (p. 364). Compare also his enumeration of five agreements against Mk 1,9-11: without analysis of the individual instances, or confrontation with the pertinent studies, the minor agreements are supposed to be "highly unlikely ... fortuitous coincidence" (p. 367).

126. Cf. *Evangelica II*, p. 40.

Biblical Interpretation Series 8 (1994) 149-165

8

LUKE 10,25-28: A FOREIGN BODY IN LUKE?

The topic for this paper was suggested to me by a recent essay on Matthean Foreign Bodies in Luke written by R.H. Gundry, with "thanks to Goulder for corrections and suggestions"[1]. Gundry, who himself expects the existence of Q to stand firm against recent attacks, concurs with M.D. Goulder's argument for Luke's dependence on Matthew based on "the Matthean and un- or anti-Lucan character" of the minor agreements with Matthew against Mark in some sections of Luke; and one of these foreign bodies in Luke is 10,25-28[2].

A first reason for my choice of this section can be seen in my own acquiescence with both scholars in denying Luke's use of the second source Q in 10,25-28[3]. My second reason is the appearance in 1993 of H. Schürmann's *Das Lukasevangelium*, Part II/1, in which he retracts his earlier view and points out that Luke 10,25-28 "sich nicht Q, sondern mit grösserer Wahrscheinlichkeit der luk R von Mk 12,28-34 verdankt"[4]. Schürmann can refer to the discussion of the literary-critical problem of Mark 12,28-34 and parallels by J. Kiilunen (1989)[5]. More recently, the love commandment has received new and extensive treatment by M. Ebersohn (1993)[6].

---

1. R.H. GUNDRY, *Matthean Foreign Bodies in Agreements of Luke with Matthew against Mark: Evidence that Luke Used Matthew*, in *The Four Gospels 1992*. FS F. Neirynck (BETL, 100), Leuven, University Press - Peeters, 1992, pp. 1467-1495. See esp. p. 1468 n. 4.

2. *Ibid.*, pp. 1480-1482. See also his *Mark*, Grand Rapids, MI, Eerdmans, 1993, p. 606; and *Matthew*, Grand Rapids, MI, Eerdmans, 1982, pp. 447-450; [2]1993, Compare M.D. GOULDER, *Luke. A New Paradigm* (JSNT SS, 20), Sheffield, JSOT, 1989, pp. 484-487.

3. Cf. F. NEIRYNCK, *The Minor Agreements and Q* (1992), in R.A. PIPER (ed.), *The Gospel Behind the Gospels. Current Studies on Q* (NTSup, 75), Leiden, Brill, 1995, pp. 49-72 [= 241-262, esp. 252-255].

4. H. SCHÜRMANN, *Das Lukasevangelium. Zweiter Teil. Erste Folge: Kommentar zu Kapitel 9,51–11,54* (HTKNT, 3: 2/1), Freiburg-Basel-Wien, Herder, 1993, pp. 129-140, esp. 139. The minor agreements in Lk 10,25-28 are discussed on pp. 138-139.

5. J. KIILUNEN, *Das Doppelgebot der Liebe in synoptischer Sicht. Ein redaktionskritischer Versuch über Mk 12,28-34 und die Parallelen* (AASF, B/250), Helsinki, Suomalainen Tiedeakatemia, 1989. Cf. *ETL* 67 (1991), pp. 432-433 (F. Neirynck); *SNTU* 16 (1991), pp. 151-168 (A. FUCHS, *Die Last der Vergangenheit*).

6. M. EBERSOHN, *Das Nächstenliebegebot in der synoptischen Tradition* (Marburger Theologische Studien, 37), Marburg, Elwert, 1993, pp. 143-247, esp. 144-150, on the minor agreements (with reference to Kiilunen, p. 150 n. 42).

I. Νομικός

 Schürmann's most remarkable shift of opinion concerns the term νομικός. In 1969, on the basis of its occurrence in Lk 10,25 = Mt 22,35, he considered Luke's use of the term in 7,30; 11,45.46.52; 14,3 to be Q usage, "Sprachgebrauch der Redequelle"[7]. This view is now expressly corrected: the six occurrences in Luke are all redactional and νομικός in Mt 22,35 is a scribal assimilation to Lk 10,25[8]. The elimination of νομικός from the text of Matthew is of course the most radical 'solution' to the problem of the minor agreements: cf. C.H. Turner, B.H. Streeter, J. Schmid, et alii[9]. In this case Goulder is on their side for an understandable reason. The word νομικός, unique in Matthew, has its place in Goulder's list of *Lukan Vocabulary* and is quite the opposite to un-Lukan and characteristically Matthean[10]. Gundry shows no such sign of defeatism in defending the influence of Matthew on Luke: "Because Luke has not imported the Pharisees, … he lacks Matthew's reason for substituting νομικός"[11]. Matthew omits Mark's statements, ἀκούσας αὐτῶν συζητούντων, ἰδὼν ὅτι καλῶς ἀπεκρίθη αὐτοῖς: "This omission occurs also in Lk 10,25-28 and therefore supports 'lawyer' as another such agreement in the original of Matthew's text"[12]. And all Goulder's faults are corrected. Goulder had cited Metzger's comment on the absence of νομικός "from family 1 as well as from widely scattered versional and patristic witnesses"[13]. Gundry's reply: "But this textual evidence is weak". Goulder agrees with Schmid that the phrase εἷς ἐξ

---

7. *Das Lukasevangelium I*, 1969 (²1982), p. 422 n. 96. See also *BZ* 5 (1961), p. 276; = *Traditionsgeschichtliche Untersuchungen zu den synoptischen Evangelien*, Düsseldorf, Patmos, 1968, p. 218: "ursprüngliche Sprechweise von Q". Compare R. PESCH, *Das Markusevangelium II* (HTKNT, 2/2), 1977, pp. 244-246, esp. 245: on γραμματεύς and νομικός (Q) as translation variants.

8. *Das Lukasevangelium II/1* (n. 4), pp. 131 n. 12, 138 n. 64. See also p. 318 n. 93 (Lk 11,45), 332 n. 200, and the radical reversal regarding γραμματεῖς in 11,53 (p. 330; cf. below n. 41). See also vol. I/2 in the same series: J. GNILKA, *Das Matthäusevangelium II* (1988), p. 258.

9. Cf. F. NEIRYNCK, *Luke 14,1-6. Lukan Composition and Q Saying*, in C. BUSSMANN and W. RADL (eds.), *Der Treue Gottes trauen. Beiträge zum Werk des Lukas. Für Gerhard Schneider*, Freiburg-Basel-Wien, Herder, 1991, pp. 243-263, esp. 250; = *Evangelica II. Collected Essays* (BETL, 99), Leuven, University Press - Peeters, 1991, pp. 183-204, esp. 191-192.

10. *Luke* (n. 2), p. 486 (and 806).

11. *Matthean Foreign Bodies* (n. 1), p. 1480.

12. *Matthew* (n. 2), p. 448.

13. B.M. METZGER, *A Textual Commentary on the Greek New Testament*, London - New York, United Bible Societies, 1971, p. 59. The word νομικός is bracketed in the text of UBS¹ (1966), with rating C; unchanged in UBS³ (1975) and UBS⁴ (1993).

αὐτῶν νομικός is 'remarkably overladen'[14]. Reply: "we should judge the variant omission of νομικός a scribal assimilation of Matthew to Mark, an assimilation perhaps prompted by a feeling that Matthew's phrase is overloaded". And on Luke's predilection for νομικός: "But νομικός never occurs in Acts, whereas γραμματεύς occurs here four times; and apart from the present passage νομικός never substitutes for γραμματεύς in Luke's gospel"[15]. Νομικός is unique in Matthew, but "Matthew likes the cognate νόμος well enough to insert it without parallel six times in paralleled pericopes"[16].

The weakest point in Gundry's argument is his statement that Luke lacks Matthew's reason for substituting νομικός, without taking into consideration the possibility that Luke may have had his own reason. Both the defense of the genuineness of νομικός in Mt 22,35 and its redactional explanation have received support in recent investigations (Kiilunen, Ebersohn). Echoes for his thesis of Lukan dependence on Matthew are less apparent. Those who accept the genuineness of νομικός in Mt 22,35 usually prefer to give the same status to the word in Matthew and Luke: either independent redaction of Mark's εἷς τῶν γραμματέων or dependence of both on a common source Q[17] (or, for some, dependence on Deutero-Mark[18]).

But the text-critical debate on [νομικός] is not closed. While I some argue that the brackets should be removed from the text in Nestle-Aland and UBS[19], others hold that the bracketed word is printed in the text "zu

14. J. SCHMID, *Matthäus und Lukas* (BSt, 23/3-4), Freiburg: Herder, 1930, p. 146: "klingt ... merkwürdig überladen".

15. *Matthean Foreign Bodies*, p. 1480. In note 27 (*ibid.*), first line, read: νομικός (instead of γραμματεύς).

16. *Ibid.* Cf. *Matthew*, p. 448: ἐν τῷ νόμῳ in 22,36 "reflects Matthew's special diction" and "echoes 'lawyer' in v 34".

17. Cf. above, n. 7. See, e.g., C.M. TUCKETT, *The Temptation Narrative in Q* (below n. 56), p. 485 n. 30. He finds Kiilunen's argument unconvincing: "the fact that the word is not used elsewhere in Matthew still makes a MattR origin here hard to conceive". Cf. *The Revival of the Griesbach Hypothesis* (SNTS MS, 44), Cambridge, University Press, 1983, pp. 125-133, esp. 131 (on νομικός as "source element"). – On the Q-origin of νομικός in Mt 22,35 as permutation from Q 11,46.52 according to W. SCHENK, *Die Sprache des Matthäus*, Göttingen, Vandenhoeck & Ruprecht, 1987, p. 65, see my *Luke 14,1-6* (n. 9), p. 251 (= 192).

18. A. FUCHS, in *SNTU* 16 (1991), p. 167 n. 37; A. ENNULAT, *Die 'Minor Agreements'. Ein Diskussionsbeitrag zur Erklärung einer offenen Frage des synoptischen Problems*, Diss., Bern, 1989, p. 274; (WUNT, 2/62), Tübingen, 1994, p. 287.

19. A. LINDEMANN, *Erwägungen zum Problem einer "Theologie der synoptischen Evangelien"*, in *ZNW* 77 (1986) 1-33, esp. p. 26 n. 102: "kein Anlass, es ... zu streichen oder seine Ursprünglichkeit ... auch nur ernsthaft zu bezweifeln"; and, with reference to Lindemann's note, A. ENNULAT, *Die 'Minor Agreements'*, p. 273 n. 44 ("mE mit Recht"); J. KIILUNEN, *Das Doppelgebot*, p. 37 n. 9. See also M. EBERSOHN, *Das Nächstenliebegebot*, p. 147 n. 20; D. LÜHRMANN, in *The Four Gospels 1992*, p. 2244 n. 20: "besser belegt als die eckige Klammer bei Nestle[26] vermuten lässt".

Unrecht"[20]. The witnesses for the omission are: f^1 205 e sy^s arm geo^2 Origen^{gr,lat}, and the methodological issue of the importance of versional evidence (Old Syriac and Old Latin) is part of the discussion[21]. Gundry's explanation of the shorter reading as a scribal assimilation to Mark is not very convincing. The omission of νομικός after εἷς ἐξ αὐτῶν (cf. v. 34 οἱ Φαρισαῖοι) could be an assimilation to Mark's εἷς τῶν γραμματέων only for copyists who were unaware of the distinction between Matthew's hostile Pharisee and Mark's friendly scribe[22]. Moreover, the phrase, with ἐπηρώτησεν preceding in Matthew, is separated from its following verb by ἀκούσας ..., ἰδών ... in Mk 12,28. A harmonizing addition is less difficult to conceive. The obvious similarities between Mt 22,35-36a and Lk 10,25 prepare for further assimilation:

> Lk νομικός τις ... ἐκπειράζων αὐτὸν λέγων· διδάσκαλε, ...;
> Mt εἷς ἐξ αὐτῶν [] πειράζων αὐτόν· διδάσκαλε, ...;

Harmonization did not stop with the insertion of νομικός in apposition to εἷς ἐξ αὐτῶν. Byzantine uncials read νομικός τις and the influence of Luke's λέγων could explain the variant reading καὶ λέγων in Mt 22,35 (𝔐, Textus Receptus)[23]. If transcriptional probability is taken into account, one can understand that, in spite of the widespread testimony supporting the presence of I νομικός in the text of Matthew, the UBS Committee "had difficulty in deciding which variant to place in the text" (rating C).

The canon formulated by F. Wheeler that "the textual decision must be made before the question of literary relationship is asked"[24] may seem attractive, but is it realistic? Critics who hold the Q hypothesis as

20. H. SCHÜRMANN, *Das Lukasevangelium II*, p. 138 n. 64. This is, I think, what is meant by "aber doch wohl zu Unrecht" (but the words "mit N" in the same note should be deleted).

21. Cf. C.H. Turner's principle of 'modern criticism' (after Hort) in *JTS* 10 (1909), p. 179: "the versions not infrequently enable us to restore the true reading against the consensus of the leading Greek uncials".

22. If Matthew introduced νομικός because he wanted a substitute for Mark's reference to "one of the scribes", is it then not a strange "assimilation to Mark" when copyists omit νομικός and retain only "one of them (= Pharisees)"?

23. Νομικός τις: E* F G H 0233 *pc*; καὶ λέγων: D W Θ ... (cf. apparatus UBS⁴, N²⁷). Note also Mt 22,37 καὶ ἐν ὅλῃ τῇ ἰσχύϊ σου added before καὶ ... διανοίᾳ (Θ 0107 *f*¹³ *pc*), cf. Lk 10,27.

24. F. WHEELER, *Textual Criticism and the Synoptic Problem: A Textual Commentary on the Minor Agreements of Matthew and Luke against Mark*, Diss., Baylor University, Waco, TX, 1985, p. 401. But see C.M. TUCKETT, *The Minor Agreements and Textual Criticism*, in G. STRECKER (ed.), *Minor Agreements. Symposium Göttingen 1991* (GTA, 50), Göttingen, Vandenhoeck & Ruprecht, 1993, pp. 119-142. – For Wheeler's view on νομικός in Mt 22,35 "to be explained as an early and widespread harmonization to the text of Luke", cf. *Textual Criticism*, pp. 215-218.

a ready solution for the minor agreements in Lk 10,25-28 may possibly be influenced by their literary theory in their acceptance of νομικός in the parallel text of Matthew. And the same can be true for those who hold the alternative solution of Luke's dependence on Matthew. It is at least in this sense that Gundry's statement can be read: the omission of Mk 12,28bc in Luke "supports 'lawyer' as another such agreement in the original of Matthew's text"[25]. But is it correct to speak of "this omission" in Matthew which "occurs also in Luke 10:25-28"? Mk 12,28bc functions in Mark as a connection with the preceding pericope which ends on Jesus' words to the Sadducees without any comment by the evangelist:

Mt 22	Mk 12
23-32	18-27
33 καὶ ἀκούσαντες οἱ ὄχλοι	—— cf. 11,18b
ἐξεπλήσσοντο ἐπὶ τῇ διδαχῇ αὐτοῦ.	
34 οἱ δὲ Φαρισαῖοι	28 a καὶ προσελθὼν εἷς τῶν γραμματέων,
ἀκούσαντες	b ἀκούσας αὐτῶν συζητούντων,
ὅτι ἐφίμωσεν τοὺς Σαδδουκαίους,	c ἰδὼν ὅτι καλῶς ἀπεκρίθη αὐτοῖς,
συνήχθησαν ἐπὶ τὸ αὐτό,	
35 καὶ ἐπηρώτησεν	d ἐπηρώτησεν
εἷς ἐξ αὐτῶν [νομικὸς]	
πειράζων αὐτόν·	αὐτόν·

Ι Gundry's commentary starts from a different synoptic presentation with Matthew's καὶ ἐπηρώτησεν (v. 35) in parallel to Mark's καὶ προσελθών, and Mt 22,34 printed without parallel in the column of Mark[26]: "προσελθών drops out and ἐπηρώτησεν takes its place by advancing from a later position in Mark"[27]. Again and again Gundry insists on the "importation" of the Pharisees in Mt 22,34 as Matthew's reason for substituting νομικός: "his importation of the Pharisees made him want a substitute for the scribes of Mk 12,28"[28]. In reality, Matthew's substitute is Mt 22,34, as indicated in the synopsis above, and after the replacement of "the scribes" with "the Pharisees" in v. 34 Matthew can refer to "one of them" as the subject of ἐπηρώτησεν in v. 35. An appositional νομικός may perhaps be added, but it can hardly be argued that the word is needed to substitute for Mark's εἷς τῶν γραμματέων.

25. Cf. above, n. 12.
26. Cf. Aland's Synopsis. The Greek Synopsis of Boismard-Lamouille (1986) has this same arrangement. Contrast Huck's *Synopse* (and followers).
27. *Matthean Foreign Bodies*, p. 1481 (see also *Matthew*, p. 448).
28. *Ibid.*, p. 1480.

The importation of the Pharisees is also supposed to be the reason for Matthew's dropping of προσελθών, which is habitually used by Matthew to connote respectful approach to Jesus. Luke does not have Matthew's Pharisees but agrees with Matthew in dropping προσελθών: thus, for Gundry, this also has the scent of Matthean influence on Luke[29]. Gundry refers to J.R. Edwards's study of προσέρχεσθαι but seems to neglect his observation that "In ten instances, those who approach Jesus come with intent to test or trap him"[30]. Compare, e.g., the question of the Sadducees in 22,23 (προσῆλθον αὐτῷ), and more particularly 16,1 (καὶ προσελθόντες οἱ Φαρισαῖοι καὶ Σαδδουκαῖοι πειράζοντες ἐπηρώτησαν αὐτόν) and 19,3 (καὶ προσῆλθον αὐτῷ Φαρισαῖοι πειράζοντες αὐτόν). What really happened in Matthew is not dropping προσελθών and advancing ἐπηρώτησεν but replacement of προσελθών with συνήχθησαν ἐπὶ τὸ αὐτό.

I will not elaborate here on Matthean style in Mt 22,33.34[31]. My point is that, on close examination, "Matthew's reason" for the insertion of νομικός and for the omission of Mark's προσελθών and his statements in 12,28bc, suggested by Gundry and supposed to be absent in Luke, cannot be verified in the Gospel of Matthew itself.

Before turning to νομικός in Lk 10,25 a few words should be added on Gundry's observation regarding Lk 20,39-40: "seems to have been added under influence from Matthew"[32]. Once more, Gundry is influenced by the current synoptic arrangement of Lk 20,39-40 in parallel to Mt 22,33 (instead of parallel to Mk 12,28-34)[33]. The location of Lk 20,39 (the reaction of τινες τῶν γραμματέων) is parallel to Mk 12,28 (εἷς τῶν γραμματέων)[34]. Compare καλῶς εἶπας in Luke with ἰδὼν ὅτι καλῶς ἀπεκρίθη αὐτοῖς in Mk 12,28c; and:

---

29. Ibid., p. 1481; Matthew, p. 448.

30. Mt 4,3; 15,1; 16,1; 19,3; 21,23; 22,23; 26,49.50.60bis. Cf. JBL 106 (1987), p. 67. Compare Gundry's own comment (Matthew, p. 55) on Matthew's προσελθὼν ὁ πειράζων in 4,3, diff. Luke: "the same combination of προσέρχομαι and πειράζω for the Pharisees and Sadducees" in 16,1, diff. Mark (with introduction of προσελθόντες), and 19,3, par. Mark; and even "the proximity of the two verbs in 22.18,23,35", i.e., πειράζετε, προσῆλθον, and πειράζων (!).

31. I can refer to Gundry's notes (in Matthew) on ἀκούσαντες, the contrast between οἱ ὄχλοι and οἱ Φαρισαῖοι, the introduction of the Pharisees (for "the scribes"), the association of Pharisees and Sadducees, the verb συνάγεσθαι ...

32. Matthew, p. 447.

33. Cf. Benoit-Boismard (1965) § 285; Boismard-Lamouille (1986) § 307; Denaux-Vervenne (1986) § 293.

34. "The statement ... seems to be a generalisation of the sentiments expressed by one scribe in Mk. 12:28 ..." (I.H. MARSHALL, ad loc.).

Mk 12		Lk 20	
32a	καὶ εἶπεν αὐτῷ	39	ἀποκριθέντες δέ
	ὁ γραμματεύς·		τινες τῶν γραμματέων εἶπαν·
	καλῶς, διδάσκαλε,		διδάσκαλε,
	ἐπ᾿ ἀληθείας εἶπες ...		καλῶς εἶπας.
34b	καὶ οὐδεὶς οὐκέτι ἐτόλμα	40	οὐκέτι γὰρ ἐτόλμων
	αὐτὸν ἐπερωτῆσαι.		ἐπερωτᾶν αὐτὸν οὐδέν.

For the interpretation of Lk 10,25-28 it is important to note that Luke knew the text of Mk 12,28-34, including vv. 32-34, and no doubt also v. 28bc. The context is different in Lk 10, and without the preceding question of the Sadducees the omission of ἀκούσας αὐτῶν συζητούντων, ἰδὼν ... is quite natural to Luke and completely irrelevant in a discussion of possible dependence on Matthew.

Νομικός τις (Lk 10,25) is the substitute for Mark's εἷς τῶν γραμματέων, and in Gundry's opinion there is no other apparent | reason for this substitution than Matthean influence on Luke. His list of the occurrences of γραμματεύς in Luke par. Mark (eight times)[35] and in Acts (four times) does not include Lk 20,39 (cf. Mk 12,28). His statistics also show two more serious defects: there is no mention of Luke's use of the term νομοδιδάσκαλος (Lk 5,17; Acts 5,34) and no distinction is made between the singular ὁ γραμματεύς in Acts 19,35 and the plural οἱ γραμματεῖς elsewhere in Luke-Acts. The singular in Acts 19,35 is used for the 'town-clerk', whereas in Acts 5,34 νομοδιδάσκαλος is used for the Jewish 'scribe' Gamaliel. Luke has the same term νομοδιδάσκαλοι (teachers of the law) at the first mention of the "scribes" in Lk 5,17. The only reference to "a scribe" (singular) in the Gospel of Mark is εἷς τῶν γραμματέων and ὁ γραμματεύς in 12,28.32, and Luke may have chosen to use here in Lk 10,25 the term νομικός (like νομοδιδάσκαλος in Acts 5,34) to avoid the Greek sense of a clerk or secretary[36].

Is it true that "apart from the present passage νομικός never substitutes for γραμματεύς in Luke's gospel"[37]? In the second Sabbath debate (Lk 6,6-11; par. Mk 3,1-6) Luke inserted the mention of Jesus' opponents in v. 7: οἱ γραμματεῖς καὶ οἱ Φαρισαῖοι (cf. Mk 3,6 "the Pharisees"). The equivalent to his expression is given by Luke in 14,3,

---

35. *Matthean Foreign Bodies*, p. 1480 n. 27: Luke adopts Mark's γραμματεύς in Lk 5,21.30; 9,22; 19,47; 20,1(sic).46; 22,2.66.

36. See my *Luke 14,1-6*, p. 249 (= 191). Cf. T.W. MANSON, 1937; J. KIILUNEN, 1989. See also SCHÜRMANN, *Redekomposition* (below n. 40), p. 59 n. 77: "Lk 'übersetzt' mit νομικός ... νομοδιδάσκαλος ... für das hellenistische Verständnis seiner Leser".

37. *Matthean Foreign Bodies*, p. 1480.

εἶπεν πρὸς τοὺς *νομικοὺς* καὶ Φαρισαίους (cf. 6,9)[38]. This case of Mk 3,6 ("Pharisees") and the Lukan parallel "scribes and Pharisees" (6,7 γραμματεῖς; 14,3 νομικοί) can be compared with Mk 2,6 ("some of the scribes") and the parallel "scribes and Pharisees" in Luke (5,21 γραμματεῖς; 5,17 νομοδιδάσκαλοι). – Gundry thinks that τοῖς νομικοῖς in Luke 11,46.52 (diff. Matt) comes from the common source Q[39]. It may be right that "the scribes" were the addressees of these sayings in Q, but his supposition that the term νομικοί and not γραμματεῖς was used is unprovable. Schürmann has recently suggested that Mt 23,4.6b-7a.13; par. Lk 11,46.43.52 formed an original unit "against the scribes"[40], and the fact that, in the conclusion he I adds to the sermon in 11,53-54, Luke refers to οἱ *γραμματεῖς* καὶ οἱ Φαρισαῖοι (v. 53, in contrast to νομικοί in 11,45.46.52) is seen by Schürmann as an indication of the pre-Lukan usage of γραμματεῖς in the sermon[41]. D. Kosch proposes a different reconstruction of Q 11,39-52, closer to the sequence of the text in Luke and with two woes against the scribes (11,46.52), but he adopts Schürmann's argument: "Die Gesetzeslehrer wurden sehr wahrscheinlich *grammateis* genannt"[42].

In sum, none of the pieces of evidence for Gundry's thesis on "the νομικός, whom Luke has gotten from Matthew"[43] stands up under analysis. It can be added that, in contrast to the appositional νομικός in Mt 22,35, the word is grammatically indispensable in Luke's sentence: καὶ ἰδοὺ νομικός τις ἀνέστη ...

38. *Luke 14,1-6*, p. 251 (= 193); in reply to Goulder's suggestion of Luke's dependence on Mt 23,2.

39. *Matthew*, pp. 455, 460.

40. *Die Redekomposition wider "dieses Geschlecht" und seine Führung in der Redequelle (vgl. Mt 23,1-39 par Lk 11,37-54). Bestand - Akoluthie - Kompositionsformen*, in SNTU 11 (1986) 33-81, esp. pp. 43-48; *Das Lukasevangelium II/1*, pp. 303-335, esp. 329.

41. *Redekomposition*, p. 60 n. 79; *Das Lukasevangelium II/1*, pp. 329-330: "der ungewöhnliche Sprachgebrauch (γραμματεῖς)" is supposed to be "die Redeweise der Redenquelle" (p. 330). His observation on the reversed order in the expression scribes-Pharisees (in contrast to the Lukan sequence in Lk 11,39-44.45-52) is a more speculative argument.

42. D. KOSCH, *Die eschatologische Tora des Menschensohnes. Untersuchungen zur Rezeption der Stellung Jesu zur Tora in Q* (NTOA, 12), Freiburg/Schw., Universitätsverlag; Göttingen, Vandenhoeck & Ruprecht, 1989, pp. 62-104 ('Die Weherede'), esp. 104. On γραμματεῖς (in the redactional verses Lk 11,53-54), cf. p. 99: "Indiz dafür ..., dass Lk dieses Wort in seiner Vorlage fand". On this "reminiscence" see also p. 74 n. 57: "Dies ist *ein m.W. bisher nicht beachtetes Argument* für die Annahme, dass Lk in Q *grammateis* und nicht *nomikoi* las" (italics mine). This statement is surprising because in the same chapter there are numerous references to Schürmann's *Redekomposition* (1986). – Note: the variant readings with νομικοί (for γραμματεῖς) in Lk 11,53 are generally considered later assimilations to Luke's usage in 11,45.46.52. But see G.D. KILPATRICK, in *JTS* 1 (1950), p. 56, and the reply by R. LEANEY, in *JTS* 2 (1951), pp. 166-167.

43. *Matthean Foreign Bodies*, p. 1481.

II. Agreements and Disagreements

The term νομικός is the first in a series of agreements with Matthew in Lk 10,25-28, all cited as "evidence that Luke used Matthew". Goulder, who judged differently and more correctly Luke's use of νομικός ("He takes over Mark's scribe, whom he renders by his customary νομικός") now keeps Gundry's company. To begin with, Luke adopts "Matthew's opening, deceitful διδάσκαλε"[44]. In Gundry's commentary: "Matthew adds 'Teacher', | which echoes vv 16 and 24, ... and again agrees with Luke against Mark. The term is a Mattheanism"[45]. The inference is more explicit in 1992: the insertion in Lk 10,25 "cannot have the echoing function which Matthew's insertion has. Thus is suggested Matthean influence on Luke". In this case a more nuanced parenthesis is added[46]:

> (though here only suggested, because Luke uses διδάσκαλος seventeen times in his Gospel and once in Acts over against twelve times in Matthew and twelve times in Mark; so disregarding the immediately surrounding other agreements of Matthew and Luke against Mark we might think of an independent insertion of διδάσκαλε by Luke).

The insertion of διδάσκαλε in Mt 22,36 is rightly seen in connection with Mt 22,16.24 (Mk 12,14.19)[47]. But no mention is made of possible influence of the scribe's διδάσκαλε in Mk 12,32. This is all the more amazing since Gundry has emphasized that such "compensation" of omissions is characteristic of Matthew's style[48]. On the side of Luke, the total numbers of the occurrences of διδάσκαλος in Matthew (12) and Luke (17) change to Matthew (6) and Luke (12) if we consider the address διδάσκαλε. As indicated above, the possibility of combined influence of Mk 12,28 and 32 is shown in Lk 20,39. The observation that "the echoing function" of Matthew's διδάσκαλε is absent in Luke 10 becomes meaningless once we recognize that the real source of Lk 10,25b is Mk 10,17b: διδάσκαλε ἀγαθέ, τί ποιήσω ἵνα ζωὴν αἰώνιον κληρονομήσω; (ἀγαθέ om.; ποιήσας for ποιήσω ἵνα, cf.

---

44. *Luke*, p. 485.
45. *Matthew*, p. 448.
46. *Matthean Foreign Bodies*, p. 1481.
47. It is less evident indeed that διδάσκαλε in Lk 10,25 can be connected with Lk 20,21.28. Ctr. SCHÜRMANN, *Das Lukasevangelium II/1*, p. 138: "schon der vorstehende Kontext ... legte beiden Evangelisten gemeinsam diese Anrede nahe".
48. See, e.g., *Matthew*, p. 355. See also p. 450, on Matthew's omission of Mk 12,31-34; and p. 452, on Mt 22,46 which "comes from Mark 22:34b". It can be added to his comment that the first half of Matthew's double clause contrasts with Mk 12,34a (ἀπεκρίθη).

Lk 18,18)⁴⁹. This parallel, not mentioned by Gundry, is at least partially acknowledged by Goulder: "the similarity of the two stories has no doubt had its effect"⁵⁰. Jesus' | counterquestion in v. 26 can be compared with τὰς ἐντολὰς οἶδας in Mk 10,19 (Lk 18,20), and his reply in v. 28b resumes the formulation of the question: τοῦτο ποίει καὶ ζήσῃ (cf. v. 37 ποίει)⁵¹.

Matthew's formulation of the question remains close to Mark: ποία (ἐστὶν om.) ἐντολὴ μεγάλη ἐν τῷ νόμῳ (for πρώτη πάντων, cf. Mark's μείζων in v. 31). The structure of Mt 22,34-36.37-40 is the question-and-answer structure of Mk 12,28.29-31. The more complex structure of Lk 10,25-28 can be compared with Mk 12,28-34, including vv. 32-34:

Lk	10,25	question	Mk	12,28	scribe
	26	counterquestion		29-31	Jesus
	27	answer		32-33	scribe
	28	final reply		34	Jesus

In contrast to the answer given by Jesus in vv. 29-31 of Mk (vv. 37-40 of Mt), the answer is spoken by the scribe/lawyer himself in Mk 12,32-33 and Lk 10,27, and he receives approval from Jesus: he saw that he answered wisely, νουνεχῶς ἀπεκρίθη (Mk 10,34a), ὀρθῶς ἀπεκρί-θης (Lk 10,28). The distinction between first and second commandment (Mk 12,29 πρώτη ἐστίν, 31 δευτέρα αὕτη; Mt 22,38 αὕτη ἐστὶν ἡ μεγάλη καὶ πρώτη ἐντολή. 39 δευτέρα δὲ ὁμοία αὐτῇ) is lacking in Lk 10,27. Luke's formulation of the two commandments fused into one (ἀγαπήσεις ... καὶ ...) comes closer to that of Mk 12,33 (τὸ ἀγαπᾶν ... καὶ τὸ ἀγαπᾶν ..., in contrast to sacrifices).

As a consequence of these contacts with Mk 10,17 and 12,32-34, the story in Lk 10,25-28 is significantly different from Mt 22,34-40. But in both stories the question is addressed to the "teacher" by someone

49. See, among others, KIILUNEN, Doppelgebot, p. 58. He also compares Lk 10,25 with the redactional verse Lk 11,45, τις τῶν νομικῶν (νομικός τις) and διδάσκαλε (n. 26).
50. Luke, p. 485: with reference to the formulation of the question τί ποιήσας ... (see also p. 486), but, curiously enough, not regarding "Matthew's [sic] ... διδάσκαλε". The qualification "deceitful" is also contestable ... and contested by Gundry: "Matthew's putting of the term as an address to Jesus in the mouth of opponents does not represent a denigration of the title, but a use of those opponents to express an aspect of Matthew's own Christology" (p. 67); cf. p. 448: "emphasizes Jesus' didactic authority".
51. Schürmann also suggests that Lk 10,26a ὁ δὲ εἶπεν πρὸς αὐτόν (diff. Mk 12,29a) depends on Mk 10,18a ὁ δὲ Ἰησοῦς εἶπεν αὐτῷ / Lk 18,19a εἶπεν δὲ αὐτῷ ὁ Ἰησοῦς (pp. 137, 139). But see below.

trying to test him, πειράζων in Mt 22,35, ἐκπειράζων in Lk 10,25. Matthew's change of "one of the scribes" to "one of them (the Pharisees)" and his insertion of | πειράζων accord well together. Matthew adopted Mark's πειράζοντες in 16,1 and 19,3, and his πειράζων in 22,35 echoes the Pharisees' question in 22,15-22, with Jesus' reply in v. 18: τί με πειράζετε (par. Mk 12,15). Luke does not have the Pharisees in 10,25 and therefore his agreement with Matthew in inserting ἐκπειράζων is cited as evidence that Luke used Matthew[52]. Four observations are in order. First, Luke has the designation οἱ νομικοί always in association with the Pharisees: 7,30 (οἱ δὲ Φαρισαῖοι καὶ οἱ νομικοί); 11,45.46.52 (preceded by the woes against the Pharisees); 14,3 (τοὺς νομικοὺς καὶ Φαρισαίους). Second, Lk 10,25-28 is followed by the example of the Samaritan, with a Lukan frame repeating the structure of question-counterquestion-answer-reply, 10,29.(30-)36.37a.37b. The introduction of the lawyer's new question in v. 29, ὁ δὲ θέλων δικαιῶσαι ἑαυτόν (cf. 16,15 οἱ δικαιοῦντες ἑαυτούς, said to the Pharisees; see also 18,9; 20,20) seems to confirm the hostile intent of the testing question in v. 25. Third, Mk 8,11 has only a weak parallel in Lk 11,16 (ἕτεροι δὲ πειράζοντες). Mk 10,2(-9) has no parallel in Luke and τί με πειράζετε (Mk 12,15) is omitted in Lk 20,23, but in Mk 10,3 and 12,15 Jesus replies to the testing question with a counterquestion, and so he does in Lk 10,26[53]. Fourth, Lk 10,25 differs from the parallel in Matthew (ἐπηρώτησεν ... πειράζων αὐτόν) by using the compound verb and replacing Mark's ἐπηρώτησεν:

Mk   προσελθὼν ... ἐπηρώτησεν αὐτόν·
Lk   ... ἀνέστη ἐκπειράζων αὐτὸν λέγων·

For Goulder Luke uses ἐκπειράζειν "in piety to Deut 6:16" which is cited by Luke in his rewriting of the Matthean Temptation narrative[54]. Οὐκ ἐκπειράσεις κύριον τὸν θεόν σου in Lk 4,12 (cf. Mt 4,7) forms an inclusio with πειραζόμενος ὑπὸ τοῦ διαβόλου (4,2): "By placing this temptation last, Luke shows that it is Satan, not Jesus, who is not to tempt the Lord his God"[55]. A first remark can be made on Goulder's suggestion of the influence of Mt 4,7 | (through Lk 4,12) on Luke's

---

52. GUNDRY, *Matthew*, p. 448; *Matthean Foreign Bodies*, p. 1481; GOULDER, *Luke*, p. 485.
53. SCHÜRMANN, *Das Lukasevangelium II/1*, p. 138: "es gibt eine Tendenz, nach der Streitgespräche 'gelegentlich auf andere Stücke' abfärben" (with reference to BULTMANN, *Geschichte*, p. 53).
54. *Luke*, pp. 485, 486.
55. *Ibid.*, pp. 294, 298; cf. p. 296, on Matthean authorship of the Temptation narrative.

ἐκπειράζων in 10,25. For Gundry and other scholars who assign the Temptation narrative to the common source Q this indirect dependence on Matthew is of course nonexistent[56]. My second remark concerns the meaning of οὐκ ἐκπειράσεις: "On the analogy of the preceding quotations [Lk 4,4.8] it is to be understood as a command to be obeyed by Jesus"[57]. Οὐκ ἐκπειράσεις ... is a warning against tempting God, while πειράζειν is used in Acts 5,9 (πειρᾶσαι τὸ πνεῦμα κυρίου) and 15,10 (τί πειράζετε τὸν θεόν). Variation is not un-Lukan and the old wisdom is still valid: "Ἐκπειράζω idem significat, quod simplex πειράζω, nam ἐκ in compositis haud raro abundat" (Schleusner)[58]. It is far from evident that the compound verb for "testing" in Lk 10,25 alludes to Deut 6,16 and means here "tempting God" and "blasphemy"[59]. At the extreme opposite, M. Klinghardt defends a neutral sense of ἐκπειράζων: "als Schüleranfrage gut denkbar", and he adds: "jedenfalls ergibt der Kontext keinen Hinweis auf das Gegenteil"[60]. As indicated above, the context in Lk 10,25-37 can be evaluated somewhat differently. But from Klinghardt's one-sided approach[61] we can retain a sound reaction against too easy associations of the lawyer's testing question with the temptation of Jesus by Satan[62].

56. Cf. C.M. TUCKETT, The Temptation Narrative in Q, in The Four Gospels 1992 (n. 1), pp. 479-507. See also GUNDRY, Matthew, p. 53: "he sticks to the non-Markan source he shares with Luke".

57. MARSHALL, Luke, p. 174. Cf. A. LOISY, Luc, 1924, p. 152: "une réponse directe à la suggestion du diable, une réfutation de cette proposition, non une condamnation du procédé dont use le diable envers Jésus".

58. Ἐκπειράσεις in Deut 6,16 LXX for tempting God: compare Ps 77 LXX: 18 ἐξεπείρασαν τὸν θεόν, 41 (and 56) ἐπείρασαν τὸν θεόν (cf. Ex 17,2.7; Num 14,22). Contrast Gnilka's suggestion of a special nuance in ἐκ-πειράζειν (Das Matthäusevangelium, p. 89, at Mt 4,7). See also 1 Cor 10,9 μηδὲ ἐκπειράζωμεν τὸν Χριστόν (v.l. κύριον), καθώς τινες αὐτῶν ἐπείρασαν (v.l. ἐξ-).

59. Cf. SCHENK, Die Sprache des Matthäus (n. 17), p. 160: "Blasphemie, Provokation, mit dem Kern-Sem Verhöhnung Gottes" (with reference to W. POPKES, art. πειράζω, in EWNT 3, p. 153).

60. M. KLINGHARDT, Gesetz und Volk Gottes (WUNT, 2/32), Tübingen, Mohr, 1988, p. 138 (and n. 9).

61. "ME zeigt auch die Eingangsfrage, dass der Gesetzeslehrer nicht in böswilliger Absicht fragt: Die Frage 'was soll ich tun?' is typischer Bestandteil der Bekehrung" (ibid., n. 11).

62. GUNDRY, Matthew, p. 448: "Testing" [in 22,35] echoes 4,1.3; 16,1; 19,3 and therefore casts the Pharisaic lawyer in a Satanic role"; see also p. 55, on 4,3 (ὁ πειράζων). With much emphasis: W. WILKENS Die Versuchung Jesu nach Matthäus, in NTS 28 (1981-82) 479-489: "Immer wieder tritt – verhüllt in die Gestalt der Führer Israels – der 'Versucher' an Jesus heran mit der Frage nach der Vollmacht seiner Sendung" (p. 483). But see also, e.g., U. LUZ, Das Evangelium nach Matthäus (EKK, 1/2), 1990, p. 445. Contrast H. SEESEMANN, art. πεῖρα κτλ, in TWNT 6, pp. 28, 36: "es geht nicht an, hier von einem in den Worten der Fragesteller versteckten Angriff des Satans zu reden" (p. 36).

Ἐν τῷ νόμῳ is also cited as one of the Matthew-Luke agreements. The phrase is used by Matthew (22,36) in his parallel to the scribe's question in Mk 12,28 (cf. above) and can be assigned to Matthean redaction (cf. v. 40)[63]. Ἐν τῷ νόμῳ in Lk 10,26 is not strictly parallel[64]: it occurs not in the lawyer's question but in Jesus' reply, the counterquestion:

ἐν τῷ νόμῳ τί γέγραπται;
πῶς ἀναγινώσκεις;

For Goulder the phrase ἐν τῷ νόμῳ is uncharacteristic of Luke: "it never recurs in Luke-Acts, despite 26 uses of νόμος" and Luke almost always qualifies νόμος ('of Moses', 'of the Lord' etc.)[65]. In his commentary on Lk 2,22-40 Goulder emphasizes Luke's triple use of the phrases κατὰ τὸν νόμον Μωϋσέως (v. 22), καθὼς γέγραπται ἐν νόμῳ κυρίου (v. 23), κατὰ τὸ εἰρημένον ἐν τῷ νόμῳ κυρίου (v. 24)[66]. Besides κατὰ τὸν νόμον κυρίου in v. 39, a fourth variation can be added, in which νόμος is used without qualifier: κατὰ εἰθισμένον τοῦ νόμου (v. 27). "The law of the Lord" (Lk 2,23.24.39) is found only here in Luke-Acts. Luke's use of "the law of Moses" (Lk 2,22; 24,44; Acts 13,38; 15,5; 28,23) deserves our attention in Lk 24,44: τὰ γεγραμμένα ἐν τῷ νόμῳ Μωϋσέως καὶ τοῖς προφήταις καὶ ψαλμοῖς. Compare "the law of Moses and the prophets" in Acts 28,23, and its variations "*Moses* and the prophets" (Luke 16,29.31; 24,27)[67] and "*the law* and the prophets" (Lk 16,16 Q; Acts 13,15; 24,14).

We can translate the double question in Lk 10,26: "In the law, what is written? what[68] do you read"? For Goulder, the use of I ἐν τῷ νόμῳ with ἀναγινώσκεις is another indication of Matthean influence. Matthew's additional verses 12,5-7 (diff. Mk 2,23-28) left no trace in the parallel text of Lk 6,1-5, but in 10,25ff. Luke has again "the Matthew 12

63. GUNDRY, *Matthew*, p. 448: "reflects Matthew's special diction (νόμος – 6,0)", but neither here nor in *Matthean Foreign Bodies* Gundry examines Luke's diction.
64. As is acknowledged by Gundry: "in a slightly later position and in Jesus' mouth" (p. 448); cf. *Matthean Foreign Bodies*, pp. 1480-1481.
65. *Luke*, p. 486.
66. *Ibid.*, p. 255.
67. Cf. Acts 26,22. See also Acts 15,21 Μωϋσῆς ... ἀναγινωσκόμενος and 13,27 τὰς φωνὰς τῶν προφητῶν ... ἀναγινωσκομένας (Moses and the prophets read in the synagogue on the sabbath); compare 13,15 μετὰ δὲ τὴν ἀνάγνωσιν τοῦ νόμου καὶ τῶν προφητῶν.
68. On πῶς = τί, cf. H. LJUNGVIK, in *Eranos* 62 (1964), p. 31. Cf. BLASS-DEBRUNNER-REHKOPF, § 436,3 (ctr. B-D); BAUER-ALAND, art. πῶς, 1a (ctr. Bauer); W. SCHENK, in *EWNT*, art. πῶς, 3 ("gg. Bauer hier nicht modal"). – On the double question in Luke, cf. T.A. FRIEDRICHSEN, *Minor and Major Matthew-Luke Agreements against Mk 4,30-32*, in *The Four Gospels 1992* (n. 1), pp. 649-676, esp. 662-675.

stories in front of him" and Luke's phrase in 10,26 can be compared with ἢ οὐκ ἀνέγνωτε ἐν τῷ νόμῳ in Mt 12,5[69]. This introduction of the scriptural argument is attributable to Matthean redaction (cf. 19,4; 21,16), though ἢ οὐκ ἀνέγνωτε here repeats οὐκ ἀνέγνωτε of 12,3 (par. Mk 2,26 οὐδέποτε ἀνέγνωτε)[70] and Matthew's addition of ἐν τῷ νόμῳ is probably reminiscent of Mk 12,26 οὐκ ἀνέγνωτε ἐν τῇ βίβλῳ Μωϋσέως (cf. v. 24 μὴ εἰδότες τὰς γραφάς) and its anticipation in Mt 21,42 οὐδέποτε ἀνέγνωτε ἐν ταῖς γραφαῖς (diff. Mk 12,10)[71]. The suggestion that Luke has Mt 12 "in front of him" starts from a consideration of Lk 10,21-22 par. Mt 11,25-27, disregarding the intervening section Lk 10,23-24 (Mt 13,16-17), which has been cited as "a classic counter-example undermining the theory that Luke used Matthew"[72].

In "Matthean Foreign Bodies", Gundry's final paragraph on Lk 10,25-28 repeats almost *ad litteram* his 1982 comment on Mt 22,37. The sentence on the tempter "who in Matthew and Luke immediately receives from Jesus the OT commandment" is now rightly changed to "in Matthew immediately hears from Jesus ..." and "in Luke, Jesus elicits from the lawyer a quotation of this commandment". It is not quite correct that "both Matthew and Luke omit 'The first is'": in Matthew, πρώτη ἐστίν is transferred to v. 38. Gundry is now more explicit on the omission of "Hear Israel, the Lord our God is our Lord": "Luke, writing for Gentiles, cannot take monotheism for granted; so his agreement with Matthew ... favors Matthean influence"[73]. This argument is at least reversible, however. A commentator like J.A. Fitzmyer, who is so impressed by the differences between Mark and Luke that he thinks that the Lukan form of the story should be ascribed to L, makes an exception for the omission of Deut 6,4 (cf. Mk 12,29b) which "could easily be explained by Luke's redactional concern for the predominantly Gentile audience for whom he was writing"[74]. The omission of the first part of the Shemaᶜ should not be isolated from its immediate context in Luke. The lawyer's initial question was about eternal life (what must I do?) and in v. 27 he answers this question on doing with Deut 6,5 and Lev 19,18 combined into a single love command: ἀγαπήσεις ... Luke

69. *Luke*, p. 485. Cf. p. 487: "Luke's Greek is strained, under influence of Mt. 12.5".
70. Par. Lk 6,3 οὐδὲ τοῦτο ἀνέγνωτε ὅ. On "reading" of the Scriptures, cf. n. 67 (Acts 13,15.27; 15,21); see also Lk 4,16; Acts 8,28.30.32.
71. Cf. W. SCHENK, *Die Sprache des Matthäus* (n. 17). p. 145.
72. D.R. CATCHPOLE, *The Quest for Q*, Edinburgh, Clark, 1993, p. 238 (cf. pp. 54-55).
73. *Matthean Foreign Bodies*, pp. 1481-1482; *Matthew*, pp. 448-449.
74. *Luke*, pp. 877-878.

had no need to address the problem of the two commandments "since he uses a quite different form of question"[75].

The 'minor' agreements against Mk 12,29a, listed by Gundry, are not taken into consideration by Goulder: ὁ δέ for ὁ Ἰησοῦς, ἔφη and εἶπεν for ἀπεκρίθη, αὐτῷ and πρὸς αὐτόν added. It can suffice here to note that, following the counterquestion in Lk 10,26, ἀπεκρίθη receives an equivalent in Luke's introduction to the lawyer's answer: ὁ δὲ ἀποκριθεὶς εἶπεν (v. 27a)[76]. Gundry and Goulder emphasize Luke's conflating Mark and Matthew in v. 27b: ἐκ, ἐν, ἐν, ἐν[77]. Luke no doubt starts with Mark's ἐξ + gen., but does he depend on Matthew in writing ἐν + dat. (diff. Mark, LXX)? Luke can be influenced by an alternative version of Deut 6,5, in conformity with the Hebrew בְּ (cf. 2 Kgs 23,25 ἐν ὅλῃ καρδίᾳ αὐτοῦ καὶ ἐν ὅλῃ ψυχῇ καὶ ἐν ὅλῃ ἰσχύϊ αὐτοῦ). But Luke retains Mark's four phrases (though with ἰσχύς before διάνοια) and the transition to ἐν + dat. can be Lukan stylistic improvement[78]. It can be added that the difference between ἐξ (1) and ἐν (2-3-4) is not restricted to the use of the prepositions if we are to adopt the reading of P[75] B: om. [τῆς] before καρδίας and om. καί before the first ἐν[79].

CONCLUSION

I J. Kiilunen wrote his 1989 monograph on the "minor agreements" in Lk 10,25-28 in response to the Two-Gospel hypothesis (Griesbach) and the *Parallelversion* hypothesis (Q or another source besides Mark)[80]. He devoted just one little footnote to the hypothesis of subsidiary Matthean influence[81]. Now, five years later, a supplementary essay was needed.

75. This is correctly observed by J. NOLLAND, *Luke 9:21–18:24* (Word Biblical Commentary, 35B), Dallas, TX, Word, 1993, p. 583.
76. Cf. Lk 10,28: ὀρθῶς ἀπεκρίθης. Cf. H. SCHÜRMANN, *Das Lukasevangelium II/1*, p. 139: "Lukas lässt Jesus VV 26.28a einen gewichtigen Ausspruch (εἶπεν) tun, den Gesprächspartner dagegen nur 'antworten' V 27a (vgl. V 28b)".
77. GUNDRY, *Matthew*, p. 449; *Matthean Foreign Bodies*, p. 1482; GOULDER, *Luke*, p. 486: "There is no clear example of Luke's knowledge of the Heb". (in contrast to Matthew's citations).
78. Cf. SCHÜRMANN, *Das Lukasevangelium II/1*, p. 139.
79. Cf. KIILUNEN, *Doppelgebot*, p. 66: "mit ἐν und zweimaligem καί werden die drei letzten Komponenten zusammengezogen, während die erste mit ἐκ und ohne Artikel und ohne weiterführendes καί wie eine Schlagzeile hervorgehoben wird".
80. *Doppelgebot*, esp. pp. 79-89: "Kritische Überlegungen zu konkurrierenden Hypothesen". See also his introduction, pp. 13-18.
81. *Ibid.*, p. 17 n. 7. He refers to E. Simons (1880), R.T. Simpson (1966) and E.P. Sanders - M. Davies (1989). M. Ebersohn's brief survey of *Lösungsversuche* depends on Kiilunen and dependence on Matthew is not even mentioned (p. 144 n. 3).

By concentrating on Gundry-and-Goulder[82] the discussion also covers other current "solutions" since both Q and Deutero-Mark often come to us in Matthew's clothing.

ADDENDUM

In his recent volume on *The Four Gospels*, 2000 (cf. below, p. 339, note) M. Hengel proposes the perfect reversal of Gundry's (and Goulder's) Matthean Foreign Bodies in Lk: Matthew is later than Luke and, "In taking over the text of Mark, Matthew here and there also took a look at Luke and sometimes allowed himself to be influenced by Luke" (186; "... in small details of narrative, language and style").

"Only here does Matthew have the rare term νομικός. This is a typical 'minor agreement' which in my view can most sensibly be explained by the dependence of Matthew on Luke. In my view he has taken this over, including the address διδάσκαλε, from the Lukan version ... He wanted to avoid Mark's positive judgment on the scribe..., and instead chose the more negative introduction in Luke" (196).

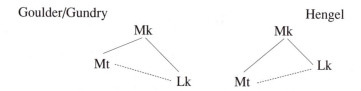

Goulder/Gundry   Hengel

With regard to the reconstruction of Q', Hengel disagrees with the principle that sayings in Matthew and Luke which show an almost verbatim agreement in wording quite certainly belong to Q (P. Vassiliadis): "Precisely here we must ask whether Matthew did not take over such passages from Luke" (310 n. 696). Hengel adopts the opposite procedure: "specifically in cases of word-for-word agreement we have to reckon with a use of the earlier Luke by the later Matthew..." (179). Thus in the case of Q 3,7-9 he conjectures a dependence of Matthew on Luke (182). Compare, for a similar approach, M.-É. Boismard's argument for Proto-Luke. See my reply, "A New Debate: Q or Proto-Luke", in D.L. DUNGAN (ed.), *The Interrelations of the Gospels* (BETL, 95), Leuven, 1990, pp. 108-114. Cf. below, 402 (nn. 11-12).

---

82. The Goulder-Neirynck debate is much older. The SNTS Seminar on the Synoptic Problem has been our annual meeting place in the years 1971-1982, and I remember that a lively discussion on Lk 10,25-28 took place in Aberdeen, 1975.

ETL 71 (1995) 151-160

9

THE MINOR AGREEMENTS AND LK 10,25-28

In a recently published essay[1] I studied the minor agreements used by some scholars for expanding Q to triple-tradition passages. I examined Q 3,2-4; 3,21-22; 6,12-16; 10,25-28; 12,1b; 17,2; 17,31 as possible candidates for inclusion in Q and had to conclude that "in none of them the Matthew-Luke agreements against Mark seem to provide conclusive evidence"[2]. One of these passages, the pericope of the Great Commandment, was studied again, and more extensively, with regard to the alternative theory of Luke's use of Matthew[3]. It is to this last essay that R.H. Gundry now responds with a Rejoinder[4].

1. THE GOULDER-GUNDRY TEAM

It could be no surprise that I contributed to the M.D. Goulder Festschrift with an essay on minor agreements. Goulder's thesis is well known: the phenomenon of the minor agreements demands Luke's knowledge and use of Matthew and, therefore, there is no need for Q[5]. Gundry disagrees on the rejection of Q but concurs with Goulder's explanation of the minor agreements. At the opening of his "Matthean Foreign Bodies" he declared: "In this essay I shall join arms with M.D. Goulder...", and he expressed thanks to Goulder "for corrections and suggestions"[6]. Starting

---

1. F. NEIRYNCK, *The Minor Agreements and Q*, in R.A. PIPER (ed.), *The Gospel Behind the Gospels: Current Studies on Q* (NovTSup, 75), Leiden, Brill, 1995, pp. 49-72. The manuscript of this paper was completed in December 1991. Its conclusion was rewritten and supplemented in 1994 (pp. 71-72).

2. *Ibid.*, p. 72. Cf. pp. 61-64: "Luke 10:25-28 (Mk 12:28-34 / Mt 22:34-40)".

3. F. NEIRYNCK, *Luke 10:25-28: A Foreign Body in Luke?*, in S.E. PORTER – P. JOYCE – D.E. ORTON (eds.), *Crossing the Boundaries: Essays in Biblical Interpretation in Honour of Michael D. Goulder* (Biblical Interpretation Series, 8), Leiden, Brill, 1994, pp. 149-165.

4. R.H. GUNDRY, *A Rejoinder on Matthean Foreign Bodies in Luke 10,25-28*, in *ETL* 71 (1995) 139-150.

5. See my *The Minor Agreements and Q* (n. 1), p. 53. Cf. *Evangelica II*, p. 144; see also p. 115 n. 116. On Goulder's *Luke* (1989), cf. *ETL* 65 (1989) 390-394; 67 (1991) 434-436. On the existence of Q, see now the responses by D. CATCHPOLE, *Did Q Exist?*, in ID., *The Quest for Q*, Edinburgh, 1993, pp. 1-59; C.M. TUCKETT, *The Existence of Q*, in *The Gospel Behind the Gospels* (n. 1), pp. 19-47.

6. R.H. GUNDRY, *Matthean Foreign Bodies in Agreements of Luke with Matthew against Mark. Evidence that Luke Used Matthew*, in *The Four Gospels 1992* (BETL, 100), 1992, pp. 1467-1495, esp. 1468 (and n. 4).

with Lk 6,13 he treats a long list of minor agreements, twenty-four passages in the order of Luke's gospel through Lk 24,9; and some more
examples are briefly discussed in his *Matthew* (1982, [2]1994) and now
also in his *Mark* (1993)[7]. Thus I thought it was quite natural that Gundry
and Goulder were brought together in an essay on Lk 10,25-28. The
choice of this pericope was facilitated by my own acquiescence with
both scholars in denying Luke's use of Q in 10,25-28[8].

2. Mk 12,28: "Was Mark's Scribe Friendly?"

I The topic of Gundry's investigation in "Matthean Foreign Bodies"
and now in his Rejoinder on Lk 10,25-28 are the supposedly "non- and
anti-Lucan features" in Luke's agreements with Matthew against Mark.
The text of Mk 12,28-34, common source of Matthew and Luke, is not
directly his theme of study. Nevertheless, he refers to a phrase of mine
on "Mark's friendly scribe" and replies by quoting a paragraph from his
Mark: "We have no good reason to think that the scribe approaches
Jesus any less antagonistically than did the Pharisees or the Sadducees"[9]. This amazing and unusual[10] comment is more or less corrected
in the commentator's own Notes where he mentions "the contrast
between the favorable portrayal of the scribe in this pericope and the
unfavorable portrayal of scribes elsewhere in Mark"[11]. He also notes:

7. On *Matthew*, see my review in *ETL* 63 (1987) 408-410; on *Mark*, cf. *ETL* 69
(1993) 183-186 (on the minor agreements, see the list of references on p. 183).
    8. On the supposition of a Q-Vorlage, cf. *The Minor Agreements and Q* (n. 1), p. 62
n. 72. K. Kertelge's essay (1985) is now reprinted: *Das Doppelwort der Liebe im
Markusevangelium*, in *TTZ* 103 (1994) 38-55 (cf. p. 44 n. 17). See also J. LAMBRECHT,
The Great Commandment Pericope and Q, in *The Gospel Behind the Gospels* (n. 1),
pp. 73-96. In contrast to the hypothesis of parallel traditions (Kertelge, *et al.*) Lambrecht
proposes the Q passage as the common source behind the three Synoptics: "there is no
need for supposing another text as source for Mark than the Q passage" (p. 95). Compare
now also M.-É. BOISMARD, *L'Évangile de Marc: Sa préhistoire* (Études Bibliques, N.S.,
26), Paris, 1994, pp. 175-177: Mark depends here on Q through Matthean tradition (contrast *Synopse II*, 1972).
    9. *Rejoinder*, p. 140 (and n. 5). Cf. *Mark*, p. 710. See also p. 712.
    10. A few illustrations from the commentaries on Mk: "Mc. clearly regards the scribe
who questioned the Lord as free from malicious intent" (Swete); "The friendly attitude
of the scribe ... is distinctive of the Markan story" (Taylor); "The stress on the friendli-
ness of the scribe" (Cranfield); "in no hostile spirit" (Nineham); "zeigt den Fragesteller
von Anfang an in einer positiven Haltung gegenüber Jesus" (Pesch); "Die Frage ... is
nicht in böser Absicht gestellt" (Lührmann).
    11. *Mark*, p. 714; referring, without contest, to A.M. Ambrozic. Cf. *Hidden Kingdom*,
p. 177: "Vs. 28a cannot be urged against this, for Mark obviously composed or reworked
it with the story in mind".

"Saying that the scribe weakens Jesus' statement ... does the scribe an injustice. Jesus' compliment gives him better press (v 34)"[12]. Gundry's evidence for the view that "the scribe started out antagonistic to Jesus" is scarcely convincing. He compares the phraseology of Mk 12,28 with that of the Sadducees' question in 12,18: Mark uses the same verb ἐπερωτάω and προσελθών parallels ἔρχονται ... πρός. However, the same verb ἐπερωτάω is used in Mk 7,17; 9,28; 10,10; 13,3, where the interlocutors are Jesus' disciples, and also in 10,17, where "the man's kneeling exceeds the reverence shown to an ordinary teacher and thereby highlights for Mark's audience the divine sonship of Jesus"[13]. It is certainly not the use of this verb which denotes "initial failure to address Jesus respectfully"; in contrast to 10,2, the scribe is not said to "test" Jesus. In 12,18 ἔρχονται ... πρὸς αὐτόν opens a new pericope: "Sadducees ... came to him and asked him a question", and some translators tend to give the same function to προσελθών in 12,28: "And one of the scribes came up and heard them disputing..." (RSV). A more satisfactory rendering of the interconnection with the preceding pericope is provided in REB: "Then one of the scribes, who had been listening to these discussions and had observed how well Jesus answered, came forward and asked him..."[14]. Elsewhere I in Mk προσελθών occurs within a pericope (1,31; 14,45) and, following Gundry's commentary, προσελθόντες in 6,35 and 10,2 marks a new shift within a larger unit (6,30-44; 10,1-12)[15].

Gundry now at least considers a view of Mark's scribe as friendly. Instead of judging the omission of νομικός in Mt 22,35 "a scribal assimilation of Matthew to Mark" he now suggests a copyist of Matthew having in mind Matthean pairing of scribes with Pharisees or a sense of overload "with no thought of assimilation to Mark"[16].

With regard to Matthew's reason for omitting προσελθών Gundry explicitly acknowledges the correction: "So I shall propose an answer other than my earlier one". There follows a remarkable parenthesis: "Failure to answer the question [why Matthew omits προσελθών here in 22,35] ... weakens Neirynck's argument", and then he continues: "The answer is that Matthew has replaced Mark's participial motion in προσελθών with the motion of a main verbal phrase, συνήχθησαν ἐπὶ

12. *Mark*, pp. 716-717.
13. *Ibid.*, p. 552.
14. Compare: "Und ein Schriftgelehrter, der..., trat heran und fragte ihn..." (J. Gnilka).
15. On Mk 10,2 προσελθόντες Φαρισαῖοι (om. Metzger, Boismard-Lamouille, *et al.*), see Gundry's comment in *Mark*, pp. 535-536.
16. *Rejoinder*, p. 140.

τὸ αὐτό"[17]. This looks like a palimpsest of the "answer" I gave: "What really happened in Matthew is not dropping προσελθών and advancing ἐπηρώτησεν but replacement of προσελθών with συνήχθησαν ἐπὶ τὸ αὐτό"[18]. As I indicated, my point there was that "Matthew's reason ... suggested by Gundry and supposed to be absent in Luke, cannot be verified in the Gospel of Matthew itself"[19]. With regard to the "omission" of προσελθών in Luke, I may refer to my presentation of the parallels[20]:

Mark   προσελθών ... ἐπηρώτησεν αὐτόν·
Luke   ... ἀνέστη   ἐκπειράζων αὐτὸν λέγων.

Some clarification is needed on Luke's omission of Mk 12,28bc. I quote Gundry's observation in *Rejoinder*[21]:

Nor have I argued for Lucan dependence on Matthew because Luke omits Mark's ἀκούσας αὐτῶν συζητούντων, ἰδών..., so that Neirynck's | comment that this omission is "completely irrelevant in a discussion of possible dependence on Matthew" is itself irrelevant.

But compare his comment in *Matthew*[22]:

[Matthew] now omits Mark's statements that one of the scribes "heard them [Jesus and the Sadducees] arguing and saw that Jesus answered them [the Sadducees] well." *This omission occurs also in Luke 10:25-28 and therefore supports* "lawyer" *as another such agreement in the original of Matthew's text.*

---

17. *Ibid.*, p. 144.
18. *Luke 10:25-28*, p. 154. My text continues on p. 155: "I will not elaborate here on Matthew's style in Matt 22:33,34", with reference to Gundry's *Matthew*, p. 447, where he notes the phraseology of Ps 2,2 LXX (now in his text: *Rejoinder*, p. 144).
19. *Luke 10:25-28*, p. 155. Compare the synopsis on p. 153. Unfortunately, the printed text did not show the alignment of the parallels:

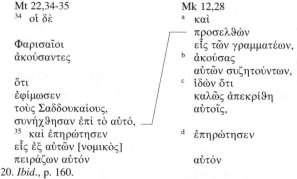

Mt 22,34-35   Mk 12,28
[34] οἱ δὲ   a καὶ
                                       προσελθών
Φαρισαῖοι   εἰς τῶν γραμματέων,
ἀκούσαντες   b ἀκούσας
                                       αὐτῶν συζητούντων,
ὅτι   c ἰδὼν ὅτι
ἐφίμωσεν   καλῶς ἀπεκρίθη
τοὺς Σαδδουκαίους,   αὐτοῖς,
συνήχθησαν ἐπὶ τὸ αὐτό,
[35] καὶ ἐπηρώτησεν   d ἐπηρώτησεν
εἷς ἐξ αὐτῶν [νομικὸς]
πειράζων αὐτόν   αὐτόν

20. *Ibid.*, p. 160.
21. *Rejoinder*, p. 145 n. 30. The text refers to my *Luke 10:25-28*, p. 155.
22. *Matthew*, p. 448 (emphasis mine). Cf. *Rejoinder*, n. 30: "How could I"!

3. Νομικός IN LUKE

The split in the Goulder-Gundry team is manifest on νομικός in Luke: "He takes over Mark's scribe, whom he renders by his customary νομικός" (Goulder); "we have many reasons to believe that apart from Matthean influence Luke would not have substituted νομικός τις at 10,25 for εἷς τῶν γραμματέων in Mark 12,28" (Gundry)[23].

Gundry has now corrected the three lacunae I noted in his survey of Lukan parallels to γραμματεύς in Mark: Lk 20,39 "some of the scribes", similar to Mark's "one of the scribes" (12,28); the use of νομοδιδάσκαλος (Lk 5,17; Acts 5,34); the distinction between the singular ὁ γραμματεύς in Acts 19,35 and the plural elsewhere in Luke-Acts[24]. There is still the case of ὁ γραμματεύς in Mk 12,32 which apparently may not see the light. It is mentioned in a list of "remaining Marcan instances of γραμματεύς (which) have no proper Lucan parallels (see Mark 9,11; 12,32 and possibly 15,1)"[25], without saying that, as usual in Mark, the plural is used in 9,11 and 15,1 and that ὁ γραμματεύς in 12,32 is Mark's unique use of the singular. Gundry now accepts Luke's adoption of (τινες) τῶν γραμματέων in 20,39 from (εἷς) τῶν γραμματέων in Mk 12,28 ("Luke is not adverse to the expression"), but he treats "(one) of the scribes" as a plural without noting that this "one of the scribes" is "the scribe" in 12,32, and thus Luke's νομικός τις is parallel to εἷς τῶν γραμματέων / ὁ γραμματεύς[26]. The information I that

---

23. *Rejoinder*, p. 142. On νομικός in Luke, see pp. 141-143 (nn. 12-21). There is no mention of Goulder's divergent opinion (*Luke*, p. 485). The only "authority" he refers to (n. 21) is I.H. Marshall (*Luke*, 1978; add p. 499, on νομικός in 11,45: "possibly pre-Lucan"); Marshall's argument at 10,25: "Nowhere else does Luke make this alteration to Mark's wording" (p. 441; see also p. 299). – Apart from authors I mentioned in *Lk 10:25-28* (his nn. 13, 20, 43, 49, 52; and n. 18, more general), his note 21 (on Marshall) is the only reference to secondary literature in *Rejoinder*.

24. *Luke 10:25-28*, p. 156.

25. *Rejoinder*, p. 142. – On p. 142, line 28, read: Mark 3,32.

26. Cf. *Luke 10:25-28*, p. 155, on the combined influence of Mk 12,28 and 32a in Lk 20,39 (unnoticed by Gundry); p. 159, on the influence of Mk 12,33 and 34a in Lk 10,27 and 28a (Gundry's comment, p. 147: "both incorrect and irrelevant"). But (1) his own comment on the two commandments simply repeats my own observation: "Luke's formulation of the two commandments fused into one (ἀγαπήσεις ... καὶ ...) comes closer to that of Mark 12:33 (τὸ ἀγαπᾶν ... καὶ τὸ ἀγαπᾶν ...)"; I did not say: are fused in Mark! (2) His explanation of ὀρθῶς ἀπεκρίθης in Lk 10,28a ("has to do with scriptural correctness") does not exclude a reminiscence of νουνεχῶς ἀπεκρίθη (Mk 12,34a); this is widely accepted, by Goulder (p. 487) as well as by upholders of the Q hypothesis (cf. above, n. 8): K. Kertelge (1994, p. 44: "ein 'Nachklang'"), J. Lambrecht (1995, p. 78). Irrelevant ("it would not matter if...") means here: "is not to disprove Matthean influence" (p. 147).

Luke uses γραμματεύς in Acts several times[27] is misleading as long as it is not added that the singular appears only in 19,35 where γραμματεύς has the meaning "town clerk"; in 5,34 Luke refers to an individual scribe, the Pharisee Gamaliel, and uses the expression νομοδιδάσκαλος.

"Neirynck notes the equivalence of 'the lawyers and Pharisees' in Luke 14,3 to 'the scribes and the Pharisees' in Luke 5,21; 6,7"[28]. More correctly, the expression "the lawyers and Pharisees" in 14,3 is the equivalent of Luke's own "scribes and Pharisees" in Lk 6,7 (diff. Mk 3,2, cf. "the Pharisees" in v. 6)[29]. This defense of Luke's redactional use of νομικός in 14,3 (and response to Goulder's view: the Lucan equivalent of "scribes and Pharisees" in Mt 23,2) remains without reply[30]. The *Rejoinder* moves straight to the conclusion: "νομικός in Luke 7,30; 11,45.46.52; 14,3 may derive, or probably does derive, from Q and perhaps Lucan special material"[31].

For Gundry, "he (= Neirynck) still cannot cite any other instance of Luke's substituting νομικός for a Marcan γραμματεύς, as Luke does at 10,25 in agreement with Matthew"[32]. In my judgment, careful examination of Lk 10,25 and 14,3 shows that in both cases νομικός is used redactionally by Luke in Markan material: Lk 14,1-6 is a "secondary" parallel to Mk 3,1-6 and Lk 10,25-28 is parallel to Mk 12,28-34. Also in Lk 7,30 and 11,45.46.52 νομικός can be ascribed to Lukan redaction. Lk 7,30 receives no further comment in *Rejoinder*. With regard to Lk 11,45.46.52 Gundry observes in general that Luke was reluctant to alter dominical sayings[33]. To this general principle I am tempted to reply in Gundry's style that it is incorrect and irrelevant in this case. The use of νομικός for "scribes" here has to do much more with order and arrangement than with the content of the traditional sayings. Lk 11,45 is not a dominical saying: ἀποκριθεὶς δέ τις τῶν νομικῶν

27. *Rejoinder*, p. 142; see also p. 143.
28. *Ibid.*, p. 142. Cf. *Luke 10:25-28*, p. 156.
29. See my *Luke 14,1-6: Lukan Composition and Q Saying*, in C. BUSSMANN – W. RADL (eds.), *Der Treue Gottes trauen. Beiträge zum Werk des Lukas. FS G. Schneider*, Freiburg-Basel-Wien, 1991, pp. 243-263; = *Evangelica II* (BETL, 110), 1991, pp. 183-204, esp. 190-193 (on νομικός).
30. For Gundry's view on Lk 14,1-6, see my *Luke 14,1-6*, p. 245 (= *Evangelica II*, p. 185). Cf. GOULDER, *Luke*, p. 586: "Gundry thinks Matthew has borrowed details from the dropsy story, which he has omitted. If we follow Schürmann and Gundry, Q becomes an enormous and speculative catch-all".
31. *Rejoinder*, p. 143.
32. *Ibid.*, p. 142.
33. *Ibid.*, p. 142. To W.G. Kümmel's text, quoted in n. 18, Gundry gives an application which goes far beyond what is meant by Kümmel. Compare, for instance, in the same *Introduction*, pp. 138 (Amen sayings), 139 (Lk 23,46), 144 (Lk 16,16).

λέγει αὐτῷ· διδάσκαλε, ταῦτα λέγων καὶ ἡμᾶς ὑβρίζεις. Compare Jesus' reply, καὶ ὑμῖν τοῖς νομικοῖς οὐαί (v. 46), and again in v. 52, οὐαὶ ὑμῖν τοῖς νομικοῖς (contrast v. 47 οὐαὶ ὑμῖν). I can agree with Gundry that Lk 11,53-54 is likely to be an editorial conclusion, but D. Kosch's suggestion I referred to only concerns the possible presence of a reminiscence in v. 53 ("the scribes")[34].

Critical analysis of Luke leads to the conclusion that, whatever may be the outcome of the text-critical discussion of Mt 22,35, it will not be possible to call I Luke's νομικός in 10,25 a Matthean foreign body in Luke. It is certainly helpful for the debate on Mt 22,35 that Gundry recognizes that strong or weak external evidence is not necessarily the decisive factor in textual judgments (cf. Mt 27,16.17)[35]. I also note the acceptance of scribal assimilations of Matthew to Luke (the readings τις and καὶ λέγων)[36]. This is perhaps a first step toward the recognition that copyists who saw the similarity between

| Matthew | εἷς ἐξ αὐτῶν | πειράζων αὐτόν· | διδάσκαλε |
| and Luke | νομικός τις ... | ἐκ πειράζων αὐτὸν λέγων· | διδάσκαλε |

possibly heightened the similarity[37] by adding νομικός in Matthew.

The new edition of *The Greek New Testament* ([4]1993) did not change the rating C of νομικός in Mt 22,35[38]. If original, νομικός can be read in the light of ἐν τῷ νόμῳ (v. 36), ὅλος ὁ νόμος ... καὶ οἱ προφῆται (v. 40; cf. 5,17; 7,12), and Matthew's liking of the cognate νόμος – ἀνομία, but it is much more doubtful to include νομίζω in this cognateness[39]. It is less evident that Gundry's emphasis on Matthean awkwardness and

34. Cf. *Luke 10:25-28*, p. 157; in Gundry's language: a compensation for the omission in the woe-sayings.

35. *Rejoinder*, p. 141.

36. *Ibid.*, pp. 140-141.

37. In discussing transcriptional probability of the two readings in Mt 22,35 one should evaluate what is more likely, the copyist's addition of νομικός (assimilation to Luke) or the copyist's omission of νομικός (for Gundry: assimilation to Mark). Gundry seems to neglect that in the copyist's text of Mark "the intervening ἀκούσας..., ἰδών..." were still there. Cf. *Rejoinder*: "wherein lies a problem?" (p. 140). In describing the "Matthean phrase in other respects more like Mark's than like Luke's" (p. 140) he curiously neglects the otherwise overemphasized agreements with Luke in the following words: πειράζων αὐτόν· διδάσκαλε.

38. On revised ratings in GNT[4], cf. *ETL* 69 (1993), p. 420. As far as I know, M.D. Goulder, who in other respects is Gundry's ally, did not change his opinion (cf. *Luke 10:25-28*, p. 150). Note also the comment by H.B. Green, another defender of Luke's use of Matthew: "this word ... has probably crept in through assimilation to Lk 10,25" (*Matthew*, 1987 = 1975, p. 185). Recent commentators who defend the Q solution make an exception for νομικός: "it may have been inserted from Luke 10:25" (D.J. HARRINGTON, *Matthew*, 1991, p. 315); "could have come in from Luke" (J. NOLLAND, *Luke*, 1993, p. 583).

39. Cf. *Rejoinder*, p. 143.

Lukan stylistic improvement⁴⁰ will increase the likelihood of νομικός in Matthew. It is hardly understandable how Luke's (νομικός) τις can be a substitute for Matthew's εἷς (ἐξ αὐτῶν)⁴¹ and not for Mark's εἷς (τῶν γραμματέων). On the side of Matthew, "one of them, a lawyer" is a substitute for Mark's "one of the scribes". In this connection Gundry now develops the new argument of Matthew's "consistent distinction between scribes and Pharisees": "Matthew shies away from equating 'one of the scribes' with one of his imported Pharisees [v. 34] and defines 'one of them' as 'a lawyer'"⁴². Because of Matthew's radical differentiation it is unthinkable that his Pharisaic 'lawyer' could be a Pharisaic 'scribe'⁴³. Unfortunately, Gundry does not elaborate any further on this ad hoc definition of νομικός. On the side of Luke, no such problem arises: Mark's scribe, εἷς τῶν γραμματέων (ὁ γραμματεύς), can be replaced by νομικός τις.

4. OTHER AGREEMENTS WITH MATTHEW

I Over and above νομικός (1) the following agreements are discussed in *Rejoinder*:

(2) Ἐκπειράζων (Mt πειράζων)

My intention, in the four points I made, was to show that independent Lukan redaction is a valid alternative to Matthean influence⁴⁴. (1) The

---

40. *Ibid.*
41. *Ibid.*, p. 145.
42. *Ibid.*, p. 144.
43. Contrast Gundry's comment on Mt 23,2 in *Matthew*: "by pairing the scribes and Pharisees repeatedly, Matthew leaves the impression that he is writing only about scribes who belong to the Pharisaical sect" (p. 454; see the reference in *Rejoinder*, n. 25).
44. And by the same: an alternative to Deutero-Mark or Q. On Deutero-Mark, see the references to A. Ennulat's dissertation (1989) in *The Minor Agreements and Q*, pp. 61-64 (and 56 n. 40); *Luke 10:25-28*, p. 151 n. 18 (and 152 n. 19). See now A. ENNULAT, *Die "Minor Agreements". Untersuchungen zu einer offenen Frage des synoptischen Problems* (WUNT, 2/62), Tübingen, 1994, pp. 278-287: "58. Mk 12,28-34parr". Compare the list of minor agreements in F. NEIRYNCK, *The Minor Agreements in a Horizontal-Line Synopsis* (SNTA, 15), 1991, pp. 70-71; *The Minor Agreements*, 1974, pp. 157-158 (§ 77). On the minor agreements and Q in Lk 10,25-28, cf. J. LAMBRECHT, *The Great Commandment* (n. 8), pp. 79-81. Like Ennulat, he makes a distinction between some "very minor" which "could have been the result of mutually independent but identical or similar rewriting of the Markan text" and other agreements "too striking to be explained by mere coincidence": his nos. 1, 2, 4, 5 in an enumeration of ten agreements (p. 81). Just one remark on his no. 2, "They have no parallel to Mk 12:32-33" (p. 79): see p. 77: "It is not impossible that in 'fusing' the two quotations Luke was influenced by Mk 12:33"; p. 78, on the parable about the good Samaritan: "The idea ... perhaps came to Luke's mind from reading Mk 12:33b"; on Lk 10,28b and Mk 10,34a, cf. above, n. 26. See also p. 79, on the title διδάσκαλε (no. 3): "subsequently in 12:32". Νομικός (no. 4) is cited

association of lawyers and Pharisees is found elsewhere in Luke. (2) The question in v. 29 indicates that the initial 'testing' question is not un-Lukan. (3) The structure (with counterquestion) corresponds to that of Markan stories with "testing" question, known to Luke. (4) In replacing Mark's ἐπηρώτησεν Luke differs from Matthew[45].

A few remarks on Gundry's reaction to these four points: (1) "Matthean influence", if not excluded, is unnecessary. (2) What is wrong with "to confirm the hostile intent..."? Plainly said: the new question in v. 29 confirms the interpretation of the first question as hostile. (3) Lk 11,16 is not a "strong" parallel because this displaced motif is separated from its original context (Mk 8,11-13; cf. Lk 11,29-30). The lack of a Lukan parallel to Mk 10,2-9 is neither irrelevant nor harmful. The influence of Mk 10,1 (and 11) on Lukan composition is well known and Mk 10,2-9 shows how Luke may conceive a story with testing question and counterquestion. (4) My treatment of ἐκ-πειράζων (cf. Goulder) is not restricted to a dialogue with Gundry, although one would like to know whether he still maintains the "Satanic role" of the lawyer[46].

(3) Διδάσκαλε

The title in Lk 10,25 may be influenced by Mk 12,32: "the possibility of combined influence of Mark 12:28 and 32 is shown in Luke 20:39". However, the question in Lk 10,25b has its real source in Mk 10,17, including διδάσκαλε. For l this address in the mouth of the Lukan "lawyer", compare Lk 11,45 (τις τῶν νομικῶν...· διδάσκαλε)[47].

In reply to *Rejoinder* one may observe that there is really no need for a demonstration that "Luke habitually compensates for omissions" since the evidence of reminiscences of Mk 12,32-34 in Lk 10,25-28 speaks for itself[48]. A somewhat sophisticated list of minor agreements could include, beside διδάσκαλε Mt 22,35 / Lk 10,25 (diff. Mk 12,28), also διδάσκαλε Mt 19,16 / Lk 10,25 (diff. Mk 10,17; Lk 18,18 διδάσκαλε ἀγαθέ), but not without adding the redactional explanations of the omission of ἀγαθέ in their respective context, Mt 19,16 (τί + ἀγαθόν) and Lk 10,25 (a lawyer's question).

in contrast to "one of the scribes" in Mk 12,28, but no mention is made of ὁ γραμματεύς in Mk 12,32 (cf. above); neither is there any reference to the other instances of νομικός in Luke. Cf. p. 74: "the minor agreements ... should be brought together and carefully analyzed"! Ἐκπειράζω is merely listed as no. 5 (p. 80). On his no. 1, cf. below (5).
45. *Luke 10:25-28*, pp. 159-161. Cf. *Rejoinder*, p. 146.
46. Cf. *Luke 10:25-28*, p. 161 n. 62.
47. *Luke 10:25-28*, pp. 157-159. Cf. *Rejoinder*, p. 147.
48. See above, nn. 26 and 45. Cf. *Luke 10:25-28*, pp. 158-159 (and 156).

(4) Ἐν τῷ νόμῳ

This phrase ἐν τῷ νόμῳ in Lk 10,26[49] is not strictly parallel to the phrase in Mt 22,36: μεγάλη ἐν τῷ νόμῳ (Mk πρώτη πάντων) in the lawyer's question. The parallel in Mt 12,5 (Goulder) is apparently not taken into consideration by Gundry. As recognized in *Rejoinder*, Luke's phrase is part of "a redactionally created counterquestion", but "Neirynck cannot deny the nonrecurrence of ἐν τῷ νόμῳ in Luke-Acts". Yet, the similarity between ἐν τῷ νόμῳ τί γέγραπται and Lk 24,44 τὰ γεγραμμένα ἐν τῷ νόμῳ Μωϋσέως καὶ τοῖς προφήταις καὶ ψαλμοῖς (together with the variations "the law of Moses", "Moses", and "the law" in Luke-Acts)[50] remains impressive and, in my opinion, counterbalances the absence of other instances of "die 'nackte' Formel" (Ennulat). Gundry is probably not unaware of the significance of this parallel; this could at least explain the concealment of the full phrase of Lk 24,44 in his survey of references. In any case, from his discussion of νομικός in Mt 22,35 we know that the singular occurrence is not always an obstacle for the acceptance of redactional usage.

(5) The omission of Mk 12,29b

Without opening here a Gundry-Fitzmyer debate on Luke's omission of the monotheistic introduction[51], I prefer to quote my own words and leave judgment to the reader[52]:

> The omission of the first part of the Shemaʿ should not be isolated from its immediate context in Luke. The lawyer's initial question was about eternal life (what must I do?) and in v. 27 he answers this question on doing with Deut 6,5 and Lev 19,18 combined into a single love command: ἀγαπή-σεις.... Luke had no need to address the problem of the two command-ments "since he uses a quite different form of question" (J. Nolland).

(6) Ὁ δὲ εἶπεν πρὸς αὐτόν

Ι Is there really need for a demonstration of Lukan redaction in this phrase (10,26a)? It may suffice here to add the illustration of ὁ Ἰησοῦς replaced by ὁ δέ in Lk 21,8: ὁ δὲ εἶπεν (and διδάσκαλε added in v. 7).

---

49. *Luke 10:25-28*, pp. 162-163. Cf. *Rejoinder*, pp. 147-148.

50. *Luke 10:25-28*, p. 162.

51. On the Shema in Mark, see now J. MARCUS, *Authority to Forgive Sins upon the Earth: The Shema in the Gospel of Mark*, in C.A. EVANS – W.R. STEGNER (eds.), *The Gospels and the Scriptures of Israel* (JSNT SS, 104), Sheffield, 1994, pp. 196-211. Cf. p. 196 n. 3, on the omission of Deut 6,4 in Matthew's and Luke's redaction of Mk 12,28-34: "For them, apparently, the emphasis on the oneness of God is not as important as it is for Mark".

52. *Luke 10:25-28*, p. 164.

(7) Ἐν ... ἐν ... ἐν ...

Gundry cannot see how the P⁷⁵ B reading in Lk 10,27 could help my argument[53]. The suggestion of Lukan stylistic improvement can perhaps be made more clear by quoting the text:

ἐξ ὅλης καρδίας σου,
    ἐν ὅλῃ τῇ ψυχῇ σου
    καὶ ἐν ὅλῃ τῇ ἰσχύϊ σου
    καὶ ἐν ὅλῃ τῇ διανοίᾳ σου.

To conclude, the thesis of the Goulder-Gundry team has special attractiveness in a case like Lk 10,25-28 because it turns away from the easy solution of a non-Markan source. But their Luke, "with one eye on Mark and another on Matthew", needs surgery. I recommend a new redaction-critical treatment.

My surrejoinder was written when I received the new edition of Gundry's *Matthew* (publication date: December 1994)[54]. The text of the commentary is reprinted without changes and no endnotes to Mt 22,34-40 are added[55]. There is one sentence in the new Preface[56] that I can make mine: "Better criticized than ignored!" Gundry seems to ask for more critical reaction: "I have tried to force attention to the last of these items (Luke's secondary use of Matthew) with my essay, *Matthean Foreign Bodies*..."[57]. In the opening section of his *Rejoinder* he does not exclude "the loss of one passage", but he concludes by referring to "the many further passages in Luke that appear to contain Matthean foreign bodies"[58]. The remark I made in my review of *Matthew* can be applied to *Matthean Foreign Bodies*[59]:

> Quant à l'argument des traits matthéens, il est plus apparent que réel parce que G. ne se demande presque jamais dans quelle mesure il s'agit d'un trait exclusivement matthéen. Indépendamment de Matthieu, Luc peut avoir la même raison ou une raison semblable pour changer le texte de Marc. La démonstration a été faite pour plusieurs passages, mais G. ne semble pas en tenir compte dans son commentaire.

---

53. *Rejoinder*, p. 150.
54. See my review in *ETL* 71 (1995) 218-221.
55. The text of his note 18 on W.G. Kümmel (*Rejoinder*, p. 142; cf. *above*, p. 155 n. 33) is reproduced in "Preface to the Second Edition" (pp. xi-xxx), p. xv. Note the references to his essay, *Matthean Foreign Bodies*, and his thesis of Luke's secondary use of Matthew, on pp. xii, xv, xvi, and in the Endnotes, nn. 3, 9, 59.
56. *Ibid.*, p. xii.
57. *Ibid.*
58. *Rejoinder*, pp. 139 and 150.
59. *ETL* 63 (1987), p. 409.

| To conclude, I quote one example, taken from the last passage, Lk 24,9 (diff. Mk 16,8)[60]:

> Luke will carry no allusion to Ps 22,23(22) which this clause can antici-pate; so despite the occurrence of ἀπαγγέλλω eleven times in Luke over against eight and five times in Matthew and Mark, it seems probable that the clause as a whole reflects Matthew (cf. GOULDER, *Luke*, p. 776, where it is noted that Luke "could have used a much more common word like εἶπαν [Mk. 16.7] or ἔλεγον [Luk. 24.10]").

Reference could be made to my 1980 note on "Mc 16,8 et l'accord Mt/Lc"[61]. In the text quoted from Goulder the first part of the sentence is dropped: "ἀπαγγέλλειν is a word congenial to Luke"; compare his comment at Lk 8,20 (Mk λέγουσιν); 8,36 (Mk διηγήσαντο); 8,47 (Mk εἶπεν)[62]. Goulder has no comment on the more significant parallel to Lk 24,9 (diff. Mk 16,8) in Lk 9,36: οὐδενὶ ἀπήγγειλαν ... οὐδὲν ὧν ἑώρακαν (cf. Mk 9,9 ἵνα μηδενὶ ἃ εἶδον διηγήσωνται). In order to explain Luke's use of ἀπαγγέλλειν in 24,9, there is really no need for a later allusion to Ps 22. By the way, the verb is not used in Ps 21,23LXX, and the allusion in Mt 28,10 may be less evident than it was suggested by Gundry in 1967[63].

---

60. *Matthean Foreign Bodies*, p. 1493. See also *Matthew*, p. 590, on Mt 28,8: "ἀπαγγεῖλαι, which replaces Mark's εἶπαν, anticipates the allusion to Ps 22:23(22) in v 10". The reference should be to Ps 22,23(LXX 21,23). Cf. GUNDRY, *The Use of the Old Testament in St. Matthew* (NTSup, 18), Leiden, 1967, pp. 146-147.

61. *ETL* 56 (1980) 78-80 (= *Evangelica I*, pp. 261-263; see also p. 309). For an extreme example of Gundry's neglect of Lukan style, see his treatment of the Mt/Lk par-allels to Mk 16,5: "Essentially, ἐμφόβων δὲ γενομένων ... in Lk 24,5 agrees with Matthew against Mark. But Luke has no guards to have provoked the change (his words apply to the women instead): so it is probably due to Matthew's influence on him" (*Matthean Foreign Bodies*, p. 1492). Of course, ἐμφόβων γενομένων in Lk applies to the women (like Mk's ἐξεθαμβήθησαν); compare the Lukan phrase ἔμφοβοι γενό-μενοι in Lk 24,37 and ἔμφοβος γενόμενος in Acts 10,4 and 24,25. Cf. *ETL* 67 (1991), p. 89 (= *Evangelica II*, p. 67).

62. *Luke*, p. 419.

63. Ps 21,23: διηγήσομαι (!) τὸ ὄνομά σου τοῖς ἀδελφοῖς μου,
        ἐν μέσῳ ἐκκλησίας ὑμνήσω σε.
On the citation in Heb 2,12 (ἀπαγγελῶ...), cf. H.-F. WEISS, *Der Brief an die Hebräer* (KEK, 13), Göttingen, 1991, p. 216: "der Autor des Hebr (liest) bewußt anstelle von διηγήσομαι (Ps 21,23LXX) ἀπαγγελῶ (und [betont] damit noch mehr als in LXX den Parallelismus zu ὑμνήσω)". On "my brothers" in Mt 28,10 (cf. 12,49), see *Evangelia I*, pp. 288-289.

– Supplementary note: U. MELL, *Die "anderen" Winzer. Eine exegetische Studie zur Vollmacht Jesu Christi nach Markus 11,27–12,34* (WUNT, 77), Tübingen, 1994, pp. 312-353 (Mk 12,28-34), esp. 314-319: "Exkurs: *Die Frage nach dem obersten Gebot nach der Logienquelle Q (Mt 22,35-40; Lk 10,25-28)*". Mell proposes pre-Mk (12,28-36b*) and Q as two independent traditions. The evidence for Q are the Mt/Lk agreements against Mk; they are listed once more (p. 314 n. 15) and are declared to be "gravierend" (n. 14) without being studied in light of Matthean and Lukan redaction: "ein metho-disches Defizit"?

ETL 75 (1999) 123-132

10

LUKE 9,22 AND 10,25-28
THE CASE FOR INDEPENDENT REDACTION

As it may appear from the bibliographic footnotes to R.H. Gundry's article[1] the author defends his thesis of subsidiary Matthean influence in reply to contributions published in *ETL* 1989, 1996 (Lk 9,22) and 1995 (Lk 10,25-28). In my own response I will treat his Parts I and II in the same order.

I

The first agreement of **Lk 9,22** with Mt 16,21 against Mk 8,31 is the substitution of ἀπό for Mark's ὑπό. Not mentioned before by Gundry, its treatment now in the first section of his article (p. 105-106) is the only topic that is new in reference to *Matthean Foreign Bodies* (1992). Gundry's approach is less statistical than Goulder's. His main argument is to observe that there is no other occurrence of Luke's substituting an agential ἀπό for ὑπό. He regards independence from Matthew's ἀπό as unlikely "for a number of reasons", but the seven reasons he enumerates all concern aspects of the use of the ὑπό of agency with passive verbs in Luke–Acts. Such a sevenfoldness not necessarily makes a complete argument. – His second reason: "Once he [Luke] writes such a ὑπό where the double tradition lacks it (Lk 3,7)". Strangely enough, Gundry abandons here his own interpretation of βαπτισθῆναι ὑπ᾽ αὐτοῦ as pertaining to the tradition behind Lk 3,7a, which Matthew revised "because of his changing the crowds to Pharisees and Sadducees" (*Matthew*, 50). However, it is a more satisfactory solution that not "the double tradition" but Mk 1,5 is the source of Lk 3,7a (cf. ἐξεπορεύετο ... καὶ ἐβαπτίζοντο ὑπ᾽ αὐτοῦ)[2]. Thus the category n° 2 can be dropped; read: ten occurrences in n° 3 (add 14,8b), and three in n° 4 (add 3,7a). Total number in Lk: 24.

---

1. *The Refusal of Matthean Foreign Bodies to be Exorcised from Luke 9,22; 10,25-28*, in *ETL* 75 (1999) 104-122, nn. 1-6. On his *Matthew* (n. 1), see my review in *ETL* 63 (1987) 408-410; 71 (1995) 218-221. On Lk 9,22 (n. 6), cf. T.A. FRIEDRICHSEN, *Luke 9,22 – A Matthean Foreign Body?*, in *ETL* 72 (1996) 398-407; M.S. GOODACRE, *Goulder and the Gospels. An Examination of a New Paradigm* (JSNT SS, 133), Sheffield, 1996, 96-98.

2. See my *The First Synoptic Pericope: The Appearance of John the Baptist in Q?*, in *ETL* 72 (1996) 41-74, esp. 72-73.

Gundry recognizes that in Acts, with 38 occurrences of such a ὑπό, Luke writes five or six times a similar ἀπό. His emphasis on *"only* five or six occurrences"[3] is scarcely justified, since it is well known that ὑπό is the usual Greek | preposition to express agency with a passive verb. If, from this proportion in Acts, any conclusion can be drawn with regard to the Gospel, it would be that one may expect in Lk some four occurrences of ἀπό (against 24 ὑπό's). Such a ἀπο is never used in Mark and only once in Lk's second source Q (= Lk 7,35). The five other occurrences in Lk can be redactional: Lk 1,26; 6,18; 8,43; 9,22; 17,25.

1,26 ἀπεστάλη ... **ἀπὸ** τοῦ θεοῦ. For Gundry the preposition ἀπό in the text of Lk means either "by" (agency) or "from" (separation) and the variant reading ὑπό (TR Vogels) either exhibits an original ἀπό = *by* or corrects a ἀπο = *from* to the substitute ὑπό (*by*). Though undecided[4], Gundry seems to have no objection against the first of these alternatives.

6,18 οἱ ἐνοχλούμενοι **ἀπὸ** πνευμάτων ἀκαθάρτων. Ac 5,16 (ὀχλουμένους ὑπὸ πνευμάτων ἀκαθάρτων) illustrates the equivalency of ἀπό and ὑπό phrases. It shows Lukan "repetition and variation" rather than reverse substitution because of his preference for ὑπό.

8,43 ἀπ᾽ οὐδενὸς θεραπευθῆναι (var. ὑπ᾽ TR von Soden), par. Mk 5,26 πολλὰ παθοῦσα ὑπὸ πολλῶν ἰατρῶν. Gundry objects that there are differences of order and content: "Mark's phrase has to do with suffering, whereas Luke's phrase has to do with healing". Yet, Luke's phrase is not about healing, but about *not* being healed (with a double negative: οὐκ ἴσχυσεν ἀπ᾽ οὐδενός...). Suffering under many physicians and not being healed by any one (of those physicians): could it be more closely parallel? Luke's substituting ἀπό for an agential ὑπό cannot be an exception to "the rule that Luke never rejects ὑπό ... for a similar ἀπό" simply because there is no such "rule".

9,22 πολλὰ παθεῖν καὶ ἀποδοκιμασθῆναι **ἀπὸ** τῶν πρεσβυτέρων..., par. Mk 8,31 ὑπό. Readers of Gundry's note 17, "We may conjecture..." (*"ibid.,* p. 45 n. 7"), will retain the impression that it was my suggestion that Luke writes ἀπό "under the influence from the prefix in

3. Ac 2,22; 4,36; 11,19; 12,20 (indication of source?); 15,4 (var. ὑπό); 20,9. Note: 15,4 ἀπό N[27] N H, ὑπό rl. Compare G. SCHNEIDER: 2,22; 4,36; 15,4; 20,9 (*EWNT*, art. ἀπό 4.b.6); J.A. FITZMYER: 2,22; 4,36; 10,33; 15,4; note 10,33 ὑπό: ἀπό P[74.75] ℵ A C D *pc.* (*The Acts of the Apostles*, New York, 1998, 254, at 2,22; *Luke*, 1981, 343); BDR § 210,2: Ac 4,36; 15,4; 20,9. Cf. C.K. BARRETT: "Causal use of ἀπό occurs three times in Acts: 11.19; 12.14; 22.11. This recalls the LXX use of ἀπό to render causal מִן" (*Acts*, II, 1998, XLVII). But see BAUER-ALAND, art. ἀπό V (causal): 1 (gener.: Ac 11,19; 22,11); 3 (motive: Ac 12,14); 6 (with passive verb: Ac 2,22; 4,36; 20,9).

4. Gundry's view is different from the position of those who read ἀπό = from, *von ... her, de la part de*, and take the variant reading ὑπό as a correction to *by*. See e.g. the commentaries by F. Bovon (*Lukas*, 72 n. 12; *Luc*, 73 n. 50) and J. Nolland (*Luke*, 40).

ἀποδοκιμασθῆναι and in ἀποκτανθῆναι". This was clearly not the intention of my reference to F. Bovon (incorrectly cited here by adding ἀποκτανθῆναι). What Gundry rightly refutes in his n. 17 is nothing more than his own conjecture.

In the Matthean-foreign-body theory one may expect some definition of a Matthean motive in using ἀπό which "does not apply in Luke". No such definition is found in Gundry's earlier comments on Mt 16,21 (1982, 1992). In *Refusal* he now rightly observes that "in Matthew the agential phrase follows the verb of suffering" (in contrast to Luke who retains Mark's verb of rejection). Therefore he refuses R.E. Brown's statement that Matthew *and Luke* "are letting the verb 'suffer' dominate the grammatical relationship" (n. 19)[5]. It is less understandable that he is also critical of J. Nolland's comment that Matthew's use of ἀπό is "differently motivated (ὑπό would not fit after 'suffer')" (n. 18). The "good reason" for Luke's changing Mark's ὑπό to ἀπό in 9,22 is given by Nolland: "the developing interchangeability of these terms".

17,25 δεῖ ... πολλὰ παθεῖν καὶ ἀποδοκιμασθῆναι ἀπὸ... "The wording [of 17,25] is verbally an extract from 9:22 and has almost certainly been introduced from there by Luke" (Nolland).

⎮ The causal meaning of ἀπό in Lk 16,18 is less certain[6], and its use in Lk 7,35 / Mt 11,19 stems from Q. Gundry's search for redactional instances in Mt (other than Mt 16,21 diff. Mk 8,31) is rather unsuccessful. The case of Mt 28,4 ἀπὸ δὲ τοῦ φόβου αὐτοῦ (p. 106) is different[7]. In sum, the so-called Matthen foreign body in Lk 9,22 (ἀπό for ὑπό) appears to be more "foreign" to Matthew than it is to Luke.

Second agreement: the definite article before πρεσβυτέρων is not repeated before ἀρχιερέων and γραμματέων (p. 107-113). As a conclusion "redactional relevance" Gundry cites his 1992 observation that "of all the instances where Luke writes only one definite article, none besides Lk 9,22 represents the omission of a further definite article presented to him by Mark"[8]. He must have overlooked the case of Lk 22,52 (cited already in my 1989 list)[9]:

5. See *Note on Luke 9,22*, 45 n. 8: in reference to Goulder and Bauer's *Lexicon*.
6. Lk 16,18 ἀπολελυμένην **ἀπὸ** ἀνδρός. Cf. FITZMYER, 1981, 343: [?]; S. ANTO-NIADIS, *L'évangile de Luc*, Paris, 1930, 202 ("il y a ici en plus une idée d'éloignement"); NJB: divorced *by* her husband; French translations: répudiée *par* son mari; Dutch: *door haar man verstoten*. – Variant reading in Lk 10,22 παρεδόθη ὑπό: ἀπό D.
7. "For fear of him" (NRSV), "because of fear of him" (GUNDRY, *Matthew*, 588). Cf. BDR § 210,1; BAUER-ALAND, art. ἀπό, V.3.
8. GUNDRY, 1992, 1478; quoted in *Refusal*, 113 (n. 46).
9. Lk 22,52 εἶπεν δὲ Ἰησοῦς πρός..., par. Mk 14,48 ...εἶπεν αὐτοῖς, cf. v. 43 (the tripartite group). Compare Lk's στρατηγοὺς τοῦ ἱεροῦ (for τῶν γραμματέων in Mk)

Mk 14,43	Lk 22,52
παρὰ τῶν ἀρχιερέων	πρὸς τοὺς ... ἀρχιερεῖς
καὶ τῶν γραμματέων	καὶ στρατηγοὺς τοῦ ἱεροῦ
καὶ τῶν πρεσβυτέρων	καὶ πρεσβυτέρους

I present here a few remarks on Gundry's references to Lk 23,13; 17,25, and 18,32 (in the order of *Refusal*, 107-109).

Lk 23,13 τοὺς ἀρχιερεῖς καὶ τοὺς ἄρχοντας καὶ τὸν λαόν. First, before any arguing, an accurate description of the evidence is needed, here with τὸν λαόν as the third group. Second, the addition of τὸν λαόν ("did not force to repeat...") and τοῦ λαοῦ used with πρεσβύτεροι in Mt 21,23; 26,3.47; 27,1 ("does not force the repetition...") should remain distinguished. Third, the variant reading in Θ (om. τούς[2]) and a fortiori a vague reference to variant readings in the other passages are scarcely relevant in this discussion.

Lk 17,25 ... τῆς γενεᾶς ταύτης. Gundry rightly stresses the eschatological context and Luke's broad use of "this generation" in 7,31; 9,41; 11,29-32; 11,50-51; 21,32; Ac 2,40: the phrase designates "the people as a whole"[10] and Jesus' adversaries are "members of it". That it exhibits "a Lucan desire to weld together Jesus' adversaries" is not my own formulation[11]. Our note in 1989 referred to M. Goulder, Gundry's ally in this question, who takes "this generation" in 17,25 as an abbreviation for the elders, chief priests, and scribes. Gundry I does not contest that Lk 17,25 (... δεῖ αὐτὸν πολλὰ παθεῖν καὶ ἀποδοκιμασθῆναι ἀπό) echoes verbatim the wording of Lk 9,22 (cf. Mk 8,31). One step further is enough for me: elders – chief priests – scribes replaced by "this generation"[12].

Lk 18,32 παραδοθήσεται ... τοῖς ἔθνεσιν. Friedrichsen's suggestion that the reader may think of the tripartite group of 9,22 as implied agents is quickly answered by Gundry: "The answer is no". I can understand his refusal of the argument with regard to the Mt-Lk agreement in 9,22, but is he not overreacting? "Lk 18,32 substitutes a vague passive..."

with Lk 22,4 τοῖς ἀρχιερεῦσιν καὶ στρατηγοῖς (cf. Mk 14,1 οἱ ἀρχιερεῖς καὶ οἱ γραμματεῖς). Note also Lk 22,52 παραγενομένοις ἐπ' αὐτόν and Mk 14,43 παραγίνεται.

10. More correctly: "the non-responsive part of the Jewish people". Cf. C.M. TUCK-ETT, *Q and the History of Early Christianity*, Edinburgh, 1996, 201, on "this generation" in Q (in reply to D. Lührmann's "Israel as a whole").

11. See *Refusal*, 107 (five times); 110, on "welding" and "the attempt to make Luke a welder".

12. On Lk 17,25.31.33 and Mk, see my *Saving/Losing One's Life: Luke 17,33(Q?) and Mark 8,35*, in R. HOPPE – U. BUSSE (eds.), *Von Jesus zum Christus. Christologische Studien* (BZNW, 93), Berlin - New York, 1998, 295-318, esp. 312-313.

(108): actually Lk 18,32 (τῷ υἱῷ τοῦ ἀνθρώπου·) παραδοθήσεται γὰρ τοῖς ἔθνεσιν combines two phrases from the parallel Mk 10,33, ὁ υἱὸς τοῦ ἀνθώπου παραδοθήσεται and παραδώσουσιν αὐτὸν τοῖς ἔθνεσιν. – On "Luke's suppressing the information in Mk 10,33 that it will be the chief priests and the scribes who give Jesus over to the Gentiles" (ibid.), cf. Carroll and Green: "one should not place too much weight on Jesus' silence about Jewish authorities in the third passion prediction (Luke 18:31-32). That passage focuses on the Gentile role in Jesus' death and simply does not address Jewish involvement (already established in the first passion prediction, 9:22)"[13]. That Luke's "omitting the chief priests and the scribes altogether in Lk 18,31" shows that Luke had no desire "to weld such groups together into a united front"[14] is, it seems to me, a gratuitous assumption.

The recent debate about the omission of the second and third τῶν in Lk 9,22 started in 1989 with Goulder's Luke (49). He had found three other instances in which Luke drops the second article (two in Lk and one in Ac), but, what is more significant, he also noticed sixteen counter-instances (eleven in Lk and five in Ac). In a critical note of the some year (Neirynck and Friedrichsen) we could observe that the examples of a second article in Lk 5,21.30; 6,7; 7,30; 11,53; 15,2; 19,47; 20,1; 22,2; 23,10ᶜ; 24,20 (plus 20,19) are all in the nominative, in contrast to the oblique case where the second article is omitted: Lk 14,3; 22,4 (plus 22,52), and 9,22. Our observation was confined to references to Jesus' adversaries in the Gospel of Luke, and it was meant to be (and I think it still is) a valid response to Goulder's arguing against Lukan redaction in 9,22. In his Matthean Foreign Bodies (1992, 1475-1478), and now in Refusal, Gundry has given a double extension to the discussion, first by including references to other groups of persons and to other dual expressions and, second, by taking into consideration the instances in Acts. The restriction to Jesus' adversaries (the Jewish authorities) is the reason why instances referring to the crowds/people are not included (1989, n. 12): 23,2 πρὸς τοὺς ἀρχιερεῖς καὶ τοὺς ὄχλους and 23,13 τοὺς ἀρχιερεῖς καὶ τοὺς ἄρχοντας καὶ τὸν λαόν. There are two instances of anarthrous nominatives: 5,17 and 22,66 (1989, n. 13), noted by Gundry as contradicting Luke's supposed pattern to repeat the article in the nominative (110). However, one should not neglect that Φαρισαῖοι καὶ νομοδιδάσκαλοι in 5,17 is the first reference in Lk to

---

13. J.T. CARROLL – J.B. GREEN, The Death of Jesus in Early Christianity, Peabody, MA, 1995, 196.
14. GUNDRY, 1992, 1475 (italics F.N.); quoted by FRIEDRICHSEN, 399; GUNDRY, Refusal, 112.

Pharisees and to scribes ("teachers of the law") and I will be followed in v. 21 by the anaphoric οἱ γραμματεῖς καὶ οἱ Φαρισαῖοι. In 22,66 Luke's reference to the *presbyterion* is followed in apposition by the names of its constituent groups: τὸ πρεσβυτέριον τοῦ λαοῦ, ἀρχιερεῖς τε καὶ γραμματεῖς. The connecting τε καί is frequently used by Luke, and indeed, with the exception of a first article in Ac 14,5 and 26,3, "the definite article does not appear even a single time" with τε καί[15].

But "if one author wrote both Luke and Acts..." (112)? The unity of Luke–Acts cannot mean an a priori decision that patterns in Lk should be transferable to Acts without alteration[16]. Finally, Gundry seems to agree "that the lack of articular repetition in oblique cases is not un-Lukan" (113). To conclude, he returns to Lk 19,47; 20,1; 22,2 (par. Mk), the three examples of Luke's retaining definite articles he cited in 1992 at the opening of his discussion of Lk 9,22 (1475). That these and other instances of a second definite article in Lk are in the nominative is not even mentioned.

Third agreement: τῇ τρίτῃ ἡμέρᾳ ἐγερθῆναι (diff. Mk 8,31 μετὰ τρεῖς ἡμέρας ἀναστῆναι). I may mention Gundry's distinction between δεῖ interpreted in terms of "scriptural and therefore divine necessity" and God's agency expressed by the passive ἐγερθῆναι (114). In addition to our earlier *Note* I cite here Brown's comment: Matthew and Luke "are using a well-established kerygmatic formula"[17].

II

The debate on **Lk 10,25-28** is becoming a multi-stage story: Gundry's *Matthew*, 1982 (447-450); Goulder's *Luke*, 1989 (483-487); Gundry, *Matthean Foreign Bodies*, 1992 (1480-1482); Neirynck, *Luke 10:25-28*,

---

15. Τε καί in Lk 12,45; 21,11; 22,66; Ac 1,1; 2,9.10.11; 4,27; 5,14; 8,12; 9,2.15.18.24.29; 14,5 (τῶν ἐθνῶν τε καὶ Ἰουδαίων); 15,9.22; 19,10.17; 20,21; 21,12; 22,4; 24,3.15; 26,3 (πάντων τῶν...).20.22.

16. For a simple illustration how the style of Lk and Acts can differ, compare the respective frequence in the use of τε καί (cf. n. 15). Note in accordance with the pattern in Lk: the nominative οἱ ἀρχιερεῖς καὶ οἱ πρεσβύτεροι (Ac 4,23; 25,15) and the oblique case τῶν Φαρισαίων καὶ Σαδδουκαίων (23,7); diff. Ac 4,5; 6,12 (but preceded by τὸν λαόν); 23,15.

17. R.E. BROWN, *The Death of the Messiah*, New York, 1994, 1468-1491 ("Jesus' Predictions of His Passion and Death"), here 1476 n. 9.

1994 (149-165)[18]; Gundry, *Rejoinder*, 1995 (139-150); Neirynck, *Minor Agreements*, 1995 (151-160); Gundry, *Refusal*, 1999 (115-122); and now my turn for a provisional conclusion, *The Case for Independent Redaction*[19].

The Scribe in Mk

Gundry's Part II takes an 'antagonistic' start. It is now clear enough that the reference to "the favorable portrayal of the scribe in this pericope" (A.M. | Ambrozic: "the depiction of a scribe in a favorable light" in contrast to the scribes "in the rest of the Gospel") in no way mitigates his view on the intention of the scribe: he "started out antagonistically"[20]. Gundry's main argument for an antagonistic approach by the scribe is the parallelism with 12,18-19. It is undeniable that in 12,18 the Sadducees show antagonism toward Jesus. One may add that "their antagonism is expressed in οἵτινες λέγουσιν ἀνάστασιν μὴ εἶναι and in the content of their question", not in ἔρχονται ... πρὸς αὐτὸν ... καὶ ἐπηρώτων αὐτόν. It is a significant step that Gundry now quotes these words and confirms them with his "Agreed" (116).

It is less evident that the contextual factor, 12,28-34 following right after 12,18-27, allows for further assimilation. One cannot make "the desire to do a better job" the link between the Sadducees and the Pharisees and between the scribe and the Sadducees. No link is expressed in 12,18, whereas 12,28 clearly alludes to the preceding pericope: [b] ἀκούσας αὐτῶν συζητούντων, [c] ἰδὼν ὅτι καλῶς ἀπεκρίθη αὐτοῖς. That "the reference to disputation may lend an antagonistic tone to the scribe's question"[21] has no foundation in the gospel text.

18. See also my *The Minor Agreements and Q* [1992], in R.A. PIPER (ed.), *The Gospel Behind the Gospels: Current Studies on Q* (NTSup, 75), Leiden, 1995, 49-72, esp. 61-64 "Luke 10:25-28" [cf. 252-255].

19. For full references see Gundry's footnotes 1-5 and 63. The private correspondence he mentions (104) includes Gundry's response to my *ETL* article (November, 1995), my answer (December 12, 1995; January 2, 1996), and Gundry's new response (April 1, 1996), and his "A Parting Shot for Subsidiary Matthean Influence in Luke 10,25-28" (May 7, 1997), which now finally appears here above in a revised version as Part II of his *Refusal* (115-121).

20. I mention here two commentaries, both published after Gundry's *Mark* (1993): S. LÉGASSE, *L'évangile de Marc* (LD-C, 5), Paris, 1997, 746: "le scribe, bien qu'il fasse progresser l'entretien, apparaît du début à la fin comme 'l'élève docile du maître Jésus' (K. Kertelge)"; B.M.F. VAN IERSEL, *Mark: A Reader-Response Commentary* (JSNT SS, 164), Sheffield, 1968, 379: the scribe "has chosen the side of Jesus, if not after Jesus' answer to the Sadducees, then now [at v. 32] after Jesus' answer to his own question", and: "In either case the reader meets a scribe who agrees with Jesus' answer about the resurrection of the dead" (378).

21. Gundry's response, April 1, 1996 (see now 115).

"Needing to play down the verbal parallelism..."? More assertive than argumentative, indeed. I have no problem (how could I) with the assertion that the link of 12,28-34 with 12,18-27 "hardly means that a new pericope does not start at 12,28". But this cannot mean that there is no difference in function between προσελθών + ἀκούσας ... ἰδών... in 12,28 and the simple ἔρχονται πρὸς αὐτόν in 12,18. Gundry's "Likewise, the coming of the Sadducees..." indicates that pericopes follow one after another, but it is 'misleading' (the banned word!) because it plays down the unparalleled linkage in 12,28.

The statement that 12,34c "implies that the scribe's question was daring, and therefore antagonistic" (116) seems to neglect that καὶ οὐδεὶς οὐκέτι ἐτόλμα αὐτὸν ἐπερωτῆσαι is not so much the conclusion of 12,28-34 (note the contrast with v. 34ab) but the more general conclusion of a series of 'questions':

> The final sentence has no direct bearing on the episode with the scribe but rather closes the whole series of discussions begun in 11.27. (van Iersel)
> En notant que 'nul n'osait plus l'interroger', Marc laisse entendre que la série des entretiens est close et qu'elle culmine avec un triomphe de Jésus. (Légasse)

By stating (in italics) that "the daring of the scribe makes unnecessary an explicit earlier reference to his 'testing' Jesus or to some theological error on his part" Gundry confesses that there is a lack of evidence for his position on the antagonistic scribe.

⏐ The absence of the address διδάσκαλε in 12,28 is a disturbing factor in Gundry's theory. Given the so much stressed parallelism between the Sadducees and the scribe, both antagonistic, one would expect that the Sadducees' guileful use of διδάσκαλε has its parallel in 12,28. But the address is lacking there. No need for Gundry: the lack of address is evidence of the scribe's disrespect and the parallel in 12,19 (and 12,14) is given up for a more distant parallel in 11,28. On the same page (117) he makes a more likely suggestion: "διδάσκαλε in 12,18 is guileful and Mark wishes to save a truly respectful διδάσκαλε for 12,32"; but there is no need to add: "so as to highlight the scribe's change of heart". "It does not seem to dawn on Neirynck ... that the scribe's attitude toward Jesus has changed" (117). The reader should know: Neirynck is not alone (cf. S. Légasse, *et multi alii*).

Mk's προσελθών

I never contested Gundry's statement that συνήχθησαν ἐπὶ τὸ αὐτό in Mt 22,34 is "a typically Matthean quotation of the OT, in particular of Ps 2:2" (*Matthew*, 447), and my own comment on Matthew's "replacement of προσελθών with συνήχθησαν ἐπὶ τὸ αὐτό" (1994, 154) anticipated what Gundry now presents as the reason "why Matthew made this change" (117). When I wrote in 1994 that "Matthew's reason" for the omission of προσελθών cannot be verified, this was meant with reference to the reason then proposed by Gundry: "the respectful connotation that attaches to προσέρχομαι"[22]. With regard to Luke, his argument remained unchanged: either respectful προσέρχομαι or predilection for OT phraseology, it is Matthean usage, and therefore the omission in Lk is due to Matthean influence. However, also the context of the omission and its respective substitute[23] should be taken into consideration:

Mk 12,28 καὶ *προσελθὼν* εἷς τ. γ. [ ]   ἐπηρώτησεν αὐτόν·
Lk 10,25 καὶ ἰδοὺ νομικός τις *ἀνέστη*   ἐκπειράζων αὐτὸν λέγων·

The case of Mk 12,28bc may serve to illustrate how successive confrontation can lead to some clarification of the debate[24]. However, as a reader of *Refusal* I realize how frustrating implicit allusions and fragmentary quotations can be[25].

Νομικός in Lk
1 "To make Luke's νομικός parallel with Mark's γραμματεύς (12,32), Neirynck has to posit Luke's reaching forward in Mark's text" (118). I may refer to the presentation of the contacts with Mk 12,32-34 in my

22. *Luke 10:25-28*, 155. Cf. Gundry's *Matthean Foreign Bodies*, 1481; *Matthew*, 448 (= [2]1994). See his *Rejoinder* (1995), 144: "So I shall propose an answer other than my earlier one". Note the inverted order in *Refusal*, 117: my "Matthew's reason..." (= 1995, after the *Rejoinder*) is cited first, followed by "Neirynck reasserts" referring to the earlier statement (= 1994, before *Rejoinder*).

23. On ἀνέστη, cf. *Refusal*, n. 76: "My point has to do with the absence of Mark's προσελθών from both Matthew and Luke". Yet ἀνέστη is a much more likely substitute for προσελθών than Matthew's συνήχθησαν... "Luke's reason" can be a different one and independent from Matthew's.

24. See *Matthew*, 448 (uncorrected in [2]1994; no reference to Mt 22,34-40 in the added endnotes); my *Luke 10:25-28*: "quite natural to Luke and completely irrelevant in a discussion of possible dependence on Matthew" (155); Gundry's *Rejoinder*: "Nor have I argued for Lucan dependence..., so that Neirynck's comment ... is itself irrelevant" (sic; 145 n. 30); my surrejoinder (153-154); and finally his *Refusal*: "at this point my *Rejoinder* was meant to correct my commentary" (118).

25. Thus, e.g., on νομικός: "There is still the case of ὁ γραμματεύς in Mk 12,32" (118). Compare the preceding context in *ETL* (1995): "Gundry has now corrected the three lacunae I noted in his survey of Lukan parallels to γραμματεύς in Mark" (154). As another example I mention the 'misleading' information, explicitly referring to his 'argument' in *Rejoinder*, 143: "Luke ... never uses νομικός in Acts but does use γραμματεύς several times there". See his correction in *Refusal*: "his using *the plural of* γραμματεύς".

Luke 10:25-28. In addition to Lk 10,25 νομικός τις ... διδάσκαλε and Mk 12,32 ὁ γραμματεὺς ... διδάσκαλε, "the structure of Lk 10,25-28 can be compared with Mk 12,28-34, including vv. 32-34:

Lk 10,25	question	Mk 12,28	scribe
26	counterquestion	29-31	Jesus
27	answer	32-33	scribe
28	final reply	34	Jesus

In contrast to the answer given by Jesus in Mk 12,29-31, the answer is spoken by the scribe/lawyer himself in Mk 12,32-33 and in Lk 10,27, and he receives approval from Jesus: he saw that he answered wisely, νουνεχῶς ἀπεκρίθη (Mk 10,34a), ὀρθῶς ἀπεκρίθης (Lk 10,28). The distinction between first and second commandment (Mk 12,29.31) is lacking in Lk 10,27. Luke's formulation of the two commandments fused into one comes closer to that of Mk 12,33" (159).

The link with the preceding pericope in Mk 12,28bc receives a most distinctive rewriting in Mt 22,34: οἱ δὲ Φαρισαῖοι ἀκούσαντες ὅτι ἐφίμωσεν τοὺς Σαδδουκαίους συνήχθησαν ἐπὶ τὸ αὐτό (cf. v. 41a συνηγμένων δὲ τῶν Φαρισαίων) and εἷς τῶν γραμματέων is changed to εἷς·ἐξ αὐτῶν (i.e., one of the Pharisees) νομικός. Is it then thinkable that, if Luke had thought of the lawyer "solely in terms of its occurrence in the parallel Mt 22,35", there would be no trace in Lk of Mt 22,34? Is the objection against Matthean influence not taken too lightly by simply stating that "the Pharisees and Sadducees mentioned in Mt 22,34 seem not to have captured Luke's attention"? Can it really be maintained that on the contrary Matthean influence "is favored by the absence of Pharisees here in Luke" (120)?

As to νομικός in Mt 22,35, Gundry declares that "Neirynck tries to get rid of this agreement by defending the possibility that νομικός does not belong to Matthew's original text" (n. 60). Yet my state of mind is somewhat different: "whatever may be the outcome of the text-critical discussion of Mt 22,35, it will not be possible to call Luke's νομικός in 10,25 a Matthean foreign body in Luke"[26]. Scholars who regard νομικός as original in Mt can hardly avoid confrontation with the alternative opinion[27]. For Gundry, "Matthew himself could | have put

26. *ETL* 1995, 155-156. See also: "If original, νομικός can be read in the light of ἐν τῷ νόμῳ..." (156). The inclusion of νομίζω in the group of νόμος cognates (and now the addition of νόμισμα) is only a marginal question, though "the breadth of meanings" in other families of cognates (120) is scarcely a decisive argument.

27. See, e.g., the latest commentary, W. WIEFEL, *Das Evangelium nach Matthäus* (THNT, 1), Leipzig, 1998, 385: "Die Lesart ... könnte unter Einfluß der Parallele Lk 10,25 hier eingedrungen sein". For earlier representatives, see *Evangelica II*, 1991, 191-

νομικός here just as easily as a later copyist might have done" (119). Perhaps not quite "as easily", since a later copyist could be influenced by Luke's undisputed νομικός τις (compare the readings τις and καὶ λέγων) while, in Gundry's theory, Matthew's redactional εἷς ἐξ αὐτῶν νομικός solely relies on εἷς τῶν γραμματέων in Mk. One may appreciate Gundry's understatement in his comment on his own emphasis upon Matthean awkwardness: "at this point I was not offering an argument for my view" (120). Matthew's distinction between scribes and Pharisees is cited to explain the appositive νομικός, again with his comment: "I did not offer an elaboration... Ultimately, however, it is Matthew who does not elaborate the distinction".

On the side of Luke, "νομικός in Lk 7,30; 11,45.46.52; 14,3 may derive, or probably does derive, from Q and perhaps Lucan special material"; Gundry's principal argument against Lukan redaction: "apart from the passage in question and against expectations for a favorite word, Luke never substitutes νομικός for γραμματεύς in Marcan material" (*Rejoinder*, 143). The added qualification leaves an open possibility for Lk 10,25 νομικός τις as substitute for εἷς τῶν γραμματέων / ὁ γραμματεύς in Mk 12,28.32 (cf. above). Besides this passage under debate we can considere here the phrase τοὺς νομικοὺς καὶ Φαρισαίους in Lk 14,3. Lk 14,1-6 is a secondary synoptic parallel to Mk 3,1-6 / Lk 6,6-11. Compare the subject added by Luke in 6,7: οἱ γραμματεῖς καὶ οἱ Φαρισαῖοι (diff. Mk 3,2; cf. οἱ Φαρισαῖοι in v. 6) and Lk 14,3: πρὸς τοὺς νομικοὺς καὶ Φαρισαίους. Gundry remarks that "we would expect 14,3 to have 'the scribes and the Pharisees'" (119), but what Luke has, and what counts for us, is νομικοί, Luke's substitute for γραμματεῖς. Gundry calls in question Luke's indirect use of Mk because "the differences are so great...". Note, however, the correspondence between Jesus' question in Mk 3,4 καὶ λέγει αὐτοῖς· ἔξεστιν...; οἱ δὲ ἐσιώπων (Lk 6,9 εἶπεν δὲ ὁ Ἰησοῦς πρὸς αὐτούς· ... εἰ ἔξεστιν...;) and Lk 14,3 καὶ ἀποκριθεὶς ὁ Ἰησοῦς εἶπεν πρὸς τοὺς νομικοὺς καὶ Φαρισαίους λέγων· ἔξεστιν...; [4] οἱ

192; *ETL* 70 (1994), 172 (H. Schürmann); 71 (1995), 156 n. 38 (D.J. Harrington, J. Nolland, B.M. Metzger). Cf. recent commentaries on Mt: D.A. Hagner (II, 1995): "the text is questionable" (646); W.D. Davies – D.C. Allison (III, 1997): "one might regard it as assimilation to Luke... But the textual evidence favours retention" (239 n. 28); U. Luz (III, 1997): the minor agreement νομικός is "wirklich schwierig für Mt"; "wäre allenfalls bei Lk als Red. erklärbar" (271 n. 15 and 18; cf. 269 n. 1: "Nur ganz wenige Textzeugen [f¹, e, sy^s, arm, geo, Or] streichen νομικός"). Note his comment that "die 'Agreements' between Mt und Lk oft keine vollständigen sind" (271). One could regard εἷς ἐξ αὐτῶν νομικός (Mt) and νομικός τις (Lk) as an *incomplete* agreement.

δὲ ἡσύχασαν[28]. The original order of the woes in Q 11 is a much debated question[29]. It is much less debated that the arrangement in two series of three woes, first to the Pharisees and then to the lawyers, is due to LkR and that the transition in 11,45 is a Lukan insertion. That makes it difficult to argue, as does Gundry, for traditional language in vv. 45 (τίς τῶν νομικῶν), 46 and 52 (τοῖς νομικοῖς). Here too νομικοί is most likely Luke's substitute for γραμματεῖς. Once more in Lk 7,30 (οἱ δὲ Φαρισαῖοι καὶ οἱ νομικοί) the | Lukan word νομικοί stands for γραμματεῖς one would expect if it were a Q text[30].

In response to Gundry's doubt about the argumentative value of the distinction between the singular and the plural (119 n. 84)[31] I recapitulate here the following data. In contrast to the plural οἱ γραμματεῖς (the Jewish 'scribes': 14 times in Lk and 3 times in Ac), the singular is used only once in Luke–Acts, referring not to a Jewish scribe but to the town clerk in Ephesus (Ac 19,15). In Ac 5,34 where one could expect that the singular γραμματεύς be used in the reference to the scribe Gamaliel, Luke writes νομοδιδάσκαλος ("a teacher of the law"), which is the explicative Luke uses in Lk 5,17 in preparation of the first mention of γραμματεῖς: Lk 5,17 καὶ ἦσαν καθήμενοι Φαρισαῖοι καὶ νομοδιδάσκαλοι..., cf. Mk 2,6 ἦσαν δέ τινες τῶν γραμματέων ἐκεῖ καθήμενοι (par. Lk 5,21 οἱ γραμματεῖς καὶ οἱ Φαρισαῖοι). In Mk the unique occurrence of the singular γραμματεύς is εἷς τῶν γραμματέων and ὁ γραμματεύς in 12,28.32, with a double parallel in Lk 20,39 τινες τῶν γραμματέων (plural!) and 10,25 νομικός τις. It would be most exceptional in Luke–Acts if Luke had adopted here the singular γραμματεύς while the singular νομικός can be compared with Luke's redactional τις τῶν νομικῶν in 11,45.

28. See my *Luke 14,1-6: Lukan Composition and Q Saying* [1991], in *Evangelica II*, 183-203, esp. 190-193; cf. *ETL* (1995), 155. See now also F. BOVON, *Das Evangelium nach Lukas* (EKK, 3/2), 1996, 469: "Die Sequenz [Lk 14,3-4] ist eine redaktionelle Adaptation der Parallele von Mk 3.4-5 // Lk 6,9-10. Lukas baut sie zweifellos als Wiederholung seines eigenen vorausgehenden Textes, der Erzählung vom Mann mit der verdorrten Hand, auf". Contrast C.M. TUCKETT, *Q* (n. 10): "Luke never introduces νομικός in a Marcan context" (417 n. 81). But in both Lk 10,25 and 14,3 it is "in a Marcan context" that Luke substitutes νομικός for γραμματεύς.

29. See my *The Sources of Matthew: Annotations to U. Luz's Commentary*, in *ETL* 74 (1998) 109-126, esp. 117-119.

30. See, e.g., F. BOVON, *Lukas* I, 1989, 378: "das redaktionelle Summarium (VV 29-30)"; n. 54: "Das von Lukas propagierte Wort νομικός entspricht dem γραμματεύς der synoptischen Tradition".

31. See also TUCKETT, *Q* (n. 10), 417 n. 81.

ETL 73 (1997) 84-93

11

GOULDER AND THE MINOR AGREEMENTS

Mark S. Goodacre's book on *Goulder and the Gospels* has a 42-page chapter on the minor agreements (MAs)[1]. The author notices that "Goulder's own statements on his methodology have been a little ambiguous" and he proposes "to look more closely at the way in which Goulder argues the case"[2]. Goulder's thesis is Lukan dependence on Matthew, and Goodacre distinguishes five different arguments on the MAs: 1. Matthean, un-Lukan wording; 2. Order; 3. Clusters of not very Lukan words; 4. Luke's dependence on Matthew's redaction; 5. Undoubtable links and coincidence of *hapax* (92-101). Special attention is given to the case of Goulder's "key MA" at Mk 14,65 (101-107). Then, Goodacre argues more personally on six examples "featuring language characteristic of Matthew and uncharacteristic of Luke" (at Mk 3,10; 4,41; 6,2; 6,33; 12,22; 14,43) and concludes that "in at least six different MAs, Goulder's criteria are satisfied" (107-117). Finally, he proceeds to some sort of control text: is it possible to point to MAs featuring language characteristic of Luke and uncharacteristic of Matthew? He presents two counter-examples, at Mk 6,44 (ὡσεί) and 12,28 (νομικός, but the textual evidence in Mt 22,35 is inconclusive for G.): "there is at least one MA which satisfies the converse of Goulder's criteria" (117-122). I quote his general conclusion (125):

> The problem with Goulder's approach is that several of his examples are not clearly Matthean and un-Lukan so his 'test' has not proved entirely convincing. Our six examples of MAs which do satisfy the relevant criteria are not enough, then, to demonstrate that Luke knew Matthew. These are striking examples but there are not enough of them and there is at least one impressive counter instance.

1. M.S. GOODACRE, *Goulder and the Gospels. An Examination of a New Paradigm* (JSNT SS, 133), Sheffield, 1996, pp. 89-130: "The Minor Agreements and Characteristic Language" (Chapter 3). Here cited: G.
2. Quoted from pp. 94 (n. 15) and 92. His main sources are: M.D. GOULDER, *On Putting Q to the Test*, in *NTS* 24 (1978) 218-234 (= *Test*); ID., *Luke: A New Paradigm* (JSNT SS, 36), Sheffield, 1989 (= *LNP*; cf. my review in *ETL* 67, 1991, 434-436); ID., *Luke's Knowledge of Matthew*, in G. STRECKER (ed.), *Minor Agreements: Symposium Göttingen 1991* (GTA, 50), Göttingen, 1993, pp. 143-160 (= *Knowledge*; cf. *ETL* 67, 1991, 361-372: "A Symposium on the Minor Agreements"). – On Goulder's theory, see T.A. FRIEDRICHSEN, *The Matthew-Luke Agreements against Mark. A Survey of Recent Studies: 1974-1989*, in F. NEIRYNCK (ed.), *L'Évangile de Luc – The Gospel of Luke* (BETL, 32), Leuven, 1989, pp. 335-398, esp. 371-384 ("Luke Used Mark and Matthew but no Q Source").

1. GOODACRE'S EXAMPLES

G.'s list of six examples shows a strange variety. One of his examples is usually found in the lists of significant minor agreements (diff. Mk 6,33). But G. has to note on another case (diff. Mk 6,2): "This MA is not listed by Neirynck and is rarely, if ever, discussed as a MA". It is discussed in Goulder's *LNP* but "drops out of the discussion in *Knowledge* without comment" (111). About his first I example (diff. Mk 3,10) he observes that "Goulder does not comment on this MA" (110). Six examples are "not enough" for Goodacre, but can he really call them "striking" examples?

Diff. Mk 3,10; 6,2; 6,33

Mk 3,10 πολλούς: Mt 12,15 / Lk 6,19 **πάντας**.

Πᾶς used of the sick (7/1/1+0): "strongly characteristic of Matthew and markedly uncharacteristic of Luke" (109-110).

Goulder does not comment on this MA. G. could have added that for Goulder pleonastic πᾶς is a congenial Lukan word: "As at Mk. 1.34; Lk. 4.40, Mark's πολλούς becomes πάντας" (*LNP*, 345). Contrast G.'s comment: "In his parallel to Mk 1.32 Luke uses ἅπας (Lk. 4.40) and Luke uses this again in the same way in Acts 5.16" (110). My first observation: there is the textual variation ἅπαντες/πάντες in Lk 4,40 and elsewhere in Lk-Acts (cf. TR T [S] V: πάντες in 4,40). Second, Luke's use of, for instance, ἅπαν τὸ πλῆθος (Lk 8,37; 19,37; 23,1; Acts 25,24) does not make πᾶν τὸ πλῆθος (Lk 1,10; Acts 6,5; 15,12) un-Lukan. Third, there is ample reason for combining the Lukan parallels to Mk 1,32-34 and 3,7-12 (cf. Lk 4,41b) and, in both passages, for attributing to Luke the change of "many" to "all".

Πᾶς "used of the sick" is however not an adequate definition of the minor agreement. In Mt 4,23; 9,35; 10,1 (all R) πᾶς is used of *healing* all the sick (θεραπεύειν) and this is the case also here: Mt 12,15 ἐθεράπευσεν αὐτοὺς *πάντας* (Mk 3,10 πολλοὺς γὰρ ἐθεράπευσεν)[3]. Mt 4,24 "MK" can be corrected to Mt 4,24 "R", like Mt 8,16 R:

4,24	8,16	Mk 1,32.34
προσήνεγκαν αὐτῷ	προσήνεγκαν αὐτῷ	[32]ἔφερον πρὸς αὐτὸν
πάντας τ. κ. ἔχ.	κ. πάντας τ. κ. ἔχ.	πάντας τ. κ. ἔχ.
κ. ἐθεράπευσεν αὐτούς	ἐθεράπευσεν	[34]κ. ἐθεράπευσεν
		πολλοὺς κ. ἔχ.

---

3. Mt 14,35 is different: προσήνεγκαν αὐτῷ πάντας τ. κ. ἔχ. (diff. Mk) is followed by ὅσοι ἥψαντο in v. 36 (par. Mk).

Mt 4,24 πάντας ... καὶ ἐθεράπευσεν αὐτούς: compare Lk 4,40 ἑνὶ
ἑκάστῳ αὐτῶν ... ἐθεράπευσεν αὐτούς (diff. Mk 1,34)[4]. Although this
is not an agreement in the actual Greek words used for "all", the similarity with Mt 12,15 / Lk 6,17 (diff. Mk 3,10) is undeniable.

Mk 6,2 ἐν τῇ συναγωγῇ:
Mt 13,54 / Lk 4,15 + **αὐτῶν**.
"The only difficulty for Goulder [*Test*, 221] is the question of the legit-
imacy of reading the parallel" (111-113).
    The parallel between Mk and Mt is evident enough:

    Mk   6,1   ... καὶ ἔρχεται εἰς τὴν πατρίδα αὐτοῦ, ...
           2 καὶ ... ἤρξατο διδάσκειν ἐν τῇ συναγωγῇ
    Mt 13,54 καὶ ἐλθὼν εἰς τὴν πατρίδα αὐτοῦ
                 ἐδίδασκεν αὐτοὺς ἐν τῇ συναγωγῇ αὐτῶν
| Compare Lk 4,16: καὶ ἦλθεν εἰς Ναζαρά, ...
                    καὶ εἰσῆλθεν ... εἰς τὴν συναγωγὴν ...

However, Goulder's (and G.'s) parallel in Lk is taken from the summary
statement in 4,15 with "their synagogues" in plural, the origin of which
can be found in Mk 1,39 (and not in Mk 6,2): κηρύσσων εἰς τὰς
συναγωγὰς αὐτῶν,

    Mt 4,23 διδάσκων ἐν ταῖς συναγωγαῖς αὐτῶν καὶ κηρύσσων ... (= 9,35)
    Lk 4,15 ἐδίδασκεν ἐν ταῖς συναγωγαῖς αὐτῶν.

For MA-hunters I may refer to my *Minor Agreements* (§ 12: 2.1), but
here the agreement against Mk is not in the use of αὐτῶν. It cannot be
my intention to contest the Matthean wording of "their synagogue(s)"
(4,23; 9,35; 10,17: plural; 12,9; 13,54: singular). But neither the statistical data 5:1 nor the absence of αὐτῶν in Lk's direct parallels to Mk
1,23.39 should prevent us from reading the summary in Lk 4,14b-15 in
the light of Mk 1,23.39[5]:

> The Nazareth pericope, though it is placed before the day in Capernaum,
> refers back to the γενόμενα εἰς τὴν Καφαρναούμ (4,23) and it is said
> that Jesus went to the synagogue on the sabbath day κατὰ τὸ εἰωθὸς αὐτῷ
> (4,16). This seems to suggest that we can interpret the preceding summary

----

4. The parallel in Lk 4,40 concerns ἑνὶ ἑκάστῳ (and not ἅπαντες). See my *Minor Agreements*, 1974, p. 63 (1991, § 10, no. 5). Cf. HAWKINS, *Horae Synopticae*, p. 117: "Passages [in Mk] seeming to limit the power of Jesus" (Mt 8,16 / Lk 4,40; Mt 12,15 / Lk 6,19).
5. Cf. *Matthew 4:23–5:2 and the Matthean Composition of 4:23–11:1*, in D.L. DUNGAN (ed.), *The Interrelations of the Gospels* (BETL, 95), Leuven, 1990, pp. 23-46, esp. 30.

in Lk 4,14b-15 in the light of the Capernaum episode: the φήμη ... περὶ αὐτοῦ has to do with Jesus' reputation as a miracle-worker (Mk 1,28) and ἐδίδασκεν ἐν ταῖς συναγωγαῖς αὐτῶν is a generalization of Mk 1,21-22 (cf. v. 23 ἐν τῇ συναγωγῇ αὐτῶν), probably under the influence of Mk 1,39.

Mk 6,33 ἐπέγνωσαν πολλοὶ καὶ ... προῆλθον αὐτούς:
Mt 14,13 καὶ ἀκούσαντες **οἱ ὄχλοι ἠκολούθησαν** αὐτῷ
Lk 9,11 **οἱ** δὲ **ὄχλοι** γνόντες **ἠκολούθησαν** αὐτῷ
"There are three differences between Matthew/Luke and Mark here: οἱ ὄχλοι, an aorist participle (ἀκούσαντες/γνόντες) and ἠκολούθησαν... Here, then, is a combination of words strongly characteristic of Matthew and uncharacteristic of Luke" (113-115).

In one note G. refers to "the force of the argument over the plural οἱ ὄχλοι" (n. 60), but clearly states in his previous note: "It is certainly not uncharacteristic of Luke and οἱ ὄχλοι on its own in this MA is not sufficient to excite attention" (n. 59). Goulder's statement that "Luke rarely writes οἱ ὄχλοι in the way that Matthew does without introducing them" is quoted in the text without being documented (114). Is it not "without introducing them" that Luke writes for the first time τοῖς ὄχλοις in 3,7? There can be no doubt for Goulder that "the Lucan version [3,7a] is quite typical of Luke": "οἱ ὄχλοι come in 4,42 R; 8,42 R; 8,45 R; [and!] 9,11 R" (*LNP*, 273, 279). G. refers to ὄχλοι plural at 4,42; 8,42.45; 9,18; 23,48 (all R) and (besides 7,24; 11,14 QC) at 3,7 QD; 3,10 L; 5,3 L; 5,15 R (or MA)[6]; 12,54 QD; 14,25 L (or QD); 23,4 R (or L). All these references can and should be corrected, or clarified, by writing R. Thus it is not Luke's use of οἱ | ὄχλοι (for πολλοί in Mk) that can be un-Lukan in 9,11. I may repeat here my earlier observation[7]:

> Luke's use of the plural οἱ ὄχλοι (9,11a) and the singular in the same section (v. 12 τὸν ὄχλον, v. 16 τῷ ὄχλῳ: Mk αὐτούς, αὐτοῖς) can be compared with the Lukan usage in the last narrative section before 9,1-9: the singular ὁ ὄχλος in 8,40 (= Mk) and the plural in vv. 42 and 45 (singular in Mk).

Compare also Lk 5,1 τὸν ὄχλον, 3 ἐδίδασκεν τοὺς ὄχλους (Mk 4,1 ὄχλος, ὁ ὄχλος 2 ἐδίδασκεν αὐτούς).

---

6. It is unclear how this could be a MA. Lk 5,15-16 is parallel to Mk 1,45 (without parallel in Mt): καὶ συνήρχοντο ὄχλοι πολλοί (cf. Mk 1,45d καὶ ἤρχοντο πρὸς αὐτὸν πάντοθεν), possibly influenced by Mk 2,1-2 (v. 2 καὶ συνήχθησαν πολλοί).
7. See my *The Minor Agreements and the Two-Source Theory*, in *Evangelica II*, 1991, pp. 5-42, esp. 29-34 ("The Introduction to the Feeding Story"), here 32; = G. STRECKER (ed.), *Minor Agreements* (n. 2), 1993, pp. 25-62, esp. 51-55, here 53.

The aorist participle ἀκούσαντες/γνόντες is mentioned as an agreement without one word of comment, not even Goulder's note on γνόντες in Lk: "from Mark's ἐπέγνωσαν" (LNP, 434). One statement seems to be decisive for G.: "outside of this context, the combination ἀκολουθέω + ὄχλοι comes only in Matthew, and always redactionally" (Mt 4,25; 8,1; [12,15]; 19,2; 21,9). More precision is needed here. Matthew's stereotyped phrase is ἠκολούθησαν αὐτῷ ὄχλοι πολλοί. The case of Mt 21,9 is different: in parallel to Mk 11,9 οἱ προάγοντες καὶ οἱ ἀκολουθοῦντες, Matthew added the subject: οἱ δὲ ὄχλοι. Mt 14,13 too shows some variation: καὶ ἀκούσαντες οἱ ὄχλοι ἠκολούθησαν αὐτῷ. The different word order and the participle added here make the combination less "strongly characteristic". It is important not to neglect the parallel text in Mk 6,33[8]:

> The verbal agreement between Mt 14,13 and Lk 9,11 is a change of Mark's "they *preceded* them" to "the crowds *followed* him". In Matthew, the phrase is stereotyped and more or less in conflict with ἐν πλοίῳ and v. 14a: "when he came ashore, he saw a great crowd" (= Mk). Luke brings a more consistent account of the return of the disciples and the initiative of Jesus (καὶ παραλαβὼν αὐτούς...): the crowds followed him and Jesus welcomed them (ἀποδεξάμενος αὐτούς).

Diff. Mk 4,41; 12,22; 14,43

There is some similarity in these three examples. They are instances of verbal agreement: the use of the plural for the singular ὁ ἄνεμος in Mk 4,41 (Mt 8,27 / Lk 8,25); the substitution of ὕστερον for ἔσχατον in Mk 12,22 (Mt 22,27 / Lk 20,32); the insertion of ἰδού after the genitive absolute in Mk 14,43 (Mt 26,47 / Lk 22,47). The same type of argument is applied: ἄνεμοι plural only here in Lk and five times in Mt (including 8,26 R); ὕστερον only here in Lk and seven times in Mt (including 21,37 R; 26,60 R); ἰδού after a genitive absolute only I here in Lk and eleven times in Mt (including 9,10.18.32; 12,46; 17,5: R). The conclusion is invariable: characteristic of Matthew and uncharacteristic of Luke; with a climax in the last instance: markedly characteristic

---

8. *Ibid.*, p. 32 (= 53). On Luke's use of ἀκολουθέω (here in contrast to Mk's προῆλθον), see my *The Matthew-Luke Agreements in Mt 14,13-14 / Lk 9,10-11 (par. Mk 6,30-34). A Response to M.-É. Boismard*, in ETL 60 (1984) 25-43, esp. pp. 34-35; = *Evangelica II*, pp. 75-94, esp. 85-86. It is strange that statements such as "foreign to Luke's style" continue to be quoted (114 n. 61) without informing the reader how they can and have been answered.

of Matthew and un-Lukan. The three MAs are listed in my *Minor Agreements*[9] and for all three G. could refer to Goulder's *LNP*[10].

In these cases there is no problem on the side of Matthew[11] and for each of them we can agree also with the statement: "only here in Lk". But the discussion must go beyond statistics. A usage that is unique in Luke is not necessarily un-Lukan: it can be meaningful Lukan redaction or, more simply, Luke's use of better Greek.

Mt 8,27 καὶ **οἱ** ἄνεμοι   καὶ ἡ θάλασσα   αὐτῷ ὑπακού**ουσιν**
Mk 4,41 καὶ   ὁ ἄνεμος   καὶ ἡ θάλασσα   ὑπακούει   αὐτῷ
Lk 8,25 καὶ **τοῖς** ἀνέμοις ἐπιτάσσει καὶ τῷ ὕδατι, καὶ ὑπακού**ουσιν** αὐτῷ.

The agreement in changing Mk's verb ὑπακούει (with the dual subject ὁ ἄνεμος καὶ ἡ θάλασσα) to the plural ὑπακούουσιν is scarcely significant (compare the plural ἐπαύσαντο in Lk 8,24). The change of Mk's ὁ ἄνεμος to the plural is a more intriguing agreement, particularly in light of the preceding τοῖς ἀνέμοις in Mt 8,26, diff. Mk 4,39 τῷ ἀνέμῳ (= Lk 8,24). At first glance one may think of Lukan dependence on Mt 8,27 (110-111). However, the transition from the singular in Lk 8,24 to the plural in v. 25 can be understood quite satisfactorily as Luke's own rewriting of Mk 4,35-41 (cf. 1,23-27):

Mk 1	Lk 8
25 ἐπετίμησεν αὐτῷ	24 ἐπετίμησεν τῷ ἀνέμῳ
27 καὶ τοῖς πνεύμασι...	25 καὶ τοῖς ἀνέμοις
ἐπιτάσσει	ἐπιτάσσει...
καὶ ὑπακούουσιν αὐτῷ.	καὶ ὑπακούουσιν αὐτῷ.

As in Mk 1,27 (= Lk 4,36) the activity of commanding is made explicit in the generalizing present tense ἐπιτάσσει and it is for the interests of generalization that Luke uses here the plural τοῖς ἀνέμοις (in contrast to τῷ ἀνέμῳ in v. 24)[12]. Note also the difference between καὶ τῷ κλύδωνι τοῦ ὕδατος (v. 24) and καὶ τῷ ὕδατι in v. 25. This distinction between the story itself and the *Chorschluß* is completely neglected by G.

---

9. *The Minor Agreements*, 1974, pp. 97, 156, 175 (1991, § 31: 14.1; § 76: 6; § 97: 1.1), and in the Classification: no 33c (singular/plural); no 32 (changes in vocabulary); no 25 (ἰδού).

10. *LNP*, pp. 421 (ἄνεμοι), 699 (ὕστερον), 746 (ἰδού). Goodacre notes that Goulder does not comment on the genitive absolute + ἰδού construction (p. 116 n. 72). As far as I see, Luke's uses of the genitive absolute are completely neglected in *LNP*. Matthew's "favourite ὕστερον" is apparently one of Goulder's favourite MAs: it is his first example in Chapter Two ("The Minor Agreements", pp. 47-5, here 48; quoted by G., p. 115).

11. Cf. my *Literary Criticism, Old and New*, in C. FOCANT (ed.), *The Synoptic Gospels* (BETL, 110), Leuven, 1993, pp. 11-38, esp. 16-18 ("The Minor Agreements and Lukan Redaction"): "in some instances Matthean redaction is likely and the problem is on the side of Luke" (p. 17).

12. See, e.g., J. NOLLAND, *Luke 1–9,20* (WBC, 35A), Dallas, TX, 1989, p. 401.

That Luke shows "a marginal preference for the singular" (111) is hardly demonstrable either in Lk (7,24 Q; 8,23.24 MK) or in Acts. Goulder's comment I on the plural in Acts 27,4: "where the sense requires it" can be applied more fittingly to the singular in Acts 27,7.14.15.

As an illustration how independent redaction of Mk can lead to similarities and dissimilarities I quote here one of the other MAs in the same pericope[13]:

Mt 8,24 καὶ ἰδοὺ   σεισμὸς μέγας   ἐγένετο ἐν τῇ θαλάσσῃ
Mk 4,37 καὶ γίνεται λαῖλαψ μεγάλη ἀνέμου
Lk 8,23 καὶ κατέβη λαῖλαψ   ἀνέμου   εἰς τὴν λίμνην

Mt 22,27 ὕστερον δὲ πάντων   ἀπέθανεν ἡ γυνή.
Mk 12,22 ἔσχατον   πάντων καὶ ἡ γυνὴ ἀπέθανεν.
Lk 20,32 ὕστερον   καὶ ἡ γυνὴ ἀπέθανεν.

The figures for ὕστερον (G., 115) are impressive: 7/0/1+0. In four of the seven occurrences in Mt the adverb is used in the comparative sense of 'later', 'afterwards' (4,2; 21,29.32; 25,11), but the superlative 'finally' is well attested in 21,37 (diff. Mk 12,6: αὐτὸν ἔσχατον!) and 26,60 (diff. Mk 14,57)[14]. Yet Mt's phrase ὕστερον πάντων remains close to Mk's ἔσχατον πάντων (last of all) and is unique in Mt (and in the NT). The adverbial ἔσχατον (Mk) is little used (only once in the New Testament, 1 Cor 15,8: the same phrase ἔσχατον πάντων) and the coincidence of an identical substitute in Mt and Lk cannot be excluded. That Luke writes ὕστερον (and not ὕστερον πάντων like Mt) may indicate independent redaction.

Mt 26,47 καὶ   ἔτι αὐτοῦ λαλοῦντος ἰδοὺ Ἰούδας ... ἦλθεν
Mk 14,43 καὶ εὐθὺς ἔτι αὐτοῦ λαλοῦντος παραγίνεται Ἰούδας ...
Lk 22,47   ἔτι αὐτοῦ λαλοῦντος ἰδοὺ ὄχλος καὶ ὁ λ. Ἰούδας ...
                                                                προήρχετο αὐτούς.

G.'s figures for ἰδού (116: 62/17/57) need correction (7 in Mk) and also further precision by concentrating on the use of ἰδού in narrative: 33 in Mt, 16 in Lk, and none in Mk. All MAs are in narrative material: Mt 8,2 / Lk 5,12 (diff. Mk 1,40); Mt 9,2 / Lk 5,18 (diff. Mk 2,3); Mt 9,18 / Lk 8,41 (diff. Mk 5,22); Mt 17,3 / Lk 9,30 (diff. Mk 9,4); Mt 26,47 / Lk 22,47 (diff. Mk 14,43); I include also Mt 12,10 / Lk 14,2 (cf.

---

13. On the possible link of τοῖς ἀνέμοις resp. τῷ ἀνέμῳ with the description of the storm as σεισμός in Mt and as "Fallwind" in Lk, cf. W. SCHENK, in G. STRECKER (ed.), *Minor Agreements* (n. 2), p. 112.

14. A. Ennulat's reservations regarding MtR in 21,37; 22,27; 26,60 can be neglected. Cf. *Die "Minor Agreements". Untersuchungen zu einer offenen Frage des synoptischen Problems* (WUNT, 2/62), Tübingen, 1994, pp. 265 [9], n. 29; 276 [11], n. 24.

Mk 3,1) and Mt 28,2 / Lk 24,4 (cf. Mk 16,5). After elimination of the occurrences of ἰδού in the Sondergut (Mt 1,20; 2,1.9.13.19; 9,32; 28,9.11; Lk 2,25; 7,12.37; 13,11; 19,2; 24,13) and of Mt 15,22 (diff. Mk 7,25: not in Lk), we retain as occurrences in common Markan material: 24 in Mt and 10 in Lk, seven of which are MAs[15]. The disparity in the number of occurrences seems to confirm the theory of Luke's dependence on Mt. But close examination of the evidence may lead to a different conclusion. Matthew's ἰδού is so overwhelmingly present in the Markan material of Mt 8–9 (8,2.24.29.32.34; | 9,2.3.10.18.20)[16] that a more moderate use of ἰδού in a parallel redaction almost unavoidably creates minor agreements. The three instances in Lk (par. Mt 8,2; 9,2.18) mark the beginning of new sections, in Lukan style[17], and are clearly related to Mk:

Lk 5,12 καὶ ἐγένετο ... καὶ ἰδοὺ ἀνὴρ πλήρης λέπρας
   Mk 1,40 καὶ ἔρχεται πρὸς αὐτὸν λέπρος
Lk 5,18 [17]καὶ ἐγένετο ... [18]καὶ ἰδοὺ ἄνδρες φέροντες...
   Mk 2,3 καὶ ἔρχονται φέροντες πρὸς αὐτόν
Lk 8,41 [40]ἐν δὲ τῷ ὑποστρέφειν ... [41]καὶ ἰδοὺ ἦλθεν ἀνὴρ ...
   Mk 5,22 καὶ ἔρχεται εἷς τῶν ἀρχισυναγώγων.

G. rightly draws attention to the genitive absolute + ἰδοὺ construction. The construction occurs ten times in Mt (correct his "eleven times in all")[18]: six times in Sondergut and four times diff. Mk. In the Sondergut passages the genitive absolute functions as a transitional formula resuming the content (and wording) of the previous paragraph:

1,20 ταῦτα δὲ αὐτοῦ ἐνθυμηθέντος
2,1 τοῦ δὲ Ἰησοῦ γεννηθέντος ἐν Βηθλέεμ τῆς Ἰουδαίας
  ἐν ἡμέραις Ἡρῴδου τοῦ βασιλέως
2,13 ἀναχωρησάντων δὲ αὐτῶν
2,19 τελευτήσαντος δὲ τοῦ Ἡρῴδου
9,32 αὐτῶν δὲ ἐξερχομένων
28,11 πορευομένων δὲ αὐτῶν.

---

15. Mt 3,16.17; 4,22; 8,2*.24.29.32.34; 9,2*.3.10.18*.20; 12,10*.46; 17,3*.5ᵃ.5ᵇ; 19,16; 20,30; 26,47*.51; 27,51; 28,2*; Lk 5,12*.18*; 8,41*; 9,30*.38; 10,25; 14,2*; 22,47*; 23,50; 24,4* (* = MA).

16. On Matthew's use of (καὶ) ἰδού, cf. *ETL* 50 (1974), pp. 223-230; = *Evangelica I*, pp. 789-796, with critical evaluation of P. FIEDLER, *Die Formel "Und siehe" im Neuen Testament* (SANT, 20), München, 1969; A. VARGAS-MACHUCA, *(Kαὶ) ἰδού en el estilo narrativo de Mateo*, in *Bib* 50 (1969) 233-244. See esp. p. 230 (= 796), n. 51.

17. Compare καὶ ἰδού + ἀνήρ (9,38; 19,2; 23,50); ἄνδρες δύο (9,30; 24,4); ἄνθρωπος (2,25; 14,2); γυνή (7,37; 13,11).

18. Mt 9,10 is different: the genitive absolute is preceded by καὶ ἐγένετο and is followed by καὶ ἰδού (καί — T).

All four instances diff. Mk use the same expression:

9,18 ταῦτα αὐτοῦ λαλοῦντος αὐτοῖς   (Jesus speaking: 9,15-17)
12,46 ἔτι αὐτοῦ λαλοῦντος τοῖς ὄχλοις (Jesus speaking: 12,39-45)
17,5 ἔτι αὐτοῦ λαλοῦντος   (Peter speaking: 17,4)
26,47 καὶ ἔτι αὐτοῦ λαλοῦντος   (Jesus speaking: 26,45-46).

Differing from the varying formulations in the Sondergut passages, this last example also differs from the other three diff. Mk. In none of them is the standard formula "while he was still speaking" supplied by the parallel text in Mk as it is in Mt 26,47 ("only here in Matthew"!)[19].

Both Matthew and Luke have taken over the genitive absolute from Mk. They omitted (καὶ) εὐθύς, probably as redundant with "while he was still speaking". Matthew added ἰδού, inverted Mk's verb-subject order, and wrote ἦλθεν for | παραγίνεται (see the reverse in Mt 3,13 par. Mk 1,9). Luke too added ἰδού, but is it a sign of dependence on Mt? Ἰδού (without καί) can be used by Luke in narrative. Cf. Acts 10,17 ὡς δὲ ..., ἰδοὺ οἱ ἄνδρες ... ἐπέστησαν ἐπὶ τὸν πυλῶνα (the ὡς δὲ... clause functions here like the genitive absolute in Lk 22,47). Ἰδοὺ ὄχλος without verb is not unlike Lk 5,12.18; 13,11; 19,2; 23,50. Mark's sentence on "Judas ... and with him a crowd" underwent a radical change in Lk: the ὄχλος comes first (and will be described in v. 52 as "the chief priests and officers of the temple and elders" παραγενομένους ἐπ᾽ αὐτόν) and Judas is placed at the head of them (προήρχετο αὐτούς). Throughout the Gospel of Luke (καὶ) ἰδού is used to introduce new characters: here ἰδοὺ ὄχλος, and not "the one named Judas" (cf. 6,9; 22,3).

2. GOULDER'S KEY MA

Mk 14,65: Mt 26,68 / Lk 22,64 + **τίς ἐστιν ὁ παίσας σε;**
Goodacre concludes his discussion of this MA as follows (107)[20]:

> Goulder's general argument from wording characteristic of Matthew but uncharacteristic of Luke is unsatisfactory for the MA at Mk 14.65. Although the language is congenial to Matthew, it is also, if anything, more congenial to Luke. Nevertheless, Goulder's underlying argument about the

19. In Mt 9,18 the use of ταῦτα αὐτοῦ λαλοῦντος αὐτοῖς (par. Mk 5,22 καὶ ἔρχεται εἷς τῶν ἀρχισυναγώγων) can be influenced by Mk 5,35: ἔτι αὐτοῦ λαλοῦντος ἔρχονται ἀπὸ τοῦ ἀρχισυναγώγου. — On Mt 17,5 (and Lk 9,34), see my *The Minor Agreements Matthew–Luke in the Transfiguration Story* (1973), in *Evangelica I*, pp. 797-810, esp. 804-808.

20. For "the key modern defence from a hardline 2ST perspective" (p. 102 n. 32), G. refers to my *ΤΙΣ ΕΣΤΙΝ Ο ΠΑΙΣΑΣ ΣΕ: Mt 26,68 / Lk 22,64 (diff. Mk 14,65)*, in *ETL* 63 (1987) 5-47; = *Evangelica II*, pp. 95-138.

unlikelihood of coincidence or independent redaction is valid here, particularly as both Matthew and Luke coincide in using the *hapax* παίω. This argument, from the unlikelihood of coincidence, is accepted by two-source theorists like Neirynck and Tuckett in that they conjecturally emend the text at Mt. 26.68 to remove the MA.

This confrontation of the two solutions is not new: τίς ἐστιν ὁ παίσας σε either original in Mt or original in Lk. G.'s personal note concerns the hapax παίω. In reply to Goulder he says that the MA is "a little more Lukan in style than it is Matthean", "the language is a little more congenial to Luke than it is to Matthew" (106, 107)[21], but παίω is the exception: the word is un-Matthean and also un-Lukan. The verb occurs "shortly before" in Mk 14,47 and Goulder thinks that its use in Mt 26,68 is a reminiscence of Mk 14,47[22]. Yet the influence of Mk 14,47 (ἔπαισεν) can be at work in Lk 22,64 as well as Mt 26,68, and even more likely because the mocking comes here before the trial (22,66 καὶ ὡς ἐγένετο ἡμέρα) and has closer connections with the arrest. One may agree that "Luke is fond of verbs of hitting" (*Test*, 227), but this can hardly justify the suggestion that in 22,64 he could have written his "favourite τύπτειν" (*LNP*, 750).

The question τίς ἐστιν ὁ παίσας σε in Mt 26,68 is problematic because of the omission of the blindfolding. G. paraphrases Goulder's first argument (103):

I   Just as Matthew in 27.29 specifies that when the soldiers mocked Jesus they put a crown of thorns 'on his head' and a rod 'in his right hand', so here he presses the detail: the soldiers spat 'in his face'.

For G. "Goulder's point here is sound" because the parallels depict the mocking of Jesus (104). But how can he say that the "clarifying additions" in 27,29 are "similar" to the confusing "omission" in 26,68?

Goulder's second point is his 'muddle' argument: "by omitting the blindfolding of Jesus' 'face', Matthew involves himself in a muddle, as often" (103). For G. this is "a brilliant move": "the 'oversight' here is evidence that Matthew himself redacted the verse" (104)[23]. Cf. *Knowledge*

21. Question beginning with τίς/τί ἐστιν and ὁ with participle: "the style is just as Lukan as it is Matthean" (p. 105); both occur together in Lk 20,2 τίς ἐστιν ὁ δούς σοι (diff. Mk 11,28); cf. Lk 8,45 (diff. Mk 5,30); 20,17 (diff. Mk 12,10) (p. 106).

22. Cf. p. 105 n. 41: G. refers to *Test*, p. 227. See also *Knowledge*, p. 153: "under the influence of Mk 14.47, where he has just read it".

23. Contrast C.M. Tuckett's reaction (cf. below, n. 25): "to accept such 'oversights', or what is almost incoherence, as a constant feature of Matthew's redaction is something of a hostage to fortune: if one is not careful, it allows almost anything to happen and to be acceptable as MtR without having to account for it in any way beyond saying that it is an 'oversight'" (p. 140 n. 72).

(153 n. 28): "the oversight consists in first elaborating the spitting with 'in his face', and then overlooking Mark's 'covering his face', which is an essential element in the story". Goulder at least recognizes that "an essential element" is lacking in Mt 26,68[24].

Finally, G. cannot accept conjectural emendation removing the MA at Mt 26,68 "because there is no manuscript evidence for the omission in Matthew and because, as Goulder has shown, it is at least possible to regard the addition of τίς ἐστιν ὁ παίσας σε; as Matthew's own" (124, cf. 107). On this second point, I may refer to my 1987 essay and later supplements. His first point is a definition of conjectural emendation, not a justification of its rejection in the case of Mt 26,68. As I noted in 1992: "The debate is not closed, but I see a growing number of scholars for whom an exceptional instance of conjectural reading is no longer methodologically unacceptable"[25].

3. THE MINOR AGREEMENTS AND Q

A last section in G.'s chapter on the MA is devoted to critical reactions to Goulder's 1978 short study: "On Putting Q to the Test" and its conclusion: "The evidence from the agreements shows that Luke knew Matthew, and that Q is | therefore no longer a valid hypothesis" (*Test*, 234). The reaction I formulated at the 1981 Colloquium is here quoted once more (127)[26]:

---

24. Goulder's classic example of 'oversights' is in Mt 14,3-12. For a reaction, see my *Evangelica II* (n. 7), p. 28 (= pp. 49-50).

25. *Literary Criticism* (n. 11), p. 18; with reference to *The Four Gospels 1992*, pp. 326 (B. Aland), 1548 (A. Vanhoye). Cf. C.M. TUCKETT, *The Minor Agreements and Textual Criticism*, in G. STRECKER (ed.), *Minor Agreements*, 1993 (n. 2), pp. 119-141, esp. 135-138; see now also his *Q and the History* (below n. 26), 1996, pp. 17 n. 41; 24 n. 59 (reply to Goulder's appeal to K. Popper).

I add here a more recent comment on Mt 26,68 by S. LÉGASSE, *Le procès de Jésus. La passion dans les quatre évangiles* (LD Commentaires, 3), Paris, 1995: "Chez un écrivain soigneux comme notre évangéliste une inconséquence aussi lourde étonne. Les explications fournies par ceux qui veulent l'en excuser sont bien fragiles. Ainsi quand on laisse entendre que Matthieu suppose chez ses lecteurs la connaissance du texte de Marc (dont il a précisément supprimé ce qui est indispensable pour comprendre la question finale!), ou quand on suggère que la question portait non sur un personnage que Jésus ne voyait pas (ayant la tête voilée) mais sur un inconnu de lui. Reste une solution qui, tout bien pesé, est la meilleure: quoique toute garantie manuscrite lui fasse défaut, elle consiste à envisager que le texte de Matthieu a été glosé sous l'influence de celui de Luc et que c'est par cette voie que la question devinette y est entrée" (pp. 205-206).

26. *Recent Developments in the Study of Q* (1982), in *Evangelica II*, pp. 409-455, esp. 411-415 ("Q and the Synoptic Problem"), here 414 (= 1982, p. 34). Similar observations were made in 1984 by C.M. Tuckett and in 1989 by T.A. Friedrichsen (both referred to

If Lukan knowledge of Matthew would be the conclusion to be drawn from the minor agreements, then Luke would have used Mark notwithstanding his knowledge of Matthew, and the inference could only be that elsewhere, where Luke is using another source, a similar subsidiary influence of Matthean reminiscences can be expected.

A few colleagues have understood this passage as a declaration for the Simons-Morgenthaler-Gundry hypothesis. Therefore, in a more recent reference, I wrote: "If [*dato non concesso*]..."[27], although I think no such clarification was needed for those who read the continuation of my text:

> It is not my conviction that Luke knew Matthew but I would support R. Morgenthaler in his reaction against the Farrer fallacy. In his view, "Lk gab grundsätzlich Mk und Q den Primat, berücksichtigte aber gelegentlich den Mt-Text. So entstanden die 'minor agreements'. Es wäre ein prinzipieller Fehler, anhand dieser 'minor agreements' Q in Frage zu stellen".

In response to Goulder's "A House Built on Sand" (1985) I added in 1987[28]:

> Let us take it more simply: the reasoning from analogy cannot go beyond the limits of the similarity. If there is any subsidiary dependence upon Matthew in the triple tradition, how can this prove that there is anything more than subsidiary dependence in the double tradition?

This note is also quoted by G. (127 n. 92). Nevertheless G. maintains (128):

> Goulder's argument works quite legitimately by attempting to demonstrate that the MAs show Lukan knowledge of Matthew, and that this knowledge *makes* the theory of *primary Lukan dependence* on Matthew in double tradition material *likely* [emphasis mine].

With reference to my text (quoted above) he replies: "This would be a possible inference but not the only possible inference" (128). I have to repeat, I think: the inference from the acceptance of subsidiary Matthean influence cannot be "*primary* Lukan dependence"[29].

by G.). See now also D.R. CATCHPOLE, *The Quest for Q*, Edinburgh, 1993, pp. 1-59 ("Did Q Exist?"), esp. 1-2; C.M. TUCKETT, *Q and the History of Early Christianity*, Edinburgh, 1996, pp. 1-39 ("The Existence of Q"), esp. pp. 17-18 and nn. 42-43.

27. *The Minor Agreements and Q*, in R.A. PIPER (ed.), *The Gospel Behind the Gospels* (NTSup, 75), Leiden, 1995, pp. 49-72, here 53.

28. *ΤΙΣ ΕΣΤΙΝ* (n. 20), p. 25 (= 115), n. 116.

29. See also TUCKETT, *Q and the History* (n. 26), pp. 17-18 n. 43. This note was added to the text that appeared in PIPER, *The Gospel* (n. 27), 1995 (not available to G.?), pp. 19-47, here 32-33: "the MAs might show at most a subsidiary use of Matthew by Luke in Markan material; from this one might perhaps deduce a subsidiary use of Matthew in non-Markan material. But the MAs themselves cannot show, even on Goulder's presuppositions, that Luke used Matthew alone where Mark was not available".

ETL 70 (1994) 406-416

12

GOSPEL ISSUES IN THE PASSION NARRATIVES

The title of this note is taken from the Introduction to R.E. Brown's *The Death of the Messiah*, § 2: "General Gospel Issues Pertinent to the Passion Narratives"[1]. Raymond E. Brown is an influential New Testament scholar and "A Commentary on the Passion Narratives in the Four Gospels" (second subtitle) is one of the major publications in 1994 in the field of Gospel studies. In this commentary "From Gethsemane to the Grave" (first subtitle) he decided to work through the passion "horizontally", studying each episode in all four Gospels simultaneously. He calls it a "controversial decision" (Preface, viii).

Such an undertaking has to face a number of serious inconveniences. It begins with the delimitation of the extent of the PNs. Brown decided "on practical grounds" to commence the "passion" with Gethsemane (139; 37: the choice was "dictated ... by practicality"). He has to caution his readers that "the evangelists themselves may have had a different understanding of what constituted Jesus' passion" (37). It is only in John that the demarcation is relatively clear (Jn 18–19). Beginning with the episode of Mk 14,26-31 "causes a sharper division than the Synoptic evangelists intended between the Last Supper and what followed on the Mount" (139). Jesus' prediction of Peter's denials (Mk 14,29-31, par. Mt) has its parallel in Lk at the Last Supper (22,31-34). The PNs end with Mk 15|16, Mt 27|28, Lk 23|24, Jn 19|20. Lk 23,56b is placed together with Mt 27,62-66 in the last paragraph of the PN (§ 48), although the half-verse from Lk is better understood as the beginning of a new section (par. Mk 16,1)[2]. Brown perfectly knows that one can argue for Mt 26,1–27,56 as "the passion unit in Matt's own view of the structure of the Gospel" (39)[3], and in fact he defends the Matthean structure of the burial/resurrection account in 27,57–28,20 (1301-1303). Nevertheless the Commentary treats the burial of Jesus (27,57-61) and the

---

1. R.E. BROWN, *The Death of the Messiah. From Gethsemane to the Grave* (The Anchor Bible Reference Library), New York, Doubleday, 1994. 2 vol., XXVII-877, XIX-(879-)1608 p. In this note I use the abbreviations PN = Passion Narrative and BDM = *The Death of the Messiah*, in the style of Brown's own abbreviations for his earlier works: BBM = *The Birth of the Messiah*, 1977, ²1993; BGJ = *The Gospel According to John*, 2 vols., 1966, 1970; BEJ = *The Epistles of John*, 1982 (all at Doubleday).

2. *Evangelica II*, p. 404 n. 40. Cf. Greeven, UBS GNT.

3. Cf. D.P. SENIOR, *The Passion Narrative according to Matthew. A Redactional Study* (BETL, 39), Leuven, 1975, ²1982.

guard at the tomb (27,62-66) as parts of the last scene of the passion (§§ 46-47 and 48).

A second inconvenience of "horizontal" readings is the possible suspicion that they may have some harmonizing goal. A commentary on the Four Gospels PNs might remind the readers of earlier work on the passion "nach den vier Evangelien ausgelegt" (J. Belser). Brown himself is not unaware of it: "Let me assure those alarmed..." (viii). He repeatedly declares that "the primary concern I of a commentary is making sense of what the biblical writers have given us", and he warns the readers of his commentary that they "should not jump to conclusions about historicity when they read (his) judgment that there is preGospel tradition underlying some detail mentioned in the narrative" (22). But there is still the possibility of a harmonizing touch in judgments on pre-Gospel tradition.

1. A NEW COMMENTARY

Brown's two-volume commentary comprises an Introduction (1-106); the Commentary proper (107-1313), divided into four "Acts", three of which have two scenes: I. Prayer/arrest: Mk 14,26-52 (26-42.43-52); II. Jewish trial: 14,53–15,1 (53-64.65–15,1); III. Roman trial: 15,2-20a; IV. Crucifixion/burial: 15,20b-47 (20b-41.42-47); nine Appendixes (1315-1524); and three rather sophisticated Indexes (80 pages): Bibliographical Index of Authors (1527-1555), referring to the full titles of books and articles, which are found for the most part in the General Bibliography (94-106) or in one of the sectional bibliographies printed at the beginning of each section; Index of Subjects (1556-1581), with "a few authors ... listed here ... because there is a discussion of their views" (in fact, only three names of scholars are included: M. Dibelius, H. Lietzmann, M. Smith); Gospel Passage Index (1583-1608), a sequential (very literal) translation of the four PNs, with the addition of references to the treatment of every passage. Since the commentary follows the Markan order, this "Index of Principal Comments" in an adjacent column is particularly useful with regard to some Lukan or Johannine passages. In addition to the PNs in the Canonical Gospels a fifth Gospel is included in the Commentary: "*The Gospel of Peter* - a Noncanonical Passion Narrative", in Appendix I (1317-1349; with a new translation: 1318-1321) and in the pertinent sections in the course of the commentary[4].

---

4. See my note *The Historical Jesus: Reflections on an Inventory*, in *ETL* 70 (1994) 221-234, pp. 226-229: "The Gospel of Peter", on GP and Mk (in reply to BDM, 1327-1328).

I would like to draw special attention to Appendix IX, by M.L. Soards: "The Question of a PreMarcan Passion Narrative" (1492-1524). Soards presents first an annotated list of thirty-five authors and then a detailed analysis of their hypotheses in a Table surveying the verses in Mk 14,32–15,47 these authors attribute to the pre-Markan PN. The article was first published in 1985 and is reprinted here in an updated version. A few corrections I suggested in a letter to the author (19.09.93) are introduced in the new version (L. Schenke: 14,33.38.40.41). Six scholars are newly added: X. Léon-Dufour (1960), S.E. Johnson (1966), R. Pesch (1977), T.A. Mohr (1982), D. Lührmann (1987), M. Myllykoski (1991). Mohr's complex subdividing of the verses is not reproduced in the Table. No analysis of the works of J. Gnilka and R. Pesch was included in 1985 and "persons interested" were referred to *ETL* 57 (1981) 144-162 (= *Evangelica*, 618-636, esp. 634-635: Gnilka). This is still the case with Gnilka (n. 4). Pesch's position (not Gnilka's!) is now introduced in the Table. One may ask, however, what can be the relevance of printing the letter A invariably I for all these 87 verses. Further improvements of Soards's table are possible. K.G. Kuhn's two sources in 14,32-42 are included (1496, 1504), but it is not indicated that Kuhn is one of those scholars who think that the PN originally began with the arrest (246: "e.g., K.G. Kuhn"). The argument that "one of the twelve" in 14,43 suggests that Mark is using a source now seems to be retracted (n. 13). It would be a significant improvement of Soards's tool if the alphabetical order could be replaced by a chronological one, showing possible dependences and ready to be supplemented with more recently suggested reconstructions. One such reconstruction is that of A.Y. Collins: 14,32a.33b-35a.36-37.42 I 43*-46.50 I 53a; 15,1*-5.15b I 16-20a I 20b-27.29a.31b-32 I 33-34a.37b-38 (now in *NTS* 40, 1994, 503, and already in *Studia Theologica* 43, 1993, 21-22). The name of A.Y. Collins is never mentioned in BDM, not even her 1992 essay on "The Passion Narrative of Mark". Some bibliographical references to commentaries on Mk were not mentioned in BDM before this last Appendix. Other commentaries are simply cited in the General Bibliography (BDM 98) by the author's name and the year of publication: e.g., R. Pesch (1976); read: (1976-1977)!

Yet, there can hardly be complaints about insufficient Bibliography. Some 1500 authors are listed in the Index, many of them with more than one title (occasionally up to fifteen different titles). ETL and BETL have not been neglected. Senior's book on the PN in Mt (BETL 39) and the Gospel studies in BETL 60 and 99 and BETL 100 and 101, both in 1992, appear in the list of abbreviations (SPNM, NEv 1.2, FGN, DJN).

In reference to J. Duplacy on Lk 22,43-44 (1981; BDM 116) I note here that this essay has been published in a more complete version in BETL 78 (1987: 349-384). I also noted some rather curious mistakes, 318: Qui sais-je? = Que...; 321: Romantische Abteilung = Romanistische; 323: Baltenweiser = Baltensweiler; Nederuits = Nederduits; 895, 1531: Cerfaux, Les Saintes = Les Saints[5]. A Bibliographical Index, however useful it may be, has obvious limitations. It is not a complete Index of Modern Authors (as provided, for instance, in AB 28A), and readers who might be interested to know whether (and where!) Brown is treating a particular author's view will miss this information. Another limitation in BDM is probably due to Brown's concern to serve a variety of audiences (ix: "probably most readers will not be students of the Greek NT"). Only unavoidable Greek words are cited in the text (always in transliteration)[6], and even variant textual readings happen to be cited in English translation.

Already in 1970, when he wrote his commentary on John, Brown was convinced that "The Passion Narrative supplies the best material for a study of the | relationship of the Fourth Gospel to the Synoptic Gospels" (BGJ 787). He began his general remarks on the Johannine PN with the relations to the Synoptic accounts (787-791) and what he now calls "certain stances about the genesis of the Synoptic PNs" (36 n. 1). He made his point quite clear: "The Johannine Passion Narrative is based on an independent tradition that has similarities to the Synoptic sources", but "John does not draw to any extent on the existing Synoptic Gospels or on their sources as reconstructed by scholars" (791). As to the PN in Mk, he was very much impressed by Taylor's theory of the two sources A and B and, referring to Bultmann, Jeremias and Taylor, he accepted without hesitation that "one of Mark's chief sources was an earlier consecutive account of the passion" (789). With regard to the PN in Lk, he thought that "a solid defense can be made for the thesis that Luke drew on a truly independent, non-Marcan source" (790).

5. Other corrections in the Bibliographies, xx, xi: Auftragè; 86, 87, 1538: Heekerens; 95, 1536: letzten; 97, 553: quatres; 112: verbale; 172, 1538: Hammerton-Kelly; 239: ecclésiastique; 316: Straffprozessordnung; 563: Neuchâtel; 668: Hérode; 671: Freiburg; 886: Der = Die Kreuzesstrafe; 892: Förderung; 1528: Jésus; 1534: De Visscher; 1543: Lövestamm; 1545: Moffatt. In the text, p. 1222 line 23: Matt, read: Mark.

6. The use of transliteration seems to be Anchor Bible style (contrast, e.g., the Word Biblical Commentary). Also the Greek words in bibliographical references are given in transliteration; e.g., 324 ἀχειροποίητος: acheiropoëtos (sic).

As can be seen in the quotations in the text above, Brown now adopts throughout the closed style in English compounds with prefix and a capitalized word (preGospel, preMarcan, antiJewish, etc.).

Brown now makes clear, particularly in reply to the Griesbach hypothesis (43-44), that there can be no doubt about his adherence to Markan priority: Mk 14,26–15,47 is used independently by Matthew and Luke. He no longer holds the hypothesis of a special source for the PN in Lk (64-67): additions in Lk as well as omissions, transpositions, and substitutions can be explained without positing a continuous non-Markan source (67-75). I welcome this retraction. What I wrote on this topic in BETL 110 (1993) apparently came too late for BDM[7].

There is another important shift in BDM. Brown is now skeptical about the possibility of reconstructing a pre-Markan PN (53-57). He came to this new position a posteriori because of the lack of agreement among scholars who propose reconstructions and a priori because of the inapplicability of the criteria used by these scholars (Mk-Jn parallels, Markan style, stylistic differences and seams). He decided therefore not to attempt a pre-Markan reconstruction but to write a commentary on *Mark*'s PN. "We do not have the tools to reconstruct *detailed* preGospel traditions; and so even when the existence of preGospel tradition can be detected, I shall practically never attempt to be precise about its wording" (23; cf. 223, 306, etc.). Before the differences in the 35 reconstructions expounded by Soards (Appendix IX) he even takes a prophetic tone: "the project is self-defeating, for no theory will ever get wide or enduring acceptance" (23). The first and most explicit treatment of this problem is found in his commentary on the Gethsemane scene, where he concludes in a final "Analysis": "granted such uncertainties I shall not attempt any detailed reconstruction of a preMarcan source" (223). In my own study of "Duality in Mark" I warned against the source-critical use of doublets and referred to K.G. Kuhn's 1952 article, "Jesus in Gethsemane", as "perhaps the best known example" of using duplication as criterion for identification of sources in Mk[8]. The discussion of Kuhn's two-source approach to the Gethsemane scene plays a decisive role in I BDM (57, 218-223) and I cannot blame Brown for noting that "Mark shows a penchant throughout the Gospel for doublets of various types" (224 n. 11)[9].

7. *Literary Criticism: Old and New*, in C. Focant (ed.), *The Synoptic Gospels* (BETL, 110), Leuven, 1993, pp. 11-38, esp. 20-27. Cf. already *La matière marcienne dans l'Évangile de Luc*, in F. Neirynck (ed.), *L'Évangile de Luc* (BETL, 32), 1973, pp. 157-201, esp. 195-199 (²1989, 105-109; *Evangelica I*, 75-79). See also ETL 49 (1973), 806-808 (= 759-761), on "Transpositions in Luke"; 48 (1972) 570-573 (review of G. Schneider, *Verleugnung*).
8. *Duality in Mark* (BETL, 31), Leuven, 1972 (²1988), pp. 30-32 and 63-64 (= ETL 58, 1972, 167-168, 200-201).
9. On Mk 14,35.36, "The twofold Marcan prayer in indirect and direct discourse", cf. BDM 165-167. On E.P. Sanders's statistics (165 n. 3) see however my critical observations in *Duality*, pp. 67-69.

If for Brown Mark did not construct his PN by copying from a source, he remains convinced that "there were sequential narratives of the passion before Mark wrote" (55): there may have been a general passion sequence and "various ways of fleshing out that sequence"; and there are some episodes in the PN which "could not have circulated outside a passion context" (54). The search for pre-Gospel tradition is a constant concern in BDM, and in particular serious consideration is given to the possibility that "the agreement between Mark and John might tell us about ... detectable preGospel items in the tradition" (224). Thus, "when Mark and John present a common sequence, that sequence may well be quite old in Christian tradition" (426).

2. THE MINOR AGREEMENTS

"Markan priority and the minor agreements" is the main issue in the section on the interrelationships of the Synoptic Gospels (40-46). Brown is not the first to use the minor agreements "as an argument to controvert Griesbach" (43). Cf. T.A. Friedrichsen (with reference to C.M. Tuckett): "The minor agreements violate the general principle of how Mark as a conflator is supposed to have worked: rather than following his sources when they agree, Mark departs from his sources"[10]. It is more important that in Brown's judgment some minor agreements "force us to modify the thesis of Marcan priority through the introduction of orality" (44).

But is this word not too strong, and too polemical[11], tending to create a somewhat artificial contrast between "Neirynck ... and his student Senior" on the one hand and Brown and his student Soards on the other? In a later section of the same § 2 one can read: "True, some instances in which Matt and Luke agree with each other against Mark are difficult to explain according to the theory of dependence on Mark; but these instances are so few when compared with the overwhelming similarities that they can be written off as examples of our ignorance of how ancient authors worked" (82). When I read through the commentary of BDM I find a number of references to minor

---

10. *The Matthew-Luke Agreements against Mark. A Survey of Recent Studies: 1974-1989*, in F. NEIRYNCK (ed.), *L'Évangile de Luc - The Gospel of Luke* (cf. above n. 7), pp. 335-392, esp. 349.

11. The text of sections 1*-5* (42-46) was submitted to the SNTS Seminar in 1993 (Chicago, August 10). The phrase "resists sternly the introduction of oral dependence" is now changed to "greatly distrusts..." (44).

agreements[12] but, apart from the case mentioned in the Introduction (45: diff. Mk 14,65), it is rare to find an appeal to oral tradition:

| **Mk 14,30**: cf. 14,72a.b.   **14,35**: "Both of them omit the prayer about the hour that was phrased in indirect discourse, perhaps judging Mark to be tautological" (171; cf. 59 n. 57: reused in Mt 26,42).   **14,36**[1]: "Matt and Luke, who do not report the transliterated Aramaic form, prefer the more normal Greek vocative form *pater*" (172 n. 12; 175 "a further development where the foreign Semitic term is dispensed with in praying"). **14,36**[2]: "Both Matt and Luke avoid Mark's initial *alla*, perhaps to avoid having that word twice, a few words apart, within such a short clause" (176; n. 23: "Thrall comments on their both preferring *plēn* to Mark's *alla*").   **14,36**[3], Lk 22,42b / Mt 26,42: "Both employ the noun *thelēma* and a form of the verb *ginesthai*" (176: "Soards attributes these agreements to the influence on the evangelists of common oral prayer tradition. The Lord's Prayer was surely part of that tradition").   **14,43**: "Granted that Matt and Luke use *idou* differently here, the fact that they both have that word versus Mark's *euthus* is not a significant agreement" (245 n. 5). **14,45+**: "The other evangelists seem to have felt the need to supply a response, perhaps because they found such a response in their tradition and/or because they felt the need for theological commentary" (256). **14,47+**: Jesus' reaction to sword-wielding "in different wording": "Matt drew on Christian tradition (not a written source)" (275).   **14,51-52**: "a culminating example of the failure of the disciples. It was omitted by Matt and Luke as too harsh for their outlook on the followers of Jesus" (309; cf. 43; 44: "too scandalous a scene"; 303: "ignominious", "this harsh"; 1222: "found the scene too scandalous a portrait of a disciple to retain"; 295: cf. below n. 13).   **14,62**[1]: "Luke's 'You [pl.] say that I am' has the appearance of combining Matt's 'You [sg.] have said it' with Mark's 'I am'. Luke's *hymeis legete*, however, is not the same as Matt's *sy eipas*... Luke is combining two Marcan answers [15,2; 14,62]" (492).   **14,62**[2]: "we should see the appended temporal phrase [ἀπ' ἄρτι / ἀπὸ τοῦ νῦν] as independent efforts of Matt and of Luke to clarify the imminent futurity of Jesus' triumph as already taking place. Each evangelist has done this in his own style" (561: cf. Mk 14,25 Mt/Lk).   **14,65**: cf. below.   **14,68** [καὶ ἀλέκτωρ ἐφώνησεν]: "The omission is the 'harder' reading and should be preferred" (601).   **14,72a.b** (and 14,30): "Presumably Matt and Luke omitted the Marcan 'twice' as a needless complication or considered such exact numbers poor rhetorical style" (137; cf. 44 n. 20; 59 n. 57). **14,72c**: "One solution [missing in the text of Lk]... More plausibly, Soards suggests that ... both evangelists were influenced by oral tradition" (609).   **15,20b**: "The agreement of Luke and Matt here in employing *apagein* against Mark's *exagein* is not significant" (618 n. 14).   **15,21**: "names of the sons of Simon" om. (43, 44; no comment *in loco*).   **15,22**: "Matt and Luke use *erchesthai*"; "avoided" Mk's φέρειν (936).   **15,25**: |

---

12. Only some of them are listed in the Index, s.v. Luke: relations to Matt('s) PN. For a more complete description of agreements diff. Mk 14,26–15,47, cf. *The Minor Agreements*, 1974, §§ 95-108 (pp. 172-192). See now also A. ENNULAT, *Die "Minor Agreements"* (cf. below n. 29), 1994, pp. 344-409.

"The absence of both elements ... in Matt and Luke is best explained as deliberate omission" (961). **15,26**[1]: "the position of the inscription, Luke: over [*epi*] him; Matt: put up [*epitithenai*] above [*epanō*] his head" (963). **15,26**[2] the inscription: "Matt and Luke simply expand on it [Mark's form]" (967 n. 79). **15,32**: τοῦ θεοῦ Lk 23,35, cf. Mt 27,40 (988, 992, 993: "Matt's preference for 'Son of God'"). **15,43**: "*Houtos* ... is scarcely significant... *Proselthōn* ... is an obvious improvement that could have occurred to each evangelist independently" (1229). **15,44-45**: "Like Matt, but presumably independently, Luke omits the material..." (1229; cf. 43, 44, 59 n. 57, 1222: "that independently such a reaction could have been caused each evangelist to omit this passage from Mark is not a perfect solution; but in my judgment it is more likely..."). **15,46**[1]: "Independently Matt and Luke may have turned to it [ἐντυλίσσειν] in preference to Mark's matter-of-fact 'tie up'" (1252; cf. 1255; 44: "perhaps independently finding this verb more customary and reverent"). **15,46**[2] κατέθηκεν (1246): "Matt and Luke ... also agree in using the normal *tithenai* instead of Mark's rare *katatithenai*; did they find a pejorative tone in that verb, one of the connotations of which is to rid oneself of a burden?" (1252; cf. 1255). **16,1**, Mt 27,62-66 / Lk 23,56b: "Both the evangelists who drew on Mark fill in by mentioning what took place on the Sabbath..." (1286).

| Brown's comment at Lk 23,52 (Mk 15,43) is most characteristic: "This ... brings some scholars to posit that Matt and Luke have a source independent of Mark. Others posit the influence of oral tradition on the two evangelists. In general I am more favorable to the latter solution, but appeal to it is probably unnecessary in the present instance..." (1229). The influence of oral tradition is a theoretical assumption which is scarcely documented in particular passages. In fact, in almost all his comments (and not only on negative agreements which are "easier to deal with")[13] he defends independent redaction by Matthew and Luke.

It is somewhat unclear when at the outset he declares that "an appeal to oral influence makes better sense than ad hoc hypotheses about written sources" (45). I am on his side in his critique of hypothetical sources independent of Mk. It is less evident what is meant by "oral influence" as *the* explanation of minor agreements. One can observe, for instance, that "Matt and Luke [diff. Mk 8,31] prefer the set kerygmatic formula 'raised [*egeirein*] on the third day'" (BDM 1475) and in this sense one

---

13. BDM 44: the model of a common omission is Mk 14,51-52. See references above; the inversion: "The fact that Matt and Luke omitted the passage ... suggests strongly that it was understood to refer to complete nakedness and thus was a bit scandalous" (295) is a more delicate argument. – The combination of negative and positive agreements in the same pericope is not mentioned as a special difficulty (BDM 44). It is remarkable how Brown strongly defends Mt's and Lk's independent redaction in the burial story, with the common omission of Mk 15,44-45 and the agreements against 15,43.46[1].46[2] (cf. above).

can speak, with J. Schmid, of influence of oral tradition "wenigstens in diesem Fall..."[14]. But is it "once again" that "this illustrates the influence of oral tradition even when copying from a written Gospel"[15]? In his analysis of Luke's special material in Lk 22,39-71 Soards considers Mt-Lk agreements influenced by oral tradition in Lk 22,42.48.51.62.64[16]. In Lk 22,42 (diff. Mk 14,36) he treats the three agreements "viewed together", but Brown explains πλήν as avoidance of Mk's ἀλλά. If oral influence here means that both Matthew and Luke are possibly influenced by a prayer tradition in their independent rewriting of Mk, this should not imply the existence of an oral-tradition variant of the Gethsemane story. In Lk 22,48 (diff. Mk 14,45+) Brown himself emphasizes the evangelist's need for theological commentary ("safeguarding the exalted character of Jesus"). The case of Lk 22,51 (add. Mk 14,47+) shows how unsubstantial the supposed oral tradition can be: "it became known *that* Jesus rebuked his disciples" but "Luke himself composed the particular form of the rebuke"[17]. Lk 22,62 καὶ ἐξελθὼν ἔξω | ἔκλαυσεν πικρῶς (diff. Mk 14,72c) and 22,64 τίς ἐστιν ὁ παίσας σε; (diff. Mk 14,65) are the two much debated instances of Mt-Lk agreement in the PN[18]. With regard to Lk 22,62 Brown repeats Soards's suggestion, without really discussing the textual problem[19]. He supposes that in the oral tradition "an emotional phrase like this was already fixed" (609); "an oral memory of the preGospel

14. Cf. *Evangelica II*, 47.
15. BDM 1475-1476, in Appendix VIII: "Jesus' Predictions of his Passion and Death" (1468-1491). On the minor agreements diff. Mk 8,31, see also 1476, nn. 9 and 10 (ἀπό and the repetition of the definite article), in reply to W.R. Farmer. Cf. my *Evangelica II*, 43-48 ("Note on Luke 9,22: A Response to M.D. Goulder"), 49-58 ("Note on a Test Case: A Response to W.R. Farmer"). – Corrigendum: it is not true that Luke *always* prefers ἐγείρειν (BDM 1475): cf. Lk 18,33. But see *Evangelica II*, 47-48, on Lukan usage.
16. M.L. SOARDS, *The Passion Narrative according to Luke: The Special Material of Luke 22* (JSNT SS, 14), Sheffield, 1987, pp. 97-106 (cf. 72, 73, 75, 78). The "uncertain" cases are not included here. Cf. Lk 22,60 (Mk 14,72a.b δίς): "... or the continued influence of oral tradition" (p. 78); Lk 22,70 "you say" (Mk 14,62¹): "perhaps from oral tradition. Here, however, there can be no real certainty" (p. 104). Cf. the same five instances of Mt-Lk agreement in the PN listed by Soards in *BZ* 31 (1987), p. 114.
17. *Ibid.*, p. 99.
18. F. NEIRYNCK, *ΤΙΣ ΕΣΤΙΝ Ο ΠΑΙΣΑΣ ΣΕ*, in ETL 63 (1987) 5-47 (= *Evangelica II*, 95-138); C.M. TUCKETT, *The Minor Agreements and Textual Criticism*, in G. STRECKER (ed.), *Minor Agreements. Symposium Göttingen 1991* (GTA, 50), Göttingen, 1993, pp. 119-142.
19. Cf. TUCKETT, pp. 132-134: "The theory of a textual corruption of the text of Luke, with a harmonizing addition being made fairly early, still seems to be the best solution" (p. 134). See *ΤΙΣ ΕΣΤΙΝ*, p. 19 (= 109) n. 85 (list of those supporting this view); also pp. 7 (= 97) n. 19; 45-46 (= 135-136). On the internal grounds for omission, see now also A. VANHOYE, *L'intérêt de Luc pour la prophétie* (below n. 23).

tradition survived even after Mark's written account" (611 n. 43). However, the problem is that (in contrast to BGJ 837) Brown now judges Luke to be dependent on Mark in the account of Peter's denials. He sees "no need for an independent source" (611) and indicates no other survival of an earlier tradition than this five-word clause. An appeal to Fitzmyer's commentary (582 n. 17) is scarcely helpful. Quite unconvincingly, Fitzmyer ascribes v. 62 to L, "which is going to be the source in the following verses [63-65]"[20], whereas Brown rightly agrees "with those who think the Lucan [mockery] scene can be explained as a free rewriting and reorganization of the Marcan account" (583). We turn now to this scene in Mk 14,65 and the other five-word agreement against Mk in Mt 26,68 / Lk 22,64.

The case is treated by Brown with a certain agitation. After referring to a first "desperate theory" and then to an "equally desperate suggestion" he continues: "Senior once more opts for a desperate solution...", and he concludes as follows: "Having reluctantly indulged in the distraction of arguing..., let me now return to commenting on the Matthean text" (578-579). Speaking for myself I can say that in $TI\Sigma$ $E\Sigma TIN$ (1987) I tried to confine the discussion to the real problem[21]: how can in Mt Jesus be asked "Who hit you?" without being blindfolded? In Brown's judgment there is a simple solution: "Matt could drop Mark's 'to cover his face' because when he added 'Who is it that hit you?' he was giving the readers perfectly clear information" about the game of blindman's buff Mark was spelling out (579, cf. 578). The game was known "under the rubric of the question" (579), and this identification of the game as τίς ἐστιν ὁ παίσας σε was added also in Lk "from set oral usage" (583). The blindman's buff game[22] here developed to become the key for the understanding | of the mockery scene. Brown depends on D.L. Miller (*JBL* 1971) without noting that it was suggested by Miller in reference to the account of Luke (with blindfolding and

20. *Luke*, p. 1458. For critical remarks on Fitzmyer's theory of L passages in Lk's PN, see my *Literary Criticism* (above n. 7), pp. 22-25.

21. My $TI\Sigma$ $E\Sigma TIN$ anticipates Brown's rejection of a number of "desperate" theories: the reading ἡμῖν χριστέ, τίς ἐστιν ὁ παίσας σε in Mk (BDM 572, 579), the omission of καὶ περικαλύπτειν αὐτοῦ τὸ πρόσωπον in Mk (45 n. 24, 572, 574 n. 6, 578), the originality of Lk or Lk's special source (572, 583), the understanding of the question in Mt not in the sense "Who is the *unseen* person..." but "tell us the name..." (578). Cf. $TI\Sigma$ $E\Sigma TIN$, pp. 96-99, 99-104, 104-118, 129-130. The list of scholars in BDM 574 n. 6 is taken from $TI\Sigma$ $E\Sigma TIN$, p. 100; read: Tucker = Tuckett 1984. See now also J.B. GREEN, *The Death of Jesus* (WUNT, 2/33), Tübingen, 1988, p. 67 n. 191. Brown also agrees with my interpretation of οἱ δέ ("some of them") in Mt 26,67 (BDM 578 n. 10).

22. In $TI\Sigma$ $E\Sigma TIN$ it was mentioned in a footnote (n. 234) with reference to D. Flusser (1976) and D.L. Miller (1971).

question united in v. 64). In BDM it is applied to Mt and even to Mk: "the Marcan phrase about covering the face is quite intelligible in light of a game that would have been known to the readers" (574). Mk's προφήτευσον is read in light of the Lukan parallel without giving due consideration to a possible shift from "Deliver a prophetic oracle!" in Mk to "Exercise the prophetic gift of second sight!" in Lk[23]. Brown rightly notes that for Mt/Mk the challenge 'Prophesy' "made sense on the storytelling level because Jesus was connected with prophecies at the trial [Matt by mentioning the Messiah makes the connection clearer], but in Luke the trial is yet to come" (584, cf. 580). Brown's unanswered questions about the context in Lk (585) have received a satisfactory response in A. Vanhoye's study of Lk 22,60-61(62)[24].

Here again Brown refers to Soards's oral-tradition approach (579). In this case, however, Soards had to observe that the five-word question "differs from previous instances [of Mt-Lk agreement: Lk 22,48.51] where oral tradition created the idea that Jesus spoke but the evangelists filled in the words"[25]. Therefore Brown supplies here an ad hoc hypothesis: "'Who hit you?' may have been the set question in this game" (45); "The question is so set that it immediately signals the name of the game" (579). The evidence he provides is what one can hear on American playgrounds... Brown restricts the oral-tradition element to τίς ἐστιν ὁ παίσας σε (cf. 585: "a minor influence from oral tradition"). Is this meant to be a correction of Soards's presentation[26]? In any case, if

---

23. *ΤΙΣ ΕΣΤΙΝ*, p. 26 (= 116): "Luke understands προφήτευσον as referring to the gift of second sight and by adding the question 'who struck you' he gives a coherent picture of the mocking". See now also A. VANHOYE, *L'intérêt de Luc pour la prophétie en Lc 1,76; 4,16-30 et 22,60-65*, in *The Four Gospels 1992* (BETL, 100), 1992, pp. 1529-1548, esp. 1547-1548: "l'examen de la composition révèle que la question: "Quel est celui qui t'a frappé?" est à sa place dans le texte de Luc et ne l'est pas dans celui de Mt".

24. *Ibid.*, pp. 1543-1547. Lk 22,60: "Jésus se fait connaître par lui (Pierre) comme prophète qui a dit vrai" (p. 1546); 22,62: "il détourne l'attention du thème de la prophétie. Ce texte long correspond donc beaucoup moins bien aux caractéristiques de Luc".

25. *The Passion Narrative*, p. 102.

26. Although Soards finally concludes that only verse 64d (= the question) comes from oral tradition, his description of "the same non-Markan tradition" is that of an oral-tradition variant of Mark's story: "the dissimilarities between the accounts of Luke and Matthew make it unlikely this tradition was written. Therefore, it seems justified to conclude that Luke and Matthew had access to the same oral tradition in Greek. We may infer that in retelling the incident of Jesus' mockery, after the challenge to Jesus to prophesy was narrated, early Christians made clear *what* Jesus was dared to say. Luke and Matthew had heard this clarification of the command to prophesy and independently added *tis estin ho paisas se* to their versions of the story" (*The Passion Narrative*, p. 102; *BZ* 31, 1987, p. 113). Contrast BDM 579: "Matt was giving the readers ... information about the game in a way more familiar to them" (and Luke did the same).

"independently, ... the two evangelists may have supplied that question instinctively as they recognized the game, or in order to help reader recognition of the game, or both" (45), this is not far away from a redactional explanation of the minor agreement (not only in Lk, as I would say, but also in Mt), and I see no ground in it for an attack against "overly bookish explanations demanded by attributing everything to desktop copying" (sic; *ibid.*). After all, the fact remains that "the originality of the question in the text of Luke is supported by | the presence of the veiling, the use of ἐπερωτάω and the construction τίς ἐστιν ὁ + participle. None of these reasons apply to the Gospel of Matthew. On the contrary, the normal antecedent of the question (περικαλύπτειν) is lacking in Matthew, and if we remove the words τίς ἐστιν ὁ παίσας σε, the text of Mt 26,67-68 can be explained as a consistent editorial rewriting of Mk 14,65"[27]. The possibility of an exceptional case of conjectural emendation of the Gospel text cannot be denied in a sound textcritical methodology[28].

A. Ennulat, in his recently published dissertation[29], studied some 1000 minor agreements and, although the oral-tradition hypothesis is not neglected in his survey[30], he had to write in his conclusion: "nur sehr selten (legte sich) der Einfluß mündlicher Überlieferung nahe"[31]. He proposes a deutero-Markan redaction, used by Matthew and Luke, as the only acceptable solution in 4% of the minor agreements. Mk 14,65 is one of the three (or four) instances in the PN[32]. In this case, however, Deutero-Mk (as well as oral tradition) is an unnecessary hypothesis on

27. *ΤΙΣ ΕΣΤΙΝ*, p. 31 (= 121). Cf. TUCKETT (n. 18), pp. 135-141; VANHOYE (n. 23), 1992, pp. 1547-1548. See also my *The Minor Agreements and the Two-Source Theory*, in *Evangelica II*, pp. 5-41, esp. 27-28; reprinted in G. STRECKER, *Minor Agreements* (n. 18), 1993, pp. 25-63, esp. 49-50 (with additional note); review *Minor Agreements*, in *ETL* 69 (1993) 428-429, p. 429 (in answer to M. Goulder).

28. *ΤΙΣ ΕΣΤΙΝ*, pp. 42-47 (= 132-137); TUCKETT (n. 17), on "mutual interaction between the disciplines of textual criticism and source criticism" (p. 138). Cf. B. ALAND, in *The Four Gospels 1992*, p. 325 n. 1.

29. A. ENNULAT, *The "Minor Agreements". Untersuchungen zu einer offenen Frage des synoptischen Problems* (WUNT, 2/62), Tübingen, 1994 (diss. Bern, 1990, under U. Luz). On the unpublished dissertation, see my note in *ETL* 67 (1991), p. 369, and an extensive review by T.A. FRIEDRICHSEN, *ibid.*, 373-385. The published text appears with a new pagination but is otherwise unchanged; it contains no bibliographical references beyond 1988.

30. See, e.g., the references to Soards on pp. 335 n. 39, 358 n. 69, 367 n. 45, 376 n. 68, 377 n. 87, 380 n. 13.

31. *Ibid.*, p. 417. He cites there (n. 1) one example: λέγων in Mt 26,27 / Lk 22,20 (Mk 14,24 καὶ εἶπεν αὐτοῖς). But how can he attribute Mt's λέγων to "pln Traditionseinfluß" if "λέγων vor direkter Rede ist eine mt VZWendung" (341[10], n. 52)?

32. Mk 14,65 (p. 381); 15,26¹ (p. 395); 15,(30)32 (p. 398): all in BDM (see list above). See also Mk 14,43 om. εὐθύς (p. 353; but not in the Index, p. 469).

the side of Luke and it does not solve the problem of Matthew's omission of the blindfolding.

3. GENERAL GOSPEL ISSUES

Since Brown accepts "the thesis that Matt knew Mark's PN and followed it so closely that many times there is no major difference in what they narrate" (57), this leaves no much room for oral tradition in Mt's PN, at least not in the Markan material. But "Matt increased the orality of its PN" through the addition of his special material, for which he drew on "a consistent body of tradition marked by orality and imaginative reflection on the OT" (57-64; cf. 61, 74 n. 87). He notes that "against that position, Senior (SPNM) ... would regard this nonMarcan material as a Matthean creation"[33].

Brown also stresses the signs of orality in the Gospel of Mark: "orality is manifested not only in what Mark took over but in the way he presents it" (51). I In rejection of W.H. Kelber's outlook he prefers a model of combined orality and textuality (50).

In the last section of the General Gospel Issues (75-92) Brown formulates his position on the Johannine PN: "John did not use any of the Synoptic PNs in writing his own account... Whether or not a preJohannine PN had already been shaped is not possible to determine... Since Mark and John wrote independently of each other, the agreement of their PNs is often an important indicator of preGospel order and stories" (92). His thesis on John's independence of Mk is not new (cf. BGJ), but he proposes it here with new rigidity: "Throughout the commentary I shall come again and again to what I regard as a completely illogical result if John knew Mark"[34]. I will reserve for a later issue the continuation up to 1994 of my survey of studies on "John and the Synoptics"[35]. Here I just

33. Cf. D. SENIOR, *Matthew's Special Material in the Passion Story*, in *ETL* 63 (1987) 272-294. See now his *Revisiting Matthew's Special Material in the Passion Narrative: A Dialogue with Raymond Brown*, in *ETL* 70 (1994) 417-424.

34. BDM 82. In a footnote, he mentions the possibility that the final redactor of John knew Mark, with reference to BGJ: "but I prefer not to appeal to that" (426 n. 39). – When discussing common factors in John and Mark as pre-Gospel elements he stresses the importance of independent material: therefore, "Johannine independence of Mark is a key issue" (554).

35. Cf. BETL 101 (1992) 3-62: "John and the Synoptics: 1975-1992". Brown mentions the case of Lk 24,12 and Jn 20,3-6 (sic) and "scholars like Neirynck and Dauer who do micro-comparisons of vocabulary" (88 n. 119). But is the structure and wording of a passage like Jn 20,3-10 not a "macro-comparison"? On this discussion, see now my *Once More Lk 24,12*, in *ETL* 70 (1994) 319-340.

indicate which are the examples for "those who wish to anticipate" (82). The example he cites again and again is Jn 18,1: "If John is dependent on Mark, he has changed the Mount of Olives (better known) to 'across the Kedron valley'". The common source is an older (pre-Gospel) appeal to the picture of David in 2 Sam 15: vv. 23 διέβη τὸν χειμάρρουν Κεδρων and 30 ἀνέβαινεν ἐν τῇ ἀναβάσει τῶν ἐλαιῶν (125-126; cf. 82 n. 103, 143 n. 41, 154, 177). I may cite my own comment (1979): "Quant à la traversée du Cédron, il n'est nullement besoin de recourir à une interprétation typologique (ou à une donnée de topographie précise du document primitif). En parlant de la traversée du Cédron, Jn emploie une terminologie assez courante pour dire que Jésus quitte la ville pour se rendre au mont des Oliviers (Lc 22,39)"[36]. Compare BGJ: "John's use of the correct terminology for the Kidron is not necessarily a proof that the Gospel is drawing on an authentic Palestinian tradition, for 'winter-flowing' is the usual designation of the Kidron in LXX. Loisy, Lagrange, and others think that John is subtly alluding here to the story of David's flight before Absalon in II Sam xv. Guilding relates the Johannine narrative to I Kings ii (37: the warning of Solomon to Shimei).... However, the reference to the Kidron is not obviously symbolic" (806).

---

36. *Jean et les Synoptiques*, p. 150 (and n. 303; e.g., Josephus, *Bell.* 5,504: ἔνθεν διὰ τοῦ Κεδρῶνος ἐπὶ τὸ Ἐλαιῶν ὄρος). For an older, less respectful comment, see B. WEISS, *Johannes*, ⁹1902: "Die typologischen Beziehungen (Luthardt nach älteren: auf David, welcher von Ahitophel verraten, denselben Weg gegangen, II Sam 15,23...) sind Spielerei" (p. 475 n. 1). On Jn 18,1, see now also M. HENGEL, *The Johannine Question*, London-Philadelphia, 1989, p. 209 n. 14: "This information supplements very precisely that of Mark 14.26,32"; S. LÉGASSE, *Le procès de Jésus: L'histoire* (Lectio Divina, 156), Paris, 1994, p. 35: "Le mot χωρίον a pour correspondant en Jn 18,1, κῆπος, plus précis. Également d'après Jean, ce jardin se trouvait 'au-delà du torrent du Cédron', information sans le moindre portée religieuse qu'on n'a pas de peine à retenir". Cf. *ETL* 70 (1994) 458-459.

SUPPLEMENTARY NOTE: Raymond E. Brown, S.S. (1928-1998) died of a heart attack on August 8, 1998. Cf. F. NEIRYNCK, *L'exégèse catholique en deuil: R.E. Brown - J. Dupont*, in *ETL* 74 (1998) 506-516. His last major work was published in 1997: *An Introduction to the New Testament*, New York, Doubleday, 1997, XLV-878 p. (The Anchor Bible Reference Library). See my review in *ETL* 73 (1997) 443-445.

ETL 67 (1991) 361-372; 69 (1993) 428-429

13

A SYMPOSIUM ON THE MINOR AGREEMENTS

On the invitation of Professor G. Strecker, and under his chairmanship, a group of New Testament scholars met in Göttingen, July 26-27, 1991, for a Symposium on the Minor Agreements. The program comprised five main papers, each followed with a response by one of the participants and a general discussion, in this order: F. Neirynck, The Minor Agreements and the Two-Source Theory (response by D.B. Peabody); M.D. Goulder, Luke's Reconciliation of the Order of Mark and Matthew (response by D.L. Dungan); W.R. Farmer, The Minor Agreements and the Two-Gospel Hypothesis (response by U. Luz); A. Fuchs, Mk 4,35-41 parr (response by W. Schenk); C.M. Tuckett, The Minor Agreements and Textual Criticism (response by F. Wheeler)[1]. The main options with respect to the minor agreements were represented at the meeting: on the one hand, priority of Mark and independent redaction by Matthew and Luke (Neirynck); priority of Mark and Luke's dependence on Matthew (Goulder); priority of Mark and the hypothesis of a Deutero-Mark, source of Matthew and Luke (Fuchs); priority of Mark occasionally combined with a deutero-Markan recension and oral-tradition variants (Luz); and, on the other hand, the neo-Griesbachian hypothesis of Markan posteriority: Matthew is copied by Luke and both are conflated in Mark (Farmer). Tuckett's paper concentrated on the possibility of conjectural emendation, particularly in the case of Mt 26,68.

In addition to G. Strecker and the ten members directly involved in the discussion, the list of twenty-four participants included some younger scholars who did research on the minor agreements in their doctoral work: F. Kogler and C. Niemand (dir. Fuchs); T.A. Friedrichsen (dir. Neirynck); A. Ennulat (dir. Luz), who unfortunately had to cancel at the last moment. The so-called "Two-Gospel team" was present in full: Farmer, Dungan, Peabody, and also L. Cope, A. McNicol, P.L. Shuler (all from U.S.). An important group of *Göttinger* attended the

---

1. G. STRECKER (ed.), *Minor Agreements. Symposium Göttingen 1991* (GTA, 50), Göttingen, 1993. See my review in *ETL* 69 (1993) 428-429. The volume includes the five main papers delivered by F. Neirynck (25-63), A. Fuchs (65-92), C.M. Tuckett (119-142), M.D. Goulder (143-162), W.R. Farmer (163-208), and two responses: the reply to Fuchs by W. Schenk (93-118) and the reply to Farmer by U. Luz (209-220). These responses and Fuchs's article are written in German, the other articles are in English; each contribution is followed by a summary in the other language. No responses by Peabody, Dungan, and Wheeler are included in the 1993 volume.

sessions of the Symposium: prof. em. E. Lohse, prof. H. Hübner, Dr. F.W. Horn, Dr. G. Löhr, and U. Schnelle (Erlangen), M.E. Boring (Fort Worth, TX).

The massive presence of the "Farmer school" (less respectfully, Dungan uses the appellation "Griesbach Mafia"; cf. below) did not contribute to a real confrontation of both theses, priority of Mark and posteriority of Mark. Peabody's response to the two-source paper was entitled "The Minor Agreements and the Two-Gospel Hypothesis", and his main concern was to show that minor agreements can be "consistent with the Two-Gospel hypothesis". Dungan, on his turn, did not reply to Goulder but took the opportunity to step down from the scientific debate and read an insipid persiflage of the two-source theory. Farmer's oral presentation was extremely brief, and, through the presidency, he suggested that the discussion would concentrate on Luz's *Korreferat*. Nevertheless, neo-Griesbachian optimism remained imperishable. Cf. Peabody, on minor agreements in the feeding story: "I am convinced that the Two Gospel Hypothesis will be making some interesting contributions to this I discussion in the near future"; Dungan, in a written response to Goulder: "the literature does not contain any systematic account of the Lukan redaction on the basis of the Griesbach hypothesis ... However, the 'Griesbach Mafia' are working on one and a provisional discussion will soon be available"[2]. At the Göttingen meeting, however, even their use of the name "*the* Two Gospel Hypothesis" did not escape contestation: "you can call it *a* two-gospel hypothesis, but not *the* two-gospel hypothesis; also my hypothesis is a two-gospel hypothesis, Luke using Mark and Matthew" (Goulder)[3].

My paper, *The Minor Agreements and the Two-Source Theory*, which was written for the meeting in Göttingen, first appeared in *Evangelica II* (1991)[4] and was reprinted in the Symposium volume (1993)[5]. In my oral

2. See the papers published in *SBL Seminar Papers*, 1992 (98-120); 1993 (303-333); 1994 (516-573); 1995 (636-669); collected in A.J. McNicol (ed. with D.L. Dungan and D.B. Peabody), *Beyond the Q Impasse – Luke's Use of Matthew. A Demonstration by the Research Team of the International Institute for Gospel Studies*, Valley Forge, PA, 1996.
3. Cf. *Minor Agreements* (n. 1), p. 143.
4. *Evangelica II*, 3-42. The article is followed by critical notes on alternative theories by M.D. Goulder (43-48), W.R. Farmer (49-58), and H. Koester (59-73). Corrigenda: on p. 19 n. 98, second line, "in all editions", add: "Greeven reads ἐδυνήθησαν in Lk and ἠδυνάσθησαν in Mt". On p. 37, line 19: ἔτι, add: αὐτοῦ.
5. *Minor Agreements*, 25-63: Introduction (pp. 25-27); I. Current Solutions (pp. 27-31); II. Significant Agreements, esp. diff. Mk 5,27; 9,19; 4,11; 14,65 (pp. 32-50); III. Independent redaction: diff. Mk 6,30-34; 9,2-10, esp. Mt 17,5a / Lk 9,34a (pp. 50-61); Epilogue (pp. 61-72); Zusammenfassung (p. 63). Updating additions are found here in the footnotes (esp. nn. 23, 36a, 146a). – *Minor Agreements* was announced by the publisher

reply to D.B. Peabody I could clarify what I meant by *Markan priority* theories, in which the MAs are post-Markan, having their origin in redaction(s), revision, or even corruption of the text of Mark[6]. Peabody seemed to neglect the distinction between pre-Markan and post-Markan. With regard to the agreement at Mk 14,65, two hypotheses ("In our view and in that of Professor Goulder") are assimilated as "a source theory that posits direct literary dependence between Luke and Matthew". But in Goulder's theory the text of Matthew is post-Markan, and the anomaly in Mt 26,67-68 can be explained by "oversight". This solution is simply not possible in Peabody's hypothesis of Matthean originality.

Only the second part of Goulder's paper, entitled *Luke's Knowledge of Matthew*, is reproduced in the 1993 volume (143-162). The printed text is a re-examination of the twelve passages he discussed in *NTS* 1978: the transposition of Markan material in Lk 4,16-30 (no. 1); and diff. Mk 2,3 (no. 3); 3,16-17 (no. 4); 1,2 (no. 5); 14,65 (no. 8); 14,72 (no. 9); 15,43-46 (no. 11); 15,42 (no. 12). Nos. 6, 7, and 10 are cancelled: "lack probative force". Since the formal response to Goulder that was expected to be given by Dungan did not come about, the discussion mainly concentrated on two problematic minor agreements, the spelling Ναζαρά in Mt 4,13 and Lk 4,16[7], and the question τίς ἐστιν ὁ παίσας σε in Mt 26,68 and Lk 22,64. Much attention was given to my view on Mt 26,68 as an exceptional case of conjectural emendation[8]. In his published text Goulder cites two new examples of "oversight": Matthew introduces the Pharisees and Sadducees at 3,7a "who are then *by oversight* promised baptism with Holy Spirit in 3,11". Other example: Mt 3,17 and 11,2ff. But in both instances Matthew returns to his source, Mk or Q, and this is quite different from τίς ἐστιν ὁ παίσας σε added to Mk in Mt 26,68 after the omission of blindfolding in v. 67. Goulder now calls this addition in v. 67 "an *independent* expansion",

as containing "eine umfangreiche Liste der *minor agreements* in ihren jeweiligen Kontexten". This is apparently a description of my *The Minor Agreements in a Horizontal-Line Synopsis* (SNTA, 15), 1991, which was prepared for the Göttingen Symposium. But this list is not included in the volume! The title of the book appears on p. 221, followed on pp. 221-230 by two lists taken from its Appendix, without indication of the original pagination (93-102). The lists of variant readings, N/N[26] and N[26]/Greeven, presuppose the cumulative list, where all agreements are actually cited "in ihren jeweiligen Kontexten". McLoughlin's list of significant agreements (229-230) can be replaced by my own selection on pp. 32-33 (= *Evangelica II*, 10-11).

6. See *Minor Agreements* (n. 1), p. 30, additional note (n. 36a). Cf. *ETL* 67 (1991), p. 362.

7. Cf. below, my "*NAZARA* in Q: Pro and Con".

8. *ETL* 63 (1987) 5-27; = *Evangelica II*, 95-138. Cf. *Minor Agreements* (n. 1), pp. 49-50 (Neirynck); 135-141 (Tuckett); contrast 153-155 (Goulder).

but in so doing he "changes the data" by treating v. 68 in isolation from the preceding v. 67, par. Mk 14,65.

In his essay on *The Minor Agreements and Textual Criticism* (119-142, with special attention to the MAs diff. Mk 14,65 and 14,72), C.M. Tuckett further examines the possibility of conjectural emendation. I quote a few sentences[9]:

> The 'gospels' concerned are not texts which we have available as pure data upon which we can test our different source-critical theories. ... We are in fact working with hypothetical reconstructions by textual critics who can only claim that their proposed texts are *as good an approximation to the texts of the originals as our evidence will allow us to achieve*. For the only 'facts' we possess are texts from the second century on, written *after* a period which included the writing of the autographs *and* a considerable period of copying of the texts by a series of scribes. All this means that ultimately we cannot hope to separate textual criticism and source criticism entirely.

W.R. Farmer's paper, *The Minor Agreements of Matthew and Luke against Mark and the Two Gospel Hypothesis: A Study of These Agreements in Their Compositional Contexts* (163-208) is a reprint of his article in *SBL 1991 Seminar Papers* (773-815). Part One (which was produced "in close collaboration with D.B. Peabody") is entitled "Markan Networks Absent in Matthew and Luke: πάλιν used retrospectively uniting two or more separated pericopes as evidence of Mark's compositional activity". My critical reaction to the source-critical conclusions of this study was anticipated in a note on "Πάλιν in Mk 10,32"[10]. U. Luz, in his *Korreferat* in response to Farmer (209-220), has a similar statement:

> Den redaktionellen Charakter dieser markinischen πάλιν-Stellen bestreitet aber kein Vertreter der Zwei-Quellen-Theorie ... Die Weglassung von πάλιν mit entfernterem Rückbezug erfolgt bei den Großevangelisten konsequent ... Ein Rückgriff auf Deutero-Markus ist daher nicht nötig. Die Weglassung ... entspricht also der matthäischen und lukanischen Redaktionssprache (211-212).

The study of πάλιν is not really relevant in a confrontation between the two-source theory and the Griesbach hypothesis. Both the use of πάλιν in Mark and the omission of πάλιν in Matthew and Luke can be redactional (stalemate). The two-source theory (priority of Mark) can only be falsified by showing the improbability of redactional changes of Mark in Matthew and Luke. Luz examines the contexts where πάλιν is used in

---

9. See p. 137 (Tuckett's emphasis).
10. *ETL* 67 (1991) 73-81, esp. 77-79 (= *Evangelica II*, 54-56).

Mark and omitted in Matthew and Luke: Mk 2,1-4; 2,13-16; 3,1-4; 3,20-23; 4,1-4; 5,21; 10,1; 10,9-11 (4,10-11; 9,33-34; 7,17-18; 9,28-29); 10,32-34; 11,27-28. Conclusion (219-220):

> Ich habe keinen Text gefunden, dessen Erklärung durch die Zwei-Evangelien-Hypothese leichter wäre als durch die Zwei-Quellen-Hypothese. Neben manchen Texten, wo beide Hypothesen möglich sind, fand ich verschiedene Texte, die der Zwei-Quellen-Hypothese geringere Schwierigkeiten bieten. Die Minor-Agreements bleiben aber auch ein Argument gegen eine einfache Zwei-Quellen-Theorie. Sie kann m.E. weder die durchgehende Fülle, noch in manchen Fälle ihre konkrete Gestalt wirklich erklären. Hier greife ich zur Erklärung zu einer Rezensionshypothese (am ehesten mit Ennulat ein von Mk leicht verschiedener Deuteromarkus). Die untersuchten Stellen haben aber keinen Hinweis darauf ergeben, daß eine Deuteromarkus-hypothese sich wirklich zwingend nahelegt. Sie hat für mich weithin eher den Charakter einer Verlegenheitshypothese[11].

Luz's *Korreferat* contains the proposal of a new terminology: MA = Minor Agreements of Matthew and Luke (against Mark); MnA = Markan Non Agreements (p. 2). In its usual acception MA means: "Matthew-Luke agreement against Mark" *and* "Markan non agreement". Compare the neutral use of addition / omission in literary criticism (source criticism) and in textual criticism. In such a neutral sense, MA can be used in all theories. Is there then really need for innovation? The discussion at the Göttingen meeting has revealed that it can be confusing to use the letter M both for Minor (MA) and for Markan (MnA). In the printed text Luz refers to MA as "Marcan non-agreements / minor agreements", but the abbreviation MnA is no longer used[12].

In A. Fuchs's essay, *Die "Seesturmperikope" Mk 4,35-41 parr im Wandel der urkirchlichen Verkündigung* (65-92)[13], all Matthew-Luke agreements against Mk 4,35-41 are treated one by one as evidence for Deutero-Mark. A response was presented by W. Schenk, *Zur Frage einer vierten Version der Seesturm-Erzählung in einer Mt/Lk-Agreement-*

---

11. Summary in English: "The passages ... have not provided any indication ... Therefore, such a hypothesis should be used only as a last resort" (220). Cf. Luz's *Das Evangelium nach Matthäus*, vol. I (1985), II (1990), III (1997), and my reviews in *ETL* 63 (1987) 410-413 (esp. 411); 67 (1991) 169-171 (esp. 170: list of MAs in Mt 8–17); 74 (1998) 109-126 (cf. below: *The Sources of Matthew: Annotations to U. Luz's Commentary*; esp. 110-115: "The Markan Source").

12. On the problem of the definition of minor agreements, raised by Tuckett, cf. *ETL* 67 (1991), p. 368.

13. The text was first published in *SNTU* 15 (1990) 73-99, itself a revised form of the original version in FS A. Stöger (St. Pölten, 1990, 59-86) and in *Estudios Biblicos* 48 (1990) 433-460 (in Spanish translation). On additional footnotes in 1993 (= *SNTU* 1990), see *ETL* 67 (1991), p. 366 n. 9.

Redaktions-Schicht ('Dt-Mk'): Versuch einer textsemiotischen Geltungs-prüfung von A. Fuchs 1990 (93-118). Not all readers will be happy with Schenk's semiotic language and stylistic idiosyncrasies (1VitaJesu = Mk; 2VitaJesu = Mt; 3VitaJesu = Lk), but his paper contains serious criticisms of Fuchs's approach. I mention here one aspect, perhaps the most important one, his description of the minor agreements is "zu atomistisch": "beschränkt sich auf die Komparatistik von isolierten Text-Elementen" (113). Agreements *against Mk* become less striking if the context in Mark is taken into consideration. Thus, e.g., Fuchs's nos. (1) and (2), diff. Mk 4,36: ἐμβάντι αὐτῷ εἰς / ἐνέβη εἰς, cf. Mk 4,1 αὐτὸν εἰς πλοῖον ἐμβάντα. No. (3), diff. Mk 4,36: οἱ μαθηταὶ αὐτοῦ / οἱ μαθηταὶ αὐτοῦ ("völlig neu..."), cf. Mk 4,34 τοῖς ἰδίοις μαθηταῖς. On the other hand, the agreements should be read in their respective Matthean and Lukan contexts. Thus, no. (6), diff. Mk 4,37: ἐν τῇ θαλάσσῃ / εἰς τὴν λίμνην ("eine Gemeinsamkeit gegenüber Mk" ... "keineswegs naheliegend"). But compare the parallels to Mk 4,37a:

Mk 4,37 καὶ <u>γίνεται</u> <u>λαῖλαψ</u> <u>μεγάλη</u>   <u>ἀνέμου</u>
Mt 8,24   καὶ ἰδοὺ   σεισμὸς <u>μέγας</u>   <u>ἐγένετο</u>
Lk 8,23   καὶ κατέβη <u>λαῖλαψ</u>   <u>ἀνέμου</u>

Schenk's comment: "Beim Fallwind [Lk] ist εἰς τὴν λίμνην die redundante logische Ergänzung seines κατέβη. Beim red. Beben [σεισμός, Mt] ist ἐν τῇ θαλάσσῃ eine lokale Neuinformation, die erst verdeutlichend zu der Aussage führt, daß es sich um ein See-Beben handelt" (98). Etc.

In the revised version, Fuchs characteristically adds the following note:

> Der Versuch, die Übereinstimmungen gegen Mk mit dem Hinweis auf schriftstellerische Tätigkeit des Mt bzw. des Lk zu entschärfen, leidet an der ... Kurzschlüssigkeit, daß man nicht apodiktisch ihnen zurechnen darf, wofür *prinzipiell* auch schon jemand vor ihnen in Frage kommen kann. Neirynck und Friedrichsen nehmen nicht zur Kenntnis, daß die *direkte* Abhängigkeit des Mt und Lk von Mk *nachzuweisen*, nicht vorauszusetzen ist (71 n. 22).

But is it not "apodiktisch" to hypothesize a lost document and to refuse as unacceptable ("völlig deplaziert") any question about traces of this document in the "Textgeschichte" (n. 84)? And is it not "kurzschlüssig" to suggest Dmk as a possible solution for some striking agreements between Mt and Lk and then expand this solution to all types of agreements against Mark? And in all that reject the *onus probandi*! – I conclude this note on Fuchs with a plea for sober language. See on p. 88:

"das tradierte 'Dogma' der Zweiquellentheorie"; cf. nn. 46, 49. Should we then apply this language to "the system of Dmk", and call it "das Linzer Dogma"? Compare his reference to the Two-Gospel hypothesis: "Immer noch kommt es ... darauf an, ob nur viel Lärm gemacht wird oder die Argumente auch etwas taugen" (*SNTU* 14, 241).

G. Strecker and A. Fuchs, "both Markan priorists", are cited together in Dungan's recent survey of "Current Developments in the Two Source Hypothesis": "Strecker and Fuchs decided that these networks [of minor agreements] were clear-cut evidence that Matthew and Luke had copied from *a slightly revised version of Mark* that later disappeared"[14]. However, in his Introduction to *Minor Agreements*, G. Strecker seems to mitigate his sympathy for Deutero-Mk[15]:

> Als ein Ergebnis des Göttinger Symposions ist festzuhalten, daß dem Problem der *minor agreements* eine wichtige Funktion im Kontext der synoptischen Frage eingeräumt werden muß... Eine erwägenswerte Möglichkeit bleibt die Deuteromarkushypothese, auch wenn sie im Zusammenhang der *minor agreements* bisher nur auf den Einzelfall anwendbar zu sein scheint.

SUPPLEMENTARY NOTE: Dungan (n. 14) refers to the Göttingen Symposium as "the most recent discussion of the issue from a number of different perspectives" (509 n. 78). But once more we are told that "a fuller discussion will have to be undertaken elsewhere" (391). Meanwhile, a new perspective is now added to the discussion by M. Hengel: νομικός in Mt 22,35 is "a typical 'minor agreement' which in my view can most sensibly be explained by the dependence of Matthew on Luke". Cf. *The Four Gospels and the One Gospel of Jesus Christ. An Investigation of the Collection and Origin of the Canonical Gospels*, London, 2000, 196 and 318 n. 767 (Lk 10,25 "one of the most striking minor agreements"). Cf. also 307 n. 677 (other examples: Lk 3,21-22; 9,29-30; 22,62.64). See his conclusion: Matthew "used Luke eclectically as a secondary source" (205) and "the question of the striking 'minor agreements' is solved" (206). "The problem of the minor agreements disappears if one assumes that Matthew used Luke, which seems to me to be fairly certain". Although I do not think that there is a future for the theory of Matthew's dependence on Luke (see above, p. 282), this is another explanation of the MAs as post-Markan. Cf. below, p. 358 (C.G. Wilke, 1838).

---

14. D.L. DUNGAN, *A History of the Synoptic Problem*, New York, 1999, p. 387.
15. *Minor Agreements*, p. 10. Cf. p. 16: "applicable only in isolated cases of the *minor agreements*".

III

THE SYNOPTIC PROBLEM

BETL 95 (1990) 3-22

14

THE TWO-SOURCE HYPOTHESIS

The Jerusalem Symposium 1984

INTRODUCTION[1]

The Two-Source Theory can be summarized in a few sentences: the Gospel of Mark was written first and it has been used by the other Synoptics as a written source for the so-called triple-tradition material. The Q document is the second common source of Matthew and Luke: it includes the double-tradition sayings material and it has been employed independently by both evangelists. In confrontation with the two other theories which are promoted to competing theories in this Symposium, the Two-Source Hypothesis is in a middle position. It combines interdependence of the Gospels and the use of one hypothetical source: "La théorie du juste milieu".

Our discussion on the relations of the Synoptic Gospels is the continuation of a long-standing debate. It began in the 18th century with a confrontation of the traditional view of Matthean priority with the (modern) theory of the priority of Mark. For some time the Griesbach theory took the relief of the "Augustinian" hypothesis (Mt-Mk-Lk) as the leading synoptic theory. The Gospel of Luke now received the rank of an earlier gospel. Much more than Luke, the Gospel of Mark was at the center of the discussion. To the priority of Mark the Griesbachians opposed its secondary character as an abbreviation, combination and conflation of Matthew and Luke. The decisive debate engaged in the middle of the 19th century, from the thirties to the sixties. As a result, the Markan hypothesis became the predominant scholarly opinion. The Griesbach theory tended to disappear or at least to fossilize.[2]

---

1. This Introduction was delivered at the opening session of the Symposium, April 9, 1984. The paper was first published in the volume *The Interrelations of the Gospels* (1990; cited as *Interrelations*) and is reprinted here in the style of the original edition.

2. Cf. F. NEIRYNCK and F. VAN SEGBROECK, "The Griesbach Hypothesis: A Bibliography," in B. ORCHARD and T.R.W. LONGSTAFF (eds.), *J.J. Griesbach: Synoptic and Text-critical Studies 1776-1976* (SNTS MS, 34), Cambridge, 1978, 176-181. Cf. B. Reicke's note, *ibid.*, 200 (n. 56). As can be seen from this Bibliography, the Griesbach hypothesis continued to be defended in the years after Strauss and Baur, also by Roman Catholics, who tended to correct the hypothesis by the assumption of Mark's contact with an original Petrine tradition. H. Pasquier (1911) was a late representative of this approach.

In the midst of our century a new development took place in some quarters of New Testament scholarship, repeating over a much shorter period of time the same successive stages of gospel criticism. First, objections were raised against the two-source theory, mainly by Catholic scholars pleading for the priority of Matthew in the form of a Proto-Matthew (L. Cerfaux, L. Vaganay) or, in the pure Augustinian tradition, of the canonical Matthew (J. Chapman, B.C. Butler). None of them gave serious attention to the Griesbach theory.[3] Nevertheless, Butler's book (1951) is at the origin of an anti-Streeter reaction in British and American gospel study and it has contributed much to W.R. Farmer's new defence of the Griesbach hypothesis as an alternative to Markan priority (1964). Once more, the Augustinian hypothesis found its successor in Griesbach (redivivus).[4] An active cell of new Griesbachians is now definitely present in the field of gospel criticism. But, at the same time, the proliferation of redaction-critical studies in the last decades gave reassurance to the two-source theory. If we look at the scholarly production and the university teaching of our days, it appears that the theory still holds its position. It is even fair to say that through redaction criticism the theory has received a new development and an expansion it never had before.

It should be added, however, that within this fundamental solution, adopted by so many scholars, a considerable amount of variety can be observed. The assumption that Mark is the first Gospel does not close the debate about its composition and its sources (the pre-Markan passion narrative, pre-Markan collections or individual pericopes and sayings), about the unity of its style and its theology. Mutatis mutandis, such questions are raised also concerning the Q source. The Q hypothesis is in some sense a subsidiary hypothesis – subsidiary to Markan priority – and there is a great diversity with regard to the unity of the source, its nature and its extent.

All agree that there are some overlappings of Mark and Q, but Mark's knowledge of Q is a point of dispute. In the more common view the sayings in Mark and Q rely on parallel traditions, probably with a common *Vorlage*, but the precise reconstruction of this *Vorlage* will often remain a most delicate performance.

3. Cf. B.C. BUTLER, *The Originality of St Matthew. A Critique of the Two-Document Hypothesis*, Cambridge, 1951, 5: "Every serious scholar recognizes that to explain Mark as a conflation of Matthew and Luke is a surrender of critical principles"; L. VAGANAY, *Le problème synoptique. Une hypothèse de travail*, Tournai, 1954, 6: "l'école de Tubingue tourna le dos à la critique littéraire ... en soutenant le système de J.J. Griesbach."

4. Cf. C.M. TUCKETT, *The Revival of the Griesbach Hypothesis. An Analysis and an Appraisal* (SNTS MS, 44), Cambridge, 1983.

The special material of Matthew and Luke gives rise to new divergences. Some *Sondergut* sayings are included in the common source, or are combined with Q in a pre-Matthean or pre-Lukan redaction, or, more radically, the Q source is combined with Lukan *Sondergut* in one Proto-Lukan Gospel. This, of course, affects the evangelist's redaction of Q and, in this last instance, it even has a considerable effect upon Luke's use of Mark.

The more central thesis of Matthew's and Luke's independent use of Mark is sometimes mitigated by the acceptance of tradition variants or by a combination of Luke's dependence upon Mark with a subsidiary acquaintance with Matthew. And, of course, there is an almost constant temptation to find a solution for the problem of the Matthew-Luke agreements against Mark by changing the text of Mark (Urmarkus, textual corruption, text recension, Deuteromarkus). With all that, the two-source theory becomes a very large house with many dwelling-places, or a big family with many family quarrels. A great deal of the discussion that is going on with other theories is taking place also within the two-source theory.

Such a comprehensive two-source theory is certainly not what I am pleading for. It is at least not my opinion that there is an urgent need for important modifications or mitigations of our hypothesis. The basic conviction of the Markan hypothesis can be seen in the fact that the Gospel of Mark has so much in common with Matthew and Luke that a literary relationship, not only of individual pericopes but of the gospel as such, is undeniable and that the most adequate solution resulting from a comparative study of the language, the style and the content of the Synoptic Gospels is the use of Mark as a common source by Matthew and Luke. The theory has its antecedents in the 18th century, but when it took its more definite form in the middle of the 19th century, it was proposed as an alternative to the more commonly accepted Griesbach hypothesis, arising from a dissatisfaction with the treatment of Mark as a secondary gospel on the basis of the phenomena of order and conflation. In the discussion of the last twenty years we are now again confronted with the theory of Markan "zig-zag" (as some new Griesbachians continue to call Mark's alternation between Matthew and Luke) and with the interpretation of Mark's duplicate expressions as combinations of Matthew and Luke, or, as recently suggested, of Proto-Matthew and Proto-Luke. The argument from order and the dual expressions in Mark are inevitably among the items to be discussed at our Conference.

A third item of discussion, equally unavoidable, and as old as the Markan hypothesis itself, is that of the minor agreements of Matthew and Luke against Mark. Within the hypothesis of Markan priority almost all modifications of the basic theory had their starting point more or less with the Matthew-Luke agreements in the triple tradition. With Vaganay (1954), Farmer (1964) and, in the line of Vaganay, M.-É. Boismard (1972), a new prestige has been given to these "minor agreements". Not so much because of the difficulty of some individual cases, but much more because of their high number, their concentration in particular passages, and the conjunction of negative and positive agreements, they are cited now as objection number one against the priority of Mark. The advocates of the two-gospel hypothesis add to that: "if these 'minor agreements' demonstrate that Mt and Lk were not independent of one another, then the need for 'Q' is also obviated". But this last conclusion is valid only for those who exclude other possibilities, such as indirect dependence or the combination of Lukan dependence on the leading source (Mk) with a subsidiary dependence on Matthew.[5]

In our hypothesis Matthew and Luke depend on a second source. The usually cited indications for the Q source are the very existence of the double-tradition material in Matthew and Luke, the high degree of verbal agreement in some of these passages, the presence of primitive elements in both versions, the more or less common order of pericopes which, with a few exceptions, are found in different Markan contexts, and, more specifically, the so-called source doublets in Matthew and Luke. In the history of the Q hypothesis since Weisse much consideration has been given to the phenomenon of the doublets and, as it can be seen from the papers submitted to this Conference, the doublets in Matthew and Luke are still now cited as an important piece of evidence. In order to avoid misunderstanding, let me recall once more that the Q source is a second source and, in some sense, a secondary hypothesis: for those who hold the priority of Mark the "proof from doublets" can become a real proof for the existence of a second source. Never in the history of the Q hypothesis has the argument from the doublets been separated from the assumption of the priority of Mark (or some Proto-Mark): one form of the doublet is recognized as Markan and the other is non-Markan.

The phenomenon of order, duality in Mark, minor agreements of Matthew and Luke against Mark, and the source doublets in Matthew and Luke: those are the four aspects of the synoptic problem which we

5. Cf. F. NEIRYNCK, "Recent Developments in the Study of Q," in J. DELOBEL (ed.), *Logia* (BETL, 59), Leuven, 1982, 29-75, 31-35: "Q and the Synoptic Problem."

have to discuss and about which at least some clarification can be expected from this Conference.

1. *The Phenomenon of Order*

With regard to the phenomenon of order, I would like to make only some introductory remarks.

1. The Markan material appears to a large extent in the same order in the three synoptic Gospels. This is, I think, a common statement in our three theories, although the multiple-stage hypothesis sometimes tends to become a multiple-source hypothesis in which each section of the gospel and each pericope can get its own synoptic theory. Such a fragmentizing approach is, to say the least, not recommended by the common order in the triple tradition.

2. Concerning the differences in order the main literary-critical solutions to the synoptic problem (Markan priority, Augustinian hypothesis, Griesbach hypothesis) agree about one statement: the absence of Matthew-Luke agreement against Mark. On the assumption of Markan priority the absence of agreement between Matthew and Luke against Mark becomes an indication for the independence of Matthew and Luke in their use of Mark. However, by itself, this statement allows for no other conclusion than the medial position of the Gospel of Mark. This had been emphasized long before Butler by 19th century defenders of Griesbach (Maier, Schwarz), and the participants of the SNTS Seminar on the Synoptic Problem at the Southampton meeting in 1973 will remember that the leading neo-Griesbachians then solemnly declared that this was also their own position.[6]

3. The argument from order for Markan priority is nothing more, and nothing less, than the demonstration that the differences of the order in Matthew and Luke receive a plausible explanation as changes of Mark which are consistent with the general redactional tendencies and the compositional purposes of each gospel. It is clear that in this area, as in any other area of the synoptic problem, our method should be a | joint effort of source criticism and redaction criticism (or composition criticism).

---

6. Cf. F. NEIRYNCK, "The Argument from Order and St. Luke's Transpositions," *ETL* 49 (1973) 784-815 (790-799: "The Absence of Agreement and its Significance"); reprinted in *The Minor Agreements* (n. 13), 291-322; = *Evangelica*, 1982, 737-768 (743-752). See also, "The Griesbach Hypothesis: The Phenomenon of Order," *ETL* 58 (1982) 111-122; and C.M. TUCKETT, *The Revival*, 26-40; "The Argument from Order and the Synoptic Problem," *TZ* 36 (1980) 338-354; "Arguments from Order: Definition and Evaluation," in ID. (ed.), *Synoptic Studies. The Ampleforth Conferences of 1982 and 1983* (JSNT SS, 7), Sheffield, 1984, 197-219.

2. Duality in Mark

The duplicate expressions in Mark are much more than a mechanical combination of two single expressions.

1. Even on the two-gospel hypothesis only a portion of Mark's dual expressions can be explained as combinations of Matthew and Luke and our conclusion that duality is a feature of Markan style is an acceptable view also in other hypotheses.

2. The instances which in the Griesbach hypothesis can be seen as combinations (A in Mt, B in Lk, and AB in Mk) become, on the assumption of Markan priority, indications of Matthew's and Luke's independent use of Mark. It has been said that "selon la Théorie des Deux Sources, Matthieu et Luc auraient simplifié le texte de Marc, choisissant, comme par hasard, chacun ce que l'autre rejetait". According to the two-source theory it is not a selection made at random, by chance, but in many instances the choice of each evangelist can be explained in light of the redactional context and in accordance with the more general tendencies of the gospel.

The most famous example is Mk 1:32a, ὀψίας δὲ γενομένης, ὅτε ἔδυ ὁ ἥλιος. It continues to be cited, with the use of the particle δέ in the first element, as a clear sign of its Matthean origin. However, it should be observed, that the use of δέ (instead of καί) in Mk 1:32 is less un-Markan than it is supposed to be. It is rightly noted that καί is used at the opening of the Markan pericopes in 1:21-39, but it is less correct to split the unit of verses 29-34 into two pericopes. The locale of the story is provided in v. 29 (the entry in the house: εἰς τὴν οἰκίαν Σίμωνος...) and it is maintained in v. 33 (πρὸς τὴν θύραν: at the door of the house); the new section will begin with v. 35 (ἐξῆλθεν καὶ ἀπῆλθεν εἰς ἔρημον τόπον). Within the unit of verses 29-34, the healing story starts with ἡ δὲ πενθερὰ Σίμωνος (v. 30) and a new subsection begins in v. 32: ὀψίας δὲ γενομένης. The formula-like character of Matthew's ὀψίας δὲ γενομένης has been overemphasized. A substitution of δέ for καί in Mt 14:15 (Mk καὶ ἤδη ὥρας πολλῆς γενομένης); 14:23 (Mk καί); 26:20 (Mk καί); 27:57 (Mk καὶ ἤδη) (see also Mt 20:8; but see Mt [16:2] ὀψίας γενομένης, at the opening of direct discourse) is a far too general Matthean characteristic to be significant. In the context of Mt 8:16 the specific reason for the motif of the sunset (the sabbath day of Mk 1:21-34) has disappeared and ὅτε ἔδυ ὁ ἥλιος could be omitted. In the composition of Matthew, the link with the scene in the house of Simon (8:14-15) has not been retained, *and* there is an overlapping of the evening time of Mk 1:32 (the day of Capernaum) and Mk 4:35 (the day of the parables, with another example of Mark's double-step expressions: ἐν ἐκείνῃ τῇ ἡμέρᾳ ὀψίας γενομένης; before the crossing of the lake: cf. Mt 8:18). – In Luke the sunset at the end of the day in Capernaum retains its full meaning. Luke has never I adopted Mark's ὀψίας γενομένης (diff. Mk 1:32; 4:35; 14:17; 15:42; om. Mk 6:47). It is omitted here also, although it may have influenced Luke's use of the genitive absolute in 4:40 (δύνοντος δὲ τοῦ ἡλίου) and again in 4:42

(γενομένης δὲ ἡμέρας, diff. Mk 1:35 πρωΐ: compare Lk 22:66 καὶ ὡς ἐγένετο ἡμέρα, diff. Mk 15:1 πρωΐ; genitive absolute in Acts 12:18; 16:35; 23:12; cf. 27:33,39 ὅτε).

Boismard has made the objection that in some instances one expression in Mark is typically Matthean, and therefore borrowed from Matthew, and the other expression is typically Lukan, and therefore borrowed from Luke. But what is meant, in this connection, by Matthean style? Boismard's treatment of Mk 3:7ff. is most typical. He quotes the verb ἀναχωρέω in v. 7: only here in Mark and 9 times elsewhere in Matthew. No consideration is given to the possibility of Matthean redaction in some or in all these instances and to the possible influence of Mark's significant use of ἀνεχώρησεν for Jesus' retirement (Mk 3:7, cf. v. 6).[7] In his study of double-tradition passages in Matthew, such as Mt 3:7-10, Boismard has noted quite correctly that "Matthieu avait tendance à systématiser certaines expressions qu'il lisait dans ses sources".[8] To accept Matthean systematization with regard to double-tradition texts and to refuse this possibility with regard to the Markan text is, it seems to me, an unjustifiable dichotomy in the study of Matthew.

3. P. Rolland's list of "expressions doubles" (or minor doublets) is not a list of duplicate expressions in the strict sense.[9] It includes a considerable number of so-called "conflations" of a Matthean and a Lukan element which do not necessarily form a unit in the text of Mark. What I call a Markan double-step expression is a much more specific stylistic phenomenon, *one* double expression and something more than the sum of two single phrases.[10] Therefore, the designation by the name of "minor doublets" ("doublets mineurs") is quite inadequate and even misleading. The Markan expression is not a mechanical combination of two parts but a stylistic unit with a progression to greater precision in the second half of the expression, and, in my view, is pointing to the originality of Mark.

7. Cf. F. NEIRYNCK, "Urmarcus redivivus? Examen critique de l'hypothèse des insertions matthéennes dans Marc," M. SABBE (ed.), *L'évangile selon Marc* (BETL, 44), Leuven, 1977, ²1988, 103-145 (132-134); reprinted in *Jean et les Synoptiques. Examen critique de l'exégèse de M.-É. Boismard* (BETL, 49), Leuven, 1979, 319-361 (348-350).
8. *Interrelations*, 274.
9. P. ROLLAND, "Marc, première harmonie évangélique," *RB* 90 (1983) 23-79 (35-79: "Expressions doubles chez Marc"); *Les premiers évangiles* (Lectio Divina, 116), Paris, 1984, esp. 109-128. See also *infra*, n. 21. Cf. F. NEIRYNCK, "Les expressions doubles chez Marc et le problème synoptique," *ETL* 59 (1983) 303-330; cf. *infra*, n. 10.
10. F. NEIRYNCK, *Duality in Mark. Contribution to the Study of the Markan Redaction* (BETL, 31), Leuven, 1972, ²1988 (with a Supplement on "Duplicate Expressions and Synoptic Problem," 227-235).

3. The Minor Agreements of Matthew and Luke against Mark

On many occasions it has been argued that numerous minor agree-ments are in fact not so striking and that for most of the so-called sig-nificant agreements a satisfactory redactional explanation can be given. Nevertheless the objection is raised again and again: you can be right with your explanation of the individual agreements but, as a whole, the phenomenon of the minor agreements remains unexplained. If this is something more than a polite way of avoiding the "textual discussion", such a reaction reveals that the minor agreements are taken as *one* phe-nomenon; and I have no objection, at least in this sense: the minor agreements share one common characteristic, they are all post-Markan. That is the truth in A. Fuchs's *Deuteromarkus* hypothesis.[11]

1. The minor agreements are first of all agreements against Mark and the first cause of the common change in Matthew and Luke is the text of Mark. Mark's Greek style has not always been rightly evaluated, and Matthew and Luke are not alone in their feeling that there is an overuse of καί, of historic presents, pleonasms, etc. Jesus who asks questions, the disciples who remain unintelligent, and many other motifs in Mark are "corrected" in Matthew and Luke. A priori it is not unlikely that two independent redactions on the basis of Mark will show some coinci-dences. Someone has written that "if Matthew omits something it is unattractive to him for some reason and what is unattractive to one Christian author has by that very fact an *increased* chance of being unat-tractive to another".[12] In any case it is not enough to list the Matthew-Luke agreements, and certainly not simply to count them. The parallel text in Mark and the possibilities of understanding and misunderstanding should be studied more than is usually done in the literature on the minor agreements.

2. In the volume on Minor Agreements I have added, in Part III, "A classification of stylistic agreements with comparative material from the triple tradition".[13] Reviewers and users of the book are usually more interested in the cumulative list of the agreements (Part II) than in the comparison with other triple tradition material. In my view, however,

11. Cf. F. NEIRYNCK, "Deuteromarcus et les accords Matthieu-Luc," *ETL* 56 (1980) 397-408; = *Evangelica*, 769-780.

12. S. McLOUGHLIN, in *The Downside Review* 90 (1972) 201-206, 202. Cf. "Les accords mineurs Mt-Lc contre Mc et le problème synoptique," *ETL* 43 (1967) 17-40; = I. DE LA POTTERIE (ed.), *De Jésus aux évangiles* (BETL, 25), Gembloux-Paris, 1967, 17-40.

13. F. NEIRYNCK (with T. HANSEN and F. VAN SEGBROECK), *The Minor Agreements of Matthew and Luke against Mark, with a Cumulative List* (BETL, 37), Leuven, 1974, 198-288 (11-48: "The Study of the Minor Agreements"; 49-195: "A Cumulative List").

I the description of the minor agreements is only one part of the evidence. The word "atomization" has been used with reference to the various explanations of the agreements, but there is also the atomization of the evidence by concentrating on one passage and collecting all sorts of agreements without studying each type of agreement together with all other similar changes of Mark elsewhere in the Gospel. Many times the minor agreement works like a signal: it draws our attention to Matthean or Lukan non-coincidental parallels and I have the impression that without those cases of coincidence some aspects of Matthean and Lukan usage would have remained partially unexplored. The minor agreements force us again and again to study each passage in the light of the whole Gospel. Without undertaking such a full-scale examination of the gospel redaction, the use of the minor agreements as an objection against Markan priority will remain quite inoffensive.

3. It is, of course, not a reasonable expectation that in every instance a redactional explanation can be made acceptable for all Markan priorists. Some will be inclined to ascribe one or another agreement to the influence of Q. Others will reckon here and there with oral tradition and the possibility of tradition variants. Others will give more importance to the textual factor, textual corruption and harmonization. But these various explanations given to residual "difficult cases" do not at all modify our general synoptic hypothesis. M.D. Goulder's contention that some agreements are Matthean in style but characteristically un-Lukan has been answered by C.M. Tuckett.[14] Boismard has made a similar observation with regard to Lk 9:10-11, and I have attempted to give a response in the paper submitted to this Conference. I quote here one sentence from the conclusion: "The examination of the minor agreements of Matthew and Luke in the light of their context in each gospel leads us to the conclusion that these agreements imply a certain amount of disagreement." This conclusion can be applied to many other instances. Similar phrases can become very dissimilar in their respective contexts and such a dissimilarity in the agreements is in fact an argument for Matthew's and Luke's independence.

4. The Source Doublets in Matthew and Luke

I I can quote here the team advocating the two-gospel hypothesis: "The question of 'doublets' within the Synoptic gospels clearly requires

14. M.D. GOULDER, "On Putting Q to the Test," NTS 24 (1977-78) 218-234; C.M. TUCKETT, "On the Relationship between Matthew and Luke," NTS 30 (1984) 130-142. See now also F. NEIRYNCK, "ΤΙΣ ΕΣΤΙΝ Ο ΠΑΙΣΑΣ ΣΕ. Mt 26,68 / Lk 22,64 diff. Mk 14,65," ETL 63 (1987) 5-47.

further research and that research needs to begin with a definition of the term"; and "When all of the evidence from 'doublets' is taken into consideration there is almost twice as much evidence (20/12) in support of some other hypothesis as there is in support of the Two-Document Hypothesis, assuming, of course, that here is a valid argument for Markan priority from the appearance of Doublets."[15] The assumption is, of course, not that there is an argument for Markan priority but rather that the doublets offer "the decisive evidence for a common, written source for Mt and Lk" (W.G. Kümmel). As to the requirement that we should begin with a definition of the term, J.C. Hawkins (and others before him) has given at least some definition of doublets: "repetitions of the same or closely similar sentences in the same gospel" (1898). He has added a footnote in [2]1909: "I have thought it best to restrict the name 'doublet' to such important cases as are collected here, and not to include under it smaller similarities as some other writers would do." In a later Additional Note he refers to T. Stephenson (1918): "He distinguishes between the doublets which are 'due to the editors,' and those which are doublets in the sources themselves".[16] Taken together, these three utterances give a workable definition of the term doublet. Editorial repetitions or "redactional doublets" (Vaganay: "doublets-répétition") have no direct source-critical relevance. The notion of "source doublets" (Vaganay: "doublets-source") applies when the saying appears twice, e.g., once in the form and the context of Mk and once in a different form and context. It can be extended here as to include also the "conflations" of sources in one passage (Vaganay: "doublets condensés").

The probative force of the doublets is contested by the advocates of the two-gospel hypothesis (not by the defenders of the multiple-stage hypothesis). But is it not so that, in the hypothesis of Matthean priority, similar questions must arise about the repetitions in Matthew? As long as the use of sources and traditions in Matthew is not completely ignored, critical analysis will have to make the distinction between merely editorial repetitions, editorial repetitions of a saying borrowed from a source, and repetitions resulting from the use of more than one source. At least in this description of the phenomenon there is a lot of similarity with our approach.

The proof from the doublets is accepted as a valid argument by the advocates of the multiple-stage hypothesis. Within this Conference such

15. Quoted from the 1984 paper, "A Response," 16, 18.
16. J.C. HAWKINS, *Horae Synopticae*, Oxford, 1898, 64; [2]1909, 80, n. 1; Note, cf. "Hawkins's Additional Notes," *ETL* 46 (1970) 78-111, 91.

an agreement among two groups is certainly not a minor one. Of course, the reconstruction of the source will not be the same, but the existence of a hypothetical sayings source is a common assumption. For Rolland the distinction between the triple tradition and the double tradition is an essential part of his theory. A new suggestion is offered by Boismard who now ascribes the double-tradition passages to Proto-Luke. In my view, however, it is more than doubtful whether the presence of some words and phrases which are attested as "Lukanisms" elsewhere in Luke and Acts can prove the case! A more or less isolated use of the same word in the source is not necessarily Lukan usage.

In connection with Proto-Luke we should mention here also the problem of the Lukan omission of Mk 6:45 – 8:26. It has been cited as one of the principal weaknesses of the two-source theory. But I find it a curious way of arguing to present first as a difficulty the common omission in Matthew and Luke of Mk 7:31-37 and 8:22-26 and then also the omission of the whole section in Luke.[17] In the same way the common omission of Mk 4:26-29 (the seed growing secretly) is cited, although in Luke the entire section of Mk 4:26-34 has no parallel in chapter 8. And can we say that there is no acceptable explanation for the Lukan omission of Mk 6:45 – 8:26? When it is agreed that Luke could have omitted the second feeding story, the consequence of this omission cannot be overlooked. We can do our guess-work about Luke's possible intentions in omitting this section, but in this stage of the discussion it is more important to study the reminiscences of Mk 6:45 – 8:26 in Luke, in the immediate context of the omission (9:10 Bethsaida; 9:18 Jesus praying κατὰ μόνας), and elsewhere in Luke (e.g., 11:16; 11:38) and in Acts (e.g., 5:15-16). From these reminiscences we conclude that Luke knew that section of Mark and there is no need for a Proto-Luke or an Urmarkus without Mk 6:45 – 8:26.

In the course of the preparation of this Conference it has been decided that preference should be given to the Textual Discussion, with a concentration on triple-tradition texts. It is indeed in the study of the text that our different approaches can be tested and that agreements and disagreements will become manifest, much better than in an abstract statement and in the elaboration of a sort of grammar of source-critical criteria.

---

17. *Interrelations*, 234-235. On Luke's omission of Mk 6,45 – 8,26, cf. F. NoËL, *De compositie van het Lucasevangelie in zijn relatie tot Marcus: Het probleem van de "grote weglating"* (Klasse der Letteren, 150), Brussel, Koninklijke Academie, 1994.

The phenomenon of order, and particularly the relative order of Mt 4:23 – 13:58 / Mk 1:21 – 6:13, is a major issue in the discussion of the synoptic problem. For that reason, our analysis will concentrate on the crucial passage of Mt 4:23 – 5:2 and the problem of dislocations in Mt 4:23 – 11:1. Cf. *Interrelations*, 23-45: "Matthew 4:23–5:2 and the Matthean Composition of 4:23–11:1".

We add here, to conclude this Introduction, two more preliminaries: a brief survey of the assumptions of the two-source theory compared with the other hypotheses and a short presentation of the argument from order.

I. THE ASSUMPTIONS OF THE TWO SOURCE THEORY COMPARED WITH THE OTHER HYPOTHESES

1. It is a common assumption in our three solutions to the synoptic problem that the important similarities between the synoptic Gospels imply a literary relationship, direct or indirect. A pure oral tradition hypothesis and the fragment hypothesis are rejected as inadequate.

2. If not all adherents of the three solutions, at least Boismard, Farmer and Neirynck agree that the Fourth Gospel is later than the Synoptic Gospels and that the fourth evangelist (for Boismard: Jn II-B) knew and used the Synoptics. However, John's use of the Synoptics is a special problem and should be treated separately.[18]

3. The Markan hypothesis holds the priority of Mark, i.e., the literary dependence of Matthew and Luke upon Mark with regard to the triple-tradition material. The double-tradition material and the Matthean and Lukan Sondergut are not directly concerned.

a. Although the priority of Mark is quite the opposite to the assumption of Griesbach, both theories place Mark in a medial position: "Er ist also das Bindeglied, und zwar bestimmter entweder die Quell- oder die Schlußeinheit seiner Mitreferenten".[19]

Mk   Q   Mt   Lk

Mt   Lk   Mk

18. Cf. "John and the Synoptics. A Response to P. Borgen", *Interrelations*, 428-450 (= *Evangelica II*, 699-711).

19. F.J. Schwarz (1844), quoted in "The Argument from Order" (*supra*, n. 6), 793 (= 746), n. 29.

The two theories can concur, for instance, in the description of duplicate expressions in Mark of which one element is found in Matthew and the other in Luke. This same phenomenon can be interpreted either as conflation of two sources or as an original feature of Markan style. A similar observation can be made concerning the relative order of pericopes.

One of the new developments in the neo-Griesbachian two-gospel hypothesis is the emphasis given to Luke's dependence upon Matthew:

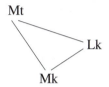

With regard to the triple tradition, Luke's use of Matthew can be compared with the use of Mark in the Markan hypothesis. In passages with a similar text in Matthew and Mark, the definition of distinctive Lukan redaction will be more or less the same in both theories.[20]

b. The Griesbach solution appears in an adapted form ("un Griesbach déguisé") in the multiple-stage hypotheses represented at this Conference. This is clearly the case with P. Rolland: Mark is a conflation of Proto-Matthew and Proto-Luke.[21]

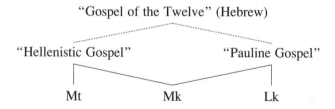

20. Cf. 77-80, "Note on the Eschatological Discourse." See also C.M. TUCKETT, *The Revival*, 167-185 ("The Apocalyptic Discourses"), esp. 167: "Matthew and Mark are very close here. Hence, many of Farmer's explanations of Luke's procedure have the implicit agreement of many other scholars. For example, the differences in Lk xxi.20-24 can be (and are) explained as due to Luke's writing after the fall of Jerusalem, and this accounts for the differences between Luke and Mark just as well as those between Luke and Matthew."

21. Cf. *supra*, n. 9. See now also P. ROLLAND, "La question synoptique demande-t-elle une réponse compliquée?" *Biblica* 70 (1989) 217-223 (on Boismard's interpretation of Mk 6:14-16). For a reply, see F. NEIRYNCK, "Marc 6,14-16 et par.," *ETL* 65 (1989) 105-109.

This theory shows only a weak analogy with the priority of Mark in the suggestion of one primitive Gospel at the origin of the triple-tradition material.

Boismard's theory is much more a combination of the two-gospel hypothesis with the Markan hypothesis. The "Mark" Matthew and Luke are using as a source is not our Gospel of Mark but a Proto-Mark ("Mc-intermédiaire"). The final Mark is a later redaction ("l'ultime Rédacteur marcien") on the basis of Proto-Mark but also influenced by Proto-Matthew ("les insertions matthéennes dans Marc") and Proto-Luke.

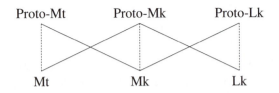

In some sections and in particular sentences the Proto-Mark used by Matthew and Luke is almost identical with the text of our Mark and in these cases Boismard's solution scarcely differs from Markan priority.

4. The Q hypothesis can be accepted without difficulty by Rolland and, at least in principle, by Boismard.[22] The two-gospel theory, however, assumes Luke's dependence upon Matthew, including the double-tradition passages, and refuses the existence of Q as an unproven and unnecessary hypothesis. But not all use of pre-synoptic sources can be denied. Thus, for example, in A. McNicol's opinion, "the author of Matthew composed his gospel by utilizing pre-existing source materials; perhaps some 'collections' like Mt 5:7 – 7:29; 10:5-42; 13:3-50; 18:1-35; 23:1-39, and 24:1 – 25:46", and in his central section (9:51 – 18:14) "Luke seems to have preferred the order and structure of his non-Matthean source".[23] With these presuppositions, if not a common source, at least some overlapping of sources seems to be unavoidable. W.R. Farmer has made a significant observation regarding Lk 17:23-37: "That section of Luke constitutes a special problem. In all probability Luke had access to a special source which contained apocalyptic material parallel to material in Matthew 24. Luke 17:26-30 ... is probably in a more original form than its parallel in Matthew 24:37-39" (1964: 272). In "A Fresh Approach to Q" (1975), he is even more

22. Cf. "A New Debate: Q or Proto-Luke" (*Interrelations*, 108-114).
23. "The Composition" (*Interrelations*, 160, 161).

explicit: "it seems to me that the Lucan form of that material is more original than the form of the material in Matthew 24. Therefore, I cannot derive that apocalyptic material in Luke 17 from Mt 24. At that point it is necessary for me to hypothecate ... another source, an apocalyptic source, that Luke has copied".[24] The recognition of non-Markan, common material in Matthew and Luke, more original in Luke than in Matthew, and not derived from Matthew: is this not the basis for the acceptance of Q?

5. The two-source theory is sometimes modified or supplemented with subsidiary hypotheses to explain literary phenomena such as,

(1) the minor agreements of Matthew and Luke against Mark in the triple tradition (Luke's subsidiary dependence on Matthew, Proto-Mark, Deutero-Mark):

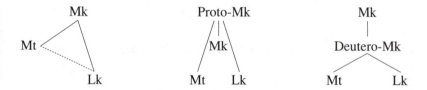

(2) the existence of extensive special material in Matthew and Luke (Four-document hypothesis):

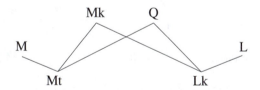

(3) the combination of Q and L (Proto-Luke):[25]

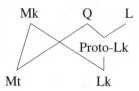

24. J. NEUSNER (ed.), *Christianity, Judaism and Other Greco-Roman Cults. FS M. Smith*, vol. I (Studies in Judaism in Late Antiquity, 12), Leiden, 1975, 39-50, esp. note 4 (46-48).

25. It should be noted that Boismard's Proto-Luke differs from this classic notion of Proto-Luke (L + Q).

(4) the differences in the double tradition material of Matthew and Luke (Q^{Mt}, Q^{Lk}):

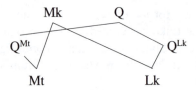

(5) the overlappings of Mark and Q (Mark's use of Q):

Some scholars firmly defend the priority of Mark but prefer to "dispense with Q":

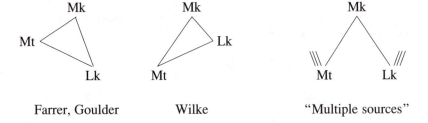

Farrer, Goulder   Wilke   "Multiple sources"

C.G. Wilke (1838): add now M. Hengel (2000). Cf. above, p. 282 (and 339).

In L. Vaganay's Proto-Matthew hypothesis the sayings source is restricted to double-tradition passages in Lk 9:51 – 18:14
(S = "Seconde Source Synoptique Supplémentaire"):

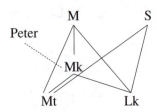

II. The Phenomenon of Order

1. *The Absence of Matthew-Luke Agreements*

Much has been written on the relative order of pericopes in the triple tradition, starting from two statements. "Marcus ... ordinem a Matthaeo observatum ita retinuit, ut, sicuti ab eo recederet, Lucae vestigiis insisteret et hunc ordinemque narrationis eius κατα ποδα sequeretur" (Griesbach). "Sed narrationum evangelicarum ordinis non tanta est quanta plerisque videtur diversitas; maxima sane si aut hos scriptores eadem conplexione omnes aut Lucan cum Matthaeo conposueris, exigua si Marcum cum utroque seorsum" (Lachmann). The same phenomenon can be described more formally as Mark's alternating support or as absence of Matthew-Luke agreements wherever Matthew or Luke departs from Mark's order. This absence of agreement has been acknowledged repeatedly by Markan priorists,

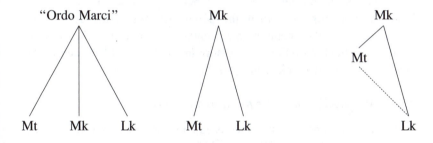

as well as by adherents of the Griesbachian and the Augustinian hypothesis (Matthean originality),

Logically, any synoptic diagram with Mark (or the order of Mark) as the linking middle term can provide a valid explanation.

Occasionally, one or another pericope has been noted as a possible exception to the rule, but none of these coincidences between Matthew and Luke is really convincing[26] and the "exception" is unable to modify the general statement. In the case of the cleansing of the temple[27] Luke omits the fig tree episode, Mk 11:12-14, 20-25, but there is no real change of Mark's order.

Much more significant is the undoing of Butler's correction of logical error by opposing now again "authorial intent" (in the two-gospel hypothesis) to "literary accident due to random chance" (in the two-source hypothesis). Do we really need either the deliberate intention of a writer (Mark) or a "concerted action" (of Matthew and Luke) to explain this absence of agreement? As I wrote already in 1973: "The significance of the phenomenon of order may become questionable with a more concrete approach. ... In Luke the alterations of the Markan order are limited in number and the transpositions in Matthew are confined to Mt 4:23 – 11:1. Emphasis on alternating support seems to imply that agreements and disagreements with the relative order of Mark are treated as comparable quantities. In fact, the disagreement against Mark is the exception and the absence of concurrence between Matthew and Luke is less surprising than the somewhat misleading formulation 'whenever the other departs' may suggest". I repeated this warning against "abstract reasoning" once more in 1982[28] and it has been further developed by C.M. Tuckett in 1984.[29]

2. The Argument from Order for Markan Priority

The real argument from order is not that abstract logical inference based upon the absence of Matthew-Luke agreements. The phenomenon of order cannot be taken in isolation from the general comparative study of the Gospels.

26. See my critique of Sanders's list of Mt-Lk agreements, in "The Argument from Order" (1973). With regard to Mk 3:13-19 (Mt 10:2-4; Lk 6:12-16), I can repeat my observation that in Lk 6:*12-16*,17-19 there is merely an inversion of order within the same section of Mk 3:7-12,*13-19* (ctr. TUCKETT, 1984, 204, 215 n. 27).

27. W.R. FARMER, The Synoptic Problem, 1964, 212. Cf. L. VAGANAY, Le problème synoptique, 1954, 59.

28. "The Argument from Order" (1973), 791-792 (= The Minor Agreements, 298-299; Evangelica, 744-745); "The Griesbach Hypothesis" (1982), 114. – The paper on the argument from order has been presented at the Southampton meeting in 1973 (cf. "Introduction", 7; here 347).

29. "If one restricts attention to strict changes in order of the same material, then the number of changes made by Matthew and Luke, assuming Markan priority, is relatively small." In his counting, "Luke changes the order of 4 Markan pericopes, Matthew changes the order of 6;" and: "There is no reason for thinking that the phenomenon of order poses a positive problem for Markan priority, as Farmer and Dungan have suggested" (204-205).

Can it be "methodologically incorrect ... to focus initially upon Matthew and Mark on the one hand, and then Luke and Mark on the other" (*173*)? And what does it mean that the three synoptic Gospels "be perceived together"? Of course, it would be incorrect to exclude a priori any possible relationship, but is it not a normal and unavoidable procedure to compare the agreements and disagreements of the individual Gospels one by one?[30] Lachmann's statement may seem uncomfortable for a Griesbachian: "exigua [diversitas], si Marcum cum utroque seorsum [conposueris]", but a true Griesbachian arrives at the same conclusion: "Noch grössere und anhaltendere Übereinstimmungen in der Aufeinanderfolge und Verknüpfung einzelner Begebenheiten finden wir, wenn wir zwei dieser Evangelisten mit einander vergleichen, besonders den Marcus im Verhältniss sowohl zum Matthäus als zum Lucas."[31]

The changes of Mark's order in the Gospel of Luke are found more particularly in the passion narrative (Lk 22:15-18, 21-23, 24-27, 33-34, 56-62, 63-65, 66-71; 23:26-49 passim). There are also some transferences of pericopes, within the same context:

Mk	Lk	Mk	Lk	Mk	Lk
1:16-20		3:7-12		3:31-35	(8:1-3)
1:21-39	4:31-44	3:13-19	6:12-16	4:1-25	8:4-18
	5:1-11		6:17-19		8:19-21

or into a more distant context:

Lk		
4:16-30	←	Mk 6:1-6a
7:36-50	←	Mk 14:3-9
10:25-28	←	Mk 12:28-31

Lachmann and many after him have shown that there is an acceptable redactional explanation for these *traiectiones* in Luke.[32]

In Matthew, the alterations of the Markan order are restricted to the section of Mk 1:21 – 6:13. All dislocations are anticipations: Mt 4:23 – 5:2 (summary); 8:2-4; 8:18-34; 9:18-26 (miracles); 9:35; 10:1-14 (disciples). As indicated below, they find a quite satisfactory explanation

---

30. See my response to "The Composition" (*Interrelations*, 77).
31. F. BLEEK, 1862, quoted in *ETL* 58 (1982), 115, n. 19.
32. Cf. "The Transpositions in Luke" (1973), 804-814 (= *The Minor Agreements*, 311-321; *Evangelica*, 757-767).

in the analysis of Matthew's unique editorial composition of Mt 4:23 – 11:1.[33]

Lachmann rightly concentrated his study on the variations in order between Matthew and Mk 1:21 – 6:13. And before him, Griesbach correctly indicated the problem of order for Markan priorists: "si statuas, Marcum consultum fuisse a Matthaeo et Luca, obscurum manet, cur v.c. Matthaeus ea, quae habentur Marc. 1,21 – 3,6. partim omiserit, partim in alium ordinem redegerit." In this case, Griesbach's own solution is far too simple: "omnia a Matth. 4,23 ad cap. 12,14 Marcus transsilierat."[34]

Note: The Markan Order in the Proto-Gospel

Boismard does not treat explicitly the problem of the relative order of pericopes. In *Synopse* II he seems to suppose that Proto-Mark had the order of Mark. The Matthean redactor followed this order, especially from ch. 13 on. The Matthean redaction is also responsible for the separation of Mt 9:1-17 and 12:1-14 (cf. Mk 2:1 – 3:6) and for the composition of Mt 8 – 9.[35]

In Vaganay's hypothesis the Markan order of the triple-tradition material in M is explicitly acknowledged: his "Proto-Matthew" has the order of Mark![36]

33. Cf. "La rédaction matthéenne et la structure du premier évangile," *ETL* 43 (1967) 41-73, 63-72; = I. DE LA POTTERIE (ed.), *De Jésus aux évangiles* (BETL, 25), Gembloux-Paris, 1967, 41-73, 63-72 (*Evangelica*, 1982, 3-35, 25-34).

34. *Commentatio* (ed. J.B. Gabler, 1825), 398, 373.

35. *Synopse* II, 35, 36, 37 (cf. 106).

36. *Le problème synoptique*, 59: "A considérer l'ordonnance particulière des péricopes dans les livrets, on peut justifier les différences entre Mt. - Mc. - Lc. en partant de l'ordre de Mc. – La plupart des arrangements propres à Mt. et à Lc. (additions, omissions, transpositions) trouvent une raison valable dans l'hypothèse où leurs auteurs ont connu un ordre à peu près semblable à celui de Mc. ... Inversement, en manière de contre-épreuve, on ne saurait justifier l'ordre de Mc., si l'on suppose qu'il a travaillé d'après Mt. ou Lc." – This aspect of Vaganay's theory seems to be neglected in B. REICKE, *The Roots of the Synoptic Gospels*, Philadelphia, 1986, 19 (*Interrelations*, 312).

ADDITIONAL NOTE:

See now also F. NEIRYNCK, art. "Synoptic Problem," in *The New Jerome Biblical Commentary* (1990), 587-595.

— On synopsis construction, cf. F. NEIRYNCK, "The Order of the Gospels and the Making of a Synopsis," and "Once More: The Making of a Synopsis," in *ETL* 61 (1985) 161-166; 62 (1986) 141-154 (= *Evangelica II*, 357-362, 363-376).

ETL 73 (1997) 386-392

15

THE ARGUMENT(S) FROM ORDER

I

The phenomenon of order has played an important role in the development of the Synoptic problem. More particularly since the revival of
the Griesbach hypothesis in the 1960's, the relative order of pericopes in
the first three gospels is one of the central questions in the new debate[1].
David J. Neville (Perth, Western Australia) has written a comprehensive
historical survey of the discussion, with critical analysis of the pertinent
literature up to 1989[2]. His book is divided into three parts. 1. The origin
of an argument from order: J.J. Griesbach, K. Lachmann; 2. The role of
the arguments from order within the developing consensus in English-
speaking synoptic criticism, 1890-1924: F.H. Woods, W.C. Allen and
J.C. Hawkins, H.G. Jameson and J.F. Springer (two voices of dissent),
B.H. Streeter; 3. The reassessment of arguments from order and the
reopening of the synoptic problem: B.C. Butler (H.G. Wood, G.M.
Styler), W.R. Farmer, C.M. Tuckett. The book concludes with a recapitulation (223-226) and the identification of "Issues relevant for analyzing
the phenomenon of order" (226-237).

Neville deliberately uses the plural in the title of his book: Arguments
from order. At the very outset he proposes to distinguish between two
basic types of arguments from order (Introduction, 8-11). The first type,
the *formal* argument from order, is based on merely formal considerations (particularly the absence of agreement in order between Matthew

1. See F. NEIRYNCK, *The Argument from Order and St. Luke's Transpositions*, in *ETL*
49 (1973) 784-815 (= *Evangelica I*, 737-768); *The Sermon on the Mount in the Gospel
Synopsis*, in *ETL* 52 (1976) 350-357 (= *Evangelica I*, 729-736); *The Griesbach Hypothesis: The Phenomenon of Order*, in *ETL* 58 (1982) 111-122 (= *Evangelica II*, 281-292).

2. D.J. NEVILLE, *Arguments from Order in Synoptic Source Criticism: A History and
Critique* (New Gospel Studies, 7), Macon, GA, 1994, XIV-270 p. The Foreword is written
by D.L. Dungan (VII-IX). A first draft of this monograph was presented as a B.D. thesis at
Murdoch University (Perth): "The Significance of the Phenomenon of Order for a Solution of the Synoptic Problem: An Historical-Critical Survey", 1988, 179 p., in mimeo-
graphed form; a copy of this thesis was sent to me in 1988 by W.R. Farmer (Dallas, TX).
The supervisor of Neville's work is Richard K. Moore of the Perth College of Divinity.
The Preface is signed November 1990. His Bibliography (245-258) contains only one
1990 title, my *NJBC* article "Synoptic Problem", referred to in the Introduction (6 n. 30;
11 n. 41). No later literature is considered here by Neville (cf. below, n. 19). But see this
footnote in his Conclusion: "I am currently engaged in my own analysis of the phenomenon of order..." (232 n. 19).

and Luke against Mark). The second type, called *compositional*, argues on the basis of language, style, and redaction, and attempts to provide plausible reasons for agreements and disagreements in the narrative sequence of the gospels. I quote from his last chapter[3]:

> Tuckett demonstrated that at least two distinct arguments from order have been advanced for Marcan priority... The argument that Butler failed to I consider was the one that tries to provide plausible reasons why differences in order may be attributed to the editorial activity of one of the gospel writers rather than another. Tuckett seems to have taken this lead on this particular argument for Marcan priority from Frans Neirynck. In his article, "The Argument from Order and St. Luke's Transpositions" (1973), Neirynck defended Lachmann against the charge of fallacious reasoning by demonstrating that Lachmann's argument was not the one that Butler showed to be fallacious...

Neville's *History* has obvious limitations, in Part 2, restricted to English-speaking synoptic criticism, but not only there. Griesbach's *Commentatio* (1790; ET by B. Orchard) and Lachmann's *De ordine narrationum in evangeliis synopticis* (1835; ET by N.H. Palmer) are quoted (and studied?) in English translation. The Bibliography includes no German titles and only one reference in French, A. Gaboury's *La structure des évangiles synoptiques* (but no analysis is provided)[4]. Neville is conscious of certain gaps: "Most notable of all is the lack of attention to German figures after Lachmann" (XI). Very few German colleagues, I think, will be satisfied with Neville's compensation by referring to H.-H. Stoldt's *History* (1977; ET by D.L. Niewyk, 1980)[5].

Such a limitation is not without consequences. As can be expected, Butler's chapter on "The Lachmann Fallacy" (1951) is described as the beginning of the post-Streeter era. Following Farmer, he also refers to J.F. Springer (1924)[6]:

> ... the history of gospel criticism reveals that a quarter of a century passed before critics were wakened from their scholarly slumber by one who simply reiterated some of Springer's criticisms, although without reference to

3. *Ibid.*, 192. Cf. below, n. 20.
4. See my *The Gospel of Matthew and Literary Criticism: A Critical Analysis of A. Gaboury's Hypothesis* (1972), in *Evangelica I*, 691-723.
5. Cf. Index: 22 references (261). There is no mention of the new edition of the German original *Geschichte und Kritik der Markushypothese*, [2]1986, expanded with "Griesbach-Korrektur" (239-264). See my review in *ETL* 62 (1986) 427-428.
6. On his indebtedness to Farmer for the reference to Springer's study of 1924, see p. 169 n. 7. In contrast to Farmer who "had not read other articles in Springer's fourteen-part study of 'The Synoptic Problem'" (169), Neville discusses the whole series of articles in *BS*, 1922-1927, of which the first five dealt with the phenomenon of order (112-123). The text quoted above is taken from the conclusion of that section (123).

Springer himself. For the next twenty-five years the inadequacy of a particular argument from order for Marcan priority went unnoticed...

Neville himself is not wholly free of "scholarly slumber". He frequently
mentions my *The Griesbach Hypothesis* (1982), but one passage
remained unnoticed[7]:

A century before Butler, an adherent of the Griesbach hypothesis had
already warned against such a logical error. The passage I quote is from the
Introduction to the New Testament by Adalbert Maier [1848]. He refers to
the middle position of Mark and considers two possible explanations, the
Griesbachian and the Augustinian:
"Auch hat eine allgemeinere Erscheinung in dem Markusevangelium ... für
sich allein keine entscheidende Beweiskraft, – die thatsächliche Erscheinung nämlich: dass Markus in seiner Sachordnung eine mittlere Stellung
I zwischen Matthäus und Lukas einnimmt, abwechselnd mit dem einen und
dem andern übereinstimmend erzählt, und sich auch in dem Texte jenem
Nebenevangelisten, mit welchem er ein längeres Stück weit zusammenhält,
näher anschliesst. Dieses Verhältniss der abwechselnden Uebereinstim-
mung lässt sich zwar sehr leicht begreifen, wenn Markus als der letzte
angenommen wird, aber es nötigt nicht zu dieser Annahme, weil es auch
mit der andern Abfolge der beiden Evangelisten möglicherweise vereinbar
ist. Wenn wir nämlich voraussetzen, dass Markus je wieder selbständig von
Matthäus abgegangen sei, und Lukas als der spätere den Markus in solchen
Stücken zum Führer genommen, so wird die in Rede Erscheinung gleich-
falls erklärt".

Butler was not the first indeed, and the anticipation of his analysis
among 19th-century Griesbachians[8] is noteworthy for more than one reason. First, Neville has repeatedly drawn attention to Farmer's claim that
there is a positive correlation between agreement in order and agreement
in wording (177-178, 187, 188, 226, 230; cf. *The Synoptic Problem*,
217-219: Step VIII). This observation on the correspondence between
order and wording is not new (cf. Maier: "sich auch in dem Texte jenem
... näher anschliesst"). What is new with Farmer is the contention that
only on the Griesbach hypothesis there is "a ready explanation" for this
phenomenon[9]. Second, notwithstanding the now usual lip service to Butler's analysis[10], recent utterances of neo-Griesbachians can be contrasted

7. *The Griesbach Hypothesis*, 113 (= 283).
8. See also the quotation from F.J. Schwarz (1844), in my *The Argument from Order*
(n. 1), 793 (= 746), n. 29. Cf. below, n. 12.
9. It is less clear what is meant by Neville: "If Farmer's contention can be verified
scientifically" (230). I can agree with G.M. Styler and see "no embarrassment to Marcan
priorists".
10. At least with regard to Markan priority: "Relying upon Butler's analysis of 'the
Lachmann fallacy' Farmer dismissed the argument from order for Marcan priority as
inconclusive" (169).

to the position of a 19th-century Griesbachian like Maier. I quote D.L. Dungan (1989): "All who think that this statement also supports the bland conclusion that 'Mark is merely the middle term' between Matthew and Luke (e.g., Neirynck and Tuckett) are totally mistaken in a fundamental point of logic" (*sic*)[11]. Even for Neville, Dungan is here guilty of "fallacious reasoning" (213 n. 50). Contrast also Farmer's own words: "the argument from order affords no proof of Marcan priority, but merely suggests that Mark stands in some sense as the 'middle term' between Matthew and Luke" (cited by Neville, 200). But the problem is that he relies on Butler with regard to Markan priority, and not in relation to the posteriority of Mark[12]: "Farmer and others had tried to wrest this flag from the two-document camp and unfurl it from the top of their own mast" (201).

II

I Neville observes that Farmer devoted comparatively little attention to the phenomenon of order and he regards his own work as complementing Farmer's book on *The Synoptic Problem* (7-8 n. 34; 200). In Step VI (*SP*, 211-215) Farmer asserted that Matthew and Luke "almost never" agree in order against Mark: "with very few exceptions"; "the most striking agreement in order ... is the placing of the Cleansing of the Temple on the same day as the Triumphal Entry" (212). This statement, with the same example, has been sharpened by Neville: "with one possible exception" (9, and n. 37)[13]. Later on he also mentions that according to Tuckett there is at least one pericope where Matthew and Luke both rearrange Mark's order: Mk 3,13-19. In this case, however, the parallel in Lk 6,12-16 can be seen as an inversion within the same section of Mk 3,7-19 (205)[14]. In the parallels to Mk 11,11-25 Matthew transferred the cleansing to the first day (21,10-17) but Luke has no second day and the "agreement" is the result of omission.

11. *Biblica* 70, 557. — Dungan's specific contribution to the debate, the much quoted testimony of Arrian, is also mentioned by Neville (212: "Although Dungan overstated his case").

12. Contrast F.J. SCHWARZ (above, n. 8), on Mark as "Mittelglied": "Er ist also das Bindeglied, und zwar bestimmter entweder die Quell- oder Schlusseinheit seiner Mitreferenten..." (307).

13. Compare Streeter's one exception, the section Mk 3,31-35 "alone" (131; 132: "difficult to ascertain...").

14. With reference to my *The Argument from Order* (n. 1), 789 (= 742); see also 808-811 (= 761-764). Neville refers to the reprint in *The Minor Agreements of Matthew and Luke against Mark* (BETL, 37), 1974, 291-322, here 296; see also 315-318.

Farmer begins his Step VI with the phenomenon of order, and then continues: "A similar statement can be made concerning the content of Mark" and he treats indiscriminately order and content, disagreements in order and omissions. Despite some warnings against the confusion of two distinct phenomena, Farmer is now supported by Neville (78 n. 36; 205-206). However, the two examples mentioned above have shown that the deviations from Mark's order may include transpositions to another context, inversions within the same context, and omissions of Mark's stories; three phenomena of which the source-critical relevance is undeniable but far from identical. The observation that "the 'argument from order' under consideration here has always been confined in the past to changes in order" (Tuckett) should not be dismissed as some kind of "strategy" (206 n. 33)[15].

The distinction between the absence of Matthew/Luke agreements against Mark and the pattern of alternating agreement in order between Matthew/Mark and Mark/Luke is presented by Neville as "Farmer's essential point concerning order":

> The absence of agreement in order between *Matthew* and *Luke* against *Mark* is a corollary of the pattern of alternating agreement in order between *Matthew/Mark* and *Mark/Luke* and not simply another way of describing precisely the same phenomenon. Both Neirynck and Tuckett seem to have made a logical error...[16] (187; cf. 9, 132-133).

I Yet Neville at least recognizes that both arguments are similar: "the mode of argumentation is the same. Both 'arguments' are actually inferences based on purely formal considerations..." (9). The notion of "corollary", cherished by Neville, can hardly be applied to Farmer's treatment in Step VI, first "the fact that Matthew and Luke almost never agree..." and then "the fact of alternating support...", with the same objection against Markan priority which excludes a concerted action of Matthew and Luke.

Farmer's fundamental fact is that "both Luke and Matthew *frequently* deviate from Mark" (*SP*, 213; quoted by Neville, 186, 204). Neville is

---

15. Is it consistent that omissions are treated together with disagreements in order (206), while "unique pericopes ... do not alter any gospel's narrative outline" (32)?

16. "... similar to the inference that all women are mothers because all mothers are women, or that all men are bachelors because all bachelors are men" (*sic*). Our debate concerns Synoptic triple-tradition pericopes in which either Matthew or Luke departs from the order of Mark. Not all women are mothers, but here absence of agreement in order between Matthew and Luke (i.e., if Mt ≠ Mk, then Lk = Mk; and if Lk ≠ Mk, then Mt = Mk) implies alternating agreement with Mark (unless Mt≠Mk and Lk≠Mk were conceived as no more than two blocks of pericopes).

not unaware of a certain objection: "Neirynck and Tuckett pointed to the relative infrequency of such disagreements", and he knows what their reason was: "because it is easier to accept the coincidence on the Marcan hypothesis ... if it is conceded that they [Matthew and Luke] did not disagree all that often" (206-207). Is he therefore justified to declare that their observation is "irrelevant"? Of course, I agree without reserve: "Disagreements in order must be explained irrespective of their frequency" (206). But it is not by moving to compositional considerations that Farmer's use of the *formal* argument from order against Markan priority can receive confirmation[17]:

> The absence of agreement is presumed to be a significant literary fact, explainable only by deliberate intention of a writer. The significance of the phenomenon, however, may become questionable with a more concrete approach. The basic statement remains the common order Mark-Matthew and Mark-Luke. In Luke the alterations of the Marcan order are limited in number and the transpositions in Matthew are confined to Mt IV,23–XI,1. Emphasis on the alternating support seems to imply that agreements and disagreements with the relative order of Mark are treated as comparable quantities. In fact, the disagreement against Mark is the exception and the absence of concurrence between Matthew and Luke is less surprising than the somewhat misleading formulation 'whenever the other departs' may suggest.

III

│ In his Conclusion, Neville comments upon the first part of this passage: "Neirynck's claim that Lachmann's approach was 'more concrete' is odd" (233)[18]. There is something amazing in Neville's reaction if we

---

17. *The Argument from Order*, 791-792 (= 744-745; *The Minor Agreements*, 298-299). Neville, following Tuckett, 1984, 204, and Dungan, 1984, 71 (below, n. 19), quotes the second paragraph, "Emphasis..." (205). "Treated as comparable quantities": a new illustration is provided by Farmer in *Interrelations* (below, n. 19), 143: "Where they depart from one another in order, *he* (Mark) *even-handedly follows* now the order of one and now the order of the other" (my emphasis). Neville can hardly maintain that "Farmer did not rely on the observation that Matthew's and Luke's orders do not agree together against Mark's" (188). He is rather unhappy with my observation that Griesbach's argument "tends to develop into abstract consideration of Mark's frequent transitions from one gospel to another" (35 n. 38). But Neville himself refers to "his [Griesbach's] formal argument from alternating agreement in order between *Matthew/Mark* and *Mark/Luke*" as being in need "to be reassessed" (38; cf. 228: "... not as precise and consistent as Griesbach claimed"). See my *The Griesbach Hypothesis*, esp. 115-119 (= 285-289).

18. A few lines further Neville writes: "One can be as concrete with three gospels as with two" (233), giving to my phrase "a more concrete approach" a sense it never had. See the passage quoted above.

take into account his own preference for "a more concrete type of argument from order" (9). How can he then ask: "More concrete than what?" (233). Is there any other way of evaluating the absence of Matthew-Luke agreements in order against Mark? Is it not by a concrete comparison of Matthew-Mark and Luke-Mark that the real significance of this phenomenon can be determined?

Five pages of Neville's Conclusion are devoted to what he calls "the most fundamental methodological issue to have arisen in synoptic studies this century" (232-236, here 232). Compare Dungan's Foreword: "most importantly of all, Neville raises the question of where to begin a comprehensive analysis of the Gospels" (IX), and Dungan's own methodological recommendation "to begin by viewing all three Synoptic Gospels together simultaneously, not by separating them into two groups, such as Mark//Matthew and Mark//Luke"[19]. However, it should be clear that a neutral and objective study of the relative order must begin by comparing the individual Gospels: Matthew/Mark, Luke/Mark, *and* Matthew/Luke, without a priori assumption on literary relationship. This also means: *without deciding a priori that all three Synoptic Gospels should be interrelated.* That Griesbach "was able to grasp and comprehend the interrelatedness of all three ... in a single synthetic judgement" might be seen as an advantage of his theory[20], but his *solution* to the synoptic problem cannot be taken as the starting point "viewing all three together simultaneously". For Neville, Lachmann's method contains "a bias against Griesbach's hypothesis" because it "disallows any literary connection between Matthew's and Luke's Gospels" (234). However, it was in response to Griesbach's view on Mark's borrowing simultaneously from Matthew and Luke that Lachmann wrote his demonstration of Matthew's and Luke's relation to the order of Mark: "exigua (diversitas) si Marcum cum utroque seorsum (conposueris)". But on Matthew/Luke there was no real dispute with Griesbach[21] and Lachmann could quietly write: "maxima sane (diversitas) si ... Lucan cum Matthaeo conposueris" without being blamed for

19. *Two-Gospel Hypothesis*, in *ABD* 6 (1992) 671-679, here 673. Cf. Neville (234) refers to Dungan's *A Griesbachian Perspective on the Argument from Order*, in C.M. TUCKETT (ed.), *Synoptic Studies. The Ampleforth Conferences of 1982 and 1983* (JSNT SS, 7), Sheffield, 1984, 67-74, esp. 70.
20. W.R. FARMER, *Modern Developments of Griesbach's Hypothesis*, in *NTS* 23 (1977) 275-295, here 294.
21. Neville notes that "Griesbach originally maintained that Luke used Matthew" (234, without documentation), but also: "Griesbach never attempted to provide a detailed analysis of Luke's use of Matthew's Gospel" (36). In contrast to Lachmann (42, 234) Griesbach is not criticized for his "assumption".

that by the 19th-century Griesbachians[22]. Still now, though the 'formal' argument from order is rightly criticized, the consensus remains on the literary datum of the absence of I agreement in order between Matthew and Luke against Mark, i.e., Matthew and Luke disagree in order except where both agree with Mark: "maxima sane diversitas".

Neville was favorably impressed by the statement on the criterion of coherence at the Jerusalem Symposium in 1984 (198, 231)[23]. Therefore I may conclude with a related statement of my own: "an adequate discussion of the relative order of the gospels should take place in the larger context of a redaction-critical examination of each gospel" (1973)[24]; and its echo at the Jerusalem Symposium[25]:

> The argument from order for Markan priority is nothing more, and nothing less, than the demonstration that the differences of the order in Matthew and Luke receive a plausible explanation as changes of Mark which are consistent with the general redactional tendencies and the compositional purposes of each gospel. It is clear that in this area, as in any other area of the synoptic problem, our method should be a joint effort of source criticism and redaction criticism (or composition criticism).

22. On De Wette and Bleek, see Neville (36; cf. 73), with reference to my *The Griesbach Hypothesis*.

23. Cf. D.L. DUNGAN (ed.), *The Interrelations of the Gospels: A Symposium Led by M.-É. Boismard – W.R. Farmer – F. Neirynck, Jerusalem 1984* (BETL, 95), Leuven, 1990, here 609. — The volume was apparently not available to Neville in 1990: he quotes the statement from A.J. McNICOL, *The Two Gospel Hypothesis under Scrutiny: A Response to C.M. Tuckett's Analysis of Recent Neo-Griesbachian Gospel Criticism*, in *PSTJ* 403/3 (1987) 5-13, here 7.

In my Introduction at the Jerusalem Symposium I could refer to Butler's statement (on the medial position of Mark): "the participants of the SNTS Seminar on the Synoptic Problem at the Southampton meeting in 1973 will remember that the leading neo-Griesbachians then solemnly declared that this was also their own position" (*Interrelations*, 7). Farmer's intervention in 1984 (143) and finally the inclusion of "the phenomenon of order" among the areas of disagreement (609) show a neo-Griesbachian regression in this question of which Neville seems to be unaware.

24. *The Argument from Order*, 794 (= 747; *The Minor Agreements*, 301). Quoted by Neville (193), with following comment: "In 1976 he (N., in *IDBS*, 846) clarified his position by saying of Lachmann: 'His argument for the priority of Mark's order is still a valuable one insofar as an acceptable explanation can be given for Matthew's and Luke's transpositions, and no good reason has been found why Mark would change the order of Matthew or Luke'"; see also 192, on Tuckett's compositional argument.

25. *Interrelations*, 7-8.

— Besides *The Two-Source Hypothesis: Introduction* (reprinted above, 3-22, here 343-362) my contributions to the 1984 Symposium include:

Matthew 4:23–5:2 and the Matthean Composition of 4:23–11:1 (23-46)

Note on the Eschatological Discourse (77-80)

Response to the Multiple-Stage Hypothesis:

    The Introduction to the Feeding Story (81-93)

    The Healing of the Leper (94-107)

    The Eschatological Discourse (108-124); *Evangelica II*, 493-510.

John and the Synoptics: Response to P. Borgen (438-450); *Evangelica II*, 699-772.

Note on Patristic Testimonies (605-606)

16

THE SOURCES OF MATTHEW

ANNOTATIONS TO U. LUZ'S COMMENTARY

U. Luz's monumental EKK commentary on Matthew will comprise four volumes: Mt 1–7 (1985), Mt 8–17 (1990), Mt 18–25 (1997), and Mt 26–28, "hoffentlich in etwa drei Jahren" (cf. VIII)[1]. The Preface to the third volume is signed September 1995; and works published in the 1990s up to 1994 are included in the Bibliography. For example, references to Ennulat's 1990 dissertation in vol. II are now updated in vol. III with references to the published text (1994)[2]. D. Hagner's second volume (Mt 14–28, 1995) is not mentioned. Compare now also the ICC commentary by W.D. Davies and D.C. Allison, vol. III (Mt 19–28, 1997)[3].

1. Text

As indicated in my review of the first volume (410), Luz's text-critical notes are appended to his translation of the gospel text. His textual options in vol. I rarely differ from N-A²⁶ (cf. 6,33: [τοῦ θεοῦ] om.). There are more deviations from N-A²⁶ in vol. II: 9,32 om. ἄνθρωπον Ι 10,25 Βεεζεβούλ (= 12,24) Ι 11,7-9 (7 ἔρημον; 8 ἐξήλθατε; 9 ἐξήλθατε;) Ι 12,10 θεραπεύειν Ι 12,15 om. [ὄχλοι] Ι 13,35 + Ἡσαΐου[4] Ι 13,44 [πάντα] Ι 14,15 + [οὖν] Ι 14,30 om. [ἰσχυρόν] Ι 15,14 om. [τυφλῶν] Ι 15,30 (uncertain order) Ι 16,2b-3 om. [ὀψίας...] Ι 16,13 + με Ι 17,15 ἔχει (for πάσχει). I note now in vol. III: 18,7 + [ἐστίν], + [ἐκείνῳ] Ι 18,15 εἰς σέ (for []) Ι 18,19 om. [ἀμήν], συμφωνήσουσιν (for -ωσιν) Ι 18,24 προσήχθη (for -ηνέχθη) Ι 20,15 ἤ (for [] Ι 20,17 om. [μαθητάς] Ι 20,30 om. [κύριε] Ι 21,1 πρός (for εἰς²) Ι 21,4 + ὅλον ("vielleicht") Ι 21,32 οὐ (for οὐδέ) Ι 21,44 (for [verse]) Ι 22,21 [αὐτῷ] Ι 22,35 νομικός (for []) Ι 22,39 om. δέ Ι 23,4 καὶ δυσβάστακτα (for []) Ι

---

1. Ulrich LUZ, *Das Evangelium nach Matthäus. 3. Teilband: Mt 18–25* (Evangelisch-Katholischer Kommentar zum Neuen Testament, I/3.) Zürich-Düsseldorf, Benziger; Neukirchen-Vluyn, Neukirchener Verlag, 1997 (16×24), XII-561 p. See my reviews in *ETL* 63 (1987) 410-413 (vol. I); 67 (1991) 169-171 (vol. II). Cf. below, 393-398.
2. Cf. below, n. 13.
3. Cf. *ETL* 73 (1997) 448-450.
4. Cf. *ETL* 72 (1996), p. 51 n. 81.

23,8 διδάσκαλος/καθηγητής Ι 24,31 + φωνῆς (possibly) Ι 24,33 ταῦτα
πάντα (for 2 1) Ι 24,38 om. [ἐκείναις] Ι 24,43 διορυχθῆναι/
διορυγῆναι Ι 25,1 αὐτῶν/ἑαυτῶν, ὑπάντησιν/ἀπάντησιν (= 6) Ι 25,16
+ [τάλαντα] Ι 25,17 + καί. About forty other notes in vol. III are written
in support of N-A²⁶ readings.

Although the characteristic style and vocabulary of Matthew play an
important role in Luz's commentary, he is far from adopting the principles of a thoroughgoing eclecticism. The external evidence is never
neglected: "besser bezeugt ... und darum ursprünglich" (13,40); "textkritisch besser bezeugt" (19,11); "fehlt Ι bei den besten MSS" (15,14);
"der Kurztext (ist) von den besten Handschriften bezeugt" (16,2b-3);
but also: "nur in ägyptischen Texten bezeugt" (16,21), "eine fast aus-
schließliche ägyptische Lesart" and therefore secondary (19,3); and:
"ich plädiere für den längeren Text, da er von allen Textfamilien
vertreten wird" (18,15). Typical of his approach is his comment on
17,15: "Obwohl die idiomatische Wendung κακῶς ἔχειν lectio facilior
ist, muß das Gewicht der Handschriften ausschlaggebend bleiben".
Matthew's style and vocabulary are used to explain the origin of secondary readings (lectio facilior!) in 12,15: "Ὄχλοι ist m.E. sekundäre
Zufügung aufgrund der ähnlichen Wendungen 4,25; 8,1; 19,2, vgl.
20,29", and in 20,17: "Ich rechne damit, ... daß spätere Abschreiber das
sonst bei Mt übliche μαθηταί einfügten (vgl. 10,1; 11,1; 26,20)". Compare Metzger's *Textual Commentary* on both passages. See also 9,32:
"Ἄνθρωπον (Nestle²⁶) ist vielleicht doch eher späterer, mt Diktion
entsprechender Zusatz", and 18,24: "Das Hap.leg. προσήχθη (B, D)
dürfte trotz der schwächeren Bezeugung ursprünglicher sein als das
typisch mt προσηνέχθη". In all four instances Luz returns to Nestle²⁵.
This is the case also in 22,35: "Daß ... die Herausgeber des GNT und
von Nestle²⁶ νομικός in [] setzen, ist textkritisch unbegreiflich" (269
n. 1). However, he notes later on: "Νομικός ist bei Mt Hap.leg. und
wäre allenfalls bei Lk als Red. erklärbar" (271 n. 15), though without
mentioning Metzger's comment: "It is not unlikely, therefore, that copyists have introduced the word here from the parallel passage in Lk
10.25"⁵. Luz also deletes the brackets in 23,4 καὶ δυσβάστακτα. Here
Metzger had suggested as his personal opinion that these words (added
after βαρέα) may be an interpolation from Lk 11,46⁶. Harmonizations
with the Lukan parallel ("Anpassung an Lk") are taken into consideration by Luz for instance in his notes on 11,19 (τέκνων), 12,10

---

5. Cf. below, n. 26.
6. See also DAVIES-ALLISON, 271 n. 39: "The best-attested reading. But this is from
Luke, as Origen observed".

(θεραπεῦσαι), 13,7 (ἀπέπνιξαν), 19,24 (τρήματος, εἰσελθεῖν), 19,29 (ἢ γυναῖκα, πολλαπλασίονα); but not in the case of the hapaxlegomena in 22,35 and 23,4. Once more external attestation seems to be the decisive factor: "Nur ganz wenige Textzeugen" for the shorter reading in 22,35 and "zu schlecht bezeugt, um Urtext zu sein" in 23,4. Likewise the text of verse 21,44 (cf. Lk 20,18) is retained without brackets[7]: "Die textliche Bezeugung ist überwältigend gut" (217 n. 11)[8].

2. The Markan Source

The order of the Markan source behind Mt 18–25 can easily be reconstructed: Mk 9,33-37.(38-41).42-47(48.49-50); 10,1-52; 11,1-33; 12,1-39.(40.41-44); | 13,1-32.(33-37)[9]. There is only one significant rearrangement of order: Mk 11,12-14 "nach hinten verschoben" (177), or, more correctly, Mk 11,15-19 "nach vorne geschoben" in Mt 21,1-17 (cf. 198)[10]. In Luz's opinion, "Das entspricht vielleicht der Reihenfolge der alten, vormarkinischen Passionsgeschichte" (177). At the same time, however, he notes that Matthew is not fond of intercalations: "Nur Mk 5,21-43 und 14,1-11.53-72 bleiben erhalten" (n. 7).

Yet, Luz thinks that a simple hypothesis of Matthew's use of Mark is not satisfactory. Already in vol. I he declared that we need a Deutero-Mark in order to cope with the evidence of the minor agreements (30), and in vol. II he provided ample illustration[11]. His DtMk recension is only slightly different from Mark and "should be used only as a last resort (*Verlegenheitshypothese*)"[12]. In vol. III the presence of minor agreements is briefly discussed in nine pericopes, with rather moderate statements on the DtMk hypothesis:

7. Contrast DAVIES-ALLISON, 186 n. 65: "Lk 20.18 can be regarded as the source of Mt 21.44... If v. 44 was original, why was it omitted?". Luz regards Mt 21,44 / Lk 20,18 as a Deutero-Markan addition to Mk 12,10-11: Luke omits Mk 12,11 (uniting Lk 20,17+18), and Matthew inserts his 21,43, separating 21,42 and 44 (218).

8. This is almost an "implicit" quotation from ALAND, *Text*, 1982, 240-241: "Die äußere Bezeugung ist also außerordentlich stark, sie *wäre überwältigend, wenn* uns das Zeugnis eines der großen alten Papyri zur Verfügung stände..." (241; emphasis mine: note the shift in Luz's comment). For Aland, there remains "ein leichter Zweifel" (single brackets).

9. To the units omitted in Mt (references in parentheses) one can add the verses Mk 9,35; 10,12; 10,15 (Mt 18,3); 10,49b-50; 11,16; 11,25 (Mt 6,14).

10. On Matthew's editorial anticipation, cf. *Evangelica*, 21-22; *Interrelations* (BETL, 95), 40.

11. See the list in my review (1991, 170); here 396-397.

12. From the conclusion of Luz's contribution in G. STRECKER (ed.), *Minor Agreements. Symposium Göttingen 1991* (GTA, 50), Göttingen, 1993, 209-220 (esp. 220).

18,1-5: Die einfache Zweiquellenhypothese ohne Zuhilfenahme einer weiteren Rezension erklärt hier also den Befund am besten (10). **19,16-30**: Die meisten [MA] sind ohne weiteres als unabhängige mt und lk Redaktion zu erklären (120). **21,1-17**: (könnten) auf eine deuteromk Bearbeitung von Mk 11,1-17 ... zurück-gehen. Ganz schwer zu beurteilen ist, ob ... die Großevangelisten oder eine deu-teromk Rezension verantwortlich sind (177). Angesichts der vielen Minor Agree-ments [in 21,12-13] bleibt unsicher, für welche Änderunger er [Mt] und für welche eine deuteromk Quelle verantwortlich ist (179). **21,23-27**: Viele [MA] können durch voneinander unabhängige Redaktion der Großevangelisten erklärt werden. Bei anderen ist eine deuteromk Bearbeitung des Mk-Textes eine mögli-che Erklärung (206). **21,44**: es ist gut denkbar, daß ihn [v. 44] Schriftgelehrte in einer deuteromk Textstufe zufügten (217-218). **22,23-33**: ... einige "Minor Agreements", die sich manchmal relativ einfach als unabhängige mt und lk Redaktion erklären lassen (262). **22,34-40** [cf. below]. **22,41-46**: Die ... gering-fügigen Veränderungen stammen mit Ausnahme eines kleinen Minor Agree-ment von Mt (286). **24,1-2**: Das auffällige Minor Agreement am Schluß von Mk 13,2 parr ist kaum erklärbar (386).

Luz's position in this question is not free of a certain ambiguity. On the one hand, minor agreements that can be explained by the evange-lists' independent redaction are not retained as evidence for DtMk. On the other, "schwer erklärbar bleibt ihre große Zahl"; here with reference to the 40 agreements in Mt 19,16-30 listed by Ennulat (120 n. 13)[13]. In fact, Ennulat's list contains twenty-two entries of category III ("lassen sich in der Regel ... als mt/lk Redaktion ... interpretieren"). For instance, the omission of διδάσκαλε in Mt 19,20 / Lk 18,21, "schwerer verständlich" to Luz (120 n. 12)[14], is a "III" case for Ennulat:

I   kann entweder als Straffung des MkTextes verstanden werden, oder aber steht in Zusammenhang mit dem mtlk Fehlen dieser Anrede gegenüber Mk 4,38; (9,38; 10,35;) 13,1. In diesem Fall wäre die Anrede als nicht passend im Mund eines (potentiellen) Jüngers zu interpretieren (225).

On the contrary, on ἔτι in Mt 19,20 / Lk 18,22 (Ennulat: "I"), compare Luz's own comment in n. 12 (and n. 9: "noch ca. 4mal red." in Mt). The case of ὅτι in Mt 19,28 / Lk 18,29 (Ennulat: "I") is not even mentioned by Luz[15].

13. Cf. A. ENNULAT, *Die "Minor Agreements". Untersuchungen zu einer offenen Frage des synoptischen Problems* (WUNT, 62), Tübingen, 1994. Diss. Bern (dir. U. Luz), 1990. Cf. review in *ETL* 67 (1991) 373-385 (T. FRIEDRICHSEN).

14. Διδάσκαλε: "für Mt sehr passend; vgl. 8,19". Cf. II.22 n. 7: "als Anrede von Außenstehenden".

15. The same is true elsewhere for "I" agreements between more or less distant par-allels: Mt 19,1 / Lk 17,11 (Γαλιλαία); Mt 21,5 / Lk 19,38 (ὁ βασιλεύς); Mt 21,17 / Lk 21,37 (αὐλίζομαι), or for "ein Mt und Lk gemeinsam vorliegendes εὐθέως" in Mk 10,52 (Ennulat, 241).

Luz concludes the section Mt 21,1-17 with his *Fazit* on the Markan source "in einer vermutlich leicht bearbeiteten Textfassung" (180). However, for at least two of the twelve Mt/Lk agreements cited in the commentary, Luz accepts that independent redaction is plausible (177 n. 9: the omissions of Mk 11,15a.17b). He is most explicit on the omission of πᾶσιν τοῖς ἔθνεσιν: "Die Auslassung durch Mt/Lk ist … red. erklärbar. Nach der Zerstörung des Tempels konnte dieser kein Bethaus für die Heiden mehr sein" (179 n. 25)[16]. — The phrase ἐν τῇ ὁδῷ in Mt 21,8 / Lk 19,36 (for εἰς τὴν ὁδόν in Mk 11,8) is simply cited as possibly Deutero-Markan (177). Ennulat observes that "weder Mt noch Lk von sich aus ἐν τῇ ὁδῷ schreiben" (249: "I/II"). One would expect here at least a reference to C.H. Turner's Note on εἰς and ἐν in Mk (1925): "The verb 'to strew' might be conceived as implying motion, 'strewed their garments on to the road'… But in view of the evidence here accumulated, it is by far the simpler view that he [Mark] meant 'on the road'. So certainly Matthew and Luke understood it, since both substitute ἐν τῇ ὁδῷ. This is the first occasion on which we find them agreeing on ἐν for εἰς; but see also below, no. 20"[17]. — In the case of ἐρεῖτε ὅτι in Mt 21,3 / Lk 19,31 (for εἴπατε in Mk 11,3) Luz argues against Matthean redaction: "ὅτι recitativum ist für Mt und Lk untypisch. Statt ἐρεῖτε wäre bei Mt in Anlehnung an das Zitat eher εἴπατε zu erwarten" (177 n. 8). Both observations are taken from Ennulat (247), who in addition refers to the use of εἴπατε in Mt 26,18 (= Mk 14,14); he could have added that the parallel in Lk 22,11 reads ἐρεῖτε (and in 22,13 εἰρήκει for εἶπεν in Mk). B.S. Easton's suggestion seems to be forgotten: in Mt 21,3 "the repetition of εἰπεῖν is avoided"[18]. There are other examples in Mt where the monotony of Mk's εἰπεῖν is somewhat corrected (e.g., Mt 20,21-23: εἶπεν, λέγει, εἶπεν, λέγουσιν, λέγει). For the use of ἐάν τις ὑμῖν εἴπῃ – ἐρεῖτε, compare Mt 21,24 ἐὰν εἴπητέ μοι – ἐρῶ (cf. Mk 11,29); 21,5 ἐὰν εἴπωμεν – ἐρεῖ (Mk 11,31). — Some other instances of minor MAs are mentioned by Luz as undecided: diff. Mk 11,2 ἀγάγετε, 7 ἤγαγον, 8 (ὑπ)ἐστρώννυον, 16 om., and: 17 οὐ + question, αὐτόν before verb (both Ennulat: "III").

16. Cf. ENNULAT, 255: "III/II", with references in n. 24: Haenchen, Schmithals, Schneider, Fitzmyer, Suhl, Luyten, Strecker, Roloff. See also DAVIES-ALLISON, 133: "the words had become potentially problematic".

17. *JTS* 26 (1925), 19 (in J.K. Elliott's reprint, p. 20). Turner's no. 20: Mk 13,16 ὁ εἰς τὸν ἀγρόν, par. Mt 24,18 ὁ ἐν τῷ ἀγρῷ and Lk 21,21 οἱ ἐν ταῖς χώραις (p. 20); add: Lk 17,31 ὁ ἐν ἀγρῷ. On Lk 17,31, cf. below, n. 32.

18. *Luke*, 1926, 286.

19. It is hardly convincing that "lk red eine Formulierung mit καλούμενος zu erwarten gewesen (wäre)" (n. 32).

I note here also Ennulat's explanation of the individual agreement in Mt 24,2 / Lk 21,7, diff. Mk 13,2 οὐ μὴ καταλυθῇ (Luz: "auffällig" and "kaum erklärbar"):

| Bei Mt und Lk ist wie häufiger die doppelte Verneinung gemieden. Entsprechend dieser Änderung wird auch statt des *AorKonj* καταλυθῇ die *fut.* Form καταλυθήσεται gesetzt. Die Textentwicklung geht dabei deutlich vom MkText aus. "III" (297).

There is a striking agreement between Ennulat and Luz on καλεῖ in Mt 22,45 / Lk 20,44 (for λέγει in Mk 12,37): "καλέω in der Bedeutung 'benennen' ist weder lk noch mt red gut verständlich zu machen" (Ennulat, 290: "I")[19]; "Καλεῖ kann weder als mt noch als lk Red. erklärt werden" (Luz, 286 n. 4)[20]. Contrast W. Schenk (1987)[21]:

> *Bezeichnung, Benennung:* Dies war nur 21,13 (= Mk Erfüllungszitat LXX-Jes 56,7) vorgegeben. Obwohl auch Lk diese Verwendung favorisiert, so treffen beide doch darin noch nie in Q-Stoffen zusammen; wenn Lk 20,44 mit der Verwendung par. zu Mt 22,45 in der Abweichung von Mk zusammentrifft, so erklärt sich das aus der beiderseitigen Favorisierung dieses LXX-bedingten Verwendungstyps unabhängig voneinander hinreichend.

The comparison of Luz's commentary with Ennulat's monograph on the minor agreements is particularly interesting in the section on Mt 22,34-40 ("Die großen Gebote"). First, in contrast to Ennulat[22], Luz can now write: "In neuester Zeit haben sich verschiedene Autoren dafür stark gemacht, daß auch hier Mk die einzige Quelle von Mt/Lk sei" (270)[23]. Second, on Ennulat's main argument for DtMk, "eine dreifache Übereinstimmung im Gebrauch von νομικός, (ἐκ)πειράζων und der

---

20. In Luz's opinion Mt 22,41-46 can be explained as Matthean redaction of Mk 12,35-37a+34b, with no other exception than καλεῖ in v. 45. This seems to imply that the first καλεῖ in v. 43 (which is not mentioned in the commentary) is "mt red.": secondary to the Deutero-Markan use of καλεῖ in v. 45? Compare 23,7b (καὶ καλεῖσθαι ὑπὸ τῶν ἀνθρώπων ῥαββί), the redactional transition to 23,8-10 (297: "red. Überleitung"). Cf. I.42: "καλέω + 2× Red." (i.e., 22,43 and 23,7b?). See also καλεῖν τὸ ὄνομα αὐτοῦ in 1,21.23.25: "Von ihm [Mt] stammt das Reflexionszitat V22f" (I.100).
21. W. Schenk, *Die Sprache des Matthäus*, Göttingen, 1987, 316-317 (art. καλέω).
22. Cf. 281 n. 30: "Eine voneinander unabhängige MkBearbeitung durch Mt und Lk wird ... eher selten angenommen".
23. In addition to J.-G. Mudiso Mbâ Mundla and J. Gnilka (cf. Ennulat), Luz can refer to J. Kiilunen (1989) and M. Ebersohn (1993). On Kiilunen (correct spelling!), cf. review in *ETL* 67 (1991) 432-433. See also F. Neirynck, *Luke 10:25-28: A Foreign Body in Luke?*, in S.E. Porter, *et al.* (eds.), *Crossing the Boundaries.* FS M.D. Goulder, Leiden, 1994, 149-165; *The Minor Agreements and Q*, in R.A. Piper (ed.), *The Gospel Behind the Gospels. Current Studies on Q* (NTSup, 75), Leiden, 1995, 49-72, esp. 61-64; *The Minor Agreements and Lk 10,25-28*, in *ETL* 71 (1995) 151-160.

Anrede διδάσκαλε" and the addition of ἐν τῷ νόμῳ[24], contrast Luz (270-271):

> Die Änderungen im Mt-Text sind mehrheitlich leicht als Red. erklärbar... Wirklich schwierig sind für Mt nur Nr. 1 [νομικός] und vielleicht Nr. 6 [ἐν, for ἐκ]. Auch die übrigen kleineren Änderungen gegenüber Mk sind red.

I Third, Luz, who like Ennulat rejects the hypothesis of a Q doublet[25], finally opts nevertheless for a non-Markan tradition (271):

> Bei Lk lassen sich nicht alle diese Änderungen gegenüber Mk als Red. erklären. Die Annahme einer Sondertradition drängt sich m.E. mindestens für Lk auf... Daß Mt diese Sondertradition auch kannte (vielleicht aus mündlicher Überlieferung?), ist gut möglich.

But Matthean contact with such a *Sondertradition* is not what one may conclude from Luz's own analysis. Since he regards νομικός as redactional in Lk (271 nn. 15 and 18), a pre-Lukan *Sondertradition* cannot solve his difficulty no. 1 in Mt[26]. The use of ἐν (for ἐκ) in the quotation of Dt 6,5 is another difficulty in Mt ("vielleicht") and in Lk (n. 18: "kaum red."). But Luz rightly notes that the agreement is not complete:

Mt		Mk 12,30	Lk
ἐν	——	ἐξ ὅλης τῆς καρδίας σου	ἐξ
ἐν	——	καὶ ἐξ ὅλης τῆς ψυχῆς σου	ἐν ——
ἐν	——	καὶ ἐξ ὅλης τῆς διανοίας σου	ἐν ——
		καὶ ἐξ ὅλης τῆς ἰσχύος σου	ἐν ——

---

24. Cf. 284: "die Übereinstimmungen gegen den MkText (sind) derart massiv, daß kaum anders als von einer bereits veränderten MkVorlage zur Erklärung ausgegangen werden kann. 'I'. — Der mtlk Zusatz ἐν τῷ νόμῳ ... ist weder mt noch lk red plausibel zu machen. 'I'".

25. Cf. Ennulat, 280, 287: "Ein Rückgriff auf eine Q-Tradition bzw. eine andere vormk Tradition ... ist nicht notwendig bzw. möglich". See also 278 n. 2 ("Den größten Zuspruch..."); J. Lambrecht (1995: Mark used Q) is added to the list by Luz (270 n. 8). Cf. DAVIES-ALLISON, 236: the agreements "are yet insufficient to let us speak confidently of Q". F. BOVON, *Das Evangelium nach Lukas. 2. Teilband: Lk 9,51-14,35* (EKK, III/2), 1996, 84: Q and Sondergut combined; no serious examination of the redactional interpretation (cf. above, n. 23): neither J. Kiilunen nor my *Luke 10:25-28* (1994) are mentioned.

26. Luz reads νομικός in the text of Mt 21,35 (cf. above). Matthean redaction (cf. R.H. Gundry, in *BETL* 100, 1992, 1481; *ETL* 1995, 139-150) is not even considered, although ἐν τῷ νόμῳ (v. 36) is "mt Red.", and: "Das Stichwort νόμος (V. 36.40; vgl. νομικός in V. 35) bildet eine Inklusion um das ganze Gespräch" (270). — On the textual and redactional problem of νομικός in Mt 22,35 and Lk 10,25, cf. *Evangelica II*, 190-193, and later articles (cf. above, n. 23): 1994, 150-157; 1995, 61-64; 1995 (*ETL*), 154-156.

Cf. Dt 6,5 LXX: three items with ἐκ + genitive. The traditional triadic form appears in Mt and Lk with ἐν + dative (compare LXX 2 Reg 23,25 = 2 Chron 35,19b, with καρδία – ψυχή – ἰσχύς)[27], and we can conclude with Ennulat that "die mt/lk Textformen des Zitates ... aus dem MkText selbst ableitbar sind" (286).

The minor agreements are treated nowhere else in Luz's vol. III as they are here in Mt 22,34-40. The phenomena are carefully described (nos. 1-7), with due attention to disagreement and variation (in the case of the omission of Mk 12,32-34: "so daß man gar nicht von einer 'Übereinstimmung' sprechen sollte") and without applying the standard solution of DtMk[28].

In sum, Luz's commentary on Mt 18–25 has reduced the number of significant minor agreements that in this part of the Gospel could attest to the use of a DtMk recension, and their number is further reducible below the minimum that is | required to constitute a "recension" (or revised text) of Mark. The example of Mt 22,34-40 has shown that DtMk is not Luz's only alternative to independent redaction of Mk by Matthew and Luke. Mt 22,23-33 is another example: "bei diesem Text (käme) am ehesten die Möglichkeit in Frage, daß Lk Mt als Nebenquelle benutzt hätte" (262 n. 4)[29]. The influence of the Q-source in triple-tradition passages (cf. below) is still another factor in Luz's theory on the minor agreements (I.30; ET, 48):

> ... the minor agreements do not necessitate a basic revision of the two-source hypothesis. Since they do not show a clear common linguistic and/or theological profile, it is not necessary to limit their explanation to one single hypothesis. Rather, depending on the passage, one may cite various hypotheses.

3. The Sayings Source Q

In connection with the preceding section I mention first that in vol. I Luz has made use of minor agreements in his reconstruction of the Q

---

27. On the structure ἐξ, ἐν ἐν ἐν in Lk 10,27 (P[75] B: om. τῆς[1], καί[1]), cf. *ETL*, 1995, 159.

28. Ennulat's "deuteromk Textrezension" is mentioned by Luz in his survey (270 n. 9) without further consideration. Compare Ennulat's own survey referring to A. Fuchs, 1982 (279 n. 12); see now *SNTU* 16 (1991) 151-168 (ctr. J. Kiilunen); 19 (1994) 77-86 (ctr. H. Schürmann, 1993).

29. As far as I can see, the suggestion of Luke's use of Mt is most exceptional in Luz's commentary. On the factor "oral tradition", cf. below, p. 120 (diff. Mk 9,33-35).

text (Q 3,3; 3,21-22; 4,16)[30]. In vol. III there is at least one more example[31]: Mt 24,17-18 τά, ἐν τῷ ἀγρῷ / Lk 17,31 αὐτά, ἐν ἀγρῷ, diff. Mk 13,15-16 τι, εἰς τὸν ἀγρόν (409 n. 20; cf. 404, 447: Q 17,31)[32]. A similar case is Mt 18,6 / Lk 17,2, diff. Mk 9,42: "(haben) nach 'es ist besser' je einen ἵνα-Satz als Subjekt" (J. Schlosser; cf. Luz, 18: "eine Q-Variante, die Lk 17,2 zugrunde liegt")[33]. In the same context, Luz repeats his view on the influence of Q (= Mt 5,29-30!) in Mt 18,8-9, par. Mk 9,43-47 (cf. I.261-262)[34]. From these three cases, Mt 5,29-30; Lk 17,2; Lk 17,31, one may retain the impression that Luz is inclined to expand the extent of Q beyond the double-tradition passages. Rather the contrary is true. I mentioned already his reservation concerning Mt 22,34-40 / Lk 10,25-28, but it is more significant that Mt 18,12-13; 19,28; 22,2-10; 25,14-30 are not assigned to Q. In my previous descriptions of the extent of Q I have always included these four pericopes[35], and I am not alone in doing so. The names of D. Catchpole, J.D. Crossan, R.A. Edwards, J.A. Fitzmyer, P. Hoffmann, J.S. Kloppenborg, D. Lührmann, A. Polag, W. Schenk, W. Schmithals, S. Schulz, D. Zeller (and IQP) may suffice to call it a majority view. With regard to the two parables of the great supper and the talents/pounds (Q 14,16-24 and 19,12-26) most authors will agree with C.M. Tuckett: "the great verbal dissimilarity between Matthew and Luke I makes it difficult to be certain about the Q wording", but "the general similarity in the outline of the story in the two gospels makes it highly likely that we do indeed have Q material here"[36]. In the case of Mt 22,2-10 Luz decides against "die Mehrzahl der Autoren" (n. 12) and regards Lk 14,16-24 as "literarisch unabhängige Variante" (233)[37]. Likewise, he assumes that Mt 25,14-30 "aus Sondergut stammt" and regards Lk 19,12-26 as "eine unabhängig

---

30. Cf. my review of vol. I in *ETL* 63 (1987), 411. For a critical reaction, see my *The Minor Agreements and Q* (n. 23), 65-72 ("The Beginning of Q"); on Mt 3,5 / Lk 3,3, cf. *The First Synoptic Pericope: The Appearance of John the Baptist in Q?*, in *ETL* 72 (1996) 41-74, esp. 62-70.

31. On Lk 20,46, cf. below, n. 48.

32. For criticism, cf. *The Minor Agreements and Q*, 54-56 ("Luke 17:31"). On ἐν for εἰς, cf. above, n. 17.

33. For criticism, cf. *ibid.*, 57-59 ("Luke 17:2"). Note Luz's reserve: "ihr Einfluß auf Mt ist aber nirgendwo spürbar" (18).

34. For criticism, cf. *Evangelica*, 817-818; *Evangelica II*, 426.

35. *New Testament Vocabulary*, 1984, 493-494; *Q-Synopsis*, 1988; *Evangelica II*, 416 (= 1982, 36).

36. *Q and the History of Early Christianity*, Edinburgh, 1996, 146, 147.

37. In n. 12 he has a strange reference to Polag's *Fragmenta*: "führt den Text nicht einmal bei den 'unsicheren Texten' auf". Lk 14,16-24 is indeed printed as no. 57 (p. 70), and of course not in the Appendix with the "uncertain texts".

überlieferte Variante" (495)[38]. He stresses the exceptional length of these two parables (233: "gibt es sonst in Q keine mehr"; 495: "Q enthält sonst keine langen Parabeln") and their position in contexts without Q material: their placement in Mt 22 and 25 is redactional, Lk 14 has no other Q-verses than 14,26-27.34 (233), and Lk 19 comes after the eschatological discourse in Q 17 where "es überhaupt keine sicheren Q-Texte mehr gibt" (495). The position of the text is also important in the case of the parable of the lost sheep (Mt 18,12-13 / Lk 15,4-7)[39]: "Eine klare Plazierung des Textes in Q ist weder von Mt noch von Lk her möglich" (26). Neither can the location of the saying on Judging Israel (Mt 19,28 / Lk 22,28.30) be determined: "über einen möglichen Ort des Logions in Q können wir nur rätseln" (121)[40]. Finally Luz collects his statements on the lack of Q-context in the four pericopes (n. 14), together with his previous comments on Mt 5,18 (Lk 16,17); 5,32 (Lk 16,18); 11,12-13 (Lk 16,16)[41]: "es gibt ... keinen sinnvollen Ort in der Logienquelle..." (with variations), and in general: "Lk 16,16-18 steht nicht in einem Q-Zusammenhang und ist in Q nicht sinnvoll zu plazieren" (II.172).

M. Sato's global statement[42] that the double-tradition sayings in Lk 14,16-24.26-27.34-35; 15,4-7; 16,16-18; 17,1.3-4.6 (the "scattered fragments" between Lk 13,35 and 17,23, with one exception: 16,13) are all uncertain, has not been adopted as such in Luz's commentary. Mt 5,13 (Q 14,34-35); 10,37-38 (Q 14,26-27); 17,20 (Q 17,6) and now also 18,7 (Q 17,1b) and 18,15.21-22 (Q 17,3-4) are treated as Q-sayings without question mark. Nevertheless he still regards "die in Lk 14–16

---

38. In this case he adds in n. 11: "Heute scheint sich die These, daß kein Q-Text vorliegt, mehr und mehr durchzusetzen". In addition to A. Weiser (1971), V.K. Agbanou (1983), and A.D. Jacobson (1992), he mentions M. Sato (1988; diss. Bern, 1984) and C. Riniker (1991, unpublished diss. Bern). — See now HAGNER, 733 ("by no means certain"; "no direct literary dependence upon Q"); DAVIES-ALLISON, 376: "many – we include ourselves – hesitate" ("M and Q or L"); cf. also 194: Mt 22,1-14 assigned to M (oral tradition).

39. Here too he concludes that "Mt und Lk diesen Gleichnisstoff unabhängig voneinander der mündlichen Überlieferung verdanken" (26). Contrast: DAVIES-ALLISON, II.768; HAGNER, 525.

40. "Anders als die meisten wage ich es nicht, das Wort der Logienquelle zuzuweisen" (121). Contrast HAGNER, 563; DAVIES-ALLISON, 55. For a recent critique of the majority view, cf. R. URO, Apocalyptic Symbolism and Social Identity in Q, in ID. (ed.), Symbols and Strata. Essays on the Sayings Gospel Q (PFES, 65), Helsinki-Göttingen, 1996, 67-118, esp. 78 n. 32; Uro's first observation: "The saying does not appear in a Q context in either gospels".

41. See 121 n. 14: Mt 5,18 (I.229); Mt 5,32 (I.269); Mt 11,12-13 (II.152: read 172).

42. Q und Prophetie, 1988, 23 and 43-44 (= 1984, 25-26 and 49-50). See the references "Q[?]" in his more recent contribution, Wisdom Statements in the Sphere of Prophecy, in R.A. PIPER (ed.), Gospel (above, n. 23), 1995, 139-158.

verstreuten (*m.E. sogenannten*) Q-Stücken" as the most difficult part in
l the reconstruction of Q (293); "der lk Kontext 14,1-14 (stammt) *sicher*
... nicht aus Q" (297 n. 15; emphasis mine). The disputed sayings are
Lk 14,5 / Mt 12,11 and Lk 14,11; 18,14 / Mt 23,12[43]. Both are treated
by Luz as traditional sayings, the first without referring to Q (II.237) and
the second with a firm rejection of its origin in Q (III.297 n. 15: "m.E.
unmöglich")[44]. The Q-context (and sequence)[45] of the sayings is always
an important criterion in Luz's discussion of their inclusion in Q. In the
case of 14,11, some scholars think that a Q-context can be detected in
Mt 23,6-7a, immediately followed with 23,12. If, as Catchpole has suggested, τὴν πρωτοκλισίαν ἐν τοῖς δείπνοις was part of Q 11,43 (Mt
23,6-7a)[46], Luke could have dropped this item "in order to exploit the
idea in 14,7-10", just before Q 14,11. It can be objected that "the first
seat at suppers" in Mt 23,6-7a comes from Mk 12,38-39, and not from
Q 11,43[47]. But if Luke used Mk 12,38-39 as his "source" in 14,7-10, we
have to reckon with a certain contamination of Mark–Q overlaps in Lk
(φιλούντων in 20,46!)[48]. — Lk 14,5 is a traditional saying used by
Luke in his composition of 14,1-6. Because of its substantial agreement
with Mt 12,11 it can be regarded as a Q saying[49]. It has been argued that

43. KLOPPENBORG, *Q-Parallels*, 160, 162. Cf. SATO, *Wisdom* (n. 43), 143 nn. 18-19:
"hardly Q-sayings" (1984: "höchst unwahrscheinlich").
44. In reply to J. Gnilka's comment on Mt 23,11-12: "isolierte Logien... Möglicherweise stand letzterer auch in Q" (1988, 273).
45. His repeated comments on the "Q-Zusammenhang Q 17,1-6" are noteworthy:
"Daß ein Q-Text vorhanden war, ergibt sich also nicht aus den Übereinstimmungen im
Wortlaut, sondern nur aus der Abfolge" (III.61 n. 4; cf. II.520 n. 15). See also I.29, on
"Q-Reihenfolge".
46. *The Quest for Q*, Edinburgh, 1993, 263-264 (= 1991, 321-322). See also H. FLED-
DERMANN, *Mark and Q*, 1995, 187 (= 1982, 59).
47. Cf. my *Assessment* (in *Mark and Q*), 291 n. 154. See also IQP, Luz (297), Davies-
Allison (274 n. 58), *et al.* It is widely accepted that Mt 23,6-7a is a combination of Mk
12,38-39 and Q 11,43. On Luke as the "author" of 14,7-10, cf. W. BRAUN, *Feasting* (n.
49), 47.
48. Lk 20,46 has τῶν θελόντων... (= Mk 12,38) and adds καὶ φιλούντων... (cf. Mt
23,6 φιλοῦσιν). Ἀγαπᾶτε in Lk 11,43 is probably LkR for φιλεῖτε in Q (Polag, Sato,
Fleddermann, Catchpole, IQP, *et al.*). Note Luz's hesitation concerning φιλέω: "Stammt
es aus einer deuteromk Rezension von Mk 12,38 oder doch aus dem Q-Text?" (297 n. 8).
Bovon (484) regards Lk 14,8-10 (Sondergut) as a third tradition besides Lk 11,43 (Q) and
Lk 20,46 (Mk).
49. See D. KOSCH, *Die eschatologische Tora des Menschensohnes. Untersuchungen
zur Rezeption der Stellung Jesu zur Tora in Q* (NTOA, 12), Freiburg(Schw.) – Göttingen,
1989, 200-210 ("Zum Sabbat-Wort Lk 14,5; Mt 12,11"); F. NEIRYNCK, *Luke 14,1-6:
Lukan Composition and Q Saying*, in *Evangelica II*, 183-204 (= FS G. Schneider, 1991).
Cf. W. BRAUN, *Feasting and Social Rhetoric in Luke 14* (SNTS MS, 85), Cambridge,
1995 (review in *ETL* 72, 1996, 448-452), 25: "the story is an item of exclusively Lukan
material which contains one saying (14.5) that may have had a prior life (cf. Matthew
12.11)".

"14,5 by itself has no obvious point unless it is connected with another saying"[50]. But if the answer to the rhetorical question is supposed to be self-evident, it is less clear that the saying cannot have existed as an isolated logion. "Dass das Logion in Q so lange ohne festen Kontext tradiert werden konnte, mag mit der Eigenart der τίς ἐξ ὑμῶν-Logien zusammenhängen, die für sich sprechen und nicht auf einen grösseren Kontext angewiesen sind"[51].

The section of woe sayings in Mt 23 comes second in order of difficulty: "Nur darum, weil die Q-Hypothese in den beiden Großevangelien im ganzen plausibel | ist, lege ich sie auch hier der Analyse zugrunde" (293). With the exception of Q 11,42 (before 11,39b-41) Luz adopts the Lukan order of Q 11,39-52 (cf. Kloppenborg, IQP, et al.)[52]:

Catchpole	Mt			Lk	Q Luz	
[4]		4	23,23-24	2	11,42	Tithes
[5]		5	23,25-26	1	11,39-41	Washing
[3]	23,6-7a			3	11,43	Seats
[6]		6	23,27-28	4	11,44	Graves
[2]	23,4			5	11,46	Burdens
[7]		7	23,29-33	6	11,47-48	Prophetic tombs
			34-36		49-51	
[1]		1	23,13	7	11,52	Key
		(2)	23,15			
		(3)	23,16-22			

Matthew added nos. 2 and 3 and relocated Q 11,43.46 (in Mt 23,2-12: om. woe) and Q 11,52 (first woe in Mt). His nos. 4, 5, 6, 7 follow the relative order of Q. There is much uncertainty on the wording of the woe sayings[53]. Luz hesitates between MtR and Q[Mt] (318, 323, 330, 335, 342)[54]. MtR are: 23,16a.21fin.22.28.32-33, and Q[Mt]: 23,24.(29c.30?) and the variants ἄνηθον, ἀφιέναι (23), παροψίς, ἀκρασία (25). I mention here a few notable options: Q 11,52 ἤρατε τὴν κλεῖδα τῆς γνώσεως (the kingdom saying in Mt 23,13 is redactional)[55]; Q 11,49-51: the Q-text (= Lk) includes σοφούς and υἱοῦ Βαραχίου (Mt

---

50. KLOPPENBORG, Q-Parallels, 160. Cf. C.M. TUCKETT, Q and the History, 415: "the saying must have been part of a wider context".
51. KOSCH, Tora, 204. Cf. my Luke 14,1-6, 201-202.
52. Cf. 318-319; here column Q = Luz. For comparison, see the column of Catchpole's more Mt-like alternative; cf. Quest, 259-261.
53. Cf. DAVIES-ALLISON, 283: "we despair of reconstructing a common Q source".
54. On the recension Q[Mt] in Luz's commentary, cf. Evangelica II ("Q[Mt] and Q[Lk] and the Reconstruction of Q"), 477 (vol. I), 480 (vol. II); and now in vol. III, 39-40: Mt 18,15-17 (Luz: 18,15-16a.17.18).
55. "Gegen die Mehrzahl der Exegeten; mit Polag" (320 n. 23). See also MARSHALL, 507; GUNDRY, 460; KOESTER (cf. GThom 39) 80; IQP (1992); DAVIES-ALLISON, 286.

23,34.35)[56]. A major problem for the interpreter is the position of Q 13,34-35 (the lament over Jerusalem) in Mt 23,37-39, after the doom oracle Mt 23,34-36 (Q 11,49-51): "Ich halte die mt Stellung für redaktionell... Lk hat dagegen das Logion nicht red. plaziert" (377)[57].

Luz can make two general observations. On the one hand, Luke is more faithful to the original order of Q. Here Luke only inverted nos. 1 and 2: 11,39-41 (om. woe) is placed first "da er zur red. Gastmahlszene am besten paßte (Lk 11,38f)". On the other hand, "Mt hat in allen seinen Reden die Tendenz, Stoff aus Mk möglichst an den Anfang zu stellen"; this can explain his placing Q 11,43 = Mk 12,38-39 in the introductory section. Much more problematic is Luz's treatment of Q 11,52. Cf. 319: "keine große Schwierigkeit"! Yet I quote a few opinions[58]:

I   The anti-climactic nature of the woe after the powerful invective of 11:49-51, and the fact that the saying fits well into the present Lukan arrangement as generalising conclusion to the series of woes, suggests that Luke's ordering may well be secondary here.

"Es bleiben auf alle Fälle große Unsicherheiten" (319); also, I would add, regarding the location of Q 13,34-35 (Mt 23,37-39)[59].

It is less difficult to trace the Q texts in Mt 24:

26-27.28.	37-39.	40-41.	43-44.45-51
Q 17,23-24.37.	26-27.30.	34-35.	12,39-40.42-46

The placement of Q 17,37b in Mt 24,28 is accepted by most authors as its original location in Q, for good reasons, but unconvincing to Luz (409 n. 19; cf. 404). In connection with Q 17,23ff., Luz defends the presence in Q, and omission by Matthew, of Lk 17,20-21.28-29.31 (446-447). But Lk 17,20-21 and 28-29 are Sondergut texts and their ascription to Q is doubtful[60]; Lk 17,31 is Lukan redaction of Mk 13,15-

---

56. "Gegen die Mehrzahl der heutigen Ausleger" and "Gegen fast alle Forscher" (368). For both, cf. S. LÉGASSE, in *BETL* 59 (1982), 242, 244 (and 245).

57. "Ich rechne ... damit, daß Lk die Verse 13,31-33 aufgrund des Stichworts Ἰερουσαλήμ in einen ihm vorgegebenen geschlossenen Q-Zusammenhang Q 13,23-29.34f eingefügt hat" (378). But see below, n. 59.

58. TUCKETT, *Q and the History*, 166 (cf. CATCHPOLE, *Quest*, 260; SCHÜRMANN, *Lk* II/1, 329). Compare KOSCH, *Tora*, 89 (and 104): Q 11,52 before 11,47-48.49-51; JACOBSON, *Gospel*, 184: "strangely anticlimactic after the prophecy in Q 11:49-51"; his solution: "Q 11:52 did not conclude Q 11:49-51 but rather introduced Q 12:2-3" (185).

59. Cf. *Evangelica II*, 446. See also BOVON, 446: "Die Lokalisierung bei Matthäus ... dürfte die richtige sein". Cf. below, 122 (Allison); n. 93 (Robinson).

60. On Lk 17,28-29, cf. *ETL* 72 (1996), 70. Luz's argument is hardly convincing: "Ein großes Interesse an Q 17,26-30 kann Mt nicht gehabt haben... Außerdem dürfte Mt 24,39b von Q 17,30 inspiriert sein" (447 n. 7). It is far from evident that Matthew would

16[61]. Likewise, in the context of Q 12,39-46, Luz regards as belonging to Q Lk 12,35-38 before and 12,49-56 after. Only Q 12,51-53 has a parallel in Mt (10,34-36). Q 12,49-50 and Q(?) 12,54-56 are omitted by Matthew (452 n. 5: "ersatzlos gestrichen"). Note however that in vol. II Luz did not exclude the possibility that Mt 10,34 may contain reminiscences of Q 12,49 (II.134 n. 1: "Non liquet"). In his view Mt 16,2b-3 (par. Lk 12,54-56) is not original in the text of Mt (II.443-444)[62]. Q 12,35-38 is omitted by Matthew "zugunsten von 25,1-12" (cf. 468, on the use of Q 13,25 in Mt 25,10fin-12).

4. Oral Tradition

As said already, Mt 18,12-13; 19,28; 22,2-10; 25,14-30 (and their parallels in Lk) are not considered to be Q material. Luz compares 22,2-10 and 25,14-30 with the Sondergut parables in 18,23-35; 20,1-16; 25,1-12; 25,31-46. In all these pericopes the Matthean style is undeniable, but Luz tries to show that none of them is simply redactional creation[63]. He looks for distinctions between redaction and | tradition: in 18,23-35, βασιλεύς in the introductory v. 23 and ὁ κύριος in the story (66); in 20,1-16, the application in v. 16 referring to the last and the first, a secondary motif in v. 8b (141); in 25,1-13, the refrain in v. 13 (cf. Mk 13,35) and the parable (468); in 25,31-46, the introductory vv. 31-32a, replete of mattheanisms, and the less "Matthean" vv. 32b-46 (318). The solution he proposes for 18,23-35 also applies to the other parables (66):

> Der Text weist durchgehend einen sehr hohen Anteil an redaktionellen
> Vorzugsvokabular auf... Ich nehme deshalb an, daß Mt eine bisher nur

be interested in the example of the days of Noah (vv. 26-27) and not in that of the days of Lot (vv. 28-29). Matthew's use of Q 17,30 in Mt 24,39b (after 24,37-39a = Q 17,26-27) scarcely argues for knowledge (and omission) of 17,28-29.

61. See above, n. 32. — On Lk 17,33 (Mt 10,39), cf. III.447: "vermutlich aus einem anderen Q-Zusammenhang" (II.134: after Q 14,26-27). But see my *Saving/Losing One's Life* (below, n. 92).

62. "Ist V 2aβ-3 ein Zusatz, so stammt es nicht aus Q = Lk 12,54-56" (444). — On *Q 12:49-59*, see now the *Documenta Q* volume (1997; cf. *ETL* 73, 1997, 458-459), with references to "Luz 1990" on Mt 10,34 and 16,2b-3 (12 and 172-173).

63. Some names of defenders of the MtR alternative ("redaktionelle Neukreation") are cited in the footnotes to Mt 18,23-35: Goulder, Breukelman, Gundry (66 n. 12); Mt 25,1-13: Donfried, Goulder, Gundry (468 n. 12); Mt 25,31-46: Cope, Haufe, Weren, Kretzer, Gundry, Gnilka, Lambrecht (517 n. 10: "Mt hat sonst nie einen so langen Text neu entworfen"). — Likewise, on Mt 21,28-32: Merkel, Gundry, Schlosser (exc. v. 31c); with the more general statement that "Mt sonst m.E. nie Gleichnisse erfindet, aber aufgrund von mündlichen Traditionen erstmals schriftlich formuliert" (206 n. 19, 207).

mündlich überlieferte Geschichte erstmals schriftlich formuliert hat. So ist
es auch bei einigen anderen Gleichnissen.

In like manner Mt 18,12-13; 19,28; 21,28-32[64]; 22,2-10; 25,14-30 and
their parallels in Lk are treated as independent oral-tradition variants.
A more sophisticated use of oral tradition is suggested in Mt 18,1-5:
Mt 18,3 could depend on an oral-tradition variant of Mk 10,15 and the
influence of a pre-Markan variant of Mk 9,36-37 behind 9,33-37 could
explain Matthew's (and Luke's) abbreviations of Mk 9,33-35 (10: "Mt
and Lk haben sich offenbar an die mündliche Tradition erinnert"). But
Luz's own comment offers a quite satisfactory explanation of their independent redaction of Mk. – Traditional sayings are used by Matthew in
18,10b; 18,19(-20)[65]; 19,12.

Mt 19,12 is a Jesus saying about celibacy which is used by Matthew
in a new sense with reference to Jesus' teaching on divorce in v. 9 (107;
n. 109: of this 'Eheauslegung', "ihr wichtigster 'Vater' ist Dupont").
Luz also adopts J. Dupont's interpretation of the *porneia*-clause. The
divorce pericope (19,3-9) has no other source than Mk 10,2-12 (91: any
existence of a *Nebenquelle* is superfluous). Μὴ ἐπὶ πορνείᾳ in 19,9 is
probably the evangelist's insertion, but παρεκτὸς λόγου πορνείας
("sprachlich anders formuliert") in 5,32 "lag Mt schon vor" (I.269):
"Die Unzuchtklausel von V 9 halte ich der Sache nach für Tradition der
mt Gemeinde" (91 n. 8). Matthew's exception clause reflects the practice of his community. It also expresses "ein eigenes theologisches
Interesse des Evangelisten": "die Scheidebriefregelung von Dtn 24,1-4
(wird) ernstgenommen" (97). However, such a Matthean interest ("das
er aber nicht explizit macht!") is scarcely provable. Moreover, it is
hardly conceivable how it can be combined with (Dupont's and) Luz's
interpretation of ἀπολύειν (in the case of πορνεία = adultery) in the
new sense of separation only[66]. Cf. Davies-Allison: "The Jewish
divorce bill contained the clause, 'You are free to marry again.' To
obtain a divorce was to obtain permission to remarry" (III.17); and
referring to Mt 1,19: "it is also possible to find in Matthew's gospel
itself the reason for the evangelist having added 'except for adultery'"
(I.531).

---

64. Cf. Lk 7,29-30. See n. 63.
65. Added by Matthew to Q^Mt 18,15-17.18 (v. 16b = Dt 19,15 can be redactional).
66. In contrast to Luz's approach (divorce saying in Q very uncertain; and "separation" in the case of adultery), see my *The Divorce Saying in Q 16:18*, in *Louvain Studies*
20 (1995) 201-218; *De echtscheidingslogia in de evangeliën*, in *Academiae Analecta –
Letteren* 58 (1996) 21-42.

Speaking of Matthew's sources, one may argue that the first to be mentioned should be Matthew's Bible[67]. One of Matthew's *Erfüllungszitate* is the quotation in Mt 21,15. It can be placed under the rubric "oral tradition" in view of Luz's statement that Zech 9,9 "sicher schon vor Mt als Weissagung des Einzugs Jesu in Jerusalem entdeckt worden (ist)"[68]; "Erst Mt hat es aber in den Mk-Text eingefügt" (178)[69]. He refuses the existence of a traditional story in which there were two donkeys (diff. Mk) as well as the influence of biblical texts other than Zech 9,9: "Beides verkompliziert die Sache unnötig" (179)[70]. Mt 21,14 and 15-16, peculiar to Mt, are "sprachlich mt", and the possibility of "eine vormt Erzählvariante" (180) can scarcely be suggested by Jn 12,17-19.

5. *U. Luz and D.C. Allison's Retrospect on Q*

The diachronic analysis is not the most typical aspect of Luz's commentary. I can cite his own words saying that he has attempted to write a "history of influence" commentary of the Gospel of Matthew[71]. *Wirkungsgeschichte* is indeed the final part of each section, but it is preceded by *Analyse* and *Erklärung* (interpretation) and Analysis comprises

---

67. Cf. H. FRANKEMÖLLE, *Das Matthäusevangelium als heilige Schrift und die heilige Schrift des früheren Bundes. Von der Zwei-Quellen zur Drei-Quellen-Theorie*, in C. FOCANT (ed.), *The Synoptic Gospels* (BETL, 110), Leuven, 1993, 281-310.

68. However, the evidence of the parallel in Jn 12,15 is less convincing than Luz's reference to Menken (1992) would suggest (n. 12). See my response to M. Menken in *BETL* 101, 28 and *ETL* 72 (1996), 453.

69. Cf. n. 11: "ich rechne nicht damit, daß Sach 9,9 auf die vormk oder mk Einzugsgeschichte einwirkte" (ctr. Gnilka).

70. Cf. nn. 22 and 23. The quotation in Mt 21,5 has received the attention of two Dutch scholars: M.J.J. MENKEN, *Old Testament Quotations in the Fourth Gospel* (CBET, 15), Kampen, 1996, 79-97 (= *ZNW* 80, 1989, 193-209); *The Quotations from Zech 9,9 in Mt 21,5 and in Jn 12,15*, in A. DENAUX (ed.), *John and the Synoptics* (BETL, 101), Leuven, 1992, 571-578; W. WEREN, *Jesus' Entry into Jerusalem: Mt 21,1-17 in the Light of the Hebrew Bible and the Septuagint*, in C.M. TUCKETT (ed.), *The Scriptures in the Gospels* (BETL, 131), Leuven, 1997, 117-141. Weren rejects Menken's association of Zech 9,9 with 2 Sam 16,1-4, but he links Zech 9,9 to both Gen 49,8-12 (Blenkinsopp) and Gen 49,14-15 (Derrett). Cf. Luz's comment on such "intertextual network": "Der bibelkundlichen Phantasie ist keine Grenze gesetzt!" (n. 23).

71. U. LUZ, *The Final Judgment (Matt 25:31-46): An Exercise in "History of Influence" Exegesis*, in D.R. BAUER – M.A. POWELL (eds.), *Treasures New and Old: Recent Contributions to Matthean Studies* (SBL Symposium Series, 1), Atlanta, GA, 1996, 271-310, esp. 273. The article is a slightly adapted version (ET by D.J. Weaver) of III.515-544, with the section "Wirkungsgeschichte" (521-530) translated as "History of Interpretation and History of Influence of Matt 25:31-46" (273-286). On *Auslegungsgeschichte* and *Wirkungsgeschichte*, cf. I.78-82 (ET, 95-99: "On the History of Influence and the Intention of This Commentary").

Aufbau, *Quellen*, and *Traditionsgeschichte und Herkunft*. In the two-source theory a commentary on Matthew constitutes the first chapter of the *Wirkungsgeschichte* of Mark and Q. Mt 26–28 par. Mk 14–16 remain to be treated in vol. IV, but with regard to Matthew's use of Q the commentary is now complete, or at least all relevant passages are commented upon. D.C. Allison, the other commentator of Matthew (in three | volumes: 1988-1991-1997), in the year he finished his commentary, has written a book on Q, and it can be instructive to compare his views on Q with those of Luz[72].

1. Q 12,54-56; 14,11; 14,16-24; 15,4-7; 16,17; 16,18; 19,12-26; 22,28-30, excluded by Luz, are all assigned to Q (26-27; contrast Davies–Allison on Mt 22,1-14 and 25,14-30). Allison also includes a few Sondergut verses: Lk 9,61-62 (Luz: probably not in Q); Lk 12,32 (Luz: Q^{Lk}, and Mt 6,34 Q^{Mt}); Mt 10,5b-6 and 23 (Luz: Q^{Mt})[73]. In 1988 Allison thought that "there was a notice of the baptism" in Q (I.329; with reference to Luz, I.150-151), but in 1997 he notes his retraction: "I now think my reasons inadequate" (8 n. 40)[74].

2. The 42 units of Q are presented in the Lukan order, with only one exception[75]: 11,45-51 + 13,34-35 + 11,52. In vol. III Davies and Allison were very hesitant about the structure of the seven woes: "we can know neither their order nor number, and the original wording likewise often eludes us" (283). Allison cites again the IQP reconstruction (= Luz), but now adds: "Luke is probably even closer to Q than this reconstruction indicates. Luke's redactional introduction (11:37-38) ... shows us that 11:39-41 introduced Q's series of woes. Further, Luke's triadic arrangement reminds one of other triads in Q" (16 n. 68). With regard to Q 13,34-35 he repeats his comment on its original location (19; cf. III.312). "If [in this case] the best guess is that Matthew's order is the order of Q, then Q 13:34-35 belong with the polemical discourse in Q 11:37-52" (202)[76].

---

72. Dale C. ALLISON, JR., *The Jesus Tradition in Q*, Harrisburg, PA, Trinity Press International, 1997, XII-243 p. The book contains a first chapter on "The Compositional History of Q" (1-66) and eight chapters on particular passages: (2) 6,20-49 (cf. *ETL* 64, 1988, 205-214); (3) 6,20-23; (4) 10,2-16 (cf. *ETL* 61, 1985, 369-375); (5) 11,24-26; (6) 11,34-36; (7) 12,7a; (8) 13,28-29; (9) 13,34-35.

73. *Jesus Tradition*, 26-27, 11 n. 50, 22 n. 91, 11 n. 52.

74. With reference to my *The Minor Agreements and Q* (1995). The case of "Q" 3,3 is not even mentioned. Cf. above, n. 30.

75. There is no indication on the placement of Lk 17,33 (Mt 10,39?) and Lk 17,37 (Mt 24,28). — On Lk 17,33, see n. 61.

76. Allison is not unaware of the difficulty of the anticlimactic final woe in 11,52: "Some, however, would argue that Q 11:52 was moved to its final place by Luke. Cf. Tuckett" (60 n. 272). Cf. above, n. 58.

3. Allison is critical of Kloppenborg's stratigraphy of Q (3-7) and offers a new theory of Q's compositional history. He divides the Q materials into five sections and proposes his own thesis of a three-stage composition:

Q¹		9,57-11,13		12,2-32	
Q²		9,57-11,13		12,2-32	12,33-22,30
Q³	3,7-7,35	9,57-11,13	11,14-52	12,2-32	12,33-22,30
	I	II	III	IV	V

Q¹ was a document addressed to itinerant missionaries (sections II + IV). In Q² it was expanded with paraenetical materials at the end (section V) in view of a new audience of disciples in the broader sense. Q³ is a new updating with the addition of section I at the beginning and the interpolation of section III; it is characterized by polemic against outsiders, by its interest in christology and in John the Baptist and by an apologetical interest in Scriptures (30-35). Besides the addition of large blocks we have to reckon with smaller additions and retouches in the text. For example, Q 10,13-15 should be attributed to Q³ (35, 40)[77]. Allison also conjectures that Q 22,28-30 originally followed 12,32 and thus concluded Q¹ (40).

Originally Allison envisaged his study of Q as a collective critique of the various compositional theories: "... I soon found myself the author of my own compositional history of Q. I ended up doing what I once thought should not be done" (Preface, ix). His chapter 3 on the Beatitudes appears here for the first time and it can serve to illustrate the development of Allison's exegetical opinion[78].

4. In their commentary on the first three beatitudes Davies and Allison noted several unanswered questions. On the order of the second and third beatitudes, Matthean or Lukan: "We prefer to confess ignorance" (436). On Mt's third person plural or Lk's second person plural: "No agreement has been reached" (445); "the clouds of doubt still hang over the issue; we still await a decisive observation" (446). On the verb πενθοῦντες in Mt "probably from the Q source": "But it may also be that neither Matthew nor Luke has preserved the wording of Q" (447).

---

77. Q 10,12 is attributed to Q¹ (35 n. 151, 52: Sodom; 61 n. 276: 10,3-12 originally composed as a unit). But see my *Evangelica II*, 445 (and 434, 449); *Literary Criticism*, 32: QR (in reply to Catchpole); and J.S. KLOPPENBORG, *The Sayings Gospel Q: Literary and Stratigraphic Problems*, in URO (ed.), *Symbols and Strata* (n. 40), 1-66, esp. 19 n. 75: 10,12 redactional, patterned on v. 14 (Hahn, Hoffmann, Jacobson, Kloppenborg, Laufen, Lührmann, Neirynck, Sato, Schenk, Schmithals, Uro, Vaage). See also LUZ: "vermutlich in Q eine sekundäre Bildung aufgrund von Lk 10,14" (II.89, 192); ctr. BOVON, II.48.
78. Chapter 3: "Four Beatitudes, Q 6:20-23: A Unified Composition" (96-103).

They seemed to be certain on one issue: "The first three [beatitudes] circulated on their own for a time before someone added the fourth" (435: "Stage II: a fourth beatitude ... is added or composed"). But this is now corrected with Allison's new thesis on the unified composition of the four beatitudes. In the light of the Qumran text 4Q525 he questions the arguments for dissociating Q 6,22-23 from 6,20b-21: the different introductory formula and differences of form, content, and setting in life. His first and main reason for holding the original unity is the fact that Q 6,20-23 "in its entirety" should be read against the background of Isaiah 61 (102):

> It is not just the first and third beatitudes that allude to Isaiah [61:1,2]: so seemingly does the fourth. Its theme of rejoicing is paralleled in Isa 61:3 and 61:10. This is perhaps some reason for postulating the unity of Q 6:20-23. Moreover, if Q 6:20-23 blesses the poor, those who mourn, and those who are hated, excluded, reproached, and spoken evil of, in Isaiah the poor and those who mourn are oppressed, despised, forsaken, and hated (Isa 60:14-15). The correlation is probably not coincidence.

The clouds of doubt apparently disappeared: the first three beatitudes are cited in the second person[79] and in the Lukan order, but Matthew's wording of the third beatitude (the second in Mt 5,4) is original in Q: "Blessed are those who mourn, for you will be comforted" (102 n. 27; cf. 7 n. 33). In a recent study of Q 6,20b-21 I rather argued that the influence of Isa 61,2 on the wording and location of Mt 5,4 should be assigned to MtR[80]. Contrast Luz's statement on pre-Matthean origin: "Die von Jes 61,2 her erfolgte Neuformulierung ... ist eindeutig vor–lmatthäisch" (I.200). But for both, as for most interpreters, the four beatitudes were not originally a literary unit.

5. Allison also discusses another "commonplace of contemporary scholarship", J. Jeremias's interpretation of Q 13,28-29 (Mt 8,11-12): those coming from east and west identified as Gentiles and "the sons of the kingdom" as the Jewish people; and the saying understood as a warning against Israel: "Annahme der 'vielen' Heiden, aber Ausschluß Israels" (Luz, II.14). Already in an article of 1989 (and in Davies–Allison, II.27-31)[81] Allison made the proposal that the many from east and

---

79. In the text quoted above: "for *you* will be comforted", although Allison still speaks of a switch from third to second person (98: "a rhetorical pattern").

80. *Q 6,20b-21; 7,22 and Isaiah 61*, in C.M. Tuckett (ed.), *The Scriptures in the Gospels* (n. 70), 27-64, esp. 29-45.

81. Chapter 8: "From East and West, Q 13:28-29: Salvation for the Diaspora" (176-191); expanded version of *Who Will Come from East and West? Observations on Matt 8:11-12 = Lk 13,28-29*, in *Irish Biblical Studies* 11 (1989) 158-170. Cited with approval by D. Catchpole, *Quest*, 306 (reprint from BETL 100, 1992, 538-539).

west are not Gentiles but diaspora Jews. He concludes "against Jeremias and so many others (that) Q 13:28-29 originally had nothing to say about Gentiles... It took up the stock theme of the eschatological ingathering of dispersed Jews in order to threaten certain Jews in the land with judgment" (189).

As for the saying in Q, I refer here to Tuckett's comment on Q 13,28-29 as the climax of the section 13,24-29[82]:

> The picture of vv. 28f. is of Jews excluded from the eschatological banquet. [ ] it is a warning of what may happen if people do not respond. The violent imagery thus serves to highlight the importance of the present call and makes that call all the more urgent.

Allison now draws attention to "a well-established habit of speaking of early Christians as though they were the Jewish Diaspora": Matthew may have interpreted 8,11-12 as a prediction of "the arrival of the Christian church, made up of Jews as well as Gentiles" (190-191).

6. Allison's well-known article on Q 13,35b is included in the last chapter of his book[83]: "The conditional interpretation commends itself by finding a middle ground that avoids the pitfalls of the alternatives... We have here a call to repentance. When the holy city recognizes its error and accepts the Messiah, he will come" (201). The alternative interpretations are either a statement of utter rejection or an unqualified announcement of salvation. Luz opts for the first possibility (*Gerichtswort*), mainly because of the judgement theme in the context (III.384). Although he admits that the meaning of ἕως ἄν can be conditional ("sprachlich möglich"), he states that here it is "in sich unlogisch". But is it not more difficult to understand that not an expression of fear and trembling but the words of Ps 118,26 εὐλογημένος ... come "from the lips of those for whom the messianic advent must mean only damnation"? Compare the reactions by Catchpole[84] and Tuckett[85].

---

82. *Q and the History*, 203-204. See also 395-397, Excursus on Catchpole's interpretation of Q 7,1-10 (esp. 396 n. 15).

83. Chapter 9: "The Forsaken House, Q 13:34-35: Jerusalem's Repentance" (192-204). Reprint (with supplement on "The Location and Function of Q 13:35b in Q", 201-203) from *Matthew 23.39 = Luke 13.35b as a Conditional Prophecy*, in *JSNT* 18 (1983) 75-84 (= *The Historical Jesus: A Sheffield Reader*, 1995, 262-270). The interpretation of Q 13,35b as a conditional sentence was first suggested by H. VAN DER KWAAK, *Die Klage über Jerusalem (Matth. xxiii 37-39)*, in *NT* 8 (1966) 156-170, esp. 168-170. Cf. DAVIES–ALLISON, III.323-324.

84. *Quest*, 274 (= 1991, 322): "Allison has convincingly demonstrated...".

85. *Q and the History*, 205, on "the positive outlook reflected in 13:35b": "this saying apparently opens up a chink of light and seems to envisage the prospect of future salvation for those addressed".

Less persuasive, however, for both Catchpole and Tuckett (and many others) is Allison's argument that v. 35b is integral to the oracle 13,34-35 and not a secondary expansion: "an expansion is extremely probable"[86]; "the half-verse looks very much like a secondary addition to the original saying"[87]. Luz disagrees: he rejects such decomposition (III.378) and in this he comes close to Allison.

POSTSCRIPT

When I concluded my survey of the EKK commentary on Matthew with a reference to Allison I thought this may incite Luz to write his own retrospect on Q. It now appears that at that very moment his "Matthew and Q" was already with the printer[88]. It contains in a first section a summary presentation of the extent of Q. His criteria for inclusion of sayings in Q are their agreements in wording, correspondence in order, and also their position in a Q context. Thus, for instance, Q 11,39-52 can be ascribed to Q as part of the larger Q-complex 11,2–12,59. But Lk 15,3-7; 22,28-30; 14,16-24; 19,11-27 (Mt 18,12-13; 19,28; 22,1-10; 25,14-30) are excluded: "keines der drei Kriterien (ist) erfüllt" (204). Luz briefly discusses Q(?) 16,13.16.17.18 and concludes: "Ich muß bei einem (allerdings sehr skeptischen!) Non-liquet stehen bleiben" (203-204)[89]. In a few instances he reckons with the possibility of Matthean omission: Q 10,4b; 12,49-50; 12,54-56(?)[90]; 17,20-21.28-31(?)[91]. His

---

86. CATCHPOLE, 274 n. 63, 273.

87. TUCKETT, 175; the saying receives "a powerful redactional addendum" in Q (*ibid.*). Catchpole and Tuckett refer to *Evangelica II*, 446 (= *Recent Developments*, 1982, 66). See also KLOPPENBORG, 1996 (n. 77), 20 and 21 n. 72.

88. U. LUZ, *Matthäus und Q*, in R. HOPPE – U. BUSSE (eds.), *Von Jesus zum Christus: Christologische Studien*. FS P. Hoffmann (BZNW, 93), Berlin – New York, 1998, 201-215.

Part IV of FS P. Hoffmann ("Logienquelle", 189-318) includes seven essays on Q, in this order: O. Merk (W.G. Kümmel on Q), U. Luz (Mt and Q), J. Schlosser (Q 11,23), J.M. Robinson (Q 13,34-35: cf. below, n. 93), C. Heil (Q 13,27c), R. Hoppe (Q 14,16-24), F. Neirynck (Q? 17,33: cf. below, n. 92).

89. This skeptical *non liquet* notwithstanding Q 16,13.16.17.18 is included without question mark in his survey on p. 208: "Mt 6,24; 5,18; 11,12f; 5,32"; read: 6,24; 11,12f; *5,18.32* (cf. p. 203). — Other corrections in the same *Übersicht*: line 10, Mt 9,37, read: 9,37-38; line 19, Q 12,2-12, read: 12,2-9 (Mt 10,26-33); line 22, Mt 24,39-46, read: 24,43-51 (Q 12,39-46); line 25, Mt 13,[30-33], read: 13,31-33. Either B 23 or B 13,31-33 should take an asterisk (diff. Q order).

90. "Neben Q 12,49f hat er wohl auch Q 12,54-56 weggelassen" (204 n. 16). But see n. 17: "Das Urteil bleibt hier aber ganz unsicher!". Cf. above, n. 62.

91. On Lk 17,28-29 (204), cf. above, n. 60; on Lk 17,31 (205 n. 18, 210), cf. above, n. 32. See now also *Saving/Losing* (n. 92), 312 nn. 111 and 114.

list of Q^{Mt} sayings comprises Mt 5,5.7-9; 5,19(?); 5,41; 6,34; 7,6(?); 10,5-6(?); 10,16b; 10,23(?); 10,41(?); 18,15b-17.18; 23,15(?).

Matthew has two ways of using Q, either by adopting blocks of sayings from Q (*Blocktechnik*) or by bringing together individual sayings from different contexts in Q (*Exzerpttechnik*). The second part of the mission discourse is cited by Luz as an illustration of how Matthew "fortlaufend exzerpiert" (209): the original sequence of the sayings in Q is preserved in Mt 10,24-25.26-33.34-36.37-38.39 = Q 6,40; 12,2-9; 12,51-53; 14,26-27; [Lk 17,33]. The location of the I saying in Lk 17,33 is Lukan indeed, but I think it is less certain that its placement in Mt 10,39, after 10,37-38 = Q 14,26-27, relies on Q (cf. Mk 8,35!)[92]. Mt 7,13-14.22-23; 8,11-12 = Q 13,23-24.25-27.28-29 is another example of "fortlaufendes Exzerpt" (211). However, it is a more doubtful suggestion that Q 13,23-29 + 34-35 (Mt 23,37-39) constituted an original unit in Q (208, 212)[93].

In a last section on the theological significance of Q for Matthew, Luz emphasizes their historical continuity and he concludes with a reformulation of his observations on "eine tiefe Krise der Israelmission" and the "relativ späte Redaktion" of Q (III.370 n. 18) in the line of Hoffmann's approach[94].

---

92. It is not unlikely that both Lk 17,33 and Mt 10,39 depend on Mk 8,35. See my *Saving/Losing One's Life: Luke 17,33(Q?) and Mark 8,35*, in FS P. Hoffmann (above, n. 88), 295-318.

93. Cf. above, nn. 57 and 59. See now J.M. ROBINSON, *The Sequence of Q: The Lament over Jerusalem*, in FS P. Hoffmann (above, n. 88), 225-260, on Q 11,49-51 + 13,34-35 in Q: "the last Woe about 'killing the prophets' (Q 11,47-48) provided the original context for appending both Sophia's Saying and the Lament over Jerusalem" (258); with reference to *Evangelica II*, 446 (260 n. 66). Robinson attributes the final position of Q 11,52 to Lukan redaction and places this Woe in sixth position before 11,47-48 in Q (228, 256). Compare D. Kosch's solution (above, n. 58) emphasizing the connection between 11,46 and 11,52: "aufgrund der genannten Adressaten und der inhaltlichen Verwandtschaft" (89). See also P. HOFFMANN, art. *Die Logienquelle*, in *LTK*³ 6 (1997) 1019-1021: Q 11,39-44.46.52.47-51 (col. 1020). On this connection, but in reverse order, cf. J. Gnilka (282 n. 9) and D. Catchpole (261): first and second Woe in Q (11,52.46).

The location of Q 11,52 and Q 13,34-35 before and after 11,47-48.49-51 (both diff. Luz) are proposed by Robinson as corrections of the general presumption in favor of Lukan sequence in Q (227-232). His list of instances of Mt=Q order includes: Q 4,5-8; 11,39b-41; 13,29.28; 17,33; 17,37 (= IQP); Q 11,16; 11,52 (= General Editors minus Kloppenborg); Q 6,29-31.27-28; 16,16 following on 7,28; 12,33-34(?); and Q 13,34-35 (= Robinson). On the order of Q 6,29-30.27-28, see my *Evangelica II*, 547 (and n. 188). The case of Q 17,33 is a more dubious one: cf. n. 92. The other instances of Mt=Q in IQP are widely acknowledged.

94. P. HOFFMANN, *QR und der Menschensohn. Eine vorläufige Skizze*, in *The Four Gospels 1992* (BETL, 100), 1992, 421-456, esp. 450-456. On his date of Q, cf. *ETL* 71 (1995), 463; 72 (1996), 444 (A. Vögtle); 73 (1997) 176 (C.M. Tuckett).

Ulrich LUZ. *Das Evangelium nach Matthäus. 1. Teilband Mt 1-7*. (Evangelisch-Katholischer Kommentar zum Neuen Testament, I/1.)
Zürich-Einsiedeln-Köln, Benziger Verlag; Neukirchen-Vluyn, Neukirchener Verlag, 1985. xi-420 p.

Le livre de U. Luz n'est qu'un premier tome. Il contient une introduction de
82 pages et le commentaire sur les sept premiers chapitres de Matthieu (p. 83-
420). La date de la parution des deux volumes couvrant les vingt-et-un chapitres
de Mt 8-28 n'est pas encore annoncée. Publié en 1985, le commentaire sur Matthieu fut précédé dans la même série par le commentaire sur Marc de J. Gnilka
en 1978/79 (voir *ETL* 57, 1981; = *Evangelica*, 609-613; cf. p. 630-636: «The
Redactional Text»). Le nouveau commentaire se distingue de celui de Gnilka par
la place réservée à la *Wirkungsgeschichte*. Gnilka avait annoncé la *Wirkungsgeschichte* comme un aspect nouveau de son commentaire, mais ce qui chez lui
ne fut qu'une section spéciale en appendice au commentaire (voir nos remarques:
p. 613) est introduit ici dans le commentaire même (cf. p. 78-82). Voir U. LUZ,
*Wirkungsgeschichtliche Exegese. Ein programmatischer Arbeitsbericht mit Bei-
spielen aus der Bergpredigtexegese*, in *Berliner Theologische Zeitschrift* 2 (1985)
18-32; cf. p. 23: «nicht Anhang, sondern Voraussetzung»; p. 27: «für mich (ist)
Wirkungs- und Auslegungsgeschichte zentral». Qu'on me permette cependant de
présenter ici la dimension historico-critique du commentaire.

La critique textuelle n'y tient que peu de place. C'est, semble-t-il, le texte
grec de N[26] qui est à la base de la traduction allemande. Une dizaine de
variantes sont signalées en note et brièvement discutées: 1,18; 4,13; 5,4/5.30.44;
6,1.25(!).28(!); 7,13.14(!). Dans deux cas, L. semble traduire le texte de N[25] plutôt que celui de N[26]: Mt 4,24 «Besessene» (p. 178), cf. N[26] [καὶ] δαιμονιζο-
μένους (voir Mc 1,32!); Mt 6,33 «nach dem Reich und seiner Gerechtigkeit»
(p. 364, n. 4: «das attributlose βασιλεία»), cf. N[26] βαλιλείαν [τοῦ θεοῦ].

En critique littéraire, L. défend la théorie classique des deux sources. En ce
qui concerne l'ordre (marcien) des péricopes, il adopte une position qui est pratiquement identique à celle exposée ici dans *ETL* 1967 (= *Evangelica*, 20-34).
J'ai plus de réserves à propos de l'hypothèse des «recensions», d'abord dans la
triple tradition, où, à cause des accords mineurs, l'on devrait accepter que Matthieu et Luc ont connu Marc dans une recension «die an manchen Punkten
gegenüber unserem Mk sekundär ist» (p. 30), et puis dans la double tradition,
où des différences entre Matthieu et Luc devraient s'expliquer par l'existence
des l recensions QMt et QLc (p. 29). Il n'est pas encore clair dans quelle mesure
le commentateur aura recours à l'hypothèse d'une recension de Marc. Dans le
premier tome, des accords mineurs sont signalés dans les notices sur le Baptiste
(3,5 πᾶσα ἡ περίχωρος τοῦ Ἰορδάνου), le baptême de Jésus (3,16
βαπτισθείς, Ἰησοῦς, ἠνεῴχθησαν, ἐπ') et la venue à Nazareth (4,13
Ναζαρά), chaque fois pour suggérer l'existence possible d'un récit parallèle
dans Q (p. 143, n. 1; 151, n. 2; 168). L. attribue à QMt les versets de Mt 5,5.7-
9.14b.41 (p. 291: peut-être omis par Luc); 6,23d(?).34; 7,2a (p. 376). 7,6 (p.
355 et 382!), et à QLc les versets de Lc 6,24-25.37b-38b. Il est moins clair sur
Lc 6,39.40/Mt 15,14; 10,24-25: «es gibt m. E. keinen sicheren Anhaltspunkt
dafür, daß Mt sie in seinem Q-Exemplar gelesen hat» (p. 376). Il se montre
sceptique également à l'égard de Mt 6,9-13/Lc 11,2-4 et Mt 7,7-11/Lc 11,9-13:
attribution à Q «moins certaine» (p. 187, n. 6); dans le commentaire même, il

ne parle pas de Q à propos du Pater, mais il traite Mt 7,7-11 tout simplement comme un «Q-Text» (p. 383). Il est plus formel en ce qui concerne Mt 5,18/Lc 16,17 (p. 229); Mt 5,32/Lc 16,18 (p. 269); Mt 6,24/Lc 16,13 (voir cependant p. 354: ?): «ganz unsicher bis unwahrscheinlich» (p. 187, n. 6). Par contre, Mt 5,29-30, sans parallèle aucun dans Luc, serait «vielleicht aus Q» (p. 261). Ce sont là des points pour le moins fort discutables. Voir, par exemple, *Evangelica*, 817-819 (Mt 5,29-30); 824-829 (Lc 16,18).

Ce n'est pas la source Q qui est la première source du Sermon sur la Montagne mais une source écrite propre à Matthieu: 5,21-24.27-28.33-37; 6,2-6.16-18, c.-à-d. une combinaison traditionnelle des trois antithèses dites primaires et des trois règles sur l'aumône, la prière et le jeûne. Voir, avec différents degrés d'affirmation, p. 31 («?»), 187 («wahrscheinlich»), 245 («vielleicht»), 321 («denkbar»). Quant au *Sondergut* de Mt 1-2, la généalogie en 1,2-17 serait traditionnelle (p. 91: «wahrscheinlich»), tandis que les récits de 1,18-25 et 2,1-12.13-23 remontent à un cycle oral mis en écrit par Matthieu. Voir surtout à propos de 1,18-25: «Daß diese Geschichte [von der Namengebung] zu einem vormatthäischen mündlichen Erzählungskranz gehörte, in dem Josef eine zentrale Rolle spielte, ist wahrscheinlich» (p. 101; cf. 113, 126). Matthieu aurait ajouté 1,18a.22-23 et 2,22-23, mais les citations de 2,5-6.15.17-18 lui seraient parvenues dans le contexte du récit traditionnel.

L. tient compte de la correspondance entre Mt 3,1-4,22l7,28b-29 et Mc 1,1-20l22 et situe correctement le Sermon sur la Montagne en parallèle à Mc 1,21 (p. 197, 415). Cf. *ETL* 1976 (= *Evangelica*, 729-736). Il est moins convaincant lorsqu'il découvre des traces de Q dans Mt 3,5.16; 4,13 (cf. *supra*) ou suggère l'utilisation de «traditions» en 3,14 (questions du Baptiste); 4,13 (Capharnaüm) et 4,15-16 (citation). À l'intérieur du Sermon sur la Montagne, L. tient Mt 5,31-32 pour «ein Musterbeispiel für völlig traditionsbezogene Redaktion!» (p. 269). Il y admet une influence de Mc 10,2-9 sur la formulation du v. 31. D'autres réminiscences de Marc auraient pu être notées: Mc 9,43.47 (Mt 5,29-30: cf. *supra*), mais également Mc 9,38-39 (Mt 7,22); Mc 9,49-50 (Mt 5,13 ἁλισθήσεται); Mc 4,24 (Mt 7,2b ἐν ᾧ); et surtout Mc 11,25 (Mt 6,14: cf. J. Schlosser, dans Mélanges J. Dupont, 1985, p. 292).

«Matthäus war ein konservativer Autor» (p. 382). C'est un thème majeur du commentaire de L.: «kein 'freier' Schriftsteller», «ein traditionsorientierter Evangelist», «der konservative Evangelist». Cette insistance nous rappelle le commentaire de R. Pesch sur l'évangile de Marc. Dans la mesure où L. souligne l ainsi la fidélité de Matthieu à ses sources dans l'utilisation de Marc et Q, on ne peut qu'applaudir notre commentateur. Il est beaucoup moins certain qu'on puisse en faire une règle pour l'interprétation du *Sondergut* matthéen. L. le reconnaît: «Wenn eine Überlieferung vom Evangelisten zum ersten Mal verschriftlicht worden ist, sind die Chancen, über die Überlieferungsgeschichte noch einigermaßen Sicheres sagen zu können, von vornherein gering» (p. 114). La *Verschriftlichung* matthéenne devrait rendre compte des traits matthéens dans 1,18-2,23 (p. 100, n.8; 113, n.4; 120, n.3), et la même solution est annoncée déjà dans l'Introduction pour des récits insérés dans le contexte marcien (p. 31: Mt 17,24-27; 27,3-10). L. admet la présence de caractéristiques matthéennes dans la triade de 6,2-4.5-6.16-18 (p. 321, n. 10) mais il la considère néanmoins comme une source écrite. Il la traite même avec une certaine déférence, car la troisième strophe (6,16-18) est le seul texte pour lequel le commentaire ne suit pas l'ordre de l'évangile (p. 319). J'ai le sentiment que L. sous-estime quelque peu l'importance des matthéanismes dans 6,1-18. Une répartition entre communauté matthéenne et rédaction matthéenne peut donner l'impression d'une exégèse à la carte. L. signale le point de vue de Gundry à propos de ce texte (p. 321, n. 10), mais au lieu de dire que selon Gundry «Mt ihn verschriftlicht habe», il fallait parler de «composition» matthéenne. En ce qui concerne les antithèses en 5,21-24.27-28.33-37, la parole originelle sur les serments devrait être reconstituée à l'aide de Mt 5,34-35.37a et Jc 5,12; la forme antithétique y serait introduite d'après 5,21-22 et 27-28, les deux anti-thèses dont L. admet qu'elles peuvent remonter à Jésus. L. écarte l'hypothèse rédactionnelle comme «la moins probable» (p. 246). Il rejette un peu vite, me semble-t-il, le parallèle de 19,9 (n. 8).

Le premier problème que L. aborde dans l'Introduction est celui de la struc-ture de l'évangile. Il a raison de rappeler «daß man nicht bei der Strukturanalyse diachrone Fragen ausklammern kann» (p. 16). J'approuve pleinement sa cri-tique des hypothèses des cinq livrets, de la structure concentrique et de la divi-sion en deux parties (4,17ss.; 16,21ss.). Cf. *ETL* 1967. On notera surtout son opposition à la dernière théorie prônée maintenant par J. Kingsbury et autres. Il fait commencer la première partie (4,23-11,30) avec le sommaire de 4,23-25 (cf. p. 178, n. 2: «Eigentlich müßte man 4,23-5,2 als *eine* Perikope fassen») et pro-pose une division des chapitres 12-20 à 16,12/13 (p. 25). Je voudrais y appor-ter une correction et situer à 4,12 la césure entre le prologue et le corps de l'évangile. Il est vrai que ἀπὸ τότε relie 4,17 avec 4,12-16 mais c'est précisé-ment une des raisons pour considérer 4,12-17 comme une péricope d'ouverture. — Dans le Sermon sur la Montagne, L. distingue trois sections, entourées de 5,17-20 et 7,12, dans une construction concentrique autour du Pater:

(5,17-20) 5,21-48 I 6,1-6.7-*15*.16-18 I 6,19-7,11 (7,12).

On se mettra assez facilement d'accord sur la délimitation des trois unités, mais on peut avoir des doutes sur la correspondance entre 5,21-48 et 6,19-7,11 (56 lignes de Nestle).

L'étude des caractéristiques de vocabulaire et de style est un des aspects les plus soignés du Commentaire, dans les notes sur la rédaction matthéenne au début de chaque section et surtout dans l'Introduction générale (p. 31-56). Elle comporte une double liste de *Vorzugsvokabular* et de *zurücktretende Wörter*. Pour dresser ce dernier catalogue (p. 54-55: 38 mots), L. a pu se servir entre autres de notre ouvrage sur *The Minor Agreements* (1974). C'est surtout le *Vorzugsvokabular* qui retiendra l'attention (p. 35-53). Les listes antérieures de I Goulder (1974) et de Gundry (1982) contiennent, dit-il, trop de mots qui ne sont pas vraiment significatifs. La nouvelle liste qu'il propose compte environ 400 entrées dont quelque 300 se trouvent déjà dans la liste de Gundry; une dizaine d'autres mots sont cités par Goulder. L. ajoute des mots comme κατα-δικάζω (2 réd.) et παρέρχομαι (9 fois; 3 réd.), mais la plupart des nouveau-tés sont des emplois spécifiques. Ainsi, par exemple, il reprend ὅστις (29 fois; 18 réd.) et ajoute ὅστις = ὅς (6 réd.) et πᾶς ὅστις (3 réd.); voir ἀπέρχομαι: ἀπελθών (12 fois; 4 réd.; γινώσκω: γνούς (4 fois; 3 réd.); ποιέω: ποιέω ὡς/καθώς (4 réd.), etc. Le nombre des emplois rédactionnels est une estima-tion provisoire qui devra se confirmer dans le commentaire même. Pour cer-tains mots, le nombre des occurrences est à corriger (cf. *ETL* 62, 1986, p. 139, n. 3).

Un mot encore sur la réception de Matthieu dans le christianisme primitif, la plus ancienne *Wirkungsgeschichte*. À propos des Pères apostoliques, L. renvoie à la dissertation de W.D. Köhler (dans la ligne de Massaux: voir la citation dans *ETL* 62, 1986, p. 402-403). En outre, L. tient compte de la possibilité que la *1ᵃ Petri* puisse fournir un premier témoignage de l'évangile de Matthieu (p. 76; 215, n. 117; 220, n. 8).

ETL 67 (1991) 169-171

Ulrich Luz. *Das Evangelium nach Matthäus. 2. Teilband: Mt 8–17* (Evangelisch-Katholischer Kommentar zum Neuen Testament, I/2.) Zürich, Benziger Verlag; Neukirchen-Vluyn, Neukirchener Verlag, 1990. XIII-537 p.

J'ai pu présenter dans *ETL* 63 (1987) 410-413 le premier tome du commentaire, publié en 1985 (²1989), et entre-temps déjà traduit en anglais: *Matthew 1–7: A Commentary*, Minneapolis, Augsburg, 1989. Pour ne pas oublier l'essentiel, notons tout d'abord les quatre excursus dans ce deuxième tome, sur le Fils de David (59-61), les paraboles (366-375), Pierre (467-472), et le Fils de l'homme (497-593), et surtout les notes, parfois fort longues, sur la *Wirkungsgeschichte*. Trois sont signalées dans la Table des matières: «Zur Bedeutung ... heute», à propos de *Wundergeschichten* (68-73), *Jüngerrede* (156-161), *Gleichnisrede* (376-380), mais presque chaque section du commentaire aboutit sur la *Wirkungsgeschichte*. Voir plus spécialement les dix pages à propos de Mt 16,17-19 (472-483): ce fut le thème de la conférence de Luz au Congrès de la SNTS à Milan en juillet 1990: «Mt 16,17-19 in wirkungsgeschichtlicher Sicht». Je resterai cependant dans la ligne de mon premier compte rendu et je me concentrerai ici sur la critique littéraire.

| Les chapitres 8–17 de Matthieu contiennent une très large part de matière marcienne. À quelques exceptions près, l'ensemble de Mc 1,29–9,33 (et 10,46-52; 13,9-13) y est repris dans une rédaction matthéenne. Si je devais encore écrire en 1987: «Il n'est pas encore clair dans quelle mesure le commentateur aura recours à l'hypothèse d'une recension de Marc» (411), nous sommes maintenant fixés sur ce sujet. Les accords mineurs retiennent particulièrement l'attention du commentateur, dans le texte et surtout dans les notes: pp. 8-9[2-4], 18[3], 22[9], 31[3], 36[7], 41, 51-52[7], 58[4], 83[6], 228-229[8-15], 237[3], 254-255[12.22], 286[3], 296[3], 301-302[6.10-11.19-22], 327[5], 384[6], 389[4], 396[7-8], 453[10], 487[6], 506[9-11], 519-520[5-14]. Un bon nombre de ces accords peuvent s'expliquer par la rédaction indépendante de Matthieu et de Luc, mais déjà à propos de la première péricope (Mt 8,1-4; par. Mc 1,40-45) on peut lire: «Die Häufigkeit solcher 'unabhängiger' Verbesserungen ... macht diese These problematisch» (9[4]); et un peu plus loin à propos de Mt 9,1-8 (Mc 2,1-12): «Auffällig bleibt die große Zahl der MA in unserem Text» (36[7]). Le mot qui revient le plus souvent est «zahlreich» («überaus zahlreich», «überhaupt sehr zahlreich», «allerdings so zahlreich»). Certains cas individuels sont notés comme difficilement explicables, spécialement du côté de

la rédaction lucanienne (!): 8,2 om. ὅτι (!), 3 om. σπλαγχνισθείς; 9,2 ἐπὶ κλίνης (!), εἶπεν, 4 εἶπεν, 6 ἐπὶ τῆς γῆς / ἀφιέναι ἁμαρτίας, τὴν κλίνην; 9,16 ἐπιβάλλει, 17 γε, ἐκχεῖται; 12,3 εἶπεν, om. οὐδέποτε, om. χρείαν ἔσχεν, 4 μόνοις, v. 7 om. Mk 2,27; 12,47 ἑστήκασιν (!), 48 ὁ δὲ ἀποκριθεὶς εἶπεν (!); 13,3 om. ἀκούετε, 4 om. ἐγένετο (!); 13,10 μαθηταί, 11 δέδοται γνῶναι τὰ μυστήρια, 13 om. τὰ πάντα γίνεται, om. μήποτε ...; 13,18 om. οὐκ οἴδατε ... καὶ πῶς πάσας τὰς παραβολὰς γνώσεσθε, 19 ἐν τῇ καρδίᾳ αὐτοῦ, 23 οὗτος (!); 8,25 om. οὐ μέλει σοι, 26 om. ἐκόπασεν ὁ ἄνεμος, 27 οἱ ἄνεμοι plur. (!); 9,20 προσελθοῦσα, τοῦ κρασπέδου (!), 23 ἐλθὼν ... εἰς τὴν οἰκίαν (!), v. 26 par. Lk 4,14b; 14,13 om. Mk 6,31, οἱ ὄχλοι ἠκολούθησαν αὐτῷ (!), 14 ἐθεράπευσεν, 15 βρώματα, 17 οὐκ ἔχομεν ..., 19 συμπόσια συμπόσια, om. καὶ τοὺς δύο ἰχθύας ἐμέρισεν πᾶσιν (20 om. καὶ ἀπὸ τῶν ἰχθύων), 20 τὸ περισσεῦον; 16,21 ἀπό, τῇ τρίτῃ ἡμέρᾳ ἐγερθῆναι (!); 17,1 om. τόν, om. μόνους, 2 τὸ πρόσωπον αὐτοῦ, om. στίλβοντα, om. οἷα γναφεὺς ἐπὶ τῆς γῆς οὐ δύναται οὕτως λευκᾶναι, 3 Μωϋσῆς / καὶ Ἠλίας, 5 ἔτι αὐτοῦ λαλοῦντος, ἐπεσκίασεν αὐτούς, 6 ἐφοβήθησαν; 17,16 ἠδυνήθησαν (!), 17 ἀποκριθεὶς δὲ ὁ Ἰησοῦς εἶπεν, καὶ διεστραμμένη, om. Mk 9,23-24. Luz y voit «die deutliche Hinweise für die Existenz einer deuteromk Rezension» (52). Il renvoie fréquemment à la dissertation de A. Ennulat (Bern, 1990), qui préconise cette solution du problème des accords mineurs. Luz se sépare expressément de A. Fuchs (254¹²) et de F. Kogler (327⁵) en admettant une variante de Mc 3,22-27 et de 4,30-32 dans la source Q. Même la solution de Ennulat ne le satisfait pas toujours (302¹⁹, 384⁶, 520¹⁶). Il se prononce parfois avec beaucoup de réserve, et finalement l'indécision semble devenir systématique: «Eine Entscheidung [à propos de Mt 17,14-20] ist mir nicht möglich und vielleicht auch nicht nötig. Man kann z.B. einen redigierten Mk-Text *und* Einfluß mündlicher Tradition annehmen. Jedenfalls hat Mt selbst am Text auch intensiv gearbeitet» (520). Autre exemple: le récit de la transfiguration, où une recension dite *dmk* «nicht ausgeschlossen scheint. Sicherheit ist aber nicht zu gewinnen» (506). Cette modestie ne manque pas de charme, mais elle s'appuie, au moins dans ce commentaire, sur une série de déclarations telles que «kaum erklärbar», «nicht lukanisch», etc., sans examen plus fouillé de la rédaction lucanienne.

| Luz reconnaît dans plusieurs cas que, du côté de Matthieu, il peut s'agir de rédaction indépendante («unabhängige Redaktion des Mk durch Mt»), à commencer par l'omission de ὅτι en 8,2: «Sie entspricht mt, nicht aber unbedingt lk Sprachgebrauch» (p. 9, n. 4). Par contre, l'omission de σπλαγχνισθείς reste «ganz unverständlich» (cf. 9,36). Mais sans faire appel à la leçon ὀργισθείς en Mc 1,41 (n. 5: «Textkritisch unwahrscheinlich!»), on peut se demander si les formules lapidaires sont la façon appropriée de traiter ce problème. Dans le même récit, ἐμβριμησάμενος αὐτῷ est également omis par Matthieu et Luc, mais Luz sait parfaitement que sa présence dans Mc 1,43 est attestée par ἐνεβριμήθη αὐτοῖς en Mt 9,30. Il dira sans doute que σπλαγχνισθείς n'a précisément pas de parallèle dans Mt 9,27-31. Mais cet argument est pour le moins ambigu. Le récit des deux aveugles est un doublet rédactionnel de Mt 20,29-34 (Mc 10,46-52), où un σπλαγχνισθείς ajouté par Matthieu (v. 34) répond aux cris répétés des aveugles, ἐλέησον ἡμᾶς, κύριε, υἱὸς Δαυίδ (vv. 30.31, cf. Mc). Comparer, dans la parabole propre à Matthieu en 18,23-35, σπλαγχνισθείς au v. 27 et ἐλεῆσαι ... ὡς κἀγὼ σὲ ἠλέησα au v. 33. La prière des aveugles est la

même en 9,27 (ἐλέησον ἡμᾶς υἱὸς Δαυίδ), mais σπλαγχνισθείς n'y apparaît pas. L'argument du silence est délicat à manier. Luz renvoie à Mt 9,36, mais on peut en tirer aussi autre leçon. L'emploi de ἐσπλαγχνίσθη y est une reprise de Mc 6,34, où la phrase ὅτι ἦσαν ὡς πρόβατα μὴ ἔχοντα ποιμένα est omise dans le texte parallèle de Matthieu et de Luc: «Den mk Vergleich ... brachte Mt bereits in 9,36» (p. 396; cf. p. 77: rayer le point d'interrogation).

À propos de la structure de l'évangile, j'avais écrit en 1987 (p. 412) que j'approuve pleinement sa critique de la division en deux parties (4,17ss.; 16,21ss.): voir tome I, p. 25 (la division de Mt 12–20 à 16,12/13), p. 168 (son analyse de 4,17), et surtout les notes aux pp. 18 (n. 12) et 19 (n. 15). J'invite le lecteur à confronter ces pages avec la division proposée dans le tome II: (I) 1,1–4,22; (II) 4,23–11,30; (III) 12,1–16,20; (IV) 16,21–20,34; (V) 21–25; (VI) 26–28 (voir p. 485, à propos de 16,21: «Ich folge damit dem heute am verbreitesten 'narrativen' Gliederungsmodell des Mt-Ev»). Il modifie le modèle de Kingsbury (et Bauer) en repoussant l'unité de la seconde moitié de l'évangile (16,21–28,20) et l'idée du titre en 16,21a. Je me suis expliqué *in extenso* sur ce problème dans *ETL* 64 (1988) 21-59 et je me contente ici de renvoyer le lecteur à cet article. Je tiens cependant à noter cette phrase de Luz: «Der Übergang zum neuen Hauptabschnitt erfolgt nicht durch eine Zäsur» (p. 485). En effet, ce qu'il écrit sur le lien entre 16,13-20 et 16,21-28 (p. 453) et sur le rôle de Pierre (p. 485) est de nature à confirmer la division à Mt 16,12/13 qu'il proposa encore dans le tome I.

En ce qui concerne la source Q, on notera la possibilité d'une recension de Q^Mt en Mt 10,5-6 (p. 88) et 10,34-36 (p. 134). L'appartenance à Q est douteuse pour les logia de Lc 6,39-40 (pp. 119, 417: Mt 10,24-25,14); une reconstruction du texte de Q n'est guère possible pour Mt 11,12-13 / Lc 16,16 (p. 172). Mt 16,2b-3 est une glose secondaire (p. 444). Il se sépare de M. Sato à propos de Lc 17,1-6: «dürfte ein Q-Zusammenhang sein» (p. 520 n. 15). Cf. *ETL* 66 (1990) 385-390.

ETL 71 (1995) 166-175

17

URMARCUS RÉVISÉ

La théorie synoptique de M.-É. Boismard nouvelle manière

«... nous nous sommes aperçu que les influences lucaniennes sur l'évangile de Mc étaient beaucoup plus importantes que nous l'avions soupçonné dans notre commentaire sur les évangiles synoptiques, à une époque où nous étions encore trop influencé par la théorie des Deux Sources (et oui!). D'où une importance nettement plus considérable que nous donnerions maintenant à l'activité du Rédacteur marco-lucanien.» C'est par ces mots que M.-É. Boismard présente au lecteur l'essentiel de la thèse qu'il développe dans son nouveau volume sur l'évangile de Marc[1].

1. *Le proto-Marc*

Le Rédacteur marco-lucanien a gardé son nom, mais le Mc-intermédiaire reçoit maintenant le nom plus commun de proto-Marc. Avec le nom, il semble avoir perdu sa fonction d'intermédiaire. Dans cette «préhistoire» de l'évangile de Marc, il est fort peu question des sources évangéliques A, B et C. La différence entre le proto-Marc et le Document B «tend à s'estomper au point que l'on pourrait se demander s'il faut encore les distinguer» (8). Le Mc-intermédiaire devenu proto-Marc se voit réduit au rôle de précurseur: ἐκεῖνον δεῖ αὐξάνειν... Il est en effet fort diminué et même décapité: «il nous paraît certain que le proto-Marc ne contenait pas les récits de la passion et de la résurrection» (241). Mc 14,26–16,8 appartient entièrement au Rédacteur marco-lucanien et celui-ci se voit même coiffé de la conclusion longue (16,9-20): «il ne fait aucun doute que cette finale de Mc ... fut rédigée par le Rédacteur marco-lucanien, comme les récits de la passion et de la découverte du tombeau vide» (241).

En conclusion de l'ouvrage, le texte du proto-Marc tel que Boismard a cru pouvoir le reconstituer est cité en grec (243-259) et en traduction française (261-275). En voici les références[2]:

1. M.-É. Boismard, *L'évangile de Marc: sa préhistoire* (Études Bibliques, n.s., 26), Paris, Gabalda, 1994, 308 p. – Le commentaire auquel il renvoie dans la citation (*Avant-propos*, p. 8) est celui de la *Synopse des quatre évangiles en français*, t. II, Paris, 1972.
2. La délimitation des péricopes est celle de Boismard (voir particulièrement 1,14; 10,1; 11,17; 12,28; 14,10). J'ai précisé, ou corrigé, les références 1,34; 2,17; 6,2; 6,45.48; 8,14.18.29; 14,12.

1,4a.5-6 9-11 12.13b 14a.16a.19b-20 21-22a.27b.23-26.27a.c 29a.30-31
32b.34 35-38 39 40a.41a.43 **2**,1a.3.5.11-12 15-17a 23-26a **3**,1.3a.5b 13-19
22a.23a.28-29 32-33a.35 **4**,1a.2b.3-9 30-31a.32b.d 35-41 **5**,1.2b-3a.5b-
8.13b.18-19a.20 22-25.27-29.38a.40b-43a **6**,1-2c.6b 7-9a.10-11.12-13³
14a.16b 32-33.34c-44 45a-b.47-48c.51-52 53-56 **7**,24a.25.26b.29-30 31a.32-
37 **8**,11-13 14a.16-18a 22-26 27a.29.30 31 34-38 **9**,1 2-10 14.16-17.25-27
30-31 33-35 **10**,1.13.14b.15-16 | 23a.24c.24a.26b-27 46-47.51-52 **11**,1-
4a.6b.7-8a.9a.10a 11a.17a;**12**,1b-5a.6.8-9.12 18-24a.25.27b.28a.32a.34b
13,1-2.3b.4-8.24-27.33 **14**,1.10 12a.13-16 17-18a.22b-24a.25.

En contraste frappant avec le Mc-intermédiaire dans *Synopse II* (cf.
Introduction, 17-23), le présent ouvrage ne contient aucune description
des caractéristiques du proto-Marc. Seulement en appendice Boismard
présente une liste de ˙parallèles qui se lisent dans le proto-Marc (277-
290). Il imprime cette liste sous le titre "Les deux documents". Est-ce
pour rappeler les deux sources du Mc-intermédiaire, les Documents A et
B?

(1)	1,21-22.27b / 6,1-2	Cf. *Synopse II*: B/A
(2)	1,23-26 / 5,1.2b.3a.6-8.13b; 1,25.27 / 4,39-41	
(3)	1,39 / 6,6b	B/A
(4)	3,13-15 / 6,7	B/A
(5)	6,8-9a.12-13 / 6,10-11	
(6)	˙6,32a.33a.d.34c / 6,32a.33b.c	A/B
(7)	6,35-44 / (8,1-9)	A/B
(8)	6,45.47-48.51 / (8,10) 4,35-37.39.41a	
(9)	6,52 / 8,14a.16-18a	
(10)	6,53-56 / 6,(32).33b.c; (1,32); 5,28	
(11)	9,30-31 / 8,31	A/B*
(12)	10,23a.24c.24a.26b-27 / 10,23a.(23b).(25)	B/A

Les parenthèses signalent des fragments du texte du Rédacteur marco-
lucanien qui sont inclus dans ce tableau[4]. Le cas de 8,1-9 (n° 7) est assez
particulier: le récit a été omis par le proto-Marc, mais il doit l'avoir
connu puisqu'il en a inséré un fragment dans le premier récit de multiplication des pains: 6,37b-38 (cf. 8,4-5)[5]. Dans la reconstruction du texte
du proto-Marc (283), Mc 6,37b-38 est remplacé par Mt 14,17-18.

---

3. Dans le proto-Marc, Mc 6,10-11.12-13 se lisait aussitôt après 3,14-15 (pp. 90 et
113). À la page 281, on corrigera les références 6,10-13; 6,8-9 en 6,8-9a.12-13 et 6,10-
11.

4. Voir n° 10; ajouter les parenthèses aux n°ˢ 8 et 12. Les indications globales de péricopes ont été remplacées par des références plus précises.

5. Cf. *Synopse II*, p. 223.

2. *Le Rédacteur marco-lucanien*

«Le proto-Marc» figure comme titre courant dans l'ouvrage (47-275), mais c'est avant tout sur l'activité du Rédacteur marco-lucanien que se porte l'attention de Boismard. Il lui consacre son premier chapitre: «Position du problème» (13-46). Il y expose ses vues sur la rédaction à l'aide de quelques exemples (cf. 13: «nous allons prouver notre thèse...»!): la présence de «lucanismes» dans le texte de Marc (16,9-20; 15,16-20; la formule ἐγένετο; les liaisons par δέ); des récits d'origine lucanienne (1,4b; 12,41-44); deux récits qui mettent en évidence les influences matthéennes (5,1-20; 9,14-27) et «un texte de synthèse»: la fusion d'un texte de tradition matthéenne avec un texte de tradition lucanienne (3,7-12).

Voici la liste des additions du Rédacteur dans le premier chapitre de Mc: **1**,1.2-3.4b.7-8 13a 14b-15 16b-19a 22b.28 29b 32a$^\beta$.33 40b.41b-42.44.45. Pour le reste de l'évangile, je me contente de citer ici les péricopes ajoutées par le Rédacteur[6]: **2**,13-14.18-22; **3**,7-12.20-21.23b-27; **4**,1b-2a.10-12.13-20.21-25.26-29.33-34; I **6**,2b-6a.17-29.30-31; **7**,1-23; **8**,1-10; **9**,11-13.38-41.42-50; **10**,2-12.17-22.28-31.32-34.35-45; **11**,11b-16.17b-25.27-33; **12**,13-17.28b-34a.35-37a.37b-40.41-44; **13**,9-23.28-32.34-37; **14**,3-9.18b-22a; **14**,26–**16**,8; **16**,9-20.

Il est à noter que par «l'influence de traditions matthéenne et lucanienne» Boismard entend parler d'influences qui se sont exercées à partir d'un proto-Matthieu et d'un proto-Luc qui, à côté du proto-Marc, sont les principales sources du Rédacteur. Mc 8,1-10 est un cas exceptionnel où il utilise une source que le proto-Marc a dû connaître. Le Rédacteur ne semble pas avoir eu un accès direct à la source Q.

3. *La source Q*

Dans certains cas d'insertion matthéenne (ou lucanienne), il s'agit d'un texte que Boismard fait remonter à la source Q: 7,1-23 (131); 8,15 (138); 10,17-19 (153); 10,21 (154); 10,28-31 (155); 12,28-34 (176-177); 12,38-40 (181; cf. Lc 20,45-47); 13,15-16 (183). Quant à Mc 8,15 (Mt 16,6; Lc 12,1b); Mc 12,28-34 (Mt 22,34-40; Lc 10,25-28); Mc 13,15-16 (Mt 24,17-18; Lc 17,31), je me permets de renvoyer le lecteur à un examen récent du problème de leur appartenance à Q[7]. Dans quatre

---

6. À l'aide du contenu du proto-Marc (voir la liste ci-dessus, pp. 174-175), l'on peut se faire une idée des additions à l'intérieur des péricopes.

7. F. NEIRYNCK, *The Minor Agreements and Q*, in R.A. PIPER (ed.), *The Gospel Behind the Gospels* (NTSup, 75), Leiden, 1995, pp. 49-72, esp. 54-56 (Lc 17,31), 60-61

cas, le rapprochement du parallèle matthéen avec un passage lucanien est trop aventureux pour être pris en considération: 7,1-23 (Lc 11,37-38)[8]; 10,17-19 (Lc 10,25-28)[9]; 10,21 (Lc 12,33); 10,28-31 (Lc 14,25-26). Un seul de ces cas est largement admis comme un doublet de Mc et Q: Mc 12,38-39 et Q 11,43, mais selon Boismard c'est «un doublet fantôme» (180). Le texte de Q (Mt 23,6-7a; Lc 11,43) serait repris et amplifié par le proto-Luc (Lc 20,45-47), et du proto-Luc, il serait passé dans le Mc actuel grâce au Rédacteur marco-lucanien: «Il ne s'agit plus d'un doublet, mais d'une seule et unique tradition (Q)» (181)[10]. On se demande pourquoi la fusion de traditions parallèles serait propre au Rédacteur marco-lucanien et refusé au Rédacteur lucano-lucanien. Lc 20,45 en serait un bel exemple: θελόντων (= Mc) et φιλούντων (= Q).

Boismard tient à rappeler que sur un point «qui n'affecte pas l'évangile de Marc» il a modifié sa théorie: «Lorsque les textes de Mt/Lc sont très differenciés, nous pensons qu'ils proviennent effectivement de la source Q (exemple: Mt 25,14-30 / Lc 19,12-27). Mais lorsqu'ils sont quasi identiques, leur caractère lucanien nous semble certain et nous pensons qu'ils proviennent de la tradition | lucanienne (proto-Lc) d'où ils seraient passés dans l'ultime rédaction matthéenne (exemple: Mt 3,7b-10 / Lc 3,7-9)» (8[-9] n. 3)[11]. Cette nouvelle théorie fut lancée par Boismard en 1984 et je crois lui avoir répondu[12]. Ma réponse reste toujours valable.

4. À l'abri de la critique?

À propos de «bien des remarques faites par Neirynck», on peut lire chez Boismard: «il s'appuie sur la distinction que nous avons faite entre

(Lc 12,1b), 61-64 (Lc 10,25-28). Voir aussi *The Minor Agreements and Lk 10,25-28*, in *ETL* 71 (1995) 151-160, nn. 8 et 44.

8. Un rapport de dépendance de Lc 11,37-39 vis-à-vis de Mc 7,1-2.5 est sans doute plus probable.

9. Sur la dépendance de Lc 10,25 vis-à-vis de Mc 10,17, cf. F. NEIRYNCK, *Luke 10:25-28: A Foreign Body in Luke?*, in S.E. PORTER, P. JOYCE and D.E. ORTON (eds.), *Crossing the Boundaries*. FS M.D. Goulder (Biblical Interpretation Series, 8), Leiden, 1994, pp. 149-165, esp. 158-159.

10. En fait, c'est la même solution, «une seule et unique tradition (Q)», qu'il propose à propos de Mc 12,28-34: Matthieu et Luc tiennent cet épisode de la source Q et c'est de la tradition matthéenne qu'il est passé dans Mc (177). Voir n. 9. Les seuls éléments de Mc 12,28-34 qu'il attribue au proto-Marc sont vv. 28a.32a.34b (177). On corrigera les indications à propos des vv. 28b (συζητεῖν) et 34a (le scribe félicité par Jésus) (38).

11. Cf. «Les sections communes à Mt/Lc», in D.L. DUNGAN (ed.), *The Interrelations of the Gospels. A Symposium Led by M.-É. Boismard – W.R. Farmer – F. Neirynck, Jerusalem 1984* (BETL, 95), Leuven, 1990, pp. 267-274. Cf. above, 282.

12. «A New Debate: Q or Proto-Luke», in *Interrelations* (n. 11), pp. 108-114.

Mt-intermédiaire et ultime rédaction matthéenne. Mais notre argumentation garde toute sa valeur dans la perspective de la théorie des Deux Sources, qui ne fait pas une telle distinction» (41[-42] n. 1). Et encore: «Nous avons renoncé ... à reprendre en détail toutes ces discussions ..., parce que notre façon d'envisager le problème synoptique n'est plus exactement ce qu'elle était lors de la composition de ce volume [*Synopse II*]» (12).

De quoi s'agit-il? Aux Journées Bibliques de Louvain, le 1er septembre 1971, Boismard a présenté sa théorie synoptique dans une conférence intitulée «Influences matthéennes sur l'ultime rédaction de l'évangile de Marc»[13]. La conférence fut suivie d'un séminaire consacré à «Marc et le problème synoptique». Après la publication de *Synopse II* (1972), j'ai donné un prolongement à nos discussions de 1971 dans l'article «Urmarcus Redivivus? Examen critique de l'hypothèse des insertions matthéennes dans Marc»[14]. Dans *Synopse II*, des insertions matthéennes sont notées aux endroits que voici: Mc 1,2-3*.5.8.15.32.40-45; 2,10.19b.28; 3,6.7-8*; 4,8.11.16.18.20.24b; 6,2b-6a; 7,9-13*.22; 8,27a.37; 9,22.41; 10,2.6-8a.11; 11,25*; 12,18.23.28-31; 13,11; 14,13.47.54; 15,3-5.41[15]. Ma réaction s'est concentrée sur Mc 1,2-3; 8,27a; 13,11; le récit de la passion (14,13.47.54; 15,3-5) et les sommaires de 1,32-34 et 3,7-12. Je reprends ici quelques phrases de la conclusion de l'article[16]:

> Ces insertions matthéennes semblent jouer un rôle capital dans la théorie synoptique de M.-É. Boismard. Elles doivent fonder l'hypothèse du double niveau rédactionnel de Mc (n. 214).
>
> Dans plusieurs cas, l'argument de la statistique du vocabulaire a pu être corrigé et nuancé à partir de l'exégèse des passages parallèles que défend l'auteur lui-même.
>
> Plus spécialement, dans le jugement sur le style matthéen, il se base souvent sur un nombre total des emplois dans l'évangile, sans trop se préoccuper du sens du mot, ni surtout de la distinction entre tradition et rédaction. La chose est particulièrement délicate quand le mot 'matthéen' devient

---

13. Cf. M. SABBE (éd.), *L'évangile de Marc. Tradition et rédaction* (BETL, 34), Leuven, 1974, ²1988, pp. 93-102.

14. «*Urmarcus Redivivus*», in *L'évangile de Marc* (n. 13), pp. 103-145; repris dans F. NEIRYNCK, *Jean et les Synoptiques. Examen critique de l'exégèse de M.-É. Boismard* (BETL, 49), Leuven, 1979, pp. 319-361.

15. L'astérisque marque les passages discutés dans *Influences matthéennes* (n. 13). On observera que la plupart de ces insertions matthéennes ont gardé le même statut littéraire en 1994. J'ai noté quelques exceptions, non signalées comme telles par Boismard: 1,5 ἐν τῷ Ἰορδάνῃ ποταμῷ, ἐξομολογούμενοι τὰς ἁμαρτίας αὐτῶν (cf. p. 23); 1,43 ἐμβριμησάμενος; 4,8 καὶ ἐδίδου καρπόν, καὶ ἓν ἐν ἑξήκοντα καὶ ἐν ἑκατόν; 8,27a Καισαρείας τῆς Φιλίππου; 8,37(?); 12,18 verset; 14,13 ὑπάγετε εἰς τὴν πόλιν. Il attribue maintenant les six (ou sept) textes au proto-Marc.

16. *Urmarcus Redivivus* (n. 14), pp. 144, 145 (= 360, 361).

indice d'insertion matthéenne dans un évangile dont on admet qu'il avait (au moins sous la forme du Mc-intermédiaire) une influence prépondérante sur la rédaction matthéenne.

Ce fut en effet une faiblesse majeure de l'argumentation de Boismard qu'il parle trop souvent indistinctement de «tradition matthéenne» et de vocabulaire «matthéen» (ou «typiquement matthéen»), alors que la distinction entre le Mt-intermédiaire et l'ultime Rédacteur matthéen (qui dépend du Mc-intermédiaire) est une donnée essentielle de sa théorie. Le verbe ἀναχωρεῖν (10/1/0/0/2)[17] est un exemple frappant. Boismard semble maintenant reconnaître qu'il y a là un problème: «Neirynck conteste notre argumentation en faisant remarquer que, dans la perspective du tome II de notre Synopse, ce verbe se trouve 6 fois dans des textes que nous attribuons au Rédacteur matthéen, et qui seraient donc postérieurs à la rédaction marcienne» (41 n. 1).

La réponse de Boismard, déjà citée plus haut, est double. D'abord, «dans la perspective de la théorie des Deux Sources, ... cette objection tombe puisque cette théorie ne distingue pas plusieurs niveaux rédactionnels dans Mt. Il s'agirait donc bien d'un verbe typiquement matthéen et non marcien puisque Marc ne l'utilise jamais ailleurs» (41[-42] n. 1). Par cette réponse, Boismard paraît se cantonner délibérément dans l'ambiguïté, car il sait pertinemment que le «matthéen rédactionnel» de la théorie des Deux Sources[18] ne se confond nullement avec une «tradition matthéenne» qui aurait pu été utilisée par un Rédacteur marco-lucanien[19]. Pour sa part, il continue de parler, comme il l'a toujours fait, du verbe ἀναχωρεῖν qui «revient 10 fois dans les traditions matthéennes» (41).

Puis, il fait valoir que sa théorie synoptique n'est plus la même. Il suffit en effet de parcourir les indications dans les brèves notes en bas de

17. *Synopse II*, p. 121: «Le verbe 'se retirer' (*anachôrein*) est typiquement matthéen (10/1/0/0/2/0)»; cf. pp. 221, 236. Voir aussi *NTS* 26 (1979-80), p. 6: «typical of his vocabulary (10/1/0/0/2/0)»; et encore ses contributions [1984] dans *Interrelations* (n. 11), 1990, p. 263: «ne se lit qu'ici chez Marc [3,7] mais 9 fois ailleurs chez Matthieu»; p. 245: «le verbe *anachôrein* est très matthéen (10/1/0/1[!]/2)». Il est à noter que le verbe se lit en Jn 6,15 (ἀνεχώρησεν), mais Boismard préfère la leçon φεύγει (cf. *Synopse II*, p. 178; *Synopsis Graeca*, p. 167).

18. Sur l'ἀναχωρεῖν matthéen, voir *Urmarcus Redivivus*, pp. 132-134 (= 348-350). Cet examen ne se limite pas, comme semble suggérer Boismard (41 n. 1), aux six emplois en Mt 2,12.13.14.22; 4,12; 27,5 (rédactionnels dans *Synopse II*); la même conclusion s'impose en 9,24; 14,13; 15,21 (diff. Mc) et 12,15 (repris de Mc 3,7). Mais même dans la perspective de *Synopse II*, «il convient de donner chances égales à Mc 3,7 et Mc 12,15 quand on discute la question de la priorité» (p. 134 = 350).

19. Dans *Synopse II*, il lui arrive de faire la distinction. Voir, par exemple, sur μεταβαίνειν en Mt 15,29: «de saveur matthéenne sans doute (5/0/1/3/1) mais qui, dit de Jésus, trahit plutôt le vocabulaire de l'ultime Rédacteur matthéen (11,1; 12,9)» (p. 236). On corrigera: six(!) fois dans Mt; voir 8,34 (diff. Mc 5,17); 17,20bis (cf. Lc 17,6).

page pour se faire une idée du changement: au lieu de récits du Mc-intermédiaire qui seraient | passés dans l'ultime rédaction de Mt (la solution de *Synopse II*) l'on y trouve souvent un Marc qui est secondaire par rapport à la tradition matthéenne. Les exemples sont fort rares où «le Rédacteur matthéen a complété le texte du Mt primitif en y insérant des textes repris du proto-Mc» (136: «beaucoup plus rarement»)[20]. L'ultime Rédacteur matthéen n'intervient presque pas dans le commentaire sur le proto-Marc. Boismard hésite même à attribuer au Rédacteur matthéen les clauses de Mt 19,3 et 9 (149)[21].

À propos des objections que j'avais faites concernant Mc 1,2-3, Boismard note explicitement qu'elles «ne sont plus valables puisque nous attribuons maintenant toutes les citations explicites de l'AT au Rédacteur marco-lucanien» (51 n. 1). Mes objections, si elles étaient valables contre l'exégèse de *Synopse II* (et j'en prends acte), ne le seraient plus maintenant. Notons que la première observation de Boismard disant que «dans Mc, c'est le seul cas où une citation explicite de l'AT est faite par l'évangéliste lui-même» (51) n'a plus la force d'argument qu'elle avait en 1972 puisque toutes les citations sont maintenant attribuées au même Rédacteur; cela doit être un résidu de *Synopse II*[22]. L'élément neuf à ce propos est un jugement assez global sur les discussions à partir de l'AT qui «ont leur origine dans la tradition matthéenne» (52). Quant à la formule «un tel le prophète» (qui «ne se lit nulle part ailleurs dans Mc»), Boismard cite les occurrences dans Mt et Lc sans se poser des questions sur le caractère rédactionnel de ces emplois. En ce qui concerne l'expression γέγραπται ἐν qui «ne se lit nulle part ailleurs dans Mc», je rappelle qu'en Mc 12,(24)26 on peut au moins voir une formule qui équivaut à celle de Mc 1,2[23].

Somme toute, le Mc-intermédiaire a fait place à un texte reconstitué du proto-Marc, mais «la tradition matthéenne» est laissée dans un flou artistique. Si le volume a vocation de devenir «une œuvre pleinement élaborée» (11), un effort de précision s'imposera du côté de Matthieu.

---

20. J'en cite deux: Mc 3,35 (49) et 1,13 καὶ οἱ ἄγγελοι διηκόνουν αὐτῷ (57: «pourrait»).
21. «Il est difficile de trancher»: on notera le contraste avec *Synopse II*, p. 308.
22. Sur l'Écriture citée «seulement par Jésus» (Mc 7,6.10; 11,17; 12,10.26.36), cf. *Synopse II*, p. 70. Voir maintenant p. 51: «Ailleurs, ces citations explicites sont mises dans la bouche de Jésus *ou des interlocuteurs*» (sic). Les mêmes références sont citées (on corrigera 12,20=10 et 12,39=36), avec deux ajouts: 10,4-7 et 10,19 (on peut corriger 10,4-7=6-8a, et biffer les «interlocuteurs»).
23. Sur Mc 1,2-3, cf. *Urmarcus Redivivus*, pp. 115-117 (= 331-333).

5. Le récit de la passion

En ce qui concerne Matthieu, la situation est à première vue plus claire dans le récit de la passion, Mt 26,30–28,10 par. Mc 14,26–16,8. Un certain nombre d'épisodes y sont attribués à l'ultime rédaction matthéenne: 27,3-10.19.24 (219); 27,52-53 (229); 27,62-66; 28,(1-)4 (236)[24]. Mais le commentaire parle couramment du *texte* matthéen et de la *tradition* matthéenne sans faire la distinction entre un proto-Matthieu et le niveau de l'ultime rédaction matthéenne. L'appellation du «proto-Matthieu (notre Mt-intermédiaire)» n'apparaît pratiquement que dans la conclusion générale (Synthèse, 242). L'on peut supposer que Boismard attribue Mt 28,11-15.16-20 à l'ultime rédaction, mais on se demande alors comment il | conçoit les rapports entre «Matthieu» et le Rédacteur marco-lucanien qui aurait rédigé Mc 16,9-20 et qui en 16,15-18 «devait s'inspirer de Mt 28,18» (237, 239). Cette «fausse note» ne l'empêche pas de déclarer formellement que selon sa théorie «l'ultime rédaction marcienne ne dépend pas du Mt actuel, mais d'un proto-Matthieu» (213 n. 2). Cela permet de reconnaître dans le texte de Marc «des traits archaïques abandonnés dans l'ultime rédaction matthéenne». Il cite l'exemple du titre de «fils du Béni» en Mc 14,61 (Mt 26,63: «fils de Dieu»). Il est à regretter qu'il n'a pas poursuivi cette piste. Elle devait le reconduire au Mc-intermédiaire, source du Mt actuel[25]. Y aurait-il donc tout de même du vrai dans cette détestable théorie des deux sources? Retenons en tout cas que, malgré la déclaration qu'«il n'y a plus aucune influence de Mc sur Mt», présentée comme le résultat de ses nouvelles recherches (8), il peut accepter dans le texte de Marc «des traits archaïques abandonnés dans l'ultime rédaction matthéenne»!

À partir de Mc 14,26 il n'existe plus de proto-Marc. Le Rédacteur marco-lucanien reprend ici la tradition matthéenne, mais s'en distingue par un style plus lucanien et par des emprunts à la tradition lucanienne. D'abord, la liaison des phrases: «les liaisons par καί alternent avec les liaisons par δέ, ce qui *pourrait* convenir au style de Lc» (22). Boismard note les liaisons par δέ, surtout en 15,2-15, et se demande: «Où sont les καί chers au proto-Marc?» (220)[26]. Il aurait pu ajouter que d'autres sections ne se prêtent pas à une telle observation:14,32-42; 15,16-21 (δέ: 16a.25); 15,42-47 (δέ: 44.47); 16,1-8 (δέ: 6). Dans la logique de son hypothèse, peut-il se contenter de compter les δέ

---

24. Voir aussi Mt 27,34 (diff. Mc 15,23): «C'est possible, mais...» (224).
25. Cf. *Synopse II*, p. 404.
26. Voir aussi Mc 14,43-52 (208, cf. 21); 14,55-64 (213, cf. 21); 15,33-39 (229); 15,40 (230).

dans Mc sans se soucier du texte parallèle dans Mt²⁷? Cf. Mc
14,29^Mt.31a.31b.44^Mt.46.47.*52*.55^Mt.61^Mt.62.63.64^Mt.68^Mt.70.71;
15,2^Mt.4.5.6^Mt.7^Mt.9.11^Mt.12^Mt.13.14a^Mt.14b^Mt.15.16.*25*.36.37^Mt.39^Mt.*44*.
47^Mt; 16,6^Mt.

En second lieu, il y a les détails stylistiques de tonalité lucanienne:
14,29 ὁ δὲ Π. ἔφη, εἰ καί, 31 ὡσαύτως δὲ καί, 43 παραγίνεται, 44
ἀσφαλῶς, 53 συνέρχονται, 57 ἀναστάντες, 58 χειροποίητον, 68
ἐπίσταμαι; 15,6 παρῃτοῦντο, 7 ὁ λεγόμενος Β., 15 βουλόμενος τῷ
ὄχλῳ τὸ ἱκανὸν ποιῆσαι, 16 συγκαλοῦσιν, 19 τιθέντες τὰ γόνατα,
20 ἐξάγουσιν, 22 φέρουσιν, ὅ ἐστιν μεθερμηνευόμενος, 43
εὐσχήμων, προσδεχόμενος, εἰσῆλθεν πρός, 46 κατέθηκεν; 16,1
καὶ διαγενομένου τοῦ σαββάτου, 4 ἀναβλέψασαι, 5 περιβεβλημέ-
νον, στολήν, 8 ἔκστασις. — Prenons le premier exemple (203), ὁ δὲ
Π. ἔφη (14,29): les références (Lc 16,37; 22,28.58) sont à corriger (Ac
16,37; 22,28; Lc 22,58); la formule, si elle «ne se lit nulle part ailleurs
dans Mc», est attestée en Mt 19,18 (H W N M) et 27,11: ὁ δὲ Ἰησοῦς
ἔφη. — La formule εἰ καί qui «ne se rencontre ailleurs qu'en Lc 11,8
et 18,4»: on peut y ajouter Lc 11,18 εἰ δὲ καί; mais ce «menu détail
stylistique» est-il suffisant pour y voir «le style du Rédacteur marco-
lucanien»? Voir le parallèle en Mt 26,33 εἰ πάντες et v. 35 καὶ πάντες.
— Quant à ὡσαύτως δὲ καί en 14,31 (Mt ὁμοίως καί), Matthieu écrit
ὁμοίως en parallèle à ὡσαύτως également en 22,26 (ὁμοίως καὶ ὁ
|δεύτερος καὶ ὁ τρίτος, cf. Mc 12,21 καὶ ὁ τρίτος ὡσαύτως); voir
aussi Mt 27,41 ὁμοίως καί (= Mc). D'autre part, ὡσαύτως n'est certainement pas plus lucanien que matthéen (Mt 20,5; 21,30.36; 25,17).
Reste l'emploi de δέ en Mc 14,31b (om. Mt). On aurait tort de l'isoler
du contexte: vv. 30 καί (Mt asyndeton) et 31a δέ (Mt asyndeton). — Le
verbe παραγίνεται (14,43) «est typique du style de Lc» (208), mais le
présent historique est sans parallèle dans Lc-Ac. Remplace-t-il ici un
ἰδού de la tradition matthéenne? Si on tient compte du ἰδού en Mt 9,18;
12,46; 17,5, le ἰδού après καὶ ἔτι αὐτοῦ λαλοῦντος s'explique facilement comme rédactionnel. Puis, la double «arrivée» de Judas en Mc
14,43 (παραγίνεται) et 45 (ἐλθών) est simplifiée dans la rédaction matthéenne: ἰδού ... ἦλθεν. — L'adverbe ἀσφαλῶς en 14,43 (208) est une
occurrence unique dans les évangiles. Le lucanisme des mots de même
racine en Lc-Ac, y compris ἀσφαλίζειν (Ac 16,24), serait à nuancer

---

27. Dans la liste qui suit, 17 cas (^Mt) ont la liaison par δέ dans le texte parallèle de
Mt; trois textes sont propres à Mc (14,52; 15,25.44). Les autres parallèles dans Mt
s'expliquent facilement par le style du rédacteur matthéen: 14,31a (asyndeton). 31b
(asyndeton). 46 (τότε). 47 (καὶ ἰδού). 62 (asyndeton). 63 (τότε). 70 (καί). 71 (τότε);
15,4 (τότε). 5 (καί). 9 (οὖν). 13 (asyndeton). 15 (τότε). 16 (τότε). 36 (καί).

quelque peu par l'emploi matthéen du verbe en 27,64.65.66. L'omission de καὶ ἀπάγετε ἀσφαλῶς après κρατήσατε αὐτόν en Mt 26,48 s'explique à la lumière de καὶ ἐκράτησαν αὐτόν (Mc 14,46 = Mt 26,50)... J'arrête ici cet exercice, car je n'ai pas à refaire un travail qui a été fait, et bien fait, dans la dissertation doctorale de D.P. Senior (1972)[28].

En troisième lieu, il y a des harmonisations sur le texte parallèle de la tradition lucanienne: 14,48 ἀποκριθεὶς ὁ Ἰησοῦς εἶπεν, 54 συγκαθήμενος, πρὸς τὸ φῶς, 67 ἐμβλέψασα αὐτῷ, 69 ἐξ αὐτῶν, 70 Γαλιλαῖος εἶ, 71 ὃν λέγετε; 15,11 ἀνέσεισαν τὸν ὄχλον (Lc 23,5), 21 τινα Σ. Κ. ἐρχόμενον ἀπ' ἀγροῦ, 26 ἐπιγραφή, 32 ὁ χριστός, 33 ὥρας ἕκτης, ἐφ' ὅλην, 37 ἐξέπνευσεν, 38 om. ἡ γῆ ἐσείσθη, 39 ἰδὼν δέ, ὁ π. ἐξ ἐναντίας (Ps 38,12), 43 βουλευτής; 16,1 ἀρώματα; et encore 14,57-58 (cf. Ac 6,12-13); 15,17 (cf. Lc 16,19). La liste ne contient guère du neuf. Ces rapprochements sont bien connus et il ne suffit pas de les énumérer pour en faire un argument contre la dépendance lucanienne par rapport à Mc.

6. *Le retour du proto-Luc*

Mc 14,26 marque «une rupture fondamentale» dans les rapports entre Mc et Lc. Luc qui jusque-là dépendait étroitement du proto-Mc («qui semble bien être sa source principale»), suit maintenant une tradition très différente: «sa source principale devient un document (pour nous un proto-Lc) qui offre des affinités évidentes avec le quatrième évangile» (201). À ce propos je me permets de citer un passage de mon analyse de *Synopse III* (1977)[29]:

> C'est surtout le *proto-Luc* pour qui la nouvelle hypothèse aura des conséquences fâcheuses. ... C'est la *retractatio* de loin la plus importante signalée dans le Commentaire: «ayant maintenant une meilleure connaissance des problèmes littéraires posés par le quatrième évangile, nous avons cru pouvoir situer à deux niveaux différents les rapports entre Jn et Lc: Jean II-A et le proto-Lc dépendent de la même source, tandis que Jean II-B a utilisé l'ultime rédaction lucanienne en même temps que Mc et Mt. N'ayant pas fait cette distinction dans le tome II, nous avions cru devoir attribuer au proto-Lc tous les accords Lc/Jn contre Mt/Mc» (*Synopse III*, 426). Cette observation I concerne ... Jn 18,28–19,16 qui fut en 1972 «le passage où la dépendance de Jn à l'égard du proto-Lc est la plus évidente». ... Les

---

28. Cf. D.P. SENIOR, *The Passion Narrative according to Matthew: A Redactional Study* (BETL, 39), Leuven, 1975, ²1982.

29. *Jean et les Synoptiques* (n. 14), pp. 19-20 (= *ETL* 53, 1977, pp. 380-381).

accords Lc/Jn constituent le premier argument en faveur de l'existence du proto-Lc. On voit mal comment le proto-Lc pourra encore se maintenir sans le soutien johannique. Le commentateur lui-même a déjà, du moins pour certains passages, tiré la conclusion qui s'impose.

Je m'en tiens ici à un seul exemple[30]: l'accord entre Lc 22,67 et Jn 10,24-25.

1972: «Le récit actuel de Lc devait se trouver déjà, substantiellement, dans le proto-Lc, comme le prouvent les nombreux accords de Lc avec Jn 10,24ss. Comme Lc, Jn fait interroger Jésus par l'ensemble des chefs religieux (les «Juifs»), et non par le seul Grand Prêtre. Comme Lc, Jn distingue un double problème: Jésus est-il le Christ (v. 24, cf. Lc 22,67), Jésus est-il le Fils de Dieu (vv. 33-36, cf. Lc 22,71)? Enfin et surtout, la formulation litté- raire de Jn 10,24b-25 est proche de celle de Lc 22,67s.» (406)

1977: «C'est avec le récit de Lc que celui de Jn offre le plus de contacts littéraires. Le plus net est entre Jn 10,24b-25a et Lc 22,67... Jean II-B dépend donc étroitement du récit de Lc (et non de celui du proto-Lc comme nous l'avions dit dans le tome II de la Synopse.» (273)

1994: «Ce dernier [Lc] ajoute un dialogue entre le grand prêtre et Jésus (vv. 67b-68) inconnu de Mt/Mc... Dans Lc, les deux questions sont nettement séparées... Or il se trouve qu'un certain nombre des particularités du texte de Lc trouvent un excellent parallèle en Jn 10,24-36. ... Les rapports entre Lc et Jn sont ici évidents. Jn a transféré au chapitre 10 les éléments du procès de Jésus devant le Sanhédrin qu'il lisait dans la source suivie aussi par Lc. ... Dans ce récit..., nous retrouvons les caractéristiques des récits de la pas- sion: ... Lc suit une tradition différente, connue aussi de Jn.» (212-213)

---

30. La signification de cet accord est fortement soulignée par R.E. Brown dans *The Death of the Messiah*, 1994 (voir la recension dans *ETL* 70, 1994, 406-416). Sans adop- ter l'hypothèse d'un proto-Lc, il admet que Luc y suit «a tradition similar to John's» (493; cf. 88, 467, 486). Il cite l'opinion de S. Légasse (*RTL*, 1974) à propos de Lc 22,67 (486: «not the usual Lucan style»); voir cependant *Le procès de Jésus*, 1994 (recension dans *ETL* 70, 1994, 458-459): «Le contact entre Lc 22,67 et Jn 10,24-25 n'est une preuve de l'indépendance de Luc par rapport à Marc que si Jean n'a pas utilisé les synoptiques» (p. 72 n. 12; cf. 30, 74). Sur la rédaction lucanienne et la dépendance johannique, cf. *John and the Synoptics 1975-1990*, dans A. DENAUX (ed.), *John and the Synoptics*, 1992, p. 40 n. 181 (W. Radl, 1988; F.J. Matera, 1989; M. Sabbe, 1991; A. Dauer, 1992). Cf. BROWN, p. 554: «Actually Dauer thinks the dependency was already on the preJohannine level, but the thrust of the argumentation is applicable on the evangelist's level as well». L'étude de Dauer (dans *John and the Synoptics*, pp. 307-339), présentée par Brown à pro- pos de Marc et Jean, concerne avant tout Lc 22,54a.66-71 (pp. 320-336).

Par ce retour en fanfare du proto-Lc dans le récit de la passion, le nouveau Boismard opte pour le revirement à contre-courant[31]. S'il défend l'authenticité de Lc 24,12, c'est encore pour l'attribuer au proto-Lc (234-235)[32]. On s'étonnera plus d'une conclusion tirée du rapprochement entre Mc 16,2.4a.5 et Jn 20,1.12: «Mc est beaucoup plus proche de Jn que de Lc. ... Malgré un vocabulaire en partie I différent, les thèmes sont identiques. Cette séquence ne nous donnerait-elle pas un écho du proto-Lc?» (236).

Dans les récits de la passion et de la résurrection, le proto-Lc prend la relève du proto-Mc comme source principale du Rédacteur marco-lucanien. Celui-ci a harmonisé le proto-Mc sur les deux autres évangiles «en puisant tantôt dans un proto-Matthieu, tantôt aussi, bien que moins souvent, dans un proto-Lc», et à partir de Mc 14,26, il a effectué une compilation des deux traditions, celle de Mt(Mc) d'un côté et celle de Lc/Jn de l'autre. Le Boismard «nouvelle manière» se range ainsi plus ouvertement du côté de Griesbach.

Mc 3,7-12 (et 1,32-34)

Les passages classiques de la théorie griesbachienne ne manquent pas à l'appel: Mc 3,7-12 (39-44: «un texte de synthèse») et 1,32-34 (65-68); cf. M.-É. BOISMARD, *Étude sur Mc 1,32-34*, dans *The Four Gospels 1992*, pp. 987-995. Mc 3,7-12 reçoit un traitement de faveur en conclusion de la «Position du problème»: «Le Rédacteur marco-lucanien ... a entièrement composé le présent passage en s'inspirant de textes qu'il reprenait aux traditions matthéennes et lucaniennes» (42). Comme en 1972, B. attribue à l'ultime Rédacteur la fusion de deux sommaires différents aux vv. 7-8 et l'ajout des vv. 9-10. Mais le Mc-intermédiaire s'est évadé. B. parle maintenant d'un texte «de tradition lucanienne» et il n'est plus question d'un sommaire «en provenance du Mc-intermédiaire». La finale du récit (vv. 11-12) est attribuée à l'ultime Rédacteur et ne remonte plus au Mc-intermédiaire. Voir également *Interrelations*

---

31. Cf. *ETL* 70 (1994), pp. 409 (R.E. Brown) et 459 (S. Légasse). Voir *Literary Criticism Old and New*, in C. FOCANT (ed.), *The Synoptic Gospels* (BETL, 110), Leuven, 1993, pp. 11-38, spéc. 20-27.
32. Il se réfère à mes articles de 1978 et 1984. On ajoutera maintenant *Once More Luke 24,12*, in *ETL* 70 (1994) 294-318.

(n. 11), 1990 (1984), pp. 259-265: «Pour ce texte précis, nous donnerions ... raison à la *Two-Gospel Hypothesis*» (259). Sur ses positions défendues en 1972 et 1984, voir mes remarques dans *Urmarcus Redivivus* (n. 14), pp. 132-144 (= 348-360); *Matthew 4:23–5:2*, in *Interrelations*, pp. 23-46, spéc. 30-33, 42-46. – J'ajoute ici une remarque sur le sort réservé au verset final. En 1972, la consigne de silence est «de saveur marcienne», et du Mc-int. elle est passée dans l'ultime rédaction matthéenne; Luc l'a transférée en 4,41 (122). En 1984, «il faut [encore] admettre que la consigne de silence, ici d'origine marcienne, est passée de Marc dans Matthieu» (264). Mais en 1994, il faut l'attribuer au Rédacteur marco-lucanien qui s'inspire de Lc 4,41 (44); il n'est plus question de saveur marcienne, malgré 1,34b; 5,43a; 7,36; 9,9 tous présents dans le texte reconstitué du proto-Marc. – À propos de la nomenclature des régions (3,7b-8), il faut nuancer l'affirmation: «Si l'on voulait faire dépendre Mt et Lc du texte de Mc, il faudrait admettre que Lc aurait repris du texte de Mc juste les éléments par lesquels il se distinguait de celui de Mt. De même, Mt aurait repris du texte de Mc juste les éléments par lesquels il se distinguait du texte de Lc» (43). Ainsi l'essentiel des parallèles risque de nous échapper: la mention de la Judée et de Jérusalem, la donnée qui est commune aux trois évangiles (et l'omission de l'Idumée, commune à Mt et Lc). Mt se tient près de Mc: la Galilée - Jérusalem, Judée, la Transjordane (cf. Mt 3,5); il complète la mention de la Galilée par celle de la Décapole, et après la mention de la Syrie en 4,24a il peut se passer de Tyr et Sidon au v. 25. À sa manière, Luc semble répondre à un même besoin d'envisager l'ensemble du pays: «toute la Judée», la Galilée comprise (cf. 4,44). – Il y a plusieurs façons de répliquer à une objection. La question: «Qui se laissera convaincre par cet argument?» en est une. C'est donc au lecteur de répondre (à propos de l'emploi de πλῆθος). Voir encore *Étude*, p. 991, à propos de la particule δέ en 1,32. Qui laisse le jugement au lecteur devrait au moins citer l'argument. Voir ma note sur Mc 1,32 (δέ) dans *The Two-Source Hypothesis*, in *Interrelations*, pp. 3-22, spéc. 8: «it is less correct to split the unit of verses 29-34 into two pericopes. The locale of the story is provided in v. 29 (the entry into the house: εἰς τὴν οἰκίαν Σίμωνος...) and it is maintained in v. 33 (πρὸς τὴν θύραν: at the door of the house)...». Assez curieusement, pour B. il s'agit d'une autre porte: «*à la porte,* celle de la ville évidemment» (p. 992). Pour une fois, B. semble avoir négligé une leçon Occidentale: πρὸς τὴν θύραν αὐτοῦ (D c ff² q).

M.-É. Boismard. *L'évangile de l'enfance (Luc 1–2) selon le proto-Luc.*
(Études Bibliques, n.s. 35.) Paris, Gabalda, 1997, 280 p.

Les livres de M.-É. Boismard se suivent à un rythme effréné. Ses récents
travaux sur les évangiles témoignent d'un intérêt commun: de l'évangile de Jean
il remonte à un évangile pré-johannique, de l'évangile de Marc à un proto-Marc,
et de l'évangile de Luc au proto-Luc. Seul le proto-Matthieu (anciennement le
Mt-intermédiaire), qui lui est si cher, échappe encore au *remake*.

Dans le volume sur Lc 1–2, il commence par présenter le résultat de son
étude: le texte reconstitué du proto-Luc imprimé en parallèle à celui de Luc,
avec les traductions fançaises en regard (15-61: Les deux Luc). Là une première surprise nous attend: malgré l'assurance que le texte qu'il adopte ici
est celui de «la dernière édition de Nestle-Aland» (12), il y glisse, sans
commentaire, un grand nombre de variantes du Textus receptus (voir
1,5.6.13.27.38.42.61.66.67; 2,4bis.11bis.15.37.39bis.52bis). Dans son vocabu-
laire, il parle couramment du | «Luc actuel» comme «le second Luc» à dis-
tinguer du «proto-Luc» (qu'il appelle aussi «la première rédaction» de Luc).
Les variantes entre les deux textes sont «considérables»; ce qui nous met en
présence d'un problème «qui ne relève pas de la critique textuelle, mais de la
critique littéraire» (9).

Il expose sa théorie littéraire dans la section suivante: «Trois récits succes-
sifs» (63-95). Il part de l'hypothèse d'un Document d'origine johannite racon-
tant diverses scènes qui se rapportent à la naissance de Jean-Baptiste: l'annonce
faite à Zacharie, la visitation, la naissance elle-même, puis la circoncision et
l'imposition du nom. – Ces récits furent repris par le proto-Luc qui en dédouble
la forme littéraire pour composer des récits parallèles concernant Jésus, mon-
trant la supériorité de Jésus sur Jean et celle de Marie sur Zacharie. – La rédaction du second Luc tend à rendre acceptables à des lecteurs chrétiens les récits
concernant le Baptiste.

Ce n'est pas la source baptiste ou le sens des récits parallèles en Lc 1–2 qui
nous retiendra ici. Ce qui constitue le propre de l'hypothèse de Boismard c'est
la reconstitution d'un texte intermédiaire, assez différent du texte du Luc actuel.
Ainsi, par exemple, Zacharie ne demande pas κατὰ τί γνώσομαι τοῦτο (1,18),
mais il met en doute la puissance de Dieu: πῶς δύναται εἶναι τοῦτο, et l'ange
lui reprochera: οὐκ ἐπίστευσας καθὼς ἔδει ποιεῖν (1,20). Le proto-Luc a transposé le verbe δύναται au v. 29, à propos de Marie, où il n'indique plus le doute
quant à la puissance divine: πῶς δύναται ὁ ἀσπασμὸς οὗτος ἐλθεῖν πρὸς
αὐτήν. Dans le récit du proto-Luc, elle ne voit pas l'ange, elle entend seulement
sa parole (ἀκούσασα) et se demande «comment peut» venir à elle cette saluta-
tion (80). Autre exemple: la visitation. Dans le proto-Luc, le tressaillement de
l'enfant n'est pas le signe qui permet de reconnaître que Jésus est «Seigneur»,
mais le signe auquel Élizabeth reconnaît qu'elle est enceinte, et c'est elle qui
prononce le *Magnificat* (89).

Mais la question doit se poser: sur quoi se base-t-on pour reconstituer ainsi le
texte du proto-Luc, et donc aussi de la source johannite? Boismard n'hésite pas:
les documents qu'on doit utiliser sont les harmonies évangéliques médiévales,
avant tout l'harmonie de Pepys (97-121: Les documents). On se souvient ici
d'une phrase de l'Avant-propos: «La quasi totalité des exégètes haus[s]eront les
épaules à la seule idée de vouloir retrouver un texte grec hypothétique à partir

d'un texte anglais du moyen-âge, traduit du français, traduit du latin, traduit du grec. N'est-ce pas de la folie?» (7). Et d'ajouter en note: «Ce 'quasi' est même probablement de trop» (n. 4). En effet, lorsqu'il s'agit de définir sa position (102-103: Notre propre position), il reprend l'hypothèse de l'harmonie évangélique connue de Justin qui serait le fond commun de nos harmonies médiévales, et le seul devancier qu'il peut citer est l'auteur du livre *Le Diatessaron*, 1992. Dans le cas du proto-Luc, il s'agit d'un texte hypothétique, précanonique, à reconstituer à partir des harmonies médiévales. Il s'y applique dans la dernière section du livre: Choix des variantes (123-243). Pour chaque verset de 1,5 à 2,52 (à l'exception du texte du Magnificat et du Benedictus, omis dans Pepys), il cite d'abord le texte classique de Luc selon le Textus receptus, puis il présente les témoins, surtout Pepys, Venise, Toscan, Liège, Heliand et Persan comme témoins de l'Harmonie SL, à partir desquels il propose la reconstitution du texte de son proto-Luc. Il est plutôt rare qu'il fait appel à d'autres témoins, si ce n'est le cas curieux d'un Pseudo-Chrysostome (PG 50, 790) qui aurait utilisé le texte du proto-Luc «qu'il devait connaître par cœur» (121). Mais peut-on se fier au l jugement de l'Auteur? Je me contente ici de l'exemple cité déjà plus haut: 1,18 πῶς δύναται εἶναι τοῦτο (Pepys: hou it migͨth be). N'est-il pas plus simple, et plus vraisemblable, d'y voir l'influence de Lc 1,34 πῶς ἔσται τοῦτο (Pepys: Hou schold that [b]e). Voir 1,18 selon le Pseudo-Chrysostome: πῶς ἔσται μοι τοῦτο. Les analyses de Boismard verset par verset résultent dans la reconstitution du texte de proto-Luc pour l'ensemble de Lc 1,5–2,52. Le nombre des versets sans correspondant aucun dans le proto-Luc est fort limité (1,6.42c-45; 2,23).

Boismard n'est pas un auteur qui lance des théories et puis s'étonne de les voir discutées; la contestation semble même lui procurer un certain plaisir. Mais dans le cas présent il s'y mêle un trait de masochisme: c'est lui-même qui se charge d'une démolition de sa théorie, fraîchement lancée.

1. Mise à part la phrase εὐλογημένη σὺ ὑπὲρ τῶν γυναικῶν en 1,28, sa reconstitution du texte de l'annonce faite à Marie reste très proche de Lc 1,26-38, v. 27 πρὸς παρϑένον... et les vv. 34-35 inclus (26-30, 162-166). À la fin du même livre, il insère un excursus sur «La conception virginale» (265-271), où il fait intervenir un éditeur anonyme (il l'appelle aussi «l'ultime rédacteur de l'évangile»). C'est cet «éditeur» qui aurait précisé que Marie était vierge (v. 27) et qui aurait inséré dans le récit de l'annonce les versets 34-35. Contrairement à ce qui est exposé antérieurement, ces versets ne remontent donc pas au proto-Luc (ni d'ailleurs au second Luc), et cela malgré le fait qu'ils se lisent dans Pepys!

2. Dans *Enfance*, il n'apparaît pas le moindre doute à propos de l'appartenance au proto-Luc du récit de 2,41-52, Jésus parmi les docteurs (56-60, 230-243). Cinq mois plus tard, les choses ont changé. Voir *En quête du proto-Luc* (octobre 1997), 35-36. Les notes lucaniennes, dont onze (sur quatorze en 2,41-52) sont attestées dans le texte du proto-Luc, sont maintenant l'argument principal contre le proto-Luc:

> Ce récit fut composé par Luc lui-même et ne se lisait pas dans le proto-Luc. On notera d'ailleurs que le verset 51b n'est qu'un décalque de 2,19 et que le verset 52 ne fait que reprendre, sous une forme un peu différente, le thème exprimé au verset 40; c'est une reprise rédactionnelle qui indique l'insertion des versets 41-51 dans la trame d'un récit plus ancien.

3. «Celui que nous avons appelé le proto-Luc est bien Luc lui-même»: telle est la position de Boismard dans *Enfance* (95; cf. 65, 83). Voir maintenant *Proto-Luc*, 336-337:

> Il ne semble pas que le même auteur soit à l'origine des deux niveaux de rédaction que nous avons attribués au document L (donc au proto-Luc) et à Luc... Le style de Luc est beaucoup plus 'lucanien' que celui du proto-Luc... Il est difficile de penser que le même auteur ait pu changer la signification de certains faits. Ayant attribué le Magnificat à Élizabeth, comment aurait-il pu ensuite l'attribuer à Marie?

4. Les harmonies évangéliques médiévales et plus particulièrement celle de Pepys, témoin préféré du texte de proto-Luc en 1,5–2,52, ne jouent plus aucun rôle dans l'analyse de Lc 3–24. Boismard en prend congé dans l'Avant-propos et n'en parle plus. Voir *Proto-Luc*, 8:

> Mais la méthode sera tout à fait différente. Nous ne nous appui[e]rons plus sur les harmonies évangéliques médiévales, assez décevantes malgré les promesses qu'elles semblaient donner dans les évangiles de l'enfance...

Devant ce revirement, il y aura sans doute des lecteurs qui se demandent si le poids extraordinaire accordé aux harmonies médiévales dans *Enfance* n'est pas également à revoir, comme Boismard lui-même l'a fait à propos de 1,34-35 et 2,41-52.

M.-É. Boismard. *En quête du proto-Luc.* (Études Bibliques, n.s. 37.) Paris, Gabalda, 1997, 364 p.

| Ce livre sur le proto-Luc, qui fait suite à *L'évangile de l'enfance*, est d'une approche plus classique, basée sur une analyse des textes «tels que nous les connaissons actuellement». Le résultat est présenté dans la deuxième partie: «Le proto-Luc», la reconstitution du texte, en grec et en traduction française (262-323), suivie d'un exposé sur la «Structure du document L» (324-332). Il s'agit d'un document «remarquablement bien construit et parfaitement cohérent», structuré en sept sections: (A) Jean-Baptiste, (B) Débuts de la vie publique, (C) Le discours inaugural, (D) L'activité de Jésus, (E) Ministère en Galilée, (F) La passion du Christ, (G) Le triomphe du Christ. Pour commencer, Boismard parle du «document L», qui comprend les matériaux propres à Luc, mais en conclusion il opte pour le titre de «proto-Luc», car le document court tout au long de l'évangile de Luc, à commencer par l'évangile de l'enfance, et se poursuit dans les Actes des apôtres. Il se réclame des «pionniers en ce domaine que furent B. Weiss et P. Feine» (335). Le rôle de pionnier joué par Johannes Weiss semble lui avoir échappé. Il croit devoir noter, citation à l'appui, que «Weiss a changé ses positions entre les huitième et neuvième éditions de son commentaire» (40 n. 1). Seulement la huitième édition (⁸1892) à laquelle B. Weiss fait allusion en 1901 fut l'œuvre de son fils, Johannes Weiss.

Le proto-Luc de Boismard diffère d'autres types de *Proto-Luke* (Q+L) qui débutent par Lc 3,1-2 et se limitent à l'évangile. Quant à la source Q, l'Auteur distingue la source Q1, utilisée par Matthieu et Luc, et la source Q2, utilisée par le proto-Luc (176). Il se sépare encore de ses devanciers, ainsi que de sa propre théorie antérieure, par l'hypothèse d'un troisième niveau de rédaction (un Rédacteur final) et l'identité des trois niveaux en Luc et Actes (333):

```
          Proto-Luc    Act I
             |            \
            Luc            \    Act II
             |              \  /
          Rédacteur        Act III
```

Les péricopes du proto-Luc suivent l'ordre de l'évangile de Luc, à une exception près. Le début de la section F se place après 10,25–17,4 (Ministère en Galilée): FA 9,28-45; 13,31-33 (Jésus doit souffrir à Jérusalem); FB 9,51-56; 10,1-2a.10-11.16b (En route vers Jérusalem; suite: 17,11-19; 19,1-10). Pour certains passages, le contexte primitif est difficile à préciser: 11,5-8; 18,1-8 (236); voir aussi 6,4+ (196).

La méthode que Boismard emploie dans *Enfance* n'est pas complètement abandonnée (cf. 8). Ici c'est le codex de Bèze qui est cité comme témoin du texte pré-canonique en 3,16; 6,4+; 21,7; 22,16; 23,35 (voir 47 n. 1). Signalons que l'Auteur défend l'authenticité du texte lucanien (= L) en 22,43-44; 23,17; 23,34a; 24,12 et sa propre reconstitution de 3,21-22 (cf. *Le Diatessaron*: ἐλθεῖν τὴν λαμπρότητα τοῦ οὐρανοῦ ... ἐν εἴδει περιστερᾶς καὶ ἐπιπτῆναι...).

Dans le premier chapitre, «Les caractéristiques stylistiques» (15-39), l'Auteur se base sur l'inventaire des caractéristiques communes à Luc et Actes de Boismard-Lamouille (1984), notamment les caractéristiques des catégories Ab et Bb, classées par verset (cf. *ETL* 61, 1985, 304-339; = *Evangelica II*, 243-278). Sa conclusion est assez réservée (39):

> Les textes repris du document L (propres à Luc) offrent peu de caractéristiques stylistiques lucaniennes. Lorsqu'un texte propre à Luc offre un nombre important de notes lucaniennes, c'est ou bien qu'il aura été entièrement composé par Luc lui-même, ou bien qu'il proviendrait du document L, mais fortement remanié par Luc.

Une certaine parenté de style le fera conclure que le proto-Luc et Luc sont de même école (337) et que le Rédacteur devait être disciple de Luc (124).

Les analyses commencent par le discours de 21,5-36, «La ruine de Jérusalem» (40-62), que j'examine ici brièvement par manière d'exemple de l'approche de l'Auteur. Ce n'est évidemment pas nouveau qu'il y défend l'hypothèse du proto-Luc, mais il propose maintenant un texte plus restreint. L'exemple de 21,34-36 est frappant: «Cet appel à la vigilance ne peut certainement pas provenir du document L; il fut composé par Luc lui-même» (60). Comparer son explication dans *Synopse II* (1972): la finale du discours en proto-Luc (modifiée en 1984, mais toujours du proto-Luc: cf. BETL 95, 286). Dans le discours même (21,20-28), le v. 23b n'appartient plus au document L: il est ajouté par Luc en dépendance de la tradition synoptique (46; cf. Mt 24,21). Autre nouveauté: les ajouts lucaniens aux vv. 21a (Mc 13,14c), 23a (Mc 13,17) et 27 (Mc 13,26) sont maintenant attribués au Rédacteur (61; cf. 44-45: insérés maladroitement, malencontreusement). Troisième particularité de la nouvelle exégèse de Boismard: l'utilisation de la leçon du codex de Bèze en 21,7, «Quel (sera) le signe de ta venue» (τῆς σῆς ἐλεύσεως). Je note simplement qu'il n'a pas tort de rapprocher la leçon de D l et Mt 24,3 (τί τὸ σημεῖον τῆς σῆς παρουσίας), mais il est sans doute plus vraisemblable de voir l'influence en sens inverse, de l'expression matthéenne (παρουσίας) à ἐλεύσεως / *adventus*.

Le discours sur la ruine de Jérusalem permet d'envisager la question de la date (62). Puisque, selon lui, le document L reprend l'expression «désolation» au prophète Jérémie, et non pas à Marc, et la description au v. 20 n'offre aucun trait qui rappelle la prise de Jérusalem par les Romains, Boismard croit devoir opter pour une datation du document L *avant* la ruine de Jérusalem en 70. – Sur Lc 21, cf. *Evangelica I*, 57-59 (= 1973); *Evangelica II*, 493-510 (= 1984); voir aussi J. Verheyden, dans *BETL* 32, ²1989, 491-516: «The Source(s) of Luke 21».

Le facteur qui domine la discussion à propos de Lc 21 est celui de l'influence marcienne sur l'évangile de Luc. Un autre facteur apparaît dans le très long chapitre «Passion et Résurrection» (63-161, sur Lc 22–24): les contacts thématiques et littéraires entre les évangiles de Luc et de Jean, qui peuvent apporter la confirmation qu'un texte propre à Luc doit remonter à L (64-65; cf. 335). L'auteur le plus souvent cité ici est F.L. Cribbs (1973), avec lequel il se sent souvent «en plein accord» (65). Il y a peu de références à *Synopse II*, et encore moins à *Synopse III* (voir *ETL* 53, 1977, 380-381; *Jean et les Synoptiques*, 19-20). Le proto-Luc de 1997 est en effet assez différent de celui de 1972. Pour citer un exemple, les Outrages à Jésus (22,63-65), le texte de proto-Luc en 1972: vv. 63b-64; en 1997: vv. 63.65. Autre exemple, non moins significatif: Les femmes au tombeau (24,1-11). En 1972 seuls les vv. 1-2 (excepté «portant les aromates qu'elles avaient préparés», faisant suite à l'addition de 23,55-56) sont attribués au proto-Luc, tandis qu'en 1997 c'est l'ensemble de 23,55-56; 24,1-11 (à l'exception des vv. 7b et 10) qu'il fait remonter au proto-Luc. Sans entrer dans le détail, il peut être instructif d'énumérer les 115 versets et demi-versets de Lc 22–24 qui sont attribués au proto-Luc, FD: **22**,1-3a.4.6c|8.14-16|21.23|24-25a.26-27|28-30|31-34|36-38| FE:39-41.43-45|47-54a|54b-5.58.60b-31|63.65|66-70|**23**,1-3a.13a.14.16-23|FF:26|27-31|32-34|35-43|46.48|50a.53-54a.55-56| GA: **24**,1-7a.8-9.11|12|36.38a.39a.41.45-49| GB:50-53. Deux épisodes y manquent en entier: l'apparition aux disciples d'Emmaüs (24,13-35), qui est une composition de Luc, et la comparution de Jésus devant Hérode (23,6-12, avec son écho au v. 15), qui est une insertion du Rédacteur.

| Je m'arrête ici. Les lecteurs des *ETL* comprendrons que j'ai de nettes réserves à propos d'une répartition de la rédaction lucanienne aux trois niveaux de proto-Luc, de Luc et du Rédacteur. (Sur le récit de la Passion dans Luc, voir *Evangelica I*, 75-80; *BETL* 110, 1993, 19-27.) Quant aux contacts entre les évangiles de Luc et de Jean, le proto-Luc n'est qu'une des solutions possibles, et non la meilleure.

NOTE: Jay M. HARRINGTON, *The Lukan Passion Narrative: The Markan Material in Luke 22,54–23,25. A Historical Survey 1891-1997* (NTTS, 30), Leiden, 2000, XIII-1003 p.

IV

THE SAYINGS SOURCE Q

ETL 71 (1995) 421-430

18

Q: FROM SOURCE TO GOSPEL

What's in a name? Sayings Source Q is a common translation of *Logienquelle*, *Rede(n)quelle*, or *Spruchquelle*. In recent years some North American scholars have suggested introducing the term "gospel" in the designation of Q, with its full name: the Sayings Gospel Q. Volumes on Q now receive titles such as *The First Gospel* (Jacobson, 1992), *The Lost Gospel* (Mack, 1993), ... *the Sayings Gospel* (Kloppenborg, 1994), *The Gospel Behind the Gospels* (Piper, 1995). The use of the new term originated in the SBL Q Seminar[1] and was strongly promoted by its presidents, James M. Robinson and John S. Kloppenborg. The latter used the title "The Sayings Gospel Q" in the edition of his English translation of Q (1990)[2] and subsequently in several other publications on Q[3]. Robinson pleaded for the use of "gospel" in the Foreword to *Q–Thomas Reader* (1990) and then more expressly in *The Four Gospels 1992* ("The Sayings Gospel Q"). Following the *Q–Thomas Reader*, Sayings Gospel Q became an accepted usage in the Scholars Version and in the publications of the Jesus Seminar[4].

1. See J.S. Kloppenborg's notice in *The Shape of Q* (n. 25 below). The first appearance of the title "the Sayings Gospel Q" that is known to me is found in an unpublished paper prepared by Kloppenborg for the session of the Q Seminar at the SBL Meeting of 1988 (Chicago, November 22). It was announced as "Redactional Stratigraphy and Social History *in Q*" (S155), but the title in the manuscript (September 12) reads: "Redactional Strata and Social History *in the Sayings Gospel Q*" (emphasis mine), and throughout the text (31 p.) "the Sayings Gospel" alternates with "Q". — See already J.D. CROSSAN, *In Fragments: The Aphorisms of Jesus*, San Francisco, 1983, p. X: "I consider that Q is a discourse gospel" (p. X: "the gospel Q"). Cf. W.H. KELBER, *From Aphorisms to Sayings Gospel and from Parable to Narrative Gospel*, in *Forum* 1/1 (1985) 23-30: "Crossan suggested the existence of three types of gospel: the cluster gospel (= sayings gospel), the dialogue gospel, and the narrative gospel" (p. 28). Cf. below, n. 49.

2. J.S. KLOPPENBORG, *The Sayings Gospel Q*, in ID., et al., *Q–Thomas Reader*, Sonoma, CA, Polebridge, 1990, pp. 1-74 ("Translation & Notes", pp. 35-74). M.G. STEINHAUSER (in his *Introduction*, pp. 3-27) simply notes that "scholars now refer to 'Q' as a gospel" (p. 3): "This source today is commonly referred to as the Sayings Gospel Q" (p. 10). See my review in *ETL* 69 (1993) 175-177.

3. In *Semeia* 49 (1990) 71-99; 52 (1990) 145-160; 55 (1991) 1-14. See now also *The Sayings Gospel Q: Literary and Stratigraphic Problems*, announced for *ANRW* II.

4. *The Complete Gospels: Annotated Scholars Version* (ed. R.J. MILLER), Sonoma, CA, 1992, pp. 249-300: "The Sayings Gospel Q" (with an introduction by A.D. Jacobson); *The Five Gospels: The Search for the Authentic Words of Jesus* (eds. R.W. FUNK – R.W. HOOVER), New York, 1993, pp. XX, 12-16. Cf. my reviews in *ETL* 69 (1993) 421-424; 70 (1994) 160-162. See now also W. Barnes TATUM, *John the Baptist and Jesus: A Report of the Jesus Seminar*, Sonoma, CA, Polebridge, 1994, pp. 35-37 ("Sayings Gospel Q: Character and Origin of Q").

This shift from Q-source to gospel is most remarkable. A few years earlier, none of these same authors had used the term "gospel" in their writings on Q. The International Q Project, which is now presented by Robinson under the title "A Critical Text of the Sayings Gospel Q", was first announced in 1983 as a project on "Q: A Lost Collection of Jesus' Sayings"[5]. Kloppenborg published in 1984 an article on "Tradition and Redaction in *the Synoptic Sayings Source*"[6] and his dissertation, in the same year, was entitled: "The Literary Genre of | *the Synoptic Sayings Source*" (published in 1987 as *The Formation of Q*). H. Koester, in his *Introduction to the New Testament* (1982), used the traditional "so-called Synoptic Sayings Source" and "sayings source Q" (for *die Spruchquelle 'Q'*)[7] and he maintains this designation in his later work[8]. Nevertheless, it is in Koester's writings that the term "sayings gospel" has its roots.

I

Robinson's 1964 essay on λόγοι σοφῶν (sayings of the wise) as a designation of the *Gattung* of Q[9] gave a new orientation to the study of the genre of Q, but one cannot say that the use of "gospel" as a title for Q was suggested there. With regard to the Gospel of Thomas he observes that the term λόγοι was at home in the sayings tradition and

5. See my note on IQP in *ETL* 69 (1993) 221-225; reprinted in *Q-Synopsis* (SNTA, 13), Leuven, ²1995, pp. 75-79, here p. 75 (= 221).

6. In *CBQ* 46 (1984) 36-42 (emphasis mine).

7. *Introduction to the New Testament*, Vol. 2: *History and Literature of Early Christianity*, Philadelphia - Berlin and New York, 1982, pp. 45-46. See my reviews in *ETL* 57 (1981) 357-358 (*Einführung*, 1980); 59 (1983) 364-365. Koester is one of the rare scholars who still understand Papias' remark on Matthew as "a reference to the Synoptic Sayings Source": "the author of the Synoptic Sayings Source would then have claimed the authority of 'Matthew' for his writing" (p. 172). Cf. *Ancient Christian Gospels* (n. 8): "In spite of major and weighty objections, this hypothesis has merits" (p. 166). D. Lührmann's recent statement, in *Q: Sayings of Jesus or Logia?* (cf. below, n. 46): "Nobody today argues for the existence of Q on the basis of the Papias quotation in Eusebius" (p. 101) is apparently not quite correct.

8. *Ancient Christian Gospels: Their History and Development*, London-Philadelphia, 1990, pp. 128-171: "The Synoptic Sayings Source". For more bibliographical references up to 1990, cf. B.A. PEARSON (ed.), *The Future of Early Christianity*. FS H. Koester, Minneapolis, MN, 1991, pp. 477-487 (D.M. Scholer).

9. J.M. ROBINSON, *ΛΟΓΟΙ ΣΟΦΩΝ. Zur Gattung der Spruchquelle Q*, in E. DINKLER (ed.), *Zeit und Geschichte*, Tübingen, 1964, pp. 77-96; = *LOGOI SOPHON: On the Gattung of Q*, in ID. – H. KOESTER, *Trajectories through Early Christianity*, Philadelphia, 1971, pp. 71-113. The last part, "Jewish Wisdom Literature and the Gattung LOGOI SOPHON" (pp. 103-113) is now reprinted in Kloppenborg's *The Shape of Q* (n. 25), pp. 51-58.

was taken up into the incipit: "These are the secret sayings which the living Jesus spoke out and which Didymus Judas Thomas wrote down". A second title is appended at the end: "The Gospel according to Thomas", but the term "gospel" is completely lacking elsewhere in the work and the subscription is probably secondarily added. Robinson compares this title with "The Gospel of Truth", a Nag Hammadi tractate "that is not a gospel in terms of its gattung" (likewise, The Gospel of Philip, The Gospel of the Egyptians) and he notes that "at the time when the canonical gospels and hence the title 'gospel' had gained wide acceptance, ... the term 'gospel' was popular in a polemical and apologetic context as a flag under which various kinds of writings circulated"[10]. In Robinson's view the Gattung *logoi sophon* shows "gnosticizing proclivity" and this is blocked by Matthew and Luke: "Q is embedded in the Marcan outline | by Matthew and Luke and continues to be acceptable in the orthodox church only in the context of *this other Gattung*, that of *'gospel'*"[11].

Robinson's conclusion is adopted by Koester: "Such critical evaluation of the Gattung, *logoi*, was achieved by Matthew and Luke through imposing the Marcan narrative-kerygma frame upon the sayings tradition represented by Q" (1965)[12]. However, Koester shows less reserve in using the term "gospel"[13]:

> The term *gospel* in the strict sense belongs only to such writings as Mark and John and to those which are dependent upon these earliest "gospels".

10. *Trajectories*, pp. 76-79 (orig., pp. 80-81): "man (wird) eher in dem Begriff λόγοι die ursprüngliche Gattungsbezeichnung suchen dürfen" (p. 81). This passage in Robinson's essay is apparently misread by D. Dormeyer. Cf. *Das Neue Testament im Rahmen der antiken Literaturgeschichte: Eine Einführung*, Darmstadt, 1993, p. 216, on the Gospel of Thomas ("des frühen 2. Jh."): "dieses Evangelium (hat) die urchristliche Gattung 'Spruchsammlung' als 'Evangelium' fortgesetzt... Die Gattung 'Worte' = Spruchsammlung wurde der Großgattung Evangelium zugerechnet (Robinson 1964, 81)"; and on Q: "die Spruchsammlung (konnte) im 2. Jh. auch als Evangelium bezeichnet werden" (sic). Cf. below, n. 26.

11. *Ibid.*, p. 113 (cf. orig., p. 96), emphasis mine. See also *USQR* 20 (1965), p. 135.

12. *GNOMAI DIAPHOROI* (1965), in *Trajectories*, pp. 114-157, here 135. On the Robinson-Koester-Robinson trajectory, see Robinson's essay *On Bridging the Gulf from Q to the Gospel of Thomas (or vice versa)*, in C.W. HEDRICK – R. HODGSON, JR. (eds.), *Nag Hammadi, Gnosticism and Early Christianity*, Peabody, MA, 1986, pp. 127-175. Cf. p. 164, on Q: "a gospel of a different kind than the canonical Gospels".

13. *One Jesus and Four Primitive Gospels* (1968), in *Trajectories*, pp. 158-204, here 162 n. 12. The section "Collection of Sayings" (pp. 166-187) is now reprinted in Kloppenborg's *The Shape of Q* (n. 25) under the title: "The Synoptic Sayings Source and the Gospel of Thomas" (pp. 35-50). – On the term "gospel", see KOESTER, *From the Kerygma-Gospel to Written Gospels*, in *NTS* 35 (1989) 361-381; *Ancient Christian Gospels* (n. 8), 1990, pp. 1-48 ("The Term 'Gospel'"). Cf. p. 20, on the term in the Gospel of Thomas: "occurs only in the colophon of a scribe or translator". Cf. below, n. 40.

It is only here that the kerygma of the cross and resurrection — Paul's "gospel," 1 Cor. 15:1ff. — has shaped and determined the form of this new literary genre. In speaking of *other written documents as "gospels,"* however, we are not merely following long-established usage. *Such a use seems legitimate* because we are concerned with other writings which contain traditions that have been incorporated into Mark and other gospels of the kerygma type.

The sayings collection, from which the Gospel of Thomas is derived, is an "earlier genre of 'gospel' literature", a "sayings gospel", and "the source 'Q', used by Matthew and Luke, was a secondary version of such a 'gospel'"[14]. In later writings Koester further developed his view on Q[15]:

> If the genre of the wisdom book was the catalyst for the composition of sayings of Jesus into a *gospel*, and if the christological concept of Jesus as the teacher of wisdom and of the presence of heavenly Wisdom dominated its creation, the apocalyptic orientation of the *Synoptic Sayings Source* with its christology of the coming Son of man is due to a secondary redaction of an older wisdom book.

The counterpart in German of his *Apocryphal and Canonical Gospels* (1980) appeared in a more elaborate survey-article on *Frühchristliche Evangelienliteratur* in *ANRW* (1984)[16]. In the section "Das Spruchevangelium und seine Auslegung" the Synoptic *Spruchquelle* is treated as "das älteste christliche Spruchevangelium"[17]. |

In 1980 Koester presents five apocryphal gospels which are "significant witnesses for the formation of the gospel literature in its formative stages": the Gospel of Thomas, the Dialogue of the Savior, the Unknown Gospel of Papyrus Egerton 2, the Apocryphon of James, and the Gospel of Peter[18]. Together with the Synoptic Sayings Source (Q), these "earlier gospels" form the principal topic of his *Ancient Christian Gospels* (1990). The corpus of gospel literature is much larger than the

---

14. *Ibid.*, p. 186 (cf. 165).

15. *Apocryphal and Canonical Gospels*, in *HTR* 73 (1980) 105-10, here p. 113. See also the passage on "three early gospels": "the canonical gospels ... used several written sources which must be classified as *gospels*. Three of these can be clearly identified: the *Synoptic Sayings Source*, the Johannine *Semeia Source*; and a *Passion Narrative*" (pp. 111-112).

16. *Überlieferung und Geschichte der frühchristlichen Evangelienliteratur*, in *ANRW* II.25.2 (1984), pp. 1463-1542. For the text on "the wisdom book" (quoted above), cf. pp. 1514-1515.

17. *Ibid.*, pp. 1512ff., esp. 1515.

18. On the influence of Koester's approach to noncanonical gospels, see my article *The Apocryphal Gospels and the Gospel of Mark* (1989), in *Evangelica II*, pp. 715-772, esp. 716-724; with references to J.D. Crossan's *Four Other Gospels* (1985) and R. Cameron's *The Other Gospels* (1982).

Markan kerygma gospel: Koester's definition includes "all those writings which are constituted by the transmission, use, and interpretation of materials and traditions from and about Jesus of Nazareth"[19]. They are classified as collections of the sayings of Jesus (Gos. Thom.; Q), dialogue gospels (Dial. Sav.; Apocr. Jas.), and collections of narratives about Jesus (Pap. Eg. 2; Gos. Pet.). It is in the same line that Robinson can write his Foreword to the *Q–Thomas Reader* (1990): "it is appropriate to designate these gospels as sayings gospels"[20].

II

"It is appropriate to refer to Q not only as a source, but as a gospel – the Sayings Gospel Q" (W.B. Tatum). His first reason seems to echo Robinson's argument: "... Forms of the Greek verb for preaching the good news (*euangelizomai*) are found on Jesus' own lips in Q 7:22 [...][21], supporting the notion that this reconstructed document consisting primarily of Jesus sayings can appropriately be called a gospel, the Sayings Gospel Q". He adds a second reason: "the so-called Gospel of Thomas unearthed in Egypt in 1945 also consists primarily of sayings attributed to Jesus. Sayings Gospel Q now has a literary companion which has been preserved in documentary form – the sayings Gospel of Thomas. ... There are therefore sayings gospels as well as narrative gospels"[22]. Whereas Robinson's original argument had brought Q together with GTh under the term λόγοι, without endorsing the secondarily added subscription[23], Q and GTh here become associated under the title "Gospel".

19. *Ancient Christian Gospels*, p. 45-47: "Criteria for the Definition of a 'Gospel'" (here p. 46).

20. "Foreword", pp. VII-X, here p. VIII. Robinson's argument for Q as a sayings *gospel* (p. VII-VIII; cf. below, n. 26) is summarized by M.W. Meyer in *Semeia* 52 (1990), p. 162.

Note: *Semeia* 52, ed. D.E. Smith, 1990, © 1991, contains four papers on the canonical gospels presented at a regional SBL meeting in Dallas, March 1989. To this collection, entitled *How Gospels Begin*, two papers were added in the published volume: one by J.S. Kloppenborg on ... the *Beginning of the Sayings Gospel (Q)*, pp. 145-160, and a paper by M.W. Meyer on *The Beginning of the Gospel of Thomas*, pp. 161-173 (p. 161: "In contrast to the four canonical gospels, Q and the Gospel of Thomas are often considered to be sayings gospels").

21. The reference "and Q 16:16" is deleted here. The verb εὐαγγελίζεται is Lukan and has no part in Robinson's argument. Cf. IQP: ἡ βασιλεία τοῦ ϑεοῦ βιάζεται (in *JBL* 113, 1994, p. 499). Cf. below, n. 26.

22. W.B. TATUM, *John the Baptist and Jesus* (n. 4), p. 36.

23. Cf. *Q–Thomas Reader* (n. 4), p. 90: "written by a scribe in subscript fashion. As such it was probably added secondarily" (S.J. Patterson).

A motive for "the shift from regarding Q as a 'source' to regarding it as a 'gospel'" can also be given without referring to the Gospel of Thomas[24]: |

> The intent in using the term "gospel" is to treat Q not as raw material for the "real" gospels or as a mere collection of Jesus' sayings which, one typically assumes, presupposed knowledge of Jesus' death and resurrection. The word "gospel" is used provocatively to suggest that Q by itself represents a view of Jesus, a view which did not necessarily have its principal focus on Jesus' death and resurrection. The use of the word "gospel" suggests that Q and the canonical gospels are comparable entities. Simply calling Q a source does not make this point.

Kloppenborg too considers the comparison with the canonical gospels[25]:

> The SBL Q Seminar has introduced "Sayings Gospel," in part to avoid the term *source*, which inevitably obscures Q as a document of intrinsic interest in its own right (much like calling the second Gospel "the Markan source"). And in part, this designation is intended to convey the notion that Q represents a "gospel" as much as do the narrative Gospels.

Robinson has taken a new course: "the trajectory *beginning already within Q* that moves toward the designation of it as a 'Gospel'". His considerations "inherent in Q" are as follows[26]:

> The noun εὐαγγέλιον does not occur in Q. Yet the synonym κήρυγμα does occur at Q 11:32 to characterize the speech of Jonah, whereas according to this saying there is present something greater than Jonah (πλεῖον Ἰωνᾶ), presumably Jesus' κήρυγμα. Q 12:3 uses the verb κηρύσσειν to urge that what the followers of Jesus have heard from him they are to

24. A.D. JACOBSON, *The First Gospel. An Introduction to Q*, Sonoma, CA, 1992, pp. 3-4. See my review in *ETL* 69 (1993) 177-179. Jacobson's defense of "the applicability of the term gospel" is quoted in R.A. PIPER, *In Quest of Q: The Direction of Q Studies*, in ID. (ed.), *The Gospel Behind the Gospels. Current Studies on Q* (NTSup, 75), Leiden, 1995, pp. 1-18, here p. 11 n. 30.

25. *Introduction*, pp. 1-21 (here p. 1-2 n. 1), in J.S. KLOPPENBORG (ed.), *The Shape of Q: Signal Essays on the Sayings Gospel*, Minneapolis, MN, 1994. See my review in *ETL* 70 (1994) 163-164: "Note, however, that this term is used in none of the ten essays" (p. 164).

26. ROBINSON, *The Sayings Gospel Q*, in *The Four Gospels 1992*. FS F. Neirynck (BETL, 100), Leuven, pp. 361-388, esp. 370-372 ("εὐαγγελίζονται Q 7,22") and 388; *The Incipit of the Sayings Gospel Q*, in *RHPR* 75 (1995) 9-33 (FS É. Trocmé), esp. pp. 32-33 (text quoted above from p. 32). See already his argument in *Q–Thomas Reader*, 1990, pp. VII-VIII (Foreword).

Compare D. DORMEYER, *Literaturgeschichte*, 1993 (n. 10): the designation of Q as a gospel (but see n. 10 above) "liegt ... auch an der Verwendung des Verbs *euaggelizo* in Q" (p. 216); on Q 7,22: "(in Q) nimmt dieser einmalige Gebrauch eine zentrale Stellung ein", and: "*Über Robinson hinaus* [sic] läßt sich festhalten, daß der Evangeliumsbegriff bereits in Q zentral verankert ist..." (p. 217, emphasis mine). Robinson's work he refers to is the 1964 article!

proclaim widely. That is to say, the *sayings* of Q are the *kerygma* of the Q community. The verb *evangelize* occurs in the clause in Q 7:22 πτωχοὶ εὐαγγελίζονται (derived from Isa 61:1), to refer back to the *incipit* of the Sermon, the Beatitude for the Poor (Q 6:20b). Thus Q 7:22, as a kind of *inclusio* referring back to what has been ascribed to Jesus thus far, tends to designate the Sermon as *evangelizing* (with the Healing of the Centurion's Lad in Q 7:1-10 standing for the various healings also mentioned in Q 7:22).

The outcome of "the trend already at work in Q itself" is found in Matthew: κηρύσσων τὸ εὐαγγέλιον τῆς βασιλείας in 4,23 and 9,35; τοῦτο τὸ εὐαγγέλιον | τῆς βασιλείας in 24,14 and τὸ εὐαγγέλιον τοῦτο in 26,13. "When Matthew in the latter two cases also adds to the Marcan τὸ εὐαγγέλιον his own τοῦτο, he would seem to be designating his book as τὸ εὐαγγέλιον τῆς βασιλείας"[27]. Can we therefore conclude that "Matthew seems already to have recognized 'gospel' as an appropriate designation for Q" (cf. 4,23; 9,35) and "Q understood itself and was understood by Matthew to be a gospel in its own right"[28]?

1. My first reservation concerns the link with Q in Mt 4,23: κηρύσσων τὸ εὐαγγέλιον (representing Q 7,22 εὐαγγελίζονται) τῆς βασιλείας (alluding to Q 6,20b ὅτι ὑμετέρα ἐστὶν ἡ βασιλεία τοῦ θεοῦ)[29]. The phrase in Mt 4,23 is Matthew's compensation for the omission of Mk 1,14 κηρύσσων τὸ εὐαγγέλιον τοῦ θεοῦ (15 ἤγγικεν ἡ βασιλεία τοῦ θεοῦ), and neither "QMt" nor "a kind of Proto-Matthew" is to be brought up here[30].

2. The influence of Isa 61,1 in Q 7,22 (πτωχοὶ εὐαγγελίζονται) is widely accepted, but it is less evident that this same influence is also

---

27. *The* Incipit, p. 33. Cf. G.N. STANTON, *Matthew: βίβλος, εὐαγγέλιον, or βίος?* in *The Four Gospels 1992*, pp. 1187-1201, esp. 1190-1195 ("Matthew: the first to refer to his writing as a εὐαγγέλιον"). See also H. FRANKEMÖLLE, *Evangelium – Begriff und Gattung: Ein Forschungsbericht* (SBB, 15), Stuttgart, ²1994, pp. 171-180: "das vorliegende 'Buch der Geschichte Jesu Christi' (1,1) [ist] mit 'Evangelium' im Sinne des Matthäus (24,14; 26,13) zu identifizieren, ohne daß der Begriff nach Matthäus darauf reduziert werden kann, da auch er weiterhin am Begriff 'Evangelium' als Verkündigungsbegriff der Heilsbotschaft von Gottes Handeln festhält" (p. 180).

28. *Q–Thomas Reader*, pp. VII-VIII.

29. *The Sayings Gospel Q*, p. 368; cf. IQP: [ὑμετέρα] ... (*JBL* 111, 1992, p. 501). Contrast *The* Incipit, p. 33: αὐτῶν ἐστιν.

30. It is most amazing to read that "the idiom τὸ εὐαγγέλιον τῆς βασιλείας ... may reflect a Q-like expansion of Q 3–7 into Matt 3–11..." (*The* Incipit, p. 33). Are we then in synoptic criticism to start again from the very beginning? See my *Matthew 4,23–5,2 and the Matthean Composition of 4,23–11,1*, in D.L. DUNGAN (ed.), *The Interrelations of the Gospels* (BETL, 95), Leuven, 1990, pp. 23-46. Cf. *La rédaction matthéenne et la structure du premier évangile*, in *ETL* 43 (1967) 41-73; reprinted in *Evangelica I*, pp. 3-36.

reflected in the first Beatitude (Q 6,20b οἱ πτωχοί)³¹. One may find the language of Isa 61,2 in Matthew's second Beatitude but Robinson himself does not suggest that πενθοῦντες and παρακληθήσονται in Mt 5,4 are from Q³². The Q Beatitudes show no cogent evidence of contacts with Isa 61,1-2: "Wer wollte einen Bezug zur messianischen Prophezeiung in Jes 61,1f einzig und allein durch das Wort 'die Armen' als erwiesen ansehen?"³³.

3. No more convincing is the statement that πλεῖον Ἰωνᾶ in Q 11,32 "would seem to refer to the message of Q as itself κήρυγμα"³⁴. Καὶ ἰδοὺ πλεῖον | Σολομῶνος/Ἰωνᾶ ὧδε is part of the double saying on Solomon's wisdom and Jonah's preaching (Q 11,31-32) and in the Q context the πλεῖον phrase appears to be "under the control of 11,29-30" (the Son of Man saying): "This causes the word πλεῖον almost inevitably to become personalized in spite of itself"³⁵.

4. Robinson rightly observes that the list of healings in Q 7,22 is almost completely attested in Isaiah³⁶. The first and the last item, τυφλοὶ ἀναβλέπουσιν and πτωχοὶ εὐαγγελίζονται, can come from Isa 61,1 LXX: εὐαγγελίσασθαι πτωχοῖς ... τυφλοῖς ἀνάβλεψιν. But see also

---

31. *The Sayings Gospel Q*, p. 368: "a scriptural basis for a self-designation of the Q movement, which, not by coincidence, also came to expression in the definition of the blessed at the opening of the Inaugural Sermon".

32. *The Sayings Gospel Q*, p. 369: "if it originally read κλαίοντες". Cf. IQP: μακάριοι οἱ [κλαί]οντες, ὅτι γελάσετε (*JBL* 111, 1992, p. 502).

33. H. FRANKEMÖLLE, *Evangelium* (n. 27), p. 146 (see already *BZ* 15, 1971, p. 60); cf. p. 129: "allein das Wort οἱ πτωχοί, das hier wie dort auftaucht (dazu noch in einem anderen Kasus), belegt noch keine Abhängigkeit". See also I. BROER, *Die Seligpreisungen der Bergpredigt* (BBB, 61), Königstein/Ts.-Bonn, 1986, pp. 64-67: "der Einfluß von Jes 61 beschränkt sich auf Mt 5,4" (p. 67). More recently, FRANKEMÖLLE, *Jesus als deuterojesajanischer Freudenbote?* in ID. – K. KERTELGE (eds.), *Vom Urchristentum zu Jesus.* FS J. Gnilka, Freiburg-Basel-Wien, 1989, pp. 34-67, esp. 49-50 (Q 6,20), 50-53 (Q 7,22), with a critique of the assimilation in Hebrew (S.T. Lachs, 1980) or Aramaic (G. Schwarz, 1985) of both phrases on "the poor" in Q 6,20 and 7,22 (pp. 51-52).

34. *The Sayings Gospel Q*, p. 370. Cf. above, n. 26: "presumably Jesus' κήρυγμα".

35. D.R. CATCHPOLE, *The Quest for Q*, Edinburgh, 1993, p. 247. On Q 11,29-30+31-32, see my *Assessment* (1995, cf. below n. 46), p. 281. A.Y. Collins stresses the use of the neuter: "When the sayings circulated independently, the referent of the *pleion* was most likely the Holy Spirit. Another possible referent is the proclamation of the early church (*to kerygma*; this term is used in v. 32)". Cf. *The Son of Man Sayings in the Sayings Source*, in *To Touch the Text.* FS J.A. Fitzmyer, New York, 1989, pp. 369-389, here 378. But can we neglect τὴν σοφίαν(!) in the parallel v. 31? Anyway, in the context of Q 11,29-32 "kann das πλεῖον ὧδε nicht mehr auf die Botschaft Jesu gehen, sondern nur auf seine Person" (R. BULTMANN, *Geschichte*, p. 137). Collins rightly defends the reference to the future, apocalyptic Son of Man in v. 30 (p. 377 n. 41; cf. Schürmann, ctr. Vielhauer). See now also P. Hoffmann (1992, p. 437) and A. Vögtle (1994, p. 155), in reply to A.D. Jacobson (1992, p. 418; *The First Gospel*, p. 71: "not the apocalyptic figure, but simply Jesus").

36. *The Sayings Gospel Q*, p. 364.

Isa 29,18-19: ἀκούσονται ... κωφοί, οἱ ... ὀφθαλμοὶ τυφλῶν βλέψονται, καὶ ἀγαλλιάσονται πτωχοί... and U. Luz's comment: "Beide Stellen bilden so den Rahmen für Mt 11,5. Es ist also voreilig, einseitig Jes 61,1 (und die damit vielleicht [!] verbundene Erwartung eines eschatologischen Propheten) zum 'Oberthema' der Antwort Jesu zu machen"[37].

One can understand that some scholars are tempted to read Q 7,22 in light of the use of this Q saying in Matthew and Luke. The redactional compositions of Mt 8–9 (cf. 11,2 τὰ ἔργα τοῦ Χριστοῦ) and Lk 7,1-10+11-17 and v. 21 prepare for the answer of Jesus in Mt 11,5 and Lk 7,22, whereas in Q there was only the Healing of the Centurion's Boy, which "fits so well" the conclusion of the Inaugural Sermon and "is not form-critically a miracle story"[38]. With regard to the allusion to Isa 61,1 in Mt 11,5 and Lk 7,22, one can refer to possible contacts with Isa 61,1-2 in Matthew's Beatitudes and Luke's quotation in Lk 4,18-19, but this allusion is less certain in Q[39]. The uniqueness in Q of both the references to Jesus' miracles and the use of εὐαγγελίζονται may invite us to a more cautious reading of Q 7,22.

III

To conclude, Robinson repeats his initial observation on the Gospel of Thomas: "it is evident that the title is secondary", but nevertheless he now defends "the scholarly custom"[40]: |

---

37. *Das Evangelium nach Matthäus (Mt 8–17)* (EKK, 1/2), Zürich-Neukirchen, 1990, p. 169 n. 38 (ctr. P. Stuhlmacher and W. Grimm).

38. ROBINSON, *The Sayings Gospel Q*, p. 365. The statement that the boy was actually healed (Robinson: "if in Q at all") is probably a redactional addition (Mt 8,13; Lk 7,10); cf. *Jean 4,46-54: Une leçon de méthode*, in *ETL* 71 (1995) 176-185, p. 179. See now IQP, Q 7:10 καὶ [[]] <...> (*JBL* 114, 1995, p. 479). This conjectural unreconstructable reading can be corrected to Q̶ ̶7̶:̶1̶0̶.

39. The ascription to Q of both Mt 5,4 and Lk 4,18-19 on the basis of the allusion to Isa 61,1 in Q 7,22 (C.M. Tuckett, et al.) is, in my view, a more doubtful alternative.

40. *The Sayings Gospel Q*, p. 372. On other Nag Hammadi tractates, cf. *ibid.*, and *The Incipit*, pp. 10-11. — Without great conviction ("perhaps") he also refers to the "other gospel" in Gal 1,6-9, where "one should recognize ... some awareness of this preeminence given to the designation 'Gospel' already in the Q–Matthew trajectory" (*The Sayings Gospel Q*, p. 372).

On the Gospel of Thomas and "gelegentliche (Selbst-)Bezeichnung apokrypher Schriften als Evangelien", cf. G. STRECKER, *Literaturgeschichte des Neuen Testaments* (UBT, 1682), Göttingen, 1992, p. 129 n. 26: "die formalen Unterschiede (sollten) eine differenzierte Terminologie veranlassen. Diese Selbstbezeichnung stellt also keinen Einwand dar gegen eine Verwendung des Begriffs 'Evangelium' (entsprechend seinem verbreiteten Gebrauch) an erster Stelle für die Gattung, die in den kanonischen Evangelien

The title *The Gospel of Thomas* has however established itself in modern usage and only for that reason will no doubt be retained, with as little justification as has the equally well established title Q(uelle).

Although the Sayings *Gospel* Q is not (or not yet?) an established usage on the Continent, the trajectory from "sayings of the wise" to "sayings gospel" is represented by D. Dormeyer. His position comes close to that of J.S. Kloppenborg[41] who recognizes in the addition of the temptation narrative "one step" in the direction of "a biographical genre for Q"[42]:

> *1989*: So kann unter Umständen Q als das Zwischenstadium zwischen einer Sammlung von gattungsgleichen thematisch zusammenhängenden Reihungen und einer originär gestalteten Biographie 'Evangelium' angesehen werden.
>
> *1993*: Der Redaktor von Q ... hat in Analogie zu frühjüdischen und hellenistischen Spruchsammlungen unter Einbeziehung der atl. Ideal-Biographie eine eigene Gattung der Ideal-Biographie geschaffen: das *Spruch-Evangelium* mit der Einsetzung als Erzählrahmen und weiteren Erzählungen im Hauptteil.

In this connection U. Schnelle has reintroduced a notion of *Halbevangelium*: "Auf die Gattung 'Evangelium' entwickelte sich die Logienquelle zu, so daß sie aus dieser Perspective als 'Halbevangelium' gelten kann"[43].

In the German-speaking area and beyond[44], "Logienquelle" remains the most I usual designation of the Synoptic Sayings Source[45]. Both D.

begegnet". – On the Gospel of Thomas, cf. C. Tuckett, *Das Thomasevangelium und die synoptischen Evangelien*, in *Berliner Theologische Zeitschrift* 12 (1995) 185-200: "Das ThEv sollte man nicht als ein sehr frühes Evangelium betrachten... Es wirft Licht auf eine Epoche des Frühchristentums, aber dies ist eine spätere Epoche als die der kanonischen Evangelien" (200). See also H.T. Fleddermann, *Mark and Q* (cf. below, n. 48).

41. *The Formation of Q*, 1987, p. 326.

42. *Evangelium als literarische und theologische Gattung* (Erträge der Forschung, 263), Darmstadt, 1989, p. 189; *Literaturgeschichte*, 1993 (n. 10), p. 219 (in confrontation with M. Sato's theory on the Gattung "Prophetenbuch": pp. 213-220). Cf. Id., in *NTS* 33 (1987), p. 463: "Q hat die Gattung 'Logoi Sophon' realisiert".

43. *Einleitung* (n. 45), p. 229.

44. Note, however, this confession in the mouth of a French scholar: "L'hypothèse de l'existence d'une source des *logia* de Jésus, dite "source Q", n'a peut-être pas mobilisé comme elle l'aurait dû les efforts des exégètes français". This is the opening sentence of a recent article by M. Trimaille, *Jésus et la sagesse dans la "Quelle"*, in J. Trublet (ed.), *La Sagesse biblique. De l'Ancien au Nouveau Testament* (Lectio divina, 160), Paris, 1995, pp. 279-319. In the course of the article he refers to "la source des *logia*", "la *Quelle*", "la source Q", or simply "Q". Other writers in French prefer "le document Q" (in English: the Q document); thus, M. Devisch, in *BETL* 29 and 34 (1972, 1974), but see also his *La source dite des* Logia *et ses problèmes*, in *ETL* 51 (1975) 82-89. D. Lührmann mentions the use of the term *Logia* in the title of *BETL* 59 (ed. J. Delobel, 1982), "the collective volume on Q" (*Q*, p. 103; cf. below n. 46). But, although Q was the major topic of the volume, the editor who chose this title had in mind "the broad field of the

Lührmann and Robinson have recently recalled to mind its 19th-century origin and the shift, at the end of the century, from Λ (Papias' λόγια) to the more neutral siglum Q (= Quelle)[46]. Of the various designations of the source[47], this symbol Q, used alone or in combination with *Logien-quelle/Spruchquelle*, "sayings source", or "sayings gospel", is now clearly the less contested one. Personally, I consider it to be an advantage of the full designation "(Synoptic) Sayings *Source* Q" that it reminds us of the fact that we have no direct access to the text of Q: it remains a hypothetical source text that we are to reconstruct from

Logia in early Christian tradition" (p. 26). It should be clear that this use of the term *logia* implies no reference to Papias. Compare, e.g., J.-C. INGELAERE, *La tradition des* logia *de Jésus dans l'Évangile de Jean*, in *Revue des sciences religieuses* 69 (1995) 3-11 (p. 3: "des sentences assez brèves [à] caractère autonome").

45. See its use in recent handbooks: U. SCHNELLE, *Einleitung in das Neue Testament* (UTB, 1860), Göttingen, 1994, pp. 214-233 ("Die Logienquelle"); (H. CONZELMANN –) A. LINDEMANN, *Arbeitsbuch zum Neuen Testament* (UTB, 52), Tübingen, [11]1995, pp. 73-80 ("Die Logienquelle Q"). Cf. Robinson's response to M. Sato in the (German) *Evangelische Theologie* 53 (1993) 367-389: *Die Logienquelle: Weisheit oder Prophetie?* Contrast Robinson's use of the title "*das Spruchevangelium Q*" in a public lecture (Bamberg 1993): *Die Bedeutung der gnostischen Nag-Hammadi Texte für die neutestamentliche Wissenschaft*, in L. BORMANN, et al. (eds.), *Religious Propaganda and Missionary Competition in the New Testament World*. FS D. Georgi (NTSup, 74), Leiden, 1994, pp. 23-41, esp. 33ff. Cf. p. 33: "das Thomasevangelium ... auf einer gattungsgeschichtlichen Ebene mit dem Spruchevangelium Q".

In this paper Robinson emphasizes once more the independence of Mark and John and presents the Johannine Signs Source in association with Q (pp. 33-38). Cf. G. VAN BELLE, *The Signs Source in the Fourth Gospel: Historical Survey and Critical Evaluation of the Semeia Hypothesis* (BETL, 116), Leuven, 1994, pp. 83-84, 172-174. By the way, one may ask why Robinson still calls this source the *Semeiaquelle* and not *das Zeichenevangelium SQ*.

46. D. LÜHRMANN, *Q: Sayings of Jesus or Logia?* in R.A. PIPER (ed.), *The Gospel* (n. 24), 1995, pp. 97-116, esp. 98-102 (p. 100 n. 9); ROBINSON, *The* Incipit (n. 26), esp. pp. 19-28 (p. 24 n. 55); with references to *ETL* 54 (1978) 119-125; 55 (1979) 382-383 (= *Evangelica I*, 1982, 683-690). See also the quotation in *The Oxford English Dictionary*, vol. 12, [2]1989, p. 951 (art. *Q, III. As a symbol, 2. Theol.*): "It seems to be a fair conclusion that he (*sc.* J. Weiss) substituted Q (= *Quelle*) for Λ (= Λόγια)" (from 1978, p. 123). But see now my *Note on the Siglum Q*, in *Evangelica II*, 1991, p. 474: "As far as I see, the work of E. Simons, published ten years before J. Weiss's *TSK* article, has not yet been mentioned in the discussion on the siglum Q". Cf. Eduard SIMONS, *Hat der dritte Evangelist den kanonischen Matthäus benutzt?* (Abhandlung, Strassburg), Bonn, C. Georgi, 1880. On p. 22: "Q. (Die apostolische Quelle nach W.)", and thereafter passim referring to B. Weiss's *Quelle* as "Q." or "die Q." (up to p. 95: "die W.'sche Q."); occasionally: Λ (resp. Q.), Λ (Q), Λ ("Q."); cf. pp. 29, 30, 111. Both Robinson and Lührmann continue to refer to J. Weiss ("in 1890 ... for the first time") without mentioning his antecessor.

47. On the terminological trajectory in H. Schürmann's writings on Q: first *Mt/Lk-Tradition* or *Q-Tradition* (1953), then *Spruchsammlung* or *Logiensammlung* (1960), corrected to *Redequelle* (1960's) and finally *Redenquelle* or *Reden-Quelle* (cf. BETL 59, 1982, p. 121 n. 2: "Als 'Logienquelle' ist diese nicht richtig bestimmt"), see *ETL* 70 (1994) 163-164 (cf. above n. 25).

Matthew and Luke[48]. I miss this nuance in the title Sayings *Gospel* Q. Moreover, without necessarily restricting the use of the term to canonicity, there is undeniably a strong tradition of scholars for whom narrativity is an essential characteristic of the gospel genre[49]. |

Corollary: The IQP Text

The last section of the IQP text has now appeared in *JBL*[50]. The cumulative list includes the complete list of the reconstructed texts. Q passages with only a lower grade of probability (C or D) are marked by double square brackets [[C]] or by question marks (?D?). References of rejected verses are also marked (e.g., ~~Q 3:1~~, ~~Q 3:4~~). The results of Robinson's inconclusive discussion of the *Incipit* of Q are printed as follows[51]:

?Title?   <..>

[[~~Q 3:0~~ **Incipit**]] ≪<words>≫ [[<’Ιησου..>]] ≪transition to John≫.

A few observations on the reconstruction of Q are called for. All double-tradition passages which are normally ascribed to the minimal extent of Q are included, but the Lukan Sondergut passages in Lk 6,24-26; 7,29-30; 9,61-62; 12,13-14.16-21; 12,35-38; 17,28-29 are all rejected[52]. Two references to Matthew are included: ?Mt 5,41?[53] and [[Mt 6,19]], but Mt 10,5b-6; 10,23 (as well as 8,18; 25,15b-16) are rejected. Regarding the

---

48. On the use of Mark in the reconstruction of Q, cf. *Recent Developments in the Study of Q* (1892), in *Evangelica II*, pp. 409-464, esp. 428-433, and now my critical *Assessment* in H.T. FLEDDERMANN, *Mark and Q: A Study of the Overlap Texts* (BETL, 122), Leuven, 1995, pp. 261-307.

49. Cf. H. FRANKEMÖLLE, *Evangelium* (n. 27), p. 149: "für die literarische Gattung *Evangelium* (bleibt) ihre durchgehende und eindeutige Narrativität bestimmend". See also my article *Gospel, Genre of*, in B.M. METZGER – M.D. COOGAN (eds.), *The Oxford Companion to the Bible*, New York - Oxford, 1993, pp. 258-259: "The narrative framework, typical of the Gospel form, is lacking in this sayings collection, and designations such as 'wisdom gospel' or 'aphoristic gospel' are inappropriate... The Markan Gospel's general outline is preserved in both (Matthew and Luke), with an expansion of the biographical element in the birth stories and the genealogies at the beginning and the appearances of the risen Lord at the end" (p. 259).
Contrast J.D. Crossan's split into Passion-Resurrection Gospels and Sayings Gospels (1988, p. 407) and his "two-source" theory: the *Cross Gospel* and the *Q Gospel*. "I term it, to give it full honor, the Q Gospel because I do not think of it as just somebody else's source" (*Who Killed Jesus?* 1995, p. 25).

50. *JBL* 114 (1995) 475-485. The references on p. 475 should be corrected: (1994) 495-499 (not 500); (1995) 475-485 (not 501-511).

51. Cf. *The Incipit*, pp. 19, 28, 31.

52. A few corrigenda in the cumulative list on p. 485 can be noted: Lk 7,29-30, cf. p. 479: ~~Q 7:29-30~~; Lk 12,[[13-14.16-21]], cf. p. 481: ~~Q 12,13-14; 12,16-21~~. In the other direction: Q 12,11-12, cf. 481: [[12:11-12]]; Q 14,5, cf. (1992), p. 506: [[Q 14:5]]; Q 14,16-21.23, cf. (1992), pp. 506-507: [[Q 14:16-21.23]].

53. Cf. (1994), p. 497; not in the cumulative list.

ascription to Q of passages such as Q 3,3 (πᾶσα ἡ περίχωρος τοῦ Ἰορδάνου) and ⟪Q 3:21-22⟫ (text unreconstructable) I have already expressed some doubt[54]. More recently, the evaluation of H.T. Fleddermann's forthcoming book on the Mark-Q overlaps gave me the opportunity to reexamine ⟪11,21-22⟫; [[13,30]]; 17,2; and 17,33[55].

Together with the publication of the revised critical text of Q, the publication has now been announced of a series of fascicles entitled *Documenta Q* (Peeters, Leuven) with excerpts and evaluation of "all relevant comments by scholars over the past century", following the suggestion I made to the IQP committee when I was present at the meeting in Toronto, 6-8 August 1993. Such a documentation, collected by a large group of collaborators, will no doubt constitute a welcome tool of study for researchers on Q.

Published volumes, in order of appearance: *Q 11:2b-4* (1996); *Q 4:1-13,16* (1996); *Q 12:49-59* (1997); *Q 12:8-12* (1997); *Q 22:28,30* (1998). See below, nos. 19, 20, and 21.

---

54. Cf. *The Minor Agreements and Q*, in R.A. PIPER (ed.), *The Gospel* (n. 24), pp. 49-72, esp. 67-71. On Lk 7,10, cf. above n. 38.

55. *Assessment* (n. 48), p. 297; cf. pp. 271-273 (Lk 11,21-22); 283-284 (Lk 17,33); 286-287 (Lk 17,2); 289 (Lk 13,30).

ETL 72 (1996) 418-424

19

DOCUMENTA Q: Q 11,2b-4

The International Q Project (here IQP) has led to the reconstruction and publication of a critical text of Q (*JBL* 1990-1995)[1]. The Editorial Board including the three general editors, J.M. Robinson (Claremont, CA), P. Hoffmann (Bamberg), and J.S. Kloppenborg (Toronto), is now in charge of a revision of this recently established text (to be published in a single volume). The IQP database will be published by the managing editors S.D. Anderson, S.G. Bjorndahl, S. Carruth, and C. Heil in a series of individual volumes, *Documenta Q*, of which this preliminary volume on the Lord's Prayer (Q 11,2b-4) is presented as a sample[2]. "The future volumes are to appear preferably in their Q sequence" (VII).

I

The database of Q 11,2b-4 is divided by verse into three sections, each of them beginning with a reproduction of the Greek texts in three parallel columns:

Mt	6,7-10	Q	11,2b	Lk	11,1-2a.2b
	6,11		11,3		11,3
	6,12-13		11,4		11,4

The sigla used in the Greek text are explained in the Introduction (IX-X). The variation units are numbered and for each unit the database comprises four sequences: *Luke Pro* (= Q), *Con* (≠ Q); *Matt Pro* (= Q), *Con* (≠ Q). This analysis of the scholarly literature is followed by *Evaluations* in which S. Carruth, J.M. Robinson, and, for Q 11,3.4, also J.S. Kloppenborg (in this order) bring to expression their own conclusions (date: 1995). The relative degree of certainty is indicated by the letters {A}, {B}, {C}, {D}, {U}. The volume concludes with a Bibliography of some two hundred titles.

---

1. See my note *The International Q Project*, in *ETL* 69 (1993) 221-225; reprinted in *Q-Synopsis* (SNTA, 13), Leuven, [2]1995, 75-79. See also "Corollary: The IQP Text", in *ETL* 71 (1995), 430.
2. Shawn CARRUTH, Albrecht GARSKY, and (volume editor) Stanley D. ANDERSON, *The Database of the International Q Project: Q 11:2b-4* (Documenta Q: Reconstructions of Q Through Two Centuries of Gospel Research Excerpted, Sorted, and Evaluated), Leuven, Peeters, 1996, XII-206 p.

There are two obvious lacunae in this preliminary volume. First, as indicated above, the Greek texts are printed by verse (pp. 3, 128, 145) but a presentation of the entire section is lacking. In the Synopsis here below the reconstruction of the Q text is marked by boldface and under-linings (and by the use of the sign □ in Lk). |

Mt 6,9-13		Lk 11,2-4	
9a	οὕτως οὖν **προσεύχεσθε** ὑμεῖς □³	2b	<u>ὅταν</u> □ **προσεύχησθε** □ λέγετε³
b	**πάτερ ἡμῶν**⁴ **ὁ ἐν τοῖς οὐρανοῖς**⁵	c	**πάτερ** □⁴ □⁵
c	**ἁγιασθήτω τὸ ὄνομά σου**	d	**ἁγιασθήτω τὸ ὄνομά σου**
10a	**ἐλθέτω ἡ βασιλεία σου**	e	**ἐλθέτω ἡ βασιλεία σου**
b	γενηθήτω τὸ θέλημά σου		□⁶
	ὡς ἐν οὐρανῷ καὶ ἐπὶ γῆς⁶		
11a	**τὸν ἄρτον ἡμῶν τὸν ἐπιούσιον**	3a	**τὸν ἄρτον ἡμῶν τὸν ἐπιούσιον**
b	<u>**δὸς**</u>¹ **ἡμῖν** <u>σήμερον</u>²	b	δίδου¹ **ἡμῖν** τὸ καθ᾽ ἡμέραν²
12a	**καὶ ἄφες ἡμῖν** <u>τὰ ὀφειλήματα</u>¹ **ἡμῶν**	4a	**καὶ ἄφες ἡμῖν** τὰς ἁμαρτίας¹ **ἡμῶν**
b	<u>ὡς</u>² **καὶ** <u>ἡμεῖς</u>³ <u>ἀφήκαμεν</u>⁴	b	**καὶ** γὰρ² αὐτοὶ³ ἀφίομεν⁴
	<u>τοῖς</u>⁵ <u>**ὀφειλέταις ἡμῶν**</u>⁶		παντὶ⁵ ὀφείλοντι ἡμῖν⁶
13a	**καὶ μὴ εἰσενέγκης ἡμᾶς**	c	**καὶ μὴ εἰσενέγκης ἡμᾶς** -
	εἰς πειρασμόν		**εἰς πειρασμόν**
b	ἀλλὰ ῥῦσαι ἡμᾶς ἀπὸ τοῦ πονηροῦ⁷		□⁷

Secondly, the consultation of the book is seriously encumbered by the absence of a Table of Contents. The volume now ends with six blank pages; two of them would suffice for an analysis of its contents:

Q 11,2b-4

pages
4-18   Variant reading Lk 11,2 ἐλθέτω τὸ πνεῦμά σου...
    Pro (4-10), Con (10-17). — Evaluations (18).
19-33   [0] Was the Prayer in Q?
    Pro (19-26), Con (27-31). — Evaluations (31-33).

Q 11,2b
34-50   [1] Position of the Prayer in Q
    Lk: Pro (34-38), Con (38-41).
    Mt: Pro (41-42), Con (42-49). — Evaluations (49-50).
51-69   [2] Introduction: Lk 11,1-2a / Mt 6,7-8
    Lk: Pro (51-56), Con (57-63).
    Mt: Pro (63-66), Con (66-67). — Evaluations (67-69).
70-74   [3] Lk ὅταν προσεύχησθε λέγετε / Mt οὕτως οὖν προσεύχεσθε
    ὑμεῖς
    Lk: Pro (70), Con (70).
    Mt: Pro (71), Con (71-72), Undecided (72). — Evaluations (73-
    74).
75-92   [4] Lk πάτερ / Mt + ἡμῶν
    Lk: Pro (75-80), Con (80-82).

Mt: Pro (82-84), Con (84-91). — Evaluations (91-92).
93-105   [5] Lk — / Mt ὁ ἐν τοῖς οὐρανοῖς
Lk: Pro (93-95), Con (95-97).
Mt: Pro (97-99), Con (99-104). — Evaluations (104-105).
106-127 [6] Lk — / Mt γενηθήτω τὸ θέλημά σου...
Lk: Pro (106-107), Con (107-109).
Mt: Pro (110-112), Con (112-126). — Evaluations (126-127).

Q 11,3
128-136 [1] Lk δίδου / Mt δός
Lk: Pro —; Con (128-132).
Mt: Pro (133-134), Con (135). — Evaluations (135-136).
137-144 [2] Lk τὸ καθ' ἡμέραν / Mt σήμερον
Lk: Pro (137), Con (137-141).
Mt: Pro (141-142), Con (143). Undecided (143). — Evaluations
(143-144). |

Q 11,4
145-155 [1] Lk τὰς ἁμαρτίας / Mt τὰ ὀφειλήματα
Lk: Pro (145-146), Con (146-151).
Mt: Pro (151-153), Con (154). — Evaluations (154-155).
156-160 [2] Lk γάρ / Mt ὡς
Lk: Pro (156), Con (156-158).
Mt: Pro (158), Con (158-159). — Evaluations (159-160).
161-163 [3] Lk αὐτοί / Mt ἡμεῖς
Lk: Pro (161), Con (161-162).
Mt: Pro (162), Con (162). — Evaluations (162-163).
164-170 [4] Lk ἀφίομεν / Mt ἀφήκαμεν
Lk: Pro (164), Con (164-167).
Mt: Pro (167-168), Con (168-169). — Evaluations (169-170).
171-175 [5] Lk παντί / Mt τοῖς
Lk: Pro (171), Con (171-173).
Mt: Pro (173-174), Con (174). — Evaluations (174).
175-177 [6] Lk ὀφείλοντι ἡμῖν / Mt ὀφειλέταις ἡμῶν
Lk: Pro (175), Con (175-176).
Mt: Pro (176), Con (176). — Evaluations (176-177).
178-194 [7] Lk — / Mt ἀλλὰ ῥῦσαι...
Lk: Pro (178-179), Con (179-181).
Mt: Pro (181-183), Con (183-193). — Evaluations (193-194).

The citations in the database are presented in chronological order.
The date normally refers to the first edition. In some instances the citation from the original German edition is followed by the English translation: Harnack 1907, ET 1908; Jeremias 1967, ET 1964; 1971, ET
1971; Luz 1985, ET 1989; Schnackenburg 1984, ET 1995; Schrenk
1954, ET 1957; Schweizer 1973, ET 1975. Besides German and English
literature there is a minority of excerpts in French (no other languages):
Loisy 1907-1908, 1924; Lagrange 1921, 1923; Dupont 1958, 1973;

Bonnard, 1963; Schlosser 1980; Magne 1988; Philonenko 1995[3]. Printing mistakes are extremely rare[4]. Dupont's long note on "Notre Père, qui est dans les cieux" (1958, 65-66 n. 1) is correctly cited with reference to Mt's ὁ ἐν τοῖς οὐρανοῖς as *Luke Con* (96) and *Matt Pro* (98), and with reference to Mt's ἡμῶν as *Matt Pro* (83), but less correctly as *Luke Pro* (76): the text quoted there ("A noter enfin...") is Dupont's fourth and last reason of the "différentes raisons d'attribuer la priorité à l'invocation longue" (see *Matt Pro*, 83). Another correction concerns the references to Klostermann 1927, 1929, i.e., *Das Matthäusevangelium*, ²1927, and *Das Lukasevangelium*, not the fifth (Bibliography, 200) but the second edition: cf. the database on Q 11,3¹·².4¹ (129 = 133; 138 = 142; 147 = 152). See already Klostermann's *Matthäus*, first edition: "δίδου ... τὸ καθ' | ἡμέραν Korrektur des Lc", and ὀφειλήματα "ursprünglich, Lc hat es durch ἁμαρτίας ersetzt" (1909, 200) and the first edition of his *Lukas* (1919, 486; the enigmatic number in Q 11,4 *Matt Pro* is this page number of the never mentioned first edition). In Q 11,3² *Matt Pro*: add Klostermann 1929 (142). The relocation of Klostermann in the chronological order may be an appropriate suggestion for improvement (VII). The inclusion of the first edition could reveal certain developments. Thus, the explicit comment on the variant reading in Lk 11,2 "wohl authentischer Text des Lc" (6) was added in ²1929.

The arrangement of the database in four sequences is not unproblematic. Two (or more) variation units can be closely connected and the authors' comments can concern more than one unit. For instance, Q 11,2b⁴ (Mt's ἡμῶν) and 2b⁵ (Mt's ὁ ἐν τοῖς οὐρανοῖς) can be treated together as secondary amplifications of πάτερ (= Q) and then the same comment should be cited as *Matt Con* in 11,2b⁴ (84-91) and 2b⁵ (99-104). Instead of repeating the citation in 11,2b⁵, the procedure adopted in the database is to refer back to 11,2b⁴: "See Q 11:1 2a.2b⁴ Matt = Q, Con". This rather complex formula is used no less than twenty-two times in 11,2b⁵ *Matt Con*: von Dobschütz, Hirsch, Schmid 1956, Knox, Jeremias 1967, Jeremias 1971, Schweizer, Edwards, Schürmann, Gundry, Gerhardsson, Schnackenburg 1984, Schneider, Gnilka, Davies

---

3. Suggestions for insertion in a revised edition: J. Dupont, *Le Notre Père: Notes exégétiques* (1966), in Id., *Études sur les Évangiles synoptiques* (BETL, 70), Leuven, 1985, 832-861; M.-É. Boismard, *Synopse II*, Paris, 1972, 274-276, esp. 274-275 ("provient du Document Q").

4. Corrigenda, 71: Mell ... Matt = Q, Pro (= Con, cf. 67); 80, 180 bis: Lagrange, read: texte; 108: Dupont, read: de Luc; 138: Klostermann 1927, 56 (= 58); 159: Schürmann, read: Ursprungs; 163: J. Weiß, read: unsrerseits; 169: Noland (= Nolland); 182: Dupont, (...): add semicolon; 201: Magne, read: réception, variante; Müller, read: ihre. Cf. below, nn. 10 and 14.

and Allison, Taussig, Stritzky, Trudinger, Catchpole, Hagner, Nolland, Meier (99-104). Moreover, ten citations in that section are strictly identical to the text cited in 11,2b[4] *Matt Con*: Loisy 1907, Loisy 1924, Bussmann, Bacon, Creed, Manson, Kilpatrick, Schulz, Schneider, Marshall. These repetitions are apparently a mistake for "See...". Another example of connected units are Q 11,3[1] δός and 3[2] σήμερον (Lk δίδου and τὸ καθ' ἡμέραν). The formula "See Q 11:3[1] Luke = Q, Con" is used nine times here (137-141: B. Weiß 1878, J. Weiß, Manson, Jeremias 1967, Jeremias 1971, Luz, Taussig, Wiefel, Catchpole), but there are also (by mistake?) twelve identical citations: Harnack, B. Weiß 1907, McNeile, Lagrange, Klostermann 1929, Schmid 1930, Wrege, Schulz, Schweizer, Lambrecht, Evans, Nolland.

The fourfold division of the material within each variation unit implies that the same option is cited twice, as *Luke Pro* and *Matt Con* or as *Luke Con* and *Matt Pro*. See, for instance, Q 11,3[1]: the citation of Klostermann 1927, 56 is given twice, whereas for Lagrange 1921, Creed 1930, Schmid 1930, Schürmann 1994 phrases from the same passage are divided over *Luke Con* and *Matt Pro*. The rationale of such a division could be that specific statements on Lukan or Matthean redaction are cited respectively in *Luke Con* or *Matt Pro*, but general statements such as "In V 11f hat Mt in allem den primären Text" (Schmid 1930) can be cited, and indeed are cited, as *Luke Con* (147) as well as *Matt Pro* (133). Since the purpose of the database in *Documenta Q* is the reconstruction of Q, and not the study of Matthean or Lukan redaction, one may suggest to join together on the one hand *Matt Pro and Luke Con* and on the other *Luke Pro and Matt Con*. If reduced to these two sequences, the arrangement in chronological order will be really helpful for those who are interested in the historical development of the Q reconstructions.

II

The reconstruction of Q 11,2b-4 in *Documenta Q* does not include the introductory material Lk 11,1-2a or Mt 6,7-8 (51-69). To the reference "Reconstruction: no introduction" (Schenk, IQP, Mack, Mell) I may add my own *Q-Synopsis* I (1988, ²1995, 30-31)[5]. — One of the sigla in *Documenta Q* is "Q 11:1-2a.2b-4", i.e., "Luke 11:1-2a par. is not in Q, but Luke 11:2b-4 par. is" (x). The siglum is used throughout the volume

_____

5. See also "The Reconstruction of Q", in *Recent Developments in the Study of Q* (1982), in *Evangelica II* (BETL, 99), 1991, 416 (cf. 418); *New Testament Vocabulary* (BETL, 65), 1984, 491.

(e.g., "Q 11:1 2a.2b"), but in the running title from p. 70 it is replaced by the more elegant "Q 11:2b".

The new critical text differs from IQP (1990)[6] in the introduction (51-74):

> 1990   <. . .> προσεύχεσθε
> 1995   [ὅταν] προσεύχ[η]σθε [λέγετε]   {C}.

Cf. Evaluations, 73-74: "Since both Matthew and Luke attest a form of the verb προσεύχομαι, we may be sure a form of this verb was in Q here... Luke may also be dependent on Q for his introduction" (Carruth, 73). Robinson argues that "there must have been some transition in Q to the Prayer (73). He is critical of Schürmann's suggestion that ὅταν προσεύχησθε in Mt 6,5 might be a reminiscence of the Q text (Lk 11,2b). However, there is some confusion in his argument on the fluctuation from singular to plural (74, italics mine):

> For the *singular* ... occurs in the opening formulation only in the *third* item (Matt 6:16). Thus it is the minority usage of the *singular* in this opening of the *third* item that, if anything, calls for some explanation or derivation. It may in fact echo the singular used in the second part of each of the three items.

But the singular occurs in the first item: 6,2 ὅταν ποίης. Mt 6,16 reads ὅταν νηστεύητε and this plural can echo the plural used in Mt 6,7-8.14-15. — This is one of the rare cases where the database has the rubric "Undecided" (here, 72: Katz 1973; see also 143: Schnackenburg, on σήμερον)[7]. The grade {C} represents "a hesitant possibility" (XI). For anything that goes beyond some form of προσεύχομαι I would sign "undecided".

The evaluations are unanimous about the supplementary material in Matthew: 6,9b ἡμῶν, ὁ ἐν τοῖς οὐρανοῖς, 10b γενηθήτω τὸ θέλημά σου ὡς ἐν οὐρανῷ καὶ ἐπὶ γῆς, 13b ἀλλὰ ῥῦσαι ἡμᾶς ἀπὸ τοῦ πονηροῦ, all added to Q (= Lk) {A}, and about Matt = Q in 6,11-12: δός, σήμερον, τὰ ὀφειλήματα {A}, ὡς, ἡμεῖς {B}, ἀφήκαμεν {A}, τοῖς, ὀφειλέταις ἡμῶν {A/B}. Only in the last items the evaluators' decisions show some variation in the grade they assign to the Q text:

---

6. Published in *JBL* 109 (1990), 500. The siglum IQP (for International Q Project) I am using here can be recommended for stylistic improvement (cf. 68, first paragraph).

7. The rubric *"Pro"* is used in a very broad sense. Schulz is cited as *Luke Pro*: "Sicherheit ist hier allerdings nicht zu gewinnen, da Lk möglicherweise auch V 2a formuliert haben könnte" (70). Is he not rather "undecided"? One other example: Bussmann, cited as *Luke Pro*: "wird schwer auszumachen sein" (145).

τοῖς   Carruth {A}; Robinson, Kloppenborg {B}
ὀφειλέταις ἡμῶν   Carruth {A}, Robinson {B}, Kloppenborg {A}.

According to their analysis, the evidence is two-fold: Matthean expansions in Mt 6,9³⁻⁵.10b.13b, and a text of Q that is better preserved in the shorter version of Lk, but also changes of Q in Lk 11,3¹⁻².4¹⁻⁶ that in Goulder's hypothesis are explicable as Luke's changes of Mt⁸. It is not insignificant that the Q origin of these | eight variations in Lk 11,3-4 is defended by R.H. Gundry⁹. As can be seen in the database, this is rather a minority position:

3¹ δίδου. *Lk Pro*: —. *Mt Con*: Gundry.
3² τὸ καθ᾽ ἡμέραν. *Lk Pro*: Mack. *Mt Con*: Bussmann, Gundry, [Meier]¹⁰.
4¹ τὰς ἁμαρτίας. *Lk Pro*: Bussmann, Wrege, Ernst. *Mt Con*: Gundry.
4² γάρ. *Lk Pro*: Easton, Jeremias, Davies-Allison, Mack. *Mt Con*: Bussmann, Gundry, Davies-Allison, Schürmann¹¹.
4³ αὐτοί. *Lk Pro*: J. Weiß¹², Davies-Allison, Mack, Schürmann. *Mt Con*: Bussmann, Gundry.
4⁴ ἀφίομεν. *Lk Pro*: Plummer¹³, Mack, Schürmann. *Mt Con*: Bussmann, Gundry, Davies-Allison.
4⁵ παντί. *Lk Pro*: Wrege, Jeremias, Mack, Schürmann. *Mt Con*: Gundry.
4⁶ ὀφείλοντι ἡμῖν. *Lk Pro*: Davies-Allison, Mack, Schürmann. *Mt Con*: Gundry, [Schneider]¹⁴, Davies-Allison.

---

8. Cf. M.D. GOULDER, *The Composition of the Lord's Prayer*, in *JTS* 14 (1963) 32-45; *Luke. A New Paradigm* (JSNT SS, 20), Sheffield, 1989, 495-502. Although for Goulder the Lord's Prayer in Mt 6,9-13 is created by the evangelist, his view on Luke's edition of the Prayer in Lk 11,1-4 could be included in the database. Compare the references to B. Weiß's Q = Mt as *Matt Pro* and/or *Luke Con* in Q 11,2b³·⁴·⁵·⁶.3¹·².4¹·²·³·⁴·⁵·⁶·⁷. Not all scholars referred to in the volume regard the Lord's Prayer as a Q text. Cf. "Was the Prayer in Q?" (27-31: "Con"). Cf. D.R. CATCHPOLE, *The Quest for Q*, Edinburgh, 1993, 1-59: "Did Q Exist?" (against Goulder), esp. 28-31.
9. *Matthew*, 1982, ²1994. Cf. *ETL* 71 (1995), 151 ("The Goulder-Gundry Team").
10. Meier 1994 is incorrectly cited here with the reference: "See Q 11:3¹ *Matt* = Q, Con" (143). See "*Luke* = Q, Con": "Luke's modification of the wording..." (132). Meier is significantly omitted in Carruth's recapitulation (Evalutations, 143).
11. Schürmann 1994, 198 n. 178: "καὶ γάρ ... muß hier ... nicht unbedingt ... luk Ursprungs sein"; cited with the comment: "Note his hesitation" (159).
12. J. Weiß 1892, 467: "Note that he is talking about Q^Luke" (161; cf. XI: LQ = Q^Luke). The siglum can be misleading: LQ (= L + Q) is more than a Q^Lk recension. Cf. *Evangelica I*, 687 (= *ETL* 54, 1978, 123). J. Weiß's opinion on Lk 11,1 can be added as Luke Con (57): "Lk wird nicht direkt aus Q, sondern aus der ihm zugänglichen Form von Q (LQ) geschöpft haben, wo die kleine Einleitung (V. 1) ... hinzugekommen ist" (464 n. 2).
13. Plummer 1896, 297: "If this is correct, ἀφίομεν is closer to the original [in the future] than ἀφήκαμεν is. But the connexion is the same...".
14. Schneider 1985, 69: "... Lk 11,4b ist in seinen Abweichungen von Mt 6,12b im ganzen sekundär" (176). This should be cited as *Luke Con* (175).

This list illustrates how confusing a distinction between *Lk Pro* and *Mt Con* can be. Bussmann 1929 appears in both *Lk Pro* (4[1]) and *Mt Con* (3[2].4[2.3.4]) but Gundry's argument regarding 4[1] (*Mt Con*) reformulates the observation made by Bussmann (*Lk Pro*): "Matthew changes sins to debts in order to match the debtors in the last part of the petition". Mack 1993 is cited as *Lk Pro* in 3[2].4[2-6] on the basis of his reconstruction of Q in English translation: "Give us each day our daily bread. Pardon our *debts*, for we ourselves pardon everyone indebted to us" (176). No justification is provided other than his "guide to the English translation": "In order to arrive at a unified Greek text, I have consulted the scholarship on the reconstruction of the original text as well as the work of the Q project at Claremont" (71). But, with the exception of 4[1] ("debts"), all Mack's textual options in Q 11,3-4 differ from the IQP text. Davies and Allison 1988 are cited as *Lk Pro* on the basis of their tentative reconstruction of Q (591: 4[2.3.6]) and as *Mt Con* on the basis of their comments on possible Matthean redaction (4[2.4.6]), in one case (4[4] ἀφήκαμεν) against their l reconstruction. Schürmann 1994 appears as *Lk Pro* (4[3-6]) and *Mt Con* (4[2]). Only Gundry is a constant witness for Lk 11,3-4 = Q (*Mt Con*: 3[1-2].4[1-6]).

My final remark concerns the *Evaluations*: Carruth 1995, Robinson 1995, Kloppenborg 1995. They are presented as three independent conclusions ("their own conclusions") and references such as Kloppenborg's "above, Robinson 1995" (136) are most exceptional. It is hard to imagine how, after so many common discussions and work sessions, this personal independence of the three evaluators can be more than a stylistic exercise. True, some distinctive traits can be noted: Carruth's summaries of the database, Robinson's emphasis on the evangelists' usage, Kloppenborg's attention to parallels in Q. And there are some nuances in their judgment. For Carruth, "it is difficult to establish a Matthean preference for ὡς καί on the basis of three occurrences" (159), but Robinson notes: "ὡς is quite frequent in Matthew. ὡς καί is in Matt 6:12; 18:33; 20:14, never in Mark or Luke... Both γάρ and ὡς could be secondary" (160). The observation that "σήμερον is attested once in minimal Q (12:28), whereas the parallel Lukan expression is not" is typical of Kloppenborg (144). But in many instances the observations are about the same (e.g., the consistency within the Prayer). Therefore, I may suggest that the three evaluators examine the possibility of combining their conclusions into one common statement at the end of each variation unit.

ETL 73 (1997) 94-102

20

NOTE ON Q 4,1-2

Only a few months after *The Lord's Prayer* a new volume in the Reconstructions of Q series has appeared, on The Temptations of Jesus (Q 4,1-13) and the one-word fragment Ναζαρά (4,16)[1]; and already a volume on Q 12,49-59 has been announced for 1997[2]. The prospectus that the volumes are to appear "preferably in their Q sequence", beginning with the problem of an *Incipit* and the sayings of John in Q 3, now seems to be given up.

The preliminary volume on Q 11,2b-4 circulated as a sample issue with the invitation to send suggestions for improvement to the Editorial Board. It may be instructive to compare the new volume with my observations (made available before publication in *ETL*)[3]. There is now a Table of Contents (x-xiii) and the resultant critical text of Q 4 is printed at the end (463: the unformatted Greek text, with English, German and French translations). Overlapping quotations as *Luke Pro* and *Matt Con* or as *Luke Con* and *Matt Pro* are now avoided. Instead of repeating comments on connected units a reference system has been used (referring to unit and page numbers). In a final remark on the *Evaluations* I made the suggestion that "the three evaluators examine the possibility of combining their conclusions into one common statement at the end of each variation unit". This has not (or not yet?) been done in the present volume. It is simply noted in the Introduction: "The original Evaluations have been updated and those of the General Editors composed in an informal dialogue of those involved" (VIII).

The first part, entitled "Q 4:1-4.9-12.5-8.13. The Temptations of Jesus", constitutes the main body of this volume (1-389; Database author: S. Carruth). The Introduction (VII) indicates that the first Evaluation was prepared by Carruth (4,1-13) and further Evaluations came from D.D. Turlington and J.M. Robinson (for 4,1-4) and from P.J. Hartin and A. Chang (for 4,5-13). This information is somewhat incomplete: also in 4,5-13 there is always a last evaluation by Robinson. Furthermore a number of units include an evaluation by P. Hoffmann: 4,1-2 (4,

1. Shawn CARRUTH, James M. ROBINSON, and (volume editor) Christoph HEIL, *Q 4:1-13,16. The Temptation of Jesus – Nazara* (Documenta Q), Leuven, Peeters, XVIII-479 p.
2. Cf. C. Heil's short paper on Q 12,51-53 at the Colloquium Biblicum Lovaniense, 1996.
3. *Documenta Q: Q 11,2b-4*, in *ETL* 72 (1996) 418-424.

6, 7, 8, 10, 11); 4,12 (2, 3); 4,8 (2, 4). The second part, "Q 4:16,~~31~~. Nazara" (note: the marked-through reference ~~31~~!), is almost an appendix (391-462; Database author: Robinson). The central question "Is (at least) Ναζαρά from Q?" (410-441) is answered unanimously by the four evaluators: the place name is from Q {B} (Robinson, Carruth, Kloppenborg, Hoffmann).

The resultant critical text of Q 4,1-13.16:

1 ⟦ὁ⟧ δὲ Ἰησοῦς ⟦ἀν⟧ήχθη ⟦εἰς⟧ τὴ⟦ν⟧ ἔρημ⟦ον⟧ ⟦ὑπὸ⟧ τ⟦οῦ⟧ πνεύμα⟦τος⟧ **2** πειρα⟦σθῆναι⟧ ὑπὸ τοῦ διαβόλου. καὶ... ἡμέρας τεσσεράκοντα... ἐπείνασεν. **3** καὶ εἶπεν αὐτῷ ὁ διάβολος· εἰ υἱὸς εἶ τοῦ θεοῦ, εἰπὲ ἵνα οἱ λίθοι Ι οὗτοι ἄρτοι γένωνται. **4** καὶ ἀπεκρίθη ⟦αὐτ<ῷ>⟧ ὁ Ἰησοῦς· γέγραπται ὅτι οὐκ ἐπ' ἄρτῳ μόνῳ ζήσεται ὁ ἄνθρωπος. **9** παραλαμβάνει αὐτὸν ⟦ὁ διάβολος⟧ εἰς Ἰερουσαλὴμ καὶ ἔστησεν αὐτὸν ἐπὶ τὸ πτερύγιον τοῦ ἱεροῦ καὶ εἶπεν αὐτῷ· εἰ υἱὸς εἶ τοῦ θεοῦ, βάλε σεαυτὸν ⟦⟧ κάτω· **10** γέγραπται γὰρ ὅτι τοῖς ἀγγέλοις αὐτοῦ ἐντελεῖται περὶ σοῦ **11** καὶ ἐπὶ χειρῶν ἀροῦσίν σε, μήποτε προσκόψῃς πρὸς λίθον τὸν πόδα σου. **12** καὶ ⟦ἀποκριθεὶς⟧ εἶπεν αὐτῷ ὁ Ἰησοῦς· ⟦⟧ γέγραπται· οὐκ ἐκπειράσεις κύριον τὸν θεόν σου. **5** καὶ παραλαμβάνει αὐτὸν ὁ διάβολος εἰς ὄρος ⟦ὑψηλὸν λίαν⟧ καὶ δείκνυσιν αὐτῷ πάσας τὰς βασιλείας τοῦ κόσμου καὶ τὴν δόξαν αὐτῶν **6** καὶ εἶπεν αὐτῷ ⟦⟧· ταῦτά σοι πάντα δώσω, **7** ἐὰν προσκυνήσῃς μοι. **8** καὶ ⟦ἀποκριθεὶς⟧ ὁ Ἰησοῦς εἶπεν αὐτῷ· γέγραπται· κύριον τὸν θεόν σου προσκυνήσεις καὶ αὐτῷ μόνῳ λατρεύσεις. **13** καὶ ⟦⟧ ὁ διάβολος ἀφίησιν αὐτόν. **16** ... Ναζαρά ...

Compare IQP (1993, 1995)[4]:
Apart from 4,1-2 (cf. below) the differences concern the degree of certainty.

3⁵   ⟦οἱ⟧ λίθ⟦οι⟧ ⟦⟧ οὗτ⟦οι⟧ ἄρτο⟦ι⟧ γέν⟦ω⟧νται
4⁴   conjectural emendation ⟦αὐτ<ῷ>⟧ om.
9⁶   εἰς ... (undecided)
9⁸   ...ε... (for εἶπεν, not λέγει)[5]
12²   καὶ ε... αὐτῷ (om. ἀποκριθείς)[6]
5³   ⟦ὁ διάβολος⟧
8²   καὶ ὁ Ἰησοῦς (om. ἀποκριθείς)[7]
8⁴   ...ε... αὐτῷ (for εἶπεν)[8].

---

4. *JBL* 112 (1993), 502 (4,1-4); 114 (1995), 477-478 (4,5-13).
5. Ctr. 211: εἶπεν/λέγει undecided.
6. Ctr. 232: καὶ ... αὐτῷ undecided. See also 234 (12³): "Although it is not obvious from this printed reconstruction, the International Q Project favored Luke's verb at a D grade". But see the obvious reading in *JBL* 1995, 478 (ε = εἶπεν).
7. Cf. 340, *Matt Pro*: add IQP.
8. Cf. 344, *Luke Pro*: add IQP.

Q 4,1-2

The first set of variants opens with a question regarding 4,1-2: "Is the framework of the story here and at 4:13 from Q or Mark?" (4). The answer of the three evaluators is unanimous: "Matt and Luke = Q {A}" (28). This question "Q or Mark" comes up here for the first time in *Documenta Q*. The arrangement of the Database in *Luke*: *Pro, Con*; *Matt*: *Pro, Con* has been conceived for double-tradition texts (major agreements Mt-Lk) and the classification of reconstructions of Q (= Lk, Mt), Q (= Lk, diff. MtR), Q (= Mt, diff. LkR), or Q (diff. LkR, MtR). Is it due to a lack of routine in handling Mark-Q overlaps that the question "from Q or Mark" concerning 4,1-2 and the problem of the Q-origin of the temptation story (the three temptations) are not treated as two different questions in the database? To cite one example: under the title "Q 4:1-2 ... Luke and Matt = Q, Pro", the name of "Wernle 1899" should be cancelled (4; cf. 20). It is even less I understandable that the list of Q-*Pro*'s ends with "Klein 1996" and an explicit quotation: "Die Arbeitsweise des Mt läßt sich also folgendermaßen beschreiben: Den Inhalt des Mittelteils übernimmt Mt von Q, gestaltet aber den Rahmen von Mk her" (19; cf. 372).

Instead of the disjunction "from Q or Mark" (and the two classes "= Q" and "= Mark") not a few scholars could have been classified under the heading "Lk 4,1-2 / Mt 4,1-2: from Mk and Q". An author like G. Schneider (*Lk*, 1977) is now found under "Luke and Matt = Q, Pro": "Der Anfang der Perikope (4,1f.) folgt hauptsächlich Mk 1,12f.; wenn es auch wahrscheinlich ist, daß die Versuchungen schon in Q wenigstens mit einer einleitenden Bemerkung über Jesu Fasten und Hungrigsein eingeleitet waren" (12; without reference under "= Mark").

In a quotation from Holtzmann (1901) "der Zusammenstoß zweier Quellen" in Lk 4,2 is apparently understood as the combination of Mk and Q (4). However, Holtzmann places the beginning of Q at Q 7,18-28.31-35 and the "two sources" in Lk 4,2 are Mk and Mt (1901, 17). A modern form of this theory is upheld by M.D. Goulder; he is cited in the section on Q 4,16 (435, 436-437) but his hard-line position is not mentioned here, either as "Luke and Matt = Q, Con" (20-22) or as "Other" (24-27: i.e., other source than Q or Mk).

In the case of Q 4,1-2, the division into two separate sections, "Luke and Matt = Q, Con" (20-22) and "Luke and Matt = Mark, Pro" (22-24), is scarcely justifiable.

Variation units in 4,1-2

			Grade
0	Framework: from Q or Mk?	Q	{A}
1	Lk δέ / Mt τότε	Lk	—
2	Lk — / Mt ὁ	Mt	{C}
3	Lk πλήρης πνεύματος ... Ἰορδάνου, καί / Mt —	Mt	{A}
4	Lk — / Mt ἀν-	Mt	—
5	Lk ἤγετο / Mt -ήχϑη	Mt	—
6	Lk spirit – wilderness / Mt wilderness – spirit	Mt	{C}
7	Lk ἐν + dat. / Mt εἰς + acc. (wilderness)	Mt	—
8	Lk ἐν + dat. / Mt ὑπό + gen. (spirit)	Mt	—
9	Lk ἡμέρας τεσσ. before πειρ. (+ ἐν τ. ἡμ. ἐκ) / Mt after πειρ.	Mt	{B}
10	Lk πειραζόμενος / Mt πειρασϑῆναι	Mt	—
11	Lk οὐκ ἔφαγεν οὐδὲν ... καί / Mt νηστεύσας	...	{U}
12	Lk — / Mt καὶ νύκτας τεσσεράκοντα	Lk	{A}
13	Lk συντελεσϑεισῶν / Mt ὕστερον	Mt	{D}

Different grades assigned to the Q text (cf. Table, last column):

		Carruth	Turlington	Robinson	Hoffmann
1	Lk	Lk {B}	Lk {C}	Lk {D}	
4	Mt	Lk {C}	Lk {D}	Mt {C}	Mt {C}
5	Mt	Lk {C}	Mt {C}	Mt {C}	Mt {C}[9]
7	Mt	Lk {C}	Lk {C}	Mt {C}	Mt {C}
8	Mt	Mt {A}	Mt {A}	Mt {C}	Mt {C}
10	Mt	Mt {B}	Mt {B}	Mt {C}	— {C}
11	Mt	Lk {C}	Lk {C}	... {U}	Mt {C}
	Note on 4 and 5:	Carruth	ἤ⟦γετο⟧		
		Turlington	ἤ⟦χϑη⟧		
		Robinson	⟦ἀν⟧ή⟦χϑη⟧	cf. Hoffmann[9].	

---

9. Cf. 51-52 (4,1-2⁴). See also the references to 4,1-2⁵ (read: 4,1-2⁴): 60, 63.

I noted a few corrigenda and addenda; read: Ursprünglichkeit (52); IQP ε̣...τ̣η... ἐρημ... (62); Sand's (66); wie Lukas (86); διαφυλάξαι (222); προσκόψῃς (463); Anointed (466); Mémorial (467); Frans (474). — M. Sabbe's 1954 article (26) is reprinted in his *Studia Neotestamentica*, 1991, 3-12; J. Delobel's 1973 article (431-433) is reprinted in *L'Évangile de Luc – The Gospel of Luke*, ²1989, 133-154 (with additional notes, 306-312); J. Dupont 1985 (419-420), add: 1st ed. 1978 ("Evangelizare pauperibus").

I do not treat in this note on Q 4,1-2 the problem of Ναζαρά in Q 4,16, which is a quite different question than the Temptations in Q. One may observe here that the inclusion of the 70 pages on Nazara in the same volume with the Temptations was not a necessity. If we consider the opinions of recent defenders of its origin in Q (Catchpole: a geographical reference in a transition formula; Robinson: the name Jesus ἀπὸ Ναζαρά), this section in Documenta Q could be combined either with the opening of the Sermon or with the *Incipit* of Q. For Catchpole, *The Anointed One*, see 423-424: here and in the Bibliography, read 1993 (!) instead of 1989; for Robinson 1992, see 424-427 (= *The Four Gospels 1992*, 361-388, esp. 379) and again in his Evaluation, 438-441, esp. 440.

Compare IQP (1993): **1** ⟦ὁ⟧ Ἰησοῦς δὲ ⟦⟧ἤ... ⟦ὑπὸ⟧ τ⟦οῦ⟧ πνεύματ⟦ος⟧ ε... τη ... ἐρημ...
2 πειρασθῆναι ὑπὸ τοῦ διαβόλου, καὶ ⟦οὐκ ἔφαγεν οὐδὲν⟧ ἡμέρας τεσσεράκοντα,.. ἐπείνασεν.

Differences: 4 (Lk), 5 (Lk), 6 (Lk), 7 (undecided), 11 (Lk), 13 (undecided).

"From Q or Mark?"

The database on Q 4,1-2 includes seven quotations under the heading "Luke and Matt = Q, Con" (20-22). It begins with Holtzmann's *Urmarcus* (1863): καὶ εὐθὺς τὸ πνεῦμα αὐτὸν ἐκβάλλει εἰς τὴν ἔρημον καὶ ἦν ἐν τῇ ἐρήμῳ ἡμέρας τεσσεράκοντα πειραζόμενος ὑπὸ τοῦ διαβόλου καὶ οὐκ ἔφαγεν οὐδέν. The *Urmarcus* theory is a common-source hypothesis[10] and, like Mg, should be located with "Other" (neither Q nor Mk), as has been done in the units 1, 2, 4, 5, 6, 8[11]. The list of quotations "Q, Con" ends with an excerpt from *ETL* (1984) comparing the reconstruction of Q 4,1 Ἰησοῦς ἀνήχθη/ἤγετο ὑπὸ τοῦ πνεύματος ἐν τῇ ἐρήμῳ (Schulz, Polag, Schenk) with the text of Mk 1,12-13a: "ne faisons pas abstraction de Mc et voyons la réaction que peut avoir suscitée le texte de Mc 1,12-13a"[12]. A later essay on "The Minor Agreements and Q" (1995) resumes one aspect of the argument, the connection with the Baptism (Q?)[13]:

> The connection with πνεῦμα is a much weaker argument. The Mt/Lk agreement in the narrative introductions, Mt 4:1 (ἀνήχθη εἰς τὴν ἔρημον ὑπὸ τοῦ πνεύματος) and Lk 4:1 (ἤγετο ἐν τῷ πνεύματι ἐν τῇ ἐρήμῳ), can be the result of independent redaction (cf. Mk 1:12 τὸ πνεῦμα αὐτὸν ἐκβάλλει εἰς τὴν ἔρημον) and is too easily accepted in reconstructions of Q. Together with Jesus' 'fasting' and hunger the location in the wilderness can be an appropriate setting for the first temptation in Q, but the link with the account of Jesus' baptism and the motif that 'he was led by the Spirit' may derive from Mk 1:12.

10. Holtzmann's A text differs from Mk 1,12-13a in ἡμέρας τεσσεράκοντα (Lk/Mt, for τεσσ. ἡμ.), διαβόλου (Lk/Mt, for σατανᾶ), and οὐκ ἔφαγεν οὐδέν (Lk; cf. Mt νηστεύσας).

11. Cf. pp. 32, 34, 51, 57, 59, 66. Ctr. 3, 7 (42, 62): Matt = Q, Pro; 9, 10, 11, 12 (67, 73, 79, 88): Luke = Q, Pro.

12. F. NEIRYNCK, *L'arrière-fond sémitique des évangiles synoptiques. Réponse à P. Rolland*, in *ETL* 60 (1984) 363-366, esp. 363-364; = *Evangelica II* (BETL, 99), Leuven, 1991, 320-329, esp. 320-321 (cited in Database, 21-22).

13. F. NEIRYNCK, *The Minor Agreements and Q*, in R.A. PIPER (ed.), *The Gospel Behind the Gospels* (NTSup, 75), Leiden, 1995, 49-72, esp. 66.

From this quotation it may be clear enough that I am not delighted to be placed in a database on Q 4,1-2 as "= Q, Con". Compare the Q reconstruction in my *New Testament Vocabulary* (1984): "Lc 4,2b-13 / Mt 4,2b-11a" (489; note: 4,2b!) and ἐπείνασεν printed in bold in my *Q-Synopsis* (1988).

Concerning the point I made on Lk 4,1-2a / Mt 4,1-2a and the alleged Q-connection with the Baptism, see also R. Uro's observation (in the same volume)[14]:

> Moreover, it is not perfectly clear whether the absolutely used τὸ πνεῦμα derives from Q... Q has 'the Holy spirit' elsewhere (3:16; 12:10; 12:12?). In Matthew, τὸ πνεῦμα for God's Spirit appears only in these two Markan contexts (the Baptism and the Temptation) and Luke's ἐν τῷ πνεύματι seems to be Lukan (cf. Lk 2:27; 4:14; Acts 19:21; 20:22 and Acts 16:18; 19:1). Therefore, one has to consider the possibility that Matthew follows Mark in using the absolute 'Spirit' in Mt 4:1 and Luke modifies Mark with his own favourite expression.

To start with Lk 4,1-2a, the suggestion of Lukan redaction in dependence upon Mk 1,12-13a combined with the influence of Deut 8,2 (cf. *ETL*, 1984) now finds more than one confirmation in the General Editors' Evaluations of the Documenta Q volume.

Mk 1,12-13a		Lk 4,1-2a	
12	καὶ εὐθὺς	1	Ἰησοῦς δὲ
	τὸ πνεῦμα		πλήρης πνεύματος ἁγίου
	αὐτὸν ἐκβάλλει		ὑπέστρεψεν
	εἰς τὴν ἔρημον.		ἀπὸ τοῦ Ἰορδάνου,
13a	καὶ ἦν		καὶ ἤγετο ἐν τῷ πνεύματι
	ἐν τῇ ἐρήμῳ		ἐν τῇ ἐρήμῳ
	τεσσεράκοντα ἡμέρας	2a	ἡμέρας τεσσεράκοντα
	πειραζόμενος		πειραζόμενος
	ὑπὸ τοῦ σατανᾶ		ὑπὸ τοῦ διαβόλου.

1 Deut 8,2 πᾶσαν τὴν ὁδόν, ἣν **ἤγαγέν σε** κύριος ὁ θεός σου **ἐν τῇ ἐρήμῳ**, ὅπως ἂν κακώσῃ σε καὶ ἐκπειράσῃ σε...

---

14. R. URO, *John the Baptist and the Jesus Movement. What Does Q Tell Us?*, in PIPER, *Gospel* (n. 13), 231-257, esp. 238.

The Piper volume (1995) on Q does not appear in the Database on Q 4,1-13 (but see 428, on Q 4,16). In more than one unit the list of quotations concludes with E. Sevenich-Bax, 1993 (*Israels Konfrontation*, 50-67) and J.B. Gibson's reconstruction (*The Temptations*, 1995, 36-37). All Evaluations are dated in the year of the appearance of the volume (1996) and there are also some occasional references to works published in 1996; I noted: Klein (19, 105, 112, 387), Moses (91, 182, 270, 275), Kollmann (178, 387), Müller (178, 196), Tuckett (178).

Hoffmann

Schon durch 4:1a – in Verbindung mit 4:14-15 – hat Lk[R] eine übergeordnete Rahmenangabe geschaffen, die den Weg Jesu von der Taufe im Jordan zurück nach Galiläa beschreibt. Die Versuchungsgeschichte wird dadurch zu einer – allerdings entscheidenden – Episode auf diesem Weg. [51]
Nach Lukas wurde Jesus *im* Geist *in* der Wüste vierzig Tage lang (herum)geführt. Das lukanische ἤγετο (Imperfekt) entspricht dem markinischen καὶ ἦν ἐν τῇ ἐρήμῳ. Lukas benutzt die markinische //Chrset7 220// Vorgabe zu seiner Ausgestaltung der Exposition der aus Q übernommenen drei Versuchungsszenen. (...) Die sicher lukanische Wendung συντελεσθεισῶν αὐτῶν bestätigt, daß Lukas es war, der im Rückgriff auf Markus die Szene geschaffen hat. (...) Da Lukas die vierzigtägige Dauer des Wüstenaufenthalten herausstellt, geht auch das Imperfekt auf ihn zurück.
Die Anspielung auf Dtn 8:2 in der Lukas-Fassung beweist nicht deren Ursprünglichkeit. Sie läßt sich durchaus dem LXX-Kenner und LXX-Imitator Lukas zutrauen. [51-52]
Die Wendung ἐν τῷ πνεύματι entspricht dem Sprachgebrauch des Lukas und generell seiner Vorstellung vom Wirken des Geistes in der Geschichte Jesu und der Kirche. [66]
Lk 4:2 (nennt) in Übereinstimmung mit Mk 1:13a nur das Faktum der Versuchung: πειραζόμενος ὑπὸ τοῦ διαβόλου. Die Übereinstimmung mit Markus in der Partizipialkonstruktion (...). Da sich Lukas in 4:1-2 auch sonst von Markus beeinflußt zeigt, liegt in der Tat der Verdacht eines Markus-Einflusses nahe. [76]

Robinson

[δέ] Luke's redactional use of δέ is sufficiently common to make it suspect of being redactional here. It occurs in Luke 4:3[1] to replace καί. [33]
['Ιησοῦς] ... the probability of extensive redactional expansion of the reference to Jesus by Luke suggests it may be Luke who made the change. [35]
[πλήρης πνεύματος ἁγίου ὑπέστρεψεν ἀπὸ τοῦ 'Ιορδάνου] This is in style and content clearly a Lukan addition, needed to connect back to the Baptism, from which the Temptation had been separated by the Lukan genealogy. ὑπέστρεψεν also performs a framing function for the Temptations in Luke, for Luke uses it both in 4:1 and in 4:14. [44, cf. 60]
[ἤγετο] Luke, building on Mark, could, with a second verb (see Mark) have shifted (...) to a more vague circulating (the imperfect without the

prefix: ἤγετο), much as Mark moves from ἐκβάλλει in 1:12 to ἦν in 1:13. (...) Luke moves directly to Mark 1:13a at the end of Luke 4:1 and the first part of Luke 4:2, in which parts he follows Mark almost verbatim. [53]

Mark is followed by Luke's presentation, where Jesus is led around (imperfect, without prefix) during 40 days of temptations. [57]

[ἐν τῷ πνεύματι] Mark's beginning with τὸ πνεῦμα (as subject of the verb) (...) is more likely to have influenced Luke's πλήρης πνεύματος ἁγίου ... ἤγετο ἐν τῷ πνεύματι in Luke 4:1. Luke's order of a verb of motion followed by ἐν τῷ πνεύματι ἐν τῇ ἐρήμῳ is similar to the redactional text Luke 4:14, ἐν τῇ | δυνάμει τοῦ πνεύματος εἰς τὴν Γαλιλαίαν, whose ὑπέστρεψεν has already been noted (4:1[5]) as completing Luke's framing of the Temptations. [60; cf. 44]

[ἐν τῇ ἐρήμῳ] Luke is here following in sequence and wording Mark 1:13a, both in this motif of wandering rather than entering, and in the corresponding use of the dative. [62]

[πειραζόμενος...] Luke follows Mark. [75]

In spite of all that Robinson continues to treat Lk 4,1-2a as a witness of Q. The first reason is probably the paradox of the minor agreements. It is far from unique in the discussions of minor agreements that notwithstanding the evidence of redactional explanations authors remain impressed by the number of agreements (cf. 28). The second reason is a more specific one. Although Robinson concedes that "the immediately preceding context in Q is quite uncertain" (32), the mirage of a Q sequence from the Baptism to the Temptation still has its effect (53: Q's ἀνήχθη "effects the basic shift of location from the low Jordan valley to the high wilderness").

However, there is an important shift from Carruth's evaluation to that of Hoffmann: from ἤγετο and ἐν τῇ ἐρήμῳ = Q {C} for Carruth (51, 62) to LkR (cf. Mk) for Hoffmann (51-52). Even more significant is Hoffmann's position on πειρασθῆναι (Matt = Q, {B} for Carruth and Turlington, {C} for Robinson):

> Weder das lukanische πειραζόμενος ὑπὸ τοῦ διαβόλου noch das matthäische πειρασθῆναι ὑπὸ τοῦ διαβόλου stammt aus Q. [76]
> Da (...) bei beiden Evangelisten mit dem Einfluß des Markus gerechnet werden muß, bietet sich als die plausiblere Lösung der Vorschlag von Schulz an, daß sowohl Matthäus als auch Lukas das Verb aus Markus übernommen haben. [77]

Hoffmann's suggestion can probably be extended and considered also with regard to Lk 4,2b (+ Mk):

Mt 4,2	Lk 4,2b
καὶ νηστεύσας	καὶ οὐκ ἔφαγεν οὐδὲν
ἡμέρας τεσσεράκοντα	ἐν ταῖς ἡμέραις ἐκείναις
καὶ νύκτας τεσσεράκοντα,	
ὕστερον	καὶ συντελεσθεισῶν αὐτῶν
ἐπείνασεν.	ἐπείνασεν.

The evaluations are divided on οὐκ ἔφαγεν οὐδὲν ... καί Lk = Q {C} (Carruth, Turlington); νηστεύσας Mt = Q {C} (Hoffmann); Indeterminate {U} (Robinson). All agree on ἐν ταῖς ἡμέραις ἐκείναις and συντελεσθεισῶν αὐτῶν LkR; Mt's ὕστερον receives the {D} grade, i.e., "without enough certainty to include the reading in the text". In this last case all Carruth can say is: "Since both evangelists have something here, we may suspect that Q had something as well" (95). The only firm evidence in Lk 4,2b is ἐπείνασεν. Perhaps F. Bovon's suggestion deserves more consideration than it has received in the evaluations: "Könnte sowohl νηστεύσας (Matthäus) als auch οὐκ ἔφαγεν οὐδέν (Lukas) redaktionelle Erweiterung der Logienquelle sein, die nur von Hunger Jesu (ἐπείνασεν [bei Matthäus und Lukas]) gesprochen hat?" (84).

None of the evaluators excludes the possibility of "a coincidence where Q and Mark agree" (cf. 53, 60: εἰς τὴν ἔρημον; 63: ἐν τῇ ἐρήμῳ), but more I than once Mt's lesser similarity to Mk tips the scales in favour of Q: "Luke's dependence on Mark indicates that Matthew probably reflects Q..." (60). However, the question of Mt's relation to Mk cannot simply be treated as it is done in this context by Robinson: "Mark's beginning with τὸ πνεῦμα (as subject of the verb) is clearly not the source of the positioning of Matthew's ὑπὸ τοῦ πνεύματος after εἰς τὴν ἔρημον" (60). See the Mt-Mk synopsis:

	Mt 4,1-2.11b		Mk 1,12-13
1	τότε	12	καὶ εὐθὺς
			τὸ πνεῦμα
	ὁ Ἰησοῦς ἀνήχθη		αὐτὸν ἐκβάλλει
	εἰς τὴν ἔρημον		εἰς τὴν ἔρημον.
	ὑπὸ τοῦ πνεύματος		
	πειρασθῆναι ὑπὸ τοῦ διαβόλου.		
2	καὶ νηστεύσας	13a	καὶ ἦν ἐν τῇ ἐρήμῳ
	ἡμέρας τεσσεράκοντα		τεσσεράκοντα ἡμέρας
	καὶ νύκτας τεσσεράκοντα		
			πειραζόμενος ὑπὸ τοῦ
			σατανᾶ,
	ὕστερον ἐπείνασεν.		
	[3-11a καὶ προσελθὼν...]	b	καὶ ἦν μετὰ τῶν θηρίων,
11b	καὶ ἰδοὺ ἄγγελοι προσῆλθον καὶ		καὶ οἱ ἄγγελοι
	διηκόνουν αὐτῷ.		διηκόνουν αὐτῷ.

Mt's ἀνήχθη or Lk's ἤγετο, Mt's εἰς τὴν ἔρημον or Lk's ἐν τῇ ἐρήμῳ, Mt's ὑπὸ τοῦ πνεύματος or Lk's ἐν τῷ πνεύματι: these are the questions studied in the database. Mt's relation to Mk is dismissed as unlikely: "It is not probable that Matthew's agreement with Mark (...) is a matter of dependence of Matthew on Mark (ἐκβάλλει εἰς τὴν ἔρημον becoming ἀνήχθη εἰς τὴν ἔρημον)" (Robinson, 60). The passive form of the verb is listed as one of the divergences from Mark which make it clear that a framework of the Temptations was in Q (28). No consideration is given to the fact that there are other instances of a change to the passive in Mt[15]:

	Mk			Mt
1,31	ἤγειρεν αὐτήν		8,15	ἠγέρθη
5,40	ἐκβαλὼν πάντας		9,25	ἐξεβλήθη ὁ ὄχλος
6,28ª	ἤνεγκεν τὴν κεφαλὴν αὐτοῦ		14,11ª	ἠνέχθη ἡ κεφαλὴ αὐτοῦ
6,28ᵇ	ἔδωκεν αὐτήν		14,11ᵇ	ἐδόθη
7,19	ἐκπορεύεται		15,17	ἐκβάλλεται
8,36	ὠφελεῖ ἄνθρωπον		16,26	ὠφεληθήσεται ἄνθρωπος
9,43	ἀπελθεῖν		18,8	βληθῆναι
9,50	αὐτὸ ἀρτύσετε		5,13	ἁλισθήσεται
10,13	προσέφερον ... παιδία		19,13	προσηνέχθησαν ... παιδία
13,20ª	ἐκολόβωσεν ...		24,22ª	ἐκολόβωσαν
	τὰς ἡμέρας			αἱ ἡμέραι ἐκεῖναι
13,20ᵇ	ἐκολόβωσεν ...		24,22ᵇ	κολοβωθήσονται
	τὰς ἡμέρας			αἱ ἡμέραι ἐκεῖναι
14,53	συνέρχονται		26,57	συνήχθησαν
15,13	σταύρωσον αὐτόν		27,22	σταυρωθήτω
15,14	σταύρωσον αὐτόν		27,23	σταυρωθήτω
15,27	σταυροῦσιν δύο λῃστάς		27,39	σταυροῦνται ... δύο λῃσταί

"There may be a christological development of elevating Jesus from subservient control by the Spirit, in Mark, where the Spirit drives Jesus out into the wilderness, to Jesus being led into the wilderness by the Spirit...": that is the development indeed, not from Mark to Q (Robinson, 63), but more probably from Mark to Matthew.

"Reducing the shared Markan/Matthean text to ὑπὸ τοῦ" (78): this phrase looks like a reductionist interpretation of Mt's parallel to Mk,

πειραζόμενος   ὑπὸ τοῦ σατανᾶ
πειρασθῆναι   ὑπὸ τοῦ διαβόλου.

---

15. *The Minor Agreements*, 1974, 251: "Active or middle voice in Mark and Passive in Matthew and Luke" (Mt/Lk: diff. Mk 1,12; 8,36; 9,50; 14,53; 15,14).

It is immediately corrected by noting: "The Matthean infinitive could be redactional, as the comparison with the redactional Matthean text 3:13 could suggest" (78). Compare Hoffmann's comment:

> Durch die Infinitiv-Konstruktion wird dem Leser schon in der Exposition das Ziel der Erzählung deutlich gemacht. Aus den drei Versuchungen der Q-Vorlage wird *die* Versuchung Jesu durch den Teufel, hinter der der Wille Gottes steht. Der Infinitiv des Zweckes korrespondiert dem τοῦ βαπτισθῆναι ὑπ' αὐτοῦ in 3:13 (diff. Mk 1:9) ... [76]
> Daß beide (Mt und Lk) das markinische σατανᾶ durch διάβολος ersetzen, läßt sich leicht durch den Einfluß der aus Q übernommenen Versuchungsgeschichte erklären. [77]

With only a few exceptions[16] all authors agree that Mt's καὶ νύκτας τεσσεράκοντα is redactional: "There is no reason to doubt that Matthew has redacted in the direction of Moses typology by the addition of καὶ νύκτας τεσσεράκοντα which recalls the fasting of Moses in Ex 34:38 and Deut 9:9,18" (Carruth, 91)[17]. In this connection, note also R.H. Gundry's comment on ἀνήχθη in Mt 4,1: "Matthew wants to display Jesus as a new and greater Moses who goes up into the mountainous part of the wilderness just as Moses went up Mount Sinai in the wilderness"[18].

In sum, I retain the impression that the resultant text of Q 4,1-2 in Documenta Q is too Matthean-like and anyway goes beyond what I am inclined to conclude from Matthew's and Luke's redaction of Mk 1,12-13. The Q-introduction one may reasonably deduce from Q 4,3-13 can be little more than the location in the wilderness and the motif that Jesus was hungry.

16. Harnack, Loisy, and more recently Gibson's reconstruction. Cf. Database, 88-91. Textual variant in T M N: τεσσεράκοντα νύκτας. Cf. B. Weiss (1907): "mit betonter Voranstellung [*sic*] des τεσσεράκοντα" (quoted with *sic* in the database, 5). The textual variant is not mentioned and Weiss's comment is apparently not understood.

17. Cf. D.C. ALLISON, Jr., *The New Moses. A Matthean Typology*, Edinburgh, 1993, 166-169 (not in the Database). Cf. 167: "the insertion must serve some purpose other than promotion of the Israel typology. Observe further that Matthew, in contrast to Luke, has temptation come to Jesus *after* forty days and forty nights. This also differentiates Jesus from Israel, for Israel's temptations came *during* her forty years sojourn"

18. *Matthew*, 54 (Database, 49-50).

BETL 96 (2000) 159-169

21

NAZAPA IN Q: PRO AND CON

The *Documenta Q* volume *Q 4:1-13,16* (1996) includes a database on Ναζαρά in Matt 4,13 and Luke 4,16. Twenty-six authors, from B. Weiss to C.M. Tuckett, are cited with a positive answer to the question: Is (at least) Ναζαρά from Q? The four evaluators, J.M. Robinson, S. Carruth, J.S. Kloppenborg, and P. Hoffmann, unanimously formulate their conclusion: "The unusually spelled place-name shared by Matthew and Luke is from Q {B}, Ναζαρά"[1]. They confirm the IQP reconstruction (1991) and raise its probability from {C} to {B}[2]. In Kloppenborg's *Q Parallels* (1988) and in his reconstruction of Q in *Q – Thomas Reader* (1990) there was no mention at all of Luke 4,16-30 or 4,16. This is now corrected in his more recent survey with a reference to [4,16] as a possible, though uncertain, Q text according to A. Polag, M. Sato, and... Kloppenborg[3].

I

Tischendorf was the first who read Ναζαρά in both Matt 4,13 and Luke 4,16 (*Editio octava*, 1869)[4]. Nothing indicates that Tischendorf himself had in mind the possibility of a common gospel source when he changed Ναζαρέθ to Ναζαρά in these two places. Already in [7]1859 he

---

1. C. HEIL (ed.), *Q 4:1-13,16. The Temptation of Jesus – Nazara* (Documenta Q: The Database of the International Q Project), Leuven, 1996, pp. 391-462: *Q 4:16,31. Nazara* (Database author: J.M. ROBINSON); see esp. 410-429 (Pro), 438-441 (Evaluations). Cited here as *DQ* (and page number). – On the first part of the volume, *Q 4:1-4,9-12,5-8,13. The Temptation of Jesus*, pp. 1-389, cf. F. NEIRYNCK, *Note on Q 4,1-2*, ETL 73 (1997) 94-102.

2. IQP: [Ναζαρά...]. See *JBL* 110 (1991), p. 495. The database was prepared by Robinson, Carruth, and Kloppenborg (New Orleans, 1990). Mention of this IQP reconstruction can be added in the *DQ* volume (p. 424).

3. J.S. KLOPPENBORG, *The Sayings Gospel Q. Literary and Stratigraphic Problems*, in R. URO (ed.), *Symbols and Strata: Essays on the Sayings Gospel Q* (PFES, 65), Helsinki–Göttingen, 1996, pp. 1-66, esp. 62. See A. POLAG, *Die Christologie der Logienquelle* (WMANT, 45), Neukirchen-Vluyn, 1977, pp. 156-157: Luke 4,16-21(22a) in Q (only "eine Vermutung"); *Fragmenta Q*, 1979, p. 84: Ναζαρά in bold among the uncertain Q texts (in note: B. Weiss, H. Schürmann). M. SATO, *Q und Prophetie* (WUNT, 2/29), Tübingen, 1988, p. 24: "Gang Jesu nach Ναζαρά" in Q ("man könnte fragen..."); cf. p. 58: Luke 4,16-30 uncertain Q[Lk] text.

4. Cf. *DQ*, 394-396: "Text Critical Issue: Is Ναζαρά in Matthew and Luke?" (esp. 394).

mentioned the witness of B* Z 33 for -ρα in the apparatus to Matt 4,13, and in 1867 he corrected his reading of Luke 4,16 in B: "ναζαρα a prima manu certissimum est. Ex Miconis et Birchii silentio ναζαρεϑ coniiciendum videbatur, Maius vero ναζαρεϑ a prima, ναζαρετ ab altera esse dixit. Ad illud per manifestam incuriam delapsus est"[5]. In the meantime he had published the readings of Codex Sinaiticus: Luke 4,16 ναζαρα, and Matt 4,13 ναζαρεϑ, here with the annotation: B ναζαρα[6]. Tischendorf's assembling of textual evidence from his Sinaiticus and in the first place from the Vaticanus may explain his option for -ρα in [8]1869:

Matt 4,13 ℵ[b] B* Z 33 k Or[4,179] Cf. N-A[27]: ℵ[1] B* Z 33 k mae

Luke 4,16 ℵ B* Ξ 33 e Or[4,161] Cf. N-A[27]: ℵ B* (Δ) Ξ (33) pc e sa[mss] Or

However, the internal criteria are not completely absent. In [7]1859: "Observare tamen certe hoc licuit, ut evangelistarum quisque suum conservaret scribendi modum. Ita igitur ναζαρετ ubique in Iohanne, ναζαρεϑ ubique in Matthaeo edidimus"[7]. Tischendorf's observation on the language of the evangelists will be adapted by C.R. Gregory according to the text of [8]1869: "Ναζαρέϑ (exceptis Mt 4,13 et Lc 4,16 Ναζαρά) usurpatur a Matthaeo et Luca (etiam in Actibus), Ναζαρέτ a Marco et Iohanne, iudice Tischendorfio"[8].

B. Weiss was the first who, in his commentary on Matt 4,13, combined the exceptional spelling Ναζαρά and the broadly parallel context of its use in Matthew and Luke:

Ti[schendorf] liest hier nach B Z, wie Luc. 4,16 nach ℵ B: Ναζαρα, wohl mit Recht. Da diese Namensform nur an diesen beiden Stellen und beidemale beim Uebergange von der Versuchungsgeschichte zum Lehramt Jesu ursprünglich, so könnte *an dieser Stelle in der Quelle* Nazara und zwar mit dieser Namensform erwähnt gewesen sein. (1876)[9].

---

5. *Novum Testamentum Vaticanum post Angeli Maii aliorumque imperfectos labores ex ipso codice edidit*, Leipzig, 1867, p. XXXVII (Commentarius), at Luke 4,16, with reference to the collations by Mico (1720) and Birch (1780) and Mai's edition (1857, 1859).

6. *Novum Testamentum Sinaiticum*, Leipzig, 1863, p. XLIII, n. 21.

7. [7]1859, pp. LIV-LV, n. 3.

8. C.R. GREGORY, *Novum Testamentum Graece*, vol. III: *Prolegomena*, Leipzig, 1894, p. 120. Cf. Tischendorf, [8]1869: Matt 4,13; Luke 4,16: -ρα; Matt 2,23; 21,11; Luke 1,26; 2,4.39.51; Acts 10,38: -ρεϑ; Mark 1,9; John 1,45.46: -ρετ. Diff. N-A[27]: Matt 2,23 -ρετ.

The *Vollständige Konkordanz* combines the three forms in one article and provides no information about the readings in editions other than N[26] and ς (all -ρετ). The twelve occurrences are listed here in the style and order of *VK* (N[26] N M V B S T H ς): Mt 2,23 -ρετ (-ρεϑ N B T); 4,13 -ρα (-ρετ M V S ς, -ρεϑ B); 21,11 -ρεϑ (-ρετ ς); Mc 1,9 -ρετ (-ρεϑ N); Lc 1,26; 2,4.39.51 -ρεϑ (-ρετ S H ς); 4,16 -ρα (-ρετ V[4] ς); Jo 1,45.46 -ρετ (-ρεϑ N B); Ac 10,38 -ρεϑ (-ρετ ς).

9. B. WEISS, *Das Matthäusevangelium und seine Lucas-Parallelen*, Halle, 1876, p. 121 (cf. *DQ*, 410; emphasis F.N.). In *Die vier Evangelien*, Leipzig, 1900, Ναζαρά is treated as "älteste Bezeichnung der Stadt", "die älteste Form" (pp. 30, 303).

H.J. Holtzmann's alternative to this common-source hypothesis was Lukan dependence on Matthew:

> ... die 4,16-30 folgende Antecipation der Scene in Nazaret, auf welche Lc wieder durch die Parallele Mt [4,]13 καταλιπὼν τὴν Ναζαρά (so B) geführt war. (1889)
> ... lediglich die Parallele Mt 4,13 hat die Anreihung dieser Perikope veranlasst; daher nur dort und [Lc 4,]16 die Form Ναζαρά. (1901)[10].

Luke's dependence on Matt 4,13 is now represented in *DQ* by M.D. Goulder:

> There are thus two reasons for thinking that Luke knew Matthew here: first, they coincide in the unique spelling Ναζαρά, and second, the presence of the phrase καταλιπὼν τὴν Ναζαρά in Matthew could have given Luke the idea of moving the story of Jesus' withdrawal from Nazareth from Mark vi / Matt. xiii to this context (1978)[11].

The database on Ναζαρά "from Q?", with Tuckett (1996) as last name in the list of the pro's and Goulder (1989)[12] as the last in the list of the con's, echoes its beginning in the 19th century with Weiss versus Holtzmann.

B. Weiss has a leading position in the database on Ναζαρά in Q. His 1876 comment on Matt 4,13 will be reiterated in the KEK commentary on Matthew[13]. On the side of Luke Ναζαρά is well attested in 4,16 ("entscheidend beglaubigt")[14], but 4,16-30 stems from L: how can it then be "ein Beweis für Q"[15]? In 1908 Weiss is finally forced to face this question in a note on the Nazareth pericope in Luke[16]:

10. H.J. HOLTZMANN, *Die Synoptiker – Die Apostelgeschichte* (HCNT, 1), Freiburg, 1889, p. 71 (= ²1892, 70); ID., *Die Synoptiker* (HCNT, 1/1), 1901, p. 331 (not in *DQ* – *Nazara*). Cf. Holtzmann's student E. SIMONS, *Hat der dritte Evangelist den kanonischen Matthäus benutzt?*, Bonn, 1880, on the anticipation of the Nazareth pericope: "Den Anlass aber zu dieser Umstellung gab die Lektüre des Mt", without mention of the spelling of the name (p. 28, cf. p. 106).

11. *NTS* 24 (1977-78), p. 220 (= *DQ*, 435). See also M.S. ENSLIN, *Luke and Matthew. Compilers or Authors?*, ANRW II.25.3 (1985) 2357-2388, esp. p. 2367 (not in *DQ*).

12. *Luke: A New Paradigm* (JSNT SS, 20), Sheffield, 1989, pp. 299-310 (*DQ*, 436-437). Cf. below, n. 40.

13. ⁸1880, ⁹1898, ¹⁰1910: "Da nur hier (durch B Z) und Luk. 4,16 die Namensform ναζαρα entscheidend bezeugt ist und zwar beide Male bei dem Uebergange von der Versuchungsgeschichte zum Auftreten Jesu, liegt der Gedanke nahe, dass an dieser Stelle *die beiden gemeinsame Quelle* die Heimath Jesu unter diesen Namen erwähnte" (p. 82 n. 2; emphasis F.N.).

14. ⁹1901, p. 340 n. 1; but see on Luke 4,16-30: "eine dem Lk ganz eigenthümliche Ueberlieferung, daher wahrscheinlich aus derselben Quelle, wie die Vorgeschichte (L)" (p. 339). See also *Die Quellen des Lukasevangeliums*, Stuttgart-Berlin, 1907: on the one hand, 4,16 Ναζαρά from Q (p. 193: fragment cited in *DQ*, 410) and on the other 4,16-30 from L (pp. 200-202, 279).

15. Cf. *Quellen*, 1907, p. 193 (see above, n. 14).

16. *Die Quellen der synoptischen Überlieferung* (TU, 32/3), Leipzig, 1908, p. 106 n. 2a. This volume is not mentioned in *DQ*.

Daß sie aus einer Quelle stammt, erhellt daraus, daß nur aus einer solchen der nur hier gebrauchte Name Ναζαρά erhalten sein kann; und daß diese Quelle L war, aus der Anknüpfung an die Jugendgeschichte Jesu. Die Namensform kann hier also nicht aus Q herrühren, wie noch S. 193 vermutet[17]; es muß die ältere Form gewesen sein, die noch in den beiden ältesten Quellen gebraucht war, ehe durch Mrk. die Form Ναζαρέτ üblich ward.

In Matt 4,13 and Luke 4,16 "stimmen selbst so verschiedenartige Quellen, wie Q und L, im Ausdruck überein" (p. 190). This means, however, for Weiss and for those who rely on him, that the argument for Q, viz., the unique spelling Ναζαρά at the same position in both Matthew and Luke, has lost much of its strength.

At the extreme opposite to Lukan dependence on Matthew (Holtz-mann) there has been some contestation of the reading Ναζαρά in Matt 4,13: "Es ist nicht ausgeschlossen, daß sie von dem lukanischen Text abhängig ist" (G. Strecker)[18]. Von Soden (1913), Vogels (1920, ²1922), and Merk (1933) read Ναζαρέτ in Matt 4,13; Klostermann (1909), Lagrange (1926) and Bover (1943) prefer Ναζαρέθ, but all read Ναζαρά in Luke 4,16[19]. Compare J. Schmid (1930): "Textangleichung an Lk ist demnach bei Mt jedenfalls ernsthaft zu erwägen"[20]. J. Delobel (1973), J. Gnilka (1986), and W. Wiefel (1988) are listed in *DQ* together with G. Strecker (396: Ναζαρά not in Matthew), although their views on Ναζαρά show greater complexity[21]. Secondary assimilation to Luke

17. Reference to *Quellen* (Lk), 1907. Weiss's correction should be added in *DQ*, 410.

18. G. STRECKER, *Der Weg der Gerechtigkeit* (FRLANT, 82), Göttingen, 1962, p. 65 n. 1. Cf. *DQ*, 396.

19. H.J. Vogels changed his text of Luke 4,16 in later editions: Ναζαρέτ in ³1949, ⁴1955, without annotation in the apparatus. E. Klostermann refers to the variant reading Ναζαρά in Matt 4,13 within brackets (p. 177) and with question mark (1919, p. 425). M.-J. Lagrange: *Synopsis Evangelica*, 1926, cf. *Luc*, 1921, p. 137; *Matthieu*, 1923, p. 67: "Mt. ne peut avoir changé si tôt son écriture aussi complètement (cf. II, 23)".

20. *Matthäus und Lukas*, p. 86 n. 1 (with reference to von Soden, Vogels, and Lagrange). Even H. Schürmann (*DQ*, 411, 413) was hesitant in 1964: "wenn die Textgeschichte uns hier nicht irreführt" (1968, p. 77); compare his "wenn" in 1969 (p. 228 n. 46) and 1970 (p. 201: "Wenn N. ursprüngliche Textüberlieferung ist"; and n. 4).

21. J. DELOBEL, *La rédaction de Lc. IV,14-16a et le 'Bericht vom Anfang'*, in F. NEI-RYNCK (ed.), *L'évangile de Luc* (BETL, 32), Leuven, 1973, pp. 203-223, esp. 217 (= ²1989, pp. 113-133, esp. 127), on Ναζαρά in Matt 4,13: "on pourrait considérer cette lecture comme une adaptation secondaire au texte de *Lc.*"; in Tuckett's understanding: "J. Delo-bel... argues that the reading Ναζαρά in Mt 4,13 is a later assimilation to the text of Luke" (1982, p. 344 n. 7). But see Delobel's additional note (1989, pp. 306-312): "Je ne me suis pas rallié à cette position" (p. 310); this note is not mentioned in *DQ*. In the line of Delo-bel, compare J. DUPONT 1978: "peut-être *Mt.* 4,13, où quelques manuscrits portent aussi 'Nazara'. Si l'on admet que cette lecture est originale chez Matthieu..." (*DQ*, 420; cf. below, n. 28). – J. GNILKA, *Das Matthäusevangelium* (HTKNT, 1/1), Freiburg, 1986, p. 95: "Für V 13 ist Nazara vielleicht zu bevorzugen"; in his translation: "Nazara (Nazaret?)". But see *Jesus von Nazaret*, 1990, p. 75 n. 4: "Ναζαρα (Lk 4,16; Mt 4,13 v.l.)". – W. WIEFEL, *Das Evangelium des Lukas* (THKNT, 3), Berlin, 1988, p. 228: "die in späterer Zeit ortsübliche (syrische) Form..., die hier einkorrigiert wurde". But see n. 22.

4,16 is now suggested anew by the late Wiefel (1998)[22], but there is a firm critical consensus for the acceptance of Ναζαρά as the harder reading in Matt 4,13 (diff. 2,23; 21,11).

The *DQ* list of the pro's includes the name of J. Jeremias (1980) who regards the form Ναζαρά as pre-Lukan tradition and is therefore cited as supporting "this side of the argument"[23]. In this category of unspecified "tradition", non-Markan and possibly oral, more names of authors could be added. I cite here one of them, A. Ennulat (1994): "Mt und Lk werden diese Namensform unabhängig voneinander aus der nebenmk (mdl?) Trad entnommen und an jeweils unterschiedlichen Ort zugesetzt haben"[24].

II

Our examination of Ναζαρά in Q can start once again with B. Weiss. I quote from his analysis of the *Matthäusquelle* (Q)[25]:

> Natürlich muß in Q irgend ein Übergang von der Vorgeschichte [3,1–4,11] zu der öffentlichen Wirksamkeit Jesu [5,1 ἀνέβη εἰς τὸ ὄρος] gemacht sein... Eine Spur davon findet sich nur in dem καταλιπὼν τὴν Ναζαρά.

Many other commentators have repeated the observation that in the order of the Q material the reference to Ναζαρά comes after the Temptations and before the Inaugural Sermon. They conjecture that "after the temptation scene Q contained at least a transitional sentence which named Ναζαρά" (Davies-Allison). Compare:

> It would look as if Q had a brief notice of the change of scene in which the name Ναζαρά occurred. (Streeter)
> L'hypothèse la plus simple serait celle qui supposerait, dans la source qui contenait les tentations, une notice finale mentionnant 'Nazara'. (Dupont)
> Das auffällige Ναζαρά in V 13 könnte eine Reminiszenz an einen verlorengegangenen Satz in der Logienquelle sein, dessen Spur sich auch Lk 4,16 noch findet. (Luz)

M. Dömer remains very much in the line of B. Weiss (and Matthew's καταλιπὼν τὴν Ναζαρά):

---

22. Though with hesitancy: "Nazara könnte... die älteste Lesart sein, wenn man nicht annehmen will, daß es aus Lk 4,16 hier eingedrungen sein soll"; in *Das Evangelium nach Matthäus* (THKNT, 1), Leipzig, 1998, p. 66.
23. *DQ*, 416. Same remark on J.M. Nützel 1980 (417).
24. *Die "Minor Agreements"* (WUNT, 2/62), Tübingen, 1994, p. 158. Not in *DQ*.
25. *Quellen*, 1908, p. 4 n. 1. Cf. above, n. 16: not in *DQ*.
26. Cited with approval in M. KORN, *Die Geschichte Jesu in veränderter Zeit* (WUNT, 2/51), Tübingen, 1993, pp. 61-62.

... die Übereinstimmung in der Namensform (dürfte) so zu erklären sein, daß in der Logienquelle im Anschluß an die Versuchungsgeschichte und vor der großen Rede Jesu in einer kurzen Überleitungsbemerkung ausgeführt wurde, daß Jesus zu seiner Verkündigung Ναζαρά verlassen habe[26].

D. Catchpole rather concentrates on the phrase in Luke 4,16:

... the obvious explanation of ἦλθεν εἰς Ναζαρά is in terms of Q (cf. ἦλθεν εἰς Καφαρναούμ, Q 7.1). This will incidentally have the virtue of responding to the need for a transition in Q from the temptation tradition (Q 4.1-13) to the inaugural discourse (Q 6.20-49), matching the transition from the discourse to the centurion tradition which follows[27].

Text and context of these quotations are found in the *DQ* database on *Nazara*[28]. The question of the verb associated with Ναζαρά is discussed there as variation unit n° 2: "Luke's ἦλθεν εἰς or Matthew's καταλιπών" (443-446). P. Hoffmann, one of the four evaluators, defends a minority view: Matt καταλιπών = Q {C}. No justification of this "hesitant possibility" (grade C) is provided under *Hoffmann 1996* (446), but in his own evaluation Robinson too seems to argue for καταλιπών in Q. Robinson will finally conclude that "only the word Ναζαρά has a strong enough case to be included in the critical text of Q" (438) and "the reconstruction of Jesus *leaving* Ναζαρά is much less certain than is some undefined mention of Ναζαρά" (445). Yet his consideration of καταλιπών probably functions as the unexpressed argument behind Hoffmann's option:

The fact that the structure shared between Matt 4:12-14 and Matt 2:22-23 has no place for καταλιπών τὴν Ναζαρά may give some preference to assuming this term for *leaving* also came from Q. (445)
... precisely what is not structurally duplicated in Matt 2:22-23 is καταλιπών τὴν Ναζαρά... this whole phrase thus has some claim to represent Q. (438)

Robinson relies on Delobel's presentation of Matthew's parallel pattern[29]:

27. D.R. CATCHPOLE, *The Anointed One in Nazareth*, in M.C. DE BOER (ed.), *From Jesus to John*. FS M. de Jonge (JSNT SS, 84), Sheffield, 1993, pp. 231-251, esp. 235-236. – DQ, 423 (cf. 466, read: A̲nointed, 19̲9̲3̲).

28. *DQ*, 410-429 (Pro), in chronological order: Streeter 1924, Dörner 1978, Dupont 1985 (cf. below), Luz 1985, Davies-Allison 1988, Catchpole 1989 (sic; see above, n. 27: 1993). Cf. J. DUPONT, *Jésus annonce la bonne nouvelle aux pauvres*, in A.B.I. (ed.), *Evangelizare pauperibus*, Brescia, 1978, pp. 127-189, reprinted in *Études*, 1985, pp. 23-85.

29. *DQ*, 438, cf. 431 (= 1973, p. 206 n. 2). On the parallel between 2,2-23 and 4,12-16 before and after Matt 3,1 – 4,11, see my *The First Synoptic Pericope*, in *ETL* 72 (1996) 41-74, esp. 55 n. 60.

4,12	ἀκούσας δὲ ὅτι	2,22	ἀκούσας δὲ ὅτι
	Ἰωάννης παρεδόθη		Ἀρχέλαος βασιλεύει ...
	ἀνεχώρησεν		ἀνεχώρησεν
	εἰς τὴν Γαλιλαίαν		εἰς τὰ μέρη τῆς Γαλιλαίας
13	καὶ **καταλιπὼν τὴν Ναζαρὰ**	23	καὶ
	ἐλθὼν κατῴκησεν		ἐλθὼν κατῴκησεν
	εἰς Καφαρναοὺμ τ. π. ...		εἰς πόλιν λεγομένην Ναζαρέτ·
14	ἵνα πληρωθῇ τὸ ῥηθὲν		ὅπως πληρωθῇ τὸ ῥηθὲν
	διὰ Ἠσαΐου τοῦ προφήτου		διὰ τῶν προφητῶν
	λέγοντος		ὅτι

The striking similarity is undeniable, but does it justify to single out καταλιπὼν τὴν Ναζαρά as a phrase from Q? The ellipsis in v. 22 (line 2) cannot be let out of consideration: τῆς Ἰουδαίας ... ἐφοβήθη ἐκεῖ ἀπελθεῖν... Jesus' return to Galilee and his move from Nazara to Capernaum in 4,12-13 can be compared with the return εἰς γῆν Ἰσραήλ (2,21) and the change of destination: not to Judea but to Galilee (Nazareth). Matthew uses twice καταλιπὼν αὐτούς diff. Mark: Matt 16,4 (for ἀφεὶς αὐτούς) and 21,17 (add.)[30].

Robinson persists:

> ... nothing actually takes place in Ναζαρά. Hence its inclusion in Matthew is hardly redactional, but must be due to it having already been here in Q. (445)

Nothing takes place in Nazara indeed. What Matthew stresses in 4,13 is ἐλθὼν κατῴκησεν εἰς Καφαρναούμ (Jesus taking residence in Capernaum), and in light of ἐλθὼν κατῴκησεν εἰς πόλιν λεγομένην Ναζαρέτ in 2,23 (and of Mark 1,9) it was almost unavoidable to mention that Jesus left his former residence in Nazareth:

> For the sake of clarity, then, Matthew is obliged to mention Nazara expressly to signal that Jesus ... is abandoning his former residence in Nazara to take up residence in Capernaum which, for Matthew, is another fulfilment of Scripture. This being the case, καταλιπών is undoubtedly Matthaean. (Kloppenborg: *DQ*, 446)

The rubric ἦλθεν εἰς = Q is left empty in *DQ*, 443. This looks strange since scholars who assign Lk 4,16-30, or at least part of it, to Q (H. Schürmann, C.M. Tuckett, W.O. Walker) usually include 4,16 in their source reconstruction. However, if all agree about the Q-origin of

---

30. Cf. W. Schenk, *Die Sprache des Matthäus*, Göttingen, 1987, p. 211: "(Jesus) + καταλιπών + (-ἔρχομαι) + (Zeitangabe)" in Matt 4,13; 16,4; 21,17 (with some overemphasis: "Für Mt ist das ganze Syntagma ... ein wesentliches makrosyntaktisches Gliederungssignal").

the term Ναζαρά[31], they are less explicit regarding ἦλθεν εἰς. For many others Luke's dependence on Mk 6,1 ἔρχεται εἰς τὴν πατρίδα αὐτοῦ is a ready solution for the phrase ἦλθεν εἰς (Ναζαρά) in Lk 4,16. Catchpole offers a different approach: he treats 4,16a apart from the body of Lk 4,16-30 and regards ἦλθεν εἰς Ναζαρά as a transition in Q from the Temptations to the Inaugural Sermon, like ἦλθεν εἰς Καφαρναούμ in Q 7,1 is a transition from the Sermon to the Centurion[32].

Catchpole did not tell how he understands "entering Nazara" as transition to the Sermon. Compare Robinson's suggestion: on the assumption that Ναζαρά functioned already in an earlier edition of Q beginning with the Sermon, one can imagine that "Ναζαρά may have been in Q not as a geographical reference, but only in the name of Jesus" "as a toponymic for Jesus" Ἰησοῦς ἀπὸ Ναζαρά, an idiom that is possibly reflected in Matt 21,11; John 1,45; Acts 10,38[33] and allows Robinson to speculate on "such a prominent designation in the *incipit* of the basic text of the Jesus movement in Syria" (*DQ*, 440-441, 444)[34]. The reference to Ναζαρά "could well have given way to a more spatial meaning of leaving or entering Ναζαρά, once (it) was no longer in an *incipit*" (444). In an almost desperate attempt to locate the Nazara phrase in Q, Robinson refers to John 2,12 for "a similar phenomenon" of a fragment that leaves the impression of a visit to a town where nothing takes place[35]. At the end "some undefined mention of Ναζαρά" is assigned to Q, although "just how the Q context referred to Ναζαρά remains unclear" (*DQ*, 445). The majority view of the evaluators ("Indeterminate") is formulated by Carruth:

31. *DQ*, 411 (cf. 413), 418 (cf. 428), 421. I note here as a supplement to the database (*DQ*, 410) A.H. McNEILE, *Matthew*, 1915: "If Q was the source of the (? vernacular) form Nazara here [4,13] and in Lk. iv.16 where alone it recurs, Q possibly placed at this point a visit on which Lk. iv.16-30 is based, and Mt. shews a reminiscence of it" (p. 43).

32. Cf. above, n. 27. Catchpole should at least be mentioned in *DQ*, 443: "Luke = Q: [ἦλθεν εἰς]² Pro". His writing Q 7,1 ἦλθεν is probably a mistake: see his reconstruction of Q 7,1 in *The Quest for Q*, Edinburgh, 1993, p. 285 (= *The Four Gospels 1992*, p. 521): εἰσῆλθεν.

33. On Acts 10,38, see my *Luke 4,16-30 and the Unity of Luke–Acts*, in J. VERHEYDEN (ed.), *The Unity of Luke-Acts* (BETL, 142), Leuven, 1999, p. 385 n. 121.

34. Cf. *DQ*, 424-426 (= *The Four Gospels 1992*, pp. 377-379). But see his *The Incipit of the Sayings Gospel Q*, in *RHPR* 75 (1995) 9-33. On "Jesus of Nazara" in an earlier draft of Q, "from which it was carried over to the *incipit* of a later draft": "such conjectures are too hypothetical to be included in the critical text of Q" (p. 31). See also on p. 32 his reference to my *The International Q Project*, in *ETL* 69 (1993) 221-225, esp. 224.

35. According to the Semeia Source hypothesis John 2,12 had been broken loose from 4,46-54. For a different approach, see *Evangelica II*, pp. 679-688. On the function of 2,12: "Der sehr kurze Aufenthalt in Kapernaum zeigt, daß es Jesus nach Jerusalem drängt" (U. SCHNELLE, *Das Evangelium nach Johannes*, 1998, p. 63).

Robinson points to the difficulty what activity of Jesus Q intended to designate. Coming to Nazareth fits the redactional setting in Luke and leaving Nazareth fits Matthew's purpose. It becomes, thus, impossible to determine whether Jesus was said to come to or to leave the town in Q (*DQ*, p. 446)[36].

III

The *DQ* database contains two attempts to explain the spelling Ναζαρά as redactional creation of the evangelists. The first is a suggestion by U. Busse in his essay on Luke 4,16-30 (1978)[37]:

> Lukas schreibt normalerweise alle hebräischen Eigennamen nach der Septuaginta-Form. (n. 33: Vgl. *Sparks*, Semitism 133.) Aber in diesem Fall konnte er nicht zwischen zwei konkurrierenden Schreibweisen wählen und sie im Sinne der Septuaginta korrigieren. (n. 34: Nazareth wird in der LXX nicht erwähnt.) Er wählt eine Anpassung an die hellenistische Schreibweise bedeutender Städte mit semitischen Namen (vgl. Gadara, Gerasa).

On the contrary, for M.D. Goulder Ναζαρά is un-Lukan and redactional in Matthew (1989)[38]:

> He (Matthew) is working here from Mk 1, with Ναζαρηνός at 1.24 and could have formed Ναζαρά on the analogy of Γαδαρηνός/Γαδαρα, Μαγδαληνός/Μαγδαλα. It may well be Matthew who introduced the variant spelling[39].

Goulder's argument for "Matthew's own redaction, copied by Luke" is further developed in 1993[40]:

36. The database *Q 4:16,31* includes, besides Ναζαρά (Matt 4,13 / Luke 4,16), the parallel text of Matt 4,13a / Luke 4,16a / Mark 6,1-2 and Matt 4,13b / Luke 4,16b / Mark 1,21, divided into ten variation units: Luke 4,16 ¹καὶ ²ἦλθεν εἰς ³(Mt τὴν) **Ναζαρά**, ⁴οὗ ἦν τεθραμμένος ⁵καὶ εἰσῆλθεν κατὰ τὸ εἰωθὸς αὐτῷ ἐν τῇ ἡμέρᾳ τῶν σαββάτων εἰς τὴν συναγωγὴν καὶ ἀνέστη ἀναγνῶναι. 4,31 ⁶καὶ ⁷κατῆλθεν ⁸εἰς Καφαρναοὺμ ⁹πόλιν τῆς Γαλιλαίας. ¹⁰καὶ ἦν διδάσκων αὐτοὺς ἐν τοῖς σάββασιν. All decisions are unanimous: not in Q, U(ndecided): 1, 2; grade B: 3; grade A: 4-10; with the exception of Hoffmann's minority opinion on ²καταλιπών (Matt: cf. above) and ⁷κατῆλθεν: Luke = Q {D} (*DQ*, 457: no justification). It is, however, not a very useful exercise to set up a database on Luke 4,31 and then conclude: "The possibility that Luke 4:31 reflects Q has not been raised in the literature and is purely speculative" (Kloppenborg: *DQ*, 457).

37. U. Busse, *Das Nazareth-Manifest Jesu. Eine Einführung in das lukanische Jesusbild nach Lk 4,16-30* (SBS, 91), Stuttgart, 1978, p. 32 (= *DQ*, 435; notes added here).

38. Goulder (cf. above, n. 12), p. 307 (*DQ*, 437). See already in 1978, *NTS* 24 (n. 11), p. 220: "at least in Matthew redactional" (= *DQ*, 435). Cf. Tuckett's reply in *NTS* 30 (1984), p. 131: "but he offers no proof of this", and Goulder's response in 1989 and again in a more extensive form in 1993 (see n. 40).

39. On the suffix -ηνός and particularly "Ναζαρά: Ναζαρηνός", cf. Moulton-Howard, *Grammar*, vol. II, p. 359 (and p. 150).

40. *Luke's Knowledge of Matthew*, in G. Strecker (ed.), *Minor Agreements. Symposium Göttingen 1991* (GTA, 50), Göttingen, 1993, pp. 142-162, esp. 144-148. Not in *DQ*.

Matthew may well have felt that the alternative feminine ending was suitable for the noun; for the Hebrew may form both Gibeath (Josh 18.28) and Gibeah (Jos 15.58), both Ajath (Isa 10.28) and Aja (Neh 11.31)[41].

It is to Goulder's merit to have drawn attention to Mark 1,24 in connection with Ναζαρά in Matt 4,13. Unfortunately he did not pay the same attention to the parallel in Luke 4,34. The occurrences of Ναζαρηνός in Mark are at 1,24; 10,47; 14,67; 16,6, and in Luke at 4,34 (= Mark 1,24) and 24,19 (vv. 19-20 τὰ περὶ Ἰησοῦ τοῦ Ναζαρηνοῦ ... ἐσταύρωσαν αὐτόν can be seen as a possible, though uncertain, reminiscence of Mark 16,6 Ἰησοῦν ... τὸν Ναζαρηνὸν τὸν ἐσταυρωμένον). In parallel to Mark 14,67, μετὰ τοῦ Ναζαρηνοῦ ... τοῦ Ἰησοῦ is changed to σὺν αὐτῷ (22,56), and in parallel to Mark 10,47 Ἰησοῦς ὁ Ναζαρηνός Luke has Ἰησοῦς ὁ Ναζωραῖος (18,37; cf. Acts 2,22; 3,6; 4,10; 6,14; 22,8; 26,9). Thus Luke 4,34 not only offers the first occurrence of Ναζαρηνός/Ναζωραῖος in Luke–Acts, its use of Ναζαρηνός is unique in that it strictly corresponds to the parallel in Mark: τί ἡμῖν καὶ σοί, Ἰησοῦ Ναζαρηνέ; It makes, however, a significant difference that Luke 4,31-37 (par. Mark 1,21-28) is preceded by Luke 4,16-30 in a redactional diptychon of synagogue visits: καὶ ἦλθεν εἰς Ναζαρά..., καὶ κατῆλθεν εἰς Καφαρναούμ... The Nazareth-Capernaum antithesis is expressed in 4,23 referring to Capernaum from the standpoint of Nazareth. In 4,34 Jesus is identified from the topographical standpoint of Capernaum as Ἰησοῦ Ναζαρηνέ[42]. The interconnection of Ναζαρά and Ναζαρηνός in Luke 4,16.34 can lessen the strength of the classic objection against a redactional Ναζαρά: why here and never elsewhere (cf. Luke 1,26; 2,4.39.51; Acts 10,38: Ναζαρέθ)[43]?

The objection takes a more radical form where it concerns Matthew[44]:

Matthew seems to have avoided *any* reference to Jesus as Ναζαρηνός. Mark 1,24 is part of a whole pericope omitted by Matthew; and in Mark

---

41. With reference to H.P. Rüger, 1981, p. 259 (= *DQ*, 408). Goulder mentions here again Μαγδαληνός, Γεργασηνός, Γαδαρηνός, and Ναζαρηνός = "from Nazara". It is less understandable how he can argue for Matthean redaction on the basis of orthographic variations in the Genealogy and of Matthew's use of Ἱεροσόλυμα and Ἱερουσαλήμ (23,37!) and of Ἰουδαία and Ἰούδα (sic).

42. Cf. J.A. Weatherly, *Jewish Responsibility for the Death of Jesus in Luke-Acts* (JSNT SS, 106), Sheffield, 1994, p. 125: "Just as in Nazareth [Nazara] Jesus refers to Capernaum (v. 23), in Capernaum he is identified as a Nazarene (v. 34)" (bracketed word added, F.N.).

43. C.M. Tuckett, *Luke 4,16-30, Isaiah and Q*, in J. Delobel (ed.), *Logia* (BETL, 59), Leuven, 1982, pp. 343-354, esp. 344 n. 7 (ctr. Busse); Id., *Q and the History of Early Christianity. Studies on Q*, Edinburgh, 1996, pp. 226-237 ("Luke 4:16ff."), esp. 228 n. 64 (ctr. Goulder); D.R. Catchpole, "Anointed" (n. 27), p. 235.

44. Tuckett, *Q and the History*, p. 228 n. 64 (*DQ*, 428).

10,47; 14,67; 16,6, Matthew appears deliberately to avoid just this adjective.

In parallel to Mark 10,47 (ὁ Ναζαρηνός) and 16,6 (τὸν Ναζαρηνόν) the adjective is simply omitted indeed, but in parallel to Mark 14,67 (μετὰ ᾿Ιησοῦ...) it has a double substitute, τοῦ Γαλιλαίου and τοῦ Ναζωραίου (Matt 26,70.71). Due consideration should also be given to the omitted pericope[45]. The doubling of the demoniac in Matt 8,28-34 compensates for the omission of the exorcism: Matt 8,29 (diff. Mark 5,7): ἔκραξαν λέγοντες: τί ἡμῖν καὶ σοί,... ἦλθες ... βασανίσαι ἡμᾶς (cf. Mark 1,24). The parallels of Mark 1,21 (ἐδίδασκεν) in Matt 5,2, of Mark 1,22 in Matt 7,28b-29, of Mark 1,28 in Matt 4,24a, and the anticipation of Mark 1,21a (εἰς Καφαρναούμ) in Matt 4,13 are almost undisputed. In this context we can be confident that Matthew was well acquainted with the adjective Ναζαρηνός, and we have to reckon with the possibility that it influenced his use of Ναζαρά in combination with Capernaum: καὶ καταλιπὼν τὴν Ναζαρὰ ἐλθὼν κατῴκησεν εἰς Καφαρναούμ.

Since it remains debated whether or not Ναζαρά could reflect a Semitic form of the name[46], it may be that the influence of Mark's Ναζαρηνός does not concern the redactional 'creation' of Ναζαρά but Matthew's and Luke's having chosen to use here this form instead of Ναζαρέτ/έθ.

---

45. Omission is not necessarily redactional avoidance. See e.g. Matt 3,13 om. Ναζαρέτ (Mark 1,9) and Matthew's use in 2,23 (-ρετ); 4,13 (-ρα); 21,11 (-ρεθ): "ganz von Mk 1,9 abhängig, obwohl er dort den Ausgangsort zur Taufe ausliest" (SCHENK, *Sprache*, p. 108).
46. Cf. *DQ*, 401-409: "The Derivation of the Spelling Ναζαρά".

Louvain Studies 20 (1995) 201-218

22

THE DIVORCE SAYING IN Q 16,18

During his twenty-five years at the faculty, Raymond F. Collins has never neglected the device of one of his colleagues: "nulla dies sine linea". In the last ten years of his stay in Leuven he has added a complement of his own: "et nullus annus sine libro". First Thessalonians has his preference, but his published work includes the Synoptics and the Fourth Gospel as well as Hebrews and the Pauline Pseudepigrapha. I chose to comment here on *Divorce in the New Testament*[1]. This book provides a comprehensive treatment of the topic and the author fully realized that in a number of exegetical issues he "had to make a decision" (5).

1. *The Study of the Divorce Sayings*

My choice also has a more personal reason. In 1957, after defending my doctoral dissertation on Luke 1–2, I was charged with the course of sacramentology at the Seminary in Bruges, 1957-1960. I had to start the three-year cycle with "De Matrimonio" and it was in the course of this first year of teaching (1957-58) that I published my first exegetical article: the prohibition of divorce in the Gospels[2]. As I wrote in the Descamps volume (1987) there is a little story connected with the preparation of this publication[3]:

> À ce propos, j'ai gardé une lettre de Descamps, du 19 février 1958, adressée au président du séminaire de Bruges. Celui-ci avait envoyé au professeur Descamps le manuscrit d'un article à paraître dans les *Collationes*. Aujourd'hui il est devenu courant parmi les exégètes catholiques d'expliquer la clausule matthéenne au | sens d'une vraie exception (cf. R. Schnackenburg, dans *Die sittliche Botschaft des Neuen Testaments*, t. 1, 1986, p. 152 n. 228). Ce ne fut pas encore le cas en 1958, et J. Dupont par exemple fera l'association que voici: "L'hypothèse ... est séduisante, qu'on la lise sous la plume de Loisy ou telle que la présente M. Neirynck" (*Mariage et divorce dans l'évangile*, 1959, p. 130). L'on comprend donc la réaction du censeur diocésain. Descamps lui répond qu'il approuve le

1. R.F. COLLINS, *Divorce in the New Testament* (Good News Studies, 38), Collegeville, MN, The Liturgical Press, 1992 ("A Michael Glazier Book"), xv-389 p.

2. F. NEIRYNCK, *Het evangelisch echtscheidingsverbod*, in *Collationes Brugenses et Gandavenses* 4 (1958) 25-46.

3. See my *Note de l'éditeur*, pp. XV-XVIII, in A. DESCAMPS, *Jésus et l'Église. Études d'exégèse et de théologie* (BETL, 77), Leuven, 1987. Text quoted from pp. XVI-XVII.

contenu de l'article ("Voor wat de inhoud betreft, ben ik persoonlijk van mening dat de oplossing die voorgesteld wordt juist is, en zeker, in onze huidige kennis van de zaken, de beste"), mais il suggère d'insérer un petit exposé sur l'inspiration et l'inerrance du texte évangélique. Suite à cette lettre, j'ai récrit la conclusion de l'article et cette nouvelle conclusion semble avoir plu à Descamps: il s'y réfère encore en 1980[4].

J. Dupont replied in his 1959 monograph[5] with a new defense of the traditional (Catholic) solution: the exceptive clauses are added by Matthew but the traditional saying of Jesus already used the verb ἀπολύειν in the new meaning of separation, not divorce with right to remarriage[6]. My critical evaluation appeared in *Collationes* (1960)[7]. |

Some ten years later[8], a colloquium on marriage and divorce to be held at the faculty in 1971 gave me the opportunity to return to "the sayings of Jesus on divorce"[9], with an assessment of recently published studies (one of those studies was B. Schaller's 1970 essay)[10] and a

4. In his essay, *Les textes évangéliques sur le mariage* (1980), in *Jésus et l'Église* (n. 3), pp. 510-583, esp. 554 (cf. n. 50). This essay was first published in *RTL* 9 (1978) 259-286; 11 (1980) 5-50 (see p. 21); ET, *The New Testament Doctrine on Marriage*, in R. MALONE – J.R. CONNERY (eds.), *Contemporary Perspectives on Christian Marriage. Propositions and Papers from the International Commission*, Chicago, IL, Loyola University, 1984, pp. 217-273 (endnotes: 347-363).

5. J. DUPONT, *Mariage et divorce dans l'Évangile. Matthieu 19,3-12 et parallèles*, Bruges, 1959, pp. 136-157.

6. Cf. COLLINS, *Divorce*, pp. 200, 317-318. In n. 99 he associates R. Schnackenburg with Dupont on the basis of his *Moral Teaching of the New Testament*, London, 1965, p. 141: "The 'classical' solution is perhaps still the most acceptable" (German original, ²1962; cf. 1954, p. 92). In 1969 Schnackenburg was inclined to follow J. Bonsirven: cf. *Die Ehe nach dem Neuen Testament* (1969), reprinted in his *Schriften zum Neuen Testament*, München, 1971, pp. 414-433 (esp. 419-420). But in his *Nachwort* (1971) he is already more hesitant (pp. 433-434: "kein sicheres Urteil"). See now *Die sittliche Botschaft des Neuen Testaments*, vol. 1, Freiburg, 1986, p. 152: "So neigen heute die meisten Exegeten (darunter auch katholische) einer wirklichen Ausnahme im Fall von Ehebruch seitens der Frau zu"; he refers to G. Schneider, R. Pesch, P. Hoffmann, J.B. Bauer, C. Marucci, and adds: "... diese Auffassung, der auch ich mich anschließen möchte".

7. *Huwelijk en echtscheiding in het evangelie*, in *Collationes Brug. Gand.* 6 (1960) 123-130. Cf. p. 129: "De 'verjonging' die S. (= J. Dupont) aan de klassieke verklaring had beloofd, lijkt dan ook vooralsnog haar effect te missen. *Apoluein* bewaart zijn gewone betekenis in het Jezuswoord, en ook in de redactie van Mt".

8. I can mention here one of the STL dissertations under my direction in the early sixties: F. POTTIE, *Het synoptisch echtscheidingslogion in de hedendaagse exegese*, 1965, 97 p.

9. *De Jezuswoorden over echtscheiding*, in V. HEYLEN (ed.), *Mislukt huwelijk en echtscheiding. Een multi-disciplinaire verkenning* (Sociologische verkenningen, 2), Leuven, 1972, pp. 127-142. Reprinted in *Evangelica I* (BETL, 60), Leuven, 1982, pp. 821-833 (Additional Note: 833-834).

10. B. SCHALLER, *Die Sprüche über Ehescheidung und Wiederheirat in der synoptischen Überlieferung*, in E. LOHSE (ed.), *Der Ruf Jesu und die Antwort der Gemeinde. FS J. Jeremias*, Göttingen, 1970, pp. 226-246.

reconstruction of the divorce saying in Q. The reprinted text in *Evangelica I* (1982) is supplemented with an additional note on supposed evidence from Qumran for πορνεία understood as marriage within forbidden degrees of kinship (J.A. Fitzmyer 1976, 1978)[11].

At the Colloquium Biblicum Lovaniense 1984 (published in 1986) I delivered a paper on "Paul and the Sayings of Jesus" including the command of the Lord in 1 Cor 7,10-11 and its synoptic parallels[12]. More recently, at the Colloquium on the Corinthian Correspondence (1994), 1 Cor 7,10-11 was considered again[13], and with regard to 1 Cor 7,10-11 and 12-16 I could now refer to Collins's *Divorce*, chapters 1 and 2[14]. In this contribution I will concentrate on the Q saying[15]. |

2. The Reconstruction of the Q Saying

At the end of his section on the divorce saying[16] Collins proposes a reconstruction of the saying in Q (Mt 5,32 / Lk 16,18):

a πᾶς ὁ ἀπολύων τὴν γυναῖκα αὐτοῦ ποιεῖ αὐτὴν μοιχευθῆναι,
b καὶ ὁ ἀπολελυμένην γαμῶν μοιχεύει.

In his view "there is a strong possibility that Matthew's 'involves here in adultery' better reflects the inflected form of Q's statement about adultery than does Luke's 'commits adultery'"[17]: Luke substituted μοιχεύει for ποιεῖ αὐτὴν μοιχευθῆναι and added καὶ γαμῶν ἑτέραν in 16,18a and ἀπὸ ἀνδρός in v. 18b. The exceptive clause in Mt 5,32a, παρεκτὸς λόγου πορνείας, is a Matthean addition. Matthew also

---

11. J.A. FITZMYER, *The Matthean Divorce Texts and Some New Palestinian Evidence*, in *Theological Studies* 37 (1976) 197-226; reprinted in his *To Advance the Gospel: New Testament Essays*, New York, 1981, pp. 79-111; ID., *Divorce among First-Century Palestinian Jews*, in *H.L. Ginsberg Volume. Eretz-Israel* 14, Jerusalem, 1978, pp. 103*-110*. See now also his *Responses to 101 Questions on the Dead Sea Scrolls*, New York - Mahwah, NJ, 1992, § 82, pp. 133-140; *Qumran. Le domande e le risposte essenziali sui Manoscritti del Maro Morte*, Brescia, 1994, pp. 197-206.

12. *Paul and the Sayings of Jesus*, in A. VANHOYE (ed.), *L'Apôtre Paul. Personnalité, style et conception du ministère* (BETL, 73), Leuven, 1986, pp. 265-321, esp. 311-320: "1 Cor 7,10-11"; reprinted in *Evangelica II* (BETL, 99), Leuven, 1991, pp. 511-567 (esp. 557-566).

13. *The Sayings of Jesus in 1 Corinthians* (cf. above, 93-128).

14. Ch. 1: "A Problem at Corinth" (on 1 Cor 7,10-11), pp. 9-39 (notes: 233-246); ch. 2: "A Related Matter" (on 1 Cor 7,12-16), pp. 40-64 (notes: 246-259).

15. In a *Mededeling* at the Academy, Brussels (Klasse der Letteren, January 21, 1995), "Het Nieuw Testament over echtscheiding", I treated the Gospel sayings on divorce in general, and particularly the Matthean exceptive clauses: *De echtscheidingslogia in de evangeliën*, in *Academiae Analecta* 58 (1996) 21-42.

16. Ch. 5: "An Old Saying", pp. 146-183.

17. "The Q Saying", pp. 181-183, esp. 183.

changed ὁ ... γαμῶν to ὃς ἐὰν ... γαμήσῃ and μοιχεύει to μοιχᾶται in v. 32b.

If I recollect my own utterances on this topic, I find a repeated defense of Lk 16,18 as the original Q form of the saying with a possible Lukan addition of ἀπὸ ἀνδρός and a possible Lukan use of ἑτέραν for ἄλλην[18]:

a πᾶς ὁ ἀπολύων τὴν γυναῖκα αὐτοῦ καὶ γαμῶν (ἑτέραν) μοιχεύει
b καὶ ὁ ἀπολελυμένην [ἀπὸ ἀνδρὸς] γαμῶν μοιχεύει.

The similarities between Mt 5,32 and Lk 16,18 are the main reason for assigning the saying to Q. According to the IQP reconstruction, the verbal agreements are[19]:

a πᾶς ὁ ἀπολύων τὴν γυναῖκα αὐτοῦ [] μοιχεύ[ει],
b καὶ ὁ[] ἀπολελυμένην [] γαμ[ῶν] μοιχ.... |

Some scholars, however, rather emphasize the differences. Thus, for U. Luz, "it is very uncertain (*recht unsicher*) to assume a Q text. Neither can the wording be reconstructed exactly nor can the logion be situated in Q in a meaningful context"[20]. Nevertheless, he stresses that Mt 5,32b and Lk 16,18b belong to the original saying[21]. D.A. Hagner is even more critical: "The similarity ... is not sufficient... More likely Luke 16:18 is derived from Mark 10:11"[22]. For M. Sato, the Q origin of all the scattered sayings between Lk 14,26 and 17,6 (including Lk 16,18) is uncertain, although he does not exclude the possibility of Q^Mt and Q^Lk [23]. J.S.

18. *Jezuswoorden* (1972), in *Evangelica I*, pp. 826, 832; *Paul and the Sayings of Jesus* (1986), in *Evangelica II*, p. 560. Cf. *Recent Developments in the Study of Q*, in J. DELOBEL (ed.), *Logia* (BETL, 99), Leuven, 1982, pp. 29-75, esp. 52 (= *Evangelica II*, p. 432): "In my opinion the phrase (perhaps with ἄλλην for ἑτέραν) is part of the original saying, and the traditional logion known by Mark was probably very similar to Lk 16,18".
19. Cf. *JBL* 109 (1990), p. 501. Compare the reproduction of the parallel texts in my *Q-Synopsis* (1988), pp. 56-57: the common elements are printed in bold; ὃς/ὁ and μοιχ-αται/μοιχεύει are marked as synonyms (*), and omissions are marked with the sign □. Cf. F. NEIRYNCK, *Q-Synopsis. The Double Tradition Passages in Greek*. Revised Edition with Appendix (SNTA, 13), Leuven, 1995; in Appendix: pp. 65-73: "A Synopsis of Q" (= *ETL* 64, 1988, 441-449); pp. 75-79: "The International Q Project" (= *ETL* 69, 1993, 221-225).
20. U. LUZ, *Das Evangelium nach Matthäus* (EKK, I/1), 1985, p. 269; ET, *Matthew 1–7*, Minneapolis, MN, 1989, p. 300.
21. *Ibid.*, p. 270 (= 301).
22. D.A. HAGNER, *Matthew 1–13* (Word, 33a), Dallas, TX, 1993, p. 123.
23. M. SATO, *Q und Prophetie. Studien zur Gattungs- und Traditionsgeschichte der Quelle Q* (WUNT, 2/29), Tübingen, 1988, pp. 23-24 (diss., Bern, 1984, pp. 25-26). But see D. KOSCH, *Die eschatologische Tora des Menschensohnes. Untersuchungen zur Rezeption der Stellung Jesu zur Tora in Q* (NTOA, 12), Freiburg/Schw. - Göttingen, 1989, pp. 262 (and n. 235), 429, 432 (reconstruction). See my essay on *Q^Mt and Q^Lk and the Reconstruction of Q*, in *Evangelica II*, pp. 475-480 (= *ETL* 66, 1990, 385-390), p. 478

Kloppenborg (1988) simply notes on Q 16,18: "In Q: Most authors"[24], and, with the few exceptions I mentioned, this remains basically correct. Although scholarly opinion is divided in reconstructing the Q saying either according to Lk 16,18 or on the basis of the parallel text in Mt 5,32, scholars think almost unanimously that Matthew's exceptive clause should be eliminated from the Q text[25]. But even on this point the alternative position has its defenders. K. Berger (1972)[26] and W. Stenger (1984)[27] propose an original form of the divorce saying | ("commits adultery") and two adaptations in Q: the change to ποιεῖ αὐτὴν μοιχευθῆναι and the addition of παρεκτὸς λόγου πορνείας[28]. Matthew's version in 5,32 then scarcely differs from Q, and their view on Lukan redaction in Lk 16,18 comes close to the thesis of Luke's dependence on Matthew of those who dispense with Q[29].

(= 388): "But he (Kosch) departs from Sato with regard to the 'scattered fragments' in Lk 14–17. Already in his dissertation, he takes issue with Sato's theory and argues that Lk 14,5; 14,26.27; 16,16.17.18 derive from Q. In his *FZPT* article, Kosch reverses Sato's argument (absence of the characteristic Lukan composition in alternating blocks) by accepting a pre-Lukan *Verschmelzung* of Q and Sondergut material". Cf. D. KOSCH, *Q: Rekonstruktion und Interpretation*, in *FZPT* 36 (1989) 409-425, p. 417.

24. J.S. KLOPPENBORG, *Q Parallels: Synopsis, Critical Notes & Concordance*, Sonoma, CA, 1988, p. 180. Kloppenborg's "opinion" is incorrectly rendered by Collins as referring to the reconstruction of the Q text: cf. *Divorce*, pp. 181-182 (and n. 163), 183. See now Kloppenborg's essay, *Alms, Debt and Divorce: Jesus' Ethics in their Mediterranean Context*, in *Toronto Journal of Theology* 6 (1990) 182-200, pp. 193-196 ("Marital Ethics and Androcentric Honour"); and *Jesus and the Parables of Jesus in Q*, in R.A. PIPER (ed.), *The Gospel Behind the Gospels: Current Studies on Q* (NTSup, 75), Leiden, 1995, pp. 275-319, esp. 315-316 (p. 315 n. 124: the IQP reconstruction of Q 16,18).

25. A. HARNACK, *Sprüche und Reden Jesu. Die zweite Quelle des Matthäus und Lukas*, Leipzig, 1907, p. 44: "bei Matth. (ist) die Phrase παρεκτὸς λόγου πορνείας zu tilgen" (see below, n. 38). Cf. COLLINS, *Divorce*, p. 181: "In the reconstruction of the Q tradition, one can begin with the elimination of the exceptive clause from the Q-text".

26. K. BERGER, *Die Gesetzesauslegung Jesu* (WMANT, 40), Neukirchen-Vluyn, 1972, p. 567: "die sog. Klausel in Mt 5,32 (ist) ursprünglich".

27. W. STENGER, *Zur Rekonstruktion eines Jesusworts anhand der synoptischen Ehescheidungslogien (Mt 5,32; 19,9; Lk 16,18; Mk 10,11f.)*, in *Kairos* 26 (1984) 194-205; = ID., *Strukturale Beobachtungen zum Neuen Testament* (NTTS, 12), Leiden, 1990, pp. 104-118, esp. 111-112, 116. This precision can be added to the description of Stenger's "very personalized opinion" in COLLINS, *Divorce*, pp. 217-218.

28. Compare H.-T. WREGE, *Die Überlieferungsgeschichte der Bergpredigt* (WUNT, 9), Tübingen, 1968, p. 68: "die Klausel in 5,32 (hängt) aufs engste mit dem ποιεῖ αὐτὴν μοιχευθῆναι zusammen. ... Παρεκτὸς λόγου πορνείας gehört ... wie ποιεῖ αὐτὴν μοιχευθῆναι zum zwar sekundären, aber längst vor-mt, palästinischen Kolorit unseres Wortes". But Wrege excludes a common Q-origin of Mt 5,32 and Lk 16,18: "Eine gemeinsame, schriftliche Vorlage kann den Fassungen Mt 5,32 / Lk 16,18 ... nicht zugrundeliegen" (p. 67). Cf. below, n. 71.

29. Lk 16,18 represents a conflation of Mt 5,32 and 19,9 (W.R. Farmer). Cf. M.D. GOULDER, *Luke*, 1989, p. 632: "Being a radical, he (Luke) drops Matthew's 'except' clause".

3. Matthew 5,32

H. Greeven (1969)[30] was the first of a series of authors who all opt for Mt 5,32 (minus the exception clause) in their reconstruction of Q: G. Schneider (1971)[31], R. Pesch (1971)[32], S. Schulz (1972)[33], H. Hübner (1973)[34], G. Lohfink (1974)[35], H. Merklein (1978)[36], | and more recently R. Schnackenburg (1986)[37] and D. Kosch (1989)[38]:

a πᾶς ὁ ἀπολύων τὴν γυναῖκα αὐτοῦ ποιεῖ αὐτὴν μοιχευθῆναι,
b καὶ ὃς ἐὰν ἀπολελυμένην γαμήσῃ μοιχᾶται.

Greeven did not hesitate to suggest a reconstruction of the double saying in Aramaic with a strong *parallelismus membrorum*; in his German translation:

> Jeder-Entlassende　seine-Frau　　veranlaßt-ihren-Ehebruch,
> und-der-Heiratende　eine-Geschiedene　begeht-Ehebruch.

30. H. GREEVEN, *Ehe nach dem Neuen Testament*, in *NTS* 15 (1968-69) 365-388, esp. pp. 382-384; also in G. KREMS – R. MUMM (eds.), *Theologie der Ehe*, Regensburg-Göttingen, 1969, pp. 37-79. Cf. ID., *Zu den Aussagen des Neuen Testaments über die Ehe*, in *Zeitschrift für Evangelische Ethik* 1 (1957) 109-125.
See also E. SCHWEIZER, *Das Evangelium nach Markus*, 1967, p. 114: "die ursprüngliche Form" in Mk 5,32a. But see *Das Evangelium nach Matthäus*, 1973, p. 76, on Mt 5,32b: "Ob dies (zwei Partizipien in Lk 16,18) die ältere Form oder nachträgliche Angleichung ist, ist nicht auszumachen"; and finally, *Das Evangelium des Lukas*, 1982, p. 171: "V. 18 ist in der Q-form angefügt, erwähnt aber eine doppelte Möglichkeit der Schuld des Mannes und ist damit noch typischer jüdisch als Mt 5,31f.".
31. G. SCHNEIDER, *Jesu Wort über die Ehescheidung in der Überlieferung des Neuen Testaments*, in *Trierer Theologische Zeitschrift* 80 (1971) 65-87, esp. pp. 70-71 (with references to Greeven, 1969). Cf. ID., *Das Evangelium nach Lukas*, 1977, p. 338: "Lukas hat den Q-Text des Logions (vgl. Mt 5,32) an Mk 10,11 angeglichen".
32. R. PESCH, *Freie Treue: Die Christen und die Ehescheidung*, Freiburg, 1971, pp. 12-13. Cf. ID., *Die neutestamentliche Weisung für die Ehe*, in *Bibel und Leben* 9 (1968) 108-121, p. 209; *Das Markusevangelium* II, 1977, p. 126.
33. S. SCHULZ, *Q: Die Spruchquelle der Evangelisten*, Zürich, 1972, pp. 116-117. Cf. COLLINS, p. 309 n. 168: "I generally concur with Schulz in this regard", i.e., as far as Mt 5,32a (and not 32b) is concerned.
34. H. HÜBNER, *Das Gesetz in der synoptischen Tradition. Studien zu einer progressiven Qumranisierung und Judaisierung innerhalb der synoptischen Tradition*, Witten, 1973, pp. 42-47.
35. G. LOHFINK, *Jesus und die Ehescheidung. Zur Gattung und Sprachintention von Mt 5,32*, in H. MERKLEIN – J. LANGE (eds.), *Biblische Randbemerkungen*. FS R. Schnackenburg, Würzburg, 1974, pp. 207-217, esp. 208: "Die wahrscheinlich älteste Überlieferung".
36. H. MERKLEIN, *Die Gottesherrschaft als Handlungsprinzip. Untersuchung zur Ethik Jesu* (Forschung zur Bibel, 34), Würzburg, 1978 ([3]1984), pp. 275-291, esp. 276-278.
37. *Die sittliche Botschaft* (n. 6), p. 149. Contrast *Die Ehe nach dem Neuen Testament*, in *Theologie der Ehe*, 1969 (n. 30), pp. 9-36; = 1971 (n. 6), p. 415: "Die älteste wahrscheinlich ursprüngliche Form ist bei Lk 16,18 erhalten".
38. *Die eschatologische Tora* (n. 23), p. 432. Cf. A. HARNACK, *Sprüche und Reden Jesu* (n. 25), pp. 44, 101.

In an Aramaic retroversion the complex expression ποιεῖ αὐτὴν μοιχευθῆναι can be simplified[39], and the subject in the second member can be the same as in the first ("und wenn er ... heiratet...")[40]. For Greeven, this last possibility could explain the insertion of "and marries another" in Mk 10,11 which forms a sort of conflation of Mt 5,32a and b[41]. Very few have espoused Greeven's bold theory on the original form of the saying and the origin of Mk 10,11. H. Merklein remains in the line of Greeven's interpretation when he considers Mk 10,11 "die Umformung von Mt 5,32" in a combination of divorce (32a) and marriage (32b), but he rightly regards Mt 5,32a (*Entlassung der Frau*) and 32b (*Heirat einer Entlassenen*) as two independent cases ("voneinander unabhängige Rechtsfälle")[42]. In his view, however, he has to admit that Mark changed marrying a divorced woman to marrying "another" (the man's remarriage). He supposes that Mark's μοιχᾶται | is taken from Mt 5,32b and that his (μοιχᾶται) ἐπ᾽ αὐτήν ("ihr gegenüber") is reminiscent of the *Schuldigerklärung* in Mt 5,32a[43]. If we can assume that Mt 5,32 is a Matthean adaptation of the Q-saying, Merklein's last observation may be reversible.

Greeven's emphasis on the Jewish-Palestinian coloration of Mt 5,32 has received a favorable echo[44]. A statement like Lk 16,18 blaming the man who divorces and remarries would not be compatible with the legal status of the husband in a Jewish polygamous society. On the contrary, Mt 5,32a concurs with the wife's status in Judaism by making the wife instead of the husband the one explicitly guilty of adultery[45]. One may ask, however: is it then not foreign to Jewish law that the man who divorces his wife is made responsible for her adultery?

---

39. *Ehe* (n. 30), p. 383: it can be expressed in Aramaic "durch das Afel (zum Beispiel von *gār*) mit Pronominal-Endung". And: "Da *gār* wie hebr. *nā'af* sowohl von der Frau wie vom Manne gebraucht wird, erübrigt sich eine passivische Konstruktion" (n. 1). See now also U. Luz, *Matthäus* (n. 20), p. 269 n. 3.

40. *Ibid.*, p. 284.

41. The addition of Mk 10,12 restores the original *Doppelheit* of the saying (*ibid.*).

42. *Die Gottesherrschaft*, p. 278. – Modern versions of Mt 5,32 normally translate v. 32b: "and whoever", "and anyone who", or some equivalent. Contrast P. Bonnard's exceptional translation: "et *lui-même* commet l'adultère, s'il épouse une répudiée" (*L'Évangile selon saint Matthieu*, 1963, p. 67; without comment).

43. *Die Gottesherrschaft*, p. 278.

44. *Ehe*, p. 382. Cf. G. SCHNEIDER, *Jesu Wort*, p. 70: "besser [than Lk 16,18] von jüdischen Voraussetzungen zu verstehen". See also H.-T. WREGE, *Bergpredigt* (n. 28), p. 67: "Hier spiegelt sich deutlich die bevorzugte Stellung des Mannes im jüdisch-palestinischen Eherecht".

45. For a discussion, see R. GUELICH, *The Sermon on the Mount: A Foundation for Understanding*, Waco, TX, 1982, p. 200.

Since we can safely assume that the thesis-antithesis is Matthew's own formulation, the Matthean version of the divorce saying in v. 32 should be read in antithesis to v. 31, i.e., in contrast to and in light of the command of Moses: ὃς ἂν ἀπολύσῃ τὴν γυναῖκα αὐτοῦ, δότω αὐτῇ ἀποστάσιον (cf. 19,7; Mk 10,4)[46]. By referring to the certificate of divorce, the status of the divorced woman is taken into consideration in v. 31 and, by contrast, in v. 32a: the result for the divorced woman is not that she is freed to remarry but that she is to become an adulteress. Moreover, a change of μοιχεύει (Q?) to ποιεῖ αὐτὴν μοιχευϑῆναι would not be unrelated to the second half of the saying in v. 32b (= Lk 16,18b) on marrying a divorced woman: "This warning provides the basis of the preceding insertion: Matthew has deduced that if a man makes himself an adulterer by marrying a divorced woman, the divorced woman herself also commits adultery by remarrying"[47].

Apart from Luke's additional ἀπὸ ἀνδρός, there are only two, rather stylistic, differences between Lk 16,18b and Mt 5,32b: Matthew uses the conditional relative construction ὃς ἐὰν ... γαμήσῃ (instead of the participle ὁ ... γαμῶν) and the Doric verb μοιχᾶται (instead of μοιχεύει). Conflation of doublets is a well attested feature in the I Gospel of Matthew, and here too the variations in Mt 5,32b may reflect the influence of Mk 10,11 / Mt 19,9 (ὃς ἂν ... γαμήσῃ ... μοιχᾶται). The phrase ὃς ἐὰν... in v. 32b makes an inclusion with ὃς ἂν... in v. 31, ὃς ἂν ἀπολύσῃ τὴν γυναῖκα αὐτοῦ (= Mk 10,11; Mt 19,9). It has been objected by R. Guelich that the different expressions of the exceptive clauses in 5,32a and 19,9 show no such verbal "influence"[48]. One could reply that the very presence of the πορνεία clauses in both passages is more important than those variations. Guelich suggested that μοιχᾶται was used in the original saying and he assigned the change to μοιχεύειν in Mt 5,32a and Lk 16,18a.b to the redaction of the respective evangelists: Luke desires to use the more common Greek verb and Matthew desires to align the saying with the context of 5,27-28 through the catchword μοιχεύειν[49]. The author was less assertive regarding the differences between ὃς ἐὰν... in Mt 5,32b and ὁ plus participle in Lk 16,18b: "the origins (are) indeterminable"[50]. Since he assigned the πᾶς ὁ

46. Mt 19,7 Μωϋσῆς ἐνετείλατο δοῦναι βιβλίον ἀποστασίου καὶ ἀπολῦσαι αὐτήν (Mk 10,4 β. ἀ. γράψαι; cf. Deut 24,1 γράψει αὐτῇ β. ἀ. καὶ δώσει...). Compare Mt 5,31.32 with the rearrangement of Jesus' reply into a Moses-Jesus antithesis in Mt 19,8 (Moses, cf. Mk 10,5) and 9 (λέγω δὲ ὑμῖν ὅτι, cf. Mk 10,11).
47. GUNDRY, *Matthew*, p. 90. Cf. G. DELLING, in *NT* 1 (1958), p. 268.
48. GUELICH, *Sermon*, pp. 199-200.
49. *Ibid.*, p. 200.
50. *Ibid.*, p. 210.

ἀπολύων construction in Mt 5,32a and Lk 16,18a to the Q-saying[51], he could have given the same origin to their agreement in using the verb μοιχεύειν.

Commentators on Matthew who consider ὃς ἄν... in 5,31 and ὃς ἐάν... in 5,32 to be redactional cite three types of argument. First, ὃς ἄν/ἐάν is statistically characteristic of Matthew. Second, the phrase in Mt 5,31.32 echoes the first antithesis in 5,21.22. Third, as emphasized above, both 5,31 and 32 may be influenced by 19,9 (Mk 10,11)[52]. A few remarks are in place. For Gundry, ὃς ἄν/ἐάν (33 21 20) is characteristically Matthean, a Mattheanism, one of the easily recognizable Mattheanisms; it represents Matthew's style, typifies Matthew's diction: "14,1", i.e., fourteen occurrences in Matthean insertions in paralleled material and one in a passage peculiar to Matthew (18 occurrences are shared with Mk or Lk). The total number of occurrences in N[26] is 35 (and not 33)[53], and Gundry's classification can be improved. The 18 occurrences shared with one of the other synoptics are identified by W. Schenk: 14 =Mk; 3 =Q (he differs from Gundry in rejecting Mt [21,44] = Lk 20,18 in the text of I Matthew)[54]. Mt 12,32a (=Mk) is a rather complex case. Mt 12,32 combines Lk 12,10(Q) and Mk 3,29: καὶ ὃς ἐὰν εἴπῃ λόγον (v. 32a) corresponds to καὶ πᾶς ὃς ἐρεῖ λόγον (Lk 12,10a), but ἐὰν εἴπῃ is used in parallel to ὃς δ' ἂν εἴπῃ in v. 32b (diff. Lk 12,10b τῷ δὲ ... βλασφημήσαντι), cf. Mk 3,29 ὃς δ' ἂν βλασφημήσῃ[55]. More problematic is Gundry's grouping "14,1". Which might be this unique instance in a passage peculiar to Matthew, and how "insertions in paralleled material" are distinguishable from "peculiar material"? This same difficulty applies to Schenk's categories (+Q), fourteen instances, and (+Mk), three instances. It is quite confusing that Mt 15,5[a] (diff. Mk 7,11) and Mt 21,24 (diff. Mk 11,29) are found together with Mt 20,4 in the same category (+Mk); in this last case the "insertion" in Mk is the parable Mt 20,1-16, peculiar to Matthew. Mt 16,19[a.b] is classified (+Q) as duplication of Mt 18,18 ("+Q von V. 15 her

51. *Ibid.*, p. 199.
52. GUNDRY, *Matthew*, pp. 89 and 90; LUZ, *Matthäus*, p. 269 (and p. 46).
53. Cf. K. ALAND, *Vollständige Konkordanz*, art. ὅς: g ὃς (δ') ἄν, ἐάν (add g at 21,24). Compare Gundry's figures (33/21/20) with Luz's: 35/19/20. W. Schenk cancels verse 21,44 in the text of Mt ([N[26]], om. Greeven; ctr. Gundry) and counts 34 instances ("kennzeichnend mt"). Cf. W. SCHENK, *Die Sprache des Matthäus*, Göttingen, 1987, p. 376: art. ὅς.
54. SCHENK, *Die Sprache*, p. 24, art. ἄν: "un-mt, sofern kein Bedingungssatz und die Verwendung im Nachsatz vorliegen"
55. Cf. GUNDRY, *Matthew*, p. 237. Cf. SCHENK, p. 376, art. ὅς: "13,32a (=Mk)"; but see p. 26, art. ἐάν: "12,32a (+Q statt Lk πᾶς)". – Note: Mk 6,23 (par. Mt 14,7 ὃ ἐὰν αἰτήσηται) reads ὅ τι (N[26], written Ὅτι in H) or ὅτι ὃ...

dupl.")⁵⁶. Mt 5,32 ὃς ἐάν (diff. Lk 16,18) is located in the same category (+Q) as Mt 5,31⁵⁷ and 5,19.21-22; 18,19; 23,16.18, all peculiar to Matthew.

The occurrences of ὃς ἄν/ἐάν in Matthew are cited with their synoptic parallels in the following table:

5,19ᵃ	ὃς ἐάν	–
5,19ᵇ	ὃς δ᾽ ἄν	–
5,21	ὃς δ᾽ ἄν	–
5,22ᵃ	ὃς δ᾽ ἄν	–
5,22ᵇ	ὃς δ᾽ ἄν	–
5,31	ὃς ἄν	– (cf. Mk 10,11)
5,32	καὶ ὃς ἐάν	Lk 16,18ᵇ καὶ ὁ Q
10,11	εἰς ἣν δ᾽ ἄν	= Lk 10,5 Q
10,14	καὶ ὃς ἄν	= Mk 6,11
10,42	καὶ ὃς ἄν	= Mk 9,41
11,6	... ὃς ἐάν	= Lk 7,23 Q
11,27	καὶ ᾧ ἐάν	= Lk 10,22 Q
12,32ᵃ	καὶ ὃς ἐάν	Lk 12,10 καὶ πᾶς ὃς Q
12,32ᵇ	ὃς δ᾽ ἄν	= Mk 3,29
14,7	... ὃ ἐάν	(=) Mk 6,23 ὅ τι ἐάν (v.l. ὅτι ὁ ...)
15,5ᵃ	ὃς ἄν	Mk 7,11 ἐὰν ... ἄνθρωπος
15,5ᵇ	... ὃ ἐάν	= Mk 7,11
16,19ᵃ	καὶ ὃ ἐάν	–
16,19ᵇ	καὶ ὃ ἐάν	–
16,25ᵃ	ὃς γὰρ ἐάν	= Mk 8,35ᵃ
16,25ᵇ	ὃς δ᾽ ἄν	= Mk 8,35ᵇ
18,5	καὶ ὃς ἐάν	= Mk 9,37ᵃ (ἄν)
18,6	ὃς δ᾽ ἄν	= Mk 9,42 (καὶ...)
18,19	... οὗ ἐάν	–
19,9	ὃς ἄν	= Mk 10,11
20,4	καὶ ὃ ἐάν	–
20,26	ὃς ἐάν	= Mk 10,43 (ἄν)
20,27	καὶ ὃς ἄν	= Mk 10,44
21,24	... ὃν ἐάν	Mk 11,29 καί
[21,44]	ἐφ᾽ ὃν δ᾽ ἄν	= Lk 20,18 MA
23,16ᵃ	ὃς ἄν	–
23,16ᵇ	ὃς δ᾽ ἄν	–
23,18ᵃ	ὃς ἄν	–
23,18ᵇ	ὃς δ᾽ ἄν	–
26,48	ὃν ἄν	= Mk 14,44

56. SCHENK, p. 376; cf. p. 25, art. ἐάν. Mt 16,19 ὃ ἐὰν δήσῃς, καὶ ὃ ἐὰν λύσῃς: cf. 18,18 ὅσα ἐὰν δήσητε, καὶ ὅσα ἐὰν λύσητε (ἐάν v. 15 = Q).

57. SCHENK, p. 376. In art. ὃς (ibid.) Mt 5,31 and 5,32 (both +Q) are treated separately as ὃς ἄν (19 in Mt) and ὃς ἐάν (15 in Mt). Contrast art. ἄν, where 5,31 is mentioned together with "Zusätze zu Mk" in Mt 15,5 (ὃς ἄν) and 21,22 (ὅσα ἄν): "sowie die Dubl. 5,31 (zu 19,9)" (p. 24); and art. ἐάν: Mt 5,32b "(+Q mit Permutation von Mk 10,12 in der weiteren Konkretisierung nach V. 32a πᾶς)" (p. 26).

Some observations can be made. With two or three exceptions[58], all references are to sayings of Jesus. The occurrences in Matthew's peculiar material are mainly concentrated in 5,19.21-22 and 23,16.18[59]. Only three are taken from Q, and at least thirteen are taken from Mark[60]. Markan influence can be observed in 12,32a (diff. Lk) and is likely to be admitted also in 5,32b (cf. Mk 10,11)[61]. Assimilation to the first antithesis[62] may have played a role but is probably not the dominant factor in the formation of Mt 5,32 πᾶς ὁ ἀπολύων ... (Q), καὶ ὃς ἐὰν ... γαμήσῃ (cf. Mk). |

4. Luke 16,18 Q

Without using the term consensus[63], we can say that the prevailing view is that Lk 16,18 comes closest to the text of Q. For D.R. Catchpole, "it appears likely that Luke has reproduced Q", and he quotes Lk 16,18 without any concession to Lukan redaction[64]. Not even the prepositional phrase (ἀπολελυμένην) ἀπὸ ἀνδρός[65] is accepted as Lukan addition. The phrase has no counterpart in Matthew, and by authors who reconstruct Q on the basis of Mt 5,32 it is assigned to Lukan redaction[66].

58. Mt 14,7: Herod (direct discourse in Mk); 26,48: Judas; and 20,4: the landowner (in the parable).

59. SCHENK, p. 24. Cf. n. 56 above.

60. Q 7,23; 10,5.22; Mk 3,29; 6,11.23; 7,11; 8,35ᵃ.35ᵇ; 9,37ᵃ.41.42; 10,11.43.44; 14,44. See also Mt 12,50 ὅστις ἄν, par. Mk 3,35 ὃς ἄν; Mt 10,33 ὅστις δ' ἄν, par. Lk 12,9 (Q* Pesch ὃς δ' ἄν), 12,8 πᾶς ὃς ἄν (Schenk, p. 24: permutation). Other instances of ὃς ἄν/ἐάν in Mk: 6,22; 8,38; 9,37ᵇ; 10,15: without par. in Mt; 10,35; 11,23; 13,11: diff. Mt.

61. Mk 10,11 ὃς ἄν ... γαμήσῃ, 12 καὶ ἐὰν ... γαμήσῃ. Cf. J. NOLLAND, Luke, 1993 (n. 92 below), p. 818: "probably Matthew [in 5,32b] has been somewhat influenced by the syntax of his Markan source". Nolland's view on Mt 5,32a is less clear: on the one hand, "it seems much more likely that it is the rather puzzling Matthean form that has been rendered more simple by Luke", but, on the other, Matthew is held responsible for "the omission of specific mention of the remarriage" (ibid.).

62. Mt 5,22 πᾶς ὁ ὀργιζόμενος, ὃς δ' ἄν εἴπῃ, ὃς δ' ἄν εἴπῃ (cf. 21 ὃς δ' ἄν φονεύσῃ).

63. Cf. COLLINS, Divorce, p. 18.

64. D.R. CATCHPOLE, The Quest for Q, Edinburgh, 1993, pp. 236-238, esp. 237. Cf. ID., The Synoptic Divorce Material as a Traditio-historical Problem, in BJRL 57 (1974-75) 92-127, esp. p. 110: Mt 5,32 is secondary as compared with Lk 16,18; see also p. 119.

65. Om. D pc syˢ·ᵖ boᵐˢ (lacuna in syᶜ). The phrase "(a woman divorced) from her husband" is felt to be redundant and is omitted in modern translations such as NIV, Living Bible, Today's English Version, etc.: "a divorced woman".

66. Cf. above, nn. 16, 30-38. See, e.g., G. Schneider (p. 70), S. Schulz (p. 116: "da ἀνήρ ein ausgesprochen lk Wort ist und die Einfügung sek verdeutlicht"); H. Merklein (p. 275: "lk Verdeutlichung"); D. Kosch (p. 432: "lk Sprache entspricht: ἀπολύω + ἀπό, ἀνήρ").

Many others agree with them on this particular point[67]. Two indications of Lukan language are cited but none of them is really convincing. Ἀπολύω + ἀπό is used only twice in the NT, here and in Acts 15,33[68], but the good wishes of the brethren ("they were sent off in peace by the believers", NRSV) is not a very close parallel to the woman divorced "from the husband". The occurrences of ἀνήρ in Luke (Synoptics and Acts: 8 4 27 100)[69] show a different proportion if, more specifically, ἀνήρ = husband is considered: Lk (1,27.34); 2,36 and 16,18[70]. In Mark ἀνήρ = husband I only occurs in the section on divorce, in combination with ἀπολύω, 10,2 (εἰ ἔξεστιν ἀνδρὶ γυναῖκα ἀπολῦσαι) and 10,12:

11 ἀπολύσῃ τὴν γυναῖκα αὐτοῦ
12 ἀπολύσασα τὸν ἄνδρα αὐτῆς.

Luke's (ἀπολελυμένην) ἀπὸ ἀνδρός is possibly a reminiscence of Mk 10,12[71].

The option for Lk 16,18a in the first half of the Q-saying and for ὃς ἐὰν ... γαμήσῃ in the second half has occasional defenders (A. Polag)[72]. Thus, P. Hoffmann considers ὁ ... γαμῶν Luke's redactional assimilation

67. See above, n. 18. Cf. FITZMYER, *Matthean Divorce Texts* (n. 11), 1976, pp. 200-202 ("Lk 16,18"), esp. 202; and p. 201: "its omission may represent the more original form of the saying" (n. 18, with reference to my *Jezuswoorden*, 1972). See also *Luke*, 1985, p. 1120: "may have been secondarily added". See also A. POLAG, *Fragmenta Q. Textheft zur Logienquelle*, Neukirchen, 1979, p. 75; W. SCHENK, *Synopse zur Redenquelle der Evangelien*, Düsseldorf, 1981, p. 116; D. ZELLER, *Kommentar zur Logienquelle*, Stuttgart, 1984, p. 69; and special studies: P. HOFFMANN, in ID. – V. EID, *Jesus von Nazareth und eine christliche Moral* (QD, 66), Freiburg, 1975, pp. 109-131 ("Jesu Stellungnahme zur Ehescheidung und ihre Auswirkungen im Urchristentum"), esp. 110: "erweckt den Eindruck sekundärer Erläuterung"; R. LAUFEN, *Die Doppelüberlieferungen der Logienquelle und des Markusevangeliums* (BBB, 54), Konigstein/Ts. - Bonn, 1980, pp. 343-360 ("Das Wort von Ehescheidung und Ehebruch"), 573-594 (notes), esp. p. 347: "eine sekundäre Verdeutlichung" (p. 579 n. 26: cf. A. Harnack, J. Schmid, S. Schulz, A. Sand); J. ZMIJEWSKI, *Neutestamentliche Weisungen für Ehe und Familie*, in *SNTU* 9 (1984) 31-78, pp. 51-53 ("Rekonstruktion der Q-Fassung"), esp. 52 (n. 137: cf. G. Schneider).

68. D. KOSCH (n. 66). Cf. J. JEREMIAS, *Die Sprache des Lukasevangeliums*, Göttingen, 1980, p. 259.

69. S. Schulz, D. Kosch (n. 66).

70. For an analysis of the 23 other occurrences, see J. JEREMIAS, *Sprache*, pp. 134-135.

71. Cf. M.D. GOULDER, *Luke*, p. 632: "Mark's ἄνδρα may have influenced his ἀπὸ ἀνδρός". But see below, on the theory of more radical dependence on Mk (and Mt). – In response to H.-T. Wrege (n. 28), p. 67 n. 7, I note here that Justin's free rendering and conflation of Lk 16,18 and Mt 5,32b in *Apol.* I,15,3 (ὃς γαμεῖ ἀπολελυμένην ἀφ' ἑτέρου ἀνδρὸς μοιχᾶται) is hardly an argument for pre-Lukan origin of ἀπὸ ἀνδρός.

72. In contrast to the reverse position of G. Schneider (n. 31), p. 70, and R. Collins (n. 16), who opt for Mt 5,32a in the first half of the saying and for Luke's ὁ ... γαμῶν in the second half.

to πᾶς ὁ ἀπολύων[73]. Although the option for relative clause or participle implies no difference of meaning in Q (and is not even traceable in the translations)[74], this case has some literary-critical significance. Two aspects of Lukan redaction are involved: Luke's use of parallelism and his preference for participles. Regarding parallelism I can refer to R. Laufen's statements: "Streng paralleler Aufbau ist für viele Sprüche der Logienquelle charakteristisch", and "Demgegenüber sind Parallelismen für Lukas nicht typisch"[75]. Further documentation is provided in A. Denaux's statistical survey (1982)[76]. At first sight Luke's preference for participles is a greater difficulty. For J. Jeremias Lk 16,18b is one of the eleven instances where a relative clause in Q (=Mt) is replaced by Luke with a participle[77]. It is important, I think, that we take separate Luke's numerous uses of participles for Mark's finite verbs with καί on the one hand[78] and participles substituted for a relative clause on the other hand. Of this last category, there are only four cases diff. Mk (and one case of the reverse: Lk 20,47). In two instances (Lk 8,8; 20,27) the Mt/Lk agreements may indicate that the change is not exclusively due to Lukan usage[79], and in Lk 8,21 and 23,49 the participles are more or less prepared for in the Markan context[80]. In parallel to Mark's ὅς (δ') ἄν/ἐάν[81] Luke retained the relative clause without change:

73. Above, n. 67 (p. 110). Cf. J. SCHMID, Matthäus und Lukas, 1930, p. 225 n. 1: "Verbesserung, die dem Partizip im ersten Glied entspricht. Zudem liebt gerade Lk das substantivierte Partizip".

74. In W. Schenk's Synopse: "Und wenn jemand eine entlassene Frau heiratet" (Q and Mt=Lk). Cf. NRSV: "and whoever marries" (Mt = Lk).

75. Doppelüberlieferungen (n. 67), pp. 346 and 578 n. 24.

76. A. DENAUX, Der Spruch von den zwei Wegen im Rahmen des Epilogs der Bergpredigt (Mt 7,13-14 par. Lk 13,23-24). Tradition und Redaktion, in Logia (n. 18), 1982, pp. 305-335, esp. (319 and) 331-335 (Appendix I, II).

77. Sprache, p. 116 n. 7; the same observation is repeated at Lk 6,29.47.48.49; 7,32; 11,51; 12,9.10; 14,11[a.b]=18,14[a.b]; 16,18[b]: "in solchen Fällen ist die Lukas-Fassung redaktionell" (p. 149). The instances are listed in J.H. CADBURY, Style, pp. 135-136. With two exceptions (6,48 οἰκοδομοῦντι, 49 οἰκοδομήσαντι), Luke uses the substantivized participle (with the article). Lk 7,32 ἃ λέγει (Mt 11,16-17 ἃ ... λέγουσιν) can be cancelled in the list.

78. See the list in The Minor Agreements, 1974, pp. 207-210 (nos. 3, 3b). It includes the 40 cases in Lk (19 MA) listed by Cadbury (Style, pp. 134-135) and a few additions: Lk 4,41; 20,28; 22,8.64.67; 23,33-34.

79. Lk 8,8 / Mt 13,9 ὁ ἔχων (Mk 4,9 ὃς ἔχει): compare the independent use of ὁ ἔχων in Mt 11,15; 13,43 and Lk 14,35 (contrast εἴ τις ἔχει in Mk 4,23; 7,16 v.l.). Lk 20,27 οἱ [ἀντι]λέγοντες / Mt 22,23 λέγοντες (Mk 12,18 οἵτινες λέγουσιν): note the variation in the agreement and the Lukan verb ἀντιλέγω (3 + 4).

80. Lk 8,21: cf. below, n. 81. Lk 23,49 αἱ συνακολουθοῦσαι αὐτῷ ἀπὸ τῆς Γαλιλαίας, for Mk 15,41a αἳ ἠκολούθουν αὐτῷ..., combines this phrase with 41b αἱ συναναβᾶσαι αὐτῷ εἰς Ἱεροσόλυμα.

81. Mk 6,22.23; 7,11; 9,41; 10,11.35; 11,23; 14,44 have no parallel in Luke; the parallels to Mk 9,42; 10,43-44; 13,11 are significantly modified. – Mk 3,35 ὃς ἄν

Mk	6,11	καὶ ὃς ἂν τόπος	Lk	9,5	καὶ ὅσοι ἄν
	8,35ᵃ	ὃς γὰρ ἐάν		9,24ᵃ	ὃς γὰρ ἄν
	35ᵇ	ὃς δ' ἄν		24ᵇ	ὃς δ' ἄν
	8,38	ὃς γὰρ ἐάν		9,26	ὃς γὰρ ἄν
	9,37ᵃ	ὃς ἄν		9,48ᵃ	ὃς ἐάν
	37ᵇ	καὶ ὃς ἄν		48ᵇ	καὶ ὃς ἄν
	10,15	ὃς ἄν		18,17	ὃς ἄν

We now turn to the double-tradition texts and Jeremias's (and Cadbury's) assumption that Luke substituted the participle for a relative clause in Q. Exegetical opinion is in fact less univocal. The IQP reconstructions are as follows[82]:

6,29	... ῥαπίζ ... σε εἰς τὴν σιαγόνα ...	
6,47	πᾶς ὁ [[ ]] ἀκού[[ων]] μου τ[[ῶν]] λόγ[[ων]] καὶ ποι[[ῶν]] αὐτούς	
6,48	... ἀνθρώπῳ, ὃς [[ ]] ᾠκοδόμησεν	Mt 7,24 ὅστις
6,49	... ἀνθρώπῳ, ὃς [[ ]] ᾠκοδόμησεν	Mt 7,26 ὅστις
11,51	... Ζαχαρίου τοῦ ἀπολουμένου ...	
12,9	ὃς δ' ἂν ἀρνήσηταί με ...	Mt 10,33 ὅστις δ' ἄν
12,10ᵇ	ὃς δ' ἂν [[βλασφημήσῃ εἰς]] ...	Mt 12,32 (cf. Mk 3,29) ǀ
14,11ᵃ	πᾶς ὁ ὑψῶν ἑαυτὸν ...	
14,11ᵇ	καὶ ὁ ταπεινῶν ἑαυτὸν ...	
16,18ᵇ	καὶ ὁ[[ ]] ἀπολελυμένην [[ ]] γαμ[[ῶν]] μοιχ...	

Matthew's relative clause is accepted in 6,48.49 (Q ὅς); 12,9.10 (Q ὃς δ' ἄν)[83], but Luke's participle is accepted in 11,51; 14,11ᵃ·ᵇ; and, with the probability rating C, in 6,47; 16,18ᵇ. In 6,29a τῷ τύπτοντί σε / Mt 5,39 ὅστις σε ῥαπίζει the exact Greek text could not be reconstructed, but see the participles in 6,29b.30a.b / Mt 5,40.42a.b (contrast 5,41 καὶ ὅστις...)[84].

ποιήσῃ τὸ θέλημα τοῦ θεοῦ is changed to (οὗτοί εἰσιν) οἱ τὸν λόγον τοῦ θεοῦ ἀκούοντες καὶ ποιοῦντες (Lk 8,21): the theme is influenced by Lk 8,11-15 (v. 11 ὁ λόγος τοῦ θεοῦ, v. 15 οὗτοί εἰσιν οἵτινες ... ἀκούσαντες τὸν λόγον κατέχουσιν); compare the participle in v. 14, par. Mk 4,18: οὗτοί εἰσιν οἱ τὸν λόγον ἀκούσαντες.
82. Cf. *JBL* (1990), p. 501; (1991), pp. 495-497; (1993), p. 506; (1994), pp. 497-498.
83. Cf. K. BEYER, *Semitische Syntax* (n. 86 below), p. 210 n. 1: "Lk 6,29a; 12,9.10b stammen die kond. Partzz. mit großer Wahrscheinlichkeit erst von Lk, da es sich hier ursprünglich – wie Mt zeigt – um *anakoluthe* kond. Relativsätze gehandelt hat". See also p. 224 on the aorist participle in Lk 12,9-10b ("griechisches Sprachgefühl").
84. Compare also the (less certain) reconstruction of Q, Mt 10,39 (diff. Lk 17,33) ὁ εὑρών, καὶ ὁ ἀπολέσας (Mk 8,35 ὃς γὰρ ἐάν, ὃς δ' ἄν): S. Schulz, J. Lambrecht, Harnack (p. 63: "Auffallend ist nur, daß Matth. in diesem Verse das Partiz. hat und Luk. das Verbum finit. (mit ὃς ἐάν); sonst ist es fast immer umgekehrt. Lukas war wahrscheinlich durch seine frühere Fassung (in c. 9,24, nach Markus) beeinflußt"); Polag: ὁ εὑρών, ὃς δ' ἄν. Contrast R. Laufen: ὃς ἐάν, καὶ ὃς ἄν (p. 321: "den Matthäus durch das Partizip vereinfachte, wie er es auch in 10,37 getan haben dürfte"). On the aorist participle, cf. n. 83 above. On Lk 17,33(Q?), cf. *Evangelica II*, pp. 428-431.

A number of sayings with relative clause in Mark have a Q doublet
with the participle attested by both Matthew and Luke:

4,25 ὃς γὰρ ἔχει   par. Mt 13,12; Lk 8,18
καὶ ὃς οὐκ ἔχει
Mt 25,29 τῷ γὰρ ἔχοντι παντί   Lk 19,26 παντὶ τῷ ἔχοντι
τοῦ δὲ μὴ ἔχοντος   ἀπὸ δὲ τοῦ μὴ ἔχοντος
9,37 ὃς ἂν ... δέξηται   par. Lk 9,48
καὶ ὃς ἂν ... δέχηται
Mt 10,40 ὁ δεχόμενος   Lk 10,16 ὁ ἀκούων, ὁ ... ἀθετῶν
καὶ ὁ ... δεχόμενος   ὁ δὲ ... ἀθετῶν
9,40 ὃς γὰρ οὐκ ἔστιν   par. Lk 9,50
Mt 12,30 ὁ μὴ ὤν   Lk 11,23 ὁ μὴ ὤν
καὶ ὁ μὴ συνάγων   καὶ ὁ μὴ συνάγων
10,11 ὃς ἂν ἀπολύσῃ   par. Mt 19,9
Mt 5,32ᵃ πᾶς ὁ ἀπολύων   Lk 16,18ᵃ πᾶς ὁ ἀπολύων

As indicated above, there is some reason for assigning ὃς ἐὰν ...
γαμήσῃ (Mt 5,32b) to Matthean redaction[85]. It appears to be more difficult to make Luke responsible for changing here a relative clause to the
participle ὁ ... γαμῶν. The more Semitic or more Greek character | of
the phrases can be a helpful criterion in the study of gospel parallels[86],
but it should be considered with circumspection because it easily
becomes a fallacious criterion in reconstructing the (Greek!) text of the
Q source.

The most substantial difference between Mt 5,32 and Lk 16,18 is the
phrase "and marries another" in the first half of the saying, absent in Mt
5,32a and present in Lk 16,18a in the form καὶ γαμῶν ἑτέραν (cf. Mk
10,11 καὶ γαμήσῃ ἄλλην). Its absence in Mt 5,32, in contrast to the
acceptance of the Markan parallel in Mt 19,9, is supposed to be a first
indication against its origin in Q. It is possibly a Lukan insertion in the
Q-saying: it can be taken by Luke from Mk 10,11 and adapted to its new
context (γαμῶν, after ἀπολύων) and to Lukan language (ἑτέραν for
ἄλλην). Thirdly, and more importantly, it looks like a secondary mitigation of an original, more radical, prohibition of divorce: πᾶς ὁ
ἀπολύων τὴν γυναῖκα αὐτοῦ μοιχεύει[87]. By adding καὶ γαμῶν

85. We can neglect here the variant readings: 5,32b ὁ γαμήσας and 19,9 + καὶ ὁ
ἀπολελυμένην γαμῶν (S V M B), ... γαμήσας (TR Greeven; "the B text", incorrectly
cited by Goulder as γαμῶν).
86. Cf. K. BEYER, Semitische Syntax im Neuen Testament. Band I: Satzlehre Teil 1
(SUNT, 1), Göttingen, 1962, esp. pp. 141-232: "Konditionale Relativsätze und Partizipien". I note here a few references to Lk 16,18: pp. 210 (conditional participle / relative
clause); 212 (πᾶς in 18a, and not in 18b); 226 (interposition of ἀπολελυμένην in 18b).
87. Cf. above n. 67: the reconstruction of Q 16,18a proposed by W. Schenk (p. 116),
J. Zmijewski (p. 53); with some hesitation (words bracketed): P. Hoffmann (p. 110; cf.

ἐτέραν Luke changes the point of the saying: what makes the man who divorces his wife an adulterer is now his remarriage[88].

In some recent studies on Q, the Lukan version of the saying including "and marries another" is said to be typical of Q. Thus, L. Schottroff, on itinerant prophetesses: "According to Q 16:18, the gospel often led to divorce, after which the woman was not permitted to remarry, but was to remain single"[89], and more directly to the theme, A.D. Jacobson's essay on "Divided Families"[90]: |

> Since remarriage is the basis of the charge of adultery in Lk 16:18b, it probably was also in 16:18a. Thus Luke's text may be taken as probably the closest to Q.
> Q 16:18 assumes that there are divorced people for whom the question now is: what about remarriage? It is remarriage that is stigmatized. Who might these divorced people be? Probably the persons to whom Jesus directed such sayings as Q 14:26, which instructed them to sunder family ties and follow him. Having left their families and joined the Jesus movement, they might now wish to marry a "believer". Q in 16:18 stigmatizes any who would do that.

I can agree with Jacobson's reaction to W. Schenk, S. Schulz, et al., who regard "and marries another" as secondarily inserted by Luke[91]. The second half of the saying is indeed about remarriage (of a divorced woman), and such is also the theme behind Matthew's "causes her to commit adultery" in parallel to Lk 16,18a[92]. The use of ἐτέραν (for

112: "erst sekundär [in Q?]"); A. Polag (p. 75). See also H. Baltensweiler (n. 88 below). Even R. Laufen, who retains the words καὶ γαμῶν ἐτέραν in his reconstruction of Q (p. 347), seems to be tempted by this hypothesis (n. 94 below). – Of course, the authors mentioned in nn. 16, 30-38 (reconstruction of Q on the basis of Mt 5,32) exclude καὶ γαμῶν ἐτέραν/ἄλλην.

88. Cf. H. BALTENSWEILER, Die Ehe im Neuen Testament (ATANT, 52), Zürich, 1967, pp. 62: "sekundäre Erweiterung und Präzisierung"; 69: "kasuistische Erweichung". Compare B. SCHALLER (n. 10), pp. 238-245: the shift from Mk 10,9 ("Jesus") to 10,11 ("Gemeinde"); pp. 243-244: "das ... apodiktische Verbot der Ehescheidung (hat man) erleichternd in ein Verbot der zweiten Ehe abgeändert".

89. L. SCHOTTROFF, Wanderprophetinnen: Eine feministische Analyse der Logienquelle, in Evangelische Theologie 51 (1991) 332-344, esp. pp. 338-339; ET by J. Reed, Itinerant Prophetesses: A Feminist Analysis of the Sayings Source Q, in R.A. PIPER (ed.), The Gospel Behind the Gospels (n. 24), 1995, pp. 347-360, esp. 354-355 ("Family Conflicts of Women"). Contrast her earlier interpretation of Lk 16,18(Q) in Frauen in der Nachfolge Jesu in neutestamentlicher Zeit (1980), in ID., Befreiungserfahrungen, München, 1990, pp. 96-133, esp. 111 n. 54 ("gegen eine Praxis ... ausserhalb der Gemeinde gerichtet").

90. A.D. JACOBSON, Divided Families and Christian Origins, in The Gospel Behind the Gospels (n. 24), 1995, pp. 361-380, esp. 369-373 ("Q 16:18"; quotations, pp. 370, 371).

91. Ibid., p. 370 n. 26.

92. Cf. J. NOLLAND, Luke 9:21–18:34 (Word, 35B), Dallas, TX, 1993, p. 818: on the assumption "in favor of the earliest source having spoken of a remarriage". But see above, n. 61.

ἄλλην) is possibly Lukan[93], but the phrase "and marries another" was most probably found in Q. Further suggestions about more primitive forms of the saying, different from Q, are not considered here[94].

Although there is much divergence in their views on the Q group between Schottroff (itinerant messengers) and Jacobson (most members were not itinerant), they concur in their interpretation of the Q-saying on divorce: "it is inappropriate to speak of Jesus | forbidding divorce. Divorce is presupposed and the ... interest is to hinder remarriage"[95]. Jacobson's "variant interpretation" has two sides and none of them is really new. The notion of divorce-separation in the light of Lk 14,26; 18,29 was proposed in the early 1960's by B.K. Diderichsen[96], and the understanding of the divorce saying as prohibition of remarriage is not uncommon: "divorce itself does not constitute adultery"[97]. But are we to differentiate between divorce and remarriage in Lk 16,18a? And can we state that only remarriage is adulterous? Our first consideration should be, I think, that in this context the verb ἀπολύω is used for divorce, and not for separation without remarriage. Secondly, the style of the protasis is "casuistic" in the sense that it describes the concrete case of someone who divorces and remarries, without implying that only

93. J. JEREMIAS, *Sprache*, p. 259; cf. pp. 110-111 (ἕτερος in Lk: "mit Vorliebe"); 142 (ἄλλος: "lukanisches Meidewort"). For ἕτερος as substitute for ἄλλος in Mk, see Lk 8,3.6.7.8; 20,11. But, in contrast to the complete absence of the word in Mark, ἕτερος occurs in Q 9,59; 11,26; 16,13a.b (par. Mt) and possibly even in Q 7,19 (Mt, diff. Lk ἄλλον!) and 7,32 (Mt, diff. Lk ἀλλήλων); its use in Lk 14,19.20; 17,34.35; 19,20 (diff. Mt) is probably Lukan (but see Schenk: 14,19 Q; Polag: 19,20 Q). "Möglich, wenn auch ... nicht beweisbar": this is R. Laufen's comment on the possible substitute in Lk 16,18 for an original ἄλλην (p. 578 n. 16).

94. An original form of the saying without "and marries another" is not excluded, for instance, by R. Laufen: "allerdings nicht völlig auszuschließen" (p. 584 n. 58). For others, "and marries another" was part of the original prohibition (J.A. FITZMYER, *Matthean Divorce Texts*, p. 201: "almost certainly") but Lk 16,18b is doubtful (p. 202: "possibly"; there is no such comment in his *Luke*, 1985); see also B. SCHALLER (*Sprüche*, pp. 236-237): the original *Einzelspruch* Mk 10,11 / Lk 16,18a. J. ZMIJEWSKI (*Weisungen*, p. 54) proposes an *Urform* without "and marries another" and in the style of Mk 10,11: ὃς ἂν ἀπολύσῃ τὴν γυναῖκα αὐτοῦ μοιχᾶται ἐπ᾽ αὐτήν (against her; contrast Schaller: with her).

95. L. SCHOTTROFF, *Itinerant Prophetesses* (n. 89), p. 354 n. 32; A.D. JACOBSON, *Divided Families* (n. 90), p. 371: "Q 16:18 does *not* say that divorce is prohibited". Note, however, that the prohibition of remarriage "has the effect of prohibiting the creation of new families within the Jesus movement, but also of effectively eliminating divorce where both spouses are members of the movement" (pp. 371-372).

96. B.K. DIDERICHSEN, *Den markianske skilmisseperikope*, Aarhus, 1962. Cf. *Evangelica* I, pp. 822-823 (and 829 n. 26).

97. Cf. above, on the insertion "and marries another". But see also *Evangelica* I, p. 827; *Evangelica II*, p. 559: on the notion of "separation" implied in the original saying (J. Dupont).

remarrying is stigmatized in the apodosis of the saying[98]. Divorce is "divorce for remarriage"[99]. To conclude, I can quote P. Hoffmann (in his reaction to B. Schaller)[100]:

> In der isolierten Fassung Lk 16,18 ist das Verdikt des Ehebruchs nicht ... auf den Fall der Wiederheirat beschränkt. Vielmehr läßt sich die Formulierung "entlassen und eine andere heiraten" auch als Bezugnahme auf die gängige Praxis verstehen, in der Entlassung und zweite Eheschließung in der Regel einander folgten. Der Spruch bringt also nicht notwendig zum Ausdruck, daß eine Scheidung ohne Wiederheirat nicht unter das Verdikt des Ehebruchs fiele.

98. See the references in n. 97.
99. Cf. J. Nolland's recent comment (n. 92), p. 822: "it is most natural to take the sense as 'divorce in order to'" (with reference to A. Descamps, in *RTL* 1, 1980, p. 16 n. 37).
100. *Jesu Stellungnahme* (n. 67), p. 112.

23

SAVING/LOSING ONE'S LIFE

LUKE 17,33 (Q?) AND MARK 8,35

The presence of doublets in Matthew and Luke has played an important role throughout the history of the Q-hypothesis. P. Wernle uses the evidence of the doublets as "Hauptargument für die Zweiquellenhypothese"[1]. For C.M. Tuckett, in his latest work on Q, it is still one of the main arguments for the existence of a Q source[2]. The one example he cites is the saying about saving/losing one's life:

Mk 8,35	Mt 16,25	Lk 9,24
Q	Mt 10,39	Lk 17,33

Q 17,33 (Mt 10,39) is classified in J.S. Kloppenborg's survey as "*In Q: Most authors*"[3] and the saying is one of the major pieces in the ongoing debate on the Mark-Q overlaps[4].

For a majority of authors, the placement in Mt following on Mt 10,37.38 (Q 14,26.27) preserves the original setting of the Q saying[5]. Mt 10,38.39 appear here in the same order as the Markan form of these sayings in Mk 8,34.35 and parallels. Moreover, ἔτι τε καὶ τὴν ψυχὴν ἑαυτοῦ in Lk 14,26 can be a reminiscence of the losing-one's-life saying which followed here in Q as it still does in Mt 10,39[6]. Lk 17,33 is supposed to be one of the exceptional instances in which Luke has dislocated a Q-saying. There is also the minority opinion of those who hold that the Lukan location is original, Lk 17,33 either being part of 17,31-33 (Q)[7] or attached to 17,28-29 (v. 29 ἀπώλεσεν)[8]. There is still a | third

---

1. *Die synoptische Frage*, 209 (cf. 111-112).
2. *Q and the History*, 10-11 (cf. *The Existence of Q*, 27): though "perhaps one of the weakest arguments". See my review in *ETL* 73 (1997) 173-177.
3. *Q Parallels*, 170.
4. H.T. FLEDDERMANN, *Mark and Q*, 142-145. Cf. my *Assessment*, 283-284; and *The Sayings Source Q and the Gospel of Mark*, 130-131.
5. See, for instance, IQP (in *JBL* 1995, 483): "Q 17:33 is to be found between 14:27 and 34".
6. See below, nn. 48-55.
7. A. POLAG, *Fragmenta Q*, 78: Q 17,31.[32].33. Cf. W. BUSSMANN, *Redequelle*, 93; J. SCHMID, *Matthäus und Lukas*, 335 n. 2; T.W. MANSON, *Sayings*, 145.
8. R. SCHNACKENBURG, *Lk 17,20-27*, 224 (1971, 232): vv. 31.32 LkR and v. 33 "schon in der Quelle"; R. GEIGER, *Endzeitreden*, 124 ("denkbar"). Cf. J.A. FITZMYER, *Lk*, 1172: in Q the saying followed on 17,26-27, but it stems from a different original context (1165).

Mt 16,25

ὃς γὰρ ἐὰν θέλῃ τὴν ψυχὴν αὐτοῦ σῶσαι
ἀπολέσει αὐτήν·
ὃς δ' ἂν ἀπολέσῃ τὴν ψυχὴν αὐτοῦ
ἕνεκεν ἐμοῦ
εὑρήσει αὐτήν.

Mt 10,39

ὁ εὑρὼν τὴν ψυχὴν αὐτοῦ
ἀπολέσει αὐτήν,
καὶ ὁ ἀπολέσας τὴν ψυχὴν αὐτοῦ
ἕνεκεν ἐμοῦ
εὑρήσει αὐτήν.

Mk 8,35

ὃς γὰρ ἐὰν θέλῃ τὴν ψυχὴν αὐτοῦ σῶσαι
ἀπολέσει αὐτήν·
ὃς δ' ἂν ἀπολέσει τὴν ψυχὴν αὐτοῦ
ἕνεκεν ἐμοῦ καὶ τοῦ εὐαγγελίου
σώσει αὐτήν.

Jn 12,25

ὁ φιλῶν τὴν ψυχὴν αὐτοῦ
ἀπολλύει αὐτήν,
καὶ ὁ μισῶν τὴν ψυχὴν αὐτοῦ ἐν τῷ κόσμῳ τούτῳ
εἰς ζωὴν αἰώνιον φυλάξει αὐτήν.

Lk 9,24

ὃς γὰρ ἂν θέλῃ τὴν ψυχὴν αὐτοῦ σῶσαι
ἀπολέσει αὐτήν·
ὃς δ' ἂν ἀπολέσῃ τὴν ψυχὴν αὐτοῦ
ἕνεκεν ἐμοῦ
οὗτος σώσει αὐτήν.

Lk 17,33

ὃς ἐὰν ζητήσῃ τὴν ψυχὴν αὐτοῦ περιποιήσασθαι
ἀπολέσει αὐτήν,
ὃς δ' ἂν ἀπολέσῃ
ζῳογονήσει αὐτήν.

opinion: the original setting of the Q-saying is no longer recoverable (P. Hoffmann)[9].

The wording of the saying in Q is also in dispute. Common words in Mt 10,39 and Lk 17,33 are accepted as derived from Q (here in bold) and almost all reconstructions prefer Mt's verb εὑρίσκω (for Lk's ζητήσῃ περιποιήσασθαι and ζῳογονήσει) and the second τὴν ψυχὴν αὐτοῦ, not in Lk (here underlined):

Mt 10,39ᵃ ὁ εὑρὼν **τὴν ψυχὴν αὐτοῦ**
ἀπολέσει αὐτήν,
ᵇ καὶ ὁ **ἀπολέσας** τὴν ψυχὴν αὐτοῦ ἕνεκεν ἐμοῦ
εὑρήσει αὐτήν.

S. Schulz simply takes Mt's text as Q[10], but opinions remain divided regarding Mt's participles, the use of καί, and ἕνεκεν ἐμοῦ[11]:

Polag 1979	ὁ εὑρών	ὃς δ' ἂν ἀπολέσῃ
Laufen 1980 (Wanke 1981)	ὃς ἐὰν εὑρήσει	καὶ ὃς ἂν ἀπολέσει
		ἕνεκεν ἐμοῦ
Fleddermann 1995	ὃς ἐὰν εὕρῃ	ὃς δ' ἂν ἀπολέσῃ

A. Polag's ὁ εὑρών (cf. Harnack)[12] and R. Laufen's καί[13] and ἕνεκεν ἐμοῦ are taken from Mt 10,39. Like Schulz, Laufen argues for ἕνεκεν ἐμοῦ in Q on the basis of the text (and context!) in Mt: "Die Logien-quelle wird es enthalten haben, da sie in Mt 10,37.38.39/Lk 14,26.27; 17,33 bereits eine geschlossene Komposition zum Thema Jüngernach-folge bot..."[14].

Thus the discussion of the wording of the saying in Q leads back to its location in Mt and to the sayings complex of Q 14,26.27; 17,33. In Kloppenborg's stratigraphy these three sayings belong together and are part of a collection in the earliest stratum of Q: 13,24 + 14,26-27;

---

9. P. HOFFMANN, *Studien*, 5: both Q 14,26-27 and Q 17,33 are "nicht mehr sicher lokalisierbare Einzelsprüche" (cf. 42: "der Kontext unbekannt"); J.D. CROSSAN, *In Fragments*, 92. See also FLEDDERMANN, *Mark and Q*, 143 n. 35. Compare I.H. MARSHALL, *Lk*, 666: an isolated saying that "appeared in different contexts in different recensions of Q".

10. *Q*, 444-445. Cf. B. Weiss, 1908. See also W. SCHENK, *Synopse*, 111; J. LAM-BRECHT, *Q-Influence*, 295; IQP (above, n. 5): brackets are used to refer to textual differences in Lk 17,33.

11. Om. ἕνεκεν ἐμοῦ: A.D. JACOBSON, *The First Gospel*, 22 n. 93; U. LUZ, *Mt* II, 135. Cf. A. HARNACK, *Sprüche*, 63. See also J. DUPONT, *Béatitudes* II, 1969, 357; SCHÜR-MANN, *Lk*, 544 n. 115 ("vielleicht"); *et al.*

12. Compare Harnack's reconstruction: ὁ εὑρὼν [ὃς ἐὰν εὕρῃ] ... καὶ ὃς ἂν ἀπολέ-σει [ὁ ἀπολέσας] ... (102).

13. However, Laufen apparently reads in Lk 17,33 καὶ ὅς (N), and not ὃς δ' (N²⁶).

14. *Doppelüberlieferungen*, 321. Cf. SCHULZ, *Q*, 445.

17,33 + 14,34-35 (Q¹)[15]. B.L. Mack includes the three sayings in his "original book of Q" as the I segment QS 52 "On the cost of being a disciple"[16]. It is disputed whether this segment can be extended to a larger block of sayings (Kloppenborg: 13,24–14,35)[17]. Some propose to restrict the cluster in Q to 14,26.27; 17,33 and suggest a pre-Q connection between two sayings, 14,27 (*Bezugswort*) and the commentary saying 17,33 (*Kommentarwort*)[18].

1. Luke 17,33

From our introductory notation of recent exegetical opinion it is clear enough that the argument for the Q-origin of Lk 17,33 mainly relies on Mt 10,39. It is less evident that the same conclusion can be held if the question is approached from the side of Lk 17,33 and its Lukan context.

1. It is a common assumption that the verb εὑρίσκω in Mt 10,39 is a distinctive element (the only one?) of the Q-saying: εὑρών/ εὕρῃ/εὑρήσει and εὑρήσει αὐτήν. The verb εὑρίσκω is absent in Lk 17,33. Yet, it has been observed that the correspondence between Lk's ζητέω and Mt's εὑρίσκω might be due to Q: "The Lukan ζήτηση ... περιποιήσασθαι is probably a rewriting of a Q-εὑρίσκω, just as in 13,24 Luke's ζητήσουσιν εἰσελθεῖν replaces the same verb... Compare also Lk 4,42 (ἐπιζητέω) with Mk 1,37 (εὗρον)"[19]. However, this last example is not a convincing parallel. Mk 1,37 has εὗρον αὐτόν indeed, but the real parallel to Lk's οἱ ὄχλοι ἐπεζήτουν αὐτόν is Mk's πάντες ζήτουσίν σε. The reference to Q 13,24 mentioned above is based on the supposition that ζητήσουσιν is LkR and εὑρίσκοντες in Mt 7,14 derives from Q (Harnack, Schenk)[20]. But it is well known that

15. *Formation*, 237: "an originally community-directed hortatory cluster of sayings". Cf. ID., *Literary and Stratigraphic Problems*, 1996, 48. For references to this cluster of sayings in (Kloppenborg's) Q¹, see, e.g., PIPER (ed.), *Gospel*, 117 n. 1 (W. Cotter); 260 n. 4 (J.M. Robinson); KLOPPENBORG (ed.), *Conflict and Invention*, 88 (L.E. Vaage).

16. *The Lost Gospel*, 79-80 (cf. 99). Ἕνεκεν ἐμοῦ is included in the text ("on account of me"). M. Myllykoski is wrong in his note on the difference between Mack and Kloppenborg regarding Q 17,33 (*Social History*, 177 n. 91).

17. D. ZELLER, *Grundschrift*, 391: "Nichts beweist, daß der Aufruf 13,24 und die Nachfolgebedingungen 14,26s einmal aufeinander folgten"; C.-P. MÄRZ, *Q-Rezeption*, 198 n. 85; TUCKETT, *Q and the History*, 71-72.

18. J. WANKE, *"Bezugs- und Kommentarworte"*, 76-81, esp. 78. Cf. C. BREYTEN-BACH, *Das Markusevangelium*, 97 (*Grundwort* and *Kommentarwort*).

19. LAMBRECHT, *Q-Influence*, 283 (and n. 33). Cf. 284 n. 37: "his choice of ζητέω [in Lk 17,33] also betrays knowledge of Q".

20. Polag's notation, εἰσὶν οἱ εὑρίσκοντες αὐτήν (Mt) "C 185* Ho 1,196" (*Fragmenta Q*, 69), is correct regarding J.M. Creed (1930: "perhaps"), but less correct regarding HOFFMANN, Πάντες, 196 (= *Tradition und Situation*, 142): "Möglicherweise ersetzt

I "opinion is sharply divided in regard to the form of the Q saying"[21]. The IQP reconstruction[22] expresses hesitation regarding εὑρίσκοντες (Mt) but includes ζητήσουσιν (Lk) in Q:

ᵃ εἰσέλθατε διὰ τῆς στενῆς θύρας,
ᵇ ὅτι πολλοὶ ζητήσουσιν εἰσελθεῖν
ᶜ καὶ ὀλίγοι οἱ...

Other reconstructions include both ζητέω (ζητήσουσιν) and εὑρίσκω (in the conjectural form εὑρήσουσιν)[23]:

ᵇ ὅτι πολλοὶ ζητήσουσιν εἰσελθεῖν [δι᾿ αὐτῆς]
ᶜ καὶ ὀλίγοι εὑρήσουσιν αὐτήν.

The difficulty in this theory is the differing meaning of the two verbs, "*try - succeed*" (ζητήσουσιν + infinitive) and "seek - *find*" (εὑρήσουσιν + αὐτήν). The suggestion that Luke's ζητήσουσιν is influenced by a Q-εὑρίσκω (Mt εἰσὶν οἱ εὑρίσκοντες αὐτήν) has to face this same difficulty[24].

One can hardly say that the verb εὑρίσκω in Mt 10,39a.b is the necessary source equivalent for the two substitutes in Lk, περιποιήσασθαι and ζῳογονήσει. By itself Mk's σῶσαι ... σώσει is not a less likely equivalent. Moreover, the phrase ὃς ἐὰν **ζητήσῃ** (τὴν ψυχὴν αὐτοῦ) περιποιήσασθαι in Lk 17,33a comes close to ὃς γὰρ ἐὰν **θέλῃ** (τὴν ψυχὴν αὐτοῦ) σῶσαι in Mk 8,35 (cf. Lk 9,24). For Luke, θέλω + infinitive and ζητέω + infinitive are almost synonymous; compare Lk 9,9 τίς δέ ἐστιν οὗτος περὶ οὗ ἀκούω τοιαῦτα; καὶ **ἐζήτει** ἰδεῖν

die Schlußwendung καὶ οὐκ ἰσχύσουσιν [Lk] eine ursprüngliche positive Parallelaussage". In his apparatus Polag himself proposes such a conjecture: καὶ ὀλίγοι δυνήσονται.

21. KLOPPENBORG, *Formation*, 223-224. For opinions on priority of Mt resp. Lk, cf. *ibid.*, n. 215; HOFFMANN, 195 (141), n. 20. For a recent discusion, see TUCKETT, *Q and the History*, 189-191.

22. *JBL* 112 (1993), 506.

23. POLAG, 1979, 68 (without δι᾿ αὐτῆς); A. DENAUX, *Spruch*, 1982, 323-326 ("Lukas 13,24") and 327. On the future tense, cf. HOFFMANN, 196 (142): "Gegenüber dem *lehrhaften* Präsens des Matthäus scheinen die Futura bei Lukas ursprünglich zu sein" (emphasis mine; ctr. Harnack, 50, on Lk's ζητήσουσιν: "*lehrhaft* gestaltet").

24. Tuckett agrees with Denaux (*Spruch*, 321-323; cf. Hoffmann, *et al.*) concerning "Matthew's imposing of the two ways scheme on an earlier tradition", but disagrees about the 'finding' reference in Q: "Nowhere is it suggested that the narrow door is hard to *find*... But just because it is narrow does not imply that it is invisible... Hence it is much more likely that the 'finding' in Matt 7:14 is due to MattR" (190-191).

In reply to Hoffmann (*Πάντες*; *Studien*, 5) Tuckett does not belief that the saying ever existed in isolation: the continuation of v. 24 is provided in v. 25 (191); "vv. 24-27 constitute a coherent sequence of sayings" (193). See also his reaction to Kloppenborg's linking of 13,24 to 14,26-27 (above, n. 17).

αὐτόν and 23,8b ἦν γὰρ ἐξ ἱκανῶν χρόνων **θέλων** ἰδεῖν αὐτὸν διὰ τὸ ἀκούειν περὶ αὐτοῦ[25].

2. "It is remarkable that both Matthew and Luke should have made the same addition from Mk., each in the context of Q material": this observation I was made by I.H. Marshall in his commentary on Lk 17,33 and has been echoed since by others in defence of the Q-origin of the saying[26]. There is a certain consistency in Marshall's position. He tries to show that 17,25 "may reflect a tradition of the passion predictions independent of Mk.". In 17,31 he finds "sufficient difference and common omissions with Mt. to make it possible that the saying originally stood also in Q" (with reference to J. Lambrecht, 1967). In sum, 17,33 illustrates Luke's "general practice of not inserting Marcan material in a Q context"[27]. Kloppenborg's position does not exhibit this same logic. He cites Marshall's observation on Lk 17,33, though he defends the more common view on 17,31: Luke inserted this saying from Mk and interpreted it in relation to Lot's wife (v. 32)[28]. Then, in contrast to what is supposed to be Luke's general practice, Lk 17,31-32+33 can be a Lukan insertion of Markan material in the context of Q (17,30 I 34-35).

Compared with Mk 8,35 and parallels, Lk 17,33 shows a number of differences: om. γάρ, ζητήσῃ ... περιποιήσασθαι in 33a, om. τὴν ψυχὴν αὐτοῦ, om. ἕνεκεν ἐμοῦ, and ζῳογονήσει in 33b, but, with the exception of the asyndeton, they are all distinctive of Lk 17,33; none of them has any positive correspondence in Mt 10,39 (Q?). Insertion "in the context of Q material" does not apply to the immediately preceding context of Lk 17,33. The cross saying of Mk 8,34 has a Q-parallel before Mt 10,39 in v. 38 but not before Lk 17,33. Therefore one can reasonably conclude: "the lack of any distinctive links [between Lk 17,33 and Mt 10,39] makes it likely that Luke has actually edited his Markan form again here rather than used language from a second form"[29].

25. In Lk 8,20 ἰδεῖν θέλοντές σε replaces Mk's ζητοῦσίν σε (3,32). On ζητέω + infinitive in Lk and the irrelevance of translation variants θέλω/ζητέω for be°a (below, n. 34), cf. *Jean et les Synoptiques*, 358 n. 209.

26. MARSHALL, *Lk*, 1978, 666. Cf. LAMBRECHT, *Q-Influence*, 283; KLOPPENBORG, *Q Parallels*, 170.

27. Quotations from *Lk*, 662, 665, 664.

28. *Formation*, 158. See also his n. 247 on "the implausible hypothesis" that 17,31 belonged to Q: "This can scarcely be justified". Cf. below, n. 114.

29. J. NOLLAND, *Lk*, 857. Cf. PIPER, *Wisdom*, 257 n. 335: "the verbal correspondence between Mt 10:39 and Lk 17:33 is slight". Less convincingly R. Morgenthaler argues for Q (Mt 10,39 / Lk 17,33) on the basis of the common omission of five words from Mk 8,35: γάρ, θέλῃ, σῶσαι, δέ, and σώσει (*Statistical Synopse*, 138). He reads Lk 17,33 καὶ ὅς (= N) instead of ὃς δ' (= N[26]) and neglects the similarity between θέλῃ/ζητήσῃ plus an infinitive and the object of the infinitive before it (cf. above, n. 25).

3. The absence of ἕνεκεν ἐμοῦ in Lk 17,33 has attracted special attention. It is the main reason why Lk 17,33 is sometimes regarded as more original than Mt I 10,39. Compare, for example, R.H. Gundry's comment on Mt 10,39[30]:

> Matthew changes "whoever seeks to keep his soul" to a substantive participle. He also changes "seeks to keep" to "finds" (εὑρών), which contrasts better with "will lose"... For parallelism he again uses a substantive participle in ὁ ἀπολέσας (contrast Luke's relative clause), writes a second "his soul" (contrast Luke's "it"), and replaces "will preserve it alive" with a second use of εὑρίσκω in "will find it". Most strikingly, he disturbs this careful balancing of the two clauses by inserting "for my sake".

More recently, in his commentary on Mk, Gundry supposes that "Mark may use a tradition more like Luke 17:33 than like Matt 10:39", but he is more reserved about the originality of the lack of ἕνεκεν ἐμοῦ[31].

Lk 17,33 is the unique Synoptic form of the saying without ἕνεκεν ἐμοῦ; hence the statement "where Luke is writing independently of Mark he has no ἕνεκεν-clause"[32]. For C.H. Dodd and some other interpreters, the absence of the ἕνεκεν-clause indicates independence and originality of the Lukan form of the saying (in Q, pre-Q, or oral tradition). This qualifying clause is also missing in Jn 12,25 and, in this respect, Lk 17,33 has been associated with the (pre-)Johannine saying in Jn 12,25: "the ἕνεκεν expression does not occur in the version which by reason of its independent attestation in Lk 17:33 and Jn 12:25 must be regarded as the oldest"[33]. In their own way, theories of translation variants, if applied to περιποιήσασθαι and ζῳογονήσει, have contributed to the acceptance of an oral-tradition origin of Lk 17,33[34]. Dodd

---

30. *Mt*, 1982 (²1994), 201.

31. *Mk*, 1993, 436. He now suggests that ἕνεκεν ἐμοῦ "has been dropped by Luke as part of a larger omission" (454). It should be clear, however, that the basis for such a solution is a less theoretical one if Mt 8,35b (Lk 9,24b) can be recongnized as the source used by Luke in 17,33: om. τὴν ψυχὴν αὐτοῦ ἕνεκεν ἐμοῦ (καὶ τοῦ εὐαγγελίου). But see below, n. 109.

32. C.H. DODD, *Historical Tradition*, 339. On Jn 12,25, 338-343 (= *NTS* 2, 1955, 78-81).

33. C. COLPE, art. ὁ υἱὸς τοῦ ἀνθρώπου, in *TWNT* 8 (1969) 446 n. 308; = *TDNT* 8 (1972) 443 n. 308. See also W. REBELL, *'Sein Leben verlieren'*, 1989, 209-210: the secondary character of ἕνεκεν ἐμοῦ "läßt sich begründen ... durch den Vergleich mit Joh 12.25 und Lk 17.33. In diesen beiden von Markus ... unabhängigen Versionen fehlt nämlich jedwede ἕνεκεν-Wendung". His parenthesis, "wie wir gezeigt haben", apparently refers to his quotation from Dodd's *Historical Tradition*, which is a statement rather than a demonstration.

34. M. BLACK, *Aramaic Approach*, ²1954, 272; ³1967, 188; J. JEREMIAS, *Theologie*, 36 n. 27; M.-É. BOISMARD, *Synopse* II, 248. These authors also explain ζητήσῃ/θέλῃ as translation variants. Cf. above, n. 25.

concludes his discussion of the saying in Jn 12,25 and its Synoptic parallels by stating in general that "the variations belong to its pre-literary history, originating, it may be, in varying attempts to translate the Aramaic in which it was first handed down"[35]. However, it is significant that for Dodd "the terms περιποιεῖσθαι, ζωογονεῖν, have a literary flavour which is unlike the generally simple vocabulary of the earliest tradition of the Sayings"[36]. On this | regard, compare also the phrases he added in 1963: "these more literary expressions are substituted for the simpler σῶσαι", "σῶσαι or some similar verb rather than Luke's more choice expressions"[37]. Dodd notes in the case of Jn 12,25: "The omission of the ἕνεκεν-clause we could understand..."[38]. What then about Lk 17,33?

4. Marshall and Kloppenborg have recourse to another "general practice": because of Luke's aversion to doublets "it is remarkable that Luke should have used the same saying from Mk. twice"[39]. Both refer to Schürmann (*Dubletten*), but at least Kloppenborg departs from Schürmann's theory of Lukan *Vergeßlichkeit*[40] by noting that some assimilation to Mk 8,35 has occurred in Lk 17,33; he mentions the use of ὃς ἐάν and ζητήσῃ/θέλῃ + infinitive[41]. Compare Lambrecht: "It is admitted that the Lukan construction probably depends on Mk 8,35... Luke seems to have conflated his Q-text [= Mt] with Mk 8,35"[42]. If it is true that Luke, through redactional variation, tries to avoid "eine zu wörtliche Übereinstimmung bei der Wiederholung"[43], this cannot be the whole truth. Lk 17,33 might show assimilation to Lk 9,24 (Mk 8,35) and such assimilations also occur in other Mk-Q overlaps (e.g., Lk 8,16/11,33:

---

35. *Historical Tradition*, 338-343, esp. 343 (= 1955, 81). Compare R.E. BROWN: "Dodd even suggests that John's form is in some ways closer to the original Aramaic saying than is any of the Synoptic patterns" (*John*, 474). This seems to refer to the concluding sentence, following on the text quoted above, in Dodd's 1955 article: "If we were permitted to speculate which of the Gospels preserves a form nearest to the common original, I believe John would be a good guess; but such speculation must always remain inconclusive" (81). This sentence is wisely cancelled in *Historical Tradition* (343)!

36. *Historical Tradition*, 339-340 (= 1955, 79).

37. *Historical Tradition*, 340.

38. *Ibid.*, 341. On the parallel in Jn, see my *Note on Jn 12,25*, in *ETL* 73 (1997).

39. MARSHALL, *Lk*, 666. Cf. KLOPPENBORG, *Formation*, 158 n. 248; *Q Parallels*, 170.

40. H. SCHÜRMANN, Dubletten (1953), 1968, 272-278, esp. 278: "mit Bewußtsein hat er wahrscheinlich keine einzige dieser [15] Dubletten eingefügt" (on Lk 17,33, esp. 276).

41. See references above, n. 39.

42. *Q-Influence*, 284 (and n. 37). Cf. LAUFEN, *Doppelüberlieferungen*, 318: "eine Angleichung der Q-Version an die Markusvariante".

43. HOFFMANN, *Studien*, 269: on Lk 9,5 / 10,10-11; and (in n. 111) 9,3 / 10,4a; 8,16 / 11,33; 17,33(!); 12,11-12 / 21,14-15.

ἵνα οἱ εἰσπορευόμενοι βλέπωσιν τὸ φῶς / τὸ φῶς βλέπωσιν)[44]. The case of Lk 17,33 is even cited by J. Dupont as an example of Luke's redactional repetitions: "Il n'hésite pas à répéter en 18,14b la sentence dont il a déjà fait état en 14,11, ou en 17,33 celle qui a été citée en 9,24"[45]. Elsewhere this same author mentions the ἔτι τε καὶ ψυχὴν ἑαυτοῦ phrase in Lk 14,26 and Luke's omission of the third saying in Mt 10,(37-38)39: "Il omet la troisième (qu'il reprendra en Lc 17,33), pour éviter peut-être de répéter ce qu'il a déjà écrit en 9,23-24"[46]. The fact remains, however, that the saying of Lk I 9,24 is repeated in 17,33, and it can hardly be convincing to reverse the general argument for the existence of Q into the statement that in all likelihood the second member of this doublet should derive from Q[47].

2. Lk 14,26 ἔτι τε καὶ τὴν ψυχὴν ἑαυτοῦ

Although ἔτι τε καὶ τὴν ψυχὴν ἑαυτοῦ is one of those phrases one would expect to find in Schürmann's list of reminiscences (1960), it was – as far as I see – in his commentary on Lk 9,24 (1969) that he mentioned it for the first time: "der Verdacht (ist) erlaubt, Luk habe das Logion in seiner Vorlage im Anschluß an 14,26.27 gelesen, zumal 14,26 τὴν ψυχὴν ἑαυτοῦ eine Reminiszenz an τὴν ψυχὴν αὐτοῦ Lk 17,33 zu sein scheint"; with reference to G. Dautzenberg (1966) as if it were a new finding[48]. In fact it was some sort of rediscovery of a "forgotten"

---

44. Compare Mk 4,21 ἵνα and Mt 5,15 καὶ λάμπει πᾶσιν τοῖς ἐν τῇ οἰκίᾳ: "Luke picks up the purpose clause form Mark 4,21, but he fills it with the content of the last Q clause preserved in Matt 5,15" (FLEDDERMANN, 77). Cf. SCHÜRMANN, *Lk* I, 467; II/1, 295: influence of Lk 8,16 "auf seine Q-Wiedergabe 11,33 (und umgekehrt)". See also Lk 8,17/12,2: "Auch V 17 ist die Mk-Wiedergabe des Luk von dem ihm wohl bekannten Q-Logion Lk 12,2 = Mt 10,26 her beeinflußt, vgl. οὐ(κ); γνωσθή(σεται)" (*Lk* I, 468). Contrast his 1953 article where he supposes that Luke "sich der Perikopen Lk 8,16-18 [...] nicht mehr recht erinnert hat" (277; but see his n. 42 on Lk 9,1-5).
45. *Béatitudes* III, 1973, 154 n. 2.
46. *Renoncer* (1971), 564; = *Études*, 1079.
47. KLOPPENBORG, *Formation*, 158 n. 248, noting that twelve cases of doublets in Lk are Mk-Q overlaps. Cf. LAUFEN, *Doppelüberlieferungen*, 557 n. 112: "so daß man *umgekehrt* sagen kann: Dubletten sind *ein wichtiges Indiz* für Doppelüberlieferung in Q und bei Markus" (emphasis mine).
48. *Lk*, 544; n. 124: "Vgl. fragend auch Dautzenberg...". Cf. G. DAUTZENBERG, *Sein Leben bewahren*, 1966, 64: "vielleicht"; n. 57: reference to E. Schweizer, in *Erniedrigung*, 1955, 14 (= ²1962, 16): "War so schon hingewiesen auf das geforderte 'Hassen des eigenen Lebens', konnte Lukas den andern Satz weglassen und 17,33 aufnehmen". The relation to Lk 17,33 remains unclear; Schweizer continues: "wo er vielleicht in der etwas veränderten Form von Lukas schon im Zusammenhang *vorgefunden* wurde"; Dautzenberg: "den ausgefallenen Spruch Mt 10,39..., der ja später noch *zweimal* erscheint" (emphasis mine). Schweizer's reference to E. Percy (n. 44 = 49) concerns the secondary

interpretation. Cf. B. Weiss: "eine Reminiscenz an Matth. 10,39"[49];
Holtzmann: "Lc arbeitet ... in dem Zusatz ἔτι δὲ καὶ τὴν ἑαυτοῦ
ψυχήν den wesentlichen Inhalt von Mt 10,39, welcher Vers in extenso
erst Lk 17,33 reproduzirt wird, ein"[50]. In 1972 J. Zmijewski did not discuss the argument in his study of Lk 17,20-37 and this will remain a
lacuna in his otherwise valuable monograph[51]. In the same year it I was
clearly formulated by S. Schulz[52] and subsequently has won an ever
growing acceptance in special studies on the location of Q 17,33 (Mt
10,39)[53]. R. Laufen calls it "ein eindrucksvoller Beweis"[54], and, more
recently, it has been adopted in the influential work on Q by J.S. Kloppenborg[55].

The standard solution given to ἔτι τε καὶ τὴν ψυχὴν ἑαυτοῦ in Lk
14,26 implies first that this phrase is a secondary (Lukan) insertion in
the traditional saying, second that τὴν ψυχὴν ἑαυτοῦ is taken from Q
17,33 / Mt 10,39 (reminiscence)[56], and third that it indicates an original
proximity of the life saying (the cluster Q 14,26.27; 17,33 / Mt

insertion of the ψυχή phrase in 14,26, "als Zusatz des Evangelisten nach 9,24 zu
beurteilen", and not its relation to Mt 10,39 (cf. *Die Botschaft Jesu*, Lund, 1953, 169-
170).

49. *Marcusevangelium*, 1872, 290 n. 2; *Matthäusevangelium*, 1876, 284; *Lk*, [6]1878,
471.

50. *Synoptiker*, 1889, 170; [2]1892, 167; [3]1901, 382; cf. 395: Lk 17,33 "Wiederholung
des 9,24 und (der Sache nach) 14,26 dagewesenen, in diesem Zusammenhang nicht recht
passenden Spruches". See also, e.g., J.M. CREED, *Lk*, 1930, 194: "ἔτι τε καὶ τὴν ψυχὴν
ἑαυτοῦ is probably taken by Luke from another saying which followed in his source as it
does still in Mt. x.39"; 221: Lk 17,33 "probably taken from Q, cf. Mt. x.39". Contrast
later hesitant formulations starting with Schweizer (above, n. 48).

51. *Eschatologiereden*, 349-350, 471-473. His dissertation was written in 1969-1970
(Bonn, under H. Zimmermann) and could not yet use Schürmann's commentary. There is
only one reference to Dautzenberg (472 n. 36) but no discussion.

52. *Q*, 447 n. 327. See also DUPONT, *Renoncer*, 1971, 563 (= 1078), n. 2, with reference to Schweizer and Dautzenberg.

53. See, e.g., R. GEIGER, *Endzeitreden*, 1973, 123: "Ersatz für das hier ausgefallene
Parallellogion zu Mt 10,39" (apparently influenced by Dautzenberg). See also n. 54.

54. *Doppelüberlieferungen*, 320. In n. 129 (559) he refers to Schweizer, Dautzenberg,
Schürmann, Schulz; and also Percy (though without good reason: cf. above, n. 48) and
H.-J. Degenhardt (*Lukas Evangelist der Armen*, 1965, 106 n. 6: "Vielleicht ... aus Lk
17,33"). — See also J. WANKE, 1981, 77 n. 7 (cf. Dautzenberg, Schweizer, Schürmann,
Laufen); J. LAMBRECHT, 1982, 283 (n. 34: cf. Dupont, Geiger, Laufen), 295. Wanke's ref-
erence to H.E. Tödt (*Menschensohn*, 37) should be cancelled: his observation concerning
Q 17,33 (Mt 10,39) does not involve the phrase in Lk 14,26.

55. *Formation*, 159; *Q Parallels*, 170 (referring to Schürmann). — See also U. LUZ,
Mt II, 1990, 134: "eine Reminiszen an den von hier 'verschobenen' Q-Vers Mt 10,39 (=
Lk 17,33!)" ("fast sicher" Lukan); J.M. ROBINSON, *The Sayings Gospel Q* (1992), 371 n.
12: "(Lk 14,26ff.), with its reference to losing one's own life, tucked into the saying
about loosing one's family, shows that Q 17,33 originally belonged with Q 14,26-27, as
indeed Mt 10,37.38.39 still attests".

56. Luke "has left behind a kind of summary of it" (JACOBSON, 221).

10,37.38.39). That the phrase in Lk 14,26 is a secondary addition[57], is now almost universally agreed in the studies on Q, although R.H. Gundry's commentary on Mt reverses the argument[58] and the commentaries on Lk by W. Grundmann[59], J. Ernst[60], and I.H. Marshall[61] | seem to support an alternative approach. Other commentators do not mention the Q-saying (Mt 10,39) as the source of the Lukan addition but refer to Lk 9,24 (Mk 8,35): "von Lukas ergänzt ... ebenso das eigene Leben (aus 9,24 = Mk 8,35)" (J. Schmid)[62]; "inspired by 9:24, which we should note follows a variant of 14:27" (J. Nolland)[63]. A more explicit reference to the Markan variant of 14,27 was provided by A. Schulz (1962)[64]:

> Wahrscheinlich hat Lk auch aus eigenem Antrieb unter dem Einfluß des verwandten Spruches in der marcinischen Überlieferung Mk 8,34 parr (= Lk 9,23), in der Jesus von seinem Schüler das ἀρνησάσθω ἑαυτόν

---

57. Cf. above, nn. 48, 52-56, and all recent reconstructions of Q 14,26 (cf. below, nn. 66-67), either as one sentence (Lk) or as a two-stich saying (Mt). Their common argument is that the phrase is not found in Mt 10,37. R.H. Stein also refers to the Gospel of Thomas (*Luke 14:26*, 191-192: Thom 55 and 101). But see Fleddermann (*Mark and Q*, 141), Fitzmyer (*Lk*, 1061), *et al.*, who rightly contest the independence of Thomas.

58. See the reversal in his comment on Mt 10,39: the reference to hating oneself, traditional in Lk 14,26 and deleted in Mt 10,37, suggested to Matthew the tradition behind Lk 17,33 (*Mt*, 201; cf. 200).

59. *Lk*, 1961, 302: "Lukas fügt noch ergänzend das eigene Leben hinzu (vgl. 9,24 Par.) — *oder sollte das allein das Ursprüngliche sein?*" (emphasis mine).

60. *Lk*, 1977, 448: "wahrscheinlich hat er [Lk] eine kürzere Vorlage, die unter Umständen nur allgemein von 'der eigenen Seele', d.h. dem eigenen Leben sprach, ergänzt". More reserved in the new edition: "es ist denkbar..." (1983, 333).

61. *Lk*, 1978, 592: "the occurrence of Luke's phrase μισεῖν ... τὴν ψυχήν in Jn. 12:25 warns against any facile conclusions, and suggests that the Lucan form was one of several similar sayings in circulation" (with reference to Dodd's treatment of Jn 12,25; cf. above, n. 35). Cf. DODD, *Historical Tradition*, 343, on Lk 14,26 (diff. Mt): "the Lucan form, with its challenging hyperbole, is surely the more original or, in other words, nearer the primary tradition. Now in this same passage of Luke the disciple is required to 'hate' his own ψυχή. The expression μισεῖν τὴν ἑαυτοῦ ψυχήν is used here in exactly the same sense as in John... It follows that ... John is moving entirely within the ideas and language of the primary tradition". See the quotations from Dodd's *Tradition* (FT, 1987, 431) in M. MORGEN, *"Perdre sa vie"*, 1995, 38.

For M.-É. Boismard the ψυχή phrase in Lk 14,26 is secondary to Mt 10,37 (= Q) but pre-Lukan: μισεῖ and τὴν ψυχὴν ἑαυτοῦ/αὐτοῦ in Proto-Lk and Jn 12,25 stem from Document C (*Synopse* II, 293).

62. *Lk*, 1940, 184; ⁴1960, 247. See also B. WEISS, *Lk*, ⁹1901, 524: "eine Reminiscenz an Mt 10,39 oder Mk 8,35" (ctr. above, n. 49: note the addition of Mk 8,35). Cf. *Die Quellen der synoptischen Überlieferung*, 1908, 46: "Mt 10,39 hat bei Luk. keine eigentliche Parallele, da der Spruch 9,24 nach Mk. gebracht war und daher in dem ἔτι δὲ καὶ τὴν ἑαυτοῦ ψυχήν nur an ihn erinnert wird, während sich 17,33 lediglich eine ganz freie Reminiszenz an ihn findet, die keine wörtliche Vergleichung zuläßt".

63. *Lk*, II, 1993, 762.

64. A. SCHULZ, *Nachfolgen und Nachahmen*, 1962, 80.

fordert, die Bestimmung von Haß des eigenen Lebens ἔτι δὲ καὶ τὴν ψυχὴν ἑαυτοῦ nachgetragen.

This reference to Mk 8,34 (Lk 9,23) and Lk 14,27 deserves further examination[65]. Concentration on the life saying in the cluster of 14,26.27; 17,33, and in the smaller unit of 14,27+17,33, should not withdraw scholarly attention from the more evident unit of 14,26-27 as a pair of discipleship sayings in Q (and in Lk).

In parallel to the single sentence in Lk 14,26, the family saying in Mt 10,37 has two sentences, first with the object father – mother and then with son – daughter. Although IQP and some other recent reconstructions of Q adopt Mt's two sentences in the original Q text[66], Matthean fondness for parallelism and the possible influence of the just preceding saying in Mt 10,34-36 (v. 35!) can explain the duplication of the original father – mother (with parallel in Lk) | in a secondary son – daughter sentence[67]. With some confidence the text of Q 14,26-27 can be reconstructed as follows:

> [26] ὃς[68] οὐ μισεῖ τὸν πατέρα αὐτοῦ καὶ τὴν μητέρα,
>   οὐ δύναται εἶναί μου μαθητής.
> [27] ὃς οὐ λαμβάνει τὸν σταυρὸν αὐτοῦ
>   καὶ ἔρχεται/ἀκολουθεῖ[69] ὀπίσω μου,
> οὐ δύναται εἶναί μου μαθητής.

In the family saying (v. 26) the object father – mother is expanded by Luke with the mention of other relatives: wife – children, brothers – sisters (probably influenced by Mk 10,29; Lk 18,29) and the phrase ἔτι τε[70]

---

65. For J. Lambrecht, A. Schulz's opinion ("although somewhat farfetched") "can be considered as supplementary" to the more common view that the phrase in Lk 14,26 "seems to be borrowed from the Q Life saying" (*Q-Influence*, 283 n. 34).

66. *JBL* 111 (1992), 507 (IQP). See also FLEDDERMANN, *Mark and Q*, 137; cf. *Cross and Discipleship* (1988), 474: J. Dupont's argument of Luke's compensation (for the omitted saying) in Lk 14,33. But see my reply, in *Study of Q*, 51 (= 431) n. 93.

67. Contrast, e.g., Polag's inclusion of "son – daughter" in the single sentence of Q 14,26.

68. IQP: [εἴ τις]; Polag: εἴ τις ἔρχεται πρός με καί (= Lk). Compare v. 27: ὅς (Mt καὶ ὅς / Lk ὅστις).

69. IQP ἀκολουθεῖ (= Mt): Harnack, Schmid, Schulz, Fleddermann; ἔρχεται (= Lk): Polag, Laufen, Kloppenborg (cf. below, n. 73).

70. B L Δ 33. 892 *pc* (H N N²⁶). Variant reading δέ: P⁴⁵ ℵ A D W Θ Ψ *f*¹·¹³ 𝔐 lat syʰ saᵐˢˢ bo Cl (TR T S V M B; Jeremias, Greeven); om.: P⁷⁵ saᵐˢ (Kilpatrick: *Diglot*). Note Tischendorf's change from τε (⁷1859; Lachmann) to δέ (⁸1879: cf. ℵ) and B. Weiss's change from δέ (= TR) to τε (= H). J. Jeremias who opts for reading δέ (*Lk*, 241; cf. 78-79, on the Lukan stylistic characteristic δὲ καί) can comment on τε καί in Lk 22,66: "Lukas bevorzugt die enklitische Partikel τε. Insbesondere ist lukanisch die Kombination τε (...) καί" (299). Compare the phrase ἔτι τε καί in Acts 21,28 and ἔτι δὲ καί in Acts 2,26 (cit. LXX).

καὶ τὴν ψυχὴν ἑαυτοῦ[71]. If the saying in Q began with ὃς οὐ μισεῖ, the conditional clause εἴ τις ἔρχεται πρός με (without parallel in Mt 10,37) can be assigned to Lukan rewriting of Q 14,26-27. Redactional changes in v. 27 are less radical: ὅστις (for ὅς), βαστάζει (for λαμβάνει), ἑαυτοῦ (for αὐτοῦ) and possibly ἔρχεται (for ἀκολουθεῖ, if original in Q)[72]. In the Markan version of the cross saying we note a similar change of ἀκολουθεῖν[73]: Lk 9,23 εἴ τις θέλει ὀπίσω μου ἔρχεσθαι. It is most likely that Luke had in mind this clause when redacting the *Doppellogion* of Q 14,26-27 (v. 26 εἴ τις ἔρχεται πρός με, cf. v. 27 ἔρχεται ὀπίσω μου)[74]; and probably also when adding ἔτι τε καὶ τὴν ψυχὴν ἑαυτοῦ (compare 9,23 ἀρνησάσθω ἑαυτόν; Mk 8,34 ἀπ-).

A. Plummer's sentence: "μισεῖν τὴν ψυχὴν ἑαυτοῦ is ἀπαρνήσασθαι ἑαυτόν (ix.23) carried to the uttermost"[75] has before it a long tradition assimilating the phrase in Lk 14,26 with the "self-denial" in Mt 16,24 (= Mk)[76]. Cf. Lucas Brugensis, at Mt 16,24: "Quo loquendi modo et nos legimus Luc. 14. v. 26. *odisse animam suam*, idem unum cum eo quod hic habemus *abnegare semetipsum*"[77]. However, if ἔτι κτλ. is

---

71. Ψυχὴν ἑαυτοῦ: P[75] ℵ B 579 (1241) *pc* (H M N N[26]; Jeremias); ἑαυτοῦ ψυχήν: P[45] A D L W Θ Ψ *f*[1.13] M; Cl (TR T S V B; Greeven). — On ἑαυτοῦ in Lk, see, e.g., the annotations in Goulder's commentary on *Lk*. Ctr. JEREMIAS, *Lk*, 78. Note however Lk 9,24 ἑαυτόν (diff. Mk 8,36 τὴν ψυχὴν αὐτοῦ); Lk 13,19.34; 14,26a.27; 19,13 (diff. Mt).

72. Here again, contrast Gundry: ὅστις, βαστάζει, ἔρχεται are original (*Mt*, 200-201).

73. Mk 8,34 ἀκολουθεῖν P[45] C* D W Θ 0214 *f*[1] 𝔐 lat sa[ms]; Or (T S V B N[26]; Greeven, Gnilka, Lührmann, Fleddermann, *et al.*); assimilation to Mt 16,24 may explain the well attested variant ἐλθεῖν (Mk's text: TR H M N; B. Weiss, Pesch, *et al.*).

74. Cf. FLEDDERMANN, *Cross and Discipleship*, 476. Note that for Dupont not only in Lk 14,26a εἴ τις ἔρχεται πρός με "l'expression fait écho à celle de *Lc* 9,23" (cf. above), but he also explains ὃς οὐκ ἀποτάσσεται in 14,33 "à la lumière de *Lc* 9,23" (!) in the sense ὃς οὐ θέλει ἀποτάξασθαι. Cf. *Renoncer*, 575 (= 1090).

75. *Lk*, 364.

76. Cf. A. FRIDRICHSEN, *"Sich selbst verleugnen"* (1936), 3: "Persönlich bin ich der Überzeugung, dass ἀπαρν. ἑαυτόν die griechische Entsprechung zu den offenbaren Aramaismus μισεῖν τὴν ψυχὴν ἑαυτοῦ ist. [n. 2] Das haben mehrere Exegeten des grossen humanistischen Zeitalters der Auslegung gesehen"; (1942), 94: "Das eigenartige ἀπαρνεῖσθαι ἑαυτόν ... eine Variante zu dem lukanischen μισεῖν τὴν ἑαυτοῦ ψυχήν (14,26)". See also O. MICHEL, in *TWNT* 4 (1942), 695 n. 27: "Man darf also μισεῖν τὴν ψυχὴν ἑαυτοῦ (Lk 14,26) mit [ἀπ]αρνεῖσθαι ἑαυτόν (Lk 9,23) zusammenstellen" (with reference to Plummer). Compare Boismard's comment on "se renier" in Mk 8,35 and par. (= Doc. B): "Lc 14,26 donne à peu près la même idée sous cette forme: '... hait ... même sa propre vie'" (*Synopse II*, 247; cf. above n. 61: Doc. C).
Fridrichsen's interpretation of ἀπαρνησάσθω ἑαυτόν is repeated by K.-G. Reploh, with some reservation (*Markus*, 1969, 126: "wenn..., wovon A. Fridrichsen überzeugt ist"), and now also by Gundry: "may represent an idiomatic Greek translation of Aramaic behind 'hate ... his own life' (Luke 14:26)" (*Mk*, 1993, 435).

77. *Mt*, [2]1712 (1606), 252.

secondarily added to the family saying (as it is now widely accepted), Lk 14,26 can no longer be cited as evidence for a traditional μισεῖν τὴν ψυχὴν ἑαυτοῦ[78]. And as long as the question of the Q-origin of Mt 10,39 is not resolved, the derivation of the ψυχή phrase in Lk 14,26 from Q remains a circular argument. The association with the cross saying (Lk 14,27) may imply that it has been influenced by ἀπαρνησάσθω ἑαυτόν of the parallel saying in Mk 8,34 / Lk 9,23, where it is followed by a string of ψυχή sayings: 8,35 τὴν ψυχὴν αὐτοῦ (bis; Lk 9,24); 8,36 τὴν ψυχὴν αὐτοῦ (Lk 9,25 ἑαυτόν); 8,37 τῆς ψυχῆς αὐτοῦ[79].

3. The Doublet in Matthew

The defence of the Q-origin of the life saying has taken two extreme forms. On the one hand, B. Weiss holds that Mt 10,39 can be assigned to Q without being supported by Lk 17,33[80]. On the other hand, for M.-É. Boismard, I whose Proto-Matthew hypothesis is otherwise not unrelated to Weiss, Lk 17,33 stems from Q while Mt 10,39 was "un simple doublet de Mt 16,25"[81]. As indicated above, the verb εὑρίσκω (Mt 10,39a.b) is generally adopted in reconstructions of the Q text, and not a few also agree with Weiss's view on εὑρήσει in Mt 16,25b (diff. Mk 8,35b): "mit diesem εὑρήσει kehrt der Evangelist zu dem änigmatischen Ausdruck der Quelle zurück"[82]. For Boismard, on the contrary, εὑρήσει in 16,25 (like 10,39) is a redactional correction of Mk's σώσει: "une correction de l'ultime Rédacteur matthéen"[83]. Word-statistical studies[84] come to the same conclusion. For U. Luz, "ca 5" of the 27 occurrences of εὑρίσκω in Mt are possibly redactional and I guess

---

78. Cf. Prov 29,24 ὃς μερίζεται κλέπτῃ, μισεῖ τὴν ἑαυτοῦ ψυχήν, נָפְשׁוֹ שׂוֹנֵא (A. SCHLATTER, *Lk*, 345). On Jn 12,25, cf. above, n. 38.

79. On the supposed "reminiscence", see also (with reference to my *Study of Q*, 50-51 = 430-431), PIPER, *Wisdom*, 151-152: "The evidence for a Q-version ... therefore appears to be ambiguous".

80. This is clearly what is meant by "eine ganz freie Reminiszenz..." (cf. above, n. 62). See also *Lk*, ⁹1901, at 17,33: "diese ganz lukan. Umbildung des bereits 9,24 nach Mk gebrachten Spruches" (569). Cf. T. STEPHENSON, *Doublets*, 6: "Mt. x 39 is from Q, and the rest is Marcan"; 3: "Lk. xvii 33 may be a repetition of the Marcan passage, with the phraseology changed, for the sake of variety".

81. *Synopse II*, 1972, 248.

82. *Mt*, ⁸1890, 296. Compare FLEDDERMANN, *Mark and Q*, 1995, 143 ("the Q verb"), 144 ("the enigmatic 'find'"). See also, e.g., LAUFEN, 556 n. 92 ("in Anlehnung an Q"); M. MORGEN, *"Perdre sa vie"*, 1995, 35 n. 23.

83. Εὑρίσκω (instead of σῴζω) with the antonym ἀπόλλυμι (*perdre*): "*égarer – trouver*" instead of "*faire périr – sauver*".

84. Εὑρίσκω: Mt 27, Mk 11, Lk 45 (Acts 35), Jn 19. Occurrences in Mt: 5 par. Mk (21,2.19; 26,40.43.60); 7 par. Lk = Q (7,7.8; 8,10; 12,43.44; 18,13; 24,46); 2 diff. Mk

10,39a.b and 16,25 are among them[85]. R.H. Gundry shows less restraint and treats as Mattheanisms the seven uses of εὑρίσκω inserted in parallel material and its eight occurrences in passages peculiar to Mt[86]. In the case of Mt 10,39; 16,25: "Matthew characteristically substitutes 'will find' for 'will save'. This substitute ... makes a better antonym to 'will lose'"[87]. W. Schenk to a large | extent agrees with Gundry's comments on redactional usage in Mt. He notes however on 10,39a.b: "+Q vorgegeben SCHULZ 1972:445 gg. [...] GUNDRY 201"[88]. But Schulz's observation on Lukan redaction in Lk 17,33 (and on possible influence of Mk 8,35 / Lk 9,24)[89] scarcely allows for any conclusion concerning the Q-origin of Mt's εὑρίσκω. Fleddermann now refers to "Luke's desire to avoid the verb εὑρίσκω which struck him as strange in this context"[90]. But no justification is provided. That "Matthew's verb εὑρίσκω is common in Q"[91] means nothing more than that this verb in Q 7,9; 11,9.10.24.25; 12,43; 15,5 is adopted by Matthew ... and by

(16,25; 27,32); 5 diff. Lk (7,14; 10,39a.b; 22,9.10); 8 in passages peculiar to Mt (1,18; 2,8; 11,29; 13,44.46; 17,27; 18,28; 20,6). Compare W. SCHENK, *Die Sprache des Matthäus*, 269: (Mk 11 − 6 + 2) + (Q 7 + 7) + (A-Mt 6). Correct the figures of +Q: 5 (instead of 7) and of red. A-Mt: 8 (instead of 6). The confusion is possibly due to a treatment of 18,28 and 20,6 as +Q: "auf jeden Fall ist es von daher [18,13 Q] red. an den beiden Folgestellen 18,28 und 20,6" (270). For similar corrections, cf. *ETL* 63 (1987) 413-419.

85. *Mt* I, 41; cf. II, 135 n. 9 (10,39: "könnte auch mt sein"); 487 n. 4 (16,25). See also 199 n. 6 (11,29); 529 n. 3 (17,27); add Mt 27,32 (+Mk). — On Mt 10,39, cf. II, 145 n. 79: "Der mt Sprachgebrauch ist vielleicht von der LXX inspiriert; vgl. Jer 45,2; vgl. 46,18 (ἔσται ἡ ψυχὴ αὐτοῦ εἰς εὕρημα = er wird leben)". — Cf. DAUTZENBERG, *Sein Leben bewahren*, 62: "vielleicht handelt es sich sogar um einen kerygmatisch-katechetischen Fachausdruck des Matthäus".

86. Cf. Gundry's figures (7,8) in the Index (*Mt*, 644) and throughout the commentary, with a variety of expressions: Mattheanism (126, 372, 438, 568), Matthean vocabulary (219), Matthew's special vocabulary (396), Matthean diction (278), his favorite diction (278). In 1,18 (εὑρέθη) and 2,8 (εὕρητε) Gundry combines Matthew's "independent liking of the verb" (30, cf. 21) with the influence of Lk 1,30 (εὗρες) and 2,12 (εὑρήσετε).

87. *Mt*, 339 (on 16,25). See also on εὑρών − εὑρήσει in 10,39: "contrasts better with 'will lose'" (201). The substitute in 16,25 "conforms to his distinctive phraseology in 10:39" (339; *Mk*, 454: "a more exact antonym"). Cf. NOLLAND, *Lk*, 478: "the Markan form [saving and losing] assumes a situation in which possession of life is under threat. The loss of this context could have produced a shift to a 'better' antithesis [finding and losing]".

88. *Sprache*, 269. Cf. *Synopse*, 111 ("finden"). However, Schenk's full text ("SCHULZ 1972:445 gg. SCHMID 1930:278...") is misleading. The opposition between Schulz and Schmid does not concern the verb εὑρίσκω but the use of the participles, original for Schulz but secondary for Schmid (as it is noted by Schulz, 445 n. 307: "Anders..."). Cf. SCHMID, 278: "Mit Ausnahme des Partizips ὁ εὑρών (für ὃς ἐὰν κτλ.)..." (and n. 4).

89. *Q*, 444 nn. 304-305 (and not 445!).

90. *Mark and Q*, 142.

91. *Ibid.*, 143 n. 32.

Luke. The evangelist who wrote νεκρὸς ἦν καὶ ἀνέζησεν, ἦν ἀπο-λωλὼς καὶ εὑρέθη in Lk 15,24.32, why would he then avoid the verb εὑρίσκω if he had found the lose-and-find language in the Q-saying (εὑρών – ἀπολέσας, or εὕρῃ – ἀπολέσῃ)?

Fleddermann departs from Schulz in that he admits that Matthew joined the losing-one's-life saying to the cross saying (10,38 Q) because he found these sayings joined in Mk 8,34-35[92], and that Matthew bor-rowed the phrase ἕνεκεν ἐμοῦ in 10,39 from Mk 8,35 / Mt 16,25. It is also true, of course, that Matthew's εὑρήσει further assimilates 10,39b and 16,25b (... τὴν ψυχὴν αὐτοῦ ἕνεκεν ἐμοῦ εὑρήσει αὐτήν). But the question then arises whether the remaining dissimilarities (viz., the use of the participles ὁ εὑρών and ὁ ἀπολέσας) still provide satisfac-tory evidence for a Q-saying different from Mk 8,35. The answer is given by Fleddermann: "Matthew uses substantival participles often, and (in 10,37-41) he creates a stylistic unit by substantival participles"[93]. The nominative participles at the head of each line in Mt 10,39 can be stressed as Matthean parallelism in contrast to Lk 17,33 (Gundry), but even so well if compared with Mk 8,35 / Mt 16,25. The "disturbing" phrase ἕνεκεν ἐμοῦ has its origin there and is incorrectly described as Matthew's *insertion* into "the tradition behind Luke 17:33"[94].

I Besides εὑρήσει (for σώσει in Mk) the only differences between Mt 16,25 and Mk are the use of ἀπολέσῃ (for ἀπολέσει) and the omission of καὶ τοῦ εὐαγγελίου, both in agreement with Lk 9,24 against Mk 8,35. The reading of the future indicative ἀπολέσει with ὃς ἄν in Mk 8,35 is not uncontested, though the variant ἀπολέσῃ (TR W S V Greeven)[95] could be due to harmonization. If ἀπολέσῃ is read in Lk 17,33b (ctr. T H M N ἀπολέσει) and from there adopted in the recon-struction of the Q-text[96], one could think of Q-influence in Mt 16,25 and Lk 9,24[97]. However, grammatical "correction" of the less usual con-struction (ὃς δ' ἄν) ἀπολέσει by both Matthew and Luke is not unlikely[98] and there is no need to speculate further about the possibility of Deutero-Mark or Matthean influence on Lk.

92. *Ibid.*, 143, and n. 35. Cf. SCHMID, *MtLk*, 276 ("Der eigentliche Grund..."); *Mt*, ⁴1959, 186.
93. *Ibid.*, 142.
94. Cf. above, n. 30.
95. See also Orchard, Fleddermann.
96. Cf. above: Polag, Fleddermann.
97. Cf. ENNULAT, *Die 'Minor Agreements'*, 198 ("denkbar?"). Note that Fledder-mann who reads ἀπολέσῃ in Q and in Mk (143) could, on this basis, argue for Mark's use of Q.
98. Cf. DAUTZENBERG, 51 n. 1; LAUFEN, 556 n. 92; ENNULAT, 198. Cf. BDR § 380, 3 (n. 5).

This last possibility is seriously envisaged by Gundry regarding the omission of καὶ τοῦ εὐαγγελίου: "Luke's agreeing with the omission despite his lacking parallels to 'on account of me' in Matthew's earlier passages suggests Matthean influence"[99]. However, if ἕνεκεν ἐμοῦ in Mt 10,39 can be explained by assimilation to 16,25[100], there are only two other occurrences in Mt: in Mt 5,11, where there is no doubt about the Q-origin of Luke's "for the sake of the Son of Man" (6,22)[101], and in Mt 10,18, par. Mk 13,9, where Luke writes ἕνεκεν τοῦ ὀνόματός μου (21,12), in partial conformity to διὰ τὸ ὄνομά μου (v. 17; = Mk 13,13), the same substitute that is used by Matthew in Mt 19,29 (diff. Mk 10,29). Anyway the problem in parallel to Mk 8,35 is not the presence of ἕνεκεν ἐμοῦ[102] but the absence of καὶ τοῦ εὐαγγελίου, and it is rather strange to argue that "'Gospel' occurs only four times in Matthew" without mentioning that it never occurs in Lk, while it is not uncommon to explain Luke's omission in 9,24 "because of his general reluctance to use that term"[103]. Gundry's more positive interpretation that the | omission "concentrates attention on Jesus" is not exclusively Matthean[104]. Unlike Matthew's ἕνεκεν ἐμοῦ in 16,25, Luke's phrase in 9,24 corresponds to με καὶ τοὺς ἐμοὺς λόγους in the same context (9,26a, from Mk), without parallel in Mt[105].

---

99. *Mt*, 339. However, there is no mention of this minor agreement in his 1992 catalogue of "Matthean Foreign Bodies" in Lk (cf. 1479), and in his *Mk* the argument of Lk's "lacking parallels" disappears: "Luke keeps the phrase at 9:24 (his proper parallel to Mark 8:35), uses phrases with ἕνεκεν at 4:18; 6:22; 18:29; 21:12, and elsewhere never drops such a phrase" (454).

100. And not, as suggested by Schenk, by assimilation to 10,18. Cf. *Sprache*, 215: "10,18 (= Mk) und rahmend V. 39 (+ Mk) dupl.".

101. Cf. TUCKETT, *Q and the History*, 180 n. 50 ("widely agreed"). See also GUNDRY, *Mt*, 74. Ctr. GOULDER, *Lk*, 353.

102. At least if, with most authors (and Gundry: above, n. 99), one reads ἐμοῦ καί in the text of Mk 8,35: om. P⁴⁵ D 28 700 it (sy^s); [H] [GNT^{1.2}], om. Bover Boismard and apparently Goulder (cf. *Lk*, 353: ἕνεκεν ἐμοῦ Mt "16.25R"; Lk: "Only at 9.24 / Mk 8.35 does he copy it in"; but no comment at Lk 9,24).

103. FITZMYER, *lk*, 783.

104. *Mt*, 339. On ἕνεκεν ἐμοῦ in Mt 10,39: "... relates the saying more specifically to persecution and yet again highlights the figure of Jesus" (201). Compare SCHÜRMANN, on Lk 9,24: "Luk arbeitet (wie Mt) den christologischen Sinn der 'Nachfolge' und des Martyriums stärker heraus, wenn er καὶ τοῦ εὐαγγελίου (Mk 8,35) fortläßt (*Lk*, 544).

105. Cf. my *The Minor Agreements and Proto-Mark*, 83-87 (= 60-64), esp. 87 (= 64). See also 85 (= 63): "Luke avoids the term εὐαγγέλιον throughout his Gospel. His substitute in 18,29 [diff. Mk 10,29] can be seen in connection with the occurrences of ἡ βασιλεία τοῦ θεοῦ in the preceding sections (18,16.17.24.25)".

4. Luke 17,33: Text and Context

For Fleddermann, in his recent *Mark and Q*, Luke substituted the verb ζητέω with the infinitive for ὃς ἐὰν εὕρῃ in Q[106]. But, as indicated above in Part 1, ὃς ἐὰν ζητήσῃ τὴν ψυχὴν αὐτοῦ περιποιήσασθαι is much closer to Mk 8,35a (Lk 9,24a) than to Mt's ὁ εὑρών or Fleddermann's conjectural ὃς ἐὰν εὕρῃ. It was probably Luke's choice to use the verbs περιποιήσασθαι and ζωογονήσει as substitutes for σῶσαι and σώσει (and not, as assumed by Fleddermann, substitutes for εὕρῃ and εὑρήσει). The two verbs do not occur elsewhere in the Gospels and are commonly regarded as Lukan LXX language[107]. Περιποιέομαι occurs in Acts 20,28 in the sense 'acquire' said of the church that God had acquired (ἣν περιεποιήσατο – cf. Isa 43,21). The occurrence of ζωογονέω in Acts 7,19, summarizing and adapting the story of Ex 1,15-22, is more significant: "... forcing them to expose their infants εἰς τὸ μὴ ζωογονεῖσθαι". Compare the order of the king of Egypt to the midwives: Ex 1,16 ἐὰν μὲν ἄρσεν ᾖ", ἀποκτείνατε αὐτό, ἐὰν δὲ θῆλυ, περιποιεῖσθε αὐτό, and to the people: 1,22 πᾶν ἄρσεν ... εἰς τὸν ποταμὸν ῥίψατε· καὶ πᾶν θῆλυ, ζωογονεῖτε αὐτό (cf. 17 ἐζωογόνουν τὰ ἄρσενα, 18 ἐζωογονεῖτε τὰ ἄρσενα). The two verbs used here for the same Hebrew חָיָה, 'let live' ('leave alive') as opposed to 'kill', are used by Luke for Mk's σῴζω ('save') in contrast to ἀπόλλυμι[108]:

> Whoever seeks to *preserve* his life will lose it;
> but whoever loses (it) will *keep* it.

It is commonly held that the christological phrase ἕνεκεν ἐμοῦ is dropped by Luke because it would not suit the context of the eschatological discourse[109]. Although the question of the context of Lk 17,33 is sometimes treated rather lightly[110], it is not without consequence in a discussion of the origin of the saying (whether derived from Q or from Mk) and of the meaning it has for Luke.

---

106. *Mark and Q*, 142.

107. On Lukan redaction, see the commentaries on Lk (e.g., JEREMIAS, 269; W. WIEFEL, 312: "in jedem Fall").

108. On the influence of Ex 1 LXX, cf. SCHMID, *MtLk*, 278 n. 4; *Lk*, 277; SCHULZ, *Q*, 445 n. 306; FLEDDERMANN, *Mark and Q*, 142 n. 31; *et al*. On the translation of the verbs in Lk, see my *Note on Jn 12,25* (n. 38).

109. "Lukas wiederholt diesen Satz aus 9,24 (= Mk 8,35), wo er Aufforderung zur Martyriumsbereitschaft – die *hier* nicht paßt – ist. Lukas hat hier den Wortlaut dem neuen Zusammenhang angepaßt und deshalb auch das hier nicht passende 'um meinetwillen' weggelassen" (SCHMID, *Lk*, 277). This is true also if the saying derived from Q: cf. SCHULZ, *Q*, 445 ("aufgrund des neuen Kontextes").

110. FITZMYER, *Lk*, 1165: "It is only loosely joined here to the rest of the context"; DAUTZENBERG, *Sein Leben bewahren*, 63: "zusammenhanglos ... eingefügt".

Leaving aside Lk 17,28-29[111] there are two major interventions by Luke in Q 17,23-37:

Mt	24,26.27.28		37-39a.	39b			40-41
Q	17,23.24.37b		26-27.(28-29).30				34-35
Lk		25				31-33	37

1. In Q the saying comparing the Son of Man to the lightning (v. 24) was probably followed by the vultures saying (Mt 24,28) and Luke moved this saying to the end of the complex (v. 37). At its place in Q he inserted the passion saying (v. 25)[112], parenthetically attached to the lightning comparison (ὁ υἱὸς τοῦ ἀνθρώπου): πρῶτον δὲ <u>δεῖ</u> αὐτὸν <u>πολλὰ παθεῖν καὶ ἀποδοκιμασθῆναι ἀπὸ</u> τῆς γενεᾶς ταύτης (slightly adapted from Mk 8,31)[113].

2. Luke's second major intervention is the insertion of vv. 31-33, with the double admonition on the basis of Mk 13,15-16 in v. 31[114], the asyndetically added clause "remember Lot's wife" (v. 32) and the saying on saving and losing one's life (v. 33). The parallel to this life saying in Mk 8,35 belongs to the same Markan context as the passion prediction (Mk 8,31), and in Lk too | the interpolations in 17,25 (Son of Man) and 33 (disciples) are not unrelated[115].

Not a few commentators read the life saying in v. 33 in light of v. 31 understood as admonition against attachment to possessions. However, a different understanding has been suggested[116]:

111. For inclusion in Q (or Q[Lk]), see the listing of authors and their arguments in KLOPPENBORG, Q Parallels, 192, 194. See now also: CATCHPOLE, Quest, 248; TUCKETT, Q and the History, 159; M. MYLLYKOSKI, Social History, 187-188. — Not in Q: Hoffmann, Schulz, et al. Cf. Evangelica II, 416, 498. See now also the IQP text (JBL 111, 1992, 508).

112. It is less evident that its reference to the suffering Son of Man can be seen as "a 'reminiscence' of 17:37b and its reference to the 'corpse'" (KLOPPENBORG, Formation, 156; cf. MORGEN, Lc 17,20-37, 310 n. 12; and 316, on Lk 17:37: "une annonce de la passion, en lien avec le dit du verset 25").

113. Compare Lk 17,25 and Mk 8,31 / Lk 9,22: αὐτόν for τὸν υἱὸν τοῦ ἀνθρώπου and ἀπὸ τῆς γενεᾶς ταύτης for ἀπὸ (Mk ὑπὸ) τῶν πρεσβυτέρων καὶ ἀρχιερέων καὶ γραμματέων. — Cf. L. HARTMAN, Reading Luke 17,20-37, 1668, on Lk 17,25 and some people who held Messianic ideas "which did not include that the Messiah had to suffer 'before' 'entering His glory' (24,26)".

114. Cf. my The Minor Agreements and Q, 54-56 ("Luk 17:31").

115. LUZ, Mt II, 134: "Vermutlich hat Lk das Logion vom Preisgeben des Lebens in die eschatologische Rede 17,33 verschoben, um das dem Leiden des Menschensohns (17,25) entsprechende Leiden der Jünger zu betonen". See also GEIGER, Endzeitreden, 122; MORGEN, Lc 17,20-37, 316: "cette clé de lecture vaut pour le Fils de l'homme lui-même (Lc 17,25) comme pour le disciple (Lc 17,33)".

116. HARTMAN, Reading Luke 17,20-37, 1669; cf. 1670: "what is at stake [in the three admonitions] is an obedient, unhesitating resolution". See also MORGEN, Lc 17,20-37, 315-316. Both refer to GEIGER, Endzeitreden, 125-126: "Auf diesen V33 führt also der gesamte Einschub hin, er ist die eigentliche Verhaltensregel für den eschatologischen Tag. 'Zusammenhanglos' kann man das eigentlich nicht nennen".

... the reader who 'remembered' Lot's wife would not only recall her turn-ing εἰς τὰ ὀπίσω but also that in the story of Gen the angels told Lot: σῴζων σῷζε τὴν σεαυτοῦ ψυχήν· μὴ περιβλέψῃς εἰς τὰ ὀπίσω μηδὲ στῆς... [19,17]. That is, the reader would realize that she disobeyed the command to the family and was not saved. In other words, the Lot story focuses on the same motif as the third, general admonition, viz. on saving one's life.

Already in the comparisons with Noah's and Lot's days Luke's use of ἀπώλεσεν in vv. 27 (Mt ἦρεν)[117] and 29 anticipates the key word of the losing-one's-life saying in v. 33.

In sum, Lk 17,33 is not an isolated saying. It functions in the compo-sition of 17,23-37 in connection with other redactional material inserted by Luke in the Q discourse and, like 17,25 and 17,31, the life saying in 17,33 is the Lukan adaptation of the saying in Mark.

---

117. Q 17,27 ἦρεν: Harnack, Schulz, Schenk, Sato, Nolland, IQP, *et al.*

BIBLIOGRAPHY

W.A. BEARDSLEE, *Saving One's Life by Losing it*, in *JAAR* 47 (1979) 57-72.

M. BLACK, *An Aramaic Approach to the Gospels and Acts*, Oxford, [2]1954, [3]1967.

M.-É. BOISMARD, *Synopse II*, Paris, 1972.

C. BREYTENBACH, *Das Markusevangelium als traditionsgebundene Erzählung?*, in FOCANT (ed.), *The Synoptic Gospels*, 1993, 77-110.

R.E. BROWN, *The Gospel according to John*, vol. I (AB, 29), Garden City NY, 1966.

W. BUSSMANN, *Synoptische Studien*. II. *Zur Redequelle*, Halle, 1929.

D.R. CATCHPOLE, *The Quest for Q*, Edinburgh, 1993.

C. COLPE, art. ὁ υἱὸς τοῦ ἀνθρώπου, in *TWNT* 8 (1969) 403-481; = *TDNT* 8 (1972) 400-477.

C. COULOT, *"Si quelqu'un me sert, qu'il me suive!" (Jn 12,26a)*, in *RevSR* 69 (1995) 47-57.

J.M. CREED, *The Gospel according to St. Luke*, London, 1930.

J.D. CROSSAN, *In Fragments. The Aphorisms of Jesus*, San Francisco, CA, 1983.

G. DAUTZENBERG, *Sein Leben bewahren. Ψυχή in den Herrenworten der Evangelien* (SANT, 14), München, 1966.

J.J. DEGENHARDT, *Lukas Evangelist der Armen*, Stuttgart, 1965.

J. DELOBEL (ed.), *Logia. Les paroles de Jésus – The Sayings of Jesus* (BETL, 59), Leuven, 1982.

A. DENAUX, *Der Spruch von den zwei Wegen im Rahmen des Epilogs der Bergpredigt (Mt 7,13-14 par. Lk 13,23-24). Tradition und Redaktion*, in DELOBEL (ed.), *Logia*, 1982, 305-335.

C.H. DODD, *Some Johannine "Herrenworte" with Parallels in the Synoptic Gospels*, in *NTS* 2 (1955-56) 75-86. Cf. *Historical Tradition*, 335-349.

—, *Historical Tradition in the Fourth Gospel*, Cambridge, 1963. FT, Paris, 1987.

J. DUPONT, *Les Béatitudes*, vol. II, Paris, 1969; vol. III, 1973.

—, *Renoncer à tous ces biens (Lc 14,33)*, in *NRT* 93 (1971) 561-582; = *Études*, 1076-1097.

—, *Études sur les évangiles synoptiques* (BETL, 70), Leuven, 1985.

A. ENNULAT, *Die 'Minor Agreements'. Untersuchungen zu einer offenen Frage des synoptischen Problems* (WUNT, 2/62), Tübingen, 1994.

J. ERNST, *Das Evangelium nach Lukas* (RNT), Regensburg, [5]1977, [6]1983.

J.A. FITZMYER, *The Gospel according to Luke* (AB, 28-28A), Garden City, NY, 1981, 1985.

H.T. FLEDDERMANN, *The Cross and Discipleship in Q*, in *SBL 1988 Seminar Papers*, 472-482.

—, *Mark and Q. A Study of the Overlap Texts* (BETL, 122), Leuven, 1995.

C. FOCANT (ed.), *The Synoptic Gospels. Source Criticism and the New Literary Criticism* (BETL, 110), Leuven, 1993.

A. FRIDRICHSEN, *"Sich selbst verleugnen"*, in *Coniectanea Neotestamentica* 2 (1936) 1-8.

—, *Zu ΑΡΝΕΙΣΘΑΙ im N.T. insonderheit in den Pastoralbriefen*, in *Coniectanea Neotestamentica* 6 (1942) 94-96.

R. GEIGER, *Die lukanischen Endzeitreden: Studien zur Eschatologie des Lukas-Evangeliums* (EHS, 23/6), Bern-Frankfurt, 1976.

M.D. GOULDER, *Luke. A New Paradigm* (JSNT SS, 20), Sheffield, 1989.

W. GRUNDMANN, *Das Evangelium nach Lukas* (THNT, 3), Berlin, 1961.

R.H. GUNDRY, *Matthew: A Commentary on His Literary and Theological Art*, Grand Rapids, MI, 1982; *Matthew: A Commentary on His Handbook for a Mixed Church under Persecution*, [2]1994.

—, *Matthean Foreign Bodies in Agreements of Luke with Matthew against Mark: Evidence that Luke Used Matthew*, in *The Four Gospels 1992. FS F. Neirynck*, 1992, 1467-1495.

—, *Mark: A Commentary on His Apology for the Cross*, Grand Rapids, MI, 1993.

A. HARNACK, *Sprüche und Reden Jesu. Die zweite Quelle des Matthäus und Lukas*, Leipzig, 1907.

L. HARTMAN, *Reading Luke 17,20-37*, in *The Four Gospels 1992. FS F. Neirynck*, 1992, 1663-1675.

P. HOFFMANN, *Πάντες ἐργάται ἀδικίας. Redaktion und Tradition in Lk 13,22-30*, in *ZNW* 58 (1967) 188-214; = *Tradition und Situation*, 135-161.

—, *Studien zur Theologie der Logienquelle* (NTAbh, 8), Münster, 1972, [2]1975, [3]1982.

—, *Tradition und Situation. Studien zur Jesusüberlieferung in der Logienquelle und den synoptischen Evangelien* (NTAbh, NF 28), Münster, 1995.

H.J. HOLTZMANN, *Die Synoptiker* (Hand-Commentar NT, I/1), Freiburg, 1889, [2]1892; Tübingen-Leipzig, [3]1901.

A.D. JACOBSON, *The First Gospel. An Introduction to Q*, Sonoma, CA, 1992.

J. JEREMIAS, *Neutestamentliche Theologie I*, Gütersloh, 1971.

—, *Die Sprache des Lukasevangeliums. Redaktion und Tradition im Nicht-Markusstoff des dritten Evangeliums* (KEK), Göttingen, 1980.

G.D. KILPATRICK, *The Origins of the Gospel according to St. Matthew*, Oxford, 1946.

J.S. KLOPPENBORG, *The Formation of Q. Trajectories in Ancient Wisdom Collections*, Philadelphia, 1987.

—, *Q Parallels. Synopsis, Critical Notes & Concordance*, Sonoma, CA, 1988.

—, *The Sayings Gospel Q: Literary and Stratigraphic Problems*, in URO, *Symbols and Strata*, 1996, 1-66.

— (ed.), *Conflict and Invention. Literary, Rhetorical, and Social Studies on the Sayings Gospel Q*, Valley Forge, PA, 1995.

J. LAMBRECHT, *Q-Influence on Mark 8,34–9,1*, in DELOBEL (ed.), *Logia*, 1982, 277-304.

R. LAUFEN, *Die Doppelüberlieferungen der Logienquelle und des Markusevangeliums* (BBB, 54), Königstein/Ts.-Bonn, 1980.

X. LÉON-DUFOUR, *Luc 17,33*, in *RSR* 69 (1981) 101-112.

U. LUZ, *Das Evangelium nach Matthäus. 2. Teilband Mt 8–17* (EKK, I/2), Zürich – Neukirchen-Vluyn, 1990.

B.L. MACK, *The Lost Gospel. The Book of Q & Christian Origins*, San Francisco, 1993.

C.-P. MÄRZ, *Zur Q-Rezeption in Lk 12,35–13,55(14,1-24)*, in FOCANT (ed.), *The Synoptic Gospels*, 1993, 177-208.

T.W. MANSON, *The Sayings of Jesus*, London, 1937; repr. 1949.

I.H. MARSHALL, *The Gospel of Luke*, Exeter, 1978.

O. MICHEL, art. μισέω, in *TWNT* 4 (1942) 687-698; = *TDNT* 4 (1967) 683-694.

M. MORGEN, *"Perdre sa vie", Jn 12,25: un dit traditionnel?*, in *RevSR* 69 (1995) 29-46.

—, *Lc 17,20-37 et Lc 21,8-11.20-24: Arrière-fond scripturaire*, in TUCKETT (ed.), *The Scriptures in the Gospels*, 1997, 307-326.

R. MORGENTHALER, *Die lukanische Geschichtsschreibung als Zeugnis* (ATANT, 14-15), Zürich, 1949.

—, *Statistische Synopse*, Zürich–Stuttgart, 1971.

M. MYLLYKOSKI, *The Social History of Q and the Jewish War*, in URO, *Symbols and Strata*, 1996, 143-199.

F. NEIRYNCK, *Jean et les Synoptiques. Examen critique de l'exégèse de M.-É. Boismard* (BETL, 49), Leuven, 1979.

—, *Recent Developments in the Study of Q*, in DELOBEL (ed.), *Logia*, 1982, 29-75; = *Evangelica II*, 1991, 409-464.

—, *Q-Synopsis. The Double Tradition Passages in Greek* (SNTA, 13), Leuven, 1988, ²1995.

—, *Evangelica II. 1982-1991: Collected Essays* (BETL, 99), Leuven, 1991.

—, *The Minor Agreements and Proto-Mark*, in *Evangelica II*, 1991, 59-73.

—, *Assessment*, in FLEDDERMANN, *Mark and Q*, 1995, 261-307.

—, *The Minor Agreements and Q*, in PIPER (ed.), *Gospel*, 1995, 49-72.

—, *The Sayings Source Q and the Gospel of Mark*, in H. LICHTENBERGER (ed.), *Geschichte – Tradition – Reflexion. FS M. Hengel. III. Frühes Christentum*, Tübingen, 1996, 125-145.

The Four Gospels 1992. FS F. Neirynck, ed. F. VAN SEGBROECK - C.M. TUCKETT - G. VAN BELLE - J. VERHEYDEN (BETL, 100), Leuven, 1992.

J. NOLLAND, *Luke 9:21–18:34* (WBC, 35B), Dallas, TX 1993.

E. PERCY, *Die Botschaft Jesu. Eine traditionsgeschichtliche und exegetische Untersuchung* (Lunds Universitets Årsskrift, 49/5), Lund, 1953.

R.A. PIPER, *Wisdom in the Q-Tradition. The Aphoristic Teaching of Jesus* (SNTS MS, 61), Cambridge, 1989.

—, (ed.), *The Gospel Behind the Gospels. Current Studies on Q* (NTSup, 75), Leiden, 1995.

A. PLUMMER, *The Gospel according to S. Luke* (ICC), Edinburgh, 1896.

A. POLAG, *Fragmenta Q. Textheft zur Logienquelle*, Neukirchen, 1979, ²1982.

W. REBELL, *'Sein Leben verlieren' (Mark 8.35 parr.) als Strukturmoment vor- und nachösterlichen Glaubens*, in *NTS* 35 (1989) 202-218.

K.-G. REPLOH, *Markus – Lehrer der Gemeinde*, Stuttgart, 1969.

B. RIGAUX, *La petite apocalypse de Luc (xvii,22-37)*, in *Ecclesia a Spiritu Sancto edocta. FS G. Philips* (BETL, 27), Gembloux, 1970, 407-438.

J.M. ROBINSON, *The Sayings Gospel Q*, in *The Four Gospels 1992. FS F. Neirynck*, 1992, 361-388.

M. SATO, *Q und Prophetie. Studien zur Gattungs- und Traditionsgeschichte der Quelle Q* (WUNT, II/29), Tübingen, 1988.

W. SCHENK, *Synopse zur Redenquelle der Evangelien. Q-Synopse und Rekonstruktion in deutscher Übersetzung mit kurzen Erläuterungen*, Düsseldorf, 1981.

—, *Die Sprache des Matthäus. Die Text-Konstituenten in ihren makro- und mikrostrukturellen Relationen*, Göttingen, 1987.

A. SCHLATTER, *Das Evangelium nach Lukas aus seinen Quellen erklärt*, Stuttgart, 1931, ³1975.

J. SCHMID, *Matthäus und Lukas. Eine Untersuchung des Verhältnisses ihrer Evangelien* (BS, 23/2-4), Freiburg, 1930.

J. SCHMID, *Das Evangelium nach Lukas*, Regensburg, [4]1960.

R. SCHNACKENBURG, *Der eschatologische Abschnitt Lk 17,20-37*, in A.L. DESCAMPS – A. DE HALLEUX (eds.), *Mélanges bibliques. FS B. Rigaux*, Gembloux, 1970, 213-234; = ID., *Schriften zum Neuen Testament*, München, 1971, 220-243.

H. SCHÜRMANN, *Die Dubletten im Lukasevangelium* (1953). *Traditionsgeschichtliche Untersuchungen zu den synoptischen Evangelien*, Düsseldorf, 1968, 272-278.

—, *Das Lukasevangelium.* I: *Kommentar zu Kap. 1,1–9,50* (HTKNT, 3/1), Freiburg, 1969.

—, II/1: *Kommentar zu Kapitel 9,51–11,54* (HTKNT, 3/2,1), 1994.

A. SCHULZ, *Nachfolgen und Nachahmen. Studien über das Verhältnis der neutestamentlichen Jüngerschaft zur urchristlichen Vorbildethik* (SANT, 6), München, 1962.

S. SCHULZ, *Q. Die Spruchquelle der Evangelisten*, Zürich, 1972.

E. SCHWEIZER, *Erniedrigung und Erhöhung bei Jesus und seinen Nachfolgern* (ATANT, 28), Zürich, 1955, [2]1962.

R. STEIN, *Luke 14:26 and the Question of Authenticity*, in *Forum* 5.2 (1989) 187-192.

C.M. TUCKETT, *The Existence of Q*, in PIPER (ed.), *Gospel*, 1995, 19-47.

—, *Q and the History of Early Christianity. Studies on Q*, Edinburgh, 1996.

— (ed.), *The Scriptures in the Gospels* (BETL, 131), Leuven, 1997.

R. URO (ed.), *Symbols and Strata. Essays on the Sayings Gospel Q* (Publications of the Finnish Exegetical Society, 65), Helsinki–Göttingen, 1996.

J. WANKE, *"Bezugs- und Kommentarworte" in den synoptischen Evangelien* (ETS, 44), Leipzig, 1981.

W. WEIFEL, *Das Evangelium nach Lukas* (THNT, 3), Berlin, 1988.

B. WEISS, *Das Marcusevangelium und seine synoptischen Parallelen*, Berlin, 1872.

—, *Das Matthäusevangelium und seine Lucas-Parallelen*, Halle, 1876.

—, *Die Evangelien des Markus und Lukas* (KEK, I/2), Göttingen, [6]1878, [9]1901.

—, *Die Quellen der synoptischen Überlieferung* (TU, 32/3), Berlin, 1908.

P. WERNLE, *Die synoptische Frage*, Freiburg, 1899.

D. ZELLER, *Eine weistheitliche Grundschrift in der Logienquelle?*, in *The Four Gospels 1992. FS F. Neirynck*, 1992, 389-401.

J. ZMIJEWSKI, *Die Eschatologiereden des Lukas-Evangeliums. Eine traditions- und redaktionsgeschichtliche Untersuchung zu Lk 21,5-36 und Lk 17,20-37* (BBB, 40), Bonn, 1972.

BETL 122 (1995) 263-303

24

MARK AND Q: ASSESSMENT

A few days after I recommended Harry Fleddermann's work for publication in BETL and promised to write a critical Assessment, I came across the following statement on the Mark-and-Q issue:[1]

> ... the case against the literary dependence of Mark on Q, or vice versa, would now seem to be closed. The following arguments are, in various places, advanced by Schüling: (1) the fact that Mark has relatively little material in common with Q and the resultant difficulty of explaining why this would be so if there was a literary relationship; (2) the fact that sometimes Mark, sometimes Q preserves the older version of sayings they have in common; (3) the absence of redactional elements from Q in Mark, or vice versa (pp. 182-83; an argument introduced by F. Neirynck in "Recent Developments in the Study of Q" [1982], 41-53, esp. p. 45); (4) the fact that forms common to Q are largely absent from Mark, and vice versa (pp. 185-186; an argument made by A. D. Jacobson in "The Literary Unity of Q," *JBL* 101 [1982] 365-89); and (5) the fact that some sayings which Mark and Q have in common were already attached to other sayings prior to their inclusion in Mark (Schüling mentions the sayings in Q 10:4, 5-7a, 10-11 par [pp. 49-50], Mark 3:23b, 27, 28-29 [p. 130], and Mark 8:34-38 [p. 138; cf. pp. 148-150]). A sixth argument, though contrary to Schüling's view, would be that the sayings Mark and Q have in common do not share a common sequence. One would therefore now seem justified in assuming that the literary independence of Mark and Q has been demonstrated.

In his book on Q, published in 1992, A. D. Jacobson assumes "literary independence of Mark and Q, as well as their use of some shared traditions." He notes that "there has been a good deal of recent research on the problem of the relation between Mark and Q."[2] He studies traditions shared by Mark and Q because "by comparing them, we can often sense more clearly what is distinctive of Q."[3] He made his point quite clear when treating W. Schmithals's proposal.[4]

---

1. A. D. JACOBSON, Review: "J. Schüling, Studien zum Verhältnis von Logienquelle und Markusevangelium, 1991," in *JBL* 113 (1994) 724-726, esp. p. 726.

Full references will be given only for works not cited previously by H. Fleddermann. His *Mark and Q* is here referred to as HF, followed by page number.

2. *The First Gospel: An Introduction to Q*, 1992, p. 62 n. 2 (= *JBL* 101, 1982, 373 n. 30). He mentions Laufen, Luz, Devisch, Schenk, Vassiliadis, and Lührmann. Fleddermann is not mentioned.

3. Mark 1,1-8; 3,20-27; 4,30-32; 6,6b-13; 8,12b: cf. *First Gospel*, pp. 67-71 (= 379-384).

4. "The doublets do not provide the weighty evidence Schmithals assumes; he has not noticed the fundamental differences between the uses made of this material by Mark and

In 1992, far from closing the debate, at least four noticeable articles in defense of Mark's use of Q were published, in vol. 55 of *Semeia* (Catchpole, Mack) and in vol. 38 of *NTS* (Catchpole, Lambrecht). In *The Four Gospels 1992* two essays on significant overlap texts argued for independence, in Mark 3,22-26 (Boring) and 4,30-32 (Friedrichsen),[5] and at the Colloquium Biblicum Lovaniense (1992) C. M. Tuckett delivered a paper on "Mark and Q." He studied Mark 1,2; 1,7-8; 4,30-32; 8,11-12, and concluded that in these passages "the view that Mark and Q represent independent versions of common traditions remains the most convincing."[6]

One of the participants at the Colloquium who expressed reservations was H. Fleddermann. Already in 1981, considering the Q parallels to Mark 9,37.40.42.50a, he had made the observation: "It is becoming increasingly difficult to deny that Mark knew and used Q."[7] Starting with the sayings in Mark 9,33-50, he subsequently examined Mark 12,38-39 (1982); 1,7-8 (1984); 13,35 (1986); 8,38 (1987); 8,35 (1988); and 4,30-32 (1989), and gradually developed his three-step procedure: (1) the reconstruction of Q; (2) Mark is secondary to Q; (3) Mark is redacting the Q text. In 1982 he noted quite modestly: "This one text cannot prove that Mark knew a document Q. All that has been proved is that in this instance Mark knew and used a Q saying."[8] Now he decided: "In this book I will study all of the overlap texts." The project is now more ambitious, but the basic intention remains the same: "Instead of general arguments progress comes from analyzing the texts."[9] And his analysis leads to three firm conclusions on the overlap texts: "(1) Everywhere ... Mark is secondary to Q. (2) Mark reflects the redactional text of Q. (3) The differences between Mark and Q ... stem from Marcan redaction. Everywhere ... starting from the Q text we can explain the Marcan text using the redactional techniques of Mark."[10]

---

by Q. Likewise, the judgment that Mark used Q is at best debatable" (*First Gospel*, pp. 52-53; with reference to W. SCHMITHALS, *Einleitung in die drei ersten Evangelien*, Berlin, 1985, pp. 384-404). Compare HF, 12 n. 42 (Schmithals's 1979 essay). See also his commentaries on Mark (1979) and Luke (1980); cf. *Evangelica I*, pp. 613-617; *Evangelica II*, pp. 422-423 (and 459, 462, 464).

5. Cf. HF, 17 n. 65; 91 n. 82. See also T. A. FRIEDRICHSEN, "Alternative Synoptic Theories on Mk 4,30-32," in C. FOCANT (ed.), *The Synoptic Gospels*, pp. 427-450.

6. "Mark and Q" (1993), p. 175.

7. "The Discipleship Discourse," p. 74. Cf. *Evangelica I*, p. 820; *Evangelica II*, pp. 425-426 (1982, pp. 45-46), p. 531 (1986, p. 285).

8. "A Warning about Scribes," p. 60 n. 37.

9. HF, 16.

10. HF, 209-214 ("Results of the Study"). Note that Fleddermann started his exegetical career with the study of Marcan redaction: *The Central Question of Mark's Gospel: A Study of Mark 8:29*, Diss. Graduate Theological Union, Berkeley, 1978; "The Flight of

This triple result needs further examination. Although Streeter was not the only one to alter his position, I am not inclined to think that Fleddermann's "everywhere..." will make people change their minds. But also for those who remain unconvinced by Fleddermann's book, reading and studying it can be beneficial.

To begin with, one can appreciate his position in the question of the extent of Q. With one possible exception in Q 17,26-30 (including vv. 28-29?) no Lucan or Matthean Sondergut texts are included in the reconstruction of Q.[11] The redaction of Q in Matthew and Luke is treated in reference to final Q without Q^{Mt} or Q^{Lk} intermediaries.[12] Minor agreements are expressly excluded. This is an important decision in studying Mark and Q. The influence of J. Lambrecht's approach, openly acknowledged elsewhere, has here some obvious limitations. Luke 10,25-28 is not part of Q,[13] and it is even more significant that he did not accept the proposal of a beginning of Q reconstructed on the basis of the minor agreements of Matthew and Luke against Mark 1,2-6 and 1,9-11.[14]

Second, Fleddermann makes a serious attempt at reconstruction of the Q text in Q 3,16-17; 6,38c; 7,27; 10,2-16; 11,10.14-15.16.17-26.29-32.33.43; 12,2.8-9.10.11-12.31b.40.51-53; 13,18-19.30; 14,26-27.34-35a; 16,17.18; 17,1b-2.6.23.33; 19,26. To these sixty-five verses involved in

a Naked Young Man (Mark 14:51-52)," in *CBQ* 41 (1979) 412-418. Compare *ETL* 55 (1979) 43-66 (cf. *Evangelica I*, p. 239 n. 301).

11. HF, 18 n. 68, 239-240 (Index: Q). See, for instance, Fleddermann's discussion of Luke 9,61-62 in "The Demands of Discipleship," 1992, pp. 548-552: "Both the theme and the vocabulary ... point to Lukan redaction" (p. 552).

12. On their introduction in some recent studies, see my "Q^{Mt} and Q^{Lk} and the Reconstruction of Q" (1990), in *Evangelica II*, pp. 475-480.

13. For recent discussion, see my "The Minor Agreements and Q," in R. A. PIPER (ed.), *The Gospel Behind the Gospels: Current Studies on Q* (NTSup, 75), Leiden, 1995, pp. 49-72, esp. 61-64; "Luke 10:25-28: A Foreign Body in Luke?" in S. E. PORTER – P. JOYCE – D. E. ORTON (eds.), *Crossing the Boundaries*. FS M. D. Goulder (Biblical Interpretation Series, 8), Leiden, 1994, pp. 149-165; "The Minor Agreements and Lk 10,25-28," in *ETL* 71 (1995) 151-160, esp. nn. 8, 44, 63. *Pace* J. LAMBRECHT, "The Great Commandment Pericope and Q," in *The Gospel Behind the Gospels* (above), pp. 73-96. K. Kertelge (cf. n. 8: 1985, 1994) is now inclined to accept the redactional interpretation of the agreements in Luke 10,25-28 (SNTS Seminar, 1995).

14. See my "The Minor Agreements and Q" (n. 13), pp. 65-72 ("The Beginning of Q"), with reference to Fleddermann's "The Beginning of Q" (p. 68 n. 104); cf. HF, 31. For the argument of the minor agreements (CATCHPOLE, "The Beginning of Q," pp. 217, 218 n. 49; LAMBRECHT, "John the Baptist and Jesus," pp. 363, 366-367), see the reply by J. M. ROBINSON, "The *Incipit* of the Sayings Gospel Q," in *RHPR* 75 (1995) 9-33, esp. pp. 14-19. But see ID., "The Sayings Gospel Q," in *The Four Gospels 1992*, pp. 361-388: although the minor agreements in the Baptism of Jesus are "notoriously inconclusive" he discusses other "more compelling" arguments for inclusion in Q (pp. 382-387). For a response, cf. R. URO, "John the Baptist and the Jesus Movement: What Does Q Tell Us?" in R. A. PIPER (ed.), *The Gospel Behind the Gospels*, pp. 231-255, esp. 237-239.

the comparison with Mark, we can add the reconstructions of Q in his earlier studies on Q 3,7-9; 9,57-60; 12,39-40.42b-46; and 22,28-30.[15] For almost all these passages we now have at our disposal the critical Q text prepared by the International Q Project,[16] and a confrontation may be instructive. I note here that, unlike the IQP texts, Fleddermann's reconstructions neither have the brackets used for less probable Q readings nor the siglum . . . used for undecided cases. Compare: Q 10,3 ὑπάγετε (IQP: ⟦ὑπάγετε⟧), ἄρνας (IQP: . . .); 16,17 πεσεῖν (IQP: π . . .); 16,18a καὶ γαμῶν ἑτέραν μοιχεύει (IQP: ⟦⟧ μοιχευ⟦ει⟧), 18b μοιχεύει (IQP: μοιχ . . .). Greater readability is an undeniable advantage of Fleddermann's Q text. Unfortunately, his printed text shows no distinction at all between words that are common to Matthew and Luke, words and forms found only in Matthew or in Luke, and conjectural Q words. Where the reconstructed texts are printed in parallel to Mark, the critical reader looks for such distinctions. Once more, when studying Fleddermann's "Mark and Q," my little *Q-Synopsis*, with its more sophisticated printing, proved to be an indispensable tool.[17]

Third, it is one of the merits of Fleddermann's work that all overlap texts are included.[18] The fact that in every instance the texts of Mark and Q are printed in juxtaposition is an improvement of the somewhat confusing presentation in J. S. Kloppenborg's *Q Parallels*. Four items are absent in Kloppenborg's collection of parallels: Mark 11,24 (§ 22); 13,12 (§ 25); 13,31 (§ 27); 14,21 (§ 17a).[19]

---

15. Q 3,7-9 ("The Beginning of Q," 1985); 9,57-60 ("The Demands of Discipleship," 1992); 12,39-40.42b-46 ("The Householder," 1986); 22,28-30 ("The End of Q," in *SBL 1990 Seminar Papers*, 1-10).

16. Cf. "The International Q Project," in *ETL* 69 (1993) 221-225; now reprinted in *Q-Synopsis*, ²1995, pp. 75-79 (with reference to *JBL*, 1990-1994). Only for Q 7,27; 10,7-16; 17,23.33 (and 22,28.30) the IQP text is not yet published (announced for *JBL* 114/3, 1995).

17. Cf. *Q-Synopsis. The Double Tradition Passages in Greek*. Revised Edition with Appendix (SNTA, 13), Leuven, 1995.

18. Cf. C. BREYTENBACH, "Vormarkinische Logientradition. Parallelen in der urchristlichen Briefliteratur," in *The Four Gospels 1992*, pp. 725-749. His survey includes Mark 4,24c; 9,42; 10,11-12 (with Q parallel). Cf. p. 748: "Um ein besseres Bild zu bekommen, wäre es nützlich, die Mk/Q-Parallelen systematisch zu vergleichen." See also ID., "Das Markusevangelium als traditionsgebundene Erzählung? Anfragen an die Markusforschung der achtziger Jahre," in C. FOCANT (ed.), *The Synoptic Gospels*, 1993, pp. 77-110, esp. 110: "*Eine systematische Auswertung der Beziehungen zwischen Q und Markus* sowie Thomas und Markus kann uns helfen, Umrisse und Motive von Teilen der von Markus literarisierten Überlieferung zu rekonstruieren und das Geflecht der vorsynoptischen Überlieferung ein wenig zu entzerren" (emphasis mine).

19. The text of Mark 4,24 (§ 7) is cited in S10 (Q 6,38c), but there is no mention of καὶ προστεθήσεται ὑμῖν (v. 24d) in S41 (Q 12,31b). Cf. "A Synopsis of Q" (1988), now reprinted in *Q-Synopsis*, ²1995, pp. 65-73, esp. 70-71 (= 446-447): "The Parallels in Mark" (with some corrections). On p. 70, Mark 9,40 should be inserted in the list of

Fourth, in "Recent Developments in the Study of Q" (1982) I mentioned Fleddermann's first contribution on Mark and Q in a concluding
paragraph:[20]

> Mark's dependence on Q may be an attractive thesis especially for those
> who study the Markan redaction. On the level of the individual saying it is
> common practice to give a tentative description of Mark's redactional activ-
> ity by comparing the saying in Mark with the Q version, but how do we
> prove Mark's dependence on Q, and not on a traditional saying or on some
> pre-Q collection of sayings? This can only be done by showing a specific
> dependence on the redaction of Q, dependence on sayings of which the cre-
> ation or at least the formulation can be attributed to the Q redactor (cf.
> Schenk), or dependence on the order of the sayings as found in a redactional
> Q arrangement (cf. Lambrecht 1966). It is not enough to observe, as several
> recent authors are doing, that Mark's version of the saying is secondary. To
> mention one example, H. Fleddermann in his article on Mk 9,33-50 (1981)
> noted that Mark made in this section an extensive use of Q material:
> 9,37.40.42.50a, and: "In each case the differences between the reconstructed
> Q saying and the Marcan saying can be accounted for by Marcan redaction."
> (74) ... No distinction is made between Q material and Q redaction.

The question whether Mark reflects the redactional text of Q is now a
central issue of Fleddermann's study:[21]

> In several places in the overlap texts Mark knows the Q redaction. We found
> two kinds of evidence. On the one hand, individual Marcan sayings reflect
> redactional features of Q. On the other hand, although the overlap texts
> appear throughout Mark, we found most of them concentrated in clusters.
> Some of these clusters consist entirely of Q texts assembled into new units.
> ... Two of the clusters show clearly that Mark had the entire Q document in
> front of him as he wrote.

Fleddermann's conclusion is unambiguous: Mark knows redactional Q;
and "since Mark knows the redactional text of Q, Mark depends on Q."
In order to verify this conclusion we will have to check its premise.

My observations, in the order of Fleddermann's paragraphs, will concentrate on some problems of his reconstruction of the Q text and on his
quest for Q redactional (QR) at the basis of Mark.

---

parallels (*Q Parallels*, p. 91: add reference to Q 11,23). — Compare R. Laufen's list:
§ § 16, 17, 17a, 20, 27 are not included (HF, 18; cf. "Recent Developments," p. 53 =
433).
    20. "Recent Developments," p. 45 (= 425). Cf. below, n. 188.
    21. HF, 211, 212.

§ 1. The Messenger

The first overlap text in the Marcan order is Mark 1,2 and Q 7,27, Fleddermann's first example of redactional Q. He describes Q 7,27 as a combination and adaptation of Exod 23,20 and Mal 3,1 and then asks the question: Who combined these two texts? "The double quotation in Q 7,27 both secures John's greatness and subordinates him to Jesus by assigning him a precise role – as Elijah he prepares the way for Jesus. The Q redactor combined the two texts to draw the two views on John together."[22] As it appears from the references to Q 7,24-26.28a for John's greatness and Q 7,28b for John's subordination, neither the entire v. 28 nor v. 28b is supposed to be redactional. It is rather strange that no mention is made of these possibilities, not even of D. Catchpole's recent defense of vv. 27 + 28b as editorial additions to an earlier tradition in 7,24-26.28a[23]. C. Tuckett's reply, though not unknown to Fleddermann, is not mentioned either:[24]

> But v. 27 scarcely gives any indication of John's *inferiority*. This is clearer in v. 28b and so it is not quite so easy to see v. 28b as coming from the same stratum as v. 27. I argued above[25] that v. 27 is unlikely to be a later modification of v. 28, if only because it comes first, and a secondary comment is more likely to follow the tradition it is seeking to modify and comment on. This makes it most likely that v. 27 is the earlier comment on vv. 24-26, to which v. 28 is added as a later addition. In fact a strong case could be made out for v. 27 being the original conclusion to vv. 24-26. Vv. 24-26 alone seem to be almost a torso and to cry out for some clarification and conclusion. V. 26 ends with the double claim that it is indeed appropriate to think of John as a prophet, but that John is also more than a prophet. To the

22. HF, 28.

23. "The Beginning of Q" (1992), pp. 207-213; = *The Quest for Q*, pp. 63-70: "Jesus' Testimony to John. Q 7:24-28."

24. "Mark and Q," pp. 165-166. See also his "The Temptation Narrative in Q," in *The Four Gospels 1992*, pp. 479-507, esp. 485 n. 29. For a slightly revised version of the passage quoted above, see his *Studies on Q*, Edinburgh, 1995, pp. 132-134.

25. See his critical remarks on J. S. Kloppenborg's theory (p. 164). For the view that Q 7,27 was inserted after v. 28 had already been conjoined to 7,24-26, see now also L. E. Vaage, *Galilean Upstarts. Jesus' First Followers According to Q*, Valley Forge, 1994, p. 184 n. 76 (Lit.). The reference to D. Zeller should be canceled; see "Redaktionsprozesse und wechselnder 'Sitz im Leben' beim Q-Material," in *Logia*, 1982, pp. 395-409, esp. 403; ET: "Redactional Processes and Changing Settings in the Q-Material," in J. S. Kloppenborg (ed.), *The Shape of Q*, Minneapolis, 1994, pp. 116-130, esp. 124: "Verse 28 as a whole may be a commentary saying on v. 27.... In view of the repeated λέγω ὑμῖν, it is scarcely likely that it was originally attached to v. 26." Cf. Tuckett, p. 166 n. 59 (see also p. 167 n. 64: "a very similar view about the tradition-history of the whole passage"). For both Tuckett and Zeller vv. 27 and 28 are "probably *pre*-redactional in Q" (Tuckett), "not inserted here by the redaction responsible for the assembling of the whole Baptist complex" (Zeller).

26. HF, 27; list of the quotations in n. 10.

question, "Is John a prophet?", the answer seems to be yes and no: he is a prophet, but he is also more. At the very least, one could say that such a claim is enigmatic! What does it mean to say that John is both a prophet and more? At one level Q 7,27 provides a perfect answer. John is described as an Elijah redivivus figure. He is then a prophetic figure in that he is an Elijah-figure, but he is also more than just any prophet: for he is the inaugurator of the new age forecast by Malachi. Thus v. 27 provides a very good conclusion to vv. 24-26 and there is no need to drive too much of a wedge between the two. There does however seem to be a seam between v. 27 and v. 28. The repeated λέγω ὑμῖν of Q 7,28 (cf. v. 26) makes it unlikely that v. 28 belongs with vv. 24-27 originally. It would appear to be a secondary comment.

Fleddermann argues that, like all the other quotations in Q, Q 7,27 depends on the Greek OT.[26] His list of quotations includes Q 4,4.8.10-11.12; 7,22; 10,15; 12,52-53; 13,19.27.29.35; 17,37; he attributes none of them to QR.[27] In two quotations, which he studied as overlap texts, Fleddermann locates the influence of the Greek OT at an earlier stage. In Q 12,53 (cf. Matt 10,35-36) the Q text "is not that close to the Sep-tuagint."[28] His comment is quite clear with regard to Q 13,19 (Dan 4,21 Theodotion): "the end of the parable quotes from the Greek OT, so the parable had already undergone Hellenistic influence before it reached Q."[29] Likewise the LXX-wording in Q 7,27 can be pre-redactional. Moreover, the influence of the Hebrew text of Mal 3,1 remains the most likely explanation of the verb κατασκευάσει (פנה piel).[30] If, as suggested by Fleddermann, the use of the quotation in Mark 1,2 shows that Mark knew the text of Q 7,27, it does not prove that Mark knew QR.

27. The analogy between Q 4,4.8.10-11.12 and 7,27 (γέγραπται, LXX) is not dis-cussed by Fleddermann. On this problem, see TUCKETT, "Mark and Q," p. 167; and "The Temptation Narrative in Q" (n. 24), pp. 480-481, 483-485 (p. 484: "In fact the evidence for the use of a Septuagintal version here is extremely thin"). — A. W. Argyle's short studies (1953, 1954) can scarcely be cited by Fleddermann (n. 10) in support of his own position. For Argyle it appears to be a feature of the OT quotations in Q that "they are *not* in the wording of the LXX:" cf. Q 10,15; 12,53; 13,27 (contrast Q 13,35; 17,27: "But in these instances the Hebrew could hardly be rendered into Greek in any other way;" 1953, p. 382). Q 7,27 is not mentioned by Argyle. Cf. below, n. 30.

28. HF, 196. Cf. 199: the influence of Micah 7,6 LXX in Mark 13,12 (ἐπαναστή-σονται). See below, p. 294.

29. HF, 94. Cf. 97 (and 95): Ezek 17,23 LXX in Mark 4,32 (ὑπὸ τὴν σκιὰν αὐτοῦ).

30. Mal 3,1 LXX ἐπιβλέψεται (פנה in *qal*): contrast Aquila: σχολάσει; Symmachus: ἀποσκευάσει; Theodotion: ἑτοιμάσει. Compare, e.g., the recent commentaries on Matt 11,10 by Gundry (1982, p. 208), Gnilka (1986, p. 415 n. 14), Luz (1990, p. 175 n. 23), Davies-Allison (1991, p. 249). With the exception of P. Wernle (but see p. 116: "mit einer Ausnahme [!] nach LXX"), the authors cited by Fleddermann (n. 10) support this view: Stendahl (p. 51), Johnson (p. 144), Schulz (p. 232). See also D. S. NEW, *Old Testament Quo-tations*, pp. 62-64. Cf. E. P. MEADORS, *Jesus the Messianic Herald of Salvation* (WUNT, 2/72), Tübingen, 1995, pp. 165, 168 ("Semitic text-form"). On Mark and Q: "the predomi-nant opinion at present favors literary independence" (p. 2; n. 8: M. Devisch, *et al.*).

In the context of Q 7,27 the pronoun σοῦ naturally refers to Jesus and for Fleddermann Mark's awkward use of this pronoun in 1,2 "certainly shows knowledge of redactional Q:"[31]

> Mark does not introduce a speaker at the beginning of the gospel, and the natural way to read v. 2 is to understand that the narrator is addressing the reader. However, this reading does not make sense...[32]

Yet, enough has been written on the function of the scripture quotation in Mark 1,2-3. I quote here M. E. Boring's comment:[33]

> [It] allows Jesus ... to be addressed "offstage" by the transcendent voice of God before the plotted narrative begins. The result is that when John appears in 1:4 his identity and significance are *already* determined by his relation to Jesus, and not vice versa. This is precisely the effect Mark intended... It is often noticed that Mark has changed the pronoun of Mal 3:1 from "my," referring to God, to "thy" (= "your") referring to the one addressed in this transcendent off-stage scene. ... by this narrative technique the reader gets to overhear the voice of God addressing *Jesus*, the one whose way is to be prepared...

It can be added that the use of the pronoun σοῦ in 1,2 prepares for God's addressing Jesus in Mark 1,11.[34]

§ 2. John and the Coming One

In this text the evidence for Mark's use of QR is "not as clear as in the first saying." Fleddermann assumes that the reference to the Holy Spirit is an addition to the original saying, ἐν (πνεύματι ἁγίῳ καὶ) πυρί, and that the Q redactor could be responsible for this interpolation. His argument: "Q presents a coherent picture of the Spirit."[35] But there are only two other references to the Spirit in Q (11,20; 12,10), or possibly

---

31. HF, 39. Cf. pp. 30, 72, 211.

32. HF, 29.

33. M. E. Boring, "Mark 1:1-15 and the Beginning of the Gospel," in *Semeia* 52 (1991) 43-82, p. 60. Cf. R. M. Fowler, *Let the Reader Understand. Reader-Response Criticism and the Gospel of Mark*, Minneapolis, MN, 1991, p. 111: "It is a hermeneutical guide to reading at the level of discourse" (see also pp. 87-89).

34. Cf. R. H. Gundry, *Mark*, Grand Rapids, MI, 1993, p. 35. See also J. Gnilka, *Markus*, p. 41 (on the "Gottessprüche"); cf. p. 44, on the quotation: "Es gibt ihm die Möglichkeit, den eben genannten Gottessohn von Gott angeredet sein zu lassen." — On υἱοῦ θεοῦ in Mark 1,1, see now A. Y. Collins, "Establishing the Text: Mark 1:1," in T. Fornberg – D. Hellholm (eds.), *Texts and Contexts*. FS L. Hartman, Oslo, 1995, pp. 111-127: "The addition probably occurred sometime in the second century" (concluding sentence). Unfortunately, the section on internal evidence mentions Mark's theme of "Jesus' sonship with God" (p. 121) without considering υἱοῦ θεοῦ in relation to "its context" (Mark 1,2 and 11).

35. HF, 37; see also 35, 39, and 69-70 (Q 12,10).

only one because the reference in Q 11,20 / Matt 12,28 is doubtful: ἐν (πνεύματι) θεοῦ (cf. § 3). Q 12,10 is supposed to have come to Mark as part of the section Q 12,2-12, in which 12,8-9 probably stems from the Q redactor. If 12,8-9 comes from the Q redactor, the commenting saying in 12,10 "does also." Thus the phrase in 3,16 and the saying in 12,10 are later additions and confirm each other: "both probably come from the same pen." But the possibility that Q 12,10 was known by Mark as an independent saying deserves more serious consideration. In the case of Q 3,16 Fleddermann's alternative could have been that the words were added in the pre-Q tradition. But there is also the alternative solution that καὶ πυρί was added to the saying (Laufen, Schüling, *et al.*).

§ 3. THE BEELZEBUL CONTROVERSY

Q 11,14-26 is one of the longest overlap texts. Luke 11,16, placed here by Luke, is rightly treated in § 11. Q 11,23 has its place here in Q but because of the parallel in Mark 9,40 it is treated in the Marcan order in § 16. This Q saying (11,23) and Q 11,19-20.24-26 are without parallel in Mark 3,22-27. It is of great importance for Fleddermann's theory that he can state that in Mark 3,22-27 "everything comes from Q."[36] But can we really say that Mark 3,27 comes from Q?

1. The main argument for the inclusion of this saying in Q is the placement of Matt 12,29 / Luke 11,21-22 between Matt 12,27-28 / Luke 11,19-20 and Matt 12,30 / Luke 11,23: this position "indicates that the parable also stood in Q at this point."[37] The problem is that Matthew adopted the wording of Mark 3,27, and those who propose a reconstruction of the Q text are to rely on the quite different version in Luke.[38] Fleddermann now recognizes Lucan composition in Luke 11,21-22.[39] In his view, however, Luke's text is not an elaboration of Mark 3,27 but derived from the Q text preserved unchanged in Matt 12,29.[40] Yet, the texts of Matthew and Mark are so similar to one another that the "solid points of contact" he notes between Luke and Matthew are in fact contacts with Mark. If, for example, Luke draws the entering motif from Q (Matt εἰσελθεῖν) and "reduces it to participle (ἐπελθών)," one should

36. HF, 213.
37. KLOPPENBORG, *Q Parallels*, p. 92. More recent commentaries can be added, on Matthew: LUZ, 1990 (II, p. 255); DAVIES-ALLISON, 1991 (II, p. 342); on Luke: NOLLAND, 1993 (II, p. 635); SCHÜRMANN, 1994 (II, p. 245).
38. POLAG, *Fragmenta Q*. Cf. LAMBRECHT, *Marcus Interpretator*, p. 43; LAUFEN, p. 131: "in einer wohl Lukas näherstehenden Fassung."
39. With reference to S. Légasse.
40. HF, 52-55.

observe that the parallel in Mark reads εἰσελθών. Fleddermann tries to explain the minor differences between Matthew and Mark as "Q flavor" on the one hand and Marcan changes of Q on the other.[41] But are they not more naturally explainable as Matthean editorial changes of Mark? The opening in Mark 3,27 ἀλλ' οὐ δύναται οὐδείς is replaced by Matthew with ἢ πῶς δύναταί τις. If the ἢ πῶς "picks up" the πῶς in v. 26, is it still relevant to look for Q flavor in Matt 7,4 (ἢ πῶς ἐρεῖς, par. Luke 6,42 πῶς δύνασαι λέγειν)? A correction of Mark's double negative is far from unique in Matthew.[42]

Fleddermann reformulates the argument based on the position of the saying into a consideration of the wording of Matt 12,29: in the Beelzebul Controversy Matthew conflates Mark and Q in 12,25-26 and 12,31-32 and between these two passages he follows his source Q word for word (vv. 27-28.29.30).[43] But the fact that in other passages such as Q 3,7-9[44] Matthew copies Q without change is scarcely a convincing argument in the case of Matt 12,29, and with regard to the preceding v. 28 it is less certain than Fleddermann suggests that Matthew's πνεύματι, and not Luke's δακτύλῳ, preserves the text of Q.[45] Anyway the lack of agreement between Matt 12,29 (= Mark 3,27) and Luke 11,21-22 may indicate that the case of the Strong Man saying differs from that of Matt 12,27-28.30 (Q 11,19-20.23). On the side of Matthew, the influence of Mark 3,23-26.27.28-29 in Matt 12,25-26(27-28)29(30)31-32 is widely accepted. But is it correctly stated that "Luke shows no definite sign of such influence" (J. Nolland)?[46] The same author does not deny that Luke 11,16 has been produced by Luke on the basis of Mark 8,11.[47] In the answer of Jesus,

41. HF, 54, 64.
42. See Matt 8,4 (om. μηδέν); 21,19 (om. μηδείς); 26,29 (om. οὐκέτι); 26,63 (om. οὐδέν). Compare the motif of inability in Mark 5,3 (καὶ οὐδὲ ... οὐκέτι οὐδεὶς ἐδύνατο), 4 (καὶ οὐδεὶς ἴσχυεν) and Matt 8,28 ὥστε μὴ ἰσχύειν τινα. See also Mark 6,5 (diff. Matt 13,58).
43. HF, 55.
44. See further the list of instances in HF, 158 n. 19.
45. He refers to C. S. Rodd, R. G. Hamerton-Kelly, J. E. Yates, A. George (early 1960's; cf. Lambrecht, *Marcus Interpretator*) and J.-M. van Cangh (1982), in contrast to T. W. Manson (1935). Compare the reference to "the more recent studies," in contrast to "earlier scholarship," in J. NOLLAND, 1993 (*Luke* II, p. 639). But see D. C. ALLISON, *The New Moses*, 1993: "I am persuaded, along with others who have examined the issue, that Luke's allusive 'finger of God' probably stood in Q" (p. 237; cf. p. 97 n. 7). Cf. LAUFEN, p. 130: "die Mehrzahl der heutigen Forscher" (p. 431 n. 49); more recent commentaries by Fitzmyer, Davies-Allison, Gnilka, Luz, *et al.* can be added. See now also E. P. MEADORS, *Jesus* (n. 30), pp. 191-192. Schürmann (1982, p. 155 n. 163, with reference to M. Hengel, *Nachfolge*, p. 73 n. 109) is now more hesitant: "keine rechte Sicherheit" (*Lk* II/1, 240).
46. *Luke* II, p. 635.
47. *Ibid.*, 637. On ἕτεροι δέ, cf. below, n. 137.

Luke 11,18b anticipates Mark 3,30 (ὅτι ἔλεγον...) in combination with the first clause of the Q saying (11,19a) and thus reinforces the coherence of 11,17-18+19-20. With regard to Luke 11,21-22, Fleddermann's demonstration of Luke's possible use of Matt 12,29 is perfectly applicable to the use of its counterpart in Mark 3,27, and the objection against independent agreement in placing the parable at Q 11,20/23 looks like an a priori statement. Considering the coherent redactional unity of Luke 11,17-20, the parable taken from Mark 3,(23-26)27 appears to be placed by Luke as soon as it was convenient; Q 11,23 was apparently understood as a concluding saying.[48]

2. The reconstruction of the Q text underlying Matt 12,25a and Luke 11,17a (εἰδὼς δὲ τὰ διανοήματα αὐτῶν εἶπεν αὐτοῖς) presents little problem for Fleddermann: Matthew changed τὰ διανοήματα to τὰς ἐνθυμήσεις and Luke added αὐτός and moved αὐτῶν to the pre-position.[49] In a second phase he considers the parallel text in Mark 3,23a: all differences result from Marcan redaction.[50] The first phase of Fleddermann's discussion of overlap texts is usually devoted to the reconstruction of the Q text from Matthew and Luke. The Marcan parallel and Matthew's and Luke's redaction of Mark are normally not considered in that first stage of his inquiry.[51] Thus, in the first section of the Beelzebul Controversy, he compares Matt 9,32-34; 12,22-24 with Luke 11,14-15, and has only one statement with regard to Mark: "Neither Matthew nor Luke show any Marcan influence...."[52] He makes an exception for Mark 3,23a in reference to the redactional interpretation of the Matthew-Luke agreement I suggested in my "Mt 12,25a / Lc 11,17a." In his response, Fleddermann describes Mark's προσκαλεσάμενος as "an adequate expression" and the participle εἰδώς in the parallel texts as an

48. For authors who reject the Q origin of the parable, see KLOPPENBORG, *Q Parallels*, p. 92. See now also A. D. JACOBSON, *First Gospel*, p. 154 n. 3, 162; L. E. VAAGE, *Galilean Upstarts*, pp. 117, 168 n. 39, 190 n. 41.

49. HF, 46-47. Contrast the pre-position of the pronoun in Q according to Polag and IQP (*JBL* 112, 1993, p. 503; cf. KLOPPENBORG, in *SBL 1985 Seminar Papers*, pp. 136, 142). But see my remarks on Lucan redaction, "Mt 12,25a / Lc 11,17a," pp. 131-133 (= 490-492).

50. HF, 62-63.

51. The exceptions are cases of redactional assimilation of the doublets by additional phrases: Matt 5,32; 19,9 (the πορνεία clause); 12,39; 16,4 (καὶ μοιχαλίς); 13,12; 25,29 (καὶ περισσευθήσεται); 17,20; 21,21 (ἐὰν ἔχητε πίστιν); Luke 8,16; 11,33 (οἱ πορευόμενοι...).

52. HF, 41-45, esp. 45. "The only possible exception" (n. 27) is ὥστε + infinitive in Matt 12,22 (cf. Mark 3,20), but he also observes, more correctly, that "the conjunction is common in Matthew" (43, and n. 16). There is no mention of a possible contact with Mark 3,21 (ἐξέστη) in Matt 12,23 (ἐξίσταντο). For a comparison of Matt 12,24 with Mark 3,22, cf. R. H. GUNDRY, *Matthew*, p. 232.

"awkward" phrase in the Beelzebul Controversy.[53] In order to avoid misunderstanding I repeat here the point I made:[54]

> Προσκαλεσάμενος αὐτούς n'est donc pas une formule typique des récits de controverse, et en lui substituant εἰδὼς δὲ τὰς ἐνθυμήσεις αὐτῶν Mt a renforcé considérablement le genre propre de l'épisode.
>
> L'influence de Mt 9,4 ne serait donc pas limitée au choix du mot ἐνθυμήσεις en remplacement du διανοήματα de la source. C'est l'expression toute entière qui serait une reprise de Mt 9,4a.

In his own way Fleddermann also refers to Matt 9,4 (Matthew's use of the *word* ἐνθυμήσεις) but in 12,25a "εἰδώς is awkward because there isn't any reference to the adversaries' commenting 'in their hearts'." But precisely in light of Matt 9,4 the *theme* of "knowing their thoughts" here "probably implies that what they had said in the preceding verse they said within themselves, not to the crowds."[55] One can hardly say that in this case Matthew "must make connections between far-flung Marcan texts in order to eliminate ... προσκαλεσάμενος." Fleddermann reads Luke 11,17a in connection with v. 15: "Only some of the crowd voiced the charge against Jesus," and he neglects the introduction of ἕτεροι δὲ πειράζοντες... That the use of πειράζοντες may suggest the theme of "knowing their thoughts" (without adding "in their hearts") *we* know from Mark 12,15 and parallels; it is not *Luke* who must make connections between far-flung Marcan texts...[56]

3. Q 11,17c καὶ οἶκος ἐπὶ οἶκον πίπτει: "Most likely Luke reflects Q... Three facts support Lucan originality."[57] Although he recognizes

---

53. HF, 47.

54. "Mt 12,25a / Lc 11,17a," pp. 127, 128 (= 486, 487). On the reading εἰδώς in Matt 9,4 (Greeven, Boismard, Gundry, *et al.*), see *ibid.*, n. 25. The variant ἰδών now receives the rating B (before C) but no new evidence is provided in Metzger's *Textual Commentary*, [2]1994, pp. 19-20.

55. R. H. GUNDRY, *Matthew*, p. 233. See also his note on Matt 12,25a / Luke 11,17a in *The Four Gospels 1992*, pp. 1482-1483.

56. The close similarity between Matt 12,25a and Luke 11,17a makes one hesitant; see my own conclusion (p. 133 = 492). Cf. H. SCHÜRMANN, *Lukasevangelium* II/1, p. 233: "Sowohl 11,17a wie par Mt 12,25a geben Lukas und Matthäus somit in eigenem Sprachstil wieder. Beide kennen das Motiv vom 'Tiefblick' Jesu aus Mk, bezeugen es aber sonst nirgends für Q. Daß aber beide das gleiche Motiv (mit je eigenen Worten) für Lk 11,17a / Mt 12,25 diff Mk bringen, kann nicht gut Zufall sein..." I may add here: "Cependant, l'étude des *minor agreements* nous a appris que des accords frappants peuvent parfois s'expliquer comme des rédactions indépendantes sur la seule base de Mc, et je crois que la question mérite d'être posée à propos de Mt 12,25a / Lc 11,17a" (p. 128 = 487). Such a possibility is not excluded by Fleddermann, at least theoretically: "We can, of course, conceive of the possibility that Matthew and Luke might agree in altering a Q text" (HF, 16 n. 63).

57. HF, 48.

that in this case "it is difficult to choose," Fleddermann has no mention of the "facts" in support of Matt 12,25c; and there is no reference to alternative reconstructions of the Q text: καὶ πᾶσα οἰκία ἐφ' ἑαυτὴν μερισθεῖσα οὐ σταθήσεται (Klauck, 1978);[58] cf. IQP: καὶ οἰκ[ία μερισθεῖσα καθ' ἑαυτῆς οὐ σταθήσεται].[59] Fleddermann simply observes: "If Luke had found a section in Q on the divided house or 'family,' he would not have omitted it as he frequently uses 'house' in the sense of 'family'." But there is more than one term that can be understood in a literal sense (ἐρημοῦται, οἰκία, οὐ σταθήσεται)[60] and may have suggested the change of the motif of the divided family to an illustration of the complete destruction of the kingdom. That in the Beelzebul Controversy Luke uses "house" only in the sense of "building" is one of the facts adduced in favor of the Q origin of Luke 11,17c. Fleddermann's translation referring to buildings is somewhat ambiguous: "and house falls *against* house" (ἐπί = upon, on; contrast the use of ἐπί = *against* in 11,17b), and here again it is not mentioned that opinions remain divided between house-building (NRSV: "and house falls on house") and house-family (REB: "and a divided household falls").[61] Cf. below, § 4.

§ 4. THE UNFORGIVABLE SIN

To begin with, the reconstructed text of Q 12,10 καὶ πᾶς ὅς...: "Although πᾶς is a favorite word of Luke, its use with the relative is attested in Q."[62] One of the two other occurrences in Q is Q 6,47, cited

---

58. H.-J. KLAUCK, *Allegorie und Allegorese in synoptischen Gleichnistexten* (NeutAbh, 13), Münster, 1978, pp. 174-179 ("Reich und Haus"), esp. 177. Cf. p. 176: "Lk hat den übergetragenen Sinn von οἰκία = Familie nicht wahrgenommen und das Zusammenstürzen von Gebäuden als passende Illustration für die Verwüstung eines Reiches angesehen. Für Q nehmen wir Mt 12,25c in Anspruch, mit Ausnahme von πόλις, das Mt eingefügt hat." On this Lucan *Mißverständnis*, see e.g. the recent commentaries by U. Luz (*Mt* II, p. 255 n. 21) and H. Schürmann (*Lk* II/1, p. 234 n. 69).

59. *JBL* 112 (1993), p. 503. Cf. KLOPPENBORG, "Q 11:14-26: Work Sheets for Reconstruction," in *SBL 1985 Seminar Papers*, pp. 133-151; p. 136, reconstruction Q 11,17c: (καὶ . . . ?); pp. 143-144 (authors pro and contra Luke = Q); "Q may have presupposed 'divided' in the second clause and οικος meaning 'household'" (p. 144).

60. Cf. SCHÜRMANN (n. 58).

61. Cf. M. D. GOULDER, *Luke*, 1989, p. 504 ("has its parallel in the five ἐν ἑνὶ οἴκῳ διαμερισμένοι"); L. T. JOHNSON, *Luke*, 1991, p. 181: "household against household"; J. NOLLAND, *Luke* II, 1993, p. 638. On this "usual rendering," see H. E. BRYANT, "Note on Luke xi.17," in *ExpT* 50 (1938-39) 525-526. See also J. A. FITZMYER, *Luke*, p. 921: "*one house falls upon another*. Or 'against' another... Here *oikos* could even mean 'family'." I. H. Marshall's reading is scarcely different: "upon another" as "one household attacking another" (p. 474). On the meaning in Q, see n. 59.

62. HF, 66 n. 115, 117.

in a note without further comment. A. Polag, for instance, reads πᾶς ὅστις ἀκούει (cf. Matt), but IQP has πᾶς ὁ [] ἀκού[ων] (cf. Luke). The second example is Q 12,8, and M. E. Boring is blamed by Fleddermann for not having investigated this Q context. But the preceding saying in 12,8 (Q πᾶς ὅς) and 9 (participle in Luke) may have influenced Luke's editing with πᾶς in 12,10a (καὶ πᾶς ὅς) and 10b (the participle τῷ βλασφημήσαντι). The text of Q 12,10b is reconstructed in parallel to 10a: ὃς δὲ ἐρεῖ λόγον εἰς τὸ πνεῦμα τὸ ἅγιον (contrast IQP: ὃς δ' ἂν [βλασφημήσῃ]). The fact that "Luke borrowed the verb 'blaspheme' from Mark" (3,28-29)[63] makes it more likely that Mark 3,27 (and not Matt 12,29 "Q") has been the source of Luke 11,21-22 (cf. § 3). "Q contains only two references to the Holy Spirit."[64] The reference to "the 'Spirit' of God" in 11,20 is not considered here (contrast his comment on 3,16 in § 2).[65] That Mark found the saying Q 12,10 in conjunction with 12,8-9 (QR) remains an unproven assumption. Cf. below, § 14.

In Mark the Unforgivable Sin logion (3,28-29) is appended to the Beelzebul Controversy, and the final comment in 3,30 forms an inclusion with the initial charge in v. 22. Mark 3,22-30 is surrounded by the True Relatives (3,20-21.31-35). This framing technique is "characteristically Marcan," "carries Mark's signature."[66] The six classic examples are listed by Fleddermann, and in particular Mark 3,20-35 and 6,7-30 receive some more special attention.[67] Two remarks can be made here. First, Mark 3,25, on the divided house, is said to be added by Mark "to refer to Jesus' split with his family."[68] Though Mark 3,22 (and 30) is related to 3,20-21, it is less likely that, at the middle of the inserted Beelzebul Controversy, the divided house saying would have such a direct connection with the framing section: "The context of a kingdom defines the house as a royal family, not an ordinary household... Strife within a royal family will open the door to usurpers."[69] My second remark concerns the framing technique in Mark 6,7-30: "For the technique to work, the outside frame must be kept short."[70] Fleddermann compares here Mark's

63. HF, 68. Cf. *Evangelica II*, 432, 442.
64. HF, 70.
65. HF, 35, 37 (cf. 50-51).
66. HF, 213, 124.
67. HF, 61-62, 73-73, 119-120, 124. The six examples are merely listed (62 n. 90; 73 n. 151, 119 n. 82; cf. *Duality*). On more recent studies, see G. Van Oyen, "Intercalation and Irony in the Gospel of Mark," in *The Four Gospels 1992*, pp. 949-974; Id., *De studie van de Marcusredactie in de twintigste eeuw* (SNTA, 18), Leuven, 1993, p. 313 n. 1213.
68. HF, 73. Cf. 64: "The framing pericope provides a concrete example of a family divided."
69. R. H. Gundry, *Mark*, p. 173.
70. HF, 119.

Mission Discourse with the Mission Discourse in Matt 10 where the disciples never return: "To avoid this problem, Mark shortens the Q discourse."[71] One has the impression that a more or less uniform framing technique is called upon to solve the problem of the "omissions" in Mark. But it is sufficient to compare Mark 6,7-13 and 30 with 3,20-21 and 31-35 to see that there is no such uniformity in Mark's intercalations.

§ § 5-8. A CLUSTER OF FOUR SAYINGS

"In the cluster of sayings in Mark 4,21-25 we find five Q sayings joined together:" 4,21 (Q 11,33); 4,22 (Q 12,2); 4,24cd (Q 6,38c; 12,31b); 4,25 (Q 19,26). "If Mark were drawing on the oral tradition, we would expect to find some non-Q material mixed in."[72] Only Mark 4,23 is not taken into consideration. The listening saying εἴ τις ἔχει ὦτα ἀκούειν ἀκουέτω ("a true Q saying" for Lambrecht[73]) is apparently regarded by Fleddermann as Marcan,[74] and Luke 14,35b, without parallel in Matthew, not ascribed to Q.[75] One can agree with Fleddermann that the sayings collection in Mark 4,21-25 is a Marcan composition and that for all four sayings there are parallels in Q. But does it mean that Mark drew on Q? It is not because the parallels are dispersed in Q that we can conclude that "Mark composed with knowledge of the whole Q document."

§ 9. THE MUSTARD SEED

The section on Mark 4,30-32 originally appeared as part of a larger essay, "The Mustard Seed and the Leaven" (1989). The text is only

---

71. HF, 120.

72. HF, 213; cf. 89, 98-99.

73. "Logia-Quellen," p. 335: "Auch dieser Vers stand wohl ursprünglich in Q^rev in dem genannten Kontext [Lk 14,35b]. Aus seiner Quelle antizipierte Markus ihn Mk 4,9;" *Marcus Interpretator*, p. 111 n. 26 ("Heeft Marcus daar de oproep gevonden en hem hierna redactioneel tot zijn voorkeurthema verheven?"); cf. p. 122 n. 50; "Redaction and Theology," p. 286 ("if it is a true Q saying, Matthew might have omitted it in V,13 for the sake of symmetry with V,14"); cf. p. 289 ("we suggested that the appeal to listen [v. 23] was also found in Q" [cf. *Lk.*, XIV,35c]). A new suggestion appears *ibid.*, p. 286: "It is also possible that the Q-expression καὶ ὃ εἰς τὸ οὖς ἀκούετε (*Mt.*, X,27; cf. *Lk.*, XII,3b) ... influenced Mark to incorporate the listening saying." Cf. "Q-Influence," p. 299 ("one should not too easily dismiss the possibility..."); cf. p. 301.

74. HF, 86: "he introduces the [Measure] saying with a double summons to hear in vv. 23-24ab." Cf. 123 n. 102.

75. Cf. § 18: Q 14,34-35a. For Luke 14,35b in Q (n. 73), cf. J. SCHMID, *Matthäus und Lukas*, p. 219 n. 1; H. SCHÜRMANN, *Traditionsgeschichtliche Untersuchungen*, p. 276 n. 33 (note: the overlap text in Mark 4,9, and not 4,23). — On Mark 4,9 (ὃς ἔχει), 23 (εἴ τις ἔχει) and Luke 14,35 (ὃ ἔχων), see C. BREYTENBACH, "Vormarkinische Logientradition" (n. 18), pp. 739-740 ("Der Weckruf").

slightly revised, somewhat rearranged[76] and supplemented with references to F. Kogler (1988) and T. A. Friedrichsen (1992). The main discussion with Friedrichsen concerns the double question in Luke 13,18.[77] For Friedrichsen it is Lucan rewriting of Mark 4,30 whereas for Fleddermann Luke 13,18-19 is uninfluenced by Mark and the double question is taken over from Q without change. Fleddermann emphasizes Luke's avoidance of double questions[78] and seems to neglect that other factors can explain why "two questions ... don't survive in Luke's redaction."[79] With regard to the possible influence of Mark 4,30 on Luke 7,31 (and 13,18), Fleddermann replies that, though Luke transfers "blaspheme" from Mark 3,29 to Luke 12,10 (Q),[80] "no other example exists of Luke taking elements from a Marcan overlap text and using them to redact a different Q text."[81] This is a rather strange limitation of possible reminiscences (permutations) in the redaction of Luke.[82] Kloppenborg has noted that the introductory formula in Q 7,31 "resembles the introductory formulae to the parables of the Mustard (Q 13:18-19; Mk 4:30) and the Leaven (Q 13:20-21)," and: "appears to imitate the interrogative introduction of the kingdom parables."[83] This observation remains valid if we read Q 7,31 τίνι (δὲ) ὁμοιώσω τὴν γενεὰν ταύτην; (cf. Matt) and attribute to Luke the insertion of τοὺς ἀνθρώπους (+ genitive) and the addition of the second question: καὶ τίνι εἰσὶν ὅμοιοι; An a priori refusal of Lucan assimilation to the double question in Mark 4,30 is hardly justifiable.

---

76. As can be seen in the numbering of the footnotes 75-115 (compared with those of 1989): 75(43), 76(7), 77(9), 78(10), 79 (11), 80(13), 81(17), 82(19+), 84(20+), 87(22), 88(23-24), 89(25), 92(26), 93(29), 94(p. 223), 95(74, p. 232), 97(46), 101(49), 102(50), 103(52), 104-105(53), 106-108(54), 109-110(61), 111(62), 113(58), 114(59), 115(60).

77. HF, 91-93. Cf. T. A. FRIEDRICHSEN, "'Major' and 'Minor' Matthew-Luke Agreements," pp. 662-675 ("The Double Question: Mk 4,30 / Lk 13,18").

78. Note that the same examples (Luke 8,25; 9,41; 20,22; 22,46; 22,71) are cited to illustrate that Luke avoids double questions (n. 83) and "eliminates double questions from Mark" (n. 84). On the other hand, Q 11,21-22 (n. 88; cf. above § 3) should be added to the six examples where Luke eliminates rhetorical questions from Q (n. 83). In Q 6,39a.39b; 6,46; 7,31b; 13,18a.18b.20 the rhetorical question is "eliminated" in Matthew (not mentioned in n. 88).

79. HF, 92 n. 84.

80. Cf. above, n. 63. See also HF, 109 (on μένετε in Luke 10,7): "If Luke can import Q expressions into Mark, he can carry over Marcan terms into Q."

81. HF, 92-93.

82. On Marcan reminiscences in Luke, see F. NOËL, *De compositie van het Lucasevangelie in zijn relatie tot Marcus: Het probleem van de grote weglating*, Brussel, 1994, pp. 191-231.

83. J. S. KLOPPENBORG, "Jesus and the Parables of Jesus in Q," in R. A. PIPER (ed.), *The Gospel Behind the Gospels*, 1995, pp. 275-319, esp. 290, 318.

§ 10. THE MISSION DISCOURSE

Fleddermann begins his analysis by comparing the Mission Discourse with the Beelzebul Controversy, the other extensive overlap text, and here too he will conclude: Mark is secondary to Q; Mark also shows knowledge of redactional Q.[84] Lambrecht's *Marcus Interpretator* was the model in § 3: "Years ago Lambrecht got it right – Mark depends on Q in the Beelzebul Controversy."[85] Throughout §§ 3–9 (Mark 3,22-30; 4,21-25.30-32) the footnotes refer frequently to Lambrecht. His name is now absent in § 10. Neither is Catchpole mentioned here, although a confrontation with his "Mission Charge" would have been most appropriate. The interlocutors here are P. Hoffmann (1971, 1972) and the more recent R. Uro (1987).[86] It is all the more surprising that the term "redactional Q," which is found in the Conclusion, is never used elsewhere in the section on the Mission Discourse.

A large part of § 10 is devoted to the detailed reconstruction of the Q text in Q 10,2-16. The Equipment Rule in 10,4a deserves special attention. His reconstruction is as follows: μὴ **λαμβάνετε ἄργυρον**, μὴ πήραν, μὴ ὑποδήματα, **μὴ ῥάβδον**. The words in bold differ from Luke's text: λαμβάνετε (for Luke's βαστάζετε), cf. Q 14,27 λαμβάνει (= Matt 10,38; βαστάζει in Luke); ἄργυρον (for Luke's βαλλάντιον), cf. ἄργυρον in Matt 10,9 and ἀργύριον in Luke 9,3; μὴ ῥάβδον (not in Luke), cf. μηδὲ ῥάβδον in Matt 10,10 and μήτε ῥάβδον in Luke 9,3. Fleddermann rightly refuses the prohibition of two tunics (μὴ δύο χιτῶνας): "the coats come from Mark."[87] But also the inclusion of "no staff" in the text of Q on the basis of Matt 10,10; Luke 9,3 is far from evident. Μηδὲ/μήτε ῥάβδον (for εἰ μὴ ῥάβδον μόνον in Mark 6,8) can be the result of assimilation to the other prohibitions. The text of Luke 10,4a remains a more secure basis for the reconstruction of Q

---

84. HF, 101-126 and 133.

85. HF 65. *Marcus Interpretator* (1969) is a collection of four articles that appeared (in the reverse order) in *Bijdragen* 29 (1968) 25-52 (Mark 4,1-34); 114-150, 234-258, 369-392 (Mark 3,20-35).

86. See now also R. URO, "John the Baptist and the Jesus Movement" (n. 14), 1995, esp. 245-246: "many of those who have worked with the Mark / Q problem think that the best hypothesis for the relationship of these two gospels is a 'common tradition' model, a hypothesis that Mark / Q overlaps are due to common tradition or sources used by the authors" (p. 245, with references to M. Devisch and R. Laufen). "Several analyses confirm that behind the Markan and Q Mission Charges one can recognize a common pattern..., which has been framed by further narrative (Mk 6:7, 12-13, 30) or sayings material (Q 10:2, 3, 12, 13-15, 16)" (pp. 245-246).

87. Mark 6,9 and Matt 10,10; Luke 9,3. Cf. HF, 105 ("tunics" rather than "coats") and n. 24, repeated in n. 25. Note that it is less certain for Hoffmann (p. 267: question mark) and Uro (p. 77: within parentheses).

(Polag, Laufen, *et al.*).[88] The mention of "silver" (Matt 10,9; Luke 9,3) is even more doubtful. Matthew really needs no second source for developing Mark's μὴ εἰς τὴν ζώνην χαλκόν into his triad χρυσὸν μηδὲ ἄργυρον μηδὲ χαλκὸν εἰς τὰς ζώνας ὑμῶν. That "Mark substitutes 'copper' for 'silver' (compare Mark 12,41)"[89] can easily be reversed: Mark's word χαλκόν is omitted in Luke 21,1 and changed to ἀργύριον, the general word for money, in Luke 9,3. Strangely, Luke 22,35-36 (ὅτε ἀπέστειλα ὑμᾶς ἄτερ βαλλαντίου καὶ πήρας καὶ ὑποδημάτων...) is not at all mentioned in Fleddermann's discussion of Luke 10,4a.[90]

Much more amazing is the fact that Fleddermann treats the Mark-Q problem in Q 10,2-16 without even referring to Catchpole's distinction between the traditional mission charge and a single redactional stratum. The most problematic verses in this repartition between tradition and redaction are vv. 12 and 16, and I have suggested correcting his hypothesis by proposing vv. 2.**12**.13-15 as redactionally added to the Q tradition (10,3.4.5-7.8-11a.**16**).[91] "If, with Catchpole, we accept traditional pre-Q material in Q 10,3-11, there may be some correspondence between its fourfold division and the contents of Mark 6,7-11: sending (7), equipment (8-9), acceptance (10), rejection (11), but this cannot be used as evidence of Mark's dependence on Q. On the other hand, because Q 10,2.12 are without parallel in Mk 6, one could argue that this Q-redactional frame [and 10,13-15] was unknown to Mark."[92] In this hypothesis, the problem of "Mark's omissions" that Fleddermann has to face[93] is considerably alleviated.

§ 11. DEMAND FOR A SIGN

"Mark's use of 'this generation' hangs in the air... Mark picks up 'this generation' from Q 11,30-32 which he omits... Mark shows knowledge of redactional Q in the expression 'this generation'."[94] Fleddermann

88. See my "Literary Criticism" (1993), p. 33 n. 106 (in reply to Catchpole). Following Hoffmann (p. 240), Fleddermann considers together "shoes" and "staff" (HF, 105, 118), but the prohibition of "shoes" is found in Luke 10,4a; the "staff" is not.

89. HF, 122.

90. Neither are alternative reconstructions of Q 10,4a such as the IQP text noted by Fleddermann. Cf. *JBL* 110 (1991), p. 496: μὴ [[βαστάζετ]]ε [[ἀργύρ. .ον, μὴ πήραν]], μὴ . . ὑποδήματα, [[μηδὲ ῥάβδον]]. The two dots indicate the variation ἀργύριον/ἄργυρον (but the accent is that of ἀργύριον!) and the possible insertion of μὴ δύο χιτῶνας. That μὴ πήραν is included [[ ]] together with ἀργύριον must be a mistake.

91. "Literary Criticism," pp. 31-33 ("Q 10,2-16 and Mark").

92. *Ibid.*, p. 33.

93. HF, 120-121.

94. Quotations from HF, 131-134 and 211: "The term does not fit smoothly in Mark... The expression does not fit naturally in Mark's passage. – In Q ... the use of 'this generation'

compares Mark 8,12 with the passage in Q without even mentioning the complex problem of the history of Q 11,29-32. He drops Luke's ἡ γενεὰ αὕτη in his reconstruction of Q 11,29, and since he proposes Mark's knowledge of QR, one may guess that he considers Q 11,30 to be redactional (cf. Lührmann, Hoffmann, Schenk, et al.: 11,30 or 29d-30 QR).[95] But other scholars think that there are good reasons for treating 11,30 as pre-redactional, either as part of the original unit 11,29-30 (Schulz, Luz) or as an explicative phrase, Deutewort or Verdeutlichungswort, added to v. 29 (Kloppenborg, Schürmann, Vögtle). They all agree that the originally independent 11,31-32 were appended at a later, still pre-redactional stage. I quote H. Schürmann:[96]

> Das Doppelwort VV 31f ist nicht als Deutewort für VV 29-30 geschaffen... Es wird schon vormals seine isolierte Tradition gehabt haben. ... die Einordnung von 11,31-32 [ist] einer späten Kompositionsstufe (aber wohl nicht erst der abschließenden Endredaktion) der Redequelle zuzusprechen.

Kloppenborg emphasizes the remarkable similarities with 11,29: "The correlative [v. 30] is constructed specifically as the explanation of 11:29, repeating the key words σημεῖον, Ἰωνᾶς and γενεὰ αὕτη." This interpretative saying 11,30 is "certainly ... not as late as the final redaction".[97]

In Fleddermann's assumption that Mark is secondary, the term "this generation" may have come to Mark in the shorter Q tradition 11,29-30 and not, as he suggested, in the longer redactional version of Q 11,29-32. The explanation that Mark has shortened this longer version may actually mean that there is no evidence that it was known by Mark.[98]

---

is more natural..., it fits naturally. 'This generation' is a key redactional expression in Q..., a redactional term that the author of Q uses to link several passages (Q 7,31; 11,31.32.51)."

95. "Recent Developments," p. 54 (= 434). Cf. TUCKETT, "Mark and Q," pp. 158-162, here 160.

96. Lukasevangelium II/1, pp. 289, 290. See now also A. VÖGTLE, 'Gretchenfrage', pp. 148-163, here 153.

97. Formation, p. 130. See also JACOBSON, First Gospel, pp. 164-169: "It seems unlikely ... that Q 11:30 was added after Q 11:29 and 11:31-32 had been brought together" (p. 166).

98. TUCKETT, "Mark and Q," p. 161: "The editorial activity of the Q redactor in bringing together different traditions (evidenced at least in the conjunction of 11,29-30 and 11,31-32) seems to have left no trace in Mark." – With regard to Fleddermann's emphasis on the pejorative "this generation" in Q, I may refer to CATCHPOLE, Quest, pp. 241-247: "the theme of 'this generation,' while firmly endorsed by Q, can be derived from Jesus" (p. 276). Cf. A. VÖGTLE: one of the "alte, von Jesus selbst stammende Elemente" (p. 151). See now also E. LÖVESTAM, Jesus and "this Generation". A New Testament Study (ConBNT, 25), Stockholm, 1995, esp. pp. 21-37.

§ 12. The Cross Saying

"Because Mark knew this Q composition, Mark knew redactional Q" or, as it is reformulated in the Conclusion: "Since Mark knows the saying, he knows redactional Q."[99] This "saying" is the overlap text Mark 8,34 / Luke 14,27 and "this Q composition" is Q 14,26a.b.27. Fleddermann's § 12 on Mark 8,34 is a revised version of his "Cross and Discipleship" (1988). He repeats his view that the Q saying in 14,27 is original, and now adds the question: "does Mark know redactional Q?" More than before he emphasizes that Q 14,26a.b.27 are conceived as "an original stylistic and conceptual unit." This observation is now his first indication that the Q saying is prior to the Marcan saying[100] and this same observation forms the proof that Mark depends on QR.

Fleddermann's statement on the original unit is not unambiguous. He also notes that 14,26.27 "draws together two separate lines of thought" and that "because Q 14,26-27 draws these two Q themes together, it comes from the pen of the author of Q." But how can he then conclude that "we cannot trace the Cross Saying any further back in the tradition than the Q cluster?"[101] If the two themes of 14,26 (family) and 27 (cross) are drawn together by QR, it would seem more natural to conclude with J. Nolland: "Vv 26-27 do not constitute an original unity. When the materials were joined, v 27 received substantial formal modification for the sake of parallelism."[102]

In Fleddermann's reconstruction the two sentences in Q 14,26 (Matt 10,37a.b) are assimilated to the relative clause ὃς οὐ in 14,27 (in contrast to the IQP text: [[εἴ τις...]] and καὶ [[εἴ τις...]] in 26a.b).[103] The conditional clause at the opening of v. 26, εἴ τις ἔρχεται πρός με, is rightly attributed to Lucan redaction: "Luke ... has in mind the conditional form of Mark's cross saying (Mark 8:34) which he redacts in 9:23 (εἴ τις θέλει ὀπίσω μου ἔρχεσθαι). The conditional clause fits the context Luke created for the saying."[104] Fleddermann adopts the thesis of Mark's knowledge of Q 14,26 (the cluster 14,26-27) but the εἴ τις construction

---

99. HF, 139, 211.
100. Compare the five indications (HF, 138) with the "three considerations" he proposed in 1988 (p. 479), now listed as nos. 2, 3, and 5, and supplemented with no. 1 (the original unit in Q) and no. 4 (the saying in Mark brought into line with the passion narrative: ἀπαρνησάσθω and ἀράτω).
101. See references in n. 99.
102. *Luke* II, p. 761. See also, e.g., Luz, p. 135: "selbständige Einzellogien;" Bois-mard, *Synopse* II, p. 292: "la liaison entre les deux parties est probablement artificielle."
103. Cf. *JBL* 111 (1992), p. 507.
104. "Cross and Discipleship," p. 476.

is banned from his Q text and in the saying itself there remains no indication of Mark's possible borrowing from Q 14,26.

It is remarkable that Fleddermann has only one reference to the treatment of Mark 8,34 in Lambrecht's "Q-Influence"[105] and has not noticed
the significant divergences in their textual options: Mark 8,34 ἀκολουθεῖν (Lambrecht: ἐλθεῖν) and in the reconstruction of Q 14,27:
ἀκολουθεῖ (Lambrecht: ἔρχεται).[106] Moreover, Lambrecht has ἔρχεται πρός με in Q 14,26a and εἴ τις, καὶ εἴ τις in 26a.b (contrast Fleddermann: ὅς, ὅς).[107] Lambrecht reads ὃς οὐ λαμβάνει in Q 14,27 but
would not a priori exclude that αἴρω (and not λαμβάνω) stood in Q:
"whether ... ἀράτω in 8,34 is due to Mark's edition is not so certain."[108]
Contrast Fleddermann: the words "deny" and "take up" in Mark "echo
the passion narrative."[109]

§ 13. Losing One's Life

Luke 17,33 differs from the reconstructed Q text (cf. Matt 10,39) in
two respects: the omission of the superfluous second τὴν ψυχὴν αὐτοῦ
and the substitutes for the verb "to find:" ζητήσῃ ... περιποιήσασθαι
for εὕρῃ[110] and ζῳογονήσει for εὑρήσει (= Matt). I can agree regarding this double redactional intervention by Luke, but his source is more
probably not Q but Mark 8,35. Mark has the relative clauses ὃς ἐάν and
ὃς δ᾽ ἂν ἀπολέσῃ, and his θέλῃ ... σῶσαι in the first half (= Luke 9,24)
is much closer to ζητήσῃ ... περιποιήσασθαι than the hypothetical
εὕρῃ (Matt ὁ εὑρών). For Luke θέλω + infinitive and ζητέω + infinitive are synonyms; compare Luke 9,9 καὶ ἐζήτει ἰδεῖν αὐτόν and
23,8b ἦν γὰρ ἐξ ἱκανῶν χρόνων θέλων ἰδεῖν αὐτόν. Luke's use of
Mark 8,35 (Luke 9,24) in Luke 17,33 is not completely isolated, since
the insertion of 17,25 in the same discourse depends on Mark 8,31 (Luke
9,22), and the saying in 17,33 is preceded by 17,31(32), taken from
Mark 13,15-16.[111]

---

105. HF, 138 n. 17: "Q-Influence," p. 282 (read: 281, on "let him deny himself"). Note,
however, that for Fleddermann the term "deny" echoes the passion narrative (fourth indication), whereas for Lambrecht ἀπαρνησάσθω would be a Q term (Q 12,9, cf. Mark 8,38).
106. "Q-Influence," pp. 279-280.
107. Ibid., p. 280 n. 18. Cf. above, nn. 103-104.
108. Ibid., pp. 281, 282.
109. HF, 138. Cf. above, nn. 100, 105.
110. HF, 142. Instead of the form εὕρῃ Laufen prefers εὑρήσει (pp. 322, 561 n. 140);
other authors read ὁ εὑρών (= Matt): Schulz, Polag, Lambrecht, et al. For Jacobson the
verb εὑρίσκειν "probably represents Q" (p. 222 n. 93). But see, e.g., G. Dautzenberg
(Sein Leben bewahren, 1966, p. 62); Boismard (1972, p. 248); Luz (Matthäus II, p. 135
n. 9: "könnte auch mt sein").

Defenders of the Q origin usually argue that the parallel Matt 10,39 is preserved in its original setting: Matt 10,37.38.39 / Q 14,26.27; 17,33; the presence of the phrase ἔτι τε καὶ τὴν ψυχὴν ἑαυτοῦ in Luke 14,26 is seen as a reminiscence of this location in Q. This last indication is not even mentioned by Fleddermann. In his view Matthew does not reflect the original Q context of the saying: "Matthew joined the Q sayings on the cross and losing one's life in 10,38-39 because he found the overlap sayings joined in Mark 8,34-35."[112] But in these conditions one may ask whether the Q origin of Matt 10,39 is still defendable. Its location depends on Mark 8,35; the phrase ἔνεκεν ἐμοῦ in the second half is taken from Mark 8,35 (par. Matt 16,25); εὑρήσει is used in Matt 16,25 in parallel to σώσει in Mark 8,35 and the use of this verb may have been extended to the first half (εὑρών); and finally the substantive participle (ὁ εὑρών, ὁ ἀπολέσας) instead of Mark's relative clauses is Matthean usage (in this context: 10,37ab.39ab.40ab.41ab).[113]

§ 14. JESUS AND THE SON OF MAN

Of the four overlap texts in Q with reference to the Son of Man, only Q 12,8-9 / Mark 8,38 (ὁ υἱὸς τοῦ ἀνθρώπου) has this reference in the Marcan parallel. Cf. Q 11,30 (om. Mark 8,12); Q 12,10 (Mark 3,28 τῶν υἱῶν τῶν ἀνθρώπων); Q 12,40 (diff. Mark 13,35). Fleddermann apparently assigns all four references to QR. His comment is most clear in § 14:[114]

> ... the Q saying on Confessing and Denying fits seamlessly in the overall Q portrayal of the Son of Man. Since it fits so smoothly in Q's christology, the saying could well come from the Q redactor. If so, then the saying shows that Mark knew redactional Q.

He anticipated this statement already in § 4, where he drew a further conclusion with regard to Q 12,10: "If the saying on Confessing and Denying comes from the Q redactor, the commenting saying on the Unforgivable Sin does also."[115] (Here and elsewhere the possibility that a commenting function could be given to previously isolated sayings has apparently not been considered by Fleddermann.) If Q 12,10 "comments on and corrects" 12,8-9, is it then likely that both sayings stem from the same redactor? Q 12,4-9 is probably a pre-Q unit and 12,8-9 "may be

111. Cf. "The Minor Agreements and Q," pp. 54-56 (Luke 17,31).
112. HF, 143. Cf. below, n. 117.
113. For authors who reject the Q origin of Mt 10,39 and Lk 17,33, see KLOPPENBORG, *Q Parallels*, p. 170. Cf. *Recent Developments*, pp. 49-51 (= 429-431).
114. HF, 151; see also 152: "The editor of Q could well have formulated the saying." Cf. "Confessing and Denying" (1987), pp. 614, 616.
115. HF, 70. Cf. above, p. 271 (§ 2).

present already in the pre-Q tradition though its concerns cohere well with other parts of Q."[116]

The sayings in Mark 8,34.35 and 38 are treated together in Chapter VI: Caesarea Philippi. The first two form a cluster in Mark bound together by θέλω. As indicated above, the order of Mark 8,34.35 (and Matthew 10,38.39), which for Lambrecht is a Q order, is regarded by Fleddermann as Marcan.[117] The argument for Mark's use of final Q built up by Lambrecht around Mark 8,38[118] has received no echo in Fleddermann's work. His own argument for Mark's knowledge of redactional Q relies directly on the Son of Man Saying and "Q's theology of the Son of Man." Unfortunately "this remains only a possibility." In his view, "the Cross Saying [8,34] definitely shows that Mark knew redactional Q," but his readers may ask how he can be so certain that the composition of Q 14,26.27 "could only go back to the Q redactor."[119] Lambrecht was rightly looking to recover larger Q contexts and had to conclude: "our way is blocked as far as these sayings are concerned."[120]

§ 15. ON ACCEPTING

According to Fleddermann the saying Matt 10,40 / Luke 10,16 forms the conclusion of the Mission Discourse in Q (in the order of Luke 10,2-16). The original wording is preserved unchanged in Matthew. Mark transferred this saying to his Discipleship Discourse and redacted it in Mark 9,37. If this hypothesis is correct,[121] one can observe that the saying used by Mark more probably may have been the conclusion of a pre-Q Mission Discourse, say Q 10,3...11a.16.

---

116. C. M. TUCKETT, "The Son of Man in Q," 1993, pp. 208-211, here 211. See also A. Y. COLLINS, "The Son of Man Sayings in the Sayings Source," 1989, pp. 369-389, esp. 378-379: Q 12,8-9 is part of a pre-Q unit (12,4-9) but vv. 2-3 and 10 were added at the same time and vv. 11-12 were possibly placed there by Luke: "If this reconstruction is plausible, ... the possibility that vv. 2-3 and 10 were added by the editor of Q cannot be ruled out" (p. 379). For Fleddermann, however, the Q composition (12,2-12) includes vv. 11-12 and then one cannot exclude that v. 10 was a pre-Q addition. Like Collins, Tuckett emphasizes the connection of v. 10 with vv. 2-3 at the compositional stage of Q, but he does not comment on 12,11-12.

117. Cf. above, n. 112.

118. "Q-Influence," pp. 298-303: "The form of Q known to Mark." In fact his overview (pp. 300-301) includes a number of uncertainties such as uncertain Q texts (11,21-22; 11,27-28; 12,1; 12,13-21) and uncertain parallels: 11,29 (μοιχαλίς); 12,3 (Mark 4,23).

119. HF, 152.

120. "Q-Influence," p. 298.

121. But see "Recent Developments," p. 47 (= 427) n. 72, on alternative reconstructions of Q (cf. Luke 10,16) and possible influence of Mark 9,37 upon Matt 10,40.

§ 16. On Tolerance

The title of § 16 refers to Mark 9,40; the saying in Q is rather exclusive and intolerant (Q 11,23). Fleddermann has indicated how Mark could have redacted this saying, if he depends on Q. Like Q 10,16 which is incorporated in the Discipleship Discourse in Mark 9,37, Q 11,23 is taken over in Mark 9,40.[122] In both cases, as also in 4,25 and 10,11-12, Mark shifted the participial construction to a relative clause.[123] That Mark's saying is more tolerant than the Q saying corresponds to a more general redactional tendency in the overlap texts.[124]

The image half of the Q saying, with the antithesis of gathering and scattering, has no parallel in Mark. The overlap text is thus restricted to Q 11,23a, a saying that shows all the characteristics of an independent aphorism: "Aphorisms have a degree of ambiguity which makes it possible to use them in various contexts with various meanings."[125] The parallel from Cicero's *Pro Q. Ligario* is referred to by Fleddermann.[126] It is less understandable that the same note refers to Mark 3,31-35 as "a Marcan parallel."

§ 17. On Scandal

There can be no dispute on the Q origin of Matt 18,7 / Luke 17,1b, in Fleddermann's reconstruction: ἀνάγκη ἐστιν **τὰ σκάνδαλα ἐλθεῖν, πλὴν οὐαὶ** τῷ ἀνθρώπῳ **δι᾽ οὗ ἔρχεται**.[127] I agree with Fleddermann about the use of Mark 9,42a in Matt 18,6a (ὃς δ᾽ ἂν σκανδαλίσῃ ἕνα τῶν μικρῶν τούτων τῶν πιστευόντων εἰς ἐμέ) and in Luke 17,2b (ἢ ἵνα σκανδαλίσῃ τῶν μικρῶν τούτων ἕνα). But in his opinion I "cut too deeply"

---

122. HF, 169, 213, 216 (conclusion, § § 15-16). Cf. 61 (§ 3), 120, 124 (§ 10).

123. HF, 88 n. 68 (Mark 4,25); 155 n. 10 (Mark 9,37); 159 n. 23 (Mark 9,40); 173 n. 9 (Mark 10,11-12).

124. HF, 209: Mark eliminates exaggerations. Cf. Mark 4,32; 6,8; 8,34; 9,40. See also Mark 10,31 (176); 11,24 (184). Mark 9,40 is a constant reference: HF 60 (§ 3), 122, 140 n. 23, 159 (§ 16), 176 n. 28, 184 n. 58, 209.

125. Cf. D. E. AUNE, "Oral Tradition and the Aphorisms of Jesus," in H. WANSBROUGH (ed.), *Jesus and the Oral Gospel Tradition* (JSNT SS, 64), Sheffield, 1991, pp. 211-265, here 241. On Mark 9,40, see pp. 237, 246 (no. 25), 250 (no. 75).

126. HF, 159 n. 22. I quote the passage: "Valeat tua vox illa, quae vicit. Te enim dicere audiebamus nos omnes adversarios putare, nisi qui nobiscum essent; te omnes, qui contra te non essent, tuos."

127. Common words are printed in bold. Contrast Fleddermann's reconstruction in "Discipleship Discourse" (1981), pp. 67-69: ἀνένδεκτον ... μή, (οὐαὶ) δέ, om. τῷ ἀνθρώπῳ (cf. Luke 17,1b). See also n. 129.

by attributing all of Luke 17,2 to the Lucan redaction of Mark 9,42.[128] I reproduce here his reconstruction of Q in parallel with the text of Mark:

Q 17,2a   Mk 9,42b
λυσιτελεῖ αὐτῷ   καλόν ἐστιν αὐτῷ μᾶλλον
εἰ περίκειται μύλος ὀνικὸς
περὶ τὸν τράχηλον αὐτοῦ
καὶ βέβληται εἰς τὴν θάλασσαν.

The text of Matt 18,6b can be left out of the picture because the reconstructed Q offers nothing that is not in Mark and could explain Matthew's redaction.[129] The only difference between Q and Mark concerns the *Tobspruch* (first line): Matthew and Luke agree in having a finite verb, συμφέρει (cf. Matt 5,29.30) and λυσιτελεῖ. Regarding Luke's λυσιτελεῖ Fleddermann refers to J. Schlosser but drops the qualification: "obwohl es, an und für sich, ein von Lk ausgesuchtes, gut griechisches Wort sein könnte."[130]

If Q did not contain Luke 17,2, then no overlap exists. In response to Fleddermann's objections it can be observed that (1) the coincidence of Matthew's and Luke's combining the woe (Q) and the millstone (Mark) has nothing extraordinary: both are sayings on scandal; (2) the suggestion that frightening punishments fit more comfortably in Q seems to neglect the association of Mark 9,42 with 9,43.45.47-48.[131]

---

128. HF, 160 (and n. 24). See now also my "The Minor Agreements and Q," pp. 57-59 (with reply to J. Schlosser, 1983).

129. Note the use of Mark's βέβληται εἰς in Fleddermann's reconstruction of Q (diff. Matt καταποντισθῇ ἐν and Luke ἔρριπται ἐν). Contrast his 1981 reconstruction: ἔρριπται and a different word order: μύλος ὀνικὸς περίκειται.

130. "Lk 17,2," here 77. The "parallel" in Luke 9,33 (HF, 161) is not the comparative καλόν ἐστιν (μᾶλλον) of the *Tobspruch* and is scarcely relevant in this discussion.

131. In reply to HF, 160-161. Still less convincing is his association of the kind of punishment with Q 17,6: "someone or something ... forcibly removed to the sea" (161). "Planting" (a tree in the sea) in Q connotes a beneficial act, whereas "throwing" in Mark connotes a destructive act (cf. GUNDRY, *Mark*, p. 652): Mark 11,23 βλήθητι εἰς τὴν θάλασσαν (cf. 9,42 βέβληται εἰς τὴν θάλασσαν). Contrast Luke 17,6 ἔρριπται ἐν τῇ θαλάσσῃ, diff. Fleddermann's conjecturally reconstructed Q (cf. above, n. 129). – For authors who reject inclusion in Q, see KLOPPENBORG, *Q Parallels*, p. 182: "Q 17:2. Not in Q." Add: BOISMARD 1972, p. 299; LAUFEN, p. 87; NOLLAND II, p. 637.

Mark 14,21 is cited in HF, 164-166, as Mark's "second overlap" with the Scandal Saying in Q (§ 17a). Cf. E. Wendling (*Entstehung*, 1908, pp. 168-169), W. Schmithals (*Markus*, 1979, p. 611, cf. 432-433); but this overlap is mentioned neither in Laufen's list nor in Kloppenborg's *Q Parallels*. The last element of Mark 14,21 (Matt 26,24), καλὸν (ἦν) αὐτῷ εἰ οὐκ ἐγεννήθη ὁ ἄνθρωπος ἐκεῖνος, is dropped out in Luke 22,22, but the scheme in Mark 14,21 and Luke 17,1b-2 is identical: the crime is set out as inevitable (it is necessary, as it is written) – woe to him – it would be better for him (to be killed, not to be born). Since the *Tobspruch* is found in Mark only in 14,21 and 9,42 (and vv. 43.45.47), Luke's combination

§ 18. On Salt

As usual, the first step is a reconstruction of the Q text from Matthew and Luke. It is only in a second phase that the reconstructed Q text will be compared with Mark. In the case of the Salt Saying, word statistics indicate that οὖν and καί in Q 14,34 were added by Luke,[132] but without documentation it is simply stated that "Luke preserves the Q introduction of the saying" (καλὸν τὸ ἅλας) and the verb ἀρτυσθήσεται "undoubtedly reflects Q" because this verb is "rare in the NT."[133] In this first phase the text of Q is reconstructed from Luke without examining the possibility that Luke's **καλὸν** τὸ ἅλας and **ἀρτυσ**θήσεται may be due to the influence of Mark 9,50.[134] In the second phase the comparison of the reconstructed Q text and Mark will inevitably lead to the conclusion that καλὸν τὸ ἅλας and the verb ἀρτύω in Mark 9,50 come from Q.

§ 19. On Divorce

I agree with Fleddermann that "Luke basically preserves the Q form of the saying."[135] The phrase ἀπὸ ἀνδρός is probably a Lucan addition, although I have some reservation about the argument based on Lucan usage. None of the two indications is really convincing. "Luke uses ἀπό with ἀπολύω in Acts 15,33," but the good wishes of the brethren (ἀπελύθησαν μετ᾽ εἰρήνης ἀπὸ τῶν ἀδελφῶν) is not a very close parallel to the woman divorced "from her husband;" and "ἀνήρ is very common in Luke," but the occurrences show a different proportion if, more specifically, ἀνήρ = husband is considered: Luke 1,27.34; 2,36 and 16,18.[136] I agree about the phrase "and marries another" which most probably was found in Q, though in contrast to Fleddermann ("ἕτερος is a good Q word") I would not exclude that ἑτέραν (for ἄλλην) is possibly Lucan.[137]

of the parallel to Mark 9,42 with Q 17,1b may have been inspired by the word about the traitor. The likelihood of such associations is shown in the combination of Matt 26,24 and 18,6 in 1 Clem 46,8: εἶπεν γάρ· Οὐαὶ τῷ ἀνθρώπῳ ἐκείνῳ· καλὸν ἦν αὐτῷ, εἰ οὐκ ἐγεννήθη, ἢ ἕνα τῶν ἐκλεκτῶν μου σκανδαλίσαι· κρεῖττον ἦν αὐτῷ περιτεθῆναι μύλον καὶ καταποντισθῆναι εἰς τὴν θάλασσαν, ἢ ἕνα τῶν ἐκλεκτῶν μου διαστρέψαι.

132. HF, 167: cf. 91 n. 77 (Luke's use of οὖν); 167 n. 60 (Luke's use of δὲ καί).

133. HF, 167.

134. Cf. "Recent Developments," p. 51 (= 431).

135. HF, 172. See now my "The Divorce Saying in Q 16:18," in *Louvain Studies* 20 (1995) 201-218, esp. 212-218 ("Luke 16:18 Q"). – On CD 4,12–5,15 (cf. HF, 172 n. 2) see also "De echtscheidingslogia in de evangeliën," in *Academiae Analecta* (1995, forthcoming).

136. "Divorce Saying," p. 212 (in reply to D. Kosch, *Die eschatologische Tora*, 1988, p. 432).

137. Compare HF, 172 n. 7 ("ἕτερος probably should be restored in seven other Q texts") with "Divorce Saying," p. 217 n. 93: Q 7,19.32 "possibly" Q, but 14,19.20; 17,34.35 (and 19,20!) probably Lucan. On 11,16 LkR, see also HF, 45, 128 (Q ἕτεροι δέ).

§ 20. The First and the Last

Matt 19,30 (= Mark 10,31) and 20,16 (cf. Luke 13,30) is treated as a classic source doublet: "Matthew uses the Marcan and Q sayings as an *inclusio* to frame the parable of the Laborers in the Vineyard."[138] Although Matt 20,16 agrees with Luke 13,30 against Mark in initially placing "last" before "first," there is much hesitation about its origin in Q.[139] Matthew's second use of the saying can be his redactional adaptation in light of the preceding parable.[140] If Matt 20,16 (with the concluding οὕτως for καί) would represent the Q form of the saying (Fleddermann), then no less than nine differences are found in Luke 13,30, and the possibility of a *Wanderlogion* freely used by Luke is to be considered.[141] The fact that it concludes a section that formed a unit in Q does not prove its Q origin: Luke 13,24.26-27.28-29 are covered by consecutive parallels in Matt 7,13-14.22-23; 8,11-12, but not Luke 13,30.

§ 21. On Faith

"The change from a mulberry tree to a mountain is intelligible, but it is inconceivable that anyone would change a mountain to a mulberry tree."[142] This is the central point in Fleddermann's position on the Faith Saying: Luke 17,6 reflects Q, and Mark's version is secondary. Although many will agree with his reconstruction of Q (= Luke 17,6),[143] it is regrettable that he restricted the discussion to some minor variations.[144] No mention is made of the alternative position of those who defend the

---

Fleddermann's argument is not wholly consistent: on the one hand he stresses the interchangeability of ἕτερος and ἄλλος (HF, 173) and on the other he argues for "the Q phrase" in 11,16 in light of "the coordinated pair εἷς ... ἕτερος that crops up from time to time in Q" (45; and 128: "pops up").

138. HF, 175. Note that Mark 9,35 is treated as "a related saying" (176), "a redactional reworking of Mark 10,43-44" (140 n. 23).

139. References in Kloppenborg, *Q Parallels*, p. 156 ("Not in Q"). Add: Laufen, pp. 88-89; Sato, p. 10.

140. See the commentaries (e.g., J. Gnilka II, p. 181). On the meaning of Matt 20,16, see the types of interpretation noted by C. Hezser, *Lohnmetaphorik und Arbeitswelt in Mt 20,1-16*, pp. 253-258.

141. Cf. D. E. Aune, "Oral Tradition," pp. 238-239: "originally an independent saying" which is used to interpret other sayings.

142. HF, 181. "Mark switches to the mountain image" (*ibid.*) and "Matthew has taken the mountain from Mark" (179).

143. Cf. IQP, in *JBL* 110 (1991), p. 498. See also recent commentaries on Matthew (Gnilka 1988, Luz 1990, Davies-Allison 1991) and Luke (Fitzmyer 1985, p. 1142; Nolland 1993) and recent studies on Q (e.g., Kloppenborg 1995, p. 316).

144. HF, 179, in response to (Schulz and) Zmijewski: ἐὰν ἔχητε (see also Catchpole) and the future tenses in the apodosis (cf. Mark's ἔσται).

originality of the mountain-moving image.[145] I also miss a reference to Catchpole who reads ἐκριζώθητι without καὶ φυτεύθητι ἐν τῇ θα-λάσσῃ, the original Q saying "bringing together ... the proverbially tiny mustard seed and the extremely deep rooted sycamine tree."[146] This would mean that we not only have to reckon with "Matthew's assimilation of the Marcan and Q sayings to each other."[147] Then Luke's version too is possibly influenced by the mountain-moving saying in Mark:[148]

ἄρθητι   καὶ βλήθητι   εἰς τὴν θάλασσαν
ἐκριζώτητι (καὶ φυτεύθητι ἐν τῇ θαλάσσῃ).

§ 22. On Asking and Receiving

Granted that Mark is secondary to Q, does Mark reflect redactional Q? Response: the author of Q joined 11,9-13 to the Lord's Prayer (11,2-4) and Mark's interpretation (προσεύχεσθε) shows that he knows this context of the saying.[149] However, dependence on QR is made unnecessary by Fleddermann's own reference to R. A. Piper's study on the pre-Q collection in 11,9-13 and to the final saying in v. 13 on "asking" the heavenly Father.[150] Moreover, Fleddermann neglects Piper's introductory remarks on the original independence of Q 11,9-10.[151]

---

145. F. HAHN, "Jesu Wort vom bergeversetzenden Glauben," in *ZNW* 76 (1985) 149-169: "συκάμινος (ist) sekundär an die Stelle von ὄρος getreten" (p. 158); D. LÜHRMANN, *Markusevangelium*, 1987, p. 195: "Die Q-Überlieferung in der Fassung von Mt 17,20 ist die ursprüngliche (Lk, der die Verfluchung des Feigenbaums ausläßt, verwendet ihren Stoff einmal in dem Gleichnis Lk 13,6-9, zum anderen, trotz der differierenden Bezeichnung συκάμινος, in seiner Fassung des Wortes vom bergeversetzenden Glauben 17,6)." See also W. SCHMITHALS, *Markus*, 1979, p. 501; W. R. TELFORD, *The Barren Temple and the Withered Tree* (JSNT SS, 1), Sheffield, 1980, p. 103 (cf. p. 101, for the view that the saying in Luke 17,6 has been modified as a result of its association with the fig-tree story: B. Weiss, Holtzmann, Wellhausen, Loisy, Harnack, Taylor, and Schweizer; cf. HAHN, "Jesu Wort," p. 156 n. 24).

146. D. R. CATCHPOLE, "The Centurion's Faith and Its Function in Q," in *The Four Gospels 1992*, pp. 517-540, here 517; reprinted in *The Quest*, p. 280.

147. HF, 179 (cf. above, nn. 142, 144).

148. On the oddity of Luke's version, see e.g. Fitzmyer's comment, p. 1144: "Two figures are obviously mixed here, 'being planted' and 'in the sea.' This is an inconsistency that does not bother Luke. In the earlier tradition it was probably a mountain that was thrown into a sea, which would be intelligible. But now a mulberry tree being 'planted' in the sea is strange, to say the least." See also HAHN, "Jesu Wort," p. 158: "So gut also das Motiv vom 'Sich-Werfen (bzw. Geworfenwerden) ins Meer' zu ὄρος paßt, so wenig paßt die Anschauung vom 'Sich-Einpflanzen ins Meer' zu συκάμινος. Hier liegt offensichtlich eine Parallelbildung zu ἄρθητι καὶ βλήθητι εἰς τὴν θάλασσαν vor, was als Argument gegen die Ursprünglichkeit der Lukasfassung gar nicht genügend beachtet wird."

149. HF, 184. See also 211: "By applying the saying to prayer Mark shows that he knows the Q context of the saying."

150. HF, 183. Cf. R. A. PIPER, *Wisdom in the Q-Tradition*, p. 19.

151. *Wisdom*, p. 16. Cf. KLOPPENBORG, *Formation*, p. 204: "vv. 9-10 and vv. 11-13 [probably] represent two originally independent traditions;" SCHÜRMANN, *Lukasevangelium*

His view on the proverb which "uses three metaphors from daily life to show that effort always attains its end" can be confronted with Catchpole's approach:[152]

> If the context presumed by v. 10 were secular, then it would be necessary to say that as a generalization (πᾶς ...) all its three parts are untrue. It is not generally true in the world at large that all asking, seeking and knocking proves successful. So a secular context can be eliminated. By a shift of main verbal form from present indicative to future passive (ἀνοιγήσεται), v. 10c contains the potential to remove all three parts of the saying away from a secular context into the context where God is at work. Then it is a religious statement about God and his reaction to human asking, seeking and knocking.

If Q 11,10-11 came to Mark in the context of the Jesus tradition, it was most probably not as secular wisdom but as "auf das Geschehen zwischen Mensch und Gott bezogen."[153]

§ 23. FIRST PLACES

The title of § 23 seems to be deliberately provocative. The phrase "first places at dinners" is found in the saying of Mark (12,39; par. Luke 20,46 and Matt 23,6) but not in Luke 11,43, and it is usually not considered to be part of the Q saying.[154] In Fleddermann's reconstruction of Q the phrase τὴν πρωτοκλισίαν ἐν τοῖς δείπνοις, "the first seat at the feasts" (NRSV: "the place of honor at banquets"), is the first of three objects of φιλεῖτε: "The phrase is found in Matthew but not in Luke. It probably stood in Q, for if Matthew had borrowed it from Mark it would appear in the plural. Luke gives a fuller treatment of the first seat in Luke 14,7-14 so he passes over it here."[155] Yet already before ch.

II/1, 221: "sowohl das Grundwort 11,9f wie das Zusatzwort 11,11ff [sind] je isoliert tradiert aus der Verkündigungssituation Jesu und der Gemeinde verständlich zu machen."

152. *Quest*, p. 219. One can make this observation without adopting Catchpole's general theory on the context in Q.

153. D. ZELLER, *Mahnsprüche*, p. 129.

154. See, e.g., the Q reconstructions by Polag, Schulz, Schenk and recent commentaries on Luke (Schürmann, II/1, p. 315 n. 77; Nolland, II, p. 666). The ascription to Q of Q 11,43 is not uncontested: cf. E. HAENCHEN, "Matthäus 23" (1951), 1965, p. 33; P. HOFFMANN, *Studien*, p. 170 n. 49; L. E. VAAGE, *Galilean Upstarts*, 1994, pp. 135-136. The evidence of Matthew-Luke agreements against Mark is regarded as unsatisfactory: (1) the verb φιλοῦσιν (Matt 23,6) / ἀγαπᾶτε (Luke 11,43), φιλούντων (Luke 20,46b: Q reminiscence), diff. Mark 12,38 θελόντων (= Luke 20,46a); (2) the order πρωτο-καθεδρίαν/ας, ἀσπασμούς, diff. Mark (the reverse). A critical note on Q 11,43 is lacking in Kloppenborg's *Q Parallels*, p. 112.

155. HF, 187. Cf. "Warning" (1982), p. 58. – Note the minor change in the reconstruction of Q: the vocative Φαρισαῖοι (cf. Matt 23,13-29) for τοῖς Φαρισαίοις (Luke 11,43) in 1982.

14 Luke shows special interest in meal-scenes, and despite his fuller treatment in 14,7-14 he will take over Mark's phrase in 20,46. The singular in Matthew (for the plural in Mark) may be due to influence of Q: φιλεῖτε τὴν πρωτοκαθεδρίαν ... καὶ τοὺς ἀσπασμοὺς... (to be followed with καὶ καλεῖσθαι... in Matt 23,7b). Πρωτοκλισίας (third in Mark 12,38-39, in plural and anarthrous) comes first and takes the place of τὴν πρωτοκαθεδρίαν in Q: φιλοῦσιν τὴν πρωτοκλισίαν...[156]

§ 24. On Confessing

The inclusion in Q is accepted by most authors. The principal indication for Q is the agreement in Matt 10,19; Luke 12,11: μὴ μεριμνήσητε πῶς ἢ τί (diff. Mark 13,11 μὴ προμεριμνᾶτε τί). Luke 12,12 is usually identified as the second half of the saying, though the final phrase ἃ δεῖ εἰπεῖν can either be dropped as Lucan (Schulz, Sato) or replaced with τί εἴπητε (Polag). Fleddermann's personal option is to take as second half Matt 10,19b (with εἴπητε for the «Marcan» λαλήσητε), and not Luke 12,12: "Luke probably introduced the Holy Spirit into the Q saying under the influence of Mark."[157]

Fleddermann's acceptance of Marcan influence in Q 12,12 invites us to reconsider his position on the Q text in 12,11: ὅταν δὲ εἰσφέρωσιν ὑμᾶς ἐπὶ τὰς συναγωγάς... (contrast Matthew's παραδῶσιν ὑμᾶς: "he follows Mark"). Can the influence of Mark be excluded in Luke 12,11? Luke's use of ἀπολογεῖσθαι in 12,11 and 21,14 (not elsewhere in the gospels)[158] is not the only contact between the two parallels to Mark 13,11. If Luke has read Mark 13,11 (καὶ ὅταν ἄγωσιν ὑμᾶς παραδιδόντες) in connection with v. 9, the prepositional phrase ἐπὶ τὰς συναγωγάς and its prolongation καὶ τὰς ἀρχὰς καὶ τὰς ἐξουσίας can be Lucan rewriting of Mark 13,9 (par. Luke 21,12 παραδιδόντες εἰς τὰς συναγωγάς...). One cannot simply say that "Luke's ἐπὶ τὰς συναγωγάς poses no problems because the noun is attested in Q (Q 11,43)."[159] Neither can the verb εἰσφέρωσιν be assigned to Q because Luke usually

156. Compare R. H. GUNDRY, Mark, p. 725, in reply to Fleddermann's "Warning." See also ibid. his critical observations on the greater originality of Q (HF, 188: "a nice climax," θέλω with noun object).

157. HF, 192. See also J. NOLLAND, Luke II, p. 680: "Luke appears to have rewritten 12:12 along the general lines of Mark 13:11c, but with his own wording." Contrast S. SCHULZ, Q, p. 442: "Lk (zeigt) in 12,11f keine Einflüsse der Mk-Fassung."

158. Cf. HF, 192. Contrast Nolland's rather strange observation that the pairing of the verbs in Luke 12,11 has a counterpart in 21,15 (ἀντιστῆναι καὶ ἀντειπεῖν) and points to the same second source (Luke, p. 680).

159. HF, 192. Luke has adopted both Q 11,43 and its overlap in Mark 12,39 (Luke 20,46). Cf. § 23.

prefers ἄγω or one of its compounds.[160] The verb εἰσφέρω in this passage probably has a particular nuance which is not well rendered in neutral translations ("lead" or "bring"): "Wenn sie euch (mit Gewalt) in die Synagogen *schleppen*."[161] If ὅταν δέ in Matt 10,19 is from Mark's καὶ ὅταν, the same can be said of ὅταν δέ in Luke 12,11. That Mark's ὅταν-clause would presuppose a more original context of the saying in Q 12,2-12 is, to say the very least, a reversible suggestion.[162] The (imperfect) agreement of order between Matt 10,26-27.28-31.32-33.(12,32).*19-20* and Luke 12,2-3.4-7.8-9.(10).*11-12* is rightly neglected by Fleddermann. The "Marcan" section Matt 10,17-22 is the context of the saying in Matthew, and the text of Mark 13,(9.)11 is also the first source of Luke 12,11-12. A reconstruction of the wording of the Q text in this case is a more arduous task than Fleddermann seems to realize.

§ 25. FAMILY DIVISION

The reconstruction of Q which here presents "enormous difficulties" is carefully discussed in a treatment that is typical of Fleddermann's approach, with due attention to the evangelists' usage and possible Q parallels. Unfortunately, recent studies on this passage are not at all referred to in § 25.[163] Thus, on the introductory verses in Luke 12,49-50: "Luke shows that he knows Matthew's clause in Luke 12,49 (πῦρ ἦλθον βαλεῖν ἐπὶ τὴν γῆν)."[164] Fleddermann may be right, but the reader should know that the Q origin of 12,49 has its defenders.[165] One can find an occasional cryptic allusion to the position of other scholars: "It might seem that Luke 12,52 is the original Q wording,"[166] but neither in the section on Mark 13,12 nor in the note on Th 16 there is any further allusion. In fact, scholarly opinion is divided, perhaps δύο ἐπὶ τρισίν, between alternative reconstructions of Q: either Matt 10,36

160. HF, 191-192. See the references in his n. 1.
161. *EWNT* 1.975 (H. Balz). Cf. K. WEISS, art. εἰσφέρω, in *TWNT* 9.66-67: "werden ... *geschleppt*" (*TDNT*: "will be *haled*"); EÜ: "Wenn man euch vor die Gerichte der Synagogen ... schleppt."
162. Cf. above, n. 116: on a possibly Lucan location of the saying in 12,11-12 (A. Y. Collins). On Lucan redaction, cf. P. HOFFMANN, *Tradition*, 1995, p. 232 n. 59: "Vielleicht hat sogar er (Lk) erst die Dublette geschaffen."
163. Cf. P. SELLEW, "Reconstruction of Q 12:33-59," in *SBL 1987 Seminar Papers*, pp. 617-668, esp. 645-653 ("Q 12:49-53"); S. J. PATTERSON, "Fire and Dissension. Ipsissima Vox Jesu in Q 12:49,51-53?" in *Forum* 5/2 (1989) 121-139. See also below, nn. 165, 167.
164. HF, 196; cf. 195, 199.
165. See C.-P. MÄRZ, "'Feuer auf die Erde zu werfen, bin ich gekommen...' Zum Verständnis und zur Entstehung von Lk 12,49" (1985), in *"... laßt eure Lampen brennen!"* (ErfTS, 20), Leipzig, 1991, pp. 9-31, esp. 9-11.
166. HF, 196.

and the three phrases of v. 35 (son, daughter, daughter-in-law) in Q 12,53 (Fleddermann) or Luke 12,52 and the doubling of the three pairs of v. 53 in Q and assimilation to Mic 7,6 in Matthew (Polag, Sellew, *et al.*).[167]

That, in this last hypothesis, the underlying Micah text is less visible in the Q saying has some weight in the study of the overlap in Mark 13,12 (with ἐπαναστήσονται from Mic 7,6 LXX). Fleddermann emphasizes that "Mark has drawn two overlap texts together into a cluster."[168] Whether the fact that "a Marcan παραδίδωμι" links Mark 13,11 and 12 has some significance for the Mark-Q relationship may be doubtful. But is it not simply irrelevant in this regard to speak of "the *clustering* of five sayings"[169] in Mark 13? The five sayings are dispersed in the Eschatological Discourse (13,11.12.21.31.35) and it is quite natural that more Mark-Q overlaps are found in the sayings material of ch. 13 than in Marcan narratives.

§ 26. RUMORS ON THE COMING

"Except for the original connective, Matthew preserves the Q"[170] (cf. Schulz, Polag, Schenk, *et al.*). In two details some authors prefer the Lucan parallel: ἐροῦσιν for ἐὰν εἴπωσιν and διώξητε for πιστεύσητε (cf. Laufen, Sato, Nolland, *et al.*). More names can be added for the second case (e.g., Marshall, Jacobson, Catchpole). Fleddermann's argument is rather weak: "Matthew had no reason to avoid (the verb διώκω)." But on the one hand διώκω in the sense "to run after, pursue" is not the most common use of the verb, and on the other Matthew's μὴ πιστεύσητε (24,26; cf. 24,23) is probably influenced by μὴ πιστεύετε in Mark 13,21.[171]

Two observations are cited to show that Mark is secondary. The same observations are repeated as evidence for Marcan redaction: Mark makes the saying explicit by adding "the Christ" and Mark also generalizes the saying with "here" and "there." Not a few scholars can agree that the Q form of the saying is more original than the saying in Mark 13,21, but they would question Fleddermann's conclusion that "Mark composes (his) discourse material with Q in front of him."[172]

---

167. See also A. D. JACOBSON, "Divided Families and Christian Origins," in R. A. PIPER (ed.), *The Gospel Behind the Gospels*, pp. 361-380, esp. 364-367.

168. HF, 199, 208, 212, 214.

169. HF, 208 (emphasis mine).

170. HF, 200. The exception is the Matthean οὖν (for καί in Luke).

171. Cf. J. LAMBRECHT, "Logia-Quellen," p. 341: "Denn es ist sehr gut möglich, dass Matthäus diesen Q^mt-Vers Mk 13,21 oder Mt 24,24 anpasste (z.B. was die ἐάν-Konstruktion und μὴ πιστεύσητε betrifft)." See also *Redaktion*, p. 103.

172. HF, 208.

§ 27. Jesus' Words

The title of § 27 refers to Mark 13,31. The saying Q 16,17, which is presented as the overlap text,[173] focuses on the Law. Fleddermann notes that the three sayings on the Law in 16,16-18 were originally independent of each other and independent also of the surrounding context in Luke. He has no further comment on the status of Q 16,17 in Q or Q redactional. Kloppenborg's theory of a nomocentric redaction of Q, with Q 16,17 as a third-stage addition together with 11,42c and 4,1-13,[174] is not even alluded to.

Fleddermann has reconstructed the Q text from Luke 16,17 with ἰῶτα ἓν ἤ and ἀπὸ (τοῦ νόμου) from Matt 5,18. His reconstruction is strictly identical with Lambrecht's and references for confirmation and documentation are mainly to Lambrecht's *Redaktion*.[175] Fleddermann observes in particular, on Matthew's verb παρέλθῃ (for πεσεῖν in Luke): "Matthew repeated the verb to bring the saying closer to Matt 24,34-35. In repeating the verb he also shifted its meaning."[176] But see Lambrecht's observation: "Es will uns scheinen, ... dass Matthäus dieses ... zweite παρέλθῃ *aus Mk 13,31* hereinholte,"[177] and on the shift of meaning ("auf Kosten einer geringen Bedeutungsänderung"): "*genau wie Mk 13,30b*: ἕως ἂν πάντα γένηται nicht mehr 'geschehen, ereignen,' sondern 'in Erfüllung gehen' bedeutet."[178] Since Fleddermann did not accept the second stage of Lambrecht's hypothesis ("Der Q^mk-Text")[179] he can have here no objection against Matthew's dependence on Mark.

§ 28. Uncertainty of the Hour

"By showing knowledge of the Householder, Mark shows knowledge of redactional Q." The Householder, i.e. the parable of the Thief (Q 12,39) and its application (12,40), was proposed by Fleddermann in

---

173. Mark 13,31; Q 16,17 is usually not included in lists of overlap texts (Van Dulmen, Polag, Laufen, Kloppenborg). Cf. above, n. 19, and my "Recent Developments," p. 53 (= 433).

174. J. S. KLOPPENBORG, "Nomos and Ethos in Q," in J. E. GOEHRING, *et al.* (eds.), *Gospel Origins & Christian Beginnings*. FS J. M. Robinson, Sonoma, CA, 1990, pp. 35-48, spec. 46.

175. *Redaktion*, pp. 213-223, on Mark 13,31: "Der Q-Text."

176. HF, 204, with reference to Lambrecht's *Redaktion*, pp. 218-219.

177. *Redaktion*, p. 219 (emphasis mine). See also *ibid.*: "ein ursprüngliches πεσεῖν..., das Matthäus under Einfluss von Mk 13,30-31 veränderte."

178. *Ibid.*; cf. p. 218: παρέρχεσθαι in Matt 5,18 first "vorbeigehen" and then "ausfallen, wegfallen."

179. There are no references to *Redaktion*, pp. 224-226; "Logia-Quellen," pp. 346-348.

1986 as Q's elaborate introduction to the parable of the Servant Left in Charge (Q 12,42b-46). He now repeats his view that the Householder is "a Q redactional formulation."[180]

Here again, more recent studies and alternative interpretations are not taken into consideration. I quote Kloppenborg (1987):[181]

> In view of the inconsistency in logic between v. 39 and v. 40 and the fact that the parable occurs elsewhere without the Son of Man saying, we must conclude that the Son of Man saying was a secondary interpretation of the parable. It must be assumed, however, that 12:40 was already attached to 12:39 prior to its association with the following materials since the basis of that association is undoubtedly the statement "You do not know in what hour (or day) the Son of Man (or Lord) is coming" (12:40,46).

On the one hand, Fleddermann emphasizes that, in contrast to Mark 13,35, the Q saying is self-contained. On the other, however, he also stresses that it forms part of the parable of the Householder and is not an independent statement: it serves to make explicit the identification of the returning Lord (12,46a) with the Son of Man. If it is true that this identification is not really needed "since Q centers so much attention on the Son of Man," the same can be said of ὁ κύριος τῆς οἰκίας in Mark 13,35 in the light of the coming of the Son of Man in 13,26.

---

180. HF, 207-208 (and 211: "The author of Q composed the Householder..."). Cf. "The Householder and the Servant Left in Charge" (1986).

181. *Formation*, pp. 149-150. Kloppenborg emphasizes the association of the parable with Q 12,33-34. Those who accept Luke 12,35-38 as part of Q can propose 12,40 as the conclusion of these verses: "Der Textbestand scheint für die ... Möglichkeit zu sprechen [daß das Diebesgleichnis nachträglich in einen Lk 12,35-38.40 entsprechenden Zusammenhang eingebracht worden wäre]. Denn der Anschluß mit καὶ ὑμεῖς (Lk 12,40) ... läßt sich zwanglos nur als Hinordnung von 12,40 auf 12,35-38 verständlich machen... Das Diebesgleichnis erscheint so in der Tat wie ein zwischengeschalteter Kontrasttext. ... Das ursprünglich isoliert weitergegebene Diebesgleichnis ist erst sekundär in den Zusammenhang eingebracht und dabei mit Lk 12,40 verknüpft worden". Cf. C.-P. MÄRZ, "Das Gleichnis vom Dieb," in *The Four Gospels 1992*, pp. 642-643. Compare also H. SCHÜRMANN: "Q 12:40 ... concludes the saying composition in Q/Luke 12:35-39, which Matthew must have also read in some other form. ... the Son of Man saying would have earlier functioned as a conclusion – a conclusion that thus would have been added prior to the redaction that added Q 12:42-46(47-48)" ("Beobachtungen zum Menschensohn-Titel," ET, pp. 87-88). — I can understand Fleddermann's choice not to include Luke 12,35-38 in his reconstruction of Q. But the question is debated (cf. KLOPPENBORG, *Q Parallels*, p. 136: S43), and its discussion can hardly be avoided by authors who make Mark 13,35 dependent on Q 12,39-40.

RESULTS AND IMPLICATIONS

A substantial part of Fleddermann's study is devoted to the reconstruction of Q texts. The reconstructions of ten Q sayings he published before are here reprinted practically without changes: Q 3,16-17; 10,16; 11, 23.43; 12,8-9.40; 13,18-19; 14,27.34-35a; 17,1b-2. There is only a minor change in Q 11,43, and more significant changes appear in 17,1b-2.[182] In four annotations I expressed reservation with regard to the inclusion in Q of the Matthew-Luke counterpart of the saying or part of it:

§ 3. Mark 3,27:	Matt 12,29	Luke 11,21-22
§ 13. Mark 8,35:	Matt 10,39	Luke 17,33
§ 17. Mark 9,42:	Matt 18,6	Luke 17,2
§ 20. Mark 10,31:	Matt 20,16	Luke 13,30

Only in a few instances is the wording of the saying strictly identical or almost identical in Matthew and Luke: Q 7,27 (+ ἐγώ MtR); 10,2 (ἐργάτας / ἐκβάλῃ LkR); 11,10 (reading ἀνοιγήσεται in Luke); 11,23; 12,31b (πάντα om. LkR); 12,40 (+ διὰ τοῦτο MtR, ὥρᾳ / οὐ δοκεῖτε LkR). Each paragraph starts with a comparative study of the two versions in Matthew and Luke. Fleddermann declares in his conclusion: "For obvious methodological reasons, I have not used Mark to reconstruct the original text of Q."[183] One can only express approval: the exclusion of Mark at this stage is a methodologically clean procedure and a significant departure from Lambrecht's method.[184] However, as a consequence of this exclusion of Mark in the reconstruction of Q, Fleddermann tends to neglect possible influences of Mark upon the Matthean and Lucan redactions of the parallel saying in Q. To cite an example, I could refer to the double question in Luke 13,18 (cf. Mark 4,30). Let us take here another example. Fleddermann's comparative study of Matt 5,13 and Luke 14,34-35a, without using Mark, leads to the reconstruction of Q, and then this hypothetical Q text is taken for granted: "We can now compare the Q saying with Mark."[185] That Luke's καλὸν τὸ ἅλας

---

182. Cf. above, nn. 127, 129, and 155.

183. HF, 215-216.

184. See, for instance, his "Q-Influence," p. 282 (on Mark 8,34): "It is not a priori excluded that αἴρω (and not λαμβάνω) stood in Q, and we will be able to use Mark's ἀπαρνησάσθω in the reconstruction of Q's Ashamed-of saying" (cf. above, n. 108); p. 285 (on Mark 8,35): "Mark's ἕνεκεν ἐμοῦ testifies to the presence of this expression already in Q (cf. Mt 10,39)." Cf. "The Great Commandment," p. 83: "we presume that Mark has known Q, and ... it it possible that some features of Q have been preserved only in Mark."

185. HF, 167. Cf. above, p. 288 (§ 18).

could depend on καλὸν τὸ ἅλας in Mark 9,50 is not mentioned, not as a suggestion made by other scholars and not even as a theoretical possibility. One has the impression that in such a case the reconstruction of the Q text anticipates Marcan dependence on Q. This is even more so in the case of conjecturally reconstructed wording of Q that happens to be the verb used by Mark (βέβληται in 9,42).[186]

As one of his findings Fleddermann proposes in the conclusion that five individual Marcan sayings reflect redactional Q elements.[187] But, as indicated above, of these five sayings in Mark (1,2; 8,12; 8,34; 11,24; 13,35; cf. §§ 1, 11, 12, 22, 28), none has been proved to depend on redactional Q. The argument of the clustering of overlap texts in Mark is scarcely more convincing. In one instance of a "small cluster" where not a few scholars accept that the sequence of the two sayings comes from Q (Mark 8,34.35), the case is dismissed by Fleddermann: "Since Matthew and Luke both moved the saying (Losing one's life) to a new context, its original position in Q can no longer be recovered."[188] It is more damaging for the thesis of Marcan dependence on "the whole Q document" that, throughout Mark and within each of the clusters, the order of arrangements differs from the order of the sayings in Q. (See the table of parallels on p. 299.)[189] I may perhaps recall my comment on Fleddermann's first contribution, on the four Q sayings in the Discipleship Discourse (1981): "no sequence [in Q] can be detected in the four sayings."[190]

Fleddermann's argument for Mark's use of Q will be read with interest by all critics who propose explanations of the overlap texts in Mark on the basis of traditional sayings identical with or similar to the sayings in Q. Observations on Marcan redaction are to some extent common ground. But not all readers will be happy with the alternative to explain Mark's text either by oral tradition or by "final Q," i.e., the complete Q document Mark had in front of him. In Fleddermann's approach, Mark can no longer be used to study the pre-history of Q and, in the absence of external control, he is extremely critical of reconstructed "earlier stages of Q." A saying like Q 3,16 where he distinguishes between pre-Q (ἐν πυρί) and QR is an exceptional case. The section on Fearless Confessing (Q 12,2-12) is said to be "a composite made of various sayings," but neither for

---

186. HF, 162. Cf. above, p. 287.
187. HF, 211.
188. HF, 143 n. 35. Cf. above, p. 284 (§ 13).
189. The "clusters" are marked with vertical lines.
190. Cf. above, n. 20.

12,8-9.10.11-12 nor for 12,2 is an earlier stage of composition taken into consideration. Special attention is given to the Beelzebul Controversy and the Mission Discourse: "we can positively rule out the oral tradition as Mark's source in the two longest overlap texts."[191] Once more, Fleddermann's alternative is either oral tradition or Q redactional. But in the case of Q 11,14-26 the overlap verses in Mark 3 can be restricted to 11,15.17b-18a. In the Mission Discourse too pre-Q is a more workable hypothesis than the oral tradition – QR alternative.

MARK-Q OVERLAPS

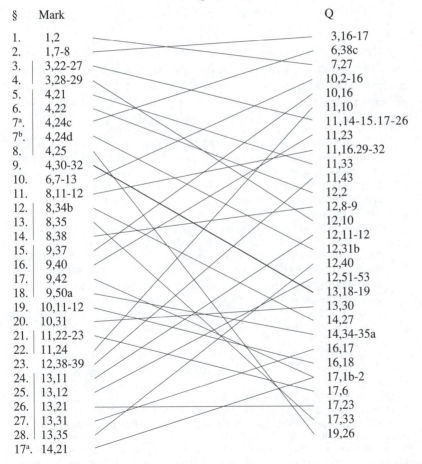

§	Mark		Q
1.	1,2		3,16-17
2.	1,7-8		6,38c
3.	3,22-27		7,27
4.	3,28-29		10,2-16
5.	4,21		10,16
6.	4,22		11,10
7ᵃ.	4,24c		11,14-15.17-26
7ᵇ.	4,24d		11,23
8.	4,25		11,16.29-32
9.	4,30-32		11,33
10.	6,7-13		11,43
11.	8,11-12		12,2
12.	8,34b		12,8-9
13.	8,35		12,10
14.	8,38		12,11-12
15.	9,37		12,31b
16.	9,40		12,40
17.	9,42		12,51-53
18.	9,50a		13,18-19
19.	10,11-12		13,30
20.	10,31		14,27
21.	11,22-23		14,34-35a
22.	11,24		16,17
23.	12,38-39		16,18
24.	13,11		17,1b-2
25.	13,12		17,6
26.	13,21		17,23
27.	13,31		17,33
28.	13,35		19,26
17ᵃ.	14,21		

191. HF, 94.

The first implication of Fleddermann's hypothesis is an adjustment of the diagram of the two-source theory (Q → Mark). His graphic presentation[192] can be slightly corrected as follows:

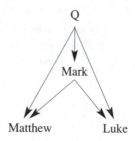

"Q stands at the beginning of the synoptic tradition as the first example of the gospel genre."[193] Fleddermann has not used Mark to reconstruct the original text of Q, but it is one of the implications that "this procedure now becomes legitimate" (sic).[194] Further reflection on this methodological issue is needed. I may refer here to I. Dunderberg's critical observations:[195]

> Q is normally reconstructed on the basis of the material shared *only* by Matthew and Luke. Furthermore, the existence of Q proves to be a good hypothesis, if a section common to all synoptics occurs in Matthew and Luke in a context that differs from Mark. To be sure, this results in a surprisingly great number of Mark–Q overlaps, for more than forty passages can be identified where Mark and Q share similar material.
>
> However, a rather odd line of reasoning would result, if these coincidences were explained by the Markan knowledge of Q. At first sight the similar divergences of Matthew and Luke from Mark give reason to believe that Mark is not their only common source. The deviations from Mark are then explained by means of Q. But as soon as Q is reconstructed, one should conclude that it was also Mark's source. So far as I see, this result simply contradicts the premise, which should consequently lead to a re-evaluation of the premise. That is to say, if Mark used Q as a source, Q can no longer

---

192. HF, 214.

193. HF, 215 (cf. 23): "The Sayings Gospel Q". See my note on "Q: From Source to Gospel," in *ETL* 71 (1995), fasc. 4.

194. HF, 216. Cf. above, nn. 183, 184.

195. I. DUNDERBERG, "Q and the Beginning of Mark," in *NTS* 41 (1995) 501-511; text quoted from pp. 502-503. (In the first paragraph, "more than forty passages" alludes to my cumulative list in "Recent Developments," p. 53 = 433.) Dunderberg's article is a critique of Catchpole and Lambrecht (*NTS*, 1992). The author is apparently unaware of similar reactions that appeared earlier in this year (cf. above, n. 14: Neirynck, Robinson). His section on Q 7,27 (pp. 508-511) can be compared with Tuckett's "Mark and Q" (above, pp. 268-269). In an additional note he refers to "a similar conclusion" in Tuckett's paper (p. 511 n. 42: "Only after having submitted this paper to *NTS* did I get access to C. Tuckett's important article.")

be reconstructed only on the basis of Matthew and Luke. Q should no longer even be defined as a sayings source used by *Matthew and Luke*.

The redefinition of the Q hypothesis as a source common to all synoptic gospels demands the re-examination of the whole synoptic question. The Markan dependence on Q immediately raises some methodological problems. Even if in a certain section Matthew and Luke seem to follow the Markan pattern, one could no longer conclude that those passages actually derive from Mark. At least two further explanations should be taken into account. In the first place, it is possible that both Matthew, Luke, and Mark draw directly on Q. Another possibility is that Matthew and Luke use Mark, but despite this fact the section may stem from Q – through Mark. On which methodological grounds could one choose between these alternatives? An extreme, but nevertheless logical consequence of the Markan knowledge of Q would be that *any synoptic passage* having triple attestation by Matthew, Mark, and Luke can derive from Q.

The alternatives in triple-tradition passages could be:

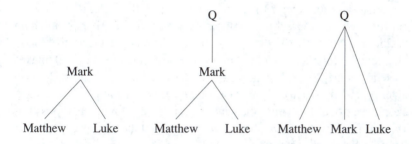

In the course of his study Fleddermann has indicated that the Gospel of Thomas showed widespread knowledge of the redactional text of all three Synoptics and he concludes that Thomas does not help us to reconstruct Q.[196] Fleddermann rightly emphasizes secondary developments in Thomas and dependence on redactional features in Matthew (seven times) and Luke (seven times). He also notes four contacts with Mark: 3,27 (Th 35); 4,25 (Th 41); 4,30-32 (Th 20); 10,31 (Th 4). I would not deny dependence on Mark,[197] although in Th 41 the evidence is not very

196. HF, 217-218; cf. 255-256 (Index: Gospel of Thomas). For the list of fourteen overlap texts with parallel in Thomas, see HF, 21, and 217 n. 15. The references in this note could be more precise: Mark 3,22-27, read: 3,27; 3,28-30, read: 3,28-29; 6,7-13, read: Q 10,2 and 10,7-9.

197. Cf. *Evangelica II*, pp. 725-732, 768-769. See also C. M. TUCKETT, "Q and Thomas," in *ETL* 67 (1991) 346-360, esp. 354-356: Q 11,52 (Th 39); 12,10 (Th 44). Contrast B. H. McLEAN, "On the Gospel of Thomas and Q," in R. A. PIPER (ed.), *The Gospel Behind the Gospels*, pp. 321-345 (cf. p. 322 n. 4: neither Tuckett 1991 nor S. J. Patterson 1993 are mentioned).

impressive (the absence of "all"). In Mark 3,27 (Th 35) and 10,31 (Th 4) the existence of an overlap text in Q is doubtful.

Though it is not resumed in the conclusions, in three instances he also examines the possibility of John's knowledge of Q. I summarize here his findings:[198]

§ 2. Mark 1,7-8: "John's saying [1,26-27] resembles the reconstructed Q form more than any other... Dependence on the synoptics could explain John's saying, but his saying makes most sense if he also had access to Q."

§ 13. Mark 8,35: "this saying [12,25] shows that John knew the redactional text of Matthew."

§ 15. Mark 9,37: "John's saying [13,20] depends either on Matthew's gospel or on Q."

In this last case, "Matthew reproduces the Q saying exactly." If Fleddermann's vocabulary analysis of John 13,20 par. Matt 10,40 is taken in combination with John 13,16; 15,20 par. Matt 10,24-25a (the δοῦλος-κύριος metaphor added to μαθητής-διδάσκαλος in Q) and with John 12,25 par. Matt 10,39, "Matthew or Q" can be changed to simply Matthew.[199] John's contact with (the reconstructed text of) Q makes sense in John 1,26-27, but the joint influence of Matt 3,11 in vv. 26a.27a (ἐγὼ βαπτίζω ἐν ὕδατι, ὁ ὀπίσω μου ἐρχόμενος) and of Mark 1,7b in the phrase about loosening the sandal strap (v. 27b) remains a possibility, also for Fleddermann: "when we allow for John's redaction, John's saying reflects the synoptic saying."[200]

---

198. HF, 38, 144-145, 156-157.

199. See my "John and the Synoptics: 1975-1990," pp. 21-25.

200. HF, 38, and n. 57. Regarding John 1,27b Fleddermann refers to the agreement with Acts 13,25 (ἄξιος, the singular ὑπόδημα), without further comment. Compare E. D. FREED, "Jn 1,19-27 in Light of Related Passages in John, the Synoptics, and Acts," in *The Four Gospels 1992*, pp. 1943-1961: Lucan variation in Acts (cf. Luke 3,16 = Mark 1,7b), and "John may well be influenced by this passage in Acts" (p. 1957). On John's dependence on Mark 1,7-8 in John 1,26-27, see in the same volume: É. TROCMÉ, "Jean et les Synoptiques. L'exemple de Jean 1,15-34," pp. 1935-1941; D.-A. KOCH, "Der Täufer als Zeuge des Offenbarers. Das Täuferbild von Joh 1,19-34 auf dem Hintergrund von Mk 1,2-11," pp. 1963-1984. For Trocmé, "ce n'est ni par une tradition orale isolée, ni par l'intermédiaire de Matthieu ou de Luc que l'auteur du IVème Évangile a connu le témoignage rendu par Jean-Baptiste à Jésus, mais bien par l'Évangile selon Marc, qui avait donné des propos du Précurseur une version abrégée et modifiée" (p. 1938). For Koch, "sämtliche Elemente des in Joh 1,26f verwendeten synoptischen Materials (sind) in Mk 1,7f vorgegeben, während dies für Mt 3,11 und Lk 3,16 jeweils nicht gilt" (p. 1978); "(die) z.T. durchaus bemerkenswerte Übereinstimmungen mit den Fassungen des Mt und Lk gegen Mk ... sind ... aus den Notwendigkeiten der eigenen Komposition des Verfassers erklärbar" (*ibid.*). See also my reference to C. K. Barrett (²1978, p. 175; in contrast to J. D. G. Dunn) in "John and the Synoptics: 1975-1990," p. 57.

Fleddermann's monograph on the overlap texts is the most complete study on the Mark-Q parallels that is available for the moment. His systematic treatment of all instances will prove to be a most useful tool for further investigation (see his Bibliography, pp. 221-238).[201] Additional references to recent secondary literature I mentioned in my annotations are collected in the Bibliographical Supplement (pp. 304-307).

---

201. For an alternative to Marcan dependence on Q, compare e.g. R.H. Gundry's statement on "contextually oriented redaction of the pre-Q tradition" (*Mark*, p. 435): "If we may suppose that Mark knows a pre-Q form of the saying [8,34] much like that in Luke 14:27..." (p. 434); "If we may suppose that Mark knows a pre-Q form of the saying in v. 35, a form much like that in Matt 10:39; Luke 17:33..." (p. 436; but see above § 13); "If we may yet again suppose that Mark knows a pre-Q form of the saying in v. 38, a form much like that in Matt 10:32-33 par. Luke 12:8-9..." (p. 438). Cf. p. 183: "On the whole, though it is likely that Mark knew sayings which Q incorporated, it is unlikely that he knew Q."

V

JOHN AND THE SYNOPTICS REVISITED

ETL 70 (1994) 319-340

25

ONCE MORE LUKE 24,12

A short "Additional Note" in *ETL* (1972)[1] has been followed by a series of studies on Lk 24,12, in *ETL* and elsewhere, over the years 1972-1992[2]. After a few indirect references in 1989 and 1990, Anton Dauer offered a formal reply to my approach in his contribution to *The Four Gospels 1992* and now again in an essay on the (in)authenticity of the Lukan verse. Such a persistent friend cannot be left without an answer, διά γε τὴν ἀναίδειαν αὐτοῦ[3].

1. *A. Dauer's Contributions on Lk 24,12*

In the Introduction to R. Schnackenburg's Commentary on John (1965) there is no mention of Lk 24,12 in the list of Johannine-Lukan parallels[4]. The case is referred to in 1970 when he treats the problem of the beloved disciple: "Of particular importance is Lk 24:12... It is true that this verse ... has long been considered to be a late interpolation based on Jn 20:3-10; but recent textual criticism has revised this opinion... I would consider a later scribal gloss based on Jn 20:3-10 to be very doubtful... A traditio-historical explanation seems to be more acceptable"[5]. A few years later, in October 1973, Robert Mahoney submitted at the Faculty of Würzburg a doctoral dissertation, written under Schnackenburg, which contains a chapter on "Luke 24,12 and the 'Western non-interpolations'"[6]. His conclusion is that "we cannot

1. F. NEIRYNCK, *The Uncorrected Historic Present in Lk. xxiv.12*, in *ETL* 48 (1972) 548-553 (= *Evangelica I*, 1982, 329-334); first published as "Additional Note" appended to *A Note on Reading Luke xxiv.12*, pp. 542-548, by John MUDDIMAN (in response to K.P.G. Curtis's interpolation theory in *JTS* 22, 1971, 512-515).

2. See the Bibliography compiled by G. Van Belle in *The Four Gospels 1992* (BETL, 100), with references to reprints and supplements in *Jean et les Synoptiques*, 1979 (no. 125: 114); *Evangelica I*, 1982 (no. 159: 79, 107, 112, 113, 121, 122); *Evangelica II*, 1991 (no. 262: 186); and no. 272 (cf. *infra*, n. 18). See the presentation by A. Dauer in his *Lk 24,12* (below n. 19), pp. 1706-1707: "Die Argumente Neiryncks".

3. Pace M. de Jonge who in 1992 (August 18) warned against overwriting about this topic.

4. *Joh I*, pp. 20-21.

5. *On the Origin of the Fourth Gospel*, in *Perspective* 11 (1970) 223-246, p. 237; = *Zur Herkunft des Johannesevangeliums*, in *BZ* 14 (1970) 1-23, pp. 16-17. See also *Der Jünger, den Jesus liebte*, in *EKK Vorarbeiten* 2 (1970) 97-117, pp. 103-104.

6. R. MAHONEY, *Two Disciples at the Tomb. The Background and Message of John 20.1-10* (Theologie und Wirklichkeit, 6), Bern-Frankfurt, 1974, pp. 41-69.

proceed on the assumption that the Fourth Evangelist had possessed such a | tradition as Luke 24,12 on which to build his own material"[7]. One would expect that this defence of the inauthenticity of Lk 24,12 was one of the points on which the Doktorvater was personally in disagreement with the results of the dissertation[8], but this does not seem to be the case. Schnackenburg will write in 1975: "Wegen dieser Unsicherheit wird man sich traditionsgeschichtlich besser nicht auf diesen Vers stützen. [n. 21:] Diese Folgerung von R. Mahoney wird man nach seiner sorgfältigen Erörterung des Pro und Contra bejahen müssen"[9].

The first reference to Lk 24,12 in the published work of A. Dauer (he too is a Schnackenburg *Schüler*, 1968/69) is a statement together with an announcement in his *Johannes und Lukas* (1984)[10]: "Auf die Parallele Joh 20,3-10 – Lk 24,12 bin ich nicht näher eingegangen, weil sie, *wie ich in einem bald zu veröffentlichen Aufsatz zeigen möchte*, keine echte Parallele ist, sondern bei Lk auf eine spätere Interpolation zurückgeht"[11]. In contrast to Mahoney who defends the same solution for Lk 24,12 and 36b.40 (Western non-interpolations)[12] Dauer opts for the authenticity of 24,36b.40[13] and against the authenticity of 24,12: "jede Stelle [ist] für sich zu beurteilen"[14].

In 1989 Dauer published an investigation on "Nachträge" in Acts. The "Anlaß" was admittedly Lk 24,12: "In der Diskussion um die Authentizität von Lk 24,12 wird zugunsten dieses umstrittenen Verses u.a. immer wieder auch darauf hingewiesen, daß Lk 24,22ff den V. 12 voraussetze" (his opening sentence)[15]. His intention was to show "daß

---

7. *Ibid.*, p. 69. Cf. p. 214: "We have in chapter two above ruled out Luke 24,12 as a likely source at this point for John".

8. Cf. Mahoney's Foreword, p. 5. Schnackenburg's reservation apparently concerns his evaluation of the figure of the beloved disciple, particularly in Jn 21 and 19,26-27 (cf. *Joh III*, pp. 451-452).

9. *Joh III*, p. 364. On Schnackenburg's phrase "textkritisch umstritten" (*ibid.*) and its echo in J. Becker's *Johannes* (1981, p. 609: "textkritisch sehr umstritten"), see my comment: "It looks like an anachronism..." (*NTS* 1984, p. 166; *Evangelica II*, p. 579). Compare now Becker's new edition: "textkritisch umstritten. Doch mehren sich die Stimmen für seine Echtheit" (³1991, p. 718).

10. *Johannes und Lukas. Untersuchungen zu den johanneisch-lukanischen Parallelperikopen Joh 4,46-54 / Lk 7,1-10 – Joh 12,1-8 / Lk 7,36-50; 10,38-42 – Joh 20,19-29 / Lk 24,36-49* (FzB, 50), Würzburg, 1984. Cf. my *Evangelica II*, pp. 205-226, 679-687.

11. *Johannes und Lukas*, p. 38 (emphasis mine). Cf. below n. 40.

12. *Two Disciples*, pp. 61-62. Cf. SCHNACKENBURG, *Joh III*, p. 383 n. 73: in Lk 24,36b "besteht ... ein starker Verdacht auf Übernahme von Joh" (no comment on Lk 24,40).

13. *Johannes und Lukas*, pp. 209-216 ("Fragwürdige Parallelen"), 412-419 (notes). Cf. my *Jean et les Synoptiques*, 1979, pp. 126-130 ("L'authenticité de Lc 24,36b et 40").

14. *Ibid.*, p. 216.

15. *"Ergänzungen" und "Variationen" in den Reden der Apostelgeschichte gegenüber vorausgegangenen Erzählungen. Beobachtungen zur literarischen Arbeitsweise des*

man aus Reden/Gesprächen in der Apg (und im Lk) nicht schließen
I kann, daß hier erwähnte Einzelheiten schon in der früheren Erzählung
vorgekommen sein müssen, und daß daher mit solchen Redenelementen
[= Lk 24,24] nicht die Authentizität einer anderen Stelle [= Lk 24,12]
bewiesen werden kann" (his concluding sentence)[16]. This essay is followed in 1990 by a small monograph with a more complete list of examples of this Lukan composition technique in Lk-Acts[17] (Lk 1,13; 4,23;
7,24.33.44b-46; 9,9.40.49; 10,13.17.19; 11,1; 13,1.4.31.34; 15,30;
22,31-32; 24,34; Acts 1,18-19*; 5,23; 6,2b.13-14*; 8,36b; 9,27b;
10,1–11,18*; 13,25-29; 19,4; 20,18-35*; 21,21; 23,27.30b; 24,17*;
25,16.18-19; 27,23-24; 28,17b-19a; 22,3-21; 26,1-29)[18].

The study on Lk 24,12 Dauer had announced in 1984 now appeared
in two issues, first on the question of Lukan redaction in *The Four
Gospels 1992* and then on the authenticity of Lk 24,12 in *ETL* (1994)[19].
His conclusion is doubly negative: he is unconvinced that Lk 24,12
could be "eine redaktionelle Bildung des 3. Evangelisten" and he maintains his opinion that the authenticity of the verse is "fragwürdig"[20]. The
most recent essay (*Authentizität*) is partially overlapping with that of
1992 (*Lk 24,12*). The first part in both is a critique of the same eight
arguments for authenticity. The discussion of Lukan redaction (*Lk
24,12*: Part 2) is not repeated as such. The two bibliographical lists of
authors against and for authenticity (*Lk 24,12*: "Anhang") are referred
to and supplemented in the footnotes 2 and 3[21]. Dauer's own view is

Lukas, in H. FRANKEMÖLLE – K. KERTELGE (eds.), *Vom Urchristentum zu Jesus*. FS J.
Gnilka, Freiburg, 1989, pp. 307-324 (on Lk 24,12: "Anlaß der Untersuchung", pp. 307-
308).

16. *Ibid.*, p. 324 (bracketed words added). See also his conclusion in *Beobachtungen*
(n. 17), p. 149 (cf. "Einleitung", pp. 9-12).

17. *Beobachtungen zur literarischen Arbeitstechnik des Lukas* (Athenäums Monografien; BBB, 79), Frankfurt, 1990. – The instances from Acts he already mentioned in
1989 are marked with * in the list above.

18. For a provisional response see my *John and the Synoptics: 1975-1990*, in A.
DENAUX (ed.), *John and the Synoptics* (BETL, 101), Leuven, 1992, pp. 3-62, esp. 43-44.

19. *Lk 24,12 – Ein Produkt lukanischer Redaktion?*, in *The Four Gospels 1992*,
pp. 1697-1716; *Zur Authentizität von Lk 24,12*, in *ETL* 70 (1994) 294-318.

20. *Lk 24,12*, p. 1713; *Authentizität*, p. 318.

21. These bibliographical supplements include works published up to 1989 and one
more recent title: G. LÜDEMANN, *Die Auferstehung*, 1994 (see below n. 113). There is no
reference to A. DENAUX (ed.), *John and the Synoptics*, 1992 (cf. above n. 18). C.F. Evans
(1990), M.C. Parsons (1986) and C.-M. Amphoux (1991) I mentioned there (in nn. 194
and 196, pp. 42-43) are more significant opponents than the rather uncommitted R.
Borger and F. Wisse (his n. 2; on S.M. Schneiders, cf. below n. 110). The same volume
includes a short study on Lk 24,12 by W.L. Craig (cf. below n. 122) and a passage on Lk
24,12 in H. Thyen's contribution (below n. 130). Dauer has no other reference to *The
Four Gospels 1992* than his own *Lk 24,12*. Here again H. Thyen can be mentioned and
also U. SCHNELLE, *Johannes und die Synoptiker* (below n. 131).

mainly developed in Part 2 ("Argumente, die gegen die Authentizität von Lk 24,12 sprechen").

2. Textual Witnesses

I Mahoney (1974), Schnackenburg (1975) and now also Dauer (1994!) rely on the apparatus in UBS GNT (1966!): "*omit verse 12 ...* syr[pal mss] Marcion Diatessaron Eusebius 1/2"[22]. Contrast GNT [3]1975 (Eusebius dropped out) and [4]1993 (all four witnesses deleted). My study of these witnesses[23] is not unknown to Dauer, but his indirect reference is extremely brief ... and misleading: "(NEIRYNCK!)" in n. 13 added to the sentence on Eusebius, "Für Eusebius wird vermutet, daß er beide Lesarten gekannt habe"[24]. Contrast my conclusion: "on peut rayer le nom d'Eusèbe dans la liste des témoins de l'omission"[25]. Dauer's observation in *Lk 24,12* is more correct: "Neirynck ... sucht nachzuweisen, daß auch Eusebius, Tatian – er zog den ausführlicheren joh. Bericht vor – und Marcion Lk 24,12 gekannt haben" (followed by a reference to "seine Beobachtungen zur syrischen Überlieferung")[26]. But without any attempt at refutation of my conclusions (and ignoring the new apparatus in GNT[4]) Dauer simply continues to cite syr[pal mss], Marcion, Diatessaron, and Eusebius in support of the omission of Lk 24,12.

Dauer recognizes the strong attestation ("ausgezeichnete Bezeugung") of Lk 24,12[27]. Possible reasons why the omission in the Western text may be considered more plausible than a secondary addition of the verse are enumerated in *Lk 24,12* and again in *Authentizität*[28]. In Dauer's opinion this transcriptional probability is a too subjective argument and it is reversible. The evidence he cites in support of a secondary insertion has to do with the relation of Lk 24,12 to its context in ch. 24 (verses 11,

---

22. MAHONEY, p. 44; SCHNACKENBURG, *Joh III*, p. 364 n. 19; DAUER, *Authentizität*, p. 304 (cf. 297: Eusebius).

23. *Lc. xxiv.12: Les témoins du texte occidental*, in *Evangelica I*, 1982, pp. 313-328, esp. 315-317 ("Les canons d'Eusèbe"). The text of this SNTC lecture (1975, May 26) was first published in T. BAARDA – A.F.J. KLIJN – W.C. VAN UNNIK (eds.), *Miscellanea Neotestamentica*, I (SupplNT, 47), Leiden, 1978, pp. 45-60.

24. *Authentizität*, p. 297 (cf. *Lk 24,12*, p. 1699). Compare Mahoney ("once of the two times the passage occurs in his extant text") and Schnackenburg ("einmal von zwei Zitaten"): both are apparently unaware of the textual data behind "Eusebius 1/2" (GNT, cf. Souter 1910).

25. *Les témoins*, p. 316 (= 48).

26. *Lk 24,12*, p. 1699 n. 16.

27. He notes the minor variants concerning (κείμενα and) μόνα and rightly maintains μόνα in the text. Cf. *Authentizität*, p. 315 n. 103.

28. *Lk 24,12*, pp. 1699-1700 (no. 2); *Authentizität*, p. 298 (no. 2).

24, or 34) and to the parallel story in Jn 20,3-10. In fact, the discussion of (in)authenticity proves to be a consideration of "innere Gründe"[29].

3. Lukanisms in Lk 24,12

I Three Lukan characteristics are accepted even by Schnackenburg (1970) and Mahoney: ἀναστάς, θαυμάζων + acc., τὸ γεγονός. Only one is acceptable for Dauer (τὸ γεγονός), and this one Lukanism is neutralized by the un-Lukan historic present βλέπει[30].

His difficulty regarding ἀναστάς is the supposedly un-Lukan word-order. J. Muddiman treated this question, in my view most effectively, in his reply to K.P.G. Curtis (*ETL* 1972)[31]. Dauer now declares that this answer is unsatisfactory, but his quotation is incomplete and neglects Muddiman's consideration of the context (Lk 24,9.10-12): "Luke's exceptional order, subject + ἀναστάς, emphasises that the second corroborating visit was conducted by none other than Peter himself"[32]. It can be added in reply to Dauer's statistical approach that, of the seventeen occurrences of the participle ἀναστάς in the Gospel of Luke, there are only three instances where the subject is expressed:

   1,39   ἀναστᾶσα δὲ Μαριάμ (cf. 1,26-38)
   23,1   καὶ ἀναστὰν ἅπαν τὸ πλῆθος αὐτῶν (cf. 22,66-71)
   24,12   ὁ δὲ Πέτρος ἀναστάς.

In contrast to 24,12, the subject in 1,39 and 23,1 was resumed from the preceding paragraph.

The Lukan usage is described by Dauer as ἀναστάς followed by a *nomen proprium* and he cites four examples in Acts (5,17.34; 11,28; 13,16), without further comment[33]. But on the one hand Acts 9,39 (ἀναστὰς δὲ Πέτρος) can be added to his list, and on the other no proper noun is used in his first instance (5,17), and there are other instances of ἀναστάς with a common noun (5,6; 23,9)[34]. Two factors

---

29. *Authentizität*, p. 305: compare the motifs in no. 2 with the following nos. 3-6, and with the arguments for authenticity, nos. 3-6 and 8 (pp. 298-304). The question of historicity (no. 7) is put aside as not relevant in a debate on authenticity (cf. *Lk 24,12*, p. 1702, no. 7).

30. *Lk 24,12*, p. 1700 (no. 3); *Authentizität*, pp. 298-300 (no. 3).

31. *Note* (above n. 1), pp. 544-546. See also my *John and the Synoptics* (1977), n. 111 (= *Evangelica I*, pp. 391-392).

32. *Note*, p. 546.

33. In *Lk 24,12*, p. 1700 n. 29, and again the same list in *Authentizität*, p. 299.

34. Cf. Curtis's definition of Luke's usage.

are to be considered. First, the subject following ἀναστὰς δέ can be simply a proper name (9,39 Peter; 13,16 Paul) but more complete formulations, quite different from Lk 24,12, are found at 5,17 (ὁ ἀρχιερεὺς καὶ πάντες οἱ σὺν αὐτῷ, ἡ οὖσα αἵρεσις τῶν Σαδδουκαίων); 5,34 (τις ἐν τῷ συνεδρίῳ Φαρισαῖος ὀνόματι Γαμαλιήλ, νομοδιδάσκαλος τίμιος παντὶ τῷ λαῷ) and 11,28 (εἷς ἐξ αὐτῶν ὀνόματι Ἅγαβος). Second, ἀναστὰς δέ in Acts 5,17.34; 9,39; 11,28; 13,16 "markiert den Beginn eines Erzählabschnitts" (G. Schneider)[35], comparable to Lk 1,39 but different from Lk 24,12 (cf. Muddiman: "the I word-order, ἀναστάς + subject, would have marked off the next stage in the story")[36].

Θαυμάζων τὸ γεγονός: The use of θαυμάζειν + acc. is rather rare (Lk 7,9; Acts 7,31; there is only one occurrence in the other gospels: Jn 5,28). Dauer agrees that αὐτόν in Lk 7,9 is added by Luke but he refuses this parallel because of the accusative of person[37]. He understands αὐτόν as a christological correction: "Jesus admired him"[38]. In the widely accepted interpretation ἐθαύμασεν αὐτόν expresses Jesus' surprise: "he marveled at him"[39], and this is comparable to θαυμάζων τὸ γεγονός. Of course, one may feel that the fact of one occurrence in Lk and one in Acts is statistically not very impressive, but if τὸ γεγονός is accepted as a Lukanism, the conjunction of θαυμάζειν + acc. and τὸ γεγονός in one expression can become a valid example of Lukan style. Not unlike ὁ δὲ Πέτρος ἀναστάς, the concluding words in 24,12 should be seen in relation to the preceding context: the apostles who did not believe (v. 11: ἠπίστουν αὐταῖς) and Peter "wondering about what had happened" (θαυμάζων τὸ γεγονός). Compare the Lukan association of the verbs in 24,41: ἔτι δὲ ἀπιστούντων αὐτῶν ... καὶ θαυμαζόντων[40].

35. *Die Apostelgeschichte* I (HTKNT, 5/1), 1980, p. 398 n. 113.
36. *Note*, p. 546. On ἀναστὰς ὁ Πέτρος, see also *Evangelica I*, 392 n. 111.
37. *Authentizität*, p. 300.
38. *Johannes und Lukas*, p. 86: "Jesus wundert sich nicht, sondern bewundert den Mann". Compare BJ: "Jésus l'admire"; TOB: "Jésus fut plein d'admiration pour lui"; J. NOLLAND, 1989, with reference to A. George (*AsSeign* 40, 1972, p. 71).
39. J.A. Fitzmyer, F. Bovon, *et multi alii*. Cf. NRSV: "he was amazed at him" (7,9); "amazed at what happened" (24,12); "he was amazed at the sight" (Acts 7,31). Cf. J. JEREMIAS, *Die Sprache*, p. 155: τὸ ὅραμα 10 times in Acts; add: 9,12 [ἐν ὁράματι] (om. T).
40. Cf. *The Historic Present* (1972), p. 549 n. 4 (= *Evangelica I*, 330); and more explicitly, *John and the Synoptics* (1977), p. 99 n. 109 (= 391). See also, with reference to my *Historic Present*, J. JEREMIAS, *Die Sprache* (1980), pp. 312 (at 24,11 and 12), 321 (24,41). – For Dauer's reaction, cf. *Johannes und Lukas*, p. 456 n. 489: "nur 2 Beispiele" and "24,12 wahrscheinlich Interpolation aus Joh". Note, however, Dauer's hypothesis on 24,41: Luke changed his source's finite verb (ἠπίστησαν) to the genitive absolute ἀπισ-

Dauer presents my study of the Lukan redaction in 24,12 as argument no. 8 for the authenticity of the verse[41]. It can be observed, however, that in 1972 the question of authenticity was specifically treated by J. Muddiman, and the direct purpose of my additional note, *The Uncorrected Historic Present*, was to examine whether, given the authenticity of the ǀverse, Luke's interventions should be restricted to the addition of the three 'classic' Lukanisms (cf. J. Jeremias, R. Schnackenburg 1970, M.-É. Boismard 1972, *et al.*). A corollary of this discussion was the confrontation with the hypothesis of a common source of Jn 20,3-10 and Lk 24,12, which has been further developed in my *John and the Synoptics* (1975; BETL 1977)[42]. On account of the absence of the three Lukanisms in Jn 20,3-10, some have argued for a common-source text without ἀναστάς and θαυμάζων τὸ γεγονός. I could reply that this absence is not a valid objection against the alternative solution of Johannine dependence on Lk 24,12[43]. The pleonastic ἀναστάς is never used in Jn[44] and it may have been omitted in 20,3 or in some sense replaced by ἐξῆλθεν. Peter's reaction, θαυμάζων τὸ γεγονός in Lk, is not directly expressed in Jn, but many interpreters include these words or at least the verb ἐθαύμασεν, said of Peter, in their reconstruction of John's *Vorlage* as a traditional basis for the beloved disciple's ἐπίστευσεν in 20,8[45].

4. *Supposedly Un-Lukan Words and Phrases*

Dauer takes note of the contacts with Jn 20,3-10 in Lk 24,12: ἔδραμεν, (ἐπὶ) τὸ μνημεῖον, καὶ παρακύψας βλέπει, τὰ ὀθόνια, ἀπῆλθεν

τούντων and added θαυμαζόντων (p. 272); thus, at least in 24,41, the association of the verbs is LkR.

In *Lk 24,12* he repeats his position: the "unbelief" in v. 41 stems from the source (p. 1709 n. 66). His observation on the relation to 24,13-35 (v. 34!) was already answered in *Jean et les Synoptiques*, p. 136: "It is also possible that in the different sections of Lk 24 the evangelist wants to describe different ways in which people came from initial unbelief to belief and recognition and, therefore, cannot take into account the previous recognition scenes. He starts everytime again from unbelief and lack of recognition" (H. Hendrickx, 1978).

41. *Lk 24,12*, p. 1702; *Authentizität*, p. 303 (no. 8).
42. "Lk 24,12", pp. 98-104 (= *Evangelica I*, 390-396).
43. *Historic Present*, p. 353 (= *Evangelica I*, 334); *John and the Synoptics*, p. 395 (= 103); *Empty Tomb Stories*, pp. 174, 176-177 (= *Evangelica II*, 590, 592-593).
44. Neither its equivalent, the pleonastic ἐγερθείς (cf. *Evangelica I*, 334 n. 20; 395 n. 121).
45. See now, e.g., R.T. FORTNA, *The Fourth Gospel and Its Predecessor*, Philadelphia, 1988, p. 187: in the pre-Johannine source: "[And he wondered.]" Cf. p. 191: "Peter wondered, for they did not *yet* know..."; in the Johannine redaction: "It becomes instead an accounting for the difference between the beloved disciple and the others (*he* believed, but as yet *they* did not know...)".

πρός; three "Johannine" words (not used elsewhere in Lk-Acts): παρακύπτειν (cf. 20,11), ὀθόνιον (cf. 19,40), ἀπέρχεσθαι πρός (cf. 4,47; 6,68; 11,46); and "das für Lukas recht ungewöhnliche Praesens historicum in βλέπει"[46].

The Historic Present

I This βλέπει is the central piece in the argument for a pre-Lukan tradition in Lk 24,12 and it was in reference to that theory that in *ETL* 1972 I chose to use the title: "The Uncorrected Historic Present"[47]. Dauer makes three more specific observations: (1) Out of twelve historic presents in Lk and thirteen (sic) in Acts, nine and eleven are *verba dicendi*. (2) Beside Lk 24,12 and Jn 20,5 the only occurrences of historic presents of the verb βλέπειν are found in Jn 1,29; 20,1; 21,9.20. (3) The incongruity of the aorist participle + historic present: "Daraus ergibt sich, daß die Konstruktion παρακύψας βλέπει sicher un-lk ist"[48]. However, this conclusion may be less firm than it is formulated. Such an "incongruity" is not unique in Lk: cf. 11,45 (ἀποκριθεὶς ... λέγει); 13,8 (ἀποκριθεὶς λέγει); 16,23 (ἐπάρας τοὺς ὀφθαλμοὺς αὐτοῦ ... ὁρᾷ); 17,37 (ἀποκριθέντες λέγουσιν); Acts 19,35 (καταστείλας ... φησίν)[49]. The predominance of *verba dicendi* is less amazing if we realize that 75 of the 151 historic presents in Mk and 68 of the 94 in Mt are *verba dicendi*, and 27 of the 29 historic presents in Mt diff. Mk are *verba dicendi*[50].

The comparison with Mt is instructive indeed. Though less radical than in Lk, the avoidance of Mk's historic presents[51] is combined with a specific Matthean usage of λέγει/λέγουσιν. From the fact that Luke

46. *Authentizität*, pp. 305-309 (on βλέπει, see also *Lk 24,12*, pp. 1705, 1710). On the parallel ἔδραμεν (Jn 20,3 ἔτρεχον ... προέδραμεν) Dauer simply cites Dillon's comment: "not overly compelling" (n. 54). But see my own comment: "Un récit traditionnel sur Pierre qui 'vint' au tombeau [B-L; now also Fortna 1988] ne contient aucun point d'attache pour y insérer le thème de l'autre disciple qui se montre meilleur que Pierre. En revanche, si Pierre 'courut' au tombeau, on introduit plus facilement l'autre qui court plus vite et arrive le premier. De même, dans le parallèle de Jn 18,15-16..." (*ETL* 53, 1977, p. 440; = *Jean et les Synoptiques*, p. 82).

47. The irony in this title (see the reference to Muddiman in the first paragraph) seems to be misread by Dauer. Cf. below n. 59.

48. *Authentizität*, p. 309. Dauer's total number (13 in Acts) is that of Hawkins; add: φησίν in 2,38; 26,25.

49. Lk 17,37 and Acts 19,35 are not mentioned by Dauer: his "nur noch" should be corrected.

50. See the lists in my *The Minor Agreements*, 1974, pp. 223-229: no. 10 (Historic Present).

51. Of the 151 historic presents in Mk, 32 have no parallel, 21 are retained in Mt, 98 are changed to aorist, participle, imperfect or (καὶ) ἰδού (of these 98, there are 42 positive agreements and 28 negative agreements with Lk).

retains only one of Mk's 151 historic presents (or more correctly, of the about 100 with parallel in Lk), can we then infer that all use of the historic present should be banned from the Lukan redaction? "Quand il n'a plus à corriger Mc, Lc sait employer cette construction à bon escient. 'Luc s'en sert surtout pour montrer la vivacité de la réplique' (S. Antoniadis)", with verbs of saying, but: "Le verbe 'il voit' ... joue un rôle analogue" (J. Dupont, 1973)[52].

I It is far too simple to treat this question with a quotation from H. Schürmann (1953): "nirgends setzt es Luk ... nachweislich von sich aus"[53]. Schürmann now thinks differently concerning Lukan redaction in Lk 11,37 and 11,45[54], and for other commentators the historic present is Lukan in 7,40 (J. Nolland); 11,37 (J.A. Fitzmyer); 11,45 (W. Schmithals); 17,37 (I.H. Marshall); 24,12 (W. Schmithals). But for J. Jeremias it is "lukanische Meidewendung" and "Wo es trotzdem auftaucht, stammt es aus der Tradition"[55]. Dauer adopts this position in the case of Lk 24,36b: he defends the authenticity of καὶ λέγει αὐτοῖς· εἰρήνη ὑμῖν and assigns the "un-Lukan" λέγει to pre-Lukan tradition[56]. In my view the suggestion that the redaction of Lk 24,36-43 was influenced by the recognition scene in Mk 6,45-52 is still valid[57]. The

52. See quotation in *John and the Synoptics*, p. 99 n. 107 (= *Evangelica I*, 391). – On Matthean usage, cf. *Jean et les Synoptiques*, p. 129 n. 243 (W. Schenk). – Is it by inadvertence that Luke retained one of Mk's historic presents in 8,49? Cf. J. Jeremias: "ganz offensichtlich versehentlich" (*Die Sprache*, p. 169). Yet, Luke's redactional intervention can be seen in the change of Mk's vague plural ἔρχονται ἀπὸ τ. ἀ. λέγοντες to the singular ἔρχεταί τις παρὰ τ. ἀ. λέγων. The vividness of the historic present is well fitting here after ἔτι αὐτοῦ λαλοῦντος, and Mk 5,35 is in some sense unique in Mk. Contrast the other occurrences, almost always as καὶ ἔρχεται/-ονται at the beginning of a paragraph (and sometimes followed by one or two other historic presents, marked here with the plus sign): 1,40; 2,3.18+; 3,20+.31; 5,15+.22+; 6,1+.(48); 8,22+; 10,46; 11,15.27+bis; 12,18; 14,32+.37+.41+; (καὶ ... ἔρχ.): 10,1+; 14,17.66; 16,2. Perhaps we should speak less indistinctively about the avoidance of historic presents.

53. *Johannes und Lukas*, p. 261. Cf. *Authentizität*, p. 308 n. 67.

54. *Das Lukasevangelium II/1*, 1994, pp. 308-309, 318.

55. *Die Sprache*, p. 170. The five historic presents in parables are not included in Jeremias's statistics (p. 169: 7 in Lk). In his commentary 13,8 and 19,22 are marked as *trad.*; there is no comment at 16,7.23.29. To the 14 instances in Acts (p. 169), φησίν in 2,38 [N26] can be added. It is rather strange, and quite unusual for Jeremias, that the instances of φησίν in Acts were unable to mitigate his opinion. Cf. J. Nolland's comment at Lk 7,40: "φησίν probably Lukan (historic present φησίν is found eleven times in Acts)" (1989, p. 355); cf. *Jean et les Synoptiques*, p. 129 n. 243 (J. Delobel, 1966). Jeremias's treatment of the historic presents in Lk is exclusively statistical (one of the main weaknesses in *Die Sprache*), without considering the contexts of their occurrences. See my observations (*ibid.*) on 16,23.29 (Lukan style in 16,19-31); 16,7 and 19,22 (variation in Luke's style).

56. *Johannes und Lukas*, pp. 261, 451 n. 420 (cf. Schürmann, Jeremias, Marshall).

57. Or at least not attacked by Dauer. The section on "Lc 24,36-43 et Mc 6,45-52" in *Jean et les Synoptiques* (1979), pp. 130-136, is not mentioned in his *Johannes und Lukas*

historic present λέγει is considered to be part of the reminiscence in the Lukan redaction[58]:

Mk   6,50   καὶ λέγει αὐτοῖς· θαρσεῖτε,   ἐγώ εἰμι
Lk   24,36   καὶ λέγει αὐτοῖς· εἰρήνη ὑμῖν. 39... ἐγώ εἰμι αὐτός.

A more or less similar interpretation has been proposed regarding the historic present in Lk 24,12: παρακύψας βλέπει is *not* the quotation of a pre-Lukan source[59], but Lukan redaction, probably influenced | by ἀναβλέψασαι θεωροῦσιν in Mk 16,4. Understood as "and looking (when he looked) he saw"[60], παρακύψας βλέπει can be compared with ἐπάρας τοὺς ὀφθαλμοὺς αὐτοῦ (= *actio videndi*) followed by ὁρᾷ (historic present) in Lk 16,23[61]. The *verba videndi* used by Luke in historic presents, ὁρᾷ (16,23), βλέπει (24,12), and θεωρεῖ (Acts 10,11), are three common words, and there are questions such as "why βλέπει and not θεωρεῖ?" (and vice versa) that should not be asked.

Παρακύψας βλέπει

Dauer's partial agreement with regard to the meaning of παρακύψας can be singled out: "Zwar ist es sicher richtig, daß παρακύπτειν als verbum videndi verstanden werden *kann* – und in diesem Sinne häufig gebraucht wird; dafür hat Neirynck den schlüssigen Beweis geliefert"[62]. But the agreement ends there and Dauer returns to the vulgate "er *bückt* sich (ins Grab) und sieht..."[63]. His concern is clearly to maintain παρακύπτειν in Lk 24,12 in the sense it has in Jn 20,5, where "dieses Verbum ja ganz offensichtlich die Bedeutung von 'sich bücken' oder

---

(1984), and my essay *Luc 24,36-43: Un récit lucanien* (1985; *Evangelica II*, 205-226; with an evaluation of his ch. 3, "Joh 20,19-29 und Lk 24,36-49") has not yet been mentioned by Dauer (1992, 1994).

58. *Luc 24,36-43*, pp. 670-672 (= *Evangelica II*, 218-219). Cf. *Jean et les Synoptiques*, p. 134. – Note: Dauer in general admits the possibility of reminiscences from Mk 6,45–8,26, "aus der er verschiedenes an anderen Stellen unterbringt" (*Lk 24,12*, p. 1708 n. 65).

59. Dauer unjustifiably assimilates (or tends to assimilate) my position with that source hypothesis (cf. above n. 47). See *Authentizität*, p. 309 n. 70: "diese 'Traditionsnotiz' war nichts anderes als Mk 16,4", "das unbearbeitete Praesens historicum".

60. "Il *regarde* et il voit"; "hij *keek* en zag". Cf. the *Synopsis* in Dutch: "toekijkend zag hij" (Denaux-Vervenne). Cf. below nn. 64 and 73.

61. Cf. *ΠΑΡΑΚΥΨΑΣ*, pp. 144-145 (= *Evangelica I*, 432-433). "Παρακύψας peut désigner l'action de regarder, en préparation du verbe βλέπει, peut-être d'après le modèle de ἀναβλέψασαι θεωροῦσιν de Mc 16,4. Ailleurs, Luc remplace lui-même un ἐθεώρει de Mc par ἀναβλέψας εἶδεν (Lc 21,1)" (*ibid.*).

62. *Lk 24,12*, p. 1710 (no. 8). But see pp. 1711-1712, (a)-(d), four objections against this meaning in Lk 24,12.

63. *Authentizität*, p. 316.

zumindest '(von außen) hineinschauen' (hat)"[64]. This meaning is obvious indeed in Jn 20,5 (παρακύψας βλέπει ..., οὐ μέντοι εἰσῆλθεν, said of the other disciple) but Dauer has to admit that in Lk 24,12 it makes "das Verhalten des Petrus ... rätselhaft"[65]. One could ask: if Lk 24,12 should be read in the light of Jn 20,3-10 (Dauer's thesis), can we then ignore which was "das Verhalten des Petrus" in v. 6: εἰσῆλθεν εἰς τὸ μνημεῖον καὶ θεωρεῖ...?

My proposal was to read Lk 24,12 in the light of its context in the Gospel of Luke. In particular, I tried to understand the story of Peter's visit to the tomb in the light of the women's visit, as suggested in Lk 24,22-23.24. What is explicitly said in Lk 24,3 (εἰσελθοῦσαι, par. Mk 16,5) is implied in Lk 24,22-23: the women went into the tomb and it was inside the tomb they failed to find the body of Jesus. This is not contested by Dauer: εἰσελθοῦσαι is not repeated, simply because in this summary of Lk 24,1-9 "nicht jede Einzelheit ... wiederholt werden mußte"; but v. 12 is different: "es handelt sich um eine wirkliche kurze Erzählung, bei der es auch auf Details ankommt"[66]. For Luke, however, the important detail is not the (implied) act of entering but Peter's finding: παρακύψας βλέπει τὰ ὀθόνια μόνα (contrast 24,24 αὐτὸν δὲ οὐκ εἶδον). Luke's double verbum videndi is more emphatic ("une formule plus solennelle") than a simple εἶδεν. Dauer's reply: "War die Situation beim Grabbesuch der Frauen weniger feierlich als beim Grabbesuch des Petrus?" (he refers to εὗρον in Lk 24,2, diff. Mk 16,4 ἀναβλέψασαι θεωροῦσιν)[67]. In fact, the motif of the stone rolled away from the tomb is less "feierlich" in Lk than it is in Mk 16,3-4. Lk 24,2 εὗρον δὲ τὸν λίθον... prepares for (εἰσελθοῦσαι δὲ) οὐχ εὗρον τὸ σῶμα τοῦ κυρίου Ἰησοῦ (v. 3), which is the climax of the first section of the tomb story (23,56b–24,3) and the real parallel to 24,12 (τὰ ὀθόνια μόνα, not the body of Jesus). The change of θεωροῦσιν to εὗρον[68] has a parallel in Lk 8,35 (diff. Mk 5,15)[69].

---

64. Lk 24,12, p. 1712. – The meaning "hineinschauen" (not mentioned in Authentizität, p. 316) is now adopted in some recent translations of Lk 24,12: "als er hineinschaute, sah er" (W. Schmithals); in English: "he peered in and saw" (Fitzmyer, cf. NEB); "He looked in. He saw" (L.T. Johnson); in Dutch "toen hij er een blik in wierp zag hij" (NWV). See also below n. 73.

65. Authentizität, pp. 316-317.

66. Lk 24,12, p. 1711, (a).

67. Ibid., p. 1711, (b).

68. Ibid., p. 1712, (c). Dauer's question, why "ein einfaches εὗρον" for ἀναβλέψασαι θεωροῦσιν, takes no account of my description of the Lukan structure in 24,2-3 (see his own quotation, p. 1705). Lk 24,2-3 as intermediate between Mk 16,4 and Lk 24,12 is completely neglected when he observes: "Es ist auch zu bedenken, daß in Mk 16,4 mit ἀναβλέψασαι die Entfernung des Steins konstatiert wird, während nach Lk 24,12 Petrus

Finally Dauer objects that I gave no plausible explanation of how Luke's παρακύψας could be changed to "stooping or peering in from outside" in Jn 20,5 (and 11)[70]. I think that my investigation of παρακύπτειν has made clear that the meaning of the verb developed from "stooping (to look in)" and "looking in". It was never my contention that the literal meaning of this compound of κύπτειν completely disappeared[71]. Taken apart from its context in Lk, παρακύψας can be used in Jn for a first stage in the story, the other disciple looking in from outside without going in, to be followed by Peter who entered the tomb. Mahoney rightly observed that in a story where Peter came to the tomb following the women's report to see for himself how the matter stood, I Peter must have entered the tomb straightway. In such a story "there is no point in the two stages 1) peering in from outside, and 2) looking while inside"[72]. Mahoney's mistake was to read Lk's παρακύψας in the "Johannine" sense. Of course, in 1973 he was unaware of my study of Lk 24,12 and at that time it was not uncommon to translate παρακύψας in Lk by "peering in from outside" (if not, even less satisfactorily, by "stooping")[73]. Dauer now reaffirms the interpolation thesis: in Jn 20,5 it was the other disciple who "zuerst nur ins Grab bückte" and a late interpolator of Lk 24,12 transferred this trait to Peter and thus created "das rätselhafte Verhalten des Petrus"[74]. It is inherent in the interpolation theory that no effort is made to understand Lk 24,12 in the context of Lk: "eine überraschend leichte Erklärung" indeed!

die *Leichentücher* sieht" (p. 1710 n. 73). Note: ἀναβλέψασαι (looking, when they looked) is an accompanying verb of θεωροῦσιν ("konstatieren", cf. εὗρον).

69. Cf. JEREMIAS, *Die Sprache*, p. 81 n. 71: "Es ist kennzeichnend für den Stil des Lukas, daß bei ihm εὑρίσκω mit Verba videndi austauschbar ist", with reference to my *Historic Present*, p. 551. Note the number of occurrences in Lk + Acts: εὑρίσκειν 45 + 35 (176 in NT); ἀνευρίσκειν: 1 + 1 (not elsewhere in NT). – For changes of Mk's θεωρεῖν, see also Lk 23,49 ὁρῶσαι (Mk θεωροῦσαι); 23,55 ἐθεάσαντο (Mk ἐθεώρουν).

70. *Lk 24,12*, p. 1712, (d).

71. The compounds ἀνακύπτειν and συγκύπτειν are used in the literal sense in Lk 13,11, but ἀνακύπτειν is used in a figurative sense in 21,28: this observation is perhaps less irrelevant than Dauer thinks (*Lk 24,12*, p. 1711 n. 74).

72. *Two Disciples*, p. 246.

73. This is still now the German translation in EÜ: "er beugte sich vor" (Luther: "bückte sich hinein"; U. Wilckens: "bückte sich hinunter"). – The recent NRSV has the combination "stooping and looking in" (= R); see also R.E. Brown: "he bent down to peer in" (*John*, 979), and Fitzmyer's comment on this translation: "would have the best of both worlds; but is scarcely accurate" (*Luke*, 1547). Cf. above nn. 60 and 64.

74. *Authentizität*, p. 316. Note this rather uncontrolled suggestion of the interpolator's motive: "Beim Betreten des Grabes hätte Petrus die wohl noch anwesend zu denkenden (?) Engel sehen und durch sie zum Glauben kommen müssen" (*ibid.*).

"Johannine" Words

My comment could be brief: "Die Vokabeln waren durch den Stoff gegeben: von spezifisch johanneischen Sprachgebrauch kann nicht die Rede sein" (J. Jeremias)[75]. A discussion with Dauer on "Johannine" vocabulary is most uncomfortable because he does not make clear what he takes to be "Johannine" in Jn 20,3-10. From his work on the passion narrative (1972) we know that he considers the beloved disciple "redaktionell vom Evangelisten eingeschaltet"[76], and this is now confirmed in a rather vague parenthetical clause: "was sicher joh Eintrag ist"[77]. Some more precise information would be helpful. Both Boismard-Lamouille (B-L) and Fortna (1988), for example, propose a pre-Johannine source, without the other disciple, beginning with vv. 3-4 (Peter went out, and he came to the tomb)[78] and ending with v. 10 (he went home), but with significant differences in the central part, B-L: 5 καὶ παρακύψας βλέπει τὰ ὀθόνια [μόνα]; Fortna: 6b καὶ εἰσῆλθεν εἰς τὸ μνημεῖον, καὶ θεωρεῖ τὰ ὀθόνια κείμενα [καὶ ἐθαύμασεν]. 9 οὐδέπω γὰρ... In both hypotheses τὰ ὀθόνια is pre-Johannine in 19,40 and 20,5 or 6b and is added in the Johannine redaction, either 20,6 and 7 (Jn II-A and II-B) l or 20,5 and 7. For B-L παρακύψας in 20,5 is traditional and παρέκυψεν in 20,11 is Johannine (Jn II-B); and viceversa for Fortna: Johannine in 20,5 and traditional in 20,11. If I understand correctly Dauer's reference to Mahoney, his solution would come close to that of Fortna[79]. B-L's pre-Johannine source corresponds with Lk 24,12 minus the three Lukanisms. As indicated above, the absence of these Lukanisms in Jn 20,3-10 cannot be an objection against Johannine dependence on Lk 24,12[80].

In Dauer's general theory on the Gospel of John the pre-Johannine source was fused together with elements from the Synoptic Gospels. One would like to know whether this was the case also in Jn 20,3-10[81].

---

75. *Die Abendmahlsworte Jesu*, ³1960, p. 143.
76. Cf. *Die Passionsgeschichte*, 1972, p. 347.
77. *Authentizität*, p. 316.
78. Fortna (above n. 45) retains the plural in v. 3: "they came to the tomb" (i.e., Peter and Mary Magdalene). His earlier reconstruction (*The Gospel of Signs*, 1970) included v. 5 (cf. B-L) and v. 7, now both redactional, instead of v. 6b.
79. *Authentizität*, p. 316. Cf. MAHONEY, *Two Disciples*, p. 246: the evangelist "can in verse 5 have anticipated the ὀθόνια from verse 6 for reasons of composition".
80. See my *The Empty Tomb Stories*, p. 174 (= *Evangelica II*, 590): "a common source which is practically identical with the text of Lk 24,12 becomes an unnecessary hypothesis once the possibility of Johannine dependence on Luke can be envisioned".
81. Dauer again and again shows familiarity with Mahoney (*Authentizität*, nn. 55, 67, 68, 73, 74, 112, 113, 114, 118). It is interesting to note Mahoney's suggestion: "he himself (the evangelist) composed the whole scene with various elements from his tradition

5. *Lukan Composition*

More clarity is needed also in Dauer's critique of Lukan redaction in Lk 24,12[82].

(1) There is some "duplicity" in his observation on *Dublettenscheu*. Neither Schürmann's fifteen saying doublets nor the examples of the anointing and the feeding stories are to the point. Peter's inspection of the tomb, rather than "eine Dublette (im eigentlichen Sinn)", is related to 24,1-9 as a verification story (cf. 24,24)[83].

(2) The reactions of the disciples and Peter (cf. Mk 16,7) in Lk 24,11.12 are not simply "Duplizierung eines Motivs" and Peter's reaction in v. 12 is not "ganz unmotiviert": the women's story did not begin to be believed until Peter checked it himself and began to wonder. |

(3) Luke's composition of the little story in Lk 23,(54)55-56a is an interesting parallel, with the same elementary threefold structure; and this analogy is not at all spoiled because it is a substitute for Mk 15,47[84].

(4) The unbelief in v. 11 prepares for the appearance to the disciples. When Dauer maintains that v. 12 has no such a role since there is no account of an appearance to Peter[85], he grossly neglects the significance of ὤφθη Σίμωνι in v. 34.

(5) Dauer concedes that the return home is a typical motif of Lukan story-telling: "Kann man das ... auch auf eine solche kurze Szene anwenden?" He could have cited the illustration I gave in 1975, the short story in Lk 23,55-56: the women followed Joseph (to the place of the tomb), they saw how Jesus' body was laid, and they returned: ὑποστρέψασαι (v. 56; cf. 24,9)[86].

---

of the women's visit to the grave: for example, the motif of entering the tomb and the description of the tomb's interior" (p. 252); "the men took over the role of entering the tomb from the women" (p. 219); the evangelist's use of παρακύπτειν in 20,5 is "logically prior to its appearance in 20,11" (p. 246, cf. 54; for Mahoney: and in Lk 24,12).

82. *Lk 24,12*, pp. 1707-1712: "Zur Kritik an Neiryncks These". My references in this section are to his objections (1)-(7), pp. 1707-1710. His nos. (4), (6), and (7) are repeated in *Authenticity* as objections against the authenticity of v. 12.

83. Dauer compares Lk 24,12 with source doublets in Lk. A comparison with redactional duplications would be more appropriate. See, e.g., my essay on the composition of *Luke 14,1-6* (1991; = *Evangelica II*, 183-203).

84. Dauer overemphasizes the contrast with the *zusätzliche Erzählung* in Lk 24,12 and repeats his theme of *Dublettenscheu*. But see my observation on 23,54-56a: "Le parallélisme avec le récit de 24,1-9 est indéniable... Luc semble avoir développé le ἐθεώρουν de Mc 15,47 comme un premier récit des femmes au tombeau" (*Evangelica I*, 300).

85. See also below n. 103. – On 24,11.12, cf. above n. 40.

86. Cf. above n. 84. I may quote here the conclusion of my note on Ἀπῆλθεν πρὸς ἑαυτόν (1978; *Evangelica I*, 454-455): "Lc qui écrit ὑποστρέφειν εἰς τὸν οἶκον αὐτοῦ (cf. 1,56; 7,10; 8,39; 11,24), mais connaît aussi ὑποστρέφειν εἰς τὰ ἴδια (Ac 21,6), et

(6) Peter saw τὰ ὀθόνια μόνα: only the ὀθόνια, "and nothing more", not the body of Jesus. Dauer's reaction: in this interpretation of μόνα, 24,3 is supposed to be the model, "aber das ist bei unserer bisherigen Auseinandersetzung doch fraglich geworden". Is this once more a reference to *Dublettenscheu*? But without cancelling 24,3 and 23a.24(!), this can only be questionable for interpreters who read 24,12 in a Johannine rather than a Lukan context (μόνα in John's picture: lying by themselves, apart from the σουδάριον)[87].

(7) I Finally, "der Lauf des Petrus" with the parallels in Lk 1,39 (ἀναστᾶσα ... ἐπορεύθη ... μετὰ σπουδῆς) and 2,16 (ἦλθαν σπεύσαντες) and Dauer's difficulty: "weder bei Maria noch bei den Hirten (wird) vorher von Unglaube gesprochen"[88]. But in both stories the motif is the verification of the sign given by the angel(s) (1,36; 2,12): like 24,12, they are verification stories.

The Context of Lk 24,12

Dauer shows much generosity in quoting extracts from R.J. Dillon's *Eye-Witnesses* (1978)[89], on Lk 24,11, apostolic incredulity which is

exprime ailleurs le motif du retour par ἀπῆλθεν εἰς τὸν οἶκον αὐτοῦ (1,23; 5,25; cf. 2,15), se sert en 24,12 de ἀπῆλθεν πρὸς ἑαυτόν, une expression qui est plus proche du vocabulaire de la Septante que beaucoup de commentateurs récents ne semblent l'admettre" (with reference to n. 65, on ἀπέρχεσθαι in the LXX). My point was that not only the Lukan term ὑποστρέφειν (cf. 23,56; 24,9.33.52) but also ἀπέρχεσθαι is used by Luke to express the theme of return. Dauer's rendering needs to be corrected: "Neirynck erwidert, die Formulierung sei *nach Meinung vieler Exegeten* 'une expression qui est plus proche du vocabulaire de la Septante'" (p. 1709; emphasis mine).

It is even more confusing when he now notes ἀπῆλθεν πρὸς ἑαυτόν = "he went home" and (without mentioning the Lukan motif) adds the following comment: "Daß freilich *deswegen* Lk 24,12 mit dieser Wendung von Lukas selbst stamme und Johannes diesen Vers als Vorlage für 20,3-10 verwendet habe, *wie N. meint* (116ff), läßt sich m.E. *daraus* nicht schließen" (*Authentizität*, p. 308 n. 64; emphasis mine). The conclusion he refers to was a more modest one: "Si Jn dépend de Lc 24,12, il doit avoir lu ἀπῆλθεν πρὸς ἑαυτόν, et non πρὸς ἑαυτὸν θαυμάζων" (p. 453). It remains true, however, that the phrase in Jn 20,10 is without parallel in Jn (cf. p. 453, on ἀπέρχεσθαι πρός in Jn 4,47; 6,68; 11,46).

87. The question "Wie kommt Johannes dazu...?" is not only to be asked in the hypothesis of Lukan redaction (p. 1710: "nach dem Verständnis Neiryncks..."; see also *Authentizität*, p. 315, and n. 106). Compare the common-source hypothesis, with τὰ ὀθόνια μόνα in the source text (R. Leaney, *et al.*). Cf. BOISMARD-LAMOUILLE (1977): Doc. C (v. 5), Jn II-A (vv. 5 and 6); v. 7 is added (and μόνα omitted in vv. 5 and 6) by Jn II-B. Dauer (n. 106) mentions the possible influence of Jn 11,44 (but κειρίαι!) and also the suggestion that the σουδάριον is a kind of sign evoking faith in the beloved disciple (Schneiders, cf. below n. 110; now also Fortna, p. 191). "John's point however may be simply to show that the natural assumption of robbery (v. 2) was mistaken" (BARRETT, p. 563).

88. See now also *Authentizität*, p. 317 (3).

89. *Authentizität*, pp. 313-314 (notes 93-98).

prelude to apostolic verification, and on 24,12 as the climax of the tomb story, with a display of the parallel development in 24,1-9 and 12, women and Peter, ἀπορεῖσθαι (v. 4) and θαυμάζων (v. 12): "Diese Beobachtungen von Dillon sind recht interessant". Just one thing is lacking: Dillon's references to *ETL* (1972)[90].

Dauer's (indirect) assent is far from complete. He cites a series of tensions and contradictions with the context in ch. 24 which militate against the authenticity of Lk 24,12 and, of course, against the Lukan redaction of the verse. He mentions first of all the contrast between the singular in 24,12 (Peter) and the plural in 24,24 ("some of those who were with us") and surveys the various solutions which have been given to this problem[91]. But what most bothers him is the statement that 24,24 refers back to v. 12 and can be cited as evidence for the authenticity of the verse. He answers with a demonstration that "es geradezu zur literarischen Arbeitsweise des Lukas gehört, in Reden, Gesprächen etc Episoden u.ä. nachzutragen, die früher in Erzählungen noch nicht von ihm gebracht worden sind"[92]. However, Dauer himself also recognizes: "Es gibt *zahlreiche Beispiele* dafür, daß Lukas z.T. recht genau, z.T. wenigstens annähernd früher Erzähltes in der Rede / dem Gespräch I wiederholt"[93]. Both are possible in Lk, *Nachtrag* and *Wiederholung*, and Dauer's inventory of the first can scarcely become an argument *against* the authenticity of 24,12.

Lk 24,34 serves to illustrate how Luke "auch *nachträglich* neue Informationen geben kann"[94]: Luke alludes to the appearance to Peter (ὤφθη Σίμωνι) without having mentioned it before, although "er hätte sicher ... einen solchen (Bericht) aus der Traditionsnotiz V. 34 bilden können"[95]. But the case of 24,24 cannot be assimilated to a *Nachtrag* like v. 34. Verse 24 is part of 24,22-24 which provides a summary of the tomb story in 24,1-12. The relation of vv. 22-23 to 24,1-11 is undisputable[96], and v. 24 "repeats" with some variation the motif of v. 12. It

90. *Eye-Witnesses*, p. 66 n. 190 (on the climax-effect), n. 192 (on the parallel development): "N. astutely observed this pattern in the passages of Lk 24 dealing with the tomb (vv. 1-12.22-24)". – One remark, on Lk 24,10b-11 "mit dem dreimaligen καί" (p. 313): ... καὶ αἱ λοιπαὶ σὺν αὐταῖς. ἔλεγον... is the better punctuation (N[26.27], GNT[3corr.4]).

91. *Authentizität*, pp. 310-312.

92. *Lk 24,12*, p. 1702 n. 38; *Authentizität*, p. 303 n. 40. Cf. above n. 15 ("*Ergänzungen*", 1989) and n. 17 (*Beobachtungen*, 1990).

93. *Beobachtungen*, p. 11 (emphasis mine); "*Ergänzungen*", p. 308: "viele Beispiele".

94. *Beobachtungen*, pp. 63-66 (esp. 66). See also *Authentizität*, pp. 312 (2); 317 (6).

95. *Beobachtungen*, p. 66. Note that Dauer stresses the possibility that Luke "selber eine solche Geschichte bildete" (*ibid.*).

96. Cf. *Authentizität*, p. 317 (6): "eine knappe Zusammenfassung des Berichtes von 24,1-8". Add 24,9-11: cf. 24,22a ἐξέστησαν ἡμᾶς.

is only on the assumption of the inauthenticity of v. 12 that 24,24 can be classified as *Nachtrag*. The term *Wiederaufnahme* is a much better definition of the relation to v. 12, and Dauer is quite correct in stressing that one should not expect that such a recapitulation "erwähnte Einzelheiten exakt wiederholt"[97].

Dauer replies with one of his amazingly radical statements: "v. 24 dürfte v. 12 kaum voraussetzen", and: "v. 24 hat nichts mit v. 12 zu tun" (sic)[98]. In his analysis of v. 24 he emphasizes that the antecedent of καθὼς καὶ αἱ γυναῖκες εἶπον includes v. 23b, λέγουσαι καὶ ὀπτασίαν ἀγγέλων ἑωρακέναι, οἳ λέγουσιν αὐτὸν ζῆν: "Dieser Versteil wird von Neirynck einfach übergangen"[99]. There is, of course, no doubt that 24,22-23 retells the story of the women at the tomb inclusive of the vision of angels, but what counts for the travelers to Emmaus is μὴ εὑροῦσαι τὸ σῶμα αὐτοῦ and its confirmation by the disciples: αὐτὸν δὲ οὐκ εἶδον[100]. Nothing in their attitude corresponds to the angelic message "that he was alive": "The Emmaus disciples have evidently discounted their story... (They) have to minimise the importance of the visits to the tomb, which are not grounds for hope. They do this by reducing the women to anonymity, γυναῖκές τινες, and the same vague plural is used of the second visit, even though Peter went alone"[101].

I The appearance to the women also plays a role in the discussion on the relation between v. 12 and v. 34 and on the parallel between Peter's θαυμάζων (v. 12) and the women's ἀπορεῖσθαι (v. 4): "As the angelic appearance is the follow-up to this aporia, so Luke may have seen the appearance of the Lord (v. 34) as the answer to Peter's amazement"[102]. Dauer's objection concerns the *Erzählstruktur*: the appearance of the angels follows immediately in v. 4, whereas the response to Peter's amazement comes much later[103]. Two obvious observations on the structure of Luke's stories can suffice here. (1) The first section of the tomb story has its climax in οὐχ εὗρον τὸ σῶμα τοῦ κυρίου Ἰησοῦ followed by the women's perplexity: καὶ ἐγένετο ἐν τῷ ἀπορεῖσθαι αὐτὰς περὶ τούτου (v. 4a); the story of Peter's visit to the tomb

---

97. *Beobachtungen*, p. 11.
98. *Authentizität*, p. 317 (6).
99. *Ibid.*, n. 116.
100. At least this connection between vv. 24c and 23a is admitted by Dauer: "sicher richtig" (n. 116).
101. MUDDIMAN, *Note*, p. 547. See also Lk 21,5 τινων λεγόντων for λέγει εἷς in Mk 13,1 (*ibid.*).
102. *Historic Present*, p. 552 (= *Evangelica I*, 333). Cf. above n. 90.
103. *Authentizität*, p. 314 n. 100.

"repeats" their non-finding of the body and ends with Peter θαυμάζων τὸ γεγονός. (2) The tomb story is concluded with the verse on the amazement of Peter and the Emmaus story comes to its close with the reference to the appearance of the Lord to Peter. Thus, verses 12 and 34 are not structurally unrelated. Dauer's assertion that v. 12 "contradicts" v. 34[104] seems to suppose the undocumented opinion that verses 12 and 34 refer to the *same* event. But "Peter's role in seeing Jesus is not mutually exclusive with his inspection of the tomb, which was, in any case, less important"[105].

The evidence from the immediate context is Dauer's final argument. "V. 12 zerreißt den Zusammenhang zwischen v. 11 und v. 13"[106]: the story of the women at the tomb ends in v. 11 with the disbelief of the disciples and this remains the background of the Emmaus story; v. 12 has no effect on the continuation of the narrative. It would be more correct to say that the characters in this story, the Emmaus disciples, knew of an inspection of the tomb to check the women's report but did not gain any new insight from it (v. 24). Luke's reference to Peter's reaction, θαυμάζων τὸ γεγονός, is apparently not meant to be an information for the Emmaus disciples. We can call it an inside view intended to prepare the reader for the Petrine apparition in v. 34[107]. – Note that those who I stress the *Zusammenhang* between vv. 11 and 13 too easily neglect that δύο ἐξ αὐτῶν in v. 13 refers not to v. 11 (the apostles) but to the wider group of v. 9[108].

As indicated above, I propose to read ὁ δὲ Πέτρος... and θαυμάζων in close relation to v. 11 but I find it unjustified to declare that v. 12 is

104. *Authentizität*, p. 312 (2).
105. W.L. Craig's formulation (below n. 122), p. 615.
106. *Authentizität*, p. 314 (5). Cf. J. Schmid, *Lukas*, p. 354: "Der Zusammenhang zwischen V. 11 und 13 wird durch ihn (V. 12) zerrissen" (= 1940, p. 253; cf. p. 255: "V. 13 knüpft an V. 11 an", but see also the parenthesis added in ²1951 and following editions: "dort aber war nur von den Elfen die Rede, zu denen die zwei nicht gehörten"). The references to L. Brun and W.E. Bundy in n. 99 should be cancelled: none has an observation on the "Zusammenhang" between vv. 11 and 13.
107. In contrast to Dauer's comment on v. 12 (p. 314: "bleibt ohne Folgen und schwebt gleichsam in der Luft"), compare how R.C. Tannehill describes the function of Lk 24,12: "v. 12 would suggest that Peter's response is a matter of continuing interest, which might remind readers that Jesus had prayed for Peter and anticipated that he would 'turn' and 'strengthen his brothers' (22:32). This special role of Peter ... begins to be fulfilled in 24:34". Cf. *The Narrative Unity of Luke-Acts. A Literary Interpretation*. Vol. 1: *The Gospel according to Luke*, Philadelphia, 1986, p. 279.
108. Lk 24,9 πάντες οἱ λοιποί, cf. v. 18 Cleopas. See n. 106. In that sense one can call 24,10-12 "a parenthetic unit" (Muddiman). Cf. *Historic Present*, p. 549 (= *Evangelica I*, 330). See now also Fitzmyer, *Luke*, p. 1541. – Dauer's reply is an evasive "nicht überzeugend" (n. 102).

an artificial appendage and v. 11 a much better conclusion[109]. I refer once more to Lk 24,22-24 and to the role of the verification story in the Gospel of Luke[110].

6. *Lk 24,12 / Jn 20,3-10*

There is a strange dichotomy in Dauer's exegetical work. In his study of parallels to Lk in the Gospel of John he is an outspoken defender of Lukan influence on the pre-Johannine source(s), and in what we know of his text-critical options and his redaction-critical investigations there is hardly any positive direction toward the interpolation theory. Is it then the need of an alternative for "literarische Abhängigkeit von Joh 20,3-10 I von Lk 24,12"[111] which inspires his effort? The interpolator of Lk 24,12 is supposed to imitate Lukan style (τὸ γεγονός), though not very successfully (word order of ἀναστάς) and, under the influence of the occurrence of θαυμάζειν (besides ἀπιστεῖν) in 24,41, to use this verb for the reaction of Peter halfway between unbelief and the beloved disciple's ἐπίστευσεν. Dauer shows no restraint in attributing to the interpolator what he refused to accept as Lukan redaction: "man kann auch umgekehrt argumentieren"[112]. The interpolator is allowed to remove the beloved disciple and to transfer to Peter παρακύψας βλέπει in spite of

109. *Authentizität*, pp. 313-314 (4).

110. The function of the reference to Peter in the larger context of the Gospel of Luke (cf. n. 107) is completely neglected by Pheme PERKINS, *Peter: Apostle for the Whole Church*, Columbia, SC, 1994, p. 87: "This verse probably did not belong to the original text of Luke, since it conflicts with the rejection of the woman's report attributed to the apostles in Luke 24:11". (Note how lightly she evaluates the textual support for v. 12: "some ancient manuscripts...".) Contrast this same author's earlier view, in *Resurrection: New Testament Witness and Contemporary Reflection*, Garden City, NY, 1984, p. 156: "Some account of a confirmation of the women's story is required by Lk 24:24. Therefore, we presume that it is original".

Compare Sandra M. Schneiders's similar development, *The Face Veil: A Johannine Sign (John 20:1-10)*, in *BTB* 13 (1983) 94-97, p. 94: "I consider Lk 24:12 an interpolation or at least an assimilation of Luke to John" (Dauer refers to the German translation: nn. 2 and 106). Contrast *The Johannine Resurrection Narrative*, Diss. Excerpt, Rome, 1975, p. 31 (and n. 15): "the fact that it accords very imperfectly with Lk. 24:24 ... suggests that Lk. 24:12 was not created by the III evangelist", and "the plural form ... indicates that v. 12 was probably a unit before Luke used it" (mistakenly classified by Dauer as defending inauthenticity).

Still one more opinion can be added to Dauer's collection: the verse is bracketed in the Scholars Version, with the following comment, "Not only is this verse textually doubtful, it is implausible, for Peter's home was in Capernaum". Cf. R.J. MILLER, *The Complete Gospels. Annotated Scholars Version*, Sonoma, CA, ²1992, p. 172.

111. See the concluding sentence in *Lk 24,12*, p. 1713. Cf. *Authentizität*, p. 309 n. 71: "ist recht unwahrscheinlich".

112. *Ibid.*, p. 1709.

the fact that the sense it had in Jn 20,5 ("er bückte sich ins Grab") becomes "rätselhaft" in a story of Peter alone. The interpolator can omit καὶ τὸ σουδάριον, ὃ ἦν ἐπὶ τῆς κεφαλῆς αὐτοῦ, οὐ μετὰ τῶν ὀθονίων κείμενον ἀλλὰ χωρὶς ἐντετυλιγμένον εἰς ἕνα τόπον (v. 7) and simply write (τὰ ὀθόνια) μόνα, which has "seinen verständlichen Sinn" only as an abbreviation of the source text in Jn 20,6-7. But when Lk 24,12 is taken apart from Jn 20,3-10 and παρακύψας and μόνα are read in the light of the Lukan context (24,3) they are neither "rätselhaft" nor "unverständlich": Peter went into the tomb, "and when he looked he saw only the graveclothes", not the body of Jesus.

References to Dauer (*Lk 24,12*, 1992) are found in three recent studies by G. Lüdemann, M. Myllykoski, and W. Reinbold, all published in the course of 1994[113]. All three exclude the possibility of an interpolation[114] and opt for a common source used by Luke and John[115]. The | "un-Lukan" vocabulary in παρακύψας βλέπει τὰ ὀθόνια is their common argument for pre-Lukan tradition and against redactional composition by Luke. Unfortunately, they offer no discussion of the evidence if not that Myllykoski stresses the use of τὰ ὀθόνια in Lk 24,12 in contrast to σινδών in 23,53 (par. Mk 15,46)[116]. Dauer considered this

---

113. G. LÜDEMANN, *Die Auferstehung Jesu. Historie, Erfahrung, Theologie*, Göttingen, 1994, pp. 172-174; ET (cited here): *The Resurrection of Jesus. History, Experience, Theology*, London, 1994, pp. 138-139, 156 (notes, 239-240); M. MYLLYKOSKI, *Die letzten Tage Jesu. Markus, Johannes, ihre Traditionen und die historische Frage*, vol. 2 (AASF, B/272), Helsinki, 1994, pp. 78-85 (esp. 81-82), 123 (notes); W. REINBOLD, *Der älteste Bericht über den Tod Jesu. Literarische Analyse und historische Kritik der Passionsdarstellungen der Evangelien* (BZNW, 69), Berlin - New York, 1994, pp. 35, 68-69.

114. Dauer's position (cf. REINBOLD, p. 35 n. 26) is misunderstood by Lüdemann (n. 561). See Dauer's correction in *Authentizität*, n. 7 (and references to Lüdemann in nn. 2, 14, 42, 48, 68, 75). There is no mention of Myllykoski and Reinbold.

115. Cf. MYLLYKOSKI, p. 81, on Lk 24,12: "Der Vers wirkt in seinem sonst lukanischen Zusammenhang wie eine unorganisch eingestreute Einzelnachricht"; "unorganische Einfügung des traditionellen Bestandteils bei Lk" (cf. REINBOLD, p. 35: "die Einbindung in den Kontext ist alles andere als gut"). But see by the same Myllykoski, *The Material Common to Luke and John: A Sketch*, in P. LUOMANEN (ed.), *Luke-Acts. Scandinavian Perspectives* (PFES, 54), Helsinki-Göttingen, 1991, pp. 115-156, esp. 149-150: "Peter's visit to the tomb hardly formed an independent tradition... It presupposes the appearance story... On the other hand, it presupposes a description of some earlier events at the tomb". Compare Lüdemann's description of the origin of "the visit of Peter to the tomb" as a combination of the tradition of the appearance to Peter (cf. Lk 24,34) and the tradition of the visit of the women to the tomb: "The 'logic' of this combination is as follows: if the tomb was empty and Jesus appeared to Cephas, then he must have previously inspected it in order to convince himself" (p. 139). Question: is this not "more probably" the logic of Luke himself?

116. MYLLYKOSKI, p. 123 n. 28. Lüdemann and Reinbold rather emphasize the historic present: "remains a problem" (LÜDEMANN, p. 139); "vor allem" (REINBOLD, p. 35 n. 27).

"contradiction" (sic) and the possible solution that Luke drew σινδών from Mk and τὰ ὀθόνια from a different source. His question then remains "warum Lukas diese Spannung nicht beseitigte"[117]. But our primary question is to know whether, in the mind of Luke, we can really speak of contradiction between 23,53 and 24,12. The now current English translation "in a linen shroud/sheet/cloth" (Lk 23,53) probably remains too close to the parallel text in Mk[118]. "Wrapped it *in linen*" (KJV) was, I think, a better rendering of Luke's ἐνετύλιξεν αὐτὸ σινδόνι[119]. With this understanding of σινδών as designation of the material there can be no contradiction between one linen cloth on the one hand and the plural ὀθόνια on the other. That both σινδών and ὀθόνια occur in the same Gospel is less strange than it may appear. In Judges 14,12.13 LXXB τριάκοντα σινδόνας and τριάκοντα ὀθόνια are used interchangeably for the same term in Hebrew. If we take into account the occurrences of ὀθόνη in Acts 10,11; 11,5 (σκεῦός τι ὡς ὀθόνην μεγάλην), then τὰ ὀθόνια in Lk 24,12 is not a Lukan hapaxlegomenon, at least not in the strict sense. Both ὀθόνη and ὀθόνιον appear in papyri for burial clothes (P. Hib. 794,5 εἰς ταφὰς ὀθόναι; P. Giess. 68,11,25 ὀθόνια εὔωνα)[120]. Luke's phrase τὰ ὀθόνια μόνα in 24,12 repeats with greater precision the negative statement "they did not find the body of Jesus". Is it then really more likely that this phrase would stem from a hypothetical source lacking the context of 24,3 and 24,22-24? Dauer's comment on ὀθόνιον in the Gospel of John (19,40; 20,5.6.7) is twofold: its use is "sachlich bedingt", but he also notes the contrast with the burial story in Lk "wo es σινδών heißt"[121]. There is almost scholarly unanimity that τὰ ὀθόνια I in Jn 20 relies on tradition (Lk 24,12 or a source very much like Lk 24,12) and has received Johannine or redactional development in 20,5 (κείμενα τὰ ὀθόνια), 6 (τὰ

---

117. *Authentizität*, p. 313. Dauer can dispense with such questions with regard to the interpolator.

118. Although J. Blinzler (below n. 123) thinks that in the three Synoptics σινδών can be understood as "Materialbezeichnung" ("in Leinwand gewickelt"), this is less evident in Mk 15,46: καὶ ἀγοράσας σινδόνα ... ἐνείλησεν τῇ σινδόνι. See also Mk 14,51-52.

119. Compare the Dutch translations: "hij wikkelde het *in linnen*" (NBG, KBS, NWV). Contrast Mk 15,46: "Deze kocht *een linnen doek*, ... en wikkelde hem in het linnen".

120. Cf. C. SPICQ, art. ὀθόνη, ὀθόνιον, in *Notes*, vol. 2, 601-605, esp. p. 603: "sont plusieurs fois mentionnés dans les ensevelissements". Note that "ces deux substantifs sont à peu près synonymes" (p. 601). It is more doubtful whether τὰ ὀθόνια ("les linges") in Lk 24,12 should be translated as "les bandelettes" (BJ, TOB), supported by Spicq (p. 604) with reference to medical language (HOBART, 218-219) and Jn 19,40 (ἔδησεν αὐτὸ ὀθονίοις).

121. *Authentizität*, pp. 308 and 307.

ὀθόνια κείμενα), 7 (οὐ μετὰ τῶν ὀθονίων κείμενον)[122]. It is quite natural that, in preparation of 20,5-7, the Synoptic σινδών is replaced by ὀθόνια in 19,40: "eben da die ὀθόνια in Kap. 20 von Bedeutung sein sollten, hat sie der Evangelist schon 19,40 genannt"[123].

In his recent comment on Jn 19,40 R.E. Brown observes that "The Synoptics seem to picture a single burial cloth while John speaks of several cloth wrappings"[124]. Without referring to Luke's use of ὀθόνια in 24,12, he states that "there (is) nothing in the Synoptic description to suggest a plurality of burial cloths"[125]. The possible relation to the Synoptics is treated in a footnote: "I see no reason to think that John knew of the Markan *sindōn* and changed it to *othonia*, for there is no clear theological import in the latter"[126]. This last clause may surprise those who read Brown's own commentary on Jn 20,5-7: "when the Beloved Disciple was introduced into the story, the Johannine writer capitalized on the presence of the burial garments as the explanation of what led the Disciple to believe"[127]. His earlier statement about Lk 24,12 saying that "the mention of *othonia* ... indicates that the verse is an addition"[128] is now mitigated: "Whether Luke 24:12 was written by Luke or added by a later scribe, its composer sensed no contradiction..."[129].

7. Conclusion

W. Radl could write in his *Forschungsbericht* on the Gospel of Luke (1988): "Das textkritische Problem von V. 12 scheint bereinigt zu sein", and "Dabei scheint bei Lukas das ursprünglichere Stadium der Tradition

---

122. I do not consider here W.L. Craig's position on "the probability that in John's account we encounter eyewitness reminiscences of the incident" (p. 618), "the reminiscences of the Beloved Disciple" (n. 7). Cf. *The Disciples' Inspection of the Empty tomb (Lk 24,12.24; Jn 20,2-10)*, in A. DENAUX (ed.), *John and the Synoptics* (above n. 18), pp. 614-619.

123. J. BLINZLER, *Die Grablegung Jesu in historischer Sicht*, in É. DHANIS (ed.), *Resurrexit*, Rome, 1974, pp. 56-107, esp. 79. See also *Der Prozess Jesu*, Regensburg, ⁴1969, pp. 385-404 ("Die Grablegung"), esp. 397.

124. R.E. BROWN, *The Death of the Messiah*, New York, 1994, pp. 1264-1265 (p. 1265, on "John's picture of plurality"). – Cf. my review in *ETL* 70 (1994) 406-416, esp. 416, n. 35.

125. *Ibid.*, p. 1264. Cf. pp. 1244-1245, on Mk 15,46a.

126. *Ibid.*, p. 1265 n. 67.

127. *John*, vol. 2, 1970, p. 1008 (pp. 1007-1008: "What the Beloved Disciple Saw: the Burial Clothes").

128. *Ibid.*, p. 985. Cf. p. 1000: "in our opinion a redactor's addition, not a later scribe's".

129. *The Death*, p. 1265 n. 67.

| erhalten zu sein, die in Joh 20,3-10 dann entfaltet worden ist"[130]. My suggestion was to take one step further by proposing Lk 24,12 as Lukan redaction and the "source" behind Jn 20,3-10. Dauer mentions three scholars who wrote in support of this hypothesis: W. Schmithals (1980)[131], J.D. Crossan (1988) and D. Senior (1989)[132]. A few more names can be mentioned: the commentaries on Lk by J. Kremer (1988)[133] and M.D. Goulder (1989)[134], and studies on Jn by J. Kügler (1988)[135], H. Thyen (1992)[136], U. Schnelle (1992)[137], M. Sabbe (1994)[138], et al.

---

130. W. RADL, *Das Lukas-Evangelium* (Erträge der Forschung, 261), Darmstadt, 1988, pp. 1415.

131. *Lk 24,12*, p. 1702 n. 40: W. SCHMITHALS, *Das Evangelium nach Lukas* (Zürcher Bibelkommentare, 3/1), Zürich, 1980: Lk 24,11.12 "ganz redaktionell". See now also *Johannesevangelium und Johannesbriefe. Forschungsgeschichte und Analyse* (BZNW, 64), Berlin - New York, 1992, p. 223, on Jn 20,2-11a: "der ganze Einschub entfaltet die eher beiläufige Notiz Lk 24,12". Cf. my review in *ETL* 68 (1992) 166-168.

132. *Authentizität*, p. 303 n. 43: J.D. CROSSAN, *The Cross that Spoke. The Origins of the Passion Narrative*, San Francisco, 1988, p. 289; D. SENIOR, *The Passion of Jesus in the Gospel of Luke*, Wilmington, DE, 1989, p. 154 n. 3.

133. J. KREMER, *Lukasevangelium* (Die Neue Echter Bibel, 3), Würzburg, 1988, p. 238: "12 kann auf einer besonderen mündlichen Tradition beruhen (vgl. Joh 20,3-8), oder auch von Lk selbst stammen (in Ausfaltung von Mk 16,7 "und dem Petrus" und unter Berücksichtigung der Sonderstellung des Petrus: vgl. 34; 1 Kor 15,5; Apg 1,15; 2,14 u.ö.)". Cf. *Die Osterevangelien - Geschichten um Geschichte*, Stuttgart-Klosterneuburg, 1977, p. 109: "Doch kann Lukas ... das hier geschilderte Sonderverhalten des Petrus auch sehr gut frei gestaltet haben, um der alten Überlieferung, daß der Auferstandene als ersten Petrus erschienen ist ... Rechnung zu tragen"; p. 106: "Nicht ohne Sinn steht hier das Präsens historicum βλέπει (sieht). Petrus wird damit dem Leser ganz besonders als Zeuge des leeren Grabes vor Augen gestellt"; see also p. 179, on Jn 20: "(unter Benützung des Lukasevangeliums?)".

134. M.D. GOULDER, *Luke. A New Paradigm* (JSNT SS, 20), Sheffield, 1989, pp. 776-779: "a Petrine visit is likely to be a Lucan construction" (one reservation: the influence of Mt 28,8 ἔδραμον ἀπαγγεῖλαι; cf. *Evangelica I*, 261-263).

135. J. KÜGLER, *Der Jünger, den Jesus liebte* (SBB, 16), Stuttgart, 1988, pp. 347-348.

136. H. THYEN, *Johannes und die Synoptiker. Auf der Suche nach einem neuen Paradigma zur Beschreibung ihrer Beziehungen anhand von Beobachtungen an Passions- und Ostererzählungen*, in A. DENAUX (ed.), *John and the Synoptics* (above n. 18), 1992, pp. 81-107, esp. 105: "Lk 24,12 ... ist ein textkritisch gesicherter Bestandteil des dritten Evangeliums (vgl. 24,24). Wie auf seine Weise Mt 28,8-10, so ist auch Lk 24,12 *redaktionelle Bildung*"; see also *Die Erzählung von den bethanischen Geschwistern (Joh 11,1-12,19) als "Palimpsest" über synoptischen Texten*, in *The Four Gospels 1992* (above n. 2), pp. 2021-2050, esp. 2046, on Jn 20: Lk 24,12 "die lukanische Vorlage unserer Erzählung" (cf. p. 2023 n. 5).

137. U. SCHNELLE, *Johannes und die Synoptiker*, in *The Four Gospels 1992* (above n. 2), pp. 1799-1814, esp. 1812: "Johannes übernahm dieses Motiv aus Lk 24,12... Textkritisch darf heute die Ursprünglichkeit von Lk 24,12 vorausgesetzt werden" (cf. n. 63).

138. M. SABBE, *The Johannine Account of the Death of Jesus and Its Synoptic Parallels (Jn 19,16b-42)*, in *ETL* 70 (1994) 34-64, p. 53, on Jn 19,40: "ὀθόνια is taken over from Lk 24,12" (cf. n. 60). See also *Studia Neotestamentica. Collected Essays* (BETL, 98), 1991, pp. 368 (n. 70), 382 n. 126.

ETL 72 (1996) 425-430

26

A SUPPLEMENTARY NOTE ON LK 24,12

In Memoriam Anton Dauer 1933-1996

I

Shortly after the publication of A. Dauer's essay on Lk 24,12 in *ETL* (1994)[1], a new contribution on the Luke–John relationship appeared in *JTS*, written by Barbara Shellard[2], with special attention to Lk 24,12:

> It is generally acknowledged that the connections between Luke and John are most apparent in their resurrection narratives (91). The most notable example of all, the one that suggests most strongly that Luke is using John at this point, rather than vice versa, is Luke 24:12 (93).

In my approach, too, Peter's visit to the tomb in Lk 24,12 is a most impressive test case, though not of Luke's use of John. I quote Shellard:

> Neirynck argues that the repetition of πρός in John 20:2, and the singular verb ἐξῆλθεν in 20:3, even though the subject is actually plural (Peter and the 'other disciple'), are evidence that the presence of the beloved disciple is a secondary insertion (94).

Shellard refers to my collected essays in *Evangelica I* (1982) and *Jean et les Synoptiques* (1979)[3], but the double argument she cites can scarcely be found there. First, regarding the use of πρός in Jn 20,2, she may have read[4]:

---

1. A. DAUER, *Zur Authentizität von Lk 24,12*, in *ETL* 70 (1994) 294-318; with my response: F. NEIRYNCK, *Once More Luke 24,12*, ibid., 319-340.

In the course of 1996 A. Dauer published his last work (Vorwort: October 1995): *Paulus und die christliche Gemeinde im syrischen Antiochia. Kritische Bestandsaufnahme der modernen Forschung mit einigen weiterführenden Überlegungen* (Bonner Biblische Beiträge, 106), Weinheim, Beltz Athenäum Verlag, 1996, (16,5×24), 299 p. (Text, 9-128; Anmerkungen, 129-275; Literaturverzeichnis, 277-299). ISBN 3-89547-106-2. I quote from the conclusion: "Antiochia erweckt den Eindruck eines paulinischen Traumas! ... Es spricht vieles dafür, daß Paulus sich in dieser Auseinandersetzung mit Kephas, einem Großteil der Gemeinde und Barnabas nicht durchsetzen konnte, sondern eine bittere Niederlage erlitt" (127).

2. B. SHELLARD, *The Relationship of Luke and John: A Fresh Look at an Old Problem*, in *JTS* 46 (1995) 71-98. On Lk 24,12, esp. 93-96.

3. More recent studies can be added: *John and the Synoptics: The Empty Tomb Stories*, in *NTS* 30 (1984) 161-187, esp. 172-178 ("Jn 20,1-10 and Lk 24,12"), reprinted in *Evangelica II*, 1991, 571-600, esp. 588-595; *John and the Synoptics: 1975-1990*, in A. DENAUX (ed.), *John and the Synoptics* (BETL, 101), Leuven, 1992, 3-62, esp. 42; and: *Once More Luke 24,12* (cf. above, n. 1).

4. *Jean et les Synoptiques*, 76-77; = *ETL* 53 (1977), 435-436.

Ce redoublement insolite [de πρός] confirme l'insertion des mots: 'et à l'autre disciple'". Boismard note que c'est le "seul cas dans Jn.

This quotation of Boismard's opinion is followed by extensive discussion and refutation. I quote here my conclusion: |

> Par la répétition de la préposition: "*vers* Simon Pierre et *vers* l'autre disciple...", les deux disciples sont mentionnés *séparément*. L'évangéliste peut très bien le faire de propos délibéré, puisque le rôle du v. 2 est de préparer le récit des vv. 3-10 sur les deux disciples en "concurrence". Le trait stylistique du redoublement de la préposition se justifie pleinement dans ce contexte, et on ne peut le citer comme indice d'une insertion dans un récit primitif.

Second, the same is true with regard to the singular ἐξῆλθεν in Jn 20,3[5]:

> La reconstruction du Document C ... se base aussi sur un argument d'ordre grammatical. En Jn 20,3, "le premier verbe est au singulier, malgré le double sujet, mais le second verbe est au pluriel" (Boismard, 311).
> En effet, l'anomalie est réelle dans une traduction littérale du texte: "Sortit donc Pierre, et l'autre disciple, et ils venaient..." (20,3). Mais en grec la construction n'a rien d'anormal. Qu'on se rappelle ses lectures classiques... En ce qui concerne Jn, E.A. Abbott présente le dossier complet du verbe au singulier précédant un double sujet: 1,33.45; 2,2.12; 3,22; 4,53; 12,22; 18,1.15; 20,3.

The passage "Neirynck argues..." in Shellard's article can be cancelled: it is a distortion of my way of arguing. In fact the evidence I decline is apparently accepted by her when she continues: "It seems indeed an insertion".

Shellard strongly defends the authenticity of Lk 24,12[6]. In a first section (93-94)[7] she discusses the supposedly 'Johannine' vocabulary (ὀθόνια, μνημεῖον, παρακύψας), the historic present βλέπει, and the Lukan touches: θαυμάζων, τὸ γεγονός, ἀναστάς. In a later section (95-96) she treats the manuscript evidence[8] and the relation to the

---

5. *Ibid.*, 81-82 (= 440-441). On Jn 18,15, see also *Evangelica I*, 359; = *ETL* 51 (1975), 137.

6. In reply to K.P.G. Curtis (1971) and R. Mahoney (1974); without mentioning A. Dauer's more recent essays: *Lk 24,12 – Ein Produkt lukanischer Redaktion?*, in *The Four Gospels 1992*. FS F. Neirynck (BETL, 100), Leuven, 1992, 1697-1716; *Zur Authentizität von Lk 24,12* (above n. 1).

7. With references (nn. 110, 114) to J. MUDDIMAN, *A Note on Reading Luke xxiv.12*, in *ETL* 48 (1972) 542-548, a response to K.P.G. CURTIS, *Luke xxiv.12 and John xx.3-10*, in *JTS* 22 (1971) 512-515.

8. She explicitly notes: "Neirynck, too, regards Luke 24,12 as authentic" (n. 116), with reference to my *Lc xxiv.12: Les témoins du texte occidental* (1978), in *Evangelica I*,

context in Lk 24 (vv. 11.24.34). In the conclusion of the article Shellard emphasizes again the importance of Lk 24,12:

> If we accept the weight of manuscript evidence, and uphold the authenticity of Luke 24:12, the case is much stronger. Luke knew and used John, and not vice versa (98).

The hypothesis of a Johannine interpolation is rejected by Shellard, but some of the arguments reappear in her own proposal. Παρακύψας is "not really relevant to Luke, which could suggest that it is secondary", in contrast to Jn 20,5 where "it delays matters until Peter arrives..." (94). The verb ἔδραμεν is irrelevant in Lk and therefore "it could be secondary", in contrast to προέδραμεν in Jn 20,4 which "is necessitated by his account, where the other disciple outruns Peter..." (95). The σουδάριον "was irrelevant to Luke, and so he dropped I it", in contrast to Jn 20,6 where "the headcloth was essential to the comparison John wished to make between Jesus and Lazarus" (95). In this last case at least she mentions the alternative ("it is equally possible") that "the mention of the headcloth was suggested to John by Luke's τὰ ὀθόνια μόνα, by which Luke meant 'only the gravecloths', i.e. not the body". She could also have mentioned that there is an alternative to her suggestion that the plural in Lk 24,24 "seems to reflect John's account" and "The content of the original source is discernible in this later verse, just as the language of that source may be apparent in the verb βλέπει" (95, 96). To conclude without becoming redundant I may refer the readers of *ETL* to the answer I anticipated in my "Once More Luke 24,12" (1994).

II

In the new edition of B.M. Metzger's *Textual Commentary* (1994), the note on Lk 24,12 remained unchanged[9], except that the degree of certainty (the letter D in 1971) is now adapted according to the Fourth revised edition (1993) of GNT: "include verse {B}". The "Note on Western Non-Interpolations" with the mention of the minority view is reprinted without change (following Lk 24,53). This minority view

---

313-328. But see my treatment of Marcion (320-321) and the Syriac versions (322-327): contrast her statement that Marcion (though with a critical remark: "perhaps not surprisingly") and some Syriac texts do not contain the verse (95).

9. B.M. METZGER, *A Textual Commentary on the Greek New Testament*, Stuttgart, ²1994. Cf. *ETL* 71 (1995) 453-454.

recently came to expression in the margin of a Colloquium on the Codex Bezae[10].

For Bart D. Ehrman, "Hort's discussion can be faulted on only one ground: it failed to provide an adequate accounting for these interpolations into the second-century text. In fact, every one of them appears to have functioned as a kind of anti-docetic polemic"[11]. "This includes ... the longer account of Peter's visit to the tomb in Luke 24:12, which emphasizes that Jesus was buried and raised in the body, an actual physical resurrection attested by the chief of the apostles"[12].

In the context of the 1994 Colloquium it can be interesting to compare this approach with C.-B. Amphoux's theory on the text of Lk 24. Starting from the "Western non-interpolations" he regards the Codex Bezae as a testimony of an earlier state of the text ("la tradition textuelle du *codex de Bèze*")[13]. | For Amphoux, Lk 24,12 is a later addition (cf. Jn 20,3-10) and its role is to add Peter to the group of witnesses of the empty tomb[14]. Likewise Lk 24,40 (cf. Jn 20,20) is a later insertion. But, with or without the following v. 40, the meaning of v. 39 remains the

10. D.C. PARKER – C.-B. AMPHOUX (eds.), *Codex Bezae. Studies from the Lunel Colloquium, June 1994* (NTTS, 22), Leiden, Brill, 1996. For the renewed interest in the study of the manuscript, see D.C. PARKER, *Codex Bezae. An Early Christian Manuscript and Its Text*, Cambridge, University Press, 1992.

11. B.D. EHRMAN, *The Text of the Gospels at the End of the Second Century*, in *Codex Bezae* (n. 10), 95-122, here 105. See his *The Orthodox Corruption of Scripture: The Effect of Early Christological Controversies on the Text of the New Testament*, New York - Oxford, 1993 (reprint 1996), esp. 211-221, on the subgroup of anti-docetic variants "Christ, Raised Bodily from the Dead", in this order: Lk 24;12 (212-217); 24;40 (217-219); 24,3 (219); 24,6 (219-220); 24,36 (220-221); followed by an Excursus on the Western non-interpolations (223-227) and Lk 24,51-52 (227-232).

12. *The Text*, 106.

13. *Le texte*, in *Codex Bezae* (n. 10), 337-354, esp. 347-349. Cf. ID., *Le chapitre 24 de Luc et l'origine de la tradition textuelle du* codex de Bèze *(D.05 du NT)*, in *Filología Neotestamentaria* 7 (1991) 21-49.

14. *Le chapitre 24*, 29. Cf. 41, on Lk 24,12.36b.40: "il semble que ce soient des emprunts à Jn". Compare M.C. PARSONS, *A Christological Tendency in P75*, in *JBL* 105 (1986) 463-479, here 477: "due to a scribal harmonization for doctrinal reasons"; 476: "the scribe of P75 was able ... to provide apostolic confirmation of the empty tomb (24:12)". In Amphoux's view, the Bezan text has two groups of women, a first group of two anonymous women (23,55 δύο D it) and the larger group mentioned in 24,10. In the Alexandrian text the women form one group and, by adding in v. 12 "un groupe de témoins... en la personne de Pierre", "le déficit dans les traditions qui confondent les deux groupes de femmes est comblé" (29). Amphoux does not consider the possibility of harmonizations in D (δύo in 23,55: cf. Mt 27,61; 28,1). In Lk 24,9 and 10 he distinguishes between "deux témoignages: d'une part, celui des 'deux femmes' (23,55)...; d'autre part, celui des compagnes des disciples, nommées au v. 10" (29). But in v. 9, subsequently to Lk 24,1 (variant: καί τινες σὺν αὐταῖς), is it still this group of only two women, apart from the larger group?

same: "d'une part, les mains et les pieds sont le signe de l'identité de Jésus [39a]; d'autre part, les disciples peuvent constater qu'il est corporel [39b]"; "sans lui [le v. 40], le signe (v. 39a) a été dépassé (v. 39b) et on n'y revient pas: c'est donc la corporalité de Jésus qui prend toute l'importance"[15]. One may leave aside this forced distinction in the theme of Lk 24,39, first the sign of Jesus' identity and then the reality of Jesus' body[16]. The point, however, is that the "anti-docetic" theme was present in the text of Luke from the beginning (v. 39, before the supposed interpolation of v. 40). Even Ehrman concedes: "Not that most interpreters would doubt the point [the physicality of Jesus' resurrected body], even without the verse, given verse 39 ('Handle [me] and see...')"[17]. But how then can the "heightened emphasis" in v. 40 become solid ground for regarding the verse as an interpolation? One thing is to say that Lk 24,39-40 may have "functioned" in a second-century anti-docetic polemic[18], but it is quite another thing to suggest that this polemic accounts for the origin of Lk 24,40. "The investigation, then, must be moved to the realm of internal evidence"[19]. I may recall my earlier comment on Lk 24,36-43: "L'insistance sur la réalité corporelle du Ressuscité (est) une nuance proprement lucanienne... La réalité corporelle de Jésus, visible et palpable (39-40), trouvera une confirmation | dans la *manducatio* (41-43)"[20]. I quote here A. Dauer's observation on the parallel structure[21]:

> Für lk Redaktion des ganzen V. 40 spricht auch seine parallele Struktur mit V. 43: Beide Male wird eine an sich überflüssige Beschreibung des eben gesagten gegeben:
> καὶ τοῦτο εἰπὼν ἔδειξεν αὐτοῖς...
> καὶ λαβὼν ἐνώπιον αὐτῶν ἔφαγεν.
> Da V. 43 von Lukas stammt, wird Gleiches für V. 40 anzunehmen sein.

---

15. *Ibid.*, 36, 37.

16. Cf. F. NEIRYNCK, *Luc 24,36-43: un récit lucanien* (1985), in *Evangelica II*, 1991, 205-226, esp. 222: "Au niveau du texte de Luc, la distinction entre reconnaissance (v. 39a) et démonstration de la réalité du corps (v. 39b) ... est difficilement défendable... 'Il leur montra ses mains et ses pieds' ... ajoute le geste à la parole du v. 39 sans qu'on puisse faire deux actes distincts de ἴδετε et ψηλαφήσατε".

17. *Orthodox Corruption* (n. 11), 218.

18. See my *Luc 24,36-43* (n. 16): "Le témoignage d'Ignace d'Antioche" (219-222); and 226: note on W.R. Schoedel, 1985). On the phrase πρὸς τοὺς περὶ Πέτρον, regarded by Ehrman as an indication that the incident was known independently by Ignatius, see *ibid.*, 221.

19. Ehrman, on Western non-interpolations in general, in *Orthodox Corruption* (n. 11), 199.

20. *Luc 24,36-43*, 222, 224. See also *Jean et les Synoptiques* (BETL, 49), Leuven, 1979, 131-132 (cf. 126-130: "L'authenticité de Lc 24,36b et 40").

21. *Johannes und Lukas* (FzB, 50), Würzburg, 1984, 269. Καὶ τοῦτο εἰπών +

Lk 24,40 is correctly described, I think, as stressing Jesus' bodily resurrection, but it cannot be treated as an intrusion in the context[22].

The case of Lk 24,12 opens Ehrman's discussion of the Western non-interpolations in Lk 24: "I will try to show that this emerging consensus (in favor of the longer text) is wrong"[23]. The intrinsic evidence[24] comes first, to begin with pleonastic ἀναστάς: "the usage in Luke 24:12 is absolutely *atypical*" (sic); it is "anomalous", "failing to reverse the sequence of the pleonastic participle with the subject in accordance with his [= Luke's] consistent style" (213, 214). The objection is not new, but the answer that has been given is simply neglected by Ehrman: "Luke's exceptional order, subject + ἀναστάς, emphasises that the second corroborating visit was conducted by none other than Peter himself"[25]. In my response to Dauer, I could add that "of the seventeen occurrences of the participle ἀναστάς in the Gospel of Luke, there are only three instances where the subject is expressed", and "in contrast to 24,12 the subject in 1,39 (Μαριάμ) and 23,1 (ἅπαν τὸ πλῆθος αὐτῶν) was resumed from the preceding paragraph"[26]. Regarding θαυμάζων τὸ γεγονός that is reduced to "the common stock of the New Testament writings" (213), three remarks are in order: (1) not the θαυμα- word group but the use of θαυμάζειν + acc. (Lk 7,9; Acts 7,31) is cited as Lukan; (2) the fact that one of the four instances of τὸ γεγονός is borrowed from Mk (213: Lk 9,35, read: 8,35) does not prevent characteristically Lukan use; (3) the conjunction of both terms in one phrase creates a valid example of Lukan style.

I Ehrman then comes to "*non*-Lukan features" (the historic present βλέπει, παρακύψας, τὰ ὀθόνια, and ἀπῆλθεν πρὸς ἑαυτόν) and their

verbum finitum: cf. Lk 19,28; 23,46 (δέ); Acts 1,9; 7,60; 19,40; 20,36; 27,35 (δέ). The intrinsic issue is neglected in Ehrman's treatment of Lk 24,40.

22. For a reaction to (Parsons and) Ehrman, cf. A.W. ZWIEP, *The Text of the Ascension Narratives (Luke 24.50-3; Acts 1.1-2,9-11)*, in *NTS* 42 (1996) 219-244, here 230: "the supposed 'expansions' bear an uncomfortable resemblance to what we otherwise know of the theological outlook of the author of Luke-Acts".

23. *Orthodox Corruption* (n. 11), 212-217 (here 213). Lk 24,12 is discussed first as "one of the thorniest and most debated texts" (212).

24. Ehrman recognizes "the presence of the verse in a wide range of textual witnesses", with referece to my 1978 article: "has convincingly shown that Marcion, the Diatessaron, and the Palestinian Syriac cannot be cited in support of the Western text here, despite their appearance in most of the apparatuses" (254 n. 129).

25. J. MUDDIMAN, in *ETL* 48 (1972), 546.

26. *ETL* 70 (1994), 323.

parallels in Jn 20, without adding really new data to the debate[27]. The most striking statement is perhaps his dismissal of Johannine dependence on Lk "in view of the growing consensus..." (255 n. 137)[28].

27. Cf. *ibid.*, 325-331: "Supposedly Un-Lukan Words and Phrases". On Luke's use of the historic present in passages that he did not take over from Mark (255 n. 135: "also traditional?" and "nearly all of these involve verbs of 'saying'", see esp. 326-328.

28. Contrast A. DENAUX (ed.), *John and the Synoptics* (n. 3): "the comment of non other than D. Moody Smith: 'The consensus (on the independence of John) is gone'!" (Denaux's Introduction, XV).

ETL 71 (1995) 161-165

27

NOTE ON MT 28,9-10

In the new edition of R.H. Gundry's *Matthew* (1994) the passage on Mt 28,9-10 is reprinted as it first appeared in 1982, without supplement whatsoever in the Endnotes[1]. What makes Gundry's comment on 28,9-10 so different from that of other commentaries is the fact that he not only notes some degree of Matthean redaction in 28,9-10 (as most commentators do) but provides specific indications on the Mattheanisms in these verses[2]:

9 καὶ <u>ἰδοὺ</u> Ἰησοῦς <u>ὑπήντησεν</u> αὐταῖς <u>λέγων·</u> χαίρετε.
   αἱ <u>δὲ</u> <u>προσελθοῦσαι</u> ἐκράτησαν αὐτοῦ τοὺς <u>πόδας</u> καὶ <u>προσεκύν-</u>
   <u>ησαν</u> αὐτῷ.
10 <u>τότε</u> <u>λέγει</u> αὐταῖς ὁ <u>Ἰησοῦς·</u> μὴ φοβεῖσθε· ὑπάγετε ἀπαγγείλατε
   <u>τοῖς ἀδελφοῖς μου</u> ἵνα <u>ἀπέλθωσιν</u> εἰς τὴν Γαλιλαίαν, <u>κἀκεῖ</u> <u>με</u>
   <u>ὄψονται.</u>

It is amazing, at least to me, that notwithstanding his emphasis on Matthean redaction throughout these two verses Gundry can identify Mt 28,9-10 (and 16-20) as the lost ending of Mark[3].

1. R.H. GUNDRY, *Matthew*, Grand Rapids, MI, [2]1994, pp. 590-591. Only the reference to "John 20:7" (p. 591) is corrected to "20:17" (and two lines of text reset). See my review in *ETL* 71 (1995) 218-221.
2. The words he discusses as redactional are marked here by underlining. Some of these words (italicized) are mentioned as such in his *Mark*, 1993, p. 1021; see my review in *ETL* 69 (1993) 183-186. – On the supposed allusion to Ps 22,23 in v. 10, see my reservation in *ETL* 71 (1995), p. 160 n. 63 (and 60).
3. *Matthew*, p. 591: "in vv 9-10 and 16-20 Matthew edits Markan material no longer available to us"; *Mark*, p. 1021: "To reconstruct the lost ending of Mark, ... probably redactional elements [n. 2 above] will need omission or, more difficultly, replacement with characteristically Marcan diction".
Contrast my own approach (first presented in a paper read at the SNTS meeting in Gwatt, 1967): "Matt. xxviii.1-10 ne suppose aucune tradition évangélique autre que Marc xvi.1-8 et la christophanie des femmes (*vv*. 9-10) s'explique au mieux à partir du message angélique de Marc xvi.6-7" (p. 190 = 295); in *Les femmes au tombeau: Étude de la rédaction matthéenne (Matt. xxviii.1-10)*, in *NTS* 15 (1968-69) 168-190, reprinted in *Evangelica* I (BETL, 60), 1982, pp. 273-295; esp. section III, on Mt 28,9-10 (pp. 176-184 = 281-289); see also section IV, on Jn 20,17 (pp. 184-189 = 289-294). – For updating and dialogue with more recent studies, cf. *John and the Synoptics* (BETL 44, 1977), in *Evangelica* I, 1982, pp. 365-398, esp. 388-390: ".Mt 28,9-10" (additional note, p. 296); *John and the Synoptics: The Empty Tomb Stories* (*NTS* 30, 1984), in *Evangelica II* (BETL, 99), 1991, pp. 571-599, esp. 579-588: "Jn 20,11-18 and Mt 28,9-10" (additional note, p. 600); *John and the Synoptics: 1975-1990*, in A. DENAUX (ed.), *John and the Synoptics* (BETL, 101), 1992, pp. 3-62, esp. 33-35; *Literary Criticism Old and New*, in C. FOCANT (ed.), *The Synoptic Gospels* (BETL, 110), 1993, pp. 11-38, esp. 19-20.

Other commentators, though less accurate in their description of Matthean redaction and less precise in their definition of Matthew's source, also hold that I these two verses "despite the Matthean vocabulary" go back to pre-Matthean tradition[4]. In his recent monograph on *The Resurrection of Jesus* (1994) G. Lüdemann declares that in his view this way of understanding Mt 28,9-10 is to be preferred[5]. Somewhat unexpectedly, he argues on the basis of C.H. Dodd's structural study of the appearance stories: "the structure makes one think"[6]. Dodd distinguished two classes among the appearances, "concise" narratives and "circumstantial" narratives. The three concise narratives are Mt 28,8-10; 28,16-20; Jn 20,19-21. In each of them he recognized a common pattern comprising the following elements: (a) the situation: Christ's followers bereft of their Lord; (b) the appearance of the Lord; (c) the greeting; (d) the recognition; (e) the word of command. Dodd conceives this class I "to represent the 'formed' tradition, stereotyped through relatively long transmission within a community"[7].

One may ask, however, whether Dodd's standard pattern of concise narratives is really helpful in a discussion on pre-Matthean tradition in Mt 28,9-10. Does it really bear "the marks of a tradition shaped ... in the process of oral transmission"[8]? Even Dodd had to note that Mt 28,8-10 differs from the two other concise narratives (which are "complete in themselves", with an abrupt beginning): "In Matt. 28,8 there is no similar beginning [as Mt 28,16a and Jn 20,19a]: a connection exists with what has preceded"[9]. Since for Lüdemann Mt 28,16-17 proves to be a

4. References can be found in footnotes and additional notes to my earlier contributions on this topic, up to 1993 (n. 3 above). See also Kühschelm's recent survey in *Angelophanie*, 1993 (cf. n. 18 below).

5. G. LÜDEMANN, *Die Auferstehung Jesu: Historie, Erfahrung, Theologie*, Göttingen, 1994; Stuttgart, ²1994; ET by J. Bowden, *The Resurrection of Jesus: History, Experience, Theology*, London, 1994, pp. 130-132, esp. 131.

6. *Resurrection*, p. 237 n. 527. Cf. C.H. DODD, *The Appearances of the Risen Christ: An Essay in Form-Criticism of the Gospels*, in D.E. NINEHAM (ed.), *Studies in the Gospels*. FS R.H. Lightfoot, Oxford, 1955, pp. 9-35; reprinted in *More New Testament Studies*, Manchester, 1968, pp. 102-133. German translation (quoted by Lüdemann): *Die Erscheinungen des auferstandenen Christus: Ein Essay zur Formkritik der Evangelien*, in P. HOFFMANN (ed.), *Zur neutestamentlichen Überlieferung von der Auferstehung Jesu* (n. 21 below), pp. 297-330. Dodd has summarized his essay in *Historical Tradition in the Fourth Gospel*, Cambridge, 1963, pp. 142-150 ("The Appearances of the Risen Christ"), esp. pp. 143 (the pattern) and 146 (Mt 28,9-10).

7. *Appearances*, pp. 11-13, 22. Cf. LÜDEMANN, *Resurrection*, p. 27 (and 131).

8. *Appearances*, p. 13. Dodd's assumption of a common pattern leads to undue assimilation of the motifs. Thus, he compares the fact that the women touch Jesus' feet (Mt 28,9) with the sight of his wounds in Jn 20,20 and Jesus' assurance in Mt 28,18, "All authority is given to me" (p. 12).

9. *Appearances*, p. 13. Therefore, Dodd admits that there has been "some editorial manipulation" (*ibid.*). Compare his note on "the signs of editorial work" in *Historical*

Matthean redactional introduction[10] and Jn 20,19-21 may be explained from a use of Lk 24,36-43[11], how can he then argue from Dodd's (supposedly traditional) structure in the case of Mt 28,9-10? The I encounter with Jesus cannot be separated from the tomb story and the structure of Mt 28,9-10 should not be studied in isolation of its closest parallel, Mk 16,5-7 (Mt 28,5-7)[12].

But Lüdemann's proposal is a more specific one: "If this structural scheme is correct, it means that at the stage of the tradition, Matt. 28,9-10 is not necessarily about the women, as in its Matthaean context, but about the eleven (or twelve) or another group of disciples"[13]. Lüdemann seems to suggest (and it was explicitly said before by S. Heine) that this is part of Dodd's theory[14]. I quote here Dodd's own words[15]:

> In the Gospel narratives of Class I ... the witnesses are usually the apostolic body as a whole (whether identified as 'the Eleven', or 'the Eleven and those with them', or in other ways). *Names of individuals are not mentioned*. An apparent exception is Matt. 28,9-10, where, in view of 28,1, the reader identifies the women as Mary Magdalen and 'the other Mary' (whoever she may have been). But if we were right in isolating 28,9-10 as an independent *pericopé*, the individual names may not have been present originally.

The point made by Dodd is that "these *pericopae* do not mention individual names"[16]. It is clear from his comments in *Historical Tradition in the Fourth Gospel* (1963) that he thinks of an originally independent story about "some women" (γυναῖκές τινες), and not about "the

---

Tradition, p. 146 n. 2 (cf. 147 n. 3: "a truncated unit whose introduction has been replaced by a re-writing of Mark xvi.8b"). He suggests a beginning of the original independent *pericopé* such as: καὶ ἰδού (γυναῖκές τινες ἐπορεύοντο, καὶ) Ἰησοῦς ... (p. 146 n. 2).

10. *Resurrection*, pp. 132-134. Cf. my *Evangelica* I, p. 12 (and 125, 802); *Evangelica II*, pp. 123-126 ("οἱ δέ in Mt 28,17").

11. *Resurrection*, pp. 161-162. Cf. *Evangelica II*, pp. 206-213 ("Jn 20,19-20").

12. Dodd's treatment of Mt 28,9-10 without even mentioning Mk 16,5-7 presupposes its original existence as independent tradition.

13. *Resurrection*, p. 131. See also p. 157: "there are good reasons for disputing this", viz. that Mt 28,9-10 "derives from a christophany to women".

14. S. HEINE, *Eine Person von Rang und Namen. Historische Konturen der Magdalenerin*, in D.-A. KOCH, et al. (eds.), *Jesu Rede von Gott und ihre Nachgeschichte im frühen Christentum*. FS W. Marxsen, Gütersloh, 1989, pp. 179-194, esp. 186: "(es) wurde vermutet, es handle sich in Vers 9 um die Elf" (cf. n. 38: reference to DODD, *Erscheinungen*, p. 324).

15. *Appearances*, pp. 29-30 (emphasis mine). Both Heine and Lüdemann are referring to the German translation (*Erscheinungen*). Compare "eine *auffallende* Ausnahme" (p. 323) with the original: "an *apparent* exception".

16. *Appearances*, p. 33.

Eleven"[17]. Of course, one is free to imagine a tradition about a group of disciples, but Lüdemann did not uncover which are his "good reasons" for assuming that Mt 28,9-10 actually relies on such a tradition.

A recent survey of studies on Mt 28,9-10 (up to 1992) is provided in R. Kühschelm's paper, *Angelophanie-Christophanie*[18]. Under the cover of a rather comprehensive title, and apparently uncommitted, he presents a catalogue of *Lösungsvorschläge*, but the central interest of the paper is an attack on the | redactional interpretation of Mt 28,9-10, presented in the form of a questionnaire[19]. My first remark is a methodological one. Kühschelm begins with questions on John-Matthew (nos. 1, 2, 5, 6). Such questions can only be answered after having previously discussed the problem of Matthean redaction in 28,9-10, and 28,1-8 par. Mk 16[20]. Kühschelm's option for "alte Tradition" seems to be predetermined by the view that "*Frauen* ... nach jüdischem Recht nicht als zeugnisfähig galten" and that therefore "die Tradition ... ihren Einfluß eher zurückzudrängen sucht" (nos. 8, 9, 10). Unbiased reading of Mt 28,1-10 is the best response to this kind of generalizations. Matthew's story of the women at the tomb begins in 28,1 (diff. Mk 16,1-2): ἦλθεν (Μαριὰμ ἡ Μαγδαληνὴ καὶ ἡ ἄλλη Μαρία) θεωρῆσαι τὸν τάφον. I may quote my 1967 comment[21]:

17. *Historical Tradition*, p. 146 n. 2 (see above, n. 9). See also p. 147 n. 3, on Jn 20,11-17 and Mt 28,9-10: "it is possible that the two stories were originally distinct, the one telling how Mary Magdalene saw the Lord at the tomb, the other telling how *other* women, having left the tomb, were met by the Lord".

18. R. KÜHSCHELM, *Angelophanie - Christophanie in den synoptischen Grabesgeschichten Mk 16,1-8 Par. (unter Berücksichtigung von Joh 20,11-18)*, in C. FOCANT (ed.), *The Synoptic Gospels* (n. 3), 1993, pp. 556-565. See pp. 557-561: "Lösungsvorschläge".

19. *Ibid.*, pp. 561-563: "Anfragen an die rein redaktionskritische Deutung" (thirteen questions). The "neutrality" of the question form does not conceal his personal option for "eine alte Tradition". – Already in n. 7 (p. 558), the bibliographical references he cites are to those who "Kritik an Neirynck üben", including the commentaries on John by R.E. Brown (1970), B. Lindars (1972), R. Schnackenburg (1975), etc. The presentation would have been more balanced if he had also mentioned my responses (1977, 1984). Cf. above, n. 3.

20. I may refer here to my first essay on Mt 28,9-10 and Jn 20,14-18: "il me paraît parfaitement justifiable de donner la priorité méthodologique à un examen de la péricope du point de vue de la rédaction matthéenne" (*Evangelica* I, p. 281; 1969, p. 176).

21. *Evangelica* I, pp. 280-281 (1969, pp. 175-176). See now also P. HOFFMANN, *Das Zeichen für Israel* (1988), p. 436: "Offenbar zielt die Wahl dieses Begriffs [θεωρῆσαι], den er schon 27,55 (zusammen mit Markus) für die Zeugenschaft der Frauen bei Jesu Tod verwendete, in 26,61 aber (gegen Markus) wegließ, auf die Zeugenfunktion der Frauen bei den folgenden Ereignissen"; p. 438, at 28,6: "Die Frauen werden ausdrücklich aufgefordert (δεῦτε ἴδετε), sich davon zu überzeugen. Die in V. 1 angegebene Absicht, das Grab zu sehen, erfährt hier eine überraschende Weiterführung". Cf. *Das Zeichen für Israel. Zu einem vernachlässigten Aspekt der matthäischen Ostergeschichte*, in ID. (ed.),

Une seule fois encore, Matthieu utilise le verbe θεωρεῖν: en dépendance de Marc, dans la notation sur les femmes qui de loin sont témoins de la mort de Jésus (27,55). Toujours à propos des femmes, Marc l'emploie encore deux fois dans ce contexte: lors de l'ensevelissement, ἐθεώρουν ποῦ τέθειται (15,47) et puis au tombeau, θεωροῦσιν ὅτι ἀνακεκύλισται ὁ λίθος (16,4). Les femmes voient, elles constatent, elles sont témoins. Dans le récit matthéen, l'ange invite les femmes avec une insistance particulière: δεῦτε ἴδετε τὸν τόπον ὅπου ἔκειτο (28,6). Serait-ce téméraire que de supposer que, pour Matthieu, déjà θεωρῆσαι τὸν τάφον exprime cette même nuance et devient en quelque sorte le titre du récit sur la constatation du tombeau vide?

Lüdemann correctly observes that "there is no universal ancient view that women are incompetent witnesses"[22], and Kühschelm, who tries to justify his position | with a reference to M. Hengel[23], is invited to consider the complete statement of his competent witness: "Für die Gemeinde in der hellenistischen Welt, die in den Leidens- und Auferstehungsberichten der Evangelien primär angesprochen wurde, hatte das Zeugnis der Frauen dagegen eher Aussagekraft"[24].

The existence of some contact between Jn 20,17 and Mt 28,9-10 is undeniable. It is recognized by scholars who are not in favor of Johannine dependence: "Ohne einen Blick auf Mt 28,9 wird nun das Folgende (V 17) kaum verständlich"[25]. The solution they propose is a traditio-historical connection through a pre-Johannine tradition: "Do not cling to me, but go to my brothers and tell them: (I have seen the Lord)" (R.T. Fortna)[26]; or, with some variation: "Rühre mich nicht an, denn ..., gehe jedoch zu meinen Brüdern und sagt ihnen: (Sie werden mich sehen)!" (J. Becker)[27]. Their tentative reconstructions scarcely offer a more agree-

Zur neutestamentlichen Überlieferung von der Auferstehung Jesu (Wege der Forschung, 522), Darmstadt, 1988, pp. 416-452; reprinted in ID., Tradition und Situation. Studien zur Jesusüberlieferung in der Logienquelle und den synoptischen Evangelien (NTAbh., NF, 28), Münster, 1995, pp. 313-340, esp. pp. 328, 329. – Cf. GUNDRY, Matthew, p. 582, on 27,61: the omission of the verb "which Matthew reserves till 28:1 for a special purpose".

22. Resurrection, p. 158 (Auferstehung, ²1994, p. 176); "Die Zeugenunfähigkeit der Frau gilt nur für das antike Judentum" (ibid.).

23. Angelophanie, p. 562 n. 23.

24. M. HENGEL, Maria Magdalena und die Frauen als Zeugen, in O. BETZ, et al. (eds.), Abraham unser Vater. Juden und Christen im Gespräch über die Bibel. FS O. Michel (AGSU, 5), Leiden, 1963, pp. 243-256, esp. 246-247.

Kühschelm also refers to F. BOVON, Le privilège pascal de Marie-Madeleine, in NTS 30 (1984) 50-62, pp. 50-52; now reprinted in ID., Révélation et écritures (Le monde de la Bible, 26), Genève, 1993, pp. 215-230, esp. 215-220. But see ETL 71 (1995), p. 218.

25. J. BECKER, Johannes, ³1991, p. 725.

26. The Fourth Gospel and Its Predecessor, 1988, p. 188 (and 189).

27. Johannes, p. 726. – Lüdemann (Resurrection, pp. 156-157) holds that the nucleus of the christophany to Mary Magdalene may go back to an independent tradition but he

able pre-Johannine "source" than does the text of Matthew (28,9-10). The argumentation for Johannine dependence upon Mt 28,9-10 is aptly summarized by G. Schneider (1992)[28]. To conclude, I quote the final words of his essay[29]:

> The ἀναβαίνω saying in John is in some sense an expansion of the traditional phrase 'my brothers'". Diese "Erweiterung" der Erwähnung von Jesu Brüdern erfolgte im Sinne der johanneischen Erhöhungschristologie. Vielleicht darf man darauf hinweisen, daß das Logion 20,17c wenigstens implizit die gedankliche Struktur von Mt 28,7 bzw. 28,10 aufweist: *Jesus geht* als der Auferstandene *den Seinen voraus* (προάγει). Vgl. Joh 14,3.6. Jesu Vater ist auch der Vater seiner Brüder.

refuses any traditio-historical connection with Mt 28,9-10: "possible only if Matt. 28,9f. derives from a christophany to women" (!). Cf. above, n. 13.

28. G. SCHNEIDER, *Auf Gott bezogenes "Mein Vater" und "Euer Vater" in den Jesus-Worten der Evangelien. Zugleich ein Beitrag zum Problem Johannes und die Synoptiker*, in *The Four Gospels 1992*. FS F. Neirynck (BETL, 100), 1992, pp. 1751-1781, esp. 1779-1781.

29. *Ibid.*, p. 1781. His first sentence is quoted from *Evangelica II*, p. 585 (1984, p. 170).

ETL 71 (1995) 431-434

28

SHORT NOTE ON JOHN 19,26-27

R.E. Brown's commentary on "The Mother of Jesus and the Beloved Disciple (John 19,26-27)" in *BDM*[1] refers to "the opposing positions taken in lively controversy by Neirynck (*'Eis'*) and de la Potterie ('Parole' and 'Et à partir')" regarding the last part of Jn 19,27: From that hour the disciple took her to his own. The abbreviation "*Eis*" stands for my note on εἰς τὰ ἴδια in *ETL*, 1979[2]. In response to I. de la Potterie's reaction ("Et à partir", 1980)[3] a fuller treatment of the translation problem in Jn 19,27b appeared in *ETL*, 1981[4]. Now, fifteen years after "*Eis*", Brown declares he takes a stance "between the two positions". On the one hand, "Neirynck shows through grammatical and vocabulary parallels what the text could mean if one ignores Johannine theology... On the other hand [...] one does not need to invoke 'interior and spiritual space' to understand 'his own'"[5]. Brown's comment seems to suggest that it was my intent to deny any theological significance to the passage in John. I may recall that my note on εἰς τὰ ἴδια was written as a corollary to an article on ἀπῆλθεν πρὸς ἑαυτόν ("he went home")[6] and that the problem I discussed in Jn 19,27b was a translation problem. This is clearly said in the Conclusion of the first article[7], and the title of the

---

1. R.E. BROWN, *The Death of the Messiah*, New York, 1994, pp. 1019-1026, esp. 1023-1024. See my presentation of Brown's commentary of the passion narratives (here referred to as *BDM*) in *Gospel Issues in the Passion Narratives: Critical Note on a New Commentary*, in *ETL* 70 (1994) 406-416.

2. *ΕΙΣ ΤΑ ΙΔΙΑ. Jn 19,27 (et 16,32)*, in *ETL* 55 (1979) 357-365. Reprinted in *Evangelica* (BETL, 60), 1982, pp. 456-464. This note was written in reply to I. DE LA POTTERIE, *La parole de Jésus "Voici ta Mère" et l'accueil du Disciple (Jn 19,27b)*, in *Marianum* 36 (1974) 1-39; in German translation: *Das Wort Jesu 'Siehe, deine Mutter' und die Annahme der Mutter durch den Jünger (Joh 19,27b)*, in J. GNILKA (ed.), *Neues Testament und Kirche*. FS R. Schnackenburg, Freiburg, 1974, pp. 191-219; in Spanish: *Las palabras de Jesús "He acqué tu madre" y la acogida del discipulo (Jn 19,27b)*, in ID., *La verdad de Jesús* (BAC, 405), Madrid, 1979, pp. 187-219.

3. I. DE LA POTTERIE, *"Et à partir de cette heure, le Disciple l'accueillit dans son intimité" (Jn 19,27b). Réflexions méthodologiques sur l'interprétation d'un verset johannique*, in *Marianum* 42 (1980) 84-125.

4. *La traduction d'un verset johannique: Jn 19,27b*, in *ETL* 57 (1981) 83-106. Reprinted in *Evangelica*, 1982, pp. 465-488. This article is not mentioned in *BDM*, p. 1023; but see the Bibliography on p. 891.

5. *BDM*, pp. 1023-1024.

6. *ΑΠΗΛΘΕΝ ΠΡΟΣ ΕΑΥΤΟΝ: Lc 24,12 et Jn 20,10*, in *ETL* 54 (1978) 104-118. Reprinted in *Evangelica*, 1982, pp. 441-455.

7. Conclusion, p. 365 (= 464): "Le but de cette note n'est cependant pas de discuter l'interprétation symbolique de la scène de Jn 19,25-27. Je me suis placé plus modestement

second article was deliberately chosen: *La traduction...* It was my impression that the "natural" sense of the words was neglected in de la Potterie's translation, first: "le disciple l'accueillit dans ses biens" (*inter spiritualia bona*); then: "l'accueillit dans son intimité"[8]. |

It is quite common in studies on Jn 19,26-27 to distinguish between two levels of understanding[9]. In Brown's own commentary (*John* II, 1970) the translation of εἰς τὰ ἴδια is discussed in the Notes: "*into his care*. Literally *to his own...* Here it has the connotation *to his own home*, as in Esther v 10, III Macc vi 27; Acts xxi 6. Yet the phrase implies care as well"[10]. The deeper meaning ("something more profound than filial care") is treated apart in a detailed Comment. Brown begins by questioning "Dauer's contention that the Beloved Disciple is more important in this episode than the mother of Jesus", and then formulates his own key for interpretation: "After all, the mother of Jesus is addressed first; and her future, and not that of the Beloved Disciple, is considered at the end of vs. 27"; therefore, "whatever symbolism is involved must be centered on Jesus' mother's becoming the mother of the Beloved Disciple". And he concludes: "By way of summary, we may say that the Johannine picture of Jesus' mother becoming the mother of the Beloved Disciple seems to evoke the OT themes of Lady Zion's giving birth to a new people in the messianic age, and of Eve and her offspring. This imagery flows over into the imagery of the Church who brings forth children modeled after Jesus..."[11]. In *BDM* Brown adopts the literal translation: "took her *to his own*"[12], and he now observes: "In advocating such symbolic interpretations [Lady Zion, Eve, the figure of the church] some scholars make no distinction between what may have been intended in a 1st-cent. milieu by the evangelist and the usage made of the passage to

---

"auf der Ebene der erzählten Welt des Textes", pour m'interroger sur le sens des mots εἰς τὰ ἴδια. On peut s'en tenir, je crois, à la traduction courante: 'Et depuis cette heure-là, le disciple la prit chez lui' (TOB)".

8. This new translation was proposed in 1980 (after my first article). See also I. DE LA POTTERIE, *La passion de Jésus selon l'évangile de Jean* (Lire la Bible, 73), Paris, 1986, pp. 144-167 ("La maternité spirituelle de Marie: 19,25-27"), esp. 160-165: "Le verset de conclusion" (cf. p. 163).

9. Cf. *ΕΙΣ*, p. 365 (= 464): "die Ebene der erzählten Welt" and the symbolic sense (H. Thyen); *Traduction*, p. 106 (= 488): "un sens humain" and "un sens symbolique" (A. Feuillet). See also J. ZUMSTEIN, *Miettes exégétiques* (Le monde de la Bible, 25), Genève, 1991, pp. 229 and 275.

10. *The Gospel of John* II, p. 907. See also p. 923: "if the scene is historical, filial care may have been its original import".

11. *Ibid.*, pp. 922-927 (Jn 19,25-27), esp. 923, 925, 926. On A. Dauer, see below n. 23.

12. Contrast the more common "into his home" (REB, NAB, NJB) or "into his own home" (NRSV).

meet the needs of the subsequent church"[13]. With regard to the untorn tunic (Jn 19,23-24) he remains undecided: "A decision about exactly what type of symbolism John had in mind may not be possible"[14], and: "that is true too of other Johannine symbolisms". Though he does not hesitate in the case of Jn 19,26-27: "What is peculiar to the beloved disciple, what is *his own*, is neither his house nor his spiritual space but the fact that he is the disciple par excellence. *His own* is the special discipleship that Jesus loves"[15]. The discipleship interpretation he initiated at our Colloquium on John in 1975 has now come to full development.

A first step in the direction of this interpretation already appears in 1970 in an "appended observation": "Loisy has captured *an element of truth* in comparing the Johannine episode at the foot of the cross to the incident in Mark iii 31-35 where Jesus says that his true mother and his true brothers are those who do the will of God"[16]. The name of Loisy is no longer mentioned in 1975 when he I proposes to see in the Johannine scene "John's equivalent to a positive interpretation of a scene similar to Mk 3,31-35 (Lk 8,19-21)": "In 19,26 the mother of Jesus is made the mother of the Beloved Disciple, and thus her physical motherhood is reinterpreted *in relation to* discipleship"[17]. The proposal was made quite modestly: "I am pointing out *one* symbolism that has echoes in the Synoptics"[18]; here and in later studies he continued to refer to his *John* for the "many symbolisms that John may have intended his reader to associate with the mother of Jesus"[19]. In *BDM* Brown now concentrates on

13. *BDM*, p. 1022. Contrast Brown's earlier utterances on symbolisms (below, nn. 18-19).

14. *BDM*, p. 958. He rightly notes: "In either reading [the tunic as the high priest vestment or as symbolizing unity] one is still forced to deal with the symbolic import of having this undivided tunic *taken away* from Jesus". See also G. BEASLEY-MURRAY, *John*, 1987, p. 347, *et al.*

15. *BDM*, p. 1024.

16. *John*, p. 927 (italics mine). Brown uses here the word "comparing" (but see n. 28) because he would not subscribe to Loisy saying that "Jean a transposé et interprété la scène des Synoptiques...". Cf. A. LOISY, *Le quatrième évangile*, 1903, p. 880; ²1921, p. 488. See also M. SABBE, *The Johannine Account of the Death of Jesus and Its Synoptic Parallels (Jn 19,16b-42)*, in *ETL* 70 (1994) 34-64, p. 39: "John has his own reasons... Perhaps some Synoptic sayings have inspired him...", with reference to Mk 3,31-35; cf. p. 36 n. 7 (on Brown's reference to Loisy: "not clear to me"; but Brown cites Loisy's second edition).

17. *The "Mother of Jesus" in the Fourth Gospel* (1975), in M. DE JONGE, *L'Évangile de Jean* (BETL, 44), Leuven, 1977, pp. 307-310, esp. 310.

18. *Ibid.*: "I do not claim that for John this is the only or even the principal symbolism of the 'woman' of 19,25-27". In n. 13 he refers to his discussion of "other symbolisms" in *John*, 1970, pp. 924-927.

19. Cf. *Roles of Women in the Fourth Gospel*, in *TS* 36 (1975) 688-699, reprinted in *The Community of the Beloved Disciple*, New York, 1979, pp. 183-198, esp. 194 n. 349;

"the type of theological issue that a 1st-cent. evangelist might be interested in": "The significance of this episode lies in the new relationship between the mother of Jesus and the beloved disciple, not in symbolism attached to Mary through the history of interpretation"[20]. And now for the first time Brown refers to H. Schürmann's essay on Jn 19,26-27[21]:

> Perhaps the most serious exegetic difficulty about these symbolic approaches has been pointed out by Schürmann: The scene does not primarily concern the two figures in themselves but the new relationship that exists between them.

There is also another reference to Schürmann, placed in a footnote and apparently less fitting with Brown's own approach[22].

> Schürmann argues that the task is *not* mutual: Mother, care for your son; Son, care for your mother. Rather it means: Mother, see the son who will care for you; Son, see the mother you will care for.

In fact, already before A. Dauer wrote down his observation that "der Ton auf dem Jünger liegt und nicht auf Maria" (1967)[23], Schürmann had anticipated the answer to Brown's 1970 statement[24]: |

> So bleibt die Notiz Joh 19,27b eben doch der kontextmässige Schlüssel für das Verstehen der Worte Jesu, weil sie die Interpretation des Evangelisten am ehesten erkennen läßt. In ihr ist aber Johannes als der künftige "Ernährer" die Hauptperson, der Maria anvertraut wird, nicht umgekehrt! – Und auch V. 26a ("Siehe da, dein – dich nun ernährender – Sohn!") ist das nicht anders.

ID., et al., *Mary in the New Testament*, Philadelphia - New York, 1979, pp. 206-218: "The Mother at the Foot of the Cross (19:25-27)", esp. p. 214, on "symbolisms that need not contradict the primary symbolism based on the family of discipleship".

20. *BDM*, p. 1024.

21. *Ibid.*, p. 1023. See also p. 1024: "I remarked above that I agree with Schürmann..." (above n. 20). Cf. H. SCHÜRMANN, *Jesu letzte Weisung: Jo 19,26-27a*, in *Sapienter ordinare*. FS E. Kleineidam (Erfurter Theol. Studien, 24), Leipzig, 1969, pp. 105-123; reprinted in ID., *Ursprung und Gestalt. Erörterungen und Besinnungen zum Neuen Testament*, Düsseldorf, 1970, pp. 13-28, here p. 20 n. 39 (in reply to A. Dauer): "'Das Hauptinteresse des Evangelisten' gilt nicht dem 'Lieblingsjünger' als solchem, freilich auch nicht Maria, sondern *dem neugestifteten Verhältnis*, nach dem Maria an den Jünger verwiesen wird und dieser sie aufnehmen soll" (italics mine).

22. *BDM*, p. 1021 n. 88. Cf. *Weisung*, p. 15.

23. A. DAUER, *Das Wort des Gekreuzigten an seine Mutter und den "Jünger, den er liebte". Eine traditionsgeschichtliche und theologische Untersuchung zu Joh 19,25-27*, in *BZ* 11 (1967) 222-239; 12 (1968) 80-93; esp. p. 236. Revised version in ID., *Die Passionsgeschichte im Johannesevangelium* (SANT, 30), München, 1972, pp. 318-332; esp. p. 318.

24. Review: "T. Gallus, Die Mutter Jesu im Johannesevangelium, 1963", in *TPQ* 112 (1964) 345-346, p. 346 (note: "Johannes", read: "der Lieblingsjünger"). Cf. *Weisung* (above, n. 21), p. 13 n. 2 (reference to the book review where "die hier ausgearbeitete These schon formuliert war") and pp. 14-15.

There is still one other passage to be considered, which is neglected by Brown[25]:

> Freilich muß ein *hintergründiger* Sinn so bestimmt werden, daß er in der "Verlängerung" des *natürlichen* Sinnes der Weisung Jesu liegt und diesen nicht – in reinem Symbolismus – überspringt oder verwischt.

In comparison to the mariological symbolisms, Brown's discipleship interpretation has evident advantages. In his view, however, there seems to be no room for the "natural" sense of the scene. "Absolutely incredible" and "extravagant" are the words he uses: the idea of "providing lodgings" is "a question of this earth"[26]. It can suffice to reply with Brown's own(?) warning: "This formula [19,27b] should not be taken too literally..., as if the beloved disciple left Calvary immediately before Jesus died", and "we need not be too literal in thinking that the beloved disciple had a house in Jerusalem where he could take Mary"[27].

In support of his interpretation of Jn 19,26-27, Brown cites the fact that the precise issue of how to relate Jesus' natural family to a family of discipleship "was one that the Synoptic evangelists struggled with" (Mk 3,31-35 par.): "The Synoptics have that scene during the public ministry and so John may have adapted it and brought it into a new setting at the cross"[28]. One gets the impression that at least in this case Brown would not deny that this is an example of Johannine "creativity on a Markan theme"[29].

---

25. *Weisung*, p. 16 (italics mine).
26. *BDM*, pp. 1023-1024.
27. *Mary* (n. 19), p. 214 n. 472.
28. *BDM*, p. 1029 n. 106; cf. p. 1025.
29. Cf. his interlocutor's phrase in J.D. CROSSAN, *Who Killed Jesus? Exposing the Roots of Anti-Semitism in the Gospel Story of the Death of Jesus*, San Francisco, 1995, p. 186. See my review in *ETL* 71 (1995) 455-457.

ETL 71 (1995) 176-184

29

JEAN 4,46-54

Une leçon de méthode

Après l'annonce d'un ouvrage sur *Das Verhältnis des Johannes-evangeliums zu den Synoptikern* à paraître dans les *Beihefte zur ZNW*, l'on s'étonne de recevoir une plaquette de quelque 70 pages. Stephan Landis est un nom nouveau dans ce secteur des études néotestamentaires et la Préface du livre nous apprend qu'il s'agit d'un travail d'étudiant (*Akzessarbeit*) préparé à Zürich en 1992 sous la direction de H. Weder. Dans l'Introduction, l'auteur se réfère au Colloquium Biblicum Lovaniense de 1990 (*John and the Synoptics*, 1992) pour déclarer ensuite: «Das Neuaufflammen [sic] der Diskussion über die Beziehungen zwischen Johannes und den Synoptikern ist der Anlass für die Entstehung der vorliegenden Arbeit» (2). À part les trois pages de cette Introduction, le livre traite exclusivement de Jn 4,46-54 et ses parallèles synoptiques (4-72). La conclusion sera claire et sans ambages: «Es besteht hier ... keine literarische Abhängigkeit zwischen Joh und den Synoptikern (Mt/Lk). Dasselbe gilt auch für die jeweiligen Quellen, die SQ einerseits, Q und das lk Sg anderseits» (71)[1].

I

L'exposé de S. Landis s'ouvre par une réflexion de méthode. Il renonce à traiter de ce que Jean et les Synoptiques ont en commun avant tout: leur structure d'ensemble et le genre «évangile»[2]. Landis se propose d'étudier la question de la dépendance littéraire par un examen *eigenständig* d'une seule péricope. Le critère doit être la présence ou l'absence d'éléments rédactionnels synoptiques chez Jean. Étant donnée

1. Stephan Landis, *Das Verhältnis des Johannesevangeliums zu den Synoptikern. Am Beispiel von Mt 8,5-13; Lk 7,1-10; Joh 4,46-54* (BZNW, 74), Berlin - New York, de Gruyter, 1994, xi-76 p.
2. À la suite de C. Riniker, mais sans parler de convention littéraire, il se réfère à l'emploi de πολλοί dans le prologue de Lc (p. 1 n. 3). Cf. Christian Riniker, *Jean 6,1-21 et les évangiles synoptiques*, in J.-D. Kaestli, e.a., *La communauté johannique et son histoire*, Genève, 1990, pp. 41-67, spéc. 66-67. Landis note les ressemblances de son travail avec celui de Riniker sur Jn 6,1-21: même méthode (p. 2 n. 8), même critique (p. 32 n. 21; 40 n. 6), même conclusion (p. 71 n. 1). Sur les remarques de Riniker à propos de Jn 4,46-54 (pp. 61-63), voir cependant *infra*, n. 9.

la *Mehrschichtigkeit* des évangiles, l'examen ne peut se limiter à la rédaction ultime: la question des rapports littéraires se pose à chacun des niveaux (3). Dès lors, Landis se livrera d'abord au travail préalable de reconstituer les sources évangéliques. La première moitié du livre y est consacrée: la source Q (4-18), la tradition du Sondergut lucanien (18-27), la Semeiaquelle (28-37).

Je reproduis ici le texte de Q tel qu'il est reconstitué par Landis (17)[3]:

8,5 εἰσῆλθεν εἰς Καφαρναούμ. καὶ ἦλθεν πρὸς αὐτὸν ἑκατοντάρχης παρακαλῶν αὐτόν 6 καὶ λέγων· κύριε, ὁ παῖς μου (κατάκειται) δεινῶς | βασανιζόμενος. 7 καὶ λέγει αὐτῷ· ἐγὼ ἐλθὼν θεραπεύσω αὐτόν; 8 καὶ ἀποκριθεὶς ὁ ἑκατοντάρχης ἔφη· κύριε, οὐκ εἰμὶ ἱκανὸς ἵνα ὑπὸ τὴν στέγην μου εἰσέλθῃς, ἀλλὰ εἰπὲ λόγῳ, καὶ ἰαθήσεται ὁ παῖς μου. 9 καὶ γὰρ ἐγὼ ἄνθρωπός εἰμι ὑπὸ ἐξουσίαν, ἔχων ὑπ᾽ ἐμαυτὸν στρατιώτας, καὶ λέγω τούτῳ· πορεύθητι, καὶ πορεύεται, καὶ ἄλλῳ· ἔρχου, καὶ ἔρχεται, καὶ τῷ δούλῳ μου· ποίησον τοῦτο, καὶ ποιεῖ. 10 ἀκούσας δὲ ὁ Ἰησοῦς ἐθαύμασεν καὶ εἶπεν τοῖς ἀκολουθοῦσιν· λέγω ὑμῖν, οὐδὲ ἐν τῷ Ἰσραὴλ τοσαύτην πίστιν εὗρον. 13 καὶ εἶπεν τῷ ἑκατοντάρχῃ· ὕπαγε, Heilungszusage, Bericht von der Heilung ἐν τῇ ὥρᾳ ἐκείνῃ.

La reconstruction, présentée par Landis comme «unsere Rekonstruktion der Q-Fassung», ne diffère que fort peu de celle de U. Wegner (1985)[4]. Deux tiers des notes aux pages 6-16 sont des renvois à Wegner (dans le style: *So* ou *S.* Wegner, Hauptmann)[5]. Un renvoi global aurait pu suffire, et au lieu de se contenter d'une réimpression abrégée de l'exposé de Wegner, l'auteur aurait pu se concentrer plus utilement sur les points de divergence. Certaines différences entre les deux sont plus apparentes que réelles: v. 6 + κύριε (Landis, 7: «Ungewiss...»); βέβληται/κατάκειται (Wegner, 270 n. 5); ἐν τῇ οἰκίᾳ om. (Landis, 8: «dürfte allerdings traditionell sein»); v. 7 εἶπεν/λέγει (Wegner, 270 n. 6). Je crois que Landis a raison de refuser παραλυτικός (v. 6). Pour renforcer son argument, il aurait pu signaler une influence possible de la séquence parallèle en Mc: Mt 8,2-4 / Mc 1,40-45; Mt 8,5-13 / Mc 2,1-12 (cf. Mt 9,1-8). D'autre part, il concède peut-être trop facilement le caractère traditionnel de βασανιζόμενος: cf. 4,24 βασάνοις

---

3. Les éléments communs y sont soulignés. Cf. F. NEIRYNCK, *Q-Synopsis*, ²1995, pp. 20-21.

4. U. WEGNER, *Der Hauptmann von Kafarnaum (Mt 7,28a; 8,5-10.13 par Lk 7,1-10). Ein Beitrag zur Q-Forschung* (WUNT, 2/14), Tübingen, 1985, spéc. pp. 91-276. Voir pp. 270-271, la reconstruction de Q.

5. *Verhältnis*, pp. 6-16: notes 6, 9, 11, 12, 13, 15, 16, 17, 19, 20, 23, 25, 26, 27, 28, 29, 31, 32, 33, 34, 35, 36, 37, 41, 42, 44, 45, 46, 47, 48, 49, 51, 55, 56, 57, 59, 60, 64. La référence «S. Schulz, Q» est à peu près la seule à rompre la monotonie.

συνεχομένους ... καὶ παραλυτικούς. Au v. 10, il a sans doute raison de supprimer ἀμήν⁶. Par contre, entre παρ' οὐδενὶ τοσαύτην πίστιν ἐν τῷ Ἰσραήλ (Wegner: cf. Mt) et οὐδὲ ἐν τῷ Ἰσραὴλ τοσαύτην πίστιν (Landis: cf. Lc) le choix restera difficile⁷. Dans le dernier verset, Landis se sépare de Wegner à propos de ἐν τῇ ὥρᾳ ἐκείνῃ, qu'il tient pour traditionnel. Mais je reviendrai plus loin sur la finale du récit (v. 13).

D'après cette reconstruction de (Wegner et) Landis, le récit de la source Q est fort semblable au texte de Mt 8,5-10.13. Lc 7,1-10 s'en distingue surtout par l'addition des deux délégations (7,3-6b.7a). Landis fait remonter la délégation des anciens des Juifs à une *Sondertradition* mais attribue à Luc la délégation d'amis et la jonction avec le dialogue de Q (6a ὁ δὲ Ἰησοῦς ἐπορεύετο σὺν αὐτοῖς. 6c ἔπεμψεν φίλους, 7a διὸ οὐδὲ ἐαυτὸν ἠξίωσα πρὸς σὲ ἐλθεῖν)⁸. Sur ce point, Landis corrige l'hypothèse de Wegner⁹, mais ici encore c'est à partir de l'analyse I de Wegner¹⁰ qu'il reconstitue le texte de la *Sonderquelle* lucanienne: 7,2-5 (... δοῦλος κτλ.), 6b (... ἤδη δὲ αὐτοῦ οὐ μακρὰν ἀπέχοντος ἀπὸ τῆς οἰκίας...), 10b (... εὗρον τὸν δοῦλον ...)¹¹. J'y reviendrai.

Passons à Jn 4,46-54 et la reconstruction de la source SQ¹²:

4,46 καὶ ἦν τις βασιλικὸς οὗ ὁ υἱὸς ἠσθένει (ἐν Καφαρναούμ). 47 (οὗτος) ἀκούσας ὅτι Ἰησοῦς ἥκει ἀπῆλθεν πρὸς αὐτὸν καὶ ἠρώτα ἵνα (ἔρχηται) καὶ ἰάσηται αὐτοῦ τὸν υἱόν, ἤμελλεν γὰρ ἀποθνήσκειν. 50 λέγει αὐτῷ ὁ Ἰησοῦς· πορεύου, ὁ υἱός σου ζῇ, καὶ ἐπορεύετο. 51 ἤδη δὲ αὐτοῦ (πορευομένου) οἱ δοῦλοι αὐτοῦ ὑπήντησαν αὐτῷ λέγοντες ὅτι ὁ παῖς αὐτοῦ ζῇ. 52 ἐπύθετο τὴν ὥραν παρ' αὐτῶν ἐν ᾗ" κομψότερον ἔσχεν· εἶπαν αὐτῷ ὅτι ὥραν ἑβδόμην ἀφῆκεν αὐτὸν ὁ πυρετός. 53 Konstatierung der Gleichzeitigkeit von Heilungszusage und Heilung [ἐν] ἐκείνῃ τῇ ὥρᾳ ... καὶ ἐπίστευσεν

---

6. Cf. *Evangelica II*, p. 449.

7. Cf. D. CATCHPOLE, *The Centurion's Faith and Its Function in Q*, in *The Four Gospels 1992. FS F. Neirynck* (BETL, 100), Leuven, 1992, pp. 517-540, spéc. 537-539; = ID., *The Quest for Q*, Edinburgh, 1993, pp. 280-308 («Faith»), spéc. 304-307: il exprime une légère préférence pour la version de Mt (p. 539=306).

8. *Verhältnis*, p. 11 (v. 7a), 24 (v. 6a.c); et surtout p. 19 n. 73, en réaction contre l'hypothèse de Wegner (combinaison pré-lucanienne de la *Sondertradition* et Q).

9. Et de Riniker (p. 18 n. 71). Cf. *Jean 6,1-21* (n. 2), p. 62: les deux délégations appartiennent à la couche pré-lucanienne, «la forme spécifique qu'a prise la source Q avant d'arriver chez l'évangéliste (QLc), ou bien le résultat du développement de la source Q dans le milieu du Sondergut lucanien».

10. Voir notes 77, 78, 79, 81, 82, 84, 85, 86, 88, 89, 90, 92, 93, 94, 96, 97, 98, 99, 100, 106.

11. *Verhältnis*, pp. 19-26. Au v. 3: (σώσῃ?), Lc διασώσῃ (p. 21); au v. 10: le sujet «les anciens» (p. 25).

12. *Verhältnis*, pp. 36-37 (cf. pp. 29-37).

αὐτὸς καὶ ἡ οἰκία αὐτοῦ ὅλη. 54 τοῦτο [δὲ] δεύτερον σημεῖον ἐποίησεν ὁ Ἰησοῦς.

Landis retient le motif de la constatation au v. 53a mais pas les mots (ἔγνω οὖν ὁ πατὴρ ὅτι et ἐν ᾗ εἶπεν αὐτῷ ὁ Ἰησοῦς· ὁ υἱός σου ζῇ), il supprime les deux οὖν au v. 52 et πάλιν au v. 54 et maintient ἐν Καφαρναούμ au v. 46 (Wegner: ἐκεῖ). Pour le reste, il a les mêmes certitudes et les mêmes hésitations que Wegner[13], et l'on se demande encore une fois quelle est la raison d'être des pages 19-26.

À première vue, il est de bonne méthode de faire la séparation entre tradition et rédaction dans les récits de Mt 8,5-13 / Lc 7,1-10 et Jn 4,46-54 avant d'aborder le problème des rapports entre Jean et les Synoptiques. À y regarder de près, on constate cependant que l'hypothèse du récit pré-johannique oriente déjà les options synoptiques. Mt 8,13 est un premier exemple. Landis compare ἐν τῇ ὥρᾳ ἐκείνῃ avec ἀπὸ τῆς ὥρας ἐκείνης en Mt 9,22; 15,28; 17,18, et insiste sur la différence entre cette formule rédactionnelle «*von* jener Stunde *an*» et le *Stundenmotiv* «*in* jener Stunde» qui serait traditionnel («ein kleines Reststück aus der Tradition»). Cela le mène tout droit à la conclusion que la source Q «im Ausdruck ἐν τῇ ὥρᾳ ἐκείνῃ die Erinnerung daran bewahrt (hat), daß der Junge in der ursprünglichen Erzählung genau in jenem Moment gesund wurde, in dem Jesus zum Hauptmann sprach». Landis n'y fait pas mention de Jn 4,53, mais, avant même d'examiner le parallèle johannique, le lecteur est fixé: le motif est pré-johannique[14]. Landis n'est probablement pas un lecteur assidu des *ETL* et je me permets de lui signaler un exposé sur la formule matthéenne dans *ETL* 57 (1981), p. 103-105[15]. Le sens de l'expression ἀπό + gén. ne diffère guère de celui de ἐν + dat.: «instantly» (NRSV), «zu derselben Stunde» (Luther)[16], et «les | parallèles matthéens sont là pour nous rappeler qu'en Mt il s'agit d'une formule typique de conclusion, *Fernheilung* (15,28) ou non (9,22; 17,18). Ce n'est qu'en Jn 4,52-53 que la formule de Mt 8,13 devient l'expression caractéristique de la constatation d'une guérison à distance»[17].

---

13. *Hauptmann*, p. 32 (cf. pp. 22-32).
14. *Verhältnis*, pp. 15-17. Au risque de se contredire, il signale que la formule en Mt 15,28 et 17,18 vient à la place d'un récit plus long en Mc: il se peut donc que le récit de Q ait été abrégé par Matthieu «zur bloss feststellenden Formel» (15).
15. *Evangelica I*, 1982, pp. 485-487 (en rapport avec la traduction de Jn 19,27).
16. Cf. J. JEREMIAS, in *ZNW* 42 (1949) 214-217: «Wörtlich: 'er (sie) wurde geheilt seit jenem Augenblick', während der Sinn ist: 'in diesem Augenblick, sofort'» (p. 216).
17. *Evangelica I*, p. 487 (= 105) n. 59.

Landis retient le mot ὕπαγε dans sa reconstruction de Q: «der einzige traditionelle Ausdruck» en 8,13b (15). Il me semble qu'il se fie ici trop facilement à la statistique de Wegner qui, pour sa part, souligne le fait que, des six emplois dans des récits de miracle en Mc, Matthieu n'en reprend que deux[18]. Et Landis de généraliser: «oft streicht er es aus seinen Mk-Vorlagen» (15). Les deux participes en Mc 6,31.33 mis à part, on compte treize emplois (dont douze à l'impératif): 1,44 (= Mt 8,4); 2,11 (= Mt 9,6); 5,19 (vv. 18-20 sans par.); 5,34 (phrase sans par.); 6,38 (phrase sans par.); 7,29 (cf. infra); 8,33 (= Mt 16,23); 10,21 (= Mt 19,21); 10,52 (phrase sans par.); 11,2 (Mt 21,2 πορεύεσθε; voir 26,18); 14,13 (= Mt 26,18); 14,21 indic. (= Mt 26,24); 16,7 (Mt 28,7 πορευθεῖσαι; = Mt 28,10). Dans deux cas seulement, Matthieu remplace un ὑπάγετε par un autre verbe: πορεύεσθε en 21,2 (mais une phrase similaire en Mc 14,13 est laissée inchangée); πορευθεῖσαι en 28,7 (mais il écrit ὑπάγετε dans le doublet au v. 10). Les «omissions» dans les récits de miracle ne concernent jamais le seul verbe ὕπαγε (Mc 5,19.34; 6,38; 7,29; 10,52; Matthieu introduit un ὑπάγετε en 8,32, diff. Mc 5,13)[19]. Le ὕπαγε de Mc 7,29 n'est pas repris en Mt 15,28, mais on aurait tort de restreindre le rapprochement entre Mt 8,13 et 15,28 au seul motif de l'heure (καὶ ἰάθη ὁ παῖς ἐν τῇ ὥρᾳ ἐκείνῃ / καὶ ἰάθη ἡ θυγάτηρ αὐτῆς ἀπὸ τῆς ὥρας ἐκείνης). Comparer le motif de la foi et ὡς ... γενηθήτω σοι / γενηθήτω σοι ὡς ... Il n'est nullement téméraire de voir dans le ὕπαγε en Mt 8,13 le parallèle secondaire de Mc 7,29 (διὰ τοῦτον τὸν λόγον) ὕπαγε. D'ailleurs, Landis lui-même le dira lorsqu'il fait le rapprochement entre ὕπαγε (Q) et πορεύου (SQ): «ὕπαγε (scheint) sekundär zu sein, da es wahrscheinlich Mk 7,29 nachgebildet wurde» (49). On cherche donc en vain les traces d'une conclusion traditionnelle au v. 13 et, comme l'ont proposé M. Dibelius e.a., la péricope dans la source Q n'a probablement jamais eu une telle conclusion au-delà du v. 10. Quoi qu'il en soit, c'est le caractère entièrement rédactionnel de Mt 8,13 qui nous intéresse ici. À ce propos, Landis se montre mal informé lorsqu'il reproche à ceux qui admettent la dépendance johannique un manque de méthode (parlant du critère des éléments *rédactionnels* synoptiques): «Dieses methodisches Prinzip (wird) von jenen Forschern, die eine joh Abhängigkeit von den Synoptikern behaupten, ... kaum konsequent angewendet» (2 n. 8). C'est plutôt le

---

18. *Hauptmann*, p. 224.
19. Emplois du verbe dans Mt en dehors de la matière marcienne: 4,10 (+Q, cf. Mc 8,33); 5,24; 5,41 (Q?); 8,13 (+Q, cf. Mc 7,29); 13,44; 18,15 (+Q); 20,4.7.14; 21,28; 27,65.

contraire qui est vrai[20] et c'est précisément cela qui explique la remon-
tée que cette thèse connaît aujourd'hui. |

En ce qui concerne Lc 7,2-6b.10, je me range du côté de D. Catchpole. Je crois en effet qu'il y a de bonnes raisons pour y voir une rédaction lucanienne[21]. Qui tient la (seule) délégation des anciens des Juifs
pour traditionnelle, dans la source Q ou dans une Q élargie (F. Bovon,
e.a.), se voit confronté avec la difficulté d'un centurion qui fait demander à Jésus de venir (v. 3) et qui se rétracte par après (Q). La théorie de
Landis permet d'échapper à cette difficulté: il considère Lc 7,2-5
comme le début d'un récit de miracle complètement indépendant de Q.
Mais dans ce cas c'est la suite du récit qui fait problème. Landis n'a
d'autre solution que le recours à Jn 4,50 (la parole de guérison) et Jn
4,51 (cf. Lc 7,6b)[22]. Ce n'est qu'une «Vermutung» (26), mais, par anticipation, elle risque de compromettre l'exégèse de Jn 4,46-54.

Après le relevé des éléments que Landis retient comme rédactionnels
dans Mt 8,5-13 et Lc 7,1-10, nul ne doutera encore du résultat d'une
comparaison avec Jn 4,46-54. Il est préparé d'avance: aucun («keine

20. Sur le cas de Mt 8,13, voir A. DAUER, *Johannes und Lukas* (FzB, 50), Würzburg,
1984 (sur Jn 4,46-54: pp. 39-125, 315-366), pp. 78-80 («Der redaktionelle Charakter von
Mt 8,13»; p. 81: «sicher ... redaktionelle Bildung») et pp. 108-109 (Mt 8,13 et Jn
4,50.53); F. NEIRYNCK, *John 4,46-54: Signs Source and/or Synoptic Gospels*, in *ETL* 60
(1984) 367-375 (= *Evangelica II*, pp. 679-688); p. 373 (= 685): Mt 8,13 + 15b et Jn 4,50-
52; I. DUNDERBERG, *Johannes und die Synoptiker. Studien zu Joh 1–9* (AASF, 69),
Helsinki, 1994 (sur Jn 4,46-54: pp. 73-97), p. 86 (Mt 8,13 «als Ganzes der redaktionellen
Tätigkeit von Mt zuzuschreiben») et p. 91.

21. *The Centurion's Faith* (n. 7), pp. 528-532 (= 293-298), on «The Intermediaries»:
«Given the formal, verbal and theological relationships..., it can be inferred without risk
that Luke 7,3-6a.7a do indeed owe their existence to LukeR. They did not belong to Q or
to any pre-Lucan recension of Q» (p. 532=298). Voir aussi I. DUNDERBERG, *Johannes und
die Synoptiker* (n. 20), pp. 87-89; P. JUDGE, *Luke 7,1-10: Sources and Redaction*, in
F. NEIRYNCK (ed.), *L'Évangile de Luc – The Gospel of Luke* (BETL, 32), Leuven, ²1989,
pp. 473-489, esp. 484-486 (U. Busse, J.A. Fitzmyer, e.a.). Cf. R.A.J. GAGNON, *The Shape
of Matthew's Q Text of the Centurion at Capernaum: Did It Mention Delegations?*, in
NTS 40 (1994) 133-142.

22. Lc 7,6b, présenté d'abord comme «ein isolierter Rest» (24), est ainsi replacé dans
le contexte narratif du retour des anciens et d'une rencontre «auf der Heimreise, *unweit
des Hauses...*», semblable à celle entre le père et les serviteurs en Jn 4,51. Mais, en premier lieu, il n'est guère possible de retirer ἤδη δὲ αὐτοῦ οὐ μακρὰν ἀπέχοντος ἀπὸ τῆς
οἰκίας du contexte rédactionnel de Lc. Sur la rédaction lucanienne (cf. 15,20 ἔτι δὲ
αὐτοῦ μακρὰν ἀπέχοντος), voir DAUER, *Johannes und Lukas*, p. 116; DUNDERBERG,
Johannes und die Synoptiker, p. 88: «die zweite Gesandtschaft (wäre) ohne die lk
Zwischenbemerkung unmotiviert». Puis, l'interprétation de Dauer et Dunderberg serait à
compléter par le constat d'une transposition de Lc 7,6 en Jn 4,50-51: ce qui est dit de
Jésus y est transféré sur le père. Cf. *John 4,46-54* (n. 20), p. 372 (= 684). R.A.J. Gagnon
(n. 21) note correctement «the verbal similarity» et la présence, des deux côtés, du
«travel motif» et du motif de la délégation, mais exclure toute dépendance directe parce
que les motifs ont des fonctions différentes dans les deux récits (p. 137) me paraît injus-
tifié.

einzige») de ces éléments rédactionnels «wird von Joh bzw. seine SQ rezipiert» (43). Un seul trait parallèle a encore droit à une mention, pour être refusé (n. 11): Mt 8,13 ἰάθη (cf. Jn 4,47) ὁ παῖς αὐτοῦ (Jn 4,51). Les autres traits communs se situent au niveau des sources: le *Entlassungsmotiv* ὕπαγε (Q 8,13) et πορεύου (SQ 4,50) et le *Stundenmotiv* ἐν τῇ ὥρᾳ ἐκείνῃ (Q 8,13) et ἐν ἐκείνῃ τῇ ὥρᾳ (SQ 4,53). Mais même si, *dato non concesso*, le motif de l'heure était traditionnel en Q 8,13, son emploi au niveau rédactionnel en Mt 8,13 ne pourrait être négligé dans une étude comparée. Mt 8,13 (... ἐν τῇ ὥρᾳ ἐκείνῃ) est suivi d'un récit de guérison dont l'expression ἀφῆκεν αὐτὴν ὁ πυρετός (v. 15) est employée en Jn 4,52 dans la notice sur l'heure de la guérison: ὥραν ἑβδόμην ἀφῆκεν αὐτὸν ὁ πυρετός[23]. Les motifs communs en Mt 8,13 (ὁ παῖς αὐτοῦ et ἐν τῇ ὥρᾳ ἐκείνῃ) reçoivent ainsi, au niveau de la rédaction matthéenne, une «valeur ajoutée» | non négligeable[24]. C'est ce contact de Jn 4,52 avec Mt 8,15 qui a permis I. Dunderberg de conclure: «Man kann sich kaum des Eindrucks erwehren, daß der joh Redaktor wenigstens Mt kannte, als er Joh 4,46-54 verfaßte»[25].

II

Pour les partisans de la source SQ il ne peut y avoir de doute: Jn 4,48-49 n'appartiennent pas au récit traditionnel. Landis se réfère à Bultmann, Schnackenburg, Fortna et Becker[26] et stigmatise de «methodische Sorglosigkeit» ma défense de l'unité littéraire de Jn 4,46-54. Il résume ma position par ces mots: «Der Vers [4,48] stellt eine joh 'harmonisation' des unterschiedlichen Erzählverlaufs bei Mt und Lk mit Hilfe von sprachlichem Material verschiedener mk Stellen (Mk 7,26-29; 8,11f; 9,19; 13,22) dar» (31 n. 21). J'ai l'impression qu'une mise au point s'impose à ce propos.

23. Cf. *Jean et les Synoptiques* (n. 29), p. 233 n. 555; *John 4,46-54* (n. 20), p. 373 (= 685); voir n. 32, en réponse à A. Dauer.

24. Voir l'insistance de M.-É. Boismard sur les trois contacts avec Mt 8,13b.15 en Jn 4,51.52.53: *Synopse III*, p. 149; cf. *Parallèles* (n. 28), p. 256.

25. *Johannes und die Synoptiker* (n. 20), p. 95. Cf. p. 94: l'observation que ce contact entre Mt et Jn «normalerweise völlig übersehen (wird)» (n. 94) s'applique encore au livre de Landis (à la suite de Wegner, *Hauptmann*, pp. 36 et 49). Sur Boismard, cf. n. 23. Voir aussi M.D. GOULDER, *Luke*, 1989, p. 380 (référence à *ETL* 1984), et maintenant dans *John and the Synoptics* (n. 28), 1992, p. 237.

26. Voir G. VAN BELLE, *The Signs Source in the Fourth Gospel. Historical Survey and Critical Evaluation of the Semeia Hypothesis* (BETL, 116), Leuven, 1994, esp. pp. 31, 95, 122, 215, et passim (cf. Index, p. 498: «4,46-54»).

Landis se présente encore une fois comme l'écho de Wegner. La liste des références marciennes et sa réflexion «zur Problematik des methodischen Verfahrens Neiryncks» nous rappelle le (bref) exposé de Wegner sur «Joh 4,46-54 und das MkEv»: «Neirynck bedient sich eines äußerst selektiven bzw. ekklektizistischen Verfahrens in der Heranziehung von Texten und Stellen...»[27]. En plus, Landis se voit confirmé par une réaction plus récente de M.-É. Boismard: «... est-il raisonnable d'imaginer Jean s'inspirant de quatre passages de l'évangile de Marc pour rédiger ses seuls vv. 48-49?»[28].

De quoi s'agit-il? Le passage incriminé est une sous-section du chapitre VI dans *Jean et les Synoptiques*, et pour autant que le volume d'un texte est jugé être indicateur du poids qu'il reçoit dans l'argumentation, on notera que ce passage n'occupe qu'une seule page[29]. Traitant des vv. 48-49 en dialogue avec M.-É. Boismard, j'avais pris comme point de départ son observation que ces versets «n'offrent aucun parallèle dans les Synoptiques»[30]. Une telle observation ne pouvait que nous étonnner venant d'un commentateur qui attribue les versets au Jn II-B dont il est dit qu'il «puise volontairement dans *chacun* des trois | Synoptiques» et qu'ici même il veut «se rapprocher de la façon de voir des Synoptiques»[31]; cela devait nous étonner d'autant plus que le même commentateur avait écrit en 1962 que le reproche de 4,48 «se situerait plutôt dans la perspective des évangiles synoptiques» (avec citation de Mc 8,11-12 et parallèles), et qu'il avait lui-même signalé l'emploi de l'expression σημεῖα καὶ τέρατα en Mc 13,22 par.[32]. À aucun moment, je n'ai parlé de dépendance littéraire vis-à-vis de ces textes (Wegner: «literarische Abhängigkeit») et j'ai clairement indiqué qu'ils ne sont pas des «parallèles» au même degré que Mt 8,5-13 et Lc 7,1-10: «les différentes références synoptiques ont pu chacun *inspirer dans une certaine mesure* la rédaction de Jn 4,48-49. Mais celle-ci doit surtout se comprendre en fonction de la rédaction personnelle de l'évangéliste

---

27. *Hauptmann*, p. 33.

28. M.-É. BOISMARD, *Jean 4,46-54 et les parallèles synoptiques*, in A. DENAUX (ed.), *John and the Synoptics* (BETL, 101), Leuven, 1992, pp. 239-259, spéc. 242-245 (citation: p. 245).

29. *Jean et les Synoptiques. Examen critique de l'exégèse de M.-É. Boismard* (BETL, 49), Leuven, 1979, chap. VI, pp. 93-120 (= *ETL* 53, 1977, 451-478), spéc. 99-100 (= 465-466). Le chapitre VI fut préparé avec la collaboration de T. Snoy et G. Van Belle. Cf. G. VAN BELLE, *Jn 4,48 et la foi du centurion*, in *ETL* 61 (1985) 167-169; *The Signs Source* (n. 26), esp. pp. 394-398: «Seeing Signs and Believing».

30. *Synopse III*, 1977, p. 148.

31. *Ibid.*, pp. 47, 150.

32. M.-É. BOISMARD, *Saint Luc et la rédaction du quatrième évangile (Jn, IV,46-54)*, in *RB* 69 (1962) 185-211, pp. 191, 195.

confronté à une certaine divergence entre les récits de Mt 8,5-13 et Lc 7,2-10 *qui lui servent de sources*»[33].

Encore aujourd'hui, je suis d'avis que le rapprochement avec les quatre «parallèles» synoptiques peut nous aider à comprendre Jn 4,48. On aurait tort d'y voir une opinion isolée, datant de 1977 et restée sans lendemain. Je cite deux exemples:

> John 4:48 laments the lack of faith without seeing «signs and wonders,» but it is couched in the *plural* – addressed to the *public* through the officer (cf. Mark 9:19 for a remarkable parallel, addressed to a father requesting his son's healing).
> We should recall here the Markan story of the healing (at a distance) of the Syro-Phoenician woman's daughter (Mark 7,24-30), which has a similar form and content; the approach of the woman meets with an apparent objection from Jesus, but is followed by affirmation of faith and the granting of healing. In view of these parallels the common notion that the Evangelist was responsible for modifying a straightforward narrative by his insertion of vv 48-49 is to be queried. (BEASLEY-MURRAY, 1987)[34]

> In V. 48 ... mit der Abweisung von σημεῖα καὶ τέρατα steht Johannes in der Tradition der Synoptiker. Auch sie kennen die Ablehnung der Zeichenforderung (vgl. Mk 8,11-12...), und das Motiv des angesichts der Not indifferenten Wundertäters findet sich ebenfalls in der synoptischen Wunderüberlieferung (vgl. Mk 6,48; 7,27). Wie in 2,4 ... weist (Johannes) nicht das Wunder als solches zurück, sondern die *Forderung* nach Zeichen und Wundern. (SCHNELLE, 1987)[35]

Le background des deux auteurs est assez différent, l'un a tendance à intégrer 4,48 dans un récit de tradition johannique dont les motifs et le vocabulaire «are akin to synoptic traditions», l'autre est enclin à y voir une insertion rédactionnelle se situant «in der Tradition der Synoptiker», mais les deux proposent une lecture de Jn 4,48 à la lumière des références synoptiques. |

Est-ce par hasard que ni Beasley-Murray ni Schnelle ne figurent dans la Bibliographie de Landis? Par contre, Boismard est cité: «Quand ils [ces parallèles] existent réellement, ils restent superficiels et n'atteignent pas le sens substantiel des récits»[36]. Landis ne semble pas avoir lu la deuxième partie de l'article de Boismard. Il aurait pu constater que le récit de Mc 7,24-30, un de ces parallèles «superficiels», est au centre de

---

33. *Jean et les Synoptiques*, pp. 108-109. Voir aussi *John 4,46-54* (n. 20), p. 371 (= 683), n. 23, en réponse à A. Dauer. Landis ne semble pas connaître cet article; il date de 1984.

34. G.R. BEASLEY-MURRAY, *John* (WBC, 36), Waco, TX, 1987, p. 71. – Cf. *ETL* 65 (1989) 166-167.

35. U. SCHNELLE, *Antidoketische Christologie im Johannesevangelium* (FRLANT, 144), Göttingen, 1987, p. 98 (ET: *Antidocetic Christology in the Gospel of John*, Minneapolis, MN, 1992, p. 85).

36. *Verhältnis*, p. 32 n. 21 (cf. BOISMARD, *Parallèles*, p. 245).

l'exposé. Boismard y reproche à Dodd, Brown et Barrett qu'«ils n'ont pas utilisé (le récit) de la fille de la Syro-phénicienne pour essayer de reconstituer la source pré-johannique»[37]. L'évangéliste dépend d'une tradition «dont le schéma est très proche de celui que l'on retrouve en Mc 7,25-29»; «les principaux contacts littéraires ... se font avec le récit de Mc 7,25-29»; par contre, «les vv. 48-49 de Jn n'offrent aucun parallèle...»[38]. Suivant le récit johannique, verset par verset, Boismard note la présence de contacts «extrêmement précis», mais quand il arrive à Jn 4,48 une cécité passagère semble l'avoir frappé: la correspondance entre Jn 4,48 et Mc 7,27 dans le schéma du récit («an apparent objection from Jesus») est passée sous silence.

Quant au v. 49, Landis aurait pu lire chez Boismard qu'une reprise rédactionnelle (*Wiederaufnahme*) «n'est pas forcément la preuve d'une insertion faite dans un récit primitif»[39]. D'autre part, ce n'est pas sans raison qu'il a négligé l'emploi du terme παιδίον au v. 49 (et non pas υἱός comme au v. 47), cité par Boismard comme un indice stylistique en faveur de l'insertion[40]. Boismard observe correctement que «le mot υἱός [v. 47] se lisait déjà au v. 46b et se retrouvera aux vv. 50 et 53»[41]. De la part d'un commentateur qui s'empresse de noter le moindre contact de «la source pré-johannique» avec le récit de Mc 7,24-30, l'on comprend qu'il signale que «le υἱός de Jn ... correspond au θυγάτριον de Mc 7,25 (cf. θυγάτηρ aux vv. 26 et 29)»[42]. On comprend moins bien que, dans le cas de παιδίον en Jn 4,49, il ne croit pas devoir signaler un emploi parallèle de παιδίον en Mc 7,30 (par rapport à θυγάτριον, θυγάτηρ). Dans la logique de leur hypothèse, Boismard et, de manière plus explicite, Landis[43] rejettent la suggestion de R.T. Fortna qui, à la place du v. 47b, adopte le v. 49 dans la source pré-johannique:

47b	καὶ ἠρώτα	49	λέγει πρὸς αὐτὸν ὁ βασιλικός·
	ἵνα καταβῇ		κύριε, κατάβηθι
	καὶ ἰάσηται αὐτοῦ τὸν υἱόν,		
c	ἤμελλεν γὰρ ἀποθνήσκειν.		πρὶν ἀποθανεῖν τὸ παιδίον μου.

---

37. *Parallèles*, p. 250.

38. *Ibid.*, p. 254.

39. *Ibid.*, p. 241.

40. *Ibid.* Cf. *Jean et les Synoptiques*, p. 100; DUNDERBERG, *Johannes und die Synoptiker*, p. 79 n. 27.

41. *Parallèles*, p. 241.

42. *Ibid.*, p. 252.

43. *Verhältnis*, p. 30. Boismard signale l'hypothèse de Fortna (p. 249) mais ne la discute pas. Cf. R.T. FORTNA, *The Gospel of Signs*, 1970, p. 41; *The Fourth Gospel and Its Predecessor*, 1988, pp. 59 et 62-63.

Landis fait remonter le verset 47c au récit traditionnel[44]. Pour Boismard, ce serait une précision ajoutée par l'évangéliste sous l'influence de Lc 7,2 (ἤμελλεν τελευτᾶν)[45].

| Ce sont là des questions que je compte reprendre dans une étude sur Jn 4,46-54 pour laquelle j'ai voulu quelque peu déblayer le terrain par la présente note. En guise de conclusion, je fais encore remarquer que le désaccord sur Jn 4,48 ne concerne pas son caractère johannique. Il y a, je crois, un large accord sur sa «joh. Prägung»[46]. C'est plutôt le contexte hypothétique d'une source pré-johannique qui pose problème.

44. *Verhältnis*, p. 31.

45. *Parallèles*, p. 257 (cf. 254). Sur la nouvelle reconstitution du texte pré-johannique de Jn 4,46-54 dans *Un évangile pré-johannique*, vol. 2 (1994), voir le compte rendu dans *ETL* 70 (1994) 462-463.

46. *Verhältnis*, p. 32. Sur la structure johannique du récit, voir M.W.B. STIBBE, in *NTS* 40 (1994), p. 40 («request-rebuke-response») et la note sur Jn 2,1-12; 4,46-54 (cf. 11,1-44) dans G. VAN BELLE, *Signs Source* (n. 26), p. 392 n. 78: «(1) Someone comes with a request (2,3; 4,47; cf. 11,3); (2) Jesus seems to refuse the request (2,4; 4,48; cf. 11,6); (3) The questioner persists (2,5; 4,49); (4) Jesus grants the request».

Une note encore à propos de la Bibliographie de S. Landis: voir déjà p. 183. Il se réfère à deux numéros de BETL (49, 1949; 101, 1992) mais ne semble pas connaître les études reprises dans *Evangelica II* (BETL 99, 1991) ni les articles qui ont paru dans *The Four Gospels 1992* (BETL 100, 1992): B. LINDARS, *Capernaum Revisited. Jn 4,46-54 and the Synoptics*, pp. 1985-2000; D. CATCHPOLE, *The Centurion's Faith* (n. 7). Voir maintenant aussi C. BURCHARD, *Zu Matthäus 8,5-13*, in *ZNW* 84 (1993) 278-288, et la publication simultanée de trois articles de R.A.J. GAGNON, *The Shape of Matthew's Q Text* (n. 21); *Statistical Analysis and the Case of the Double Delegation in Luke 7:3-7a*, in *CBQ* 55 (1993) 709-731; *Luke's Motives for Redaction in the Account of the Double Delegation in Luke 7:1-10*, in *NT* 36 (1994) 122-145.

ETL 74 (1998) 386-397

30

JOHN AND THE SYNOPTICS
IN RECENT COMMENTARIES

In the survey article on John and the Synoptics I delivered at the Colloquium Biblicum Lovaniense 1975 I had to observe that Johannine
independence of the Synoptics was a predominant view in the commentaries on the Fourth Gospel[1]. Fifteen years later, surveying the years
1975-1990, I could mention a new trend in a significant number of special studies, showing that "Johannine dependence on the Synoptics is
not an idiosyncracy of Leuven"[2]. Along the same line several additional
references up to 1992 were included in the published text of the paper[3].

Three full-scale commentaries on the Gospel of John now appeared in
the first half of 1998. Francis J. Moloney's commentary in the *Sacra
Pagina* series is largely dependent on his narrative-critical reading of the
gospel of John[4]. His position is briefly formulated in the Introduction:
"it is impossible to trace any direct literary relationship between John's
gospel and the synoptic gospels", with reference to P. Gardner-Smith
(1938) and with no other justification than the alleged "complexity of
the suggestions of Neirynck, Boismard–Lamouille, and Brodie" (3)[5]. A
different approach is found in two German commentaries by Ulrich

---

1. *John and the Synoptics*, in M. DE JONGE (ed.), *L'évangile de Jean. Sources, rédaction, théologie* (BETL, 44), Leuven, 1977, 73-106, pp. 75-76; = *Evangelica* (BETL, 60),
Leuven, 1982, 365-400, pp. 367-368.
2. *John and the Synoptics: 1975-1990*, in A. DENAUX (ed.), *John and the Synoptics*
(BETL, 101), Leuven, 1992, 3-62, p. 8.
3. See pp. 61-62: Supplementary Note (n. 278), list of contributions in *The Four
Gospels 1992. FS F. Neirynck* (BETL, 100), Part VI: "The Gospel of John", and several
essays in *John and the Synoptics* (BETL, 101). Cf. below, n. 22.
4. F.J. MOLONEY, *The Gospel of John* (Sacra Pagina, 4), Collegeville, MN, 1998. Cf.
ID., *Belief in the Word: John 1–4; Signs and Shadows: John 5–12; Glory and Dishonor:
John 13–20(21)*, Minneapolis, MN, 1993-1996-1998. — For a note on the signs source,
see p. 86 (but there is no mention of G. Van Belle's monograph, *The Signs Source in the
Fourth Gospel*, 1994).
5. His references are: F. NEIRYNCK, *Jean et les Synoptiques. Examen critique de
l'exégèse de M.-É. Boismard* (BETL, 49), Leuven, 1979; M.-É. BOISMARD and A. LA-
MOUILLE, *L'Évangile de Jean* (Synopse, 3), Paris, 1977; T.L. BRODIE, *The Quest for the
Origin of John's Gospel. A Source-Oriented Approach*, New York, 1993. — On "complexity" see D.M. SMITH, *John among the Gospels. The Relationship in Twentieth-Century Research*, Minneapolis, MN, 1992, 139-176 ("The Dissolution of a Consensus", not
mentioned by Moloney): "Perhaps after diagraming Boismard's complex theory of
Gospel origins, Neirynck could not at this point resist diagraming his own, which is sim-
plicity itself" (151).

Wilckens and by Udo Schnelle, the first replacing S. Schulz in *Das Neue Testament Deutsch*[6] and the latter in replacement of J. Schneider in *Theologischer Handkommentar zum Neuen Testament*[7].

I

| 1. U. WILCKENS's introduction opens with a first section on "John in relation to the other gospels" (1-5). I quote here a few illustrative passages:

> Als Gesamtbild ergibt sich: Einerseits ist an einigen Stellen zwingend zu erweisen, daß der Joh.evangelist Mk wie auch Lk gekannt und benutzt hat. Ob auch Mt, muß offen bleiben, weil es eindeutige Textbeobachtungen nicht gibt und bei den meisten mit Mk parallelen Vergleichsstellen nicht entscheidbar ist, ob nun Mk oder Mt zugrundeliegen. Man kann nur allgemein vermuten: Weil zur Zeit der Herausgabe des Joh in der frühen Kirche des Ostens wie des Westens Mt die anerkannteste und verbreitetste Evangelienschrift gewesen ist, wäre es seltsam, wenn es dem Joh.evangelisten gänzlich unbekannt geblieben sein sollte. Andererseits zeigt sich überall dort, wo synoptische Stoffe vorliegen, ein hohes Maß johanneischer Eigenständigkeit. Es ist völlig klar, daß darin die Hand des vierten Evangelisten zu erkennen ist, der sowohl literarisch wie theologisch ganz eigene Wege zu gehen pflegt. (3)

Not only the significance of Mt in the early church is taken into consideration. Wilckens also compares Jn with the composition of apocryphal gospels:

> so zeigt sich schon früh und je länger je mehr eine literarische Benutzung der neutestamentlichen Evangelien. Und die Tendenz geht dahin, die Verschiedenheiten zwischen diesen auszugleichen (zu "harmonisieren"), und vielfach auch neue Erzählungen zu konstruieren durch Kombination von Einzelzügen aus den Evangelienschriften. Auf ähnliche Weise kann sehr wohl bereits der Joh.evangelist mit den ihm vorgegebenen synoptischen Evangelien verfahren sein. (4)

Wilckens's most important observation concerns the evangelist's communication with his readers:

---

6. U. WILCKENS, *Das Evangelium nach Johannes* (NTD, 4), Göttingen, 1998. His new commentary represents a fourth generation in *NTD*: F. Büchsel (1936-[5]1949), H. Strathmann ([6]1951-[11]1968), S. Schulz ([12]1972-[16]1987), U. Wilckens ([17]1998). The commentary is written in the *NTD* style with a concise *Einleitung* (1-17) and only general *Literaturhinweise*, predominantly in German (352-353; Schnelle's *Christologie* is included).

7. U. SCHNELLE, *Das Evangelium nach Johannes* (THNT, 4), Leipzig, 1998. See also L. SCHENKE, *Johannes. Kommentar*, Düsseldorf, 1998: "in Kenntnis und unter Verwendung aller Synoptiker abgefaßt" (432).

Der entscheidende Grund, warum ich diese Annahme [einer eigenwilligen
Benutzung der synoptischen Evangelien] in der Regel bevorzuge, ist eine
Einsicht, die sich mir in der Einzelauslegung des Joh ergeben hat: Der
Joh.evangelist setzt bei seinen Lesern die Kenntnis dieser Evangelienschriften, ja ihr Vertrautsein mit diesen, voraus. In der Art seiner Darstellung ist überhaupt die ständige Kommunikation mit seinen Lesern ein
wesentliches Mittel. (4)
Alle 'synoptischen Parallelen' setzen nicht nur Leser voraus, die die synoptischen Evangelien kennen, sondern die zugleich in der Lage sind, die
z.t. tiefgreifenden Veränderungen im Joh als theologisch-vertiefende Interpretation zu verstehen. (8)[8]

2. In particular the parallels to four Synoptic stories can be cited:

Jn 4,46-54, par. Mt 8,5-13; Lk 7,1-10

Der Joh.evangelist hat beide Versionen gekannt und benutzt, geht jedoch in
seiner Erzählung eigene Wege. (89) |

Jn 6,1-15.16-24 (30.68-69), par. Mk 6,30-44.45-52 (8,11; 8,27-28)

Seine Vorlage ist also der Mk-Bericht. ... Der Joh.evangelist könnte sehr
wohl die beiden parallelen Speisungsberichte seiner Mk-Vorlage zusammengezogen und sich durch den Kontext von Mk 8 zu dem kritischen Dialog mit "den Juden" und zu dem Abschluß mit dem Petrusbekenntnis
haben anregen lassen. (95)

Jn 12,1-8, par. Mk 14,3-9; Lk 7,36-50; 10,38-42

Die Formulierung in V.2a zeigt freilich an, daß der Joh.evangelist die verschiedenen Fassungen der Erzählung im Mk und Lk als seinen Lesern
bekannt voraussetzt... Da die folgende Erzählung von der Salbung deutlich
an Lk 7,36ff. anklingt, ist es möglich, daß der Joh.evangelist das
Nebeneinander von Marta und Maria aus Lk 10,38ff. entnommen hat und
es hier benutzt, um die in der synoptischen Salbungsgeschichte namenlose
Frau mit Maria zu identifizieren. (185)
Der Joh.evangelist hat in höchst auffälliger und eigenartiger Weise die beiden verschiedenen Erzählungen von Mk 14 und Lk 7 so kombiniert, daß
zwar der Vorgang als solcher seine konkrete Handlungsplausibilität ver-
liert, aber dadurch zugleich eine theologische Symbolik gewinnt, die als
solche sehr tiefsinnig ist. (186)

Jn 12,12-19, par. Mk 11,1-10 parr.

˙ ... man vermutet, daß auch hier der Joh.evangelist nur die drei synoptischen
Evangelienschriften gekannt, diese aber in ungleich stärkerem Maß nach

---

8. "Unter dieser Voraussetzung lassen sich einige besonders auffallende Unterschiede
zwischen Joh und den synoptischen Evangelien erklären" (4-5): Jn 2,13-22 placed at the
beginning; no mention of Jesus' baptism in Jn 1 and of the Eucharist in Jn 13; the
chronology of Jesus' death in Jn 19.

eigenem Konzept benutzt hat, als Mt und Lk ihrerseits das Mk-Evangelium. Vermutet man zudem, daß er deren Kenntnis bei seinen Lesern voraussetzt, dann erklärt sich die Freiheit seines Umgangs mit ihnen: Sein Evangelium soll als ganzes eine theologische Vertiefung dessen sein, was seine Leser von der Geschichte Jesu schon wissen. (188)

3. Right from the beginning of the gospel narrative in Jn 1,19-34 Wilckens describes John's use of the Synoptics as an alternative to the theories of oral tradition or some special written source:

eine bewußte Umgestaltung von Lk 3,15f. ... Das ist nicht als eine Traditionsvariante, sondern nur als literarische Gestaltung des Joh.evangelisten under der Überschrift von 1,19 zu verstehen. ... [E]r hat keine anderen Quellen gekannt und benutzt als die synoptischen Evangelien, hier vor allem Lk. (45)

Special emphasis is given to the contact with Lk 22,33-34:

Joh 13,37f. ist eine der Stellen im Joh, wo die Nähe zum Lk so deutlich ist, daß von daher die Annahme sehr wahrscheinlich ist, daß der Joh.evangelist Lk gekannt hat. (219)

Wilckens also stresses the parallelism of order between Jn and Lk in the trial of Jesus before Pilate:

Lk 23,1. (2). 3a.   3b.   4.   (6-12). 13-15. 16. 18. 19. 20. 21.   22. 23. 24-25a. 25b.
Jn 18,28. – 33.37a. 37b. 38b. –   (19,4). 39. 40a. 40b. – 19,6a. 6b. 15. –   16a.
Solche Entsprechung – nicht nur hier und da im Wortlaut, sondern in der Reihenfolge des Berichteten – legt die Vermutung nahe, daß es hier das Lk ist, an dem der Joh.evangelist seinen Bericht orientiert. (278)[9] |

On the parallels to Lk in Jn 20, see below, section IV.

Wilckens also mentions possible contacts with Mt such as Jn 1,41b.42 / Mt 16,16.17 (48); Jn 11,49-53 / Mt 26,3-4 (182-183); and less explicitly Jn 13,16.20; 15,20 / Mt 10,24-25a.40 (209, 210).

4. Finally, the sayings of Jesus in Jn 12,25-26 and 27 can be mentioned,

die Annahme (ist) wahrscheinlich, daß der Joh.evangelist beide Lk-Sprüche kombiniert: In V.25 zieht er Lk 17,33 und Lk 14,26 zusammen; und bei der Anfügung von V.26 an V.25 orientiert er sich an der Spruchfolge in Lk 14,26f. (192)

---

9. See the table of parallels (278), slightly corrected here: Jn 18,37a, read 37b; 19,65, read 6b; 19,16, read 16a. The table is taken from J. Becker (559f., read: ³1991, 666), who without good reason excludes direct dependence: "Die Angaben machen deutlich, daß Joh zu einem Teil der Sonderform des lk PB folgt" (666).

> Alle drei Elemente (Mk 14,34 par; 14,36 parr; 14,41) sind in Joh 12,27 aufgenommen, jedoch charakteristisch verändert. ... So ist Joh 12,27 ein Konzentrat der synoptischen Getsemaniszene. (193)

and the prayer in Jn 17:

> Seine zentralen Motive freilich finden sich in einem Lobpreisgebet Jesu wieder, das in Lk 10,21f.; Mt 11,25-27 überliefert wird... Dieses Gebet Jesu war für das Gebet Joh 17 eine wichtige Vorlage. (260)

Wilckens's essays on Jn 6,51c-58, on the Paraclete and the Church, and, more recently, on Jn 19,26-27 are well-known[10], but there was no mention of Wilckens in earlier surveys on John and the Synoptics. Neither does his name appear in G. Van Belle's book on the Signs Source (1994). Schnelle's commentary, available in July 1998, now already includes references to his critique of the Signs Source[11] and to his position on John's use of the Synoptics[12].

II

In contrast to the case of Wilckens, U. SCHNELLE's commentary is not his first publication on this topic. It started with a critical examination of the Signs Source in his *Habilitationsschrift* (1985, published in 1987)[13]. His section on "Das zweite Wunder in Kana 4,46-54" in *Das Evangelium nach Johannes* (95-99), with *Exkurs 2*, "Die Wunderzählung im Johannesevangelium" (99-100), is a slightly revised reprint of his 1987 text (*Christologie*, 96-100 and 105-108); only the original subsection, "Joh 4,46-54 im Verhältnis zu Mt 8,5-13 / Lk 7,1-10" (101-104), is left

---

10. Cf. FS R. Schnackenburg (1974), FS G. Bornkamm (1980), and FS K. Kertelge (1996). On the Beloved Disciple as *Symbolfigur* (1980, 199-203; 1996, 264: "bislang überwiegend abgewiesen"), see my *John 21*, in *NTS* 36 (1990) 321-336, p. 335 (= *Evangelica II*, 614-615).

11. SCHNELLE, 14 n. 60: "*U. Wilckens*, Joh. 9f." (also 100 n. 198). See WILCKENS, 10: "Die Hypothese einer Wunderquelle entbehrt so jeder überzeugenden Begründung"; cf. 319: "muß fraglich bleiben" (at 20,30-31).

12. SCHNELLE, 17 n. 30: "*U. Wilckens*, Joh. 2-5".

13. U. SCHNELLE, *Antidoketische Christologie im Johannesevangelium. Eine Untersuchung zur Stellung des vierten Evangeliums in der johanneischen Schule* (FRLANT, 144), Göttingen, 1987 (= *Antidocetic Christology in the Gospel of John. An Investigation of the Place of the Fourth Gospel in the Johannine School*, Minneapolis, MN, 1992). See especially chapter 3: analysis of redaction and tradition in Jn 2,1-11; 4,46-54; 5,1-9ab; 6,1-15; 6,16-25; 9,1-41; 11,1-44; and 20,30-31 (87-167) and "Einwände gegen die Annahme einer 'Semeia-Quelle'" (168-182).

out in the commentary[14]. Jn 4,46-54 has its own tradition history and "eine literarische Abhängigkeit besteht nicht" (*Christologie*, 104, 170). His evaluation of Jn 6,1-15.16-21 (par. Mk 6,32-44.45-52) was a more positive one: "Speisung und Seewandel lassen erkennen, daß die joh. Tradition das Markusevangelium kannte, so daß auch für den Evangelisten diese Annahme nicht abwegig ist" (130); and then he added: "In der neueren Forschung wird wieder zu Recht vermehrt mit einer Kenntnis der Synoptiker durch Johannes gerechnet" (n. 226)[15].

For Schnelle, "die von Johannes gewählte Gattung 'Evangelium'" is the decisive argument for dependence. It was clearly stated in his concluding chapter:

> Der Evangelist schuf sein Evangelium nicht unabhängig von Markus... Es ist m.E. sehr unwahrscheinlich, daß Markus und Johannes unabhängig von einander innerhalb einiger Jahrzehnte die Gattung 'Evangelium' schufen. (1987, 250-251, n. 7)[16]

The question is expressly treated in 1992 (*Johannes und die Synoptiker*) and again in 1994 (*Einleitung*)[17]. The reception of the gospel genre by John comes first:

> Vielmehr verlangt die Einzigartigkeit und Neuheit der Gattung Evangelium ein Erklärungsmodell, bei dem das Markusevangelium als die einzig existierende mögliche Vorlage für Johannes miteinbezogen wird. (1992, 1802)

It was rephrased in 1994 (567) and finally corrected in the commentary:

> Vielmehr weisen die Einzigartigkeit und Neuheit der Gattung Evangelium auf Markus als die einzig existierende Vorlage für Johannes. (1998, 16)

Schnelle is more hesitant with regard to coincidences in details and verbal resemblances between John and the Synoptics: "die beachtlichen Übereinstimmungen im Detail (sind) immer verschiedenen Interpretationen zugänglich" (1998, 16 = 1994, 566; cf. 1992, 1801: "... den immer

---

14. Likewise the comparisons of Jn 6,1-15 / Mk 6,32-44 par. (119-122) and Jn 6,16-21 / Mk 6,45-52 (126-130) are not reprinted in the commentary. But see p. 116 n. 8 (on Jn 6,1-15).

15. In this note (1987, 130 n. 226) Schnelle refers to my *John and the Synoptics* (1977) and *Jean et les Synoptiques* (1979), though his personal emphasis seems to be on the use of Mk as *Vorlage* in the pre-Johannine tradition. See 122 n. 189, 129, 170.

16. Compare 1992: "Historisch muß es als unwahrscheinlich gelten..." (1801) and 1994 (566) = 1998 (16): "... allerdings als sehr unwahrscheinlich...". See references in n. 17.

17. *Johannes und die Synoptiker*, in *The Four Gospels 1992*. FS F. Neirynck (above, n. 3), 1799-1814; ID., *Einleitung in das Neue Testament* (Uni-Taschenbücher, 1830), Göttingen, 1994 (²1996), 558-571 (8.5.7: "Das Johannesevangelium: Traditionen, Quellen").

mehrdeutigen Befund der Einzeltexte")[18]. In 1987 he described the combined evidence of "die für Johannes außerordentlich großen wörtlichen Übereinstimmungen" in Jn 6,1-15, the unit of the feeding | story and the walking on the sea, and its extension to the sequence of "Speisung (Mk 6,32-44 / Joh 6,1-15), Seewandel (Mk 6,45-52 / Joh 6,16-21), Überfahrt (Mk 6,53f; 8,10 / Joh 6,22-25), Zeichenforderung (Mk 8,11-13 / Joh 6,26) und Petrusbekenntnis (Mk 8,27-30 / Joh 6,66-71)" (1987, 121)[19]. In 1992 and 1994 this agreement in order between Mk and Jn was cited as an example of *Kompositionsanalogie* and supplemented with a long list of "analogies" in the composition of the passion narrative. In his *Fazit* there was only a secondary mention of Lk and no mention at all of Mt:

> Bei der Ausgestaltung der Passionsgeschichte nahm Johannes markinische Kompositionselemente und lukanische Motive auf und integrierte sie in seinen umfassenden theologischen Gestaltungswillen. (1992, 1813)

Compare now the general introduction to his commentary:

> ... die Rezeption der Gattung Evangelium und die Kompositionsanalogien (weisen) auf Markus als die grundlegende synoptische Vorlage des Johannesevangeliums hin... Der Evangelist rezipierte in unterschiedlicher Intensität das Markus- und Lukasevangelium... das Markus- und (in abgeschwächter Form) das Lukasevangelium. (1998, 16-17)

For a discussion of Jn 18–20 I refer to sections III and IV. Here a few comments on passages from the first part of the Gospel are in order.

Jn 4,46-54. Schnelle rightly repeats his earlier observation on 4,48: "In V. 48 äußert sich keine spezifisch joh. Wunderkritik, sondern mit der Abweisung von σημεῖα καὶ τέρατα steht Johannes in der Tradition der Synoptiker. Auch sie kennen die Ablehnung der Zeichenforderung, und das Motiv des angesichts der Not indifferenten Wundertäters findet sich ebenfalls in der synoptischen Wunderüberlieferung" (97; cf. 1987, 98). See *Jean et les Synoptiques*, 107-108; *ETL* 71 (1995), 182. Less convincing is his form-critical argument on the basis of Mt

---

18. In his commentary an annotation like that on Jn 1,26-27 is rather exceptional: "Die Antwort des Täufers lehnt sich eng an die synoptischen Berichte an. Die Wendung ἐγὼ βαπτίζω ἐν ὕδατι dürfte auf Mark. 1,8par. zurückgehen, V. 27a berührt sich mit Matth. 3,11, und V. 27b zeigt eine deutliche Nähe zu Mark. 1,7b par." (49). References to parallels in Mt are rare. But see his note on "Pharisees" in Jn 18,3: "Nur Matthäus erwähnt im Zusammenhang mit der Passion Jesu noch die Pharisäer (vgl. Matth. 21,45; 27,62), beide Belege sind redaktionell; zu beachten ist die Nähe von Joh. 11,47-53 zu Matth. 26,3-5" (195 n. 199). See also Jn 19,2: "Dennoch sind die Übereinstimmungen beachtlich; Joh. 19,2a entspricht fast wörtlich Matth. 27,29a" (277 n. 80; = 1992, 1809 n. 51). Cf. below, n. 23 (Jn 18,11a).

19. Note, however, that the parallel (and contrast) to Mk 6,53a can be seen in Jn 6,21 (the second miracle). For the request for a sign, read 6,30 (rather than v. 26).

8,13 for assigning Jn 4,51-52.53a to pre-Johannine tradition (98; cf. 1987, 99-100). See *ETL* 72 (1996), 455 (on Mt 8,13.15; review I. Dunderberg).
Jn 5,8. "Das Befehlswort zeigt beachtliche Übereinstimmungen mit Mark. 2,11; ob eine direkte literarische Abhängigkeit vorliegt oder ein Einzellogion aus der mündlichen Überlieferung verarbeitet wurde, läßt sich nicht mehr mit Sicherheit entscheiden" (103). Cf. 1987, 111: "an eine direkte literarische Abhängigkeit (ist nicht) zu denken". See now the addition in n. 12: "anders *F. Neirynck, John 5,1-18 and the Gospel of Mark*, in: *ders.*, Evangelica II, 703-708" (see also my note on Jn 5,8: 1992, 53). — On Jn 5,8, cf. M. LABAHN, *Eine Spurensuche anhand von Joh 5.1-18. Bemerkungen zu Wachstum und Wandel der Heilung eines Lahmen*, in *NTS* 44 (1998) 159-179, p. 163: "Obgleich einige enge Parallelen zwischen Joh 5.8 und Mk 2.9b,11 bestehen, ist kein sicherer Nachweis für die Abhängigkeit vom synoptischen Text zu führen". But the parallels in the Greco-Latin literature (esp. Lukian: Midas ἀράμενος τὸν σκίμποδα, ἐφ᾽ οὗ ἐκεκόμιστο) make the close verbal resemblances with Mk in Jn 5,8-9 rather more impressive. The evidence of the structural correspondences between Jn 5,1-18 and Mk 2,1–3-6 is "beeindruckend" indeed.
Jn 6,1. "Für die Brotvermehrung erscheint Jesu Gang zum anderen Ufer des Sees nicht notwendig, wohl aber für den folgenden Seewandel, ein Hinweis darauf, daß beide Perikopen bereits auf vorjoh. Ebene verbunden waren" (115; with reference to Schnider-Stenger in n. 3); "Eine eigenständige joh. Traditionsgeschichte des Speisungswunders I (und des Seewandels) ist damit keineswegs ausgeschlossen, sondern sehr wahrscheinlich" (116 n. 8). In 1987 Schnelle's position on Jn 6,1-15.16-21 was not quite clear: "traditionsgeschichtlich und literarisch von Mk 6,32-52 abhängig" (170). This seems to imply the evangelist's use of Mk in combination with "die Benutzung ... durch die joh. Tradition" (170). The formulation remains ambiguous in the commentary. In any case the argument that is taken from F. Schnider – W. Stenger (1971) concerns "die Quelle des Johannes" (143; cf. Schnelle: "auf vorjoh. Ebene").
Jn 11,1. "Die luk. und joh. Traditionen über Maria, Martha und Lazarus weisen Übereinstimmungen auf" (186 n. 153). Cf. 1987: "Auf eine literarische Abhängigkeit lassen die Übereinstimmungen nicht schließen, wohl aber sind Berührungen in der mündlichen Tradition zu vermuten" (142-143). This comment is now dropped and replaced with a reference to H. Thyen's interpretation: "eine Collage aus verschiedenen luk. Texten (speziell Luk. 7,11-17; 10,38-42; 16,19-31" (n. 153; cf. *The Four Gospels 1992*, 2038).
Jn 12,1-8. "Eine sichere Entscheidung ... ist kaum möglich; für eine direkte literarische Abhängigkeit von Markus und Lukas sprechen allerdings sprachliche und inhaltliche Übereinstimmungen" (200; n. 12: M. Sabbe 1992; I. Dunderberg, including Mt 26,11 / Jn 12,8).
Jn 12,27-28. "Der Evangelist greift die Gethsemane-Tradition auf, wobei er die mark. Überlieferung voraussetzt (V. 27a / Mk 14,33b.34a; V. 27c / Mk 14,36a; V. 27c / Mk 14,35b.41c; V. 28a / Mk 14,36c)" (204).
Jn 13,16. "... eine eigenständige joh. Traditionsgeschichte..., deren Ausgangspunkt das matth. Logion war" (217; compare my note on Mt 10,24: 1992, 21-26).
Jn 13,33. "Die joh. Version der Verleugnung des Petrus (V. 33.36-38) dürfte dem Evangelisten vorgelegen haben, wofür insbesondere die für das Evangelium singuläre Anrede τεκνία und die offenkundige Nähe zu Luk. 22,31-34 sprechen" (225).

In general there is a large measure of agreement between Wilckens and Schnelle in questions of literary criticism. Both defend the unity of Jn 1–20. Chapter 21 is treated as an appendix, but neither the Beloved Disciple passages nor the Last Discourses in Chapters 15–17 are assigned to secondary redaction. Schnelle (13) rightly criticizes the displacement of Jn 6/5 + 7,15-24; ctr. Wilckens, 91-92: "wird heute von einer Mehrheit der Ausleger vertreten" (sic). Both defend the location of Jn 15–17 at 14,31 (see Schnelle's *Exkurs* 9, 237-238: par. Mk 14,42 and v. 43 ἔτι αὐτοῦ λαλοῦντος "ein *literarischer* Ort ... für den 4. Evangelisten")[20].

III

As indicated above, Schnelle has anticipated his commentary on the passion narrative in Jn with a list of "Kompositionsanalogien zwischen Markus und Johannes" (1992, 1805-1813; cf. 1994, 567-568). In his bibliographical note on John and the Synoptics (1998, 17 n. 70) and passim through the commentary he refers to Manfred LANG's unpublished dissertation on Jn 18–20 (Halle, 1997)[21]. | The main body of Lang's work is a verse-by-verse analysis of tradition and redaction in Jn 18–20 (Part II: *Redaktionsgeschichtliche Einordnung*, 43-271). The gospel text is divided into sections (nine) and subsections; each has its three parts: *Kontext und Aufbau – Analyse – Interpretation*, and each time again the question is asked: "In welcher Weise sind die Synoptiker für die Exegese von Joh 18–20 von Bedeutung?"[22]. In contrast to A. Dauer's

---

20. Cf. U. SCHNELLE, *Die Abschiedsreden im Johannesevangelium*, in *ZNW* 80 (1989) 64-79, esp. 71-72.

21. M. LANG, *"Mein Herr und mein Gott" (Joh 20,28). Aufbau und Struktur von Joh 18,1–20,31 vor dem Hintergrund von Mk 14,43–16,8 und Lk 22,47–24,43*, Diss. (under U. Schnelle), Halle, 1997, 375 p. Besides the bibliographical notes (*) on pp. 263, 265, 269, 283, 297, 304, 305, Schnelle's references to M. Lang are mostly about tradition and redaction (266, 274, 275, 289, 302) and once about Jn and the Synoptics: Jn 18,39-40 "in Kenntnis von Mark. 15,6-13 und Luk. 23,16-20 komponiert" (276 n. 75).

22. In addition to my 1975-1990 survey (n. 2), see Lang's note on John and the Synoptics (41, n. 230). "Neuerdings (ab 1990) vermuten eine Kenntnis": F.J. Matera (1990), H. Thyen (1990, 1992, 1992a), U. Schnelle (1992, 1994), E.W. Stegemann (1990), M. Sabbe (1991, 1994, 1995), M. Hengel (1993), K. Beckmann (1994), D. Dormeyer (1995), H.-Chr. Kammler (1996).

At the end of the discussion of each verse, Lang refers to scholarly opinions in a concluding footnote. Unfortunately, the classification he uses there (*Tradition*; *Redaktion*) can be misleading. Traditional material of the Johannine community and John's redactional (!) use of the Synoptics are cited together under the rubric *Tradition*. Thus in the case of Jn 18,39, where Dauer (123 n. 135) distinguishes between *Aus den Synoptikern* (Finegan, Barrett, *et al.*) and *Aus dem Bericht der joh Quelle* (Schniewind, Bultmann, Dodd, Borgen, *et al.*), Lang has no such distinction (136 n. 183: all *Tradition*).

Passionsgeschichte and other studies on the "Passionsbericht" (PB) Lang's redaction-critical commentary includes Jn 20 together with Chapters 18–19.

If we concentrate for the moment on Jn 18–19, it appears that no parallels to Mt are retained by Lang: "In der bisherigen Untersuchung hat das MtEv an keiner Stelle ein Mehr geboten, so daß sich eine literarische Abhängigkeit vom MtEv nahegelegt hätte" (252 n. 851, cf. 234 n. 778). Only one of the parallels to editorial phrases in Mt (diff. Mk) is briefly discussed[23]: Jn 18,11a βάλε τὴν μάχαιραν εἰς τὴν θήκην / Mt 26,52a ἀπόστρεψον τὴν μάχαιράν σου εἰς τὸν τόπον αὐτῆς. Lang's comment: "nur entfernt vergleichbar, eine direkte Abhängigkeit besteht kaum" (62). But setting and content of the command could hardly be more identical. Lang argues that "der in Joh 18,11 beschriebene Vorgang häufiger belegt ist" (n. 88, with reference to Josephus' use of θήκη for sheath). This can only weaken Lang's argument based on the NT hapaxlegomenon. Anyway it could have been of some help for the late R.E. Brown who saw "no way of telling about rephrasing by John"[24]. — The specific parallel in Mt is not mentioned in the case of Jn 18,11b τὸ ποτήριον ὃ δέδωκέν μοι ὁ πατὴρ οὐ μὴ πίω αὐτό; (62 n. 90: "ich rechne mit dem direkten literarischen Einfluß des MkEv"). It should be noted that Mt 26,39 (par. Mk 14,36) is repeated in Mt 26,42 and only there we read ... ἐὰν μὴ αὐτὸ πίω (cf. Wilckens, 272). Mk 10,38-39, which is cited as supplementary evidence (63: πίνω τὸ ποτήριον), has its parallel in Mt 20,22-23, with ὑπὸ τοῦ πατρός μου added to ἡτοίμασται. — Four other instances are just mentioned to be refused: Jn 18,16 / Mt 26,69a (73 n. 128); Jn 18,27b / Mt 26,74 (91 n. 192); Jn 19,16b / Mt 27,27 (181 n. 560); Jn 19,19 / Mt 27,37 (186 n. 585)[25]. — "Joh 19,2 ... stammt aus Mk 15,17" (150). There is no comment on the striking verbal similarities in Mt 27,29 (πλέξαντες στέφανον Ι ἐξ ἀκανθῶν ἐπέθηκαν ἐπὶ τῆς κεφαλῆς αὐτοῦ). In the question of Mt's influence on Jn Lang does not seem ready to compromise. Schnelle, too, does not treat Mt as a source or *Vorlage* of Jn, but it is clear from a case like Jn 19,2 that he does not espouse Lang's radical refusal of Matthean influence[26].

---

23. For a list of agreements with Mt in Jn 18–19 (A. Dauer, *et al.*), see my 1975-1990 survey (n. 2), 16-18, n. 69. On Jn 18,11a / Mt 26,52a, see WILCKENS, 272; SCHNELLE, 264 n. 16; cf. SABBE, *Arrest*, 229-230 (*Studia*, 381-382).

24. *The Death of the Messiah*, 275.

25. All four are taken from SABBE, *Denial*, 235, 239; *Death*, 55, 57.

26. Cf. above n. 18.

The criterion applied to parallels in Lk is apparently less severe. Lang refuses the contact with Mt in Jn 18,11a, but defends the Lukan origin of τὸ δεξιόν in Jn 18,10 (ἀπέκοψεν αὐτοῦ τὸ ὠτάριον) τὸ δεξιόν / Lk 22,50 (ἀφεῖλεν τὸ οὖς αὐτοῦ) τὸ δεξιόν. There is no mention of the paraphrase of ἐξέπνευσεν (Mk/Lk) in Mt 27,50 ἀφῆκεν τὸ πνεῦμα / Jn 19,30b παρέδωκεν τὸ πνεῦμα, while Jesus' last word in Jn 19,30a is put in parallel to Lk 23,46a (204). Compare Jn 18,10b.38b.40; 19,4.6.12.15.18 in Dauer's list[27], all adopted by Lang (add Jn 19,41 / Lk 23,53).

Lang summarizes the results of his investigation in a graphic presentation (313-317). The material in Jn that stems from Mk comprises in *Jn 18,1-11*: Mk 14,36.45.47; *Jn 18,12-27*: Mk 14,54.65.66-67.70-71.72; *Jn 18,28–19,16a*: Mk 15,1a.2b.6.9.13.14.15b.16-17.18.19-20; *Jn 19,16b-30*: Mk 15,20b.21b.22.24a.b.26.27.36.40; *Jn 19,(31-37)38-42*: Mk 15,43.45.46. Lang's references to more distant contexts are not included in his table. See Jn 18,3 σπεῖρα, cf. Mk 15,16; Jn 18,6 ἔπεσαν χαμαί, cf. Mk 15,19 (48-49). His list contains verbal similarities such as Jn 18,22 ἔδωκεν ῥάπισμα, cf. Mk 14,65 ῥαπίσμασιν αὐτὸν ἔλαβον (82), but also cases like Mk 14,45 (ῥαββί): "die Tatsache, daß die Verhaftung selbst nicht wortlos vonstatten ging" (54); here, too, there is no mention of Mt.

IV

Jn 20 was included in Schnelle's 1992 essay (1811-1813) and is also part of Lang's investigation (226-265). In the prolongation of the treatment of Jn 20 in my own work on John and the Synoptics[28] I will examine here more closely this chapter in the two commentaries (Wilckens, 303-319; Schnelle, 297-313).

Jn 20,3-10 / Lk 24,12

They agree about the textual authenticity of Lk 24,12[29] and about its influence upon Jn 20,3-10. In their view, however, it is the *Vorlage* or (pre-)Johannine tradition that depends on Lk: "der vorjohanneische Bericht", "die Vorlage, die nur von Petrus erzählt hat" (Wilckens, 305,

---

27. See my 1975-1990 survey, 36-38, n. 168 (list of agreements with Lk in Jn 18–19).
28. Schnelle and Lang refer to *John and the Synoptics: The Empty Tomb Stories*, in *NTS* 30 (1984) 161-187 (= *Evangelica II*, 571-600), here quoted as *Tomb*; and *Once More Luke 24,12*, in *ETL* 70 (1994) 319-340 (in reply to A. Dauer).
29. With reference to *ETL*, 1994: LANG, 230-231; SCHNELLE, 299.

307); "Luk. 24,12 (bildete) den Ausgangspunkt für die Petruserzählung der joh. Tradition" (Schnelle, 301).

The traditional story of Peter's visit to the tomb is supposed to begin with the singular verb ἐξῆλθεν in 20,3: cf. Wilckens (305), Schnelle's more explicit remarks (298, 299 nn. 8 and 9) and his translation: "Da machte sich Petrus auf und der andere Jünger, und sie gingen zum Grab". But see my *Jean et les Synoptiques*, 81-83: "en grec la construction n'a rien d'anormal"; the verb preceding | the two subjects is in the singular (ἐξῆλθεν, see also ἠκολούθει in 18,15) and the subsequent verb is plural (καὶ ἤρχοντο). Compare Wilckens's translation of v. 3a: "Da gingen sie hinaus, Petrus und der andere Jünger". His translation of v. 3b is less satisfactory: "und *kamen* zum Grab" (also EÜ *et al.*). Lang (n. 757) rightly refers to Bauer's comment: ἤρχοντο is used "von der unvollendeten Handlung" (contrast v. 4c: ἦλθεν ... εἰς τὸ μνημεῖον). There is no need for a *Vorlage* of Jn 20,3 other than Lk 24,12a ὁ δὲ Πέτρος ἀναστὰς ἔδραμεν ἐπὶ τὸ μνημεῖον. For v. 5a, cf. Lk 24,12b καὶ παρακύψας βλέπει τὰ ὀθόνια μόνα[30], and for v. 10, cf. Lk 24,12c καὶ ἀπῆλθεν πρὸς ἑαυτόν. Both commentators agree that the other disciple and the race motif are brought in by the evangelist (vv. 4.5b-6.8) but regard vv. 7 and 9 as traditional. One may observe that these distinctive elements in Jn show some connection with Lk 24,12: for v. 7, cf. τὰ ὀθόνια μόνα understood as "by themselves", lying apart from other things, and for v. 9, cf. Peter's θαυμάζων, "unausgesprochen vorausgesetzt" in Jn (Wilckens, 306), in contrast to ἐπίστευσεν in v. 8[31].

It is important to note that, by taking Peter's visit to the tomb in Lk 24,12 as the starting point and Jn 20,3-10 as the final stage, Wilckens and Schnelle on the one hand decline the hypothesis of a primitive gospel text[32]

---

30. Instead of Jn 20,5a (Schnelle, Lang, *et al.*) Wilckens takes v. 6b (καὶ θεωρεῖ τὰ ὀθόνια κείμενα, said of Peter) as traditional (304). But the verbal similarity to Lk 24,12 is much closer in v. 5a: καὶ παρακύψας βλέπει κείμενα τὰ ὀθόνια, said of "the other disciple", the evangelist's substitute for Peter.

31. On Jn 20,9 (οὐδέπω γὰρ ᾔδεισαν...) see my comment in *Tomb*, 177 (= *Evangelica II*, 594), with reference to Haenchen in n. 120: "Die Unkenntnis der Schriftstelle macht beides verständlich: daß der eine Jünger zum Glauben kam und der andere nicht". On the Lukan inspiration of v. 9, see *Tomb* (*ibid.*). See also Lang's conclusion: "Joh 20,9 ist daher aus Lk 24,6-8.44-46 entnommen" (237), but can it therefore be called "traditional" (cf. n. 22)?

For Wilckens and Schnelle the motif of Lk 24,12d θαυμάζων τὸ γεγονός also has its place in the pre-Johannine *Vorlage*, where it is followed by Jn 20,9, the singular ᾔδει referring to Peter: "erstaunt, weil er das Auferstehungszeugnis der Schrift noch nicht kannte" (WILCKENS, 305; cf. SCHNELLE, 301).

32. Cf. SCHNELLE, 1992: "Die These einer Lukas und Johannes gemeinsamen Tradition vermag an dieser Stelle den Textbefund nicht zu erklären, denn zu offensichtlich sind die inhaltlichen, sprachlichen und kompositionellen Parallelen" (1812).

and on the other refuse the theory of post-Johannine redaction[33]. But it is not proven that we | need a Johannine (or "pre-Johannine") tradition as intermediary stage between Lk and Jn[34].

Jn 20,11-18 / Lk 24,4 (Mk 16,5); Mt 28,9-10

In v. 11 Mary Magdalene is back at the tomb "ohne daß ihre Rückkehr berichtet wird"[35], and "die Engelszene ist für die nachfolgende Begegnung zwischen Jesus und Maria Magdalena ohne Bedeutung": the traditional story, which was resumed in v. 11, is interrupted again by the evangelist's insertion of vv. 12-13 (Schnelle, 298, 302)[36].

One can, with Schnelle, recognize in 20,12-13 the evangelist's redactional composition, but it is less evident that it should be regarded as an

---

33. Contrast now M. THEOBALD, *Der Jünger, den Jesus liebte. Beobachtungen zum narrativen Konzept der johanneischen Redaktion*, in H. LICHTENBERGER (ed.), *Geschichte – Tradition – Reflexion*. FS M. Hengel, *III. Frühes Christentum*, Tübingen, 1996, 218-255, esp. 234-239: the story of Peter's visit to the tomb (vv. 3*.6*.7.9.10, originally after 20,18) relocated and the Beloved Disciple added by R (all BD passages are assigned to R). Theobald rejects dependence on Lk 24,12 but reconstructs an original sequence in E of a hypothetical story like Lk 24,1-11 followed by a Peter story like Lk 24,12 (cf. P. Seidensticker, 1967; D. Zeller, 1986: this 'Lukan' sequence in the source of E). He argues against John's use of the Synoptics with the *Farbkästen* argument. Cf. M. THEOBALD, *Der johanneische Osterglaube und die Grenzen seiner narrativen Vermittlung (Joh 20)*, in R. HOPPE & U. BUSSE (eds.), *Von Jesus zum Christus. Christologische Studien*. FS P. Hoffmann (BZNW, 93), Berlin - New York, 1998, 93-123, esp. 102 n. 31. See my reply to D. Zeller (and J. Becker) in *ETL* 62 (1986) 404, and in my 1992 survey (15 n. 62).
On the Beloved Disciple in 1,35-40 and 18,15-16 (Theobald: R), note that the identification is accepted by Schnelle (already in 1987, 28-30) but refused by Wilckens. On 18,15-16, see my *The 'Other Disciple' in Jn 18,15-16*, in *ETL* 51 (1975) 113-141; = *Evangelica I*, 335-362 (pro) and on 1,35-40, *The Anonymous Disciple in John 1*, in *ETL* 66 (1990) 5-37; = *Evangelica II*, 617-649 (contra; cf. WILCKENS, 49: "Wer immer mit dem anderen Jünger von V. 37 gemeint sein mag, — mit dem späteren 'Jünger, den Jesus liebte', hat er nichts zu tun").
34. One can agree with Schnelle: dependence on the Synoptics in the Johannine source or tradition cannot be a reason for refusing the evangelist's dependence (1992, 1814 n. 72: the *Hauptschwäche* in Dauer's position). However, if on the contrary it is agreed that the evangelist used the Synoptics, is there then still a good reason for anticipating the dependence on the Synoptics in Johannine tradition?
35. Compare the analogous verse 11,39. Cf. *Tomb*, 178 (= *Evangelica II*, 595). See now also LANG, 239 n. 796. Note that Lang and Schnelle regard 20,11a as "joh. Redaktion".
36. More precisely, according to Schnelle, vv. 12aβ-14a, with καὶ θεωρεῖ (v. 12aα) repeated in v. 14b: "ein sandwich-agreement" (302 n. 31). The term "sandwich-agreement" (LANG, 72, 92, 228, 229, 245; cf. SCHNELLE, 266 n. 26) was first (?) used in German by J. Gnilka as a designation of Mk's intercalations (1979; cf. *ETL* 57, 1981, 164; = *Evangelica I*, 610), instead of the more usual "sandwich arrangement" (*Verschachtelung*). — On the intercalation in Jn 18,15-18.19-24.25-27, see SCHNELLE, 266 n. 26: "geht auf den Evangelisten Markus zurück"; LANG, 92: "dem zuerst im MkEv begegneten Verfahren des sog. sandwich-agreement nachgebildet". See *ETL* 51 (1975), 129-132 (= *Evangelica I*, 351-354) and my 1992 survey, 47-49.

Einschub. My reply was anticipated in *Tomb*, 171-172; = *Evangelica II*, 586-588 ("Jn 20,11b-14a"): "the angelophany is a preparation for the christophany, and not a superfluous episode... Verse 14a indicates the end of the episode, not necessarily the end of an interpolation" (587, 588).

Schnelle emphasizes, "die Engel waren dem Evangelisten durch Lukas vorgegeben" (302 n. 31); cf. 1992: Jn 20,12-13, "dessen Grundmotiv sich Lk 24,4 verdankt" (1812). Lang (239) rightly adds the reference to the parallel in Mk 16,5 (cf. Jn 20,12 two angels *in white, sitting*...)[37]. His comment on Jn 20,14b-16 is less convincing: "Johannes gibt ... unverändert seine der Gemeinde entstammende Tradition wieder" (242). Contrast Wilckens: "Der Joh.evangelist hat den Dialog zwischen Maria und Jesus ausgestaltet, vor allem in V. 17" (305)[38].

I "Redaktionell dürfte ... das Verbot an Maria sein, Jesus zu berühren", "erst Thomas darf den Auferstandenen berühren" (Schnelle, 1992, 1813). The parallel in Mt 28,9-10, not mentioned by Schnelle, is refused by Lang: "Mt sagt nichts von einer abgewiesenen Berührung" (243 n. 813). Wilckens has the correct translation: "Halte mich nicht fast!" and the presupposition Lang requires: "Offenbar ist sie (Maria) ihm bei seinem Anruf zu Füßen gefallen (... so Mt 28,9)" (309)[39].

Jn 20,19-29 / Lk 24,36-49

The appearance to the disciples (Jn 20,19-23) has close parallels in Lk 24,36-49. See A. Dauer's detailed analysis (1984) and my discussion of Jn 20,19-20 (cf. Wilckens, 311; Schnelle, 304)[40].

The scene with Thomas (Jn 20,24-25.26-29), assigned to the evangelist's redaction, has "keinerlei synoptische Parallele" (Wilckens). Note, however, Lang's observation:

> Den literarischen Ausgangspunkt, d.h. die 'Idee', zu einer solchen Geschichte dürfte der Evangelist jedoch aus Lk 24,38f.41b-43 entnommen

---

37. Compare also the young man "sitting on the right" (Mk 16,5) with the position of the two angels "sitting ... one at the head and the other at the foot". Theobald connects this differentiation with the position of the *soudarion* "that had been on Jesus' head ... in a place by itself": traditions "aufeinander abgestimmt" (*Jünger*, 236 n. 95); or both 20,7 and 20,12 the evangelist's elaboration.

38. Cf. THEOBALD, *Osterglaube*, 102: "Der vierte Evangelist hat die Szene der Christophanie vor Maria Magdalena 20,14-18 stilistisch und theologisch selbst gestaltet".

39. See *Tomb*, 166-171 (= *Evangelica II*, 579-586). On Jn 20,17, cf. THEOBALD, *Osterglaube*, 100-116 (esp. 102: on direct or indirect dependence on Mt 28,9-10).

40. A. DAUER, *Johannes und Lukas*, esp. 283-288 ("Folgerungen für das Verhältnis von Joh 20,19-29 zu Lk 24,36-49"), and, in addition to Lang's bibliography, my *Luc 24,36-43: Un récit lucanien*, in *À cause de l'évangile*. FS J. Dupont (LD, 123), Paris, 1985, 655-680; = *Evangelica II*, 205-226, esp. 206-213 ("Jn 20,19-20").

haben... Der Evangelist hat Joh 20,27 selbst gebildet, er verdankt die Anregung aber Lk 24,41b-43. (254, 257)

Compare *Luc 24,36-43*, 660 (= 209):

On concédera volontiers que Jn 20,24-29 ne peut avoir existé indépendamment de Jn 20,19-23, mais cela n'exclut nullement une composition parallèle des deux récits à partir d'une tradition préexistante qui ne serait autre
que Lc 24,36ss. La dualité des deux apparitions en Jn 20,19-23.24-29 peut
s'inspirer directement de la double démonstration en Lc 24,37-40 et 41-43
(v. 41 ἔτι δὲ ἀπιστούντων αὐτῶν...).

SUPPLEMENTARY NOTE (2000)

M. Lang's dissertation, *"Mein Herr und mein Gott" (Joh 20,28)*, which was
presented in *ETL* 74 (1998) 392-394 (here above, 609-611), is now published in
a slightly revised form and under a new title: *Johannes und die Synoptiker. Eine
redaktionsgeschichtliche Analyse von Joh 18–20 vor dem markinischen und
lukanischen Hintergrund* (FRLANT, 182), Göttingen, Vandenhoeck & Ruprecht,
1999; see my review in *ETL* 75 (1999) 481. The middle paragraph of the review
is reprinted hereafter.

One can observe a certain tension between the main title speaking of *the* Synoptics and the more precise subtitle: "vor dem markinischen und lukanischen
Hintergrund". The general statements on Mt he made in the dissertation (234
n. 778: "der direkte literarische Einfluß des MtEv [konnte] bisher nicht
wahrscheinlich gemacht werden"; 252 n. 851: "In der bisherigen Untersuchung
hat das MtEv an keiner Stelle ein Mehr geboten, so daß eine literarische
Abhängigkeit vom mtEv nahegelegt hätte") are now cancelled (267 n. 799; 386
n. 876), but he remains critical with regard to possible influences of Mt (94
n. 129; 113 n. 193; 209 n. 571; 251 n. 598; cf. dissertation: 73 n. 128; 91
n. 192; 181 n. 560; 186 n. 585). The footnote on Mt 28,9-10 (diss., 243 n. 813:
"Neirynck meint...") is now printed in the text (275) and a reference to
W. Reinbold is added (n. 832). Lang's principal objection: the women's
προσεκύνησαν αὐτῷ "gerade nicht in Joh 20,16f vorausgesetzt" has been
answered by Wilckens: "Offenbar ist sie ihm bei seinem Anruf zu Füßen
gefallen" (309; cf. 315: likewise in Jn 20,28 "als Geste des Bekenntnisses zu
ergänzen").

ETL 76 (2000) 122-132

31

THE QUESTION OF JOHN AND THE SYNOPTICS

D. Moody Smith 1992-1999

The reader of my two survey articles on John and the Synoptics 1960-1975 (1977) and 1975-1990 (1992) may have noticed that D. Moody Smith (Duke University, Durham, NC) appears to be one of the principal interlocutors in this debate[1]. In 1992 I could include at the last minute a reference to the monograph he published in the same year, *John among the Gospels*[2].

In the volume of essays presented to Smith in 1996, *Exploring the Gospel of John*, R. Kysar gave a description of Smith's contributions to the question of sources, ending with a quotation of the conclusion of *John among the Gospels*[3]. Apart from J.D.G. Dunn's article on the difference between John and the Synoptics "at the theological level", the volume contains only a few occasional allusions to John/Synoptics[4].

---

1. F. NEIRYNCK, *John and the Synoptics* [1960-1975], in M. DE JONGE (ed.), *L'évangile de Jean. Sources, rédaction, théologie* (BETL, 44), Gembloux-Leuven, 1977 (Leuven, ²1987), 73-106; = *Evangelica I* (BETL, 60), Leuven, 1982, 365-400, esp. 365 n. 1; *John and the Synoptics: 1975-1990*, in A. DENAUX (ed.), *John and the Synoptics* (BETL, 101), Leuven, 1992, 3-62, esp. 12-13.

2. *Ibid.*, 61-62 ("Postscript"). Cf. D.M. SMITH, *John among the Gospels: The Relationship in Twentieth-Century Research*, Minneapolis, MN, 1992. See my review in *ETL* 68 (1992) 442-444. Smith's subsequent works on John before 1999: *Historical Issues and the Problem of John and the Synoptics*, in M.C. DE BOER (ed.), *From Jesus to John: FS M. de Jonge* (JSNT SS, 84), Sheffield, 1994, 252-267; *The Theology of the Gospel of John*, Cambridge, 1995; *John*, in J. BARCLAY – J. SWEET (eds.), *Early Christian Thought in the Jewish Context: FS M.D. Hooker*, Cambridge, 1996, 96-111; *Prolegomena to a Canonical Reading of the Fourth Gospel* [1992], 169-182; *What Have I Learned about the Gospel of John?* [1994], 217-235, in F.F. SEGOVIA (ed.), *"What Is John?" Readers and Readings of the Fourth Gospel* (SBL Symposium Series, 3), Atlanta, GA, 1996 (see my review in *ETL* 72, 1996, 457-458). His earlier essays are collected in *Johannine Christianity. Essays on Its Setting, Sources, and Theology*, Columbia, SC, 1984, esp. 128-144: "John and the Synoptics: de Solages and Neirynck" (= *Bib* 62, 1982, 102-113: review of my *Jean et les Synoptiques*, 1979). See my review in *ETL* 61 (1985) 400-402.

3. R.A. CULPEPPER – C.C. BLACK (eds.), *Exploring the Gospel of John: FS D. Moody Smith*, Louisville, KY, 1996: R. KYSAR, *The Contribution of D. Moody Smith to Johannine Scholarship*, 3-17 (esp. 6-8). In the same volume: D.M. Smith's *Selected Bibliography 1943-1995*, compiled by Kysar (xvi-xxvii).

4. See my review in *ETL* 72 (1996) 456-457. Note in Dunn's essay (*John and the Synoptics as a Theological Question*, 301-313) his statement on John's use of the Gospel genre: "does not necessarily imply his knowledge of Mark in particular" (312 n. 32: "*pace* ... Smith, *John among the Gospels*, 179-80").

"One could argue that Smith's own position has changed only slightly since his 1963 article" (Kysar, 8). But it would be a mistake to think that the time to repose had come. Now, in 1999, we can quote the Preface of his *John* in the ANTC series[5]:

> While I continue to believe, along with P. Gardner-Smith (1938), C.H. Dodd (1963), and R.T. Fortna (1970, 1988), that John knew and used important traditions or sources independent of the other canonical Gospels, Frans Neirynck (1992) and his Louvain colleagues have made us again take seriously the question of John and the Synoptics, as I believe this commentary will show.

I

Let us begin our analysis with Smith's reference to the Synoptics in his comment on the final verse of the Gospel.

> **21,25**: the mention of other books ... rather clearly suggests that other Gospels are known to exist. Arguably, knowledge of one or more of the Synoptics is reflected in the latest editorial layer of the Gospel, whatever its origin. Thus certain statements can be viewed as editorial notations intended to reconcile the accounts (e.g., 3:24; 4:2; 6:59: 18:24,28). [372]
>
> **3,24**: The evangelist's, or an editor's, note in verse 24 presumes knowledge of John's imprisonment, which is recounted in the Synoptics (cf. Mark 1:14), but not in this Gospel. [104]
>
> **4,2**: This rather awkward interjection looks like an effort to square John's account with the Synoptics (cf. 3:24). [110]
>
> **18,24**: ... the evangelist perhaps intends the reader to supply the scene [of the trial] from Mark (or Matthew)... there are similar statements elsewhere in John that have the effect of bringing this Gospel into line with the Synoptics, while breaking the flow of the narrative (cf. 2:12; 3:24: 4:2: 6:59). [336]
>
> **2,12**; **6,59** Capernaum: "Perhaps here John indirectly acknowledges the synoptic Gospels or tradition". [86; cf. 161]

In each instance, however, there follows a "yet" or a "but". At 3,24: "Yet, John's imprisonment and execution were widely known facts" (104); 4,2: "Yet even there [in the Synoptics] we do not read that Jesus' disciples baptized" (110); 18,24: "but such an expectation and assump-

---

5. D.M. SMITH, *John* (Abingdon New Testament Commentaries), Nashville, TN, 1999: Preface (13-15; here, 14), Introduction (21-45), Commentary (47-406), Select Bibliography (407-418), Index (419-428). With four exceptions (A. Dauer 1992, M. Hengel 1993, K.L. Schmidt 1923, H. Thyen 1971) all works cited in *John* are in English, including the translations of three German commentaries (R. Bultmann, E. Haenchen, R. Schnackenburg). On "John and the Synoptic Gospels", see the Introduction, 29-32; and "Other Sources", 32-33.

tion would be rather strange in John" (336; cf. 333). — On Jn 18,19-24 and the trial before the Sanhedrin, cf. below[6]. On Jn 3,24; 4,2; 6,59; 21,25 and Johannine style, see G. Van Belle's study of the parentheses[7]:

> if Van Belle's analysis of the *hermeneiai* as being consistent with the language world of the gospel as a whole be correct (*Les parenthèses*, 206-10), it makes less convincing any argument that appeals to a later different editor, since syntax, vocabulary, and style are a major part of the evidence that helps one to isolate a different redactional hand[8].

II

I   For Smith, to read the Gospel of John "in the light of the Synoptics" is "a reading that sometimes fits but just as often jars" (72). He speaks of similarities between John and the Synoptics in general or between John and Mark in particular, and "the many similarities unique to Luke and John" (374). But also **Matthew** is not out of the picture[9]. In *John among the Gospels* my position on John's dependence upon Mt 28,9-10 is described as follows[10]:

> In an earlier article [1969], Neirynck had shown how Matthew 28:9-10, the story of Jesus' encounter with the women outside the tomb, can be understood as a Matthean editorial composition. The principal argument against

6. See below, section III. On Jn 18,24, cf. my *Parentheses in the Fourth Gospel*, in *ETL* 65 (1989) 119-123 (= *Evangelica II*, 693-697), esp. 120-122 (= 694-696): "Jn 18,24". My note was meant to be a supplement to G. Van Belle's historical survey (n. 7) rather than a new defence of the pluperfect; ctr. M. LANG, *Johannes und die Synoptiker* (below, n. 9), 107 n. 172. But see R.E. BROWN (*The Death of the Messiah*, 407): "This rendition is unusual but not impossible in an independent clause (Gardiner)". F. GARDINER, *On the Aorist ἀπέστειλεν in Jn. xviii.24*, in *JBL* 6 (1886) 45-55, can be added to my historical survey.

7. G. VAN BELLE, *Les parenthèses dans l'Évangile de Jean* (SNTA, 11), Leuven, 1985: 3,24 (69, 108[4], 112[14]); 4,2 (70, 111[12]); 6,59 (77, 108[5]); 21,25 (104, 111[13], 112[15]). Cf. *JBL* 106 (1987) 719-721 (review by C.W. Hedrick).

8. C.W. HEDRICK, *Authorial Presence and Narrator in John: Commentary and Story*, in J.E. GOEHRING, et al. (eds.), *Gospel Origins & Christian Beginnings: FS J.M. Robinson*, Sonoma, CA, 1990, 74-93, here 85. Cf. 82 (3,24[v]; 4,2[v]; 6,59[i]; 21,25[v]). Neither van Belle's *Parenthèses* nor Hedrick's essay is mentioned by Smith.

9. Contrast the view of some interpreters who accept Johannine dependence upon Mk and Lk but not upon Mt. Thus, recently, M. LANG, *Johannes und die Synoptiker. Eine redaktionsgeschichtliche Analyse von Joh 18–20 vor dem markinischen und lukanischen Hintergrund* (FRLANT, 182), Göttingen, 1999: cf. *ETL* 75 (1999) 481 (review). See also my *John and the Synoptics in Recent Commentaries*, in *ETL* 74 (1998) 386-397, esp. 393-394.

10. *John among the Gospels*, 157; with references to *Les femmes au tombeau: Étude de la rédaction matthéenne (Matt. xxviii.1-10)*, in *NTS* 15 (1968-69) 168-190 (= *Evangelica I*, 273-296) and *John and the Synoptics: The Empty Tomb Stories*, in *NTS* 30 (1984) 161-187 (= *Evangelica II*, 571-600).

this view always refers to the existence of John 20:11-18, the appearance to Mary Magdalene, said to be based on a similar and related tradition. Now [1984] Neirynck seeks to show that the Johannine account can be read more intelligibly as an elaboration and retelling of the Matthean story. The logic of his argument is impeccable: if Matthew composed 28:9-10 on no traditional basis, and if John can best be understood against that background, John must have known Matthew's Gospel, and other putative sources become superfluous. John has carried forward what was already occurring in Matthew, the displacement of the angelophany (John 20:11-13) by the appearance of Jesus himself. As one can observe by noticing Neirynck's underlinings in the text above[11], essential elements of Matthew's brief narrative recur in that of John, albeit mostly in different forms. It is, of course, scarcely possible that Matthew redacted and compressed John; on the other hand, that John created his dramatic narrative and gave to Mary Magdalene the central role is easily imaginable.

Smith now focuses his comment on μή μου ἅπτου in NRSV and most modern translations: "Do not hold on to me" (RSV: Do not hold me):

> Arguably, the narrative of Matthew 28:9-10, where the women take hold of the feet of Jesus, is assumed, for John has not said that Mary attempted to hold him.

Curiously enough, in contrast to his 1992 translation ("Touch me no more") he now turns to the old KJV (and Bultmann), "Touch me not":

> ... this meaning is not impossible for John... If this interpretation is followed, there is an even neater contrast between Jesus' prohibition here and his invitation to Thomas (20:27). In this case also the relationship to the Matthean version is less compelling, *although still possible*. [377; emphasis mine]

I Jn 1,41-42 is another passage where "affinities with the Synoptics, and especially Matthew, are striking":

> First of all, Peter is present at the announcement that Jesus is the Messiah... Then in Matthew and John alone Jesus bestowes on Simon the name Peter... Moreover, he describes him as "son of...": in Matthew "son of Jonah" (16:17); in John "son of John". [74][12]

That the identification of Jesus as the Messiah is attained already at the beginning of the Fourth Gospel can be seen as the evangelist's editorial composition. In this context Smith mentions also the power of binding and loosing in Mt 16,19 (18,18) and Jn 20,23 (74, cf. 380). Yet

---

11. Jn 20,16-17 in Smith's translation, 154. For a detailed analysis, see *NTS* 30 (1984), 166-171: "Jn. 20.11-18 and Mt. 28.9-10" (= 579-586).

12. Cf. *Jean et les Synoptiques. Examen critique de l'exégèse de M.-É. Boismard* (BETL, 49), Leuven, 1979, 188-194 ("Jn 1,41-42 et Mt 16,16-18").

"scattered in John and united in Matthew" does not necessarily mean more original in Jn and secondary in Mt. Note that Smith applies the rule differently with regard to Jn 6: what is scattered in the Synoptics is consolidated in Jn (145).

The observation that "for agreements between John and Mark/Matthew there is at least a theoretical possibility that the contact with Mark took place via Matthew"[13] can be extended to Smith's references to Matthew/Luke (Q).

3,22-30 and Q 7,18-35:

> This second appearance of John [during Jesus' ministry] ... presumably represents a remote agreement of John and Q. [105][14] Once again the Johannine narrative has a point of contact with the Synoptics, although in substance the accounts are quite different. [103]

3,31-36 and Q 7,28:

> One could perhaps see here a kind of Johannine analogy to what is found in Matthew and Luke. John is praised, but is clearly placed in the old age rather than the new, that is, the kingdom. The comparison is, so to speak, temporal and eschatological. Here, in the Fourth Gospel, it would be spatial (from above and from below; cf. Isa 55:9-11) – again a typically Johannine transposition of a synoptic perspective. [106]

4,34 and Q 4,4:

> The Matthean version of the Deuteronomy quotation that gives the contrast between living by bread alone or "by every word that comes from the mouth of God" (4:4) is reminiscent of the statement of Jesus in John. It is conceivable that John knows and reflects the Matthean account... [120][15]

4,36-38 and Q 10,2:

> | Probably we are dealing with independently transmitted versions of the same or related sayings. As the Synoptics speak of laborers, John has sowers and reapers who labor. [120]

12,25 and Mt 10,39; Lk 17,33 "presumably a Q-source parallel" (238):

> When we see the parallels in the Synoptics, the Johannine form of the same saying is easily recognizable as such. It could have been derived from the Synoptics... On the whole we seem to be dealing with common tradition,

13. *John and the Synoptics* (1992), 35.

14. "In the Synoptics John asks, through his disciples, whether Jesus is the one to come; in the Fourth Gospel he tells his disciples that Jesus is. The difference is, of course, typical of John in comparison with the Synoptics" (*ibid.*).

15. Smith adds: "or an earlier tradition of it". But see *DQ*: ἀλλ' ἐπὶ παντὶ ῥήματι ἐκπορευομένῳ διὰ στόματος θεοῦ = MtR (*Q 4:1-13,16*, 1996, 142-147).

also found in Q, rather than with John's use of other canonical Gospels. [239][16]

13,16; 15,20a and Q 6,40 (Mt 10,24-25a)[17]
13,20 and Q 10,16 (Mt 10,40):

> But there are distinctive agreements with Matthew as well: for example, the saying of Jesus in John 13:20 is closer to that of Matthew 10:40 than to the (possible Q) parallel in Luke 10:16. [*John among the Gospels*, 180]

4,46-54 and Q 7,1-10 (Mt 8,5-13):

> In the synoptic version the point of the story hinges upon the fact that the man is a Gentile. Whether or not John knows that version, his point is different. [125]
> Here John deliberately avoids saying or implying that he is a Gentile. This is particularly significant if the evangelist knows the Synoptic (apparently Q) version of the story. [91]

Without speaking of deliberate avoidance[18] one can agree that John's point is different: "The question of faith is raised here ... in a different and typically Johannine way" (126). For a discussion of the relationship of the Johannine and synoptic versions, Smith refers to Brown "1966"(!), without mentioning his own presentation of A. Dauer's analysis in *John among the Gospels*. His comment on the story's ending is most typical:

> In the Synoptics, the result – the lad's healing – is very briefly recounted; in John it is told in considerable detail (vv. 51-53), with particular attention to the time at which Jesus had spoken and the time the boy began to recover. [127]

He refers no more to the "striking similarities" (1992, 163) between John and Mt 8,13 and there is no mention at all of Mt 8,15[19]:

16. But the Q-origin of Lk 17,33 (Mt 10,39) is not certain. See my *Saving/Losing One's Life: Luke 17,33 (Q?) and Mark 8,35*, in *Von Jesus zum Christus: FS P. Hoffmann* (BZNW, 93), Berlin - New York, 1998, 295-318.

17. See *John and the Synoptics* (1992), 21-26. See now also U. SCHNELLE, *Joh*, 217: "Während die Q-Überlieferung οὐκ ἔστιν μαθητὴς ὑπὲρ τὸν διδάσκαλον (Matth. 10,24a; Luk. 6,40a) aufgrund des fehlenden zweiten Oppositionspaares wahrscheinlich nicht der traditionsgeschichtliche Ausgangspunkt für das überlieferte joh. Logion ist, kommt der vorliegende Matthäus-Text dafür in Frage".

18. Contrast U. Schnelle's comment: "Die meisten Kommentatoren beziehen βασιλικός auf einen Juden, wobei übersehen wird, daß Johannes dies an keiner Stelle ausdrücklich sagt" (96 n. 169).

19. See *Jean et les Synoptiques*, 1979 (n. 12), 223 n. 555 (cf. 142 n. 275). Compare BOISMARD-LAMOUILLE, 1977: "les mots 'à cette heure-là' et 'la fièvre la quitta' se trouvent là à deux versets d'intervalle seulement!" (149). See also *John 4,46-54: Signs Source and/or Synoptic Gospels*, in *ETL* 60 (1984) 367-375 (= *Evangelica II*, 679-687),

Jn 4		Mt 8	
51c	ὁ παῖς αὐτοῦ ζῇ.	13b	καὶ ἰάθη ὁ παῖς [αὐτοῦ]
52a	... τὴν ὥραν ... ἐν ᾗ...		ἐν τῇ ὥρᾳ ἐκείνῃ.
b	... ἀφῆκεν αὐτὸν ὁ πυρετός	15	καὶ ἀφῆκεν αὐτὴν ὁ πυρετός

It is rather rare in *John* that Smith refers to his earlier works on John, but he has explicit references to the 1975-1976 essays on the signs source: 10,40-42 at the end of the signs source (203) and 12,37-40 the nexus between signs source and passion (242). From the outset he repeats his support for R.T. Fortna's position (32: "Quite possibly the author drew upon an earlier collection of miracle stories already joined to a passion narrative"), and in his comment on 20,30 he will conclude: "that John drew on a source of miracle stories *different from the Synoptics* is an entirely plausible hypothesis" (385, emphasis mine). The classic argument is developed in the comment on 4,46-54, enumerated in v. 54 as the second sign. Here too the signs source functions as an alternative to Johannine use of the Synoptics: "this would explain the source of John's miracle tradition without recourse to the other Gospels" (124). Unfortunately there is no mention in *John* of G. Van Belle's book and other critical evaluations of the semeia hypothesis[20].

here 373 (= 685); *John and the Synoptics* (1992), 19; *Jean 4,46-65: Une leçon de méthode*, in *ETL* 77 (1995) 176-184, here 180-181. The argument on the basis of Mt 8,15 closely following on 8,13 is adopted by I. DUNDERBERG, *Johannes und die Synoptiker. Studien zu Joh 1–9* (AASF, 69), Helsinki, 1994, 93-95 (95: "Man kann sich kaum des Eindrucks erwehren, daß der joh Redaktor wenigstens Mt kannte, als er Joh 4,46-54 verfaßte"); *Johannine Anomalies and the Synoptics*, in J. NISSEN – S. PEDERSEN (eds.), *New Readings in John* (JSNT SS, 182), Sheffield, 1999, 108-125, esp. 116 n. 29.

Note that the πυρετός clause in Jn appears in A. Dauer's list of the *Unterschiede*, which is resumed in *John among the Gospels*: "The differences between John's and Matthew's versions are nevertheless real, for example, in John the *huios* lies near death of a fever, while in Matthew the *pais* is lame (paralyzed)" (103; cf. DAUER, *Johannes und Lukas*, 1984, 43, without referring to Mt 8,15).

20. G. VAN BELLE, *The Signs Source in the Fourth Gospel: Historical Survey and Critical Evaluation of the Semeia Hypothesis* (BETL, 116), Leuven, 1994 (on D.M. Smith, see esp. 194-197). Cf. my *The Signs Source in the Fourth Gospel: A Critique of the Hypothesis*, in *Evangelica II*, 651-677; *John and the Synoptics in Recent Commentaries* (above, n. 9), 389 n. 11 (U. Wilckens, U. Schnelle). See now U. SCHNELLE, *Ein neuer Blick: Tendenzen gegenwärtiger Johannesforschung*, in *Berliner Theologische Zeitschrift* 16 (1999) 21-40, esp. 26 (and n. 17): "auf internationaler Ebene bezweifelt heute eine deutliche Mehrheit der Exegeten die Existenz dieser 'Semeia-Quelle'". — Note that in Smith's earlier essays the signs source is designated as *semeia*-source (cf. Bultmann) and now in *John* as "sign source" (or miracle source).

III

The **Passion Narrative** (chaps. 18–19) is "by far the longest section in which John runs side-by-side with the Synoptics" (322). Yet the order of the episodes in the Passion Narrative, betrayal - arrest - trial(s) - execution - burial, can scarcely be changed: "So the common order of the episodes does not necessarily imply a | common source" (326). For Smith, 1 Cor 11,23 indicates that Paul "apparently knows, and presumes knowledge of, a narrative of Jesus' death" (325); and "Mark and John could well represent two separate, if not unrelated, responses to the need for such a narration" (32). As I noted elsewhere[21], the tradition quoted by Paul "is hardly thinkable without some knowledge of the events of the passion", but can the reference to the Last Supper and the giving over of Jesus be said to suggest the existence of a pre-Gospel passion story? "Wie weit die geschichtliche Kenntnis vom Passionsgeschehen bei Paulus oder gar den Korinthern reicht, läßt sich nicht sagen" (W. Schrage)[22].

Smith clearly states his method in dealing with John's PN:

> This commentary will not ... assume John's knowledge of other Gospels, but relationships will be examined and tested at every relevant points. [325]
>
> Our procedure will be to read John's narrative alongside the Synoptics, particularly Mark, but without assuming John's dependence upon any one of them. In this way the significant similarities and differences will be noted. [333]

Perhaps the most significant difference is John's omission of the trial before the Sanhedrin: "the Markan account ... fits so well the Johannine Jews' case against Jesus, its absence is remarkable" (336). As noted above, Smith declines the suggestion that the transfer of Jesus to Caiaphas (18,24) could evoke the synoptic scene (336). Nevertheless, he is not unaware of the counterarguments:

> Officially, condemnation of Jesus by "the Jews" has already occurred more than once (beginning in 5:18) and will continue into the trial before Pilate. [337]
>
> Of course, the Jewish authorities in John have long since condemned Jesus because of his view of his own dignity and role in relation to God and sought to put him to death (cf. 5:18; 7:19; 8:40; 10:31-39). [336] |

21. *Paul and the Sayings of Jesus* (1986), in *Evangelica II*, 541.
22. *Der erste Brief an die Korinther*, vol. 3 (EKK, 7/3), 1999, 32. On παραδιδόναι, cf. 31: "sozusagen eine auf ein einziges Wort verdichtete Kurzformel für die gesamte Passion Jesu".

11,47-53: John's account of the plotting of the priests corresponds to the brief notice in the synoptic Gospels (Mark 14:1-2 par.). In John, Caiaphas takes the leading role in the proceedings. In Matthew and Mark the high priest Caiaphas (named only in Matthew) plays such a role when Jesus himself is arrested and brought before the council. No such formal trial, with a culminating death sentence, is found at the same point in John. Yet John will here depict the council pronouncing such a sentence on Jesus in absentia, before he is arrested. [228]

If John knew an account of Jesus' appearance before the Sanhedrin, he has suppressed it in order to focus entirely upon the one trial before Pilate, in which the Jews, in condemning Jesus, also condemn themselves. [338]

Smith's comment on 10,22-39 is worth noting:

The Jews' questioning of Jesus about his possible messiahship is reminiscent of the high priest's question to Jesus at the (synoptic) trial before the Sanhedrin (Mark 14:61). When in Mark, Jesus affirms that he is the Messiah, the Son of the Blessed One, the confession leads directly to his condemnation to death because of blasphemy (Mark 14:64). Similarly here, the question and ensuing discussion lead to the Jews' trying to stone Jesus to death because of his blasphemy (10:33). I Not surprisingly, Anton Dauer suspects that the synoptic account of the Jewish trial of Jesus has influenced the formation of John 10. [212][23]

The Sanhedrin trial is not simply omitted in John's Passion Narrative:

Mark 14:55-65 has a counterpart of diminished significance in John (18:19-24), which does not have the same pivotal function in the narrative. At the same time the Johannine version of this episode cannot be explained as derivative of Mark. [338][24]

This last statement receives some mitigation in Smith's own comment on Jn 18,20:

Jesus' response (v. 20) is remarkably similar to what he says at the point of his arrest in the Synoptics (Mark 14:49 par.). [335]

Compare the words of Jesus at the arrest in Mk 14,48-49: καθ' ἡμέραν ἤμην πρὸς ὑμᾶς ἐν τῷ ἱερῷ διδάσκων (v. 49a) and ἐγὼ πάντοτε

---

23. To my surprise, there is no mention at all of Lk 22,67 and its striking parallel in Jn 10,24-25a. Cf. A. DAUER, *Spuren der (synoptischen) Synedriumsverhandlung im 4. Evangelium*, in *John and the Synoptics*, 1992 (n. 1), 307-339, esp. 310 and 316. The parallel is not noted in Aland's *Synopsis* (§§ 257, 332). But see R.E. BROWN, *The Death of the Messiah*, New York, 1994, 460 and 484 (cf. 471, on the separation of Messiah and Son of God in Lk 22,67.70a and Jn 10,24.36). Cf. M. SABBE, *John 10 and Its Relationship to the Synoptic Gospels* (1991), in ID., *Studia Neotestamentaria. Collected Essays* (BETL, 98), Leuven, 1991, 443-464, esp. 443-455 (Jn 10,22-39). On A. Dauer's essay, see 454 n. 24, 465 (additional note).

24. Slightly adapted from Smith's text on both Mk 8,27-30 (Jn 6,66-69) and Mk 14,55-65 (Jn 18,19-24), in the plural.

ἐδίδαξα ἐν συναγωγῇ καὶ ἐν τῷ ἱερῷ, ὅπου πάντες οἱ Ἰουδαῖοι συνέρχονται (Jn 18,20b). "Probably the whole reply was composed by John, perhaps on the basis of Mark 14.49" (Barrett)[25]. Like the Markan trial before the Sanhedrin, the arraignment before Annas ends with the abuse of Jesus: Mk 14,65 καὶ οἱ ὑπηρέται ῥαπίσμασιν αὐτὸν ἔλαβον (v. 65b) and Jn 18,22 ... εἷς παρεστηκὼς τῶν ὑπηρέτων ἔδωκεν ῥάπισμα τῷ Ἰησοῦ (cf. 19,3c καὶ [οἱ στρατιῶται] ἐδίδοσαν αὐτῷ ῥαπίσματα). Both Mk 14,55-65 and Jn 18,19-23 are bracketed within the story of Peter[26]:

| Mk 14,54 | 55-64.65 | 66-72 |
| Jn 18,15-18 | 19-21.22-23[24] | 25-27 |

If one includes the misunderstanding of Jesus' temple saying in Jn 2,19-22, then the major elements found in the Markan trial can be accounted for[27]: |

temple charge	Mk 14,58	Jn 2,19-22
messianic question	61	10,24
Jesus' affirmation	62a	36
charge of blasphemy	64a	33.36
condemnation	64b	11,47-53

Unexplained omissions also play an important role in Smith's interpretation of the narrative of the crucifixion and the death of Jesus (Jn 19,28-30):

> Conceivably John knows an independent tradition that is less elaborate and omits the second mocking. [356] There will be no cry of dereliction, nor will Jesus utter a loud cry as he expires. [361] John ... omits certain features found in Mark. The omission of Jesus' pained outcries is understandable. Yet John also omits mention of the darkness at noun, the rending of the temple veil, and the centurion's confession... Such omissions make it difficult to understand John as having worked from a Markan or synoptic source. Rather, it seems more likely that he employed a source or tradition that did not contain these features. [362]

---

25. See F.J. MATERA, *Jesus before Annas: John 18,13-14.19-24*, in *ETL* 66 (1990) 38-55, here 48; M. SABBE, *The Denial of Peter in the Gospel of John*, in *Louvain Studies* 20 (1995) 219-240 (219-229: "The Interrogation of the High Priest").

26. See F. NEIRYNCK, *The 'Other Disciple' in Jn 18,15-16*, in *ETL* 51 (1975) 113-141 (= *Evangelica I*, 335-364), here 131 (= 353). On Jn 18,18b and 25a (cf. Mk 14,54 and 66a): "It is an inadequate expression – and a somewhat misleading presentation of the evidence – to say that 18,19-24 is inserted in between the first and the second denial. The (Markan) interweaving of the stories is one thing, the transposition of the first denial *within* the Peter story (diff. Mk) is another". Cf. *John and the Synoptics* (1992), 47-49.

27. Cf. MATERA (n. 25), 54.

There is, however, an alternative understanding of John's omissions[28]:

> One main contrast between the Synoptic Gospels and John is that the great dramatic picture of the dying Jesus is transformed into a scene full of majestic calm and symbolic meaning. No darkness over the whole land, no mockery, no dereliction, no opening of tombs, no earthquake nor splitting of rocks, but a prophetic victorious Jesus in full control, completing his mission.

IV

A few remarks on John and **Mark**. In Jn 3,29 John the Baptist speaks of Jesus metaphorically as the bridegroom: "Again there is a relation to the Synoptics (Mark 2:18-20), where Jesus refers to himself as the bridegroom" (105). In his comment on Jn 4,44 (par. Mk 6,4 "recognizably the same saying"), Smith inserts a general statement on Johannine sayings:

> Except in a few cases where they are integral to a narrative, Johannine sayings of Jesus with synoptic parallels are never found in the same context in John, probably an indication of their separate traditional origins. [122]

Compare his comment on the healing story in Jn 5,1-9:

> That John's story is a rewriting of Mark's seems on the face of it unlikely. They evince similarities, but in different narrative contexts. [130]

Yet I may refer the reader to my presentation of "the striking parallelism between the structure of Jn 5,1-18 and Mk 2,1-12; 2,23–3,6"[29]:

> The seeking to kill Jesus is indeed "central in Jn", but in John and Mark the motif appears here for the first time (Jn 5,18; Mk 3,6) and in both gospels it is connected with the violation of the sabbath and in both gospels too it is found at the conclusion of the same pattern: first the healing, then a controversial sabbath case in the action of people who are related to Jesus: the healed man and the disciples, and finally Jesus' healing activity as a violation of the sabbath. No modern interpreter of the gospel of Mark can blame the Fourth Evangelist for having made the connection between Mk 2,1-12 and Mk (2,23-28) 3,1-6. – Three other features in Jn 5,10-18

---

28. M. SABBE, *The Johannine Account of the Death of Jesus and its Synoptic Parallels (Jn 19,16b-42)*, in *ETL* 70 (1994) 34-64, here 60. Compare also, on the next scene in Jn 19,31-37, U. WILCKENS, *Joh* (NTD, 4), Göttingen, 1998, 299: "Zu dieser Szene gibt es in den synoptischen Evangelien keinerlei Parallelen. Daher liegt die Annahme nahe, daß sie vom Joh.evangelisten gebildet worden ist, ohne daß ihm dafür ein Bericht vorgelegen hat".

29. *John 5,1-18 and the Gospel of Mark*, in *Evangelica II*, 699-712, esp. 705-708 (in response to P. Borgen, 1984).

can be explained in the light of Mk 2,1-12: the healing as immediate execution of Jesus' command (5,12, cf. vv. 8.9); healing and forgiveness of sin
(5,14); the accusation of blasphemy (5,18).

Chapter 6 is mentioned by Smith as "one of the three places in the
Gospel where its narrative runs close to the Synoptics" (1,24-34; 6,1-
71; 18–19; one can add chap. 20).

> Definitely parallel with Mark are the stories of the feeding (vv. 1-15) and
> Jesus' walking on the water of the Sea of Galilee (vv. 16-21), as well as
> Peter's confession (vv. 66-71). More remotely parallel are the discourse
> on bread (vv. 25-58) and the mention of signs (v. 26). [144]
> Whether John brought these materials together (following Mark) or
> worked with a traditional complex has been difficult for exegetes to
> decide. [145, cf. 150]

Smith rightly observes that the motif of the barley loaves in Jn 6,9
recalls the scene of 2 Kgs 4,42-44 (147). It is less certain that this parallel ("almost too striking to be coincidental") suggests that the story
belongs to an independent tradition[30].

With regard to chaps. 5 and 6, Smith's opinion seems to be that the
present order is not the original one, because "If the order of these chapters is reversed, the connection is better" (28; cf. 146: "Conceivably";
210: "presumably").

V

In the ANTC commentaries, "the New Revised Standard Version of
the Bible is the principal translation of reference for the series", but
"when necessary (the authors) provide their own original translations of
difficult terms or phrases" (the General Editor's Foreword, 12). Smith's
notes on translation, in particular on NRSV compared with RSV, constitute
a most valuable aspect of his commentary on John.

For illustration see *ETL* 76 (2000) 131-132.

---

30. See my *Jean et les Synoptiques* (n. 12), 186-187.

SUPPLEMENTARY NOTE (2000)

The issue of John and the Synoptics is briefly treated by Joel Marcus in his recent commentary on the Gospel of Mark[1]. He recognizes, "it must be admitted that the number and influence of the advocates of dependence of John on one or more of the Synoptics have been growing in recent years"[2], but in his own view "convincing evidence for Johannine usage of Synoptic redaction" has still not been presented. My 1984 essay on Jn 20,1-18 par. Lk 24,12 and Mt 28,9-10 is cited as an example of "too slight a base to support the thesis of dependence on Lukan and Matthean redaction" (54). Compare the critical Notes reprinted in this Part V of my essays. I prefer to consider here the examples taken from Mark[3].

In the course of the commentary Marcus refers back to his initial statement: "Since John seems to be literarily independent of the Synoptics..." (414); "If, as I have argued, John is literarily independent of Mark..." (436). With such an antecedent, parallel sequences in Jn and Mk (cf. above, 51-53) are unavoidably explained by shared dependence on a pre-Gospel source[4]:

Jn 6,1-15	Mk 6,34-44	cf. 8,1-9	Feeding miracle
6,16-21	6,45-52	cf. 8,10.13	Sea-crossing
6,24-25	6,53		Landing
6,30		8,11-12	Demand for a sign
6,35-59		8,14-21	Discussion about bread
6,60-69		8,29-30	Peter's confession
6,70-71		8,31-33	Passion, betrayal

Contrast, however, U. Wilckens, 95 (quoted above, 603).

The relationship in the passion narrative between Jn 18,18.25 and Mk 14,54.66-67 (above, 48-51) is discussed by J.D. Crossan as an example of Markan intercalation[5]. The six classic cases are Mk 3,20-35; 5,21-43; 6,7-30; 11,12-21; 14,1-11; 14,54-72. Two cases are added by Marcus: 1,4(5-6)7-8 and 2,1-5(6-10a)10b-12, and in all instances Mark is held responsible for creating the sandwich structure: "This framing technique is typically Markan"; "The 'sandwich' like most if not all of the Markan intercalations, is probably Mark's editorial creation" (278, 385). As Marcus includes Mk 14,54-72 in all his lists of intercalations in Mk, he can hardly disagree with Crossan's conclusion[6]:

> John accepts fully the Markan intercalation and even the "warming himself" duplication in John 18:18 and 18:25. In fact, he even intensifies the Markan purpose and effect because he puts the first denial *before* and the last two denials *after* Jesus' confession...
>
> My conclusion is that there is one unit that John took from Mark and in a fairly direct, literary manner. After all, my working hypothesis is that John's passion narrative itself is dependent on Mark.

---

1. J. MARCUS, *Mark 1–8. A New Translation with Introduction and Commentary* (AB, 27), New York, Doubleday, 2000: "Mark and John" (53-54).

2. With reference to D.M. Smith's "excellent survey of the contemporary discussion" (1992).

3. Cf. above, 46-55: "John and Mark".

4. Cf. 256, 414, 436, 486, 492 (with slight variation).

5. J.D. CROSSAN, *Who Killed Jesus?* San Francisco, 1995, 100-105 ("Mark's Literary Fingerprints"); *The Birth of Christianity*, San Francisco, 1998, 106, and 565: "Markan intercalation ... is a quite uniquely Markan phenomenon. But that intercalation is also found in John 18:13-27".

6. *Who Killed*, 102. Cf. above, 613 (n. 36: Schnelle, Lang) and 625 (n. 26).

VI

THE GOSPELS AND JESUS

ETL 70 (1994) 221-234

32

THE HISTORICAL JESUS

REFLECTIONS ON AN INVENTORY

The series of supplementary volumes to Herders New Testament commentary already comprises two Jesus-books, one by J. Gnilka in the style of the historical-Jesus research (1990)[1] and now also a synthetic work by R. Schnackenburg on the christologies of the four evangelists (1993)[2]. In his concluding Perspective (*Ausblick*) Schnackenburg glorifies the tetramorphous gospel as "the four streams flowing from Eden"[3] and emphasizes the contrast with the later noncanonical gospels: "Was in den apokryphen Evangelien im zweiten, dritten und vierten Jahrhundert erzählt wird, kann sich mit den vier kanonischen Evangelien nicht messen. Diese apokryphen Darstellungen sind von Legenden und zum Teil phantastischen Erzählungen überlagert"[4]. Gnilka's methodological introduction also contains such a statement: "später kam es zu Wucherungen und Fehlentwicklungen, die teils der erzählerischen Phantasie, teils der Irrlehre entsprangen und zur Ausbildung der apokryphen Evangelien geführt haben. Das gnostische Thomasevangelium ... ist hierfür ein besonders sprechendes Beispiel"[5].

The problem of the sources of our knowledge about the historical Jesus is treated more explicitly in the first volume of J.P. Meier's Jesus-book (1991)[6]. He has a special chapter 5 on the agrapha, the apocryphal

---

1. Joachim GNILKA, *Jesus von Nazaret. Botschaft und Geschichte* (HTKNT, Supplementband 3), Freiburg-Basel-Wien, Herder, 1990, ²1991, 331 p. For an appraisal, cf. R. SCHNACKENBURG, in *MüTZ* 42 (1991) 395-401; J. SCHLOSSER, in *BZ* 36 (1992) 138-140, p. 139: "Im allgemeinen dürfte G. in Sache Authentie doch ein wenig zu optimistisch sein".

2. Rudolf SCHNACKENBURG, *Die Person Jesu Christi im Spiegel der vier Evangelien* (HTKNT, Supplementband 4), Freiburg-Basel-Wien, Herder, 1993, 357 p. Each gospel receives a separate treatment: Mark (28-89), Matthew (90-151), Luke (152-244), John (245-326), with a comparative last chapter: "Das viergestaltige Evangelium als vielfältiges und doch einheitliches Christuszeugnis" (327-354). On the comparison between John and the Synoptics (269-272), cf. his more extensive essay in *The Four Gospels 1992* (BETL, 100), pp. 1723-1750: *Synoptische und johanneische Christologie. Ein Vergleich*.

3. "Ausblick", 355-357, esp. 356, on Irenaeus' image of the four-column building (cf. 24-25) and his own more dynamic image of the four *Paradiesesströme*.

4. *Ibid.*, p. 355.

5. *Jesus*, pp. 22-34: "Methodisches", esp. p. 25.

6. John P. MEIER, *A Marginal Jew. Rethinking the Historical Jesus. Volume One: The Roots of the Problem and the Person* (The Anchor Bible Reference Library), New York,

gospels, and the Nag Hammadi material[7], and his conclusion is quite clear: "The four canonical Gospels turn out to be the only documents containing significant blocks of material relevant to a quest for the historical Jesus. ... I do not think that ... the *agrapha*, the apocryphal gospels, and the Nag Hammadi codices (in particular | the *Gospel of Thomas*) offer us reliable new information or authentic sayings that are independent of the NT"[8].

"Contrary to some scholars" (Meier): one of these scholars is the author of *Four Other Gospels* (1985) and *The Cross That Spoke* (1988)[9]. J.D. Crossan's book *The Historical Jesus*[10] became available by the end of 1991[11], and it is this work, more particularly its Part III[12], that I will consider here.

1. *Overture: The Gospel of Jesus*

"If we ask which of all the words placed on his lips actually go back to the historical Jesus, it is possible to offer at least a reconstructed inventory" (xiii). There follows a list of 104 sayings of Jesus (in English translation, as all citations in this book). They are cited without

Doubleday, 1991, x-484 p. The first volume is mainly devoted to prolegomena, including the cultural background of Jesus. Volume Two is occupied with the public ministry proper: *Mentor, Message, and Miracles*, 1994.

7. *Ibid.*, pp. 112-141; notes, pp. 142-166.

8. *Ibid.*, pp. 139-140.

9. John Dominic CROSSAN, *Four Other Gospels. Shadows on the Contours of Canon*, Minneapolis, MN, Winston Press, 1985, 208 p. (four parts: The Gospel of Thomas, Egerton Papyrus 2, The Secret Gospel of Mark, The Gospel of Peter); *The Cross That Spoke. The Origins of the Passion Narrative*, San Francisco, CA, Harper & Row, 1988, xv-437 p. (pp. 409-413, Appendix: Strata in the *Gospel of Peter*).

For an assessment, see my essay *The Apocryphal Gospels and the Gospel of Mark*, in J.-M. SEVRIN (ed.), *The New Testament in Early Christianity* (BETL, 86), Leuven, 1989, pp. 123-175; reprinted in *Evangelica II* (BETL, 99), 1991, pp. 715-767, with Additional Notes, pp. 768-772.

10. *The Historical Jesus. The Life of a Mediterranean Jewish Peasant*, San Francisco, CA, HarperCollins, 1991, xxxiv-505 p.

11. Crossan's and Meier's books are parallel and independent works, both published in 1991. Crossan refers to Meier (*CBQ* 52, 1990, 76-103; now Chapter 3: *Josephus*, pp. 56-88) and adopts his views on the *Testimonium Flavianum* (372-374). Contrary to Meier, Crossan has chosen not to discuss divergent opinions: "In quoting *secondary* literature I spend no time citing other scholars to show how wrong they are" (xxxiv).

12. The first half of the book is a social-historical study of the Mediterranean society (cf. the subtitle): Part I, "Brokered Empire" (1-88); Part II, "Embattled Brokerage" (89-224). Part III, directly on Jesus, is entitled "Brokerless Kingdom" (225-416; with Epilogue, 417-426). It contains five chapters: 11. John and Jesus (227-264); 12. Kingdom and Wisdom (265-302); 13. Magic and Meal (303-353); 14. Death and Burial (354-394); 15. Resurrection and Authority (395-416).

references, not numbered, and without justification of the order in which they are given. The unwarned reader may think these are secret sayings, or at least this is a hidden list of sayings: "as you read them, recall that ... these words are not a list to be read" (xiii). And: "Once again, those words are not a list to be read" (xxvi). The 104 sayings may remind him of the 114 secret sayings in the Gospel of Thomas. And J.S. Kloppenborg can be delighted: the sayings gospel genre is still alive. More industrious readers will find out that the key to this preliminary inventory is provided in Appendix I: "An Inventory of the Jesus Tradition by Chronological Stratification and Independent Attestation" (427-450). Textual complexes are listed there in the order of stratification and independent attestation (522 items), and sayings that Crossan judges to be from the historical Jesus are marked with a plus (+) sign. | Those are the items listed in the Overture (xiii-xxvi)[13]: **I.** 1, 4, 8-10, 15, 19-24, 27, 31, 32, 34-36, 38, 40, 43, 44, 46, 48-51, 53, 55, 57, 59, 63, 71, 72, 74-76, 78-82, 84-90, 94-98, [99], 101-108, 113, 114, 121, 124, 126 | 140, 145-147, 149, 150, 159, 160, 168, 172, 178. **II.** 191, 199 | 290, 295, 297, 303, 311, 320, 321. **III.** 371, 372, 379 | 418, 419, 427, 428, 447, 449, 454, 461, 462, 464-466, 471, 473, 474.

In a first analysis of this list we should observe that Crossan holds the classic two-source theory: Q and Mark are used by Matthew and Luke; there is no direct Matthew-Luke dependence. Also Q and Mark are mutually independent and sayings that appear in both are counted as double attestations. Crossan separates two layers in Q. The Gospel of Jesus includes the following Q-texts[14]: **6**,20b^1.21a^1.b^1.22-23^{1+2}.27-28^1.29^1.30^1. 34^1.35a^1.b^1.39^1.41-42^1; **7**,24-27^2.28^2; **9**,58^1.59-60^1.61-62^1(?); **10**,2^1.3^1.**4a. 5a.8b.9^1.16^1**; **11**,4a^1.**9-10^1**.11-13^1.14-**15.17-18^2**.19-20^2.**23^2**.27-28^1(?).**33^2**. 39-40^2.**43^2**.52^2; **12**,2^1.3^1.6-7^1.**10^2**.13-15^1(?).16-21^1(?).22-31^1.[33^1].34^1. 49^1(?).51-53^2.54-56^2; **13**,18-19^{1or2}.20-21^{1or2}.**30^2**; **14**,15-24^2.25-26^1.**27^1**. **34-35a^1**; **15**,3-7^1; **16**,13^{1or2}.16^{1or2}.**18^{1or2}**; **17**,4^{1or2}.20-21^1(?).**23^2.33^1**; **19**,12-24^2.**26^2**.27^2. Out of these 56 items only twelve are not supported by

13. Roman numbers indicate Stratum I (30-60 A.D.), II (60-80), III (80-120). The vertical line | separates plural attestation and single attestation. Two items are incorrectly placed: 57 between 63 and 71; 150 between 121 and 124 (xvi, xix). Nos. 461 and 462 are combined in one item, Lk 14,28-30.31-32 (xxiv). No. 99+ (p. 440) is not in the list (by mistake?).

14. The list includes six passages of Lukan Sondergut (with question mark in Appendix 1). The layers 1Q and 2Q are marked in superscript. References in bold have a parallel in Mark (plural attestation). On Q 12,33, added here within brackets, see n. 13 (no. 99). – Note that the sayings of John the Baptist (nos. 115+ and 137+: 3,7-9a^2.16-18^2) are not included in this inventory of Jesus' sayings.

extracanonical attestation[15] and in 36 cases the Gospel of Thomas is cited as independent attestation of the saying. Some fifty Q-sayings have received the minus (–) sign (that is, less likely to come from the historical Jesus), nineteen with plural attestation[16]: 6,31^1.(32-35)^1.37a^1.38bc^1.40^1.43-45^1.46^1; 7,1-10^2; 10,21^1.22^2.23-24^2; 11,2-4a^1.29-30^2.34-36^2; 12,8-9^2.11-12^1.39-40^2; 13,28a^2; 17,34-35^2; and thirty with single attestation: 3,9b^2; 4,2b-13^3; 6,36^1.47-49^1; 7,18-23^2.31-35^2; 10,12-15^2; 11,24-26^2.31-32^2.42^2.44^2.45-46^2.47-48^2.49-51^1; 12,42-46^2.57-59^2; 13,23-24^1.25^2.26-27^2.28-29^2.34-35^2; 16,17^{1or2}; 17,1^{1or2}.3^{1or2}.5-6^{1or2}.24^2.26-27^2.28-30^2.37^2; 22,28-30^2.

Crossan's "basic database" (434) is the list of complexes with plural attestation in the first stratum. As indicated above, independent attestation in the Gospel of Thomas is cited for 36 Q-sayings. This is also the case (with one exception)[17] for 22 other instances of sayings assigned to the first stratum: Mk 2,18-20.21-22; 3,27.31-35; 4,3-8.9.26-29; 6,3; 7,15; 10,13-16; 12,1-9.12.13-17; 14,58/15,29; Mt 5,14a.14b; 10,16b; 13,24-30.44.45-46.47-48; Lk 5,39. And in more than one instance Jesus' voice in the reconstructed Inventory is the voice of Thomas (cf. below). Moreover, seven sayings singly attested in I Thomas are accepted in this Gospel of Jesus (Th 25, 42, 47^1, 58, 77, 97, 98)[18]. None of them is mentioned in the Complex Index of the discussed passages (506-507):

> Love your neighbour like your soul; guard your neighbour like the pupil of your eye. [290]
> Become passersby. [295]
> It is impossible to mount two horses or to stretch two bows. [297]
> Blessed is the one who has suffered. [303]
> Split a piece of wood, and I am there. Lift up the stone, and you will find me there. [311]

---

15. Single attestation in Q: 6,29; 9,59-60.61-62; 10,3; 11,11-13.14-15.17-18^{mk}.19-20.43^{mk}; 12,6-7.34; 14,34-35a^{mk}; 17,4.12-24.27. Q 17,33^{mk} can be added (but see p. 438: no. 63 independently attested in Jn 12,25-26). No. 379+, Mt 23,12 and Lk 14,11; 18,14 is not assigned to Q (p. 447).

16. Independent attestation in Mark: 11,29-30; 12,11-12; in John: 7,1-10; only six items with parallel in the Gospel of Thomas: 6,31.43-45; 10,22.23-24; 12,39-40; 17,34-35. Note: 6,32-35 = "Better than sinners".

17. No. 113, Eating with sinners (Mk 2,13-17a): cf. P. Oxy. 1224 (p. 440).

18. In the second stratum: nos. 290, 295, 297, 303, 311, 320, 321. (Since Th 110 and 111 are not accepted in the reconstruction I suppose that nos. 324 and 325 should take a minus sign on p. 446.) Singly attested sayings in Matthew and Luke are assigned to the third stratum: Mt 18,23-34; 19,10-12a; 20,1-15; 21,28-32; Lk 10,29-37; 11,5-8; 13,6-9; 14,28-30.31-32; 15,8-10.11-32; 16,1-7.19-31; 18,1-8.9-14. Instances of double attestation are Mt 5,23-24 (*Did.* 14,2) and Mt 5,33-37 (James 5,12); on Mt 23,12, see n. 15. Mk 10,23-27 (Herm. *Sim.* 9.20) is assigned to the second stratum. Less convincing is the triple independent (!) attestation in no. 191: (1) Mk 9,33-35; 10,41-45: (2) Lk 22,24-27; (3) Jn 13,1-17.

The Kingdom is like a certain woman who was carrying a jar full of meal. While she was walking on the road, still some distance from home, the handle of the jar broke, and the meal emptied out behind her on the road. She did not realize it; she had noticed no accident. When she reached her house, she set the jar down and found it empty. [320]

The Kingdom is like a certain man who wanted to kill a powerful man. In his own house he drew his sword and stuck it into the wall in order to find out whether his hand could carry through. Then he slew the powerful man. [321]

2. The Canonical Gospels and Their Sources

In their latest publication (1993)[19] the members of the Jesus Seminar, or at least the editors, seem to adhere to a scholarly consensus on the chronology of the four Gospels: Mark around 70, Matthew before 90, Luke around 90, and John towards the close of the first century[20]. In Crossan's more personal view the date of Mark is by the end of the seventies, Matthew around 90, Luke in the nineties, and John very early in the second century[21].

The relatively late date of Mark is connected with Crossan's theory regarding *Secret Mark*: the Gospel of Mark that was composed in the early seventies contained the SG fragments (Dead Man Raised, after 10,32-34; Raised Man's Family, after 10,35-46a) and our Mark is a later expurgated version of that first gospel[22]. Crossan maintains his theory that canonical Mark dismembered the SG story and that 14,51-52 and 16,1-8 are Mark's redactional creation. He now adds a new element: "My proposal is that the original version of Mark's Gospel ended with the centurion's confession in 15:39. What comes afterward, from 15:40 through 16:8, was not in *Secret Mark* but stems from canonical Mark"[23]. I As indicated elsewhere, I agree with Crossan as to the text of (our) Mark used by Matthew and Luke[24], but I still hold the view that "when we accept a secondary formation on the basis of the canonical gospels,

---

19. R.W. FUNK - R.W. HOOVER (eds.), *The Five Gospels*, New York, 1993. Crossan is co-chair of the Jesus Seminar (p. 533). See my review in *ETL* 70 (1994) 160-162.

20. *Ibid.*, pp. 545-546 (and 18).

21. *The Historical Jesus*, pp. 430-431.

22. *Ibid.*, pp. 328-332, 411-416. Cf. Inventory, nos. 130, 255 (see also no. 92, Mk 4,10-12).

23. *Ibid.*, pp. 415-416 (on Mk 15,40.47; 16,1 and the three women in SG). For Mk 15,39 as the conclusion of the pre-Markan passion narrative, see, e.g., F.C. GRANT, *The Earliest Gospel*, New York, 1943, p. 179.

24. *The Minor Agreements and Proto-Mark. A Response to H. Koester*, in *ETL* 67 (1991) 82-94 (= *Evangelica II*, 59-73).

the Secret Gospel of Mark becomes a less exceptional literary product, not very much different from ... other noncanonical gospels fragments of the mid-II century"[25]; and: we can get rid of "proleptic Carpocratians" (430).

The edition of the Gospel of John (Jn I) was followed in the fourth stratum (120-150) by a second edition (Jn II: ch. 21; 1,1-18; 6,51b-58; 15–17; the Beloved Disciple passages). John is dependent on the Synoptics for the passion and resurrection account (and probably for the Baptist traditions)[26]; the pre-Johannine signs source is presented as undisputed. More important for the study of the historical Jesus is the existence of an earlier Collection of Miracles, a common source that lies behind Mark and John (310-313):

Sickness and Sin	Mk	2,1-12	Jn	5,1-18
Bread and Fish		6,33-44		6,1-15
Walking on Water		6,45-52		6,16-21
Blind Man Healed		8,22-26		9,1-7
Dead Man Raised	SG	1v20-2r11a		11,1-57

However, Crossan's argument is extremely weak: "That common sequence could, of course, be sheer coincidence, but, at least hypothetically, I hold on to it as the only evidence we have for early collections of miracles ..." (312). It is rather amusing that he sees redaction of the final author in 2,11 and 4,54 (editorial backwards linking like 21,14) and in so doing excludes from the collection the two Cana miracles which are the classic starting point of all Signs Source hypotheses[27]. The counterpart in Mark of the five (that is, 7 – 2) can be reduced to Mk 6,33-44.45-52. The addition of Mk 2,1-12 and 8,22-26 to form a traditional sequence has no justification whatsoever and the SG miracle can only function within Crossan's own theory of Secret Mark[28].

---

25. *Evangelica II*, pp. 760-762, esp. 762. See also pp. 68-73 (cf. n. 24). Compare now also R.E. BROWN, *The Death of the Messiah* (cf. below, n. 34), pp. 295-297: "an expansion of Mark in imitative Marcan style" (p. 296), using "material picked up from hearing or reading at times past other canonical Gospels, especially John"; was composed "most likely ca. 125 when Carpocrates was active (Hadrian's time)" (p. 297). Cf. below, n. 47.

26. The Inventory indicates the following passages as possibly dependent on the Synoptics Jn 1,19-23.24-31.31-34 [= nos. 51, 115, 58; cf. p. 234]; 2,12 [215, 218]; 4,1-3 [214]; 6,67-69 [73]; 12,1-8 [192]; 12,9-19 [257]; 12,27 [205]; 13,27a [267]; 13,36-38 [25]; chs. 18–19 [5, 70, 131, 269-274]; 20,1.11-18 [275]; dependent on Lk 24: 20,2-10 [6]; 20,18-22 [18, 479].

27. Cf. *Evangelica II*, pp. 651-678: *The Signs Source in the Fourth Gospel. A Critique of the Hypothesis*. Cf. G. VAN BELLE, *The Signs Source in the Fourth Gospel* (BETL, 116), Leuven, 1994.

28. Cf. p. 332: "It seems most probable that John [ch. 11] is an intensely redacted version of the same story found in *Secret Mark*, although no direct relationship need be postulated. I presume that *Dead Man Raised* was simply the last in the collection of miracles used alike and independently by Mark and John".

In Crossan's judgment there is one common source used in the passion and resurrection accounts of all four canonical Gospels: the Cross Gospel, embedded in the Gospel of Peter: "Composed by the fifties C.E., and possibly at Sepphoris in Galilee, it is the single source of the intracanonical passion accounts" (429).

3. *The Gospel of Peter*

I Crossan's presentation of the Gospel of Peter in English translation (1988: 409-413) is reprinted in his new volume as Appendix 7: "Strata in the *Gospel of Peter*" (462-466)[29]. He proposes the following summary table:

Original Stratum	Redactional Stratum	Intracanonical Stratum
Crucifixion and Deposition	Request for Burial	→ Joseph and Burial
1-2.5b-22	3-5a	23-24
Tomb and Guards	Arrival of Youth	→ Women and Youth
25.28-34	43-44	50-57
Resurrection and Confession	Action of Disciples	→ Disciples and Apparition
35-42.45-49	26-27.58-59	60 ...

The original stratum, or Cross Gospel, is the original passion narrative (cf. 385-387: "Innocence Rescued"), used by the four canonical evangelists[30]. The other parts of the GP text (middle second century) are later "intracanonical" insertions (dependent on the canonical Gospels)[31] and redactional connections; in the order of GP: ...1-2.**3-5a**[R].5b-22.**23-24**.25.**26-27**[R].28-34.35-42.**43-44**[R].45-49.**50-57.58-59**[R].**60**...

Already in the first presentation of his composition theory, Crossan contended that the unit *Women and Youth* (GP 50-57, with its redactional preparation in 43-44) "is dependent on the intracanonical gospels, that is, essentially on Mark" (1985: 157-160). And again in 1988 he argued that GP 50-57 is a redactional composition on the basis of the structural sequence of Mk 16,1-8 combined with some elements of Johannine influence (1988: 281-290). The case is now simply mentioned in the Inventory: "275-. The Empty Tomb: (1a) Mark 16:1-8 = Matt. 28:1-10 = Luke 24:1-11, (1b) John 20:1,11-18, (1c) *Gos. Pet.* 11:44; 12:50–13:57"[32]. My own essay, *The Apocryphal Gospels and*

---

29. On the translation, see below, n. 34.

30. In the Inventory: nos. 5, 17, 29, 65, 70 (2a), 180-186.

31. Inventory, nos. 70 (2d): GP 3-5a.23-24; 275 (1c): GP 44.50-57 (single, no. 387: GP 56b).

32. Parenthetically I may suggest that our North American colleagues decide to abandon the double reference system and simply use the Harnack division. Cf. *Evangelica II*, p. 733 n. 103.

the Gospel of Mark, contains a section on GP 50-57 and Mk 16: "GP 50-57 is undoubtedly the most 'Markan' section in the Gospel of Peter"; and "Crossan rightly emphasizes the Johannine background of the material added to Mk 16"[33]. R.E. Brown, in his recent commentary on the passion narratives (1994)[34], I considers this question again and declares to disagree: "In my judgment, the tomb-story similarities leave too slim a basis for positing *GPet* dependence on Mark"[35]. By the way Brown's reference to Crossan is rather confusing: "Only in the story of the women at the tomb ... does *GPet* come close to vocabulary peculiarities in Mark", and having cited a few similarities he concludes that they are "insufficient to show that *GPet* was a primary written source for the Marcan evangelist (Crossan's thesis) or, in the other direction, that the author of *GPet* had Mark before him as he wrote"[36]. It is clear that regarding GP 50-57 and Mk 16 Crossan's thesis goes "in the other direction"!

Brown has solid reasons for placing the Gospel of Peter in the second century (rather than in the first), and the first of these reasons is "the likelihood ... that the author used echoes from the canonical Gospels of Matt, Luke, and John"[37]. As for GP 50-57 he admits that the author "was influenced by canonical Gospel material; there are echoes of Luke and of John, and of passages where Mark and Matt agree ... But is there evidence that the author of *GPet* used Mark?"[38] Brown sees three major difficulties. (1) "Even Neirynck has to state that this is the most 'Markan' section in *GPet*". There can be no disagreement about this

33. *Evangelica II*, pp. 735-744 (1989, 143-152), esp. 736, 737.

34. R.E. BROWN, *The Death of the Messiah. From Gethsemane to the Grave. A Commentary on the Passion Narratives in the Four Gospels* (The Anchor Bible Reference Library), New York, Doubleday, 1994, pp. 1317-1349: "Appendix I: *The Gospel of Peter* – a Noncanonical Passion Narrative".

The author offers a new "Literal Translation of *GPet*" (1318-1321). For the Greek text I may refer the reader to my presentation of the text in sense-lines in *Evangelica II*, pp. 763-767 (1989, 171-175). The English translation used by Crossan (and also by R. Cameron, R.W. Funk, *et al.*) is that of *NT Apocrypha*. Another new translation, prepared by A.J. Dewey, is included in the Scholars Version (1992). As an illustration of these translations I take the textual corruption at GP 2 (παρ[αλη]μφθῆναι, cf. *Evangelica II*, p. 732 n. 102): And then Herod the king commanded that the Lord should be marched off (Crossan); ... orders the Lord to be [taken away] (SV); ... orders the Lord to be taken [sent?] away (Brown; but see p. 856: "to be marched off"). Another example, the subject οἱ πρεσβύτεροι in GP 29: The elders were afraid (Crossan; but *NTA*: – were afraid); they became frightened (SV); feared (especially the elders) (Brown).

35. *The Death*, p. 1328 (conclusion of his treatment of GP and Mark, pp. 1327-1328).

36. *Ibid.*, p. 1327.

37. *Ibid.*, p. 1342. Mark is deliberately omitted (cf. p. 1335: "I see no compelling reason ...").

38. *Ibid.*, p. 1328 n. 16.

statement[39], though for Brown this should "alert readers to how little distinctively Marcan is found in the rest of *GPet*"; and he quotes P. Gardner-Smith (1926): "if the author of *GPet* had read Mark, he had certainly forgotten the details"[40]. But if these details are present in GP 50-57, the interpreter's logic can go in two directions: either one can isolate this section in GP as a later stage of composition (Crossan) or one can argue, as I would prefer to do, that what happened in GP 50-57 with Mk 16 is not without analogy with GP's redaction elsewhere on the basis of other traditional texts, especially Matthew[41]. It is less understandable how Brown can argue against dependence on Mark in GP 50-57 because little distinctively Markan is found in other parts of GP, since he admits a consecutive pre-GP account of the guard at the tomb in GP 28-49 and a separate pre-GP women-at-the-tomb story in GP 50-57[42]. And how can he accept echoes of Matthew in GP 28-49 and radically exclude echoes of Mark in GP 50-57? (2) The differences between GP and Mark "should not be overlooked in studying the comparison Neirynck makes between the two: He has had to make changes in the Marcan verse sequence to draw attention to the parallels". First, the changes in sequence I "had to make" are clearly indicated in my synoptic presentation and the reader can judge there how minimal they are[43]. Second, I since Brown "has postulated that the Matthean and Lucan evangelists did work directly on Mark's passion narrative"[44], and I do not see why things should be different in parallel to Mk 16,1-2, the inversion of Mk 16,2a and 1b at GP 50 (ὄρθρου δὲ ... Μαριὰμ ...: cf. Mt 28,1 and Lk 24,1) is scarcely a significant change in internal sequence. And the same is true for changes in order in GP 51 (ὅπου ἦν τεθείς), 53 (εἰσελθοῦσαι), 56 (ἴδετε ... ὅτι οὐκ ἔστιν). In GP 54 μέγας γὰρ ἦν ὁ λίθος (where "the word order is different"), "not a misunderstanding but a correct understanding of Mk 16,4 may be at the

---

39. See the text quoted above at n. 36. Cf. R.E. BROWN, *The* Gospel of Peter *and Canonical Gospel Priority*, in *NTS* 33 (1987) 321-343, p. 332: "close to Mark" (n. 48: "in this section ... closest to Mark").

40. In 1987 he mentioned Gardner-Smith's solution: "the author knew an earlier form of the women's visit story than that found in Mark" (p. 342 n. 48). On the influence of Gardner-Smith, cf. J. VERHEYDEN, *P. Gardner-Smith and "The Turn of the Tide"*, in A. DENAUX (ed.), *John and the Synoptics* (BETL, 101), 1992, pp. 423-452, esp. 434.

41. Cf. *Evangelica II*, p. 745 (= 153): "B.A. Johnson's description of the redaction in GP 28-49 (the guard at the tomb) shows much similarity with the redaction in GP 50-57 (the women at the tomb)".

42. *The Death*, p. 1306 (and n. 47). See also p. 1301 n. 35.

43. *Evangelica II*, pp. 736-737 (= 144-145).

44. *The Death*, p. 83 n. 107. Cf. pp. 40-66, on "Interdependence among the Synoptic Gospels".

origin of the change of order and even of the introduction of the clause into the words of the women"[45]. In GP 57 φοβηθεῖσαι ἔφυγον ("again in different order") may be a correct rendering of Mark's use of γάρ. (3) The third difficulty is the vocabulary statistic: out of 200 words in GP 50-57 and 140 in Mk 16, there are only 30 shared words, and the author of GP could have got two-thirds of these 30 words from either Matthew or Luke. But is it not so that, in comparing texts and their derivatives, the configuration of the words is more important than their total number? It can hardly be denied, for instance, that there is a significant resemblance between GP 53-54 and the women's question in Mk 16,3 (τίς ἀποκυλίσει ἡμῖν ...)[46]. Brown insistingly observes that for words that GP shares only with Mark "we must keep in mind the possibility of noncanonical origin". The example he cites is νεανίσκος: "SGM also portrays a *neaniskos* in the tomb, and so the image of the young man did circulate in apocryphal tradition". If, however, one judges the *Secret Mark* account to be "an amalgam of Synoptic details" and "secondary borrowing, above all, from Mark" which reminds us of the empty tomb story[47], I really do not see how the echoes of Mark can be refused in GP 50-57 which is so much closer to the tomb-story in Mk 16[48].

I In the course of Brown's commentary it is repeatedly said that GP "draws on the canonical Gospels", that the author "was familiar with he

45. *Evangelica II*, pp. 743-744 (= 151-152).
46. See *The Death*, p. 1327. Cf. 1987, p. 333: one of the few instances that are "sufficiently long and close to offer significant vocabulary identity".
47. R.E. BROWN, *The Relation of "the Secret Gospel of Mark" to the Fourth Gospel*, in *CBQ* 36 (1974) 466-485, pp. 484, 469, 476 n. 23. Cf. *The Death*, p. 296: "I still hold the views expressed in my 1974 article" (cf. above, n. 25).
48. Brown adds in a footnote: "Neirynck would increase the basis for dependence by sheer hypothesis" (p. 1328 n. 17). He refers to my consideration of GP 56: "The return to Galilee (Mk 16,7) is replaced by the return 'thither whence he was sent' and this, too, has a Johannine background (Jn 20,17)" (*Evangelica II*, 738 = 146). Sheer hypothesis? Or is it a too condensed argument? The Johannine background is Jn 20,17, par. Mt 28,10 (Mt 28,7 / Mk 16,7). Cf. *Evangelica II*, pp. 584-586 (= 1984, 169-171). See also G. SCHNEIDER, in *The Four Gospels 1992*, pp. 1780-1781: "Während nach Matthäus die Jünger *nach Galiläa* gehen sollen, um dort den Auferstandenen zu sehen (Mt 28,10; vgl. 28,7!) entfällt dieser Auftrag bei Johannes ... Johannes (mußte) die Botschaft an die Jünger umprägen. ... Vielleicht darf man darauf hinweisen, daß das Logion 20,17c wenigstens implizit die gedankliche Struktur von Mt 28,7 bzw. 28,10 aufweist: *Jesus geht* als der Auferstandene *den Seinen voraus* (προάγει)". GP 56 can be understood in the light of this intertextual reading:
GP   ζητεῖτε ... τὸν σταυρωθέντα ... ἀνέστη καὶ ἀπῆλθεν
Mk 16,6 ζητεῖτε ... τὸν ἐσταυρωμένον· ἠγέρθη, οὐκ ἔστιν ὧδε
GP   ἀνέστη καὶ ἀπῆλθεν ἐκεῖ ὅθεν ἀπεστάλη
Mk 16,7 (Mt ἠγέρθη) προάγει ὑμᾶς εἰς τ. Γ.· ἐκεῖ αὐτὸν ὄψεσθε.
Such a connection is far from unique in GP. Brown can draw attention to the combination of Mt 27,24 and Jn 19,7 in GP 46 (p. 848 n. 49).

canonical Gospels". His expressions are more reserved in the Appendix: the author of GP "was familiar with Matthew because he had read it carefully in the past and/or had heard it read several times in community worship ... Most likely he had heard people speak who were familiar with the Gospels of Luke and John"[49]. Only the Gospel of Mark is completely left out of the picture, without good reason.

Brown's refutation of Crossan's theory exempts me here from further examining the Cross Gospel hypothesis[50]. GP is a second-century folk-gospel, without reliable knowledge of first-century Palestine, overtly antiJewish, with "echoes" of canonical Gospels developed and combined with popular traditions[51]. Brown emphasizes orality and distant memory; he is allergic to literary dependence "with the ms. before him"[52]. He comes close to Crossan's *Cross Gospel* in his approach to the guard-at-the-sepulcher story (GP 28-49): the author knew an independent form of this long story, and a less developed pre-Matthean form of the same story is preserved in the Gospel of Matthew. But this holds together with his more general approach to the special material in Matthew's Gospel[53].

4. *Papyrus Egerton 2*

The name has changed from Papyrus Egerton 2 (1985)[54] to Egerton Gospel, and there is a remarkable contrast between the ascending line of the date of the manuscript: 130-165 in 1985, now "dated from the early second to the early third century", and the descending line of the original

49. *The Death*, pp. 1334-1335. Compare, e.g., pp. 781, 1001.

50. Just one remark: in Crossan's proposal of the fivefold structure of the *innocence rescued* genre (p. 386; cf. 1988, 297-334) it is rather inconvenient that he must place the first two themes in the lost materials: (1. Situation; 2. Accusation); 3. Condemnation; 4. Deliverance; 5. Restoration.

51. Brown has stated that it was not his purpose to write a commentary on GP in *The Death*. Yet, a 33-page Appendix, some subsections on segments of GP (esp. pp. 1056-56, 1089-91, 1232-34, and 1305-09), and numerous references throughout make as a whole some sort of commentary. The translation of GP is cited together with the canonical texts (at the beginning of each §): pp. 863 (GP 7-9); 983 (13); 1032 (15-19); 1097 (20-22); 1142 (14.21.25-29); 1205 (3-5); 1243 (24-32); 1285 (28-34.35-49).

52. Cf. pp. 1333-1334. He stresses the multiplicity of omissions, additions, changes ('switching' of details). Not all evidence he cites for his thesis is convincing. Thus, e.g., the omission of Simon of Cyrene (*ibid.*): "The absence of the attractive figure of Simon from *GPet* may reflect the antiJewish thrust of that apocryphon" (p. 929).

53. For an alternative interpretation of *Matthew's Special Material*, cf. D.P. SENIOR, in *ETL* 63 (1987) 272-294.

54. *Four* (n. 9), pp. 63-75 and 77-87 ("The Question about Tribute"). Cf. *The Historical Jesus*, pp. 428 and 321-323 ("A Leper Cured").

composition: from 80/90-120 to "as early as the fifties C.E." (428). It remains unchanged that P. Eg 2 is "independent of all the intracanonical Gospels" (*ibid.*), but Crossan is now willing to withdraw his earlier proposal that Mark may be dependent on P. Eg 2 (321). In his Inventory nos. 55 and 110 Egerton 2 and Mark are cited as independent attestation[55].

| There is no discussion of no. 55+, *Caesar and God*: (1) Th 100; (2) Eg 50-57a (3) Mk 12,13-17 parr., but the reconstructed text in "The Gospel of Jesus" is that of Th 100:

> They showed Jesus a gold coin and said to him, "Caesar's men demand taxes from us."
> He said to them, "Give Caesar what belongs to Caesar, give God what belongs to God".

Crossan noted in 1985 that *Thomas* simply added a final phrase ("and give me what is mine"), and also: "One watches the dialogue steadily shorten from Eger P 2, to Mark, to Luke, to *Thomas*, and see a dialogue slowly tending to become an aphorism"[56]. The fact that Crossan now quotes the wording of Th 100 seems to suggest a reverse development. Anyway the text in Egerton lines 50-57a corresponds to Mk 12,13-14, but the parallel ends there[57] and Egerton is not an independent attestation of Jesus' saying itself (Mk 12,17).

More attention is given to no. 110+, *A Leper Cured*[58]. Egerton 35-47 and Mk 1,40-44 are proposed as independent attestations of a common

---

55. Inventory, nos. 42 (Eg 1), 55 (Eg 3a), 56 (Eg 3c), 109 (Eg 2a), 110 (Eg 2b), 111 (Eg 3b), 132 (Eg 4). To avoid confusion, Crossan should have said that this numbering 1, 2, 3, and 4 is not the same as that of "the fragments 1, 2, 3" in the order of Bell and Skeat (428). The following little survey of the numbering of fragments and lines can be useful:

Bell and Skeat	1v	1r	2r	2v	3v	3r
	1-21	22-41	42-59	60-75	76-81	82-87
Daniels	1-24	25-48	49-66	67-82	83-87	89-94
[Crossan]	[1]	[2a, b]	[3a, b, c]	[4]		
Gronewald	1v	1r	3r	3v	2v	2r
(order: 3r v, 2v r)	1-24	25-48	77-94	61-76	55-60	49-54

Crossan adopts the standard order of fragments 2 and 3 (why is it "more neutral"?). A discussion of the order 1v, 1r would be more promising. Cf. *Evangelica II*, p. 756 (= 164), n. 220: the order 1r, 1v reconsidered in the light of P. Köln 255 (1r last line). See now also D. LÜHRMANN, *Das neue Fragment des PEgerton 2 (PKöln 255)*, in *The Four Gospels 1992*, pp. 2239-2255, esp. 2249.

56. *Four*, pp. 77 and 86.

57. Cf. *Evangelica II*, pp. 756-759 (= 164-167): "Crossan rightly emphasizes that P. Eg 2 and Mk 12,13-17 are not unrelated but the direction of the influence is, I think, from Mark to P. Eg 2" (p. 759).

58. *The Historical Jesus*, pp. 321-323. Crossan refers to my study in *ETL* 61 (1985) 153-160 ("some acquaintance with the three Synoptic Gospels") and in *BETL* 86 (1989) 163-164 (on P. Köln 255), without mention of the reprints in *Evangelica II*, 773-780, 755-

source. The original healing story showed Jesus' power and authority: Jesus can both cure and declare cured. This is rectified in the common source, where the injunction is added: "go, show yourself to the priest ..." and the story is adapted to make Jesus an obedient observer of levitical purity regulations. Markan redaction intensifies the thrust of the original story. Jesus is not a law-observant Jew: "as a witness to (against) them" means confrontation to the priests. Egerton develops the story in a different direction: the leper's autobiographical account is added and "Jesus' final admonition, 'sin no more,' indicates that Jesus does not agree with such 'sinning'" (322).

That Jesus actually "touched" the leper could be a Markan addition. It could also have been part of the original story: "The *Egerton Gospel* would then have omitted it while Mark retained it" (323). The acceptance of redactional additions (lines 35b-39a and 47) and omissions ("touched him") may indicate that Crossan is on a move to a new evaluation of the story in Egerton. The evidence I of independence is becoming doubtful[59]. In a more recent presentation of the healing of the leper in Mk 1,40-44 references to Egerton are characteristically absent. In the original story, by touching the leper, Jesus refuses to accept official sanctions against the diseased person[60].

5. First-Century Noncanonical Gospels?

The Gospel of Thomas (first layer, by the fifties), the Egerton Gospel (as early as the fifties), the Cross Gospel (by the fifties), and the Secret Gospel of Mark (in the early seventies) are not the only extracanonical "gospels" in Crossan's stratification of first-century writings (427-430: nos. 5, 6, 13, 15). Both the Gospel of the Hebrews (by the fifties) and the Gospel of the Egyptians (possibly by the sixties) are independent of the intracanonical Gospels (nos. 9 and 14). Other independent sources are: P. Vindob. G. 2325 (the Fayum Fragment), P. Oxy. 1224, P. Oxy. 840,

---

756, and the Additional Notes (1991), *ibid.*, pp. 771-772, 780-783 (in dialogue with J.B. Daniels, *et al.*).

59. Contrast J.B. DANIELS, *The Egerton Gospel: Its Place in Early Christianity*, Diss. Claremont, 1989, esp. pp. 140-155: "Egerton's author shows no knowledge ... of Jesus' touching him [the leper]" (p. 150). Regarding the Mt/Lk agreement diff. Mk 1,43 (*ibid.*, n. 2), Daniels's suggestion can scarcely be reconciled with Crossan's position on minor agreements (1991, p. 413; cf. 1985, p. 120; 1988, p. 357).

60. J.D. CROSSAN, *Jesus. A Revolutionary Biography*, San Francisco, Harper, 1994, pp. 77-84: "To Touch a Leper" (esp. 83-84: "Event and Tradition"). On Crossan's notion of "healing the illness without curing the disease" ("change in the social world"), see p. 82.

and the Dialogue Collection isolated by H. Koester in the Dialogue of the Savior (nos. 7, 8, 17, 19).

Crossan has placed the Dialogue Source in the second stratum (60-80; Koester-Pagels: "in the last decades of the first century"); and about forty items in his Inventory include references to "independent attestation" in *Dial. Sav.*[61]. Only two cases receive some comment; they can suffice to show how problematic is on the one hand the identification of the parallels and on the other the thesis of independence. In *Dial. Sav.* 16 the allusion to Gen 1,2 (Creation myth) is followed by: "And I say [to you, ...] ... you seek ... [...] inquire after ... [...] within you ..." (Emmel's translation), and this is cited by Crossan as a parallel to Lk 17,20-21[62]. Mt 10,10b, *Didache* 13,1, and *Dial. Sav.* 53b are supposed to be independent attestations of the proverbial saying, "the laborer deserves his *food*" (342-344). The full paragraph 53 contains references to three sayings, all three present in Matthew: 6,34 (Sv); 10,10b (diff. Lk 10,7b); 10,25a (Lk 6,40)[63]: |

> Mary said, "Thus with respect to 'the wickedness of each day,' and 'the laborer is worthy of his food,' and 'the disciple resembles his teacher.'" She uttered this as a woman who had understood completely.

In this case at least the possibility of Matthean influence on the Dialogue should be taken into consideration[64], pace Koester and Pagels and their statement on "the absence of any evidence for the use of the canonical gospels"[65].

The dating of the writings fragmentarily preserved in the papyri mentioned above cannot be more than a guess. This can be an educated guess such as "sometime before 200 C.E." (P. Sellew, on P. Oxy. 840), or more imaginative guesswork such as "as early as the 50s" (R.J.

---

61. Plural attestation: nos. 1, 4, 8, 14, 21, 37, 52, 59, 61, 125, 194, 195, 206, 208-211; single attestation: 328-348. With only a few exceptions the references are to the Dialogue Source (*Dial. Sav.* 4-14, 19-20, 25-34a, 41-104a). Crossan refers to the paragraph numbers (in nos. 1 and 14 the precise references to the page and line numbers of the codex are added). Some items are mentioned twice: *Dial. Sav.* 73-74 (Love and Goodness) in nos. 337=340; also nos. 208=335.

62. Inventory no. 8; and pp. 282-283: "When and Where". Cf. The Gospel of Jesus (= Lk 17,20-21), p. xiv.

63. Emmel's translation (p. 79). See his note on "resembles": "*tense of the verb uncertain, poss. due to corruption; or poss. understand* the disciple *deserves* to resemble his teacher; *or poss. emend to* the disciple is 'not' like his teacher" (*ibid.*). Compare the translation "resembling" (H.W. Attridge), "gleicht" (B. Blatz). The phrase seems to be closer to Mt 10,25a than 10,24a (and the much quoted parallel Jn 13,16).

64. Cf. J.-M. SEVRIN, in *Logia* (ed. J. DELOBEL), 1982, p. 523.

65. *NHS* 26 (1984), p. 15.

Miller, on P. Oxy. 1224)[66]. Crossan treats those papyri as independent sources[67]. The saying *For and Against* (no. 57) is apparently cited in the P. Oxy. 1224 version: "Who is not against you is for you"[68]. His Gospel of Jesus even includes *Eating with Sinners* (no. 113) in the version of P. Oxy. 1224:

> The scribes and elders and priests were angry because he reclined at table with sinners.

The more usual restoration reads: οἱ δὲ γραμματεῖς κ[αὶ Φαρισαῖ]οι καὶ ἱερεῖς ... (cf. the Pharisees in the Synoptic story)[69]. It is rather strange that Crossan's list of sayings "the Gospel of Jesus" includes this (narrative) accusation against Jesus without following saying[70]. All other items are sayings or parables[71].

The six fragments of the Gospel of the Egyptians are preserved by Clement of Alexandria. One saying, the encratite "The Two Become One", is discussed by Crossan: "I agree that this complex does not stem from the historical Jesus" (298)[72]. I see no reasonable basis for dating Gos. Eg. "by the sixties". W. Schneemelcher's proposal is more realistic: in the second century, "wahrscheinlich das erste Drittel" (1959), "vermutlich in die erste Hälfte" (1987).

Crossan rightly distinguishes between the Gospel of the Nazoreans and the Gospel of the Hebrews[73], but again I see no justification for

66. Cf. R.J. MILLER (ed.), *The Complete Gospels. Annotated Scholars Version*, Sonoma, CA, 1992, pp. 412 (Sellew), 416 (Miller).

67. P. Vindob. G. 2325: no. 25; P. Oxy. 1224: nos. 112, 113, 114, 133; P. Oxy. 840: nos. 204, 276, 277.

68. Ὁ γὰρ μὴ ὢν [κατὰ ὑμ]ῶν ὑπὲρ ὑμῶν ἐστιν. Compare Q 11,23 (ὁ μὴ ὤν) and Mk 9,40 / Lk 9,50 (κατά, ὑπέρ): "This is an indication that GOxy 1224 did not use any of the NT gospels as a written source" (MILLER, n. 66, p. 418; cf. p. 416: "none of their redactional elements are discernible"). In addition, compare ὑμῶν with ἐμοῦ in Q and ἡμῶν/ὑμῶν in Mk/Lk. If we read ἡμῶν in Mk and ὑμῶν in Lk (diff. TR), this Lukan "redactional element" could be "discernible" in P. Oxy. 1224.

69. On "elders" as possible alternative, cf. MILLER (n. 66), p. 417. The triple designation (obviously secondary in this context) "might have originally been an attempt to designate the three groups in the Sanhedrin" (*ibid*).

70. Ὁ δὲ Ἰῆ ἀκούσας [εἶπεν· οὐ χρείαν ἔχ]ουσιν οἱ ὑ[γιαίνοντες ἰατροῦ] ...

71. In a few instances with a narrative introduction (cf. Q and Th): nos. 55 (Th 100, cf. above); 97 (Th 72,1-2; cf. Lk 12,13-14 Q); 106 (Th 104; cf. Mk 2,18-20); 121 (Lk 11,14-15 Q); 145 (Lk 9,59-60 Q); 146 (Lk 9,61-62 Q?); 172 (Lk 17,4 Q); 191 (Lk 22,25).

72. "Two as One" (no. 13: Gos. Eg. 5b), pp. 295-298. For the sayings 1, 2, 3, 4, 6, see Inventory, no. 195 (Woman and Birth).

73. Cf. A.F.J. KLIJN, *Jewish-Christian Gospel Tradition* (Suppl. Vigiliae Christianae, 17), Leiden, 1992, pp. 31-32. See also *ANRW* 25,5 (1988) 3997-4033. Contrast D. VIGNE, *Christ en Jourdain. Le Baptême de Jésus dans la tradition judéo-chrétienne* (Études Bibliques, n.s. 16), Paris, 1992 (Diss. Rome 1992, dir. T. Špidlék): "il n'y a aucune différence à chercher entre l'*Évangile des Hébreux* et celui des Nazaréens" (p. 28);

dating Gos. Heb I "by the fifties C.E.": "Because it [Gos. Heb.] was already known to Clement we can suggest a date about the year 150"[74]. Crossan's Inventory of the Jesus tradition contains eighteen complexes concerning John the Baptist: "The first and most important complex is, necessarily, 58 *John Baptizes Jesus*" (232-234). "The earliest text is in the Gospel of the Hebrews"[75]. Crossan's comment concentrates on the problem of superiority and inferiority (cf. Mt 3,14-15). However, this is absent in Gos. Heb. 2 and most likely also in the account of Jesus' baptism which may have preceded. With "the heavens opened" and "a voice" being absorbed in "fons omnis spiritus sancti"[76], the theophany of Mk 1,10-11 (ascendens de aqua, spiritum descendentem [et manentem], tu es filius meus ...) and the prophecy "et requiescet super eum spiritus Domini" (Is 11,2) may form the components of Gos. Heb. 2[77]:

> Factum est autem cum ascendisset Dominus de aqua, descendit fons omnis Spiritus Sancti, et requievit super eum, et dixit illi: fili mi, in omnibus prophetis expectabam te, ut venires, et requiescerem in te. Tu enim es requies mea, tu es filius meus primogenitus, qui regnas in sempiternum.

6. *The Earliest Gospel*

Crossan separates two layers in the Gospel of Thomas. Sayings with independent attestation elsewhere are assigned to the earlier layer ("composed by the fifties C.E.") and are placed as *Gos. Thom*. I in the first stratum of the Inventory[78]. Sayings that are unique to this collection are assigned to the later Thomas-layer ("added possibly as early as the sixties or seventies") and are placed as *Gos. Thom*. II in the second

---

"*Évangile des Hébreux* ou *des Nazaréens* sont un seul évangile, distinct de celui des Ébionites" (p. 29).

74. KLIJN (n. 73), p. 30. Cf. P. Vielhauer - G. Strecker: first half of the second century.

75. See in the Inventory, separated from Mk 1,9-11 and the six texts dependent on Mk: "(1) *Gos. Heb.* 2; (2a) Mark 1:9-11 = Matt. 3:13-17 = Luke 3:21-22; (2b) *Gos. Naz.* 2; (2c) *Gos. Eb.* 4; (2d) John 1:32-34; (2e) Ign. *Smyrn.* 1:1c; (3) Ign. *Eph.* 18:2d" (p. 438: No. 58+).

76. On this expression, see D. VIGNE (n. 73), pp. 169-184.

77. See the text in KLIJN (n. 73), p. 98 (no. XXI). In Klijn's "Text and Commentary" the seven Gos. Heb. fragments are numbered as follows: 1 = XLIV; 2 = XXI; 3 = II; 4 = I; 5 = XIV; 6 = XXII; 7 = XV.

78. Th 2+ 3,1+ 4,2+ 5,2+ 6,3a 6,4+ 8,1+.2+ 9+ 10+ 12± 13 14,2+.3+ 16+ 17 20,1-2+ 21,3+.4+.5+ 22,1-2+.3-4 24,1-3+ 26+ 30 31+ 32+ 33,1+.2+ 34+ 35+ 36+ 37 38,2 39,1+.2+ 40 41 44+ 45 46+ 47,2+.3+.4+ 51+ 52 54+ 55,1-2a+.2b+ 57+ 61,1.4 62,1.2 63,1+.2+ 64,1-2+ 65,1+.2+ 66 68+ 69,2+ 71+ 72,1-3+ 73+ 76,1+.2+ 78+ 79,1-2+.3 86+ 89+ 90 91,1-2+ 92,1+ 93 94+ 95+ 96,1+.2+ 99+ 100+ 101 102+ 103 104+ 107+ 109+ 113+

I stratum[79]. This is a "rather crude stratification" indeed. It is less clear to me how that stratification "emphasizes how much of this collection is very, very early" (428). The primary argument for an early date is the assumption of independence of the canonical Gospels, and for the thesis of independence Crossan refers to his earlier work (*Four Other Gospels*, 1985, with case studies on Th 64 and 65-66), S.L. Davies (1983) and especially S.J. Patterson (1988). As indicated above, seven sayings of *Gos. Thom.* II are judged to be from the historical Jesus. To take one of them, Th 42 "Be passersby":

> The saying occurs only in Thomas. It can therefore also be understood as a creation of Thomas in which this evangelist counsels detachment from the world, one of his favorite themes. On this understanding, it does not merely *reflect* a certain lifestyle, it *dictates* one ... The Fellows who took this view voted gray or black.

In this case Crossan may have voted with the other half of the Fellows[80]. The Jesus Seminar has shown that there is divergent opinion regarding singly attested sayings. Users of Crossan's Inventory of the Jesus tradition should know also that, in the chronological stratification of plural attestation, the first rank given to the Gospel of Thomas, in accord with a recent trend especially among American scholars, is not an uncontested position.

---

79. Th 1 3,2 4,1 5,1 6,1.2.3b 7 11,1-2a.2b 14,1 15 18 19,1.2 21,1-2 23 25+ 27 28 29 38,1 42+ 43 47,1+ 48 50 53 56 58+ 59 60 61,2-5 67 70 74 75 77,1.2+ 80 81 82 83 84 85 87 88 92,2 97+ 98+ 105 106 108 110 111,1.2 112 114. For five of these sayings there is a second independent attestation: 1 3,2 11,1-2a 75 111,1.

80. *The Five Gospels* (n. 19), p. 496.

SUPPLEMENTARY NOTE (2000)

Crossan's more recent book, *The Birth of Christianity* (1998) contains a further adaptation of the original Inventory, now with specific tabulation of "Common Sayings Tradition in the *Gospel of Thomas* and the *Q Gospel*"[81]. Out of 132 units in Th and 101 units in Q, Crossan counts 37 common units which he presents in the order of Th (numbered 1-37). I give them here in the order of Q: 6,20. 21a. 22-23. 30 34 35b. 31. 39. 41-42. 43-45; 7,24-27. 28; 9,57-58; 10,2. 4-11. 22. 23-24; 11,9-10. 21-22. 33. 39-40. 52; 12,2. 3. 10. 22-31. 33. 39-40. 51-53; 13,18-19. 20-21; 14,15-24. 25-26. 27; 15,3-7; 16,13; 17,23. 34-35; 19,26. Only units "with secure attestation in both Matthew and Luke" are included. Lukan Sondergut which was noted as "Q?" in 1991 is now cancelled (compare above, in the Gospel of Jesus: 9,61-62; 11,27-28; 12,13-15; 12,16-21; 12,49; 17,20-21)[82]. Two other units are omitted (12,54-56; 13,30) and one is added (11,21-22). In all three cases Crossan refers to the IQP text, though without justifying the contrast he himself introduces. IQP has ⟦13,30⟧ on the one hand and ⟦«11,21-22»⟧ on the other; Q 12,54-56 is a special case because of the uncertain text in Mt 16,2b-3. The Critical Edition of Q (2000) uses double brackets in all three, and ⟦< >⟧ in the case of 11,21-22 for a Greek text that could not be reconstructed[83].

---

81. *The Birth of Christianity: Discovering What Happened in the Years Immediately After the Execution of Jesus*, San Francisco, CA, Harper, 1998, 587-589 (Appendix 1). Crossan prefers to call Q the *Q Gospel*: "That serves to respect its textual and theological integrity (Q as gospel) but also to remind us that we know it only by scholarly reconstruction (Q as source)" (110; but compare my critical note above, 419-439).

82. The same rule is applied in the list of the 64 sayings in Q without parallel in Th (Appendix 2B, 595-596). One critical remark: "(61) *As with Lot*: Luke 17:28-30 = Matt. 28:39b"; read Lk 17,30 par. Mt 24,39b as part of (60) *As with Noah*: Lk 17,26-27.30 par. Mt 24,37-39, and Lk 17,28-29 as Lukan Sondergut. – All units are given in the Lukan order (1-64), with only one exception Lk 17,33 (50); but, as indicated above (480-499), its origin in Q is disputable (cf. Mk 8,35). Lk 11,16 is (rightly) treated as Markan, and so could be also Lk 17,2 (above, 252-255).

83. For criticism of the ascription to Q, see my *The Sayings Source Q and the Gospel of Mark*, in H. LICHTENBERGER (ed.), *Geschichte – Tradition – Reflexion*. FS M. Hengel. *III. Frühes Christentum*, Tübingen, Mohr (Siebeck), 1996, 125-145, esp. 127-131 (Lk 11,21-22; 13,30; 17,2; 17,33).

INDEXES

INDEX OF CROSS-REFERENCES

EVANGELICA III

INDEX OF AUTHORS

LIST OF EDITORS

The names of editors are not included in the list of authors. Cf. *Evangelica II*, 830-831. The numbers in superscript refer to the footnotes. BETL volumes are marked with an asterisk.

BARCLAY, J. – SWEET, J. (FS M. Hooker) 616[2]
BAUER, D.R. – POWELL, M.A. (Mt Studies) 386[71]
BEST, E. – WILSON, R.McL. (FS M. Black) 8[32] 30[137]
BETZ, O. (FS O. Michel) 583[24]
*BIERINGER, R. (1-2 Cor) XIII
BEUTLER, J. – FORTNA, R.T. (John 10) 41[181] 77[54] 624[23]
BORMANN, L. (FS D. Georgi) 429[45]
BUSSMANN, C. – RADL, W. (FS G. Schneider) 89[120] 258[78] 268[9] 288[29]
CARROLL, J.T. – COSGROVE, C.H. – JOHNSON, E.E. (FS P.W. Meyer) 13[56]
CASTELLI, E.A. – TAUSSIG, H. (FS B.L. Mack) 165[n]
CHARLESWORTH, J.H. (Qumran) 155[109]
CHILTON, B. – EVANS, C.A. (Historical Jesus) 96[16]
COGGINS, R.J. – HOULDEN, J.L. (Dictionary) 66[4]
COLLINS, A.Y. (FS H.D. Betz) 194[117]
*COLLINS, R.F. (1-2 Thess.) 93[1]
CULPEPPER, R.A. – BLACK, C.C. (FS D.M. Smith) 616[3]
CULPEPPER, R.A. – SEGOVIA, F.F. (Fourth Gospel) 62[274]
DAUTZENBERG, G. (Geschichte) 79[60]
DAUTZENBERG, G. (Die Frau) 118[112]
DE BOER, M.C. (FS M. de Jonge) 189[105.107] 456[27] 616[2]
*DE JONGE, M. (Jean) 3[1] 587[17] 601[1] 616[1]
*DE LA POTTERIE, I. (Évangiles) 350[12]
*DELOBEL, J. (Logia) 81[74] 87[103.105] 89[119] 132[17] 147[82] 168[5] 245[1] 346[5] 428[44] 436[5] 460[43] 474[76] 484[23] 500 570[122] 571[136] 601[2] 644[64]
DE LORENZI, L. (1 Cor 12–14) 110[78]
*DENAUX, A. (John and Syn.) 63[1] 75[53] 77[63-66] 386[70] 551[18.20] 572[3] 578[28] 579[3] 597[28] 616[1] 624[23] 639[40] XIII
DHANIS, É. (Resurrexit) 570[123]
*DIDIER, M. (Matthieu) 134[25] 364[4] 428[44]
DORIVAL, J.-D. – MUNNICH, O. (FS M. Harl) 107[65]
*DUNGAN, D.L. (Interrelations) 14[57] 68[9] 165[159] 214[24] 250[27] 282[n] 309[5] 370[23] 402[11]
*DUPONT, J. (Jésus) 247[14]
EBERT, K. (FS A. Weyer) 113[89]
ELTESTER, W. (Jesus in Nazareth) 184[74]
EPP, E.J. – MACRAE, G.W. (Modern Interpreters) 13[55]
EVANS, C.A. – STEGNER, W.R. (Gospels and Scriptures) 292[51]
FARMER, W.R. (New Synoptic Studies) 143[65]
*FOCANT, C. (Synoptic Gospels) 229[88] 249[26] 312[11] 323[7] 410[31] 500 508[18] 579[3]
    XIII

BIBLIOTHECA EPHEMERIDUM THEOLOGICARUM LOVANIENSIUM

SERIES I

* = Out of print

*1. *Miscellanea dogmatica in honorem Eximii Domini J. Bittremieux*, 1947.

*2-3. *Miscellanea moralia in honorem Eximii Domini A. Janssen*, 1948.

*4. G. PHILIPS, *La grâce des justes de l'Ancien Testament*, 1948.

*5. G. PHILIPS, *De ratione instituendi tractatum de gratia nostrae sanctificationis*, 1953.

6-7. *Recueil Lucien Cerfaux. Études d'exégèse et d'histoire religieuse*, 1954. 504 et 577 p. Cf. *infra*, nos 18 et 71 (t. III).   25 € par tome

8. G. THILS, *Histoire doctrinale du mouvement œcuménique*, 1955. Nouvelle édition, 1963. 338 p.   4 €

*9. *Études sur l'Immaculée Conception*, 1955.

*10. J.A. O'DONOHOE, *Tridentine Seminary Legislation*, 1957.

*11. G. THILS, *Orientations de la théologie*, 1958.

*12-13. J. COPPENS, A. DESCAMPS, É. MASSAUX (ed.), *Sacra Pagina. Miscellanea Biblica Congressus Internationalis Catholici de Re Biblica*, 1959.

*14. *Adrien VI, le premier Pape de la contre-réforme*, 1959.

*15. F. CLAEYS BOUUAERT, *Les déclarations et serments imposés par la loi civile aux membres du clergé belge sous le Directoire (1795-1801)*, 1960.

*16. G. THILS, *La «Théologie œcuménique». Notion-Formes-Démarches*, 1960.

17. G. THILS, *Primauté pontificale et prérogatives épiscopales. «Potestas ordinaria» au Concile du Vatican*, 1961. 103 p.   2 €

*18. *Recueil Lucien Cerfaux*, t. III, 1962. Cf. *infra*, n° 71.

*19. *Foi et réflexion philosophique. Mélanges F. Grégoire*, 1961.

*20. *Mélanges G. Ryckmans*, 1963.

21. G. THILS, *L'infaillibilité du peuple chrétien «in credendo»*, 1963. 67 p.
                    2 €

*22. J. FÉRIN & L. JANSSENS, *Progestogènes et morale conjugale*, 1963.

*23. *Collectanea Moralia in honorem Eximii Domini A. Janssen*, 1964.

24. H. CAZELLES (ed.), *De Mari à Qumrân. L'Ancien Testament. Son milieu. Ses écrits. Ses relectures juives* (Hommage J. Coppens, I), 1969. 158*-370 p.   23 €

*25. I. DE LA POTTERIE (ed.), *De Jésus aux évangiles. Tradition et rédaction dans les évangiles synoptiques* (Hommage J. Coppens, II), 1967.

26. G. THILS & R.E. BROWN (ed.), *Exégèse et théologie* (Hommage J. Coppens, III), 1968. 328 p.   18 €

*27. J. COPPENS (ed.), *Ecclesia a Spiritu sancto edocta. Hommage à Mgr G. Philips*, 1970. 640 p.

28. J. COPPENS (ed.), *Sacerdoce et célibat. Études historiques et théologiques*, 1971. 740 p.   18 €

29. M. DIDIER (ed.), *L'évangile selon Matthieu. Rédaction et théologie*, 1972.
    432 p.   25 €
*30. J. KEMPENEERS, *Le Cardinal van Roey en son temps*, 1971.

SERIES II

31. F. NEIRYNCK, *Duality in Mark. Contributions to the Study of the Markan
    Redaction*, 1972. Revised edition with Supplementary Notes, 1988. 252 p.
                                                                             30 €
32. F. NEIRYNCK (ed.), *L'évangile de Luc. Problèmes littéraires et théologiques*,
    1973. *L'évangile de Luc – The Gospel of Luke*. Revised and enlarged
    edition, 1989. X-590 p.   55 €
33. C. BREKELMANS (ed.), *Questions disputées d'Ancien Testament. Méthode
    et théologie*, 1974. *Continuing Questions in Old Testament Method and
    Theology*. Revised and enlarged edition by M. VERVENNE, 1989. 245 p.
                                                                             30 €
34. M. SABBE (ed.), *L'évangile selon Marc. Tradition et rédaction*, 1974.
    Nouvelle édition augmentée, 1988. 601 p.   60 €
35. B. WILLAERT (ed.), *Philosophie de la religion – Godsdienstfilosofie. Mis-
    cellanea Albert Dondeyne*, 1974. Nouvelle édition, 1987. 458 p.   60 €
36. G. PHILIPS, *L'union personnelle avec le Dieu vivant. Essai sur l'origine et
    le sens de la grâce créée*, 1974. Édition révisée, 1989. 299 p.   25 €
37. F. NEIRYNCK, in collaboration with T. HANSEN and F. VAN SEGBROECK,
    *The Minor Agreements of Matthew and Luke against Mark with a Cumu-
    lative List*, 1974. 330 p.   23 €
38. J. COPPENS, *Le messianisme et sa relève prophétique. Les anticipations
    vétérotestamentaires. Leur accomplissement en Jésus*, 1974. Édition
    révisée, 1989. XIII-265 p.   25 €
39. D. SENIOR, *The Passion Narrative according to Matthew. A Redactional
    Study*, 1975. New impression, 1982. 440 p.   25 €
40. J. DUPONT (ed.), *Jésus aux origines de la christologie*, 1975. Nouvelle
    édition augmentée, 1989. 458 p.   38 €
41. J. COPPENS (ed.), *La notion biblique de Dieu*, 1976. Réimpression, 1985.
    519 p.   40 €
42. J. LINDEMANS & H. DEMEESTER (ed.), *Liber Amicorum Monseigneur W.
    Onclin*, 1976. XXII-396 p.   25 €
43. R.E. HOECKMAN (ed.), *Pluralisme et œcuménisme en recherches théolo-
    giques. Mélanges offerts au R.P. Dockx, O.P.*, 1976. 316 p.   25 €
44. M. DE JONGE (ed.), *L'évangile de Jean. Sources, rédaction, théologie*,
    1977. Réimpression, 1987. 416 p.   38 €
45. E.J.M. VAN EIJL (ed.), *Facultas S. Theologiae Lovaniensis 1432-1797.
    Bijdragen tot haar geschiedenis. Contributions to its History. Contribu-
    tions à son histoire*, 1977. 570 p.   43 €
46. M. DELCOR (ed.), *Qumrân. Sa piété, sa théologie et son milieu*, 1978.
    432 p.   43 €
47. M. CAUDRON (ed.), *Faith and Society. Foi et société. Geloof en maat-
    schappij. Acta Congressus Internationalis Theologici Lovaniensis 1976*,
    1978. 304 p.   29 €

68. N. LOHFINK (ed.), *Das Deuteronomium. Entstehung, Gestalt und Botschaft / Deuteronomy: Origin, Form and Message*, 1985. XI-382 p.   50 €
69. P.F. FRANSEN, *Hermeneutics of the Councils and Other Studies*. Collected by H.E. MERTENS & F. DE GRAEVE, 1985. 543 p.   45 €
70. J. DUPONT, *Études sur les Évangiles synoptiques*. Présentées par F. NEIRYNCK, 1985. 2 tomes, XXI-IX-1210 p.   70 €
71. *Recueil Lucien Cerfaux*, t. III, 1962. Nouvelle édition revue et complétée, 1985. LXXX-458 p.   40 €
72. J. GROOTAERS, *Primauté et collégialité. Le dossier de Gérard Philips sur la Nota Explicativa Praevia (Lumen gentium, Chap. III)*. Présenté avec introduction historique, annotations et annexes. Préface de G. THILS, 1986. 222 p.   25 €
73. A. VANHOYE (ed.), *L'apôtre Paul. Personnalité, style et conception du ministère*, 1986. XIII-470 p.   65 €
74. J. LUST (ed.), *Ezekiel and His Book. Textual and Literary Criticism and their Interrelation*, 1986. X-387 p.   68 €
75. É. MASSAUX, *Influence de l'Évangile de saint Matthieu sur la littérature chrétienne avant saint Irénée*. Réimpression anastatique présentée par F. NEIRYNCK. *Supplément: Bibliographie 1950-1985*, par B. DEHAND-SCHUTTER, 1986. XXVII-850 p.   63 €
76. L. CEYSSENS & J.A.G. TANS, *Autour de l'Unigenitus. Recherches sur la genèse de la Constitution*, 1987. XXVI-845 p.   63 €
77. A. DESCAMPS, *Jésus et l'Église. Études d'exégèse et de théologie*. Préface de Mgr A. HOUSSIAU, 1987. XLV-641 p.   63 €
78. J. DUPLACY, *Études de critique textuelle du Nouveau Testament*. Présentées par J. DELOBEL, 1987. XXVII-431 p.   45 €
79. E.J.M. VAN EIJL (ed.), *L'image de C. Jansénius jusqu'à la fin du XVIIIᵉ siècle*, 1987. 258 p.   32 €
80. E. BRITO, *La Création selon Schelling. Universum*, 1987. XXXV-646 p.   75 €
81. J. VERMEYLEN (ed.), *The Book of Isaiah – Le livre d'Isaïe. Les oracles et leurs relectures. Unité et complexité de l'ouvrage*, 1989. X-472 p.   68 €
82. G. VAN BELLE, *Johannine Bibliography 1966-1985. A Cumulative Bibliography on the Fourth Gospel*, 1988. XVII-563 p.   68 €
83. J.A. SELLING (ed.), *Personalist Morals. Essays in Honor of Professor Louis Janssens*, 1988. VIII-344 p.   30 €
84. M.-É. BOISMARD, *Moïse ou Jésus. Essai de christologie johannique*, 1988. XVI-241 p.   25 €
84ᴬ. M.-É. BOISMARD, *Moses or Jesus: An Essay in Johannine Christology*. Translated by B.T. VIVIANO, 1993, XVI-144 p.   25 €
85. J.A. DICK, *The Malines Conversations Revisited*, 1989. 278 p.   38 €
86. J.-M. SEVRIN (ed.), *The New Testament in Early Christianity – La réception des écrits néotestamentaires dans le christianisme primitif*, 1989. XVI-406 p.   63 €
87. R.F. COLLINS (ed.), *The Thessalonian Correspondence*, 1990. XV-546 p.   75 €
88. F. VAN SEGBROECK, *The Gospel of Luke. A Cumulative Bibliography 1973-1988*, 1989. 241 p.   30 €

89. G. THILS, *Primauté et infaillibilité du Pontife Romain à Vatican I et autres études d'ecclésiologie*, 1989. XI-422 p.   47 €
90. A. VERGOTE, *Explorations de l'espace théologique. Études de théologie et de philosophie de la religion*, 1990. XVI-709 p.   50 €
*91. J.C. DE MOOR, *The Rise of Yahwism: The Roots of Israelite Monotheism*, 1990. *Revised and Enlarged Edition*, 1997. XV-445 p.
92. B. BRUNING, M. LAMBERIGTS & J. VAN HOUTEM (eds.), *Collectanea Augustiniana. Mélanges T.J. van Bavel*, 1990. 2 tomes, XXXVIII-VIII-1074 p.   75 €
93. A. DE HALLEUX, *Patrologie et œcuménisme. Recueil d'études*, 1990. XVI-887 p.   75 €
94. C. BREKELMANS & J. LUST (eds.), *Pentateuchal and Deuteronomistic Studies: Papers Read at the XIIIth IOSOT Congress Leuven 1989*, 1990. 307 p.   38 €
95. D.L. DUNGAN (ed.), *The Interrelations of the Gospels. A Symposium Led by M.-É. Boismard – W.R. Farmer – F. Neirynck, Jerusalem 1984*, 1990. XXXI-672 p.   75 €
96. G.D. KILPATRICK, *The Principles and Practice of New Testament Textual Criticism. Collected Essays*. Edited by J.K. ELLIOTT, 1990. XXXVIII-489 p.   75 €
97. G. ALBERIGO (ed.), *Christian Unity. The Council of Ferrara-Florence: 1438/39 – 1989*, 1991. X-681 p.   75 €
98. M. SABBE, *Studia Neotestamentica. Collected Essays*, 1991. XVI-573 p.   50 €
99. F. NEIRYNCK, *Evangelica II: 1982-1991. Collected Essays*. Edited by F. VAN SEGBROECK, 1991. XIX-874 p.   70 €
100. F. VAN SEGBROECK, C.M. TUCKETT, G. VAN BELLE & J. VERHEYDEN (eds.), *The Four Gospels 1992. Festschrift Frans Neirynck*, 1992. 3 volumes, XVII-X-X-2668 p.   125 €

SERIES III

101. A. DENAUX (ed.), *John and the Synoptics*, 1992. XXII-696 p.   75 €
102. F. NEIRYNCK, J. VERHEYDEN, F. VAN SEGBROECK, G. VAN OYEN & R. CORSTJENS, *The Gospel of Mark. A Cumulative Bibliography: 1950-1990*, 1992. XII-717 p.   68 €
103. M. SIMON, *Un catéchisme universel pour l'Église catholique. Du Concile de Trente à nos jours*, 1992. XIV-461 p.   55 €
104. L. CEYSSENS, *Le sort de la bulle Unigenitus. Recueil d'études offert à Lucien Ceyssens à l'occasion de son 90ᵉ anniversaire*. Présenté par M. LAMBERIGTS, 1992. XXVI-641 p.   50 €
105. R.J. DALY (ed.), *Origeniana Quinta. Papers of the 5th International Origen Congress, Boston College, 14-18 August 1989*, 1992. XVII-635 p. 68 €
106. A.S. VAN DER WOUDE (ed.), *The Book of Daniel in the Light of New Findings*, 1993. XVIII-574 p.   75 €
107. J. FAMERÉE, *L'ecclésiologie d'Yves Congar avant Vatican II: Histoire et Église. Analyse et reprise critique*, 1992. 497 p.   65 €

108. C. Begg, *Josephus' Account of the Early Divided Monarchy (AJ 8, 212-420). Rewriting the Bible*, 1993. IX-377 p.   60 €
109. J. Bulckens & H. Lombaerts (eds.), *L'enseignement de la religion catholique à l'école secondaire. Enjeux pour la nouvelle Europe*, 1993. XII-264 p.   32 €
110. C. Focant (ed.), *The Synoptic Gospels. Source Criticism and the New Literary Criticism*, 1993. XXXIX-670 p.   75 €
111. M. Lamberigts (ed.), avec la collaboration de L. Kenis, *L'augustinisme à l'ancienne Faculté de théologie de Louvain*, 1994. VII-455 p.   60 €
112. R. Bieringer & J. Lambrecht, *Studies on 2 Corinthians*, 1994. XX-632 p.   75 €
113. E. Brito, *La pneumatologie de Schleiermacher*, 1994. XII-649 p. 75 €
114. W.A.M. Beuken (ed.), *The Book of Job*, 1994. X-462 p.   60 €
115. J. Lambrecht, *Pauline Studies: Collected Essays,* 1994. XIV-465 p.   63 €
116. G. Van Belle, *The Signs Source in the Fourth Gospel: Historical Survey and Critical Evaluation of the Semeia Hypothesis,* 1994. XIV-503 p.   63 €
117. M. Lamberigts & P. Van Deun (eds.), *Martyrium in Multidisciplinary Perspective. Memorial L. Reekmans*, 1995. X-435 p.   75 €
118. G. Dorival & A. Le Boulluec (eds.), *Origeniana Sexta. Origène et la Bible/Origen and the Bible. Actes du Colloquium Origenianum Sextum, Chantilly, 30 août – 3 septembre 1993*, 1995. XII-865 p.   98 €
119. É. Gaziaux, *Morale de la foi et morale autonome. Confrontation entre P. Delhaye et J. Fuchs*, 1995. XXII-545 p.   68 €
120. T.A. Salzman, *Deontology and Teleology: An Investigation of the Normative Debate in Roman Catholic Moral Theology*, 1995. XVII-555 p.   68 €.
121. G.R. Evans & M. Gourgues (eds.), *Communion et Réunion. Mélanges Jean-Marie Roger Tillard*, 1995. XI-431 p.   60 €
122. H.T. Fleddermann, *Mark and Q: A Study of the Overlap Texts*. With an Assessment by F. Neirynck, 1995. XI-307 p.   45 €
123. R. Boudens, *Two Cardinals: John Henry Newman, Désiré-Joseph Mercier*. Edited by L. Gevers with the collaboration of B. Doyle, 1995. 362 p.   45 €
124. A. Thomasset, *Paul Ricœur. Une poétique de la morale. Aux fondements d'une éthique herméneutique et narrative dans une perspective chrétienne*, 1996. XVI-706 p.   75 €
125. R. Bieringer (ed.), *The Corinthian Correspondence*, 1996. XXVII-793 p.   60 €
126. M. Vervenne (ed.), *Studies in the Book of Exodus: Redaction – Reception – Interpretation*, 1996. XI-660 p.   60 €
127. A. Vanneste, *Nature et grâce dans la théologie occidentale. Dialogue avec H. de Lubac*, 1996. 312 p.   45 €
128. A. Curtis & T. Römer (eds.), *The Book of Jeremiah and its Reception – Le livre de Jérémie et sa réception*, 1997. 331 p.   60 €
129. E. Lanne, *Tradition et Communion des Églises. Recueil d'études*, 1997. XXV-703 p.   75 €

130. A. DENAUX & J.A. DICK (eds.), *From Malines to ARCIC. The Malines Conversations Commemorated*, 1997. IX-317 p. 45 €
131. C.M. TUCKETT (ed.), *The Scriptures in the Gospels*, 1997. XXIV-721 p. 60 €
132. J. VAN RUITEN & M. VERVENNE (eds.), *Studies in the Book of Isaiah. Festschrift Willem A.M. Beuken*, 1997. XX-540 p. 75 €
133. M. VERVENNE & J. LUST (eds.), *Deuteronomy and Deuteronomic Literature. Festschrift C.H.W. Brekelmans*, 1997. XI-637 p. 75 €
134. G. VAN BELLE (ed.), *Index Generalis ETL / BETL 1982-1997*, 1999. IX-337 p. 40 €
135. G. DE SCHRIJVER, *Liberation Theologies on Shifting Grounds. A Clash of Socio-Economic and Cultural Paradigms*, 1998. XI-453 p. 53 €
136. A. SCHOORS (ed.), *Qohelet in the Context of Wisdom*, 1998. XI-528 p. 60 €
137. W.A. BIENERT & U. KÜHNEWEG (eds.), *Origeniana Septima. Origenes in den Auseinandersetzungen des 4. Jahrhunderts*, 1999. XXV-848 p. 95 €
138. É. GAZIAUX, *L'autonomie en morale: au croisement de la philosophie et de la théologie*, 1998. XVI-760 p. 75 €
139. J. GROOTAERS, *Actes et acteurs à Vatican II*, 1998. XXIV-602 p. 75 €
140. F. NEIRYNCK, J. VERHEYDEN & R. CORSTJENS, *The Gospel of Matthew and the Sayings Source Q: A Cumulative Bibliography 1950-1995*, 1998. 2 vols., VII-1000-420* p. 95 €
141. E. BRITO, *Heidegger et l'hymne du sacré*, 1999. XV-800 p. 90 €
142. J. VERHEYDEN (ed.), *The Unity of Luke-Acts*, 1999. XXV-828 p. 60 €
143. N. CALDUCH-BENAGES & J. VERMEYLEN (eds.), *Treasures of Wisdom. Studies in Ben Sira and the Book of Wisdom. Festschrift M. Gilbert*, 1999. XXVII-463 p. 75 €
144. J.-M. AUWERS & A. WÉNIN (eds.), *Lectures et relectures de la Bible. Festschrift P.-M. Bogaert*, 1999. XLII-482 p. 75 €
145. C. BEGG, *Josephus' Story of the Later Monarchy (AJ 9,1–10,185)*, 2000. X-650 p. 75 €
146. J.M. ASGEIRSSON, K. DE TROYER & M.W. MEYER (eds.), *From Quest to Q. Festschrift James M. Robinson*, 2000. XLIV-346 p. 60 €
147. T. RÖMER (ed.), *The Future of the Deuteronomistic History*, 2000. XII-265 p. 75 €
148. F.D. VANSINA, *Paul Ricœur: Bibliographie primaire et secondaire - Primary and Secondary Bibliography 1935-2000*, 2000. XXVI-544 p. 75 €
149. G.J. BROOKE & J.D. KAESTLI (eds.), *Narrativity in Biblical and Related Texts*, 2000. XXI-307 p. 75 €
150. F. NEIRYNCK, *Evangelica III: 1992-2000. Collected Essays*. 2001. XVII-666 p. 60 €
151. B. DOYLE, *The Apocalypse of Isaiah Metaphorically Speaking. A Study of the Use, Function and Significance of Metaphors in Isaiah 24-27*, 2000. XII-453 p. 75 €
152. T. MERRIGAN & J. HAERS (eds.), *The Myriad Christ. Plurality and the Quest for Unity in Contemporary Christology*, 2000. XIV-593 p. 75 €
153. M. SIMON, *Le catéchisme de Jean-Paul II. Genèse et évaluation de son commentaire du Symbole des apôtres*, 2000. XVI-688 p. 75 €

154. J. VERMEYLEN, *La loi du plus fort. Histoire de la rédaction des récits davidiques de 1 Samuel 8 à 1 Rois 2*, 2000. XIII-746 p.   80 €

155. A. WÉNIN (ed.), *Studies in the Book of Genesis. Literature, Redaction and History*, 2001. XXX-643 p.   60 €

156. F. LEDEGANG, *Mysterium Ecclesiae. Images of the Church and its Members in Origen*. 2000. XVIII-722 p.   84 €

157. J.S. BOSWELL, F.P. MCHUGH & J. VERSTRAETEN (eds.), *Catholic Social Thought: Twilight of Renaissance?* 2000. XXII-307 p.   60 €

158. A. LINDEMANN (ed.), *The Sayings Source Q and the Historical Jesus*. 2001. XXII-776 p.   60 €

159. C. HEMPEL, A. LANGE & H. LICHTENBERGER (eds.), *The Wisdom Texts from Qumran and the Development of Sapiential Thought*. 2001. X-486 p. Forthcoming.

PRINTED ON PERMANENT PAPER • IMPRIME SUR PAPIER PERMANENT • GEDRUKT OP DUURZAAM PAPIER - ISO 9706

ORIENTALISTE, KLEIN DALENSTRAAT 42, B-3020 HERENT